Sajjilu Arab American

Critical Arab American Studies
Carol W. N. Fadda, *Series Editor*

Critical Arab American Studies

Syracuse University Press is pleased to announce the launch of a new series, Critical Arab American Studies. The series features cutting-edge scholarship that adopts interdisciplinary, intersectional, feminist, transnational, and comparative frameworks of inquiry to develop the study of Arab Americans across various fields of research, including history, gender and sexuality studies, critical race and ethnic studies, anthropology, literature, film and media studies, and sociology, among others.

Arab Americans in Film: From Hollywood and Egyptian Stereotypes to Self-Representation
Waleed F. Mahdi

Arab American Women: Representation and Refusal
Michael W. Suleiman, Suad Joseph, and Louise Cainkar, eds.

Breaking Broken English: Black–Arab Literary Solidarities and the Politics of Language
Michelle Hartman

Interrogating Secularism: Race and Religion in Arab Transnational Art and Literature
Danielle Haque

Sajjilu Arab American

A Reader in SWANA Studies

Edited by
Louise Cainkar,
Pauline Homsi Vinson,
and Amira Jarmakani

Syracuse University Press

First Edition 2022

22 23 24 25 26 27 6 5 4 3 2 1

∞ The paper used in this publication meets the minimum requirements of the American National Standard for Information Sciences—Permanence of Paper for Printed Library Materials, ANSI Z39.48-1992.

For a listing of books published and distributed by Syracuse University Press, visit https://press.syr.edu.

ISBN: 978-0-8156-3735-6 (hardcover)
978-0-8156-3721-9 (paperback)
978-0-8156-5522-0 (e-book)

Library of Congress Cataloging-in-Publication Data

Names: Cainkar, Louise, editor. | Vinson, Pauline Homsi, editor. | Jarmakani, Amira, 1974– editor.
Title: Sajjilu Arab American : a reader in SWANA studies / edited by Louise Cainkar, Pauline Homsi Vinson, and Amira Jarmakani.
Description: First edition. | Syracuse, New York : Syracuse University Press, 2022. | Series: Critical Arab American studies | Includes bibliographical references and index. | Summary: "'Sajjulu Arab American' is a carefully curated multi-disciplinary collection of scholarly writings in Arab American studies. Written by both recognized and emerging scholars, the collected essays utilize a wide range of theoretical frames and analytic lenses that are essential to understanding the field"— Provided by publisher.
Identifiers: LCCN 2021041097 (print) | LCCN 2021041098 (ebook) | ISBN 9780815637356 (hardcover) | ISBN 9780815637219 (paperback) | ISBN 9780815655220 (ebook)
Subjects: LCSH: Arab Americans—Social conditions. | Muslims—United States—Social conditions. | United States—Race relations. | United States—Ethnic relations.
Classification: LCC E184.A65 S245 2021 (print) | LCC E184.A65 (ebook) | DDC 305.892/7073—dc23
LC record available at https://lccn.loc.gov/2021041097
LC ebook record available at https://lccn.loc.gov/2021041098

Manufactured in the United States of America

Contents

Illustrations

Preface

The Critical Arab American Studies (CAAS) book series showcases innovative scholarship that develops cutting-edge theoretical and thematic engagements in Arab American and Southwest Asian and North African (SWANA) studies. At the core of this book series is an investment in raising and addressing key questions about the politics of producing radical antiracist, anti-imperial, and feminist knowledges about Arab American and SWANA communities as well as their connections to other racialized communities in the United States and in the global South more broadly. *Sajjilu Arab American: A Reader in SWANA Studies* directly attends to such critical investments in radical and decolonial knowledge production, investments that continue to be articulated and solidified in response to ongoing racial and gendered violence and to evolving imperial agendas and military projects.

As this reader goes through its final stages of production, the devastating impact of such entrenched structures of violence are in full evidence in the United States and throughout the world. The COVID-19 global pandemic has starkly laid bare how racial inequities and lack of access to adequate health care for marginalized communities determine who lives and who dies. Such inequities and the effects of COVID-19 have been compounded in the United States by the continuance of lethal anti-Black and anti-Asian gendered racism, oppressive immigration policies, as well as the interlocking systems of power informing police brutality, hate crimes, gendered violence, homophobia, and transphobia. Globally, vulnerable and underserved populations in the global South have to contend with the ravaging impact of COVID-19 in the midst of crumbling economic infrastructures, struggling health-care and medical sectors, and corrupt political systems, as made evident by the devastating COVID-19 crisis in India, Brazil, and other parts of the global South. The intertwined nature of such forms of violence and the deadly effects of settler-colonial and imperial states' hegemony have been starkly evident in the latest ruthless Israeli bombardment of the Gaza Strip and the forced expulsion of Palestinians from Sheikh Jarrah and other East Jerusalem neighborhoods amid continued expansions of illegal settlements in the West Bank; in the reverberating economic crash in Lebanon and the disastrous explosion in Beirut on August 4, 2020; and in the continued brutal effects of the imperial and proxy wars across the Middle East and North Africa region, including in Iraq, Syria, and Libya. Movements such as Black Lives Matter call on us to resist anti-Blackness in local, national, and transnational contexts and to confront how the death and devastation caused by US racist structures have touched the lives of so many not only within the classed, racialized, and gendered framework of the United States but in the global South more broadly.

These interconnected global and transnational landscapes remind us that as scholars, artists, writers, activists, and cultural workers, we are urgently responsible for developing and mobilizing a critical language that interrogates and challenges multiple and ongoing oppressions and inequities that repeatedly target the lives of the most vulnerable. At this political and historical juncture, feminist, queer, antiracist, abolitionist, anti-imperialist, and antimilitaristic movements converge to trace solidarities across racial and global boundaries, thus rethinking these boundaries and their structures altogether. The curtailment of such critical projects of knowledge production nevertheless abounds, as made evident by the censoring of the Arab American studies section planned for the Ethnic Studies Model Curriculum in California, an act that highlights the violent erasure of Arab experiences in the United States as evoked and reified by the state.

The editors of *Sajjilu Arab American* and its contributors take seriously the urgency of producing critical mappings of Arab American and SWANA studies to show what collective futures become possible when we attend to the specificities, histories, and genealogies of racialized experiences of violence and Othering within the United States and beyond. This reader emphasizes what becomes tangible and immediate when we render visible the shifting, emergent, and complex connections across racial, geopolitical, national, and spatial divides. Edited by Louise Cainkar, Pauline Homsi Vinson, and Amira Jarmakani, *Sajjilu Arab American* encompasses some of the foundational work in the field, showcasing a set of important and insightful essays spanning decades of scholarship, covering a wide range of vibrant thematic engagements, and reflecting the field's exciting and defining interdisciplinary commitments. In encompassing such various disciplines, thematic foci, historical timelines, sociocultural contexts, and geopolitical frames, this first-of-its-kind reader marks a crucial field-forming moment in Arab American and SWANA studies: it features a rich and wide-ranging critical mass of scholarship and research that has defined and continues to define the field and direct it in new directions. In doing so, it centers fluid, anti-institutionalized approaches to field-formation projects that are here understood as living archives.

A much-needed and timely reader like this one is exciting, but it can at the same time be challenging. Delineating and demarcating "the origin stories of the field" and the temporal, historical, and thematic framings can invariably also pin down and delimit a fixity to the story of the field's development, as the editors rightfully point out. Rather than asserting that the field of Arab American studies has finally "arrived," what this collection brilliantly confirms are the ways in which scholars, thinkers, writers, artists, activists, and community builders, among others, have explored and continue to explore, articulate, and redefine Arab American and SWANA experiences in ways that reimagine our individual and collective futures. Thus, instead of signaling an end point that punctuates the field's beginning or asserting fixed temporal, spatial, or thematic framings that animate the field's interventions and investments, *Sajjilu Arab American* clearly and evocatively highlights ongoing conversations, unfolding trajectories, and developing investments firmly grounded in past and contemporary, complex and unfolding historical, cultural, social, imperial, settler-colonial, and geopolitical contexts.

Insisting on such an open-ended approach to the field that privileges explorations rather than fixed determinations of past and future field developments and trajectories is integral not only to this collection but to the Critical Arab American Studies series as a whole, as evinced by the growing list of the series' featured books. Such a fluid approach highlights the inevitable porosity of fields of study and their shifting boundaries, which are constantly negotiated in light of political turns, national and transnational priorities, as well as ongoing global crises. Such negotiations ultimately and necessarily place Arab American and SWANA studies in conversation with other adjacent and related fields of study, including critical race and ethnic studies, Muslim American studies, Asian American studies, Indigenous studies, and transnational Middle East studies, among others. This relational lens calls on us to readjust our understanding of how knowledges are produced not only within but also across these interrelated and overlapping fields and through the multiple, intersecting, and imbricated experiences they address.

The six parts around which this reader is organized attend to the ongoing development of such a critical language grounded and immersed in the grammars of intersectionality and transnationality. In these parts, the focus on legibility, migration, racialization, representation, imperialism, and cross-coalitional solidarity movements in relation to Arab American and SWANA communities in the United States and beyond foregrounds the shifting parameters and evolving self-definitions characterizing our communities. By weaving together these sections, the reader places important and necessary conversations in relation to one another, refusing their seeming separateness and revealing the overlapping geographies (real and imagined) that highlight the pervasive mechanisms of nation and empire.

This reader is essential reading for anyone who is interested in gaining a critical understanding of Arab

American and SWANA communities as shaped by wide-ranging yet at the same time specific and contextualized knowledges. It invites students and scholars from different disciplines and research backgrounds to trace connections, historical continuities, and geographic intimacies in what are often presented as dissimilarities and ruptures. It also invites readers to challenge institutional and structural racism in and across various related communities and national boundaries as well as to highlight the visible and covert effects of US empire and military projects on Arab, SWANA, and Muslim communities within and beyond the US settler-imperial state. It does so by foregrounding how the challenge to racism and imperialism is an ongoing, multipronged commitment that should simultaneously attend to multiple oppressions and marginalizations. Although inviting proximity and comparison, the reader never erases the specific realities and experiences of individual groups and communities. It instead invites us to consider multiple, ongoing, and future knowledge-production projects, an investment echoed in the Critical Arab American Studies series as a whole and its commitment to fostering the exciting and urgent developments of the field.

Carol W. N. Fadda
Syracuse, New York
June 7, 2021

Acknowledgments

The vision for this reader—the first of its kind in the field—grew out of the Arab American Studies Association Conference of 2017. Prior to the conference, I (Louise) had spoken to Suzanne Guiod at Syracuse University Press about editing a volume of the conference papers. But after the conference, I came to two important realizations: that as a social scientist I needed a partner with expertise in literature and the arts and that the field needed more than another edited volume. It needed a body of work that would stand up and shout, "WE EXIST: our voices and our scholarship will no longer be ignored!" The clear and obvious choice for editing partner was Pauline Homsi Vinson; once she was on board, the ambitious vision for the project solidified and grew. At a certain point we decided that another lens was needed to give full expression to all of the beauty and breadth that was contained under the rubric of Arab American studies. At that point, we invited Amira Jarmakani, who brought her expertise in gender, cultural, and American studies to the table. Carol Fadda has been an ardent advocate to bring this vision to fruition, and there really are no words to express the depth of our gratitude for her indefatigable support. Both Carol and Suzanne Guiod at Syracuse University Press offered unwavering support, meeting with us at conferences and following up through emails as we crafted and honed the vision. Deborah Manion later stepped into Suzanne's role at the press and continued to provide rigorous advice and encouragement.

Books are always the product of a series of thought collaborations, and a reader takes such collective scholarly work to yet another level. This reader would not be possible without the years of work and the steadfast endurance of scholars in the field to carve space in the academy for Arab American and critical SWANA studies. In this sense, credit is owed not only to each of the contributors to the reader but also equally to all of the scholars—cited and not cited—whose work created and enriched our field/s.

During early brainstorming about what should be included in the reader, we did a preliminary survey of what was being taught in the field. We are grateful to those who shared their syllabi with us (also named in note 3 of the introduction): Ghassan Abou-Zeineddine, Evelyn Alsultany, Leila Ben-Nasr, Umayyah Cable, Meiver De La Cruz, Carol W. N. Fadda, Sarah M. A. Gualtieri, John Tofik Karam, Charlotte Karem Albrecht, Randa Kayyali, Akram Khater, Waleed Mahdi, Michael Malek Najjar, Therí Pickens, Mejdulene B. Shomali, and Nina Shoman-Dajani. We learn, teach, and think alongside all of the scholars, teachers, and activists who intentionally bring our field to light.

The tremendously labor-intensive project of compiling the manuscript for this reader would have been impossible without the support of several graduate research assistants, including Deena Naime, Yazan Zahzah, W. G. Ellis, Amanda Brown, Nawal Zahzah, and Alan Chavoya. Special thanks go to Yazan Zahzah for their truly masterful pdf-conversion labor—not to mention cunning contributions to the pod—that aided in assembling all the essays into one coherent manuscript. Many thanks also to all of the contributors for the labor they put into copyediting previously published pieces, particularly given the onerous task of trimming them down. Much gratitude also goes to those contributors who offered newly crafted pieces and for their dedication and patience throughout the review and editing process. Copyediting is a labor of both love and precision; we hold a deep well of appreciation for the dexterous, attentive, and engaged copyediting of Annie Barva. For advice, expertise, and the invaluable labor of indexing, we give thanks to Lisa DeBoer. We are grateful to Nadine Sinno, Nader Uthman, and Shadi al-Khatib for quick responses to our frantic texts as we were debating possible titles, and we owe much gratitude to Miles Laith Vinson and Sally Homsi for helping us envision a book cover to match the title. Finally, many thanks again to Deborah Manion and to the whole team at Syracuse University Press—Mona Hamlin, Fred Wellner, and Kelly Balenske—for supporting this project in so many concrete ways.

In addition to compiling and editing our contributors' work, we, as editors, collectively wrote the introduction to the reader as well as the framing essays for each thematic part. Our process for cowriting was both intensive and adaptive—a process that evolved along the way. We took turns taking the lead on writing part introductions; we all collectively edited these introductions, rotated who rewrote each introduction, and collectively edited the whole work again. In this way, we honored each of our areas of expertise while simultaneously making room for fresh perspectives on each topic. In the sometimes overwhelming—and constantly growing!—set of comments that spindled down the right-hand side of our shared Google docs, we challenged, supported, and uplifted one another. Throughout this truly feminist and transformative writing process, we learned many things about the field, given our varied content areas of expertise; we learned a great deal about writing and editing; we validated each other's experience of being marginalized in the academy; and we learned a great deal about each other. Our hope is that at least some of this transformative process translates to the volume's readers as well.

In the same collective, feminist spirit, we are also grateful to people who read early drafts of our introductions to both the volume and its thematic parts and who were in conversation with us about them. Among them are Evelyn Alsultany, Carol W. N. Fadda, Therese Saliba, Deena Naime, Layla Zbinden, and the anonymous peer reviewers for the press. We are particularly indebted to Evelyn Alsultany and Carol W. N. Fadda for their careful, engaged reading, crucial feedback, and ongoing consultations throughout the process.

Most of all, our deep respect goes to the anonymous shrew, who always knew when to show up.

Louise

Although I never considered quitting, I want to thank all of the people who encouraged me to continue writing in Arab American/SWANA studies despite its lack of socially recognized reward. They include not only some of the early scholars in the field, such as Barb Aswad, Yvonne Haddad, Elaine Hagopian, and Michael Suleiman, as well those who embraced me from the emerging next generation, especially Nadine Naber and Evelyn Alsultany, but also the activists who saw scholarship as an integral component of the struggle for Arab American recognition and freedom from racism. That line runs from those who were already fighting when I started, such as Jim Zogby, Abdeen Jabara, Edward Said, Janet Abu-Lughod, and Ibrahim Abu-Lughod, through the Union of Palestinian Women's Associations and especially their visionary leader, Camille Odeh, to my comrades at Chicago's Arab American Action Network. It is only because of your unwavering commitment to fighting for justice in the United States and throughout the world that my work has meaning. I have been deeply touched by the productive, supportive, and inspiring sisterhood of this project. To Pauline Homsi Vinson and Amira Jarmakani: thank you! We experienced a wide range of joys and struggles in the course of this multiyear process; we congratulated and comforted each other; and we made each other better in so many ways. Finally, I thank my family, especially Hassan and Anwar, for providing me with the extensive times of peaceful silence required to bring this project to fruition.

Pauline

No work is done without the support of others, both named and unnamed. I am grateful to Louise Cainkar for inviting me to coedit this volume and to Amira Jarmakani for agreeing to join us. I am equally grateful to both Louise and Amira for their good humor and the camaraderie we built as we worked to finalize the project in the midst of a pandemic, surrounded by so much uncertainty, illness, and loss. As each work builds on what has come before it, I am also grateful to Elie Chalala, Sarah M. A. Gualtieri, Carol W. N. Fadda, Nawar al-Hassan Golley, Suad Joseph, and Nadine Sinno for deeply stimulating conversations that have influenced the development of my work. Thanks also for past collaborative work that has sustained my work in the field, including the effort to form AASA led by Suad Joseph, with Rita Stephan, Randa Kayyali, and Lutfi Hussein, and with Hatem Akil and Carol Fadda to form GAAM at the MLA. I am fortunate to have the love and support of my family. I am especially grateful for the inspiring legacies of my mother, Mutia Homsie, and my eldest sister, Lily Asfour, both of whom left this world too soon, and for the sustaining care and ready laughter of my sisters, Nelly Saliba, Sally Homsi, and Mary Koussa, each of whom set the bar high for me to follow but also has held me up along the way. My husband, Michael, has been a steady and avid supporter of my work. My three grown children—Laila, Yasmeen, and Miles—keep me grounded in what matters even as they inspire me with their own brilliance and give meaning to my work. It is my hope that this reader, with the work it highlights and the future work it might generate, contributes to a climate where future generations of Arab Americans are seen in their diversity and no longer forced to explain who they are.

Amira

I am so grateful to have been brought in to the vision that Louise and Pauline had already labored to put forward—many humble thanks to both of you for seeing in me a partner with whom to collaborate. Louise, I deeply admire and am inspired by your drive to realize the vision of this reader and to write its truths into existence. Pauline, I admire your fastidious work precisely because it is grounded in a deep ethical commitment to the people to whom this reader is devoted. Though sometimes diminutively understood as a superfluous "attention to detail," your careful dedication to getting the words right reinspires my own reverence for words and their power. My commitment to our field/s has been meaningfully sustained by several organizing collectives. Among them are the Arab Women's Solidarity Association (AWSA), the Radical Arab Women's Action Network (RAWAN), the organizing collective that planned the Arab Movement of Womxn Arising for Justice (AMWAJ), the Movement to End Israeli Apartheid–Georgia, the Palestinian Feminist Collective, and the Stop LAPD Spying Coalition. It would be impossible to truly acknowledge how the work of these organizations and collectives have transformed me, but lately I have been thinking a great deal about a conversation with Joe Kadi and Katherine Acey while AMWAJ was being organized. In a word, they made me feel like enough at a moment when being a queer Arab scholar activist seemed impossible, and that feeling has been a reservoir of enough over the years. In no particular order, I also want to name individuals whose presence and/or support throughout time and/or at a critical moment has sustained me through the academy and/or COVID and/or life: Nadine Naber, Evelyn Alsultany, Mimi Kirk, Stephanie Abraham, Mej Shomali, Carol Fadda, Joe Kadi, Therese Saliba, Lara Kiswani, Deb Najjar, Irene Lara, Jess Whatcott, Priscilla Wathington, Nadine Sinno, Tiffany King, Umayyah Cable, Juliana Ramírez, Andrea Miller, Mary Gage Davidson, Lara Deeb, Heba Nimr, Karina Bidaseca, Deena Naime, Leigh Miller, Julie Kubala, Janet Jakobsen, Catherine Clune-Taylor, Anne Donadey, Nader Uthman, Hartlyn Haynes, Astin Wangel-Brown, Asako Yonan, Ale Gomez, Yazan Za3za3, Wes Paláu, Donna Troka, Sig/Sara Giordano, Sarah Gualtieri, Margaret Koehler, Kim Segna, Nawal Zahzah, Suzy Goldsmith, Ruby, Griffin, Mardaqush, and the peeps. I am grateful for family in all of its formations, among whom I include Jay Jarmakani, Brenda Jarmakani, Ramona Bruno, Yara Bruno, Savannah Bruno, Diego Bruno, Jeff Jarmakani, Tahereh Aghdasifar, and Mel Boyajian. I particularly want to uplift Ramona, Yara, and Savannah as the pulse that sustains me. Their collective feisty spirit—perhaps symbolized by the fire that Savannah accidentally lit during one of our many editorial conference calls—inspires this work. May this reader light the world on fire in surprising and unexpected ways, and may that fire simultaneously find the shelter for it to be nurtured toward generative burning and guided away from useless and violent destruction.

Sajjilu Arab American

Introduction

Sajjilu Arab American: A Reader in SWANA Studies

LOUISE CAINKAR, PAULINE HOMSI VINSON, and AMIRA JARMAKANI

"Mostly my stories choose me, I do not choose them" (Majaj 2007, 406). The words of the Arab American scholar and poet Lisa Suhair Majaj resonate with the aims of this project—namely, to tell the story of Arab American studies not as a single defining account but as a narrative that reflects the complexity, tensions, and richness of the field. As the storytelling metaphor suggests, our process has been to engage the origin stories of the field, to think about the themes that dominate how those stories have been told, and to reveal the political and institutional contexts that have shaped Arab American studies. Insofar as origin stories operate as creative fictions, we have also sought both to disrupt and to build on the narrative logics that have so far framed the field, with the aim of stimulating conversation about the formation of the field of Arab American studies and also about the possibilities for its future directions.

From a young age, we are taught to understand stories through the narrative coherence of a beginning, middle, and end. The problem with such narrative neatness is that it obscures the messiness of a good story, smoothing over shifts in perspective and temporal anomalies, normalizing experiences, and heightening particular aspects over others for dramatic effect. In relation to the story about the field of Arab American studies, when the privileging of narrative coherence takes the shape of a chronological arc, it can flatten the sorts of tensions that make the field more interesting and vibrant. In our telling of the story of Arab American studies in this introduction, we aim to strike a balance between the coherence of a neat story and the generative potential of messiness in telling a complex and ever-expanding tale.

At the same time, because linearity can have the benefit of providing an organizing structure on which to hang an overall understanding of what has been at stake in field formation, we begin this introduction with an overview of some of the dominant themes and narratives in Arab American studies. In other words, we describe some of the common stories about the field, and then we point to some of the problems with these sorts of origin stories and the ways they can inadvertently produce and solidify orthodoxies even as they also miss important strands within the field. We then describe our rationale for organizing the reader thematically, a structure that foregrounds our aim to bring attention to cyclical patterns, disruptions, continuities, and divergences in the process of field formation.[1]

In keeping with the spirit of storytelling with which we began this introduction, we round out our discussion by telling our own academic stories in relation to the field of Arab American studies. Our academic trajectories are inextricably bound up in the gradual formation of the field, and we tell our stories as a way of contextualizing three of the major obstacles that impeded field formation:

1. A similar point is emphasized in the introduction to "Arab/Americas: Locations & Iterations," a special issue of the *Amerasia Journal*, where Sarah M. A. Gualtieri and Pauline Homsi Vinson advocate looking beyond the chronological wave model that has characterized the study of Arab immigration and consider instead "how the recent iterations of Arabness . . . intersect with or negotiate differences from past articulations . . . depending on location or in relation to other racialized groups" (Gualtieri and Homsi Vinson 2018, x).

struggles to render the field legible, resistance to framing Arab Americans as racialized, and a general climate of censorship in relation to work on Palestine and on Arabs more generally. The title we have chosen for this collection, *Sajjilu Arab American: A Reader in SWANA Studies*, speaks to these three obstacles in that it demands recognition for the field. From the Arabic word *sijil*, سجل, which carries the meanings of both "recording" and "registering," the word *sajjilu* intentionally echoes the opening lines of Mahmoud Darwish's poem "Identity Card," or "Bitaqat Hawiyyah," which begins, "sajjil ana 'arabi" (سجِّل انا عربي). Using the imperative form of the verb, the opening line means, "Register/Record/Write Down: I am Arab." First published in 1964 and composed while Darwish was in an Israeli prison, his poem replays an exchange at an Israeli checkpoint and gives voice to the Palestinian speaker's defiant challenge to the absurdity of having to be registered by a state institution that would also erase his identity and deny his claim to the land.[2] Choosing the plural imperative in place of a universal masculine singular, our title both echoes and expands on the opening words of Darwish's poem. While the imperative demands recognition and simultaneously insists on the idea of having our histories recorded and recognized, the plural invites a broader coalition into that demand. Though our reader focuses on Arab American studies, our subtitle also locates this work within the broader umbrella of critical Southwest Asian and North African (SWANA) studies, and it addresses the multiple conflations that affect the overlapping, contingent, and historically situated experiences of SWANA Americans. Our intent is to highlight our collective efforts to record our own stories in their multiplicity and variety, to foreground the importance of decolonizing geographies, and to acknowledge the historic invisibility of Arab American studies even as we have faced the hypervisibility of domestic surveillance and policing of our communities. These struggles of recognition, racialization through surveillance, and racialized exclusion affect everyone from the larger SWANA region—Arabs, Iranians, Turks, Assyrians, Kurds, Chaldeans, Imazighen, and Armenians, among others.

The cover image we have chosen further communicates the complexity of resistance and control that we signal in our title. The image is of two mirror halves of a passport photo of Elaine Hagopian, a central figure in the development of Arab American studies, who has donated her photos to the Arab American National Museum and has generously agreed to allow us to use her image on the cover. Resonant on multiple levels, this image evokes the refusal to be boxed in even as it directly references state efforts to control and manage us—for instance, in government registries, identity documents, FBI files, and border crossings. The image also invokes a symmetry that eludes closure, as one half is in color, and the other is in grayscale, suggesting a dichotomy that is unstable and inviting a refusal of sorts and an alternative within. Together, the title and cover image carry the force of an injunction to inscribe that which has been elided even as each captures a central tension between the constraints of institutional mechanisms and the possibilities for escaping them. *Sajjilu Arab American: A Reader in SWANA Studies* registers and reflects on major developments and central concerns within the field of Arab American studies, its intersections with the fields of US Muslim and SWANA American studies and in relation to fields such as Asian American, transnational, American, Middle Eastern, race and ethnic, and migration studies.

Our Goals and Process

Our goals for the reader are to communicate key works in the field, foreground the complexities and paradoxes of these conversations, and invite conversations not yet imagined. Our thematic organization offers clusters—not teleological narratives—that are meant to stimulate conversation and debate rather than reproduce uniformity and linearity. We arrived at our particular themes

2. See Khalidi 2008. Darwish's poem was first published in *Awraq al-zaytun* (Olive Leaves, 1964). Copies of Arabic and English translations of the poem are frequently recited, and many can be found online. For a published English translation, see Hilmy 2017, which translates *sajjil* as "write down." For a recording of a recitation of the poem in Arabic, see *Sajjil Ana Arabi—Mahmoud Darwish* 2012.

after carefully reviewing a range of syllabi[3] from scholars teaching in Arab American studies and related fields as well as after reading capaciously in the growing body of scholarship related to Arab American studies, which necessarily includes US Muslim and Muslim American studies. Arabs and Muslims are conflated in culture talk and represented as the same, their bodies similarly acted upon by punitive agents.[4] Our review of the literature and course syllabi revealed clusters of interest, which we developed into themes, as well as gaps in scholarship, which helped us identify new essays to solicit. The lack of a linear trajectory in the reader, however, should not be read as ahistorical—we recognize that subjectivities, theoretical perspectives, and grounded experiences are historically contingent and subject to change over time. In choosing a thematic approach, we foreground key questions and debates, weave a complex story about what the field includes and what it has (perhaps unintentionally) excluded, and reveal implicit and explicit collaborations that transverse disciplines of study.

Our initial list of essays for potential inclusion in the reader well exceeded even the most generous possible page limits. In undertaking the difficult task of selecting what to keep, we strove both to honor the work that has been done and to avoid the ossification of ideas that sometimes accompanies canonization. As a consequence, we took a relational and layered approach in which we (1) weave discussions of early work in Arab American studies into our general introduction and part descriptions; (2) include essays that cite and build upon earlier work; and (3) present new and emerging scholarship in the field. With the aim of including a wide range of contributions, we also trimmed pre-published essays (with cuts indicated by ellipses). Reflecting the richness of scholarship in this highly interdisciplinary field, the reader intends to be useful to scholars working from a range of disciplinary perspectives and teaching a variety of courses related to the study of Arab Americans, including studies of SWANA diasporas, historic and contemporary imbrications of Islam and Muslims in the Americas, and, more broadly, race and racialization. Our intention is to engage with work that has shaped Arab American studies across the disciplines while pointing to new directions taking shape. In other words, while gathering a large number of important previously published works, we include both past contributions that have informed the field as well as new scholarship that invites us to reflect on elisions and orthodoxies that appear to be taking shape within the still emerging field of Arab American studies. In short, the mode of this reader is not one of canonization but rather of inquiry and exploration.

Overview of the Field

Linear narratives of Arab American studies, which we have chosen to disrupt in this reader, are US-focused and follow chronological threads of time and dominant markers of change. These narratives emphasize the significant early migration of persons—not all of whom were Arabs—from (former) Greater Syria: their migratory movements, social status, institution building, social contexts, and patterns of work and creative productions. The typical wave model of immigration also attends to growth, geographic spread, and generations, making it important to note that early communities of "Syrian" immigrants and their children were widely spread across the United States and had grown to some one hundred thousand persons by the early 1920s (Hitti 1924) before immigration was severely curtailed by quotas, the Great Depression, and World War II, after which movement began again, subject to policy limitations. These narratives tend to deploy a decontextualized sense of fresh start or new beginnings, at once presenting Arab Americans as perpetual new arrivals (but in different groups at different times) and eliding the fact that Arabs, Muslims, and persons broadly from the "East" have been for centuries represented as uncivilized, threatening, and exotic others in white-supremacist societies, as scholars

3. Many thanks to the following for sharing their syllabi: Ghassan Abou-Zeineddine, Evelyn Alsultany, Leila Ben-Nasr, Umayyah Cable, Meiver De La Cruz, Carol W. N. Fadda, Sarah M. A. Gualtieri, John Tofik Karam, Charlotte Karem Albrecht, Randa Kayyali, Akram Khater, Waleed Mahdi, Michael Malek Najjar, Therí Pickens, Mejdulene B. Shomali, and Nina Shoman-Dajani.

4. See Mamdani 2005, chapter 1: "Culture Talk; Or, How Not to Talk about Islam and Politics" (17–62).

such as Edward Said (1978) and Ella Shohat and Robert Stam (1994) so eloquently demonstrate. The wave model thus suggests that Arab Americans would ultimately be spared some of the severe consequences of racial othering. In this period, for example, Arab Americans were able to lay claim to naturalized citizenship, a legal benefit of whiteness, although in certain areas they had to wage court battles to do so, as laid out in Sarah M. A. Gualtieri's contribution to this reader. Likewise, Arab Americans in this early era were economically successful partly because they did not face the segregation and labor subjugation that impeded subordinated peoples of color in the United States. The possibilities opened by proximity to white privilege contextualized many of the post–World War II studies of Arab Americans, which were framed by assimilation theories and a tone of aspiring to whiteness—work that was later critiqued for its heteronormative silences, naive optimism concerning the US racial order, and lack of complexity.

In addressing important markers of change, the wave model of migration and linear narratives about Arab Americans highlight the serious challenges that emerged for Arab Americans after 1967, following the Israeli military occupation of East Jerusalem, the West Bank, Gaza, and parts of Egypt and Syria. It was at that time that Arab Americans were effectively transformed from exotic outsiders associated *with* the Holy Land into monstrous outsiders who *threatened* the Holy Land, both of which marshaled the orientalist ideas that were always lurking in the background. This transformation was operationalized through deployment of an us/them binary that represented Arabs as uncivilized human beings and Israelis as "people like us," and it cemented overwhelming US political, media, and popular support for Israeli conquests. The representation of Arabs as threatening others was reinforced through marketing strategies that utilized racialized tropes and through the proliferation of the "Arab terrorist" stereotype in mass media. These efforts were buttressed by the criminalization of dissent enforced by US government agencies through surveillance and deportation; the practices that purported to screen out "Arab terrorists" were codified under President Richard Nixon as Operation Boulder (Bassiouni 1974). All of these tactics, aimed at manufacturing consent (Herman and Chomsky 1988) for the policies of the United States and allied governments, forged growing dissent among Arab Americans and their allies, culminating in Arab American institution building. The next decades would witness the rise of organizations such as the Association of Arab American University Graduates (AAUG, 1967), the Arab Community Center for Economic and Social Services (ACCESS, 1971), the Palestine Human Rights Campaign (PHRC, 1977), the American Arab Anti-Discrimination Committee (ADC, 1980), and the Arab American Institute (AAI, 1985).

The following decades were marked by a series of civil, belligerent, and imperialist wars in the region (e.g., the Lebanese Civil War, the Israeli invasion of Lebanon, the US military intervention in Libya, the Iraqi invasion of Kuwait, the US and US allies' first invasion of Iraq and related expulsions of Arab workers from Persian Gulf states, the second Gulf War, and the war in Yemen) that not only inflicted substantial economic losses, physical and ecological damage, and death but also increased Arab migration to the United States—most notably of Palestinians, Lebanese, Egyptians, Iraqis, and Yemenis. The door to these movements had been opened by changes in US law, including the Immigration and Nationality Act of 1965, the Refugee Act of 1980, and the Diversity Visa Lottery program of 1990. The wave model of migration collapses all of these newcomers under the rubric of post-1965 immigrants, overlooking the substantial differences among and between them.

Scholarship on Arab Americans during the latter decades of the twentieth century consistently demonstrated the wide range of systemic social, cultural, political, and academic exclusions faced by Arab Americans. This scholarship also revealed the affinities and intersections between Arab Americans and similarly racialized, othered, or marginalized groups both in the United States and across the world. These findings eventually congealed into assertions by scholars that Arab Americans had been racialized as nonwhite others and like other marginalized groups in the United States were affected by threat narratives, policing, vulnerability, and peril. Yet this claim largely went unnoticed as scholarship on Arab Americans had been relegated to outsider status in the academy.

Scholars of Arab Americans have faced substantial challenges to being heard, hired, and published. In response, they have worked tirelessly to forge a place to teach and learn in the academy as well as for recognition of their work in race and ethnic studies, critical race scholarship, literary studies, gender and sexuality studies, and American studies. However, the ambiguous state of being positioned both inside and outside of whiteness—a state referred to as being "ambiguous insiders" by Nadine Naber (2000) and "not quite white" by Helen Hatab Samhan (1999)—was a complexity that made Arabs illegible within the dominant paradigms of race that had emerged in the United States by the late 1960s. This racial ambiguity was further aggravated by the official categorization of Arabs as "white" (a "white" person is officially defined as "a person having origins in any of the original peoples of Europe, the Middle East, or North Africa") by the US Office of Management and Budget in its 1977 Directive 15.[1]. While the directive sought better documentation of the status of "racial and ethnic minorities" with regard to civil rights and employment, it effectively obscured data on Arab Americans, who were buried among Euro-Americans on the US Census and all US government forms. This bureaucratic whiteness concealed the de facto racialized status of Arab Americans, and it was augmented by the earlier history of Arab American economic success as well as by the desires for whiteness and the push for assimilation among some Arab Americans. Add to this concoction the active efforts by elites (scholarly, cultural, political) and government agents to silence Arab American voices, and it becomes evident that Arab American studies' struggle for recognition and a place at the race and ethnic studies table was as complicated as it was political.

Then the attacks on New York City and Washington, DC, happened on September 11, 2001 (9/11). Though the attacks were not committed by Arab or Muslim Americans, the massive government repression and popular backlash that ensued after they occurred—built on decades of silencing, stereotyping, and criminalizing—made daily life highly tenuous for Arab and Muslim Americans. The conflation of Arabs and Muslims as well as the denigration of Arab and Muslim women widely propagated in the mass media long prior to these attacks played out in gendered hate crimes and widespread discrimination against both Arab and Muslim Americans (Cainkar 2009; Jarmakani 2008; Naber 2012). The post-9/11 project of finding the terrorists "hiding in our communities," in the words of Attorney General John Ashcroft, was launched using a broad range of policies and tactics. Yet even after years of surveillance, FBI interviews, arrests, registrations, and deportations, the US government uncovered no domestic terrorists, but it did disrupt millions of lives (Cainkar 2009). These new facts on the ground could not go unnoticed. Scholarship on Arab and Muslim Americans finally received some recognition and funding, and many new scholars joined the field, even though they had few mentors and had to search for academic homes. Although decades of scholarship on Arab Americans had demonstrated that 9/11 was not the starting point of racist stereotyping, extralegal violence, systematic exclusion, and government surveillance of Arab Americans, some scholars new to the field erroneously marked 9/11 as the beginning of Arab American racialization, thus introducing a distortion in the field.

Narratives about the period after 9/11 emerged that contributed to the idea that it represented a new historical marker in the treatment of Arab, SWANA, and Muslim Americans. Implicit in the 9/11 start date is the assumption that anti-Arab/Muslim racism was triggered by Arab (and/or Muslim) terrorism. There are multiple problems with this logic: it introduces a blame-the-victim scenario, common to historic racism, and it disengages anti-Arab/Muslim racism from its larger structural interests, in this case its ties to imperial projects. The idea that 9/11 caused anti-Arab (and anti-Muslim) racism, like the "race-relations" paradigm, conveys a myopic and parochial understanding of racialization that is comfortable for many scholars because it makes it possible to avoid considerations of racialization's global structural dimensions and thus to avoid politically controversial territory. In addition, endorsing this post-9/11 theme becomes complicit in silencing the decades of scholarship on Arab Americans that preceded 9/11, the very work that informed the struggle for scholarly recognition of anti-Arab racism and its global dimensions. Rather than the beginning of anti-Arab and anti-Muslim racism, 9/11 more precisely signals the commencement of the broad scholarly recognition of that racism (as argued in Cainkar 2018).

This recognition, together with the emergence of Arab American studies from the shadows of whiteness and the politics of silencing, opened up spaces for Arab American scholarship to be published and taught. Growth in both scholarship and the number of scholars led to efforts to solidify the field, as in the formation of the Arab American Studies Association (AASA) in 2012, the founding of *Mashriq & Mahjar: Journal of Middle East and North African Migration Studies* in 2013, and the Critical Arab American Studies series at Syracuse University Press in 2015. In the academy, Arab American studies has witnessed incremental growth; its work is taught within race/ethnic, gender, literary, queer, disability, and American studies, among other fields, and a number of Arab American studies programs have been established.[5]

Parallel to increasing recognition and scholarship, and despite a hostile context of reception, Arab migration to the United States continued to rise in the decades after 2001, with some dips and upswings relevant to different groups, maintaining a pattern of growth that had begun in earnest in the 1990s. Most notable among the demographic changes brought about by this movement is the increase in the number of Iraqis (including Chaldeans, Assyrians, and others) and Egyptians, who by 2020 had become the largest Arab *immigrant* groups in the United States (Migration Policy Institute [2020] analysis using American Community Survey data on the foreign born through 2018). Nonetheless, persons claiming Syrian and Lebanese ancestry still constitute the largest number of Arab Americans by "national origin," according to American Community Survey data. Other notable shifts include the sharp rise in Yemeni and Syrian migration beginning in 2016, both movements propelled by war. Although Yemenis migrated largely through family reunification and Syrians as refugees, both of these flights for safety were sharply curtailed by President Donald Trump's executive order in 2017, "Protecting the Nation from Foreign Terrorist Entry into the United States," known commonly as the "Muslim Ban" (Cainkar 2020).

As this brief overview reveals, linear narratives of Arab American studies can highlight important milestones and moments in the development of the field by following migration patterns, markers of change, and scholarly receptivity. At the same time, as we argue, such a linear narrative offers a deceptively neat and homogenizing view of both Arab American experiences and Arab American scholarship, obscuring tensions among Arab Americans and within the field, especially those around gender, sexuality, religion, national origin, class, and ethnicity. Our thematic organization expands on the key topics of the linear narrative by centering conversations at the intersection of multiple disciplines, including fruitful overlaps between Arab American, US Muslim American, race and ethnic, Indigenous, and transnational migration studies.

Themes in Arab American Studies

Dominant stories about Arab American studies often invoke its precarity; for decades, it was perilously situated on the scholarly and artistic outside, neither part of the Eurocentric mainstream nor included in the race and ethnic studies counter to Eurocentrism. Such precarious positioning in academic disciplines and within scholarly institutions fostered the field's productive interdisciplinary evolution. Our thematic grouping of readings reflects this thriving interdisciplinary interchange of ideas among Arab American scholars. We place scholars in conversation with one another around six themes: (1) legibility and naming; (2) migration and transnational

5. Among them are the Arab and Muslim American Studies Program in the Department of American Culture at the University of Michigan, Ann Arbor; the Center for Arab American Studies at the University of Michigan–Dearborn; and the Arab and Muslim Ethnicities and Diaspora Studies Program at San Francisco State University. A number of academic programs have created specialties in Arab and Muslim studies—including the Global Asian Studies Program at the University of Illinois, Chicago; the Department of American Studies and Ethnicity at the University of Southern California; and the Arab and Muslim American minor at Marquette University. Indicative of the subspecializations within the field of Arab and Muslim American studies is the Moise A. Khayrallah Center for Lebanese Diaspora Studies at North Carolina State University, which focuses research on Lebanese migrants in the United States and throughout the world.

configurations; (3) racialization and the limits of liberal multiculturalism; (4) representation and epistemological formations; (5) imperialism and the war on terror; and (6) solidarities and intersectionalities across movements for justice among people of color. We ultimately decided on these six themes because we felt they reflect current sites of scholarly inquiry; they highlight the kinds of interdisciplinary approaches that are moving the field forward in promising new directions; and they emphasize critical expansions in Arab American studies. We have included work that intentionally deploys the lenses of queer, critical race, disability, and transnational American studies, and we have placed this work alongside contributions that apply decolonial theory and situate US imperialism in relation to anticolonialist movements waged by what Vijay Prashad (2007) calls the "darker nations." In the part on migration, for example, we read a canonical article such as Alixa Naff's "The Early Arab Immigrant Experience" alongside Charlotte Karem Albrecht's "Narrating Arab American History: The Peddling Thesis" to acknowledge simultaneously the dominant narrative about Arab American immigrants and their experiences in the United States and to note the inevitable silences of this sort of historical archive that privileges assimilationist and heteronormative narratives. In the part on imperialism and the war on terror, we highlight the relationships between structural racism, Islamophobia, and empire; and in the part on solidarities and intersectionalities across movements for justice among people of color, we explore both forgotten and currently vibrant solidarities among Indigenous, Black, Arab, South Asian, Asian, and Latinx communities.

Our thematic choices also allow us to grapple with the intermingling and disentangling of race, religion, and ethnicity and to reassess the problems inherent in both liberal multiculturalism and articulations of cultural belonging. In the part on racialization, for example, we explore the tensions and contradictions of US Arab Americans' historical claims to whiteness and its privileges in the context of their more recent racialization and conflation with Muslims. These explorations build on prior work to further our understanding of how both internal racial hierarchies and US imperialism have shaped Arab experiences in the Americas. For example, in the part on epistemologies we address how Arabs in the Americas are racialized in particular ways within different nation-state formations even as they are uniformly orientalized for the purposes of global white supremacy. The essays in the reader also challenge the growing normative view that Arab and Muslim American racialization emerged in response to the 9/11 attacks and instead highlight its much earlier origins in American imperial aspirations and alliances going back to the mid–twentieth century as well as to the emergence of what Hisham Aidi (2003) has called the "Moorish Atlantic" and the European conquest of the Americas.

The reader is decidedly transnational because the field of Arab American studies has largely been so. Scholars have argued for decades that the racialization of Arab Americans cannot be understood solely through a limited focus on the United States, the traditional scope of US American race and ethnic studies. The field is also transnational in recognition of a nuanced understanding both of diaspora and of continuities and discontinuities across the Americas. We highlight scholarship—such as Carol W. N. Fadda's work—that pushes beyond a simple definition of the transnational as denoting movement across national borders and instead moves toward a conceptualization of transnational homelands that can simultaneously encompass historic homelands as well as the fabric of homes and communities intentionally made in the Americas. We engage scholarship—such as the work by Christina Civantos, Ella Shohat, John Tofik Karam, Leslie Quintanilla, and Jennifer Mogannam, among others—that focuses on Arabs and wider SWANA movements, migrations, and communities in Mexico as well as Central and South America.

Although a thematic organization foregrounds the crystallizing of nodes of conversation in the field, it can also lend itself to an artificial division between topics that actually overlap and intersect with one another. Placing particular essays in certain thematic sections does not preclude their engagement with other themes in the reader. It is our hope that the reader as a whole will be taken as an opportunity to generate multiple conversations based on the ideas highlighted within each thematic section as well as across the six thematic clusters we have gathered.

Further Considerations

Although this reader highlights important themes in Arab American studies, there are some things it does not do that deserve mention. Our selection methodology biases the reader toward areas of research and exploration that are experiencing the largest growth, such as American studies, while giving less visibility to important work in more quantitative fields witnessing less expansion, such as sociology and political science. We encourage our readers to continue looking outside this volume for additional important scholarship on Arab Americans, both by authors included and by scholars whose work we could not include within the book's parameters. The reader is notably thin on issues of social class, a highly relevant variable for Arab Americans that shows significant variations by and within "immigrant" and "ancestry" groups and that distinguishes Arab Americans from both the white majority and from groups officially recognized as "racial minorities." Overall, some Arab American communities have high socioeconomic status as measured by median incomes, whereas others have troubling levels of economic disadvantage. In 2017, a report authored by Arab American studies scholars Jen'nan Ghazal Read and Kristine Ajrouch based on the US Census Bureau's American Community Survey found that "at the national level, Arab Americans are younger, more likely than Whites to be unemployed, to live in poverty, and to lack private health insurance, despite having higher rates of college completion" (3). With regard to internal differences, they note: "Particularly striking is the disadvantaged socioeconomic status of Iraqis and Yemenis at both the national and local levels. They have among the highest rates of poverty, greatest reliance on public health insurance, lowest rates of educational attainment, and lowest levels of English fluency," which contrasts with the rates "of more established Arab ancestry groups (e.g., Lebanese, Egyptian, Syrian) and underscores the need to disaggregate Arab Americans from Whites" (4). As with all nonwhite and white groups in the United States, social class has meaningful implications for a person's identity, health, quality of life, mobility, political views, and personal security. In the case of Arab Americans, social class as well as religious affiliation play a part in racial identification.

A number of texts in the reader point out that Arab Americans of all religious affiliations suffer from anti-Arab and anti-Muslim racism. It is nonetheless important to highlight that Arab Americans are religiously quite diverse, perhaps to a higher degree than most US (ethnic and racial) groups and especially as compared to Euro-white Americans. Research shows that religion intersects with social class to play a role in racial identification. For example, Randa Kayyali's (2018) research indicates that Christian Arab Americans living in wealthier suburbs of Washington, DC, were more likely than other Arab Americans to identify as white, even as they were generally assumed to be Muslim and face anti-Muslim bias based on this misconception. Other research suggests that not only social class but also US region and membership in a religious congregation may affect racial identification. The Detroit Arab American Study Team (2009) found that 73 percent of Arab and Chaldean Christians identified as white compared to 50 percent of Muslims. In Texas, surveys conducted by Jen'nan Ghazal Read (2008) at an Arab mosque and Arab church found that only 5 percent of Muslim Arab Americans (more likely to be foreign born than Christian Arab Americans) identified as white, compared to 34 percent of Christian Arab Americans. In Read's study, more Muslim Americans than Christian Arab Americans reported experiencing discrimination prior to 9/11, although 44 percent of Christians said they had experienced some. With regard to membership in a congregation, Amaney Jamal (2005) found that American Muslims who worship in mosques are more likely to be locally and nationally politically engaged than "the unmosqued." Her findings suggest that communal participation may play a role in racial identification, and they rebuke the Islamophobic trope that the more religious a Muslim is, the more alienated and threatening that person appears to non-Arabs and non-Muslims. We invite our readers to consider questions of class, religion, institutional membership, and local context while exploring the essays we have gathered in this reader.

We also want to recognize important research conducted in the field of Arab American health, broadly defined, especially because this work is made all the more difficult by the near-universal absence of a category for

Arab Americans in statistical reporting.[6] Indeed, a primary goal of the recent census effort in the United States (see the part three introduction) was to end the invisibility of Arab Americans in data collected by all sectors of US society, including in hospital, health, and school statistics as well as in police and hate-crime reporting. Substantial research on Arab American health indicators, aging, disability, and adolescence has been conducted by Kristine Ajrouch (Ajrouch 2008; Ajrouch and Antonucci 2017; Ajrouch and Fakhoury 2013), among others, and work on schools has been carried out by Nina Shoman-Dajani (2016). Similarly, groundbreaking work by the psychologists Mona Amer and Germine Awad appears in their edited volume *Handbook of Arab American Psychology* (2016). Research on Arab Americans in these fields is important because we know that racism, fear, and trauma take severe physical and mental-health tolls on their targets. We recognize and honor the increasing breadth, depth, and multidisciplinary growth of the field of Arab American studies, and we hope this reader spurs further conversations in the field. Most importantly, we want to acknowledge that many persons who have contributed in important ways to the field of Arab American studies are not represented in the reader, including scholars, artists, and activists, and to emphasize that the goal of this reader is neither to offer a "best of" or a "definitive collection of" Arab American scholarship. Rather, our aim is to provide opportunities for rigorous explorations of the field by highlighting critical scholarship and a number of salient intellectual debates within it.

We started this introduction with a quote from Lisa Suhair Majaj that captures how our stories choose us rather than the other way around. Her remark highlights the way that our political and institutional contexts shape our experiences and influence our understanding of what we mean by "Arab American." Although Arab American studies is an institutional and collective formation, the story of the field is also shaped by the lived realities of individual scholars. For that reason, we include our situated stories in this introduction not to claim that they are representative of the experiences of all scholars in Arab American studies but to provide perspective on how the field has been mediated both by the range of obstacles that were in place at an institutional level and, paradoxically, by the collaborations and activism that these obstacles generated. These obstacles include but are not limited to (1) the illegibility of the field in dominant academic formations; (2) the invisibility of Arab Americans as a racialized group; and (3) censorship of those working on issues related to Palestine, a censorship that at one time included anything related to Arabs. Our narratives demonstrate how these three barriers have permeated academia and influenced our own im/possibilities. By interweaving personal anecdotes about our scholarly trajectories with the larger scholarly and institutional narratives shaping Arab American studies, we hope to illustrate the multifaceted and intersecting dimensions that have contributed to and continue to shape the formation of the field.

Louise's Story

Building from a Context of Censorship: Palestine and Arab America

While pursuing my doctoral degree in sociology at Northwestern University (1980–88), I visited Morocco with some colleagues. That experience, so different from any that I had before on many levels, awakened my sociological imagination (Mills 1959), and upon my return to school I was thirsty to deepen my knowledge. I suddenly realized that after some six years of university "training" I had not learned anything about the world outside of the West (which speaks poorly but accurately about sociology at the time). Seeking book knowledge, I found the collections of the Northwestern University library totally unhelpful. Its holdings exposed a stark disjuncture between what I had observed on my trip and how Arabs were spoken about in the social science literature, which reeked of a blatant racism that even the uninformed couldn't miss. This finding prompted me to change the direction

6. The absence of an "Arab American" category in data gathering on COVID-19 illnesses and deaths in Illinois is a case in point (Assad, Tucker, and Hacker 2021a). Only after demands for being counted arose from the Arab American community did the situation change, and data gathering on Arab American vaccination rates in Illinois began (Assad, Tucker, and Hacker 2021b).

of my dissertation research and to conduct an ethnographic study of Arabs living in metropolitan Chicago (a summation of a much longer process of discernment). I eventually focused on Palestinians because they were the largest Arab group present in the city. It seemed only natural that I would seek the mentorship of Northwestern's prominent urban sociologist Janet Abu-Lughod. Although Abu-Lughod was not a scholarly expert on Arab immigration or Arab Americans—not only was it not her field, but there was also not that much scholarly literature available, especially sociological—she offered finely honed methodological skills, conceptual critique, political insight, and emotional support for traversing an unexpected minefield. Throughout my long and deep relationship with Janet and her husband, Ibrahim, a political science professor at Northwestern, I was mentored through the global, domestic, transnational, and hostile political terrain I needed to comprehend.

After having built ties within the Palestinian community, I attended an invigorating and powerful concert by Marcel Khalife in 1982, my first community-wide event. Three months later, the Israeli military invaded Lebanon. Driving with a friend to California at the time, I was appalled at the way this violence was portrayed by the US media I observed in truck stops, restaurants, and motel lobbies. The bomb-dropping planes swooping over their victims relayed a fantasy of visual excitement; the persons around me expressed thrill at the spectacle. I learned in a visceral way that somehow I was no longer one of "them." I was in pain. I called Janet from a phone booth in the Arizona desert and asked her if I should go back to Chicago, to which she replied, "Oh, honey, there will be much more like this." The Israeli siege of Beirut followed and culminated in the Phalangist-led, Israeli-facilitated massacre of Palestinians at the Sabra and Shatila refugee camps. Other notable events occurring during my research phase included the (weakly investigated) murder of the ADC Los Angeles regional director Alex Odeh, the US Immigration and Naturalization Service's (INS) attempt to denaturalize and deport two Chicago Palestinian activists, the FBI arrests of the "LA 8" activists on (false) charges of terrorism (a case in which defense attorneys asked me to testify), and the release of an INS working document proposing a US internment camp for "alien terrorists and undesirables"—non-US citizens from a list of Arab and Muslim countries. There was also a US military attack on Libya, during which I observed a "kill the Arabs" banner hung from a dorm at a nearby university. These events and many others brought tangible anguish to members of the community I was researching and distinctly colored their American experience. As my interlocutors repeatedly stated, "If supporting this is what being American means, I decline!" (thus exposing the parochial narrowness of dominant assimilation theory). A couple of things became clear: that the lives of Arab Americans could not be understood without reference to matters global and that Arab Americans had been racialized by intent in order to facilitate and gain popular consent for the global aspirations of the US government and its allies: US empire. The structural relationship between, on the one hand, the production and maintenance of a domestic climate of anti-Arab and anti-Muslim racism—generated through deployment of the barbarism frame and "the terrorist" and "oppressed women" tropes—and, on the other, the interests of US, US-proxy, and Israeli military, economic, and social engineering projects could not be clearer. The purpose of this racial project was (and remains) to justify aggression and to silence dissent. These ideas and research findings were totally at odds with race theory of the time, especially as I argued for recognizing the intersection of domestic and global systems of racialized subordination tied to empire, and so they would suffer in the silences imposed by scholarly gatekeepers.

Navigating Silencing and Censorship

The Abu-Lughods had warned me of the climate of academic censorship that existed around Arab and Arab American points of view (especially concerning Israel/Palestine) and had alerted me to the fact that I would find both publishing and academic employment a difficult challenge because of my focus on Palestinians. I distinctly recall Janet saying, "You will never get an academic job if you pursue this topic." As I had entered this research project knowing nothing about Palestinians, it took a while for me to comprehend why an ethnographic study of Palestinians would be so threatening to the academy, a peril perhaps crystalized in my department chair's request that I take down a poster of Palestinians in my office because some faculty found the display of "terrorists" offensive. These minor but persistent reprimands did not sidetrack my research; rather, they ignited my spirit of struggle, making this counterhegemonic work even more important to me. *Nothing* in my years of field research among Palestinians, Arabs, and Muslims had resonated with the stereotypes of them so widely promoted. The relationship between knowledge and power was laid bare. Over time I saw that much sociological production was vested in racial hierarchy and empire, even when it stated otherwise. Indeed, social theory tells us that we should expect pushback precisely *because* of the strength of the relationship between knowledge and power.

In academia, this pushback has characterized the struggles to be legible by scholars rejecting orientalist frameworks that systematically racialize and denigrate "people from the East" both within Middle East (area) studies and within ethnic studies, critical race studies, and American studies. In an important but unpublished piece, Yvonne Haddad (2010) documents Arab American scholars' many contributions to the field of Middle East studies, which, she says, radically altered the way the "Middle East" was thought about and studied. Without them, she argues, orientalists à la Bernard Lewis and Martin Kramer would have remained dominant in the Middle East Studies Association (MESA) for another few decades, irrespective of the publication of Edward Said's paradigm-shattering book *Orientalism* in 1978. The AAUG, driven by Arab American scholars, played an important developmental role in these changes as it provided a scholarly forum for methodologies, ideas, and research that challenged dominant writing and teaching about Arabs and the Arab world. Its role was especially crucial as it "became clear" that the American Oriental Society and MESA "would not accommodate [these Arab American scholars'] ideas or allow them to read papers or publish their research" (Haddad 2010, 11). The imperial incentives behind this type of censorship are ongoing, as discussed later.

During my graduate school days and prior to them, Arab Americans established their own presses to make writings on Arabs and Arab Americans legible, circumventing the substantial mainstream barriers to publishing their work. For example, the AAUG Press published, among other scholarly books, *The Civil Rights of Arab Americans: The Special Measures* (Bassiouni 1974) and *Arab Americans: Continuity and Change* (Abu-Laban and Suleiman 1989) as well as the journal *Arab Studies Quarterly*, founded by Ibrahim Abu-Lughod and Edward Said. Other presses included Medina University Press, established by Ibrahim Abu-Lughod, which copublished with AAUG *The Arab Americans: Studies in Assimilation* (Hagopian and Paden 1969) and *Arabs in America: Myth and Reality* (Abu-Laban and Zeady 1985); the American Arab Affairs Council, which published Edmund Ghareeb's edited volume on US media representations of Arabs, *Split Vision*, in 1983 and Janice Terry's *Mistaken Identity: Arab Stereotypes in Popular Writings* in 1985; and the short-lived Amana Press, which published Michael Suleiman's *Arabs in the Mind of America* in 1988. Still actively publishing are the Institute for Palestine Studies, which publishes monographs and the *Journal of Palestine Studies*; Interlink Publishing, which publishes Arabic literature in translation as well as history and current-affairs titles under its imprint Olive Branch Press; and Post-Apollo Press.

In the 1980s, a handful of books on Arab Americans were available outside of Arab American venues, but none by major university presses. They included Abdo Elkholy's *The Arab Moslems in the United States* (1966), published by College and University Press; Barbara Aswad's *Arabic Speaking Communities in American Cities* (1974), published by the Center for Migration Studies; Philip Kayal and Joseph Kayal's *The Syrian-Lebanese in America: A Study in Religion and Assimilation* (1975), published by Twayne; Sameer Abraham and Nabeel Abraham's *Arabs in the New World: Studies on Arab-American Communities* (1983), published by Wayne State University Press; Alixa Naff's *Becoming American: The Early Arab Immigrant Experience* (1985), published by Southern Illinois University Press; and, although not on Arab Americans but rather on representations of them, Jack Shaheen's path-breaking book *The TV Arab* (1984), published by Bowling Green State University Popular Press. In addition, the left-leaning *Middle East Report* devoted a special issue (number 34) to Arab American auto and farmworkers in 1975 and published articles on Yemenis in the United States in 1977 and 1986.

This early body of literature on Arab Americans was highly interdisciplinary and displayed varying methods and writing styles; nonetheless, some prominent themes stand out. One might be called "we exist" as scholars made the repeated claim that Arab Americans were an unknown, almost hidden population to both scholars and the public.[7] This theme coexisted with another prominent claim, "you know us wrongly," referencing the extensive stereotyping of Arabs as terrorists in US mainstream media and popular culture. Scholars highlighted the contradiction of being simultaneously invisible and hypervisible, yet the co-constitutive relationship between these two states and their larger political meaning were largely left unquestioned. Scholars believed that their work exposing negative representations and their punitive outcomes (e.g., harassment, hate crimes, civic and political exclusion) and creating visibility by conducting ethnographies, community studies, and surveys of Arab American points of view, which highlighted the varied histories and internal complexities of Arab Americans, were the answer to the visible/invisible predicament. The Arab American community studies conducted by the ADC Research Institute were part of this trend (Hooglund 1985, 1987; Zogby 1984). Similarly, making evident internal diversity fought back against the flattening, monolithic racist stereotypes so prevalent at the time. Yet the bracketing off of Arab American studies from larger bodies of mainstream scholarship meant that those who stood to benefit most from this knowledge would never see it.

"Historic change" was another common theme in the scholarly literature of the time in terms of demography, identities, and what might be called "modes of adaptation," expressed through terms such as *assimilation*, *resurgent ethnicity*, and *marginalization*. Scholarship produced a pre- and post–World War II narrative that identified significant differences between who came before and after the war, with the latter being much more diverse in country of origin, social class, level of education, occupation, and religion and therefore more differentiated in positionalities, interpretations, and performances of being an Arab in America. One of the most important changes observed by these scholars was the significant increase in the number of Muslims among Arab Americans. Here the joined description "Arab and Muslim" begins to unfold in Arab American studies, not only because of its demographic fact but also in recognition of these two groups' conflation in popular discourses and representations and of the parallels between them in the operations of the US national-security state and its military. The Iranian Revolution of 1979 had brought about new, postnationalist challenges to US hegemony in the region; representations followed suit by flattening Arabs and Muslims into a singular terrorist stereotype. This representational fusion provoked (and continues to provoke) popular violence against Arabs, other brown people whether they are Muslim or not, and Muslims whether they are Arab or not, making it difficult to conceptually separate these groups when examining patterns of racist attacks. The work of Nabeel Abraham (1994) on anti-Arab racism and violence was especially poignant on these points.

Finally, the rise of a panethnic Arab American identity was another theme of the scholarship of this era, observed as a significant change from prior localized identities and attributed mainly to pan-Arabist ideologies prevalent at the time, the Israeli conquest of the rest of Palestine, the racist anti-Arab US media, and domestic efforts to organize dissent. Bassiouni's civil rights monograph of 1974, with significant contributions from Abdeen Jabara, although not a work of social science (both Bassiouni and Jabara were attorneys), remains important because it anchors the commencement of the US government's securitization of Arab Americans and aggressive deportation policy, both under the pretext of terrorism, in the decades long before the 9/11 attacks and locates these measures as mainly efforts to stifle dissent and freedom of speech. The name "Arab American" is therefore rooted in global political formations that aspired to strength in Arab unity, domestic antidiscrimination work, and dissent to pro-Zionist politics. "Arab American" emerged

7. Students in the University of Michigan system have been using #WeExist as their campaign slogan in advocating for a "Middle East and North Africa" category on university forms.

as a countername to "Middle Easterner," an imposed appellation few Arabs have identified with because of its orientalist origins. Yet "Arab American" is also embraced within other conceptualizations, such as SWANA, that bind broader swaths of land and people and epistemologically shift mainstream understandings of Arab Americans and their homelands.

Much of this early work on Arab Americans bears the imprint of an immigrant generation of scholars who saw the "problem" for Arabs in America as one that could be fixed with greater knowledge production, dedicated outreach strategies, and better leadership, here and abroad. Once provided with accurate information, the US American public would see the truths about Palestine. Once legible, Arab Americans could provide a "bridge of understanding" (Suleiman and Abu-Laban 1989, 13) between the US American public and the US government that would steer US foreign policy in a more humane and just direction. The problem with these dominant themes, designed to make Arab Americans visible for who they *really* were and to fix the problems of global misrepresentation, was that their focus detached the study of Arab Americans from the larger domestic context of racial oppression. Although many Arab American activists and some scholars drew connections between Arab Americans' experiences and those of other people of color, the institutional barriers noted earlier prevented any kind of scholarly solidification of these ideas (see Cainkar 2018).

The aforementioned themes are thus notable for the ideas they did not fertilize: that Arabs were one among many oppressed groups in the United States with shared experiences of white supremacy, including its binary notions of who was civilized and who was not.[8] Although Said's *Orientalism* (1978) had exposed the ways in which the degradations invented by imperialism are systemic and thus not defeated by greater knowledge or the "truth," much of this generation of scholars of Arab America remained optimistic that their work could make a difference, where "making a difference" was directed toward the goals of inclusion and anti-imperialism. Their optimism assumed that attitude change could occur absent structural change, a faulty premise laid bare in critical race theory.

At the same time, we must recognize that dominant social science theorizing at the time—its focus on attitudes, majority-minority "relations," modernity, and development instead of on intersecting structures of oppression—was a by-product of white supremacy (as well as of patriarchy and heteronormativity) and provided little opening for the kinds of critique that would later unfold in Arab American studies. The last thing scholars of Arab America felt they needed to produce in their struggle for recognition was work unintelligible to the purveyors of mainstream paradigms. It was the next generation of scholars, emerging in parallel to the rise of intersectional frameworks and critical race, feminist, and queer studies, who explored the systemic nature of the relationships between, on the one hand, white supremacy and imperialism and, on the other, invisibility/hypervisibility, extralegal violence, state surveillance, and negative representations, thus inching the field of Arab American studies closer to an intersectional critical race perspective.

Circuitous Routes: Out of Academia, into Activism and Advocacy, Back to the Academy

Janet Abu-Lughod was right; I found no reception for my scholarship in mainstream sociology. My ideas—such as that domestic racism could be deployed to serve global (in addition to domestic) interests or that research on refugees in the United States would benefit from including persons not officially deemed refugees by the US government (e.g., Palestinians, some Lebanese)—were rejected outright. I was seemingly unqualified for teaching positions or postdocs in race and ethnic studies because the people I studied were both invisible (seen as neither white ethnics nor people of color) and upsetting, and my research proposals went unfunded (some came back to me with comments such as "What do Arabs have to teach us about anything?"). At the same time, published leaders in the field whom I met at MESA conferences or at conferences focused on Arab Americans (the few spaces we could speak)—especially Michael Suleiman, Barbara

8. There are multiple reasons for this. See the introduction to part three, "Race, Religion, and the Discourse of Multiculturalism."

Aswad, Yvonne Haddad, and Elaine Hagopian—brought me into the Arab American studies fold. I continued to publish from my dissertation, using more acceptable paradigms of social class and gender in the next series of edited volumes on Arab Americans that were beginning to find receptivity in university presses. These texts included collected volumes such as Earle Waugh, Sharon Abu-Laban, and Regula Qureshi's *Muslim Families in North America* (1991), published by the University of Alberta Press; Ernest McCarus's *The Development of Arab-American Identity* (1994), published by the University of Michigan Press; and Barbara Aswad and Barbara Bilgé's *Family and Gender among American Muslims* (1996) and Michael Suleiman's *Arabs in America: Building a New Future* (1999), both published by Temple University Press. The shifting terrain of Arab American studies is notable in that two of these volumes had "Muslim" in their title and included chapters on Turks and Iranians. These collections as well as Joe Kadi's volume *Food for Our Grandmothers* (1994) and Evelyn Shakir's monograph *Bint Arab* (1997) marked the next decade of publishing in the field, as reflected in my coeditors' narratives.

Although my dissertation (1988) focused on Palestinian Muslim women in the US and their everyday acts of political resistance to "keep Palestine alive," a presentation of my scholarship at a National Women's Studies Association (NWSA) meeting elicited substantial hostility from scholars in the audience.[9] Arab/Muslim women, especially Palestinian women, were not permitted a voice, these scholars argued, because their men were so patriarchal and oppressive. At a reception, a subsequent conversation with a top sociologist, feminist, and Asian American studies scholar rendered the same verdict. Rather than being allowed to speak, I had to defend! Key writings of Arab American feminists in this reader testify to their struggles for recognition as they found themselves censored by both mainstream white feminists and women of color. I learned only later that Arab American women scholars were also shouted down by feminists at NWSA meetings, unable to discuss their research papers, and instead forced to account for "Arab misogyny." In addition, because my research was on people who happened to be Muslim, I sought to speak and publish in scholarly venues whose interests were religious studies, only to find a similar outcome. Muslims could be spoken about only as an exotic religious group, not as human beings or as women with agency. In the end, I left academia's unwelcome climate for a while and thus missed out on the solidarity that could be found working with the rising group of Arab American studies feminist scholars such as Evelyn Shakir, Carol Haddad, Joe Kadi, Lisa Suhair Majaj, Nada Elia, Therese Saliba, Nadine Naber, and the coeditors of this volume. Had I known these feminists then, my NWSA experience would not have been so powerfully rejecting and isolating. Indeed, feminist scholars have been at the forefront of Arab American studies and were the ones most responsible for exposing the direct relationship between representations and silencing, white supremacy, and imperialism. (Tearing down patriarchy in the field of Middle East studies also required a feminist revolution; see Joseph 2021). Nonetheless, I was not totally isolated: I experienced an incredible embrace from the Palestinian women I interviewed in Chicago as well as from the members of the Union of Palestinian Women's Associations, especially its president, Camille Odeh, who gave voice to my work at its annual conferences, helped me build strong ties in Palestine, and invited me to lead the first women's solidarity delegation to Palestine. These relationships eventually led to my being a founding board member of Chicago's community-based Arab American Action Network. But what is perhaps most important is that whereas my work was silenced by those who dominated the scholarly world, it was lifted up by Palestinian women.

9. My other mentor was Arlene Kaplan Daniels, a noted feminist scholar and activist at the time. She encouraged me to focus on "the everyday" in Palestinian women's lives, which is precisely where I located acts of resistance and sovereignty. Janet Abu-Lughod had recommended Daniels for my committee as one of the few department faculty who would not be hostile to my work on Arabs/Palestinians. Daniels's research concerned gender, social class, and occupations, and she was a strong fighter for women's equity at Northwestern and in sociological associations and journal editorships. Earlier in her career, she had joined other faculty at San Francisco State in support of a student strike over demands for Black studies and ethnic studies programs and, as a result, was denied tenure there. Nonetheless, her theoretical perspective notably excluded race and would be considered white liberal feminist today.

As for my trajectory, I did other work (and writing) that had meaning. Ibrahim Abu-Lughod and Edward Said introduced me to the Chicago-based Palestine Human Rights Campaign (founded in 1980 by Jim Zogby) and its director Don Wagner, and I spent a number of years documenting, writing about, and speaking on conditions for Palestinians living under Israeli rule. I later partnered with the Jerusalem-based Palestine Human Rights Information Center and its Palestinian fieldworkers (who were former prisoners) to more systematically document the Israeli government's population-control and removal policies. With the first US invasion of Iraq, I conducted fieldwork in Iraq and Kuwait and published research on the impacts of that invasion, of economic sanctions on Iraqis, and of the expulsions of Palestinians and Jordanians from Kuwait (Yemenis, too, were expelled from Saudi Arabia). Then, the climate for research that lifted the narratives of the oppressed and global progressive ideas and activism radically changed following the end of the Cold War and the first Gulf War (a story too long to tell here). I attempted again to locate a university job, at times applying for positions in Asian American studies, but my specialty was still not what any sociology department was interested in; Arab Americans were still illegible, and study of them found no place in the academy. I turned to conducting community-based research and advocacy on the lives and struggles of immigrants in the United States and eventually became a program director at the Illinois Coalition for Immigrant and Refugee Rights. Each of these choices outside of the academy was a product of the strong mentorship of the politically engaged Abu-Lughods. I was able to return to academia only when the gates were opened by those who thought it was important to know how Arab and Muslim Americans were faring in the post-9/11 onslaught of hate, surveillance, incarceration, deportation, and immigration restrictions. Yet, still, it is interesting to note that I was hired to teach in a social justice major at Marquette University and not by a sociology program; sociology's openness was yet to come. Entering through that gate did not mean that the struggle against a climate of censorship had ended, but it did provide a better position from which to argue for making Arab American studies legible within academia.

Pauline's Story

Institutionalizing Arab American Studies: Cultural and Academic Pathways

The theme of storytelling that we have adopted for this introduction points to the ways in which stories give shape and meaning to experience, however selective and incomplete. Though idiosyncratic, the story of how I came to participate in Arab American studies also dovetails with the story of the field's emergence from relative obscurity to growing, if still insufficient, recognition within academia. It also points to the impact of world events and of cultural as well as political institutions on the field's development.

As an undergraduate at the University of California at Berkeley in the 1980s, I was still a relatively recent newcomer to the United States from Lebanon, and Arab American studies was not yet to me a recognizable academic field. To my mind, the writers of the *mahjar*, those early immigrants to the Americas who participated in literary production, were linked to their place of origin and epitomized by Kahlil Gibran, whose home and museum—a cavelike space filled with ethereal drawings, love letters, and metaphysical writing—I had visited in the mountains of North Lebanon as a child. Though I did come across Gibran's *The Prophet* in American bookstores, I did not see course listings that explored either his works or those of his contemporaries, let alone anything by more recent Arab American writers. With a few exceptions, most comparative literature departments were still largely Eurocentric, and area studies focused on language and politics, or so it seemed to my inexperienced eyes then. Drawn to literary studies, I settled on Shakespeare and English Renaissance drama, in part because I found this work fascinating but also because Berkeley offered interesting courses in that field by exciting scholars who were focusing on gender, representation, and historical/cultural materialism—modes of analysis that engage me to this day. While considering graduate studies in literature, I contemplated exploring Arab responses to Shakespeare's plays but was dissuaded from doing so, perhaps too easily, by an offhand remark from a professor in a program I was considering. However, when I was a graduate student at Northwestern University, then visiting feminist Shakespearean scholar Constance Jordan asked me why I wasn't doing anything that drew on my knowledge of Arabic and interest in comparative studies. In that same period, the chair of the English Department, Martin Mueller, invited me to teach a seminar on Arabic literature in translation. This course offering was possible because of a departmental policy that allowed graduate students to teach outside their immediate research projects. The course also seemed timely because of the sudden interest in Arabic literature that arose after Naguib Mahfouz received the Nobel Prize in Literature in 1988, the first time the award was given to an Arab writer. This experience would prove instrumental, leading to my first published article, a piece that appeared in the book *Etel Adnan: Critical Essays on the Arab-American Writer and Artist* edited by Lisa Suhair Majaj and Amal Amireh (2001a). This work was also a fitting entrée into the burgeoning field of Arab American studies. As Majaj and Amireh observe in their introduction to the book, "Adnan occupies a central role for a transnational community of writers and artists" because she "helped to link Arab and Arab-American artists and writers, and to bring Arab cultural production into the space of American and European literature, philosophy and art" (2001b, 1). Tellingly, the English translation (from French) of Adnan's work was released by an independent publisher, the Post-Apollo Press, founded by Adnan's lifetime partner and fellow artist, Simone Fattal. Adnan's work, its publication in translation by a small press, and my trajectory toward it reflect the development of Arab American studies at the intersection of—but also marginal to—conventional fields within academia. My experience as a graduate student also demonstrates the importance of creating recognizable fields of study that undergraduate students can explore and that universities can support through course offerings and faculty hiring.

Unconventional Movements and Migrations: Weaving a Way toward the Field

Like my entry into the field, my work in it has developed outside the conventions and along the periphery. My dissertation, for example, is not on Arab American literature, and my teaching appointments have included a number of temporary positions in English departments at colleges in the United States, Southeast Asia, and Arab countries, mirroring, in a way, the migrant experiences of so many transnational and diasporic academics as well as the multidirectional movement of Arab Americans from and to Arab and non-Arab countries, what Carol W. N. Fadda has called "returns and rearrivals" (Fadda-Conrey 2014, 68). And though such a peripatetic life necessarily brought with it academic precarity, it also proved liberating, affording me the freedom to teach and explore topics that did not fall within a predefined institutional track. This meant I could include work from the growing body of Arab American writing in many of my literature courses while also exploring avenues for scholarship outside standard academic pathways.

One of these unconventional avenues to Arab American scholarship opened up when I discovered the magazine *Al Jadid: A Review and Record of Arab Culture and Arts* in the early 2000s. Launched in 1995 by Elie Chalala, *Al Jadid* provided a space for me and a number of others to engage critically with both Arab and Arab American intellectual and cultural production. For a time, I became a regular contributor, producing articles, book reviews, and translations from Arabic to English for the magazine. During this same period and through my work with *Al Jadid*, I started discovering an ever-growing body of Arab American literature, much of which had not yet made its way to university libraries, though some of it was beginning to attract major publishers. It was this new body of Arab American literature, along with the cultural institutions supporting it, that articulated many of the themes that would come to occupy the field and inspired my own participation in it.

Although Arabs in the United States in particular and in the Americas at large have actively participated in literary production for more than a hundred years, the designation "Arab American literature" did not emerge until the 1980s (Majaj 2012, 42; Pickens 2010), and it was not until the 1990s that writing by self-identified Arab Americans entered the mainstream. One of the earliest works to highlight Arab Americans' experiences published by a mainstream US press is Diana Abu-Jaber's *Arabian Jazz*, a novel that was first released in 1993 by Harcourt Brace and then republished in 2003 by Norton, two powerful publishing companies. Unevenly received by Arab Americans for its depiction of Arab characters that some audiences felt reinforced stereotypes of Arabs, the novel nonetheless marks a turning point in its presentation of characters who grapple with their Arab American identities and whose struggles are articulated in relation to US racial and ethnic discourses. Naomi Shihab Nye's *Words under the Words* (1995), which combined three of Nye's earlier collections from 1980 on, was published by the more specialized Eighth Mountain Press and featured a woman in traditional Palestinian dress on its cover. Joe Kadi's highly impactful collection *Food for Our Grandmothers: Writings by Arab-American & Arab-Canadian Feminists* (1994), published by South End Press, would mark a turning point in Arab American writing. Drawing on traditions developed in feminist and ethnic studies, the collection gathered various voices that combined poetry with personal accounts and included both creative and critical reflections centered in Arab American and Arab Canadian experiences. Rabih Alameddine's novel *Koolaids: The Art of War* (1998), which takes the reader back and forth between San Francisco at the height of the AIDS epidemic and Lebanon in the midst of the civil war, was published by Picador, a division of St. Martin's Press. These contributions by Arab American writers not only made inroads into mainstream American publishing spheres but also delineated important themes that remain resonant to this day and that are reflected in this reader: questions of naming; representation; maps and location; ethnic identity; food and grandmothers; invisibility/visibility; anti-Arab and anti-Muslim racism; Arab, American, and transnational belonging; feminism and queer critique; orientalism; migration; and cross-racial affiliation.

A prominent theme that cannot be ignored in Arab American writing of the early 2000s has to do with the tragedy of 9/11 and the consequent atmosphere of suspicion, surveillance, and detention of Arabs and Muslims in the United States. One of the first lyrical expressions in response to 9/11 is Suheir Hammad's "first writing since," a poem that went viral online and was later published on YouTube as a performance for Def Poetry (Hammad 2011). Longer works would soon follow, including Laila Halaby's *Once in a Promised Land* (2007) and Rajia Hassib's *In the Language of Miracles* (2015). Philip Metres's *Sand Opera* (2015) confronts the horrors of torture of those held at Abu Ghraib, while Diana Abu-Jaber's *Crescent* (2003b) reminds us that the treatment of Arabs and Muslims as suspect terrorists long preceded the trauma of 9/11.

Yet another prominent theme in Arab American writing has to do with the tradition of Arab oral storytelling, especially in relation to the tales of *The Thousand and One Nights* and the figure of Shahrazad, with at least ten or more works alluding to it published in the span of thirty years. This preoccupation with *The Thousand and One Nights* in Arab American literature and its entanglement with questions of orientalism, gender, and heteronormativity are addressed in this reader by the contributions from Matthew Jaber Stiffler (chapter 26), and me (chapter 27; see also Sabry 2011, Sawires-Masseli 2018, and Shomali 2018).

As the theme of storytelling highlights, it is through the stories we tell about ourselves that we begin to shape both how we come to see and understand ourselves and how we render ourselves legible to the world around us. And, indeed, it is through the stories told by and about Arab and Arab American writers that the field of Arab American studies has come to be shaped. These are issues that Joe Kadi and Michelle Hartman take up in their contributions to this reader (see chapters 1 and 5). With few exceptions, however, these stories are rarely afforded space in college curricula, and where they are, they are often framed through orientalist frameworks that position Arabs and Muslims as "others" whose experiences revolve around some sort of binary and inevitable clash: modernity/tradition, religious fanaticism/tolerance, women's oppression/liberation, terrorism/freedom. Such narrow framing is accomplished through what we might call the politics of inclusion, which operates on two levels: one is through the stories chosen to be told and retold, and the other is through the paratexts that accompany the stories (various introductions, explanations, and editorial explanations that frame our understanding of those stories)—a topic that Dima Ayoub (2020) explores in her work on translations of Arabic literature and that Michelle Hartman addresses in chapter 5 (see also Amireh 2000; Hartman 2012).

Moving from Tokenized Inclusion toward Self-Definition

Through their paratexts and selections from Arab and Arab American writers, many, if not most, literary anthologies geared toward college writing and introduction-to-literature courses tend to reproduce this politics of inclusion in that, unlike most anthologies of the 1980s, they now include work by Arab and Arab American writers, but those works selected tend to repeat hackneyed themes and perpetuate the association of Arabs with inferiority, oppression, and violence.[10] The repetition of particular themes in relation to narratives about Arabs and Arab Americans reproduces "the dangers of a single story" (Adichie 2009), limiting and homogenizing how Arab Americans are seen and understood. As such, this repetition operates in the guise of inclusion to further advance exclusionary practices that justify US military interventions abroad (Alsultany 2012; McAlister [2001] 2005; Naber 2008) as well as domestic surveillance and detention at home (Abraham, Howell, and Shryock 2011; Cainkar 2018; Jarmakani 2011; Naber 2008). Evelyn Alsultany addresses this point in her discussion of media representations of Arabs, which, she says, offer "simplified complex representations" that repeatedly equate Arabs with threats to security even if the media appear unbiased in the way they "seek to balance a negative representation with a positive one" (2012, 14; see also chapter 21). Clearly, inclusion is not in itself sufficient to challenge negative representations of Arabs.

In my own classes, I eschew such anthologies and assign texts of my own choosing. However, it is clear that more needs to be done to support historically grounded, theoretically nuanced, and richly varied approaches to teaching and scholarship in Arab American studies—hence, the importance of producing our own anthologies and cultural institutions as critical interventions in the discourse on Arab Americans within both academic and cultural arenas. Indeed, one can argue that anthologies have been critical in advancing the field of Arab American studies, reflecting both the collaborative character of this field and the need to intervene and redefine ways of seeing (Berger 1972) and listening to Arabs and Arab Americans.[11] This realization has driven my own

10. It is important to note that this growing inclusion is not universal. For example, no work by Arab- or Arab American–identified writers is included in the *Norton Anthology of Short Fiction* (2020) edited by Richard Bausch and R. V. Cassill. It was only in 2020 that the popular *Norton Reader*, edited by Melissa Goldthwaite and others, added a selection by an Arab American writer, which is a piece by Diana Abu-Jaber titled "Lamb Two Ways," a humorous and personal account that nonetheless highlights differences in cultures as it relates the culinary rivalry between Abu-Jaber's Irish Catholic grandmother and her Jordanian-born father. Similarly, only one short poem titled "To Manage" by Naomi Shihab Nye is included in the 1,500-page-long ironically named *Compact Bedford Introduction to Literature*, edited by Michael Meyer and D. Quentin Miller published in 2020. Two pieces appear in the anthology *Globalization* (2013) edited by Maria Jerskey and published by Oxford University Press, which is aimed at American college-writing courses; one is Leila Ahmed's "Reinventing the Veil" and the other is Latif Nasser's "Do Some Cultures Have Their Own Ways of Going Mad?" The 2017 edition of Cengage's *The New World Reader* edited by Gilbert Muller offers an exception and includes two pieces by Arab American writers, "Deportation Order" by the pugnacious Randa Jarrar and the prose piece "To Any Would-Be Terrorists" by the poet Naomi Shihab Nye, and one piece by American-born British Libyan writer Hisham Matar called "The Light." Matar's piece is included in a section titled "The Clash of Civilization: Is Conflict Avoidable?" Nye's is under a section titled "The Challenge of Globalization: What Are the Consequences?," and Jarrar's is in a section titled "New American Mosaic: Are We Becoming a Universal Nation?" Framed to stimulate discussion, these section divisions nonetheless place Arab writing within the framework of pro/con debates, topics that require some sort of defense to prove their legitimacy. The Pearson anthology *Writing Situations* (2015) edited by Sidney I. Dorbin includes Anwar Accawi's "The Telephone," which describes the advent of the telephone to his village in Lebanon in the 1950s. Admittedly, each of these pieces is worthwhile and compelling in its own right, yet when taken in isolation they perpetuate associations of Arabs with incidents of terror, backwardness, religious conservatism, and the veiling of women.

11. A number of Arab American anthologies in the overarching fields of the humanities and the social sciences have long played an important role in providing compelling interventions that disrupt homogenizing discourses of Arabs and Arab Americans, and several offer groundbreaking contributions to how we think about Arab American studies. Though it is impossible to list all titles, one might consider the following: *The Arab Americans: Studies in Assimilation* (1969) edited by Elaine Hagopian and Ann Paden, with an introduction by Ibrahim Abu-Lughod; *Arabic Speaking Communities in American Cities* (1974) edited by Barbara Aswad; *The Civil Rights of Arab Americans: The Special Measures* (1974) edited by M.

scholarship and participation in Arab American Studies and is reflected more broadly in literary and cultural associations, edited anthologies, and collaborative efforts at institution building in the field.

Perhaps because of the paucity of opportunities to develop the field within conventional academic tracks, many working within it have had to work to create it. Much of that work has included academic program development, as in the case of the collaboration between Evelyn Alsultany and Nadine Naber to develop the Arab and Muslim American Studies Program in the Department of American Culture at the University of Michigan, Ann Arbor. Others include the development of cultural organizations and literary associations outside of conventional academic frameworks. Many programs grew in concert with the blossoming of Arab American literature, and they offered invigorating alternative spaces for academics, activists, and cultural workers to meet, collaborate, and work together toward the development of Arab American studies.

The flourishing of Arab American literary and cultural production cannot be separated from either the political sphere affecting Arab Americans both before and after 9/11 or the absence of representation of Arab Americans within mainstream American culture and academia. Such a trajectory is in line with the formation of earlier Arab American associations, specifically the AAUG, which arose in response to anti-Palestinian US bias during the Six Day War of 1967 (as illustrated elsewhere in this reader—for example, by Cainkar in this introduction and by Suraya Khan in chapter 35). In its embrace of the nomenclature "Arab American," the AAUG centered itself in US multiethnic and transnational frames and endeavored to influence US foreign policy and public opinion through public engagement and the establishment of the *Arab Studies Quarterly*. In a similar vein, the cultural and literary associations that developed in the 1990s and early 2000s also endeavored to render visible Arab American concerns, influence public opinion about Arabs, and provide opportunities for scholarship. Paradoxically, as Amaney Jamal (2008) observes in the data she gathered from the Detroit Arab American Survey in 2003, the tragedy of 9/11 created both increased hostility and greater receptivity toward Arab Americans. She notes, for example, that even though non–Arab Americans were willing to "do away with the civil liberties of Arabs and Muslims" based on "perceived differences based on religious values," these differences "also paved the way for an opportunity. While worrying about the presence of the 'Other' in their midst, Americans are also attempting to learn more about this

---

Cherif Bassiouni; *Arabs in America: Myth and Reality* (1985) edited by Baha Abu-Laban and Faith Zeady; *Food for Our Grandmothers: Writings by Arab-American & Arab-Canadian Feminists* (1994) edited by Joe Kadi. Others include *Arabs in America: Building a New Future* (1999) edited by Michael Suleiman; *Grape Leaves: A Century of Arab American Poetry* ([1988] 2000) edited by Gregory Orfalea and Sharif Elmusa; *Post Gibran: Anthology of New Arab American Writing* (1999) edited by Munir Akash and Khaled Mattawa; *Scheherazade's Legacy: Arab and Arab American Women on Writing* (2004) edited by Susan Muaddi Darraj; *Dinarzad's Children: An Anthology of Contemporary Arab American Fiction* ([2004] 2009) edited by Pauline Kaldas and Khaled Mattawa; *Inclined to Speak: An Anthology of Arab American Poetry* (2008) edited by Hayan Charara; *Race and Arab Americans before and after 9/11: From Invisible Citizens to Visible Subjects* (2008) edited by Amaney Jamal and Nadine Naber; *Arab & Arab American Feminism: Gender, Violence, & Belonging* (2011) edited by Rabab Abdulhadi, Evelyn Alsultany, and Nadine Naber; *Arab Detroit 9/11: Life in the Terror Decade* (2011) edited by Nabeel Abraham, Sally Howell, and Andrew Shryock; *Between the Middle East and the Americas: The Cultural Politics of Diaspora* (2013) edited by Evelyn Alsultany and Ella Shohat; *Four Arab American Plays: Works by Leila Buck, Jamil Khoury, Yussef El Guindi, and Lameece Issaq & Jacob Kader* (2014) edited by Michael Malek Najjar; *The Edinburgh Companion to the Arab Novel in English: The Politics of Anglo Arab and Arab American Literature and Culture* (2015) edited by Nouri Gana; and *Arab-American Aesthetics: Literature, Material Culture, Film, and Theater* (2018) edited by Therí Pickens. Special issues may be counted in this category as well, and they include a number already referenced in this discussion, including a special issue of *Arab Studies Quarterly* titled "Arab Americans: Continuity and Change," with an introduction by Michael Suleiman and Baha Abu-Laban (1989) that was also republished as a book by AAUG with the title *Arab Americans: Continuity and Change* (Abu-Laban and Suleiman 1989). Other special issues include "Arab American Literature," published in *MELUS*, with an introduction by Salah Hassan and Marcy Jane Knopf-Newman (2006); a subsection of a special issue of *PMLA* titled "Writing while Arab," with an introduction by Nouri Gana (2008); a special section of *Mashriq & Mahjar* titled "New Directions in Arab American Studies" (2016) edited by Evelyn Alsultany, Louise Cainkar, and Pauline Homsi Vinson; and the special issue of *Amerasia Journal* titled "Arab/Americas: Locations & Iterations" (2018) edited by Sarah M. A. Gualtieri and Pauline Homsi Vinson and a special section of the *Journal of Palestine Studies* titled "Scholarly essays on Palestinian communities in the US and Canada" (2021), edited by Louise Cainkar.

population" (126, 127). Such a paradoxical stance toward Arab Americans might explain—at least in part—some of the new directions that cultural associations that had begun before 9/11 took in the decades after it.

Among the cultural institutions that emerged in the 1990s and that grew in number and influence in the 2000s are film festivals, theater companies, and literary associations. Film festivals include, among others, the Arab Film Festival, founded in 1996 in the San Francisco Bay Area, now expanded to become the Arab Film and Media Institute; the Chicago Palestine Film Festival, founded in 2002; the Twin Cities Arab Film Festival, founded in 2005; and the Boston Palestine Film Festival, founded in 2007. These prominent film festivals highlight uniquely Arab or Palestinian forms of expression, often in Arabic (see Cable, chapter 13, on questions of language, location, and authenticity in such festivals), but a number of pathbreaking theater groups also foreground cross-ethnic identity configurations. For example, Golden Thread, a theater company founded in 1996 by artistic director Torange Yeghiazarian in San Francisco, highlights on its website that it is dedicated to producing work from and about the Middle East. Similarly, Silk Road Rising, a theater company founded by Malik Gillani and Jamil Khoury in 2002 in Chicago, emphasizes its promotion of work by East Asian, Southeast Asian, and Middle Eastern communities. These companies' choices to adopt the designation "Middle Eastern" is instructive. Although it is rooted in a colonial past and perpetuates identity configurations developed in relation to geographical proximity to Europe and a hegemonic "West," the name "Middle East" nonetheless allows these companies to recognize cultural affinities and historical cross-cultural exchanges among multiethnic and multilinguistic groups such as Armenians, Iranians, Turks, Arabs, and Imazighen, who would not be brought together under the category "Arab" or "Arab American." Both Silk Road Rising and Golden Thread have opened opportunities for Arab American artists such as Yussef El Guindi, Andrea Assaf, Leila Buck, Betty Shamieh, Heather Raffo, and others to develop and share their work with wide audiences.

With a more US-centered focus on racialized identities, the Voices of Our Nations Arts Foundation (VONA), one of whose cofounders is Arab American writer Elmaz Abinader, was established in 1999 to offer writing workshops for writers of color, including Arab Americans, in the United States. Indicative of the way that Arab American studies straddles both the local and the global, Silk Road and Golden Thread highlight linkages between persons of Southwest Asian and North African backgrounds, while VONA forges alliances among historically marginalized communities in the United States.

The synergy between various cultural and literary associations has contributed to the flourishing of the field as well as to my own participation in it. In 2007, I participated in a conference organized by the Radius of Arab American Writers (RAWI) and held at the Arab American National Museum (AANM) in Dearborn, Michigan. This was the first conference I attended that was dedicated entirely to Arab American writing. RAWI, whose acronym means "storyteller" in Arabic, was founded in 1993 by Barbara Nimri Aziz with the aim of providing a supportive network for Arab American writers. The AANM was launched in 2005 under its founding director Anan Ameri, who has been a staunch advocate for encouraging Arab American scholarship through the museum and its available resources. Many of RAWI's members would publish their work in the journal *Mizna*. "Mizna" is a woman's name in Arabic that loosely means "desert cloud." Founded in 1999 in St. Paul, Minnesota, under the leadership of Katherine Haddad, *Mizna* was inspired by the newsletter of the Minnesota chapter of the ADC, a national organization founded in 1980 by former US senator James Abourezk and for which Haddad was local chapter president (Durrani 2002). Similarly, the AANM is an ACCESS institute. Founded in Dearborn, Michigan, in 1971 as a social service organization to assist Arab immigrants in adjusting to life in the United States, ACCESS also launched the National Network for Arab American Communities and the Center for Arab American Philanthropy. As the overlaps between these various groups reveal, the growth of Arab American studies was nurtured by the concerted efforts of a number of important collaborations. It was at the RAWI conference at the AANM in 2007 that I would begin to meet Arab American writers, activists, artists, and scholars in person, many of whom have now become dear friends and valued colleagues.

It was also from that same RAWI conference that a number of papers would get published in the subsection on "comparative racialization" titled "Writing while Arab" in the 2008 issue of *PMLA*. This issue, together with the 2006 special issue on Arab American literature in *MELUS: The Journal of the Society for the Study of the Multi-Ethnic Literature of the United States*, would mark a shift for Arab American literary scholarship from obscurity to minor recognition within US academia. No doubt this shift, as noted by Amaney Jamal (2008) and by Louise Cainkar earlier in this introduction, was impelled not only by a flourishing of scholarship in Arab American studies but also by the reception environment that evolved in the wake of 9/11. Arab American scholars found greater receptivity and avenues for publishing their work even if these opportunities were precipitated, at least in part, by suspicion of and orientalist curiosity about the Arab and Muslim "other."

Collaboration and Interdisciplinarity as Foundational to Field Formation

As is the case for others (see Cainkar's story in this introduction as well as Ameri 2011; Aziz 2004; Kadi 1994; Said 2005; Shakir 1997; and Yunis 2013, among others), my involvement in this field is motivated, at least in part, by the disconnect I have felt between my own experiences, first in Lebanon and later in the United States, and the stories about Arabs and Arab Americans perpetuated or omitted in US media and academia. The cultural, artistic, literary, and activist organizations that nurtured interdisciplinary spaces to develop the field outside academia also gave me the opportunity to participate in developing associations that would support the field within academia. For example, it was at the 2011 conference in honor of Michael Suleiman—also held at the AANM—that I would begin the collaborative, interdisciplinary work with the anthropologist Suad Joseph, the sociologist Rita Stephan, and the anthropologist Randa Kayyali to establish the AASA. Launched in 2012 with the assistance of its founding webmaster, Lutfi Hussein, a linguist, and with Suad Joseph as its founding president, the AASA would also hold its inaugural conference at the AANM in 2014. The AASA would eventually become an affiliate of both MESA and the American Studies Association (ASA), reflecting the way in which Arab American studies straddles and crosses disciplinary boundaries and academic fields of study.

My work in AASA opened a world of collaborative interdisciplinary engagement that counterbalanced the isolation I felt working in English departments, where I was often not just the only person of Arab background but also the only academic interested in Arab American studies. This isolation often contributed to feeling "out of place," as Edward Said (1999) puts it in the title of his memoir. Working collaboratively with scholars in different disciplines on projects related to Arab American studies energized me intellectually and offered me a type of scholarly home I appreciated. As a consequence, many of my projects in Arab American studies have been collaborative and interdisciplinary. For example, I coedited a number of special journal issues with the historian Sarah M. A. Gualtieri. The publications we contributed to, moreover, were not strictly in Arab American studies but also included *Amerasia*, a journal focused on Asian and Pacific Islander transcultural studies, and *The Encyclopedia of Women and Islamic Cultures*, run under the main editorial guidance of the anthropologist Suad Joseph. Similarly, *Mashriq & Mahjar*, which published a special section on Arab American studies that I coedited with the media studies specialist Evelyn Alsultany and the sociologist Louise Cainkar, is a journal of Middle Eastern and migration studies. These examples illustrate not only the productive nature of interdisciplinary scholarship but also how the illegibility and absence of academic institutional support for Arab American literary studies have contributed to its interdisciplinary character.

Such a circumstance also captures how the story of the field of Arab American studies is situated in historical moments and particular locations, and it highlights how the development of the field is linked not only to the cultural, creative, and scholarly circumstances of those working to advance it but also to the context of reception that can either invite or curtail it.

In 2014, I collaborated with Carol W. N. Fadda and Hatem Akil to form the Global Arab and Arab American Literature forum at the Modern Language Association (MLA). In a fitting coincidence, the push to gain approval for this forum was supported by then MLA president and Shakespearean scholar Margaret Ferguson, whose work I had studied at Northwestern during graduate school when I was still searching to find a way toward comparative Arab and Arab American studies. Like my coeditors Louise and Amira, I share my story to illustrate how my own trajectory in the field intertwined with one strand of the multilayered narrative of Arab American studies. Whereas the field was barely legible in the 1980s, now it is possible to find colleges and universities, albeit still few in number, that offer degrees or minors in Arab American studies.[12] A far greater number of campuses still do not provide a single course devoted to Arab American studies, suggesting that the reception environment for the field is at once facilitated and constrained by not only the creative and scholarly production within it but also by historical circumstance, reception environments, and the intersection of our individual lives and the themes we elucidate in this reader—namely, questions of migration, self-definition, race and racialization, orientalist representations of Arabs and Muslims, imperialism, and transnational and cross-ethnic affiliation and solidarities.

Amira's Story

Toward Collaboration: On Bridges and Other Solidarity Metaphors

Building on the themes of feminist collaboration so far reflected in my coeditors' narratives, I came to the field through the life-giving stories in foundational collections such as *Food for Our Grandmothers* edited by Joe Kadi, which inspired me to engage in scholarship. I found *Food* before I knew it was possible even to conceive of scholarly work on Arab Americans, much less to create a field of Arab American studies. At the time, I was working at the National Coalition against Domestic Violence and hungrily devouring feminist collections that I found at the local independent bookstore. *Food for Our Grandmothers* named an absence I had so deeply felt that it had not even been possible for me to articulate it.

The ineffable gift of creating space and possibility through naming the invisibility that, for me, had so far only been profoundly felt cannot be understated; it reverberated through other spaces of scholarly community building as well. In the same year that I applied to graduate school with the intention of studying Arab American literature, I responded to a call for contributions to what would later become *This Bridge We Call Home* (2002) edited by Gloria Anzaldúa and Ana Louise Keating and framed as a follow-up to the groundbreaking anthology *This Bridge Called My Back* (1981), edited by Cherríe Moraga and Gloria Anzaldúa. My creative essay submission was selected for inclusion in the collection, though the entire section in which my essay was to appear was abruptly cut by the publisher as the collection moved toward the copyedit phase; only a trace of my contribution remains in an epigraph to the introduction. Nevertheless, I was part of the revision process, and it was on a listserv for contributors that I became familiar with other Arab American women who understood themselves as coming to feminism through women-of-color theorizing. *This Bridge Called My Back*, a collection of writings by women of color, did not include any essays or poems by Arab Americans, and although the editors intentionally sought to include Arab American women in *This Bridge We Call Home*, our inclusion in the 2002 sequel, so to speak, was nevertheless punctuated by divisive and exclusionary politics among the contributors (and, in my case, by the ultimate excision of my essay). Tellingly, the listserv for contributors revealed how Zionism and charges of antisemitism functioned to silence, exclude, and/or alienate Arab American voices from such spaces and collections. Although the contributors who protested Zionist tactics of exclusion on the listserv—namely, Nadine Naber and Nada Elia—were not ultimately excluded from *This Bridge We Call Home*,

12. In addition to university programs mentioned earlier (see note 4) such as the University of Michigan at Ann Arbor, the University of Michigan–Dearborn, San Francisco State University, and Marquette University, it is worth mentioning that a number of campuses support faculty appointments and courses in Arab American studies. Among them are the English Department at Syracuse University, the American Race and Ethnicity Studies Program at the University of Southern California, the Global Asian Studies Program at the University of Illinois at Chicago, and both comparative ethnic studies and Asian American and Asian diaspora studies at the University of California at Berkeley.

they faced a barrage of attacks that the listserv moderators met with silence, avoidance (a passive form of censorship), and eventually marginalization. When the book project was threatened by the strife on the listserv, the moderators shut down the discussion, suggesting that it would be sidelined to a separate listserv. As Nada Elia concludes, "The centrality of the Palestinian issue to women of color generally—namely, the fact that we are a colonized people seeking to break through the distorted hegemonic narrative that either completely erases or totally misrepresents us—was once again pushed to the margins" (2011, 154). The way that marginalization and silencing played out in relation to *This Bridge We Call Home* aptly crystallizes how Zionist censorship intertwines with illegibility and the barriers that Arab and Arab American women face when organizing within women-of-color spaces. In the next subsection, I elaborate on each of these two threads to encompass a longer story and legacy of how they have played out in relation to the field of Arab American studies.

Censoring Palestine

As delineated in Louise's story, silencing and blocking research related to Palestine, to the SWANA region more broadly, and to their diasporas have a long history and a broad reach. These potent barriers manifest in the many untold stories of scholars who were sidelined or otherwise discouraged before even having the chance to enter the academy and are additionally demonstrated by the censorship, sanctioning, monitoring, and even firing of professors critical of the Zionist project. Campaigns against pro-Palestinian scholars at all stages of involvement with the academy are supported by well-funded groups such as Campus Watch, which has typically targeted professors, and Canary Mission, which has concentrated efforts more specifically on students advocating justice for Palestine. These groups often use a form of intimidation amounting to what Liz Jackson of Palestine Legal describes as "psychological warfare."[13] The case of Steven Salaita, who was "unhired" from his tenure-track appointment at the University of Illinois, Urbana–Champaign, because of his political tweets, powerfully demonstrates the material consequences of such campaigns. As Salaita (2019) notes, a theoretical commitment to academic freedom—even if it includes support from the American Association of University Professors—cannot protect academics at all levels from being fired, sanctioned, and—in Salaita's case—effectively barred from an academic position despite an extensive publishing record.

Indeed, Salaita's innovations in the field of American studies trace current forms of xenophobia, Islamophobia, and anti-Arab racism in the United States to the discourses deployed to defend the uprootings and violence perpetrated by settler colonialism. A special issue of the *American Quarterly* coedited by Rabab Abdulhadi and Dana Olwan (2015) grounds the ASA's historic vote in 2013 to endorse the Palestinian call for boycott, divestment, and sanctions (BDS) in the larger intellectual critique of the United States as a settler-colonial state. In their introduction, Olwan and Abdulhadi also situate Palestinian activism—such as Students for Justice in Palestine chapters, calls for BDS, and efforts to create connections between US and Palestinian universities, including Rabab Abdulhadi's own campus at San Francisco State University—within larger US histories of repression of student activism and academic dissent on college campuses (2015, 996–98). They build on the synergy of scholars and organizations such as the US Campaign for the Academic and Cultural Boycott of Israel[14] both to chart the material impacts of the repression of dissent as well as to highlight the importance of including comparative critiques of settler colonialism within American studies and other interdisciplinary and social-justice–oriented fields.

13. Here, Jackson is referring to data collected from interviews with more than two hundred people targeted by Canary Mission. She notes, for example, that "targets of Canary Mission have been denied entry to Palestine, fired from jobs, interrogated by employers and university administrators, and targeted with death threats and racial, homophobic misogynist harassment from Canary Mission followers. . . . People have reported their relationships with parents and business relationships being damaged. And that doesn't begin to describe the self-censorship and psychological warfare effects" (quoted in Cane 2018).

14. See also Chatterjee and Maira 2014, 2018; Deeb and Winegar 2015; Maira 2018; and Salaita 2015.

The cumulative impact of shutting down discussion and debate about Palestine undoubtedly stunted the development of Arab American studies as a field. In their essay "The Forgotten '-ism'" (2006), Nadine Naber, Eman Desouky, and Lina Baroudi explain: "Those who speak up about Palestinian rights agreed that they are often excluded, silenced, censored, and/or erased from progressive politics by the systematic, institutionalized attempts to exclude and delegitimize critiques of Israel" (104). Nevertheless, the fact that their essay appears in the collection *Color of Violence: The INCITE! Anthology* (INCITE! 2006) also speaks to the possibilities of forging connections with radical women-of-color organizations and scholarship.

Building Networks of Support

The various forms of alienation we have experienced—from the lack of support for our areas of interest to unwillingness to publish our research, challenges in finding suitable academic positions, and direct tactics of intimidation—require us to form strong networks of support. I found radical community in a group of scholars and activists—including Katherine Acey, Suzanne Adely, Yas Ahmed, Janaan Attia, Lara Deeb, Eman Desouky, Noura Erakat, Huda Jadallah, Nadine Naber, and Heba Nimr—as we came together to organize the Arab Movement of Women Arising for Justice (AMWAJ) in 2006, which welcomed upward of one hundred participants. We sought to build on the earlier work of Carol Haddad (among others), who founded the Feminist Arab-American Network (FAN), about which I say more later.

AMWAJ focused on intentionally creating space for Arab American women, inclusive of trans and nonbinary people, and intentionally welcoming queer ciswomen, trans, and nonbinary people to come together to build frameworks for dismantling structural oppression both internal to and external to our communities. Although the gathering certainly offered workshops and spaces to critique the external racism, orientalism, and imperialist sexism facing Arab women as well as trans and nonbinary people in the United States, we were also intentional about creating space to address issues internal to Arab American spaces. We adopted Audre Lorde's "eye to eye" framework to address critical issues of homophobia, internalized racism and colonialism, as well as controlling narratives of cultural authenticity that were operating within our communities. Audre Lorde's essay "Eye to Eye" ([1984] 2007) unpacks the way that internalized racism and white-supremacist hatred can recirculate as anger and hatred among Black women. She proposes as a response the practice of "being gentle with each other by being gentle with that piece of ourselves that is the hardest to hold." The AMWAJ gathering likewise privileged creating spaces in which we could, as Lorde says, "arm ourselves with ourselves and each other, and [where] we could stand toe to toe inside that rigorous loving and begin to speak the impossible—or what has always seemed like the impossible—to one another. The first step toward genuine change" (175). Aligning ourselves within a rich tradition of women-of-color theorizing, we also sought to solidify our analysis by confronting the ways we perpetuated institutionalized oppressions within Arab American feminist spaces. We considered the eye-to-eye framework a vital exercise to address internalized oppressions, but the gathering itself was also an energizing and galvanizing moment for Arab American feminist organizing and scholarship.

As Therese Saliba's essay in this reader demonstrates, such collaborative organizing existed well before the AMWAJ gathering in 2006. Though not the earliest example, the culmination of Arab and Arab American feminist organizing at NWSA conferences in the 1980s, which resulted in the founding of FAN in 1982, deserves elaboration. As Carol Haddad recounts, the NWSA conference in 1981, entitled "Women Respond to Racism," was a turning point, particularly due to debates about the relationships of both Arab and Jewish women to racism in the United States.[15] About her experience attending the conference, Haddad writes: "In the evenings, Arab American women in attendance met with one another and with women of other ethnic and racial groups to discuss [their] omission [from a panel entitled 'Anti-Semitism:

15. See also Feldman 2015, chapter 5, and Jarmakani 2011 for more on the NWSA conferences in the 1980s, Arab American feminisms, and women-of-color organizing against racism.

The Unacknowledged Racism'] and their rightful place as 'women of color.' For me that was an epiphany of sorts . . . connecting the dots between experienced childhood discrimination and systemic societal racism with permutations based upon degree of nonwhiteness" (2021, p. 250). Here, Haddad highlights two key elements in Arab American feminist organizing and scholarship: (1) finding and fostering the space to connect with other Arab American feminists as well as (2) developing critical analysis and building affiliations across feminist communities of color.

Although Haddad acknowledges AMWAJ as one example of continuity in the kind of networking that FAN sought to establish, it is critical also to mention the concurrent organizations with which AMWAJ organizers were affiliated. Many of us on the organizing committee had also been active with the Arab Women's Solidarity Association (AWSA), North America, which operated a listserv. Some of us were also part of the Radical Arab Women Action Network (RAWAN), which organized a presence at the INCITE! "Stopping the War on Women of Color" conference in 2005. Held in the Tremé district of New Orleans, one of the main historical neighborhoods of free people of color in a city that would be devastated by the levee breach during Hurricane Katrina just months later, the conference included Arab and Arab American feminist analyses of Palestine in a way that was energizing and exciting for the RAWAN members who attended. Though general engagement with these issues was mostly sidelined to a "Palestine 101" panel and the "militarism and war" track, which was poorly attended relative to the "reproductive justice" and "police brutality" tracks, the opportunity to think about these issues together was crucial. The title of the RAWAN-organized panel, "We Are Your Sisters, Too," demonstrates that this historical moment for Arab American feminisms was largely about striving to collaborate and be acknowledged as part of similar struggles with radical women-of-color organizing.[16]

Academic Institutional Legibilities and Conundra

As the examples given earlier demonstrate, there was synergy between organizing and academic spaces of Arab and Arab American feminisms, which found sustenance in collaborations with decolonial, liberationist feminisms. For me, feminist decolonial scholarship—such as *This Bridge Called My Back*—was what led me to academia. It was during this time, when I was exploring whether to pursue graduate work related to Arab American studies and feminism, that I found Evelyn Shakir's book *Bint Arab* (1997), which opened up the possibility of seeing Arab American women written into scholarship. A general orientation toward decolonial (or what used to be called "multicultural" and then "transnational") feminist scholarship as grounded in critical race studies led me to sources such as Ella Shohat's groundbreaking collection *Talking Visions: Multicultural Feminism in a Transnational Age* (1998), which I found after a library database search turned up Mervat Hatem's essay about Arab American feminisms in the 1990s, which was included in Shohat's collection.

Though Arab American feminist scholarship was totally illegible at the time, at least to my graduate program, it was growing, and I found a way to imagine my own engagement with academia through engaging it. Because I started graduate school with the intention of studying Arab American literature, Lisa Suhair Majaj played an especially influential role in my scholarly development, and I will never forget the generous gift of time and support she offered, symbolized in a manila envelope filled with photocopies of her work and other examples of Arab American literature that she mailed to me. I am also indebted to Therese Saliba, whose work I knew from *Food for Our Grandmothers*. Both Lisa and Therese made time to meet with me when I attended my first MESA conferences, which were otherwise generally spaces of profound alienation for me. Both Majaj and Saliba also had essays in the collection *Arabs in America: Building a New Future* (1999), edited by Michael Suleiman, which was

16. In the end, "We Are Your Sisters, Too" combined with another concurrently scheduled panel on a similar theme, meaning that the overall conversation ultimately did not go beyond the general, basic themes of militarization and war. RAWAN eventually affiliated with INCITE! in 2008, though it had largely dissolved by the time the next INCITE! conference took place in 2015.

published during my first year in graduate school. These encounters gave me the oxygen I needed to continue on in graduate school when faced with an institution that was telling me not only that the field I wished to pursue did not exist but also that it was unintelligible as a field. Many of the scholars in that collection were the people who populated the reference sections of my papers as I built my understanding of the history and sociopolitical realities of Arab Americans—Barbara Aswad, Janice Terry, Helen Hatab Samhan, Suad Joseph, Therese Saliba, Lisa Suhair Majaj, Kristine Ajrouch, Louise Cainkar, and, of course, Michael Suleiman himself—in addition to the scholars they cited, in particular Alixa Naff. This early scholarship, along with interventions (and teaching tools) such as the documentary *I Exist: Voices from the Lesbian and Gay Middle Eastern Community in the U.S.*, about queer Arab Americans,[17] could be aligned with two of the themes Louise mentions earlier—"we exist" and "you know us wrongly." Though my cataloging of each individual anthology, essay, film, and even manila folder filled with photocopies may seem punctilious or superfluous, I single them out because each one felt like a generous gift of recognition and possibility.

Legibility as Related to Racialization

In my early forays into Arab American studies, I grappled with questions of fit and how to understand Arab Americans in relation to critical race and ethnic studies. I felt caught between the scholarly gatekeepers in my graduate program—my early advisers and committee members in the Graduate Institute for the Liberal Arts (ILA) at Emory University—who were directing me to think about Arab Americans in relation to Karen Brodkin's book *How Jews Became White Folks and What That Says about Race in America* (in other words, to see Arab Americans as white) and my own inclinations to read Arab American feminism in relation to women-of-color feminism. Specifically, one of my early advisers pushed back on the idea that Arab Americans could be seen as anything other than a white ethnic group by telling me that a comparison between Asian American and Arab American literature was theoretically unsound. Faced with this lack of support, I eventually gave up on the project I had proposed to study—Arab American literature and Arab American studies more broadly—in favor of a dissertation focused on excavating orientalist stereotypes of Arab and Muslim femininity in the United States. Notably, I felt I first had to back up and lay the groundwork for conceiving of Arab Americans as racialized at all, and that is what led me to the project of demonstrating how Arabs were othered and racialized in stereotypical US representations. Despite the fact that my graduate department, the ILA, was an interdisciplinary program that prided itself on supporting nascent fields, my efforts to name Arab American studies as my area of interest were largely buried under suggestions that I study Arabic literature written by women or—even more depressing—under a general disinterest in my work. Ironically, though the ILA housed a specialization in American studies, it was not until much later that I would even consider going to the ASA conferences, despite the fact that my early graduate research explored overlaps between the formation of the fields of Arab American and Asian American studies.

In fact, the two conferences I did attend during graduate school, at which I presented my research on Arab American literature, only cemented the feedback I had received in my program about the illegibility of Arab American studies. At the NWSA conference in 2001, about which I write in "Mobilizing the Politics of Invisibility" (reprinted in chapter 6 in this reader), my work was read through either orientalist or xenophobic lenses, and at a smaller conference in 2002 called "Representing the Other" I was put on a panel with a white Christian woman who showed slides about her trip to the "Holy Land." While seriously considering leaving academia, I had enrolled in Beverly Guy Sheftall's "Global Black Feminisms" course, and it was there that I found the inspiration for what would become my dissertation topic. As I explain in "Mobilizing the Politics of Invisibility," I aimed to confront the paradox of being framed through orientalist and stereotypical notions about Arab women

17. Peter Barbosa and Garrett Lenoir, dirs., *I Exist: Voices from the Lesbian and Gay Middle Eastern Community in the U.S.* (Arab Film Distribution, 2003), at https://www.arabfilm.com/item/307/.

at the same time that I faced resistance in situating the study of Arab Americans as people of color. Finding no support in my institutional context to study Arab Americans as racialized in the United States, I instead turned toward the scholarly project of theorizing and contextualizing the dominant images and stereotypes of Arab womanhood within the larger contexts of US imperialism and neoliberal globalization. In this respect, I built on the scholarship of Ella Shohat (1997; Shohat and Stam 1994) and Mohja Kahf (1999), which created space for thinking about orientalist representations of Arab and Muslim womanhood in an institutional context.[18]

I share the details of my trajectory within Arab American studies to highlight the importance of dismantling orientalist representations alongside the projects of illuminating Arab American lives and realities. The project of analyzing what I came to describe as "cultural mythologies" is grounded in the ways that orientalist images violently limit the full potential of the people they purport to represent. In *Imagining Arab Womanhood* (Jarmakani 2008), I argue that the cultural mythologies of the veil, the harem, and the belly dancer "function to obscure the many layers of understanding—about the Arab and Muslim worlds, yes, but also about the vague American dreams and imaginings that have sought expression in the shorthand of caricatures rather than the longhand of thoughtful reflection and introspection" (xiii). For me, the work of analyzing representations—in other words, a cultural studies paradigm—is grounded in an ethical engagement with "honoring the lives of those obscured, maimed, and even killed in the long shadow of orientalist representations" (xiii). Also crucial, then, are analyses of US imperialism as indebted to the normalization of orientalist stereotypes. If one of orientalism's defining features is the conflation of cultures, ethnicities, and religions of the region largely imagined to be the "East," another defining feature is its grounding in colonialist and imperialist power.

US imperialist action in the war on terror exploits the orientalist move of broadly construing the enemy as a racialized Arab/Muslim subject to be surveilled. An important aspect of Arab American studies, then, is also the careful analysis of the conflation of Arabs with Muslims and with anyone perceived to be either Arab or Muslim (including Sikhs as well as non-Muslim Pakistanis, Afghans, and Iranians, just to name a few such groups), including all of the attendant misunderstandings and conflations of ethnic, regional, and religious groups therein. This conflation, in turn, has demanded analysis of anti-Arab racism (Abraham 1994; Salaita 2006), Islamophobia, anti-Muslim racism, and racialization based on religion (Bayoumi 2010, 2015; Cainkar and Selod 2018; Garner and Selod 2015; Jamal and Naber 2008; Kumar 2012; Love 2017; Maira 2009, 2016; Rana 2011, 2016). As these growing bodies of scholarship demonstrate, the racialization of Arabs in the United States is closely linked to the racialization of Muslims, as further explored in what is alternately called "American Muslim" or "Muslim American" or "US Muslim" studies (Abdul Khabeer 2017; Chan-Malik 2018; Daulatzai 2012; Grewal 2014; Kundnani 2007, 2014).[19]

Overall, my story is punctuated by the multiple impacts of the general illegibility of Arab American studies as a field. Though the obstacle of illegibility has played out differentially for my peers and colleagues, it has manifested through some common themes. Such illegibility stunted the growth of the field both in terms of the ways our research went unsupported and undermined and in terms of the research thwarted due to pro-Zionist censorship of our scholarship, as detailed in all of our stories.

18. Contributions to Arab American media and cultural studies include Jack Shaheen's *The TV Arab* (1984), which can be credited with inaugurating the field; Mohja Kahf's *Western Representations of the Muslim Woman: Termagant to Odalisque* (1999); and Melani McAlister's *Epic Encounters* ([2001] 2005), which played a pivotal role in legitimizing the study of popular culture representations of the SWANA region. With the addition of Shaheen's later books (2008, [2001] 2009), Evelyn Alsultany's *Arabs and Muslims in the Media* (2012), my own books *Imagining Arab Womanhood* (Jarmakani 2008) and *An Imperialist Love Story* (Jarmakani 2015), and Waleed Mahdi's *Arab Americans in Film* (2020), Arab American media and cultural studies should be understood not only as its own burgeoning subfield but also fundamentally as engaged with the fields of US Muslim studies, critical ethnic studies, and anti-imperialist work.

19. For a discussion about the former two terms as labels for the field, see Chan-Malik 2014.

As is also detailed in my stories, our work—and, I would argue, ultimately the field—also thrived through collaborations with other scholars who were grounded in decolonial feminist theories, critical race studies, and critical ethnic studies.

Arab American and Allied Studies

As our stories elucidate, establishing an Arab American space in the academy has not been an easy task. In part this is because the ambiguous positioning of Arab Americans in relation to categories of whiteness have rendered them structural "misfits" for race and ethnic studies. However, Arab Americans are subjected to highly racialized conditions—characterized by stereotypes, racist representations, physical attacks, and state repression (see Cainkar 2018). In the words of Nabeel Abraham, "Anti-Arab racism, like other types of racism, permeates mainstream cultural and political institutions. But unlike other forms of racism, anti-Arab racism is often tolerated" (1994, 159). Discounting Arab Americans from race and ethnic studies paradigms thus cannot be simply attributed to a poor "fit" but must also be seen as the result of both scholarly blind spots and active efforts to silence their stories.

One of the goals of this reader is to solidify Arab American studies as a robust field aligned with the broader institutional frameworks of American studies, ethnic studies, and critical race and Indigenous studies. As indicated by the fact that the AASA holds affiliate status with both the ASA and MESA, mentioned in Pauline's story, our work has long been uneasily situated at the interstices of both fields. The conflation of Arab Americans with other groups—Muslims, Iranians, South Asians, to name a few—has produced new ideas about where and how to locate Arab American studies. As we have sought to build on and grow from these affiliations, we are also mindful of the un/necessary elisions fostered by the demands to claim a name and a space under recognized terms of engagement, which can perpetuate unnecessary divisions and place barriers to collaboration between Arab American, Iranian American, Turkish American, Armenian American, and US Muslim studies, to name a few. The anthropologist Stanley Thangaraj, for example, whose work focuses on Kurdish diasporans, has participated in Arab American venues, as have scholars in Iranian studies, such as Persis Karim. The field will only be strengthened by fostering more of this type of interaction, particularly with direct and engaged conversations about frictions as well as affinities between various racialized groups from the SWANA region.

The advantages of cross-fertilization are many. For example, religious studies scholars might integrate the global political interests involved in demonizing Islam rather than narrowly seeing anti-Muslim sentiments as matters of religious difference. They might also consider the longer trajectory of shared racialization of Muslims with Arabs along with attendant conflations of Arabs with Islam. In sum, scholars of Muslim experiences in the Americas have much to gain from the study of Arabs in the Americas, and vice versa. So, too, scholars of Arab, Iranian, Turkish, and other diasporic groups might more deeply investigate shared and long-standing precapitalist, precolonial Christian religious animosities toward Muslims, the Moorish Atlantic, and slavery as well as the ways in which the treatment of US Black Muslims lies at the intersection of multiple histories, hierarchies, and hegemonies. Concerning the latter, Arab American entanglements are complex: on the one hand, Arab Americans are racially subordinated under white supremacy and empire; on the other, they adopt anti-Black racist positions and also often claim an Arab–South Asian Muslim "authenticity" in diasporic Muslim configurations, as Su'ad Abdul Khabeer (2016) demonstrates. Moreover, Arab (and South Asian) Americans are often situated as market intermediaries between white capital and Black consumption, a problematic position that has led to calls for an Arab American reckoning with anti-Blackness (Abuznaid et al. 2019; Bayoumi 2020; Beydoun 2015; Erakat 2015, 2016; Erakat and Hill 2019; Herzing 2019). All of these aspects of Arab America offer fruitful sites for inquiry—among critical race, ethnic, and Indigenous studies scholars and others—into the buy-ins and buyouts that accompany the seductions of capitalism and white supremacy. Cross-fertilizations like these have the potential to generate growth in Arab American studies, allied fields, and beyond, attending to shared histories and intersections of experience while reducing often divisive and unnecessary demarcations between people, cultures, and places.

Like Breath: Once and Future Stories of the Field

We have employed the metaphor of storytelling in this introduction because we wish to emphasize both the potential and the limits of stories to capture the complexities of experiences that lie in a field's formation. We have aimed to highlight the duality of the storytelling metaphor. On the one hand, stories both shape and reflect experiences, demonstrating how the field came to be molded through the political conditions that have shaped its formation. On the other hand, stories can convey truths that are often left out of canonical, conventional, or linear ways of thinking.

We selected the essays included in this reader with three goals in mind: to highlight the major conversations in the field, to foreground some of the key complexities and paradoxes within these conversations, and to foster further development of as yet underdeveloped conversations in the burgeoning field. Throughout the process, we have also sought to acknowledge those topics and subject areas that are excluded from the reader because of both space and the state of the scholarship. Although we have framed the story of Arab American studies in a particular way, in some respects we can also say that the stories represented here also chose us both as individuals and as a collective of scholars. In other words, as we have been arguing, Arab American studies scholarship has been shaped by larger contexts of racism, exclusion, orientalism, imperialism, transnational migrations, and life-giving solidarities that have also affected our larger field. Our greatest desire for the reader is that it will not only provide opportunities for acknowledging important developments that have shaped the field thus far but also help to open space for stories that are yet untold and unacknowledged.

As Lisa Suhair Majaj says in the interview with which we begin this introduction, "Language carries residues of meaning, and once we start allowing these subterranean layers to emerge and interact we discover that language has a movement of its own, like breath" (2007, 406). Like any scholarly field, Arab American studies should be understood as living, breathing, and constantly evolving. In crafting one narrative about it here, we also acknowledge the power and potential of language—like breath—to be life giving and to always hold open the potential of telling the story in a different way. We offer this reader as an invitation to conversation, debate, and, ideally, new and continued growth of the field.

Works Cited

Abdulhadi, Rabab, Evelyn Alsultany, and Nadine Naber, eds. 2011. *Arab & Arab American Feminism: Gender, Violence, & Belonging.* Syracuse, NY: Syracuse Univ. Press.

Abdulhadi, Rabab, and Dana Olwan. 2015. "Introduction: Shifting Geographies of Knowledge and Power: Palestine and American Studies." *American Quarterly* 67, no. 4: 993–1006.

Abdul Khabeer, Su'ad. 2016. "The Limits of Muslim Cool." In *Muslim Cool: Race, Religion, and Hip Hop in the United States*, 178–218. New York: New York Univ. Press.

———. 2017. "Citizens and Suspects: Race, Gender, and the Making of American Muslim Citizenship." *Transforming Anthropology* 25, no. 2: 103–99.

Abraham, Nabeel. 1994. "Anti-Arab Racism and Violence in the United States." In *The Development of Arab-American Identity*, edited by Ernest McCarus, 155–214. Ann Arbor: Univ. of Michigan Press.

Abraham, Nabeel, Sally Howell, and Andrew Shryock, eds. 2011. *Arab Detroit 9/11: Life in the Terror Decade.* Detroit: Wayne State Univ. Press.

Abraham, Sameer, and Nabeel Abraham. 1983. *Arabs in the New World: Studies on Arab-American Communities.* Detroit: Wayne State Univ. Press.

Abu-Jaber, Diana. [1993] 2003a. *Arabian Jazz.* New York: Norton.

———. 2003b. *Crescent.* New York: Norton.

Abu-Laban, Baha, and Michael Suleiman, eds. 1989. *Arab Americans: Continuity and Change.* Belmont, MA: AAUG Press. 1989. Previously printed as Suleiman, Michael, and Baha Abu-Laban, eds. 1989. "Arab Americans: Continuity and Change." Special issue of *Arab Studies Quarterly* 11, nos. 2–3.

Abu-Laban, Baha, and Faith Zeady, eds. 1985. *Arabs in America: Myth and Reality.* Evanston, IL: Medina Univ. Press; Belmont, MA: AAUG Press.

Abuznaid, Ahmad, Phillip Agnew, Maytha Alhassan, Kristian Davis Bailey, and Nadya Tannous. 2019. "Roundtable: On Solidarity Delegations." *Journal of Palestine Studies* 48, no. 4 (Summer): 92–102.

Adichie, Chimamanda Ngozi. 2009. *The Danger of a Single Story.* TEDGlobal, video. At https://www.ted.com/talks/chimamanda_adichie_the_danger_of_a_single_story.

Aidi, Hisham. 2003. "The Moorish Atlantic: Moors, Aztecs, and the Invention of the Americas." Paper prepared for the seminar "Modernity and Its Others," taught by Paul Gilroy, Sociology Department, Yale Univ., New Haven, CT, May.

Ajrouch, K. J. 2008. "Social Isolation and Loneliness among Arab American Elders: Cultural, Social, and Personal Factors." *Research in Human Development* 5, no. 1: 44–59.

Ajrouch, K. J., and T. C. Antonucci. 2017. "Social Relations and Health: Comparing 'Invisible' Arab Americans to Blacks and Whites." *Society and Mental Health* 8, no. 1. doi:https://doi.org/10.1177/2156869317718234.

Ajrouch, K. J., and N. Fakhoury. 2013. "Assessing Needs of Aging Muslims: A Focus on Metro-Detroit Faith Communities." *Contemporary Islam* 7, no. 3: 353–72.

Akash, Munir, and Khaled Mattawa, eds. 1999. *Post Gibran: Anthology of New Arab American Writing.* Jusoor Series nos. 11–12. Syracuse, NY: Syracuse Univ. Press.

Alameddine, Rabih. 1998. *Koolaids: The Art of War.* New York: Picador.

Alsultany, Evelyn. 2012. *Arabs and Muslims in the Media: Race and Representation after 9/11.* New York: New York Univ. Press.

Alsultany, Evelyn, Louise Cainkar, and Pauline Homsi Vinson, eds. 2016. "Special Issue: New Directions in Arab American Studies." *Mashriq & Mahjar* 3, no. 2.

Alsultany, Evelyn, and Ella Shohat, eds. 2013. *Between the Middle East and the Americas: The Cultural Politics of Diaspora.* Ann Arbor: Univ. of Michigan Press.

Amer, Mona, and Germine Awad, eds. 2016. *The Handbook of Arab American Psychology.* New York: Routledge.

Ameri, Anan. 2011. "Taking Power and Making Power: Resistance, Global Politics, and Institution Building." Interview by Nadine Naber. In *Arab & Arab American Feminisms: Gender, Violence, & Belonging*, edited by Rabab Abdulhadi, Evelyn Alsultany, and Nadine Naber, 159–65. Syracuse, NY: Syracuse Univ. Press.

Amireh, Amal. 2000. "Framing Nawal El Saadawi: Arab Feminism in a Transnational World." *Signs* 26, no. 1 (Autumn): 215–49.

Anzaldúa, Gloria, and AnaLouise Keating, eds. 2002. *This Bridge We Call Home: Radical Visions for Transformation.* New York: Routledge.

Assad, Samah, Dorothy Tucker, and Christopher Hacker. 2021a. "Across Illinois, Arab Americans Were Dying from Covid-19, but the Government Wasn't Counting. Some Say That Cost Lives." *CBS Chicago*, May 7. At https://chicago.cbslocal.com/across-illinois-arab-americans-were-dying-from-covid-19-but-the-government-wasnt-counting-some-say-that-cost-lives/.

———. 2021b. "Arab Americans in Illinois Will Finally Be Counted When They Get Their Vaccine." *CBS Chicago.* August 2, 2021. https://chicago.cbslocal.com/2021/08/02/arab-americans-in-illinois-will-finally-be-counted-when-they-get-their-vaccine/.

Aswad, Barbara, ed. 1974. *Arabic Speaking Communities in American Cities.* New York: Center for Migration Studies.

Aswad, Barbara C., and Barbara Bilgé. 1996. *Family and Gender among American Muslims: Issues Facing Middle Eastern Immigrants and Their Descendants.* Philadelphia: Temple Univ. Press.

Ayoub, Dima. 2020. "Politics of Paratextuality: The Glossary between Translation and the Translational." *Journal of Arabic Literature* 51, no. 1: 27–52.

Aziz, Barbara Nimri. 2004. Foreword to *Scheherazade's Legacy: Arab and Arab American Women on Writing*, edited by Susan Muaddi Darraj, xi–xv. Westport, CT: Praeger.

Bassiouni, M. Cherif, ed. 1974. *The Civil Rights of Arab Americans: The Special Measures.* Belmont, MA: AAUG Press.

Bausch, Richard, and R. V. Cassill, eds. 2020. *The Norton Anthology of Short Fiction.* 9th ed. New York: Norton.

Bayoumi, Moustafa. 2010. "The Race Is On: Muslims and Arabs in the American Imagination." *Middle East Report Online*, Mar. At www.merip.org/mero/interventions/bayoumi_in-terv.html.

———. 2015. *This Muslim American Life: Dispatches from the War on Terror.* New York: New York Univ. Press.

———. 2020. "Why Did Cup Foods Call the Cops on George Floyd?" *New York Times*, June 17.

Berger, John. 1972. *Ways of Seeing.* London: British Broadcasting Corporation and Penguin Books.

Beydoun, Khaled A. 2015. "Why Ferguson Is Our Issue: A Letter to Muslim America." *Harvard Journal on Racial and Ethnic Justice* 31:1–5.

Cainkar, Louise. 2009. "Whose Homeland Security?" In *Homeland Insecurity: The Arab American and Muslim*

American Experience after 9/11, 110–52. New York: Russell Sage Foundation.

———. 2018. "Fluid Terror Threat: A Genealogy of the Racialization of Arab, Muslim, and South Asian Americans." In "Arab/Americas: Locations & Iterations," edited by Sarah M. A. Gualtieri and Pauline Homsi Vinson. Special issue of *Amerasia Journal* 44, no. 1: 27–60.

———. 2020. "The Muslim Ban and Trump's War on Immigration." *Middle East Report*, no. 294 (Spring). At https://merip.org/2020/06/the-muslim-ban-and-trumps-war-on-immigration-2/.

———. 2021. "Palestine—and Empire—are Central to Arab American/SWANA Studies." *Journal of Palestine Studies*. Spring 2021 issue. Vol. L:2; Issue 198: 4–21.

Cainkar, Louise, and Saher Selod. 2018. "Review of Race Scholarship and the War on Terror." *Sociology of Race and Ethnicity* 4, no. 2: 165–77.

Cane, Alex. 2018. "'It's Killing the Student Movement': Canary Mission's Blacklist of Pro-Palestinian Activists Is Taking a Toll." *Intercept*, Nov. 22. At https://theintercept.com/2018/11/22/israel-boycott-canary-mission-blacklist/.

Chan-Malik, Sylvia. 2014. "'A Space for the Spiritual': A Roundtable on Race, Gender, and Islam in the United States." *Amerasia Journal* 40, no. 1: 17–33.

———. 2018. *Being Muslim: A Cultural History of Women of Color in American Islam*. New York: New York Univ. Press.

Charara, Hayan, ed. 2008. *Inclined to Speak: An Anthology of Arab American Poetry*. Fayetteville: Univ. of Arkansas Press.

Chatterjee, Piya, and Sunaina Maira, eds. 2014. *The Imperial University: Academic Repression and Scholarly Dissent*. Minneapolis: Univ. of Minnesota Press.

Darraj, Susan Muaddi, ed. 2004. *Scheherazade's Legacy: Arab and Arab American Women on Writing*. Westport, CT: Praeger.

Darwish, Mahmoud. 1964. "Bitaqat Hawiyyah" [Identity Card]. In *Awraq al-Zaytun* [Olive Leaves]. Haifa: Maṭba'at al-Ittihad al-Ta'awuniyah.

Daulatzai, Sohail. 2012. *Black Star, Crescent Moon: The Muslim International and Black Freedom beyond America*. Minneapolis: Univ. of Minnesota Press.

Deeb, Lara, and Jessica Winegar. 2015. *Anthropology's Politics: Disciplining the Middle East*. Palo Alto, CA: Stanford Univ. Press.

Detroit Arab American Study Team, ed. 2009. *Citizenship and Crisis: Arab Detroit after 9/11*. New York: Russell Sage Foundation.

Dorbin, Sidney I., ed. 2015. *Writing Situations*. New York: Pearson.

Durrani, Anayat. 2002. "Arab-Americans Find a Liberating Voice in 'The Cloud of the Desert.'" *Daily Star* (Lebanon), Jan. 21. At https://www.dailystar.com.lb/Culture/Art/2002/Jan-21/109002-arab-americans-find-a-liberating-voice-in-the-cloud-of-the-desert.ashx.

Elia, Nada. 2011. "The Burden of Representation: When Palestinians Speak Out." In *Arab & Arab American Feminisms: Gender, Violence, & Belonging*, edited by Rabab Abdulhadi, Evelyn Alsultany, and Nadine Naber, 141–58. New York: Syracuse University Press.

Elkholy, Abdo. 1966. *The Arab Moslems in the United States: Religion and Assimilation*. New Haven, CT: College & University Press.

Erakat, Noura, moderator. 2015. "Roundtable on Anti-Blackness and Black–Palestinian Solidarity." With Rabab Abdulhadi, Ahmad Abuznaid, Ebony Coletu, Bill Fletcher Jr., Che Gossett, Sarah Ihmoud, Robin D. G. Kelley, Aja Monet, Donna Murch, Nadine Naber, Linda Sarsour, Jared Sexton, and Nadera Shalhoub. *Jadaliyya*, June 3. At https://www.jadaliyya.com/Details/32145/Roundtable-on-Anti-Blackness-and-Black-Palestinian-Solidarity.

———. 2016. "The Nakba and Anti-Blackness." *Jadaliyya*, May 19. At https://www.jadaliyya.com/Details/33280.

Erakat, Noura, and Marc Lamont Hill. 2019. "Black–Palestinian Transnational Solidarity: Renewals, Returns, and Practice." *Journal of Palestine Studies* 48, no. 4 (Summer): 7–16.

Fadda-Conrey, Carol. 2014. *Contemporary Arab-American Literature: Transnational Reconfigurations of Citizenship and Belonging*. New York: New York Univ. Press.

Feldman, Keith. 2015. *A Shadow over Palestine: The Imperial Life of Race in America*. Minneapolis: Univ. of Minnesota Press.

Gana, Nouri. 2008. "Introduction: Race, Islam, and the Task of Muslim and Arab American Writing." In "Comparative Racialization," coordinated by Shu-Mei Shih. Special issue of *PMLA: Publication of the Modern Language Association* 123, no. 5 (Oct.): 1573–80.

———, ed. 2015. *The Edinburgh Companion to the Arab Novel in English: The Politics of Anglo Arab and Arab American Literature and Culture*. Edinburgh: Edinburgh Univ. Press.

Garner, Steve, and Saher Selod. 2015. "The Racialization of Muslims: Empirical Studies of Islamophobia." *Critical Sociology* 41, no. 1: 9–19.

Ghareeb, Edmund, ed. 1983. *Split Vision*. Washington, DC: American Arab Affairs Council.

Goldthwaite, Melissa, Joseph Bizup, Anne Fernald, and John Brereton, eds. 2020. *The Norton Reader: An Anthology of Nonfiction*. 15th ed. New York: Norton.

Grewal, Zareena. 2014. *Islam Is a Foreign Country: American Muslims and the Global Crisis of Authority*. New York: New York Univ. Press.

Gualtieri, Sarah M. A., and Pauline Homsi Vinson. 2018. Introduction to "Arab/Americas: Locations & Iterations," edited by Sarah M. A. Gualtieri and Pauline Homsi Vinson. Special issue of *Amerasia Journal* 44, no. 1: vii–xxi.

Haddad, Carol. 2021. "Second-Wave Arab American Feminist Activism: The Story of the Feminist Arab-American Network." In *Arab American Women: Representation and Refusal*, edited by Michael Suleiman, Suad Joseph, and Louise Cainkar, 247–81. Syracuse, NY: Syracuse Univ. Press.

Haddad, Yvonne Yazbeck. 2010. "Arab Christian Scholars and the Study of the Middle East in the United States." Farhat J. Ziadeh Distinguished Lecture in Arab and Islamic Studies, Univ. of Washington, May 6.

Hagopian, Elaine, and Anne Paden, eds. 1969. *The Arab Americans: Studies in Assimilation*. With an introduction by Ibrahim Abu-Lughod. Evanston IL: Medina Univ. Press International.

Halaby, Laila. 2007. *Once in a Promised Land*. Boston: Beacon Press.

Hammad, Suheir. 2011. *First Writing Since*. Def-Poetry, July 20. YouTube video, 5:48. At https://www.youtube.com/watch?v=FDyLNgLHprI.

Hartmann, Michelle. 2012. "Gender, Genre, and the (Missing) Gazelle: Arab Women Writers and the Politics of Translation." *Feminist Studies* 38, no. 1 (Spring): 17–49.

Hassan, Salah, and Marcy Jane Knopf-Newman. 2006. Introduction to "Arab American Literature." Special issue of *MELUS* 31, no. 4 (Winter): 3–14.

Hassib, Rajia. 2015. *In the Language of Miracles*. New York: Penguin Books.

Herman, Edward S., and Noam Chomsky. 1988. *Manufacturing Consent*. New York: Pantheon Books.

Herzing, Rachel. 2019. "Developing Alternatives to Policing." Arab Organizing and Resource Center, Aug. 28. At http://araborganizing.org/wp-content/uploads/2019/08/AROC_Build-the-Block-Alternatives-to-Policing.pdf.

Hilmy, Salman. 2017. "'ID Card' by Mahmoud Darwish—a Translation and Commentary." *Washington Report on Middle East Affairs*, Nov.–Dec. At https://www.wrmea.org/017-november-december/id-card-by-mahmoud-darwish-a-translation-and-commentary.html.

Hitti, Philip Khuri. 1924. *The Syrians in America*. New York: George H. Doran.

Hooglund, Eric. 1985. *Taking Root: Arab American Community Studies*. Washington, DC: ADC Research Institute.

———. 1987. *Crossing the Waters: Arabic Speaking Immigrants in the US*. Washington, DC: Smithsonian Institution Press.

INCITE! Women of Color against Violence, ed. 2006. *Color of Violence: The INCITE! Anthology*. Cambridge, MA: South End Press.

Jamal, Amaney. 2005. "The Political Participation and Engagement of Muslim Americans: Mosque Involvement and Group Consciousness." *American Politics Research* 33, no. 4: 521–44.

———. 2008. "Civil Liberties and the Otherization of Arab and Muslim Americans." In *Race and Arab Americans before and after 9/11: From Invisible Citizens to Visible Subjects*, edited by Amaney Jamal and Nadine Naber, 114–30. Syracuse, NY: Syracuse Univ. Press.

Jamal, Amaney, and Nadine Naber, eds. 2008. *Race and Arab Americans before and after 9/11: From Invisible Citizens to Visible Subjects*. Syracuse, NY: Syracuse Univ. Press.

Jarmakani, Amira. 2008. *Imagining Arab Womanhood: The Cultural Mythology of Veils, Harems, and Belly Dancers in the U.S.* New York: Palgrave.

———. 2011. "Arab American Feminisms: Mobilizing the Politics of Invisibility." In *Arab & Arab American Feminisms: Gender, Violence, & Belonging*, edited by Rabab Abdulhadi, Evelyn Alsultany, and Nadine Naber, 227–41. Syracuse, NY: Syracuse Univ. Press.

———. 2015. *An Imperialist Love Story: Desert Romances and the War on Terror*. New York: New York Univ. Press.

Jerskey, Maria, ed. 2013. *Globalization: A Reader for Writers*. London: Oxford Univ. Press.

Joseph, Suad. 2021. "Arab American Women: Intersectional Genealogies and Trajectories." In *Arab American Women: Representation and Refusal*, edited by Michael Suleiman, Suad Joseph, and Louise Cainkar, 1–18. Syracuse, NY: Syracuse Univ. Press.

Kadi, Joe, ed. 1994. *Food for Our Grandmothers: Writings by Arab-American & Arab-Canadian Feminists*. Boston: South End Press.

Kahf, Mohja. 1999. *Western Representations of the Muslim Woman: From Termagant to Odalisque*. Austin: Univ. of Texas Press.

Kaldas, Pauline, and Khaled Mattawa, eds. [2004] 2009. *Dinarzad's Children: An Anthology of Contemporary Arab American Fiction*. Fayetteville: Univ. of Arkansas Press.

Kayal, Philip, and Joseph Kayal. 1975. *The Syrian-Lebanese in America: A Study in Religion and Assimilation*. Woodbridge, CT: Twayne.

Kayyali, Randa. 2018. "Race, Religion, and Identity: Arab Christians in the United States." *Culture and Religion* 19, no. 1: 1–19.

Khalidi, Rashid. 2008. "Remembering Mahmud Darwish." *Journal of Palestine Studies* 38, no. 1 (Autumn). At https://www.palestine-studies.org/en/node/42080.

Kumar, Deepa. 2012. *Islamophobia and the Politics of Empire*. Chicago: Haymarket Books.

Kundnani, Arun. 2007. "Integrationism: The Politics of Anti-Muslim Racism." *Race and Class* 48, no. 4: 24–44.

———. 2014. *The Muslims Are Coming! Islamophobia, Extremism, and the Domestic War on Terror*. New York: Verso.

Lorde, Audre. [1984] 2007. "Eye to Eye: Black Women, Hatred, and Anger." In *Sister Outsider: Essays and Speeches*, 145–75. Berkeley, CA: Crossing Press.

Love, Erik. 2017. *Islamophobia and Racism in America*. New York: New York Univ. Press.

Mahdi, Waleed F. 2016. "Post-Oriental Otherness: Hollywood's Moral Geography of Arab Americans." *Mashriq & Mahjar* 3, no. 2: 35–61.

———. 2020. *Arab Americans in Film: From Hollywood and Egyptian Stereotypes to Self-Representation*. Syracuse, NY: Syracuse Univ. Press.

Maira, Sunaina. 2009. *Missing Youth, Citizenship, and Empire after 9/11*. Durham, NC: Duke Univ. Press.

———. 2016. *The 9/11 Generation: Youth, Rights, and Solidarity in the War on Terror*. New York: New York Univ. Press.

———. 2018. *Boycott! The Academy and Justice for Palestine*. Berkeley: Univ. of California Press.

Majaj, Lisa Suhair. 2007. "Fragments of Hope: An Interview with Lisa Suhair Majaj." Interview by Deborah al-Najjar. *International Journal of Politics* 9, no. 3 (Sept.): 402–9.

———. 2012. "Transformative Acts: Arab American Writing/Writing Arab America." PhD diss., Univ. of Michigan. At https://deepblue.lib.umich.edu/handle/2027.42/91383?show=full.

Majaj, Lisa Suhair, and Amal Amireh, eds. 2001a. *Etel Adnan: Critical Essays on the Arab-American Writer and Artist*. Jefferson, NC: McFarland.

———. 2001b. "Introduction: Biographical and Career Highlights." In *Etel Adnan: Critical Essays on the Arab-American Writer and Artist*, 15–24. Jefferson, NC: McFarland.

Mamdani, Mahmood. 2005. *Good Muslim, Bad Muslim: America, the Cold War, and the Roots of Terror*. New York: Pantheon Books.

McAlister, Melani. [2001] 2005. *Epic Encounters: Culture, Media, and U.S. Interests in the Middle East 1945–2000*. Berkeley: Univ. of California Press.

McCarus, Ernest, ed. 1994. *The Development of Arab-American Identity*. Ann Arbor: Univ. of Michigan Press.

Metres, Philip. 2015. *Sand Opera*. Farmington, ME: Alice James Books.

Meyer, Michael, and D. Quentin Miller, eds. 2020. *The Compact Bedford Introduction to Literature: Reading, Thinking, and Writing*. 12th ed. Boston: Bedford/St. Martins.

Migration Policy Institute. 2020. "U.S. Immigration Trends." Apr. 13. At https://www.migrationpolicy.org/programs/data-hub/us-immigration-trends.

Mills, C. Wright. 1959. *The Sociological Imagination*. London: Oxford University Press.

Moraga, Cherríe, and Gloria Anzaldúa, eds. 1981. *This Bridge Called My Back: Writings by Radical Women of Color*. San Francisco: Kitchen Table/Women of Color Press.

Muller, Gilbert H., ed. 2017. *The New World Reader: Thinking and Writing about the Global Community*. 5th ed. South Melbourne, Australia: Cengage Learning.

Naber, Nadine. 2000. "Ambiguous Insiders: An Investigation of Arab American Invisibility." *Ethnic and Racial Studies* 23, no. 1: 37–61.

———. 2008. "'Look, Mohammed the Terrorist Is Coming!': Cultural Racism, Nation-Based Racism, and the Intersectionality of Oppressions after 9/11." In *Race and Arab Americans before and after 9/11: From Invisible Citizens to Visible Subjects*, edited by Amaney Jamal and Nadine Naber, 276–304. Syracuse, NY: Syracuse Univ. Press.

———. 2012. *Arab America: Gender, Cultural Politics, and Activism*. New York: New York Univ. Press.

Naber, Nadine, Eman Desouky, and Lina Baroudi. 2006. "The Forgotten '-ism': An Arab American Women's Perspective on Zionism, Racism, and Sexism." In *Color of Violence: The INCITE! Anthology*, edited by INCITE! Women of Color against Violence, 97–112. Cambridge, MA: South End Press.

Naff, Alixa. 1985. *Becoming American: The Early Arab Immigrant Experience*. Carbondale: Southern Illinois Univ. Press.

Najjar, Michael Malek, ed. 2014. *Four Arab American Plays: Works by Leila Buck, Jamil Khoury, Yussef El Guindi, and Lameece Issaq & Jacob Kader.* Charleston, SC: McFarland.

Nye, Naomi Shihab. 1995. *Words under the Words.* Portland, OR: Eighth Mountain Press.

Orfalea, Gregory, and Sharif Elmusa, eds. [1988] 2000. *Grape Leaves: A Century of Arab-American Poetry.* New York: Interlink Books.

Pickens, Therí. 2010. "Presently Reading the Past: A Look at Early Arab American Literature." *Al Jadid* 16, no. 63: 18–19, 24.

———, ed. 2018. *Arab-American Aesthetics: Literature, Material Culture, Film, and Theater.* New York: Routledge.

Prashad, Vijay. 2007. *The Darker Nations: A People's History of the Third World.* New York: New Press.

Rana, Junaid. 2011. *Terrifying Muslims: Race and Labor in the South Asian Diaspora.* Durham, NC: Duke Univ. Press.

———. 2016. "The Racial Infrastructure of the Terror-Industrial Complex." *Social Text* 34, no. 4: 111–38.

Read, Jen'nan Ghazal. 2008. "Multiple Identities and Post 9/11 Discrimination: A Comparison of Muslim and Christian Arab Americans." In *Race and Arab Americans before and after 9/11: From Invisible Citizens to Visible Subjects,* edited by Amaney Jamal and Nadine Naber, 305–17. Syracuse, NY: Syracuse Univ. Press.

Read, Jen'nan Ghazal, and Kristine Ajrouch. 2017. *Executive Summary of the Pilot Census Study Report Submitted to the Arab Community Center for Economic and Social Services (ACCESS) Arab American Research Initiative.* Dearborn, MI: Arab Community Center for Economic and Social Services (ACCESS).

Sabry, Somaya Sami. 2011. *Arab-American Women's Writing and Performance: Orientalism, Race, and the Idea of* The Arabian Nights. London: I. B. Tauris.

Said, Edward. 1978. *Orientalism.* New York: Vintage Books.

———. 1999. *Out of Place: A Memoir.* New York. Vintage Books.

———. 2005. "Transcript: Edward Said On 'Orientalism.'" Interview by Sut Jhally. Media Education Foundation. https://www.mediaed.org/transcripts/Edward-Said-On-Orientalism-Transcript.pdf

Sajjil Ana Arabi—Mahmoud Darwish / سجل انا عربي - محمود درويش | / *Record!... I'm an Arab—Mahmoud Darwish.* 2012. YouTube video. At https://www.youtube.com/watch?v=mzfKQ4PFfPE.

Salaita, Steven. 2006. *Anti-Arab Racism in the USA: Where It Comes from and What It Means for Politics Today.* London: Pluto Press.

———. 2015. *Uncivil Rites: Palestine and the Limits of Academic Freedom.* Chicago: Haymarket Books.

———. 2019. "The Inhumanity of Academic Freedom: A Transcript of the 2019 TB Davie Memorial Lecture at the University of Cape Town, Delivered August 7, 2019." At https://stevesalaita.com/the-inhumanity-of-academic-freedom/.

Samhan, Helen Hatab. 1999. "Not Quite White: Race Classification and the Arab-American Experience." In *Arabs in America: Building a New Future,* edited by Michael W. Suleiman, 209–26. Philadelphia: Temple Univ. Press.

Sawires-Masseli, Marie-Christin. 2018. *Arab American Novels post 9/11: Classical Storytelling Motifs against Outsidership.* Heidelberg, Germany: Unversitätsverlag Winter.

Shaheen, Jack G. 1984. *The TV Arab.* Bowling Green, KY: Bowling Green State Univ. Popular Press.

———. 2008. *Guilty: Hollywood's Verdict on Arabs after 9/11.* New York: Olive Branch Press.

———. [2001] 2009. *Reel Bad Arabs: How Hollywood Vilifies a People.* New York: Olive Branch Press.

Shakir, Evelyn. 1997. *Bint Arab: Arab and Arab American Women in the United States.* Westport, CT: Praeger.

Shohat, Ella. 1997. "Gender and Culture of Empire: Toward a Feminist Ethnography of Cinema." In *Visions of the East: Orientalism in Film,* edited by Matthew Bernstein and Gaylyn Studlar, 19–66. New Brunswick, NJ: Rutgers Univ. Press.

———, ed. 1998. *Talking Visions: Multicultural Feminism in a Transnational Age.* Cambridge, MA: MIT Press.

Shohat, Ella, and Robert Stam. 1994. *Unthinking Eurocentrism: Multiculturalism and the Media.* New York: Routledge.

Shomali, Mejdulene. 2018. "Scheherazade and the Limits of Inclusive Politics in Arab American Literature." *MELUS* 43, no. 1: 65–90.

Suleiman, Michael W. 1988. *The Arabs in the Mind of America.* Brattleboro, VT: Amana Books.

———, ed. 1999. *Arabs in America: Building a New Future.* Philadelphia: Temple Univ. Press.

Suleiman, Michael, and Baha Abu-Laban. 1989. "Introduction." In "Arab Americans: Continuity and Change," edited by Michael Suleiman and Baha Abu-Laban.

Special issue of *Arab Studies Quarterly* 11, nos. 2–3: 1–13.

Terry, Janice. 1985. *Mistaken Identity: Arab Stereotypes in Popular Writings*. Washington, DC: American Arab Affairs Council.

US Office of Management and Budget. 1977. *Directive No. 15: Race and Ethnic Standards for Federal Statistics and Administrative Reporting*. Washington, DC: US Government Printing Office.

Waugh, Earle H., Sharon McIrvin Abu-Laban, and Regula Qureshi, eds. 1991. *Muslim Families in North America*. Edmonton, Canada: Univ. of Alberta Press.

Yunis, Alia. 2013. "Afterward: My Arabian Superheroine." In *Scheherazade's Children: Global Encounters with* The Arabian Nights, edited by Philip F. Kennedy and Marina Warner, 395–400. New York: New York Univ. Press.

Zogby, James, ed. 1984. *Taking Root Bearing Fruit: The Arab-American Experience*. Washington, DC: ADC Research Institute.

Part One

Arab American Legibility and the Question of Naming

> . . . a girl knocked,
> wanted to see the Arab.
> I said we didn't have one.
> After that, my father told me who he was,
> "Shihab"—"shooting star"—
> a good name, borrowed from the sky.
>
> —Naomi Shihab Nye, "Blood"

These simple yet powerful lines from Naomi Shihab Nye's poem "Blood" (1994) capture some of the paradoxes of Arab American identity and its legibility in US contexts. Nye's discovery of her "good" Arabic name is prompted by an inquisitive and intrusive knock on the door of her family home, an incident that illustrates both the xenophobic curiosity and the invasive surveillance that can frame Arab American life. "Shihab," the family name, means "shooting star" and connects the poet to her Arab "blood." Yet the name also denotes something brilliant and difficult to discern, implying that it can be uncovered only by language or through storytelling ("After that, my father told me who he was"). To be Arab American, Nye's poem suggests, is to be something treasured that no one can take away from you—like a shooting star or your name—but also invisible, illegible without translation, and, additionally, somehow suspect in the eyes of others.

The cluster of paradoxes in Nye's poem are directly addressed in the essays we have gathered in this opening part of the reader. Rather than ask, Who are Arab Americans?—a question that is addressed in almost every introduction to studies by and about Arab Americans—we ask: How do Arabs become legible in the Americas? What concepts have Arab Americans utilized to frame their individual and group identities? Who does this category include, exclude, make visible, or obscure? How does it manifest differently in different parts of the Americas? What names does it take, and what are some of the contradictions and pressures, both internal to Arab communities and external to them, that inform attitudes toward the category "Arab American"? How do matters of race, class, religion, ability, gender, and sexuality contribute to particular ways of marking Arab Americanness in specific national or social contexts? These questions allow us to explore the naturalization of the category "Arab American" and to foreground conversations that discuss the underlying ideological and political processes involved in demanding legibility through identity categories and discourses on racialization.

Nye's poem was included in Joe Kadi's groundbreaking collection *Food for Our Grandmothers: Writings by Arab-American & Arab-Canadian Feminists* (1994). In the introduction to that book, which is included as chapter 1 in this reader, Kadi identifies two related themes that would prove central to Arab American scholarship—namely, the question of invisibility and the problem of naming. Maintaining that Arabs are "the Most Invisible of the Invisibles" (p. 56), Kadi emphasizes the importance of naming as a means for gaining visibility, declaring: "Names are critical for a personal and communal sense of affirmation" (p. 55). Yet as Kadi also acknowledges, names can also set a group apart from others who share similar experiences, and in that sense they are problematic. Even as a name makes one group identity visible, in this case Arab Americans, it necessarily excludes persons such as Turks, Iranians, Armenians, Kurds, and Imazighen, among others, who hail from Arabic-speaking regions and don't fit neatly or comfortably into the limits inscribed by the category. In posing the question of how Arabs have become legible in the Americas, this part of the reader surveys the scholarly conversations about visibility and its paradoxes while also considering the struggles for naming and recognition, particularly in relation to both the limits and the possibilities of the category "Arab American."

Striving for Visibility

The need to map out or make visible a distinct Arab American experience is reiterated in texts produced throughout the late 1980s and up to the early 2000s. Gregory Orfalea, for example, explains the impetus for his book *Before the Flames: A Quest for the History of Arab Americans* (1988) as a desire to fill a gap. "It began to nag me," he says, "that there were no available volumes about Arab Americans" (4). More than ten years later, Michael Suleiman remarks: "There is still a dearth of information. . . . Much of the available literature on Arabs in America has not found its way into the main body of scholarship" (1999c, [xi]). What was available, Kadi reminds us, is a "social construction of 'the Arabs' that has cast us as enemy, other, fanatical terrorist, crazy Muslim. If we are women, we can add to that list veiled Woman and exotic whore" (p. 54). Barbara Nimri Aziz remarks that the accounts about Arabs "simply get it wrong. We are really not how others write us. At best we are invisible" (2004, xii). In response to this perceived invisibility and misrepresentation, Elmaz Abinader envisions her "characters [as] tiny warriors against the massive media machine that does not see them at all" (2004, 113). As these declarations demonstrate, the category "Arab American" can function as an assertion of presence and dignity in the face of invisibility, misrepresentation, and erasure.

The drive to become visible is unquestionably a political act that directly engages with the impacts of erasure on actual lives. Therese Saliba, for example, notes that the "absent Arab woman" trope "has been deployed within the U.S. media both as a resonant and as an efficient signifier of so-called Western cultural superiority over the Arab world" (1994, 126). The connection between political aims and exclusionary invisibility is also addressed by Helen Hatab Samhan (1987), who argues that anti-Arab racism is essentially a form of political racism that refuses to see Arab viewpoints, particularly when it comes to US foreign policy toward Arabs and Israel. James Zogby and Helen Samhan (1987) also note that "Arab baiting" is a strategy used to smear political opponents and exclude Arabs from political participation. Noura Erakat highlights this point in describing the silencing of dissent she experienced as a law student at the University of California, Berkeley, where attempts to suppress her activism and political views on Palestine made her "not just feel invisible; [she] felt erased" (2011, 179). To become visible is to be heard, made legible, named; in essence, it demands political recognition. To be denied a voice, to be rendered invisible and illegible, is to be denied participation in civic and political life as well as in scholarship, as we discuss in the introduction to this book.

Paradoxes of Visibility

At the same time that Arab Americans continue to experience exclusionary forms of invisibility, they nonetheless face punishing hypervisibility manifested in practices of heightened scrutiny, surveillance, and exclusion (Cainkar 2018; Hagopian 2004; Jamal and Naber 2008; Volpp 2003). This hypervisibility is demonstrated, for example, in the long-standing FBI surveillance of Arab communities in the United States, in decades of hate-crime victimization, and in the more recent so-called Muslim ban, which aimed to bar the entrance of persons from a number of predominantly Arab and Muslim-majority countries to the United States, issues we take up in greater detail in part five. Practices of hypersecuritization and the crude representations on which they rely also contribute to messy amalgamations and misinterpretations of Arab Americans. As the expression "Muslim ban" suggests, these practices are often accompanied by a conflation of the category "Arab" with the category "Muslim" in spite of the facts that not all Arabs are Muslims and the majority of Muslims are not Arab. This conflation of Arabs with Muslims is a point that a number of scholars have addressed (Cainkar 2018; Hagopian 2004; Jamal and Naber 2008). As these conflations demonstrate, visibility alone does not rectify dominant and obscuring narratives about Arabs, Muslims, and Arab Americans.

The problems of both hypervisibility and invisibility—including the conflation of Arabs and Muslims, heightened surveillance of anyone perceived to be such, and the struggle for Arab American legibility in mainstream contexts—shape what could be described as a paradox of visibility for Arab Americans. In "Ambiguous Insiders: An Investigation of Arab American Invisibility" (2000), the anthropologist Nadine Naber identifies four paradoxes that Arab Americans face in the United States. One has to do with "Arab American positioning within the US racial/ethnic classification system"—namely, the "paradox . . . that Arab Americans are racialized according to religion (Islam) rather than biology (phenotype)" (37). The other paradoxes are that "Arab Americans are a complex, diverse community, but are represented as a monolith in popular North American media images," that "Arab Americans are simultaneously racialized as whites and as non-whites," and that "the religious forms of identity that Arab immigrants bring to the US" intersect with "racial forms of identity that structure US society" (37). These paradoxes reveal that the interplay between invisibility and hypervisibility also has to do with external processes of racialization, which we discuss in more detail in part three, and that struggles for legibility can be double-edged.

In fact, as Amira Jarmakani (2011) reminds us, invisibility can also serve as a means for expressing complexity and resisting conformity to preconceived paradigms of legibility and ways of being. In an excerpt that we include as chapter 6 in part one, Jarmakani focuses on perceptions of Arab femininity and proposes strategic uses of invisibility, whereby Arab and Arab American ciswomen, trans, and nonbinary people who "are doubly silenced" by the very categories that claim to give them voice can instead "mobilize [the politics of invisibility], thereby reinventing and transforming that invisibility into a tool with which they can create transformative and liberatory futures" (pp. 107, 112). Arab Americans, Jarmakani reminds us, have the power to resist and disidentify (Muñoz 1999) with hegemonic perceptions of them and can ideally move past the false binary of visibility/hypervisibility to create supple and flexible frameworks of meaning.

Naming and Recognition

Concomitant with the question of visibility is the question of names with which we opened this discussion. Although Arabic-speaking communities have established their presence in the Americas since the 1880s, the term *Arab American* gained saliency only relatively recently. Research by Gregory Orfalea (1989), Sarah M. A. Gualtieri (2009), and Hani Bawardi (2014) reveals that usage of the term *Arab American* can be traced back to the 1940s, particularly as it was used by US citizens of Arab background who wished to influence American policy on Palestine. Prior to this period, "Arabic-speaking groups" were referred to by others as "Asians, 'other Asians,' Turks from Asia, Syrians, Caucasians, white, black, or 'colored'" (Suleiman 1999b, 12). Michael Suleiman attributes the absence of an "Arab American" identity in the United States during the late 1800s and early 1900s to several causes, one of which is that "the main bond of solidarity among [Arabic-speaking people] at that time was based on familial, sectarian, and village- or region-oriented factors" (1999b, 12). Another contributing factor was the difficulty of fitting into US racial classifications, an issue that persists to this day. We take up this matter in greater detail in part three, where we discuss the paradox of being racially classified as white by the US government at the same time as being subjected to discrimination, harassment, assault, surveillance, and exclusionary practices based on a wide range of signifiers, including religion, phenotype, dress, name, and language use (Cainkar 2018; Gualtieri 2009; Haney López 2006; Jamal 2008; Naber 2008; Samhan 1999; Zopf 2017).

In Brazil, Argentina, Mexico, and other places in Central and South America, Arabic-speaking peoples and their descendants were and in some cases continue to be labeled *turco* (Alfaro-Velcamp 2007; Civantos 2013; Karam 2013). This designation at once (1) marks the fact that initial arrivals of migrants from Southwest Asia and North Africa (SWANA) came to the Spanish-speaking Americas during the period of the Ottoman Empire and (2) consolidates a set of stereotypes about Arabs as economically shrewd and culturally backward that frames general perceptions of them in those regions.[1] For example, John Tofik Karam, whose work we excerpt in part three, explains: "*Turco* (Turk) has served as a general designation for 'Middle Easterner' in Brazil for more than a century." He adds: "Coined by late nineteenth-century Brazilian elites to denigrate Syrian and Lebanese immigrants as economic pariahs, the term of difference today continues to attribute an alleged shrewdness to Brazilians of Middle Eastern origin" (2013, 80). Christina Civantos, whose work we include in part two, demonstrates that the term *turco* in Argentina was initially used as shorthand for the stereotype of the "wily" Levantine peddler. "To this day," Civantos notes, "'*turco*' usually carries a derogatory connotation linked to the antisemitism of the first half of the twentieth century and to a second wave of anti-Arab sentiment that arose at the end of the 1980s" (2013, 111). Neither the Spanish equivalent of *Arab American* nor an alternate identity-consolidating term yet exists in Mexico, Central America, and South America, which no doubt also has to do with the common imperialist and US-centric conflation of the United States with "America."

Arab Americans' responses to the question of naming have been varied and complex. In the United States, Arab Americans have engaged with both the counterhegemonic discourse of race, illustrated by increasing self-identification as people of color, and with the more assimilationist discourse of multiculturalism, which tends to uphold nationalist mythologies about racial and ethnic harmony. Such nationalist mythologies also operate in the

1. Another common designator for Arab Americans in Latinx America, "Sirio-Libanés," also gestures to the way that an Arab American presence in the Spanish-speaking Americas was consolidated through early migration patterns, about which we elaborate in the introduction to part two.

Americas more broadly. For example, Karam has shown how Arab Brazilians have responded to the pejorative connotations of the appellation *turcos* by reproducing "nationalist notions of 'mixture' (*mestiçagem*) and 'racial democracy' (*democracia racial*) in Brazil" (2013, 80), thereby contributing to the national mythology of racial harmony through mixture. In contrast, Arab Argentines, Civantos reveals in chapter 9 of this reader, adopted the nationalist figure of the Argentine gaucho, simultaneously embracing an orientalist narrative about the figure's Andalusian origins and a nationalist narrative about the figure as "the product of *mestizaje*—of the mixture of Spanish and indigenous elements" (p. 147, citing Richard Slatta). Debates surrounding the ultimately unsuccessful effort to create the category "Middle East and North Africa" (MENA) on the 2020 US Census (see Beydoun 2016; Buchanan, Marks, and Álvarez Figueroa 2016; Kayyali 2013), which we take up in more detail in part three, demonstrate that efforts to become legible to the state are inevitably fraught with the opposing forces of political recognition versus co-optation and even rejection. These various responses reveal naming to be both necessary and overwrought; it can function as a means toward political inclusion at the same time that it draws its own boundaries for exclusion. This consequence is effected not only by internally limiting the group to those who identify with the named category but also by providing the state with more tools to manage the named group.

The Shaping of a Category

During the 1960s, a number of factors coalesced to forge the increasing adoption of an "Arab American" identity: Arab nationalism; the Israeli–Arab War of 1967 and subsequent Israeli military occupations of Arab territories; the US civil rights movement; internationalist women's, workers', and Third World alliances; and anticolonial rights movements more globally. As Gualtieri and Homsi Vinson note, the writings of Evelyn Shakir and Etel Adnan offer insights into the embrace of the category "Arab American" (2018, vii). Evelyn Shakir, for example, remarks that even though she and others in her community knew themselves as "*bint*" and "*ibn Arab*" (literally, "daughter or son of an Arab"—in other words, "an Arab"), she and other second- and third-generation US-born children of immigrants from what was formerly called "Greater Syria" publicly added the label *Arab* as a political statement after the Israeli–Arab War of 1967 (1997, 1). Etel Adnan, however, emphasizes her location in the United States and the student movements on US campuses as pivotal in her embrace of both an Arab and American identity. In Lebanon, she remarks, she "had a kind of fluid identity" that made her wonder: "Was I Greek, Ottoman, Arab, almost French?" However, she adds: "It was in Berkeley that . . . I became what I was, I became an Arab at the same time that I was becoming an American. . . . This world became a reality, in all its interplay of local identities and transnational solidarities" (2004, 56–57). As the remarks by both Shakir and Adnan illustrate, the designation *Arab American* is not just reactive to political exigency but also proactive and deployed strategically to assert an emerging sense of shared cultural, political, legal, and social identity for Arabs in the United States.

A number of scholars have argued that the development of an Arab American identity was crystallized in the formation of the Association of Arab American University Graduates in 1967 (Joseph 1999; Khan 2017 and chapter 35 in this reader; Pennock 2017; Suleiman 1999a; Terry 1999), discussed in the introduction to this reader. Responses to this crystallization, manifested by the Arab American organizations that arose after the 1960s, typically envision a break from articulations of identity at the turn of the twentieth century, a period generally associated with a *mahjar* or emigrant group identity. Recent scholarship, however, helps us tease out the continuities between these time periods as well as the differences between them. Members of the *mahjar* attempted to influence US policies toward Arab countries, in particular Palestine (Bawardi 2014; Ghareeb and Tutunji 2016; Hassan 2011); they engaged in transnational political activism and philanthropy (Balloffet 2017; Fahrenthold 2013); and they formed benevolent, cultural, and literary associations. They also spoke in Arabic and for the most part identified themselves by their places of origin. For example, while some associations of the period such as the Partido Patriótico Árabe (Hizb al-Watani al-ʿArabi) in Buenos Aires highlighted a pan-Arab political stance, others such as al-Nadi al-Homsi ([City of] Homs Club) in São Paulo and the Syrian Ladies Aid Society of New York highlighted—as evident in their chosen names—parochial or regional affiliations. Similarly, the newspaper *Kawkab Amirka* (Star [planet] of America), which was published between 1892 and 1908, espoused the aim of "bringing its eastern and western readers into closer and more intimate relations" (qtd. in Moise A. Khayrallah Center for Lebanese Diaspora Studies 2015). However, the newspaper was published largely in Arabic, with only some articles in English, and it identified its primary audience as "Ottoman subjects scattered throughout Europe, North and South America" (qtd. in Moise A. Khayrallah Center for Lebanese Diaspora Studies 2015). The writers who joined the Pen League (*al-Rabitah al-Qalamiyya*), an association first established in 1916 and then resurrected in New York City in 1920—including among its members Ameen Rihani, Mikhail Naimy, and Kahlil Gibran (Jubran Khalil Jubran)—came to be known as writers of the *mahjar*—that is, writers abroad, and their literary contributions, scholars agree, exerted a strong influence on the development of a modern literary style that broke away from classical Arabic forms and contributed to the Arab literary renaissance movement, or *al-Nahda* (El-Ariss 2018; Hassan 2011; Kayyali 2005; Ludescher 2006; Shakir 1997). Similarly, ʿAfifa Karam, who was born in Amshit, Lebanon, and lived in Louisiana, produced three novels in Arabic and contributed to a transnational feminist Arab movement through her contributions to the magazine *al-Huda* (Guidance) between 1897 and 1924 as well as to *Majallat al-'alam al-jadid al-nisa'iyya* (The New World: A Ladies Magazine), the earliest Arabic-language women's magazine published in the Americas (Ghurayyib n.d.; Gualtieri 2020, 284; Saylor 2015). Notwithstanding the contrasts in the tenor and aims between the associations that arose at the turn of the twentieth century and those of the 1960s and after, the adoption of the term *Arab American* as category and identity signals—in line with the earlier associations—the importance of maintaining transnational ties to the homelands and the key role of language in the connection to homelands.

The essays we have compiled for this opening part of the reader offer ways of understanding how there is nothing natural or complete about the category "Arab American." It excludes, for example, ethnic minorities from Arab countries and SWANA at large (e.g., Kurds, Imazighen) and may figuratively obscure religious identifications (Christian, Jewish, Baha'i) not popularly invoked by the term *Arab* because of its imagined conflation with Islam. For example, as Shohat's (2017) work on the splitting of the category "Arab" from the category "Jew" elucidates, the former is not only conflated with Islam but also distanced from Judaism, occluding shared if complex histories of interaction and cultural production. Kyla Wazana Tompkins also addresses this point when she notes that Arab Jewish identity is often rendered invisible, in part from the "occlusion of Arab Jewish history from mainstream Jewish history" and in part because "there are almost no Jews left in Arab countries," but also because "it is almost impossible to conceive of non-Muslim Arab subjects within the public sphere today, inflected as it is by anti-Arab hysteria" (2011, 129). It is important to emphasize that the category "Arab American" is in itself ecumenical in that it makes no claims about religious identity. Given that most Arab states are Muslim majority and elide distinctions between Arab ethnicity and national/political identity (where "Arab" is not only a marker of a shared culture and language but also a designation of citizenship in a group of nation-states), then it becomes understandable that the categories "Arab" and "Arab American" would be in a state of constant revision and reinvention. Indeed, if the category "Arab American" appears to occlude the experiences of certain groups, such as Arab Jews, it also subsumes groups who contest or reject it. For example, L. J. Mahoul (1994) writes about her Maronite Christian Lebanese family's resistance to the label *Arab* and their insistence on a Lebanese Maronite identity instead, a stance that is echoed by many other Lebanese Christians, as Randa Kayyali (2018) has shown. Similarly, in *The Chaldeans: Politics and Identity in Iraq and the American Diaspora* (2019), Yasmeen Hanoosh has shown how many Iraqi Chaldeans also distinguish themselves from other Arabs and Arab Americans through their identification with their religious affiliation. Not only does the category "Arab American" elide distinctions among religious groups who come from what are now Arab nation-states, but it also obscures the presence of large numbers of non-Arab ethnic and linguistic communities, among them Armenians, Kurds, Turkomen, and Imazighen, who are citizens of Arab countries. Discussions of Arabs and Arab Americans, therefore, must remain cognizant of these elisions, conflations, and distinctions among individuals who are either left out or nonconsensually subsumed within them.

Recipes for Mapping an Intersectional and Transnational Field

As the conversations about naming and legibility (including the paradoxes of visibility and hypervisibility) demonstrate, the category "Arab American" has at times operated in rigid, limited, and exclusionary ways. Scholarship in the field has also at times (and perhaps unwittingly) upheld unspoken hegemonies—for example, through reifying the implicit whiteness of the category "Arab American" and through contributing to the US-centrism of the category. The essays selected for this part aim to expand and complicate ways of seeing (after Berger 1972) the category. They build on narratives that endeavored to define and lay claim to the category "Arab American" in the 1980s and early 2000s. These works include *Becoming American: The Early Arab Immigrant Experience* (1985) by Alixa Naff; *Before the Flames: A Quest for the History of Arab Americans* (1988) by Gregory Orfalea; *The Development of Arab-American Identity* (1994) edited by Ernest McCarus; *Bint Arab: Arab and Arab American Women in the United States* (1997) by Evelyn Shakir; *Arabs in America: Building a New Future* (1999) edited by Michael Suleiman; and, more recently, *The Arab Americans* (2005) by Randa Kayyali and "Becoming Arab American" (2016) by Louise Cainkar, which articulates how transnational Arab American youth define the term. The discussions in these edited collections, monographs, and essays offer important interventions in defining the category "Arab American" by filling in gaps and silences about Arab American history and experiences. Addressing the category-defining question mentioned earlier, "Who are Arab Americans?," they laid important groundwork for exploring the themes of visibility/invisibility, religion and ethnicity, race and racialization, diaspora and mobility, multiculturalism, orientalism and representation, solidarities, empire, and self-definition. The essays we include in this part collectively build on as well as revise these earlier debates about legibility, naming, and visibility.

We open this part with the introduction from Joe Kadi's groundbreaking collection *Food for Our Grandmothers: Writings by Arab-American & Arab-Canadian Feminists* (1994). Working from a feminist tradition that recognizes "the personal is political," Kadi foregrounds questions of race, gender, and sexuality while highlighting the importance of using an intersectional lens for addressing Arab American experiences. Conceived as an homage to the important figure of the Arab or Arab American grandmother, the collection also endeavors to provide "a helpful map for women and men in our community who are struggling with issues of culture, identity, history, and activism" (p. 55). The themes articulated in Kadi's collection—invisibility/

visibility, maps, naming, home, and cooking—became central to the development of the field of Arab American studies in the 1990s and 2000s and continue to resonate today.[2]

Maps, cooking, and home are apt themes for thinking about the ways intersectional scholarship has sought to complicate and expand the field. We draw on this set of themes here as a useful point of departure for reconsidering how both the struggle for and the limitations of legibility have shaped the category "Arab American." In this sense, the theme of "home" can be an invitation to interrogate the assumptions that can shape the notions of "home" and "homelands": How might these concepts essentialize, authenticate, or elide other ways of understanding and being Arab American? How might they unintentionally conflate the United States with "America"? For example, in her contribution to this part (chapter 5), Michelle Hartman asserts that, in contrast to earlier Arab American literary anthologies, Joe Kadi's *Food for Our Grandmothers* offers an alternative to essentialist constructions of Arab American identity, and it does so through a critical engagement with both gender and race that builds alliances with other marginalized groups in Canada and the United States. Further complicating narratives of essentialism, in chapter 2 Nadine Naber explores the complexities and contradictions of "authenticity" as it functions within Arab American communities. Her contribution, "The Politics of Cultural Authenticity," interrogates the way middle-class Arabs in the United States "herald particular ideals as markers of an authentic, essential, true, or real Arab culture" (p. 57). Unpacking the discourses of authenticity in relation to the larger contexts of orientalism and US imperialism, Naber situates her analysis within the discourse of

2. Food, maps, and grandparents as conduits or links to ethnic identity are motifs that are not unique to Arab Americans or Arab American writing. On the topic of food alone, one might consider a number of special journal issues, such as the *MELUS* special issue on food in multiethnic literatures in 2007, edited by Fred Gardaphe and Wenying Xu, the special issue of *Mizna* titled "Eating the Other" in 2014, edited by Khaldoun Samman, and the *Mashriq & Mahjar* issue on food and Middle East diasporas in 2019, edited by Andrew Arsan, Lily Balloffet, and Akram Khater. Kyla Wazana Tompkins's *Racial Indigestion: Eating Bodies in the 19th Century* (2012) examines the relationship among food, visual rhetoric, whiteness, and nationalism. See also Carol Bardenstein's (2010) work on Diana Abu-Jaber's use of food metaphors in her memoir *The Language of Baklava*; Rachel Norman's (2018) essay on food and the maternal body in the work of Arab American writers in Canada, the United States, and Mexico; as well as the articles by Michelle Hartman and Matthew Jaber Stiffler that we have included in this reader (chapters 5 and 26). Similarly, the recurrence of references to maps in Arab American literature, as in the works of Randa Jarrar (*A Map of Home*, 2008) and Zeyn Joukhadar (*The Map of Salt and Stars*, 2018), among others, is in line with preoccupations with mapping in diasporic and Indigenous writing more generally (see, for example, the Vietnamese American graphic writer Thi Bui's *The Best We Could Do* [2017] and the Egyptian British writer Ahdaf Soueif's *The Map of Love* [1999], among others). The significance of the concept of mapping in Indigenous literature is captured in Mishuana Goeman's critical study *Mark My Words: Native Women Mapping Our Nations* (2013).

multiculturalism in the United States, on the one hand, and in relation to "transnational modalities of power—US Orientalist discourses and structures of colonialism and imperialism, race, class, gender, and sexuality" (p. 57), on the other. By troubling the essentializing narrative of cultural authenticity and expanding beyond a US-centric notion of Arab America, Naber's work demonstrates critical expansions in the field within the past decade.

The activity of cooking draws our attention to questions of embodiment and the ways that everyday activities shape subjectivity. How can a focus on the body and attention to the fluidity of breath and embodiment help to productively loosen the restrictive boundaries of the category "Arab American"? The insights Kadi and Hartman make possible by attending to intersectional approaches to literary production and analysis are further highlighted in chapter 3 by an excerpt we include from Therí Pickens's book *New Body Politics* (2014). Working from a disability studies perspective, Pickens analyzes how Palestinian American poet and spoken-word artist Suheir Hammad "mobilizes breath" and the fragility of the body "as an act of resistance" (p. 81). Elucidating the ways in which Hammad mixes Arab American and African American poetic traditions to complicate ideas of race, language, and the significance of bodily presence, Pickens suggests that "Hammad's work also proposes a set of cross-cultural conversations about what people of color across the globe can say to one another despite being implicated in the domination of one another often imposed by nation-states in their name (and without their permission)" (p. 83). A disability justice framework teaches us to understand racial politics as viscerally centered in the body and highlights how bodies are intersectionally affected by violent white supremacy, heteropatriarchy, ableism, and capitalism. Pickens addresses the way that body politics informs Arab American cultural production, inviting us to center the disability justice principles of coalitional sustainability and collective liberation in the work of dismantling oppressive systems (Sins Invalid 2015).

Finally, the metaphor of maps reminds us of cartography's colonialist origins, of the residue of colonialism in the unnatural boundaries of nation-states, and of the need to transnationalize the Arab Americas in their very conceptualization and to de-center the United States as synonymous with "America." The contribution by Ella Shohat on "the two 1492s" in chapter 4 establishes the firm connection between the expulsions of Muslims and Jews from Spain and the conquest of the Americas, sealing the shared fates of Europe's others: Africans, Arabs, Muslims, and Indigenous people. Shohat reminds us that the "intersectionality of regions and cartographies of knowledge allow us to redraw static maps of scholarly terrain, stretching and broadening the field" (2013, 59).

Although necessarily partial, the essays we have gathered in this opening part of the reader, when taken together, map key concerns of the field. Exploring historical constructions of the category "Arab American" across the Americas and across nations, they foreground questions of legibility in the formation of the field, explore the politics of invisibility/hypervisibility and of naming as foundational to Arab American studies, and situate Arab American studies as intersectional and transnational. The types of questions that frame part one are put forth in a spirit of open inquiry and curiosity, not as a fixed definition of an "Arab American" category.

Works Cited

Abinader, Elmaz. 2004. "The Relentlessness of Memory." In *Scheherazade's Legacy: Arab and Arab American Women on Writing*, edited by Susan Muaddi Darraj, 109–19. Westport, CT: Praeger.

Adnan, Etel. 2004. "The Itinerary of an Arab American Writer." In *Scheherazade's Legacy: Arab and Arab American Women on Writing*, edited by Susan Muaddi Darraj, 51–57. Westport, CT: Praeger.

Alfaro-Velcamp, Theresa. 2007. *So Far from Allah, so Close to Mexico: Middle Eastern Immigrants in Modern Mexico*. Austin: Univ. of Texas Press.

El-Ariss, Tarek, ed. 2018. *The Arab Renaissance: A Bilingual Anthology of the* Nahda. New York: Modern Language Association of America.

Arsan, Andrew, Lily Balloffet, and Akram Khater, eds. 2019. "Food and Middle East Diasporas." Special issue of *Mashriq & Mahjar* 6, no. 2.

Aziz, Barbara Nimri. 2004. Foreword to *Scheherazade's Legacy: Arab and Arab American Women on Writing*, edited by Susan Muaddi Darraj, xi–xv. Westport, CT: Praeger.

Balloffet, Lily Pearl. 2017. "From the Pampa to the Mashriq: Arab-Argentine Philanthropy Networks." *Mashriq & Mahjar* 4, no. 1: 4–28.

Bardenstein, Carol. 2010. "Beyond Univocal Baklava: Deconstructing Food-as-Ethnicity and the Ideology of Homeland in Diana Abu Jaber's *The Language of Baklava*." *Journal of Arabic Literature* 41, nos. 1–2: 160–79.

Bawardi, Hani. 2014. *The Making of Arab Americans: From Syrian Nationalism to U.S. Citizenship*. Austin: Univ. of Texas Press.

Berger, John. 1972. *Ways of Seeing*. London: British Broadcasting Corporation and Penguin Books.

Beydoun, Khaled A. 2016. "Boxed In: Reclassification of Arab Americans on the U.S. Census as Progress or Peril." *Loyola University Chicago Law Journal* 47:693–759.

Buchanan, Angela, Rachel Marks, and Magdaliz Álvarez Figueroa. 2016. *2015 Forum on Ethnic Groups from the Middle East and North Africa: Meeting Summary and Main Findings*. Washington, DC: US Census Bureau.

Bui, Thi. 2017. *The Best We Could Do*. New York: Abrams.

Cainkar, Louise. 2016. "Becoming Arab American." *Middle East Report* 278 (Spring): 44–46.

———. 2018. "Fluid Terror Threat: A Genealogy of the Racialization of Arab, Muslim, and South Asian Americans." In "Arab/Americas: Locations & Iterations," edited by Sarah M. A. Gualtieri and Pauline Homsi Vinson. Special issue of *Amerasia Journal* 44, no. 1: 27–60.

Civantos, Christina. 2013. "Ali Bla Bla's Double-Edged Sword: Argentine President Carlos Menem and the Negotiation of Identity." In *Between the Middle East and the Americas: The Cultural Politics of Diaspora*, edited by Evelyn Alsultany and Ella Shohat, 108–29. Ann Arbor: Univ. of Michigan Press.

Erakat, Noura. 2011. "*Arabiya* Made Invisible: Between Marginalization of Agency and Silencing of Dissent." In *Arab & Arab American Feminisms: Gender, Violence, & Belonging*, edited by Rabab Abdulhadi, Evelyn Alsultany, and Nadine Naber, 174–83. Syracuse, NY: Syracuse Univ. Press.

Fahrenthold, Stacey. 2013. "Transnational Modes and Media: The Syrian Press in the *Mahjar* and Emigrant Activism during World War I." *Mashriq & Mahjar* 1, no. 1: 30–54.

Gardaphe, Fred L., and Wenying Xu, eds. 2007. "Food in Multiethnic Literatures." Special issue of *MELUS* 32, no. 4.

Ghareeb, Edmund, and Jenab Tutunji. 2016. "Arab American Writers, the Mahjar Press, and the Palestine Issue." *Arab Studies Quarterly* 38, no. 1 (Jan.): 418–42.

Ghurayyib, Rose. N.d. "Afifa Karam: A Pioneering Lebanese Journalist." *Al-Raida Journal* 1, no. 8. At https://doi.org/10.32380/alrj.v0i0.935.

Goeman, Mishuana. 2013. *Mark My Words: Native Women Mapping Our Nations.* Minneapolis: Univ. of Minnesota Press.

Gualtieri, Sarah M. A. 2009. *Between Arab and White: Race and Ethnicity in the Early Syrian American Diaspora.* Berkeley: Univ. of California Press.

———. 2020. *Arab Routes: Pathways to Syrian California.* Stanford, CA: Stanford Univ. Press.

Gualtieri, Sarah M. A., and Pauline Homsi Vinson. 2018. Introduction to "Arab/Americas: Locations & Iterations," edited by Sarah M. A. Gualtieri and Pauline Homsi Vinson. Special issue of *Amerasia Journal* 44, no. 1: vii–xxi.

Hagopian, Elaine C., ed. 2004. *Civil Rights in Peril: The Targeting of Arabs and Muslims.* Chicago: Haymarket Books.

Haney López, Ian. 2006. *White by Law: The Legal Construction of Race.* New York: New York Univ. Press.

Hanoosh, Yasmeen. 2019. *The Chaldeans: Politics and Identity in Iraq and the American Diaspora.* London: I. B. Tauris.

Hassan, Waël S. 2011. *Immigrant Narratives: Orientalism and Cultural Translation in Arab American and Arab British Literature.* New York: Oxford Univ. Press.

Jamal, Amaney. 2008. "Civil Liberties and the Otherization of Arab and Muslim Americans." In *Race and Arab Americans before and after 9/11: From Invisible Citizens to Visible Subjects*, edited by Amaney Jamal and Nadine Naber, 114–30. Syracuse, NY: Syracuse Univ. Press.

Jamal, Amaney, and Nadine Naber, eds. 2008. *Race and Arab Americans before and after 9/11: From Invisible Citizens to Visible Subjects.* Syracuse, NY: Syracuse Univ. Press.

Jarmakani, Amira. 2011. "Arab American Feminisms: Mobilizing the Politics of Invisibility." In *Arab & Arab American Feminisms: Gender, Violence, & Belonging*, edited by Rabab Abdulhadi, Evelyn Alsultany, and Nadine Naber, 227–41. Syracuse, NY: Syracuse Univ. Press.

Jarrar, Randa. 2008. *A Map of Home.* New York: Other Press.

Joseph, Suad. 1999. "Against the Grain of the Nation—the Arab." In *Arabs in America: Building a New Future*, edited by Michael W. Suleiman, 257–71. Philadelphia: Temple Univ. Press.

Joukhadar, Zeyn. 2018. *The Map of Salt and Stars*. New York: Touchstone.

Kadi, Joe, ed. 1994. *Food for Our Grandmothers: Writings by Arab-American & Arab-Canadian Feminists*. Boston: South End Press.

Karam, John Tofik. 2013. "Turcos in the Mix: Corrupting Arabs in Brazil's Racial Democracy." In *Between the Middle East and the Americas: The Cultural Politics of Diaspora*, edited by Evelyn Alsultany and Ella Shohat, 80–95. Ann Arbor: Univ. of Michigan Press.

Kayyali, Randa. 2005. *The Arab Americans*. Westport, CT: Greenwood Press.

———. 2013. "US Census Classifications and Arab Americans: Contestations and Definitions of Identity Markers." *Journal of Ethnic and Migration Studies* 39, no. 8: 1299–318.

———. 2018. "Race, Religion, and Identity: Arab Christians in the United States." *Culture and Religion* 19, no. 1: 1–19.

Khan, Suraya. 2017. "Transnational Alliances: The AAUG's Advocacy for Palestine and the Third World." *Arab Studies Quarterly* 40, no. 1: 53–72.

Ludescher, Tanyss Carol. 2006. "From Nostalgia to Critique: An Overview of Arab American Literature." *MELUS* 31, no. 4: 93–114.

Mahoul, L. J. 1994. "Battling Nationalisms to Salvage Her History." In *Food for Our Grandmothers: Writings by Arab-American & Arab-Canadian Feminists*, edited by Joe Kadi, 24–29. Boston: South End Press.

McCarus, Ernest, ed. 1994. *The Development of Arab-American Identity*. Ann Arbor: Univ. of Michigan Press.

Moise A. Khayrallah Center for Lebanese Diaspora Studies. 2015. "Kawkab Amirka." At https://lebanesestudies.omeka.chass.ncsu.edu/collections/show/51.

Muñoz, José Esteban. 1999. *Disidentifications*. Minneapolis: Univ. of Minnesota Press.

Naber, Nadine. 2000. "Ambiguous Insiders: An Investigation of Arab American Invisibility." *Ethnic and Racial Studies* 23, no. 1: 37–61.

———. 2008. "'Look, Mohammed the Terrorist Is Coming!': Cultural Racism, Nation-Based Racism, and the Intersectionality of Oppressions after 9/11." In *Race and Arab Americans before and after 9/11: From Invisible Citizens to Visible Subjects*, edited by Amaney Jamal and Nadine Naber, 276–304. Syracuse, NY: Syracuse Univ. Press.

Naff, Alixa. 1985. *Becoming American: The Early Arab Immigrant Experience*. Carbondale: Southern Illinois Univ. Press.

Norman, Rachel. 2018. "Eating the Matriarch: Locating Identity in the Arab American Female Body." In "Arab/Americas: Locations & Iterations," edited by Sarah M. A. Gualtieri and Pauline Homsi Vinson. Special Issue of *Amerasia Journal* 44, no. 1: 128–45.

Nye, Naomi Shihab. 1994. "Blood." In *Food for Our Grandmothers: Writings by Arab-American & Arab-Canadian Feminists*, edited by Joe Kadi, 226. Boston: South End Press.

Orfalea, Gregory. 1988. *Before the Flames: A Quest for the History of Arab Americans*. Austin: Univ. of Texas Press.

———. 1989. "On Arab Americans: A Bibliographical Essay." *American Studies International* 27, no. 2: 26–41.

Pennock, Pam. 2017. *The Rise of the Arab American Left: Activists, Allies, and Their Fight against Imperialism and Racism, 1960s–1980s*. Chapel Hill: Univ. of North Carolina Press.

Pickens, Therí A. 2014. *New Body Politics: Narrating Arab and Black Identity in the Contemporary United States*. New York: Routledge.

Saliba, Therese. 1994. "Military Presences and Absences: Arab Women and the Persian Gulf War." In *Food for Our Grandmothers: Writings by Arab-American & Arab-Canadian Feminists*, edited by Joe Kadi, 126–32. Boston: South End Press.

Samhan, Helen Hatab. 1987. "Politics and Exclusion: The Arab American Experience." *Journal of Palestine Studies* 16, no. 2: 11–28.

———. 1999. "Not Quite White: Race Classification and the Arab-American Experience." In *Arabs in America: Building a New Future*, edited by Michael W. Suleiman, 209–26. Philadelphia: Temple Univ. Press.

Samman, Khaldoun, ed. 2014. "Eating the Other." Special issue of *Mizna* 15, no. 1.

Saylor, Elizabeth. 2015. "'A Bridge Too Soon': The Life and Works of 'Afifa Karam: The First Arab American Woman Novelist." PhD diss., Univ. of California, Berkeley.

Shakir, Evelyn. 1997. *Bint Arab: Arab and Arab American Women in the United States*. Westport, CT: Praeger.

Shohat, Ella. 2013. "The Sephardi-Moorish Atlantic: Between Orientalism and Occidentalism." In *Between the Middle East and the Americas: The Cultural Politics of Diaspora*, edited by Evelyn Alsultany and Ella Shohat, 43–62. Ann Arbor: Univ. of Michigan Press.

———. 2017. *On the Arab-Jew, Palestine, and Other Displacements: Selected Writings*. London: Pluto Press.

Sins Invalid. 2015. "10 Principles of Disability Justice." Sept. 17. At https://www.sinsinvalid.org/blog/10-principles-of-disability-justice.

Soueif, Ahdaf. 1999. *The Map of Love*. New York. Anchor Books.

Suleiman, Michael W., ed. 1999a. *Arabs in America: Building a New Future*. Philadelphia: Temple Univ. Press.

———. 1999b. "Introduction: The Arab Immigrant Experience." In *Arabs in America: Building a New Future*, edited by Michael W. Suleiman, 1–21. Philadelphia: Temple Univ. Press.

———. 1999c. Preface to *Arabs in America: Building a New Future*, edited by Michael W. Suleiman, [xi]. Philadelphia: Temple Univ. Press.

Terry, Janice. 1999. "Community and Political Activism among Arab Americans in Detroit." In *Arabs in America: Building a New Future*, edited by Michael W. Suleiman, 209–26. Philadelphia: Temple Univ. Press.

Tompkins, Kyla Wazana. 2011. "History's Traces: Personal Narrative, Diaspora, and the Arab Jewish Experience." In *Arab & Arab American Feminisms: Gender, Violence, & Belonging*, edited by Rabab Abdulhadi, Evelyn Alsultany, and Nadine Naber, 124–40. Syracuse, NY: Syracuse Univ. Press.

———. 2012. *Racial Indigestion: Eating Bodies in the 19th Century*. New York. New York Univ. Press.

Volpp, Leti. 2003. "The Citizen and the Terrorist." In *September 11 in History: A Watershed Moment?*, edited by Mary L. Dudziak, 147–62. Durham, NC: Duke Univ. Press.

Zogby, James J., and Helen Samhan. 1987. "Arab Baiting and the 1986 Elections." *Washington Report on Middle East Affairs*, Feb., 5–6.

Zopf, Bradley. 2017. "A Different Kind of Brown: Arabs and Middle Easterners as Anti-American Muslims." *Sociology of Race and Ethnicity* 4, no. 2: 178–91.

1

Introduction to *Food for Our Grandmothers*

JOE KADI

I sat in a wooden desk, its top scarred by the pens and knives of students who had gone before me, and stared at the map of the world hanging over the blackboard. "This represents the earth," Mrs. Gallagher said emphatically as my feet swung a few inches above the floor. "North is at the top, south at the bottom. You need to know how to read maps, so that you know where you are."

I could not challenge my teacher, but I didn't know what to make of all this. For one thing, the way I perceived towns and cities, countries and continents did not match the neat, concise way they appeared on maps. For another, even when I learned Mrs. Gallagher's basic map-reading formula, I often did not know where I was. Her formula did not answer my questions. My grandmother told me that Syria and Lebanon hadn't been separate countries when she was growing up, but Mrs. Gallagher spoke adamantly about clear boundaries between them, past and present.

Confused, I dangled my feet in silence.

My dictionary tells me a map is a representation of the earth's surface showing both physical and political features. This definition fits with what I now believe about maps: they exist in many forms, some are complicated and contradictory, and north is not always at the top. Different maps also provide us with new information about where we are. Creating a map is a powerful experience. *Food for Our Grandmothers* can also be understood as a map, representing both physical and political features of the earth's surface. Complicated and contradictory, north is not always at the top. It provides new information about where and how we locate ourselves in the world. Finally, creating this book has empowered and hopefully will continue to empower many of us.

Maps appear in different forms. Mrs. Gallagher never explained that, but I've figured it out myself. It's true that some maps are on flat paper with straight lines, and it's also true that some are twisting and winding. Braided.

I remember standing in that small bathroom watching what my Gram did with her beautiful hair. It fell past her waist. Dark grey with light silver threads and a few dark-brown ones remaining. She divided it into three even strands—no easy task.

Take those three pieces and weave, curve, twist. Do not pull so tightly that it hurts your scalp; do not weave so loosely that the hairs separate. It's hard to find that balance. There are things I once took for granted whose beauty, endurance, and usefulness now astound me.

I once took my grandmother, my Sittee, whom we called Gram, for granted. Everything I remember about her I once took for granted. Today, I am puzzled by and ashamed of this.

Gram had a loving voice, a ready laugh, a soothing touch. Her green thumb allowed her to grow any plant under any conditions. She survived poverty in her homeland only to have it follow her halfway around the world. She loved poker and never lost at cards. Gram had small, strong, gnarled hands. Work-worn hands, busy hands. I watched them kneading dough for Syrian bread. I watched them wrap a new bowl of *laban* in several towels to sit overnight. I watched them roll out spinach pies. I watched them cut freshly baked kibbeh into diamond-shaped pieces.

Introduction to *Food for Our Grandmothers: Writings by Arab-American & Arab-Canadian Feminists*, edited by Joe Kadi (Boston: South End Press, 1999), xiii–xx.

I watched those hands braid hair. Beautifully. Daily.

I know it is possible and I believe it is necessary to create maps that are alive, many-layered, multidimensional, open-ended, and braided. I watched Gram combing that long hair, dividing it into three equal parts, twisting and turning and curving the pieces. Braiding tightly enough so that each hair stays in place, but not so tightly that it hurts. It is difficult finding that balance.

It is difficult finding that balance. Take three strands—one that is Gram, one that is me, one that is the force of history—twist, turn, and curve; do not pull so tightly that it hurts; do not weave so loosely that strands escape. It is difficult finding that balance.

My grandmother's life began in the Lebanese mountains in the early years of this century. Twenty years ago an aunt told me the name of the village: Aduba Qozhaya. She only told me once. I never forgot it. I carried it with me, a small seed in my left hand. I looked on maps but never found it. It is too small for most map makers to notice.

Gram immigrated to Canada as a young girl—part of a large family looking for a better life. She married a man who had come from Beirut, and he died young, decades before my birth. I think pneumonia was the cause. I think poverty was the cause.

So Gram raised five children alone. They had little money. "But she always had food to share," my father said to me once as we drove to the shopping center. He rarely mentioned his childhood. So this story was a most unexpected gift. "All the hobos passing through on the trains during the Depression stopped at our house for dinner, and she always fed them. I thought there must have been a mark on our door, telling them to come in."

These days I am able to appreciate my grandmother's very remarkable and very ordinary beauty. I do wish I could talk to her, I have so many questions. Do transplants ever find home? Are we weakened by the ever-present feeling of not belonging in the West or the East, of having a foot in both worlds but no solid roots in either? Or are we stronger, more innovative and creative, able to make home in odd sites, able to survive in small, hard places, plants growing out of rocks? Perhaps this is our advantage, perhaps this is what we bring to the world. Find home wherever you can make it. Make home so you can find it wherever.

There are things I once took for granted whose beauty, endurance, and usefulness now astound me.

Lebanon is east of here. I am sure of this fact. After all, its location is the Middle East. An appropriate name only if one is a colonizer standing west and invading east. The Middle East. What's in a name? Quite a lot, actually.

Lebanon. I grew up tasting Lebanon and hearing its music, but not speaking and only rarely hearing its language. Often I listened to English spoken by a tongue that had first learned Arabic, a tongue that hissed the *s*'s and rolled the *r*'s. And now when I hear "broken English" it edges its way into my heart.

Lebanese. Not Black. Not white. Never quite fitting in. Always on the edge.

There are things I once took for granted whose ugliness, endurance, and uselessness now astound me.

Dig out a map of my old high school. Try to retrace those corridors, try to recast those sound waves echoing off walls lined with yellow lockers. "Oil slick." "Arab whore." "Greasy Arab."

Jokes I once laughed at, tried desperately to see the humor in. Kevin O'Reilly brazenly skipped school for a whole day, a daring act in 1973. The year of the oil embargo. Arab enemy. Kevin presented his own note to the homeroom teacher the next day. "Had to go fight the Arabs and get our oil back." Laughter.

Words of a prophet. Eighteen years later it happened. Although *fight* is not the word I would use.

As Arabs, like other people of color in this racist society, our race is simultaneously emphasized and ignored. For long periods of time no one can remember that Arabs even exist. This is the case no matter how many times non-Arabs are reminded of our presence. Of course, this forgetfulness changes once there is another "crisis" in the Middle East. Crisis: a by-product of past and current colonialism. During crises, Arabs can be reassured we exist as a distinct racial group. We will remember it, in the dark of night and the light of day. We will feel the effects of the social construction of "the Arabs" that has cast us as enemy, other, fanatical terrorist, crazy Muslim. If we are women, we can add to that list veiled Woman and exotic whore.

I cannot remember the last time I saw a newspaper headline that did not link Palestinians and terrorism,

Islam and fanaticism. Some people are surprised to learn I rarely read newspapers.

I desperately needed a map during the massacre known as the Gulf War. All Arab-Canadian and Arab-American activists—and even those who tried to stay hidden—did. Avoid that street; Arab-bashers are lurking. Don't go to that demo; too many FBI cameras. Accept this speaking engagement, but not that one. Leave your kaffiya at home tonight. Wear that button. Don't display your grief so openly—it's not the time or the place. Lock the grief inside those brown eyes and hold it there for however long it takes. Don't talk about what you know.

We can talk about what we know, we can work for radical change, we can create maps that chart new ground. I hope this collection of essays and poems offers landmarks, signposts, names, and directions not only for Arab-American and Arab-Canadian communities but for other communities of color and our allies.

Books such as this one have functioned and continue to function in those ways: I am thinking of *This Bridge Called My Back: Writings by Radical Women of Color* edited by Gloria Anzaldúa and Cherríe Moraga; *Home Girls: A Black Feminist Anthology* edited by Barbara Smith; *Making Waves: An Anthology of Writings by and about Asian American Women* edited by Asian Women United of California; *A Gathering of Spirit: A Collection by North American Indian Women* edited by Beth Brant. Books such as these help record a community's history and spirit. They are valuable maps in our struggle for liberation, offering the hope and information, sustenance and analysis, education and challenges that we need so desperately.

This book is a new map, created by writers, activists, artists, poets, teachers, a mother-and-daughter team, and two (blood) sisters. We are lesbians, bisexuals, and heterosexuals; of different generations; working class, middle class, upper-middle class; women born in the Arab world and women born here. Even with all this diversity, *Food for Our Grandmothers* is not complete because many of our experiences and histories are still to be explored. I hope many anthologies follow this one. I believe that this collection is a good beginning, however. I believe it provides a helpful map for women and men in our community who are struggling with issues of culture, identity, history, and activism.

Editing this book raised many political questions. One question I grappled with long and hard was the book's title and, in particular, the phrase "Writings by Arab-American and Arab-Canadian Feminists." Arabs are Semitic people who originated on the Arabian Peninsula. The nineteen Arab countries on the west part of the Asian continent and the northern part of the African continent are: Lebanon, Palestine, Jordan, Syria, Kuwait, Saudi Arabia, Yemen, Oman, Bahrain, Tunisia, Algeria, Egypt, Sudan, Qatar, Mauritania, Iraq, Libya, Morocco, and the United Arab Emirates. Those countries, along with the non-Arab nations of Turkey, Armenia, and Iran, are often referred to as the Middle East. In some contexts Somalia and Djibouti are also considered part of the Middle East.

Three contributors to this anthology are of Middle Eastern, but not Arab, descent: two Armenian-Americans and one Iranian-American. These women share a great many things with Arab women. It made sense to include them as contributors and offer them a chance to give voice to their experiences. Yet the title I came up with does not include them.

I tried to find a title that included all contributors to this anthology, and I did not. But as I searched, I gained a new perspective on the power of names and the effects they have on our psyches. Names are critical for a personal and communal sense of affirmation. Choosing our names and thinking through their implications, rather than accepting those given to us by the dominant culture, is an empowering act. I've come up with three possibilities for naming ourselves as a community—Arab-American/Arab-Canadian, people of Middle Eastern/North African descent, and West Asian/North African.

The term "Arab-American/Arab-Canadian" appeals to me. It allows us to reclaim the word "Arab," to force people to hear and say a word that has become synonymous with "crazy Muslim terrorists." It affirms our identity and links us to our brothers and sisters in Arab countries. However, there are two problems with this phrase. It does not link us to larger groups of people of color, that is, Asians and Africans, but rather sets us apart and in isolation. This problematic dynamic already exists because few other groups of people of color know much about or care much about Arabs. It feels important to me to disrupt and change that pattern. Second, "Arab" excludes those three countries with whom we share so much—Armenia, Turkey, and Iran.

If we use the term "people of Middle Eastern/North African heritage," then Iranians, Armenians, and Turks would be included. However, we would then have a new consideration, one that I consider an unresolvable political problem concerning the term "Middle Eastern." That term was given to the Arab world by Western (European) colonizers who named the region only as it related to their particular worldview. It's a term that could only make sense to white colonizers so certain their existence and homelands were the center of everything that they actually named huge regions of the world in relation to themselves. It is offensive to me, and not at all affirming, to use such a term to describe my identity. Using the term "Middle Eastern" feels very much like I am adopting the oppressor's language.

The third possibility, "people of West Asian/North African descent," does not feel like the oppressor's language. Further, it does include Arabs and Middle Eastern peoples. Because some Arabs now living in various European countries, such as England and France, identify as West Asian, it may increase visibility for all of us if we use the same term. It would also help forge a strong connection to other people of color, particularly South Asians, whose cultural, religious, and political heritage is similar to ours. However, it is not a perfect solution. I fear that using the term "West Asian/North African" will once again make Arabs invisible. I can safely say that in the United States and Canada people do not think of Arabs as being included with Asians or Africans. Of course, that may change in time. A few years ago, no one considered people of Indian and Pakistani descent South Asians. Now they do. Other Asians acknowledge their existence. It is entirely conceivable that this may happen with Arabs—we may become more visible and may be perceived as part of a larger group.

One reason it's hard to find an accurate name has to do with our invisibility. It's tough to name a group when most people aren't aware the group exists. I constantly meet people who can't comprehend what I mean when I identify as Arab. "What?," they repeatedly ask, even though I've spoken clearly. That's why, after one particularly bad day, I coined this phrase for our community: the Most Invisible of the Invisibles. Not only did it make me feel better, I realized it might make people stop and think about what I mean. It raises questions about who the other invisibles are and whether Arabs really are the most invisible. I believe we are. In the United States and Canada, it is not only white people who refuse to see us; it is other people of color—Latinos, Africans, Asians, Natives—who do not acknowledge our existence.

In reflecting on this book's title, I am aware that the subtitle is far from perfect and that its ambiguity reflects the current complexity and messiness we live with. By contrast, the main title, *Food for Our Grandmothers*, came to me easily and cleanly in the early days of putting this book together. Reading through a pile of manuscripts that had recently arrived in the mail, I was struck by the incredible number of them centering around our grandmothers and what they had given us. I began to conceive of the book as a way to give something back to our grandmothers and to our community. *Food for Our Grandmothers* made sense as a title both because the book is an offering back to our grandmothers/our community and because it offers *appropriate* food for our grandmothers—the Arabic food that many of them made daily. The theme of food is woven through the book. A common Arabic food is used to embody the themes connecting each section, and a recipe using that common food accompanies each section.

There are things I once took for granted whose beauty, endurance, and usefulness now astound me. Thankfully I am at a point in my life where I did not take the following stories for granted. I marveled at their beauty. I cried over their endurance. I absorbed them in my bones so their usefulness could be with me always. I offer these stories—beautiful, enduring, and useful—to our grandmothers, to ourselves, and to the generations after us.

2

The Politics of Cultural Authenticity

NADINE NABER

Arab culture is about being a certain way; knowing what is *abe* (shameful); knowing how to give *mujamalat* (flattery); knowing what you're supposed to do when someone greets you; knowing how to act at *azayim* (gatherings) and weddings; drinking *shai* (tea) or coffee; talking about politics *so* much; getting up for an older person; respecting your elders; looking after your parents and taking care of them; judging people according to what family they are from; marrying through connections; gossiping and having a good reputation; going anywhere with Arabs, with your own kind, with brothers, uncles, family, cousins, but not with Americans.

This list highlights a combination of cultural ideals taken from interviews with middle-class, second-generation young adults. Here, I interrogate what I refer to as the politics of cultural authenticity, a process by which middle-class Arab diasporas come to herald particular ideals as markers of an authentic, essential, true, or real Arab culture. I map the historical and political conditions that give rise to the concepts of Arab culture that second-generation young adults learn from their parents' generation. I provide a theoretical framework for understanding young adults' engagements with apparently "intracommunal" forms of patriarchy and the pressure for compulsory heterosexuality. I also analyze the ramifications of the politics of cultural authenticity for the lives of second-generation young adults. This chapter is based upon intensive interviews with eighty-six second-generation Arab American young adults and participant observation within a range of community-based organizations.[1] . . .

Rather than reflecting an authentic, pure Arab culture frozen in time, idealized concepts of Arab culture are best understood as cultural sensibilities that become entangled in transnational modalities of power—US Orientalist discourses and structures of colonialism and imperialism, race, class, gender, and sexuality. Dominant middle-class concepts of Arab cultural identity indeed draw upon long-standing norms about religion, family, gender, and sexuality that have circulated in the Arab region for centuries. This helps explain why idealized concepts of Arab cultural identity provide middle-class Arab diasporas with a sense of cultural and historical continuity in relation to their places of origin. Middle-class articulations of an authentic Arab culture meet desires for connection, attachment, comfort, and security that come with displacement, immigrant marginality, and the pressures of assimilation. Yet the idea that middle-class

Excerpt from Nadine Naber, "The Politics of Cultural Authenticity," in *Arab America: Gender, Culture, Politics, and Activism* (New York: New York Univ. Press, 2012), 63–110. A works cited list was added to this chapter. Reprinted with corrections and press style changes for consistency throughout the volume by permission of New York University Press.

1. These groups included the American Arab Anti-Discrimination Committee, San Francisco Chapter; Aswat (an Arabic Choir); the Arab Cultural Center; Arabic-language courses at the College of San Mateo, San Francisco State University, and the University of California–Berkeley; the Arab Women's Solidarity Association, San Francisco Chapter; the General Union of Palestinian Students (San Francisco State University); Muslims for Global Peace and Justice; the Muslim Student's Association (University of California–Berkeley); St. Anne's Arab Catholic Church's Arab American Youth Group; St. George's Church; Students for Justice in Palestine (University of California–Berkeley); St. Nicholas's Greek Orthodox Church's Youth Group; and the Zaytuna Institute for the Dissemination of Traditional Islam.

immigrants simply transmit to their children an authentic Arab culture that they brought with them from their homelands cannot explain dominant middle-class articulations of Arabness. . . .

In the San Francisco Bay Area in the 1990s, middle-class articulations of Arabness provided Arab diasporas with a framework for conceptualizing themselves that, to a certain extent, challenges US Orientalist and racist discourses about Arabs, Muslims, and the Middle East. Yet they also advance a binary struggle between what they conceptualize as good Arabs versus bad Americans, good Arab families versus bad American families, and good Arab girls versus bad American(ized) girls. This formulation resembles what diaspora studies scholars have theorized as the incorporation of conventional concepts of nationalism into concepts of community, affiliation, and belonging within historical contexts of displacement (Axel 2001; Gopinath 2005; Clarke 2004; Hall 1994). I refer to this formulation as the politics of Arab cultural authenticity.

Specifically, the middle-class politics of cultural authenticity articulates Arab cultural identity and community through the triangulated ideal of the good Arab family, good Arab girls, and compulsory heterosexuality, all in opposition to an imagined America and its apparent sexual promiscuity, broken families, and bad women. The politics of cultural authenticity, while drawing upon conventional masculinist nationalisms, conjoins with the liberal logic of US multiculturalism, a logic for imagining and performing cultural identity that becomes available to Arab diasporas upon their arrival in the United States. Liberal multiculturalism requires immigrants, people of color, and Indigenous people to craft concepts of culture that are depoliticized and ahistorical (Povinelli 2002; Moallem and Boal 1999; Lowe 1996; Prashad 2000). Vijay Prashad contends, "Whereas assimilation demands that each inhabitant of the United States be transformed into the norm, U.S. multiculturalism asks that each immigrant group preserve its own heritage. . . . The heritage, or 'culture,' is not treated as a living set of social relations but as a timeless trait" (2000, 112). Conjoining masculinist homeland nationalisms with the logics of liberal US multiculturalism, the politics of cultural authenticity posits an essentialist, authentic Arab identity that exists outside of history.

Moreover, while on the one hand many of my interlocutors articulate Arabness in terms of an authentic, unified Arab culture and community, they simultaneously reference internal communal differences based on nation of origin and religion, and they represent these differences in power-laden, hierarchical terms, such as good Jordanians versus bad Palestinians or good Christians versus bad Muslims. Dominant US discourses about Arabs, Muslims, and the Middle East shape my interlocutors' articulations of internal Arab differences. Entangled in these overlapping, contradictory discourses, the politics of cultural authenticity is best understood as a selective assimilation strategy. As it provides middle-class Arab diasporas with a meaning system for conceptualizing a sense of belonging, empowerment, and cultural grounding in the context of displacement and diaspora, the politics of cultural authenticity also supports desires for US middle-class acceptability and belonging.

In everyday life, the politics of cultural authenticity sets up various regulations and constraints that police the lives of second-generation young adults and disproportionately impact (although in different ways and to different degrees) women and queers. The politics of cultural authenticity translates conventional nationalist hierarchies between nation and diaspora into the categories "immigrant generation" and "second generation." Here, the immigrant generation represents the pure, authentic "Arab culture," while the second generation represents its potentially impure, inauthentic Other. In the San Francisco Bay Area, the politics of cultural authenticity positions the immigrant generation as cultural authorities setting the terms for belonging and unbelonging—terms that define cultural authenticity through the concepts of "good girls" and a patriarchal, heterosexual family. The politics of cultural authenticity positions the second generation as a potential threat to the survival of Arabness in America because of their apparent potentiality for transgressions of the racial, classed, gendered, and sexualized demands of middle-class Arabness. The stories of second-generation young adults elucidate different aspects of the politics of cultural authenticity in which both generations seemed to participate, although to different degrees. I consider the politics of cultural authenticity a baseline articulation of Arabness against which the alternatives that are the focus of the remaining chapters [in *Arab America*] emerge.

Arabness as Family

In the Bay Area, I spoke with second-generation young adults about the concepts of Arabness, Arab culture, and Arab cultural identity that they learned from their parents' generation. Some spoke of cultural identity in terms of music, film, and poetry. Others referenced architecture, language, and food. One thing remained consistent: nearly everyone referred to relational concepts of selfhood and family ties and attachments as among the most fundamental aspects of Arabness. People articulated Arabness through concepts of family and relationality in these terms: "Arab culture is about family and the closeness of people"; "Arab culture is family oriented"; "Arabs are supposed to have connections with cousins, brothers, sisters, aunts, uncles"; and "Arab culture is about family ties and family values—an attachment to family and the love of children."

Indeed, long-standing sensibilities about relationships, loyalty, affiliation, and belonging have organized Arab societies. For centuries, concepts of family have been at the center of social organization in the Arab region (Barakat 1985; Joseph 1993; Tucker 1993). While modern ideals about kinship are based upon heterosexual marriage and familial expansion and reproduction, Arab and Islamic societies have tolerated homosexuality "as long as the prolongation of the family tree is guaranteed and no possessions are lost in the homosexual relationship" (Becker 2010). . . . Yet, generally speaking, the normative cultural ideal has expected family members to remain closely interlocked in webs of intimate relationships, to intermarry, to uphold expectations of one another, and to hold family members responsible for each other's acts (Barakat 1985; Joseph 1993).

Second-generation young adults in the Bay Area refer to concepts of family ties, loyalty, connection, and attachment as crucial to the concepts of Arabness that they learned from their parents' generation.[2] Yet as their stories show, these concepts were significantly influenced by the conditions of diaspora. For instance, in the Bay Area, several interlocutors referred to family as a marker of an authentic Arab culture that is distinct from the way the word is used in American culture. Within their stories, while "the Arab family" supports heteronormative sexuality within the framework of marriage, a patriarchal division of labor, extended kin relations, and relational concepts of selfhood, "the American family" lacks a sense of relationality and supports sexual "deviance" (homosexuality as well as sex outside of marriage, for instance). Young adults elaborate on this apparent tension between Arab and American notions of family. Nicole grew up in San Francisco with a Palestinian community. Her life story defies nearly every US Orientalist notion about Arabs. Her parents were atheists. They did not impose many restrictions concerning dating or staying out late at night. She tells me,

> My parents were really liberal about guys. I would tell them when I had a crush on someone. I told my mom when I lost my virginity and she's the one who got me the pregnancy test. I used to go on vacations with my college boyfriend. My father knew we were staying in the same hotel room. I've even told them I've done drugs. When I was a junior, I went on a spring break with two of my girlfriends to Mexico. I met a guy there and I dated him for a year and a half. I would talk about him to my parents. I went to visit him five or six times.

Yet Nicole also speaks about family-based relationships as the most crucial site of support and security in her life.

> Arab culture means that my life is bound up in the lives of others. [M]y family and community's love . . .

2. A range of scholars has documented the permeable and shifting history of the categories "Arab" and "Muslim" (see, e.g., Eickelman 1998; Hitti 1968; Dawisha 2005; and Majid 2000).

> is my life-blood, the social glue that keeps me tied to my roots and all the networks of social relations that are my family—the ties I have to the community that nurtured me.[3]

Tony is Jordanian. He grew up in the peninsula, on the outskirts of the city of San Francisco. At the time we spoke, he was a graduate student in business administration at San Francisco State University. Tony often expressed to me a profound distaste for the strong emotive attachments he attributed to Arab culture. He told me that he had always felt overwhelmed by his interactions with "other Arabs" . . . at places like the Arab church or the Arab cultural center. In his view, "Too many people intervene in other people's lives, gossip, and pressure me to get married. They think, you're dating someone and you're going to get married. I don't want anyone to know about my personal life. I don't want to deal with all the questions."

Tony's engagements with US Orientalist and racist discourses about Arab masculinity exacerbated his desire to distance himself from "other Arabs" and US discourses that portray Arab masculinity as potentially violent and misogynist:

> American women have a bad view of Arab men. A lot of Arab guys I know don't even admit they're Arab because . . . people assume you're you treat women bad. Or they'll say, "Wow, you speak English! You don't drive a Mercedes? Does your dad wear a turban?" . . . Someone hears an Arab name and thinks you're backwards.

These sorts of experiences inspire Tony to disassociate himself from what he considered the "Arab community" and from public displays of "Arab culture." He avoids Arab community-based events, he asks his mother not to play Arabic music and to avoid speaking Arabic in public, and he swears that he will never "marry an Arab." Yet it turns out that most of his closest friends are his cousins and that forms of attachment and relationality that he attributes to "Arab culture" are crucial to his life journey and his sense of being in the world.

Like Nicole and Tony—whether or not they say they affiliate with "Arab culture" or an "Arab community"—most of my interlocutors conflate the concepts of family and Arab culture and find themselves wrapped up in familial and communal relations. In other words, the idea of "Arabness as family" is immensely important to many of my interlocutors' sense of self and to their sense of being in the world. . . .

Adel, who grew up among a Palestinian family in the East Bay, shares with me an embellished distinction between what he perceives as connected Arabs and individuated Americans. He spent most summers visiting relatives in Palestine. He worked with his father at his grocery store while attending college:

> When it comes to Americans, everyone hates their cousins. [T]here is the crazy mother-in-law and lots of divorce. People don't connect with their families or with each other in general! People can go for a year without talking to their sister or not knowing what is going on with her. People aren't close to their friends like we are.

Adel's words illustrate how the middle-class politics of cultural authenticity signified Arabness through a sense of connection, knowing what is going on with each other, and strong emotive ties. . . .

Cultural Authentication and Parental Control

Claims to cultural authenticity reinforce parental control. Many young adults found a profound sense of security and comfort in the concept of Arabness as family. Yet they also said it constrained their lives. As parents exercise their control over young adults through claims to cultural authenticity, young adults experience normative generational wars as a conflict between Arab [culture] and American culture. Many face intense emotional struggles over whether they are going to live up to the demands of what their parents' generation conceptualized as idealized "Arab culture" or [of] stereotypical "American culture." They understand that this idealized Arab

3. Volume editors' note: Ellipses in quotations from interlocutors indicate omissions (rather than pauses) in all cases.

culture requires a strong sense of family and emotional attachments and that stereotypical American culture privileges individuality, personal desires, and independence. Many refer to weekends as sites of tension between the Arab expectation to be with family and the American desire to be with friends. Jameel grew up among a Palestinian extended family and spent most of his time with his first cousins. When we talked, he was working as a physical therapist at a hospital. He says, "It was as if you don't need anyone else. If you have anything going on in your life, family always comes first. Anything that had to do with family you had to be there, you had no choice. . . . The difference between Arabs and Americans is that an American kid would tell their parents, 'I want weekends to myself.'" While Jameel desired connections beyond his extended family, he told me that his parents considered this desire irrelevant or, at best, secondary.

Young adults who desired to rebel against the normative demands of cultural authenticity explain that their parents' generation marked their rebellion as a sign of cultural loss or Americanization. Ramsy is Palestinian, was born in Saudi Arabia, and moved to the United States with his family when he was five:

> I would always get these great clothes and had a sense for fashion, but Arab men can't be fashionable. That's the rule. My sister wore all these great clothes, but if I'm around the family, my mom would tell me "pants with pleats." Nothing too flashy, nothing striped, nothing too . . .

At the time of our conversations, Ramsy was struggling with his family over whether he would continue living with them or move out and live on his own:

> I hear it from my parents and our relatives all the time . . . from everyone: "How come you don't live with them? *Kif y'ani tseeb bait ahlok* [How could you leave your parents' house?]. Ramsy? Your parents' house is empty." It's a lot of pressure. My mom's like, "Everyone is talking about us . . . they're asking me, 'Why isn't your son living with you?' Do you think we're an American family where sons move away from their parents?"

Nuha's family is from Jordan. We met at Arabian Nights, a weekly dance club in the Mission District where the DJ spins Arabian music. . . . During the time of my interviews with her, Nuha had been torn apart by what many of my interlocutors referred to as "the double life"—where she felt she lived one life with her parents and immediate family and the other with her friends and peers. When we first began talking, Nuha was graduating with a master's degree in nutrition. . . . Nuha considered her aunt someone who was "cool," who did not intervene in her life, and who could cover for her in relationship to her parents. Living with her aunt, Nuha maintained what she referred to as "living in two worlds . . . the 'Arab' world of my family . . . and the 'American' world outside of home." At the core of this struggle was her desire to marry a man of whom her parents did not approve. According to her,

> If I decide to follow my heart, I'll go and get all this freedom, but I'll be all alone. I'll be another lonely white CEO woman who's all alone and has no one; has no family, no brothers, no nothing, 'cause that's what it's like in this [American] culture. My mom keeps saying, "You better let him know how important we are to you." And I keep saying, "Whatever my relationship is with you, my relationship is with you. And then, whatever my relationship is with him, my relationship is with him." But they can't take that kind of separation—it's too American.

Nuha interprets her reality as a choice between having family and being Arab or having independence and becoming American. She articulates her Arab world as constraining and comforting and her "American world" as free while simultaneously lonely.

In Ramsy's and Nuha's stories, the politics of cultural authenticity regulates life decisions that significantly circumscribe their lives and their sense of future possibilities. The binary of good Arabs and bad Americans, central to the politics of cultural authenticity, underscores intergenerational tensions. Jameel captures the disciplinary effects of cultural authenticity when he says that his mother referred to his rebellion as "losing ourselves to the Amerikaan." Guided by a nationalist logic that queers the diaspora or renders it impure and inauthentic (Gopinath 2005), the politics of Arab cultural authenticity assumes that immigrant parents are the authentic representatives of Arab culture and that the second generation embodies the potential for cultural loss or annihilation. In this sense, many interlocutors' struggles with their immigrant parents were as much about their relationship with their families as they were about the Arab diaspora's relationship to an imagined America.

Arab Virgins and American(ized) Whores

In my own family, my parents' generation repeatedly articulated "American culture" through concepts of gender and sexuality. One December evening in 1999, while my father was asleep, I joined my mother on the couch, and we searched for something interesting to watch on TV. My mother held the remote control, flipping through the stations. On station after station, a similar picture of an Anglo-American male and female holding one another in romantic or sexual ways appeared on the screen. As she flipped the channel, my mother remarked, "Sleep, slept. . . . Sleep, slept. That is Amerika!" She continued, "*Al-sex alhum, zay shurb al-mai* [Sex for them is as easy as drinking water]." As I listened to my mother, I recalled several experiences growing up in which people referred to al-Amerikaan in derogatory, sexualized terms. Amerika was the trash culture—degenerate, morally bankrupt, and sexually perverse. Al-Arab (Arabs), on the other hand, had good families, good girls, and good morals.

My interlocutors similarly recalled stories in which individuals of their parents' generation articulated "American culture" through the language of gender and sexuality. Indeed, many second-generation young adults, like many of their parents, were invested in this articulation. Men tended to feel less constrained by idealized concepts of gender and sexuality than women, and women tended to feel less constrained than queer-identified interlocutors. However, in nearly every interview, gender and sexuality were central to discussions about idealized concepts of Arabness and stereotypical notions of Americanness in the diaspora.

Susu's family is from Jordan. Her parents owned a convenience store. When we met, she had been working as a secretary in a law firm in San Francisco's financial district. I interviewed her at a café near the law firm. As our first conversation began, Susu shared her excitement with me about her new relationship with a man who lived in England. She had met him through an online dating site for Muslims and was preparing to meet him in person the following month. She told me that her parents did not impose tremendously rigid rules on her growing up, yet they preferred that she socialize primarily with other Arabs: "I always wanted to be a singer or dancer. But my mom would say that is trashy because all the Americans are doing drugs and having sex and we have to stick with our culture." . . .

My conversations with young Arab American men most explicitly reveal the significance of gender and sexuality, and women's bodies specifically, to the politics of cultural authenticity. The regulatory demands of cultural authenticity require young men to become future husbands and require that their future wives uphold distinct concepts of womanhood. Young men are thus key recipients of a heterosexual marriage ideal and an ideal femininity. Most young men I worked with had grown up hearing that Arab girls are good girls compared to American girls. The stories they had heard illustrate that the patriarchal demands placed upon young women set the terms of marriageability. Women who fail to meet these demands are unmarriageable. In this sense, the dichotomy between Arab girls and American girls underscores a demand for heterosexuality and a dismissal of nonnormative sexualities. The relationship between patriarchy and compulsory heteronormativity has been theorized as heteropatriarchy (Smith 2006; Cohen 1999). I spoke with young men extensively about the idealized notions of Arab womanhood, marriage, and sexuality with which they had grown up.

John comes from a Catholic family from Ramallah, Palestine. He grew up in a multiracial neighborhood in San Francisco until junior high school, when his family moved to the North Bay. He worked in his father's stores while growing up. He worked hard in school because he wanted to get away from the harassment and racism he regularly experienced from his father's customers. He tells me, "Getting shit from customers because they thought we were Iranian, during the Iran/Contra affair back in the '70s, or because they just didn't want to pay you is why I don't want to have a store." He was accepted to the University of California at Davis and then became an engineer in the South Bay. I met him when he was studying Arabic at San Francisco State University. When we spoke about dating and marriage, he told me that he had been dating non-Arab women—Vietnamese, Filipinas, Mexican—for many years. "I've always identified with minorities. I never felt comfortable talking to whites. You'll never find me checking out the white women." By the time he finished college, he was interested in dating and potentially marrying an Arab woman. He said,

> Part of the reason why I didn't want to pursue these other relationships was that they were not Arab. I told myself, if I'm going to go out with anyone now, I want to marry an Arab. At some points I say, "Screw it. You're never going to meet an Arab, forget it. Just marry whoever the hell you want."

Yet he struggled in his relations with Arab women because of the ideals about Arab womanhood that he heard while growing up.

> "Arab girls don't screw around"—that is what you expect: "Arab girls are good girls." And then there's the idea that "American women are evil. Stay away from them." It was made clear. There were always discussions about how bad Americans were and how lousy American women were. Because they would divorce their husbands, they would cheat on their husbands. They wouldn't clean the house like an Arab woman. My brother was dating a Hawaiian woman, but I didn't want him to marry her. . . . I couldn't really pinpoint anything bad about her but the fact that she had a boyfriend—that she messed around sexually, put her in that category—American, bad. I've never dated an Arab girl, number one. I've never dated one because I guess in the back of your mind, Arabs are for marrying, not for dating. The non-Arabs, the Americans, are the ones you play around with. And then you settle down and get married to an Arab. I always felt that Arab women wouldn't want to hang out with Arab men because they couldn't be themselves. 'Cause they could risk being labeled as sluts and, you know, . . . their reputation would be ruined, and then they would have that reputation for the rest of their lives, and they would never marry an Arab guy. . . .

"You're the Only Gay Arab in the World"

> When I went to Folsom Street Fair I took pictures and showed them to my mother. I always try not to say anything but subtly show them something—that I am involved in a circle that could be gay like this one in the pictures. My mom took one look at the pictures and said, "My God! What are we doing in this country! Oh, look what this country did to us!" They definitely see it as an American thing. They don't know that there are a lot of gay people back home, that's underground. . . . [T]here are lots of things that they don't see. They want me to hide it.

I first met Ramsy through his cousin Heba in 1998. At the time, Heba told me, "He is very gay. . . . [E]veryone [in the extended family] knows it, but no one wants to admit it." Most people I spoke to over the years who self-identified as gay, lesbian, or queer and Arab have confronted a similar schema that defines Arabness in terms of heterosexuality and Americanness in terms of sexual transgression and promiscuity.

Consider Rabia's story. Rabia's family is originally from Lebanon. She was actively engaged in queer Arab politics during the time of my research. She told me that she was especially eager to speak out about her experience of exclusion from her immediate family as a consequence of her coming out to them as a lesbian. We made plans to meet at a restaurant in San Francisco. When I first walked in, I recognized her by the tattoo of her girlfriend's name, Amina, in Arabic script on her arm and by the Palestinian flag sewn onto her book bag. After we began talking, I learned that Rabia was the artist who graffitied the words "Queer Arabs Exist" that I had read in large print on the bathroom wall of Café Macondo, one of my favorite cafés in the Mission District. Rabia:

> My mother keeps finding ways to say I'm too Americanized, and when I tell her, "You don't know how many queer Arabs I know," she says, "They're American, they're American born, they're not Arab."

> My uncles would come and take me out to lunch. They would say, "Let's talk. This doesn't happen in our culture. You've been brainwashed by Americans. You've taken too many feminist classes. You joined NOW. You hate men. You have a backlash against men. . . ." It was like . . . "This is what this American society has done to our daughter." They blamed Western feminism. I was so strong in defending myself that they thought that too was very American. "You chose sexuality over us. Sex is more important than your family." Which goes back to the tight-knit Arab family thing. It's all about group dynamics. And I still get that. "We [Arabs] don't do that," or "You're the only gay Arab in the world."

Ramsy's and Rabia's stories point to the normative demand for compulsory heterosexuality underlying the politics of cultural authenticity. This demand operates in connection with the concept of Arabness as family and the idealization of "good Arab girls." Here we see the consolidation of heteropatriarchy through the triangulation among idealized concepts of family, patriarchy, and heteronormativity. Put differently, the ideal of Arabness as family with "good Arab women" forecloses the possibility of homosexuality. Within this logic, the survival of an imagined Arab community depends upon a good Arab family, which requires good women within the construct of heterosexual marriage. These demands and the articulation of homosexuality as distinctly Western operate as markers that distinguish good Arabs from bad Americans.

To interrogate the conflation of Arab culture and heterosexuality, we can turn to scholarship on sexuality in Arab- and Muslim-majority countries. This scholarship reveals that this conflation has no basis in historical realities but emerged as a reaction to European domination and, as I will argue, as a reaction to the pressures of immigration, assimilation, and racialization in the diaspora. The scholarship also shows that we must reorient conventional Eurocentric frameworks that ask whether or not Arab culture allows for "homosexuality" to a focus on the historically and culturally specific concepts of gender and sexuality that have been circulated in the region. Indeed, in the Arab region, same-sex desire and sexual relations have existed and have taken on varying and diverse forms and cannot be explained as simple consequences of engagements with the West or colonial or imperial impositions (Babayan and Najmabadi 2008; Najmabadi 2005; Habib 2010; Rowson 2008; Amer 2008; Traub 2008). . . .

Ramsy also plans to provide for his parents when they retire. Thus, while he is criticized by the family because of his avoidance of marriage, he can also be reworked back into the family. The extended family can allow varied possibilities of gender and sexuality to remain in the circuit. Jose Muñoz (1999) uses the term "disidentification" to refer to queer subjectivities that do not easily map onto Eurocentric US categories of sexual identity. Through this framework, he strives "to envision and activate new social relations" among minority subjects who must work with or resist the conditions of (im)possibility that the dominant culture generates (5). In Rabia's and Ramsy's stories, multiple power-laden, socially encoded scripts collide into each other—the binary of straight Arabs and promiscuous, sexually loose Americans, the discourse of US Orientalism and its sexually savage Arabs versus sexually civilized "Americans," and the more fluid Arab concepts of sexual acts and desires compared to rigid Eurocentric categories of sexual identity. Indeed, their stories cannot be explained through liberal Eurocentric frameworks that equate visibility or "coming out" with emancipation and more subtle and fluid modes of sexuality with backwardness and victimization.

Ramsy's place in his extended family parallels longstanding structures of family in the Arab world in which same-sex desire or behavior exists as long as it does not threaten the reproduction of the extended family. While he refers to his circle of friends as potentially "gay," he disidentifies with coming out. He straddles a space in between, cast out as possibly "gay" and incorporated back into the patrilineal extended family structure. . . .

A Selective Assimilation Strategy

While the triangulation of family, the good Arab woman, and compulsory heterosexuality draws on various, colliding Arab and European discourses, it is also informed by middle-class US norms and the connected US logics of liberal multiculturalism. For immigrants and people of color in the United States, middle-class acceptability requires an investment in the logic of liberal multiculturalism. This logic requires immigrants and people of color to disavow structural inequalities such as racism and exclusion and instead to promote and celebrate essentialist forms of cultural identity (Moallem and Boal 1999; Sleeter and McLaren 1995; Lowe 1996). . . .

Furthermore, a patriarchal nuclear family and compulsory heteronormativity have been fundamental to white US middle-class acceptability. Cathy Cohen (1999) explains that middle-class African American discourses have articulated concepts of cultural identity through a notion of an apparently distinct "African American" respectability. At the same time, she argues, this notion is shaped by white middle-class ideals of respectability. Middle-class African American discourses have claimed notions of respectability as Indigenous or authentic although such notions serve the interests of Black elites (see Collins 2000; Cohen 1999; Alarcón 1999). . . .

Among the middle-class Arab diasporas I worked with, dominant discourses privileged certain white middle-class norms about gender, sexuality, marriage, and family and suppressed those that may be deemed transgressive, thus providing Arab Americans with a strategy to displace racist assumptions about uncivilized and barbaric gender and sexual regimes among Arabs. In this sense, as Kevin Gaines (1996) argues, rigid structures that police gender and sexuality are, in part, an example of unconscious internalized racism. Yet the preoccupation with family, patriarchy, and heteronormativity as a strategy for acceptance has the effect of blaming individuals who do not measure up to middle-class gender and sexual norms and [of] obscuring the actual problem of gendered and sexualized racisms. By promoting white middle-class norms and avoiding a critique of US imperialism, racism, classism, sexism, and homophobia, the politics of cultural authenticity facilitates access to political, economic, and social resources (Duggan 2004; Bhattacharjee 1992, 27; Burek, cited in Bhattacharjee 1992).

While Arab cultural authenticity serves to consolidate or solidify some sense of a distinct Arab identity, it simultaneously reifies white middle-class concepts of heteronormativity and marriage, incorporating US categories of respectability into its logic. Thus, Arab cultural authenticity effectively prioritizes cultural forms that represent Arabs as similar to stereotypical white, middle-class Americans. Heterosexual marriage and the prohibition against homosexuality not only preserve an idealized concept of Arabness but also model "appropriate behavior that will lead to assimilation, acceptance, access" (Cohen 2004, 20). The dominant middle-class Arab American concepts and practices of marriage not only require heteropatriarchy but prescribe which identity categories (race, class, gender, sexuality, nationality, religion) are important and what forms of relationships, attachments, and identities deserve respect. In these very specific terms, marriage ideals facilitate white middle-class acceptability.

Although most interlocutors do not discuss socioeconomic class directly, the stories of people who felt constrained by the demands of middle-class acceptability reveal the significance of class to the politics of cultural authenticity. Ramsy and Nader relate how idealized notions of "Arab culture" pressured them to establish financial security before marriage, pointing to connections between concepts of class mobility and marriageability. Ramsy:

> My parents keep saying, "What are you waiting for? It's about time." For them, it's like, "That's it. He finished school. He has his own business. The next step would be the bride."

Nader, a disc jockey, expresses the preference to produce music over a more "acceptable" career. He encountered a code of sociability that considered financial success inseparable from marriage. In Nader's experience, his desire to produce music contradicted familial-communal norms, particularly since he was married.

> From the Arab community, I get comments every single day because I'm a DJ. Especially from women, they'll say, "I didn't think you were married." It's not that I don't act like I'm married, it's that they assume that you can't have a family and be into the arts at the same time. Some guys look at me as the enemy. They think, "What you are doing is wrong" because my brain is not locked up in what my brother and I call the real man/real job syndrome.

While men disproportionately felt pressured to uphold an arc of education, a professional career, and marriage, women shared a sense that the ideal of education and a career could be supplanted by marriage within middle-class boundaries. For many women, marrying within class boundaries took precedence over other ideals. Rime experiences the pressure to marry within class boundaries when she meets the love of her life on a trip to Jordan:

> In Jordan, my life completely turned around. I met Omar. All my life the message was that I had to marry an Arab man. I finally met an Arab man I love, but my parents are not accepting him. They say, "The guy has no money—and you're going to go live with his family." Traditionally if an Arab man is going to get married, he should furnish and open a house for the girl and then get married, not get married and then worry about that stuff. My mom and him started talking, and my mom kept asking him, "How about getting her an apartment after you guys get married?" He said, "I can't. I don't have the money." He said, "If your daughter wants to bring money and get me an apartment, I'll move the next day." My mom said, "If you have no money, you shouldn't be getting married." They hung up, and he called me back in three minutes, and my mom's in the background saying "*Batlee!* [Stop!] You're not getting married!" It all comes down to our traditions—having Arab traditions. . . .

The articulation of cultural authenticity through marriage is as much about race as it is about class. In everyday life, marriage norms also reify US racial schemas fundamental to white middle-class codes of sociability. Interlocutors and their families engage with socioeconomic class in many different ways. Some identify as people of color, some as white, and some are more open than others to marrying across racial lines. Yet most people agreed that the dominant middle-class Arab discourse promoted particular ideals about interracial dating and marriage. Before Rime went to Jordan and met Omar, she spent most of her time in high school and college socializing among Mexican and Black friends. She tells me,

> One day, my dad said to me, "I had a nightmare that my daughter would marry a Black man." That was because he owns a liquor store in the Tenderloin. All his life he's been robbed and shot at and his wife's been robbed by Blacks. He blamed poor Blacks from the Tenderloin for their situation without understanding it. He couldn't understand that I had a lot of Black friends at school and that Blacks were always the first ones out there supporting Arab student movements at school.

Rime's story points to the entanglement of Arab cultural authenticity within dominant US discourses that regulate marriage in racial and class terms (and prohibit white middle-class intermarriage with people of color). Dominant US anxieties about interracial marriage complicate Rime's references to "Arab tradition." Her father's position as a liquor store owner in the Tenderloin neighborhood shapes the racialized and gendered imperatives that policed Rime's sexuality. His nightmare over his daughter's potential marriage to a Black man represents a threat to the securing of white middle-class norms and the forging of a critical distance between the racial Other and whiteness. Many interlocutors articulate similar ideals. Tony tells me, "It would be bad to marry someone who was white. Asian is the worst. Black . . . they would think you were joking. It's not even an option. They would never get over it. You would be the topic of discussion for the next . . . I don't know how long." . . .

Kalam al-nas (Words of the People)

We have seen how Arab cultural authenticity is constituted by multiple regimes of patriarchy and heteronormativity that collide, instituting a binary between "Arab culture" and "American culture." Here, I analyze a culturally specific term, *al-nas* (the people), that operates to consolidate the boundaries of Arabness or an imagined Arab community in America and the politics of Arab cultural authenticity. My interlocutors and their parents use this term to refer to a concept of Arab people who are deterritorialized rather than living in a bounded geographic place. The concepts of *al-nas* and family reputation go hand in hand. Most second-generation interlocutors felt expected to uphold their family's reputation before *al-nas*. Women tend to discuss reputation in terms of sexuality, whereas men do so in terms of stature. Most interlocutors agree that reputation is about how other people perceive their family.

Nuha: "It all has to do with our family worrying about what other people think and how other people will perceive them, as opposed to what makes them happy. They're not just worried about family, but the entire Arab community. What I do is a reflection of them."

Muna: "My parents said, always, 'Someone is going to talk about you. *Al-nas* are going to find something to talk about.'"

Many interlocutors state that their parents respond to their desires to transgress the ideals of cultural authenticity with questions such as these: "Do you know what *al-nas* would say about you?" Or, "Where am I going to put my head? What are other people going to say?"

Most interlocutors told me that the demand to uphold their family's reputation was especially prevalent when they attended events with other Arabs. Weddings, funerals, holiday celebrations, and *azayim* (dinner gatherings) exemplify the social spaces of *al-nas*. Interlocutors reference *azayim* more than other social spaces since they take place more often and happen within the close confines of people's homes. *Azayim* bring together people considered "family"—people related to one another through blood ties or through friendships based on strong affective bonds. For people without extended family or with few extended family members in the Bay Area, *azayim* include "friends" who become "family" after immigration.

To a certain extent, interlocutors inherit the concept of *al-nas* from Arab countries. Yet the concept of *al-nas* takes on new form in the diaspora. It works as shorthand for an imagined Arab community. It enhances the possibilities for the politics of cultural authenticity to regulate behaviors by rendering transgression not only as individual rebellion but [also] as cultural loss and Americanization. The power of *al-nas* in America is that it means that one's behaviors implicate one's entire family as well as an entire "Arab people" in the United States. The concept of *al-nas* reinforces the implication of one's family within acts of transgression, cultural loss, and Americanization and thus expands the stakes placed on young adults' desires, actions, and behaviors. Its ability to police the lives of young adults lay in its reliance on the concept of an imagined community that does not require the physical presence of "the people" to which it refers.

Nicole elucidates how this sense of "Arab community" does not require the existence of "real people" but is indeed one step removed from lived realities and operates, to a certain extent on the level of the psyche, as an effective form of control and constraint. She tells me that "none of my relatives live in the Bay Area. Growing up, my family did not interact with other Arabs. But my mom would always tell me that *al-nas* are watching us. One day, I asked my mom, 'Where are the people?,' and she couldn't reply." For Nicole, the concept of *al-nas* reflects a sense of a people attached to one another in some kind of union of shared responsibilities, or what Benedict Anderson (1983) refers to as an "imagined community." . . .

Intracommunal Difference

A series of intra-Arab hierarchies takes on new significance in the diaspora and operates in tension with the ideal of an intracommunal Arab domain in the diaspora—particularly since the idea of *al-nas*, communal unity or cultural homogeneity in the face of an imagined America, is so crucial to the politics of cultural authenticity. Among these are differences of religion (Muslim and Christian) and nationality (Jordanian, Lebanese, Palestinian, and Syrian), although these do not exhaust the broad constellation of differences within and between Arab diasporas. These differences do not necessarily imply hierarchy, conflict, or tension in official or community-based Arab politics. Political regimes—whether internal or external to the Arab region—that privilege one group and demonize the other(s) have fueled national and religious tensions to varying degrees in different historical moments. In the United States, Arab national and religious categories take on new meanings in light of dominant US imperial discourses about Arabs and Muslims, Muslims and Christians, Palestine and Israel.

They also take on new meaning in a Bay Area context in which Arab migrants from diverse nations of origin interact with one another in unexpected ways and where the stakes for crafting "unimagined communities" (Ono and Sloop 2002) are particularly high. Community networks in which my interlocutors and their families participate tend to include predominantly Palestinian but also Jordanian, Lebanese, and Syrian Arabs. This context produced a contradictory situation in which multiple, coexisting affiliations constituted the term "Arab community." This was most clearly reflected in concepts and practices of marriage.

Earlier I explained that the politics of cultural authenticity privileges the idea of marrying an "Arab" (as opposed to marrying an "American"). Yet when lived, the ideal of "marrying an Arab" has multiple meanings that are hierarchical and contested. In some cases, marriage norms privilege marrying an Arab from the same nation of origin and with the same religious affiliation. Both generations similarly privilege marrying within religious categories over those of nation through a critical inheritance of the ideal of kinship-based endogamy from Arab nations. . . . Whether and to what extent families permit marrying across these boundaries depend on their political or religious beliefs and opinions. Historical realities contribute to the ways people articulate national distinctions and the values they grant to national differences. Rabia tells me that Lebanese are the least open to marrying Palestinians because, she explains, "there's an antagonism between Lebanese and Palestinians. Lebanese, especially Lebanese Christians, consider themselves more cultured. It's also because of the role the Palestinians played in the Lebanese Civil War. Palestinians, especially the Palestinian Muslims, are associated with being refugees, being radical politically, and trying to take over other Arab countries." . . .

Hashem exemplifies how long-standing conventional Jordanian nationalist stereotypes about Palestinians inform his position on marrying a Palestinian:

> I identify with being Arab and the different Arab causes . . . Palestine . . . Iraq . . . but I definitely differentiate between Palestinians and Jordanians. I'm Jordanian. Their roots aren't 100 percent like mine . . . like their women, it's like that saying, "*al Falastiniyat gawiyat*." It means they're rude and ride their husbands a little bit. I believe it. I don't think I would marry a Palestinian. Not that a wife should be submissive, but they're kinda *wighat* [rude].

Hashem's remark reflects assumptions underpinning a range of Arab discourses that conceptualize Palestinians as distinct on the basis of their distinct struggle against colonization. . . .

Histories of engagement with European and US discourses also guide norms related to marriage across religious lines. Nicole explains, "All my life the message was that I had to marry an Arab Christian man." Bassam told me, "I knew I was supposed to have children with an Arab woman with the same religion as us." Hurriya is a Palestinian American from a Muslim family. She tells me that she spent a year in conflict with her parents because she was in love with a Latino man, while they expected her to marry an Arab Muslim man. She expressed how things changed when she met an Arab Muslim whom she considered marrying: "Being with an Arab Muslim man meant all the prerequisites were gone. All we had to worry about was whether we could get along, love each other, and live together. So immediately, there was the possibility of marriage. You've jumped all the hurdles, and all you have to do is fall in love." . . .

Rabia's mother reconfigures the Arab virgin/American whore in terms of Muslim virgin/Christian whore. She associates the category "Lebanese Christian" with the classification "westernized Other." She conflates "Islam" and "Arabness" through an Arab nationalist discourse about a distinct Arab–Muslim civilization that juxtaposes notions of Arab Muslimness against the notion of a Christian West. In her mother's view, the Lebanese–Muslim self is to be protected from the corrupted, westernized Lebanese–Christian Other. Yet while distinguishing herself from the Christian West, Rabia explains, "My parents are very into the mentality of 'Arabs are white.'" Rabia's parents were open to the idea of their daughters dating before marriage yet did not support her dating men of color. Lulu explains, "My sister was really vocal about having boyfriends, and they were always Black, which was always a problem."

[Lulu's] parents' openness to talking about sex is atypical among interlocutors and their families. Yet it points to a general dilemma that most interlocutors' parents face in which the possibilities of marrying "other Arabs" is more likely when living in the diaspora, among Arabs from diverse nations of origin. The conditions of this "unimagined community" (Ono 2000) render the stakes for policing intra-Arab differences particularly high. Marriage is a crucial mechanism through which Arab diasporas negotiate a range of intracommunal differences and their varied relationships to US codes of whiteness, Orientalism, and modernity. Regulating demands about marriage necessitate negotiations over the categories "Arab," "American," "Jordanian," "Lebanese," "Palestinian," "Syrian," "Muslim," and "Christian" that take place with and through European and US discourses about Western modernity and Muslim backwardness. These negotiations emerge in a context in which the way a person is perceived in relation to any of these categories has significant implications for middle-class assimilation and acceptability.

Rabia's story elucidates that the politics of cultural authenticity works within a selective assimilation strategy. Her mother's distinction between good Muslims and bad Christians provides a sense of empowerment and cultural continuity in the diaspora. Yet her mother simultaneously reinforces codes of white middle-class acceptability in identifying as white and disapproving of her daughter's Black boyfriends. Rabia's story reflects a complex process by which both generations critically inherit categories of national and religious difference from Arab homelands and remake them with and through engagements with US categories of knowledge and the challenges of immigration, assimilation, and Americanization. To different degrees, through discourses and practices about marriage, interlocutors and their parents resist assimilation by positing particular categories of identity different from US or Western modernity. They simultaneously deploy particular categories as mechanisms for maintaining middle-class status.

This essay has interrogated the analytical and historical trajectories underpinning the politics of cultural authenticity; it relies on theorizations of diaspora that go beyond conventional notions of ethnicity and nation, theorizations that assume a purity of cultures that exist in a separate domain from politics. This diaspora studies approach transcends theories of tradition versus modernity (isolation versus assimilation; traditional gender and sexual repression versus Americanization and gender and sexual liberation). While the politics of cultural authenticity invokes a seemingly essentialist Arab cultural identity, this essay shows that the politics of cultural authenticity is motivated by economic and political conditions of cultural and geographic displacement, US Orientalism and empire, and the desire for middle-class status and acceptability. This essay also shows that normative concepts of hyphenated identity that assume a mixing of two cultures (i.e., Arab and American) cannot explain the narrative of cultural authenticity. Nor can the politics of cultural authenticity be explained by linear concepts of assimilation (Brah 1996, 241). I have explained this articulation of Arabness as a complex interaction between an imagined Arab community and an imagined America—a complex entanglement between multiple histories and discourses that are transnational in scope.

I have presented the politics of cultural authenticity as historically situated and constructed. Yet I have also shown that, for second-generation young adults for whom it is both empowering and constraining, the politics of cultural authenticity is not simply imagined or fictive. It is a grounded articulation of Arabness—embedded in historical and material realities and experiences—that has lived effects. The politics of cultural authenticity sets into play a particular approach to US politics that wittingly or unwittingly ignores social inequalities of race and class or the violences of imperialism, militarism, and war. In this sense, the politics of cultural authenticity works within a conventional middle-class immigrant approach to cultural identity: it prioritizes economic mobility and establishes a sense of cultural continuity while ignoring politics (Prashad 2000).

Keeping in mind the multiple, colliding histories that shape dominant middle-class Arab American forms of patriarchy and compulsory heterosexuality, we can now understand the limitations of an essentialist, Orientalist cultural analysis. My theoretical model, a diasporic Arab feminist critique, makes central a critique of the power structures of patriarchy and homophobia that are internal to Arab families and communities, while illustrating that these power structures are shaped by a range of intersecting histories and power relations. This approach takes seriously the varying historical circumstances that are entangled in middle-class Arab American regimes of gender and sexuality, such as the challenges of displacement, reactions to US Orientalism, desires for middle-class status, and engagements with US liberal multiculturalism. This approach also centers an analysis of the power relations that these regimes set into play—including the kinds of subjects it produces and the internal hierarchies and exclusions they enable. I have also shown that while most interlocutors find the gendered and sexualized regimes of cultural authenticity constraining, they also find claims to cultural identity and belonging comforting and empowering.

Works Cited

Alarcón, Norma. 1999. "Chicana Feminism: In the Tracks of 'the' Native Woman." In *Between Woman and Nation: Nationalisms, Transnational Feminisms, and the State*, edited by Caren Kaplan, Norma Alarcón, and Minoo Moallem, 63–71. Durham, NC: Duke Univ. Press.

Amer, Sahar. 2008. "Cross-Dressing and Female Same-Sex Marriage in Medieval French and Arabic Literatures." In *Islamicate Sexualities: Translations across Temporal Geographies of Desire*, edited by Kathryn Babayan and Afsaneh Najmabadi, 72–113. Cambridge, MA: Harvard Univ. Press.

Anderson, Benedict. 1983. *Imagined Communities: Reflections on the Origin and Spread of Nationalism*. New York: Verso.

Axel, Brian Keith. 2001. *The Nation's Tortured Body: Violence, Representation, and Formation of a Sikh "Diaspora."* Durham, NC: Duke Univ. Press.

Babayan, Kathryn, and Afsaneh Najmabadi, eds. 2008. *Islamicate Sexualities: Translations across Temporal Geographies of Desire*. Cambridge, MA: Harvard Univ. Press.

Barakat, Halim. 1985. "The Arab Family and the Challenge of Social Transformation." In *Women and the Family in the Middle East: New Voices of Change*, edited by Elizabeth Warnock Fernea, 27–48. Austin: Univ. of Texas Press.

Becker, Brian. 2010. *Will Sanctions on Iraq Be Lifted? International Action Center Urges Movement to Stay Vigilant*. New York: Workers World Service.

Bhattacharjee, Anannya. 1992. "The Habit of Ex-nomination: Nation, Woman, and the Indian Immigrant Bourgeoise." *Public Culture* 5, no. 1: 19–44.

Brah, Avtar. 1996. *Cartographies of Diaspora: Contesting Identities*. New York: Routledge.

Clarke, Kamari Maxine. 2004. *Mapping Yoruba Networks: Power and Agency in the Making of Transnational Communities*. Durham, NC: Duke Univ. Press.

Cohen, Cathy J. 1999. *The Boundaries of Blackness: AIDS and the Breakdown of Black Politics*. Chicago: Univ. of Chicago Press.

———. 2004. "Deviance as Resistance: A New Research Agenda for the Study of Black Politics." *Du Bois Review* 1, no. 1: 27–45.

Collins, Patricia Hill. 2000. "It's All in the Family: Intersection of Gender, Race, and Nation." In *Decentering the Center: Philosophy for a Multicultural, Postcolonial, and Feminist World*, edited by Uma Narayan and Sandra Harding, 156–76. Bloomington: Indiana Univ. Press.

Dawisha, Adeed. 2005. *Arab Nationalism in the Twentieth Century: From Triumph to Despair*. Princeton, NJ: Princeton Univ. Press.

Duggan, Lisa. 2004. "Holy Matrimony!" *Nation*, Mar. 14. At https://www.thenation.com/article/archive/holy-matrimony/.

Eickelman, Dale. 1998. *The Middle and Central Asia: An Anthropological Approach*. Upper Saddle River, NJ: Prentice-Hall.

Gaines, Kevin. 1996. *Uplifting the Race: Black Leadership, Politics, and Culture in the Twentieth Century*. Chapel Hill: Univ. of North Carolina Press.

Gopinath, Gayatri. 2005. *Impossible Desires: Queer Diasporas and South Asian Public Cultures*. Durham, NC: Duke Univ. Press.

Habib, Samar. 2010. *Islam and Homosexuality*. Santa Barbara, CA: Praeger.

Hall, Stuart. 1994. "Cultural Identity and Diaspora." In *Colonial Discourse and Post-colonial Theory: A Reader*, edited by Patrick Williams and Laura Chrisman, 392–403. New York: Columbia Univ. Press.

Hitti, Philip. 1968. *The Arabs in History*. London: Macmillan.

Joseph, Suad. 1993. "Gender and Relationality among Arab Families in Lebanon." *Feminist Studies* 19, no. 3 (Fall): 465–86.

Lowe, Lisa. 1996. *Immigrant Acts: On Asian American Cultural Politics*. Durham, NC: Duke Univ. Press.

Majid, Anouar. 2000. *Unveiling Traditions: Postcolonial Islam in a Polycentric World*. Durham, NC: Duke Univ. Press.

Moallem, Minoo, and Iain A. Boal. 1999. "Multicultural Nationalism and the Poetics of Inauguration." In *Between Woman and Nation: Nationalisms, Transnationalism Feminisms, and the State*, edited by Caren Kaplan, Norma Alarcón, and Minoo Moallem, 243–64. Durham, NC: Duke Univ. Press.

Muñoz, José Esteban. 1999. *Disidentifications: Queers of Color and the Performance of Politics*. Minneapolis: Univ. of Minnesota Press.

Najmabadi, Afsaneh. 2005. *Women with Mustaches and Men without Beards: Gender and Sexual Anxieties of Iranian Modernity*. Berkley: Univ. of California Press.

Ono, Kent A. 2000. "Re/membering Spectators: Meditations on Japanese American Cinema." In *Countervisions: Asian American Film Criticism*, edited by Darrell Hamamoto and Sandra Liu, 129–49. Philadelphia: Temple Univ. Press.

Ono, Kent A., and John M. Sloop. 2002. *Shifting Borders: Rhetoric, Immigration, and California's Proposition 187*. Philadelphia: Temple Univ. Press.

Povinelli, Elizabeth A. 2002. *The Cunning of Recognition: Indigenous Alterities and the Making of Australian Multiculturalism*. Durham, NC: Duke Univ. Press.

Prashad, Vijay. 2000. *The Karma of Brown Folk*. Minneapolis: Univ. of Minnesota Press.

Rowson, Everett K. 2008. "Homoerotic Liaisons among the Mamluk Elite in Late Medieval Egypt and Syria." In *Islamicate Sexualities: Translations across Temporal Geographies of Desire*, edited by Kathryn Babayan and Afsaneh Najmabadi, 204–38. Cambridge, MA: Harvard Univ. Press.

Sleeter, Christine E., and Peter L. McLaren, eds. 1995. *Multicultural Education, Critical Pedagogy, and the Politics of Difference*. Albany: State Univ. of New York Press.

Smith, Andrea. 2006. "Heteropatriarchy and the Three Pillars of White Supremacy: Rethinking Women of Color Organizing." In *The Color of Violence: The INCITE! Anthology*, edited by INCITE! Women of Color against Violence, 66–73. Cambridge, MA: South End Press.

Traub, Valerie. 2008. "The Past Is a Foreign Country? The Times and Spaces of Islamicate Sexuality Studies." In *Islamicate Sexualities: Translations across Temporal Geographies of Desire*, edited by Kathryn Babayan and Afsaneh Najmabadi, 1–40. Cambridge, MA: Harvard Univ. Press.

Tucker, Judith. 1993. *Arab Women: Old Boundaries, New Frontiers*. Bloomington: Indiana Univ. Press.

3

Excerpts from *New Body Politics*

THERÍ A. PICKENS

From the Introduction

This project is obsessed with bodies, bodies that do what a body does, no matter how mundane or embarrassing or unpredictable. Since no body exists without its owner, and no one who owns a body exists outside social and political grounding, I channel that obsession to discuss the relationship between one's corporeality and one's sociopolitical position. Specifically, I ask, what can corporeality offer social and political discourse? How do those discourses change when the bodies in question belong to Arab Americans and African Americans? How can we place Black and Arab American embodied experience in conversation around salient social and political concerns (Jarrett 2011)?[1] By way of answer, I offer the following: within narratives by and about Blacks and Arabs, embodied experience, particularly when the body announces its fragility, becomes a vehicle through which they articulate their reflections on and critiques of the world we inhabit.

At the crux of this discussion is *embodiment or embodied experience*, moments of tangible, sensory living from which humans make sense of their world. I draw from Tobin Siebers's (2008) notion of "complex embodiment," which "views the economy between social representations and the body not as unidirectional . . . but as reciprocal." That is, embodied experiences emanate from understanding and living what is sensory and tangible within social contexts. The flesh not only comprises the world and helps one make sense of that world but is also beholden to and constrained by that social, cultural, and political world. I turn to the quotidian flesh (breathing, touch, illness, pain, death) because, as Sharon Holland notes in *Erotic Life of Racism* (2012), examining the everyday not only foregrounds the "messy materiality of the body" but is also critically useful for understanding how ordinary the practice and effects of virulent discourses have come to be. The body so often (rightly or wrongly) stands in for the body politic and the family and as an allegory for the nation-state. My analysis of the everyday embodiment of Arab and Black people within the United States questions how the quotidian aspects of subjectivity and making families (among other acts) affect the political discourses to which they are often wed. The seemingly mundane aspects of embodiment allow us to unpack some of the culturally conscripted ideology mapped onto Arab and Black bodies within the United States. This is not to say that narratives about stereotypes like the supposed big Black buck or oppressed veiled Arab woman disappear. Rather, a discussion of the quotidian challenges us to consider how and where those

Excerpts from the introduction and chapter 1 of Therí A. Pickens, *New Body Politics: Narrating Arab and Black Identity in the Contemporary United States* (New York: Routledge, 2014). Full references in the original notes were converted to author-date citations in the text and notes here, and a works cited list was added. Reprinted with corrections and press style changes for consistency throughout the volume by permission of Routledge.

1. Gene Andrew Jarrett writes a provocative entreaty to scholars regarding the use of "politics" in discussions of literature in his introduction to *Representing the Race* (2011). He draws a distinction between formal political engagement and informal politics within aesthetic documents, cautioning against a slippage between the two. In my project, I contend that authors advocate for certain formal political engagement within informal media. Their aesthetic engagements, though informal, should not be easily shunted aside.

narratives buckle. Moreover, embodiment opens up the possibility for cross-cultural conversation based on fundamental human sameness, even if said conversation remains fraught with the social and political concerns that prompt and sustain divisions.

Since "the embodied subject on which this book dwells is not ethereal, transcendent, or fixed, in either form or identity, but rather palpable, porous, and motile" (Cohen 2008), I examine moments when embodiment highlights corporeal fragility. "Fragility" here is synonymous with neither strength nor weakness, but rather the wear and tear caused by being both acted upon and agentive. The moments in my analysis call attention to the aforementioned relationship between social representation and the body, the world and the flesh. Such an interplay highlights how indebted this project is to the field of disability studies. Certainly, disability studies is "a location and a means to think critically about disability, a juncture that can serve both academic discourse and social change" (Linton 1998). However, the field also bears implications for understanding "the variations that exist in human behavior, appearance, functioning, sensory acuity, and cognitive process, but, more crucially, the meaning we make of those variations" (Linton 1998). As a result, disability is both object of inquiry and analytic for this project. I examine what disability studies scholar Simi Linton (1998) terms "the critical divisions [made] in creating the normal versus the pathological, the insider versus the outsider, or the competent citizen versus the ward of the state." I analyze them from the standpoint (or more accurately sitpoint) that embodied experience matters significantly to these distinctions and the rubrics upon which they are based.

Though I explore what it means to narrate African American and Arab American embodied experience in particular, I draw from several other modes of inquiry that undergird and complement the larger field of American studies: comparative ethnic studies, literary and cultural studies, gender studies, and phenomenology. I link these embodied ways of knowing as an avenue to making sense of Black and Arab American embodied experience based on the terms delineated by the writers themselves. As such, this project's aims align with the imperative to "write or be written" (Aziz 2004), as articulated by Barbara Nimri Aziz in the edited collection *Scheherezade's Legacy*. She challenges Arab American writers to create their own stories or risk having others do so for them. As Aziz notes, the same injunction has existed for African American writing. Her injunction recalls Alain Locke's challenge to the new Negro of the early twentieth century or the Black Arts Movement's specific aims for creating and sustaining Black art. Langston Hughes's desire to depict the beauty and the ugly too echoes here as a refrain for Arab American and African American writing. In the words of Khaled Mattawa and Munir Akash (1999), "If the image of us [Arab Americans] is truly being created by the American imagination, the time has come to invalidate that image and render it unrecognizable both to ourselves and to the world." The critical conversations with which [*New Body Politics*] dialogues emphasize the social and cultural politics at stake when choosing to narrate raced, gendered, classed, and abled quotidian experience.

I contend that Arab American and African American narratives announce the body's fragility as a way to open up sociopolitical discourse. In contrast to the depiction of the raced and gendered body as exclusively able, exceptionally strong, or visibly threatening, these writers spotlight their bodies' fragility as compelling for sociopolitical commentary. These authors and cultural producers' ideas emphasize the tenuousness and unruliness of quotidian embodied experience, finding critical utility in the following conundrum: the body is an inherently mercurial object of inquiry that, at times, does not change the conversations in which people participate; nevertheless, the discussions must begin with the body itself. Each of the figures I examine attempts to debunk the idea that their embodied experiences are solely an individual matter. Instead, their work becomes an empowering and transgressive space, viable for examining and contesting their "condition[s] of alterity" (Brooks 2006). They take for granted that, regardless of how others view them, they make sense of the world, in phenomenological terms, "through processes and logic of sense-making that owe as much to [their] carnal existence as they do to [their] conscious thought" (Sobchack 2004). To my mind, their work privileges the radical potential within the diegetic capacity of embodiment, harnessing ordinary embodiment as a starting point for understanding and critiquing institutional and social practices.

. . . As Du Bois's *Souls of Black Folk* and Fanon's *Black Skin, White Masks* illuminate, the raced and gendered body must be conscious of itself in terms of how others understand it as well as how it understands itself. In short, the flesh matters.

As examples of how an emphasis on embodiment opens up the critical possibilities of reading Arab American and African American literature, I point to Ralph Ellison's novel *Invisible Man* (1952) and Joseph Geha's short story collection *Through and Through* (1990). While the characters' corporeality refutes their social invisibility, their corporeality also reveals the logics by which the characters are made socially invisible. Ellison's unnamed narrator struggles with how he is seen and understood in the context of Jim Crow America, claiming in the familiar line, "I am invisible because people refuse to see me" (Ellison [1952] 1980). In the preceding sentence, he acknowledges the irony of this invisibility in terms of his body, saying, "I am a man of substance, of flesh and bone, of fiber and liquids—and I might even be said to possess a mind." Here, Ellison's unnamed narrator wrestles against the disjuncture between the tangibility and the materiality of his body and its social fungibility and invisibility. Geha's short-fiction collection mirrors Ellison's novel in that Geha's characters demonstrate the simultaneity of being seen and not seen. In "Monkey Business," Asfoori, a deaf, palsied neighborhood vagrant, remains visible, as he is a fixture on the street, but invisible since others generally ignore his presence. Much as in Ellison's novel, the street becomes the space of contested selfhoods. Neither man receives acknowledgment of his material presence as part of a unique subjectivity. By the end of both narratives, Asfoori is dead, and the unnamed narrator is underground. Unlike the latter's community, the neighborhood does mourn Asfoori, but his funeral cannot grant him the subjectivity he has been denied all along. As David Mitchell and Sharon Snyder (2000) might describe, Asfoori's disabilities make him a "symbolic vehicle for meaning-making and cultural critique." The tragedy of Asfoori's death is that he remains invisible and largely symbolic even when his dead body is the impetus for the occasion. In Ellison's novel, it is the psychological trauma of being understood as invisible despite being physically visible that forces the unnamed narrator underground.

Ellison's and Geha's works evince the disjuncture between the way the body is understood by others and how it is experienced by the one who inhabits it. Moreover, when read in concert, their works proffer a critique of the logics that determine who gets to be a subject. For instance, Ellison contests the credibility of the world outside in determining the parameters of community and citizenship, two significant vehicles for defining a subject. Yet even with the presence of a community, as with Geha's short story, the neighborhood can still be a profoundly alienating space. Though Asfoori has found a place in the community, his character's symbolic function would indicate that space was not carved out by him but for him instead— according to the logic that invisibilizes his presence. I would venture that Geha's "Monkey Business" comments on the choice available to Ellison's unnamed narrator because Asfoori brings into sharp relief a clustered identity that includes ethnicity, gender, immigrant status, and disability. While Ellison's narrator can assert his agency by going underground, Geha's work asks, How does agency operate when bodily impairment forecloses certain possibilities? If we are to consider that Geha and Ellison also comment on the making of masculinity, then we learn that being flesh and bone significantly, but only partly, constitutes one's subjectivity, community is contested, and ability status must be foregrounded.

Reading Geha and Ellison alongside each other becomes an instructive example for how Black and Arab authors interrogate the liberatory possibility of both conceptualizing oneself in terms of embodied experience and mobilizing that conception to be at stake in wider conversation. To rely on the body as a primary way of accessing the world and to highlight the reciprocity of human interaction counter and distort existing notions about Black and Arab savagery, licentiousness, pain, and fungibility (among other narratives). The artists I examine take for granted that "departures from the norm are seen as threats to the mainstream body politic" (Bell 2011) and envision a polity that contests the accepted standard of normality, crafted as it was in the crucible of the Enlightenment. Relying on "a theory in the flesh" (Moraga

[1981] 2002) that believes "the reality of identities often comes from the fact that they are visibly marked on the body itself" (Alcoff 2005), I view their work as a challenge to and engagement with these classical ideas. They mobilize the broken, fragile, scatological, and impaired body to explode the Cartesian underpinnings of racism, sexism, and ableism.

In pairing Arab American and African American narratives, [*New Body Politics*] constructs a new cultural history of the two groups in conversation with each other. Current conversations circumscribe their relationship to one of three historically based but limited options: competition, hierarchies of whiteness, or replacement paradigms. With a brief sketch of Arab and African Americans' intertwined history, it is clear how the narratives came to be. During the twentieth century, the two groups navigated the American racial, cultural, and economic landscape, seemingly pitted against each other for resources. In the beginning of the twentieth century, Arabs in America fought to be considered legally white so that they could immigrate to the US, a series of juridical battles that socially and legally distanced them from Blacks (Gualtieri 2009; Hartman 2006; Jamal and Naber 2008; Majaj 1999a; Shalal-Esa 2003).[2] Black worry regarding immigration dates prior to this time. The debates regarding immigrants, which included Arabs during the late 1800s and early 1900s, were rehearsed in the writings of Booker T. Washington ([1901] 2003) and splashed across the pages of the NAACP's *The Crisis* in Jessie Fauset's *The Sleeper Wakes* (Ammons 2008). During the era of Jim Crow segregation, it became clear that the relationship between the two communities seemingly rested on a specific converse idea. Blacks had access to citizenship but not economic capital, while Arabs in America had access to economic capital but not citizenship (Abdulrahim 2008; Jun 2011; Shryock 2008).[3] Certainly, the terms of this inversion were vexed as African American citizenship was decidedly second class, and Arabs in America had access to the economic capital that placed them in Black neighborhoods. For instance, Nadine Naber (2012) notes that, according to Arab American businesspeople in California's Bay Area, "there is a tendency to view Arab business owners as violent and that this [limits] their business opportunities." These same businesspeople could not receive government assistance because they were not recognized as minorities. San Francisco was the first to recognize them as minorities and provide the business opportunities that accompany that status (Naber 2012). The result of such vexed competition was a growing set of tensions between the two communities, particularly in areas where they were in close contact. As Sohail Daulatzai (2012) notes, some of this competition has been manufactured. He writes, "When [America] emerged from the Cold War and the Red Scare of communism in the aftermath of World War II, Civil Rights assumed that the United States' moral standing in winning the hearts and minds of the decolonizing nations of Africa and Asia (which includes what is now the 'Middle East') was linked to its treatment of Black peoples." As a result, "the Civil Rights establishment supported an aggressive U.S. foreign policy in the name of anticommunism" (Daulatzai 2012). I do not conflate immigrant struggles with Arab American struggles lightly. However, until the third wave of Arab American immigration beginning in 1967, most of the Arab American population comprised immigrants or children of immigrants, so competition between the communities was formed (and continues, in part) on this basis.

2. In Nadine Naber's introduction to *Race and Arab Americans before and after 9/11* (Jamal and Naber 2008), she details the Arab American relationship to whiteness in legal and social terms. Amaney Jamal follows up her points in the conclusion. Sarah M. A. Gualtieri has detailed this relationship extensively in her text *Between Arab and White* (2009) regarding the first half of the twentieth century. Other scholars have started with the Arab American relationship to Blackness as a point of departure, notably Michelle Hartman, Lisa Suhair Majaj, and Andrea Shalal-Esa.

3. Shryock (2008) details the Arab American relationship to citizenship when he analyzes the way Arab Americans define their relationship to whiteness. Abdulrahim (2008) makes this point abundantly clear when discussing the base consumers of businesses in Dearborn. Helen Heran Jun's book *Race for Citizenship* (2011) underscores how Blacks' relationship to citizenship and economic capital becomes a contentious part of that community's relationship with Asian Americans. Though Jun's book mainly focuses on Chinese Americans, her analyses are instructive for thinking through this idea.

Yet, scrutiny of this competition narrative assumes a constancy regarding Arab American economic power and African American access to citizenship that is not true. Such a formulation ignores the Arab American poor, lack of cultural competency within health-care agencies for both groups, and structural inequalities that prevent African Americans from accessing resources (Aswad 1999). Moreover, the competition paradigm elides the way that Orientalism and racism become strange bedfellows with regard to citizenship and economic capital. Without relying on fiction as sociological treatise, I find it useful to point out the way fictive works have imagined these narratives and laid bare the discrepancy within them. For instance, in Mohja Kahf's novel *The Girl in the Tangerine Scarf* [2006], resentment of immigrant ambition and racial hatred collide in American suburbs; the results of such hostility are rapacious violence and constant harassment. The Muslim Cultural Center within Kahf's novel becomes one site of useful, albeit uneasy, cross-cultural unification. In urban areas where African and Arab Americans share geographical proximity, like Houston, Texas, the Greater Detroit Metropolitan Area, Michigan, and Paterson, New Jersey, xenophobia and racial prejudice can combine to deny both groups access to resources. Rabih Alameddine's *Koolaids: The Art of War* [1998] briefly depicts a friendship between two men (one Arab and one Black) during the height of the HIV/AIDS epidemic. Though the novel does not explicitly mention battles with social services, it does point to the possibility of building community in a tense and fraught social landscape.

During the mid–twentieth century, a shift in demographics prompted a change in the cultural climate such that Arab Americans forged some bonds with Blacks. Specifically, the 1967 War (also referred to as the Six-Day War) brought an influx of Arab immigrants (Jamal and Naber 2008; Ludescher 2006),[4] many of whom were more politically engaged with the Arab world and who were more culturally aware of their status as "not quite white" (Samhan 1999). However, the juridical battles that classified Arab Americans as legally white seemed to position the two groups along a hierarchy of whiteness with Blacks at the bottom. Michelle Hartman (2006) has refuted this paradigm by pointing out the way Arab Americans have used "political organizing [as] one of the primary locations for these solidarities [with African Americans]" and articulated "identification with African American arts, literature, and creative production more generally." Hartman is not alone in these ideas since her scholarship draws from Therese Saliba (1999), Helen Samhan (1987), and Lisa Suhair Majaj (1999a, 1999b, 2000)[5] and dialogues with Andrea Shalal-Esa (2003). Subscribing to the belief that the two groups exist along a hierarchy of whiteness erases the way racialization of Arabs and Blacks operates along the same volatile fault lines within US political discourse. For instance, Daniel Patrick Moynihan not only authored the infamous "Moynihan report" that pathologized Black families but also lobbied the United Nations General Assembly to rescind Resolution 3379, which linked Zionism with South African apartheid (Salaita 2006). Moynihan's uncomplicated view of both the Israel/Palestine conflict and Black life highlights the commonalities between anti-Black and anti-Arab racism stemming from an impoverished view of both cultures and histories.

I do not seek to dismiss the way the perception of the two groups along a hierarchy of whiteness has social implications and repercussions for their interaction with each other. In fact, I take up that concern at several points within [*New Body Politics*]. However, continuing to think about them within an unquestioned hierarchy of whiteness ignores the stringent critiques that both groups make vis-à-vis white privilege. Danzy Senna's

4. Scholars have pointed to this wave of immigration as the "third wave." Tanyss Ludescher (2006) describes the third wave's political awareness's effect on literature. Nadine Naber details the shifting demographic in California's Bay Area in *Arab America: Gender, Cultural Politics, and Activism* (2012). Nadine Naber also points to this phenomenon in terms of Arab Americans' vexed relationship with whiteness in the introduction to *Race and Arab Americans before and after 9/11: From Invisible Citizens to Visible Subjects* (Jamal and Naber 2008).

5. Specifically, Hartman refers to Majaj's article "Arab American Ethnicity: Locations, Coalitions, and Cultural Negotiations" (1999a). I would add that Majaj's other work highlights these connections as well.

work consistently draws attention to the way whiteness is configured as standard. In her first novel, *Caucasia* [1998], the main protagonist, Birdie, has a Black father and a white mother, and others assume she is white based on appearance. When she and her mother must go on the run from the authorities, Birdie assumes a white Jewish identity. Birdie questions the implications of her choice, not simply because it is a lie, but also because her silence allows others—her friends and possible paramour—to articulate Blackness as an aberration. *Caucasia* frustrates the idea of whiteness as normal because Birdie has difficulty assuming whiteness internally and externally (she is assumed to be other ethnicities). It makes clear Richard Dyer's (2012) assertion that "white power . . . reproduces itself regardless of intention, power dynamics, and goodwill and overwhelmingly because it is not seen as whiteness but as normal." Diana Abu-Jaber's novel *Arabian Jazz* [1993] takes up the same question when one of her Arab American characters, who others assume is white, affirms her connection to African Americans. Critic Steven Salaita's (2005) statements clarify how Diana Abu-Jaber's and Danzy Senna's works unsettle white privilege in relation to national narratives of inclusion and belonging. He defines "imperative patriotism" as a narrative that "assumes (or demands) that dissent in matters of governance and foreign affairs is unpatriotic and therefore unsavory." For him, ethnic studies and literature by people of color (including Arab Americans) "challenge centers of traditional (White) American power." Of Arab American literature, he specifically notes that the genre discusses the vexed position Arab Americans hold within the American polity, concurrently embedded within and yet isolated from it. Authors like Danzy Senna, Diana Abu-Jaber, and others function as flies in the ointment of national patriotic narratives. The way that "traditional (White) American power" can determine who is and is not legitimately American remains fundamentally tied to whiteness as it authorizes white privilege, making it antithetical to inclusion. When viewed together, Senna and Abu-Jaber's fictional works create a cross-cultural conversation about the workings of white privilege. Whiteness as a standard and arbiter of national identity deposes both Arab and African Americans from citizenship and repositions them as subordinate to whites within the national narrative.

After 9/11/2001 and the election of the first African American president, Barack Obama, media depictions of Arab Americans and the USA PATRIOT Act led some to believe that Arab Americans have replaced Blacks as the most disenfranchised group in America or that social relations in America had transformed such that the country was now supposedly postracial. There are several objections to the pervasive idea that African American and Arab Americans currently exist in a replacement paradigm in which Arab is the new Black. The first objection is based in history. Arab Americans have been in the US since the Wahab family in the 1400s and steadily came to the country beginning in the late nineteenth century (Hassoun 2005; Kayyali 2006; Orfalea 2006). Such a long history within the United States couples with a longer history of Orientalism to suggest that Arab Americans have always occupied a vexed racial position. It also elides the way the aforementioned shifts in demographic compound the hyperinvisibility of Arab Americans within the American racial landscape (Alsultany 2012). The second objection extends the first and questions the replacement paradigm on the basis of Arab American struggles with assimilation. Evelyn Shakir (1982, 1988, 1991) notes that some Arab American authors capitalized on their phenotypical proximity to whiteness to assimilate during the mid–twentieth century. True, assimilation requires eliding multiple factors of one's identity, but it can often rest on one's physical ability to pass for white. The fact is that the preference for white skin in America allowed for and encouraged some Arab Americans to erase their specific ethnic identity in favor of a white Protestant identity. Some Arab American writers, including Abu-Jaber (noted above), point out that this passing can be involuntary. In short, the replacement paradigm obscures the way that white skin privilege and assimilation facilitates the invisibility of Arab American identity. Moreover, the replacement paradigm—couched as it is in the language of fashion—adopts a progressive view of history for Blacks in America. It assumes that Black history moves forward from slavery to Barack Obama, viewing the latter as indicative of eradicated structural inequality despite Obama's consistent recourse to conservative racial politics.[6] It also assumes that liberal fights for equality have not been without their problematic homophobic, misogynist, ableist, and even racist underpinnings. Not only does a progressive view of history obfuscate the complicated nature of history itself, but it also presupposes that there have been no setbacks in the journey toward equality. As Moallem and Boal (1999) note, "Racialization remains a deep current in the politics of inequality. It has generated severe historical contradictions to the point of crisis for liberal nation-state formations, which must reconcile racial logic with the universalistic aspirations of Enlightenment ideology."

This project, by rethinking the vicissitudes of living in a Black or Arab body, unpacks the problematic ideology at the heart of our conception of the nation-state. I pair Black and Arab narratives because rethinking this ideology challenges the doxic seduction of whiteness, maleness, and able-bodiedness masquerading as normalcy. To be clear, midwifing a conversation between Blacks and Arabs makes clear the "heterogeneous nature of racism's ideological underpinnings" (Salaita 2006). Specifically, anti-Arab racism and anti-Black racism share the same "complicated (and usually discordant) discourse of oppression and resistance, capitalism and egalitarianism, stereotype and self-representation" (Salaita 2006). The two groups' relationship with institutions ranging from the medical establishment to the nation-state forces a consideration of how race, racialization, and racial hierarchy work within the United States. These conversations are made more exigent and more difficult because the two groups are not always in agreement, and the opposition proves revelatory. When Michelle Hartman (2006) rightly asks how Arab Americans engage with Blackness, such a question "reformulate[s] the positioning of Arab Americans within US racial hierarchies." Here, Hartman's analysis draws on Arab Americans as being situated within a probationary whiteness both legally and socially. Toni Morrison (1993) makes clear how Blacks born in America become suspicious of the privilege (however vexed) that relationship to whiteness affords: namely, because the price of the ticket into American culture is maltreatment of Blacks born in America. In Morrison's words, "a hostile posture toward resident blacks must be struck at the Americanizing door before it will open." As scholars seek to explore race within the United States, they cannot ignore the tension between how Arabs and Blacks have been mutually constituted, at times in opposition to one another. In scholastic terms, conversations between Blacks and Arabs challenge the way we discuss the larger fields with which this project is engaged (and I would imagine many others). In American studies and comparative ethnic studies, a robust comparison of this sort refuses to participate in the invisibilizing of Arabs and Arab Americans, constituting them as part of the American narrative.[7] Ken Warren's purposefully provocative *What Was African American Literature?* (2011) prompted scholars of African American literature to consider how to read the tradition of African American literature in the late twentieth and early twenty-first century. I would argue that reading African American literature now requires a set of cross-cultural conversations that examine the wide range of influences this art has as well as the inspiration it receives from others.

As I noted, a cross-cultural conversation between Blacks and Arabs could be contentious because of the way both groups have been enfolded and implicated within the "hegemony of normalcy" (Davis 1995; Garland-Thomson 1996).[8] Within the crevices, we find that

6. During the fiftieth anniversary that commemorated the March on Washington, Barack Obama lambasted Blacks for putatively poor behavior, citing that their complaint about racial injustice divided the country. He has routinely criticized Black men regarding their role in family life.

7. Lisa Suhair Majaj calls for this kind of discussion in her article "Arab American Ethnicity: Locations, Coalitions, and Cultural Negotiations" (1999a), realizing that this is difficult and fraught territory.

8. I reference this phrase here to draw out how the concept of normalcy relies on what disability studies scholar Rosemarie Garland-Thomson in *Extraordinary Bodies* (1996) has called the normate, "the constructed identity of those who, by way of the bodily configurations and cultural capital they assume, can step into a position of authority and wield the power it grants them."

"white supremacy is an equal-opportunity employer; nonwhite people can become active agents of white supremacy as well as passive participants in its hierarchies and rewards" (Lipsitz 2006). More specifically, Arab American battles with racism reveal African American complicity with intolerance. African American battles with racism also reveal Arab American complicity with intolerance. It becomes urgently necessary to unpack the "significant linkages that enable us to understand possibilities for social change" without "position[ing] racialized groups or individuals as somehow inadequately politicized or underdeveloped" (Jun 2011). On the one hand, African American studies occupies a peculiar, advantageous position within ethnic studies as the long-established tradition from which most scholars, critics, and authors draw inspiration. That peculiar advantage has several impacts on existing scholarship. First, it would be easy to remain solipsistic about African American issues as if they were not in dialogue with other communities. In addition, it becomes taboo to discuss African American complicity with intolerance. Lastly, when Black studies is placed into a privileged position over other ethnic studies fields, Blackness is erased even as it is relied upon as a resource to articulate progressive politics or readings. Arab American studies as a nascent field challenges this so-called advantage and forces African American studies to reconsider how it engages race and racism post–civil rights. On the other hand, African American studies has the potential to question the Arab American relationship to whiteness and the historical distance between the two communities economically and socially. Integral to mining these cross-cultural discussions for their potential is the knowledge of the way Arabs and Blacks have already sought to traverse the historical and cultural distance of difference. For instance, Alice Walker, Angela Davis, Gina Dent, Robin D. G. Kelley, June Jordan, and other Blacks have been heavily involved in boycott, divestment, and sanctions (BDS) activism against Israel. Arab American and African American women writers find common ground in their explorations of intersectional identity. Andrea Shalal-Esa (2003) notes that Arab American writers "deriv[e] strength from feminists, black theorists, and post-colonial thinkers . . . to chronicle decades of racism, oppression, and marginalization in the United States."

Instead of creating a narrative of "cross-racial dysfunction" (Jun 2011), I examine how both groups critique the national and cultural narratives that sustain various politics of inequality. This conversation does have a caveat. It assumes that "the psychic life of racism can best be read in the context of the United States in the space where black and white intersect" (Holland 2012). I concur with the idea that "regardless of how far modernist binaries may be deconstructed, regardless of how unstable their bare understanding of oppositional difference, they cannot be simply dismissed: their power may be based on an illusion, but its operation is all too real" (Shildrick 2009). However, my stance regarding the Black/white binary does not assume that the only way to approach a discussion of that "psychic life" is through the depiction of Black/white relations. Scholarship must explore how that binary affects other racial and ethnic groups. In the words of Andrea Smith (2006), we must "address the nuanced structure of white supremacy" without assuming that "if we just include more people, then our practice [and our scholarship] will be less racist." I am interested neither in erasing Blackness nor in moving beyond it but rather [in] seeking to understand how Blackness remains in dialogue with the racial landscape that includes Arab Americans and how Arabness remains in dialogue with a racial landscape whose foundation is the Black/white binary. . . .

This project also opens up a discussion between and about Blacks and Arabs in America on a wide range of issues, including Palestine, hierarchies of whiteness, double consciousness, communally sanctioned silence around illness, and the medical establishment. I examine narrative (broadly defined) because stories are never divorced from the circumstances that create them, neither can they be cleaved from the circumstances upon which they comment, nor can they be delinked from the embodied experience that architects them. I have chosen to discuss a variety of social and political concerns because politicized flesh appears in multiple places. To narrow the conversation to one topic dismisses the wide range of critiques these authors and figures make.

Moreover, this project is, I hope, the beginning of scholarship that addresses the intersection of Blackness and Arab identity.

From Chapter 1: "Respirating Resistance: Suheir Hammad's Invocation of Breath"

In 2001, Suheir Hammad closed the premiere episode of *Russell Simmons Presents DEF Poetry* by reading her poem "first writing since." The last lines were:

> there is life here. Anyone reading this is breathing,
> maybe hurting, but breathing for sure. And if there
> is any light to come, it will shine from the eyes of
> those who look for peace and justice after the rubble
> and rhetoric are cleared and the phoenix has risen.
> affirm life. affirm life.
> we got to carry each other now.
> you are either with life, or
> against it. affirm life.
> (in Simmons 2004)

For me watching on television, it was a profound moment because Suheir Hammad voiced what it meant to be an Arab American woman watching "those / buildings collapse on themselves like a broken heart" (in Simmons 2004). She spoke poignantly about being simultaneously politically aware and grief-stricken. She also alerted everyone listening to the necessity of affirming life at a time when ideology and rhetoric could overcome compassion and critical thinking. Moreover, she reminded mourning Americans of the danger posed by permitting "the obsessive focus on the Self in the United States [to obscure] the violence against the Other" (Erevelles 2011). . . .

Hammad's robust set of multicultural influences points to a sentiment expressed by Arab American literary critic Lisa Suhair Majaj (1999a): namely, that "contemporary Arab-American literature increasingly reflects the awareness of the need to forge connection beyond the insular boundaries of group identity." Yet the commentary about American poetics extends beyond the realm of the literary to how we think about inclusion. To be sure, Hammad's claims about language engage with the semiotic question of how words maintain social and political meaning and who determines that meaning. As Edward Said (1994) has remarked, the ability to prevent certain stories "from forming and emerging is very important to culture and imperialism, and constitutes one of the main connections between them." In other words, one cannot have domination of bodies without domination of discourse. Hammad focuses on the exclusion of various racialized, gendered, and classed voices. She claims that the result is language that remains ill equipped to describe, define, or discuss everyone's concerns. Hammad openly discusses the "transparent struggle that [she has] with the poem about finding appropriate language" (in Knopf-Newman 2006). She recasts words like "occupation," "liberation," and "terrorist" to examine why they are automatically ascribed to Arabs and Muslims. For instance, in "first writing since," she asks, "When we talk about holy books and hooded men and death, / why do we never mention the kkk?" (Hammad 2008). Moreover, Hammad points out that people of color do not "have the power of the narrative," so their claims on language and meaning making remain tenuous (in Knopf-Newman 2006). As a result, their words can be "neutralized under the terms 'victim art' and 'political correctness,' [so that their] incursion into territory usually secured for whiteness can momentarily be tolerated and quickly dismissed" (Dolan 2006).[20]

Yet Hammad continues to mobilize the ephemeral to explain and explore concerns that are so easily and summarily dismissed. Turning again to her appearance on *DEF Poetry*, I wish to highlight how she understands breathing as integral to the act of affirming life. Within the logic of the poem, those who are breathing make clear that "there is life here." Hammad writes, "anyone reading this is breathing" despite their hurt. She repeats "breathing" and emphasizes it with "for sure." When she underscores that life is present, she explicitly links the heft of existing after this trauma to the quotidian nature of breathing. Her call to "affirm life" is also a call to breathe and to honor those who do so. Notably, Hammad's emphasis on living and breathing does not negate the fragility of either. Instead, her injunction relies on breathing and living as evidence of all our ephemerality. Despite the clear fragility of those actions, Hammad insists upon them as urgent and necessary counterbalances to injustice and pain.

In this [chapter of *New Body Politics*], I turn to Hammad for two reasons. First, she mobilizes breath—as metaphor, image, idea, and action—as an act of resistance. Within Hammad's oeuvre, fragility does not need to be overcome or compensated for but rather embraced as a way to reconstitute the past and move into a politically and socially progressive future. Second, her poetry and essays facilitate cross-cultural conversations between Blacks and Arabs about myriad social and political issues. As noted above, she enacts these conversations within her work based on the influences of hip hop, Arab oral poetic tradition, and spoken word. Of Hammad's invocation of African American jazz traditions, critic Michelle Hartman (2006) notes that she "establishes an [Arab American] identity based on a shared cultural feature." In addition, Hammad draws inspiration from Black feminist traditions, particularly June Jordan and Audre Lorde (Hammad 1996a; Hartman 2002). Hammad finds Jordan's work "powerful and transformative" because Jordan wrote poetry about injustice in Nicaragua and Guatemala during the 1980s and linked it to other injustices in Palestine and the United States (Knopf-Newman 2006). Hammad recalls that reading Jordan transformed her understanding of what poetry can do and who can have a voice. Hammad's poetry takes up a project similar to Jordan's, discussing global injustice and also explicitly linking it back to US domestic issues with race, class, and gender.

Hammad's "first writing since" made her famous both as a spoken-word artist and as an artist responding to 9/11/2001. The latter tends toward a partial erasure of Hammad's oeuvre. Positioning herself as indebted to June Jordan and others places Hammad within a lineage of Black and Brown feminism and activism. Her first collection, *Born Palestinian, Born Black* (1996a), and her memoir, *Drops of This Story* (1996b), explore the complex interracial landscape of the United States and what it means to write oneself into existence within such a milieu. *Born Palestinian, Born Black* especially illuminates that the issues brought into sharp relief by the attacks on the World Trade Center have long histories. Her first collection includes poems that discuss and critique a wide range of issues, including interracial sexual politics, the Israeli/Palestinian conflict, and the politics of fashion. Shadowing the collection are the vexed terms of visibility that surface only to "silenc[e] critiques of state violence and the structural inequalities that produce hatred and racism" (Jamal and Naber 2008). Hammad's poetry works against the erasure through her use of breathing and respiration as a constant image and action, which insists on visibility and tangibility of a different sort.

The readings below make use of phenomenology as a way to access the texts' use of breath. Incorporated (and I use that verb deliberately) into the metaphor of breathing is the act itself. Since phenomenology understands the body as the "first way of access to the world" (Merleau-Ponty 2008), I read the metaphors of breathing by focusing on the way their function as part of embodied experience dictates how the metaphors perform in Hammad's poetry. So before thinking through how Hammad mobilizes breathing as poetic tool, it is important to consider the physiological aspects of the action. Breathing involves both voluntary and involuntary processes. The brain stem controls both since breathing is essential for life function. We breathe to exchange oxygen for carbon dioxide, ridding ourselves of excess heat and water. The respiratory process involves not only the respiratory system but also the nervous system and the circulatory system since breathing helps to regulate the heartbeat and requires that the nervous system send pulses to the diaphragm so that it can expand and contract at the appropriate time. Humans have some control over when and how much to breathe so that we can control speech or participate in activities like exercise and singing. Controlling one's breath is also integral to avoiding inhalation of noxious gases and [to] participating in certain religious practices. As a result, respiration involves physiological processes and bears implications for cultural production. Hammad's poetry highlights the interplay between breathing as a natural phenomenon and as evidence of cultural practice.

In the piece "argela remembering" (Hammad 1996a) the speaker watches the father reconstitute memory as he smokes an *argela* (water pipe). The act of breathing governs the rhythm and the logic of the poem. When one smokes an *argela*, one must inhale and exhale the smoke, taking care not to allow the smoke into the lungs. It is a process that relies on both the voluntary and involuntary aspects of breathing. As the father in the poem speaks, he remembers and retells certain aspects of history, the result of which is the tearful end of the poem. The father's breathing sets up the rhythm of the poem, "exhaling Mediterranean breezes / mid east sighs / him telling me." The father expels air both to exhale the smoke of the *argela* and to sigh. His sigh prompts the stories within the poem. On the page, the stories, which begin with the first-person plural pronoun, are center justified such that the page's layout performs the exhalation. In other words, the left-justified text appears to exhale the centered text. Since *w* is a labial consonant and requires an exhale, the poem also forces a reader to perform a round of inhalations and exhalations every time the speaker mentions "we."

What subtends the poem is the idea that the foundational story of Israel leaves out the Palestinians. In other words, the inhalation or acceptance of one story is tempered with the exhalation of another. The centered stories, the exhaled stories, present the loss of Palestine. The inhaled stories, or the left-justified verse, points to the acknowledgment of the current situation. After a series of center-justified text, the left-justified text reads:

> inhaling strawberries through
> argelas we've become a people of
> living room politics and tobacco
> stained teeth painfully reminding
> each other.
>
> (Hammad 1996a)

Echoing the page layout, the speaker inhales in order to tell a different story. Unlike the center-justified verse, this stanza is about the present, not the past. The inhalation is a painful moment of memory and, like the repetitive act of breathing, will be reenacted. It is important to note that the inhalation within the poem is by necessity. It occurs before and after "we" and as a result of moving between center-justified and left-justified text. Since the reading of the poem forces one to return to exhalation, the poem foregrounds it as the more forceful and powerful action. Nonetheless, there cannot be one without the other. However short the inhalations, they remain an opposed but necessary action for maintaining the rhythm of the poem. Here, the poem evokes the tension between Israel's story of its own foundation and Palestinian remembrance. The rhythm suggests that, unlike some real breathing, the pattern of inhale and exhale on the page is not an even exchange. Much more like the process of smoking an *argela*, the history of Palestine has gone through a process of uneven acceptances and articulations.

In "argela remembering," respiration indexes the cultural practice of smoking water pipes as evidence of Palestinian existence. The poem dovetails with Hammad's larger critique of the discourse regarding the Israel/Palestine conflict. Elsewhere, Hammad speaks of Palestinian life as a challenge to the existence of the State of Israel. She points to Golda Meir's statement, made exactly one year before her birth, "I cannot sleep at night knowing how many Arab babies are being born this night" (in Knopf-Newman 2002). Hammad contends that Meir's statement configures Palestinian existence as a "nightmare for the Israeli enterprise" (in Knopf-Newman 2002). As a result, she views her birth and all others since as an indication of Palestinian humanity in the face of the desire to deny it. In the poetry, breathing moves the poem along, but it still remains metonymic for the other acts that distinguish the human from the inhuman. Not surprisingly, Hammad spotlights independent and critical thought as central to her ability to live. She writes, "In feminist circles, where the fear of anti-Jewish racism has become a muzzle on any critique of Zionism, I can't not be me—a Palestinian whose ancestry traces itself to the 1948 territories, whose existence undermines the legitimacy of the state of Israel" (Hammad 2002). The double negative "can't not" emphasizes that her understanding of herself as a Palestinian is not a choice but an embodied reality. Immediately after her statement, she anticipates the silencing rhetoric that would attempt to erase her and her critique by asking and answering, "Complicated? Not really" (Hammad 2002). Within the logic of Hammad's oeuvre, the act of breathing constitutes a rebellion since it indicates life. . . .

In contemplating Hammad's use of breathing and embodiment as sacred, the question arises as to whether the delicacy of the body itself counteracts the narrative she attempts to create. Physically speaking, the body and its breath are inherently breakable and temporary. It would seem that a narrative based on them would also be tenuous. Nonetheless, I would argue that Hammad's work does not seek to negate the nature of embodiment but rather uses its delicacy as evidence of its value. Her poetry critiques the idea that fragility equals fungibility. . . .

In *Breaking Poems*, Hammad's poetry creatively mines the limitations of the body to expose the way violence ruptures human experience. Many of the poems break words apart and sounds apart as a way to get through to meaning. She relies on puns and what Lennard Davis (1995) has termed the "deaf moment of reading," in which readers must hear the words inside their heads rather than rely on sonic cues to determine meaning. He writes, "All readers are deaf because they are defined by a process that does not require hearing or speaking . . . reading is a silent process, and although anyone can vocalize what he or she reads, the vocalization is a second-order activity." The "deaf moment" defamiliarizes one's relationship to text because it privileges sight over sound. Hammad's collection likewise defamiliarizes one's relationship to the text, not only because it privileges sight over sound but also because it requires one to engage sight to understand sound. The text is often broken apart, indicating that the typeface and the sound create multiple and, at times, varied meanings. For example, the titles all include "break" in some way, usually at the front (e.g., "break (clean)") and sometimes in between words (e.g., "wind(break)her"). "Wind(break)her" sonically refers to the jacket that often shields wearers from environmental elements like wind or rain and provides some warmth. Textually, the title meditates on the possible relationship between a woman, brokenness, and the wind. Separate from but reliant on this "deaf moment" is the title's reliance on the literal broken body as an image. Some poems force the reader to impose a structure on the words to determine meaning. Given that all of the poems contain Arabic, which may be unfamiliar to some of her readers, the structures one can impose vary greatly depending on one's linguistic knowledge. Specifically, the last four poems don't follow a deliberate poetic structure as they are rendered in paragraph form and rely on the reader to link the words together however one sees fit. The mere act of doing so creates a rupture, forcing the reader to linguistically enact what has already been done to the people, countries, and places she discusses. . . .

. . . Hammad's work links the fragility of the body and the temporary nature of embodied experience with the construction of narratives about people groups. For her, bodily presence is neither incidental nor accidental but rather evidence of the fundamental value of human life. She ruptures language to force a reexamination of commonly used words and their attendant meanings for nationalist and imperialistic projects. Hammad's work also proposes a set of cross-cultural conversations about what people of color across the globe can say to one another despite being implicated in the domination of one another often imposed by nation-states in their name (and without their permission). . . .

Works Cited

Abdulrahim, Sawsan. 2008. "Whiteness and the Arab Immigrant Experience." In *Race and Arab Americans before and after 9/11: From Invisible Citizens to Visible Subjects*, edited by Amaney Jamal and Nadine Naber, 131–46. Syracuse, NY: Syracuse Univ. Press.

Abu-Jaber, Diana. 1993. *Arabian Jazz*. New York: Harcourt Brace.

Alameddine, Rabih. 1998. *Koolaids: The Art of War*. New York: Picador.

Alcoff, Linda. 2005. *Visible Identities: Race, Gender, and the Self*. New York: Oxford Univ. Press.

Alsultany, Evelyn. 2012. *Arabs and Muslims in the Media: Race and Representation after 9/11*. New York: New York Univ. Press.

Ammons, Elizabeth. 2008. "Black Anxiety about Immigration and Jessie Fauset's *The Sleeper Wakes*." *African American Review* 42, nos. 3–4: 461–76.

Aswad, Barbara C. 1999. "Attitudes of Arab Immigrants toward Welfare." In *Arabs in America: Building a New Future*, edited by Michael Suleiman, 177–91. Philadelphia: Temple Univ. Press.

Aziz, Barbara Nimri. 2004. Foreword to *Scheherezade's Legacy: Arab and Arab American Women on Writing*, edited by Susan Muaddi Darraj, xi–xvi. Westport, CT: Praeger.

Bell, Christopher M. 2011. "Doing Representational Detective Work." In *Blackness and Disability: Critical Examinations and Cultural Interventions*, edited by Christopher M. Bell, 1–8. Berlin: Lit Verlag.

Brooks, Daphne. 2006. *Bodies in Dissent: Spectacular Performances of Race and Freedom*. Durham, NC: Duke Univ. Press.

Cohen, William A. 2008. *Embodied: Victorian Literature and the Senses*. Minneapolis: Univ. of Minnesota Press.

Daulatzai, Sohail. 2012. *Black Star, Crescent Moon: The Muslim International and Black Freedom beyond America*. Minneapolis: Univ. of Minnesota Press.

Davis, Lennard. 1995. *Enforcing Normalcy*. London: Verso.

Dolan, Jill. 2006. "Utopia in Performance." *Theatre Research International* 31, no. 2: 163–73.

Dyer, Richard. 2012. "The Matter of Whiteness." In *White Privilege: Essential Readings on the Other Side of Racism*, 4th ed., edited by Paula Rothenberg, 9–14. New York: Worth Publishers.

Ellison, Ralph. [1952] 1980. *Invisible Man*. New York: Vintage Books.

Erevelles, Nirmala. 2011. *Disability and Difference in Global Contexts: Enabling a Transformative Body Politic*. New York: Palgrave Macmillan.

Garland-Thomson, Rosemarie. 1996. *Extraordinary Bodies: Figuring Physical Disability in American Culture and Literature*. New York: Columbia Univ. Press.

Geha, Joseph. 1990. *Through and Through: Toledo Stories*. St. Paul, MN: Graywolf Press.

Gualtieri, Sarah M. A. 2009. *Between Arab and White: Race and Ethnicity in the Early Syrian American Diaspora*. Berkeley: Univ. of California Press.

Hammad, Suheir. 1996a. *Born Palestinian, Born Black*. New York: Harlem River Press.

———. 1996b. *Drops of This Story*. New York: Harlem River Press.

———. 2002. "Composites." *Signs* 28, no. 1: 471.

———. 2008. *Breaking Poems*. New York: Cypher Books.

Hartman, Michelle. 2002. "A *Debke* Beat Funky as P.E.'s Riff: Hip Hop Poetry and Politics in Suheir Hammad's *Born Palestinian, Born Black*." *Black Arts Quarterly* 7, no. 1: 6–8.

———. 2006. "'This Sweet/ Sweet Music': Jazz, Sam Cooke, and Reading Arab American Literary Identities." *MELUS* 31, no. 4: 145–66.

Hassoun, Rosina J. 2005. *Arab Americans in Michigan*. East Lansing: Michigan State Univ. Press.

Holland, Sharon. 2012. *Erotic Life of Racism*. Durham, NC: Duke Univ. Press.

Jamal, Amaney, and Nadine Naber, eds. 2008. *Race and Arab Americans before and after 9/11: From Invisible Citizens to Visible Subjects*. Syracuse, NY: Syracuse Univ. Press.

Jarrett, Gene Andrew. 2011. *Representing the Race: A New Political History of African American Literature*. New York: New York Univ. Press.

Jun, Helen Heran. 2011. *Race for Citizenship: Black Orientalism and Asian Uplift from Pre-Emancipation to Neoliberal America*. New York: New York Univ. Press.

Kahf, Mohja. 2006. *The Girl in the Tangerine Scarf*. New York: Carol & Graf.

Kayyali, Randa. 2006. *The Arab Americans*. Westport, CT: Greenwood Press.

Knopf-Newman, Marcy Jane. 2006. "Interview with Suheir Hammad." In "Arab American Literature," edited by Salah D. Hassan and Marcy Jane Knopf-Newman. Special issue of *MELUS* 31, no. 4: 71–93.

Linton, Simi. 1998. *Claiming Disability: Knowledge and Identity*. New York: New York Univ. Press.

Lipsitz, George. 2006. *The Possessive Investment in Whiteness*. Philadelphia: Temple Univ. Press.

Ludescher, Tanyss. 2006. "From Nostalgia to Critique: An Overview of Arab American Literature." In "Arab American Literature," edited by Salah D. Hassan and Marcy Jane Knopf-Newman. Special issue of *MELUS* 31, no. 4: 93–114.

Majaj, Lisa Suhair. 1999a. "Arab American Ethnicity: Locations, Coalitions, and Cultural Negotiations." In *Arabs in America: Building a New Future*, edited by Michael Suleiman, 320–36. Philadelphia: Temple Univ. Press.

———. 1999b. "New Directions: Arab American Writing at Century's End." In *Post Gibran: Anthology of New Arab American Writing*, edited by Khaled Mattawa and Munir Akash, 67–82. Syracuse, NY: Syracuse Univ. Press.

———. 2000. "Arab Americans and the Meaning of Race." In *Postcolonial Theory and the United States: Race, Ethnicity, and Literature*, edited by Amritjit Singh and Peter Schmidt, 320–37. Jackson: Univ. of Mississippi Press.

Mattawa, Khaled, and Munir Akash. 1999. Introduction to *Post Gibran: Anthology of New Arab American Writing*, edited by Khaled Mattawa and Munir Akash, xi–xiii. Syracuse, NY: Syracuse Univ. Press.

Merleau-Ponty, Maurice. 2008. *Phenomenology of Perception*. Translated by Colin Smith. New York: Routledge.

Mitchell, David, and Sharon Snyder. 2000. *Narrative Prosthesis: Disability and the Dependencies of Discourse*. Ann Arbor: Univ. of Michigan Press.

Moallem, Minoo, and Iain A. Boal. 1999. "Multicultural Nationalism and the Poetics of Inauguration." In *Between Woman and Nation: Nationalisms, Transnational*

Feminisms, and the State, edited by Caren Kaplan, Norma Alarcón, and Minoo Moallem, 243–64. Durham, NC: Duke Univ. Press.

Moraga, Cherríe. [1981] 2002. "Entering the Lives of Others: Theory in the Flesh." In *This Bridge Called My Back: Writings by Radical Women of Color*, edited by Gloria Anzaldúa and Cherríe Moraga, 19–20. Berkeley, CA: Third Woman Press.

Morrison, Toni. 1993. "On the Backs of Blacks." *Time*, Dec. 2.

Naber, Nadine. 2012. *Arab America: Gender, Cultural Politics, and Activism*. New York: New York Univ. Press.

Orfalea, Gregory. 2006. *The Arab Americans: A History*. Northampton, MA: Interlink Books.

Said, Edward. 1994. *Culture and Imperialism*. New York: Vintage.

Salaita, Steven. 2005. "Ethnic Identity and Imperative Patriotism: Arab Americans before and after 9/11." *College Literature* 32, no. 2: 146–68.

———. 2006. *Anti-Arab Racism: Where It Comes From and What It Means for Politics Today*. Ann Arbor, MI: Pluto Press.

Saliba, Therese. 1999. "Resisting Invisibility: Arab Americans in Academia and Activism." In *Arabs in American: Building a New Future*, edited by Michael Suleiman, 304–19. Philadelphia: Temple Univ. Press.

Samhan, Helen. 1987. "Politics and Exclusion: The Arab American Experience." *Journal of Palestine Studies* 16, no. 2: 11–28.

———. 1999. "Not Quite White: Race Classification and the Arab-American Experience." In *Arabs in America: Building a New Future*, edited by Michael Suleiman, 209–26. Philadelphia: Temple Univ. Press.

Senna, Danzy. 1998. *Caucasia*. New York: Riverhead Books.

Shakir, Evelyn. 1982. "Pretending to Be Arab: Role Playing in Vance Bourjaily's 'The Fractional Man.'" *MELUS* 9, no. 1: 7–21.

———. 1988. "Mother's Milk: Women in Arab-American Autobiography." *MELUS* 15, no. 4: 39–50.

———. 1991. "Arab Mothers, American Sons: Women in Arab-American Autobiographies." *MELUS* 17, no. 3: 5–15.

Shalal-Esa, Andrea. 2003. "Arab-American Writers Identify with Communities of Color." *Al-Jadid* 9:42–43.

Shildrick, Margaret. 2009. *Dangerous Discourses of Disability, Subjectivity, and Sexuality*. New York: Palgrave Macmillan.

Shryock, Andrew. 2008. "The Moral Analogies of Race." In *Race and Arab Americans before and after 9/11: From Invisible Citizens to Visible Subjects*, edited by Amaney Jamal and Nadine Naber, 114–30. Syracuse, NY: Syracuse Univ. Press.

Siebers, Tobin. 2008. *Disability Theory*. Ann Arbor: Univ. of Michigan Press.

Simmons, Russell. 2004. *Russell Simmons Presents DEF Poetry Season 1*. New York: HBO Home Video.

Smith, Andrea. 2006. "Heteropatriarchy and the Three Pillars of White Supremacy: Rethinking Women of Color Organizing." In *The Color of Violence: The INCITE! Anthology*, edited by INCITE! Women of Color against Violence, 66–73. Boston: South End Press.

Sobchack, Vivian. 2004. *Carnal Thoughts: Embodiment and Moving Image Culture*. Berkeley: Univ. of California Press.

Warren, Kenneth W. 2011. *What Was African American Literature?* Cambridge, MA: Harvard Univ. Press.

Washington, Booker T. [1901] 2003. *Up from Slavery*. Boston: Bedford–St. Martin's.

4

The Sephardi-Moorish Atlantic

Between Orientalism and Occidentalism

ELLA SHOHAT

. . . In his book *The History of the Concept of Latin America in the United States*, Brazilian political scientist João Feres Jr. . . . usefully deploys a Saidian prism to anatomize the writings of certain US scholars working in the service of Cold War ideology, such as Samuel Huntington and Seymour Martin Lipset, who represent Latin Americans as irrational, passion-driven, pathological, and unproductive, condemned to historical immobility. Within this discourse, to cite Feres, "the Anglo-Saxon Protestant Occident constitutes the beacon of progress and human development, while Catholic Latin America is the prison which maintains its detainees frozen in the feudal past" (2005, 129).

Other Latin American studies scholars, such as Walter Mignolo, have pointed out that postcolonial discourse, by concentrating on "Orientalism" as a discursive symptom of later forms of British and French imperialism, forgets that "Orientalism" was itself preceded by "Occidentalism" (Mignolo 2005).[1] In *The Idea of Latin America* (2005), Mignolo deploys the concept of "Occidentalism" in a sense very different from that of writers such as Ian Buruma and Avishai Margalit, who use it as part of what amounts to a variation on the "reverse racism" argument vis-à-vis Said, in this case a "reverse Orientalism" argument, which suggests that Arab/Muslims have themselves subjected the West to dehumanization and pernicious stereotypes (Buruma and Margalit 2004; see also Carrier 1995). For Mignolo, in contrast, Occidentalism, as the idea of the West and its ideology of expansionism, refers to the consequences of the European Conquest in the Americas. Mignolo, in the vein of Caribbean and Latin American studies scholars in general, crucially identifies the beginnings of colonial discourse not with the post-Enlightenment era but with Columbus and 1492. In contrast to much of postcolonial studies, including Said's *Orientalism* (1978), the question of "the colonial" as embedded in 1492 requires that one examines continuities and discontinuities between early Iberian expansionism and latter-day nineteenth-century, largely British and French, imperialism.

Excerpts from Ella Shohat's, "The Sephardi-Moorish Atlantic: Between Orientalism and Occidentalism," in *Between the Middle East and the Americas: The Cultural Politics of Diaspora*, co-edited by Evelyn Alsultany and Ella Shohat (Ann Arbor: Univ. of Michigan Press, 2013), 42–64. Full references in the original notes were converted to author-date citations in the text and notes here, and a works cited list was added. Reprinted with copyediting and press style changes for consistency throughout the volume by permission of the University of Michigan Press. A shorter earlier version of this essay, entitled "On the Margins of Middle Eastern Studies: Situating Said's *Orientalism*," was presented at the plenary session of the Middle East Studies Association conference, "Celebrating the Thirtieth Anniversary of Orientalism: Critiques and New Insights" (Washington, DC, November 24, 2008), which was organized and moderated by the association's president Mervat Hatem, and was published in *Review of Middle Eastern Studies* 43, no. 1 (Summer 2009): 18–24. Part of the research here was made possible thanks to a research/lectureship Fulbright Award, University of São Paulo, Spring 2010.

1. In *Unthinking Eurocentrism* (1994), Robert Stam and I advanced a parallel critique of postcolonial theory, which focused on the "colonial" as beginning with the heights of the nineteenth-century imperial expansionism, of British and French imperialism, while tending to ignore 1492.

The Two 1492s—toward Another Beginning

At the same time, one could slightly amend both Feres and Mignolo, for different but related reasons, having to do with the question: When exactly does Orientalism begin? Feres's identification of the United States as the primal fount of Orientalism runs its own risks, some of which derive from certain omissions within Said's *Orientalism* itself. Feres's emphasis on US-style Monroe Doctrine, Big Stick Diplomacy, and Cold War Orientalism in Latin America forgets the fact that latter-day Orientalism comes superimposed on the preexisting forms of Orientalism—as a branch of colonial Eurocentric discourse—that have shaped Caribbean/Latin American history itself.

Prior to the US Orientalizing of Latin America à la Feres, the Spanish and Portuguese had already Orientalized, as it were, the Indigenous peoples—"los Indios." Columbus, in this perspective, could be regarded as the first Orientalist of the Americas, even in the sense of imagining himself, as his diaries indicate, to be actually *in* the Orient, in the land of the Great Khan. In his fanciful account, the island, supposedly off the shore of India, was peopled with wild flora, fauna, cannibals, and mermaids. In the wake of 1492, Orientalist discourse traveled to the Americas, generating the emergence of Western world order, which in turn created another base from which to disseminate Eurocentric conceptions of the world. Infused and empowered by the Americas' material wealth, Europe subsequently colonized Egypt, Algeria, and the rest of the Middle East and North Africa, subjecting these regions to an old/new kind of Orientalism. Before arriving in the Orient, then, the Orientalist imaginary had arrived in the West Indies. Columbus's spatial disorientation is thus foundational to the narrative of the beginning of Orientalism.

Although Feres assumes Said's genealogy of Orientalist discourse as dating back to latter-day European empires, Orientalist discourse as a mode of colonial/Eurocentric discourse could just as easily be traced back to the early colonization of the Americas. While extending Said's critique of post-Enlightenment Orientalism to clarify US attitudes toward Latin America is certainly productive, in other respects it overlooks the ideological conquest of the Americas generally within Orientalist paradigms. In this sense, Mignolo provides a corrective to both Feres and Said by speaking of Latin America's "double wound," first from Iberian Conquest and second by American imperialism. Yet, while in full agreement with the Latin Americanist take on the beginning of colonial discourse, by the same token, however, one might offer another genealogy that argues that Occidentalism à la Mignolo did not begin simply in one 1492 but rather simultaneously in *two* 1492s. The Conquista was itself already informed by what could be called the "proto-Orientalism" of the Reconquista, which was imbricated in Judeophobia and Islamophobia. Columbus, after all, by traveling west, intended to go to the east and intended to convert the diverse heathens, including Muslims and Jews. Orientalism, in this sense, begins with the very arrival, at the end of the fifteenth century, of Iberian theological vision in the Americas.

If we examine the circulation of tropes and metaphors as well as the discursive connections and links between the two 1492s, we afford ourselves another way to begin the story of Orientalism. To reflect on these submerged analogies, we need to think back again to the events associated with the cataclysmic moment when the beginning of the conquest of the "new" world converged with the forcing-out of Sephardic Jews and Muslim Moors from Spain. The ground for colonialist racism was prepared by the Inquisition's Limpieza de Sangre (Cleansing of Blood), by the Edicts of Expulsion against the Jews and Muslims, by the Portuguese exploration of the west coast of Africa, and by the transatlantic slave trade. Forged in the centuries of the Reconquista, fifteenth-century Spain provided a template for the creation of other racial states and for ethnoreligious cleansing. Although the Limpieza de Sangre was formulated in religious terms—by which the "problem" of Jewishness and Muslimness could be remedied by conversion—the metaphor of the purity of blood prepared the way for the biological and scientific racism of the nineteenth century. Christian demonology thus set the tone for colonialist racialization. The various "questions"—the Jewish, Muslim, "Indian," Black, and African questions—have been interwoven for centuries. Their linked trajectories can be traced, as Robert Stam and I argued in *Unthinking Eurocentrism* (Shohat and Stam 1994), back to the events associated with the cataclysmic moment summoned up by the various "1492s"—i.e., the conquest of the "new" world, the expulsion of the Moors, and the Inquisition.

In effect, discourses about Muslims and Jews armed the conquistadores with a ready-made demonizing vision, transferable from the "old" to the "new" world. Amerigo Vespucci's accounts of his own voyages invoked the familiar anti-Jewish and anti-Muslim idiom to characterize the Indigenous peoples as infidels and devil worshipers (Carew 1988). The conquest of "the Indians" of the Americas, for sixteenth-century Spanish historian Francisco Lopez de Gomara, prolonged the struggle against "the infidels" in the East. In his *Historia general de las Indias* (1552), de Gomara wrote that "the conquest of the Indians began after that of the Moors was completed, so that Spaniards would ever fight the infidels" (quoted in Fuchs 2001, 228; also quoted in Majid 2009, 10). The Hieronymite friars, for their part, referred to the inhabitants of Hispaniola as "Moors" (Weckmann 1984, quoted in Lozano 2007, 316). Shakespeare's Caliban in *The Tempest*, meanwhile, mingled the traits of African Moors and Indigenous Americans. Within a phantasmatic resemblance, both the internal non-Christian "enemy" and the external Indigenous American and African "savage" are all imagined as "sorcerers," "cannibals," and "blood drinkers." Indigenous deities (for example, the Tupi deity Tupan) and West African *orixas* (such as Exu) were diabolized to fit into a normatively Manichaean Christian schema. Antisemitism or Judeophobia, along with anti-infidelism or Islamophobia, provided a conceptual framework projected outward against the Indigenous peoples of Africa and the Americas.[2] Occidentalism (in Mignolo's sense), then, does not exist without (proto) Orientalism, just as Orientalism (in Said's sense) does not exist without earlier Occidentalism—both of which are modes of Eurocentric discourse.

Columbus's Atlantic route generated foundational paradoxes that illuminate the formation of both Occidentalism and Orientalism. In the hopes of both material riches and theological expansions in the East, Columbus's voyage moved toward the west, partly to avoid the enemy lands dominated by Muslims.[3] It is often noted that Columbus took with him an interpreter, the converso Luis de Torres, whose knowledge of Semitic languages was to facilitate encounters in the East. Although Arabic was irrelevant in the period of "the Discovery," that language arrived in the Americas with the Arabic-speaking Muslim African slaves, long before the late nineteenth-century Arab immigration from the provinces of the Ottoman Empire (Reis 1993; Gomez 2005). Apart from the innumerable traces of Arabic and Hebrew that have persisted in Portuguese and Spanish till today, the new coinages specific to the Americas were also sometimes borrowed from Arabic. The term for racial miscegenation between white and red in Brazil—*mamelucos*—for example, could be traced back to the Arab/Muslim context of the Mamluks (Nimer 2005). Conversos and Moriscos also traveled to the Americas, where the Inquisition persisted in places like Mexico (including what is now the southwestern United States) and Brazil. The various routes around the Atlantic were linked in ways that partly mirrored Europe's geopolitical landscape; some Sephardic Jews who escaped from the Inquisition to Holland ended up in the Dutch-dominated territories in the Americas. In 1654, the Sephardic Jews of Pernambuco in northern Brazil left with the withdrawing Dutch to New Amsterdam, where they established the first (Portuguese) synagogue in what is now downtown Manhattan. In light of the political battle over the Cordova Islamic Center near Ground Zero, it is also worth noting that the Muslim presence in New York goes back to the very beginnings of colonization. Historian Michael Gomez cites the case of the freeman Antonio the Turk, supposed to have been born in Morocco, who became one of the largest landowners in Manhattan (Gomez 2005, 75).

The Iberian wrestling with its legacy of "the Orient," associated with Africa and the South, and "the Occident,"

2. This argument here about the discursive links between the two 1492s is based on a series of my related publications on the quincentenary (Shohat 1992, 1992–93, 1997, [1999] 2006; Shohat and Stam 1994). See also Aidi 2003a and Majid 2009.

3. In one of his key letters, Christopher Columbus wrote to the Spanish queen: "Your Highness completed the wars against the Moors, after having chased all the Jews and sent me to the said region of India, in order to convert the people there to our holy faith" (quoted in Comby 1990).

associated with Europe and the North, persisted in the Americas. In this version, the concept of "Orientalism" functioned as a synonym for the negative view of the Moorish Muslim and Sephardic Jewish "Orientalization" of Iberia and consequently of its new territories in the Americas (Freyre 1963). In this expanding Atlantic space, the ritual legacy of the struggle between Christians and infidels, such as the equestrian combats between Spaniards and Moors, continued to be reenacted in the form of popular spectacles, featured, for example, in Brazilian street festivals on Easter Sunday. "The Christians," in the words of the Brazilian anthropologist Gilberto Freyre, "were always victorious and the Moors routed and punished. And Easter Saturday ended or began with the effigy of Judas being carried through the streets and burned by the urchins in what was evidently a popular expression of religious hatred of the Catholic for the Jew" (1963, 297). Jews were viewed, in the words of Freyre, as the "secret agent of Orientalism" (1963, 297). Thus, before the contemporary Eurocentric erasure, as it were, of the hyphen in the "Judeo-Islamic" and the insertion of the hyphen in the "Judeo-Christian," the "Jew" and "the Muslim" or "the Morisco" and "the converso" were articulated within the same conceptual space, as one allegorical unit. To speak of the Muslim Moor is therefore also to invoke the Sephardi Jew and vice versa. As a form of Iberian anxiety about its Arabization/Judaization, "Orientalism" was thus carried over to the Americas, where it participated in the shaping of emerging regional and national identities.

Yet if Iberia witnessed centuries of an ideology that justified the cleansing of the "Orientalized" Moorish/Sephardic past, Latin America, as a complex site of global cultural encounters and of ambivalence toward the colonial metropole, has also witnessed a certain nostalgia for that "Oriental" past. The tropical imaginary has partly been shaped by what I would call "the Moorish unconscious" of Latin America, where denial and desire of that forgotten origin have simultaneously coexisted. The mundane pride of some families in their Moorish "Morisco" or Sephardi "converso" lineage has been expressed in popular tales and registered in the various Latin American texts. From José Martí's exhortation "Seamos Moros!" to Carlos Fuentes's celebration of Mexico's "buried mirror," the question of the Moor never stopped haunting, even if only on the margins, the Latin American imaginary (Martí 1938; Fuentes 1992).[4] In his theorization of Brazilian identity, Freyre gives great weight to the Moorish/Sephardic cultural history of Portugal as actively shaping Brazilian customs and practices. In the early colonial era, Brazilian people maintained Moorish/Sephardic traditions such as the covering of women attending church or the preference to sit on rugs with legs crossed, and they deployed various Moorish architectural structures and artistic design, including glazed tiling, checkered windowpanes, and so forth (Freyre [1933] 1964).[5] But with the programmatic adoption of Occidental-European customs that were institutionalized with Brazil's independence in 1822 began a detachment from the Moorish/Sephardic heritage (Freyre [1933] 1964).

For Freyre (1963), the Europeanization—another word for modernization—of Brazil came through the triumph of "the Occidental" over "the Oriental." The Brazilian Occidentalization project meant a self de-Orientalization that is a cleansing of the Sephardic/Moorish traces from the veins of Latin America. Within a certain romanticism of search for lost origins, Freyre, however, developed an argument for a genealogy of Brazilian national character

4. For a historical overview of José Martí and Latin American references to the Moor, see Aidi 2003a, 2006, and his work "The Moorish Atlantic" (2003b, unpublished paper sent by Aidi to the author), which stresses the connected histories between the Muslim world and Latin America. While the term "the Moorish Atlantic" tends to refer to the Moroccan coast of the Atlantic, I use the phrase to highlight not only the positive cross-Atlantic historical, discursive, and cultural links between "the Orient" and "the Occident" but also the anxieties that such links provoked. I am also suggesting that this Muslim space must be viewed as always-already Sephardic as well, within shared cultural geographies that are part and parcel of the Americas. As already explored in "Staging the Quincentenary" (Shohat 1992–93), "Taboo Memories, Diasporic Visions" (Shohat [1999] 2006), and *Unthinking Eurocentrism* (Shohat and Stam 1994), the cross-Atlantic Sephardi/Moorish space inaugurated with the two 1492s carried over the ocean hegemonic Iberian discourses about Muslims and Jews. In short, I am interested here in the ambivalences that the Moor/the Sephardi, as a Janus-faced figure, has provoked in the Americas in ways that disturb any facile schism of Orient/Occident and North/South.

5. See especially the chapter "The Portuguese Colonizer" (in Freyre [1933] 1964) originally published in Portuguese in 1933.

whose positive traits of cultural flexibility, plasticity, and adoptability were largely traced back to Moorish/Sephardic Portugal. He also emphatically stresses the Moorish/Sephardic blood of the Portuguese that reveals a hybridity running through the veins of the colonizers even prior to their mixing with Indigenous Tupis and enslaved West Africans. Setting aside Freyre's culturalist-essentialist assumptions, his act of theorizing Brazilian identity in relation to Moorish/Sephardic heritage sheds significant light on the linked cultural histories of the two 1492s. Despite the project of de-Orientalizing Ibero-American blood and culture, it can be argued that the Moor (here also standing in for the Sephardi) never fully disappeared from Latin America, whether as a specter or [as a] figure of desire. Even if often only remaining in the shadow, the figure of the Moor has been revisited for the purpose of self-conceptualization in some Latin American texts. The highlighting of an "Oriental" genealogy in such texts stands in glaring contrast to the Reconquista/Conquista de-Orientalizing project; it turns the Moor into a kind of a return-of-the-repressed figure.

Orientalism as an ideological discourse, one could thus argue, preceded Orientalism as a field of study that emerges with the post-Enlightenment and the colonization of the Middle East/North Africa. While Said's *Orientalism* inaugurated a critique of the imaginary of the Orient in European thought, particularly British and French, in another perspective Orientalism is embedded in both the Reconquista and the Conquista. Colonial discourse in relation to the Americas, then, did not simply take in latter-day French or British or North American Orientalist discourse but rather was constituted by it. As suggested earlier, Occidentalism—in Mignolo's sense—does not exist without Orientalism, just as Orientalism—in Said's sense—does not exist without Occidentalism. Orientalism and Occidentalism (Mignolo), meanwhile, can both be seen as branches of Eurocentric epistemology; as such they are intimately connected, mutually constitutive within the same historical moment. The concept of the "Moorish unconscious" of Latin America thus helps us chart another route for tracing the genealogies of both Orientalism and Occidentalism. In this sense, one could speak, in tandem with the by now familiar "Black Atlantic" and the less familiar "Red Atlantic" and "White Atlantic," of a "Brown Atlantic" or "Arab/Muslim Atlantic" or "Sephardi/Moorish Atlantic" as part of a multiply raced "Rainbow Atlantic."[6] The history of the traffic of Orientalist ideas, thus, is not merely longer but also more multifaceted and multidirectional than might at first appear.

From Diaspora to Diasporic Readings

The last chapter of Said's book focuses on "Orientalism Now." And thirty years later, the era of transnational flows and the ongoing diasporization of Middle Eastern peoples pose a challenge to notions of reified cartographies and isolated regional units. But what analytical frameworks are available for studying these cross-border movements between regions? Can Middle Eastern studies be rethought as a more inclusive and fluid space in ways that expand the boundaries of what constitutes a legitimate object of inquiry within current area studies? And how can such a reconceptualization bypass the notion of the Middle East as a fixed sign with quarantined boundaries between East and West?—a notion that was one of the objects of Said's critique. And where do American studies, ethnic studies, and Latin American studies fit into this picture? Are there discursive spaces of mutual illuminations?

Situating the critique of Orientalism in relation to multiple geographies necessarily challenges the boundaries separating ethnic studies, presumed to study those within the nation-state "over here," and area studies, particularly the designation of study according to national or regional boundaries such as Middle Eastern studies, Latin American studies, Asian studies, and African studies. . . . In this sense both area studies and ethnic studies marginalize Middle Eastern Americans by positioning them as "foreigners" to be studied merely "over there," denying their entry into a scholarly framework of race and ethnicity in the Americas . . .

. . . Although the field of Orientalism and its critique are associated with specific geographies, they can also

6. The notion of a multiply raced Atlantic, i.e., "the Rainbow Atlantic," is taken from my work with Robert Stam, . . . *Race in Translation* (Shohat and Stam 2012).

be seen as part of a multidirectional flow connected to cross-border circuitries . . . It is not, ultimately, a question of migratory demographics, of merely following a population from its originary base into new geographical zones. Rather, it is a question of taking seriously what could be called the "diasporic turn," of thinking of all regions, including the Middle East/North Africa itself, in a profoundly diasporic manner, where geography constitutes not a point of origin or final destination but rather one terminal in a transnational network.

Works Cited

Aidi, Hisham D. 2003a. "Let Us Be Moors: Islam, Race, and 'Connected Histories.'" *Middle East Report* 33, no. 229 (Winter): 42–53.

———. 2003b. "The Moorish Atlantic: Moors, Aztecs, and the Invention of the Americas." Paper prepared for the seminar "Modernity and Its Others," taught by Paul Gilroy, Sociology Department, Yale Univ., New Haven, CT, May.

———. 2006. "The Interference of al-Andalus: Spain, Islam, and the West." In "Edward Said: A Memorial Issue," edited by Patrick Deer, Gyan Prakash, and Ella Shohat. Special issue of *Social Text* 98 (Fall): 67–88.

Buruma, Ian, and Avishai Margalit. 2004. *Occidentalism: A Short History of Anti-Westernism*. London: Atlantic Books.

Carew, Jan. 1988. *Fulcrums of Change*. Trenton, NJ: Africa World Press.

Carrier, James. 1995. *Occidentalism: Images of the West*. Oxford: Clarendon Press.

Comby, Jean. 1990. "1492: Le Choc des cultures et l'evangelization du monde." *Dossiers de l'episcopat français*, no. 14 (Oct.).

Feres, João Jr. 2005. *A Historia do conceito de "Latin America" nos Estados Unidos*. São Paulo, Brazil: Edusc.

Freyre, Gilberto. 1963. "Orient and Occident." In *The Mansions and the Shanties: The Making of Modern Brazil*, translated by Harriet de Onis, 273–301. New York: Knopf.

———. [1933] 1964. *The Masters and the Slaves*. New York: Knopf.

Fuchs, Barbara. 2001. *Mimesis and Empire: The New World, Islam, and European Identities*. Cambridge: Cambridge Univ. Press.

Fuentes, Carlos. 1992. *The Buried Mirror*. New York: Houghton Mifflin.

Gomez, Michael. 2005. *Black Crescent: The Experience and Legacy of African Muslims in the Americas*. New York: Cambridge Univ. Press.

Lozano, Tomás. 2007. *Cantemos al alba: Origins of Songs, Sounds, and Liturgical Drama of Hispanic New Mexico*. Edited and translated by Rima Montaya. Albuquerque: Univ. of New Mexico Press.

Majid, Anouar. 2009. *We Are All Moors: Ending Centuries of Crusades against Muslims and Other Minorities*. Minneapolis: Univ. of Minnesota Press.

Martí, José. 1938. "España en Melilla." In *Cuba: Letras*, vol. 2, 203–8. Havana, Cuba: Edición Trópico.

Mignolo, Walter D. 2005. *The Idea of Latin America*. Alden, MA: Blackwell.

Nimer, Miguel. 2005. *Influências Orientais na língua portuguesa*. São Paulo, Brazil: Editora Universidade de São Paulo.

Reis, João. 1993. *Slave Rebellion in Brazil*. Baltimore: Johns Hopkins Univ. Press.

Said, Edward. 1978. *Orientalism*. New York: Vintage Books.

Shohat, Ella. 1992. "Rethinking Jews and Muslims: Quincentennial Reflections." *Middle East Report*, Sept.–Oct., 25–29.

———. 1992–93. "Staging the Quincentenary: The Middle East and the Americas." In "The Wake of Utopia." Special issue of *Third Text* 21 (Winter): 95–105.

———. 1997. "Columbus, Palestine, and Arab-Jews: Toward a Relational Approach to Community Identity." In *Cultural Readings of Imperialism*, edited by Keith Ausell Pearson, Benita Parry, and Judith Squires, 88–105. London: Lawrence & Wishart in association with New Formations.

———. [1999] 2006. "Taboo Memories, Diasporic Visions: Columbus, Palestine, and Arab-Jews." In *Taboo Memories, Diasporic Voices*, 201–32. Durham, NC: Duke Univ. Press. Published earlier in *Performing Hybridity*, edited by May Joseph and Jennifer Fink, 131–56. Minneapolis: Univ. of Minnesota Press, 1999.

Shohat, Ella, and Robert Stam. 1994. *Unthinking Eurocentrism: Multiculturalism and the Media*. London: Routledge.

———. 2012. *Race in Translation: Culture Wars around the Postcolonial Atlantic*. New York: New York Univ. Press.

Weckmann, Luis. 1984. *La Herencia medieval de México*. Mexico City: Centro de Estudios Históricos, Colegio de México.

5

Grandmothers, Grape Leaves, and Kahlil Gibran

Writing Race in Anthologies of Arab American Literature

MICHELLE HARTMAN

Arab American literature began to be increasingly anthologized starting in the late 1980s and into the 1990s. Three major anthologies appeared between 1988 and 1999, making a broader range of Arab American literary works available than ever before. *Grape Leaves: A Century of Arab-American Poetry* (Orfalea and Elmusa [1988] 2000), *Food for Our Grandmothers: Writings by Arab-American & Arab-Canadian Feminists* (Kadi 1994), and *Post Gibran: Anthology of New Arab American Writing* (Akash and Mattawa 1999) are all easily accessible books, published by relatively mainstream publishers. Each of these three works embraces a significantly different focus, showing the breadth of Arab American literary production: the first focuses on poetry spanning a century; the second on different genres of writing by contemporary feminists, both US and Canadian; and the third on new writers of different genres, men and women, with an emphasis on experimentation. . . .

Like all anthologies, these three works invoke emblems of the community they represent. This serves as a gesture to the community and is also important in the symbolic representation of the group to the "outsider" or "mainstream" audience. Three important emblems of the community in these anthologies, which also recur in Arab American literature more generally, are grandmothers, grape leaves, and Kahlil Gibran. They embody familiar themes in Arab American self-identification: an emphasis on family and community, shared food and other cultural customs, and a history of cultural and literary contributions to both the Arab world and the United States. In order to understand how these three anthologies construct community identity in the United States, I will analyze the interaction of these emblems and symbols of the Arab American community in relation to race. As interest in the Arab American community and its literature grows in the United States, it is crucial to explore the terms by which Arab American identity is constructed racially. Literary anthologies are a particularly productive site of analysis of these issues as they explicitly define and delimit the identity that they claim to represent and use race and the racialization of Arab Americans strategically in these constructions. . . .

In order to contextualize how racial discourses are employed in Arab American anthologies, it is crucial to understand the complex, contradictory, and contested history of Arab American racialization in the United States.[1] To understand how Arab Americans have been inconsistently racialized in the United States, scholars of Arab America have undertaken a serious investigation of the formation of a "white" (and "not quite white") Arab American

Excerpt from Michelle Hartman, "Grandmothers, Grape Leaves, and Khalil Gibran," in *Race and Americans before and after 9/11: From Invisible Citizens to Visible Subjects*, edited by Amaney Jamal and Nadine Naber (Syracuse, NY: Syracuse Univ. Press, 2008), 170–203. A works cited list was added to this chapter. Reprinted with corrections and press style changes for consistency throughout the volume by permission of Syracuse University Press.

1. Arab American literary critics have been calling for a greater investigation of race and racialization of Arab Americans in relation to literary studies. See in particular Majaj 1999b, especially pages 72–74, and Salaita 2000. For more detail, see the discussion of these issues in Majaj 1999a, especially pages 321–22.

identity through the racial prerequisite laws (Gualtieri 2001; Majaj 2000; Massad 1993; Morsy 1994; Samhan 1999).[2] This investigation includes tracing the history of how Arab Americans were categorized as nonwhites, how they fought the categorization legally, and how their legal status changed and developed over time, particularly after they achieved "white" status through this litigation. There is a general consensus among scholars that although the identity of Arab Americans as "white" has been variously embraced and contested, the experiences of Arab Americans—individually and as a group—have very often not matched their official legal status (Gualtieri 2001; Joseph 1999a; Majaj 1999a; Naff 1985; Saliba 1999; Samhan 1999; Suleiman 1987, 1999). Therefore, many works use terminology like "honorary," "probationary," or "in between" whiteness to examine Arab American identity in the United States.[3] . . .

I seek to situate the study of race and Arab American identity and belonging in the literary field. Like [for] other racialized/ethnic groups, Arab American literary identities are crucial to claiming an acknowledged position in the United States. The theoretical underpinnings of my analysis here draw upon the critical work of Henry Louis Gates Jr., who has pointed out how race has also played a central role in the way in which literature is produced, read, and taught in the United States. In particular, he has argued that canon formation in the United States is bound up in issues of race and racialization and that this matter must be addressed in US literary studies and not only those focused on African American literature (Gates 1985; 1991, 23–32; 1992). In "The Master's Pieces: On Canon Formation and Afro-American Tradition," for example, Gates places particular importance on the role of the anthology to shape and change literary traditions and canons in the United States. His study details how African American literature has been crucial to literary realities in the United States since slavery and elaborates on how African American slave narratives were identified in 1846 as the only "authentically American" literature in distinguishing this new tradition from British literature (1991, 21–22). He also draws links to the historical context of building anthologies of Black literature since the mid-nineteenth century, while also analyzing his own experience as editor of the *Norton Anthology of African American Literature* (28–32). Gates's work is so useful here because of his attention to the dynamic interactions and relationships between canon formation, racial thinking, and the power relations between white and racialized groups in the United States.

My approach here differs from that of Gates in that I will neither draw out a history of Arab American literature nor argue for its importance and centrality within the traditions of US literary canons. Here, rather, I employ Gates's analysis to emphasize the importance of the structural relationships between building anthologies, [their] connection to establishing canons, and the need to question both of these processes in relation to how they are informed by race, even as they are taking place.[4] . . .

As interest in Arab American literature grows, the continued formation and revision of the canon of Arab American literature are taking place—in these three anthologies and elsewhere—which has an impact on how Arab American identity is shaped and reshaped. . . . The critical readings of the introductions of each text, linked to an analysis of its overall project, show that Arab

2. On the related issue of religious racialization, see Naber 2000; on political racism, see Samhan 1987.

3. A number of studies of the indeterminate status of European immigrant groups and their tenuous relationship to whiteness are particularly useful in thinking through these issues in the Arab American context: Brodkin 1998; di Leonardo 1994; Ignatiev 1995; Jacobson 1998; and Roediger 1994.

4. In this line of argument, I also hope to avoid some of the problems that would arise in submitting Arab American and African American literature to a comparison. African Americans have been considered the "prototypical" minority group; other groups have used comparisons with them to attain minority status and advantages, which has often led to the disenfranchisement of Blacks. This is part of the problem with the "Black–white" binary into which the US racial system is divided. For a detailed discussion, see chapter 5 of Delgado and Stefancic 2001, 67–83. What I hope to do here is not [to] reproduce a problematic discourse in order to prove that Arab Americans are similar to African Americans but rather to draw on some of the most important and sophisticated studies of these issues that have been developed by African American critics like Henry Louis Gates Jr. and in conjunction with African American literature.

American identity formation in the texts employs racial discourses in different ways, with different strategic goals and effects. Questioning these discourses and holding them up to scrutiny can help better achieve the working bases for solidarity and activism with other groups of color, as suggested by Majaj (1999b, 73), and such an examination can lead to determining which are best suited for continued deployment in the articulation of Arab American identities in this context.

To accomplish this analysis, my first area of inquiry in each anthology is its stated project and, in particular, how it articulates its mission. Second, I investigate how each defines "Arab American" implicitly and explicitly and the connection of this definition to race. In conjunction with these readings, the analyses of the texts treat how Arab American anthologies are carving spaces for themselves within literary canons in the United States, while negotiating not only an Arab American identity, which is informed by Arab racialization, but this identity in conjunction with and opposed to other groups in the United States—particularly but not exclusively those that are also racialized. My readings below show how these anthologies use three interrelated strategies of racialization: framing their projects, locating themselves in relation to other groups, and choosing emblems. . . .

These analyses will show that all of the anthologies use race and the racialization of Arab Americans strategically in their articulation of Arab American identity, but that they do so in very different ways. The strategy for invoking race in each anthology is closely linked to that anthology's political and social project and therefore is also linked to how this work is able to function institutionally in the building of an Arab American literary canon as well as identity more generally.

Grape Leaves: A Century of Arab-American Poetry

The seventeen-page introduction to *Grape Leaves: A Century of Arab-American Poetry* explicitly justifies the existence of the anthology itself, its value, as well as that of its individual contributions. On its first page, the introduction firmly claims a space within "ethnic" American literature. It employs the "equal time" principle in its self-validation: Arab Americans deserve a poetic "anthology of their own" because other similarly marginalized ethnic and racial groups have them (Orfalea and Elmusa [1988] 2000, xiii). . . .

It is not a surprise that the first group mentioned is labeled "black." African Americans are consistently located as the most visible, prominent, and disenfranchised "minority" group in the United States, upon which all other groups traditionally build their case for claiming minority status (Delgado and Stefancic 2001, 67). Mentioning this group first in the list, therefore, powerfully claims both an affiliation and a justification for the anthology.[5] "Hispanics" follow—a group that is often specifically linked to Black Americans as a similarly oppressed minority. The next group, "Jews," occupies a significantly different space in the US public imagination as a group with a history of discrimination but [that] has been successful in the United States. Locating this group immediately after African Americans and Latinos emphasizes the range of different experiences of groups considered minorities. In particular, Jews have been granted white status in the United States, thereby shifting the attention from Arab American racialization to their "white ethnic" belonging (Brodkin 1998). Furthermore, Jews are also the specific group to which Arabs/Arab Americans are often required to compare and/or contrast themselves in order to gain status or "equal time" for their concerns (Massad 1993; Saliba 1999). The list then continues with Indians and Chinese—two Asian groups geographically near the Arab world—and then Armenians follow. Placed last, they are another "model minority" group, like the previous three, and one with which Arabs share historical, cultural, and geographical ties.

5. The use of a lowercase *b* [in *black*], undoubtedly an editor's choice, also stands out in such a list of groups, all the rest of which are capitalized. Though some writers consciously use the lowercase *b* in order to invoke parity with the lowercase *w* in *white*, others have done the opposite and use a *W* and *b* to designate these terms in order to draw more attention to the whiteness. This debate serves as a reminder of how the continued lower status of African Americans within the United States is debated in rhetorical as well as practical ways.

Much like the complicated "racial" hierarchies that govern official US policies and institutions, the chosen groups represent different types of categorization—linguistic, racial, religious/ethnic, and national. This list demonstrates another problematic notion in identity formation in the United States—here identities are understood as exclusive; one is "black" or "Hispanic," not both. Not only is the US official confusion about categorizations reflected in this list, but [the list] also reproduces an implied hierarchy of which groups are the most oppressed and therefore perhaps the most deserving of attention. This strategy of locating Arab Americans within the complex fabric of US society relies on a general and vague notion of their place within it. Rather than clarifying or defining a specific, discrete location for Arab Americans, it juxtaposes them with a number of other groups. All of these groups are considered to be ethnic and/or racial minorities in the United States. As a strategy, therefore, this list locates Arab Americans generally within a context of other so-called minority groups but resists assigning them a more specific space. This strategy has the advantage of leaving options open for identity building but at the same time risks being so vague that it does not advance any proposal for the consolidation of an identity or how to promote specific affiliations and alliances.

. . . The third justification for the volume employs a shift in strategy, deploying the notion of Arab/Arab American exceptionalism. Here, the introduction distances itself from the other "minority," "ethnic," and/or racialized groups with which it was affiliating itself in the previous examples and rather claims exceptional, inherent qualities of Arab Americans in order to position itself in relation to canonical "white" authors. The first of the examples given in the text is the Arabs' "natural" love of poetry. This strategy of claiming an exceptional quality can be understood as a way in which to counter the discrimination identified above: Arab Americans have inherited an innate appreciation for poetry and thus are cultured and refined. The notion that poetry is "in the Arab blood" is reiterated several times. The introduction defines them as "a group whose love of poetry is native and deep: the two million Arab Americans" (Orfalea and Elmusa [1988] 2000, xiii) and proclaims that "the great Arab love of poetry had not been drained from new world veins" (xv).[6]

These three justifications for publishing an anthology of Arab American poetry follow a familiar argument about why and how ethnic or minority literatures are important in the United States: [that] oppressed/minority groups can create great art, [that] these groups have an inborn love of art/poetry, and so on, and that if one group can show its pride in these creations, others should be deemed similarly deserving of such an opportunity. . . . The logic of *Grape Leaves*'s introduction, therefore, echoes a central sentiment in African American literary development and justification. Its strategy for claiming the rightful and respected place for Arab Americans in the United States is to prove their humanity through literary production. . . .

If poetry is categorized by race or ethnic group—as it is in an anthology of Arab American poetry—to use "universal" standards for its quality is necessarily contradictory. That is to say, when we categorize literature by ethnic, cultural, or racial categories, we recognize and emphasize its difference from other groups. Logically, therefore, its content, perhaps form, and other features theoretically may be different than that of these other groups. Claims to "universality" and "universal value" therefore should be eliminated from the discussion, as these differences show their irrelevance.

Grape Leaves, however, does not reject universality or quality but rather operates within this set of contradictory assumptions. It claims a separate and distinct space for Arab American poetry while comparing Arab Americans favorably with canonical US poetry, employing the terms set by the canon. In our critical reading practices, therefore, it is important to question to what extent this project aims to reproduce the "master's voice" (as Gates would have it) and publish poetry acceptable to mainstream US society. In building a canon of Arab American literature through an anthology, how are Arab Americans positioned? Does the strategy of linking

6. See Majaj's critique of this element of *Grape Leaves* in her discussion of the politics of memory (1996).

Arab American projects to African American ones valorize, deny, or seek to transcend these experiences? Does the ambiguous Arab American position strengthen the identity formation and pride of the community or simply leave it vague and undefined?

These questions recur in relation to how *Grape Leaves* treats the question of the Arab American family: it makes the dramatic claim that for Arab Americans "family *is* self" (Orfalea and Elmusa [1988] 2000, xix, italics in the original). This broad statement can be understood in a number of contexts, including US stereotypes about ethnic/racialized families, critically inherited notions about families from Arab countries of origin, and how these ideas are connected to what scholars like Suad Joseph have called the "relational self" (Joseph 1994, 1999b). The idea here is that Arab American families somehow overshadow the individual and that one's self is always determined by one's relationship to the group. This putatively warm, loving, and unified family also evokes the gendered stereotypes about the woman of color (mother/grandmother) who nurtures the large racialized family because she is the product of her passions, emotions, and affections (di Leonardo 1994, 177–89). Furthermore, communities of color have often marked women as bearers of reproduction of the community, particularly as a reaction to white supremacy. Thus, whereas the notion of family as self is one that can be used strategically to emphasize shared cultural values and group solidarity, it is also loaded with additional meaning that can be unpacked to understand further implications.

. . . *Grape Leaves* activates stereotyped notions of the family of color, drawing on racialized and cultural nationalist tropes of women that mark the community (Williams 1996). The introduction's use of these notions conveys the message to Arab Americans not only that their identity is tied to their families but [also] that it should be, as the anthology does lay a claim to defining Arab American identity prescriptively.

An example of this collision between the family, race, and gender is even more pronounced where *Grape Leaves* conflates the Arab American relationship to poetry—identified throughout as "in the blood"—with family relations and the women's roles within them. In another attempt to show the importance of poetry to Arabs and therefore to Arab Americans, the introduction cites a quotation attributed to Ibn Rashiq, "The ancient Arabs wish one another joy but for three things—the birth of a boy, the coming to light of a poet, and the foaling of a noble mare" (Orfalea and Elmusa [1988] 2000, xv). Here, the Arab connection to poetry is proposed as natural and innate, made obvious although the metaphor used is that poetry is "still flowing in new world veins." I argue that the notion of an innate connection between Arabs and poetry is one part of the symbolic economy of how this anthology uses strategies drawing on racial logic and cultural essentialism in order to present a positive Arab American identity.

This particular example is problematic not only because it exceptionalizes Arab Americans in relation to allegedly "inborn qualities" [but] also [because it] couples this "inherent" love of poetry with an explicitly misogynistic message. The qualities that the introduction proposes to be innately connected to being an Arab are the importance of family and poetry. The putatively "Arab" focus on the family is used here to emphasize the celebration of male children only. For an anthology that partly bases its claim for existence on trying to counter stereotypes about Arab Americans, this focus seems to undermine the book's goals.[7] The glorification of an "authentically" Arab proverb that neglects Arab girls, while conflating the favoring of boys with the appreciation of poetry, reinforces the "mainstream" pathologization of Arab men as misogynistic. Understanding the alleged misogyny of Arab men as an inherent feature in Arab (and also Muslim) culture holds much currency in mainstream discourse in the United States.[8] Hence, . . . connecting a laudable characteristic, the love of poetry, with

7. This point is used to underline the Arab love of poetry by at least one reviewer, who interestingly chooses to omit the bit about the love of male children in her review in *MELUS* (Zoghby 1988, 91).

8. The literature on how Arab men are represented in mainstream US culture as pathologically misogynistic is large and growing. For some examples, see Salem Manganaro 1988 and Kadi 1994, especially pages 125–32 and 150–59. The collection of Hollywood movie plots involving Arab and Muslim characters, *Reel Bad Arabs: How Hollywood Vilifies a People*, bears out this assertion in relation to cinema (Shaheen 2001).

one that reinforces mainstream US stereotypes about Arabs, that only boys are appreciated and celebrated, contributes to a logic that posits the Arab American as not only racially Other but also inferior to whites.

Clearly, it is not the intention of *Grape Leaves* to denigrate Arab American culture by identifying it as misogynistic. However, the strategies it uses to define Arab American identity activate accepted racialized ideas about Arabs and Arab Americans, particularly in conjunction with ideas about gender and the family. The critical close reading of some salient elements of *Grape Leaves*'s introduction shows how racial discourses in the United States deeply inform the logic of this anthology. Within even the most "literary" justifications for the inclusion of certain works in the anthology, racialized discourses about mainstream and other groups and [about] essentializing qualities they share can be located. . . .

Post Gibran: Anthology of New Arab American Writing

Post Gibran rejects *Grape Leaves*'s varied strategies that draw on racialized tropes to prove American equality and to define literary quality in terms of the white American canon. Similarly, whereas *Grape Leaves* is a celebration of Kahlil Gibran and his generation of poets, *Post Gibran*, true to its title, attempts to move past this circumscription and to place an explicit emphasis on publishing works that are new and experimental. The rhetoric of comparison to the great names of the canon becomes irrelevant in this context; there is not one in its three-page introduction. Even more important to this study, *Post Gibran* employs different strategies than *Grape Leaves* to engage with issues around race and ethnicity.

This does not mean that the discourses of race, strategic essentialism, and cultural exceptionalism are totally absent here. On the contrary, *Post Gibran*'s introduction relies heavily on the notion that Arab Americans are genuinely and truly "Arabs," which is purposely defined broadly. Rather than elaborate on how Arabs are unique or draw comparisons to other so-called minority groups in the United States, *Post Gibran* deploys an even broader concept when it speaks of a generalized Arab "spirit." This appealing definition of Arabs/Arab Americans seeks to offer alternative ways to think about the question of self-definition and identity, . . . to transcend the problems of essentialism and "Arab blood" as well as comparisons with other groups, [and] to understand where Arab Americans might belong in the United States. . . .

Although *Post Gibran* does attempt to move beyond race as a category in employing the concept of "spirit," it maintains a focus and insistence on "Arabness" that suggests that there is an essence that defines people and culture. The way in which this informs *Post Gibran* can further be identified in the shift away from *Grape Leaves*'s focus on literary excellence and "quality" to its own project of identifying new writers and forms of literary experimentation. One way in which this is expressed is the explicit solicitation of pieces in genres that have been underrepresented in Arab American literary production, such as fiction and drama—one of the steps called for by Majaj in her contribution to this very anthology. In connection to this strategy, the introduction to *Post Gibran* also explicitly articulates a specific interest in and call for pieces that embrace the Arabic language and what it refers to as "Arab concerns." By not only prescribing genres but also defining Arab American identity as connected to language and the vaguely termed "concerns," the anthology prescribes two ways in which the identity [the editors] seek to define can be expressed. Therefore, at the same time that *Post Gibran* insists that its contributors embrace an "Arabness" defined as multicultural—and presumably at least vaguely cosmopolitan—an identity that is like a "bouquet of mixed flowers," there is an explicit insistence on texts that literally manifest a quite concretely defined Arabness, identified as "concerns" (topics and themes?) and language (Akash and Mattawa 1999, xii). This interest betrays the fact that the anthology does define a prescriptive notion of what it means to be an Arab in this anthology—one must show an attention to politics, culture, language, and so on. . . .

Therefore, though *Post Gibran*'s strategies for defining Arab American identity are complex, they draw on multiple techniques that can be contradictory. At the same time that it defines "Arabness" as multicultural and claims that it can encompass everyone, it nonetheless also draws on two essentialist notions that undermine this claim. First, though "Arabness" is meant to be an open and all-embracing category, it is contrasted to "Americanness," which is defined as oppositional to Arabs. This contrast leads to a necessary contradiction and difficulty for Arab Americans. *Post Gibran* suggests that Arab Americans should produce "new literature," but it is best if it somehow shows that they are "truly Arabs" in contrast to Americans (read: mainstream white Americans) by showing their "spirit" and drawing on their "origins" and language without being "secondhand" copies of American literature. Second, writers who show a connection to the Arabic language and Arab "concerns" are valorized as somehow more worthy of inclusion and part of this "spirit" than others. This can be read as encouraging Arab Americans to embrace the history and culture of their heritage, which no doubt it is. But by allowing for slippage between the Arabic language, the mainstream Arabic literary tradition, Arab concerns, and the Arab spirit—all in contrast to "Americanness" (which theoretically could participate in all of the above)—a problematic logic based in essentialist notions shows through. . . .

Food for Our Grandmothers: Writings by Arab-American & Arab-Canadian Feminists

Food for Our Grandmothers: Writings by Arab-American & Arab-Canadian Feminists has much in common with *Post Gibran* in its shift in focus away from Kahlil Gibran as the main emblematic figure of Arab American literature and toward new writers and approaches. This anthology's very existence is ignored, however, within the text of *Post Gibran*'s introduction. "Since *Grape Leaves: A Century of Arab American Poetry*, no anthology of our literature, even partial, has come out" (Akash and Mattawa 1999, xii).[9] Lack of awareness of this volume seems ironic, indeed, as *Food for Our Grandmothers* received considerable critical attention and many more reviews than *Post Gibran* and *Grape Leaves* combined.[10] Several plausible reasons for this exclusion point to features that set this work apart from the other two anthologies. The first is located in its subtitle, which identifies its specific contributors—Arab American and Arab Canadian feminists. The feminist focus and its publication by a small, nonprofit, collectively run publisher perhaps might limit its reception and/or its audience; though it received more attention than the other works, this may be limited mainly to feminist groups.[11] Linked to its feminist project is the volume's inclusion of many memoirs, essays, and personal narrations rather than poetry or generically experimental works like plays, once again raising the question of the definition of "literature." Would the pieces included in *Food for Our Grandmothers* meet the standards of "literary quality" outlined in *Grape Leaves*, for example? Like . . . other marginalized groups, feminist writers are often challenged on the basis of their works not manifesting the allegedly "universal" values of literature. Moreover, feminist voices, like others, often challenge accepted notions of community, which can contribute to their isolation.

Related to [the volume's] feminist focus, the question of race is treated explicitly from the very beginning of the *Food for Our Grandmothers* eight-page introduction; many of the individual contributions also draw and expand on this focus.[12] There is also a strong emphasis on

9. It should be noted that *Post Gibran* was published in 1999, five years after the publication date of *Food for Our Grandmothers* (Kadi 1994), presumably leaving enough time for [the latter] to be noticed. Moreover, Lisa Suhair Majaj's contribution in *Post Gibran* mentions *Food for Our Grandmothers*, to which she also contributed.

10. I base this assertion on my reading of over two dozen printed and online reviews of these works in journals and newspapers.

11. Food for Our Grandmothers was reviewed in locations where I did not locate reviews for the others, including but not limited to publications devoted to women's/feminist and/or lesbian issues: *Ms.* (Maksoud 1994); *Off Our Backs* (Douglas 1995); *Lambda Book Report* (Katz 1995); *Women's Review of Books* (Helmbold 1998); *Middle East Women's Studies Review* (Naber 1996); *Feminist Teacher* (Vandrick 1995); and *Sojourner: The Women's Forum* (Yadegar 1995).

12. Most of the narrative pieces [in *Food for Our Grandmothers*] treat this issue in some way. For some that deal very explicitly with race, see Boudakian, "Crossing Over to the Other Side"; Haddad, "In Search of Home"; Mahoul, "Battling Nationalisms to Salvage Her History"; Majaj, "Boundaries Arab/American"; Mamary, "Mint Tomatoes and the Grapevine"; Rashid "What's Not in a Name"; Saliba, "Sittee"; and Salome, "Wherever I Am."

class and the complex interconnections of race, gender, and class. The introduction asserts the dilemma faced by Arab Americans and Arab Canadians: "As Arabs, like other people of color in this racist society, our race is simultaneously emphasized and ignored" (Kadi 1994, xvi). This theme of being both racialized and ignored is central to the Arab American experience and has been explored by a number of scholars. Helen Hatab Samhan, for example, has argued that Arab American belonging in US society is often tolerated as long as it is not deemed political, at which point the mechanism of racialization is mobilized, and Arab Americans lose their rights (Samhan 1987, 1999; also Morsy 1994 [and] Naber 2000). Being "in between," or insecure within racial hierarchies because of a provisional white status, is articulated here in relation to the binary oppositions of Black and white in the United States and Canada, "Not Black. Not white. Never quite fitting in. Always on the edge" (Kadi 1994, xvi). How race is dealt with in *Food for Our Grandmothers* is particularly important in three areas: the insistence on experience, [the] naming and defining [of] the terms of the project, and the treatment of family and community.

Food for Our Grandmothers differs from *Grape Leaves* and *Post Gibran* not only in its foregrounding of race but also in its focus on Arab American writings and experience rather than on literary form. Whereas *Post Gibran* chooses works based on generic or other experimentations and *Grape Leaves* insists on "quality above all," *Food for Our Grandmothers* privileges the notion of representing the diversity of experiences of Arab American and Arab Canadian feminists, pointing out that even with this span there are still missing experiences. The contributors are defined, for example, as "writers, activists, artists, poets, teachers, and mother and daughter team, and two (blood) sisters. We are lesbians, bisexuals, and heterosexuals; of different generations; working class, middle class, uppermiddle class; women born in the Arab world and women born here" (Kadi 1994, xvii). It is within this context of experience, then, that *Food for Our Grandmothers* locates its project of community building and alliance formation.

It is from within this emphasis on the contributors' multiple social roles and their feminist identification that this anthology establishes links and bonds with other groups of color: "I hope this collection of essays and poems offers landmarks, signposts, names and directions not only for Arab-American and Arab-Canadian communities but for other communities of color and our allies" (Kadi 1994, xvii). . . . In this it takes a thoughtful stance in how it locates Arab Americans as a racialized group that can be an active partner in working with other communities of color and also benefit from these affiliations. . . .

Calling for these links once again recalls notions of universal literary value, which *Food for Our Grandmothers* effectively marginalizes along with the shadow of Kahlil Gibran. Similarly, it avoids the kind of racialized discourse that *Grape Leaves* inscribes and also the explicit rejection of these notions of value and racialized discourse in *Post Gibran*. In this way, *Food for Our Grandmothers* is able to grapple directly with the issue of race and racialization in relation to Arab Americans. Another related way in which this anthology shifts its focus away from employing vague and contradictory strategies of identity building in relation to race is in its self-definition through embracing the two other emblems framing this study—grandmothers and grape leaves. This focus is reflected in the book's very title: *Food for Our Grandmothers*. Here, these emblems emphasize both family/community and food as a specific cultural production. The introduction states that this title was easy to choose because it represents well the "incredible number of contributions" treating these themes and issues. The introduction and also individual contributions celebrate grandmothers—particularly as links to homeland and identity. This anthology is conceived explicitly as giving something back to these women, and the contributions are arranged in sections that are organized around different Arabic foods. The theme of food is not merely touched upon in a superficial way but is interwoven into the structure of the book, whose sections include olives, bread, thyme, *laban*, grape leaves, and mint. Not only idealized and simplified understandings of family are represented, though; many pieces draw out negative as well as positive sides to the traditional family structure, challenge patriarchal values, and critique the marginalization of gays and lesbians. Moreover, alternative community solidarities are highlighted—women's groups, for example.

Moreover, *Food for Our Grandmothers* is also aware of issues such as the unpaid labor involved in food preparation and the painstaking work many women have devoted in this field at the expense of others. As discussed above, the stereotype of ethnic women/women of color who hold the family together with food—the Arab women "stuck in the kitchen"—is an issue that recurs. This emphasis on food risks naturalizing these women's unpaid labor and locating it as something only to celebrate. As I have shown above in relation to *Grape Leaves*, such ideas indeed can be tied to the process of racialization of Arab women, like other women of color, and showing them as naturally tied to these activities, unable to "advance" like white women, and [as] victims of an endemically oppressive and misogynistic Arab society. In his own contribution to the volume, its editor, Joe Kadi, takes this issue on directly by identifying the labor of these grandmothers as "cultural work" and explicitly locating it as a parallel to his own cultural work, manifested in one way in the compilation of the anthology (Kadi 1994, 231–37).

By locating grandmothers' food preparation as cultural work that can be passed down and appreciated through generations, this anthology rejects a racial explanation for poetry and creative production (it is in the blood) or one vaguely linked to a spirit. It is still worthwhile to question if its emphasis on "grape leaves" and grandmothers reinscribes the very notions that [it] seek[s] to dismantle—keeping women figuratively, if not literally, in the kitchen. The framing and title of the work, though, is conceived of as a positive message, reinforcing that this anthology should be seen in some way as giving "food" back to these grandmothers who nurtured the anthology's contributors. Thus, this volume proposes that there is value in literary work that is connected to Arab American and Arab Canadian culture and heritage, and the work of Arab American and Arab Canadian grandmothers is thus also valorized by equating it with the seemingly more "intellectual" cultural work of writing and producing an anthology. In addition, Kadi's individual contribution to the volume presents a compelling argument for understanding the continuity of Arab American and Arab Canadian women's experiences as cultural work.

What sets how *Food for Our Grandmothers* treats the issue of race and the racialization of Arab Americans apart from the other two anthologies discussed in this chapter is its shift in emphasis. Here, the introduction places an emphasis on culture and specific cultural production and couples it with an explicit discussion of race and positionality of Arabs in North America. This discussion moves the definition of Arab American/Arab Canadian identity away from essentializing categories. It does not, however, ignore the question of race totally because of its centrality to the United States and systems of identity and community affiliation there. It therefore strategically uses Arab American racialization as a tool in alliance building with other groups of color, while calling racial discourses into question at the same time. In these ways, *Food for Our Grandmothers* engages with race and the racialization of Arab Americans and Arab Canadians in ways that can lead toward potentially more productive conceptualizations of Arab American identities.

Conclusions

As the analyses above reveal, the explicit and implicit strategies of the racialization of Arab Americans that these three anthologies use vary widely—some are sophisticated and linked to investigations of gender and class, others reproduce old paradigms and hierarchies, and others draw on deeply problematic essentialist notions to define the community. Particularly within the feminist framework of *Food for Our Grandmothers*, intersections of race, class, and gender are explored both in the overall project and in the introduction specifically. When such discussions are explicit, of course, they are easier to engage. Here I have shown that much of the discourse around race in Arab American literature and literary study, however, is implicit. Ideas bound up in essentialized and essentializing notions, such as that "poetry is in the Arab blood," are an integral part of the strategy of building community identity in *Grape Leaves*, for example. *Post Gibran* rejects this strategy on the surface but nonetheless proposes that there is an Arab spirit that itself can be defined, at least partly, as somehow essentially "Arab," though this itself is defined as open and multicultural. Such strategies of essentialization inform the identity-building projects of *Grape Leaves* and *Post Gibran* and are employed in many different and often contradictory ways to claim legitimacy, authenticity, and value in a racist US system. *Food for Our Grandmothers* provides both the most specific discussion of race and the positionality of Arab Americans and Arab Canadians; it also employs the most concrete and creative strategies in defining a group identity that is based in culture rather than [in] essence and complicates the positionality of Arab Americans while working toward useful conceptualizations of it. . . .

As critics, scholars, readers, teachers, and activists, it is vital for us to deepen our knowledge about how Arab American literature relates to and engages with the history of race and racism in the United States and the specific, complex, and contradictory places that Arab Americans have held in [that history] over time. One way of working with this relationship in literary terms, for example, is to explore literary links between Arab Americans and other groups, such as African Americans, in more specific detail. This is not in order simply to advocate or point out a parity or equality of experience but to build on both shared and different experiences better to understand the complexities and diversity of the literary production of these communities. In teaching and writing about Arab American literature, it is important to ask difficult questions about the impact of race and racial thinking on it—including whiteness, Blackness, and being "in between." Arab American literary publications, like these anthologies, expand the reach of Arab American voices and can be used effectively to probe these issues. Journals like *al-Jadid* and *Mizna* regularly publish pieces that investigate these questions (Dabis 2001; Shamieh 2001; Wade 2001; West 2000). In addition, it is essential to follow the lead of literary scholars and activists like Joe Kadi, Lisa Suhair Majaj, Steven Salaita, and others in pushing for gender and class to be included in these discussions and to expose the links between them in complex ways. This period of canon formation and interest in Arab American literature can be productively used to investigate the process of Arab American racialization in relation to literary studies and to complicate simple notions of what the community and its literary production are and can be.

Works Cited

Akash, Munir, and Khaled Mattawa, eds. 1999. *Post Gibran: Anthology of New Arab American Writing.* Syracuse, NY: Syracuse Univ. Press.

Brodkin, Karen. 1998. *How the Jews Became White Folks and What That Says about Race in America.* New Brunswick, NJ: Rutgers Univ. Press.

Dabis, Cherien. 2001. "Arab and a Half." *Mizna* 3, no. 3: n.p.

Delgado, Richard, and Jean Stefancic. 2001. *Critical Race Theory: An Introduction.* New York: New York Univ. Press.

Di Leonardo, Micaela. 1994. "White Ethnicities, Identity Politics, and Baby Bear's Chair." *Social Text,* no. 41: 165–91.

Douglas, Carol Anne. 1995. "Book Review: *Food for Our Grandmothers.*" *Off Our Backs* 25:10.

Gates, Henry Louis, Jr. 1985. "Writing 'Race' and the Difference It Makes." In *"Race," Writing, and Difference,* edited by Henry Louis Gates Jr., 1–20. Chicago: Univ. of Chicago Press.

———. 1991. "The Master's Pieces: On Canon Formation and Afro-American Tradition." In *The Bounds of Race: Perspectives on Hegemony and Resistance,* edited by Dominick La Capra, 17–38. Ithaca, NY: Cornell Univ. Press.

———. 1992. *Loose Canons: Notes on the Culture Wars.* New York: Oxford Univ. Press.

Gualtieri, Sarah M. A. 2001. "Becoming White." PhD diss., Univ. of Chicago.

Helmbold, Lois Rita. 1998. "No Passing Zone." *Women's Review of Books* 15, no. 4: 15–16.

Ignatiev, Noel. 1995. *How the Irish Became White: Irish Americans and African Americans in Nineteenth Century Philadelphia.* New York: Verso.

Jacobson, Matthew Frye. 1998. *Whiteness of a Different Color: European Immigrants and the Alchemy of Race.* Cambridge, MA: Harvard Univ. Press.

Joseph, Suad. 1994. "Problematizing Gender and Relational Rights: Experiences from Lebanon." *Social Politics* 1, no. 3: 271–85.

———. 1999a. "Against the Grain of the Nation—the Arab." In *Arabs in America: Building a New Future,* edited by Michael W. Suleiman, 257–72. Philadelphia: Temple Univ. Press.

———. 1999b. "Searching for Baba: Personal Notes on Rights and Responsibilities." In *Intimate Selving in Arab*

Families: Gender, Self, and Identity, edited by Suad Joseph, 53–76. Syracuse, NY: Syracuse Univ. Press.

Kadi, Joe, ed. 1994. *Food for Our Grandmothers: Writings by Arab-American & Arab-Canadian Feminists*. Boston: South End Press.

Katz, Judith. 1995. "Both Sides Now: *Lesbiot: Israeli Lesbians Tell Their Stories*, Edited by Tracy Moore, and *Food for Our Grandmothers: Writings by Arab-American and Arab-Canadian Feminists*, Edited by Joe Kadi." *Lambda Book Report* 4, no. 10: 24–25.

Majaj, Lisa Suhair. 1996. "Arab American Literature and the Politics of Memory." In *Memory and Cultural Politics: New Approaches to American Ethnic Literatures*, edited by Robert E. Hogan, Amritjit Singh, and Joseph T. Skerrett, 267–90. Boston: Northeastern Univ. Press.

———. 1999a. "Arab-American Ethnicity: Locations, Coalitions, and Cultural Negotiations." In *Arabs in America: Building a New Future*, edited by Michael W. Suleiman, 321–36. Philadelphia: Temple Univ. Press.

———. 1999b. "New Directions: Arab American Writing at Century's End." In *Post Gibran: Anthology of New Arab American Writing*, edited by Akash Munir and Khaled Mattawa, 66–77. Syracuse, NY: Syracuse Univ. Press.

———. 2000. "Arab Americans and the Meaning of Race." In *Postcolonial Theory and the United States: Race, Ethnicity, and Literature*, edited by Amritjit Singh and Peter Schmidt, 320–37. Jackson: Univ. Press of Mississippi.

Maksoud, Hala. 1994. "Food for Thought." *Ms.* 5, no. 3: 74–75.

Massad, Joseph. 1993. "Palestinians and the Limits of Racialized Discourse." *Social Text* 34:94–114.

Morsy, Soheir. 1994. "Beyond the Honorary 'White' Classification of Egyptians: Societal Identity in Historical Context." In *Race*, edited by Steven Gregory and Roger Sanjek, 175–98. New Brunswick, NJ: Rutgers Univ. Press.

Naber, Nadine. 1996. "The Most Invisible of the Invisibles." *Middle East Women's Studies Review* 11, no. 2: 6–8.

———. 2000. "Ambiguous Insiders: An Investigation of Arab American Invisibility." *Ethnic and Racial Studies* 23, no. 1: 37–61.

Naff, Alixa. 1985. *Becoming American: The Early Arab Immigrant Experience*. Carbondale: Southern Illinois Univ. Press.

Orfalea, Gregory, and Sharif Elmusa, eds. [1988] 2000. *Grape Leaves: A Century of Arab-American Poetry*. Northampton, NY: Interlink.

Roediger, David R. 1994. *Towards the Abolition of Whiteness*. London: Verso.

Salaita, Steven. 2000. "Split Vision: Arab American Literary Criticism." *Al-Jadid* 32, no. 14: 26–27.

Salem Manganaro, Elise. 1988. "Voicing the Arab: Multivocality and Ideology in Leon Uris' *The Haj*." *MELUS* 15, no. 4: 3–13.

Saliba, Therese. 1999. "Resisting Invisibility: Arab Americans in Academia and Activism." In *Arabs in America: Building a New Future*, edited by Michael W. Suleiman, 304–19. Philadelphia: Temple Univ. Press.

Samhan, Helen Hatab. 1987. "Politics and Exclusion: The Arab American Experience." *Journal of Palestine Studies* 16, no. 2: 11–28.

———. 1999. "Not Quite White: Race Classification and the Arab American Experience." In *Arabs in America: Building a New Future*, edited by Michael W. Suleiman, 209–26. Philadelphia: Temple Univ. Press.

Shaheen, Jack G. 2001. *Reel Bad Arabs: How Hollywood Vilifies a People*. New York: Olive Branch Press.

Shamieh, Betty. 2001. "Why I Am Afraid to Write This Poem." *Mizna* 3, no. 1: n.p.

Suleiman, Michael W. 1987. "Early Arab Americans: The Search for Identity." In *Crossing the Waters: Arabic-Speaking Immigrants to the United States before 1940*, edited by Eric James Hooglund, 37–54. Washington, DC: Smithsonian Institution Press.

———, ed. 1999. *Arabs in America: Building a New Future*. Philadelphia: Temple Univ. Press.

Vandrick, Stephanie. 1995. "Book Review, *Food for Our Grandmothers*." *Feminist Teacher* 9, no. 2: 98–104.

Wade, Corey. 2001. "Memoirs of a White Arab American." *Mizna* 3, no. 3: n.p.

West, Stan. 2000. "An Afrocentric Look at the Arab Community." *Mizna* 2, no. 3: 20–22.

Williams, Brackette F. 1996. *Women out of Place: The Gender of Agency and the Race of Nationality*. New York: Routledge.

Yadegar, Rebecca. 1995. "Arab-American/Arab-Canadian Anthology: An International Perspective" (book review). *Sojourner: The Women's Forum* 20:12.

Zoghby, Mary. 1988. "Book Review: *Grape Leaves: A Century of Arab American Poetry*." *MELUS* 15, no. 4: 91–101.

6

Mobilizing the Politics of Invisibility

AMIRA JARMAKANI

> If you want to hear me, you'll listen to my silences as well as my words.
>
> —Joe Kadi, "Speaking (about) Silence"

In the early 2000s I walked into a coffeehouse in Atlanta, ordered a drink, and placed the book I was reading, *Opening the Gates: A Century of Arab Feminist Writing* (cooke and Badran 1990), on the counter while I paid for my drink. "Arab feminism," the barista exclaimed. "That's just an oxymoron to me!" Her comment, cloaked as it was in certainty and self-assurance, demonstrates a particularly precarious positioning into which Arab and Arab American feminists are often thrust. Given the prevalence of popular misinformation about Arab (often conflated with Southwest Asian and North African, hereafter SWANA, and Muslim) women[1] in the United States, Arab American feminists face a complicated context that simultaneously seeks to define our realities as well as obscure the issues we consider to be pressing. The barista's comment, disarming in its nonchalance, glosses over the nefarious meaning in both the content and the tone of her statement, which quietly insinuates a rich field of feminist thought out of existence. Furthermore, far from unique, the idea that Arab (or Arab American) feminism is oxymoronic gains credibility against the backdrop of US official discourse about the "war on terror," which appropriates feminist logic in order to justify militarism and neoliberal imperialism. The barista's comment, uttered in September 2002, is indicative of the intensification of orientalism and Islamophobia following the events of September 11, 2001 (9/11); her presumed knowledge that Arab feminism could not exist was

Updated revision of Amira Jarmakani, "Mobilizing the Politics of Invisibility," in *Arab & Arab American Feminisms: Gender, Violence, & Belonging*, edited by Rabab Abdulhadi, Evelyn Alsultany, and Nadine Naber (Syracuse, NY: Syracuse Univ. Press, 2011), 227–41. The essay has been edited to update language (see footnote 1). Full references in the original notes were converted to author-date citations in the text and notes here, and a works cited list was added. Revised version printed with corrections and style changes for consistency throughout the volume by permission of Syracuse University Press.

1. The category "Arab and Arab American women" is an uncomfortably essentializing one, as is the popular orientalist image of the monolithically oppressed woman who needs to be saved by US imperialism. Particularly in relation to the stereotypes with which this essay is engaged, the category "Arab and Arab American women" makes a mess of both gender and ethnic/racial identities. The orientalist stereotype of the oppressed Arab/SWANA/Muslim woman both flattens the complexities of actual lived gender and violently collapses the already imprecise ethnic category of "Arabs" with other ethnic and national categories (e.g., Afghan, Iranian, Pakistani) as well as with the broad religious/cultural category "Muslim." Because orientalist (and therefore colonialist) narratives have conflated these categories in popular narratives, my efforts to speak from the positionality of Arab American feminism necessarily engages its overlaps with SWANA and Muslim feminisms, even as I recognize that acknowledging overlaps can further collapse distinctions and hierarchies within and between these categories. In this essay, I muck around in this messy language. I have maintained the category "women" when referring to discourses that rely on the idea of a stable and coherent category. I have broadened "Arab" to include SWANA and Muslim when discussing flattening narratives that do the same and to acknowledge similar processes of racialization of these groups in the United States. I hope the inevitable imprecisions I have introduced will nevertheless communicate my aim to contextualize the complexities of lived gender, race, culture, and religion in an imperialist, white-supremacist, heteronormative world.

framed and bolstered by the US-led invasion of Afghanistan, cast by the Bush administration as a project of liberation meant to save Afghan women from the oppression of the Taliban (see Abu-Lughod 2002; Hirschkind and Mahmoud 2002). Indeed, this one anecdotal interaction exemplifies multiple layers through which Arab American feminism tends to be perceived. At the most obvious surface level is the narrative of the imperialist-colonialist civilizing mission, which capitalizes on the image of exotic, oppressed women who must be saved from their indigenous (hyper)patriarchy. Adopting the "women's rights" civilizing mission stance, in turn, depends on an appropriation of feminist logic, yet it must be a logic that is amenable to the imperialist position. In the case of the US-led invasion of Afghanistan, for example, the US-based Feminist Majority Foundation had been advocating on behalf of (but not with) Afghan women since at least the early 1990s. In what could be called a form of "global feminism," the Feminist Majority worked from the position of savior rather than one of solidarity with feminists in Afghanistan and therefore developed a position easily appropriated in the service of militarism. Importantly, the military-imperialist and feminist-imperialist stances collude to reify stereotypical notions of Arab/SWANA and Muslim women as monolithically oppressed. They depend on a set of US cultural mythologies about the Southwest Asian and North African region, sometimes euphemistically described as "the Arab and Muslim worlds," which are often promulgated through overdetermined signifiers, like the "veil" (the English term collapsing a range of cultural and religious dress expressing modesty, piety, or identity or all three). These powerful symbols, in turn, threaten to eclipse the creative work of Arab American feminists. Because the mythologies are so pervasive, operating subtly and insidiously on the register of "common sense," Arab American feminists are often kept oriented toward correcting these common misconceptions rather than focusing on our own agendas and concerns.

Perhaps owing to its actual dynamism and flexibility across multiple historical and cultural contexts (and known by various names and practices), the cultural mythology of the veil serves as a salient example of the paradoxical framework Arab American feminists must negotiate. The image of the veil has been appropriated and deployed, as I have been arguing, by colonialist and imperialist powers to justify domination (for example, Britain in Egypt [Ahmed 1992], France in Algeria [Lazreq 1994; Fanon 1965], and the United States in Afghanistan and Iraq). It has also been utilized as a symbol of cultural authenticity in anticolonial nationalist movements and as a loaded marker in debates about "civilization," modernity, and liberal-democratic citizenship, all of which tend to obscure discussion of the ways Muslim women negotiate faith and piety.[2] With the exception of the last, most deployments of the veil eclipse the complex sociohistorical realities of the women they purport to represent. Functioning according to what Minoo Moallem has called a "semiotic war" (2005, 2), the cultural mythology of the veil easily becomes a signifying tool among competing patriarchies or imperialisms or both, a framing that constructs SWANA and Muslim women as either hidden or revealed objects rather than thinking subjects. The paradox is that, as a marker (supposedly) of invisibility and cultural authenticity, the cultural mythology of the veil renders SWANA women as simultaneously invisible and hypervisible. While Arab/SWANA and Muslim subjectivity is obscured by the mythology of the veil, the heteropatriarchal notions of oppression, tradition, and civilization become animated in the service of imperialist or nationalist agendas that render the mythology itself hypervisible. As feminists of color analyzing the impact of the faulty levees after Hurricane Katrina have pointed out, both invisibility and hypervisibility can operate as tools of oppression (Bierria, Liebenthal, and INCITE! 2007, 32). As demonstrated by my opening anecdote, the cultural mythology of the veil has largely signified invisibility in the US context in order to corroborate dominant assumptions about the oppression of Arab/SWANA (often assumed to be Muslim) women. The powerful presence of actual ciswomen, trans, and nonbinary people is therefore subsumed under the louder message of their supposedly helpless silence. As hypervisible, the mythology of the veil is so powerful and prolific in the United States that it is

2. See Gole 1996; Amin 1992; Abu-Lughod 1998; Wallach Scott 2007. For exceptions, see Deeb 2006; Hoodfar 1997; El Guindi 1999; and Mahmood 2005.

virtually impossible to talk about the realities of Arab and Arab American gendered subjectivity without invoking and necessarily responding to the looming image and story that the mythology of the veil tells.

Although I have been focusing on the US cultural construction of the "veil" so far, it is by no means the only signifier or sensationalist issue that impacts the work of Arab American feminists. Indeed, the point is not that Arab American feminists are unconcerned with the questions raised by the cultural and religious customs people negotiate in various contexts and the way these customs—and gendered subjectivity—are circumscribed within patriarchal, nationalist, imperialist, and local realities. Rather, the problem is that a range of complex, nuanced concerns are flattened into convenient symbols, which then become fodder for mainstream debates about the "death" of (US) feminism (Chesler 2005). Take, for example, the opening sentence of a 2007 article by Christina Hoff Sommers:

> The subjection of women in Muslim societies—especially in Arab nations and in Iran—is today very much in the public eye. Accounts of lashings, stonings, and honor killings are regularly in the news, and searing memoirs by Ayaan Hirsi Ali and Azar Nafisi have become major best-sellers. One might expect that by now American feminist groups would be organizing protests against such glaring injustices, joining forces with the valiant Muslim women who are working to change their societies. This is not happening.

Sommers's opening statement demonstrates a number of things. First, it reiterates the laundry list of issues—"honor killings" and "stonings," for example—that have become the primary lenses through which the gendered realities of SWANA people are filtered in popular US discourse. Second, it invokes native informants—figures like Ayaan Hirsi Ali and Azar Nafisi—who are indeed widely popular in the United States, no doubt because they corroborate the images their audiences already hold about the status of "Muslim women."[3] Finally, and perhaps most revealingly, its true focus is a critique of "American feminist groups," who are (according to Sommers's logic) supporting (Islamic) "terrorism" by failing to denounce the absolute subjugation of Muslim women. The problem, again, is in the framing of the issue. It capitalizes on the idea of Muslim (often conflated with SWANA) women's oppression, signified through overdetermined symbols (like the "veil") and sensationalized, decontextualized news stories (about "stonings" and "lashings"), in the service of another project altogether: building a case for the "war on terror" by characterizing the SWANA region as widely supporting terrorism and oppression. Notably (and significantly), any critical space for Arab American feminists is either obviated or filled by native informants who speak to the monolithic logic of absolute oppression through ready-made symbols and news stories.

Building on this idea of the way Arab American feminisms have been circumscribed within a paradoxical framework, I would also like to suggest that such a position might be put to strategic use. In his essay "Speaking (about) Silence" (2003), Joe Kadi argues that stories of silence (or being silenced) are political, a point that has much salience for the case of Arab American feminisms. While he largely frames silence as a form of oppression that can be alleviated through coming into one's voice, I want to build on his argument here to suggest that silence can also be a potential strategy (among many others) in crafting an oppositional consciousness through which to both define Arab American feminisms and build alliances and solidarities with other women-of-color feminists in the United States.

A Historical Context for Arab American Feminisms

The anecdote with which I began also demonstrates a general context of misunderstanding about and misrepresentation of "Arab women" and Arab feminisms, which helps to determine the framework for the articulation and reception of Arab American feminisms. Because Arab American feminism often finds itself necessarily engaged with an incomplete and monolithic understanding of Arab (often conflated with SWANA and Muslim) gendered subjectivity, it equally often speaks from a corrective, and therefore defensive, stance.

3. For further critique of these "native testimonials," see Mahmood 2008.

This type of oppositional stance is nothing new. In fact, it closely resembles Leila Ahmed's experience at the 1980 National Women's Studies Association (NWSA) conference as she recounts it in her article "Western Ethnocentrism and Perceptions of the Harem" (1982). Ahmed's article, though certainly not the only or the oldest example of Arab American feminism, provides a point of reference for tracing the trajectory of Arab American feminism in the United States. Since the attacks on the World Trade Center and the Pentagon in 2001, Arab American feminism has been portrayed and perceived, from a mainstream perspective, as suddenly relevant or newly forming. Yet, using the 1980 and 2001 NWSA conferences as a loose framework, I am interested in exploring the way in which Arab American feminists have been participating in critical feminist dialogue for the past few decades. Charting Arab American feminisms' intersections with women-of-color feminisms in the United States, I will be particularly exploring the development of oppositional consciousness as a defining, integral feature of Arab American feminisms. A preliminary example comes from Leila Ahmed's experience at the 1980 NWSA conference. While attending a panel entitled "Women in Islam," Ahmed was surprised to hear what she found to be an overly optimistic view of women's status in Islam. Although Ahmed agreed that "Islam had, as that panel maintained, brought about a number of positive gains for women in Arabia at the time, and had granted women certain rights," she felt that fact "still did not warrant playing down Islam's blatant endorsement of male superiority and male control of women, or glossing over the harshness of, in particular, its marriage, divorce, and child custody laws" (1982, 521). Having attended a conference devoted to critical interrogation of the status of women across multiple contexts, Ahmed was no doubt confused to find the panelists' analysis of gender oppression within Islam strikingly underdeveloped. Nevertheless, as she explains in her later reflection, she had not yet lived in the United States and, therefore, did not yet understand the defensive position from which the panelists had begun. Before discussing the rich complexity and dynamics of gender oppression within the Islamic tradition, the "Women in Islam" panelists first had to address those supposed certainties and assumptions that existed in the audience about the hyperpatriarchal and overly oppressive nature of Islam. There was no space for the panelists to offer an honest and productive critique of the status of women in Islam without first confronting US misperceptions about Islam. As Ahmed discovered, these misperceptions were (and are) deeply entrenched in the mainstream psyche: "Just as Americans 'know' that Arabs are backward, they know also with the same flawless certainty that Muslim women are terribly oppressed and degraded. And they know this not because they know that women everywhere in the world are oppressed, but because they believe that, specifically, Islam monstrously oppresses women" (1982, 522).

This type of "knowledge" about Islam, which is often conflated with an understanding of the SWANA region as the two have become virtually interchangeable in US discourse, is the same sort of certainty that has reified the cultural mythology of the veil as an all-encompassing signifier of Arab/SWANA (often conflated with Muslim) gender subjugation in the United States. As Ahmed points out, there is not simply a dearth of information about Arab and Muslim women; rather, there is a plethora of misinformation about gender oppression in Islam. Consequently, Arab American feminists often find themselves absorbed in the task of addressing and correcting this misinformation, which ultimately subverts and redirects Arab American feminist energy and analysis.

An example of such a double bind can be found in the public discourse surrounding "Islamo-Fascism Awareness Week," which was staged by the "Terrorism Awareness Project" (an affiliate of the David Horowitz Freedom Center). As described by David Horowitz (2007)[4] in the magazine *Front Page*, the goal of the October 2007 event was to "confront two big lies of the political left: that George Bush created the 'war on terror' and that

4. The articles from *Front Page* have been removed from the website since this essay's first printing. They are also unavailable in their entirety through the Wayback Machine archival search engine (inquiries are met with the message "Sorry, this url has been excluded from the Wayback Machine"), so I have provided the closest possible link. References to these events can be found in more recent *Front Page* stories. See, for example, https://archives.frontpagemag.com/fpm/islamo-fascism-and-war-against-jews-volume-iv-david-horowitz/.

global warming is a greater danger to Americans than global Jihad and Islamic supremacism." Although "Islamo-Fascism Awareness Week" mostly drew criticism for its sloppy conflation of "terrorism" and "fascism" with Islam, in part through its rhetorical use of dubious terms such as "global jihad" and "Islamic supremacism," it is perhaps most notable for its tactical deployment of gender oppression and its strategic targeting of women's and gender studies departments across the United States. Despite purporting to care about women's oppression, the argument goes, women's and gender studies departments in the United States have been inexcusably silent about "Islamic misogyny," the brutal oppression of women in the Muslim world, and "Islamic gynophobia" (Spencer 2008). If equating "the Left" with so-called Islamofascists (or, in another formulation, "feminists and Islamists") has been a clever, yet disingenuous, strategy of the David Horowitz Freedom Center to discredit widespread critique of the "war on terror" and to demonize Islam by attributing all intimate violence against Muslim women to the religion itself, its appropriation of "women in Muslim societies" (to use Hoff Sommers's phrase) in the service of its own argument is a well-worn orientalist and imperialist trope (Horowitz 2008). Most important, though, it sets up a familiar dichotomy of actors (the freedom-loving US liberators on one side . . . "feminists and Islamists" on the other, for example) warring over the presumptive task of saving Muslim women. Though I am loathe to give the Freedom Center credibility through naming it, the fact is that it is part of a larger discourse (including voices as diverse as the Freedom Center, the Bush administration, the National Organization for Women, and mainstream newspapers) that speaks about Muslim women, invoking them symbolically as part of a rhetorical strategy. Indeed, this rhetorical strategy is often so effective as to reify the false binaries of liberation and oppression forever hovering around Arab/SWANA and Muslim women as well as around everyone who can be identified as such.

Despite her seeming attempt to undercut the types of claims made by David Horowitz and Christina Hoff Sommers, for example, Katha Pollitt (2008, in "Sign the Open Letter from American Feminists") reinforces the same binary that situates Arab/SWANA and Muslim women as objects of sensationalist (cultural-religious) violence, such as "female genital mutilation (FGM), forced marriage, child marriage, spousal violence, rape." In her rush to defend US feminist organizations against the accusation that they do not support gender-justice struggles for Muslim women, she uses the same sensationalist examples that have inscribed Muslim women as victims of their culture or religion, thereby perpetuating a rhetorical framework that ultimately appropriates, objectifies, and therefore subjugates these same women for the sake of argumentative strategy. For Arab American feminists concerned with gender and social justice for SWANA ciswomen, trans, and nonbinary people worldwide, this common discursive framework does violence to the very people it purports to represent. It attempts to provide an analysis isolated from the actual conditions (for example, military occupation and global economic restructuring) that help give rise to the violences they face, while simultaneously objectifying them as convenient talking points.

The Politics of Invisibility

Given these examples of how Arab/SWANA/Muslim women become categorically objectified in popular discourse, it is no wonder that Arab and Arab American feminists often find themselves cast into a liminal space, compelled to engage in a debate constructed by a set of false binaries about whether veiling is oppressive or liberating, for example, or whether feminism is a "Western" concept. These kinds of debates consistently privilege the notion that gender oppression can be understood in isolation from other factors of oppression, and they routinely center an analysis of the individual as abstracted from larger structural axes of oppression. In short, they enact what I am describing as a politics of invisibility, where the politics of invisibility describes the systematic elision of a nuanced analysis regarding gender justice for Arab and SWANA ciswomen, trans, and nonbinary people and an overemphasis on sensationalist issues and stereotypical categories associated with Arab femininity. The politics of invisibility, then, describes how these stereotypical categories doubly silence the very people to whom they claim to give voice. Invisibility here is meant to signify both the gendered ways that SWANA people are silenced and the ways they are made hypervisible, paradoxically, as markers of invisibility, exoticism, or oppression. Far from being absent from the public domain, SWANA women are represented prolifically as veiled women, as harem slaves (particularly in the 1970s in the context of the 1973 oil embargo), and as exotic belly dancers (in contexts as varied as the popular sitcom *I Dream of Jeannie* to a 2002 Camel cigarette advertising scheme titled "Exotic Pleasures") (Jarmakani 2008). However, these popular representations serve to circumscribe gendered SWANA subjects within a totalizing shroud of silence and oppression. They speak in the shorthand of stereotypical categories. Furthermore, these categories of representation are insidious in that they present themselves as accurate and authentic reflections of reality, and they are deployed by the dominant discourse in the same way—as proof of a subjugated condition.

Because these images are so pervasive, Arab American feminist thought is often overlooked or not heard unless it engages the dominant myths and categories through which Arab femininity has been filtered in the United States. The continuous need to identify and deconstruct stereotypical images functions as a double silencing of Arab American feminists, whose energy could be better spent theorizing new spaces of possibility for Arab American ciswomen, trans, and nonbinary people rather than responding to the misinformation promulgated by the dominant discourse. To the extent that Arab and Arab American feminists have been able to carve a space in which to give voice to their own issues and concerns, they have found much of that space reluctantly yet inevitably filled with corrective responses to mainstream misunderstandings.

Even those Arab and Arab American narratives that refuse to engage stereotypical categories are often reinterpreted or translated through them. Amal Amireh gives a salient example of this phenomenon in the case of Nawal el Saadawi, a famous Egyptian feminist, whose book *Al-wajh al-'ari lil mara'a al-arabiyyah* (The Naked Face of the Arab Woman) was translated into English with the title *The Hidden Face of Eve: Women in the Arab World*, literally covering the Arab woman's face in the process of translation (Amireh 2000, 224). Though hardly the only example of the way Arab femininity gets translated through stereotypical categories (see also Darraj 2011), this one demonstrates both the power of the metaphorical cover that everywhere threatens to obscure the textured, gendered realities of SWANA people and the politics of reception that forever privileges the "cover" to the extent of eliding the contents of SWANA lives.

The complicated ways in which the politics of invisibility impacts the articulation of Arab American feminism was brought home to me during my own experience at the 2001 NWSA conference. Though I was giving a paper about Arab American literature, I was scheduled on a panel titled "Construction of Gender and Sexuality in International Literature," thereby highlighting popular US perceptions of the Arab as perpetually foreign, even (especially?) in the case of Arab Americans. The conference organizers did not seem to have a framework for understanding Arabs as ethnic Americans. Yet it was the audience response to my paper that gave the clearest indication of how Arab American feminism is affected by the politics of invisibility. Remember that I was scheduled on a panel that was meant to discuss international literature, so the US nationality of the writers was subsumed under the organizers' understanding of a dichotomy between domestic–US and foreign–Arab, eliding the possibility of a transnational framework, reinscribing Arabs as foreign within a US context, and pointing to another way in which Arab American women writers did not fit dominant conceptual categories. Moreover, the people in the audience seemed to have no frame of reference for understanding Arab or Arab American women as writers since the activity of writing requires a subjectivity that is incompatible with the stereotypical frames of reference that are widely available for understanding SWANA gendered subjectivity. Indeed, these dominant interpretive categories were clearly in play for the woman who posed one of the main questions I received, though it must be said that the overwhelming audience response to my paper was characterized by silence, despite the fact that there was ample time left in the session for discussion. It struck me as telling, then, that one of the main questions I did receive was from a white woman who wanted me to explain why Arab and Arab American women react negatively when she tells them she is a belly dancer. Her indignant tone suggested that she was asking for validation and reassurance about her performance of the belly dance as a white woman. Her question can be contextualized within a larger phenomenon of the rising popularity of American interpretations of belly dance and the increasing popularity of belly-dance exercise classes. These are further embedded in a larger history of the American belly-dance community, which has seen itself as reclaiming and honoring the belly dance as a celebration of female power since at least the 1970s and has, in some instances, presented itself as saving the dance from its excessively patriarchal cultural heritage (Jarmakani 2006). I can only assume that my questioner was coming from the righteous perspective of such good intentions when she inappropriately and rather shockingly expected me to speak for other Arab and Arab American women's reactions to her. More to my point, however, her question exemplified the fact that the only way in which Arab subjectivity can be understood is in terms of the already entrenched stereotypical markers—in this case of Arab female sexuality, particularly because I made no mention of belly dancing in my talk.

Regardless of which stereotypical category was invoked during my presentation, the fact remains that the audience had either no frame of reference for understanding Arab gendered subjectivity (in the case of Arab American women writers, for example) or could understand Arab women only through the filter of preexisting stereotypical categories (like the harem, the veil, and the belly dancer). The implications of this sort of politics of invisibility are explored by Japanese American writer Mitsuye Yamada in her contribution to *This Bridge Called My Back: Writings by Radical Women of Color*: "No matter what we say or do, the stereotype still hangs on. I am weary of starting from scratch each time I speak or write, as if there were no history behind us, of hearing that among the women of color, Asian women are the least political, or the least oppressed, or the most polite" (1981a, 71). I reference Yamada here because of the ways in which she writes about the "double invisibility" of Asian American women (Yamada 1981b, 37). As I elaborate on what I mean by the politics of invisibility in relation to Arab/SWANA American ciswomen, trans, and nonbinary people Yamada provides a useful model for analyzing the insidiousness of a stereotype that reinforces the image of Asian American—or, for my purposes, Arab American—gendered subjects as already inscribed in a space of silence or oppression. Like Yamada, I felt as if I were "starting from scratch" in that I had to name the stereotypes about Arab femininity as stereotypes before I could begin the work of dispelling them. In this regard, then, the politics of invisibility has impacted Arab American people's lives in gendered ways and, by extension, the articulation of Arab American feminism in insidious and complicated ways.

Returning to my opening example, it is not simply that Arab American women are not seen because they are, as contemporary US popular culture would have us believe, "hidden" behind the veil. Rather, as the barista's comment indicates, it is a matter of not being credited with the possibility of existence. Arab feminism appears as an oxymoron not only because Arab women are perceived to be silent and submissive according to the mythology of the veil. It is an oxymoron because Arab ciswomen, trans, and nonbinary people are not afforded the subjectivity of thinking, theorizing individuals. We are not merely silenced; we are wholly displaced and, therefore, ontologically elided by sensationalized news stories and images of oppressed and exoticized Arab women. That we are actively engaged in the process of creating and producing knowledge is incomprehensible to those individuals who understand Arab and Arab American women through the filmy lens of stereotypical categories. My own experience at the 2001 NWSA conference speaks to the ways in which Arab American feminism has gone unrecognized and unacknowledged within the mainstream movement. With no frame of reference by which to understand it, it has all too often either been ignored or been displaced by the very stereotypes it seeks to critique.

The Cutting Edge of Invisibility

Three months after the 2001 NWSA conference, following the events of September 11, the politics of invisibility would take on another dimension in relation to Arab American feminisms in the academy. The explosion of stories and images of Afghan women's brutal oppression at the hands of the Taliban (an issue that had utterly failed to garner public and widespread US interest for years) in many ways highlighted the hypervisibility of Muslim (often conflated with Arab/SWANA) gender oppression. Again, it was not a matter of not being seen. Indeed, the US public seemed to believe that it was finally seeing SWANA women in a way that it had not seen them previously. However, the seemingly sudden hypervisibility of Muslim and SWANA women's lives had, predictably, shrouded their realities even further. The sheer proliferation of the image of the veil, coupled with the way in which it was reproduced as a monolithic signifier of the oppression of SWANA women, effectively displaced any potential for understanding the complicated network of power relations, patriarchal and imperial, that impact people's lives in SWANA regions.

In September 2001, I was teaching a course at Emory University titled "American Identities," and as I struggled to acknowledge and voice the disturbing reality of violence and racism enacted against the Arab American community as a corrective to my students' assured assertions that hostility and hate crimes did not exist, I realized something about the mechanics of invisibility. Despite evidence and news stories to the contrary, my students could not see the violent and dangerous reality of Arab Americans' lives after 9/11, in part because their understanding of the Arab American community was already determined by the dominant narrative of terrorism. As with the mythology of the veil, the narrative of terrorism had prefigured my students' understanding of Arab Americans. Their knowledge about Arab Americans was informed by the prolific image of the terrorist, which was incompatible with the realities of the violent attacks the community faced in the aftermath of 9/11. The conditions of Arab Americans' lives were already displaced by the interpretive categories through which they had come to be understood.

Regrettably, my colleagues' responses to me and to my work after September also highlighted the problematic ways in which Arab Americans' realities continued to be elided. The immediate connection that my peers made to my work on representations of Arab femininity in US popular culture after the horrific events of September 11 was to suggest, with a tinge of jealousy, that my work was at least now "cutting edge." I did not, and still do not, know how to respond to heartbreaking destruction and grief with the consideration of how I might capitalize on or benefit from that destruction and grief. Yet the "cutting edge" comment once again exemplifies the way in which the hypervisibility of Arab gender oppression actually worked to further eclipse Arab and Arab Americans' realities. The assumption that my work was now suddenly interesting or useful in a way that it had not previously been participates in the construction of 9/11 as the origin story for perceptions and representations of Arab femininity and, in so doing, ignores the history of stereotypical representations about Arab/SWANA and Muslim femininity in the United States. It also suggests that an understanding of Arab gendered subjectivity is important only in relation to larger political and international conflict and achieves a moment of recognition in the shadow of such events.

Perhaps most problematic, however, is the suggestion that I can capitalize, through my research, on the increased attention given to representations of Arab femininity since the suggestion condones and reinforces an uncritical commodification of such representations. . . . In a climate in which the David Horowitz Freedom Center deploys the language of "academic freedom" to chastise women's and gender studies departments for their lack of attention to "the plight of Muslim women" and to coerce those departments into promulgating Islamophobic and simplistic lessons about women and Islam, the conversation about gendered SWANA subjectivity once again gets reduced to an obfuscating binary. In such a context, in which surveillance and privatization work in tandem, Arab American feminisms seem to be presented with two options: be appropriated or be censored and censured.

NWSA Revisited

One of the most troubling features of the politics of invisibility is precisely this ability to simultaneously silence Arab American feminist analysis and produce discourse that further obscures that analysis. As I see it, the primary task for Arab American feminisms is to find a way to reject both disingenuous appropriation as well as more insidious forms of censure. My suggestion for responding to the politics of invisibility actually brings me back to my discussion of the "Women in Islam" panel at the 1980 NWSA conference and to a recognition of the ways that Arab American feminist discourse has long been engaged in mobilizing, or deploying, the politics of invisibility as a strategy. In the context of a hegemonic white women's movement, the panelists addressing Arab women's issues at the 1980 NWSA conference spent much of their time working to dispel mainstream US feminist narratives that cast SWANA women as unwilling victims of a seemingly hyperpatriarchal society. In so doing, they were employing a critical perspective that participated in a mode of analysis that paralleled the experience of women of color at the 1981 NWSA conference, as documented by Chela Sandoval in her article "Feminism and Racism: A Report on the 1981 National Women's Studies Association Conference" (1990). Sandoval's account of the way in which women of color organized in response to the title of the 1981 NWSA conference, "Women Respond to Racism," offers a useful framework for understanding the work that has already been done by Arab American feminists. Although Arab American feminists were not clearly identified with what Sandoval calls "U.S. Third World feminists" in the context of the early 1980s feminist movement, both groups of women were clearly utilizing some of the same strategies.

In many ways, the fact that Arab American feminism has had to construct itself negatively has facilitated the development of its greatest strength: an oppositional consciousness. Sandoval's comments regarding the experiences of feminists of color at the 1981 conference can apply to Arab American feminists as well: "U.S. Third World feminists must recognize that our learned sensitivity to the mobile webs of power is a skill that, once developed, can become a sophisticated form of oppositional consciousness . . . which creates the opportunity for flexible, dynamic and tactical responses" (1990, 66–67). This sort of flexible, dynamic, and tactical response to power is what Ahmed witnessed at the "Women in Islam" panel in 1980, and it is the type of critical consciousness and resistance that Arab American feminists have continued to cultivate in response to multiple forms of oppression propagated by racism in the white feminist movement, sexism in Arab and Arab American communities, and the racist, sexist, and patronizing effects of imperialistic projects of so-called liberation. What Arab American feminists need most urgently is to continue to use the skills and tools we have gained from an oppositional consciousness in order to forge more spaces of possibility for the lives of Arab and Arab American ciswomen, trans, and nonbinary people. The work of Arab American feminists contributes to the work of those feminists, both in the United States and transnationally, who "are calling for new subjectivity, a political revision that denies any one perspective as the only answer, but instead posits a shifting tactical and strategic subjectivity that has the capacity to recenter depending upon the forms of oppression to be confronted" (Sandoval 1990, 67). Indeed, Arab American feminists demonstrate a "shifting . . . strategic subjectivity" by creatively mobilizing a politics of invisibility. Mobilizing the politics of invisibility can mean using silence as a strategy; it is a response that understands contextual clues to determine when speech will simply reinforce the false binary that frames so much of the public discourse about SWANA and gender. It employs oppositional consciousness in flexible ways and therefore does not solely operate as a counterdiscourse since counternarratives run the risk of legitimating the problematic assumptions of the very discourses they resist. Most important, mobilizing the politics of invisibility helps to disarm the notion that silence and invisibility are necessarily oppressive and opens up a wider field of intervention for Arab American feminists.

The powerful and potent shorthand of cultural mythologies (like the images of the belly dancer and the terrorist, for example) and of sensationalist stories about the "plight" of SWANA women is not going to disappear—these tropes are unfortunately too useful as interpretive categories. Simply advocating for a rejection of current stereotypical categories and narratives would inevitably lead to the establishment of equally limiting categories of representation, and spending energy to create a counterdiscourse will perhaps unwittingly reify the false binary that already frames much of public understanding. The work of Arab American feminists, then, must continue to encourage a fruitful fluidity that constantly forges new possibilities for understanding and contextualizing the complexly gendered realities of Arab and Arab American people's lives. In solidarity with social justice and liberation projects worldwide, we must mindfully utilize the tools of an oppositional consciousness in order to support the urgent work of carving and crafting new spaces for the expression of Arab American feminisms. Rather than simply resisting the politics of invisibility that have denied us a full presence, we must mobilize it, thereby reinventing and transforming that invisibility into a tool with which we can create transformative and liberatory futures.

Works Cited

Abu-Lughod, Lila, ed. 1998. *Remaking Women: Feminism and Modernity in the Middle East.* Princeton, NJ: Princeton Univ. Press.

———. 2002. "Do Muslim Women Really Need Saving? Anthropological Reflections on Cultural Relativism and Its Others." *American Anthropologist* 104, no. 3: 783–90.

Ahmed, Leila. 1982. "Western Ethnocentrism and Perceptions of the Harem." *Feminist Studies* 8, no. 3: 521–34.

———. 1992. *Women and Gender in Islam: Historical Roots of a Modern Debate.* New Haven, CT: Yale Univ. Press.

Amin, Qasim. 1992. *The Liberation of Women, The New Woman: Two Documents in the History of Egyptian Feminism.* Translated by Samiha Peterson. Cairo: American Univ. of Cairo Press.

Amireh, Amal. 2000. "Framing Nawal el Saadawi: Arab Feminism in a Transnational World." *Signs* 26, no. 1: 215–43.

Bierria, Alisa, Mayaba Liebenthal, and INCITE! Women of Color against Violence. 2007. "To Render Ourselves Visible: Women of Color Organizing and Hurricane Katrina." In *What Lies Beneath: Katrina, Race, and the State of the Nation*, edited by South End Press Collective, 31–47. Cambridge, MA: South End Press.

Chesler, Phyllis. 2005. *The Death of Feminism: What's Next in the Struggle for Women's Freedom.* New York: Palgrave Macmillan.

cooke, miriam, and Margot Badran, eds. 1990. *Opening the Gates: A Century of Arab Feminist Writing.* Bloomington: Indiana Univ. Press.

Darraj, Susan Muaddi. 2011. "Personal and Political: The Dynamics of Arab American Feminism." In *Arab & Arab American Feminisms: Gender, Violence, & Belonging*, edited by Rabab Abdulhadi, Evelyn Alsultany, and Nadine Naber, 248–60. Syracuse, NY: Syracuse Univ. Press.

Deeb, Lara. 2006. *An Enchanted Modern: Gender and Public Piety in Shi'i Lebanon.* Princeton, NJ: Princeton Univ. Press.

Fanon, Frantz. 1965. *A Dying Colonialism.* Translated by Haakon Chevalier. New York: Grove Press.

Gole, Nilufer. 1996. *The Forbidden Modern.* Ann Arbor: Univ. of Michigan Press.

El Guindi, Fadwa. 1999. *Veil: Modesty, Privacy, Resistance.* Oxford: Berg.

Hirschkind, Charles, and Saba Mahmood. 2002. "Feminism, the Taliban, and the Politics of Counter-insurgency." *Anthropological Quarterly* 72, no. 2: 339–54.

Hoff Sommers, Christina. 2007. "The Subjection of Islamic Women." *Weekly Standard* (Washington, DC), May 21.

Hoodfar, Homa. 1997. "The Veil in Their Minds and on Our Heads: Veiling Practices and Muslim Women." In *The Politics of Culture in the Shadow of Capital*, edited by Lisa Lowe and David Lloyd, 248–79. Durham, NC: Duke Univ. Press.

Horowitz, David. 2007. "Islamo-Fascism Awareness Week." *Front Page*, Sept. 21. At https://web.archive.org/web/20070923042442/http://frontpagemagazine.com/.

———. 2008. "A Response to Feminists on the Violent Oppression of Women in Islam." *Front Page*, Jan. 24. At https://web.archive.org/web/20080215151418/http://frontpagemagazine.com/.

Jarmakani, Amira. 2006. "Belly Dancing for Liberation." In *Arabs in the Americas: Interdisciplinary Essays on the Arab Diaspora*, edited by Darcy Zabel, 145–68. New York: Peter Lang Press.

———. 2008. *Imagining Arab Womanhood: The Cultural Mythology of Veils, Harems, and Belly Dancers in the U.S.* New York: Palgrave Macmillan.

Kadi, Joe. 2003. "Speaking (about) Silence." In *Sing, Whisper, Shout, Pray: Feminist Visions for a Just World*, edited by M. Jacqui Alexander, Lisa Albrecht, Sharon Day, and Mab Segrest, 539–45. Fort Bragg, CA: EdgeWork Books.

Lazreg, Marnia. 1994. *The Eloquence of Silence: Algerian Women in Question.* New York: Routledge.

Mahmood, Saba. 2005. *The Politics of Piety: The Islamic Revival and the Feminist Subject.* Princeton, NJ: Princeton Univ. Press.

———. 2008. "Feminism, Democracy, and Empire: Islam and the War of Terror." In *Women's Studies on the Edge*, edited by Joan Wallach Scott, 81–114. Durham, NC: Duke Univ. Press.

Moallem, Minoo. 2005. *Between Warrior Brother and Veiled Sister: Islamic Fundamentalism and Patriarchy in Iran.* Berkeley: Univ. of California Press.

Pollitt, Katha. 2008. "Sign the Open Letter from American Feminists." *Blog: And Another Thing,* Jan. 20. At https://www.thenation.com/article/archive/sign-open-letter-american-feminists/.

Sandoval, Chela. 1990. "Feminism and Racism: A Report on the 1981 National Women's Studies Association Conference." In *Making Face, Making Soul / Haciendo Caras,* edited by Gloria Anzaldúa, 55–71. San Francisco: Anne Lute.

Spencer, Robert. 2008. "Islamic Misogyny." *Front Page,* Jan. 4. Formerly at http://www.frontpagemag.com/Articles.

Wallach Scott, Joan. 2007. *The Politics of the Veil.* Princeton, NJ: Princeton Univ. Press.

Yamada, Mitsuye. 1981a. "Asian Pacific American Women and Feminism." In *This Bridge Called My Back: Writings by Radical Women of Color,* edited by Cherríe Moraga and Gloria Anzaldúa, 71–75. New York: Kitchen Table/Women of Color Press.

———. 1981b. "Invisibility Is an Unnatural Disaster: Reflections of an Asian American Woman." In *This Bridge Called My Back: Writings by Radical Women of Color,* edited by Cherríe Moraga and Gloria Anzaldúa, 35–40. New York: Kitchen Table/Women of Color Press.

Part Two

Structuring Migration

Moving Bodies and Shared Histories

In some ways, all scholarship on and writing by Arab Americans can be captured under the themes "moving bodies" and "shared histories." Arab Americans have physically, subjectively, and politically flowed through spaces, categories, identities, barriers, and legal statuses shared and not shared with others throughout their diasporic trajectories. So, too, Arabs, Africans, Latinx, Asians, Muslims, Europeans, Americans, and Indigenous peoples have shared histories and spaces, the complexities of which have been overwritten by dominant scholarly traditions that prefer boundedness to transnational and transcontinental fluidity, conceal shared oppressions under invented human hierarchies, and reify binaries of here and there, then and now, self and other. These dominant narratives often suggest that Arabs and Muslims (among others) have nothing to do with "America" and that their journeys to "over here" render them out of place and perpetually foreign. Such conceptualizations provide support to those who argue that Arab and Muslim Americans may legitimately be seen as alien, characterized as invasive, and justifiably subject to regulation of movement, as has occurred at various historical moments, including quite recently.

As noted in the introduction to part one, Arab American studies scholarship and indeed the study of most migrant groups typically start with an articulation of whom we are speaking about: Where did they come from? How many were they? Why did they leave? And where do we place them on demographic indices of meaning in western migration studies, such as education, occupation, religion, gender, and social class? These questions in turn direct our attention to notable historic shifts taking place in both the "sending" region and the "receiving" country's immigration policies. However, focusing solely on the emigration/immigration binary can obscure the contexts that affect the way bodies move. Indeed, as Camila Pastor notes, "moving bodies rub against the grain of the nation-state" (2017, 9), disrupting the logics of demographic indices. The essays included in this part speak to the complex realities of moving bodies: migration is fluid, not unidirectional—it may involve transnational circuits and "South–South" flows. In addition, migration is shaped not only by the conditions of "origin" and "destination" but also by circuits of movement precipitated by global capitalism, settler colonialism, climate change, environmental destruction, and imperialism as well as by corruption and political and social repression. It should be no surprise that the largest human movement between Arab countries and the United States has occurred in recent decades, a phenomenon true of all non-European migration to the United States and resulting both from changes in US laws and from disruptions caused by war and the global capitalist economy. Decontextualized demographic statistics can hide or suppress the impact of military aggression and invasion on migration. As demonstrated by the fact that Iraqis are now the largest Arab immigrant group in the United States, the movement of bodies is not infrequently the result of violent displacement. The focus on the receiving country's numbers can also obscure movement in the other direction: important to the Southwest Asia and North Africa (SWANA) region and its context of migration is the more than 2.5 million US military personnel (Wenger, O'Connell and Cottrell 2018) and countless expatriates who have moved there in the past two decades, not as migrants but largely as agents of US empire and its enterprises. In the next section of this introduction, we describe the dominant model—especially the wave model—that has shaped Arab American studies scholarship on migration, and we explain how the essays included in this part of the reader build on and revise that model to account for the more complex and fluid realities of migration.

The Wave Model and Its Undertow

Scholars of migration from Arab countries to the United States have used the concept of migratory waves to organize their understanding of demographic shifts. They have, thus far, spoken about two waves: pre– and post–World War II (Suleiman 1999); three waves: pre–World War II, post–World War II through 1965, and post-1965 (Fadda 2014; Orfalea 1988); and four waves: the three waves plus a post-1990 wave (Arab American National Museum 2019). These categorizations make sense given the demographic parameters of meaning in migration studies; when deployed, the wave models locate distinct differences in the characteristics of Arab (and Arab world) migrants across historical time. Whether using the two-, three-, or four-wave model, scholars consistently distinguish between the Syrian/Lebanese-dominated early migration (1890–1920)—which also included smaller numbers of Palestinians, Yemenis, Assyrians, and Chaldeans—that was halted by immigration quotas in the 1920s and the much more varied migrations that came later. The early group is portrayed overall as of peasant origin, not highly educated, initially mostly male, and predominantly Christian, with smaller numbers of Muslims and Druze. After a slowdown lasting some fifty years beginning in the mid-1920s, as evidenced in US immigration statistics, later migration became not only larger in number but also far more diverse in terms of countries of origin, education levels, and religious affiliations, and it is characterized by family movement, as US law currently promotes. Although such broad-brush-stroke characterizations can be useful analytically, we are also interested in scholarship that complicates and unpacks the gaps overlooked in them.

A migration studies accounting of who, from where, how many, when, and why—a system of knowing that derives from state efforts to categorize humans monolithically by "stock," "race," and, later, nation-state as well as from historic efforts to preserve religious hegemonies—is perhaps baseline material for studying diasporic groups, yet it conveys the false notion that human movement is a unidirectional, decontextualized, complete, and lateral process of detached bodily, as opposed to lived and embodied, transfer. Although accounting methods have a place, they are only a starting point and can operate in deceivingly fixed ways. Bodies move back and forth, bodies move around, and in each place bodies are contextually situated. Bodies are also clothed and host subjectivities that may be allied with multiple sites of belonging and multiple histories from which they draw resilience and power. None of these fundamental aspects of human life is laid visible by an itemization of origins or a singular concept of who someone "is"; such taxonomies privilege rigid ideas of biology, genealogy, sameness, and closure.

Arrival Stories

Narrating in significant detail a particular history of the "first wave" of "Arabic-speaking" immigrants, based on family archives and hundreds of oral history interviews, Alixa Naff's book *Becoming American: The Early Arab Immigrant Experience* (1985) is recognized as a major contribution to the field of Arab American studies. (Naff's inclusive term *Arabic speaking* is intended to encompass all persons, Arab and non-Arab, migrating from Arab regions.) Naff's account (an excerpt of which is given as chapter 7 in this reader) describes male and female "pioneers" who were hard working, independent-minded, and highly mobile; they toiled long hours as shopkeepers and peddlers who spread across the United States in trade networks that were organized by webs of suppliers. Naff argues that these admirable traits and the interactions with native-born whites afforded by the peddling occupation forged the social and economic assimilation of Arab immigrants into American culture and society. Though she pays attention to female peddlers and states that "75 to 80 percent of the women peddled during the pioneer years" (178), she left for further study an analysis of differences between male and female peddlers in a society organized hierarchically by gender, such as that of the United States, as well as of the settler colonialist assumptions behind the use of the term *pioneer*. Scholars have offered many critical expansions of Naff's important work, including by more critically examining the lives of women, placing peddling in its social context, recognizing other occupational patterns held by Arab immigrants, and highlighting the ways in which Naff's framework evidences conformity to dominant assimilationist and heteronormative modes of thinking.

The rise of feminist and queer critiques brought about new explorations and a rethinking of the early wave of Arab migration (Gualtieri 2004; Karem Albrecht 2016; Khater 2001; Shakir 1997; Tawil 2022). Scholars delving more deeply into peddling as an occupation for women observe that women tended to work locally, owing largely to family obligations, whereas men often traveled great distances and that women's peddling shifted power relations within the family. In her contribution to this part of the reader (chapter 8), Charlotte Karem Albrecht demonstrates how Naff deployed liberal multicultural frameworks in her discussion of Arab immigrants by promoting gender and sexual normativities and a commitment to capitalism (see also Karem Albrecht 2016); Karem Albrecht interprets this as an effort to prove that Syrians met the contemporaneous standards of whiteness. She argues that social workers and reformers viewed female peddling as an offense to white middle-class norms of female domesticity and ideals of the good wife; for this deviation (perhaps not solely) from hegemonic ideals, Arab women peddlers were othered by dominant whites.

Assimilation and Incorporation Stories

The focus in early scholarship, such as Naff's, on Arab Americans as highly mobile entrepreneurs tends to obscure the location of Arab Americans within the intersecting social class and racial structures of US American society at the time, making it seem as if they lived and worked independently of those structures, an approach that gives power to the story of assimilation by capital accumulation and cultural contact. Greater attention to social class structures helps us to consider different conclusions concerning Arab Americans' "assimilation." For example, Arab Americans fit nicely into what Edna Bonacich (1973) calls "middleman minorities," groups who occupy a liminal position between dominant and subordinate groups that renders them capable of trading with both. Although they may share some of the traits of assimilation, middleman minorities are always to some degree marginal. This positionality, in turn, makes them easier to vilify and cast out, as needed, by those in power. Other scholars—Eric Hooglund (1987), Akram Khater and Zoe Avery (2017), Evelyn Shakir (1997), and Matthew Jaber Stiffler (2010) among them—locate Arab Americans as blue-collar workers within the US American class structure, laboring in the textile, canning, and auto industries, in corporate agriculture, and in shipping. For example, Lebanese Muslims were drawn to Dearborn, Michigan, early in the twentieth century by the Ford auto industry (Abraham and Shryock 2000), and Yemenis worked for decades as farm laborers in California (Kelley 1986) and as ship captains and crew on the Great Lakes (Howell and Albaneh 2019). A significant body of work has also elaborated on the precarious space inhabited by the early generation of Arab Americans in the US American racial structure (Beydoun 2018; Gualtieri 2009; Haney López 2006; Tehranian 2009), particularly concerning the rights and privileges they were and were not accorded by US policies and practices. Sarah M. A. Gualtieri's contribution to part three of the reader (chapter 14) details Arab Americans' positioning in relation to whiteness and their struggles to be read as eligible for naturalization. Louise Cainkar has argued that extant scholarship has insufficiently addressed Arab American positionality vis-à-vis nonwhiteness. She notes, "While they must have observed the constraints and privileges of race, we know little about how Arabs understood their structural position in relation to groups more broadly structurally excluded, such as African Americans, Latinos, or Harlem's Bengalis" (2018, 34). Cainkar challenges the "first-wave" model premise that Arab Americans' success is owing mainly to their hard work, determination, and social capital. Although such resources are important, the argument implies that other groups did not succeed because they lacked these qualities, which plays into the meritocracy logics of white supremacy. It is not inconsequential that the male peddlers' freedom of movement across the country, which Naff describes in fine detail, was a privilege granted under white supremacy that was systematically denied to ethnic and racial groups who did not benefit from proximity to whiteness. Nor is it meaningless that all groups, white and nonwhite, had some awareness of this privilege as well as of its boundaries, a topic addressed by Karem Albrecht in chapter 8 as she describes the "otherness" of transient peddling. Uncovering the complexities that contextualize the lives of and possibilities for the earliest group of Arab Americans does the work Gualtieri and Pauline Homsi Vinson (2018) call for in their special issue on Arab Americans for *Amerasia* by moving beyond the concerns of a simple wave model of immigration.

We acknowledge that migrants do form, as the literature has demonstrated, communities (all of which are not the same) based in likenesses and shared histories, yet these communities are neither strictly mirrors of the homeland nor blank-slate vehicles of assimilation; they are deeply shaped not only by social class but also by their context of reception (Portes and Rumbaut 2016). For example, Nadine Naber explores in chapter 2 of this reader the ways in which Arab American communities create idealized notions of Arabness in order to establish their internal integrity, highlight their differences from dominant groups that oppress them, and affirm their dignity in a political climate of policing and defamation. Yet these efforts framed by idealized constructions can have punitive outcomes as they reify ideas of biological purity, rely on heteropatriarchal norms, deploy simple us/them dichotomies that are themselves a product of taxonomies of the state, and lose some of the flexibility that characterizes culture in Arab countries of origin. In other words, the construction of "who we are" creates its own outsiders, a subject addressed in this part both by Umayyah Cable, who examines the impacts of these idealized constructions on claims of authenticity that are mediated by proximity to the homeland, and by Charlotte Karem Albrecht, who confronts the heternormative and scholarly silences such constructions impose. In sum, communities can and do develop internal hegemonies shaped by their social and political contexts. We also recognize that these communities are not frozen in time, place, or capacities to engage others, that they are altered by generations and changing social contexts, and that they may not be the sole communities of meaning for individuals. Migrants are, do, and have done so much more than the concepts of ethnic group or community can communicate, an observation we build on in part three of the reader.

Complicating Movement Stories

Arab American studies scholarship has also complicated the movement stories that characterized earlier work in the field, particularly in terms of the fluidity and multiple histories of transnational migrations as well as the benefits of conceiving of conquest and colonialism in broader terms. Expanding on Naff's depiction of migrant routes across the Atlantic and the intermediaries in Europe who guided them, Rana Razek (2018) and Sarah Gualtieri (2020) have explored circuits of migration, for example, of Arabs who wound their way to the United States through Mexico and other parts of Central and South America. Akram Khater (2005), in this part of the reader, engages Arab emigrant narratives of departure, pointing out that such narratives become socially reproduced and may at times assume the form of institutional myth, a topic also addressed by Madeline Otis Campbell's work on Iraqis in this part. Khater also critiques the static notion of migration as unidirectional, lateral, and complete. Instead, he explores the repeated movements of Syrian/Lebanese migrants to and from their homelands and other places, and he demonstrates the ways in which *muhajireen* (emigrants) returning to their points of departure provoked fundamental changes "over there." Likewise, Carol W. N. Fadda demonstrates in chapter 11 how post-1990 Arab American literature disrupts the simple binary of "here" and "there," arguing (quoting Hammad 2005) that "over there is over here" (p. 166) and advocating for a dynamic and fluid model of transnational belonging. In her larger project, Fadda argues that Arab American authors and artists have been at the forefront of charting "new pathways for Arab American articulations" (Fadda-Conrey 2014, 19) of US belonging and citizenship that are transnational, transcultural, antiessentialist, and antihegemonic.

Camila Pastor describes the term *mahjar* as a "space of migration, diasporic homeland, [and] dwelling in movement" (2017, 2). In drawing attention to migration as a "space" and a "dwelling in movement," Pastor echoes contemporary scholarship that broadens focus beyond a static notion of reception and instead theorizes migration as a rich, fluid, and constantly evolving context that shapes migrants' experiences well beyond a simple move from one country to another. In short, this scholarship "reconceptualizes movement as central, rather than marginal, to human sociality" (2017, 10). Scholars of Arabs in the Latinx Americas have sought to situate "*mahjar* mobilities" in relation to the projects of nation-state formation as well as global economic shifts spurred by industrialization, both of which were shaped by colonialism (Alfaro-Velcamp 2007; Pastor 2017; Tawil 2018). In so doing, they theorize migration between the "Middle East" and the Americas as a more fluid and reciprocal "transnational public sphere," attending also to the "factors that propelled migration *within* the Americas" (Gualtieri 2020, 145, emphasis in original) and cultivating what Lily Pearl Balloffet, building on others, calls "South–South circuits" (2017, 5–6).

Led by scholarship on Arabs and Muslims in the Latinx Americas, understandings of migration within Arab American studies also benefit from an expanded conception of modernity and settler colonialism that extends from the early-modern conquest of the Americas to late nineteenth- and early twentieth-century French and British colonization of the SWANA region. This broader conceptualization of conquest and colonialism can uncover a more complex and intertwined history between Arabs, Muslims, and the Americas, as the essays in this reader do. Ella Shohat argues (in chapter 4) that the Spanish conquest of the Americas was deeply informed by ideas and practices that guided the Reconquista—territorial conquests, forced conversions, and expulsions (of Muslims and Jews). The "two 1492s"—Shohat's phrase to recognize both the Spanish Reconquista context and the context of the birth of settler colonialism in the Americas—laid the "ground for colonialist racism" (p. 87) that weaves together the shared histories of Arabs, Muslims, and Jews in Iberia and the histories of the Indigenous, nonwhite, and non-Christian peoples of the Americas and the Caribbean. More recent US efforts to limit Arab and Muslim migration and naturalization (Cainkar 2020) also find precedent in this framework. Daniel König recounts legal rulings issued beginning in 1493 that demonstrate "the Spanish Crown made great efforts to keep Muslims out of South America as soon as its discovery had taken place" (2018, 227). He also provides evidence that in addition to "these legal and practical measures taken to prevent the spread of Islam in the colonies and to extirpate all possible Islamic remnants, the colonists also introduced anti-Islamic traditions to the colonies, thus creating an ideological bulwark against Islam" (230). Christina Civantos explores in chapter 9 the "ways in which the relationship between Spain and the Arab world was transferred to the Americas" (p. 145) and continues to be invoked by South Americans of Spanish as well as Arab lineage, especially in "the figure of the Arab gaucho" (p. 145). In chapter 37 of part six, Hisham Aidi elaborates on the ways in which these shared histories are today being reclaimed and mobilized as liberatory imaginaries in Latin America, the Caribbean, the United States, Europe, and Africa. A cultural "cross-fertilization" among Arabs, Muslims, Africans, African Americans, and Latinx Americans resulting from global human flows is invoked in multiple ways: through the figure of the Moor, the lyrics of hip hop, the Arab "cultural invasion" of Latin America, and claims of membership in a transnational *umma*, "challenging or 'exiting' the white West" (p. 487) (see also Logroño Narbona, Pinto, and Karam 2015; Majid 2009).

World War Stories and the Submerged Wave

As a plethora of research in the field describes, the early flow of migration from Arab regions to the United States was all but halted by the late 1920s owing to US immigration quotas implemented in legislation intended to favor northern Europeans. The Depression and World War II substantially paused cross-Atlantic migration, at least to the United States, after which Arab migration resumed at comparatively low levels relative to before 1920 and after 1965. Immigration records show that there was a substantial flow of Arab migration between Latin America and the United States during World War I; indeed, owing to the volatilities of war, it was the primary route of Arab entry to the United States at the time (Cainkar 1988; see also Gualtieri 2020). Whether this was or was not the case during World War II and why or why not remain to be explored. Scholarly accounts of Arab migration in the period after the end of World War II through 1965 speak of a broader range of countries of origin (e.g., the beginning of Egyptian migration), of Arab American World War II veterans sponsoring their spouses' migrations (especially meaningful for groups such as Palestinians that were once largely male), and of Arab students arriving in significant numbers for university study (meaningful for the ideas they engendered), a group that Michael Suleiman and Baha Abu-Laban refer to as "neosojourners" (1989, 3), indicating their bounded temporal intentions. Indeed, a goal of many of the Arab students arriving in the United States at this time was to complete a university education and either return to their homelands or seek better opportunities elsewhere, even though many ended up staying. In addition, a few thousand Palestinians were admitted under refugee legislation of the 1950s (mainly accessible to Palestinians who lost land in the Jerusalem area). Scholars note that in general people who arrived during this period had higher levels of education and greater religious diversity and were more middle class than those who preceded them (see, e.g., Abu-Laban and Suleiman 1989). Although national origin quotas remained in place during this period, legislation in 1952 opened US naturalization to "nonwhites," removed the Asia barred zone, and implemented the recruitment of highly educated migrants for skills needed in the United States, the spur to Egyptian migration. In quantitative terms, the two decades after World War II were more significant for migration from formerly barred countries, such as by persons in East and South Asia, than from Arab countries. A migration of highly skilled workers especially from India and Pakistan altered in major ways the demographic, socioeconomic, and cultural character of the US Muslim population, heretofore mainly African American and Arab. During this era, Arabs were migrating not only to the United States but also to other destinations where they had established communities, especially across the

Americas. They were also recruited as "guest workers" for European postwar rebuilding efforts—as in the significant postcolonial *maghrebi* (North African) migration to France, among other European destinations—and for the development of emerging oil-industry-based economies in the Arab Gulf States (Cainkar 2013). With regard to the United States, a disinterested demographic accounting of this time period might simply be satisfied to note the smaller influx but greater variety of immigrants from SWANA. Attending to the fuller complexities of migration stories, however, requires the consideration of multiple points of entry, the multiplicity of reasons for migrating, and the unanticipated realities that reroute circuits of migration.

Imperialist/Colonialist Pressures on Migration

The period between the end of World War II and the mid-1960s not only had the lowest numbers of Arab migrants relative to other periods but is also the least studied by scholars of Arab Americans. Because the wave model is driven by quantification, this period's location in that paradigm is ambiguous: Suleiman (1999) collapses it into the first wave, and other scholars consider it a separate wave (Arab American National Museum 2019; Fadda 2014; Orfalea 1988). Although relatively small in number, Arab migrants who came during this period are notable for the expansiveness of the ideas they embodied, pan-Arab, anticolonial, and anti-imperial, and for their deployment of national and pan-Arab identities that expanded senses of belonging beyond the parochial. This change from the local and religious identities common to the earlier migrants to a more expansive sense of political identity is no surprise when one considers all that had occurred in the region since the 1920s—Arab nationalist independence movements and formal nation-state independence; the rise of Nasserism, Ba'athism, and socialism; European carving up of the former Ottoman Empire and colonial (mandate) rule; the establishment of Lebanon, Syria, and Transjordan as nation-states; the creation of Israel in Palestine with its attendant population expulsions and land confiscations; and US and European exploitation of regional oil resources, to name only some events. According to Suleiman and Abu-Laban (1989), the earliest Arab immigrants sought mainly to make money in the United States in order to return home (whether they did so or not); post–World War II migrants, in contrast, sought to become participants in US American democracy. Although we know from hindsight that American imperial priorities in the region (oil and Israel) would block any meaningful participation of Arabs in American politics except with regard to domestic issues, we have little detailed research on how Arab Americans actually experienced American democracy at the time. Furthermore, the literature discussing this period speaks mainly about male immigrants, leaving the character of female migration and the lives of women understudied (see, e.g., Abu-Laban and Suleiman 1989). Overall, the numerical majority of Arab Americans at this time were the second-generation children of earlier Lebanese and Syrian immigrants, of whom Naff writes: "If the political events in the post–World War II Arab world had not reactivated Arab immigration and provoked descendants of the first wave into an Arab identity, they might have assimilated themselves out of existence" (p. 135). However, as noted earlier, assimilating to whiteness can be achieved only through participating in racist/classist/gendered structures of the state, a critique to which we return in part three.

Post-1965 Migration and Changing Scholarship

Changes in US immigration law in tandem with war, occupation, political oppression, structural inequality, economic dislocations, population growth, and limited access to socioeconomic mobility in the Arab region substantially altered both the size and the demographic composition of migration from Arab countries to the United States in the last three decades of the twentieth century and into the twenty-first. The US Immigration and Nationality Act of 1965 abolished country quotas and prioritized family reunification as the basis for immigration, providing immigrant visas upon approved application to "immediate relatives" of US citizens, including spouses, parents, and unmarried children younger than twenty-one, and, through a priority system subject to annual country limits, to other qualified "sponsored" family members as well as to immediate relatives of permanent residents. The US Refugee Act of 1980 brought US refugee and asylee policy in line with United Nations definitions, eventually altering (along with the end of the Cold War) the US practice of favoring persons seeking to leave communist countries. Since Palestinians are recognized under a separate refugee regime than all others, the United Nations Relief and Works Agency rather than the United Nations High Commissioner for Refugees, they have been unable to benefit from US refugee and asylee policy, whereas large numbers of Iraqis as well as thousands of Syrians, Somalis, and Egyptians (as asylees) have.

Scholarship on Arab Americans in the 1970s, 1980s, and early 1990s was preoccupied with the demographic changes brought on by post–World War II/post-1965 migration from Arab countries and their meaning for Arab America, as signaled in the titles of collected volumes published in this period, Abu-Laban and Suleiman's *Arab Americans: Continuity and Change* (1989), Ernest McCarus's *The Development of Arab-American Identity* (1994), and Suleiman's *Arabs in America: Building a New Future* (1999). In a wide range of very meaningful ways, Arab America was shifting culturally and politically. Equally compelling to scholars were documenting and explaining the persistent upsurge of open anti-Arab racism beginning in 1967—although not everyone called it racism at the time—as well as the parallel rise in hate-crime attacks, stereotyping, government surveillance, election-cycle political shaming, media silencing, and broad censorship. (See the general introduction to this reader for more on scholarship and censorship during this period.) The continuity and intensification of these hostile conditions eventually shifted the scholarly focus away from migration waves, demography, hyphenated identities, and bounded communities and toward a full reckoning of Arab American circumstances and their inextricable connection to US global imperial designs. The recognition set in that "here" and "there" were inseparable and that domestic US conditions for Arabs (and Muslims) were a co-constitutive element of the global project of white supremacy. This awareness in turn fertilized scholarship on the ways in which Arabs and Muslims had for centuries been cast by this project as inferior, othered peoples across wide swaths of the globe (Aidi 2003; Grosfoguel and Mielants 2006; König 2018; Said 1978; Shohat 2013). In sum, boundaries of geography, history, and race that had characterized earlier scholarship were being shattered.

Current scholarship on Arab migration necessarily moves beyond the binary of host and home societies because it recognizes that the histories of these places are linked. The scholarship included in this reader builds on earlier research and invites us to think about migration beyond a unidirectional wave model. For example, Akram Khater in this part weaves together the connected histories of Arabs in different parts of the Americas; Hisham Aidi in part six explores the Moorish Atlantic and the ties that bind global South diasporas in the West; and Ella Shohat in part one demonstrates the line of continuity between 1492 and today. So, too, scholarship on Arab American identities attends to more supple and complex understandings than binaric notions of hyphenated or ancestral/former and adopted/current identities permits. It examines the ways in which the transnational and postnational senses of identity and belonging held by Arab Americans are cultivated ideologically, imaginatively, and situationally, whether through literature, organizations, relationships, solidarities, or movement to and from the "homeland." This scholarship not only helps us understand who Arab Americans are, when they came to the Americas, and what they did after arriving there, as typical wave-model migration stories do, but also expands the ways we think about migration more generally. The framework of "moving bodies" helps us understand migration processes as situated in historical, economic, and ideological circumstances and as transformative exchanges that are not fixed in either space or time.

Works Cited

Abraham, Nabeel, and Andrew Shryock, eds. 2000. *Arab Detroit: From Margin to Mainstream*. Detroit: Wayne State Univ. Press.

Abu-Laban, Baha, and Michael Suleiman, eds. 1989. *Arab Americans: Continuity and Change*: Belmont, MA: AAUG Press. Printed earlier as Suleiman, Michael, and Baha Abu-Laban, eds. 1989. "Arab Americans: Continuity and Change." Special issue of *Arab Studies Quarterly* 11, nos. 2–3.

Aidi, Hisham D. 2003. "The Moorish Atlantic: Moors, Aztecs, and the Invention of the Americas." Paper prepared for the seminar "Modernity and Its Others," taught by Paul Gilroy, Sociology Department, Yale Univ., New Haven, CT, May.

Alfaro-Velcamp, Theresa. 2007. *So Far from Allah, so Close to Mexico: Middle Eastern Immigrants in Modern Mexico.* Austin: Univ. of Texas Press.

Arab American National Museum, with Randa Kayyali. 2019. *Arab Americans: History, Culture, and Contributions.* Dearborn, MI: Arab American National Museum.

Balloffet, Lily Pearl. 2017. "From the Pampa to the Mashriq: Arab-Argentine Philanthropy Networks." *Mashriq & Mahjar* 4, no. 1: 4–28.

Beydoun, Khaled A. 2018. *American Islamophobia: Understanding the Roots and Rise of Fear.* Berkeley: Univ. of California Press.

Bonacich, Edna. 1973. "A Theory of Middleman Minorities." *American Sociological Review* 38, no. 5: 583–94.

Cainkar, Louise. 1988. "Palestinian Women in the United States: Coping with Tradition, Change, and Alienation." PhD diss., Northwestern Univ.

———. 2013. "Global Arab World Migrations and Diasporas." *Arab Studies Journal* 11, no. 1: 122–61.

———. 2018. "Fluid Terror Threat: A Genealogy of the Racialization of Arab, Muslim, and South Asian Americans." In "Arab/Americas: Locations & Iterations," edited by Sarah M. A. Gualtieri and Pauline Homsi Vinson. Special Issue of *Amerasia Journal* 44, no. 1: 27–60.

———. 2020. "The Muslim Ban and Trump's War on Immigration." *Middle East Report* 294 (Spring). At https://merip.org/2020/06/the-muslim-ban-and-trumps-war-on-immigration-2/.

Fadda-Conrey, Carol W. N. 2014. *Contemporary Arab-American Literature: Transnational Reconfigurations of Citizenship and Belonging.* New York: New York Univ. Press.

Grosfoguel, Ramón, and Eric Mielants. 2006. "The Long-Durée Entanglement between Islamophobia and Racism in the Modern/Colonial Capitalist/Patriarchal World-System: An Introduction." *Human Architecture* 5, no. 1: 1–12.

Gualtieri, Sarah M. A. 2004. "Gendering the Chain Migration Thesis: Women and Syrian Transatlantic Migration, 1878–1924." *Comparative Studies of South Asia, Africa, and the Middle East* 24, no. 1: 69–81.

———. 2009. *Between Arab and White: Race Ethnicity in the Early Syrian American Diaspora.* Berkeley: Univ. of California Press.

———. 2020. *Arab Routes: Pathways to Syrian California.* Stanford, CA: Stanford Univ. Press.

Gualtieri, Sarah M. A., and Pauline Homsi Vinson. 2018. Introduction to "Arab/Americas: Locations & Iterations," edited by Sarah M. A. Gualtieri and Pauline Homsi Vinson. Special issue of *Amerasia Journal* 44, no. 1: vii–xxi.

Hammad, Suheir. 2005. "first writing since." In *Shattering the Stereotypes: Muslim Women Speak Out*, edited by Fawzia Afzal-Khan, 90–94. Northampton, MA: Olive Branch Press.

Haney López, Ian. 2006. *White by Law: The Legal Construction of Race.* New York: New York Univ. Press.

Hooglund, Eric. 1987. *Crossing the Waters: Arabic Speaking Immigrants in the US.* Washington, DC: Smithsonian Institution Press.

Howell, Sally, and Gallal Albaneh. 2019. "The Untold History of Yemeni Sailors on the Great Lakes." *All Things Considered*, Michigan Radio, NPR. At https://www.michiganradio.org/post/untold-history-yemeni-sailors-great-lakes.

Karem Albrecht, Charlotte. 2016. "An Archive of Difference: Syrian Women, the Peddling Economy, and U.S. Social Welfare, 1880–1935." *Gender & History* 28, no. 1: 127–49.

Kelley, Ron. 1986. "The Yemenis of the San Joaquin." *MERIP* 139 (Mar.–Apr.). At https://merip.org/1986/03/the-yemenis-of-the-san-joaquin/.

Khater, Akram. 2001. *Inventing Home: Emigration, Gender, and the Middle Class in Lebanon, 1770–1920*. New ed. Berkeley: Univ. of California Press.

———. 2005. "Becoming 'Syrian' in America: A Global Geography of Ethnicity and Nation." *Diaspora* 14, nos. 2–3: 299–331.

Khater, Akram, and Zoe Avery. 2017. "Complicating the Lebanese Peddler Myth." *Khayrallah Center for Lebanese Diaspora Studies News*, May 10. At https://lebanesestudies.news.chass.ncsu.edu/2017/05/10/complicating-the-lebanese-peddler-myth/2017/.

König, Daniel G. 2018. "The Making of a Christian Atlantic: The Role of Islam in the Early Modern Emergence of 'the West.'" In *Entre mers—Outre-mer: Spaces, Modes, and Agents of Indo-Mediterranean Connectivity*, edited by Nikolas Jaspert and Sebastian Kolditz, 219–46. Heidelberg, Germany: Heidelberg Univ.

Logroño Narbona, María del Mar, Paulo G. Pinto, and John Tofik Karam, eds. 2015. *Crescent over Another Horizon: Islam in Latin America, the Caribbean, and Latino USA*. Austin: Univ. of Texas Press.

Majid, Anouar. 2009. *We Are All Moors: Ending Centuries of Crusades against Muslims and Other Minorities*. Minneapolis: Univ. of Minnesota Press.

McCarus, Ernest, ed. 1994. *The Development of Arab-American Identity*. Ann Arbor: Univ. of Michigan Press.

Naff, Alixa. 1985. *Becoming American: The Early Arab Immigrant Experience*. Carbondale: Southern Illinois Univ. Press.

Orfalea, Gregory. 1988. *Before the Flames: A Quest for the History of Arab Americans*. Austin: Univ. of Texas Press.

Pastor, Camila. 2017. *The Mexican Mahjar: Transnational Maronites, Jews, and Arabs under the French Mandate*. Austin: Univ. of Texas Press.

Portes, Alejandro, and Ruben Rumbaut. 2016. *Immigrant America*. Los Angeles: Univ. of California Press.

Razek, Rana. 2018. "Trails and Fences." In "Arab/Americas: Locations & Iterations," edited by Sarah M. A. Gualtieri and Pauline Homsi Vinson. Special Issue of *Amerasia Journal* 44, no. 1: 105–26.

Said, Edward. 1978. *Orientalism*. New York: Vintage Books.

Shakir, Evelyn. 1997. *Bint Arab: Arab and Arab American Women in the United States*. Westport, CT: Praeger.

Shohat, Ella. 2013. "The Sephardi-Moorish Atlantic: Between Orientalism and Occidentalism." In *Between the Middle East and the Americas: The Cultural Politics of Diaspora*, edited by Evelyn Alsultany and Ella Shohat, 42–64. Ann Arbor: Univ. of Michigan Press.

Stiffler, Matthew Jaber. 2010. "A Brief History of Arab Immigrant Textile Production in the U.S." Arab American National Museum Library & Resource Center.

At https://www.academia.edu/802251/A_Brief_History_of_Arab_Immigrant_Textile_Production_in_the_US.

Suleiman, Michael W., ed. 1999. *Arabs in America: Building a New Future*. Philadelphia: Temple Univ. Press.

Suleiman, Michael, and Baha Abu-Laban. 1989. Introduction to "Arab Americans: Continuity and Change," edited by Michael Suleiman and Baha Abu-Laban. Special issue of *Arab Studies Quarterly* 11, nos. 2–3: 1–13.

Tawil, Randa. 2018. "Racial Borderlines." In "Arab/Americas: Locations & Iterations," edited by Sarah M. A. Gualtieri and Pauline Homsi Vinson. Special Issue of *Amerasia Journal* 44, no. 1: 85–104.

———. 2022. "A 'Flying Carpet to Doom': Retracing Gender and Orientalism through the Transnational Journeys of a Syrian Migrant Woman, 1912–1949." *Frontiers* 43.1: 120–44.

Tehranian, John. 2009. *Whitewashed: America's Invisible Middle Eastern Minority*. New York: New York Univ. Press.

Wenger, Jennie W., Caolionn O'Connell, and Linda Cottrell. 2018. *Examination of Recent Deployment Experience across the Services and Components*. Santa Monica, CA: RAND. At https://www.rand.org/pubs/research_reports/RR1928.html.

7

The Early Arab Immigrant Experience

ALIXA NAFF

Arabic-speaking people began emigrating from the Ottoman province of Syria, which included the administrative district of Mount Lebanon, to the United States in sufficient numbers to form communities in the last quarter of the nineteenth century. Like the millions who left their homes in Europe, they were drawn to the New World by the changing character of the United States in that period. While huge tracts of land remained to be cultivated in the West and Southwest, agrarian interests began to compete with burgeoning industrial interests in the East. Among other problems, both interests faced mounting labor shortages.

Even though their numbers were small relative to the large European groups, distinct Syrian communities were identifiable by the mid-1890s. In the next ten or fifteen years, these communities would proliferate throughout the nation—the result of pack peddling, which became the immigrant occupation of most Syrians.

Arabic-speaking immigrants, now estimated at roughly 2 million, arrived in the United States in two major waves. The first, or pre–World War II wave, is distinguished from the second, or post–World War II wave, in a number of ways. The first wave overwhelmingly consisted of unsophisticated village farmers or artisans; they were relatively poor but not destitute, and they were not well schooled, if at all. The initial aspirations of these pioneers who emigrated before about 1910 did not exceed the hope of earning as much money in as short a time as possible and returning home wealthier and prouder. The second wave had, and continues to have, a very large component of educated, bilingual, politicized, and nationalistic emigrants. Having originated in numerous Arab nations that gained their independence in the aftermath of World War II, members of this second wave identified themselves as Arabs. The United States they sought had filled its borders, experienced two world wars, and become the world's leading industrial, scientific, technological, and military power; thus, this second wave experienced a radically different immigration experience than their Syrian predecessors.

How many Syrians immigrated to the United States before World War II? How many were Christians, and how many Muslims and Druze? From which strata of their society were they drawn? How many were skilled, how many were literate? All these questions have no reliable answers. Fragments of information provided by the immigrants themselves merely confound estimates in published sources and cast doubt on official data.

Immigration and census statistics are unreliable for several reasons. For example, before 1899 immigrants from the eastern Mediterranean were recorded as arriving from "Turkey in Asia." Moreover, classification of immigrants by the Bureau of Immigration did not include religion or national identity. Emigrating, as the Syrians did, from a multinational empire where country of origin did not correspond with national identity and where the

Excerpt from Alixa Naff, "The Early Arab Immigrant Experience," in *The Development of Arab American Identity*, edited by Ernest McCarus (Ann Arbor: Univ. of Michigan Press, 1994), 23–36. Full references in the original notes were converted to author-date citations in the text and notes here, and a works cited list was added. Reprinted with corrections and press style changes for consistency throughout the volume by permission of the University of Michigan Press. A copy of the book may be purchased at https://www.press.umich.edu/13258/development_of_arab_american_identity.

latter was as much determined by religion as by language and culture, Syrians were not distinguished from other Ottoman subjects.

However, in 1899, when immigration officials became aware that most of these Ottoman subjects were from Syria, they added a "Syrian" classification. This gave the Arabic-speaking immigrants a way of identifying themselves in a land teaming with immigrants from different ethnic origins. By World War I official statistics show that about 100,000 immigrated, and by World War II [Arabic-speaking] immigrants and their descendants numbered about 206,000 (see Naff 1985, 105–17).

Lacking accurate data that would identify immigrants by faith, scholars estimate that 90 to 95 percent of the pre–World War II Syrian immigrants were Christians from Mount Lebanon. The rest were Muslims and Druze. The latter were so few that they hardly warranted passing mention in the literature on Syrians at the turn of the century (see Hitti 1924; Houghton 1911; Miller [1904] 1969). Among them were a few thousand Palestinians.

In the United States, most of these immigrants, including many Palestinians, called themselves and were referred to as Syrians until the independence of Syria and Lebanon after World War II. Rarely in their homeland would they have had to refer to themselves as Syrians, even more rarely as Arabs, although they were proud of being Arab and of their Arab heritage. The Syrian and Arab references were cultural rather than nationalistic since there was no independent Syrian political entity to which nationalism could be tied. An incipient political component appeared in the identity of some Christians from Mount Lebanon after France established itself as the mandatory power over Ottoman Syria in 1920. Immigrants and their descendants debated whether to call themselves Syrian American or Lebanese American.

The most meaningful and reflexive identity factors that Syrians used among themselves were family name, religion, and place of origin—factors that were a source of factionalization and community fragmentation in the homeland as well as the new land. How the Syrians identified themselves in the United States, however, did not seem to interfere with their ability to assimilate.

Migration

Historians generally agree that in the late nineteenth century, Mount Lebanon was not a place to flee from. In the words of Albert H. Hourani, the period from 1861 to 1915 was "a period of increasing prosperity" (1954, 33). Philip K. Hitti, a native of Lebanon, noted that the people of Mount Lebanon "enjoyed a period of cultural flourish and economic prosperity and achieved a state of security and stability unattained by any Ottoman province, European or Asian. . . . It came to be acknowledged as the best governed, the most prosperous, peaceful and contented country in the Near East" (1967, 447; see also Chevalier 1968, 220, and Ruppin 1966, 272). Moreover, it enjoyed a great deal of autonomy relative to its neighbors. If there were any push factors affecting Syrian emigration, they were more evident in the harsher political and economic conditions in Syria proper. Nevertheless, far fewer emigrants, even Christians, left Syrian villages and towns.

In fact, the immigrants were attracted to the United States by its accelerating urbanization and industrialization, which required a greater workforce than was available in their country in the last quarter of the nineteenth century. Labor, therefore, was recruited from abroad by agents of industry, steamship lines, and even the less-populated western states and territories. As a result, millions of immigrants flooded to the country, triggering a virulent anti-alien movement before and especially after World War I. In response, Congress passed a series of restrictive immigration laws culminating in the Johnson-Reed Act of 1924. Syrian immigration under this quota system was restricted to one hundred annually until the repeal of the act in 1965.

The most reliable data on what triggered a mass migration of Syrians to the United States [consist of] the testimony of turn-of-the-century immigrants in interviews conducted in numerous communities in the United States and Canada.[1] Almost unanimously, they stated that they

1. Conducted by Alixa Naff during a major research project on Arab Americans, 1962 and 1980, under a grant from the National Endowment for the Humanities and included in the Naff Arab-American Collection, Smithsonian Institution, Washington, DC.

came on a two- or three-year sojourn to make money and return to the homeland, where most had left their families, to lead better lives, and to elevate their family status. They did not, they said, leave because of religious persecution or economic oppression. At that time, those who came in search of the lofty ideals of liberty and democracy were the rare exceptions.

Later, the pioneers would be joined by others. While making money continued to be the dominant attraction, some came because of personal problems at home or to escape military conscription or simply to join relatives. After World War I, they migrated because of the hardships, especially famine, that they had endured during the war.

The Immigrants

The way to the United States was opened by tradesmen and artisans who were encouraged to exhibit their wares at the Philadelphia Centennial Exposition in 1876 by the Ottoman sultan, Abdul Hamid II, a trade-minded reform tyrant. Perhaps it was these trailblazers who returned to spread the word of easy wealth or "gold in the streets." Soon, glowing letters from early adventurers describing undreamed of wealth began to draw more immigrants. The exodus was further fueled by returning villagers in serge suits and shined leather shoes, sporting gold watch fobs. Faris N., after talking with visiting cousins and learning how much could be earned in trade, left with thirty-one men and two women in 1895. That same year Mike H. left his village with seventy-two friends and relatives. Similarly large groups left from other villages, inviting the comparison with a gold rush.

The pioneers were mainly young, single, and adventurous men. Some single women and some married men and women joined them. More often than not, the men, farmers and their sons, had to augment the family income by engaging in some kind of craft or trade. It was not uncommon for a family, who considered the costs of the voyage as an investment, to borrow money or to mortgage land to send a member or two to fulfill its dream of greater wealth and status.

In America

When villagers began to stream into the Syrian port cities of Beirut and Tripoli, there emerged a host of entrepreneurial and often unscrupulous agents to book steamship passage for the unsophisticated travelers who thought they were headed for New York or at least the United States. Many, instead, found themselves in Canada, South and Central America, the Caribbean, and even Australia. Many of them smuggled themselves across Mexican and Canadian borders, making it further difficult to generate accurate demographic data.

New York and the other ports of entry through which the Syrians entered the United States were merely gateways. Generally, [Syrian immigrants] knew their specific destination and what they were going to do when they arrived there. They were going to pack-peddle merchandise from door to door in towns and cities and from farmhouse to farmhouse in the countryside. They pursued its get-rich-quick potential all over the United States. It was the major magnet that drew Syrian immigrants before about 1910. By that year, they had penetrated every state and territory of the country.[2] They covered the American continent in a network of peddling routes that radiated from a network of peddling settlements. Those few who eschewed peddling because they found it too difficult or too demeaning joined the labor force.

Settlements formed around a supplier—generally a veteran peddler who decided to settle down in a well-chosen location. He would then recruit peddlers from his village or from nearby villages. Kin drew kin and villager drew villager so that immigrants were able to group themselves by kinship, religion, sect, or place of origin as they had in the homeland. Subnetworks of settlements whose members were mainly from one village can be traced across more than one state. Immigrants of the Druze faith, an offshoot of Shiʿa Islam, had one or two subnetworks of their own.

2. See table 27, "Destination of Immigrants Admitted to the United States, Fiscal Year 1899 to 1910, Inclusive, by Race of People," 269–92, in US Immigration Commission 1911.

A peddling settlement was an open and fluid community. That is, peddlers came and went as their self-interest dictated. The supplier's settlement was the peddlers' home base and the supplier their acknowledged leader by virtue of their dependence on him. Yet no special title was attached to him; no abject obedience was demanded. He not only supplied merchandise to the peddler on credit but guaranteed credit to uncapitalized recruits to induce them to come to him. He received their mail, banked their money, even frequently godfathered their children. He also served as liaison between them and the host community. The good relations between supplier and peddler were based on the canons of tradition and on mutual economic self-interest.

In the settlements the immigrants were taught the rudiments and tricks of the trade by friends and relatives. For example, they were taught the value of US currency and how to address a woman who answered their knock. "Buy sumthin', Ma'am?" was probably the first English sentence they learned. They also learned how to ask for a place to sleep and some food when they were in the countryside. In general, they initially learned how to survive with only a rudimentary knowledge of the language and customs of the country. Consequently, newcomers could start to earn a living almost on arrival. . . . Peddlers would return to the settlements, as near replicas of the village, to revitalize their spirits after weeks or months on the road.

Immigrants were attracted to peddling because initially it required no capital, advanced training, or English-language skills. Moreover, it suited the Arabs' individualist nature and the immigrants' impermanence. Most important, it yielded quicker wealth than they had hoped for.

Peddling was the most fundamental factor in their assimilation for several reasons. It forced them to learn English quickly because learning English was critical to their success; and success, driven by the age-old native competition for family honor and status, was, in the final analysis, the engine that drove Syrians toward their goal in the United States. Peddling further enabled them to see the country and experience its way of life firsthand. It took them into US homes and raised their aspirations. It spared them the uncertainty of finding factory work, standing in long job lines, and industrial layoffs. It spared them, too, a ghetto mentality. Finally, it provided opportunities for thousands of newcomers.

Peddlers were mobile department stores, even when they peddled on foot, as most did at first. With well-packed suitcases, frequently one in each hand and one on their back, they carried almost anything a housebound urban housewife or isolated farmwife would need or desire. There were ready-made school clothes, men's work clothes, yard goods, linens, toweling, costume jewelry, and much more. There were also such special items as laces, doilies, crocheted tablecloths, embroidered bedspreads, and ribbon-decked dusting caps frequently made by the women in the peddler's family in a kind of settlement cottage industry.

In the notions case, which was the peddlers' primary and constant companion, were all the kinds of notions one would find at a Woolworth's notions counter plus icons, frames, rosaries, etc. If the peddlers' hands were full, the notions case dangled on his chest.

Some peddlers covered half a continent on foot and remained away from the settlement for months; others returned in a week or two, while usually, but not always, women and children remained closer to the settlement.

Peddling was a hazardous occupation. These villagers, accustomed as they were to hardships in their villages, never reckoned on what they would encounter on the road in the United States. Their hardships are preserved in a body of humorous anecdotes that glorify cunning and ingenuity and that acted as a psychological safety valve for their fear, fatigue, and frustration when they told them to each other. Many of the anecdotes deal with the hardships of climate, lack of knowledge of the language, and the difficulties of finding lodging. They tell about frozen extremities, parched throats, relentless heat; of being mired in mud, robbed, beaten; of killings and being lost; and of being chased by farmers with guns and dogs. "How do you tell a dog to go away if it doesn't understand Arabic?," complained an informant. One peddler, articulating the consensus, said that he "endured a lot" but enjoyed this country, and he was "free to make money."

Peddlers did indeed make money. As a whole, they averaged $1,000 annually when the US labor force was averaging about $650 annually. High earnings and unrelenting frugality allowed them to send remittances home, pay debts, and buy fares to bring other family members to the United States. They contributed to US commerce by expanding the market of small-industry products to the most remote areas of the country.

By about 1910, peddling declined as an immigrant occupation. Immigrants had outgrown it, and its services to US consumers were replaced by proliferating department stores and mail-order houses such as Montgomery Ward and Sears Roebuck.

Becoming "American"

When immigrants decided to settle down and make the United States their permanent home, they adhered to the cherished cultural ideal of being in business for one's self. They turned to family businesses in which the whole family participated, even the young. Usually, the home and the store were a staircase or a door apart. Dry goods and grocery stores were most popular, but businesses ran the gamut from banking and wholesaling and manufacturing to movie houses, pool rooms, confectionery stores, and dry cleaning. [Because they had] little or no experience in most of these endeavors, failure was common but not daunting. They simply kept trying until they succeeded. Many immigrants who arrived in the period of peddling's obsolescence and afterward in the 1920s entered the labor force. They were attracted by industry's payment of five dollars for an eight-hour day, which was initiated during the war by the Ford Motor Company and adopted by other manufacturers. This innovation coincided with the influx of Syrian Muslims. Yet many of the men who worked on assembly lines also opened stores, which were operated by their women relatives and children.

The Americanization process advanced most rapidly after World War I. Settlements, generally located in ethnically mixed low-income neighborhoods, ultimately matured into stable communities as immigrants bought homes and acquired middle-class symbols such as home appliances and cars. In general, they followed the middle-class path up the economic and social ladder. Moreover, they adopted the respective regional social attitudes, tastes, and accents and became New Englanders, southerners, midwesterners, etc.

The ethnic institutions that they established—churches, an Arabic-language press, and voluntary associations—not unexpectedly reflected the traditional identity factors and perpetuated the traditional community fragmentation. The first churches were of the Eastern-rite faiths. Most prominent among them were the Maronite, Melkite, and Eastern Orthodox. There was also a Syrian Protestant church. These were built in the early 1890s in New York City, which was the Syrian mother colony and the cultural and economic center. Churches increased slowly and unevenly across the country in the next half century. Nevertheless, vast areas were, and remain, unserved. Syrians in these areas, therefore, attended "American" churches—that is, Roman Catholic and Protestant. This accounts, in large part, for the relatively high percentage of mixed marriages before and after World War I. Syrian identity in these households, even more so in those of their descendants, was consequently diluted.

The accelerating assimilation of Syrians reduced attendance at all Eastern-rite churches. In order to arrest the defection, to reach the non-Arabic-speaking offspring, and to perpetuate the unity of the subgroup, the leaders acknowledged the inevitable. Liturgies were anglicized and shortened, chants were westernized, and choirs replaced cantors.

Americanization of the Maronite and Melkite churches had begun very early because, as affiliates of the Roman Catholic Church, they came under the administrative authority of the church in the United States. Consequently, Maronite and Melkite churches served by their own clergy spread very slowly until their independence from Roman Catholic authority after World War II.

On the other hand, the Eastern Orthodox church turned for guidance in the United States to the Russian Orthodox archdiocese. The latter, in turn, ordained the first Syrian bishop in the United States. A year after his ordination in 1904, he established a cathedral in Brooklyn. Under his leadership, Orthodox churches increased, and many adherents returned to their native faith.

Only in four Muslim communities were mosques known to have been built before World War II. Yet Muslims fulfilled their spiritual obligations without fear of perdition. For Muslims, any uncontaminated place at home or work could be a place to pray. Both Muslims and

Druze immigrants could compensate for lack of consecrated religious institutions by gathering for prayer, reading from holy books, discussing religion, or celebrating religious festivals.

The traditional identity factors prevailed in the Arabic-language press and in the formation of clubs and societies. It was in the United States that Syrians learned to organize around a common purpose or cause. They developed such a propensity for it that at any given time the number of organizations was out of proportion to the number of Syrians in the United States. Most, of course, were short-lived.

Family, religious, and village social clubs proliferated in part to counter the rate of mixed marriages and to maintain the continuity of the subgroup. If these clubs had a central and common theme, it was the underlying one of group solidarity mainly through in-group marriage. They tended, therefore, to be exclusivist. Attempts by the US-born Syrians to change this divisive custom succeeded only after World War II.

Homeland politics played little or no part in the formation of clubs until the French mandatory rule replaced the defunct Ottoman Empire in the former Syrian province in 1920. It was not so much that political clubs multiplied at any noticeably high rate as that the social clubs became embroiled in an identity controversy. France triggered the controversy by granting increased autonomy to the Lebanese, favoring Christian (and particularly Maronite) domination, and laying the foundation for the modern independent state of Lebanon by expanding its territory from Syrian lands, including major port cities. With kin pitted against kin and friend against friend, clubs hotly debated whether to call themselves Syrian or Lebanese American. Maronites formed Phoenician clubs in an effort to tie themselves historically to that ancient civilization and to distance themselves and Lebanon from Arab Syria and from Muslims whose larger population threatened Maronite domination.

An active and highly competitive Arabic-language press was centered in New York City. The impetus for its development was provided by the immigration of a few intellectuals who were graduates, for the most part, of religious and secular schools of higher education in the cities of Syria. It was coincidental and fortuitous that in New York the publishers of newspapers and journals, many of whom had had little or no prior journalistic training or experience, came together with émigré Arab writers and poets in a symbiotic relationship to form an immigrant intelligentsia.

The Syrians' penchant for publishing matched their penchant for organizing clubs and societies. Dailies, weeklies, and monthlies appeared and disappeared regularly between 1892 and 1930. Yet the press was influential and contributed significantly to the Americanization process. From its inception, it explained the US social, economic, and political life to its eager readers, albeit in fairly simple and idealized terms. It tied success to becoming "American" and encouraged and taught good citizenship. In addition, it kept immigrants informed about events in the homeland. Many Syrian immigrants became informed, for the first time, about the society, politics, history, literature, and culture of Arabs in general and of Syrians in particular. Never before had these predominantly village-centered, poorly schooled readers learned so much about their heritage even though it was filtered through sectarian biases. Having befriended the intellectuals, Syrian publishers from the start used the pages of their publications to launch, test, and advance the early literary output of a school of modern Arabic literature in the United States that was to revolutionize age-old Arabic literary forms.

Only three of several influential newspapers survived into the post–World War II period. *Al-Hoda*, published six years after *Kawkab Amrika*, the first Arabic-language newspaper, appeared in 1898 and spoke for the Maronite community. *Meraat al-Gharb*, the voice of the Syrian Orthodox and of anti-Ottoman Arab nationalists, was launched in 1899 to oppose what its publisher considered to be the political and religious biases of *al-Hoda*. *Al-Bayan*, not published until 1911, spoke for the Druze and Muslim community, although it was started by a Druze.

To its own detriment, the Arabic press, for all its complaints against fragmentation of the community, succeeded, in effect, in exacerbating the divisions. Moreover, by establishing itself on a sectarian basis, its respective publications did not address themselves objectively to the interests of the broad readership, thus limiting that readership.

The appearance in 1926 of *The Syrian World*, a monthly opinion and literary journal in English, signified the publisher's recognition of the end of an era as well as a crisis in the use of Arabic. It was aimed at the US-born generation that could not read Arabic, the generation that the publisher, Salloum Mokarzel, called the Syrian American generation. The immigration quota act limited the entry of Arabic readers and speakers at the same time that the accelerated Americanization process was eroding the use of Arabic. English increasingly replaced the native language in the homes and at the social functions of immigrants and those of their married children. Attempts by community leaders to teach Arabic to their offspring who were products of US schools and ardent consumers of such innovations as moving pictures and radio programs were defeated by the pace of assimilation. The usefulness of Arabic publications, therefore, declined, as did their numbers.

The impact of the Americanization process was most evident in the family and most significantly in the role of women. Women gained greater self-confidence and a sense of independence as they assumed responsibilities traditionally performed by the patriarch of the household. Their increased participation in the economic welfare of the family as well as in more disciplinary and decision-making responsibilities led to the gradual eroding of traditional social restrictions on women—mainly in the Christian community.

Rapid Americanization did not, however, prevent parents from inculcating their children with an important and, it seems, ineradicable set of traditional values. Most notably among them were [maintaining] strong family units, upholding the family honor, improving its status, and adhering to the family's religious beliefs. These core values drove the Syrians to achieve their primary goal in the United States and gave rise to corollary values that proved to be compatible with the most cherished US values: self-denial, thrift, initiative, perseverance, individualist attitudes, and a strong work ethic.

In their eagerness to succeed, the immigrant generation neglected to preserve their cultural heritage. Much of what that generation knew of their heritage was, in any case, centered on village life and its mythology. About the great Arab-Islamic contributions to world civilization the majority of the immigrants knew little, and what they did know was selective and refracted through traditional biases.

This village view of Arab culture left immigrant children poorly informed about their deeper historical roots. They knew little of the kind of events that in other nations produced national heroes and kindled ethnic and national pride. The void, therefore, was filled from the well of American myth and history. As a further consequence, the American-born and American-raised generations showed scant interest in or knowledge of their ethnic origins. References to Arab or Syrian culture were as remote as their parents' homeland. If the political events in the post–World War II Arab world had not reactivated Arab immigration and provoked the descendants of the first wave into an Arab identity, they might have assimilated themselves out of existence.

Works Cited

Chevalier, Dominique. 1968. "Western Development and Eastern Crisis." In *Beginnings of Modernization in the Middle East: The Nineteenth Century*, edited by William R. Polk and Richard L. Chambers. Chicago: Univ. of Chicago Press.

Hitti, Philip K. 1924. *Syrians in America*. New York: George Doran.

———. 1967. *Lebanon in History*. New York: Macmillan.

Houghton, Louise Seymour. 1911. "Syrians in the United States." Pts. 1–3. *Survey* 26 (July, Aug., Sept.); pt. 4, *Survey* 27 (Oct. 1911).

Hourani, Albert H. 1954. *Syria and Lebanon: A Political Essay*. London: Oxford Univ. Press.

Miller, Lucius Hopkins. [1904] 1969. *Our Syrian Population: A Study of the Syrian Communities of Greater New York*. San Francisco: R and E Research Associates.

Naff, Alixa. 1985. *Becoming American: The Early Arab Immigrant Experience*. Carbondale: Southern Illinois Univ. Press.

Ruppin, Arthur. 1966. "Syrien als Wirschaftsgebiet." In *The Economic History of the Middle East: 1800–1914*, edited by Charles Issawi. Chicago: Univ. of Chicago Press.

US Immigration Commission. 1911. *Statistical Review of Immigration, 1820–1910*. Vol. 3. Washington, DC: O.C.

8

Narrating Arab American History

The Peddling Thesis

CHARLOTTE KAREM ALBRECHT

> Socially, the deep satisfaction with America which accompanied their peddling success redirected their goals from those of temporary migrants to permanent citizens. In their trade, the unavoidable contacts with American society broke down resistance to learning by interacting with and imitating many aspects of American life. Any barrier that Syrian leaders would later erect against the tide of Americanization would be built on the quicksands of the peddling experience.
>
> —Alixa Naff, *Becoming American*

> The narrative of the Syrian pack-peddler is so central to the way in which the pioneer generation has been historicized that no scholarly account of the years between 1880 and 1924 exists in which the figure does not appear prominently.
>
> —Jacob Rama Berman, *American Arabesque*

Alixa Naff dedicated her life to the preservation of the stories of Arab American history. Herself the daughter of immigrants, Naff was a trained social historian and anthropologist, whose research led to the establishment of the Faris and Yamna Naff Arab American Collection at the Smithsonian Institution. In the process of undertaking her research, Naff produced an Arab American community archive of primary sources, including most notably over 2,300 hours of recorded oral history interviews as well as photographs, other documents, and artifacts donated by the families that Naff contacted for her research.

Published in 1985, *Becoming American: The Early Arab Immigrant Experience* showcases the research that Naff undertook. It is based primarily upon numerous oral history interviews that Naff conducted with first- and second-generation members of the early Arab American community. Scholarship on Arab Americans by Arab Americans themselves was especially rare at the time of Naff's work—whether that was in the 1960s when she first began collecting oral histories or in the late 1970s and into the 1980s when she conducted the bulk of her research and published *Becoming American*. This book illuminated the centrality of peddling practices in the early Syrian[1] American community and advanced Naff's thesis that peddling was the key to the social integration of early Arab immigrants into US society. Naff shows how these immigrants relied upon a dynamic network of support to begin peddling and how, through the literal routes and social connections of their work, many Syrians

Excerpt from Charlotte Karem Albrecht, "Narrating Arab American History: The Peddling Thesis," *Arab Studies Quarterly* 37, no. 1 (Winter 2015): 100–117. Full references in the original notes were converted to author-date citations in the text and notes here, and a works cited list was added. Reproduced with corrections and press style changes for consistency throughout the volume by permission of the *Arab Studies Quarterly* through PLSclear.

1. I use the term *Syrian* to denote people coming from the region of Bilad al-Sham or Greater Syria under the Ottoman Empire (the present-day regions of Israel/Palestine, Jordan, Lebanon, and Syria).

eventually settled in smaller towns and rural communities, dispersing themselves throughout the United States. Their English improved, and, particularly after they had children, they used Arabic less and less. Having been largely received with open arms by their customers and having found the ability to accumulate enough money to purchase property, Syrian immigrants abandoned their intentions of returning to Syria and eventually became Americans. Naff says that Syrian immigrants were unique because they had a "deep and broad identification with pack peddling" (1985, 130), similar to German Jewish immigrant peddlers. The high numbers of women who also peddled distinguished the Syrian community from other immigrant peddling groups.

This article considers the significance of Naff's peddling thesis and examines what it tells us about the social positioning of early Arab Americans. I focus on Naff's thesis that peddling was the key to the assimilation of the early Arab immigrant community, as advanced in *Becoming American*, because of its wide circulation among subsequent scholars. Although historians have focused more on peddling in early Arab American communities than on other forms of labor, Syrians working in textile mills were actually more numerous throughout the first wave of migration, particularly for younger, unmarried women and girls in the northeastern United States (Shakir 1997; Stiffler 2010). Despite this statistical evidence, the figure of the peddler and the economic network of peddling emerge as central features of the Arab American immigrant "success story." I will delineate how ideologies interweaving class, gender, race, and sexuality undergird this narrative. I group the discussion of ideology within *Becoming American* into three subsections: class, individualism, and capitalism; periodization and progress; and gender, sexuality, and citizenship. Then, I situate Naff's work within the traditions of US immigration history and liberal multiculturalism in order to show how these ideological currents function with regard to the peddling thesis.

Pack peddling has had a central place in Arab American historical narratives as being the key to the early Syrian immigrants' integration into US society. Peddling is the foundation of such a claim because it enabled the dispersal of Syrians beyond urban enclaves; it was a relatively quick and, at times, easy way to earn money; and it allowed for contact between Syrians and other US residents (Naff 1985). The first epigraph to this article, from Naff's *Becoming American*, exemplifies the relationship that has been articulated between peddling and Syrian assimilation.[2] While neither race, sexuality, nor gender is explicit in the description of the cultural "quicksands of the peddling experience," the categories of migrant versus citizen and Syrian versus American are dependent upon the racial, gendered, and sexual subjectivities of whiteness (Naff 1985, 199). Where class is concerned, a recurring narrative strategy in Arab American history emphasizes Syrians' entrepreneurial nature and adaptability in peddling work—peddling was seen as a temporary profession of survival that showcased Syrians' propensity for entrepreneurship and commitment to capitalism. In this narrative, peddling was viewed as a stepping-stone to more "settled" business practices and personal life—all things that were part and parcel of assimilating into Americanness.

However, pack peddling was also gendered labor and attracted scrutiny as such: peddling was cited as a venue for nontraditional living arrangements between women and as a means for unconventional family structures (Gualtieri 2009, 143–45). Such arrangements of support usually happened when long-distance peddlers, often men, were away from home for long periods of time. These types of observations about peddlers were a locus of anxiety about Syrians' deviance from white, middle-class, American norms of gender and sexuality. Non-Syrians often invoked Orientalist stereotypes of "Asians" in giving voice to that anxiety. For instance, one common view framed the Syrian peddler as exotic and manipulative. In this view, peddling was a profession that encapsulated the "true nature" of Syrians in a typical Orientalist fashion—deceitful, manipulative, and seductive. Peddlers were also seen as a threat to local business owners and were seen as too lazy to take up industrial labor (despite the fact that peddling was grueling work). A *Harper's Weekly* editorial on the New York Syrian community demonstrated these types of Orientalist ideas:

2. Scholars have challenged any simplistic view regarding this early generation and assimilation. See Gualtieri 2009; Khater 2001.

> The peddler, with a choice assortment from this worthless lot, sets out after fortune. . . . His commercial system is simple, and essentially Asiatic. He asks ten times as much for his wares as he will in reality accept, and twenty times what they are worth. He employs importunity, eloquence, mendacity, sympathy, and even fear to secure a customer, but, to his credit be it said, rewards every purchaser with a gratitude and obeisance that would be dignity itself were it not for their suggestiveness of servility. (1890, 835)

This passage reflects the virulent anti-Asian racism that was prevalent in the United States at this time. . . .

In what follows, I will examine how peddling is narrated in *Becoming American* through detailing the ideological currents regarding class, race, gender, and sexuality that have accompanied Naff's thesis. Then, I place Naff's work within the traditions of US immigration history and liberal multiculturalism in order to understand the function of these ideological currents within the peddling thesis. I focus on how the work and economies of peddling are employed in Arab American historical scholarship in order to reveal how gender and sexual normativity are used implicitly in these narratives to construct a naturalization of Syrian whiteness through economic upward mobility. In this narrative, Syrians are not "becoming" white as they are becoming American, but rather the story of their ascent in class is employed as retroactive proof of their preexisting whiteness. In framing peddling as an example of the entrepreneurial and individualistic nature of Syrians, historians have taken what was a socially unstable practice in Arab American history and repackaged it to fit the ideals of US citizenship: individualistic, entrepreneurial, and capitalist. In addition, because the major peddling period for Syrian migrants coincided with Asian immigrant struggles to naturalize as US citizens, the discussions around the merits or detractions of peddling took place in a larger context of debates about race, whiteness, and assimilation. Labor was essential to these discussions of race, as Asian immigrants were positioned as "unfree" through the figure of the Chinese "coolie," regardless of their actual employment (Jung 2005; Lowe 2006).

The Peddling Thesis

. . . Naff's use of oral history methods in *Becoming American* was an oppositional strategy. Gary Okihiro (1981) describes oral history methods as an alternative to the silencing and distorted self-perceptions that ethnic minorities have experienced under colonial oppression; Okihiro advocates for oral history as a way to recover that silenced and distorted past (47). While Naff's methodological framework is not explicitly political in the way that Okihiro articulates, she defends her decision to rely upon oral history by emphasizing its strengths as a method in "eliciting and recording for older, uneducated, or illiterate informants' primary information that would otherwise be lost" (1985, 6). Naff notes the critical bias in much of the biographies and other literature of the early Arab immigrant community, saying that the majority of the authors "looked back from an acquired, middle-class perspective" (6). Naff's method then, in the collection of data and in the overall focus of her scholarship, centers on Arab American perspectives that had been previously marginalized, particularly those of elders, Arabic speakers, and illiterate community members. Therese Saliba shows that Naff's use of oral histories, while not explicitly feminist, was influenced by methodological frameworks that women experience seriously as sources of knowledge. Naff viewed Arab American women "as political, economic, and cultural agents in their communities" (2014, 1), Saliba says, and her oral history method was central to this approach.

Class, Capitalism, and Individualism

One prominent theme that surfaces in *Becoming American* (1985) emphasizes upward economic mobility, entrepreneurship, and individualism. Naff crafts an association of peddlers with capitalism by distancing Syrians from the position of the proletariat and by framing peddlers as entrepreneurs. She writes, "In Arab American folklore . . . we have liked to think of our forebears as independent businessmen who disdained to work for others and had the courage, against all odds, to strike out on their own" (129).

Naff is aware of the tendency to romanticize peddling within the early Arab immigrant community, including the accounts of the former peddlers that she interviewed. Although she recognized that these accounts tended toward the hyperbolic, her own characterization of the peddling profession also gestured toward the dramatic. This is a moment where we can see the historian's struggle to balance the need for accuracy with the desire to tell a compelling story. For instance, on introducing the subject of Arab peddlers, she writes, "Not only did they leave their villages to follow its promise of quick wealth with a herd instinct, but they pursued that promise to every quarter of the American continent; no region was to prove too remote or forbidding" (128). This language repeats, as she calls Syrian peddlers "tenacious, roaming the most remote and forbidding sections of the country" (125). This description brings Syrian peddlers in metaphorical parallel to the early European settlers of Turtle Island, likening them to courageous explorers, striking out on their own.

Naff calls the peddlers "pioneers," and while she acknowledges the proliferation of Syrians in factory and mill work, she claims that Syrians had "an innate disdain for wage labor" (153). She calls peddlers "petty capitalists" (126) and "diehard opportunists" (129) who promoted commerce wherever they went. Naff makes the link from the antiproletariat to the capitalist by emphasizing the individualism of Syrian peddlers, saying that peddling suited Syrians' "individualistic nature and sense of impermanence" and allowed them to "operate on their own terms" (128). She reinforces this association between peddling and individualism by saying that peddlers were more motivated to succeed than wage earners. Perhaps she drew this conclusion from the numerous successful businesses that grew out of peddling practices. But it is equally plausible that peddlers were not more motivated than wage earners, so much as wage earners had little prospect of advancement in the industrial workplace hierarchy. The most emphasized aspect of this association between peddlers and capitalism is the framing of peddlers as entrepreneurs and capitalists. Naff claims that "Syrian immigration and rapid modernization were fortuitously compatible" (126) as the Syrian peddling sector "revitalized . . . an anachronistic enterprise and made it function successfully within a technologically oriented economy" (198). Interestingly, she situates Syrian peddlers as having filled a niche opened by the rapid industrialization of the late nineteenth century—the isolation of rural communities from goods and services as urban populations swelled. In linking peddling with capitalism and entrepreneurship, she renders the labor of peddling and the economy that supported it normative in the US context.

Periodization and Progress

Correlating closely with this entrepreneurial framing of peddling is a temporal notion of progress. Naff divides early Syrian migration into two periods, one from 1880 to 1910 and the other from 1910 to 1930, roughly. She refers to the former period, in which Syrians peddled in highest numbers, as the "pioneer period" and the latter as the "settled period." The pioneer period is characterized by impermanence, adventure, and colonization, whereas the settled period—marked by the arrival of more Syrian women and the move from peddling to business ownership—signifies the Syrians' "confidence in the new land" (12). In order for the binary of pioneer/settled to function, peddling must be characterized as a temporary endeavor and as a profession done out of necessity and ingenuity. For this reason, peddling is frequently referred to as a "stepping stone" toward "success and middle-class status" (130). As Naff explains the move many Syrians made from peddling to other forms of nonmobile work, she explains these changes through multiple mechanisms, such as changes in rural economies and the unsustainability of peddling long term because it was a physically demanding job. But she also cloaks these explanations in a naturalized progression of upward economic mobility. On the move of some peddlers to open stationary businesses with the capital they made in peddling, Naff terms this a "graduation" of work away from the humble origins of the peddler and calls these shifts "evolutionary stages" (169) in peddling: "They were no longer the humble pack peddler. They saw themselves and acted as 'classier salesmen dealing with classier people.' The period of adventure and impermanence had been gradually phasing into a period of permanence and community building" (145–46). Here, she also quotes one of her second-generation Arab American informants, echoing the sentiment from Syrian elites that peddling was "too demeaning" and veered too close to begging (129).

As many small Syrian communities developed across the midwestern and southern United States, produced by peddling routes, Naff calls this process the "piecemeal transition of transients into citizens" (140). This is how the settled period begins, through the class ascension, assimilation, and physical rootedness of these communities: "The Syrians moved gradually into the ranks of America's middle class and became willing subjects of the Americanization process" (12). In these ways, the overarching binary regarding class, mobility, and assimilation in Naff's narrative operates through several other articulated binaries as well: ethnic enclave/dispersed settlements, Syrian nationalist/American citizen, working class/middle class, and transient/settled or migrant/citizen. All of these binary articulations contribute to an implicit racial spectrum from Arab or nonwhite to white.

Gender, Sexuality, and Citizenship

Migration and peddling had tremendous effects on the practice of marriage within the Syrian community. Those men who migrated on their own in the early years frequently left wives and fiancées in Syria. Even if they did not, they may have been counted as a potential spouse for someone back home. But migration and peddling work brought with it possibilities for different kinds of lives than were possible in Syria, particularly where family and intimate relationships were concerned. In the Arab diasporic press, community leaders raised concerns that male peddlers would abandon their familial obligations by breaking engagements, abandoning wives and children, or maintaining multiple families in separate locales (Gualtieri 2009, 137). These fears were not paranoid worries; they were founded on reports of such stories that made it back home to the families and communities who expected migrating men to adhere to typical community practices. Some returning single men were even asked to provide proof that they had not married while in the United States (Naff 1985, 233; Gualtieri 2009, 137). Naff acknowledges the heterosexual transgressions of some male peddlers, but she reassures her readers that "the majority of single peddlers remained well within cultural bounds" (233). Those who did not, she suggests, succumbed to "nontraditional marital solutions," such as marrying outside the community, taking common-law wives, or engaging in "temporary marriages" with American girls (233). In the Syrian communities that formed in the United States, those Syrians who remained single after a particular age were heavily scrutinized. Naff attributes this to the belief among Syrians that "the state of being single was both unnatural and deplorable" (230).

While deviations from heterosexual norms were widely discussed, the prospects of homoerotic or homosexual encounters were unacknowledged in community accounts, despite both the frequent occurrence and the public outcry surrounding such encounters at the turn of the century. The expectation that "transient" peddlers should become "settled" business owners was particularly related to a heteronormative economy—a paradigm of US national culture, which permeated the Arab immigrant community as it sought to survive in a new home. Connotations in the context of the period during which Syrians migrated and public worries about "tramps," "hobos," and migrant workers mirrored the same concerns about the abandonment of heterosexual marriage and the nuclear family (Canaday 2011; Shah 2005, 2012). While Naff notes the concern of Syrian leaders about the instances of male peddlers abandoning or avoiding marital responsibilities, she overlooks the context of transience at the time and its specific implications for same-sex sexual encounters on the road. Some of the anecdotes that Naff provides of cultural misunderstandings are actually rife with unease about gendered boundaries and sexual roles. For instance, one of Naff's informants recounted a story of a Muslim peddler who employed an Arab method for imploring a local farmer to house him for the night: he kissed the man's beard. In response, the farmer beat the peddler until his peddling partner saw this and intervened (164). The possibility of an accidental homoerotic act is the silent character in this anecdote and the reason for the violence wrought upon the peddler, not merely cultural misunderstanding.

As far as women peddlers were concerned, Naff estimates that 75 to 80 percent of Syrian women migrants peddled during the pioneer period, between 1890 and 1910 (178). Like their male counterparts, the majority of Syrian women peddlers were Christians. This is in part proportional to the overall demographics of the Syrian immigrant community in the first half of the twentieth century. Naff suggests that the absence of Muslim and Druze women peddlers is owed to the timing of their migration during the decline of Syrian peddlers' heyday toward the end of the first decade of the twentieth century and to the conservatism regarding women in those religious traditions (168). However, two things should be taken into account regarding this assertion. First, there has been documentation of at least one Syrian Muslim woman peddler, who lived in the sizable Syrian Muslim community in North Dakota in the early 1900s (Curtis 2008). Second, Syrian Christian women peddlers were far from universally sanctioned. While their survival often depended on their participation in work outside the home, many in the Syrian Christian community were concerned that women working outside the home would lead to their sexual and moral decay. Still others were against this deviation from Arab cultural norms because they feared it would prevent Syrian immigrants' entry into the American middle class (Khater 2006, 93). Some Syrian Jews from this time period were also peddlers, but it is unclear if women were among their ranks (de Sola Pool 1914, 12).[3] More research is needed overall to ascertain the participation of non-Christian Syrian women in peddling economies. One of the most important contributions of Naff's work is her emphasis on the economic contributions of women in the early Arab American community. Indeed, her work shows how crucial women's labor was to the survival of the Syrian immigrant community. Naff also suggests that women peddlers were eager to leave peddling for the more respectable vocation of marriage and childrearing—and indeed, there was community pressure to do so. Naff asserts that "most gladly gave up peddling to marry and raise a family" (178), while admitting that "no one will ever know how many girls who peddled yearned for some man, any man, to free them from the drudgery" (230). In contrast to the periodization that fixes peddling's decline by 1910, numerous accounts show that Syrian women continued to peddle well into the 1930s and 1940s, especially "in times of economic crises, between pregnancies and even after the childbearing age" (178). Thus, while Syrian men began increasingly to take on nonmobile jobs, Syrian women continued to find economic opportunity and flexibility in peddling. One Syrian woman, named Aqlah Brice al Shidyaq, immigrated to the United States by herself in 1894, leaving her husband and children behind in Mount Lebanon. Arriving at West Virginia, she changed her name to "Mary" and began peddling. Despite her illiteracy, she learned rudimentary English, Italian, Polish, and Hungarian and built a base of loyal customers (Hourani 2007). She continued to peddle into her sixties, when her sons persuaded her to stop. But as the Great Depression began, she took up the profession once more to aid her family and peddled until she was almost seventy years old (Brice al Shidyaq 1997). Although some women preferred to "escape" into marriage and cease peddling, based on the same kinds of evidence it is equally plausible that women also gained pleasure, independence, and self-worth from their peddling work.

Contextualizing Naff's Work: US Immigration History and Liberal Multiculturalism

Naff published *Becoming American* within a tradition of US immigration history and during the rise of liberal multiculturalism. . . . It is within the context of the management and acceptance of certain understandings of racial difference that Naff's work and the peddling thesis must be situated. . . .

Jodi Melamed's (2011) trenchant critique of "official antiracisms" . . . argues that within the writing of ethnic history, racial liberalism demanded that racial

3. Within Arab American history, there is a dearth of information on Arab Jews, while simultaneously Arab Jews have largely been subsumed within the rubric of Ashkenazi immigration to the United States. The combination of ethnocentrism, Orientalism, and androcentrism present in the existing scholarship has largely occluded significant illuminations on the early history of Arab Jews in the United States. Thus, little is known about the laboring practices of Syrian Jewish women, particularly their relationship to peddling.

others prove their deserving of equality through demonstrating their commitment to mainstream "American" values. By the 1980s, liberal multiculturalism had become the official antiracism, beginning its incorporation into US institutions, with its epicenter at the university. The condition upon which all official antiracisms were predicated was the association of Americanness with capitalism. . . . For liberal multiculturalism in particular, the critique of material inequality along racial lines associated with the civil rights and national liberation movements of the 1960s and 1970s had to be deracinated from the critique of white supremacy (Melamed 2011). Even more so than producing a critique, liberal multiculturalism produced the validation of certain kinds of legible racial difference, predicated upon what Melamed calls the "reasonable, possible, or desirable" (2011, xvi). The maintenance of heteronormativity and US cultural and economic hegemony is central to that legibility. We can see this line of official antiracist thought in Naff's *Becoming American*. Naff emphasizes the capitalistic nature of Syrian immigrants and their quick acceptance of the United States as their new home, while simultaneously reminding the reader of their cultural difference, embedding this story of Arab Americans within liberal multiculturalism.

At the same time, Naff anchored Syrian immigrants within the tradition of immigration history. This positioned them implicitly as "white ethnics," as the concept of the United States as a "nation of immigrants" had "unified modern American whiteness" throughout the period of racial liberalism (Melamed 2011, 35). Thus, as Naff situates Arab immigrants within the immigration history tradition without contesting the color line that maintained white supremacy, this effectively associates Arab Americans with whiteness. . . . Naff contends that the contact with Americans through peddling facilitated their assimilation. Through interactions with their customers (and their eventual neighbors), Syrians learned English and developed relationships in which Americans began to see and treat them as equals. However, Syrians had to have contact with the right kind of Americans in order to access this assimilation: they had to have a widespread contact with *white* Americans. If the substantial contact Syrians gained through peddling was with nonwhite Americans or other non-European immigrants, this would likely not have led to assimilation into white standards, nor would it have likely been considered a sign of their integration into US society. Vivek Bald's (2013) work on Bengali migrants in New Orleans illustrates this very point. These South Asian migrants, many of whom were peddlers, became embedded in African American and Creole communities in the early twentieth century. However, this integration into American communities did not facilitate any access to privilege.

For Naff and many other scholars of the early Arab immigrant communities, peddling demonstrated the entrepreneurial skills and resourcefulness of Syrian migrants. This is a gesture that normalizes the labor of peddling. But the acts of labor that peddling entailed—the transience of traveling door to door, the encounter of a racialized other at the doorstep, and the women who peddled or supported peddling from within their homes—were acts of deviant labor. These laboring practices were constantly under scrutiny for the implications they wrought upon the Syrian community. What enables the normalization of peddling is not peddling at all. Rather, it is the cessation of peddling, the purchase of private property, marriage and reproduction, and the transition to small-business ownership that enable the narration of normativity in Arab American history. This narrative is dependent upon the assumption of whiteness at the center of this framework, wherein the ability of Syrian immigrants and their descendants to buy property and live among, socialize with, marry and reproduce with, and eventually identify as white Americans (for those who did) was enabled by a system of white-supremacist capitalism and settler colonialism. Naff writes,

> Syrians certainly felt no virtue in poverty, but they were generally a driven people. Quintessentially, it was a matter of honor to succeed in America. That was their strength. Their rigorous habits—hard work, thrift, self-denial—alleviated despair and spared them the entrapment at the bottom of the American economy. (1985, 192)

The emphasis on "rigorous habits" is a familiar echo of the myth of the American dream—one that erases the necessary presence of Black Americans at the bottom of the American economy and leaves unarticulated the necessary absence of Indigenous people on lands that Americans could settle. The occlusion of the Arab immigrants' contested place in the US racial hierarchy works to emphasize what Emma Pérez calls a "shared immigrant experience with . . . European immigrants in the United States" (2009, 9). . . .

Conclusion

In analyzing the experience of her grandmother as one of Naff's subjects, Therese Saliba must confront the radical potential of Naff's methodology along with the contradictory nature of some of the conclusions drawn in Naff's work (2014, 3–4). . . . Saliba pushes us to remember the significance of Naff's methods and that Naff's own intellectual and physical labor was ahead of her time. In addition, Saliba cautions that Naff did not see her work as being definitive and urged future scholars to engage with her findings. It is within this spirit that I disclose my own discomfort regarding how to engage with Naff's work. While I am critical of some of the currents within Naff's research on peddling, it is an understatement to say that I am indebted to her work. I am indebted to her not only for the archive she left behind but for the tenacity she demonstrated in pursuing knowledge production about her own community when much of the academic world seemed not to care. . . . Taking Naff's wish seriously, that scholars would continue to engage with the questions she posed in *Becoming American*, this article presses for a reexamination of how peddling practices are narrated in Arab American history, with a particular attention to the relationship between gender, sexuality, class, and race in early Arab American experiences.

Works Cited

Bald, Vivek. 2013. *Bengali Harlem and the Lost Histories of South Asian America*. Cambridge, MA: Harvard Univ. Press.

Berman, Jacob Rama. 2012. *American Arabesque: Arabs, Islam, and the Nineteenth Century Imaginary*. New York: New York Univ. Press.

Brice al Shidyaq, Edward. 1997. "Sitta 'Aqlah: A Woman of Faith, Strength, and Dignity. From Blawza to Wheeling, West Virginia." *Journal of Maronite Studies* 1, no. 3. At http://maroniteinstitute.org/ MARI/JMS/july97/Sitta _Aqlah.htm.

Canaday, Margot. 2011. *The Straight State: Sexuality and Citizenship in Twentieth Century America*. Princeton, NJ: Princeton Univ. Press.

Curtis, Edward E., ed. 2008. *The Columbia Sourcebook of Muslims in the United States*. New York: Columbia Univ. Press.

De Sola Pool, David. 1914. "The Immigration of Levantine Jews into the United States." *Jewish Charities* 4:12–27.

Gualtieri, Sarah M. A. 2009. *Between Arab and White: Race and Ethnicity in the Early Syrian American Diaspora*. Berkeley: Univ. of California Press.

Harper's Weekly. 1890. "Our Arab Colony." Oct. 25.

Hourani, Guita. 2007. "'Aqlah Brice al Shidyaq: A Woman Peddler from Northern Lebanon." *Al-Raida* 24, nos. 116–17: 52–55.

Jung, Moon-Ho. 2005. "Outlawing 'Coolies': Race, Nation, and Empire in the Age of Emancipation." *American Quarterly* 57, no. 3: 677–701.

Khater, Akram. 2001. *Inventing Home: Emigration, Gender, and the Middle Class in Lebanon, 1870–1920*. Berkeley: Univ. of California Press.

———. 2006. "Like Pure Gold: Sexuality and Honour amongst Lebanese Emigrants, 1890–1920." In *Sexuality in the Arab World*, edited by Samir Khalaf and John H. Gagnon, 85–106. London: Saqi Books.

Lowe, Lisa. 2006. "The Intimacies of Four Continents." In *Haunted by Empire: Geographies of Intimacy in North American History*, edited by Ann Laura Stoler, 191–212. Durham, NC: Duke Univ. Press.

Melamed, Jodi. 2011. *Represent and Destroy: Rationalizing Violence in the New Racial Capitalism*. Minneapolis: Univ. of Minnesota Press.

Naff, Alixa. 1985. *Becoming American: The Early Arab Immigrant Experience*. Carbondale: Southern Illinois Univ. Press.

Okihiro, Gary Y. 1981. "Oral History and the Writing of Ethnic History: A Reconnaissance into Method and Theory." *Oral History Review* 9, no. 1: 27–46.

Pérez, Emma. 2009. *The Decolonial Imaginary: Writing Chicanas into History*. Bloomington: Indiana Univ. Press.

Saliba, Therese. 2014. "From 'Becoming American' to Transnational Alliances: Feminist Methodologies and

Transformations in Arab American Studies." Unpublished paper delivered at the Arab American Studies Association Conference, Dearborn, MI.

Shah, Nayan. 2005. "Between 'Oriental Depravity' and 'Natural Degenerates': Spatial Borderlands and the Making of Ordinary Americans." *American Quarterly* 57, no. 3: 703–25.

———. 2012. *Stranger Intimacy: Contesting Race, Sexuality, and the Law in the American Northwest*. Berkeley: Univ. of California Press.

Shakir, Evelyn. 1997. *Bint Arab: Arab and Arab American Women in the United States*. Westport, CT: Praeger.

Stiffler, Matthew Jaber. 2010. "A Brief History of Arab Immigrant Textile Production in the U.S." Arab American National Museum Library & Resource Center, Dearborn, MI.

9

The Arab Gaucho

From Between Argentines and Arabs

CHRISTINA CIVANTOS

> Christopher Columbus takes the Arabized [Iberian] Jew Luis de Torres on his first voyage of discovery believing that they are going to the court of the Great Khan and that they will need someone who is fluent in Arabic to make themselves understood there. The Jew disembarks on the island of Cuba and speaks Arabic to the confused Indians: the anecdote, so picturesque today, forces us to consider the fact that the language of the Quran was one of the first to be spoken in the New World.
>
> —Luce López-Baralt, *Huellas del Islam en la literatura española*

López-Baralt's comment upon the arrival in Cuba of the Arabic-speaking Luis de Torres serves to remind us not only of the extent to which Arab culture dominated the Iberian Peninsula precisely at the time when Iberians were first encountering the Americas but also that Arabo-Jewish Spanish culture was, quite literally, taken to the Americas. What I will elaborate upon here is other ways in which the relationship between Spain and the Arab world was transferred to the Americas and also invoked by South Americans of Spanish as well as Arab lineage. Various cultural contexts inform criollo Argentines' Orientalisms; in some cases these contexts include, as part of the particular periods of nation formation that the writers lived through, the relationship to Spain—both as España and as al-Andalus. Attitudes toward Spain were particularly significant during the first century after Argentine independence from Spain, first as part of the establishment of a separate nation and later as part of the alignment of the national culture with Spanish culture. For this reason, both the history of Arab presence in Spain and the constitution of Argentina as a nation play a part in the intertwined invocations and representations of the gaucho and his pampas and [of] the Arab and his Oriental deserts in the works of two canonical criollo writers—Domingo Sarmiento and Leopoldo Lugones. Later, Arab Spain as well as Argentine nation building arise in the works of two Arab Argentine writers—Ibrahim Hallar and Juan Yaser—who reformulate Sarmiento's and Lugones's figure of the Arab gaucho.

Part of Spanish culture that has been heatedly debated from the eighteenth through twentieth centuries is the legacy of the almost nine hundred years of Arab presence in the Iberian Peninsula and the process of the Spanish Reconquista. Spain's failure to modernize, in both a political and economic sense, since the 1600s led to attempts to explain the country's so-called decadence. This created basically two intellectual camps in Spain throughout the next centuries: those who saw the expulsion of Jews and

Excerpts from Christina Civantos, *Between Argentines and Arabs: Argentine Orientalism, Arab Immigrants, and the Writing of Identity* (Albany: State Univ. of New York Press, 2006), 25–30, 73–74. Source citations were slightly reformatted, and a works cited list was added. Reproduced with corrections and press style changes for consistency throughout the volume by permission of the State University of New York Press.

Arabs and the Inquisition as the cause of this decline, and those who saw the Jews and Arabs as a negative influence on Spain that needed to be eliminated. This debate went on to produce, in the eighteenth century, positions as diverse as the resistance to the French cultural invasion and defense of Spain vis-à-vis Europe by reevaluating Spanish history and pointing to the glories of the period of Arab rule; the notion that Arabs were barbarians; and a renewed desire to conquer North Africa (earlier interest in doing so had been redirected into the conquest of the Americas). Then, in the early nineteenth century the Spanish Romantics were inspired by the history and culture of the Moors of Granada, and with the Generation of 1898 the questioning of Spain's identity reached a peak.

Domingo F. Sarmiento—a prominent Argentine statesman[1] and prolific author—as part of the Argentine Generation of 1837, had a very conflictive relationship with all things Spanish. As Andrea Pagni describes it, Sarmiento suffers from a "peculiar 'orfanhood'" because he has killed his parents, Spain—but they remain in his "cultural unconscious" (1989, 154). While anti-Spanish sentiment had stemmed, understandably, from the Latin American colonies' independence movement, it reached particular intensity later among the liberals of the Generation of 1837. These thinkers blamed the political turmoil of mid-1800s Argentina on its having been colonized by a backward country, one they saw as inferior to and distinct from Europe. In terms of Spain's own questioning of its relationship to Europe versus North Africa, although Sarmiento tended toward the strain of thought that blamed the expulsion for Spain's decline (Kovadloff 1993, 776), his different positions toward Arabs ran the gamut of the stances found in Spain. With his characteristic ambivalence as well as his Romantic leanings and readings in European Orientalism, he not only saw Arabs as the erstwhile civilizing force in Spain but also at times as barbarians and at other times as romanticized figures. . . . What I would like to argue is that Sarmiento, through textual images and mimetic acts, uses the multivalenced figure of the Arab as a way of translating the difference—the cultural identity in formation—of Argentina, for himself as well as for Europeans.

A few decades later, when Leopoldo Lugones wrote, the tide of sentiment toward Spain had completely changed. Early twentieth-century delineations of national identity in Latin America are known for their *hispanismo*, or Hispanism, a spirit of reconciliation with Spain that entailed a revalorization of Hispano-America's Spanish heritage. This period is also known for its positivism; biological determinism was central to early twentieth-century delineations of national identity in Latin America. In the case of Argentina, the ideas of the Spanish Generation of 1898 also played a major role. The Argentine search for a national tradition, influenced by the Generation of 1898's search for the essence of the Spanish "belonging," focused on the notion of defining the national "race" or soul of Argentina. In looking to the Spanish roots of Argentina to try to delineate this national soul, Lugones focused on the Arabs of Spain. As we shall see, however, he gave the Moorish element of Spanish cultural history a positive and primary position that went beyond what the Spanish thinkers of the time had granted it.

In 1962, the Arab Argentine writer Ibrahim Hallar takes up this web of relations between Spanish and Latin American searches for identity, and the Orientalist images that operate therein, in his negotiation of an Arab Argentine identity. In the late 1970s and early 1990s, another Arab Argentine, Juan Yaser, incorporates some of Hallar's ideas on the Arab heredity of the Argentine gaucho into his own additions to this textual dialogue between criollo Argentines and Arab Argentines. I focus mostly on interpreting Hallar's theories on the gaucho and the ways in which he substantiates them, while also making some references to Hallar's other works as well as Yaser's writings. My aim is to understand how Hallar constructs his Moorish gaucho and how this in turn allows him to use the Argentine search for a national identity to formulate a stronger Arab Argentine identity. In certain ways Hallar's and Yaser's renditions of the Arab gaucho are auto-Orientalist, but all the same they constitute a significant intervention in the formulation of Argentine identities. By considering the linked figures of the Arab and the gaucho, which in some cases becomes

1. Among various government posts, Sarmiento served as president of Argentina from 1868 to 1873.

the genealogically fused Arab-gaucho, in the works of the canonical Euro-Argentine writers Sarmiento [e.g., (1850) 1952, (1845) 1979, (1849) 1981] and Lugones [e.g., (1916) 1979] and in the works of Arab Argentine immigrant writers Hallar and Yaser, I consider the shared rhetoric, appropriations, and counterappropriations used in formulations of conservative nationalist as well as Arab immigrant subject positions.

In order to understand the semantic richness and cultural significance of the figure of the Arab gaucho, we must first consider the history of the gaucho as a social group and of the word *gaucho* itself. As Richard Slatta eloquently states, "The definitive social origin of the gaucho lies shrouded in the mists of the early colonial pampa and mired in the quicksands of academic polemics" (1983, 7). Not surprisingly, the debates surrounding the gaucho were most active during the period of heightened nationalism from the late 1800s through the early 1900s. Slatta explains that the proponents of the theories about the origins of the gaucho can be divided into two broad groups: the Hispanists and the Americanists. The Hispanists point to an Andalusian or Arab source for the horse-centered culture of the gauchos (1983, 7). Some of these Argentine thinkers, such as Sarmiento and Lugones and later Hallar and Yaser, relate the gaucho to the Arab, and, like the last three of these writers, they explicitly make the connection via Spain. Other Argentine intellectuals, swept up in the spirit of reconciliation with Spain, posit that the gaucho's culture of horsemanship and song grew out of Andalusian culture (and somehow manage to disconnect Andalusia from Arab civilization). Slatta elucidates that, in contrast with the Hispanist camp, the Americanists see the gaucho either as a criollo, frontier phenomenon, as derived from nomadic Native cultures, or as the product of *mestizaje*—of the mixture of Spanish and Indigenous elements (1983, 7–8). There is also disagreement about the region in which the gaucho first roamed. Though most point to the Argentine littoral, others reject the pampas as the birthplace of the gaucho and contend that it was actually the area east of the Río de la Plata or even north of the Plata (Slatta 1983, 8).

Moreover, the etymology of the word *gaucho* itself is, to this day, an open and disputed question. . . . [Nicolas] Shumway notes that "River Plate intellectuals continue arguing over the 'true' meaning of the term in a polemic that apparently will not accept the idea that words have and acquire new, even contradictory, meanings according to how, when, where, and by whom they are used" (1991, 69). Furthermore, debate surrounds not only the origin of the term but to whom exactly it refers. As Shumway points out, in its narrowest sense *gaucho* designates "the nomadic, often outlaw inhabitants of the great plains of Argentina, Uruguay and Brazil"—though because of works such as Sarmiento's *Facundo* ([1845] 1979) the gaucho is basically associated only with Argentina. In its broadest sense and according to current usage, *gaucho* refers to *campesinos*—"the rural working class" (Shumway 1991, 12).

In spite of, or perhaps precisely because of, this ambiguity, the gaucho functions as a key cultural sign in Argentina. The ambiguities surrounding the origins and very name of the gaucho make the figure of the gaucho very malleable. Thus, both the ruling-class desire for a narrative of the nation that could be adapted to different historical moments (as circumstances and elite needs changed) as well as marginalized immigrants' need for a point of insertion into the Argentine narrative have been met by the gaucho. Even when no longer an existing social actor, the gaucho has continued to function as a potent national symbol, as a national character.

The term *national character* was put into circulation by the German Romantic Johann Gottfried von Herder to refer to the distinctive qualities of a national grouping. While certain conditions can lead to particular predilections among a group of people, it is an understanding of the nation as an organic entity that underlies Herder's coinage of the term. In contrast, I would like to use *national character* here to refer to a constructed notion of a national temperament as well as to the figure that is taken to exemplify that temperament. The qualities that this figure is deemed to have—or is invested with—are in turn considered to be—or promoted as—the most authentic and distinctive qualities of a national group. In this way the double meaning of *character*—temperament as well as a fictional person in a narrative—is particularly appropriate. The national character is a self-propagating fiction; however, it is a fiction with very real functions, as this icon can be used to cultivate a specific sense of national community.

In the case of Argentina, the gaucho emerged from his history as part of the wars of independence as the national character of Argentina—a figure for the heroic yet ruggedly individualistic persona that certain Argentines wished to project. Although mixed-race cowboys known as "gauchos" (or "gaúchos" in Portuguese) have also been a part of Uruguayan and Brazilian history, it is Argentina that comes to mind when we hear the word *gaucho,* and inversely it is the gaucho that comes to mind when we hear *Argentina.* Clearly, the gaucho has been promoted in Argentina as an identificatory symbol of that which is truly Argentine. Initially, Argentine liberals, looking to Europe for cultural orientation, maintained that gauchos were uneducated masses that were influenced and controlled, to negative ends, by local leaders. But eventually, nationalists and populists romanticized the gaucho, exalting him as the authentic Argentine, "the true criollo."

The appropriation of the gaucho by the Argentine ruling classes is the topic of Josefina Ludmer's important study *El género gauchesco: Un tratado sobre la patria* (1988). Ludmer describes how the gaucho, without property, steady work, or a fixed dwelling place—and thus an outlaw or vagabond according to the law of the elites—is first demarginalized when used by the independence army. After [he is] pressed into military service and heroicized, the gaucho's voice, his oral form of expression, is used by high literary culture to form the gauchesque genre. Finally, this genre is used to place the gaucho within the bounds of liberal law. The body and voice of the gaucho are institutionally disciplined such that they become part of "civilization" (Ludmer 1988, 16–18). Thus, the gaucho came to embody the virtues of the Argentine spirit, and it was not long before immigrants, seeking to negotiate around conceptions of criollo authenticity, began to participate in the strategic use of the gaucho.

In a sort of inversion of Sarmiento's and Lugones's references to Arabs, two Arab Argentine authors—Ibrahim Hallar and Juan Yaser—make use of the established writers' work as they write Arabs into the early history of the Americas. Ibrahim Husayn Hallar, the son of Lebanese immigrants and a practicing Muslim, was born in San Luis in the Argentine interior in 1915. In his *El gaucho, su originalidad arábiga* (1962) Hallar incorporates Sarmiento's and Lugones's writings as part of the supporting evidence for his claim that the Argentine gaucho arose out of the relationships between Indigenous women and Arabs from Spain who had arrived with the Spanish to conquer and settle the New World. Juan Yaser, born in the village of Tayiba in Palestine in 1925, immigrated to Córdoba, Argentina, in 1952. In two of his publications, *Herencia arábiga en América* (1979) and *Fenicios y árabes en el génesis americano* (1992), Yaser presents basically the same argument as Hallar about the Arab origins of the gaucho with similar support, basing himself at least partially on Hallar's work.

In their works Hallar and Yaser take the similarities between Arabs and gauchos that Sarmiento and to a lesser extent Lugones base on the notion of geographically determined character and make them literal. That is, they take these notions to a concrete, biological realm. In addition, they take to its limits Lugones's description of the link between Arabs and gauchos as a biological one. Rather than a genealogy of Arabs intermingling and intermarrying with Spaniards, who then carry Arab atavisms with them to the New World, Hallar and Yaser narrate a much more immediate heredity. They point to the probable presence of Arabs among the Iberian conquerors of the Americas. According to their narrative, these Arabs, who were not under the jurisdiction of Spanish laws that forbade sexual relations between Spanish Catholics and Indigenous peoples, had children with Indigenous women. These children were the first gauchos. The histories written by Yaser and Hallar make it such that the infusion of Arab blood took place not only in the Iberian Peninsula but also more recently and on Argentine soil itself.

The basic rhetorical strategy that Hallar and Yaser deploy is the invocation of the historical connection between the Hispanic world and the Arab world in al-Andalus. The two immigrant writers literally bring this Hispano-Arab connection to Argentina to establish a direct biological link with the gaucho—the Argentine par excellence. With these narratives of a historical Arab presence in Argentina, Hallar and Yaser are able to make a space, however small, for themselves in Argentina. They are able to assert, as Hallar puts it, that "the Arab is here incognito, diluted, unrecognized, but he is here" (1959, 11).

Hallar dedicates all of *El gaucho* to presenting an alternative narrative about the gaucho. The text consists of revisionary and oppositional, albeit often convoluted, conceptions of the gaucho and of the ethnic origins of both Arabs and Argentines. Throughout the twists and turns in Hallar's argumentation, he manipulates Argentine notions of racial purity and patriotic miscegenation for the purpose of bolstering the position of Arab immigrants to Argentina from a variety of different, and often contradictory, angles. He undoes fear of ruining a preexisting racial purity, makes Arabs whiter and more European, redefines the term *white* so that it need not mean European, and says that Arab immigrants helped to "whiten" Argentina. *El gaucho*, therefore, can be understood as an attempt at shoring up the position of Arabs in Argentina through a variety of entry points into the ideologically charged issue of race and ethnicity that has played a major role in Argentine identity formation. The history of positivist concern with the racial and ethnic makeup of Argentina and the intertwined record of anti-Arab sentiment resulted in the project of literally creating a particular type of national body. This, together with economic interests, led to the rejection of certain immigrants. Hallar's and Yaser's writings must be read in light of this sociohistorical context. By expounding upon the Arab heritage of the gaucho, they attempt to maneuver around the whole issue of the great wave of immigration. The *gaucho moro* [Moorish gaucho] allows them to establish a pre-immigration Arab presence and thereby disassociate themselves from the negative image of the Semitic immigrant as they proclaim their undivided loyalty to Argentina.

Coda: Menem's Self-Stylization as Arab Gaucho

One of Argentina's most prominent descendants of Arab immigrants, Carlos Saúl Menem, also took up the figure of the Arab gaucho, not in a textual assertion of identity but in the creation of his political and public image. Menem, the son of Syrian Muslim immigrants, was born and raised in La Rioja, and until his shift from Peronist to neoliberal politics, in a variety of ways he consciously cultivated an identification between himself and the famous caudillo of La Rioja province, Juan Facundo Quiroga. For instance, at the beginning of his political career Menem used to dress and wear his hair like Facundo Quiroga. Menem invoked the nineteenth-century caudillo, the most famous populist leader of La Rioja, in order to play up and strengthen Menem's own Riojan populism and, in the process, to highlight Menem's criollo attributes. Another manifestation of Menem's homage to Facundo Quiroga is the name he gave his son: Carlos Facundo. Menem's invocation of Facundo Quiroga may in fact have its roots in Sarmiento's description of Quiroga as a sort of Arab gaucho. According to Gabriela Cerruti, Menem's personal copy of Sarmiento's *Facundo* has particular passages underlined: those in which Sarmiento describes Quiroga with Orientalist references, along with those that point to Quiroga's supreme power over La Rioja and his political charisma (1993, 15–17).

Although many aspects of Menem's political record are thoroughly reprehensible, his attempt to create a space for non-Catholics and noncriollos in Argentina is noteworthy, particularly given the Argentine context of intertwined cultural nationalism and Orientalism. Arguably the one true accomplishment of Menem's political career has been the constitutional reform regarding the eligibility requirements for the presidency. Until 1994, in order to become president of Argentina one had to be Catholic. Menem was eligible because, no doubt planning ahead, he had converted to Catholicism in the 1960s. Once he became president, he promoted the reform of the Constitution that removed religion from the requirements for candidacy and from the presidential oath (Brieger 2002).

In spite of this change in presidential eligibility requirements—or perhaps precisely because of it—Menem often disavows ever having been anything other than Catholic (although his son was openly Muslim and his son's funeral rites and burial were Islamic [Jozami 1996]). In a filmed 1999 interview, a reporter said to Menem, "You were never Muslim?" Menem answered, "No, I have always been an Apostolic Riojan—I mean, Roman-Catholic [*No, siempre fui católico, apostólico, riojano . . . digo romano*]" ("Menem y Quintero, solos en la madrugada" 1999, ellipses in original). Menem's transposition of the rhyming words *riojano* and *romano* was seen as a comical slip-up in the midst of the disavowal of something that was already public knowledge; but the verbal switch, whether conscious or not, points to Menem's understanding (or projection) of his Argentine identity. What makes him Argentine is not being Roman Catholic but, rather, being Riojan: on the one hand, simply having been born and raised in La Rioja and, on the other hand, being gaucho-like and Arab-like, in the tradition of (Sarmiento's representation of) Facundo Quiroga.

Sarmiento uses the figure of the Arab as a conceptual model, a graspable counterpart to the gaucho, and in this way formulates a national identity that balances between eschewing barbarism and embracing the gaucho as that which is most Argentine. Lugones uses the *moro* to make the conflict-ridden gaucho an Argentine icon and one that represents pre-immigration Argentina. Hallar and Yaser, and then Menem, utilize Sarmiento's and Lugones's links between Arabs and gauchos to create a deep connection between the Arab immigrant and Argentina. As part of this textual maneuver, they use auto-Orientalist images to reposition Arabs in Argentine society. In this way, the Arab Argentines turn the gesture of rejection of the immigrant—that is, the elevation of the gaucho to national hero as well as a particular form of Orientalism—into an entry point for the Arab immigrant into Argentine subjecthood. By bringing to light and examining this textual dialogue surrounding the figure of the Arab gaucho, I hope to have elucidated the ways in which Argentines have rhetorically managed and merged two figures—the *moro* and the gaucho—in their negotiation of both conservative criollo and immigrant identities.

Works Cited

Brieger, Pedro. 2002. "Latin Islam since 11 September." *ISIM Newsletter* 11:8.

Cerruti, Gabriela. 1993. *El jefe, vida y obra de Carlos Saúl Menem*. Buenos Aires, Argentina: Editorial Planeta.

Hallar, Ibrahim. 1959. *Descubrimiento de América por los árabes*. Buenos Aires, Argentina: Ibrahim Hallar.

———. 1962. *El gaucho, su originalidad arábiga*. Buenos Aires, Argentina: Ibrahim Hallar.

Jozami, Gladys. 1996. "The Manifestation of Islam in Argentina." *The Americas* (Academy of American Franciscan History) 53, no. 1: 67–85.

Kovadloff, Santiago. 1993. "España de Sarmiento." In Domingo F. Sarmiento, *Viajes por Europa, África y América 1845–1847 y Diario de gastos*, edited and compiled by Javier Fernández, 759–89. Buenos Aires: Fondo de Cultura Económica de Argentina.

López-Baralt, Luce. 1985. *Huellas del Islam en la literatura española, de Juan Ruiz a Jusan Goytisolo*. Madrid: Hyperion.

Ludmer, Josefina. 1988. *El género gauchesco: Un tratado sobre la patria*. Buenos Aires, Argentina: Editorial Sudamericana.

Lugones, Leopoldo. [1916] 1979. *El payador*. Caracas, Venezuela: Ayacucho.

"Menem y Quintero, solos en la madrugada." 1999. *La Nación*, Jan. 24. At http://www.lanacion.com.ar/99/01/24/s05.htm.

Pagni, Andrea. 1989. "Los *viajes* y el lugar de la escritura en los textos de Friedrich Gerstacker y Domingo Faustino Sarmiento." *Río de la Plata* 8:141–57.

Sarmiento, Domingo F. [1850] 1952. *Recuerdos de provincia*. Buenos Aires, Argentina: Hemisferio.

———. [1845] 1979. *Facundo o civilización y barbarie*. Buenos Aires, Argentina: Centro Editor de América Latina.

———. [1849] 1981. *Viajes por Europa, África y América*. Buenos Aires, Argentina: Editorial de Belgrano.

Shumway, Nicolas. 1991. *The Invention of Argentina*. Berkeley: Univ. of California Press.

Slatta, Richard. 1983. *Gaucho and the Vanishing Frontier*. Lincoln: Univ. of Nebraska Press.

Yaser, Juan. 1979. *Herencia arábiga en América*. Córdoba, Argentina: Juan Yaser.

———. 1992. *Fenicios y árabes en el génesis americano*. Bogotá, Colombia: Colgraphex.

10

Becoming "Syrian" in America

A Global Geography of Ethnicity and Nation

AKRAM FOUAD KHATER

An Imagined Home

Between 1889 and the beginning of World War I, around one hundred thousand immigrants left Mount Lebanon for the United States, and another two hundred thousand made their way to South America, mainly Argentina and Brazil.[1] Regardless of the reasons that prompted them to come to "Amirka," very few thought to stay long. They expected to land somewhere, work for a while to accumulate money, and return home to live the good life. Focused as they were on these straightforward goals, only the most clairvoyant among the emigrants could have anticipated that the voyage would be far more complex. Even fewer could have foretold that the days spent peddling lace and buttons, shopping for food and clothes, and strolling in the streets of their adopted communities would be transformative. Almost none would have expected that their experiences in the *mahjar* (land of immigration) would involve social and cultural contacts and dislocations necessitating a self-conscious examination of their individual and collective identities.

Yet these transformations did happen, and they began even before immigrants set foot on American soil. In Marseilles, the halfway point between Mount Lebanon and the ports of entry into the United States (or Central and South America), most immigrants self-consciously defined themselves as Christians leaving Ottoman lands to escape Muslim persecution. This served as a means to explain and facilitate their desire to enter the United States. Although not based on any immediate reality, these latter-day stories of persecution fed off narratives about the massacres in the 1860s in Mount Lebanon and earlier in Damascus, even as they embellished and perpetuated them.

Yusuf Bey, the Ottoman consul in Barcelona, remarked on this in an 1889 report to the Sublime Porte: "When questioned why they had to leave their homes in such large numbers, they invent ridiculous stories about the massacre of their wives and children . . . to increase the compassion and thus the alms they can elicit" (quoted in Akarli 1992, 115). One may be tempted to dismiss such an assessment as the selfserving remark of an Ottoman official defending his government; the fact that he was sending this internal report to Istanbul, however, makes it much less likely to be an exercise in disingenuous public relations and more likely to be an

Excerpt from Akram Fouad Khater, "Becoming 'Syrian' in America: A Global Geography of Ethnicity and Nation," *Diaspora* 14, nos. 2–3 (2005): 299–331. Author-date citations and the entries in the works cited list were reformatted in some instances. Reprinted with corrections and press style changes for consistency throughout the volume by permission from the University of Toronto Press. https://utpjournals.press. doi:10.1353/dsp.0.0010.

1. Even though the great majority of immigrants came from the historical Mount Lebanon—today part of Lebanon—I use the term *Syrian* in this essay, for two reasons: first, the overwhelming majority of immigrants used that term to identify themselves; and, second, some immigrants came from other parts of the eastern Mediterranean. However, this term is not meant to indicate the modern nation-state of Syria; rather, it denotes the geographical territory encompassed by Bilad al-Sham, which in today's geopolitical parlance would be Lebanon, Syria, Jordan, and Palestine/Israel.

objective—albeit irritated—observation. Less speculatively, various non-Ottoman sources corroborate this assessment in that they depict a Mount Lebanon that was actually quite tranquil between 1880 and the beginning of World War I, with little evidence of either political or religious persecution.[2]

Regardless of the historical veracity of these accounts, immigrant writers such as Abraham Rihbani (1914), George Haddad (1916), and Philip Hitti (1924) codified the stories of persecution in their books by portraying Christians in Mount Lebanon as defenseless victims of persecution, oppressed by ruthless "Turks" who extorted monies from them. In resorting to this explanation for their immigration, many peasants from Mount Lebanon were feeding into Orientalist notions current in America, which portrayed Islam and "Turks" (the term used for Muslims) as nefarious, violent, and repressive. For instance, in an article in the September 4, 1899, edition of the *New York Times*, Edward Riggs referred to the Muslims in Lebanon as "un-speakable" Turks who were bent on expelling all Christians from the Holy Land. The outcome of such constructions was to render all immigrants from Mount Lebanon, in popular and scholarly works, as Christians fleeing persecution, [thus] erasing the presence of a sizable number of Druze and Muslim immigrants and flattening the multidimensional reasons that drove peasants and townsfolk to leave their homes. In using such images to their advantage, immigrants began the process of reinventing themselves.

Upon arrival at Ellis Island, immigrants continued this process with two additional steps of self-representation. First, they had to decide whether they were Turks or Syrians. In the 1890s, they were invariably recorded as Turks, the only category available to them as citizens of the Ottoman Empire, which was dominated by ethnic Turks. However, the great majority who arrived after the turn of the century could choose to define themselves as either "Syrian" or "Turk." (This change came about through the efforts of immigrant interpreters working at Ellis Island, including Mr. Arbeely, whom we will meet below.) Most chose the term *Syrian* to distinguish themselves from the presumably Muslim "Turk."[3] Similarly, in Brazil most immigrants resented the label *Turcos* because, as a derogatory term, it lumped them together with Muslims and Turks, and they worked assiduously to be called *Sirios* (Duoun 1944).[4] For most immigrants, the appellation *Syrian* would have meant very little in any real sense. Certainly the term had been used—with strikingly different political meanings—since the 1860s among the literati and intellectuals of Beirut. Butrus al-Bustani, a leading member of al-Nahda (the Arab cultural and literary renaissance movement) who helped establish al-Jam'iyya al-Suriyya lil-'Ulum wal Funun (the Syrian Society for Sciences and Arts), articulated the term as defining Arab people, culture, and language united in the geographical expanse stretching across modern-day Iraq, Syria, Lebanon, Jordan, and Palestine/Israel (Rabinovich 1992; Manneh 1980). Others, like Shukri Ghanem and Georges Samne, wrote—in the second decade of the twentieth century—of a "Syria" that was distinct and separate from Arab culture and history and that embraced a Mediterranean culture founded on an imagined Phoenician past and lingering heritage (Samne 1920). Yet these various urban-based constructions of "Syria" remained distant from the rural and illiterate lives of most peasants. In other words, at Ellis Island—or any other port of entry—registering as "Syrian" was an act of expediency

2. The immediate reasons for this migration had little to do with religious persecution and much more to do with the hope for a better quality of life through the accumulation of money. In local histories of this period, like Ma'alouf 1908 and Hashi 1983, no mention is ever made of religious persecution. It is also important to note here that twentieth-century memories and stories of Ottoman persecution and oppression—enshrined in scholarly and popular books—are rooted in the terrible famine that afflicted Mount Lebanon during World War I.

3. Montie Bryan Pitts Jr. notes that in Brazil, "since immigrants from Syria and Lebanon before World War I carried passports from the Ottoman Empire, Brazilian immigration officials often classified them as *turcos* (Turks). Lebanese did not appear as a category until 1926, shortly after France separated Lebanon and Syria into separate protectorates after World War I. From 1927 onward, the number of immigrants designated as turcos decreased dramatically, from 3,370 in 1926 to only 203 in 1927" (2006, 3).

4. "In 1899, the year in which the term 'Syrian' began to be used [in the United States], 3,708 immigrants registered themselves as Syrians and only 28 as Turks" (Kaufmann 2004, 100–101).

and not an engagement with the political, economic, cultural, or ideological dimensions of the term. It was still a category that far exceeded anything they knew in their village and a choice that had little practical or emotional relevance to the lives they had left behind.

After marking themselves as "Syrian," immigrants had to list a relative as their contact person in America. One story perhaps highlights the implications of such an act; as immigrant Michel Haddy tells it,

> All who came [to the United States from Rachaya, a town in southern Lebanon] would say "I am going to my Uncle Salem Beshara in Ft. Wayne, Indiana." There was a Druze man with us, and when Mr. Arbeely [the interpreter for immigration officials at Ellis Island] asked who he was going to meet, he said "My uncle Salem Beshara." Mr. Arbeely said [in Arabic], "How is it that a Druze is related to a Christian?! But he let us through anyway because he knew who Salem was." (Haddy 1962)

This story becomes more illustrative when placed against the backdrop of the 1860 civil war that embroiled Druze and Maronite communities in a spiral of violence and generated a collective memory of distrust—and outright animosity, in some instances—between the two communities. In a single utterance, differences of family and religion—two important identifiers in Mount Lebanon—were put aside. Certainly this truce was born out of need, and it was not necessarily permanent: interreligious rivalries surfaced again and again for at least two subsequent decades in the *mahjar.* Yet it still marked a moment—and there were many like it—of ignoring boundaries that, to a greater or lesser extent, had defined the peasants before they immigrated. It demonstrates the malleability of these categories and their susceptibility to historical change when other considerations proved more important. In a literal stroke of the pen, an immigrant acquired a new identity that transcended anything she or he had known before. What this meant was hardly clear or even important, at least not yet.

. . . During subsequent sojourns of immigrants in New York, Chicago, Greenville, South Carolina, Houston, and the host of cities and towns to which immigrants journeyed, these immigrants appeared and were treated as a foreign "Other" belonging—whether as "Turk," "Arab," or "Syrian"—to the same "Orient." The clothes they wore, the language they spoke, the food they ate, and their mannerisms all came to be regarded as threateningly alien or romantically exotic. In the villages or towns of the eastern Mediterranean from which they had come, none of these would have elicited remark or any need for explanation. Within that much more intimate context, people knew each other by name, their clothes were quite similar, their language familiar but for slight variations in accents. An anecdote may help illustrate this point. After a particularly difficult day of peddling, Nasim Samaha complained to an experienced woman peddler that while all the other peddlers were having doors opened to them, he was having no such luck. She told him,

> "You are not speaking to them in the Rachaya [a town in Lebanon] accent, are you? What an ass you are! Talk to them in a Damascene accent." So he went out the next day and began using the Damascene accent, and tried to act appropriately refined to match it. He held up a pair of earrings [for a woman customer] and began to swing them back and forth, speaking all the while in the singsong intonation of the Damascene accent and finally put them to her ears. She picked up a broom and swatted him with it and chased him away. (S. Samaha 1962)

What Nasim innocently took as a helpful sales hint became a humorous prank and a painful lesson about the irrelevance in the larger American society of previously meaningful linguistic mappings. A Damascene accent no longer distinguished one person from another, as all immigrants became an amalgamated "Other" in the new territory they came to inhabit.

In some cases this otherness was regarded as exotic, as in the case of Jibran Khalil Jibran. In the late 1890s, as a young boy, he had immigrated with his mother, his brother, Butrus, and two sisters to Boston. There he attracted the attention of Helena Stuart Dudley, a social worker at Denison House, one of the "Settlement Houses" intended to provide social services to the immigrant community. Recognizing his talent in art, she turned—through a series of intermediaries—to a local Boston Brahmin, Fred Holliday Day, a millionaire, a "leader of the Boston avant-garde and the centre of a group of Young Decadent poets and artists. . . . To Day, Jibran was . . . an unspoiled genius—a type of noble savage with which Romantic America was obsessed" (Waterfield 1998, 35–37). This was not a unique incident. Rather, the Orient (exoticized, either negatively—lazy, indolent, and sybaritic—or positively—spiritual, natural, and untainted—as "uncivilized") had by the end of the nineteenth century become inscribed into the American literary landscape through travel narratives, novels, and literary magazines. Productions like *Sumrum*, a Max Reinhardt adaptation of *The Arabian Nights*, which he brought to New York in the wake of the success of another Oriental tale, *Kismet*, thrilled audiences "when the curious, murderous and sensuous fancy passed before their eyes" (Nash 1998, 35). Some immigrants traded on this exoticism and the associated Holy Land mania in America even as they constructed their own images of America and Americans (Obenzinger 1999). For instance, the tutor of Mary Amyuni, a recent immigrant, told her to "hold up the rosaries and crosses first; say they are from the Holy Land because Americans are very religious" (Amyuni 1962). . . .

In other cases, the differences were seen not as alluringly exotic but as disturbingly alien. In an article straightforwardly titled "Don't Like Arabs," which appeared in the *Cedar Rapids Evening Gazette* in July 1901, neighbors complained of "the deportment of fifty Arabians who represent the colony [of 'Syrian' immigrants] living in a building . . . at 1220 South Third Street." Then there was Congressman John L. Burnett, who proclaimed in 1907 that the "Syrians" were "the most undesirable of the undesirable peoples of Asia Minor" (Burnett 1907). The most horrifyingly tragic manifestation of this anti-Syrian sentiment occurred in Florida in 1929 when Nicholas Romey, a Syrian grocer in Lake City, was lynched "by a mob after a dispute with the local Chief of Police" (Gualtieri 2004, 63). The work of Louise Houghton—a social activist who wrote four essays about Lebanese immigrants in the United States for the socially progressive magazine *Survey*—shows that this prejudice was not restricted to the southern part of the United States. Stating the matter rather delicately, Houghton attributed the "clannishness" of the three thousand Lebanese in Boston to the fact that "even the best of Boston people . . . appear unable to appreciate certain characteristics of the Syrian nature and temperament" (1911, 492). A study issued by South End House in Boston, titled *Americans in Process*, put the matter far more bluntly, characterizing Syrians as "liars and deceivers" (Bushee 1937, 49). Such sentiments appear also to have been prevalent in Australia. During the debate about whether the 1903 Naturalisation Act should include "Syrians," Senator William Higgs declared that "Syrian hawkers in Queensland were a menace, frightening women in isolated places into buying goods"; Senator George Pearce of Western Australia concurred, adding that he considered Syrians lazy and unproductive and believed they would dilute the "White" nature of Australia (Higgs and Pearce quoted in Mansour 2002, 35).

In between those who romanticized and rejected immigrants, there were others who saw the "Syrians" as redeemable peasants who could be made into "modern Americans." Horatio Alger presaged these ideas in his 1871 book *Tattered Tom; Or, The Story of a Street Arab*:

> Arab as she was, she had been impressed by the kindness of Captain Barnes, and she felt that she should like to please him. Still, there was a fascination in the wild independence of her street life which was likely for some time to interfere with her enjoyment of the usages of a more civilized state. There was little prospect of her taming down into an average girl all at once. The change must come slowly. (104)

This passage associates an ethnicity/race (Arab) with an uncivilized state of existence—somewhat tantalizing in its independence—that can and should be tamed. Thus, to be "Arab"—or "Arabian," as in the Iowan newspaper quoted above—is to be uncivilized, a state that necessitates redemption, if at all possible. This attitude was reflected three decades later in the words of a social worker who declared that "old standards must be changed if we are sincere in our desire to attain a higher form of civilization. The strangers from across the water must be taught to discard un-American habits and conventions, and to accept new ideals" (Razovki 1917, 539). Or, as M. A. Howe wrote in 1903,

> To cope with these new conditions [the influx of immigrants] the same efforts are being made in Boston as elsewhere in America. The attempt to amalgamate the diverse elements into a common citizenship goes forward through hundreds of agencies—the public schools, the social settlements, the organization of charities, secular and religious, designed to meet every conceivable need of the unfortunate, but in such a way as to create citizens instead of paupers. (382)

In other words, immigrants could not be allowed to hover indeterminately between the "modern" and the "traditional" [or] their correlates the "American" and the "Syrian," for such a position would expose the impossibility of these ideal types and their irrelevance as either historical devices or symbols of the present world. Immigrants were expected to choose and to choose to be "American" as defined by the norms of a predominantly white, AngloSaxon, and Protestant middle class.

Being In-Between

In all these ways, immigrants experienced America's ideal and promise of absolute freedom (rights, religion, movement, values, etc.) as constrained by hegemonic social and legal boundaries that sought to locate them within categories of race and ethnicity that lie at the foundation of America. Ironically, equally restrictive and clearly distinctive boundaries were being drawn by early middle-class nationalists in the Middle East itself (Watenpaugh 2005; Kaufmann 2004).

In one argument that spanned the better part of 1905, a debate raged about where "Syrians belong." Intellectuals such as Juriji Zaydan, Shibli Shumayl, Farah Antoun, and Dawud Aoun (all "Syrian" émigrés in Egypt) argued that when the "Syrian" emigrates, "he leaves his nationality and adheres to the nationality of the people amongst whom he lives." Specifically, by "consorting with the American who is more civilized than he, the Syrian will without doubt adopt from him [the American] his habits, manners, sciences, and social arts to the point where he will forget his citizenship and join that of the American" (Bajjani 1905, 5).[5] Or, as Michel Chiha—a Lebanese nationalist who profoundly shaped the Libanist narrative—poetically put it some decades later when describing Lebanese emigration, "The butterfly does not become a caterpillar again" (1949, 63). Like American nationalists, these Middle Eastern nationalists would not allow immigrants to hover in-between states of political and cultural being.

Most "Syrian" immigrants rejected this dichotomized existence and worked to create a liminal space between the two. Ameen Rihani captures this best in his literary oeuvre *The Book of Khalid*. Written in English in 1911 for a "Western" audience, the book's preface is titled "Al-Fatihah"—the name of the first chapter of the Qur'an. From this intertextualized opening Rihani proceeds to further blur the line between "East" and "West" with his description of a fictional ancient manuscript found in the Khedivial Library in Cairo, which is the subject of the book:

> The present Editor was attracted to it [the manuscript] by the dedication and rough drawings on the cover . . . one of these is supposed to represent a New York Skyscraper in the shape of a pyramid; the other is a dancing group under which is written: "The Stockbrokers and Dervishes." (v)

The same "Editor" goes on to proclaim,

> No, there is nothing in this Work which we can call ours, except it be the Loom. But the weaving, we assure the Reader, was a mortal process; for the material is of such a mixture that here and there the raw silk of Syria is often spun with the cotton and wool of America. (v)

Interweaving threads of culture produced something totally different from either but intimately tied to both.

Other immigrants responded even more directly to attempts at the canonization of belonging. Writing from

5. Unless otherwise noted, all English translations are my own.

Paris for an Arab American newspaper—*al-Huda* (Guidance), published in New York—Abbas Bajjani took issue with the Cairo-based Syrian émigrés about the citizenship of Syrian immigrants. He engaged in the dialogue—which pitted Boston's *al-Muhajir* (The Immigrant) against *al-Munazir* (The Debater) in São Paolo, Brazil—by asserting that Syrians who become "Americanized" in customs and habits can still remain "Syrian" in political belonging—although it was still not quite clear what "Syria(n)" meant in terms of geopolitical dimensions and national identity. In fact, he contended, *inhabiting two separate worlds—physically and socially—was not only possible but actually desirable since it was the only hope for the salvation, edification, and modernization of "Syria."* To make his point, he cited the example of Yusuf Sima'an Humays, "who went [back] to the homeland and donated forty thousand [French] francs to build a tuition-free school in his town, then returned to his business in Mexico" (1905, 5).

The pursuit of individual interests in the *mahjar* did not, from Bajjani's perspective, negate or nullify the interests or rights of the Syrian immigrant as they pertained to the "homeland." Thus, he insisted that the immigrant had every right to play a role in the future of the Ottoman union, even if he did not serve in the army. In these two arguments, Bajjani first dissociated nation from a monolithic notion of ethnicity, itself defined by prescribed customs and habits. He then went one step further by separating "nation" from geography, allowing for the nation to exist simultaneously across many continents, in the hearts and minds of Syrian immigrants. Presaging Benedict Anderson's (1991) notion of the nation as an imagined community, Bajjani articulated "Syrianness" as an idea bridging past and future as well *al-balad* (homeland) and *al-mahjar* (place of settlement). In addition to the substance of the argument, what is equally striking is the global nature of the debate. In just one article, the discussion darts from Lebanon, Syria, and Cairo through Paris to New York, Boston, Mexico, and São Paolo and back, without explanation or self-consciousness: the author clearly expected the readers to see this nebulous imagined community as normal. Tellingly, even those arguing against this diffused construction of "Syria" were themselves part of the very structure they were dismissing as irrelevant. Immigrants thus created a globalized imagined community that sought to define "Syria" and "Syrians" just as those residing in Bilad al-Sham were busy articulating their vision of Syria.

It was not only immigrant intellectuals like Rihani and Bajjani who imagined a space beyond national and ethnic polarities. Ordinary immigrants also lived and built that very world. As centripetal nationalist tendencies pulled and tugged at the social fabric of their existence, immigrants became aware of the need to reweave that cloth, even as its threads frayed and became worn. In other words, they had to continue the journey—begun in the ports of Beirut and Tripoli—of (re)discovering who they "were" and reconstructing their "home" as a container of their identities. "Home" emerged as a concoction of memories of the homes they had left behind, new realities that required a place in this collective abode, and plenty of gaps in between. This was not always—if ever—a coherent or complete process, nor did it take place at one exclusive level or location. More importantly, it was a "home" that was neither "American" nor "Syrian," "traditional" nor "modern," even as it was partly all of these. It could not be landlocked within national boundaries because it existed simultaneously on several continents, in the imagination of immigrants, through their own travels between the two localities, and in the network of relations that spanned the distances across and beyond.

One of the ways of constructing a future with an eye to the past (or "walking backwards into the future," as James Clifford [2001, 475] paraphrases the Hawaiian historian Lilikala Kame'eleihiwa [1992]) was the broad spectrum of organizations established by immigrants to provide a coherent structure for their emerging identities, which ranged from the parochial to the global. Some organizations were narrowly focused on promoting the strict cohesion of a clan or of adherents of the same faith; for example, Victoria Samaha was asked—politely but firmly—to resign from the Douma Society (named after a village in northern Lebanon) after she married a non-Douma man (V. Samaha 1962). Others were organized by gender, such as the Syrian Women's Charitable Society in Brooklyn, or by interest, such as the literary society al-Rabitah al-Qalamiyya (the Pen League), which included among its members Mikhail Nu'aymeh and Jibran Khalil Jibran. Some lasted a few years (e.g., the Young Syrian Society), while others are still going. . . . Regardless of the mission or the size of such association, their boundaries were rarely fixed as their members struggled to define their communal identity in an inclusionary as well as exclusionary manner. Najla Saliba alluded to this state of flux in describing her Melkite Club in Detroit. As these Melkite Christians came from various parts of Mount Lebanon and Syria, "they couldn't get together because each was from a different village or city. Everybody wanted to come forward in the name of the place he came from" (Saliba 1962).

Religion provided another identity that stubbornly persisted despite attempts to reduce all immigrants to "Syrians." By 1920 there were ninety churches that ministered to Maronite, Melkite, and Syrian Orthodox communities in the United States. The clergy of these various churches actively sought to keep their parishioners from melting away into the larger American Christian churches. . . . The Maronite community set up churches in places like Boston, New York, and Philadelphia to maintain a separate identity from the larger Catholic churches.

This struggle to maintain a distinct religious identity also played out within the community itself, descending at times into sectarian violence. On October 14, 1905, the *New York Times* reported that "wild-eyed Syrians battled fiercely for a quarter of an hour in the lower west side" ("Syrians Riot" 1905). The "battle," which left one person dead and several injured, was the culmination of a war of words between Bishop Hawaweeny (and the elements of the Syrian Orthodox community) and Naoum Mukarzel, editor of the Arab American newspaper *al-Huda* (and elements of the Maronite community). For about a year, the pages of *al-Huda* and of the Syrian Orthodox mouthpiece, *Mira'at al-Gharb* (Mirror of the West), edited by Najib Diyab, manifested this tension at various levels. Part of it stemmed from an argument about the role that clergy—as opposed to secular leaders—should play. . . . Another element was the claim to religious authenticity. . . . A third characteristic of these newspapers was their nationalist orientation: *al-Huda*, considered pro-French even before the establishment of the Mandate in 1918, advocated for Lebanese independence, while *Mira'at al-Gharb* agitated against the French for a united and independent "Syria." The two newspapers and communities appeared to take issue with each other even over the Russo-Japanese War. . . . This controversy was thus an instance of local identity's being intimately and passionately tied to global issues, crossing myriad boundaries in the process. Indeed, news of this controversy reached beyond New York and the Arab American community in the United States to find its way into the pages of the Arab press in Brazil, Argentina, and Egypt.

Despite, or perhaps because of, such contentious moments, some immigrants continued to establish associations and organize activities (plays, picnics, parties, lectures, musical recitals, etc.) that attempted to unify their community. The size and scope of these events and organizations expanded over time as the community grew but also because, at particular historical moments and for certain purposes, the smaller groups were proving irrelevant to a United States that saw them as "Syrians," "Easterners," or "Arabs." In other words, even as the immigrant community maintained a diverse set of identities, it was forced time and again to define itself in larger ethnic and national terms and to imbue those meta-identities with "modern" and positivist aspects. As may be obvious from the preceding discussion, among the most instrumental institutions in the construction of larger concepts and frameworks of community were Arab American newspapers published before World War I. Between 1892 and 1907 there were twenty-one Arabic dailies, weeklies, and monthlies published in the United States alone. Seventeen of these were based in New York, and most did not survive long; nonetheless, when one considers that by 1907 the fifty thousand immigrants in the United States had access to eleven publications, it becomes clear that the Arabic press did indeed flourish as a new medium of communication for the community. . . .

The newspapers embodied the centripetal and centrifugal nature of community politics. Many, as noted earlier, came to represent a particular community, publishing self-serving articles and insulting diatribes. Yet the same newspapers included noteworthy discussions of social and political issues that faced the Syrian community in the "West." Moreover, each vied with the others to define the shape of that community. With titles such as *al-Huda*, *al-Muhajir*, and *Mira'at alGharb*, these newspapers clearly positioned themselves as the guideposts for the immigrant community in "Amirka." Their stated purpose was to tell their readers about the ways and habits of the "West" and to instruct them in how to become "modern." To that end, the topics covered ranged from social etiquette to parenting to women's work and their "proper" gender roles. Most such articles sought to juxtapose the "traditional" with the "modern Syrian," a category that was being constructed by immigrants in the *mahjar*. . . .

Collectively, however, these articles did not constitute a project of "Americanizing" the immigrants or of integration into the mainstream American public space; rather, they were creating a "Syrian American" public space. The same authors who were advocating new ways of being also regarded themselves first and foremost as "Syrian," with a distinct and worthy culture. In advocating the emancipation of the "Syrian" woman, 'Afifa Karam (1900) spoke as an "Eastern" woman, quite conscious of her distinction from her "Western" counterpart. Labiba Hashim, an early feminist living in Chile, published a magazine whose title was *Fatat al-Sharq* (Young Woman of the East). Naoum Mukarzel, who preached a "modern" social etiquette, never learned English and was politically engaged in creating both a distinct "Syrian" community in the United States and Mexico and, later, in establishing an independent Lebanon. They self-consciously positioned themselves between a "traditional East" and a "modern West," seeking to uplift the first and humanize the latter. Within that liminal space, they continually mixed and matched (or mismatched, for that matter) what they brought with them and what they saw in the streets and homes of the Americas. New "traditions" were created out of these combinations, in compromises that tried to straddle the cultural and class divides that separated "Syria" and peasants from the *mahjar* and immigrants [as well as] the latter from the larger Anglo-American middle-class world that surrounded them. . . . The "modern Syrian" would be cultured by reading books that reflected and created the[se] emerging ideals, attending theater productions by "Syrian" acting troupes, and visiting art galleries that displayed the works of Jibran Khalil Jibran. Thus, within the immigrant communities in the United States there arose a class whose members tried to distinguish themselves as different (culturally and socially) from middle-class America as well as from peasant "Syria" (see Khater 2001).

Globalizing Syrianness

This was not a unique phenomenon. Immigrants in South and Central America, Australia, and South Africa were creating the modern middle-class Syrian around the same time (J. Karam 2007; Lesser 1992). The similarities included occupational transformation (from peddlers to storekeepers), residential relocation (from inner cities to middle-class suburbs), educational aspirations (from illiterate parents to educated children), and material culture (from peasant clothes to westernized attire). In part, these parallel changes derived from similar experiences with hegemonic societies in which the "Syrian" was a minority. But this globalized modern Syrian was also the product of the transnational networks of immigrants. For example, even as Arab American newspapers helped create a space for immigrants within American society, they also gave their readers the means to be outside the boundaries of "Amirka"; they became the main communal means of maintaining connections with the people and places immigrants had left behind. The language of these newspapers—a "modernized" Arabic, until the close of World War I—was itself a highly evocative inscription of persisting cultural links with the "East," even if these, along with the language, were strained and changing. The articles, advertisements, and news stories published daily or weekly created an imaginary geography that could not be encompassed in one nation or another. . . .

News from the Middle East was featured regularly, maintaining a link for those who desired it—between immigrants and the "homeland." *Kawkab Amirka* (Planet America)—the first Arabic newspaper published in the United States, starting in 1892—had correspondents in the Ottoman Empire, Egypt, India, Iran, and North

Africa. Its early circulation—some thirty thousand copies per issue—sold not only in the United States but also in the Ottoman Empire. *Al-Huda*, *Mira'at al-Gharb*, and *al-Muhajir* ran daily columns under the title "News of Lebanon and Syria," which provided sundry news items from the Middle East. Thus, immigrants sitting in a Brooklyn coffeehouse or peddling in Oklahoma could have read on January 4, 1905, that the Sublime Porte was negotiating with a company to set up an electric tram service and an electric substation in Damascus. . . .

It was not only toward the "home country" that newspapers directed the attention of their subscribers and readers. They also helped inscribe an imagined community that went beyond the United States and "Syria" to Egypt, Europe, and South America, where fellow immigrants resided. For example, when the "Syrian" community in São Paolo boycotted an Italian import/export company that was discriminating against them, the news warranted mention in *Mira'at al-Gharb* (see "Akhbar" section, July 20, 1911). An advertisement in *al-Huda* by two business partners announced that

> as we have prepared to begin business in all the countries of South America and have struck agreements with the most famous factories here [the United States] to obtain all types of textiles . . . food and products that are traded by our Syrian brothers in those lands[,] we have taken out this announcement. (*al-Huda*, Jan. 4, 1905, 1)

These words reflect the mobility of immigrants across the Americas in search of family and fortune. After the Immigration Act of 1891, which prohibited immigrants with trachoma from entering the United States, Mexico became "America's 'Back Door'" (John 2001, 24, quoted in Alfaro-Velcamp 2003, 82). In 1906, concern over the crisscrossing of the US–Mexico border by "Syrian" immigrants led to an undercover investigation by the US Department of Commerce and Labor (Seraphic 1907). "Syrian" immigrants from Uruguay, Argentina, Jamaica, Haiti, and Cuba journeyed up and down North and South America, looking for work or seeking entry into the United States, all the while expanding the boundaries of this imagined community by etching, through peregrinations, links among all of these disparate places.

In these myriad ways "Syrian" immigrants contested the exclusive definitions of ethnic and national boundaries that were being drawn around them. They physically and mentally transgressed these boundaries. They wrote to and received letters from their home villages and towns, and they traveled back and forth, taking grandfather clocks with them to Mount Lebanon and bringing back *burghul* (cracked wheat). They wrote and read articles and books in Arabic while living in Chicago or New Orleans, and they established "Syrian" associations that discussed the economic and political state of "Syria." They construed the "East" as a prized spiritual space that stood in marked and welcome opposition to the materialist "West." At the same time, they saw themselves as distinct from and certainly superior to the "traditional Syrian." In the words of an "Americanized Syrian" to a "traditional Syrian," rendered through a fictional dialogue printed in *al-Huda*, "Are you still a villager? Haven't you become civilized? [*Zaraf wa fakaha*]." They criticized the bigotry and illiberal ideas rampant in an "East" dominated by traditional clergy and despotic rulers and proposed the unfettering of social and political relations. They believed that bridges, tramways, and skyscrapers were equally symbols of a modernity desirable at least as an end result, if not as a process. In other words, these immigrants not only refused to be contained—either physically or textually—in a narrowly defined cultural and political space but, in fact, proposed and lived alternative definitions of "Syrian" that were "modern" but not "American" and that pertained to a physical "Syria" but were assuredly neither contained by nor rooted to space on the map.

How the Syrians Became "White" and America "Colored"

In creating this liminal space that rendered "America" and "Syria" far less coherent than nationalists on either side proclaimed them to be, immigrants were in fact constantly redefining these very places. One of the tropes of this redefinition centered on the racial designation of "Syrians." While in the Middle East the concept of race was not self-evidently integral to the structure of societies, in the United States, South Africa, and Australia—and even in Brazil, to a certain extent—it proved essential for the very existence of "Syrians" in these territories (see J. Karam 2007 concerning Brazil and [Sarah] Gualtieri [in chapter 14 of this reader] concerning pivotal US court cases revolving around Syrians, race, and the right to naturalize). . . .

"Syrians" in South Africa and the United States sought successfully to characterize race in terms of religion—that is, to argue that they were Caucasians because they were Christians. This argument certainly was born out of necessity since most of them were—as Judge Smith of South Carolina said—"in color . . . darker than the usual person of white European descent" (*Ex parte Shahid* 1913, 3). But it is also a reflection of their preconceived conceptualization of the division of the world. Specifically, they came from a society in which the millet (religious sect) was the broadest marker of belonging and exclusion, while skin color was less pertinent. Once in South Africa, the United States, and Australia, where skin color carried more weight, they tried to reconcile the two concepts (religion and race) by making them coterminous. In doing so, they forced the legal systems of South Africa and the United States to adjust their definitions, at least enough to include ["Syrians"] as Semitic Christians. Thus, Justice Innes (one of the three Supreme Court justices ruling in the Gandur case [in South Africa]) wrote that "the Syrians though Asiatic are a White Semitic race which has been Christian, and not a Mohammedan [*sic*] from very early times" (*Gandur v. Registrar of Rand Townships* 1913, 15).

Through the association of Syrianness with "whiteness," Christianity and Syrianness became inscribed as one and the same. As anthropologist Ghassan Hage has remarked of a Christian Lebanese immigrant in Australia, "Her Christianity made her more White" (2002, 60). In this manner, the narrative of immigration/ethnicity that began in the 1890s with peasants claiming to be Christians escaping Turkish persecution became enshrined in the 1910s in the legal definition of "Syrians" as white. Marginalized in this fashion, Muslim immigrants disappeared from the narrative of immigration to the United States, South Africa, and Australia, among other places. Even among those immigrants who rejected such religious exclusion, the term *Syrian* became ethnically distinct from *Arab* or *Turk*.[6]

Conclusion

What began at ports of entry as a utilitarian label of geographical belonging became, over three decades, an identity defined and lived in communities in the *mahjar* and fiercely defended in courts, historical narratives, and newspaper editorials. What originated as a skeletal idea of Syrian ethnicity among urban intellectuals in Beirut during the 1860s was fleshed out and transformed by the lived experiences and practices of transplanted peasants in places as diverse as New York, Sydney, and Rio de Janeiro. In other words, the idea and ideation of the "Syrian" as an ethnic and national category were profoundly shaped by immigrants and their diasporic experiences. As close to two hundred thousand immigrants traveled back regularly or permanently to Mount Lebanon during the first three decades of the twentieth century, they sought to transform Mount Lebanon in the image they constructed of themselves in the *mahjar.* Remittances amounting to half the total income of Mount Lebanon altered the socioeconomic landscape of the territory, giving rise to new moneyed elites who displaced some of the old land-owning notables (Issawi 2006, 86). The departure of inordinately large numbers of men from the villages of Lebanon as well as the growing economic independence of some immigrant women combined to create a crisis in the patriarchy, necessitating renegotiations of gender roles both in the *mahjar* and in Lebanon. Social constructions of the "modern Syrian" were transported back into the new bourgeois homes that came to dot the mountains of Lebanon and stood out as symbols of *mahjar* wealth and change among the surrounding peasant homes. This physical embodiment of the immigrant identity—the "Lebanese House," with its red-tile roof, central receiving hall, separate public and private spaces, and distinct threshold between landscape and architecture—became the central motif in modern Lebanese culture (see Davie

6. [Theresa] Alfaro-Velcamp (2003) notes a similar exclusion of Muslims from the stories of immigration to Mexico.

2004). The reification of the eastern Mediterranean into a romanticized Lebanese "Mountain"—for example, in *zajal* (folk) immigrant poetry and the writings of authors like Jibran Khalil Jibran (Gibran 1952)—also emerged as a dominant theme in Lebanese popular culture through the 1970s (for discussion, see Salem 2003; Stone 2007). Equally telling is the fact that most thinkers and leaders who articulated a non-Arab nationalist ideology, from either a Libanist or a Syrianist perspective, came from the *mahjar* (e.g., Antun Saʿadeh, who was raised in Brazil, and his Syrian Social Nationalist Party; Pierre Gemayel, who grew up in Egypt, and the Lebanese nationalist Phalanges Party). Pertinently, the concept of the "Syrian" as a non-Arab Christian became the dominant narrative in Lebanon even when most people living there did not embody or even accept this idea. There is no doubt that the intersection of French colonial interests and the machinations of some Maronite religious and secular elites partly explain the hegemony of this idea; however, there is also no doubt that returning immigrants gave it substance and support. Whether as ideologues, as financial backers, or as members, immigrants played an inordinate role in those political parties of Lebanon dedicated to either a Lebanese or a Syrian brand of nationalism.

What the preceding discussion makes clear is that migrants are not a marginal element in the history of the Middle East. Rather, they were instrumental in shaping both the *mahjar* and the lands from which they came. They did so not according to some preset idea of "modernity" but, rather, by constructing their own "modern," which related genealogically to both the *mahjar* and the eastern Mediterranean but was also quite different from either. Their very existence and insistence on maintaining a set of multiple identities kept the boundaries of "America" and "Lebanon" from being hermetically sealed. Their travels and discourses perforated those borders, maintaining the notion that one can be—among other things—"Syrian" in America and "American" in Syria and thus dislocating the meanings of such categories. Their clothes, houses, mannerisms, language, schools, investments, newspapers, expectations, and images of "Syria" bumped up against those same elements in the United States and Mount Lebanon, rendering both into spaces that fluctuated in meaning and in physical contours.

On one level, this was a tension about how to define the two spaces and their peoples. But on another level it was about where "America" and "Syria" really are. Around the turn of the twentieth century, the myriad connections among immigrant communities and the Middle East created a transnational imagined community that diffused "Syria" beyond the physical place it occupied in the Middle East. "Syria," then, was as much in Brooklyn and Buenos Aires as it was "there," in the Middle East. As a contested idea, as a set of changing customs and habits, as a group of people, as a language transforming and accommodating new realities, "Syria" was not—if it ever was—contained within a set of physical boundaries. In other words, the organic and arborescent notion of a place—roots and branches—as well as the naturalized identity of a place and a people cannot be sustained against the backdrop of immigrant stories. From this perspective, the story of immigrants is not peripheral to the history of the Middle East; rather, it is an integral part of that social, cultural, and economic matrix. It is only by deploying such a transnational approach that we can fully dislocate the Middle East from its position as a historical and contemporary "Other."

Works Cited

Volume editors' note: This works cited list includes sources cited in the original publication of this chapter but not in the excerpt given here.

Akarli, Engin. 1992. "Ottoman Attitudes towards Lebanese Emigration, 1885–1910." In *The Lebanese in the World: A Century of Emigration*, edited by Albert Hourani and Nadim Shehadi, 109–38. London: Centre for Lebanese Studies, I. B. Tauris.

"Akhbar [News]." 1907. *Mira'at al-Gharb*, Apr. 12.

Alfaro-Velcamp, Theresa. 2003. "So Far from Allah, so Close to Mexico." PhD diss. Georgetown Univ.

Alger, Horatio, Jr. 1871. *Tattered Tom: Or, The Story of a Street Arab*. Boston: Loring.

Amyuni, Mary. 1962. Interview by Alixa Naff, Fall. Series 4-c-1, Naff Arab-American Collection. Smithsonian Institution, Washington, DC.

Anderson, Benedict. 1991. *Imagined Communities: Reflections on the Origin and Spread of Nationalism*. 2nd ed. London: Verso.

Bajjani, Abbas. 1905. "*Al-Munazara* bayna jaridat *al-Muhajir* wa jaridat al-munazir [Dispute between *al-Muhajir* and *al-Munahir* Newspapers]." *Al-Huda*, Jan. 8.

Batrouney, Trevor. 2005. *Unravelling Identity: Immigrants, Identity, and Citizenship in Australia.* Altona, Australia: Common Ground.

Burnett, John. 1907. Letter to the editor. *Birmingham Age-Herald*, Oct. 12.

Bushee, Frederick A. 1937. "The Invading Host." In *Americans in Process: A Study of Our Citizens of Oriental Ancestry*, edited by William Carson Smith, 43–76. Ann Arbor, MI: Edwards Bros.

Chiha, Michael. 1949. *Liban d'aujourd'hui: 1942* [Lebanon today: 1942]. Beirut: Ed. du Trident.

Clifford, James. 2001. "Indigenous Articulations." *Contemporary Pacific* 13:468–90.

Davie, May, ed. 2004. *History of the Central House in the Mediterranean.* Beirut: ELBA.

"Don't Like Arabs." 1901. *Cedar Rapids Evening Gazette*, July 16.

Duoun, Taufik. 1944. *A emigrardo sirio-libanesa cis terras de promissdo* [Syrian-Lebanese immigration to the promised lands]. São Paulo, Brazil: Tipografia Editora Arabe.

Ex parte Shahid. 1913. 205 F. 812.

Gandur v. Registrar of Rand Townships. 1913. Supreme Court of South Africa, Mar.

Gibran, Kahlil. 1952. *The Prophet.* New York: Knopf.

Gualtieri, Sarah. 2004. "Strange Fruit? Syrian Immigrants, Extralegal Violence, and Racial Formation in the Jim Crow South." *Arab Studies Quarterly* 26:63–85.

Haddad, George. 1916. *Mt. Lebanon to Vermont.* Rutland, VT: Tuttle.

Haddy, Michael. 1962. Interview by Alixa Naff. Series 4-c-1, Naff Arab-American Collection. Smithsonian Institution, Washington, DC.

Hage, Ghassan. 2002. *White Nations: Fantasies of White Supremacy in a Multicultural Society.* Sydney, Australia: Routledge.

Hashi, Salim Hassan. 1983. *Yawmiyyat lubnani fi ayam al-mutesarrifiyya* [Diary of a Lebanese during the days of the *mutesarrifiyya*]. Beirut: Dar Lahad Khatir.

Hitti, Philip. 1924. *Syrians in America.* New York: G. H. Doran.

Houghton, Louise. 1911. "Syrians in the United States." *Survey*, part 2 (Aug. 5): 656–69.

Hourani, Albert, and Nadim Shehadi. 1992. *The Lebanese in the World: A Century of Emigration.* London: Center for Lebanese Studies and I. B. Tauris.

Howe, M. A. 1903. *Boston: The Place and the People.* New York: Macmillan.

Issawi, Charles. 2006. *The Economic History of the Modern Middle East and North Africa.* New York: Taylor.

John, Sara Elizabeth. 2001. "'Trade Will Lead a Man Far': Syrian Immigration to the El Paso Area, 1900–1935." Master's thesis, Univ. of Texas at Austin.

"Kalimat *al-Huda*" [*Al-Huda*'s word]. 1905. *Al-Huda*, Jan. 18.

Kame'eleihiwa, Lilikala. 1992. *Native Land and Foreign Desires.* Honolulu: Bishop Museum Press.

Karam, 'Afifa. 1900. "Akhatar al-nisa'a" [Women's thoughts]. *Al-Huda*, Sept. 1.

Karam, John Tofik. 2007. *Another Arabesque: Syrian-Lebanese Ethnicity in Neoliberal Brazil.* Philadelphia: Temple Univ. Press.

Kaufmann, Asher. 2004. *Reviving Phoenicia: The Search for Identity in Lebanon.* Bilingual ed. London: I. B. Tauris.

Khater, Akram Fouad. 2001. *Inventing Home: Emigration, Gender, and the Making of a Lebanese Middle Class, 1870–1920.* Berkeley: Univ. of California Press.

———. 2017. "Why Did They Leave? Reasons for Early Lebanese Migration." *Lebanese Studies*, Nov. 15. At https://lebanesestudies.news.chass.ncsu.edu/2017/11/15/why-did-they-leave-reasons-for-early-lebanese-migration/.

Khatir, Lahad. 1967. *Epoque des mutassarif au Liban, 1861–1918* [The age of the *mutassarif* in Lebanon]. Beirut: Dar Lahad Khatir.

Lesser, Jeffrey. 1992. "From Pedlars to Proprietors: Lebanese, Syrian, and Jewish Immigrants in Brazil." In *The Lebanese in the World: A Century of Emigration*, edited by Albert Hourani and Nadim Shehadi, 393–410. London: Centre for Lebanese Studies and I. B. Tauris.

Ma'alouf, lskandar [*sic*] 'Issa. 1908. *Dawani al-qutuf fi tarikh bani Ma'alouf* [Approaches to the history of the Ma'alouf family]. Ba'abda, Lebanon: Al-Matba' al-'Uthmaniya.

Manneh, Butrus Abu. 1980. "The Christians between Ottomanism and Syrian Nationalism: The Ideas of Butrus al-Bustani." *International Journal of Middle East Studies* 11:287–304.

Mansour, Anne. 2002. "Whitewashed: The Lebanese in Queensland, 1880–1947." In *Arab-Australians Today: Citizenship and Belonging*, edited by Ghassan Hage, 16–36. Carlton, Australia: Melbourne Univ. Press.

Mukarzel, Salim. 1898. "Qara' al-Bab" [Knocking on the door]. *Al-Huda*, Mar. 22.

Nash, Geoffrey. 1998. *The Arab Writer in English*. Brighton, UK: Sussex Academic.

Obenzinger, Hilton. 1999. *American Palestine: Melville, Twain, and the Holy Land Mania*. Princeton, NJ: Princeton Univ. Press.

Pitts, Montie Bryan, Jr. 2006. "Forging Ethnic Identity through Faith: Religion and the Syrian-Lebanese Community in São Paulo." MA thesis, Vanderbilt Univ.

Qirqmaz, Elias. 1899. "Shaqa' al-walad al-suri fi al-mahd, wa fi al-bayt wa fi al-suq" [The misery of the Syrian child in the crib, in the house, and in the market]. *Al-Huda*, Apr. 18.

Rabinovich, Itamar. 1992. "Syria and the Syrian Land: The 19th Century Roots of 20th Century Developments." In *The Syrian Land in the 18th and 19th Century*, edited by Thomas Philipp, 43–54. Stuttgart, Germany: Steiner.

Razovki, Cecilia. 1917. "The Eternal Masculine." *Survey* 37:538–46.

Riggs, Edward. 1899. "A Missionary in Syria: The Rev. Edward Riggs Tells of Existing Conditions in That Country." *New York Times*, Sept. 4.

Rihani, Ameen. 1911. *The Book of Khalid*. New York: Dodd.

Rihbani, Abraham. 1914. *A Far Journey: An Autobiography*. Boston: Houghton Mifflin.

Salem, Elise. 2003. *Constructing Lebanon: A Century of Literary Narratives*. Gainesville: Univ. Press of Florida.

Saliba, Najla. 1962. Interview by Alixa Naff, May. Series 4-b-1, Naff Arab-American Collection. Smithsonian Institution, Washington, DC.

Samaha, Skiyye. 1962. Interview by Alixa Naff. Series 4-c-1, Naff Arab-American Collection. Smithsonian Institution, Washington, DC.

Samaha, Victoria. 1962. Interview by Alixa Naff, May. Series 4-b-3, Naff Arab-American Collection. Smithsonian Institution, Washington, DC.

Samne, Georges. 1920. *La Syrie*. Paris: Boddard.

Seraphic, A. 1907. *Report to Commissioner-General of Immigration, Department of Commerce and Labor, Immigration Service, Seraphic Report*. Document No. 51, 423–11. Record Group 85, Immigration and Naturalization Service. National Archives and Records Administration, Washington, DC.

Stone, Christopher. 2007. *Popular Culture and Nationalism in Lebanon: The Fairouz and Rahbani Nation*. London: Routledge.

"Syrians Riot in Street, and Many Are Hurt." 1905. *New York Times*, Oct. 24.

"Tahajum al-huda ʿala al-sahafa al-ʿarabiya" [*Al-Huda*'s attack on the Arab press]. 1928. *Al-lttihad alLubnani*, Mar. 28.

"To Battle, O Syrians." 1914. *Al-Huda*, Apr. 4.

Watenpaugh, Heghnar Zeitlian. 2005. "Deviant Dervishes: Space, Gender, and the Construction of Antinomian Piety in Ottoman Aleppo." *International Journal of Middle East Studies* 37:535–65.

Waterfield, Robin. 1998. *Prophet: The Life and Times of Kahlil Gibran*. New York: St. Martin's.

"Zarafwa fakaha" [Wit and humor]. 1898. *Al-Huda*, Mar. 22.

11

Representing Arabs and Muslims in the US after 9/11

Gender, Religion, and Citizenship

CAROL W. N. FADDA

In the short story "Alone and All Together" (2002) by Lebanese-American writer Joseph Geha, the teenage protagonist, Libby (an Americanized version of the Arabic name "Labibeh"), is watching the events of September 11 unfold on television in her suburban Chicago home while talking on the phone with her sister, Sally (originally Salma), in New York. Distraught by the "strip at the bottom of the screen" indicating "that everything points to the hijackers being Middle-Eastern extremists," Libby declares, "I just wish they wouldn't say it's us . . . until they're, like, sure." On hearing this, Sally fires back, "Us? . . . What us? . . . We were born here, and so were Mom and Dad, right here in Chicago, Illinois, U.S.A. . . . What I want to know . . . is when 'us' stops meaning *ibn Arab* [son of Arabs] and starts meaning American!" (Geha 2002, 53). More than merely pointing to some of the debates within Arab-American communities pertaining to the adoption of the Arab-American label,[1] Sally's and Libby's respective espousal and disavowal of a Middle Eastern, or more specifically Arab, identity become symptomatic of a divisive rhetoric that quickly dominated post-9/11 national discourse. This rhetoric separates the American from the un-American, the patriotic from the unpatriotic, with Arab and Muslim subjectivities being squarely cast in the latter category.

This chapter addresses a range of Arab-American literary and cultural texts that respond to the post-9/11 political and social terrain in the United States. They capture and challenge homogenized depictions of Arab-Americans, forging in the process what can be identified as revisionary or counterhegemonic spaces that redefine exclusionary conceptualizations of US citizenship and belonging. In addition to problematizing simplistic types of post-9/11 patriotism that demand a unilateral type of US national identity, the creation of these revisionary spaces responds to racial stereotyping, blanket labeling, and discriminatory profiling by insisting on complex representations of Arab-Americans. The focus on literary and cultural texts is meant to highlight the role of Arab-American creative production in shaping discussions of national belonging and citizenship in the United States, particularly following such an intense and traumatic crisis in the history of the nation as the 9/11 attacks.[2]

Excerpt from Carol Fadda-Conrey, *Contemporary Arab-American Literature: Transnational Reconfigurations of Citizenship and Belonging* (New York: New York Univ. Press, 2014), 139–76. Full references in the original notes were converted to author-date citations in the text and notes here, and a works cited list was added. Reprinted with corrections and press style changes for consistency throughout the volume by permission of New York University Press.

1. As I point out in the introduction [to *Contemporary Arab-American Literature*], while many Americans with Arab roots embrace the "Arab-American" or even the "Middle Eastern" label (at the same time raising questions as to who should be included under these umbrella terms), many others, in the name of safety and cultural assimilation, distance themselves from what they deem to be ultimately harmful and compromising Arab labels.

2. This is not to say that only Arab-American writers offer such a critical stance, for we find non-Arab and non-Muslim intellectuals

The attacks of 9/11, however, do not mark the first or the only event that has fomented reductive perceptions about Arab-Americans in the United States. They are in fact a recent installment in a long history of national and international crises and conflicts that have repeatedly and consistently underlined the provisional nature of US citizenship and belonging for Arab-Americans. These crises include the Six-Day War in 1967, the 1973 oil embargo, the first Gulf War, and the attacks on the World Trade Center in 1993. Such events position the formation and development of Arab-American identities within well-cemented racialized structures that hold the political relations between the United States and the Arab world at their center. These relations are dominated by US political and military hegemony. Domestic and foreign US policies underwent intense changes in the months and years after September 11 (including, for instance, the USA PATRIOT Act, the National Security Entry-Exit Registration System, and the establishment of the Department of Homeland Security).[3] These changes as well as the mobilization of extreme US military operations in Afghanistan and Iraq make evident that it is political rather than so-called civilizational or cultural factors that inform demonizing depictions of Arab identities, as they exist in the Arab world as well as in the United States.[4] Such political factors render 9/11, as pointed out by Nadine Naber and others, "a turning point, as opposed to the starting point, of histories of anti-Arab racism in the United States . . . in that representations of 'terrorism' and 'Islamic fundamentalism' have increasingly replaced other representations (that is, the rich Arab oil sheikh, belly-dancers, and harem girls) and have become more fervently deployed in anti-Arab state policies and everyday patterns of engagement than ever before" (Naber 2008a, 4). But more than being a "turning point," and notwithstanding obvious continuities in anti-Arab forms of discrimination that precede 9/11, I would argue that 9/11 constitutes a formative moment in self-iterations (literary and otherwise) that insist on portraying Arab-Americans through a transnational and antihomogeneous lens. This formative moment has mobilized more vocal, assertive, and unapologetic claims to transnational enactments of Arab-American identities that problematize the assimilative pressures inherent in dominant performances of US citizenship and belonging.[5] . . .

. . . [T]he texts analyzed in [this excerpt of the fourth] chapter [of *Contemporary Arab-American Literature*] articulate transnational Arab-American assemblages that overturn exclusionary conceptualizations of US citizenship and undercut the us-versus-them binary still pervading national discussions of 9/11. At the same time, they problematize the divisive rhetoric identifying the good Arab from the bad Arab. . . . Pointing out . . . discursive strategies that challenge the historical exceptionalism dominating US national rhetoric post-9/11, I analyze the ways in which Arab-American literary texts position the events of 9/11 along a transnational, transpolitical, transhistorical, and transgeographical continuum of aggression, violence, loss of civilian life, and conflicts that continue to plague the Arab world. The texts discussed in this section include the poems "first writing since" and

also voicing their concerns about the binary rhetoric and the violence that have typified national responses to the attacks of 9/11. See [writings by] Judith Butler (2006); Slavoj Žižek (2002); Joan Didion (2003); and Noam Chomsky (2001).

3. On September 11, 2002, the Justice Department initiated the National Security Entry-Exit Registration System. This system involves fingerprinting, interviewing, and photographing foreign or nonresident men in the United States from twenty-four Muslim-majority countries and North Korea. See [writings by] Salah Hassan (2002); Leti Volpp (2003); and Moustafa Bayoumi (2006). According to Nadine Naber, "Special registration resulted in the deportation of more than thirteen thousand individuals, none of whom was found guilty of terrorism charges" (2008b, 288). Moreover, Louise Cainkar notes that "in the seven days following September 11, Arabs and South Asians reported 645 cases of hate crimes" (2002, 22). Some of these murder victims include a Sikh man, Balbir Singh Sodhi (killed on September 15 in Mesa, Arizona), the Pakistani Waqar Hasan (killed on September 15, 2001, in Mesquite, Texas), Coptic Christian Adel Karas (killed in San Gabriel, California), and the Yemeni Ali Almansoop (killed in Detroit, Michigan). These murders were part of a 1,600 percent increase in crimes against Muslims, Arabs, or South Asians in the United States between 2000 and 2001 (Naber 2008b, 289).

4. Helen Hatab Samhan refers to such discrimination as "political racism" (1987, 11).

5. As portrayed in the other chapters [of *Contemporary Arab-American Literature*], literary iterations of transnational Arab-American subjectivities [were] in circulation well before 9/11.

"america" by Suheir Hammad and Dima Hilal, respectively, as well as the nonfictional essay "Where Is Home? Fragmented Lives, Border Crossings, and the Politics of Exile" by Rabab Abdulhadi. In depicting US and Arab lives within a transnational framework, these works debunk dominant representations of the events of 9/11 as an inexplicable attack on US freedom. Rather than condoning the 9/11 attacks, however, the push to overturn an emphasis on US innocence undercuts US historical amnesia by placing the role of a militaristic US foreign policy in the Arab world at the forefront of dominant discussions of 9/11 trauma.[6]

After addressing such issues, the chapter turns in its third and last section to examine the ways in which gender and sexual stereotypes are embedded in the us-versus-them, good-Arab-versus-bad-Arab binaries. This last section focuses specifically on how texts such as Yussef El Guindi's play *Back of the Throat* and Wafaa Bilal's performative and installation art interrogate the intersection of gendered, religious, racialized, and sexualized violence in the construction of a hegemonic narrative of US national security and citizenship post-9/11. By contextualizing the 9/11 attacks within a complex framework that privileges transnational perspectives, works such as the ones discussed in this chapter move national responses to 9/11 beyond the simplistic narratives of "you're either with us or with the terrorists" touted by George W. Bush and his administration. They also complicate rationalizations such as "they are jealous of our freedom" formulated in response to an uninformed public's bewildered "Why do they hate us?" question. . . .

"Over There Is Over Here": Positioning 9/11 within a Transnational Political Framework

With the impact of violence and trauma arriving in full force at the shores of the United States after 9/11, neat ideological and political separations between the Arab world and the United States were immediately contested. Arab-Americans collectively and individually rushed to denounce the attacks of 9/11, vehemently defining them as the acts of a handful of nonrepresentative extremist individuals. The poems by Suheir Hammad and Dima Hilal discussed in this section as well as the essay by Rabab Abdulhadi contribute an additional and crucial layer to such condemnations by viewing the events of 9/11 through a transnational lens. In doing so, these writers connect the attacks of 9/11 to Arab-Americans' direct or indirect experiences of war and conflict in the Arab world. In this way, the antihegemonic and transnational type of political citizenship espoused and enacted in these texts becomes the antithesis of . . . apolitical acquiescence. . . . It is in voicing such interrogative forms of dissent against imperial ventures overseas, then, that Arab-American literature not only imagines but also concretizes an antiamnesiac and transnational political landscape on the US domestic front, which in turn leads to transformed understandings of US citizenship and belonging.

One of the first Arab-American literary pieces to articulate this transnational, hybrid perspective is Hammad's poem "first writing since." Written a week after the attacks and widely distributed on the internet, the poem came to the attention of Russell Simmons, who subsequently signed Hammad to a deal with HBO's widely successful *Def Poetry Jam*, with which she toured for two years.[7] In this poem, Hammad widens the sphere of trauma and catastrophe resulting from the 9/11 attacks by including the perspective of Arab- and Muslim-Americans. More than doing so, Hammad places the attacks within a larger rubric of conflict and loss that transcends US national boundaries. Noting that 9/11 should in fact be regarded as part of a chain of violence to which people across the globe are repeatedly subjected, the speaker evokes places such as Gaza and the West Bank, where Palestinians have to deal with the brutal reality of loss, disruptions, and ruptures on a daily basis due to the vicissitudes of the Israeli occupation:

6. Such involvement includes the military presence in the Arabian Gulf, US sanctions against Iraq starting in 1990, and US support of Israel, to name a few. For a discussion of the history of US foreign policies in the Middle East, see Khalidi 2004 and McAlister 2001.

7. Hammad's performance of "first writing since" on the show can be viewed on YouTube: http://www.youtube.com/watch?v=SNfec7Fa2Cc.

> if there are any people on earth who understand how
> new york is feeling right now, they are in the
> west bank and the gaza strip. (Hammad 2005,
> lines 88–89)

This observation is followed by the speaker's jolting and powerful proclamation that "over there is over here" (Hammad 2005, line 121), a stark rebuttal of the neat geographical, national, and ideological categorizations (inherent in theories such as Samuel Huntington's clash of civilizations . . .) that ultimately enable facile constructions of the Other and his or her concomitant dehumanization. In doing so, Hammad enlarges the impact of the national catastrophe of 9/11 to incorporate more intricate and informed political, geographical, and human mappings of loss and trauma. By taking on a transnational approach to reading (or even reading into) 9/11, the poem overturns the markings of "true" US citizenship that distinguish between the grieving and the nongrieving or the patriotic and the unpatriotic. In this way, the claim that "over there is over here" ultimately points to the fact that 9/11 is not a starting point of suffering and trauma in contemporary US history or an inexplicable act of aggression against Americans but is in fact a continuation of worldwide acts of violence that the United States is complicit in through its foreign policy and strategic relationships with international powers as well as local governments in the Arab world. The pain and suffering that have for decades characterized thousands of lives "over there," in the Arab world, are in the poem brought to the United States, "over here," so much so that the language of trauma pervades both locales.[8] The recognition of this connectivity triggers a bittersweet sense of déjà vu for many Arab-Americans, one that brings back the memory of war and conflict in Arab homeland(s), while reminding them of their vulnerable and suspect status in their US home. What such a poetic articulation ascertains, then, is that the grafting of a similar traumatic pain onto both geographical domains ironically brings them into conversation with each other, thus challenging the neat separations between "here and there" and in turn between "us and them."

In addition to placing 9/11 within a transnational geopolitical rubric, the perspective offered in "first writing since" also challenges homogeneous conceptualizations of US citizenship by diversifying the narrative of fear propagated by the attacks, homing in on the specific fears of Arab- and Muslim-Americans. Upon hearing about the attacks, the speaker in the poem states,

> fire in the city air and I feared for my sister's life in a
> way never before. and then, and now, i fear for
> the rest of us.
> first, please god, let it be a mistake, the pilot's heart
> failed, the plane['s] engine died.
> then, please god, let it be a nightmare, wake me
> now.
> please god, after the second plane, please, don't
> let it be anyone who looks like my brothers.
> (Hammad 2005, lines 10–16)

But with the realization that the pilots who drove planes into the World Trade Center and the Pentagon do look like her Arab brothers, the speaker, and by extension Arab- and Muslim-Americans generally, had to tackle and face the divisive rhetoric that pitted the two parts of their hyphenated identities against each other. They could not adequately grieve as Americans since their Arab racial and religious attributes and affiliations connected them with what quickly and simplistically became synonymous with evil or, simply, anti-American:

> 4. ricardo on the radio said in his accent thick as
> yuca, "i will
> feel so much better when the first bombs drop over
> there. and my
> friends feel the same way."
> . . . .
> if i can find through this exhaust people who were
> left behind to
> mourn and to resist mass murder, i might be all right.
> thank you to the woman who saw me breaking my
> cool and blinking
> back tears. she opened her arms before she asked "do
> you want a hug?"

8. For a discussion of Hammad's "first writing since" in the context of contemporary trauma theory, see Rothberg 2003.

a big white woman, and her embrace was the kind
only people with the
warmth of flesh can offer. i wasn't about to say no to
any comfort.
"my brother's in the navy," i said. "and we're arabs."
"wow, you
got double trouble." word.
5. one more person ask me if i knew the hijackers.
one more motherfucker ask me what navy my
brother is in.
one more person assume no arabs or muslims were
killed.
one more person assume they know me, or that i
represent a people.
or that a people represent an evil. or that evil is as
simple as a
flag and words on a page. (Hammad 2005, lines
50–52, 65–78)

The pain induced by having one's identity unquestionably lumped with desperate extremist actions inevitably leads to anger on the part of the speaker, especially since what she conceives of as not only her American or New Yorker but specifically her Brooklyn identity is readily stripped away so that she becomes a stranger in her own city. The paradox imposed on Arab-American identity post-9/11, succinctly and beautifully captured here in the words "double trouble" describing her brother's seemingly disparate roles as a Muslim and a navy man, leads the speaker to vacillate between fear and anger: fear of the repercussions awaiting Arabs and Muslims in the United States and in the Arab world and anger that presumptions and blanket assessments become the dominant means for posttraumatic recuperation. Moreover, the speaker's refusal to succumb to polarizing reactions to the attacks leads her to turn her anger against assessments of US political and historical culpability in the Arab region that leave her no room to grieve as an Arab-American who considers the United States her home:

yet when people sent emails saying, this was bound
to happen, let's not forget u.s. transgressions, for
half a second i felt resentful. hold up with that,
cause I live here, these are my friends and fam,
and it could have been me in those buildings,
and we're not bad people, do not support
america's bullying. can i just have a half second
to feel bad? (Hammad 2005, lines 59–64)

The use of the word "we" in these lines is important, for it points to the speaker's refusal to participate in the polemics of national exclusivity propagated by the us-versus-them rhetoric. The word "we" is also a reminder that the speaker is American as much as she is Arab, with a need to mourn her "friends and fam" who died in the World Trade Center. However, this "we" that the speaker identifies with is not an uncritical collective but one that imbues US identity and citizenship with a dissenting strain that denounces "america's bullying." Acknowledging nuanced forms of citizenship and belonging necessitates a complex approach to notions of alterity and difference, an approach that maintains at its center a transnational awareness of place and experience that connects various spaces and geographies of knowledge.

The thematics exploring the transnational reach of conflict and war are also explored by Dima Hilal, another strong voice emerging from the contemporary collective of a younger generation of Arab-American poets. Hilal was born in Beirut, Lebanon, and, like Hammad, moved with her family to the United States at a young age. Echoing the historical and geopolitical continuities in narratives of war and aggression as explored in Hammad's "first writing since," Hilal's poem "america" captures the anguish of Arab-American immigrants who have left their war-torn homelands behind, only to be faced with violence and personal threats in their new home:

we fade into the fabric of these united states
pay our taxes, pledge our allegiance
lose ourselves in its thick folds
success finds us and we find success
intoxicating
until a plane carves a path though steel and glass
smoke billowing from two wounded skyscrapers,
the aftermath all too familiar
. . . .
until the sudden sidelong glance,
the step back
wait, isn't that where you're from?
let's bomb them back to the stone age

those arabs
never should have let them into our country those
arabs
. . . . .
we'll teach those turban-wearing, towel-headed,
dirty, motherfucking, camel loving, terrorists
a lesson they'll never forget
fractured skull, baseball bat,
crushed bones, clenched fists
battered bodies, a switchblade, crow bar
gun shot blast
it's us versus them
are you with us are
you with us are
you with us
or against us? (Hilal 2004, lines 11–18, 25–31, 37–48)

Here again, the speaker refutes the assumption that 9/11 constitutes the single, overarching, and transformative act of political aggression that mitigates all others in recent history, asserting instead that for many US citizens, specifically for Arabs, the attacks of 9/11 in fact are another devastating installment in the continuum of violence and oppression experienced on a daily level in the Arab world and beyond. With "the aftermath [being] all too familiar," the events of 9/11, notwithstanding the specificity of the circumstances or the political motives that brought them about, ultimately yield a disconcerting language of anguish and loss recognizable by all war-zone survivors intimately familiar with what the poem describes as "the endless sorrow / of life snatched without warning or reason" (Hilal 2004, lines 15–16).

But rather than enabling many war-weary Arab-Americans to assert their US belonging and participate in collective national healing, this sense of déjà vu in many ways links them to violent histories that are then used as justifications for regarding Arabs and Muslims (regardless of citizenship rights) as a foreign and even downright dangerous presence in US society. Demonstrating a dexterous use of poetic voice, Hilal's poem addresses the exclusionary dimensions of US citizenship as constructed and conceived after 9/11 by switching the identity of the collective evoked by the word "we" midway through the poem. She uses it first to designate an Arab immigrant collective intent on making the United States its home and then changes its ascription later on in the poem to point to a suspicious and violent faction of US society intent on upholding its patriotic post-9/11 fervor by attacking "towel-headed . . . terrorists." With this switch in the groupings signified by the word "we," the repetition of the phrase "are you with us or against us" toward the end of the poem, more than merely undercutting, through redundancy, the rudimentary logic informing such a polemical stance, is in fact further problematized by Hilal's strategic destabilization of what or whom the two terms, "you" and "us," signify. In doing so, Hilal, like Hammad, . . . embeds her work with transnational and revisionary articulations of US citizenship and belonging that reimagine homogeneity and hegemony by transforming "'the American way of life' into 'American ways of life'" (Salaita 2005, 165).

The dogged insistence on underscoring the transnational links informing Arab-American citizenship as depicted in Hammad's and Hilal's work takes on more specific dimensions in the nonfictional piece by Rabab Abdulhadi, "Where Is Home? Fragmented Lives, Border Crossings, and the Politics of Exile" (2005). In this essay, Abdulhadi, . . . originally from the city of Nablus in the West Bank, reflects on the thematic of Palestinian exile and the construction of individual and collective Palestinian identities in the United States in light of 9/11. Creating two interconnected narratives, she describes in one narrative her attempts (as a Muslim Arab) to navigate and survive the closed-off boundaries of New York City in the hours and days following the 9/11 attacks. In another narrative, she replicates the same concerns from the geographical vantage point of the Israeli-controlled Palestinian territories. In both cases, Abdulhadi portrays Arabs and Muslims as a besieged and monitored group, even if the contexts of such positionings might seem divergent at first glance.

Trying to reach her home in upper Manhattan right after the planes hit the World Trade Center, Abdulhadi finds herself suddenly engulfed by a throng of policemen and checkpoints in an area that has quickly become akin to a war zone. Sensing the rising levels of fear and paranoia, she becomes increasingly conscious of her visibly Arab features and accent. In self-censoring her actions and speech in a taxi she is sharing with other New

Yorkers trying to reach their homes (including a businessman she suspects to be Iranian[9]), she is reminded of similar restrictions faced every day by Palestinians in the West Bank and Jerusalem. These restrictions include checkpoints, unwieldy border crossings, and the overall debilitating effects of Israeli occupation on Palestinians. Using linguistic parallels to link the critical tropes of racial passing and border crossing, and pointing to the privileges and limitations entailed in both, Abdulhadi states, "My split lives are on a collision course again: I feel like such a traitor for *passing*. But wouldn't it be better to *pass* today? Do I want to identify with 'them' [meaning Arabs]? Do I want to escape the collective guilt-by-association, the fate of my fellow Arabs, Palestinians, and Muslims? Should I renege on my roots?" (2005, 74).

These questions and musings not only underscore the volatile and changeable nature of Arab-American citizenship and belonging in the United States but also point to the forever-shifting qualities of homes and homelands. Speaking of a sense of Arab belonging in the United States (which 9/11 made all the more fleeting and questionable), Abdulhadi draws on the collective experience of Palestinian dispossession, stating, "This *home* [the United States or specifically New York City] is becoming so similar to what happens back home [in Palestine]" (2005, 76). Here again, as in Hammad's poem, the transnational political lens through which Abdulhadi negotiates the post-9/11 fear and panic "over here," in the United States, incorporates dispossession and trauma as experienced "over there," specifically in the occupied Palestinian territories and the refugee camps in Lebanon.[10]

Such a perspective overturns exclusionary depictions of 9/11 that frame it as the single most defining moment of national or even international trauma. Instead, alternative models of historical and geopolitical continuities between seemingly disparate locations are placed at the forefront of 9/11 trauma, so much so that the events "over there" come to inform and bleed into crises "over here." This strategy, however, is not meant to conflate two such distinct geographical locales but is geared toward questioning the shortcomings involved in fixing identities in seemingly bounded places. Such a perspective transforms concepts and practices of homes and homelands, which, instead of being stable and solid entities, are always revised and evaluated to assess not only who is included but also who is excluded from dominant understandings of citizenship and belonging.

Further questioning the politics of containment that occlude Arab-Americans from discussions of national recuperation after 9/11, Abdulhadi asks, "Whose memories are valid? For whom are memorials built?" (2005, 82). Through such questions, what this essay and in fact many of the texts discussed in this chapter speak to is the need to acknowledge and make space for transnational articulations of US citizenship and belonging in order to acknowledge the multiple connections to and remembrances of loss and trauma that 9/11 evokes, specifically here as it applies to Arab-Americans. In doing so, these texts unveil a strong, informed, yet complex type of transnational political commitment that minimizes the ideological gulf separating "here" (the United States) from "there" (the Arab world). In doing so, they challenge the state-sponsored politics of containment and the monitoring of racialized Arab and Muslim bodies, in turn discrediting racist and exclusionary articulations of US citizenship.

Rethinking the Mobilization of Gender and Sexuality in the National-Security State

The mobilization of a transnational political framework (albeit of the imperialist, neo-Orientalist kind) has not been absent from the workings of the US security state since 9/11. In the name of securing the homeland, hypervigilant patriotism demands that the elusive threats of terrorism posed by a homogenized Muslim or Arab enemy "over there" be reinscribed on the racialized bodies of religious, ethnic, and diasporic minorities "over here." The containment of racialized bodies at home (in the United States) through surveillance, incarceration,

9. In an interesting moment of ethnic recognition, Abdulhadi and the Iranian businessman choose not to reveal each other's Middle Eastern identity to the other passengers in the taxi in order to preserve each other's and [their] own safety.

10. The essay also incorporates Abdulhadi's memories of visiting the Sabra and Shatila Palestinian refugee camp in Beirut.

and deportation becomes an extension as well as a justification of the US wars abroad, all in the name of preserving (and disseminating) US "freedoms." The rhetoric developing out of such a state-defined transnational political framework vastly differs from the one deployed in the counterhegemonic discourse evident in the Arab-American texts discussed in this [work]. Such difference becomes most obvious in the ways in which dominant US narratives eschew any acknowledgment of or responsibility for the violence, trauma, and loss of lives "over there" that are directly caused by so-called democracy or freedom projects such as Operation Enduring Freedom in Afghanistan and Operation Iraqi Freedom [in Iraq]. A specific strategy of such hegemonic transnational deployments is devising the identifiable Arab and Muslim body within the United States as the internal embodiment of the external threat posed by the distant Other. Following such logic, then, the security of the US homeland necessitates perpetuating the foreignness of Arab and Muslim bodies, with this foreignness always being a gendered one that pits the demasculinized, homosexualized, and even "perverted" figure of the Arab or Muslim man against a hypermasculine and heteronormative (or even homonormative) understanding of US nationalism and citizenship.[11] . . .

What is primarily perceived to be most insidious and threatening about Arab and Muslim men is their ability to "infiltrate" the US social fabric. Such a possibility places the US public in a policing position vis-à-vis difference and dissidence, which are then constructed at the interstices of religion, race, ethnicity, politics, and sexuality. One aspect of such positionings that is most pertinent to my discussion here is the ways in which homophobia, racism, and fear of the Arab and Muslim Other intersect in constructions of the male terrorist (suspect) as he is identified within the United States. Such constructions interweave discriminatory descriptors such as "monster, terrorist, fag," which are lumped together to form a necessary prescriptive antidote in national productions of "docile patriots" (Puar and Rai 2002, 117, 130). Hence, we find that the fight against terrorism both at home and abroad (over there and over here) necessitates not only military violence but also sexual violence that, as enacted on the male Arab and Muslim body, becomes a means to both reveal and punish its perverse identity (a rationale made evident by the torture tactics carried out at Abu Ghraib, Guantánamo Bay, and elsewhere).[12] . . . [In what follows,] I single out Yussef El Guindi's play *Back of the Throat* and Wafaa Bilal's installation art to exemplify performative destabilizations of public and governmental constructions of threatening Arab and Muslim masculinities post-9/11.

Back of the Throat was written by El Guindi and was performed in various cities across the United States, including San Francisco, Seattle, New York City, and Chicago [starting in] 2005. The play is about an American-born Muslim-Egyptian writer, Khaled, who is visited in his apartment by two federal agents, Carl and Bartlett, in the period immediately following 9/11 (the whole play takes place inside his apartment). The two agents initially claim to be following a procedural investigation and even come equipped with evaluation forms for Khaled to fill out. Their "friendly" interrogation, however, hits a turning point toward the middle of the play when Khaled realizes that the agents have already determined him to be guilty of colluding with the 9/11 attackers. Representing these attackers is Asfoor (depicted as the mastermind behind the 9/11 attacks), who haunts the whole scene and makes ghostly appearances throughout the play. Asfoor's character in fact has interesting parallels to that of Mohammad Atta, the so-called leader of the nineteen 9/11 hijackers, parallels made evident by some of the details provided in the play that I will turn to shortly. The agents visiting Khaled start constructing the narrative of his guilt by examining his political beliefs in conjunction with his sexual leaning. Searching his apartment for

11. For an in-depth analysis of the connections among heterosexuality, hypermasculinity, and patriotism, see Alexander 2006. For a discussion of homonormative nationalism, see Jasbir Puar's chapter titled "The Sexuality of Terrorism" in [her book] *Terrorist Assemblages* (2007, 37–78).

12. Thus, we find that visual representations of the terrorist figure's [so-called] perverse/failed heterosexuality abound in the period right after 9/11, with cartoons depicting Osama bin Laden, for instance, being sodomized by the Empire State Building (see Puar and Rai 2002, 126).

"clues," they come across some porn magazines, one of which features a woman "draped over a cow" (El Guindi 2006, 16). The agents read these magazines not merely as kinkiness or sexual curiosity but as material evidence of what they eventually describe as Khaled's "unnormal" character (19). In fact, it is this same abnormality (which gets paired with religious and political difference) that they also see surfacing in the titles of the books he owns. For in addition to the Qur'an, a gift from his mother that Khaled cannot even access because of his inability to read or speak Arabic, these titles include *Getting Your Government's Attention through Unconventional Means*, *A Manual for the Oppressed*, *Covering Islam*, *Militant Islam*, and *Quotations from Chairman Mao Tsetung* (17).[13] These findings provide the agents with insurmountable evidence pointing to Khaled's questionable US identity, leading Bartlett to state,

> I am frankly amazed at just how abnormal everything is in your apartment. I have actually been growing quite alarmed by what we've been finding. I mean we've already established you're a left-leaning subversive with Maoist tendencies who has a thing for bestiality and militant Islam. Throw in your research on guns and assassins and I could have you inside a jail cell reading about yourself on the front page of every newspaper before the week is out. (El Guindi 2006, 19–20, 21)

Such a pronouncement, which might seem an extreme threat, nevertheless captures the dangerous paranoia and random deductions that informed the rounding up of Arab and Muslim men by government officials right after 9/11 as well as the continued targeting and incarceration of Muslim men (many of whom are US citizens) in the name of state security.[14] Bartlett's statements, then, clearly delineate how Khaled's sexual, intellectual, religious, and political identities (or what is presented of them through the culled evidence) become incriminating links to or evidence of a threatening, antinormative type of US citizenship. Khaled's repeated and insistent reminder that he is a "citizen" throughout the "interrogation" inevitably begs the weighty but unstated question, But what *kind* of citizen is he? In fact, it becomes clear that such a question is not even a necessary or valid one, for the agents have already determined what kind of citizen Khaled is before they entered his apartment. Khaled's possessions then duly confirm to the agents that his is a type of citizenship that tears at the ideological fabric of US national identity, producing a questionable type of belonging that not only deters cultural inclusion but is a valid reason for its holder's prosecution. . . .

In *Back of the Throat* ([a title that] incidentally refers to the advice that Khaled gives the agents on how to pronounce the first letter of his name in Arabic), Khaled's repeated insistence on asserting his US citizenship is his way of (naively) seeking out just treatment. But the agents' strategy of disassembling his behavioral normalcy leads to the erosion of his citizenship and the rights that it should convey.

After all, in the post-9/11 national-security state depicted in the play, the only citizenship allowed or deemed safe is of the hetero- and homonormative, compliant, and docile kind. The erosion of Khaled's rights reaches a crescendo in the second half of the play, in which the agents implicate him in the 9/11 plots by providing flimsy evidence that he was present at a strip club the same night

13. Covering Islam, written by Edward Said, was first published in 1981 and then reprinted in 1997. *Quotations from Chairman Mao Tsetung*, or the *Little Red Book* contains some of the famous writings and sayings of Chairman Mao Tsetung and was first published in 1964. *A Manual for the Oppressed* most likely draws on works such as *Pedagogy of the Oppressed* by Paulo Freire, and *Militant Islam* might be in reference to right-wing pundit Daniel Pipes's *Militant Islam Reaches America*, published in 2003.

14. In the two months following the 9/11 attacks, over 1,100 noncitizens were detained by the Justice Department, but such figures were no longer released by the government after November 8, 2001 (Volpp 2003, 148). The detainment and incarceration of Muslim-American men in the United States (including citizens) continues, with the well-known cases of Dr. Sami Al-Arian of Temple Terrace, Florida, Dr. Rafil Dhafir of Syracuse, New York, Yassin Aref and Mohammed Hossain of Albany, New York, and Fahad Hashmi of Flushing, New York, to name a few (all of whom, except Aref, are US citizens).

1. Agents interrogate Khaled in the Silk Road Rising production of *Back of the Throat* by Yussef El Guindi. Photograph by Johnny Knight; courtesy of Silk Road Rising.

that Asfoor was there. A shadowy picture and a pay stub prove to be enough for the agents to confirm that, on "August 21st, at around 10:05" o'clock, Khaled visited the "Eyefull Tower Club," where he met with Asfoor. "Ms. Jean Sommers, aka, Kelly Cupid, 'Dancer Extraordinaire and Stripper Artiste'" (El Guindi 2006, 45), is presented as the eyewitness of this encounter. In fact, her testimony is preceded by that of two other female characters who are brought in as "witnesses" during the makeshift interrogation scene in Khaled's apartment. The first "witness" is a librarian who allegedly sees Asfoor approaching Khaled for the first time at the local library, and the second is Khaled's ex-girlfriend, Beth.[15] Kelly Cupid recounts how, after performing a lap dance on Khaled (or someone she is told was Khaled), she sees him follow Asfoor into the men's bathroom, where she "see[s] both of their legs under one of the stalls." She states, "they must have heard me, because Khaled comes shooting out and runs, just runs past me. And out saunters Mr. Creepy [Asfoor] after him. Calm as can be, like he'd just been holding a meeting in his office. . . . Might have been sucking each other off for all I know. Or shooting up. Who knows. At least one of them's dead" (in reference to Asfoor's suicide mission) (El Guindi, 2006, 48, ellipses in original). Khaled's purported disinterest in Kelly Cupid's lap-dance act (which frustrates her to the point that she breaks her professional code and makes him come) closely connects the charge of terrorism or terrorism plotting to Khaled's "failed" heterosexual desire. In fact, in some productions of the play, Kelly Cupid herself performs such an intermixture of heterosexuality and patriotism through her American-flag-inspired costume, which confirms the binary of healthy patriotic heterosexuality versus perverse homosexual terrorism.

Toward the end of the play, in a desperate last bid to collect "evidence," Agent Bartlett subjects Khaled to a violent and invasive strip search in order to find out if Khaled has a tattoo on his penis, a discovery that he thinks would thereby certify Khaled's guilt. The tattoo clue is gleaned from an email fragment allegedly sent by Asfoor in which he makes a vague reference to tattoos done "where the skin folds so you can hide it if you change your mind" (El Guindi 2006, 32). The agents interpret this reference as a way for sleeper-cell agents to recognize each other. What becomes clear in the second part of the play is that the basis of the agents' conviction of Khaled's guilt is intricately and closely related to what they perceive as his questionable nonnormative sexuality. Even though the strip search does not yield a confirmatory tattoo sighting, a guilty or innocent verdict vis-à-vis any terrorist act remains irreversibly connected to Khaled's sexuality. Bartlett, confessing that he finds the strip search extremely unappealing, states, "It still leaves us wondering what you did all that time in the bathroom with one of the more hideous individuals [Asfoor] we've come across? Now would be the time to fess up to any deviant sexual inclinations. It might get you off" (49). The multiple meanings attached to the pronouncement "get you off" cements the link between Khaled's alleged sexual and terrorist acts. The end of the play does not yield any easy answers about Khaled's guilt or innocence, with the audience (or the reader of the play) being positioned as the ultimate judge of Khaled's character and actions.

Asfoor's closing address propagates such ambiguity. Stepping out of the closet after the two agents leave Khaled's apartment, Asfoor addresses Khaled (who remains crouching on the floor after his invasive interrogation). Asking him for English lessons, Asfoor tells Khaled, "I might even teach it. . . . I will teach language back. I will make them speak their own language differently. I will have them speak words they never spoke before. . . . And soon my language will also fall on their heads. Like theirs falls on ours. Exploding in our brains 'til we can't even dream in peace. . . . I can help you [Khaled] find your voice. You've lost your way. . . . I can help. . . . I know how to inspire. I know how to inspire" (2006, 50–51, ellipses in the original). I read such proclamations not merely as an anti-imperialist statement

15. In fact, the positioning of such female characters as judges or regulators of Khaled's Arab Muslim identity has resonance with the role of women in the Abu Ghraib scandal, in which US female military personnel such as reservist Lynndie England were portrayed as primary (and independent) agents involved in torturing prisoners by using what they deemed to be nonnormative, taboo, and deviant sexual methods. For an in-depth discussion of the Abu Ghraib photographs, see Tétreault 2006; for an analysis of the role of female soldiers in the war on terror, see Riley 2006.

or as a harbinger of Khaled's possible radicalization as a result of his traumatic interrogation. They point to the inescapable branding of Khaled as a so-called terrorist at the hands of the agents so much so that he comes to embody that role, regardless of his innocence or guilt. I also read the play's open-endedness as a deliberate tactic aimed at engaging an audience (visually and discursively) in interrogations of citizenships. Such tactics, as deployed in Arab-American cultural and literary production, disrupt and defy normative models of nation and belonging by specifically underscoring the intersection of religion, sexuality, and nationality in racialized constructions of the terrorist figure. The end result of such revisionary deployments is the formation of counterpublic sites or spaces in which dissident and transnational forms of political citizenship could be imagined and enacted, which in turn pushes against (and transforms) the logic of normative and "docile" US citizenships.

2. Khaled and Asfoor in the Silk Road Rising production of *Back of the Throat* by Yussef El Guindi. Photograph by Johnny Knight; courtesy of Silk Road Rising.

Nevertheless, the various counterhegemonic articulations discussed in this chapter, in their response to simplistic and binary formulations of US citizenship after 9/11, often strategically incorporate some of the self-same oppressive language of racial, religious, and national discrimination they are seeking to undercut and refute. Such strategies, even while informing an antiessentialist and transnational Arab-American discourse, can run the risk of perpetuating a hegemonic binary structure even through disavowal. In other words, in the same way that George W. Bush's affirmation (following the 9/11 attacks) of Arab- and Muslim-Americans' "true" Americanness rendered their foreignness more vivid and immediate in the public's imagination (Salaita 2005, 151), the question becomes, Can these texts' engagement with questions of exclusionary US citizenship and belonging inadvertently reify the racialization of Arab- and Muslim-Americans in the United States?

To investigate the boundaries as well as the possibilities posed by such a question, I conclude my discussion of Arab-American literary responses to 9/11 by looking briefly at other forms of cultural interventions to seek out the various ways in which the limits of Arab-American self-representations after 9/11 can be reconfigured and renegotiated. To do so, I examine the work of Iraqi-American installation artist Wafaa Bilal, work that directly challenges and undercuts the normalization of the culture of surveillance and militarism in the United States. Ranging from photography to installation art and video, Bilal's work repeatedly defamiliarizes elements of war, combat, surveillance, and torture, all of which have become part and parcel of everyday social and cultural consciousness in the United States. Uncovering the artificiality of the ideological apparatus that serves to rationalize war atrocities and violence to a desensitized Western audience, Bilal's work is ultimately meant to disrupt the neat separation between what he calls "the comfort zone" and "the conflict zone" as captured in what I referred to earlier as the binary of over here and over there (Bilal and Lydersen 2008, 1). Some of his works that exemplify such a revisionary outlook include his 2007 month-long art installation titled *Domestic Tension*. In this installation project, performed

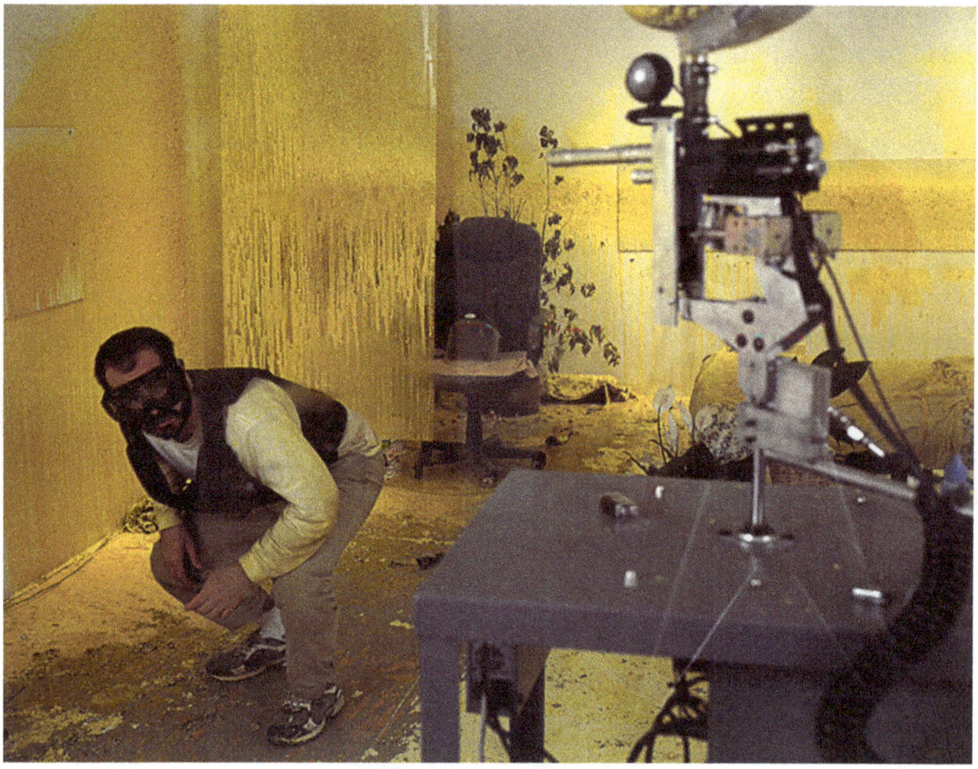

3. Wafaa Bilal, detail from *Domestic Tension*, 2007. Photograph by Wafaa Bilal.

by Bilal in a room of Chicago's FlatFile Galleries, the artist links his computer to a remote-controlled paintball gun and gives worldwide viewers free access to shoot at him around the clock with a press of a button on their computers. With very little reprieve, Bilal confined himself to that space, placing himself directly in the line of "fire" coming from his virtual shooters, resulting in eighty million hits and more than sixty-five thousand shots from 136 countries in thirty days (Becker 2008, xvi; Bilal and Lydersen 2008, i, 2). He chronicles his performance in his book *Shoot an Iraqi: Art, Life, and Resistance under the Gun* (Bilal and Lydersen 2008), which integrates two parallel narratives. One narrative follows Bilal's life in Iraq under Saddam Hussein's regime, his survival in refugee camps in Kuwait and Saudi Arabia after the first Gulf War, and his arrival to the United States in 1992 after being offered asylum. The other narrative provides a day-by-day chronicle of his *Domestic Tension* project.

Bilal's positioning of the body, specifically his male, Muslim Iraqi body, at the center of artistic investigations of national discourse constructions is also evident in another project, *. . . and Counting*, a twenty-four-hour live performance in which Bilal "turns his own body . . . into a canvas, his back tattooed with a borderless map of Iraq covered with one dot for each Iraqi and American casualty near the cities where they fell. The 5,000 dead American soldiers are represented by red dots (using permanent visible ink), and the 100,000 Iraqi casualties are represented by dots of green UV ink, seemingly invisible unless under black light. During the performance, people from all walks of life read off the names of the dead" (Bilal 2011b).

In addition to framing a particularly antiessentialist claim to the male Muslim Arab, specifically Iraqi, body, what is particularly interesting about Bilal's work is the way in which the audience or the viewer becomes an integral part of the artistic piece. In *. . . and Counting*, for instance, one camera shows the tattoos being done on Bilal's back, and the other shows the audience, which at once becomes the viewer and the viewed. Unlike in El Guindi's play, where the spectator/reader is called on to impart a judgment on Khaled's guilt or innocence despite his or her physical disengagement or removal from the action of the play, Bilal's performative pieces integrate the viewer/spectator as a central and formative element of the

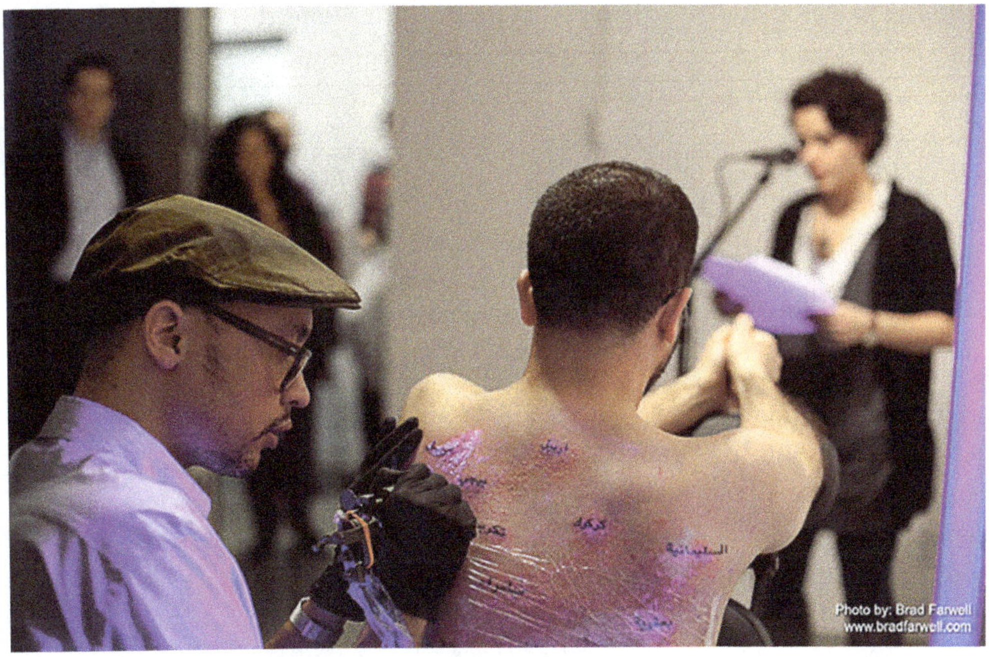

4. Wafaa Bilal, detail from . . . *and Counting*, 2010. Photograph by Brad Farwell.

counterpublic spaces that he creates. In this way, the audience becomes both spectator and participant, shaping the content and direction of such exploratory iterations.

Such panoptic methods of looking and being looked at are central to Bilal's year-long project (which started in December 2010) called *3rdi*, for which he had a camera implanted in the back of his head, taking a snapshot every minute and transmitting it to a website where viewers can access the images.[16] With Bilal calling it a form of "anti-photography" (Bilal 2011a), capturing images that his body cannot see, the project provides a platform for commenting on the insidious methods of technological surveillance that have permeated our everyday lives to such an extent that we do not see them anymore. Bilal's invitation to resee and to reassess how we see and are seen again gives the viewer the power of choice, allowing him or her to manipulate/control the images through a browsing function that can be used to scroll through the images arranged by month, day, and hour (with sixty snapshots available for each hour). This project was commissioned by the Mathaf, Qatar's new Arab Museum of Modern Art, for its inaugurating exhibition *Told/Untold/Retold: 23 Stories of Journeys through Time and Place* on December 30, 2010. In fact, the *3rdi* installation at the exhibition underscores (in more immediate and obvious ways than the online version) the role of the viewer as a central factor in shaping the specific and shifting ways in which the images are displayed. As Bilal describes the museum exhibition on the *3rdi* project's website (Bilal 2011a), the installation is divided into three connected rooms, with the middle room set up in such a way that the images shift in accordance with the viewer's movement through the space.

Other than some brief updates occasionally provided by Bilal on the webpage indicating the dates and destinations of his travel itinerary, no information accompanies the images, leaving it up to the viewer to deduce Bilal's location by piecing together the narrative itinerary of the fragmented images. In fact, these images, while literally being projected through the movement of Bilal's body, become largely disengaged from him (or at least from this viewer's perspective), except for some fleeting ones that capture Bilal's back in a mirror or glass reflection or when the dark panels indicate that it is nighttime and

16. On the project's website, Bilal describes the technological setup of the project: "Technically, the 3rdi is an automatic photographic apparatus that is comprised of three different components: a small digital camera permanently surgically mounted to the back of my head with a USB connection, a lightweight laptop which I carry on my body connected to the camera with a USB cable, and a 3G wireless connection to access the internet" (Bilal 2011a).

that Bilal is sleeping. The fact that New York University, where Bilal teaches at the Tisch School of the Arts, made him place a cap on the camera's lens whenever he was on campus (to protect its students' privacy) underscores how such interrogative redeployments of surveillance methods denaturalize their pervasiveness and emphasize their invasive and dehumanizing policing aspects, especially when applied to NYU's normative student *body*. As Bilal states in some introductory reflections on the *3rdi* project, "My work to date has been concerned with the communication of public and private information to an audience so that it may be retold, distributed" (Bilal 2011a). It is, then, the retellings and redeployments of images and information through such counterpublic spaces that give rise to new sites of knowledge that extend our understanding of identity constructions beyond imperialist projects' polemics of "us and them," "over there and over here."

Even twelve years after the attacks of 9/11, Islamophobia and Arabophobia are still widely prevalent in the United States, as evident in the anti-Muslim rhetoric that circulated in the 2008 presidential elections, the Cordoba House or Ground Zero crisis in the summer of 2010, and the March 2011 congressional hearings conducted by Rep. Peter T. King, which sought to attack the so-called radicalization of Muslims in America.[17] The revised ways of seeing, defining, and representing Arab-American identities that inform the literary and cultural interventions discussed in this chapter engender radical reconceptualizations of the hegemonic gaze that currently shapes the depiction of Arab-American subjectivities as homogeneous Others. Moreover, it is through such projects that the normalization of masculinist and imperialist agendas [is] questioned and problematized. In espousing heterogeneous, multilayered, and transnational Arab-American belongings, these texts destabilize exclusionary forms of US citizenship (extending to the racial, political, religious, and sexual) by incorporating new spaces and horizons that give rise to complex knowledges of US identities while promulgating an important awareness of the power relations that continue to inform and shape the various segments of US society.

17. Rep. King is a Long Island Republican and the chairman of the House Homeland Security Committee.

Works Cited

Abdulhadi, Rabab. 2005. "Where Is Home? Fragmented Lives, Border Crossings, and the Politics of Exile." In *Shattering the Stereotypes: Muslim Women Speak Out*, edited by Fawzia Afzal-Khan, 71–83. Northampton, MA: Olive Branch Press.

Alexander, Jacqui M. 2006. "Not Just (Any)Body Can Be a Patriot: 'Homeland' Security as Empire Building." In *Interrogating Imperialism: Conversations on Gender, Race, and War*, edited by Naeem Inayatullah and Robin L. Riley, 207–40. Basingstoke, UK: Palgrave Macmillan.

Bayoumi, Moustafa. 2006. "Racing Religion." *CR: The New Centennial Review* 6, no. 2: 267–93.

Becker, Carol. 2008. "Introduction: Drawing the Line." In Wafaa Bilal and Kari Lyderson, *Shoot an Iraqi: Art, Life, and Resistance under the Gun*, xv–xxii. San Francisco: City Lights.

Bilal, Wafaa. 2011a. "*3rdi*." Wafaa Bilal's website, Jan. 2. At https://wafaabilal.com/thirdi/.

———. 2011b. "*. . . and Counting*." Wafaa Bilal's website, Mar. 16. At https://wafaabilal.com/and-counting/.

Bilal, Wafaa, and Kari Lydersen. 2008. *Shoot an Iraqi: Art, Life, and Resistance under the Gun*. San Francisco: City Lights.

Butler, Judith. 2006. *Precarious Life: The Powers of Mourning and Violence*. London: Verso.

Cainkar, Louise. 2002. "No Longer Invisible: Arab and Muslim Exclusion after September 11." *Middle East Report*, no. 224: 22–29.

Chomsky, Noam. 2001. *9/11*. New York: Open Media.

Didion, Joan. 2003. *Fixed Ideas: America since 9.11*. New York: New York Review of Books.

Geha, Joseph. 2002. "Alone and All Together." In *Big City Cool: Short Stories about Urban Youth*, edited by M. Jerry Weiss and Helen S. Weiss, 51–63. New York: Persea Books.

El Guindi, Yussef. 2006. *Back of the Throat*. New York: Dramatists Play Service.

Hammad, Suheir. 2005. "first writing since." In *Shattering the Stereotypes: Muslim Women Speak Out*, edited by Fawzia Afzal-Khan, 90–94. Northampton, MA: Olive Branch Press.

Hassan, Salah D. 2002. "Arabs, Race, and the Post–September 11 National Security State." *Middle East Report*, no. 224: 16–21.

Hilal, Dima. 2004. "america." In *Scheherazade's Legacy: Arab and Arab American Women on Writing*, edited by Susan Muaddi Darraj, 104–6. Westport, CT: Greenwood Press.

Khalidi, Rashid. 2004. *Resurrecting Empire: Western Footprints and America's Perilous Path in the Middle East*. Boston: Beacon Press.

McAlister, Melani. 2001. *Epic Encounters: Culture, Media, and U.S. Interests in the Middle East, 1945–2000*. Berkeley: Univ. of California Press.

Naber, Nadine. 2008a. "Introduction: Arab Americans and U.S. Racial Formations." In *Race and Arab Americans before and after 9/11: From Invisible Citizens to Visible Subjects*, edited by Amaney A. Jamal and Nadine Christine Naber, 1–45. Syracuse, NY: Syracuse Univ. Press.

———. 2008b. "'Look, Mohammed the Terrorist Is Coming!' Cultural Racism, Nation-Based Racism, and the Intersectionality of Oppressions after 9/11." In *Race and Arab Americans before and after 9/11: From Invisible Citizens to Visible Subjects*, edited by Amaney A. Jamal and Nadine Christine Naber, 276–304. Syracuse, NY: Syracuse Univ. Press.

Puar, Jasbir K. 2007. *Terrorist Assemblages: Homonationalism in Queer Times*. Durham, NC: Duke Univ. Press.

Puar, Jasbir K., and Amit S. Rai. 2002. "Monster, Terrorist, Fag: The War on Terrorism and the Production of Docile Patriots." *Social Text* 20, no. 3: 117–48.

Riley, Robin L. 2006. "Valiant, Vicious, or Virtuous? Representation and the Problem of Women Warriors." In *Interrogating Imperialism: Conversations on Gender, Race, and War*, edited by Robin L. Riley and Naeem Inayatullah, 183–205. New York: Palgrave Macmillan.

Rothberg, Michael. 2003. "'There Is No Poetry in This': Writing, Trauma, and Home." In *Trauma at Home: After 9/11*, edited by Judith Greenberg, 147–57. Lincoln: Univ. of Nebraska Press.

Salaita, Steven. 2005. "Ethnic Identity and Imperative Patriotism: Arab Americans before and after 9/11." *College Literature* 32, no. 2: 146–68.

Samhan, Helen Hatab. 1987. "Politics and Exclusion: The Arab American Experience." *Journal of Palestine Studies* 16, no. 2: 11–28.

Tétreault, Mary Ann. 2006. "The Sexual Politics of Abu Ghraib: Hegemony, Spectacle, and the Global War on Terror." *NWSA Journal* 18, no. 3: 33–50.

Volpp, Leti. 2003. "The Citizen and the Terrorist." In *September 11 in History: A Watershed Moment?*, edited by Mary L. Dudziak, 147–62. Durham, NC: Duke Univ. Press.

Žižek, Slavoj. 2002. *Welcome to the Desert of the Real: Five Essays on 11 September and Related Dates*. London: Verso.

12

Arab American Refugee Subjects

MADELINE OTIS CAMPBELL

For interpreters, the refugee interview was one in a series of encounters with American soldiers, officials, and police that required situated and creative responses. . . . After taking an oath in that decisive refugee interview, Iraqi applicants would find that the most defining elements of their personal biographies became potential liabilities. In the refugee interview, identifying as a proud war veteran or widow—even if foundational to one's national or gender identity—became a red flag. On some occasions, the very events that led a family to apply for resettlement—for example, a kidnapping—resulted in problems, delays, or even denials in the immigration process. If the parents of a kidnapped child paid a ransom, for example, such remuneration constitutes material support to a terrorist organization, requiring a high-level review in Washington. Responding to these murky and, at times, arbitrary realities, young Iraqi men and women put to use the strategies they sharpened on base and on patrol in the immigration pipeline: to underscore their filial duties, their victimization in Iraq, or their mission to protect Iraqis alongside US brothers and sisters in recognizable ways. As interpreters recounted their strategies in the immigration process when I met them in New England, I was struck by the degree to which their self-described accounts during the refugee interviews were as coded as refugee officers' ears were selective in hearing them.

Excerpt from Madeleine Otis Campbell, *Interpreters of Occupation: Gender and the Politics of Belonging in an Iraqi Refugee Network* (Syracuse, NY: Syracuse Univ. Press, 2016), 145–75. A works cited list was added to the end of the excerpt. Reprinted with corrections and press style changes for consistency throughout the volume by permission from Syracuse University Press.

While they were approached instrumentally, these encounters with the US state had lasting impacts. Out of these encounters, Iraqis in the diaspora developed practices of cultural citizenship vis-à-vis the US nation and state, which would prove to be focal avenues in making claims for years to come. In the xenophobic climate that followed the 9/11 attacks, where state and society in effect (and in reality) "de-Americanized" many Arab and Muslim communities, young Iraqis found that honing such strategies of identification were as urgent as during an "us-versus-them" war in Iraq—or to ward off accusations of betrayal by fellow Iraqis. Louise Cainkar suggests that "de-Americanization revolves around the notion of perpetual foreignness and an implicit lack of national loyalty. . . . It appears that Arab and Muslim Americans were de-Americanized in gendered ways: the source of their foreignness was interpreted differently depending on whether they were men or women" (Cainkar 2009, 232–33). If a male subject's foreignness surrounded political inclinations of violent predilections, a female subject's foreignness revolved around her attachment to "culture," represented by a headscarf, among other things.

Here I consider how former military interpreters' gendered relationships to the US state and nation unfold over the course of immigration and resettlement processes. Beginning in the refugee interview, young men tend to take an assimilationist tack and claim belonging in the United States as hyphenated Americans, whereas young women identify themselves as betwixt and between Iraqi and US-based identifications. Strikingly, single Iraqi women in the United States tend to self-identify as "refugees"—managing their "foreignness" by claiming itinerant uprootedness rather than cultural rootedness;

single Iraqi men widely assert themselves as "immigrants" or "Iraqi Americans" and demonstrate this identity through their continued work for the US military, government, or paragovernmental organizations. . . .

After the refugee crisis of World War II,[1] the United Nations (UN) chartered the Convention on the Status of Refugees, outlining the definition and accordant rights for refugees worldwide. The United States signed the UN Convention on Refugees in 1967 in the midst of massive Cuban migration to the United States and as refugee displacement from the Vietnam War began to mount. After the precipitous fall of South Vietnam in 1975, the American government faced the enormous challenge of protecting the South Vietnamese who had allied with the US military. The United States airlifted thousands of South Vietnamese allies; others made their way out on commercial ships in ad hoc arrangements. This ushered in a broader refugee resettlement program for Vietnamese, Cambodian, and Laotian refugees in the late 1970s and especially in the early 1980s.

After the partial and initially improvised response to the Southeast Asian refugee crisis, the US government passed a comprehensive Refugee Act in 1980, overhauling refugee policy and outlining the procedures for US refugee admissions thereafter.[2] The Refugee Act adopted the UN definition of a refugee, which identified a refugee as someone who had been persecuted or feared persecution on the basis of race, religion, nationality, or political opinion. Thus began a chapter of rigorous refugee resettlement that prioritized "victims of communism" (as a monument outside of the Refugee Affairs Division of the Department of Homeland Security in Washington designates) from Southeast Asia, eastern Europe, and Cuba throughout the Cold War. Refugees of civil wars in Africa and Latin America, which represented proxies for the US–Soviet conflict, became top priorities for the program as well. Though considered a "humanitarian" program, the identification of priority refugee populations and the approach to refugee processing have from the beginning been a highly political matter.

Aihwa Ong's seminal work on Cambodian refugees of this period examines the contradictory experiences of cultural citizenship among resettled families in the San Francisco area (Ong 2003). Cambodian refugees' experiences of belonging in the United States reflected neoliberal economic structures that produced them as working-class individuals, on the one hand, and their interpellation into categorical racial and ethnic identifications, on the other. In Ong's assessment, refugees are schooled to become individual workers within a structure of imagined American meritocracy. At the same time, they are constructed as racialized others, outside the bounds of the "American Dream." Such "unofficial social meanings and criteria" as language, dress, or religion represent the bases for refugees' cultural citizenship, and these criteria have long been as important to refugees' lived experience in the United States as legal citizenship (Ong 2003, 70). Following Ong, I understand cultural citizenship to refer to the everyday experience of belonging or exclusion within dominant structures of social classification (relating to class, ethnicity, race, and gender).[3]

The contradictory forces that Iraqi refugees now face—which construct them as cultural beings and simultaneously discipline them as neoliberal workers—are therefore far from new. The beginning of the war on terror brought with it new trials for the waves of refugees that it displaced, however. The PATRIOT Act directly impacted the way refugees were evaluated for admission to the United States. Most obviously, federal citizenship and immigration services were moved to the newly created Department of Homeland Security, bespeaking an increased focus on national security and counterterrorism that reshaped the humanitarian program of refugee resettlement.

1. In response to the massive displacement of European Jews and others during World War II, the United States demonstrated an informal and, according to many, insufficient response. In the wake of war, assistance to refugees was far from systematic and carried out largely by faith-based organizations rather than through government programs.

2. For further history of refugee policy and the 1980 Refugee Act, see Zucker and Zucker 1992. For more on Southeast Asian refugee resettlement specifically, see Rumbaut [2001] 2005.

3. For further discussions on cultural citizenship among migrant communities specifically, see Siu 2001 and Flores 2003.

Iraqis—and Iraqi allies in particular—became a priority population for US resettlement in 2007 after the escalation of violence in the country.[4] In the course of their immigration proceedings, these "allies" were vigorously screened for Terrorism-Related Inadmissibility Grounds. Once in the United States, however, Iraqis faced surveillance, harassment, and, in some cases, imprisonment and deportation. The contradictions between neoliberal economic ideals of meritocracy and racialized realities thus took on new valences in a post-9/11 era of a surveillance state. The PATRIOT Act gave the state ever-greater power over immigrant and nonimmigrant Arab and Muslim lives, including those who had once worn a US uniform in Iraq. Louise Cainkar (2009) observes that the implementation of the PATRIOT Act's racialized policies—and the delineation of threat—was very much a matter of gender, quite like the delineation of threat functioned in Iraq (see also Jamal and Naber 2008). As they set foot on US soil at US embassies[5] for decisive refugee interviews, Iraqis found that the United States represented a continuation of gendered battlefield logics and discourses of threat rather than an escape from them.

Work proved the most viable avenue to lay claim to cultural citizenship in the United States, but neither work nor citizenship came easily or without strings attached for Iraqi refugees.[6] As we will see in Tamara's case, economic participation came with a "de-hijabing" for certain Iraqi women—sometimes voluntary, at other times under pressure from peers.

This aptly symbolizes the knot of economic and cultural pressures interpreters in the diaspora encountered. Especially in the wake of the economic recession beginning in 2008, the opportunities to "belong" by way of economic participation were already slim. That to pursue them also came with some degree of embedded violence was enough to compel many Iraqi youth to return to Iraq after only months or years in the United States. Indeed, the path for Iraqi refugees from the Middle East capital cities to US metropolitan areas—and in some cases back—has been harder than many refugees had ever imagined, not least for US allies who arguably have sacrificed the most.

Dislocations: From Ally to Refugee

After working as interpreters, young Iraqis decided to leave Iraq under a range of circumstances. Some interpreters were directly threatened, while others describe a more abstract fear in Iraq or a sense of opportunity in the United States as motivating their decisions. Anwar heard rumors from her neighbors that "her name was on a list," while Mikhaeil received a threat letter signed by a local militia member; others were spared these threats but feared that it was a matter of time before similar letters arrived on their doorstep.

Iraqi interpreters applied for refugee status in the United States through two principal channels: via a case-by-case UN referral program outside of Iraq (a "Priority 1," or P1, case) or via an expedited program in Baghdad, Amman, and Cairo if one had worked directly with US forces (a "Priority 2," or P2, case). Most interpreters took advantage of this P2 program, and many applied through "in-country processing" in Baghdad.[7] The US Congress approved an aggressive Iraqi resettlement program with ambitious admission targets after the escalation of the conflict in 2006. Between 2007, when Iraqi refugee processing began, and 2012, about 150,000 Iraqi cases were interviewed, about half that number of cases was approved for resettlement, and a total of 84,902 Iraqi refugees arrived in the United States (US Citizenship and Immigration Service 2012). The years 2009 and 2010 were

4. By contrast, the relatively modest Afghani refugee resettlement (which was the case at the time of this chapter's original publication in 2016) is due in part to the logistical challenges of refugee processing in Pakistan, where most Afghani refugees have fled. The Afghani resettlement program has been generally limited to interpreters and other allies.

5. Refugee interviews take place in embassies in certain countries, while in others the interviews are carried out in the offices of the NGO that facilitates the process.

6. Sunaina Maira has similarly shown that economic participation—as workers and American Dream aspirants—represented a key channel for South Asian immigrant youth to assert their cultural citizenship in the United States during the war on terror (Maira 2009).

7. In addition, the State Department conducted a much smaller "Special Immigrant Visa" program for five hundred interpreters annually, which several interpreters I met had utilized.

the busiest for Iraqi refugee processing as the refugee crisis widened.[8] Resettlement slowed significantly in 2011 when two recently resettled Iraqis were arrested in Kentucky on charges of terrorist activity.

In any given case—whether the case comprises an individual or a family—only one person, the principal applicant, can offer testimony. In the case of nuclear families containing a heterosexual married couple (the only type of family recognized by US Citizenship and Immigration Services), immigration officials almost always appoint the male as the "principal applicant." In this sense, men are the speaking agents, while women are often asked to leave the room during the interview. Women most often appear as the unspeaking victims in a family's "persecution story," the name given to a refugee's testimony. If the norm was a male principal applicant, refugee officers often considered the case of a single woman—in which she would necessarily be the principal applicant—the "easiest." Whereas refugee interviews with men (for whom security concerns were assumed greater) could last hours, a case with a single woman could be over in thirty minutes. Single women commonly hold special designations as "women at risk," and their admission as refugees was widely seen as a "no-brainer." While the outcome may be seen as advantageous to women, the effect of this gendered structure, based in part on caricatured views of Iraqi culture, is to silence many Iraqi women during the immigration process. This dynamic would be echoed for many women along the resettlement path, for example, with caseworkers who would "look after them" at the expense of listening to them.[9]

To resettle in the United States as refugees, Iraqi applicants had to establish that they had suffered past harm or possessed a well-founded fear of harm on the basis of their race, religion, nationality, or political opinion. These World War II–era categories were blunt tools in assessing Iraqis' lived experiences of war, violence, and apprehension about remaining in their homes. Applicants wrote a personal "persecution story" with reference to these dominant categories prior to the refugee interview, which they would then need to perform in oral testimony during the interview.[10] Given the sectarian dimensions of the conflict in Iraq, "religion" was the chief prism through which the refugee resettlement leaders that I encountered understood and appraised Iraqis' refugee claims—at least P1 cases. (P2 cases were assumed in advance to be "political opinion" or even "imputed political opinion" cases because of the applicants' affiliation with the United States.)

In other words, if someone reports that she is Sunni and is gravely afraid of her Shi'i neighbors, she establishes a refugee claim. If one reports that he is Shi'i and had credible reason to fear his Sunni neighbors, he is a refugee. If someone reports that she is Christian and fears both Sunni and Shi'i neighbors, she also meets the criteria to be considered a refugee. I recall talking to one of my refugee resettlement supervisors, who, when I questioned the logic of this approach, told me: "There's no question that it's crazy. If all you have to do is claim a sect to be a refugee, should we just pave the whole country and bring all of Iraq to America?"

Unsurprisingly, many Iraqi applicants quickly learned (from one another, the UN, the NGO that organized refugee processing, or immigration officers themselves) how the US state defines a refugee. Given this, some officers accepted the fact that what we heard in the course of our short, formulaic interviews were mostly canned "camp stories," as they called the frequently repeated stories believed to be fabrications. Many officers sympathized with the applicants as they navigated a flawed and outdated refugee process. Others believed that "rules were rules" and would deny applicants with canned stories—even if the officer had reason to believe that the individual's fear in Iraq was well founded, as any Iraqi's fear would be presumed to be by the program's inexact sectarian logic.[11]

8. I was among dozens of refugee officers hired on a temporary basis to meet the desired targets in the Middle East during those years.

9. For more on the gender dynamics in refugee processing, see "I Have a Name" (McSpadden and Moussa 1993) about East African refugees in the US resettlement process.

10. Compare Coulter's discussion of the imperative for war victims to perform their "war stories" to receive benefits from NGOs in postconflict Sierra Leone (2009, 177).

11. For an elaboration on refugee law for Iraqi refugees, see Rikoski and Finer 2009.

Officers' real job was to screen out past or future perpetrators of "terrorist activity." Terrorist activity was defined broadly as any action—willful or coerced, knowing or unknowing—that supports the efforts of a terrorist organization. A terrorist organization was defined as a group of two or more people who engaged in violent activity targeting civilians for reasons other than monetary gain. Given this definition's breadth, officers spent a large portion of interviewing exploring past political affiliations, religious views, group membership, military training, and contact with (even as the targets of) neighborhood militias or political movements. Young single men were required to give month-by-month timelines of their whereabouts and activities from 2003 until the date of the interview—sometimes the better part of a decade. The determination of Terrorism-Related Inadmissibility Grounds (TRIG) was the central objective of the refugee interview.[12] In addition to the refugee interview, refugees were subject to multiple background checks. . . . Material support to terrorist organizations, even remotely or under duress, led to delays and denials for large portions of the Iraqi refugee pool.

Apart from Terrorism-Related Inadmissibility Grounds, US refugee law bars the admission of applicants who have been involved in the persecution of others. Refugee officers spent a great deal of time inquiring about possible persecutory acts committed by anyone in Saddam's military (most Iraqi men) or in the Ba'th Party (most Iraqi students and professionals). Because military service was mandatory for all men and Ba'th Party membership was compulsory for many students, professional groups, and government servants, applicants were required to provide detailed records of military service and party activities to ensure that they had not participated in military campaigns against civilians or the punishment of political dissidents.

Finally, refugee officers had to assess the credibility of the applicant. While the definition of a credible claim was "plausible, detailed, and consistent," credibility ultimately came down to a "gut feeling," as one supervisor told me. Nearly every officer I met admitted that "instinct" or "sense" about the applicant played a significant role in the final decision to approve or deny a case. Even if an applicant did not appear to raise any red flags relating to TRIG, an officer might deny the applicant on the grounds of being "evasive" or "uncooperative" if [the officer] had a bad "gut feeling." The assignment of a case to an officer is the first of multiple rounds of roulette for Iraqi refugees in the process of resettlement.

After the refugee interview, applicants waited for weeks or months for processing of their fingerprints, background checks, and, if they worked with US forces, verification of their employment. Though theoretically an "expedited" process, the P2 program for contractors of US forces was sometimes delayed well over a year due to the need for employment verification. This was a common complaint of interpreters. Though often slow, the approval rate for P2 cases—US allies—was extremely high. If a case was approved, the applicants would be informed of their travel date and destination and would attend a "cultural orientation" that aimed to equip them for life in the United States. If a case was denied, applicants might petition the decision, though this rarely resulted in a reversal of the adjudication. . . .

Tamara: A "Liberation War" Refugee Rebuffs Salvation

Tamara does not frequently see other Iraqis. A former Terp (interpreter) for several army units involved in training the Iraqi army at Camp Victory, she applied for refugee status in the United States with two goals: to find an engineering job and to eventually petition for her mother and siblings to join her in the United States. Tamara is from a large middle-class family in Baghdad, and her mother and younger siblings had decided to stay in the family home in Iraq for the short term unless the security situation worsened. More importantly, Tamara's mom wanted to limit the impact of the move on Tamara's brother, who had a severe developmental disability. The family decided it made sense for Tamara to go ahead of them, settle down in the United States, and try to find a job.

12. Information about TRIG can be found at USCIS.gov. For a critical examination of TRIG on refugees, see the Refugee Council USA's website at rcusa.org.

Tamara, twenty-eight years old, with a surprising life history full of grit and loss, found that her most personal experiences mattered little in the refugee resettlement process. The immigration process demanded that she perform a certain kind of "persecution story." The day-to-day details about her sacrifices with US forces mattered not at all. Her own biography, views, or experiences were not vital, and her dreams for the future were of no concern at all. It was, as she said, all about "the story."

Tamara had heard about the P2 refugee program for US allies while working at Camp Victory, and she applied from Baghdad. She decided to apply because of the deteriorating security situation: she had not been directly threatened because of her work with US forces but said she could not predict if she would be in the future. Indeed, it was because she could not predict the future that she wanted to apply for refugee resettlement. In her refugee interview, she learned that this was not sufficient for refugee status. To be considered a refugee, she had to articulate a specific type of narrative in which dominant US categorizations of the conflict mattered more than her nuanced experiences.

Tamara and I frequently took long walks around the city. On one, she recounted her refugee interview to me in detail. "The officer's name, was Mr. Smith," she told me. When Mr. Smith asked if she had been a target of any violence in particular, she said no. His eyes remained downcast, focused on his notes. Any threats? No. "Is it safe to stay in Iraq?" he asked in a routine voice. She reminded him of the dangers interpreters faced in Iraq. She said it was her mom who was most fearful that something might happen. He asked why she remained in Baghdad if it were potentially dangerous. She responded curtly that she was one of the only people in her family earning an income—and it was home. It is a big decision to leave one's home. Mr. Smith probed further: "Tell me more about the danger you might be in? Who would want to target you? Can you name any terrorist organizations in particular?" And it went on like that. Tamara found herself reducing her life experiences to what she described as "headlines." She acquiesced to his line of questioning: over the course of the interview, she became a "pro-American" single woman in danger from anti-American terrorists.

When the refugee officer asked about her family's political affiliations, Tamara again spoke telegraphically. "My family has a history of supporting America," she recalls telling the officer. She explained that her uncle was imprisoned, tortured, and executed by Saddam's government due to his membership in the Dawa Party and his participation in the Shi'i intifada in 1991. Her family hoped for American intervention in support of the uprising, and when it did not come, they lived in fear. "If you're my relative, they will believe that you and I think alike. They will hold you responsible for something that I did," she explained to the officer. So, she went on, the family's loyalties remained questionable and the subject of ongoing investigations. She was hopeful when the US-led invasion took place in 2003. She did not mention to her interviewer that her dad had died of kidney failure right before the 2003 invasion and that this was what she most clearly remembered about 2003. She did not say that after his death, she deferred her dreams of attending graduate school to earn money for her family. Instead, she noted that her mom referred to the US-led war as a "liberation war." She elaborated: "I grew up watching TV against America. I began listening to radio—BBC—that connected me to outside. After my uncle died, I felt trapped in Iraq. I was dreaming of leaving." When the officer asked about any family member's possible connections to militia groups, she said her family believed in the democratic process, not violence. Tamara became a double victim in the course of her interview: her family was persecuted under Saddam Hussein—awaiting "liberation"—and they were also now targets in the new Iraq. She told me that the officer began stamping her paperwork in front of her.

When Tamara arrived in the Boston area, her caseworker, a young Iraqi man, placed her with an Iraqi couple as her sponsors. A few years older than she, the couple had two children. She described the caseworker and the couple as very "protective" of her. She had not spoken to anyone about her work in Iraq but figured they knew: single women alone were assumed to have worked with US forces. Her caseworker told her that it was important that she live with a good family because life in America was difficult alone. As it turned out, one of her greatest difficulties in the United States was the family she lived with—and the caseworker himself. Her sponsors did not approve of her going out of the house alone, and when the couple went out, they often asked Tamara to babysit. After working outside of the house for years in Iraq, being limited to four walls felt punishing. She tried to explain to her sponsors that while she appreciated being taken in as part of their family, she needed to go out and get a job to earn money for her family back in Iraq. Her sponsors acceded to her request to go out and look for work. When she did, they strongly encouraged her to wear a headscarf, which she typically did not except to pray, so that neither American men nor other Iraqis would get the "wrong idea." When she met with her caseworker about finding a job, he informally suggested that she might have more success in the interview if she took off the headscarf. She was incredulous: "This is crazy! Which way is it? Who do they want me to be?"

Tamara did not want to work at the temp agency where her caseworker placed many other Iraqis. With the amount of money she could make there, Tamara would have to stay in her sponsor's apartment forever. So she decided to look for work on her own. Time and again she hit the same wall looking for a job: she had no "work experience" in the United States. She found it deeply unfair. She reflected: "Coming to the US has always been good and bad. It got to a point where I felt like I didn't have any more good options in Iraq. I spent all my time with the military—all my time—I didn't even see my family. But here that does not count as 'work experience.' I knew coming to the US would be hard, but I thought it would create some chances for my family. Now, I can't find anything for me here." Part of what struck Tamara as unfair was the fact that the intense pressures she felt in the United States—especially from her caseworker—had seemed directly at odds. On the one hand, she was expected to become an economically independent and productive member of society. In other words, she needed a job. But, on the other hand, she was expected to live with a "good" Iraqi family and be a "good" Iraqi girl who helped out at home. How could she be both? The incident around her wearing—or not wearing—a headscarf was particularly upsetting to her. She believed it was her decision, not her sponsors' or her caseworker's, and yet it had become the test of both her acceptability in the diaspora and her employability in the United States.

Eventually, Tamara took a bolder approach. She began approaching places of business and asking to speak to the manager. She would explain that she was a refugee from Iraq, that she had to leave her home and her family, and that she was trying to restart her life in the United States. Finally, she got a job reshelving clothes at a department store. She was not guaranteed more than twenty hours a week, however, which meant that she could not yet move out of her sponsors' home. She was stuck at home with a family that was not hers. She began to speak increasingly satirically on our walks about the "liberation war." She might be stuck in an apartment, Tamara quipped, but at least she was in a "free country."

She discovered that she had to do everything for herself, adding dryly that this was "the American way." Tamara found her Iraqi caseworker overbearing and unhelpful: he gave advice rather than assistance. "Really, I don't know how he got that job," she commented. Against his advice, once she saved enough money, she finally moved out of her sponsors' home into an apartment with another young woman whom she met at the refugee agency (an Eritrean woman). Though they came from different national, ethnic, and class backgrounds, she found her new roommate far more accepting of who she was. Now across town from her former sponsors in the suburb of Chelsea, she insulated herself from the pressures and gossip of the Iraqi diaspora.

She slowly got more hours at work but also began dreaming more and more about a career in her field: engineering. Realizing that a graduate degree in the United States was her only option if she wanted a career in engineering, Tamara began studying feverishly for the GRE and would take the test four times before getting a score with which she was satisfied. She then began the years-long process of getting her college transcript certified and applying for graduate school in engineering. Graduate school became the guiding dream and central focus of Tamara's life in the United States. When we spoke about graduate school, she would furtively remind me not to tell anyone else (i.e., other Iraqis) about her plans: they were *her* plans. . . .

Though Tamara avoided Iraqis in Boston, she . . . traveled back to Iraq once a year to see her family. She brought medicines and electronics that they requested. She also took GRE test-prep books with her on the journey, she told me, and studied on the bus ride from Amman to Baghdad. She says, "I'm not really here, and I'm not really there. I'm really a refugee." Many others in her very situation—former interpreters who applied for refugee resettlement via the P2 program from Baghdad—would not identify as a "refugee." For Hussein, whom we will meet shortly, a refugee is someone who has to "flee their homes," which neither he nor Tamara did. In his mind, they simply took advantage of an immigration benefit. Yet Tamara identifies with the image of the refugee, betwixt and between, making her way through the world under challenging circumstances and more or less alone.

Tamara is uncomfortable asking for help, though she often asks for "information" and, sometimes, a fair "chance." Rather than asking other Iraqis or her caseworker for "help," Tamara opted to make her own way, negotiating with bosses and authority figures independently to get what she needs. She explained to me how she had lobbied her landlord to allow her to sublet her apartment when she returned to Iraq to visit her family and asked him not to report . . . to the refugee agency [that she had gone], so that she could continue to receive cash assistance. (Though modest, this cash assistance helped.) He agreed. She described the process of writing her graduate application, in which she identified herself as a refugee looking for an opportunity to change her life—and to give her family a chance. After reading the application myself, it struck me that Tamara's personal statement about her journey as a refugee closely mirrored the "persecution story" that she had performed for the refugee officer. She was admitted to a master's program in engineering.

From the beginning of the resettlement process, Tamara has strategically positioned herself within variations of a "persecution story." Far from a passive victim, Tamara navigates the challenges of immigration and resettlement assertively. Feeling acute pressure from other Iraqis, Tamara navigates US society on her own. Rather than asking other Iraqis for help, she negotiates power structures in the United States—employment, housing, education—by herself, asking for a "break" from a landlord or from a graduate admissions office when she needs it—not only to better herself but to give her family a "chance." Tamara identifies as a refugee both instrumentally and affectively. Her identification as a single refugee emerges as an assertion of her duty to family, a reminder of individual strength and, in an important sense, a rebuke of her Iraqi sponsors' and caseworker's "protection." While she adopts the subject-position of a refugee in her travels through US power structures, she is clear that the US government has neither "saved" nor "liberated" her. What she has been able to achieve, she achieved by her own efforts—not from the help of the US state or her refugee agency, specifically. (Indeed, she is critical of the state's lack of support for refugees and chides her caseworker's incompetence.) She says, "I can only depend on myself. And my family is depending on me." Tamara makes claims of cultural belonging not as a passive victim in need of the state's salvation but as a resourceful refugee making her way, despite and not because of the state's help, and all for the sake of family.

Though avowedly motivated by her family, Tamara responds to pressures of American individualism and neoliberal capitalist demands. Mirroring Ong's observations of Cambodian refugees, Tamara's identification as a refugee indicates her assumption of a subject-position as an individuated subject, a worker, and to some degree an aspirant toward the "American Dream." A hopeful observer might interpret her to be on the brink of fulfilling her American Dream—starting fresh in the United States, going back to school, and beginning a new life. Yet her American dreaming—and the cultural currency it garners—comes with deep criticism of the United States. She critiques the lack of systematic support for refugees and the unfairness of the American economy more broadly. Further, she describes the conditions in the diaspora in which she must seek out work, crystallized for her in the debate between her sponsors and caseworker about *her* body, as "crazy." That she was expected to be both a good Iraqi girl and an independent, employed woman—and that pursuing one made the other impossible—infuriated Tamara.

Hussein: Rebuilding Iraq as a Refugee Caseworker

In contrast, young men like Hussein may make claims of belonging in the United States by assuming roles of authority within the US state apparatus. Apart from joining the military, a common avenue for employment in state (or parastate) agencies is as a refugee caseworker. Like interpreters turned soldiers in the US military, interpreters turned caseworkers occupy a position as both Iraqi and American. They assume a role of authority as decisive gatekeepers of financial assistance within US resettlement structures, but they also are gatekeepers of the Iraqi diaspora in an important sense. They are empowered to "look after" Iraqis—precisely in the sense that Tamara did not want to be looked after. . . .

Hussein evokes a form of liberal feminism, which, coming from his positionality as an employee of a US parastate organization, appears as a sort of Western democratic doctrine. For him, "women's rights" appear as an index of acculturation to the United States—and not only of Iraqi societal shifts. As an Iraqi leader in the United States, Hussein appears to be rebuffing "Iraqi patriarchy" in favor of a liberal state-based patriarchy, in which authority figures like himself look after the "rights" and well-being of women. His goal to protect Iraqi women may be exactly the sort of project that young women reject. To hear him tell it, Hussein's earnest intention for women is far from keeping them trapped at home, despite the fact that this might be the felt effect. Yet he remains a protective, patriarchal figure in his vision of the Iraqi diaspora, and it is his real patron–client relationship in the diaspora that lends him the platform to voice it.

Hussein's view of rights, triangulated through US liberalism and based on his idealized vision of the individual, represents his mode of claim making and asserting belonging in the United States—as well as a technology of governing other people's views. The male caseworker is not the sole author of cultural scripts of claim making for Iraqi refugees, but he is an important conduit of technologies of government—"policies, programs, codes, and practices . . . that attempt to instill in citizen-subjects particular values (self-reliance, freedom, individualism, calculation, or flexibility)" (Ong 2003, 6). [In his position as a] broker of the state, his strategies of claim making are also strategies of governance by which other citizen-subjects are formed.

Gendered Citizenship

Gendered dynamics of claim making in the US resettlement process respond to orientalist biases in the US immigration system that empower men to be the spokespeople during the immigration process as well as diasporic leaders in the United States as a function of "culture" as well as histories of shifting gender ideals in Iraq. The encounter between male caseworkers and female refugees is particularly illuminating. Iraqi women like Tamara described feeling conflicting pressures: both to get a job as an independent working woman and to be a good Iraqi girl. Tamara identifies strongly as a refugee, sacrificing a great deal to start over in the United States. By contrast, male subjects like Hussein identify as Iraqi Americans, rebuilding Iraq in the United States as soldiers and caseworkers, among other state positions. Hussein becomes a spokesperson for women's rights, advocating greater "equality" among men and women. Yet in such efforts for women's rights Iraqi men remain the protectors of women's bodies.

Much like in Iraq during its back-to-back wars and under occupation, women's bodies are the site of governance by patriarchal figures in the diaspora—but here taking the form of self-described "feminist" caseworkers. Despite the suspicion that he described feeling from his clients, Hussein has sparked a positive buzz around many Iraqis I have met. His dream of opening an Iraqi cultural center has gained traction and may soon come to fruition.

Just as Hussein has laid down roots in the United States, assuming an authority position within the US resettlement infrastructure and becoming a leader of Iraqis in Worcester [Massachusetts], he has also been targeted with racial and ethnic discrimination and profiling. Because of his "complexion" and his "name," Hussein tells me, he has received several slurs and was once detained by the police for hours after a simple traffic violation. He recounted:

> One day last fall, I was driving through "Sadr City" [the Main South neighborhood of Worcester],[13] and I accidentally went through a yellow light. A police officer was nearby, and he pulled me over. He said I was speeding too, but I don't believe we were. I was with another Iraqi guy, my client, and we were headed back to the office. I guess we looked suspicious to him—you know, dark guys, dark hair, sunglasses. But, they put us in the back of the car and kept us there for two hours. And then they called backup. Backup! In the end, they didn't even give us a ticket. Really, it doesn't bother me. I explained that we were on the way to the agency, where I worked. I called him "Sir" and "Mr. Officer" and told him, "Hey brother, I am very sorry about that." I understand it is their job. But my friend was really upset. And really I understand that too. It's not fair. But, you have to know how to deal with it. He doesn't have the same experience with those sort of people that I have from working in the US military.

Hussein speculates that he and his client looked suspicious because "you know, dark guys, dark hair, sunglasses." He adds that he dealt with the officers—by apologizing and addressing them as "Sir" and "Mr. Officer." Hussein tells me that it was not "fair" that he was pulled over and detained but that he knew how to deal with the situation.

Hussein's experience is part of a broader trend in the post-9/11 United States that targets Arabs and Muslims with special attention—and targets Arab and Muslim men and women differently. As Cainkar observes,

> Gendered ideas were evident in the ways in which the American government . . . focused its policies on men. . . . American government agencies conducted widely publicized mass arrests and deported thousands of noncitizen Arab and Muslim men, who were referred to by the government as "terrorists," although they had been cleared of terrorist associations. . . . Only two females, both sixteen-year-old girls, were detained or incarcerated on suspicion of being terrorists, and women were wholly excused from the government's special registration program. Arrest, interrogation, incarceration, special registration, and removal were almost wholly implemented on male subjects. (2009, 231–32)

This gender-inflected racial profiling exemplifies a reductive and orientalist view of Arab, Muslim, Middle Eastern—often homogenized as a monolithic threat. If Iraqi interpreters enacted a form of "military orientalism" in Iraq, they are encountering legal orientalism in the United States. Further, the scrutiny that Hussein and Tamara alike face in the United States was exacerbated by the media, which reinforced images of violent Arab men and alternately sexualized or victimized Iraqi women.[14] Thus, in addition to the orientalist underpinnings in the resettlement process itself, orientalist biases in law and media also aggravated state-based surveillance and mutual suspicion among refugees in the diaspora. . . .

Works Cited

Cainkar, Louise. 2009. *Homeland Insecurity: The Arab American and Muslim American Experience after 9/11*. New York: Russell Sage Foundation.

Coulter, Chris. 2009. *Bush Wives and Girl Soldiers: Women's Lives through War and Peace in Sierra Leone*. Ithaca, NY: Cornell Univ. Press.

Flores, William V. 2003. "New Citizens, New Rights: Undocumented Immigrants and Latino Cultural Citizenship." *Latin American Perspectives* 30, no. 2: 87–100.

Jamal, Amaney, and Nadine Naber, eds. 2008. *Race and Arab Americans before and after 9/11: From Invisible Citizens to Visible Subjects*. Syracuse, NY: Syracuse Univ. Press.

Maira, Sunaina. 2009. *Missing: Youth, Citizenship, and Empire after 9/11*. Durham, NC: Duke Univ. Press.

McSpadden, Lucia Ann, and Helene Moussa. 1993. "I Have a Name: The Gender Dynamics in Asylum and in

13. Here Hussein is referring to the Main South neighborhood of Worcester, which he dubs "Sadr City" because of Main South's crowded low-income housing.

14. Iraqi American Celia Shallal has observed: "Diaspora politics get me down. . . . So-called progressive American publications foster more damage; they often regurgitate Orientalist frameworks, images of charred bodies, men holding guns, and oversexualized identities thrust upon men and women are ubiquitous" (2013, 144).

Resettlement of Ethiopian and Eritrean Refugees in North America." *Journal of Refugee Studies* 6, no. 3: 203–25.

Ong, Aihwa. 2003. *Buddha Is Hiding: Refugees, Citizenship, and the New America.* Berkeley: Univ. of California Press.

Rikoski, Jennifer, and Jonathan Finer. 2009. "Out of Iraq: The US Legal Regime Governing Iraqi Refugee Resettlement." *Rutgers Law Record* 34:46.

Rumbaut, Rubén G. [2001] 2005. "Vietnamese, Laotian, and Cambodian Americans." *Interdisciplinary Perspectives on the New Immigration: The New Immigrant in American Society* 3. Reprinted in *Asian Americans: Contemporary Trends and Issues*, new 2nd ed., edited by Pyong Gap Min, 262–89. Thousand Oaks, CA: Sage.

Shallal, Celia. 2013. "Disconnected." In *We Are Iraqis: Aesthetics and Politics in a Time of War*, edited by Nadje al-Ali and Deborah al-Najjar, 144–50. Syracuse, NY: Syracuse Univ. Press.

Siu, Lok. 2001. "Diasporic Cultural Citizenship: Chineseness and Belonging in Central America." *Social Text* 19, no. 4: 7–28.

US Citizenship and Immigration Service (USCIS). 2012. *USCIS Iraqi Refugee Fact Sheet.* At www.USCIS.gov.

Zucker, Norman L., and Naomi Flink Zucker. 1992. "From Immigration to Refugee Redefinition: A History of Refugee and Asylum Policy in the United States." *Journal of Policy History* 4, no. 1: 54–70.

13

Projections of Palestine

Negotiating Diasporic Palestinian Identity in the United States through Film Festival Participation

UMAYYAH CABLE

The Remis Auditorium in Boston's Museum of Fine Arts reverberated with laughter as Cherien Dabis's narrative film *May in the Summer* screened for a full audience on the opening night of the ninth annual Boston Palestine Film Festival (BPFF) in October 2014. In the film, three Palestinian American sisters—May, Yasmine, and Dalia—sit poolside at a Dead Sea resort in Jordan for May's bachelorette weekend. Dalia and Yasmine bicker over each other's Arabic-language skills, an argument that turns out to be less about proper pronunciation and more about whose relationship to cultural authenticity is more precarious. Eldest sister May—played by filmmaker Dabis—interjects to settle the argument, glaring with frustration over the top of her dark, oversize sunglasses. With a mix of annoyed paternalism and knowing irony, May interrupts her younger sisters: "Guys, you speak equally shitty Arabic!" In the theater's darkness, spectators emitted the kind of amused chuckles that originate from that same knowing irony. It is a bittersweet amusement produced at the intersection of insecurity and inaccessibility.

This scene and the audience's reception of it exemplify how a politics of cultural authenticity undergirds diasporic cinematic representation and, in turn, how Palestinian Americans struggle to uphold and represent that cultural authenticity in diaspora. What this scene does not reveal, however, is how Palestinian American attempts to embody or express cultural authenticity are stymied by compulsory Zionism (Cable 2020)—a form of cultural hegemony demanding support for the Israeli state that informs the context of the United States. This essay explores how diasporic film culture—by which I mean filmmaking, spectatorship, festival production, and festival participation in diaspora—offers a rich site for analyzing how Palestinian American subjectivity is produced and represented in relation to the demands of cultural authenticity and the limitations imposed by compulsory Zionism. It is through engagements with diasporic film culture that Palestinian Americans negotiate these demands and limitations in ways that produce a sense of Palestinian American *political* and *cultural queerness*.

This essay is based on participant observation and interviews with fourteen self-identifying Palestinian participants of the BPFF and investigates how concerns over identity, self-determination, and belonging within the diasporic context of the United States are represented in and projected onto Palestinian cinema and negotiated through festival participation.[1] These inter-

1. I focus on the voices of six of my interlocutors because of the overlapping themes and experiences shared among them. Of those nine participants, one identified as Palestinian, two identified as Palestinian American, one identified as "pure Palestinian," one identified as "Palestinian Palestinian," and one identified as half-Palestinian. At the time of the interviews, all had been living in the Boston area for an extended period or were residing in the Boston area temporarily as they pursued higher education. Throughout the essay, I primarily refer to my interlocutors collectively as "Palestinian Americans," with some exceptions. I do this not to minimize the nuanced differences among the identity monikers listed in this note but rather to highlight their shared identification as Palestinians and

views reveal how Palestinian Americans are drawn to Palestinian cinema and festival participation for reasons that are deeply tied to concerns over their subjectivity within the United States and their relationships with both Palestinian and American cultures and identities. By placing queer theory, critiques of settler colonialism, and diaspora studies in conversation, this essay offers new perspectives on the role of film culture in diasporic Palestinian social experience and helps to account for the increase in culture-based modes of Palestine activism in the United States, such as the proliferation of Palestine-themed film festivals.

Definition of Terms: Cultural Authenticity, Compulsory Zionism, Queerness

Diasporic Palestinian film culture has emerged as a site of contest between two polarized yet imbricated sets of cultural politics: the politics of cultural authenticity (Naber 2012) and the articulation of Palestinianness in diaspora, on the one hand, and the politics of compulsory Zionism plus the limitations of expressing Palestinian cultural identity, on the other. My interlocutors remarked often about feelings of difference, tension, and isolation they have experienced in negotiating their subjectivity between these two poles. In hearing my interlocutors articulate these tensions within the context of diasporic cinematic representation and participation, I came to understand their subjectivities as constituting a form of *cultural queerness* in relation to the intra-Palestinian politics of cultural authenticity and a form of *political queerness* in relation to the politics of compulsory Zionism. I therefore argue that for my Palestinian American interlocutors, participating in the festival as spectators, organizers, and volunteers serves as a method by which to negotiate these interrelated cultural politics and claim cultural identity in diaspora.

I conceptualize "queerness" in distinctly cultural and political ways in order to highlight the internal and external pressures placed on diasporic Palestinian subjectivity. "Queerness" here does not refer to gender or sexual orientation but rather serves as an analytic for the interrogation of socially constructed identity categories and norms. A queer analytical framing helps to account not only for the sense of "Otherness" that diasporic Palestinians may experience in the US context or in relation to historic Palestine (Cainkar 2016) but also for how that Otherness informs identity formation, cultural production, and community engagement. While cultural queerness and political queerness are not mutually exclusive, I separate them here for analytical purposes in order to emphasize the simultaneity of internal and external pressures bearing down on diasporic Palestinian subjectivity and how those pressures are in turn exerted and reflected within diasporic film culture.

"Cultural queerness" refers to how Palestinian American subjectivity at times fails to adhere to or outright challenges the politics of cultural authenticity, which Nadine Naber defines as "a narrative of Arabness that prescribes what is respectable and what is stigmatized, what is normal and what is deviant" (2012, 13). The pressure to uphold cultural authenticity is indicative of how the very concept of "diaspora" relies on "a genealogical, implicitly heteronormative reproductive logic" of nationalism that denigrates diasporic subjectivity as the inauthentic, debased "other" to the nation, or what Gayatri Gopinath refers to as "queer diaspora" (2005, 10–11). When I refer to Palestinian Americans as *culturally queer*, then, I mean that their social and geographic distance from the Palestinian homeland renders them deviant or inauthentic in relation to an idealized Palestinian national culture.

"Political queerness" refers to how Palestinian American subjectivity is regulated, condemned, and sometimes censored by the politics of compulsory Zionism. With reference to Adrienne Rich's (1980) concept of "compulsory heterosexuality" and building on Erella Shadmi's (1992) discussion of "compulsory Zionism," I theorize compulsory Zionism as culturally hegemonic to account for the ways in which the US–Israel political relationship is reproduced through cultural productions such as film and media, thereby serving as a regulatory script that informs diasporic Palestinians' social power relationships in the US context. Given these power

---

to signify their shared positionality within the geopolitical and social context of the United States at the time of the interviews. All names are pseudonyms.

dynamics, it is through confrontations with compulsory Zionism that Palestinian Americans experience a sense of *political queerness.*

Why Film Culture?

The study of cinema affords a uniquely rich site for tracing how compulsory Zionism in the United States is deeply rooted in the American settler-colonial project's identification with Israel through Christian ideology. With its canonical place in Christian and Jewish narratives of deliverance and conquest, the Exodus story, Robert Warrior asserts, has greatly shaped the American origin story. Such narratives "made their way into Americans' consciousness and ideology," resulting in the construction of "America's self-image as a 'chosen people'" (1989, 264). Taking this point further, Steven Salaita notes that "early settlers conceptualized North America as a New Canaan," indicating that settlers assumed the subjectivity of the Israelites, with North America as their Promised Land. Through this framing, the United States and Israel share an "underlying ideology" that "encompasses a teleology of divine fulfillment . . . [and] as such, the emergence of Zionism in Europe in the late nineteenth century entered a dialectic with the project of American settlement" (2014, 129–30). Indeed, Melani McAlister identifies Hollywood as a primary vector through which such narratives have been ingrained in the American psyche, naturalizing and popularizing the relationships between Christian Zionism and US settler colonialism through cinema. McAlister asserts that through films such *The Ten Commandments* (1956), *Ben-Hur* (1959), and, most importantly, *Exodus* (1960) Hollywood has played a strategic role in cultivating American political and spiritual identification with Israel, and she notes how "in *Exodus*, the Zionist story of Israel also became an American tale . . . as the American frontier had been tamed, so the desert bloomed" ([2001] 2005, 161–63).

Understanding the cinematic origins of compulsory Zionism in the United States is important for understanding how and why expressions of Palestinian identity and cultural politics have historically been disciplined in the US context, including attempts to censor Palestinian cinema.

Within such a context, the expression of Palestinian identity and cultural politics through engagements with film culture serves not merely as a method for subverting the norm but as a form of social justice activism.

Yet despite the compulsory Zionism endemic in American culture, the United States has emerged as a site of a thriving diasporic Palestinian film culture. As a city with a history of attempts to censor Palestinian cinema (Cable 2020) but now one of six major cities to host an annual Palestine-themed film festival in North America, Boston offers an interesting example of how and why Palestinian cinema has emerged as a site of cultural contest and activism in the United States. Established in 2006 and with the first festival occurring in 2007, the Boston Palestine Film Festival is an all-volunteer-run festival cosponsored by Boston's Museum of Fine Arts, which is also its permanent annual venue. From the start, the original organizers envisioned the festival as a form of activism. Mary, one of the founding Palestinian organizers, recalled: "The guiding principle was: this is not like business-as-usual in terms of political work, this is going to be different, we thought, a better way to reach a mainstream audience to hear what's happening."

The organizer's vision for the festival as a form of political work is in keeping with the literature in cinema and media studies on spectatorship, film festivals, identity, and cultural politics. Cinema has the unique ability, in the words of film scholar Miriam Hansen, to "function as a matrix for challenging social positions of identity and otherness, as a catalyst for new forms of community and solidarity" (1993, 208). Likewise, film festivals, Cindy Hing-Yuk Wong argues, "do not create social issues, but in selection, screening, and reception, they galvanize debates" (2016, 87). In a similar vein, Skadi Loist and Ger Zielinski have pointed to the emergence of lesbian, gay, bisexual, and transgender identity-based film festivals as offshoots of political movements that have "offered interventions into hegemonic representational regimes" to galvanize existing identity- and cause-based activism (2012, 50). Film festivals, therefore, afford unique possibilities through which to study how political and social interventions operate under the guise of "culture." I therefore take the BPFF as a case study for understanding how and why diasporic film culture has emerged as a terrain of struggle over both Palestinian politics of cultural authenticity and compulsory Zionism in the United States. As my interlocutors' testimonies will attest, these two sets of cultural politics—competing but also at times colluding with each other—affect the identity expression and social experiences of Palestinians living in diaspora in the US context. For my interlocutors, participation at the film festivals affords many of them an opportunity to negotiate, express, and claim their Palestinian identity amid these representational struggles.

In the following section, I address how the tensions between compulsory Zionism and cultural authenticity are brought into focus primarily around three issues: Arabic-language knowledge, geosocial proximity to historic Palestine, and ethnic lineage. Contestations over these three issues are not merely represented on screen but manifest among festival participants as conflicts over film categorization and festival curation. Studying these conflicts over representation within diasporic film culture illustrates how the politics of compulsory Zionism and the politics of cultural authenticity compete and collude to produce a sense of political and cultural queerness among diasporic Palestinians in the United States.

Language, Lineage, and Proximity to Cultural Authenticity

This essay began with a description of a scene in *May in the Summer.* Released in 2013, the film is primarily in English, but Arabic language is interwoven throughout the narrative. The film's plot revolves around protagonist May's ambivalence toward her upcoming wedding. Such ambivalence is fueled by a series of social conflicts between May and her fiancé; between May and her devoutly Christian mother, who feigns disapproval of May's engagement to a (nonpracticing) Muslim; between May's divorced parents; between May and her younger sisters; and between May and her white, American father. The conflict in the scene described at the beginning of this essay exemplifies how Arabic-language knowledge has long played a role in producing or obfuscating a sense of cultural authenticity and connectivity among Arabs more broadly in diaspora (Gualtieri 2009, 167; Hammer 2005, 201). Indeed, the festival itself promotes the idea of broader Arab American community connectivity through its mission statement, which outlines three major aims: first, "to celebrate Palestinian cinema as a cultural and artistic production of a people in exile and under occupation and siege"; second, "to reduce prejudice and discrimination against Middle Eastern people generally and Palestinians in particular" in the United States after September 11, 2001; and, third, "to instill pride in our Arab-American *community*" and "provide a *link*" to Arab heritage, culture, and history for those living in diaspora (Cook-Obregon and Hanna 2012, emphasis mine).

Conflict over language, both on- and off-screen, represents the pervasive sense of insecurity around diasporic identity and culture experienced—to varying degrees—by the festival's Palestinian American spectators, volunteers, and organizers I interviewed. Yet the described scene in *May in the Summer* and its representation of conflict over Arabic-language skills also offers a poignant example of what motivates many of my interlocutors to attend the festival in the first place. One year before the *May in the Summer* screening, I interviewed Samira, a festival audience member and Boston-based graduate student. She explained how hearing Arabic both on-screen and among spectators greatly motivated her to attend the BPFF. Having moved to Boston from a tight-knit Palestinian American community in the San Francisco Bay Area, Samira lamented:

> Without really an Arab friend base here, I hate to say it, but I feel like I lose touch with that part of me a lot here. And this week of movies allows me to reconnect with that part, allows me to hear Arabic again, hear other people speaking Arabic, and that makes me feel sort of closer to home in a sense. But it also makes me feel like I'm connecting with my identity that's—here in Boston at least—sometimes minimized in my day-to-day life. . . . Going to the festival and watching the movies, I feel like I'm making that connection.

Samira worried that she would "lose" her identity if she did not maintain it through an active practice of, exposure to, and participation in Arabic language and

Palestinian cultural events. However, her concerns over language were heightened by the fact that her engagement to a man who was neither Palestinian nor Arab had caused strife between herself and her family. Nadine Naber (2012) identifies in her ethnography of the Arab American community in the Bay Area how anxiety over women's and girls' gendered behavior and sexuality stokes the politics of cultural authenticity, which manifests, in part, as a deep preoccupation with intraethnic marriage as a primary method for the social reproduction of cultural authenticity.

In this sense, Samira's concern over her interethnic engagement is emblematic of how the politics of cultural authenticity compel Palestinian Americans—women in particular—to seek out and engage in cultural productions as a way to preserve their identities. I understand her concerns here as exemplary of an anxiety around *cultural queerness* primarily because her interethnic marriage, although heterosexual, renders her suspect with regard to the politics of cultural authenticity and to the social reproduction of Palestine in diaspora. For Samira, as for other participants, the expression of Arabic language and participation at the film festival serves as a way to maintain cultural connectivity and appease feelings of conflict resulting from other perceived infractions around failure to maintain Palestinian lineage and, more generally, to reproduce a culturally authentic Palestine. The resultant pressure to uphold cultural authenticity compounds into a form of compulsory, ethnocentric heterosexuality, the deviation from which constitutes a form of cultural queerness and thus a threat to cultural authenticity.

When I interviewed Samira again a year later and shortly after the *May in the Summer* screening, her opinion of the film surprised me. She explained her ambivalence toward the film:

> I left feeling very mixed. I wanted to like it, and I wanted to love it.... First of all, the fact that they chose a movie that was centered and revolved around Jordan was a very interesting idea. For that to be the showcase of the film festival, I had mixed opinions about that. What I really liked was the discussion with the director afterwards; some woman asked a question I thought was so brilliantly stated: that Palestine is always in the background, it's always there. I thought that is one of the most relevant statements I've ever heard about my identity. It's like this place, this region that is sometimes very abstract, is always there.... I liked that concept, but otherwise I didn't feel it was a strong Palestinian film. It was a strong refugee film. And while that's relevant to Palestine, I didn't think it was a Palestinian film.

Although Samira attends the festival primarily to maintain a sense of connection to her Palestinian identity through engagement with Arabic language, her disappointment around the film speaks to concerns around ethnic lineage and geosocial proximity to historic Palestine. A desire to hear Arabic was Samira's primary motivation for attending the festival, but English was the film's primary language, so it is understandable that she would feel ambivalent about the film's capacity to produce the sense of connectivity she sought out. Yet in her further explanation she reveals a sense of discomfort around how the film speaks to essentialist notions about mixed marriages and cultural inauthenticity: "[For me] as someone who is thinking about it a lot and who experiences it a lot, there's a message there that maybe these relationships [intraethnic and interfaith] may not be successful because of culture. Or maybe there are too many tensions for them to be successful in the end. And that upsets me a little bit." For Samira, *May in the Summer*'s setting outside of historic Palestine and representations of social conflict over Arabic language and interethnic and interfaith marriage are indicative of larger concerns about failure to adhere to the politics of cultural authenticity.

Samira's comments also raised an important question: Is *May in the Summer* a Palestinian film? Samira was quick to point out that the film is not set in Palestine, but rather in Jordan. Her opinion that *May in the Summer* is *not* a Palestinian film reflects how concerns over identity and the politics of cultural authenticity also manifest as concerns over film categorization and the very identity of the film itself. After the festival's opening screening of *May in the Summer*, filmmaker Dabis participated—by way of a video conference call—in a question-and-answer period that was dominated largely by women's voices, many of whom conveyed heartfelt gratitude to the director for bringing Palestinian women's stories to the screen and making diasporic experiences seen and heard. This feedback continued virtually on the BPFF Facebook page the day after the screening. A Facebook user posted a comment in reply to a promotional post about the film: "*May in the Summer* was fabulous! The lead actress who also wrote and directed the film is Palestinian-American—something to be truly celebrated! Bravo and thank you BPFF!!" The comment that followed this enthusiastic reception, however, represented a very different attitude toward the film, wherein another Facebook user wrote, "*May in the Summer* was an OK film—not much to do with Palestine." This second comment suggests that Dabis's film—which was not set in Palestine and was not primarily in Arabic and which featured characters of mixed ethnic heritage—was perhaps unworthy of headlining a Palestine-themed film festival.[2] In this sense, the film—in form, content, and reception—exemplifies how the representation of Palestinian American cultural queerness produces anxiety for those concerned with or subject to upholding the politics of cultural authenticity. As an institution of diasporic cultural representation, the festival is in a unique position to serve as an arbiter of that cultural authenticity. The placement of *May in the Summer* as the festival's opening film, therefore, authorizes an intervention to the politics of cultural authenticity in ways that recognize and accommodate diasporic difference.

Further, the contestations over the film's identity exemplify how the struggle over cultural authenticity can unwittingly collude with the politics of compulsory Zionism. These questions about what constitutes a Palestinian film or even whether a film is about Palestine or not are deeply embroiled in questions about what it means to be Palestinian, who is counted as Palestinian, and which voices are recognized as Palestinian. Mary, who has been a festival organizer from the start, spoke of an incident during one of the festival screenings:

> I was sitting at a table outside of a film. The filmmaker was Palestinian, the main actor was Palestinian, but the story was about a guy in Jordan. . . . And I remember sitting outside of the film when this man came out of the film with his two friends. They had purchased tickets to see the film, and it [the screening] was halfway through. He came out and started complaining to me that it wasn't a Palestinian film. And I said, "But the filmmaker is Palestinian, and the actor is Palestinian." And though he [the filmmaker] never says the nationality or these constructs in the film, it could be the story of a Palestinian just as much as it isn't. We're very divided. It's like the Zionization of our own culture. We've taken on those structures ourselves.

Here, a question around film categorization serves as a metonym for questions about identity. I take Mary's use of the word *Zionization* to indicate how compulsory Zionism has colonized the discourses on Palestinian cultural identity and authenticity. Within the context of pervasive compulsory Zionism, Palestinian Americans feel pressure to adhere to limited notions of Palestinianness that conform to the ideals of cultural authenticity. Therefore, attempts to delimit, quantify, and manage Palestinian identity in ways that demand adherence to the politics of cultural authenticity unwittingly reproduce the logic of compulsory Zionism by demanding a homogenous, singular Palestinian subjectivity, one that is ethnocentrically heterosexual, linguistically disciplined, and proximal to historic Palestine. *Cultural* queerness, therefore, is not merely about a failure to adhere to cultural authenticity but also serves as a starting point from which to choose *political* queerness in order to challenge compulsory Zionism and its attempts to quantify, limit, and exclude Palestinian subjectivity, both within the borders of historic Palestine and in diaspora.

These conflicts over categorization, identity, and cultural queerness are not limited to spectators and audience reception. Similar conflicts have dogged the festival planning and curation process. Former festival organizer Ruba spoke at length about her experiences in organizing

2. At some point after this virtual exchange took place, this entire Facebook post—along with the comments—was deleted by the BPFF Facebook page administrator. I had taken a screenshot of the original post before it was deleted.

the BPFF and the social conflicts that ensued between diasporic festival organizers based in the Boston area and Palestinian filmmakers based in historic Palestine. In what she described as an attitude of "more Palestinian than thou," Ruba explained how her positionality in diaspora placed her in conflict with a filmmaker from the West Bank in a disagreement over which films to feature in the festival: "There was always this issue of 'I'm more Palestinian than thou.' This asshole [the filmmaker] basically tried to discredit me. I don't need anybody to tell me whether I'm Palestinian or not or whether I'm Palestinian *enough* or not." In Ruba's experience, a creative disagreement over which films to include in the festival resulted in an interrogation of her cultural authenticity and an attack against her identity in order to discredit and disempower her in the curatorial process.

Ruba's experience in the early years of festival organizing exemplifies how gender informs Palestinian Americans' relationships to cultural authenticity and disenfranchisement. The gendered struggle Ruba faces—as a Palestinian woman born and raised in diaspora—to have her voice heard and counted in decisions about how to represent Palestine within diasporic film culture is mirrored in the works of Palestinian women filmmakers such as Cherien Dabis, Annemarie Jacir, and Zeina Durra, whose narrative films focus on diasporic women characters and their experiences of social conflict.

Because the BPFF has prioritized the works of women and diasporic filmmakers, culturally queer spectators are able to see themselves represented as part of Palestinian national identity. Instead of viewing culturally queer representations as a liability, the BPFF privileges them for their potential to transform the discourse on cultural authenticity and thereby produce a more inclusive sense of Palestinian national identity. The time and space of the festival grant access to a Palestinian identity that is, in Samira's words, "minimized in day-to-day life" or otherwise inaccessible, as reflected in other interlocutors' comments.

The festival thus serves as a point of access and reconnection for dispossessed Palestinian identities. For example, Lamia was born and raised in the West Bank but had been studying abroad when the Israeli occupation began in 1967, and she was thus unable to return home after college. She has lived in the Boston area and been active in the Palestinian community there since 1979 and has attended the festival as a spectator since it began in 2007. She pointed to the importance of Arabic language in drawing her to attend the festival and in turn bolstering her identification as Palestinian, which she described as something she had been "disconnected from forcibly by not being allowed to go home" after 1967. Lamia emphasized the importance of language in producing her sense of cultural connectivity, specifically in the form of what she considers to be a distinctly Palestinian sense of linguistic humor that mocks the occupation and apartheid state through sardonic word play in Arabic. For Lamia, attending the festival and seeing Palestinian films—and the humor that resides in Arabic dialogue—serves as a method of access for reconnecting with a sense of identity from which she has been forcibly disconnected.

Coming Out of Compulsory Zionism's Closet

The articulation and consumption of Arabic language may serve as a method of cultural maintenance, yet it also exposes Palestinian Americans to confrontations with compulsory Zionism. While essentializing ideas about cultural authenticity serve to delimit who can lay claim to and represent Palestinian identity in diaspora, compulsory Zionism suppresses cultural expressions—such as speaking in Arabic—that would typically be expected to affirm one's sense of cultural authenticity. My interlocutors' social experiences within the context of compulsory Zionism are often marked by confrontations with strangers, acquaintances, coworkers, and even friends over the politicization of Palestinian cultural identity. It is through these confrontations that Palestinian Americans experience a sense of political queerness in the context of compulsory Zionism. The following section addresses Palestinian American political queerness as both a social experience and a strategic choice in expressing resistance to compulsory Zionism.

These social conflicts are also a factor in motivating my interlocutors to attend the festival. As discussed earlier, Samira's motivation for attending the festival stemmed largely from a desire to maintain her sense of cultural identity through engagements with Arabic language. This language-based motivation emerged, in part, because of Samira's experiences of social conflict around her expression of Arabic language. She explained to me how her use of Arabic in public has exposed her to compulsory Zionism in her professional and personal social interactions. A doctoral candidate at the time of our interview, Samira relayed a story to me about a time she was attending an academic conference with several of her mentors. At the conference, Samira was socializing in a small group with two faculty mentors, each of whom served on her dissertation committee, and an Iranian woman who also happened to speak Arabic. As Samira and the Iranian woman began to converse in Arabic, one of Samira's dissertation committee members interrupted by asking, "What *are* you? You're speaking Arabic." In that moment, Samira—who had previously never mentioned her ethnic heritage or Palestinian identity with any of her academic mentors out of fear of this very sort of interaction—was pressed to "come out" as Palestinian. When Samira divulged her identity, she described the faculty member as having a strongly negative reaction. This incident and Samira's strong memory of it illuminate how compulsory Zionism deters Palestinian Americans from engaging in cultural expressions that are vital to their sense of identity and cultural connectivity, such as speaking Arabic. In this way, the film festival takes on greater significance as a space for the open expression of Palestinian American identity.

This type of hostile response to the expression of Palestinian American identity indicates how Palestinian culture is constituted as politically queer in that it is perceived as an affront to dominant social and political norms that are shaped by compulsory Zionism. Samira's fear of being rejected by her mentor because of her Palestinian identity mirrors, in some ways, the fear an LGBTQ-identified person might have in disclosing their sexuality within a context of compulsory heterosexuality. This sense of political queerness influences my interlocutors' decisions whether to divulge or withhold information about themselves in their everyday social interactions. The concept of political queerness is also helpful for understanding the process of consciously choosing how and when to "modulate" identity or when to "out" oneself as Palestinian. Former festival organizer Ruba described the dilemma she faced regarding how and when to express her Palestinian identity when meeting new people. She explained to me the way that she "modulates" her identity through a process of strategic outing and closeting, in large part as a way to cope with the sense of anxiety she feels as a Palestinian in the United States.

Negotiating such a process is about exercising agency and shifting the power relations that inform Palestinian social experiences in the context of compulsory Zionism. I borrow the metaphor of the closet not to connote a sense of shame around Palestinian identity but rather as a way to describe how Palestinian Americans claim agency as minority subjects in sometimes hostile environments. Ruba stressed the importance of the festival as a space for the expression of her identity and the accompanying cultural politics in light of the compulsory Zionism closet: "The festival was creating that community where we who share the same politics can just be together, celebrating and feeling like we're not isolated, we're not freaks for what we think."

What my interlocutors' experiences indicate is that to represent and express Palestinian American identity in the United States is to be politically queer within a culture of compulsory Zionism. For some, this sense of political queerness is closely reminiscent of their experiences as LGBTQ-identified and/or gender-nonconforming people within a culture of compulsory heterosexuality. For example, spectator Alma likened her experiences of strategically closeting her Palestinian identity as similar to the kinds of social modulation she performs around her sexual orientation within both the American and the Palestinian contexts of compulsory heterosexuality. She explicitly compares her experiences as Palestinian and as queer, explaining to me the frustration she feels in social situations where she is expected to passively endure anti-Arab racism: "It reminds me of a lot of being queer in straight spaces, where you're like, 'I'm going to hold back [on divulging sexual identity] so that I don't make you feel uncomfortable.'" Alma's characterization of her strategic disclosure or omission of her Palestinian identity or cultural politics as analogous to her experience as a queer-identified woman brings new meaning to my interlocutors' conscious acts of "outing" their identities. What is more, this kind of experience indicates that Palestinian cultural politics and queer sexual politics share similar subjectivities in relation to systems of power and domination.

Inclusion or exclusion from the category "Palestinian" hinges not only on Arabic-language knowledge but also on anxieties about ethnic lineage and geographic proximity to Palestinian land and society. Suha, a festival organizer, was born and raised in the United States to a Palestinian mother and a white American father. She grew up speaking Arabic and strongly identifies as "*nuss falastiniyya, nuss amrikiyya, bess* [half Palestinian, half American but] 100 percent Muslim," wherein her mixed-ethnic heritage is made whole through her faith and cultural identification as Muslim. Despite her strong sense of self, she describes numerous occasions wherein peers or extended family members ignored or delegitimized her identification as Palestinian because of her parentage or fair features or upbringing in the United States or oftentimes all three at once.

These experiences led her to, in her own words, "overcompensate" by investing significant time and labor toward organizing the film festival. Despite her Arabic-language abilities, she felt culturally illegible as Palestinian, which produced a sense of anxiety about her legitimacy as a festival organizer: "I felt this weird tension, that I can't—or they won't accept me. Or I'm not Arab *enough* or don't *look* Arab enough. Clearly I have to wear this keffiyeh!" Suha employs the keffiyeh, the traditional black-and-white Palestinian scarf, as a means to claim her space within the festival with a visual marker of her identity. As part of the festival itself, the BPFF sells Palestinian-made keffiyeh scarves at the program table outside of each film screening. While keffiyeh sales provides additional revenue for the festival's operations, they also offer Palestinian American spectators who may share Suha's insecurities the option to purchase cultural authenticity (both as a prop and by way of financially supporting Palestinian craftwork) and literally to wear their identity politics. Suha's experience offers an example of how cultural queerness compels Palestinian Americans to actively choose political queerness by engaging with film culture as a form of activism in resistance to the compounding pressures of cultural authenticity and compulsory Zionism. Positioned at the margins of cultural authenticity, Suha recuperates her sense of identity through her festival labor, which in turn supports the festival's mission, as articulated by Ruba, to "do politics though film."

Examining compulsory Zionism and the politics of cultural authenticity together highlights the cynical relationship that exists between the two, particularly regarding how Palestinian lineage is *quantified* in ways that resemble conceptions of blood quantum or is *qualified* in terms of sociogeographic proximity to historic Palestine. It is this tension that amplifies a sense of *cultural* queerness among my Palestinian American interlocutors, especially those of mixed ethnic heritage, and it is through participation in film culture that my interlocutors' attempt to mitigate that tension, choose political queerness, articulate their cultural identities, and claim their relationships to Palestine.

My interlocutors' engagements with diasporic film culture help in managing their insecurities around their identities and exemplify what Lisa Suhair Majaj has described as a process of "self-creation" through an "on-going negotiation of difference" (1984, 84). Majaj, who identifies as Palestinian American of mixed ethnicity, writes of the importance of "claiming" her Palestinian identity largely to counteract how "passing . . . wreaks implicit violence upon the lived reality of our experiences" (80). "Claiming" in this sense serves as a way simultaneously to acknowledge and to resist the cultural, political, material, and geographic dispossession that characterizes the Palestinian diaspora. A queer diasporic framing illuminates how my interlocutors' feelings of insecurity are a by-product of both the discourses on Palestinian cultural identity that reify heteronormative genealogy as well as social and geographic proximity to historic Palestine as the basis for national identification.

Queering Palestine

Examining concerns over Palestinian identity through the lens of queer theory allows for, to borrow from David Eng, "a different story about the contemporary politics of nation-building and race under globalization, along with its accompanying material and psychic processes of social belonging and exclusion" (2010, 14). Scholars working at the intersection of queer studies and diaspora studies have critiqued how the very notion of diaspora has been used to shore up heteronormative ideas about "racial descent, filiation, and biological traceability" (Eng 2010, 13). As Eng further remarks, "Configuring diaspora as displacement from a lost homeland or exile from an exalted origin can thus underwrite regnant ideologies of nationalism, while upholding virulent notions of racial purity and its structuring heteronormative logics" (13). In this sense, my interlocutors' anxieties with respect to their identities reflect Gopinath's conception of "queer diaspora" in that diasporic Palestinians, especially those who identify as ethnically mixed, are implicitly coded as ethnically inauthentic and therefore *culturally queer.* The concept of cultural queerness, therefore, accounts for the sense of cultural dispossession some Palestinians in the United States experience due to their estrangement from the land and the society that inhabits it.

In spite of these struggles with the politics of cultural authenticity and the politics of compulsory Zionism, film festival participation has become a mechanism through which Palestinian Americans "derive their power not from purity and *refusal* but from impurity and *refusion*" (Naficy 2001, 6, emphasis in original). For Palestinian Americans such as those represented in this essay, spectatorship has served as a way to affirm their cultural identities, while festival organizing and volunteering have privileged the promotion of culturally queer representations of Palestine that expressly challenge the expectations of cultural authenticity. The labor performed through this organizing helps to keep the question of queer diaspora—and all of its heterogeneity—on the table within the larger discourses on national identity and self-determination as it is represented throughout the field of the Palestinian cinematic movement.

My interlocutors' investments in diasporic film culture exemplify the dual purpose of queering both the culture of compulsory Zionism in the United States and the intra-Palestinian politics of cultural authenticity. As a diasporic site, the festival provides a productive space where these subjectivities congregate around and connect through their shared cultural politics. These engagements with film culture indicate how Palestinian Americans cultivate social and political power to imagine a fuller sense of what justice for Palestine might mean for the diaspora.

Works Cited

Cable, Umayyah. 2020. "An *Uprising* at *the Perfect Moment*: Palestine in the 1990s Culture Wars." *GLQ: Journal of Lesbian and Gay Studies* 26, no. 2: 243–72.

Cainkar, Louise. 2016. "Becoming Arab American." *Middle East Report* 278:44–46.

Cook-Obregon, Maryssa, and Katherine Hanna. 2012. "6th Annual Boston Palestine Film Festival Set for October 5–13, 2012." Boston Palestine Film Festival press release.

Eng, David L. 2010. *The Feeling of Kinship: Queer Liberalism and the Racialization of Intimacy.* Durham, NC: Duke Univ. Press.

Gopinath, Gayatri. 2005. *Impossible Desires: Queer Diasporas and South Asian Public Cultures.* Durham, NC: Duke Univ. Press.

Gualtieri, Sarah M. A. 2009. *Between Arab and White: Race and Ethnicity in the Early Syrian American Diaspora.* Berkeley: Univ. of California Press.

Hammer, Juliane. 2005. *Palestinians Born in Exile: Diaspora and the Search for a Homeland.* Austin: Univ. of Texas Press.

Hansen, Miriam. 1993. "Early Cinema, Late Cinema: Permutations of the Public Sphere." *Screen* 34, no. 3: 197–210.

Loist, Skadi, and Ger Zielinski. 2012. "On the Development of Queer Film Festivals and Their Media Activism." In *Film Festival Yearbook 4*, edited by Dina Iordanova and Leschu Torchin, 49–62. St. Andrews, Scotland: Univ. of St. Andrews Film Studies.

Majaj, Lisa Suhair. 1994. "Boundaries: Arab/American." In *Food for Our Grandmothers: Writings by Arab-American & Arab-Canadian Feminists*, edited by Joe Kadi, 65–86. Boston: South End Press.

McAlister, Melani. [2001] 2005. *Epic Encounters: Culture, Media, and US Interests in the Middle East since 1945.* Updated ed., with a post-9/11 chapter. Berkeley: Univ. of California Press.

Naber, Nadine. 2012. *Arab America: Gender, Cultural Politics, and Activism.* New York: New York Univ. Press.

Naficy, Hamid. 2001. *An Accented Cinema: Exilic and Diasporic Filmmaking.* Princeton, NJ: Princeton Univ. Press.

Rich, Adrienne. 1980. "Compulsory Heterosexuality and Lesbian Existence." *Signs* 5:631–60.

Salaita, Steven. 2014. "Inter/Nationalism from the Holy Land to the New World: Encountering Palestine in American

Indian Studies." *Native American and Indigenous Studies* 1, no. 2: 125–44.

Shadmi, Erella. 1992. "Women, Palestinians, Zionism: A Personal View." *News from Within*, Oct.–Nov., 13–16.

Warrior, Robert. 1989. "Canaanites, Cowboys, and Indians." *Christianity and Crisis* 49 (Sept. 11): 261–65.

Wong, Cindy Hing-Yuk. 2016. "Publics and Counterpublics: Rethinking Film Festivals as Public Spheres." In *Film Festivals: History, Theory, Method, Practice*, edited by Marijke de Valck, Brendan Kredell, and Skadi Loist, 83–99. New York: Routledge.

Part Three
Race, Religion, and the Discourse of Multiculturalism

Laila Halaby's lyric poem "Brown Shades of White," published in *Food for Our Grandmothers*, begins:

> Under *race/ethnic* origin
> I check *white*.
> I am not
> a minority
> on their checklists
> and they erase me
> with the red end
> of a number
> two pencil. (Halaby 1994, 204)

These opening lines of Halaby's poem capture the feeling of erasure that Arab Americans experience when they are asked to conform to institutionalized racial classifications in the United States. Arabs are white according to the US Office of Management and Budget Directive 15 (1977), whose guidelines determine not only the categories of the US Census but also those of all official forms, such as in schools, health-care facilities, places of employment, and police departments. The same guidelines define the parameters of accounting with respect to the experiences of "racial minorities" in the United States, leaving Arab Americans as well as people from Southwest Asia and North Africa (SWANA) more broadly absent from the larger institutional story of structural racism in the United States. Yet as scholars of Arab America assert, irrespective of how Arab Americans are officially categorized, they do not share the privileges of whiteness, and they have been racialized as people of color. Conflation of Arabs with other ethnic groups from Southwest Asia and South Asia as well as the imaginative association of Arabs with Islam have further complicated questions of racialization. Though only one small part of the complex story of race for the SWANA diaspora in the Americas, the question of racial boxes highlighted in Halaby's poem captures some of the main themes that have dominated conversations about the process of racialization for Arab Americans.

Tackling the question of Arab American racialization, the essays in this part of the reader address the following questions: How have Arabs been racialized at different historical periods and in different parts of the Americas? Considering the racial paradox of being "not quite white" (Samhan 1999), how have Arabs situated themselves within existing racial frameworks in the United States, including strategic assertions of whiteness and nonwhiteness and on measures of anti-Blackness? How do Arab American positionings on racial hierarchies reveal similarities and differences across various parts of the Americas? How do conflations among Arab Americans, Muslim Americans, and other racialized groups from SWANA operate, and how have they affected the lives of people? How do the demands of white supremacy and its variant, liberal multiculturalism, stifle and constrain activism and advocacy, and what limitations do they place on practices of dissent?

Processes of Racialization

Racialization signifies "the extension of racial meaning to a previously racially unclassified relationship, social practice or group" (Omi and Winant 1994, 64). Michael Omi and Howard Winant argue that race "can never be merely a concept or idea" (64); it gains salience only in social structures, where the processes of racialization are enacted. Especially in the case of Arab Americans (and of people from SWANA more widely), who lack the recognition offered by a racial category, one must highlight evidence of racialization in social structures—laws, policies, actions—in addition to dominant ideologies expressed through media and otherwise, and, indeed, plenty of evidence of such racialization can be found. Furthermore, the widespread conflation of Arabs and Muslims and the application of similar laws, policies, actions, and ideological frames to both also indicate that religious groups can be racialized (Bayoumi 2010; Cainkar and Selod 2018; Rana 2011). In sum, the racial and ethnic categories of the state should not distract us from where and how one locates racialization processes. Like race itself, these categories are particular social constructions that emerged at a particular historical moment.

The difference between Arab, SWANA, and Muslim racialization, on the one hand, and that of the officially recognized racialized "minorities," on the other, is largely one of *timing and purpose*. Omi and Winant's (1994) concept of "racial projects" provides the framework with which to understand this distinction. They explain the mechanisms through which the US domestic project of white supremacy subordinated historic minorities—Indigenous peoples, African Americans, Latinx, Asians—for the purposes of land confiscation, economic exploitation, and white capital accumulation. Early Arab American immigrants largely escaped being subsumed into this project of racial capitalism (Robinson 1983) and, as the work of Sarah Gualtieri (chapter 14 in this reader) and others shows, benefited from a liminal white status. Arab immigrants in the United States were largely able to obtain naturalized US citizenship, and for the most part Arabs were not subjected to the restrictions on movement, housing, and types of work that many other groups faced in the United States (see Cainkar 2006, 2018; Gualtieri 2009; Khater 2001; Shakir 1997). Although Arabs (and Muslims) were "cast out" (Razack 2008) by whites in numerous other ways, their status as white afforded them a privileged position that allowed them and their children the opportunity to accumulate capital (Cainkar 2006, 2018). When the mid-twentieth-century civil rights movement emerged, Arab Americans were, as a group, neither poor nor socially excluded to the same degree as other nonwhite groups; as a result, they were not included on the Office of Management and Budget's list of minority groups whose conditions would be monitored for civil rights purposes.

It was in the interests of a different but intersecting project—that of US global economic and political hegemony, itself built on white supremacy—that the racializations of Arabs, people from SWANA, and Muslims have been forged. For this racial project, domestic *economic* servitude is not required; censorship, silencing, policing, deportations, migration bans, and transnational and global efforts to control land and resources, including through weapons deals and wars, are more important. In the logic of orientalism, the mass targeting of people from SWANA and Muslim Americans operates as a "pillar of white supremacy," which imagines this entire conflated group of people as "permanent foreign threats to empire" (Smith 2006, 68). Although Arabs and Muslims were already othered peoples at the commencement of the conquest of the Americas (coterminous with the Iberian Reconquista), there is wide agreement among scholars that Arab American racialization escalated during the Israeli–Arab War of 1967 (Cainkar 2006, 2018; Jamal and Naber 2008). At that time, Arabs were persistently portrayed in the US mainstream media as uncivilized and barbaric, a description deploying an orientalist settler-colonial narrative of superior and inferior people that resonated with audiences across the United States. Such portrayals and narratives effectively endorsed Israeli conquests of Palestinian land and helped to solidify the seeming naturalness of the US–Israeli imperial alliance.

The case of Arab Americans and those with whom they are conflated demonstrates that racialization, far from being biologically based, relies on narratives that use keywords such as *culture* (Balibar 1991; Mamdani 2004) and *civilization* (Said 1978). Edward Said, whose views on orientalism we discuss at greater length in the introduction to part four, has shown how orientalism facilitated European colonialism by constructing a generalized view of the "East," which is contrasted to an idealized "West." The "East"—encompassing, collapsing, and conflating all that is east of Europe, including SWANA as well as southern and eastern Asia—is configured as indolent, violent, and uncivilized, whereas the "West," epitomized by Europe and the United States, is rational, capable of rule, and civilized (1978, 57). With his characteristically keen and caustic intellect, Said observed: "This is the problem with unedifying labels like Islam and West: They mislead and confuse the mind, which is trying to make sense of a disorderly reality that won't be pigeonholed or strapped down as easily as all that" (2001; see also Said [1981] 1997). Orientalist discourse exoticized Arabs and conflated them with all "Easterners"; the racialization of Arab Americans builds on this conflation, configuring them not only as exotic others (Hamilton 1994; Jarmakani 2008; Kahf 2011) but also as volatile, internal threats to the nation (Bayoumi 2015; Cainkar 2018) who must be subjected to policies of surveillance, detention, deportation, registration, and banning (Abraham 1994; Bassiouni 1974; Cainkar 2009, 2018, 2020; Jamal 2008; Naber 2008; Volpp 2003).

The racialization of Arab Americans intensified throughout the 1970s and thereafter through policing, censorship, political exclusion, and repeated representations of Arabs as terrorists in popular media (Shaheen [2001] 2012). As a consequence, the paradox of being defined as white but not having the privileges of whiteness bubbled to the surface of scholarship. Helen Hatab Samhan (1999) captures this paradox with the description "not quite white"; Nadine Naber (2000) describes Arab Americans as having an "ambiguous insider" status; and Ian Haney López (2006) configures such a status as "white by law." The mass collective targeting of Arabs and Muslims in the United States by both the US government and the American public after the attacks on September 11, 2001 (9/11) must be seen as *proof* (not cause) of the racialization of Arab, SWANA, and Muslim people (as well as of those who "look," "sound," or seem like them) because were it not for their racialized status, only those who actually participated in the attacks would have been held accountable (as occurred with fine-tuned investigations of the siege of the US Capitol in January 2021). Instead, millions of Arab and Muslim Americans (and persons presumed to be so) as well as hundreds of millions of Arabs and Muslims across the globe were punished for the attacks (see part six). That is precisely how race works under white supremacy.

Racialization and Conflated Categories: Islamophobia and Othering of Islam

The process of SWANA racialization works in tandem with the creation of the figure of the "terrorist," a racist formulation that effectively produces an ongoing fear-based discourse of a threat to national security, including from the "enemy within." Positing SWANA subjects as the reservoir for this imagined terrorist, the war on terror is a project that situates them as having a perpetual outsider status while also creating a racialized category that conflates Arabs, so-called Middle Easterners, Muslims, and anyone perceived to belong to these broad, imprecise categories. In his contribution to this part (chapter 16), Steven Salaita names *terrorism* as a term "used uncritically to describe anybody (of the requisite Arab background) who contests either domestic or international American hegemony" (p. 247). Likewise, Bradley Zopf, in his contribution to this part (chapter 19), concludes from interviews with Christian and Muslim Egyptians and Egyptian Americans that racialization is "a layered process in which their skin color and phenotype, ethnicity, national origin, and religion come to define Arabs and Middle Easterners as a different kind of brown: anti-American Muslim terrorists" (p. 270). These studies demonstrate the extent to which the war on terror, through its production of the specter of the terrorist, contributes to a racial project that simultaneously silences and targets Arab Americans and everyone with whom they are affiliated. Even when not overtly named, the term *terrorist* as inspiration for this racialized grouping "serves as a means of systematizing a whole set of state policies—classification, surveillance, strategies of punishment and detention, and distribution of resources—that are meted out along racial lines" (Jarmakani 2015, 128). Precisely because *terrorist* is not a racial (or, for that matter, ethnic or religious) category, the term's fluidity effectively binds together the conflated group of identities imaginatively associated with terrorism.

The imprecision of the social construction of the "Middle Eastern terrorist" allows for the disciplining of a wide range of people in the interests of the war on terror, many of whom are officially marked as white. In *Whitewashed: America's Invisible Middle Eastern Minority* (2009), John Tehranian observes that Armenians, Turks, Iranians, and others classified as "white" by official US Census criteria face systemic racial discrimination "highlighted by recent targeted immigration policies, racial profiling, a war on terrorism with a decided racialist bent, and growing rates of job discrimination and hate crime" (3). In *The Limits of Whiteness: Iranian Americans and the Everyday Politics of Race* (2017), Neda Maghbouleh demonstrates how Iranian American youth "report persistent identity-based bullying by white peers and even teachers" even though they, like Arab Americans, are "counted as legal whites in the United States" (82). This harassment, Maghbouleh reveals, "relies heavily on rhetoric drawn from the War on Terror" and "targets other sites of difference like physical appearance, familial connections to Iran and the Middle East, Persian names, and varying degrees of bilingualism" (82). The racialized conflation of those imagined to be affiliated with terrorists also relies on anti-Muslim racism. Nadine Naber, for example, has observed that "Arab Americans have become racially marked on the assumption that all Arabs are Muslim and that Islam is a cruel, backward and uncivilized religion" (2000, 52). Erik Love posits in chapter 18 that making "connections between race and Islamophobia provides, among other insights, the only plausible explanation for why Christians, Sikhs, Hindus, and people of all faiths are vulnerable to Islamophobia" (p. 261). Scholarship included in the #Islamophobia Is Racism Syllabus, which itself was inspired by earlier online antiracist syllabi such as #FergusonSyllabus, #StandingRock Syllabus, and #BlackIslam Syllabus, explores the ways in which anti-Muslim racism is a racial project.

Liberal Multiculturalism: Racialization by Another Name

The essays in this part of the reader tell the story of Arab racialization and illustrate how such officially unacknowledged but actually practiced racialization has affected Arab and Muslim Americans. In *Between Arab and White: Race and Ethnicity in the Early Syrian American Diaspora* (2009), Sarah M. A. Gualtieri reveals how Arab identification with whiteness cannot be separated from the legal constraints and immigration laws in the United States, which restricted naturalized citizenship to immigrants deemed "white" from 1790 up until 1952. Placing Arab American claims to citizenship within the discourse of race, Gualtieri examines racial perquisite cases for Syrian immigrants between 1909 and 1915 and demonstrates how Arab identification with whiteness was hard-won, strategic, and imperative, allowing Arabs to gain some of the legal rights that accrue to "whiteness," including naturalized citizenship. Yet as Lisa Suhair Majaj demonstrates in chapter 15, the category of whiteness is malleable: "At stake . . . were these questions: whether Arabs are 'white' in color; whether Arabs are Asian or Caucasian; whether whiteness is determined by race, color, geography, culture, or religion; and whether there is an intrinsic connection between Caucasian identity and whiteness" (p. 234). Meanwhile, though these questions purported to answer to scientific logic and studies, they were just as often "answered" in court deliberations and decisions with the popular white-supremacist logic of what white looked like.

These inconsistent notions of what constitutes whiteness as a race, coupled with ongoing realities of systemic discrimination regardless of legal status, have rendered Arab Americans, as Suad Joseph—echoing Samhan—puts it, "not quite citizens" (1999, 257). Yet the goal of citizenship forces those who seek it to navigate the terms of inclusion and belonging, terms that are set by a white-supremacist state and its more recent liberal multiculturalism project. Steven Salaita's concept of "imperative patriotism" suggests that only when Arab Americans stop dissenting against imperial policies that most "find invasive and unjust" will they have a chance at being "absorbed" within the nation (chapter 16, p. 243). Emily Regan Wills further notes, based on her research in Arab American communities and organizations in New York in the early 2010s, that Arab American practical and political speech is curtailed by "discursive misrecognition" (2019, 12), which (at best) ignores political participation and (at worst) punishes it. Salaita connects the tactic of imperative patriotism to a longer history of forced assimilation, one that characterizes settler societies where legal structures impose conformity on settlers so they don't ask moral questions. When some political leaders after 9/11 declared that "Arab Americans are part of us," their gesture of inclusion circulated, warns Salaita, with a demand for an imperative patriotism requiring the suppression of dissent as the price of belonging.

Indeed, narratives of inclusion and belonging uphold the logic of liberal multiculturalism, an ideological lynchpin of US imperialism rooted in white supremacy (Jarmakani 2015, 118; Melamed 2006). In her book *Arab America: Gender, Cultural Politics, and Activism* (2012), Nadine Naber illustrates how "liberal multiculturalism requires immigrants, people of color, and indigenous people to craft concepts of culture that are depoliticized and ahistorical" (65). Offering an incisive intervention in conventional diaspora theory, Naber argues that "rather than reflecting an authentic, pure Arab culture frozen in time, idealized concepts of Arab culture are best understood as cultural sensibilities that become entangled in transnational modalities of power—U.S. Orientalist discourses and structures of colonialism and imperialism, race, class, gender, and sexuality" (64). Naber's observations on the depoliticizing demands of multicultural inclusion are echoed in an excerpt we include in this part of the reader from Su'ad Abdul Khabeer's book *Muslim Cool: Race, Religion, and Hip Hop in the United States* (2016), which, among many other contributions, elaborates on forms of anti-Blackness among Arab and South Asian Muslims. In the piece "The Limits of Muslim Cool" (chapter 17), Abdul Khabeer demonstrates how "Muslim Cool" is an "alterity . . . constructed through the Black radical tradition," one that mounts challenges to the "interlocking hegemonies of white supremacy and of Arab and South Asian US American Muslims" (p. 253). Khabeer argues that although "Muslim Cool" works within a politics of resistance and dissent to forge a sense of identity for Muslim youth through "the loop of hip hop, Islam, and Blackness" (p. 250), its critical edge is undermined by the politics of inclusion, codes of civic engagement, and multicultural state discourses that place limits on the demands any group can make on the state.

The limits of a multicultural framework, in short, manifest in the ways its privileged modes, like the politics of inclusion, ultimately uphold and reinforce the logics of white supremacy. Yet racial regimes, such as the United States, produce not only racialized subjects but also racialized subjectivities. Systemic change requires proactive contestation of white-supremacist categories. Amina Zarrugh posits that "moments of racialized political shock," such as the Israeli–Arab War of 1967 or 9/11, produce backlashes that in turn become opportunities for collective organizing, thus contributing to a shift from an identification with whiteness to a call for "recognition as non-white racial subjects" (2016, 2723). Efforts to create a new census category can be understood as one step toward such recognition, particularly since the absence of a racial category for Arab Americans came to be understood by many as yet another means of silencing, as expressed in Halaby's poem, with which we open this introduction to part three. Today, Arabs and others from SWANA must continue to check "white" on the census, and the absence of a census category continues to silence Arab Americans, to make data on them hard to locate, to exclude them from racial justice accounting, and to justify their institutional exclusion.

Census efforts are ultimately embedded in a politics of inclusion, even if as a strategic move. While having a category can mobilize access to state resources, it also requires participation in the racist classification schemes of the state. Momentum for a census category unique to Arab Americans began in the 1990s and grew with the "Check It Right, You Ain't White" campaign urging Arab Americans not to check "white" on the 2010 US Census. These campaigns culminated in joint Census Bureau/community efforts to create a Middle East and North Africa (MENA) reporting category on the 2020 US Census (Kayyali 2013), a collaborative process that initially made significant headway under the Obama administration, was halted by the Trump administration's Office of Management and Budget, and resumed under the Biden administration, supplemented by community advocacy work with members of Congress. The census efforts were met with resistance from some Arab Americans, however, who feared that a category would facilitate surveillance and tracking. Preference for an ethnic rather than racial category was not without dissent among scholars and activists in the census working group but was favored by the Arab American organizations involved in the process. So, too, the decision to exclude from the MENA category predominantly Black African countries in the League of Arab States was favored by Census Bureau staff but not by all in the working group. This decision underscores the sorts of divide-and-conquer politics that promote anti-Blackness. Most importantly, it highlights the need to simultaneously "organize without a box" and to foreground working "in solidarity with other affected communities against all forms of subjugation, violence, and exclusion" (Qutami 2020, 187, 188), a project we discuss in part six.

Racialization and the "Intimacies of Four Continents"

Liberal narratives of multicultural inclusion depend on an erasure of colonialist and settler-colonialist histories and a disavowal of the way that the founding of modern nation-states in the Americas was a colonial project that relied on the genocidal expropriation of Indigenous lands as well as on the extraction of resources and exploitation of labor that is characteristic of the project of racial capitalism. Lisa Lowe uses the rubric of the "intimacies of four continents" to describe "the residual processes of settler colonialism that appropriated lands from indigenous people and the colonial logics through which men and women from Africa and Asia were forcibly transported to the Americas, who with native, mixed, and creole peoples constituted colonial societies that produced the assets for the bourgeois republics in Europe and North America" (2015, 20). This framing of the expropriating colonialist interconnections across continents invites us to investigate how modes of conquest, enslavement, violent displacement, and coerced or forced movement to extract labor enabled the existence of modern nation-states, despite their demarcation as liberal democracies. We can understand Lowe's work to be in conversation with scholarship that explores the coloniality of power—a framework that situates race within a matrix of modern-colonial-patriarchal-capitalist power formations (Dussel 1995; Grosfoguel 2006; Lugones 2010; Mignolo 2005; Quijano 2000). Extending beyond a Eurocentric paradigm of colonialism, these paradigms offer useful rubrics for better theorizing SWANA racialization throughout the Americas. For example, in their essay "Tropical Orientalism: Brazil's Race Debates and the Sephardi-Moorish Atlantic" (2014), Robert Stam and Ella Shohat observe that "the metanarrative of racial-cultural harmony through mixing" frames national Brazilian discourses about race (143). Stam and Shohat reveal, though, that rather than idealizing notions of racial democracy, it is more useful to contextualize patterns of racialization in relation to comparative colonial contexts and migration histories. If a Moorish and Sephardic presence entered Brazil through Portuguese and Dutch colonization of the Americas, they argue, Islam was introduced by enslaved Africans. Regardless of modern and contemporary narratives that romanticize racial mixing, then, Arabs, Muslims, and semitic/SWANA people more broadly are figured into the Brazilian racial landscape—and that of the Americas at large—through the contexts of conquest and colonization.

SWANA trajectories throughout the Americas reflect both their oppression by and their possessive investment in these colonial contexts. While nineteenth-century Syrian and Lebanese migration forged the construction of them as "Syrian-Lebanese-street-peddlers-turned-wealthy-businessmen" (Amar 2014, 11), Arab Brazilians have also been racialized through "tropical orientalist" (Stam and Shohat 2014) discursive associations of SWANA with exoticism as well as with war-on-terror-affiliated constructions of Arabs—especially recent migrants—as terrorists. John Tofik Karam's piece in this part of the reader, in which he observes that neoliberal policies have opened "the novel formation of Arabness in Brazil" (chapter 20, p. 275), aims to broaden the field's consideration of the way that discourses of (neo)liberal multiculturalism manifest differently through the Americas. Whether through modes of neoliberal multicultural "inclusion" or "tropical orientalist" racialization, this growing scholarship gestures to the need for critical expansions on our conceptualizations of race in relation to Arab Americans throughout the Americas.

Broadening our scope to understand how the process of racialization is bound up in the differential projects of genocide, enslavement, and "social death" (Cacho 2012; Patterson 2018) that operate in the service of racial capitalism is necessary if we are to move past the impotent and insufficient analytics of inclusion and belonging. As noted in the general introduction to the reader, most scholars of Arab America in the 1970s and 1980s were optimistic that negative attitudes toward Arabs could be changed by providing more and more accurate information about them. That perception aligned well with race studies scholarship of the time, which, according to Eduardo

Bonilla-Silva, viewed racism largely as "a purely ideological phenomenon" (1997, 465). If race works mainly on the level of ideas, the argument went, all that is required for change operates on the level of knowledge. The flaw in this logic was increasingly apparent to scholars of Arab Americans as, despite all of their work, state policies of surveillance, policing, and deportation directed at Arab Americans increased in scope, as popular attacks on them became a consistent reality, and as negative representations of them became more, not less, entrenched in American culture. Using the insights of critical race studies, scholars recognized that the denigration and policing of Arab Americans were about much more than ideas; they constituted a systemic racial project of white supremacy and empire, and so the goal of inclusion through acknowledgment by a racial regime was deeply problematic. The essays we include in this part point to the persistent need for more complex, intersectional, and structural approaches to understanding Arab Americans' experiences with race under white supremacy.

Works Cited

Abdul Khabeer, Su'ad. 2016. *Muslim Cool: Race, Religion, and Hip Hop in the United States*. New York: New York Univ. Press.

Abraham, Nabeel. 1994. "Anti-Arab Racism and Violence in the United States." In *The Development of Arab-American Identity*, edited by Ernest McCarus, 155–214. Ann Arbor: Univ. of Michigan Press.

Amar, Paul. 2014. Introduction to *The Middle East and Brazil: Perspectives on the New Global South*, edited by Paul Amar, 1–14. Indianapolis: Univ. of Indiana Press.

Balibar, Étienne. 1991. "Is There a 'Neo-racism'?" In *Race, Nation, Class: Ambiguous Identities*, edited by Étienne Balibar and Immanuel Wallerstein, 17–28. London: Verso.

Bassiouni, M. Cherif, ed. 1974. *The Civil Rights of Arab Americans: The Special Measures*. Belmont, MA: AAUG Press.

Bayoumi, Moustafa. 2010. "The Race Is On: Muslims and Arabs in the American Imagination." *Middle East Report Online*, Mar. At http://www.merip.org/mero/interventions/bayoumi_in-terv.html.

———. 2015. *This Muslim American Life: Dispatches from the War on Terror*. New York: New York Univ. Press.

Bonilla-Silva, Eduardo. 1997. "Rethinking Racism: Toward a Structural Interpretation." *American Sociological Review* 62, no. 3: 465–80.

Cacho, Lisa Marie. 2012. *Social Death: Racialized Rightlessness and the Criminalization of the Unprotected*. New York: New York Univ. Press.

Cainkar, Louise. 2006. "The Social Construction of Difference and the Arab American Experience." *Journal of American Ethnic History* 25, nos. 2–3: 243–78.

———. 2009. *Homeland Insecurity: The Arab American and Muslim American Experience after 9/11*. New York: Russell Sage Foundation.

———. 2018. "Fluid Terror Threat: A Genealogy of the Racialization of Arab, Muslim, and South Asian Americans." In "Arab/Americas: Locations & Iterations," edited by Sarah M. A. Gualtieri and Pauline Homsi Vinson. Special issue of *Amerasia Journal* 44, no. 1: 27–60.

———. 2020. "The Muslim Ban and Trump's War on Immigration." *Middle East Report* 294 (Spring). At https://merip.org/2020/06/the-muslim-ban-and-trumps-war-on-immigration-2/.

Cainkar, Louise, and Saher Selod. 2018. "Review of Race Scholarship and the War on Terror." *Sociology of Race and Ethnicity* 4, no. 2: 165–77.

Dussel, Enrique. 1995. *The Invention of the Americas: Eclipse of "the Other" and the Myth of Modernity.* Translated by Michael D. Barber. New York: Continuum.

Grosfoguel, Ramón. 2006. "World-Systems Analysis in the Context of Transmodernity, Border Thinking, and Global Coloniality." *Review* (Fernand Braudel Center) 29, no. 2: 167–87.

Gualtieri, Sarah M. A. 2009. *Between Arab and White: Race and Ethnicity in the Early Syrian American Diaspora.* Berkeley: Univ. of California Press.

Halaby, Laila. 1994. "Brown Shades of White." In *Food for Our Grandmothers: Writings by Arab-American & Arab-Canadian Feminists*, edited by Joe Kadi, 204. Boston: South End Press.

Hamilton, Marsha J. 1994. "The Arab Woman in U.S. Popular Culture." In *Food for Our Grandmothers: Writings by Arab-American & Arab-Canadian Feminists*, edited by Joe Kadi, 173–80. Boston: South End Press.

Haney López, Ian. 2006. *White by Law: The Legal Construction of Race.* New York: New York Univ. Press.

Jamal, Amaney. 2008. "Civil Liberties and the Otherization of Arab and Muslim Americans." In *Race and Arab Americans before and after 9/11: From Invisible Citizens to Visible Subjects*, edited by Amaney Jamal and Nadine Naber, 114–30. Syracuse, NY: Syracuse Univ. Press.

Jamal, Amaney, and Nadine Naber, eds. 2008. *Race and Arab Americans before and after 9/11: From Invisible Citizens to Visible Subjects.* Syracuse, NY: Syracuse Univ. Press.

Jarmakani, Amira. 2008. *Imagining Arab Womanhood: The Cultural Mythology of Veils, Harems, and Belly Dancers in the U.S.* New York: Palgrave.

———. 2015. *An Imperialist Love Story: Desert Romances and the War on Terror.* New York: New York Univ. Press.

Joseph, Suad. 1999. "Against the Grain of the Nation—the Arab." In *Arabs in America: Building a New Future*, edited by Michael W. Suleiman, 257–71. Philadelphia: Temple Univ. Press.

Kahf, Mohja. 2011. "The Pity Committee and the Careful Reader: How Not to Buy Stereotypes about Muslim Women." In *Arab & Arab American Feminisms: Gender, Violence, & Belonging*, edited by Rabab Abdulhadi, Evelyn Alsultany, and Nadine Naber, 111–23. Syracuse, NY: Syracuse Univ. Press.

Kayyali, Randa. 2013. "US Census Classifications and Arab Americans: Contestations and Definitions of Identity Markers." *Journal of Ethnic and Migration Studies* 39, no. 8: 1299–318.

Khater, Akram F. 2001. *Inventing Home: Emigration, Gender, and the Middle Class in Lebanon, 1770–1920.* New ed. Berkeley: Univ. of California Press.

Lowe, Lisa. 2015. *The Intimacies of Four Continents.* Durham, NC: Duke Univ. Press.

Lugones, María. 2010. "Toward a Decolonial Feminism." *Hypatia* 25, no. 4: 742–59.

Maghbouleh, Neda. 2017. *The Limits of Whiteness: Iranian Americans and the Everyday Politics of Race*. Stanford, CA: Stanford Univ. Press.

Mamdani, Mahmood. 2004. *Good Muslim, Bad Muslim: America, the Cold War, and the Roots of Terror*. New York: Pantheon.

Melamed, Jodi. 2006. "The Spirit of Neoliberalism: From Racial Liberalism to Neoliberal Multiculturalism." *Social Text 89* 24, no. 4: 1–2.

Mignolo, Walter D. 2005. *The Idea of Latin America*. Malden, MA: Blackwell.

Naber, Nadine. 2000. "Ambiguous Insiders: An Investigation of Arab American Invisibility." *Ethnic and Racial Studies* 23, no. 1: 37–61.

———. 2008. "'Look, Mohammed the Terrorist Is Coming!': Cultural Racism, Nation-Based Racism, and the Intersectionality of Oppressions after 9/11." In *Race and Arab Americans before and after 9/11: From Invisible Citizens to Visible Subjects*, edited by Amaney Jamal and Nadine Naber, 276–304. Syracuse, NY: Syracuse Univ. Press.

———. 2012. *Arab America: Gender, Cultural Politics, and Activism*. New York: New York Univ. Press.

Omi, Michael, and Howard Winant. 1994. *Racial Formation in the United States*. 2nd ed. New York: Routledge.

Patterson, Orlando. 2018. *Slavery and Social Death: A Comparative Study*. 2nd ed. Cambridge, MA: Harvard Univ. Press.

Quijano, Aníbal. 2000. "Coloniality of Power, Ethnocentrism, and Latin America." *Nepantla* 1, no. 3: 533–80.

Qutami, Loubna. 2020. "Censusless: Arab/Muslim Interpolation into Whiteness and the War on Terror." *Journal of Asian American Studies* 23, no. 2: 161–200.

Rana, Junaid. 2011. *Terrifying Muslims: Race and Labor in the South Asian Diaspora*. Durham, NC: Duke Univ. Press.

Razack, Sherene H. 2008. *Casting Out: The Eviction of Muslims from Western Law and Politics*. Toronto: Univ. of Toronto Press.

Robinson, Cedric. 1983. *Black Marxism: The Making of the Black Radical Tradition*. London: Zed Press.

Said, Edward. 1978. *Orientalism*. New York: Vintage Books.

———. [1981] 1997. *Covering Islam: How the Media and the Experts Determine How We See the Rest of the World*. New York: Pantheon.

———. 2001. "The Clash of Ignorance." *Nation*, Oct. 4. At https://www.thenation.com/article/archive/clash-ignorance/.

Samhan, Helen Hatab. 1999. "Not Quite White: Race Classification and the Arab-American Experience." In *Arabs in America: Building a New Future*, edited by Michael W. Suleiman, 209–26. Philadelphia: Temple Univ. Press.

Shaheen, Jack. [2001] 2012. *Reel Bad Arabs: How Hollywood Vilifies a People*. Rev. updated ed. Amherst, MA: Interlink.

Shakir, Evelyn. 1997. *Bint Arab: Arab and Arab American Women in the United States*. Westport, CT: Praeger.

Smith, Andrea. 2006. "Heteropatriarchy and the Three Pillars of White Supremacy: Rethinking Women of Color Organizing." In *Color of Violence: The INCITE! Anthology*, edited by INCITE! Women of Color against Violence, 66–73. Cambridge, MA: South End Press.

Stam, Robert, and Ella Shohat. 2014. "Tropical Orientalism: Brazil's Race Debates and the Sephardi-Moorish Atlantic." In *The Middle East and Brazil: Perspectives on the New Global South*, edited by Paul Amar, 119–61. Bloomington: Indiana Univ. Press.

Tehranian, John. 2009. *Whitewashed: America's Invisible Middle Eastern Minority.* New York: New York Univ. Press.

US Office of Management and Budget. 1977. *Directive No. 15: Race and Ethnic Standards for Federal Statistics and Administrative Reporting.* Washington, DC: US Government Printing Office.

Volpp, Leti. 2003. "The Citizen and the Terrorist." In *September 11 in History: A Watershed Moment?*, edited by Mary L. Dudziak, 147–62. Durham, NC: Duke Univ. Press.

Wills, Emily Regan. 2019. *Arab New York: Politics and Community in the Everyday Lives of Arab Americans.* New York: New York Univ. Press.

Zarrugh, Amina. 2016. "Racialized Political Shock: Arab American Racial Formation and the Impact of Political Events." *Ethnic and Racial Studies* 39, no. 15: 2722–739.

14

Claiming Whiteness

Syrians and Naturalization Law

SARAH M. A. GUALTIERI

Race in the present state of things is an abstract conception, a notion of continuity in discontinuity, of unity in diversity. It is the rehabilitation of a real but directly unattainable thing.

—Circuit Judge Lowell, *In re Halladjian et al.* (1909)

No one was white before he/she came to America. It took generations, and a vast amount of coercion, before this became a white country.

—James Baldwin

As the number of Syrians in the United States increased and people . . . found work, many began to contemplate acquiring American citizenship. Naturalization gave immigrants access to certain privileges. They could vote, travel more easily—including back and forth to Syria—and purchase property. Essa Samara noted that he chose to naturalize "to be like the people with whom we were doing business, to vote, and it was useful in case one went to Canada or back home or elsewhere" (Samara 1962). Although not entirely happy about this development, the French consul in Seattle argued that "it is natural that all these immigrants prefer to naturalize as Americans because of all sorts of advantages that result [from it]."[1]

Acquiring citizenship, however, was not so straightforward in a country that was increasingly concerned about its "foreign element." In this context, naturalization law became a key arena for determining who could and could not become an American. Because the naturalization law was limited to "aliens being free white persons, and to aliens of African nativity and to persons of African descent," the contest was, at its root, a racialized one. For Syrian immigrants, acquiring citizenship came to hinge on the question of whether they were white. It is this history that Costa Najour alluded to in an interview conducted fifty-two years after Circuit Court judge [William T.] Newman deemed him to be a "free white person," eligible for naturalization. Reflecting on the experience, he described the "great furor in some states (and especially North Carolina) that the Syrians were yellow,

Excerpt from Sarah M. A. Gualtieri, *Between Arab and White: Race and Ethnicity in the Early Syrian American Diaspora* (Berkeley: Univ. of California Press, 2009), chapter 2, "Claiming Whiteness: Syrians and Naturalization Law," 52–80. Full references in the original notes were converted to author-date citations in the text and notes here, and a works cited list was added.

1. Consul of France to Ministère des affaires étrangères (MAE), Paris, Apr. 20, 1921, Levant, 1918–40, Syrie-Liban, 1918–29, vol. 132, 43b, MAE.

not white [*min asfar laysa abyad*]" (Najour 1961). Najour, whose 1909 case helped secure the Syrian legal status as "white," seemed to understand his whiteness only in relation to a racialized Other, to a group he described as "yellow." He did not so much *affirm* his status as a "white" person as *negate* that he was something else. This chapter [in *Between Arab and White*] examines how and why Syrian immigrants, whose premigratory conceptions of difference were rooted primarily in religion, developed a new racial awareness and became increasingly invested in whiteness.

Syrians and the New Nativism

The question of whether Syrians met the racial requirement of the naturalization law did not become controversial until the first decade of the twentieth century. Syrians who had applied for citizenship before 1909 had been granted it without much deliberation.[2] Many had filed their first papers (the so-called declaration of intent to become a citizen) and were waiting the requisite time period before they could complete the application process and be sworn in as citizens. This wait became more difficult as anxieties over the United States' large immigrant population intensified and as nativists sharpened their rhetoric with demands for restriction on immigration and greater surveillance of the foreign born—particularly those born in southern Europe and Asia. The concern with controlling immigration found institutional support in 1906 with the creation of the Bureau of Immigration and Naturalization in the Department of Commerce and Labor. The bureau's responsibilities involved the administration of a new naturalization law aimed at curtailing many of the abuses that had plagued the naturalization process in the nineteenth century. The law of 1906 banned, for example, naturalization hearings held within thirty days of a general election in a court's area of jurisdiction. Such a measure would, its framers hoped, discourage political bosses from rounding up immigrants and herding them to court to secure their naturalization papers and thereafter their votes. An extensive bureaucracy that included three hundred naturalization examiners stationed throughout the country administered the newly codified law (Ueda 1980, 740).

This reinvigorated nativism produced elaborate theories of the contaminating effect of the "new immigration" from southern and eastern Europe. Members of the northern intelligentsia, for example, churned out literature on Anglo-Saxon "race suicide" and allied themselves with the proponents of eugenics. Southern whites, in contrast, were principally concerned with cracks in the color line. Particularly threatening to white southerners was the "inbetweenness" of the new immigrants (Higham 1969, 165). The ambiguous racial status of Italians, East European Jews, and Syrians stemmed from the perception that they possessed cultures and habits that were fundamentally at odds with southern traditions and values and that immigrants would not abide by the "white man's code." Southerners could point, for example, to the close relations that Italian immigrants had with Blacks with whom they worked as evidence of interracial alliances that threatened to undermine white supremacy (Higham 1969, 169). In the wake of the lynching of three Italians in Hahnville, Louisiana, in 1896, some whites feared that Italian immigrants would bond with Blacks (who were regularly the victims of lynch mobs) and seek revenge (Cunningham 1997). Nativists lashed out at the alleged "immigrant menace" in public denunciations and in behind-the-scenes schemes that involved intimidation and violence. It was in this climate of rising nativism that North Carolina senator F. M. Simmons claimed that the new immigrants were "the spawn of the Phoenician curse" (quoted in Higham 1969, 165).

Senator Simmons's use of the biological metaphor "spawn" was in keeping with the most vitriolic nativist language of the day, which linked immigration to contagion and disease. Government health officials helped fuel this prejudice by quarantining entire immigrant neighborhoods, ostensibly to control whatever disease that they believed was spread by immigrant habits (Kraut 1994). The Chinese and Russian Jews were especially pathologized in this regard, and it was possible that Syrian immigrants would suffer the same fate. Already Syrians were being refused entry into the United States at

2. New York City, for example, had approximately three hundred naturalized Syrians by 1901 (US House 1901, 445).

an increasing rate as carriers of trachoma. Caused by the bacteria *Chlamydia trachomatis*, the disease occurred at high rates in countries with a lack of clean running water and often led to blindness (Gabbert 2002). The US Public Health Service considered trachoma (along with favus, venereal diseases, parasitic infections, and tuberculosis) a "loathsome and dangerous contagious disease" warranting exclusion (quoted in Fairchild 1997, 38). In 1909, Ellis Island officials certified 103 Syrians for trachoma, and of the thirty-nine "races" listed according to numbers deported in 1909 for medical reasons, Syrians were ranked sixth at 113 cases, 35 of whom were women.[3] . . .

The fear of being excluded because of trachoma prompted many Syrians to attempt entering the United States via Mexico (S. 1997). Alice Abraham sailed on to New York from Marseilles and reached her destination of Cedar Rapids, Iowa, but her relatives went to Mexico and entered the United States from there; the journey took them four months (Abraham 1962). Some Syrians even "disguised" themselves as Mexicans by learning rudimentary Spanish and crossed into the United States from Mexico at El Paso, Texas.[4] . . .

Syrians did, then, find ways to evade authorities, but trachoma separated many of them permanently from members of their family and sent them sailing out of US ports of entry to South America and even as far away as Australia.[5] As Alan Kraut (1994) has argued, the "disease status" of a particular immigrant group, whether real or imagined, served as a gauge of the desirability of their entry both into the country and into the polity. In this context of heightened nativism, bureaucratic reform, and concern with disease, Syrian racial identity began to be challenged by politicians, academics, and, eventually, lawyers and federal judges.

One of the pillars of the nativist movement was the literacy test, a test that would restrict entry into the United States to literate persons only. Like much proposed legislation aimed at curtailing immigration, however, its proponents linked illiteracy (in English) to other undesirable traits. Popular Alabama congressman John L. Burnett, for example, proposed the literacy test as a means to control the entry of nonwhite persons into the United States. Of particular concern to him were the Syrians, Jews, Poles, and Russians, who he argued "belonged to a distinct race other than the white race" (quoted in *Birmingham Age-Herald* 1907). His comments did not fall on deaf ears, and in response a leading member of the Syrian community in Birmingham generated the first significant argument in favor of Syrian whiteness. In a carefully worded letter to the editor in the *Birmingham Age-Herald*, H. A. Elkourie, a physician and president of the Syrian Young Men's Society in Birmingham, Alabama, challenged Burnett's views on the literacy test and on racial difference (*Birmingham Age-Herald* 1907).[6] Elkourie argued that the test was an inadequate measure of a person's qualifications, and he added in good humor that "my experience has shown me that scoundrels exist among the educated in greater proportion than amongst the uneducated" (*Birmingham Age-Herald* 1907).[7] The most important issue for Elkourie was Burnett's claim that Syrians "belonged to a distinct race other than the white race." Elkourie responded by emphasizing Syrian compatibility with Western civilization and by relying

3. "Nativity and Race of Immigrants Certified for Trachoma" and "Race of Immigrants Deported on Medical Certificates," Records of the Immigration and Naturalization Service (INS), Series A, Part 3, Ellis Island, 1900–1933, microfilm roll 6, Joseph Regenstein Library, Univ. of Chicago.

4. Alexandra Stern, personal communication based on her research of the US Records of the INS, Mexican Immigration, 1906–30.

5. According to records from the Department of Commerce and Labor, 4,648 Syrians were turned back in the period between 1899 and 1907. Of these, 1,578 persons were debarred on account of trachoma. See [also] Houghton 1911, 490; "Report of Detained Immigrants," Dec. 17, 1899, and "Race of Immigrants Deported on Medical Certificates during Fiscal Year Ended June 30th, 1909," both in Records of the INS, Series A, Part 3, Ellis Island, 1900–1933, microfilm roll 6, Joseph Regenstein Library, Univ. of Chicago.

6. On Elkourie's leadership of the Cedars/Phoenician Club, see "The Cedars/Phoenician Club of Birmingham," in Southern Federation of Syrian Lebanese American Clubs 2006, in my own files.

7. This was the second of two letters written by Elkourie. The first appeared under the title "Dr. El-Kourie Defends Syrian Immigrants" in the *Birmingham Ledger*, Sept. 20, 1907. According to Nancy Faires Conklin and Nora Helen Faires, the two letters were collected in a pamphlet and distributed under the title "In Defense of the Semitic and the Syrian Especially." See Conklin and Faires 1987.

on a religious argument that would become key to Syrian understanding of whiteness.

The first step was to argue that the Syrians were Semites. Then, citing "authorities" from Edward Gibbon to *Webster's Dictionary*, Elkourie placed the Semites within a branch of the "white race." But his argument went beyond the purely ethnological, for at the core of his defense of the Semitic peoples was a description of their contribution to Western civilization. From the Phoenicians to Jesus Christ, he wrote, the "Semitic was the original civilizer, developer and intermediator of culture and learning" (*Birmingham Age-Herald* 1907). The power of this argument derived not from a claim to any special racial phenotype but from a reclaiming of a Semitic origin for the Syrians and an emphasis on the Syrian connection to the Holy Land and to Christianity. However, Elkourie's argument was not merely an attempt to emphasize religious affinity with southern whites (a difficult argument to sustain given that southerners were unfamiliar with the Eastern-rite churches to which most Syrians belonged); it was an attempt to understand difference—in this case racial difference—the way Syrians had traditionally done so, that is, in religious terms. Thus Elkourie made his argument for inclusion in the "white race" on the basis of membership in the Christian fold. Alone, this argument would not hold up in a court of law as constituting decisive proof of whiteness, but it became a pillar of Syrian legal argumentation and community self-construction. The sense of Christian entitlement to share in whiteness became markedly evident in a series of naturalization cases that soon followed the controversy around Syrian racial identity generated by Congressman Burnett.

Litigating Whiteness

Scholars of the Arab American experience have tended to assume that Syrians encountered difficulty in the naturalization process only in the "color-conscious" South, with its culture of racial segregation and Jim Crow laws. This was not the case. Syrians litigated their racial status in Massachusetts, Oregon, Ohio, Missouri, and California, in addition to South Carolina and Georgia. In fact, the first Syrian racial prerequisite case to provoke a coordinated response by Syrians was that of George Shishim, which was heard in the Los Angeles Superior Court in 1909. George Shishim immigrated from Zahle, Lebanon, to the United States in 1894. As a young man, he traveled with the "Streets of Cairo" exhibit and later settled in Venice, California, where he became a police officer. His legal battle to prove his whiteness began after he arrested the son of a prominent lawyer for disturbing the peace. The arrested man claimed that Shishim could not charge him with the crime because he was not, and could not become, an American citizen since he was not of the white race. This argument echoed the one made by a white defendant in *People v. Hall* in 1854. Convicted of murder, Hall appealed to the California Supreme Court on the grounds that the testimony against him by a Chinese witness was invalid under the provisions of an 1850 statute stating that "no Black, or Mulatto person, or Indian shall be allowed to give evidence in favor of, or against a White man" (quoted in Haney-López 2006, 51). The court ruled in favor of the defendant, reasoning that *black* was a generic term encompassing all nonwhites and that it thus included Chinese persons.

Leading members of the Syrian community in Los Angeles, including Phares Behannesey, Mike George, Elias Shedoudy, Nick Baida, Saleem Sawaya, and John Safady, pooled their resources to hire an attorney, Byron C. Hanna, and defend Shishim. Judge Frank Hutton, who ruled in the case, based his decision primarily on legal precedent. He argued that "the courts of this nation, both state and federal, have whenever called upon for more than a century, construed the term 'white person,' or members of the white race, to include the Syrians" (quoted in Haiek 1992, 21). According to the *Los Angeles Times* (1909), the decision in Shishim's favor "made every feature of his dark, swarthy countenance roseate with pleasure and hope."

Judge Hutton's argument that the courts of the nation had decided and would continue to decide in favor of Syrian whiteness was quickly undermined in the case of Costa Najour, heard in Atlanta, Georgia, in December 1909.[8] Najour was from the coastal town of Batroun,

8. On the *Shishim* case, see Haiek 1992; *Los Angeles Times* 1909.

situated north of Beirut in present-day Lebanon. He immigrated to the United States in 1902, following the lead of his mother, who had come twice before with her brothers and had returned to Batroun. After working as a clerk in Atlanta (where he had cousins), Costa purchased a dry-goods store (Najour 1967). He petitioned for citizenship in the fall of 1909 but was denied on the basis of the argument that he did not meet the requirements of the revised statute. Najour appealed, hired a lawyer, Willis M. Everett, and formed an association to assist in his effort to gain American citizenship. His case generated considerable attention in the Atlanta papers, which began covering the story in November and carried frequent articles through to the December rehearing. "Atlanta Syrians Fight for Rights," announced an early article in the *Atlanta Journal* (1909a): "[They] have formed a league and employed counsel to resist the efforts now afoot in many parts of the United States to deny their race the right of becoming American citizens on the alleged ground that they are not Caucasians."

After the first day of arguments at the Fifth Circuit Court, the same paper noted that "Costa Najour . . . is still in the dark as to whether or not he is a white man" (*Atlanta Journal* 1909b). On December 3, however, after hearing arguments of both sides and listening to the lengthy questioning of the petitioner until, as Najour phrased it, "I became as a drunk," Judge William T. Newman granted him naturalization on the basis of membership in the "white race." The rationale for Judge Newman's decision fell overwhelmingly on the side of what he considered "scientific evidence." He cited, for example, A. H. Keane's *The World's People*, which divided the world's population into four classes: Negro or Black, Mongol or yellow, Amerinds, and Caucasians. According to Keane, Caucasians hailed from "North Africa, Europe, Iran, India, Western Asia, and Polynesia." Newman relied on Keane's classificatory scheme to argue that Syrians belonged to "what we recognize, and what the world recognizes, as the white race."[9] He rejected the idea that the naturalization statute referred to skin color and was adamant that "fair or dark complexion should not be allowed to control [the decision]."[10] This construction would be used in other rulings where the judges argued that race was not to be determined by "ocular inspection alone."

Judge Newman's decision in the Najour case helped alter the discourse on racial classification by distinguishing between skin color and race (Haney-López 2006, 68). It is important to note, however, that he followed his statement on color with this caveat: "providing the person seeking naturalization comes within the classification of the white or Caucasian race."[11] In other words, color didn't necessarily matter if it could be determined by some other rationale that the applicant was white and possessed the personal qualifications deemed necessary for naturalization. In cases where personal qualifications were in doubt, and the applicant was deemed unworthy of citizenship, color continued to serve as an additional marker of ineligibility. When, for example, Judge [Henry] Smith denied Syrian applicant Faras Shahid naturalization in a South Carolina district court in 1913, he emphasized that Shahid was "somewhat darker than is the usual mulatto of one-half mixed blood between the white and the negro races."[12] Even Judge Newman, whose ruling in the Najour case seemed to move away from color as the defining marker of race, began his decision with a description of Najour as "not particularly dark." He may have distinguished between skin color and race, but a basic pattern persisted in the racial prerequisite cases: the ascription of darkness increased the chances of ineligibility, while that of lightness decreased them. The lawyer for the government in the Najour case knew as much. After four hours of testimony by Costa Najour that seemed only to confirm his eligibility to naturalize, the exasperated lawyer, desperate to prove that Najour was not white, asked him to take off his shirt and show his body to the court. Najour began to comply but was stopped in the early stages of undress by Judge Newman, who wanted no such theatrics in his courtroom (Najour 1961). What was perhaps more important in Judge Newman's ruling—as far as altering the legal discourse on racial classification

9. In re Najour, 174 Fed. 735 (1909).

10. In re Najour, 174 Fed. 735 (1909).

11. In re Najour, 174 Fed. 735 (1909).

12. Ex parte Shahid, 205 Fed. 813 (1913).

goes—was his use of the category "Caucasian." Using the literature on ethnology, he reached the conclusion that Syrians were "part of the Caucasian or white race."[13] The use of *or* was significant, for it indicated that being Caucasian and being white were held to be one and the same thing. This equation had been used in combination with other rationales in previous racial prerequisite cases.[14] What was different in the *Najour* case was that Judge Newman made it possible to use membership in something called the "Caucasian race" as the *sole* criterion for judging whether someone was white for the purposes of naturalization.

Several judges followed Judge Newman's lead, but an equal number rejected this formulation and dismissed altogether the relevance of "scientific evidence." Judge Henry Smith, for example, ruling in the *Shahid* case cited above, ridiculed the idea that being Caucasian automatically meant someone was white. The very idea of a Caucasian race was suspect to him, the result, he would later write, "of a strange intellectual hocus pocus."[15] The ultimate test of whiteness, in his view, was one of geography, and the deciding factor was whether the applicant was from Europe or a descendant of a European immigrant. There was, therefore, no need to "examine his [the applicant's] complexion with a microscope nor measure his skull or his limbs and features."[16] Since the Syrians were, in his estimation, clearly not European but "Asiatic," they were not entitled to the privileges of citizenship.[17] To arrive at this ruling that whiteness was linked to European descent, Judge Smith relied on two other rationales that would become increasingly popular in the racial prerequisite cases: common knowledge and congressional intent.

The term "congressional intent" referred to the meaning of the Naturalization Act as it was first formulated by Congress in 1790. In Judge Smith's words, "The real question is: What does the statute mean, to whom did the terms 'free white persons' refer in 1790, in the understandings of the makers of the law?"[18] He answered the question through an imaginary journey into the mind of a member of Congress at the end of the eighteenth century. Such a man, he argued, would have known nothing of the ethnological or linguistic theories that undergirded modern racial classification. He would, for example, "certainly have repudiated the idea that a black Ceylonese or dark South Persian was in the language of the enthusiastic supporters of the theory that all speakers of Aryan languages are of one race, an 'Aryan brother.'"[19]

Judge Smith was so sure of his argument that he claimed it was all something to which "an average citizen" in 1790 could agree. Appeals to the racial knowledge of the "average citizen" were made frequently in the racial prerequisite cases. James Farell, for example, assistant US attorney in the *Halladjian* case, argued against the admissibility of Armenians by appealing to the racial knowledge of the "average man." He claimed that "without being able to define a white person, the average man in the street understands what it means, and would find no difficulty in assigning to the yellow race a Turk or a Syrian with as much ease as he would bestow that designation on a Chinaman or Korean."[20] Despite Farrell's assertion that race could be determined without difficulty, the racial prerequisite cases reveal a lack of consensus about who belonged to what race and why. . . .

. . . While some judges relied on scientific evidence, others used congressional intent [or] common knowledge or some combination of all three to determine the race of an applicant for naturalization. Complicating matters was the category of personal qualifications, which, like color, was not supposed to figure prominently in the determination of race but was repeatedly used to assist in the decision. Syrian applicant Tom Ellis's religious,

13. In re Najour, 174 Fed. 735 (1909).

14. In re Ah Yup, 104 Fed. (1878), in Haney-López 2006, 210.

15. He was quoting from Thomas H. Huxley's *Methods and Results of Ethnology*. See *In re Dow*, 213 Fed. 358 (1914).

16. In re Dow, 213 Fed. 366 (1914).

17. The classification of Syrians as "Asiatic" could be deduced from the 1910 US Census, which considered Syria part of "Turkey in Asia." However, it is clear from the census that for the purpose of population statistics Syrians were considered white since immigrants from "Turkey in Asia" were listed in the category "foreign-born white."

18. In re Dow, 213 Fed. 366 (1914).

19. In re Dow, 213 Fed. 366 (1914).

20. In re Halladjian et al., 174 Fed. 838 (1909).

professional, and moral profile, for example, clearly influenced the decision on his racial eligibility in an Oregon district court in July 1910. Indeed, so intertwined were the criteria in the judge's ruling that it is difficult to discern where one ended and the other began.

Ellis, described as "a Turkish subject . . . a Syrian, a native of the province of Palestine, and a Maronite,"[21] had to counter the argument that he was ineligible for citizenship because he was not of European descent. Lawyers for the district attorney made no attempt to argue that Ellis was not "of the white race," and they openly admitted that Syrians were considered to be white by immigration authorities. The Immigration Commission, for example, which had conducted extensive studies of the immigrant population in the United States between 1907 and 1910, noted that "physically the modern Syrians are of mixed Syrian, Arabian, and even Jewish blood. They belong to the Semitic branch of the Caucasian race, thus widely differing from their rulers, the Turks, who are in origin Mongolian."[22] The argument against Ellis was that he was not the right *kind* of white: that is, he did not descend from white Europeans. The district attorney emphasized the importance of being of European descent in his interpretation of the statute, arguing that the meaning of the words "free white persons" "comprehended such only of the white races who, from tradition, teaching, and environment, would be predisposed toward our form of government, and thus readily assimilate with the people of the United States."[23]

Whereas Judge Smith had couched his preference for European immigrants in the language of congressional intent, lawyers for the government in the *Ellis* case were much more explicit in their use of race as a marker of a particular cultural and political disposition. In the logic of their argument, whiteness was linked to geography (Europe), which in their opinion produced moral and intellectual traits essential for participation in the American polity. More to the point, they assumed that white Europeans were familiar with and supportive of republican forms of government. Non-Europeans were, in contrast, deemed to be dubious products of despotic regimes, politically unsophisticated, and likely to taint the cherished pool of American citizenry. The government lawyer's insistence on the connection between whiteness and fitness for self-government was a well-worn strategy that was firmly embedded in the discourse of American citizenship (Jacobson 2003).[24] The district attorney in the *Najour* case had also used this argument, claiming that Najour, as a subject of the Muslim Ottoman sultan, was incapable of understanding American institutions and government. Judge Newman dismissed the argument and claimed that if being a Turkish subject disqualified one from naturalization, "the extension of the Turkish Empire over people unquestionably of the white race would deprive them of the privilege of naturalization."[25] Despite a ruling in Najour's favor, whiteness as fitness for self-government continued to figure prominently in the legal debates on *racial* eligibility for citizenship until the 1950s.

Fortunately for Ellis, Judge Wolverton ruled that if Congress had intended the statute to mean Europeans only, it would have specified such. He granted Ellis citizenship, but his ruling reveals how it was possible to reject the specific formulation of the government argument while accepting its underlying assumptions—that "personal qualifications" were an indication of a person's racial eligibility for naturalization. What ultimately tilted the decision in Ellis's favor was Judge Wolverton's conviction that he was "possessed of the highest qualities which go to make an excellent citizen . . . well disposed toward the principles and policies of this government."[26] Having already decided that Ellis was of "Semitic stock, a markedly white type of the race," the judge went on to extol Ellis's personal qualifications, noting that he was a "good and highly respected citizen of the community." Tom Ellis spoke English, was a practicing Christian, and was of "good morals, sober and industrious." In short, he

21. In re Ellis, 179 Fed. 1002, 1003 (1910).

22. US Industrial Commission on Immigration Commission 1911, 1:280.

23. In re Ellis, 179 Fed. 1002, 1003 (1910).

24. See also Suad Joseph's (1999) study of how representations of Arabs as "not quite free" has impeded their integration into the category of American citizen.

25. In re Najour, 174 Fed. 735 (1909).

26. In re Ellis, 179 Fed. 1002, 1003 (1910).

possessed "all the essential qualifications to entitle him to naturalization." He was, in Judge Wolverton's view, exactly the type of person Congress had intended to become a citizen. Remarkably oblivious to the debates—scientific, judicial, and congressional—that suggested otherwise, Judge Wolverton believed that the words "free white persons" were devoid of ambiguity and were of "plain and simple signification."[27] He did not pause to consider how far the "personal qualifications" of the applicant had influenced the legal construction of his whiteness.

Transnationalism and the Syrian Debate on Race

By 1909, it was clear that the Syrian naturalization cases were generating a significant, if at times contradictory, legal definition of whiteness. Syrians were themselves confused about how best to define their racial status, and they turned to various sources to answer their questions. Elkourie had used English-language dictionaries, while Najour and his supporters found standard works in ethnology convincing. Other Syrians turned to the Arabic-language press in the Middle East. Indeed, partly because of the increase in transatlantic migration, there was within elite Middle Eastern discourse in the late nineteenth and early twentieth centuries a new interest in racial classification. The Cairo-based journal *al-Hilal*, for example, devoted several issues to articles on the scientific categorization of human types, written by the editor, Jurji Zaydan, a Syrian émigré. *Al-Hilal* was a popular monthly magazine that "appealed to readers of different classes and leanings because of its interesting subject matter" (de Tarazi 1913, 87). The journal had a wide circulation in the Middle East and in the diaspora. "You will not find a country in the five continents of the world in which there are readers of Arabic and they do not read *al-Hilal*," Philip de Tarazi asserted in his comprehensive study of the Arabic press published in 1913 (87).

The articles in *al-Hilal* on human classification were drawn from [Jurji] Zaydan's book *Tabaqat al-umam* (Classes of Peoples, 1912). The book was based on the "modern sciences" of anthropology and ethnology and drew extensively (often verbatim) from a classic tome of ethnology, A. H. Keane's *The World's Peoples*. Zaydan's title, however, borrowed from the fifth-century (*hijri*) Arab judge Sa'd ibn Ahmad al-Andalusi's book of the same name. Al-Andalusi had divided the world into two types: peoples who had excelled in learning and those who had not. Zaydan set out to modernize and supplant this system by using the new "real" classificatory schemes based on "observation and research" (1912, 5). He noted that that the importance of these schemes extended beyond purely scientific realms: "The science of human classification is the basis of the philosophy of history, for it elucidates the morals of peoples and their characteristics . . . and it helps explain their decline and florescence" (5).

Tabaqat al-umam divided the world's population into four main categories arranged from lowest to highest. At the bottom were Blacks (*al-zunuj*), "the lowest and most base," followed by the Mongolian or "the yellow race," the American Indian, or "the red race," and the Caucasian, "or the white race" (Zaydan 1912, 7). Within the last category Zaydan placed the Semites, which included the "Arabs, Jews, and Aryans." To support the text, he included numerous pictures representing the different human types and, in intriguing choices to represent the Arabs, featured an Egyptian, Mustafa Kamil (1874–1908), leader of the independence movement against the British, and a "Syrian Lebanese," Yusuf Bey Karam (1823–89), a legendary Maronite leader famous for his nineteenth-century revolt against Ottoman authority in Mount Lebanon.

Zaydan's writings reflect the concerns of educated, cosmopolitan elites who were anxious to forge a modern orientation to the world by familiarizing themselves with European racial theories. Interest in racial classification also stemmed from the experience of immigrants throughout the *mahjar*, whose curiosity on matters of race emerged as they confronted new social realities in new places. Earnest queries about their racial status can be found in the less flowery, more matter-of-fact "Question and Answer" sections of *al-Hilal* and other periodicals.

In 1914, for example, Mahmud Sulayman Bu Karam wrote in from Little Rock, Arkansas, inquiring whether

27. In re Ellis, 179 Fed. 1002, 1003 (1910).

the "Phoenicians were Semites or Hamites." *Al-Hilal* responded that "it is believed they are Semites like the Arabs, Caldeans, Babylonians, Hebrews, Aramaens . . . since the language found on their ruins is very Semitic and resembles Hebrew" (*al-Hilal* 1914b, 705). From London, England, a young student informed *al-Hilal* that his fellow Egyptians considered themselves among the "colored people" (*min al-shu'ub al-mulawwana*), a designation he thought wrong. *Al-Hilal* responded, "Yes, this is incorrect. The Egyptians are Caucasian, but there are two types: white and red." For further edification, the editor referred the reader to his *Tabaqat al-umam* (*al-Hilal* 1914a, 460). On the same page of the journal, Iskandar al-Khuri wrote in asking about the racial identity of Syrians and referred to their "troubles" in the United States: "I have heard that the United States of America does not consider the Syrians among white people (*min al-shu'ub al-baida*) or Caucasians, which is a condition for entry into their country. And the Syrians have set out to prove the error of the Americans" (*al-Hilal* 1914a, 460).

These questions and responses indicate a number of things about racial ideas among Syrians at the beginning of the twentieth century. First, there was confusion over what race the Syrians belonged to as well as disagreement over its importance. Were the Syrians Phoenicians, and, if so, were they Semites, Hamites, or "white" or "red" Caucasians? While Zaydan tried to be precise about racial differences, another leading Syrian journalist of the day dismissed the whole idea of racial hierarchies. Muhammad Kurd 'Ali, editor of the Damascus newspaper *al-Muqtabas*, criticized the idea of white racial superiority, noting that it was the result of narrow-mindedness. "In reality," he argued, "there is only one race, and that is the human race" (*al-Muqtabas* 1907). Second, it is clear that the problem of racial classification in the diaspora engendered debates in the homeland—a reminder that emigration produces a flow across borders not only of bodies and resources but of ideas also.

Like Costa Najour, George Dow was born in the coastal town of Batroun, Syria, in 1862. He immigrated to the United States in 1889, entering at the port of Philadelphia. Seven years later, he filed his declaration to become an American citizen in 1896 in Evansville, Indiana, and eventually made his way to Summerton, South Carolina, where he ran a store with his wife, Saydy.[28] He filed for citizenship in 1913, initiating a legal battle that would generate various opinions on the racial status of Syrians.

Dow's testimony before the court revealed that he was unfamiliar with the US system of government and possessed poor English-language skills. To questions posed to him about US politics, for example, he responded that there were about thirty houses of Congress and that the difference between the government in Turkey and the United States was that he would like to be a citizen of the United States. It was on the basis of this lack of knowledge (and not his race) that the lawyer for the government asserted that Dow was not a worthy candidate for citizenship. However, Judge Smith ruled not on this basis but on the grounds that Dow did not meet the racial requirement of the naturalization statute. His petition refused, Dow gained the assistance of the Syrian American Association (SAA), which had been founded by Naoum Mokarzel, owner and editor of *al-Hoda* (The Guidance) in 1909. Determined to settle the question of eligibility for citizenship once and for all, the SAA and Dow's lawyers formulated an elaborate defense of Syrian whiteness.

Their argument for why Dow should be included in the category of *white persons* had five points:

1. That the term "white persons" in the statute means persons of the "Caucasian race" and persons white in color.
2. That he is a Semite or a member of one of the Semitic nations.
3. That the Semitic nations are all members of the "Caucasian" or white race.
4. That the matter has been settled in their favor as the European Jews have been admitted without question since the passage of the statute and that the Jews are one of the Semitic peoples.
5. That the history and position of the Syrians, their connection through all time with the peoples to

28. "Transcript of Court Record," Group II, Series C, Syrian-American Archival Collection (SAAC), Center for Migration Studies, Staten Island, NY.

> whom the Jewish and Christian peoples owe their religion, make it inconceivable that the statute could have intended to exclude them.[29]

This complex argument incorporated nearly all the rationales used in previous attempts to prove Syrian whiteness. There was first the three-part equation that Syrians were Semites, hence Caucasian and therefore white. . . . The second important component of the Syrian argument was cultural, an insistence that their "history and position" made them eligible for the privilege of citizenship. . . . The third part of the argument turned on legal precedent, namely that European Jews (who were also Semites) had been naturalized and that the same should hold for Syrians. . . .

Smith's views on race were of grave concern not only to the Syrian applicants but to members of the Jewish American community also. Many feared that if Syrian inclusion in whiteness were denied, it would be only a matter of time before the same would hold for Jews. Cyrus Adler of the American Jewish Committee expressed these fears in a letter to his colleague Mayer Sulzburger. Once the Syrians and Japanese were declared nonwhite, he noted, "it will not be a very far step to declare the Jews Asiatic" (quoted in Goldstein 2006, 103). There was already fierce debate within Jewish circles about whether Jews should define themselves as a race and allow government officials to designate them as such. The US Immigration Commission's practice of classifying Jews racially as "Hebrews," for example, worried those who believed that such a designation isolated Jews from white Americans (Goldstein 2006, 103). Two Jewish lawyers, Louis Marshall and Max J. Kohler, who were active in the campaign to reverse this classification and to prevent the Census Bureau from adopting a racial category for Jews on the census were also involved in the Syrian naturalization cases. They viewed the cases as an important test that could have far-reaching repercussions for Jewish citizenship. . . .

In this rehearing, Judge Smith denied Dow's petition for naturalization, which the SAA had so vigorously supported. Smith actually began his ruling with an acknowledgment of the "deep feeling manifested on the part of Syrian immigrants" but went on to argue that they had misinterpreted the decision of the court. The Syrians claimed that they had suffered "humiliation" and "mortification" in the wake of the decision that they did not belong to the "white race." Judge Smith countered that this had not been the wording of the decision; rather, "a modern Syrian was an Asiatic, and was thus not included in the term 'white persons' as contained in section 2169 of the U.S. Revised Statutes as amended in 1875."[30] He followed this clarification with a telling interpretation of the Syrian position: "The true ground of this supposed humiliation is that the applicant and his associates conceive the refusal of this privilege to mean that they do not belong to a white race but to a colored and what they consider an inferior race."[31]

The judge's musings were not without merit. Syrians did perceive exclusion from naturalization to mean that they were deficient, unwelcome, and uncultured. That is why their early arguments for inclusion in the "white race" revolved around the issue of the contribution of Semitic peoples to the Western world, especially Western Christendom. When George Shishim's eligibility was challenged in the Los Angeles Superior Court, for example, his response was to assert his Christian identity (Haiek 1992, 22). Costa Najour also based his argument for membership in the white race on the fact that he was a "pure Syrian and a Christian" (*Atlanta Constitution* 1909). In both cases, the applicants for citizenship emphasized their Christian heritage to distinguish themselves from the "Asiatic" Muslim Turks who were the sovereigns of the Ottoman Empire.

The claim that the Syrians interpreted the defeat in the courts to mean that they were "colored" and therefore members of an inferior race was different. This was a construction that was familiar to southern whites, but it had to be learned by Syrian immigrants. Elkourie in his defense of Syrian whiteness did not mention color, nor did he resort to the strategy of defining whiteness

29. In re Dow, 213 Fed. 366 (1914).

30. In re Dow, 213 Fed. 366 (1914).

31. In re Dow, 213 Fed. 366 (1914). See also *Meraat ul-gharb* 1914.

as the absence of Blackness. The "others" from which he attempted to distance Syrians were not Blacks and Asians but prostitutes and anarchists, persons whom he deemed morally, not racially, unfit for full participation in the American polity and who were among the classes excluded from entry into the United States. As refusals to naturalize Syrians increased, however, the ways in which Syrian whiteness was defined both within the community and outside it shifted. No longer did Syrians simply claim whiteness by asserting their Christian credentials. Since the majority of Syrians were either Catholic or Eastern Orthodox, doing this was not always effective in the eyes of their Protestant neighbors, who viewed their Christianity as odd and foreign (Conklin and Faires 1987; Sherman 2002, 180). Instead, Syrians began to claim whiteness in terms that explicitly excluded Blacks and Asians.

Evidence of this development can be seen in the letters that poured in to *al-Hoda* concerning the *Najour* case. Saleem Shaheen, for example, complained of the "premature rejoicing and claiming of [Najour's] victory while the main stigma has not yet been removed from us and the American people still refer to us with the stigma of Asiatic." He described how a judge in Lincoln, Nebraska, had refused to naturalize a Syrian, Mahmoud Salem, because "he is as the American newspapers referred to him an 'Asiatic' or 'Mongolian.'" Saleem Shaheen also related that he had been told by some Syrian peddlers that they had been refused entry into restaurants and taverns and that some of them had been greeted with the words "Hello, nigger." He then went on to describe another incident that revealed how Syrian racial identity was in dispute, not only in the courts but in everyday encounters as well. He related in Arabic the story of Syrian cousins, Khaleel and Rasheed Zarzoor, who entered a saloon in Chattanooga, Tennessee. When the bartender served them, one man (described by Shaheen as a "ruffian") objected and asked the bartender: "Why do you serve these Negroes [*al-'abid*] before you serve me?" The bartender responded that there were no Negroes in the bar. The "ruffian" pointed at the two Syrians and said: "Yes, these two are Negroes [*zunjian*]. . . . You and all your Syrian people are Negroes, so get out of here." At this point one of the Syrians responded, "We are not Negroes. We belong to the white race [*sulala al-baida'*] more than you do, and we are more honorable." A fight ensued between Rasheed and his detractor in which the latter was "injured plenty" and left the saloon saying, "I'll kill that negro Rasheed some day" (*al-Hoda* 1909, 5).

In the Ross area of North Dakota, [members of] the small community of Syrian peddlers, homesteaders, and store owners were often referred to as "Black Syrians," "black ones," or "Blackies." Reflecting on their childhood relationships with those who used these terms, Syrians (who now call themselves Lebanese) report that "we're now good friends." One man recalled, however, having had to "fight regularly" as a young man (Sherman 2002, 181). Whether the perception of Syrians as other than white led to discrimination depended on the context. In many instances, Syrians had supporters. One prominent white citizen of Ross objected to the attempt to declare Syrians racially ineligible for citizenship. "If Syrians are to be barred from citizenship," he declared to the local paper, "the government should not have accepted their first papers and allowed them to file on land" (quoted in Sherman 2002, 173). In 1995, an elderly resident of Crookston, North Dakota, was asked by a researcher, "How was the work performance of Syrians on the railroad crews?" He responded that they "worked every bit as good as white people" (quoted in Sherman 2002, 181).

For Syrians in North Dakota, the debate on their racial classification was ultimately about property because many intended to acquire land. To do so, one had to be a citizen or have indicated the intention to become one. In 1909, almost two hundred Syrians had filed their first papers in North Dakota. Many were anxious to acquire citizenship after learning that thirty Japanese who lived close to the Syrian settlement in Ross had lost their homesteads because the government exercised provisions of the Oriental Exclusion Act (Sherman 2002, 173). Syrian immigrants did not want to suffer the same fate.

These incidents indicate Syrian concern with racial misidentification and, in the case of Rasheed, a willingness to challenge comparisons to Black Americans. Over time and particularly as Syrians faced problems in the courts, these attempts to distance Syrians from Blacks in the discourse on race became more frequent. . . .

This shift to a more racial, rather than a purely religious or civilizational, understanding of Syrian whiteness was further evidenced in a book that appeared in the midst of the *Dow* controversy. Published in both English and Arabic, it aimed to clarify (before Dow's case went to the Circuit Court of Appeals) the racial classification of the Syrians. The book was written by Kalil A. Bishara at the urging of Naoum Mokarzel, editor and owner of *al-Hoda* and president of the SAA. The goal of the book in the . . . introduction [to the English version] was to "set forth with a fairly high degree of precision, the evidence conducive to the determination of the racial identity of the modern Syria" (Bishara 1914b, 5). The . . . introduction [to the Arabic version] dispensed with the niceties and stated the purpose more forcefully. The book was a "reply to those who have denied that the Syrian emigrant is Caucasian and have made him out to be of Mongolian origin, whereby they have made him ineligible for American citizenship" (Bishara 1914a, 5).

This was not the only place where the English version differed from the Arabic. In an impressive list of figures described as evincing the Semitic "pliability combined with iron fixity of purpose," Bishara cited Moses, Elijah, Hannibal, Amos, Paul, Peter, and John. The Arabic version was identical except that it also included the name of the Muslim prophet Muhammad. The omission was an interesting and strategic move. Having already made gains by promoting the Christian credentials of Syrian immigrants, Bishara probably did not want to jeopardize their standing by aligning them with Muslims, especially not at a time when the Anglo-American judiciary and the American public's perception of Islam was steeped in ignorance and superstition (Suleiman 1987, 45).[32] Like others before him, Bishara stressed the Syrian connections to the Holy Land, Christianity, and "Western" civilization. But the larger argument in his book (especially the Arabic-language version) conveyed a new development in the debate on Syrian racial identity. The early Syrian arguments for inclusion in the white race had emphasized industry, religiosity, and sobriety—qualities that proponents put forward as measures of a group's ability to contribute effectively to the American nation rather than of membership in the "white race" specifically. Increasingly, though, Syrians saw the denial of their whiteness to mean that they were Asian or Black and not, as Elkourie had seen it, heathens, derelicts, and drunks. Syrians thus generated a different definition of their whiteness, one that hinged on the question of who was "not white." It was this argument that carried the day in George Dow's final appeal in 1915, where it was affirmed at the federal court level that he was indeed a "white person."

The presiding judge in the *Dow* case argued that the original act of 1790 had been repealed through successive amendments and new acts. He moved away from congressional intent and argued that the decision of the court must be controlled by the "generally accepted meaning of the words used at the time of the passage of the new statute."[33] "With its amendment of 1875," he continued, "it seems to be true beyond question that the generally received opinion was that the inhabitants of a portion of Asia, including Syria, were to be classed as white persons."[34] . . .

The Problem with Being White

Taken as a whole, the Syrian racial prerequisite cases heard in federal courts between 1909 and 1915 demonstrate that buried beneath the reasoned rationales of the legal rulings lay contradictions, ambiguities, and discrepancies. Quite simply, the courts were having difficulty deciding who was a "white person." There was, however, a basic pattern amid the confusion. Judges were turning more and more to the rationales of congressional intent and common knowledge (and away from science) to determine racial eligibility for naturalization. While, for example, ethnological classification had assisted Costa

32. The most common perception was that Islam was an impediment to progress and that its adherents were prone to debauchery. These ideas could be found in the accounts of American missionaries as well as in enormously popular literary works like Robert Hitchens's *The Garden of Allah* (1904) and Mark Twain's *Innocents Abroad* (1911). See Hammons 1978.

33. Dow v. United States, 226 Fed. 147 (1915).

34. Dow v. United States, 226 Fed. 148 (1915).

Najour in his request for citizenship, it was completely discarded in *Ex parte Shahid*. This move away from scientific explanations of race was evident in other cases as well and would culminate in the 1923 US Supreme Court decision in the case of South Asian applicant Bhagat Singh Thind. . . .

"It is not without significance," Justice Sutherland wrote, "that Congress, by the Act of February 5, 1917, . . . has now excluded from admission into this country all natives of Asia within designated limits of latitude and longitude, including the whole of India. This not only constitutes conclusive evidence of the congressional attitude of opposition to Asiatic immigration generally, but is persuasive of a similar attitude toward Asiatic naturalization as well, since it is not likely that Congress would be willing to accept as citizens a class of persons whom it rejects as immigrants."[35]

The inclusion of India in the Asiatic "barred zone" had thus informed Justice Sutherland's thinking on racial eligibility for naturalization. Significantly, Syria had fallen outside the zone, a decision that furnished additional proof for the Syrian claim of whiteness. In 1923, for example, when a poorly informed Judge Smith tried once again to prevent the naturalization of a Syrian applicant, he was confronted with the same argument made by Justice Sutherland, only in reverse: Syrians were eligible to immigrate to the United States, so they were therefore eligible to naturalize. Smith was forced to naturalize the applicant, F. W. Basha, and the Syrian eligibility question never again reached the courts (Ferris 1928, 22; Samhan 1999, 217). . . .

Armed with expert lawyers, "friends of the court," and a belief in their special status as the mediators of the Christian tradition, Syrians had actively participated in arguments for their inclusion in the "white race." The exclusion of Syria from the Asiatic barred zone helped consolidate it. Thus, the legal construction of Syrian whiteness became part of a larger story of their disassociation from Asia and of the creation of a new category, the "Middle East" (which is, in fact, West Asia).

The erection of the Asiatic barred zone marks an important moment of differentiation between Europe's Asia—which included India and West Asia—and America's Asia, in which India occupied a liminal space and West Asia (the "Middle East") was absent (Menon 2006, 57).

With the ruling in *Dow v. United States* supporting Syrian whiteness, the race crisis for Syrians subsided—but only temporarily. The periodic violence inflicted upon Syrians and the popular and political characterizations of them as a suspect immigrant group suggested that their whiteness was inconclusive, particularly in a South still steeped in the politics of Jim Crow (*Syrian World* 1929, 47). Indeed, the seemingly provisional quality of Syrian whiteness, despite *Dow v. United States*, prompted Syrian immigrants (especially the elite among them) to reaffirm their coveted racial status as whites. They did not challenge the premise that whiteness was a legitimate prerequisite for citizenship and the privileges it afforded, only "that their rightful share in whiteness was being denied them" (Jacobson 2003, 239; Moore 1995, 54). . . .

"To enter the white race," Noel Ignatiev reminds us, "was a strategy to secure an advantage in a competitive society," and whiteness was, ultimately, the "result of choices made" (1995, 2). Syrians had written letters, published articles, hired lawyers, formed associations, and raised money, all to support the claim of whiteness. The legal decision in *Dow v. United States* corresponded to and was even made possible by a decision on the part of individual Syrians to think of themselves as white in the "popular" sense of the term or, as the legal phrasing of the day put it, "in the understanding of the common man." Ultimately, this demanded that Syrians construct and make sense of their whiteness in relation to others who were nonwhite, for historically whiteness had little meaning unless it stood in opposition to a racialized Other.

For Costa Najour, Slayman Nimmee (Nimmee 1962), and many other Syrians, being classified as white encouraged them to participate in the racialization of those who remained nonwhite. While this may have helped Syrians assimilate more quickly, it helped perpetuate a discourse of exclusion in which other immigrant groups were marked as "Others," ineligible for citizenship and

35. United States v. Thind, 261 US 204 (1923).

full membership in the American nation. Thus one of the unfortunate, if unintended, consequences of the Syrian struggle for whiteness was that it helped refine the legal arguments that repeatedly called into question the suitability of non-Europeans to "become American."

Works Cited

Abraham, Alice. 1962. Interview by Alixa Naff. Series 4/C, transcript, Naff Arab-American Collection. Smithsonian Institution, Washington, DC.

Atlanta Constitution. 1909. Nov. 22.

Atlanta Journal. 1909a. Nov. 21.

———. 1909b. "Najour's Nativity Still in Doubt." Dec. 2.

Birmingham Age-Herald. 1907. "Elkourie Takes Burnett to Task." Oct. 2.

Bishara, Kalil A. 1914a. *Asl al-suriy al-hadith* [The origin of the modern Syrian]. New York: Al-Hoda Publishing House.

———. 1914b. *The Origin of the Modern Syrian*. New York: Al-Hoda Publishing House.

"The Comprehensive Immigration Act of 1917." 1924. In *Immigration: Select Documents and Case Records*, edited by Edith Abbott, page numbers unavailable. Chicago: Univ. of Chicago Press.

Conklin, Nancy Faires, and Nora Helen Faires. 1987. "'Colored' and Catholic: The Lebanese in Birmingham, Alabama." In *Crossing the Waters: Arabic-Speaking Immigrants to the United States before 1940*, edited by Eric J. Hooglund, 69–84. Washington, DC: Smithsonian Institution Press.

Cunningham, George E. 1997. "The Italian, a Hindrance to White Solidarity in Louisiana, 1890–1898." In *Racial Classification and History*, edited by E. Nathaniel Gates, 68–82. New York: Garland.

De Tarazi, Philip. 1913. *Tarikh al-sihafa al-arabiyya* [History of the Arab press]. Vol. 2. Beirut: Dar Sadr.

Fairchild, Amy. 1997. "Science at the Borders: Immigrant Medical Inspection and Defense of the Nation, 1891–1930." PhD diss., Columbia Univ.

Ferris, Joseph. 1928. "Syrian Naturalization Question in the United States." *Syrian World* 2, no. 9: 22.

Gabbert, Ann R. 2002. "El Paso, a Sight for Sore Eyes: Medical and Legal Aspects of Syrian Immigration, 1906–1907." *Historian* 65, no. 1: 15–42.

Goldstein, Eric L. 2006. *The Price of Whiteness: Jews, Race, and American Identity*. Princeton, NJ: Princeton Univ. Press.

Haiek, Joseph R. 1992. *Arab-American Almanac*. 4th ed. Glendale, CA: News Circle Publishing House.

Hammons, Terry Brooks. 1978. "A Wild Ass of a Man: American Images of Arabs to 1948." PhD diss., Univ. of Oklahoma.

Haney López, Ian. 2006. *White by Law: The Legal Construction of Race*. New York: New York Univ. Press.

Higham, John. 1969. *Strangers in the Land: Patterns of American Nativism, 1860–1925*. New York: Atheneum.

Al-Hilal. 1914a. Mar. 1.

———. 1914b. June 1.

Hitchens, Robert. 1904. *The Garden of Allah*. London: Methuen.

Al-Hoda. 1909. Dec. 4.

Houghton, Louise Seymour. 1911. "Syrians in the United States." *Survey* 26, no. 14: 480–95.

Ignatiev, Noel. 1995. *How the Irish Became White*. New York: Routledge.

Jacobson, Matthew Frye. 2003. *Whiteness of a Different Color: European Immigrants and the Alchemy of Race*. Cambridge, MA: Harvard Univ. Press.

Joseph, Suad. 1999. "Against the Grain of the Nation—the Arab." In *Arabs in America: Building a New Future*, edited by Michael W. Suleiman, 257–71. Philadelphia: Temple Univ. Press.

Kraut, Alan M. 1994. *Silent Travelers: Germs, Genes, and the "Immigrant Menace."* New York: Basic Books.

Los Angeles Times. 1909. "Syrians Admitted." Nov. 5.

Menon, Sridevi. 2006. "Where Is West Asia in Asian America? 'Asia' and the Politics of Space in Asian America." *Social Text* 24 (Spring): 55–79.

Meraat ul-gharb. 1914. "On the Syrian Question." Apr. 7.

Moore, Kathleen M. 1995. *Al-Mughtaribūn: American Law and the Transformation of Muslim Life in the United States*. Albany: State Univ. of New York Press.

Al-Muqtabas. 1907. 1, no. 10.

Najour, Costa. 1961. Interview [by] Adele Younis (in Arabic). Group II, Series C, folder 203. Syrian-American Archival Collection (SAAC), Staten Island, NY.

———. 1967. Interview [by] Adele Younis, Aug. 11–12. Group II, Series A, box 8, folder 203. Syrian-American Archival Collection (SAAC), Staten Island, NY.

Nimmee, Slayman. 1962. Interview by Alixa Naff. Series 4/C, abstract, Naff Arab-American Collection. Smithsonian Institution, Washington, DC.

S., Farah. 1997. Interview, Mar. 1, transcript. Damascus, Syria.

Samara, Essa. 1962. Interview. Series 4/C, transcript, Naff Arab-American Collection. Smithsonian Institution, Washington, DC.

Samhan, Helen Hatab. 1999. "Not Quite White: Race Classification and the Arab American Experience." In *Arabs in America: Building a New Future*, edited by Michael W. Suleiman, 209–26. Philadelphia: Temple Univ. Press.

Sherman, William. 2002. *Prairie Peddlers: The Syrian-Lebanese in North Dakota*. Bismarck, ND: Univ. of Mary Press.

Southern Federation of Syrian Lebanese Clubs. 2006. *75th Diamond Jubilee Convention, 1931–2006: June 30–July 4, 2006*. San Antonio, TX: Southern Federation of Syrian Lebanese Clubs.

Suleiman, Michael W. 1987. "Early Arab-Americans: The Search for Identity." In *Crossing the Waters: Arabic-Speaking Immigrants to the United States before 1940*, edited by Eric J. Hooglund, 37–54. Washington, DC: Smithsonian Institution Press.

Syrian World. 1929. 3 (June).

Twain, Mark. 1911. *The Innocents Abroad: Or, The New Pilgrim's Progress Being Some Account of the Steamship Quaker City's Pleasure Excursion to Europe and the Holy Land*. New York: Harper.

Ueda, Reed. 1980. "Naturalization and Citizenship." In *Harvard Encyclopedia of American Ethnic Groups*, edited by Stephen Thernstrom, 734–48. Cambridge, MA: Belknap Press of Harvard Univ. Press.

US House of Representatives. 1901. *Industrial Commission on Immigration*. Vol. 15. H. Doc. 184. 57th Cong., 1st sess. Washington, DC: US Government Printing Office.

US Industrial Commission on Immigration. 1911. *Abstract of Reports*. 2 vols. 61st Cong., 3rd sess. S. Doc. 747. Washington, DC: US Government Publication Office.

Zaydan, Jurji. 1912. *Tabaqat al-umam aw al-salail al-bashariyya* [Categories of people or human classification]. Al-Fajala, Egypt: Matbaʿa al-Hilal.

15

Arab-Americans and the Meanings of Race

LISA SUHAIR MAJAJ

> Race . . . now functions as a metaphor so necessary to the construction of Americanness that it rivals the old pseudo-scientific and class-informed racisms whose dynamics we are more used to deciphering. . . . American means white.
>
> —Toni Morrison, *Playing in the Dark*

> For better or for worse, without a clear racial identity a North American is in danger of having no identity.
>
> —Howard Winant, *Racial Conditions*

> No one today is purely *one* thing. Labels like Indian, or woman, or Muslim, or American are not more than starting-points, which if followed into actual experience for only a moment are quickly left behind. . . . [J]ust as human beings make their own history, they also make their cultures and ethnic identities.
>
> —Edward Said, *Culture and Imperialism*

What does "race" mean to Arab-Americans? This question takes on increasing significance at the present time as Arab-Americans, excluded from the rosters of minorities of color as well as of white ethnic groups, debate whether to lobby for a categorization as "Arab" or "Middle Eastern" or to continue to struggle for inclusion as white Americans on other than merely "honorary" grounds.[1] Like other immigrant groups at various historical junctures, Arab-Americans occupy a contested and unclear space within American racial and cultural discourse.[2] Although classified as "white" by current government definitions, they are conspicuously absent from discussions of white ethnicity and are popularly perceived as nonwhite. Such liminality has profound implications for Arab-Americans as they attempt to assert a public identity, claim a voice within the American multiculture, and take collective action on issues of common concern. It also makes clear the inability of prevailing American models of racial and ethnic classifications to fully account for the diversity of the American multiculture.

Contested Categories

Underlying the current status of Arab-Americans is a history of inconsistent racialization. Although individual

Excerpt from Lisa Suhair Majaj, "Arab-Americans and the Meanings of Race," in *Postcolonial Theory and the United States: Race, Ethnicity, and Literature*, ed. Amritjit Singh and Peter Schmidt (Jackson: Univ. of Mississippi Press, 2000), 320–37.

1. On the term "honorary whiteness," see Joseph Massad in "Palestinians and the Limits of Racialized Discourse" (1993) and Soheir Morsy in "Beyond the Honorary 'White' Classification of Egyptians: Societal Identity in Historical Context" (1994).

2. In *Racial Formation in the United States* (1994), Michael Omi and Howard Winant use Arabs as their example of groups "whose racial category is ambiguous at present" (162 n. 3).

Arabs had traveled to the United States since before the beginning of the nation, Arabic-speaking immigration did not begin in earnest until the late nineteenth century. From the early days of their immigration there was much confusion over how to classify Arabic-speaking immigrants. As historian Alixa Naff notes, the immigrants—largely Eastern-rite Christians from Mount Lebanon, at that time part of Ottoman-controlled "Greater Syria" (present-day Syria, Lebanon, and Israel/Palestine)—were considered an "enigma" and viewed with mingled curiosity and derision (1985, 14). Initially classified on immigration forms under the category "Turkey in Asia" or "other Asians" (Naff 1985, 109), they were subsequently termed "Syrians" by immigration officials and adopted this nomenclature themselves, finding their more familiar categories of identification, according to familial, village, or religious affiliation, of little relevance in the American context. Meanwhile, they were also characterized through a variety of derogatory racial terms, including "nigger," "dago," and "sheeny" (Naff 1985, 250–51). While the immigrants' strong pride in their own cultural identity to some extent allowed them to shrug off such negative characterization as a case of "mistaken identity," the repercussions could nonetheless be serious.[3]

Arabic-speaking immigrants also had to contend with nativist rhetoric from government officials and scholars—rhetoric that was particularly worrisome within the context of legislative and judicial debates about immigration and naturalization. The Naturalization Act of 1790 had granted the right of citizenship to what it termed "free white persons." However, the definition of "white" remained a subject of intense debate. By 1899 the Bureau of Immigration had begun "to distinguish Syrians and Palestinians by 'race' from other Turkish subjects, considering them Caucasian" (Naff 1985, 109). But after 1906 immigrants from western Asia became caught up in new naturalization laws basing eligibility for citizenship on non-Asiatic identity. In 1910, Syrians, Palestinians, Turks, Armenians, and others were classified as "Asiatic" by the US Census Bureau. In 1911 the Bureau of Immigration and Naturalization ordered court clerks to "reject applications for first papers from 'aliens who were neither white persons nor persons of African birth and descent'" (Naff 1985, 253)—a ruling that targeted "Asiatics" for exclusion. A series of court cases ensued, known as the "prerequisite cases," in which petitions for naturalization were challenged and in some instances denied on the basis of whether or not petitioners qualified as "white." These cases not only decided the fate of individual immigrants but also set precedents for the inclusion or exclusion of entire ethnic groups.[4]

At stake in these cases were competing and sometimes contradictory definitions of "whiteness." As Ian F. Haney López notes, "The courts had to establish by law whether, for example, a petitioner's race was to be measured by skin color, facial features, national origin, language, culture, ancestry, the speculations of scientists, popular opinion, or some combination of these factors. Moreover, the courts also had to decide which of these or other factors would govern in the inevitable cases where the various indices of race contradicted one another" (1996, 2). The definition of whiteness was particularly an issue in the case of immigrants from South and West Asia, such as Arabs and Indians, whose darker complexion set them at odds with popular perceptions of whiteness. Although such groups were scientifically identified as Caucasian, their popular perception as nonwhite was so persuasive that courts were willing to privilege common knowledge over scientific evidence when the two were at odds, thereby upholding politically motivated assumptions about the meaning of "whiteness."[5]

This schism between scientific evidence and popular perception played a significant role in the series of prerequisite cases involving Arab applicants between 1909 and 1915 and again in the 1940s, in which courts declared

3. For example, a Syrian merchant in an Oklahoma town was warned by the Ku Klux Klan to "keep away from the town at the risk of economic boycott and his own life," while the store of another Syrian merchant "was burned down soon after he received a threat by mail ordering him to move away from the town" (see Shadid 1927, 23–24).

4. Ian F. Haney López provides a compelling analysis of these cases in *White by Law: The Legal Construction of Race* (1996).

5. See Haney López 1996, 5–9, for a discussion of the clash between common knowledge and scientific evidence.

Arab applicants to be variously white and nonwhite.[6] At stake in the cases were these questions: whether Arabs are "white" in color; whether Arabs are Asian or Caucasian; whether whiteness is determined by race, color, geography, culture, or religion; and whether there is an intrinsic connection between Caucasian identity and whiteness. The answers that emerged illustrate the contradictory and politicized meanings of race during this period of nativist xenophobia and generalized anxiety about American identity.

The arguments presented as rationale for challenging the right of Arabic-speaking applicants to naturalization included dark skin color, origin on the continent of Asia, distance (literal and metaphorical) from European culture, and cultural and geographical proximity to Islam. Despite—or perhaps because of—the difficulty of defining "whiteness," the courts' decisions were frequently made on the grounds of commonsense assumptions about race: judges were more likely to deem lighter-skinned applicants worthy of naturalization and to deny naturalization to darker-skinned immigrants even when attributing rejection to other reasons. For instance, both applicant Faras Shahid, described by the court as "walnut or somewhat darker than is the usual mulatto" (*Ex parte Shahid* 1913, 813), and applicant George Dow, described as "darker than the usual person of white European descent" (*Ex parte Dow* 1914, 487), were initially excluded from naturalization, while applicant Tom Ellis, described as Semitic but "a markedly white type of the race," was admitted (see Ferris 1928a, 4).

However, "whiteness" was understood to involve not just racial appearance and skin color but also geographical, cultural, linguistic, and religious factors. Under the "white person" prerequisite, immigrants whose cultural background and place of origin seemed to have proximity to Europe were more likely to be judged admissible than those whose cultural background and place of origin were perceived as alien to European culture. Thus, although the judge who excluded George Dow presented a discourse on the relative coloration of different West Asian peoples, he ultimately argued that in cases of ambiguous coloration "whiteness" must be construed on the basis of general affiliation with European identity. If an applicant from Syria "cannot rest on complexion," he asserted, he "must find other grounds . . . to establish any community of race with the European races assuming those last to be the white race" (*In re Dow* 1914, 363). Intrinsic to this European "community of race" was Christian identity. Although most of the early Arab immigrants were in fact Christian, this fact was obscured by the popular confusion between Arabs and Muslims. Islamic culture was viewed as diametrically opposed to western European culture and, in a conflation of religious and racial identity, was construed as intrinsically nonwhite.[7] In asserting their claims to "whiteness" and American citizenship, Syrian immigrants therefore tended to stress their Christian identity and their historical, geographical, and religious relationship to the Holy Land and to accentuate their distance from Islam. It comes as no surprise, for instance, that during Dow's rehearing one of the arguments presented on his behalf was that the Syrians' "connection through all times with the peoples to whom the Jewish and Christian peoples owed their religion, made it inconceivable that the Statute could be intended to exclude them" (*In re Dow* 1914, 357). But even though non-Christian identity weighed heavily *against* applicants seeking naturalization, the link between Christian identity and whiteness was viewed as insufficient grounds for inclusion. Indeed, arguments for naturalization on the grounds of an intrinsic Syrian connection to the birthplace of Christianity were dismissed as "emotional" and having "no place in the judicial interpretation of a statute" (*Ex parte Shahid* 1913, 816).

Although the prerequisite cases had various outcomes, most of the cases before 1920 were eventually resolved in favor of the applicants. As a result, scholars have viewed the prerequisite controversy as an anomalous period in a relatively straightforward Arab-American history of assimilation (e.g., Naff 1985, 259). Indeed, the official

6. Arab applicants were declared white in 1909 and 1910, nonwhite in 1913 and 1914, white in 1915, nonwhite in 1942, and white in 1944.

7. Nadine Naber terms this conflation the "racialization of religion" (1998, 8).

classification of Arabic-speaking immigrants as "white" seemed ensured by a 1917 decision of the Congress that drew the longitudinal and latitudinal lines of Asian exclusion along boundaries that situated immigrants from Greater Syria within the space of "whiteness" and American citizenship (see Ferris 1928b, 22–24). This inclusion seemed solidified by the 1920 census, which identified Syrians and Palestinians, separately, under the category "foreign-born white population" (Naff 1985, 117).[8]

However, the link between western, European, Christian identity and "whiteness" and the importance of this link in defining American identity persisted. So, too, did the connection between non-European, non-Christian, and nonwhite identity. A 1942 case denying naturalization to a Yemeni applicant, Ahmed Hassan, made clear the extent to which "whiteness" continued to be interpreted as a characteristic of European Christians but not of non-Europeans or non-Christians. "Apart from the dark skin of the Arabs," the judge argued, "it is well known that they are a part of the Mohammedan world and that a wide gulf separates their culture from that of the predominantly Christian peoples of Europe" (*In re Ahmed Hassan* 1942, 845). Although affiliation to Christianity had earlier been held irrelevant as a rationale for inclusion of Arabs, in this case non-Christian cultural identity was viewed as a convincing rationale for exclusion. In contrast, the judge noted that certain (non-Arab) applicants might be judged suitable for American citizenship on the basis of their relationship to Christian Europe. Although voicing "serious doubt as to whether any peoples of Asiatic stock could be considered white persons within the meaning of the statue," he noted that Armenians could be considered "white" because they were Christian and were geographically closer to Europe (*In re Ahmed Hassan* 1942, 845).[9] Through such reasoning, markers of religion were assimilated into the geographical construction of race, with Islam relegated to the opposite side of the geographical boundary separating white, western, Christian Europe from nonwhite, eastern, non-Christian Asia.[10]

The continuing association between western identity and whiteness also played a role, with different results, in a 1944 case that granted naturalization to an Arab applicant. In this case the judge argued that Arabs could be considered "white"—not in and of themselves, but because they had historically served as *transmitters* of western civilization. The basis for inclusion as white, the judge held, turned upon "whether the petitioner is a member of one of the 'races [(a)] inhabiting Europe or [(b)] living along the shores of the Mediterranean' or [(c)], perhaps, is a member of a race of 'Asiatics whose long contiguity to European nations and assimilation with their culture has caused them to be thought of as of the same general characteristics'" (*Ex parte Mohriez* 1944, 943). In contrast to earlier courts that had argued the distance of Arabs from European culture, this judge held that Arabs had accrued sufficient whiteness through their role in transmitting European civilization to be considered white. As he stated, "The Arab people stand as one of the chief channels by which the traditions of white Europe, especially the ancient Greek traditions, have been carried into the present," and therefore "the Arab passes muster as a white person" (*Ex parte Mohriez* 1944, 943).

This ruling marked the end of explicit challenges on racial grounds to the suitability of Arab immigrants for naturalization. However, the question of racial classification reemerged in a 1987 discrimination case filed by an Iraqi professor charging that he had been denied tenure on

8. Although Naff cites the 1929 census, this seems to be an error. See also Hitti, who notes that "in the reports of the fourteenth decennial census of 1920, the Syrians were for the first time treated as a separate people" (1924, 19 n. 1).

9. Indeed, in a 1909 case involving an Armenian applicant, the circuit court judge held that the applicant should be granted citizenship because Armenians may readily become westernized and Europeanized and because "history has shown that Christianity in the near East has generally manifested a sympathy with Europe rather than with Asia as a whole" (*In re Halladjian* 1909).

10. Such racialization of geography and culture, while particularly glaring in the case of Arabs and Muslims, reflected the general tenor of the times. As Omi and Winant point out, in the wake of nineteenth-century political and ideological struggles over the racial classification of southern Europeans, Irish, and Jews, "nativism was only effectively curbed by the institutionalization of a racial order that drew the color line *around*, rather than *within*, Europe" (1994, 65, emphasis in original).

the basis of being of "Arabian race" (*Saint Francis College v. Al-Khazraji* 1987, 604). The case, filed under civil rights statute 42 USC Section 1981, was initially thrown out of court because the civil rights statute assumes a nonwhite plaintiff. However, the Supreme Court subsequently determined that "although Arabs are Caucasians under current racial classifications, Congress, when it passed what is now [Section] 1981, did not limit its protections to those who today would be considered members of a race different from the defendant's. . . . [A]t a minimum, [Section] 1981 reaches discrimination directed against an individual because he or she is genetically part of an ethnically and physiognomically distinctive subgrouping of *homo sapiens*" (604). As Therese Saliba notes, the ruling not only "supports the claim of an 'Arabian race' within the arbitrary construction of racial categories" but also challenges existing racial categories—for "once 'Arabs' as a category are included in racial politics, it is not in addition to already familiar groups of people of color covered under Affirmative Action, but rather, their inclusion leads to a dismantling of those categories" (1999, 312).

Informing such legal debates both in the early period and at the present time are historical discourses of Orientalism and heathenism that situate non-Europeans and nonwhites as uncivilized and inferior to white, Christian Europeans. As Edward Said has cogently demonstrated, Orientalism, functioning as a "system of knowledge" filtering the Orient into western consciousness, has perpetuated "the idea of European identity as a superior one in comparison with all the non-European peoples and cultures" (1978, 5–7). In the Orientalist worldview, the West is "rational, developed, humane, superior," while the Orient is "aberrant, undeveloped, inferior" (Said 1978, 300). Islam fares particularly badly in Orientalist portrayals; historically represented as a "menace" to the West and to Christianity, it has more recently been caricatured as the epitome of barbarism, repression, and irrational political violence, supplanting communism as the new enemy of the "civilized" West.

American views of Arabs also draw on the racially inflected "civilized/heathen" schism that historically opposed white American colonists to Native peoples, immigrants, and enslaved Africans. As the definition of "American" became equated with the characteristics of whiteness, Christianity, European/Anglo-Saxon origin and "civilization," other groups were both racialized and hierarchically ranked in relationship to these characteristics.[11] Immigrants whose tenuous racial status compromised their ability to assimilate into white America often sought to move up the racial scale, and hence accentuate their claim to American identity, by distancing themselves from people of color. For instance, in their bid for acceptance in the American context, Irish and Italian immigrants sought to put as much distance as possible between themselves and African Americans.[12] Similarly, Arabic-speaking immigrants, recognizing that perceptions of "whiteness" turned upon relative distance from the "darker" end of the racial spectrum, anxiously sought to assert their difference from Blacks. For instance, in a 1929 Florida incident involving the lynching of a Syrian man after a car accident (see "Syrian and Wife Killed in Florida" 1929), the Syrian immigrant community responded not only with outrage but also with a defensive attempt to assert their "whiteness." A letter published in a Syrian immigrant journal declaimed, "The Syrian is not a Negro whom Southerners feel they are justified in lynching when he is suspected of an attack on a white woman. The Syrian is a civilized white man who has excellent traditions and a glorious historical background" ("Has the Syrian Become a Negro?" 1929, 42). While racist, such responses also made clear the immigrants' anxieties about their own racial identification in a context where to be nonwhite had serious consequences. As one immigrant journal warned, "*Al-Hoda* is of the opinion that the Syrians should proceed with extreme caution in

11. For instance, Mexicans in California were considered "half civilized" because they spoke a romance language, were Christian, had been "Europeanized" through their colonization by Spain, and were racially assimilable because of their "mixed-blood" ancestry (Almaguer 1994, 54).

12. Southern Italian immigrants, considered "tainted" by the "dusk of Saracenic or Berber ancestors showing in their cheeks" (a telling reflection of attitudes toward Middle Eastern peoples) and made to sit with Black congregants in church, separated themselves from Black Americans as much as possible (Orsi 1992, 318). Similarly, Irish immigrants attempted to facilitate their own transformation from "Irish" to "American" by positioning themselves in opposition to Blacks (Takaki 1993, 151).

this matter. . . . A certain feeling of prejudice undeniably exists against the Syrians in some parts of the South and any rash action on their part might tend to aggravate matters unnecessarily" ("Syrian and Wife Killed in Florida" 1929, 47–48).

At the same time, the anomalous location of Arabs within the binary framework of American race relations sometimes positioned immigrants outside of this framework altogether. For instance, Egyptian students in racially segregated regions of the United States during the 1950s and early 1960s found that their foreignness often set them outside of the Black–white racial dynamics that might otherwise have relegated them to a disadvantageous sphere. Despite their dark skin, they were welcomed as "foreign students" and assigned to "white" schools (Morsy 1994, 184). Similarly, Lebanese Catholics in racially segregated Protestant Birmingham were able to sidestep some of the implications of being "colored" in the segregated South because their Catholic identity set them apart from both Black and white Protestants (Conklin and Faires 1987, 80).[13]

In the contemporary period, perceptions of and attitudes toward Arabs draw not only upon Orientalist discourse and traditional racism but also on what has been described as "political racism" (Samhan 1987). Political racism is distinguishable from earlier, nativist strands of racism by a focus on Arab-oriented political activity, particularly activity related to the Palestinian struggle for national rights (Samhan 1987, 16). Post–World War II political events—the 1948 creation of the State of Israel, the corresponding dispossession of the Palestinians and the military response of Arab states, the 1967 Arab–Israeli War, the 1973 Arab–Israeli War, the oil boycott of the 1970s, the Israeli invasion of Lebanon in 1982, the 1990–91 Gulf Crisis, and incidents of violence, whether or not carried out by Arabs (e.g., the 1995 bombing of the Oklahoma City Federal Building, perpetrated by a white European-American but initially attributed to Arabs)—have resulted in a climate of hostility toward Arab-Americans in general and politically active individuals in particular.[14] Arab-American offices, homes, and religious centers have been bombed and vandalized, and individuals have been threatened, beaten, and murdered in politically motivated assaults.[15] In 1985, following the murder of Alex Odeh, the West Coast regional director of the American-Arab Anti-Discrimination Committee (ADC), FBI director William Webster warned that Arab-Americans and others advocating "Arab points of view have come within the zone of danger" (quoted in Abraham 1994, 165).

At the same time, however, federal government agencies have also played a role in targeting Arab-Americans. As Helen Samhan notes, "While Arab American first amendment [*sic*] rights to speak and assemble are protected by the Constitution, government agencies in varying degrees have often abused those rights in the name of security against terrorism" (1987, 17). A striking example may be seen in the case of the "LA Eight"—the seven Palestinians and one Kenyan arrested in Los Angeles on January 26, 1987, incarcerated, and publicly labeled a "terrorist threat" for legitimate First Amendment activities, who remain under threat of deportation at the present time [c. 2000] (Abraham 1994, 199–203; Naber 1998, 7). Since the passage of the 1996 antiterrorism bill, targeting of Arab-Americans has increased. In addition to being subjected to special scrutiny at airports and other public places, Arab-Americans have been singled out by the bill's provisions for arrest and detention on the basis of secret evidence. It cannot pass notice that *all* of the detainees imprisoned on "secret evidence" to

13. However, such "honorary" white status was not always reliable. Soheir Morsy points out that although some Egyptians in the United States were exempted from classification as nonwhite on the basis of being foreign, others were denied housing, told to sit in the back of the bus, and refused service in restaurants, "often after long consultations among waitresses who were audibly debating our racial identity" (1994, 184–85).

14. Nabeel Abraham argues that contemporary anti-Arab discrimination and hate crimes are rooted in three sources: traditional racism, politically motivated racism, and jingoistic racism. The first, arising when Arabs are ethnically visible, is evident throughout the history of Arabs in the United States. The second, linked to the Arab–Israeli conflict, is ideologically motivated and targets individuals who support Palestinian and other Arab causes. The third arises in the context of international unrest such as hijackings and military conflict and involves a knee-jerk lashing out at "the enemy." See his discussion in "Anti-Arab Racism and Violence in the United States" (1994).

15. See Abraham 1994 for a detailed account of such incidents.

date (twenty-five by January 1999), who face deportation without being allowed to know either the charges levied against them or the identity of their accusers, are of Arab or Muslim identity.[16]

Given these realities, whether or not Arabs are viewed as "white" or "nonwhite" matters both discursively and pragmatically. Classification and nomenclature play a role in community visibility, in political power and access to resources, as well as in the ability to claim protection from discrimination. Governmental classifications that include Arab-Americans within the majority white population have not protected Arab-Americans from targeting on the basis of ethnicity. Rather, demographic research would arguably show that this group has "suffered historic, pervasive discrimination like other minority groups" (Gregory Nojeim, quoted in *ADC Times* 1994, 11). Categorization as "white" not only obscures this history of discrimination but makes it difficult to collect accurate statistics on Arab-Americans and to assess their needs.[17] Classification as white also makes Arab-Americans culturally invisible, creates contradictions for dark-skinned Arabs who are not socially perceived as "white,"[18] and glosses over disparities between governmental as well as popular treatment of Arabs and Europeans in the American context (for instance, unequal access to the right of immigration).

The implications of this schism between official classification and popular perception emerge with particular clarity at moments of crisis, such as the 1995 Oklahoma Federal Building bombing, carried out by the European-American Timothy McVeigh. In the wake of the bombing, government officials identified the suspects as "white males." Surprised reporters, who had immediately raised the specter of Arab/Muslim terrorism, queried whether this identification excluded Middle Easterners.[19] Their disconcertion made clear their assumption that "white" and "Middle Eastern"—and, by extension, "American" and "Arab," "American" and "terrorist"—are mutually exclusive categories. Moreover, popular opinion clearly supported such views: despite the lack of evidence pointing toward Arab perpetrators, ordinary Arab-Americans across the country were harassed, threatened, assaulted, and abused in the days following the bombing.[20]

Such incidents have convinced many Arab-Americans that the designation "white," with its implications of mainstream status, does not reflect the reality of their experiences. As a result, Arab-American community leaders have begun lobbying for a specific racial or ethnic classification, even as they remain divided over whether to work toward legal identification as "Arab-Americans" or as "Middle Eastern Americans" (an identification that would include not just Arabs but also Iranians, Turks, Armenians, and others).[21] At the time of the 1990 census, national Arab-American organizations launched a concerted campaign to encourage Arab-Americans to answer the ancestry question on the "long form" by writing in an Arab country of origin rather than identifying as

16. See *ADC Times* 1998, 4.

17. For instance, ADC has reported that "due to the absence of federal, state or local guidelines requesting census data on Arab Americans, the National Education Association (NEA) does not include Arab Americans in discussions of multiculturalism in school curricula" ("The 2000 Census: Will We Count?" 1995, 12).

18. In an incident reported to ADC, a Palestinian-American girl was forbidden from attending her school prom with *either* a Black *or* a white date. She was allegedly told by her teacher, "You're a foreigner. Go with someone who has the same features as you" (*ADC Times* 1994).

19. Press conference with US attorney general Janet Reno, April 20, 1995.

20. Two hundred twenty-two incidents were reported to ADC during the three-day period immediately following the bombing. In one incident, a pregnant Arab-American woman lost her baby when her house was attacked by angry mobs. The *1995 Report on Anti-Arab Racism* states that the woman "huddled in the bathroom with her two children as angry crowds grew outside, throwing stones and other objects at her house. Believing the loud noises were gunshots and terrified for her children, she began hemorrhaging. Shortly thereafter, her child was stillborn" (Khoury, Ramadan, and Wingfield 1996, 4).

21. The category "Arab American" has been proposed by the ADC, while the Arab American Institute (AAI) has lobbied for the category "Middle Eastern." Other possible modes of classification include identifying West Asian Arabs as Asian-American and North African Arabs as African-American. However, while such categorizations have the advantage of fitting Arabs into existing classifications, they privilege geography over culture as the basis for identification, accentuate the invisibility of Arabs as they become subsumed within these larger groups, and risk dividing a community still struggling for unity.

"white" or by a religious designation.[22] And in 1994, following the decision of the federal Office of Management and Budget to review the categories used for collecting data on race and ethnicity in preparation for the 2000 census, the Arab American Institute held discussions on the question of minority status (Naber 1998, 11–12).

The increasing turn to panethnic identification among Arab-Americans has been encouraged by factors specific to the Arab-American community, including ongoing immigration from Arab countries, the increasing proportion of Muslims among Arab-Americans, and the growing politicization of Arab-Americans in response to both domestic and international events. However, it also reflects the general reliance in the American context on panethnic models of racial organization. As many scholars have argued, race, far from being a "biological" category, is "an unstable and 'decentered' complex of social meanings constantly being transformed by political struggle" (Omi and Winant 1994, 55), a fact that has long been evident in the shifting classifications of the US Census.[23] The current white–Black–Hispanic–Asian–American Indian pentagon[24] formalized during the Nixon era is a product of this political struggle between state-level ordering and community efforts to "claim or rearticulate identity" (Frankenberg 1993, 12). While panethnic categorization blurs distinctions between groups, it also helps minority groups to find a third space between specific ethnic identification and the binary opposition of Black/white relations (Winant 1994, 60).[25] Recognizing this, Arab-Americans, like other groups, have increasingly turned to panethnic delineation to confront their identity "in a political environment of heightened racial consciousness and mobilization" (Winant 1994, 61).

Literary Reflections

Arab-American literature both reflects and is situated within this history of contested racial categories. Literary texts from the first half of the [twentieth] century make clear the anxieties of Arab-Americans as they struggled for inclusion as "white" Americans. Aware of their contested racial, legal, and social status in the American context, early Arab-American authors tended to emphasize those aspects of their identities more likely to gain acceptance by white Americans and to distance themselves from those elements of Arab culture viewed as particularly foreign and less readily assimilable. In particular, they stressed their Christian identity, their geographical origin in the "Holy Land," and their "spirituality," employing biblical rhetoric and religious parallels in their attempt to engage American readers and familiarize the "exotic," while at the same time seeking to distance themselves from Islam. . . .

As the century progressed, the strident assimilation pressures characterizing the early decades of the twentieth century gave way to a greater focus on cultural pluralism and to a humanism characterized by the stance that different races and groups were "all the same under the skin." However, these shifts notwithstanding, Arab-Americans found that "American" continued to mean Christian, European, western, and white and that they were still located outside of these definitions. Meanwhile, the Orientalist stereotypes of Arabs held such sway that ordinary Arab-Americans were often viewed as not "exotic" enough to be "authentic." . . .

22. Given the diverse ways in which Arabs identify themselves, there were fears that Arab-Americans who wrote in such answers as "Maronite" or "Muslim" would not be tabulated, resulting in an undercount of Arab Americans—something that virtually all Arab-American scholars agree occurred anyway.

23. See Sharon M. Lee's discussion of census classifications in "Racial Classifications in the US Census: 1890–1990" (1993).

24. This framework was first promulgated in a 1977 Office of Management and Budget circular, "Race and Ethnic Standards for Federal Statistics and Administrative Reporting" (see Sanjek 1994, 109). David Hollinger notes that the issuing of this directive was "the single event most responsible for the lines that separate one bloc from another" (1995, 33).

25. For instance, although the category "Asian-American" obscures the linguistic, cultural, historical, and national distinctions between immigrants from different Asian countries, it also makes it possible for immigrants from these diverse countries to take action on issues that affect them *as Asians*, such as "exclusionary immigration laws, restrictive naturalization laws, labor market segregation, and patterns of ghettoization by a polity and culture that treated all Asians as alike" (Winant 1994, 60).

Whether through tactics of assimilation or through the strategic deployment of exoticism, [early] writers such as [Abraham Mitrie] Rihbany (1914, 1922) and [William] Blatty (1960) sought not to unsettle the racial categories of white America so much as to find acceptance within them. In contrast, however, contemporary Arab-American writers increasingly seek to challenge established cultural and racial boundaries in their articulation of Arab-American identity and to assert their identity on their own terms. Lebanese-American Lawrence Joseph,[26] Jordanian-American Diana Abu-Jaber,[27] and Egyptian-American Pauline Kaldas[28] provide examples of contemporary writers' efforts to grapple more directly with the racialization and politicization of Arab-American experience and to assert their Arab-American identity without apology. . . .

Indeed, contemporary Arab-American literature increasingly probes the ways in which classification as "white" serves not as a mode of inclusion but as a form of erasure. Consider, for instance, the poem "Exotic" by Egyptian-American poet Pauline Kaldas. Beginning with an invocation of markers of "exotic" beauty, the poem explores the ways in which Arab women are excluded from "white" American identity yet simultaneously recuperated into its domain through a neocolonial gesture of possession. Dark enough to be "interesting," yet white enough to be "safe," the Egyptian woman in the poem presents what Kaldas terms an "also permitted" alternative to the mainstream "golden beauty" ([1990] 1994, 168). But such "permissible" difference turns not only upon exoticism but also upon the safety of categorization. The woman is surrounded by a swirl of voices that attempt to define and contain her in an ethnic kaleidoscope:

> "Que pasa niña"
> "Hey baby!"
> "What are you—Lebanese, Armenian, Spanish,
> Puerto Rican, Italian, Mexican
> c'mon what are you?"
> "You're either Spanish or Italian."
> (Kaldas [1990] 1994, 168)

By invoking ready-made slots of identification, these efforts at containment ward off an actual engagement with the complexity of difference. As Kaldas writes, "The square edges me as it extends *White / includes People from North Africa and the Middle East*" ([1990] 1994, 168, italics in original).

The classification tensions evoked in Kaldas's poem are not dissimilar from the tensions around race that informed the prerequisite cases earlier in the century. As in those court cases, here, too, Arab identity challenges the boundaries of available racial and ethnic classification, contained only by exclusion or by extending the meanings of whiteness. But while the definition of individual Arabs as "nonwhite" in the early period reflected a politics of exclusion, the contemporary location of "Arab" in the square of "white" is felt by many Arab-Americans to obscure Arab-American realities, silencing them through a strategy of containment and rendering them invisible.[29]

The inadequacy of the category "white" to account for Arab-American experience is reflected in Kaldas's poem through images of food and embodiment that spill bodily over the square's demarcation lines. "White?" she queries.

> As fava beans stirred green with olive oil
> falafel fried sesame seeds burned black
> baklava and basboosa the aroma browned crisp in
> the oven
> White is not my breasts growing at nine
> . . . not my last menstruation at sixty.
> ([1990] 1994, 168–69)

26. Lawrence Joseph is the author of the poetry collections *Shouting at No One* (1988b), *Curriculum Vitae* (1988a), and *Before Our Eyes* (1993) and of the prose volume *Lawyerland: What Lawyers Talk About When They Talk About Law* (1997).

27. Diana Abu-Jaber is author of the novel *Arabian Jazz* (1993) [and] of essays and short stories (see Abu-Jaber 1991, 1995). . . .

28. Pauline Kaldas's poetry has appeared in *Lift Magazine*, *Michigan Review*, [the edited volumes] *Food for Our Grandmothers* (Kaldas [1990] 1994) and *The Space between Our Footsteps*, and a special Arab-American issue of *Jusoor*. She is the author of *Egyptian Compass*" (2006), a poetry collection. . . .

29. As Joe Kadi writes in the introduction to *Food for Our Grandmothers*, "One reason it's hard to find an accurate name [for Americans and Canadians of Arab, North African, and Middle Eastern origin] has to do with our invisibility. It's tough to name a group when most people aren't aware the group exists" (1994, xix).

But official categories recuperate this bodily excess, containing it within the bounds of exoticism: the ethnic-food aisle in the grocery store, the glass cases displaying mummies. Next to the identification box, which holds only a precise, anonymous X, the speaker writes her name. But her "guttural kha script / twirl[s] into ABC"; her body, its excesses contained, is wound by "lengths of cloth / mummy encased in glass" ([1990] 1994, 169). If figurations of race are modes of scripting the embodied self, whiteness here is written in standardized typeset. Converted into "the exotic," the speaker is commodified: the poem ends with the sardonic invitation, "taste a color not confined / by the squares" (169).

This recognition that Arabs constitute a "color not confined / by the squares" underlies the growing search among Arab-Americans for categories of identification able to account for their realities. As Edward Said has written, "No one today is purely *one* thing. Labels like Indian, or woman, or Muslim, or American are not more than starting-points, which if followed into actual experience for only a moment are quickly left behind" (1993, 336). The debate among Arab-Americans over how to identify—as Arab, as Middle Eastern, as Asian or North African—comes together with the community's internal diversity—religious, national, cultural, and ideological—to underscore the inadequacy of rigid categories of identification. . . .

Works Cited

"The 2000 Census: Will We Count?" 1995. *ADC Times*, May–June, 12.

Abraham, Nabeel. 1994. "Anti-Arab Racism and Violence in the United States." In *The Development of Arab-American Identity*, edited by Ernest McCarus, 155–214. Ann Arbor: Univ. of Michigan Press.

Abu-Jaber, Diana. 1991. "At the Continental Divide." *Writer's Forum* 17 (Fall): 130–53.

———. 1993. *Arabian Jazz*. New York: Harcourt Brace.

———. 1995. "Arabs and the Break in the Text." In *Scars: American Poetry in the Face of Violence*, edited by Cynthia Dubin Edelberg, 130–33. Tuscaloosa: Univ. of Alabama Press.

ADC Times. 1994. Aug–Sept.

———. 1998. Aug.–Sept.

Almaguer, Tomas. 1994. *Racial Fault Lines: The Historical Origins of White Supremacy in California*. Berkeley: Univ. of California Press.

Blatty, William. 1960. *Which Way to Mecca, Jack?* New York: Geis.

Conklin, Nancy Faires, and Nora Faires. 1987. "'Colored' and Catholic: The Lebanese in Birmingham, Alabama." In *Crossing the Waters: Arabic-Speaking Immigrants to the United States before 1940*, edited by Eric J. Hooglund, 69–84. Washington, DC: Smithsonian Institution Press.

Dow v. United States. 1915. 226 *Federal Reporter*, Sept. 14.

Ex parte Dow. 1914. 211 *Federal Reporter*, Feb. 18.

Ex parte Mohriez. 1944. 54 *Federal Supplement* 1500, Apr. 13.

Ex parte Shahid. 1913. 205 *Federal Reporter*, June 24.

Ferris, Joseph W. 1928a. "Syrian Naturalization Question in the United States: Part 1." *The Syrian World* 2, no. 8 (Feb.): 3–11.

———. 1928b. "Syrian Naturalization Question in the United States: Part 2." *The Syrian World* 2, no. 9 (Mar.): 18–24.

Frankenberg, Ruth. 1993. *White Women, Race Matters: The Social Construction of Whiteness*. Minneapolis: Univ. of Minnesota Press.

Haney López, Ian F. 1996. *White by Law: The Legal Construction of Race*. New York: New York Univ. Press.

"Has the Syrian Become a Negro?" 1929. *Ash-Shaab* (New York), May 24. Reprinted in *The Syrian World* 3, no. 12 (June 1929): 42.

Hitti, Philip. 1924. *The Syrians in America*. New York: George H. Doran.

Hollinger, David A. 1995. *Postethnic America: Beyond Multiculturalism*. New York: Basic Books.

In re Ahmed Hassan. 1942. 48 *Federal Supplement* 843, Dec. 15.

In re Dow. 1914. 213 *Federal Reporter*, Apr. 15.

In re Halladjian. 1909. 174 F. 834, Dec. 24.

Joseph, Lawrence. 1988a. *Curriculum Vitae*. Pittsburgh: Univ. of Pittsburgh Press.

———. 1988b. *Shouting at No One*. Pittsburgh: Univ. of Pittsburgh Press.

———. 1993. *Before Our Eyes*. New York: Farrar, Straus and Giroux.

———. 1997. *Lawyerland: What Lawyers Talk about When They Talk about Law*. New York: Farrar Straus and Giroux.

Kadi, Joe. 1994. Introduction to *Food for Our Grandmothers: Writings by Arab-American & Arab-Canadian Feminists*, edited by Joe Kadi, xiii–xx. Boston: South End Press.

Kaldas, Pauline. [1990] 1994. "Exotic." In *Food for Our Grandmothers: Writings by Arab-American & Arab-Canadian*

Feminists, edited by Joe Kadi, 168–69. Boston: South End Press.

Khoury, Ghada, Mary Ramadan, and Marvin Wingfield, comps. 1996. *1995 Report on Anti-Arab Racism: Hate Crimes, Discrimination, and Defamation of Arab Americans*. ADC Special Report. Washington, DC: ADC Research Institute.

Lee, Sharon M. 1993. "Racial Classifications in the US Census: 1890–1990." *Ethnic and Racial Studies* 16, no. 1 (Jan.): 75–94.

Massad, Joseph. 1993. "Palestinians and the Limits of Racialized Discourse." *Social Text* 34:94–114.

Morrison, Toni. 1992. *Playing in the Dark: Whiteness and the Literary Imagination*. Cambridge, MA: Harvard Univ. Press.

Morsy, Soheir. 1994. "Beyond the Honorary 'White' Classification of Egyptians: Societal Identity in Historical Context." In *Race*, edited by Steven Gregory and Roger Sanjek, 175–98. New Brunswick, NJ: Rutgers Univ. Press.

Naber, Nadine. 1998. "Arab-American In/Visibility." *AAUG Monitor* 13, no. 3 (Dec.): 1–16.

Naff, Alixa. 1985. *Becoming American: The Early Arab Immigrant Experience*. Carbondale: Southern Illinois Univ. Press.

Omi, Michael, and Howard Winant. 1994. *Racial Formation in the United States: From the 1960s to the 1990s*. 2nd ed. New York: Routledge.

Orsi, Robert. 1992. "The Religious Boundaries of an Inbetween People: Street Feste and the Problem of the Dark-Skinned Other in Italian Harlem, 1920–1990." *American Quarterly* 44:313–47.

Rihbany, Abraham Mitrie. 1914. *A Far Journey*. Boston: Houghton Mifflin.

———. 1922. *Wise Men from the East and from the West*. Boston: Houghton Mifflin.

Rizk, Salom. 1943. *Syrian Yankee*. Garden City, NY: Doubleday.

Said, Edward. 1978. *Orientalism*. New York: Vintage.

———. 1993. *Culture and Imperialism*. New York: Knopf.

Saint Francis College v. Al-Khazraji. 1987. 481 US 604. Although published for the Oct. 1986 term, argued on Feb. 25, 1987, and decided on May 18, 1987.

Saliba, Therese. 1999. "Resisting Invisibility: Arab Americans in Academia and Activism." In *Arabs in America: Building a New Future*, edited by Michael Suleiman, 304–19. Philadelphia: Temple Univ. Press.

Samhan, Helen. 1987. "Politics and Exclusion: The Arab American Experience." *Journal of Palestine Studies* 16, no. 2 (Winter): 11–28.

Sanjek, Roger. 1994. "Intermarriage and the Future of Races in the United States." In *Race*, edited by Steven Gregory and Roger Sanjek, 103–30. New Brunswick, NJ: Rutgers Univ. Press.

Shadid, Michael. 1927. "Syria for the Syrians." *The Syrian World* 1, no. 8: 21–24.

———. 1956. *Crusading Doctor*. Boston: Meador.

Shakir, Evelyn. 1993. "Coming of Age: Arab American Literature." *Ethnic Forum* 13:63–88.

Suleiman, Michael. 1987. "Early Arab-Americans: The Search for Identity." In *Crossing the Waters: Arabic-Speaking Immigrants to the United States before 1940*, edited by Eric J. Hooglund, 37–54. Washington, DC: Smithsonian Institution Press.

"Syrian and Wife Killed in Florida." 1929. *The Syrian World* 3, no. 12 (June): 45–48.

Takaki, Ronald. 1993. *A Different Mirror: A History of Multicultural America*. Boston: Little, Brown.

Williams, David. 1993. *Traveling Mercies*. Cambridge, MA: Alice James Books.

Winant, Howard. 1994. *Racial Conditions*. Minneapolis: Univ. of Minnesota Press.

16

Ethnic Identity and Imperative Patriotism

Arab Americans before and after 9/11

STEVEN SALAITA

. . . [I]t can be said that no single event shaped the destiny of Arab Americans more than 9/11. After 9/11, the Arab American community was thrust into the spotlight. This attention represented a drastic change from the community's previous position, for during the times that Arab Americans attempted to be noticed—times generally related to our flagship issue, Palestinian independence—it was rare for mainstream forums to acknowledge us. When Arab Americans were acknowledged, it was usually in the form of ridicule, dismissal, or an outright racism that had long been considered an unacceptable way to address other ethnic groups. It is a general rule that ambivalence will follow when a once-ignored or outright slandered community is suddenly offered unceasing attention and is asked to define and redefine itself daily. The peculiar nature of the sudden attention after 9/11 only did more to catalyze Arab Americans into serious introspective glances. That attention was simultaneously an outpouring of hostility and kindness. On the day of the attack, Rudy Giuliani and George W. Bush urged Americans not to engage in racial violence and to prevent any that might occur, as did practically every television commentator and politician of significance. For every racist comment and report of harassment, there were ten stories about "average" Americans going out of their way to make their Arab neighbors feel safe and welcome.

But what do those pronouncements actually reveal about the culture from which they were produced and the community at which they were directed? And what were their effects on both? First, while they were in some cases sincere when uttered by politicians and probably sincere in every case when uttered by ordinary citizens, the cultural impulses inspiring them cannot be considered altogether pure since they drew tacitly from a tradition of forced assimilation. (It is also problematic that such pronouncements needed constant repeating to begin with.) While the goodwill of everyday Americans cannot be called into question, one might look upon aspects of the discourse of American leaders with suspicion. They attempted to urge Arab Americans, before 9/11 generally antiassimilationist and radical, into total assimilation. In this case, it was not a forced assimilation that other ethnic groups, primarily Natives, have experienced. It took the form of the repeated statements: "They're American, too"; "They're American, just like you"; "They also love this country." The suspicion I cite should be drawn out briefly. A community can accept the call, whether or not it was solicited, to be absorbed fully into the politics of its surrounding society only if it assumes that the surrounding society's politics are amenable to the community. This has never been the case with Arab Americans because the American government has long been involved in the Arab world in a way that most Arab Americans find invasive and unjust. Moreover, draconian legislation like the USA PATRIOT Act wholly contradicts the

Excerpt from Steven George Salaita, "Ethnic Identity and Imperative Patriotism: Arab Americans before and after 9/11," *College Literature* 32, no. 2 (2005): 153–59. © 2005 John Hopkins University Press and West Chester University. Reprinted with corrections and press style changes for consistency throughout the volume by permission of John Hopkins University Press.

occasionally inclusive language of Congress and the Bush administration. . . .

The domestic environment . . . is one that terrifies many Arab Americans and keeps us from politics, especially Palestinian politics, because the fear of being harassed or arrested is more than mere paranoia. At the same time, numerous Arab Americans feel that we have no real leadership on which we can rely. Nobody genuinely speaks our concerns in the media, and nobody has adequate power to protect us from FBI investigations should our names become suspicious to American officials. Arab Americans, and many others, are under the impression that speaking too loudly against the war on terror or American support for Israel is a viable cause for suspicion. In addition, Arab Americans cannot discuss on campus the conditions of Palestinian life in the Occupied Territories without harassment, complaints of anti-Americanism, or, worse, accusations of anti-Semitism. . . .

"The American Way of Life"

Some years back, I published a column in the *Palestine Chronicle* urging Arab Americans to reformulate a self-image by rejecting the vocabulary of *terrorism* employed so uncritically in today's United States. My columns for the paper usually elicited passionate reactions, but this one provoked outright anger from a few American readers whose vocabulary I had attacked. One reader demanded to know why I "split time between the United States and the Middle East," as my author bio explained. The message claimed that discomfiting motivations were evident in my article: "Apparently your dislike for the American way of life and the [policy of the] current administration to keep it that way, even if it means war, is a problem for you."

This formulation in many ways accurately highlights the relationship between Arab Americans and the larger society in which we live. Often accused of dual sympathies, Arab Americans feel sometimes as if we are removed (of our own accord) from the Arab world but equally removed (not of our own accord) from the United States. Xenophobia certainly plays a role in the isolation many Arab Americans feel, but it would be foolish to limit our analysis to either xenophobia or racism. While the respondent to my article is most likely xenophobic and perhaps racist—Would she have objected had I split time between the United States and, say, Britain?—her sensibilities can be attributed to a more profound phenomenon dating to the settlement of the New World.

I speak about a particular type of discourse that, with technical and temporal variations, has existed continuously in the United States, which I term *imperative patriotism*. Imperative patriotism assumes (or demands) that dissent in matters of governance and foreign affairs is unpatriotic and therefore unsavory. It is drawn from a long-standing sensibility that nonconformity to whatever at the time is considered to be "the national interest" is unpatriotic. Imperative patriotism is most likely to arise in settler societies, which usually need to create a juridical mentality that professes some sort of divine mandate to legitimize their presence on Indigenous land. The juridical mentality impresses conformity on the settlers, who might otherwise demur when being asked to slaughter Indigenes or when absorbing attacks by them. Hilton Obenzinger demonstrates that this mentality existed in early America, where settlers "invested New England settlement, and by extension all of America, with a sense of religious destiny: that the new society extinguishing the various indigenous peoples' claims to land and independence was a re-creation of the scriptural narrative of covenantal, chosen-people identity" (1999, 24).

This sensibility has evolved into a detectable feature of modern American politics. When one hears George W. Bush present war on Iraq as a "war for civilization" and make statements such as "either you are for us or against us" and "God is on America's side," it becomes clear that the early settler ethos, in which the settlers had a divine mission conferred upon them, continues to influence American discourse—and, more important, American morality. Imperative patriotism arises in this context. I prefer the phrase *imperative patriotism* to the unmodified *patriotism* because the word *imperative* insinuates necessity and purpose. It further denotes a particular set of American desires (enumerated below) that connects to a historical dynamic. In modern America, while imperative patriotism functions at the levels of discourse and philosophy, it generates its strength most consistently at the level of morality. Imperative patriotism manifests itself most explicitly during wartime or domestic unrest. Ethnic nationalist movements, such as the American Indian Movement and Black Panthers, were widely considered to be inimical to American values and therefore also caused the manifestation of imperative patriotism. (Even movements using less-nationalist rhetoric, such as the SCLC [Southern Christian Leadership Conference] and Cesar Chavez's United Farm Workers, evoked fear in many Americans.) Moreover, imperative patriotism both informs and is derived from colonial discourse. Politicians frequently speak about the need to occupy Arab countries and "civilize" them by introducing the natives to "democracy." (Like the colonial discourse before it, this one rarely mentions the actual motivation for intervention: the plunder of resources, in this case oil.) Americans today hear so much about the need for their government's "leadership" in all areas of the world that most, like the Europeans before them, automatically equate colonization with generosity and moral strength.

Yet perhaps the most crucial (and discomfiting) feature of imperative patriotism is its relationship with xenophobia. While imperative patriotism has a symbiotic moral association with colonial discourse, it is more disconnected from xenophobia because it does not actually arise from xenophobia, which is a phenomenon that, to a degree, has its roots in European contact with Indians but more traditionally has resulted from animosity over (perceived or real) economic disparity. On one level, xenophobia is a less vicious form of colonial discourse, but it more often results from a certain type of fear that is generated when people feel that their economic stability (or the possibility of it) is threatened—as, for instance, when laborers battle with immigrants over blue-collar jobs or when middle- to upper-class whites complain to city councils about immigrants moving into their neighborhoods. Imperative patriotism, however, tends to inform xenophobia, a fact that is expressed in statements such as "If you don't like America, go back to where you came from"; "If you don't agree with the United States, why don't you just leave?"; and "A real American works hard and doesn't complain." These statements insinuate that "American" is a stable, fixed identity rooted in a physical and cultural whiteness for which many immigrants do not qualify. They also indicate that in xenophobia narrow political suppositions often govern social behavior: to dissent from the imagined mores of America is to forfeit identification as American. Leaving the United States then becomes the only logical option.

It is easy to see how these suppositions are played out in the reader's complaint that I "dislike the American way of life." The reader assumes that only one or a few forms of thought and/or behavior constitute "the American way of life." This sensibility has long been common in the United States and has proliferated since 9/11, in no small part because of the colonial discourse arising from hawks in Washington. And yet it would be reductionist to attribute the sensibility to a crude xenophobia informed by imperative patriotism. It is better conceptualized as an articulation of imperative patriotism that appears at first glance to be crude xenophobia, but in reality brings to mind remnants of settler discourse with its rigid juridical undercurrents. One might argue that it is impossible to define "the American way of life" since the United States is a multicultural society with thousands of subcultures (not to mention the fact that numerous Central and South Americans also consider themselves to be "American"). Nevertheless, at the popular level, it is assumed that a "true" American is (or should be) patriotic and capitalistic and, less explicitly, Christian and white.

Arab Americans exist as a composite of postmodern Americana and American subculture in this complex of issues. To various degrees, our positioning in the United States has been highly complex for some time, but 9/11 exacerbated the complexities by simultaneously endowing the community with sympathetic gestures and amplifying xenophobic outpourings of imperative patriotism, a mindset that is by its very nature antithetical to the Arab American experience. The irony of this positioning became evident when a church in Jacksonville, which has a sizeable Arab American population, posted a sign claiming that Mohammad condoned murder. While Arab Americans protested this stereotype, it was another Christian conservative, radio columnist Andy Martin of Florida, who offered the most vocal response: "I thought we were past that kind of bigotry and ignorance in Florida. But apparently not. . . . Any religious leader who fosters bigotry is not a religious leader; he or she is espousing evil." . . .

. . . If ethnic cleansing and slavery, among other odious practices, played a salient role in the physical and psychological formation of the United States, then it should be no surprise that various types of racism survive. Indeed, one could claim that the United States has a collective sickness that results from never having officially confronted its destruction of Indian nations and that this sickness accounts, however abstractly, for many persisting social problems (imperative patriotism, xenophobia, racism, sexism, discrimination). Rather than arguing whether various types of racism exist, we are better served interrogating the actual extent of their existence.

Arab Americans are in a special position to assist in that understanding. First of all, I would argue that the Jacksonville discourse is racist precisely because it cannot be decontextualized from (admittedly more noxious) incidents in the American past. When considering this sort of argument, our analytical framework should include the peculiar amalgam of premillennialism, Messianism, and extremism that marked European settlement of the New World, particularly in New England. Modern American racism developed as a result of the imagery of Indians and Africans promulgated by white settlers—a process that continues into the present—in addition to foreign intervention and biological determinism. Indeed, the covenantal Messianism with which early American settlers invested their identity invents and reinvents itself based on deeply encoded notions of racial superiority. Those notions have been modernized, sometimes disguised as pragmatism, and manage to pervade a surprisingly large portion of mainstream American discourse. The label of *racism* can thus be applied to anti-Arab vitriol independent of the severe dehumanization that occurs by construing a religious group's prophet as a murderer. If, after all, Mohammad is portrayed as subhuman, what does it imply about those who follow his religion?

Obviously, Arab Americans interact with the dominant American culture based on the specifics of Arab immigration and the subsequent development of the Arab American community. But once Arabs formed a distinct communal identity, as do all American ethnic minorities, we inherited a centuries-old history of ethnic–mainstream conflict that has yet to be assessed in detail, either before or after 9/11. Settlement, dispossession, slavery, and overseas imperialism—all are included in that inheritance. The overseas imperialism has traditionally been most resonant in the Arab American community and is the centerpiece of the community's current reorganization. Like most other minorities, Arab Americans "piggyback" the ethnic tensions that were developed uniquely in the United States based primarily on the oppression of Blacks and Indians. Imperialism, however, is the most immediate issue facing Arab Americans since much of the imperialism is directed at the Arab world (especially if we consider, as I do, Israel's occupation of the West Bank and Gaza Strip to be an aspect of American imperialism).

Based on this formulation, I reject the notion that anti-Arab racism was formed and has evolved based solely on social features (primarily geopolitics) detectable in the interaction of Arabism and Americana. We are better served looking at that racism as being on a continuum with America's roots in settler colonialism. A correlative settler colonialism in the West Bank, after all, accounts for much of the tension among the United States and Arab nations—and, by extension, Arab Americans. American racism had thrived for years before the first Arab arrived in North America; Arab Americans have faced an evolution of that racism since we began to vocally articulate a Middle Eastern identity after 1967 (which rehashed some of the tensions developed between the Founding Fathers and Muslim pirates off the Barbary Coast two hundred years earlier). It is not necessarily a modern racism, but one that has been perpetually reformulated based on contemporary popular and political sentiment and a failure by American leaders to adequately confront the past, in philosophy by apologizing and erecting monuments or in practice by eliminating colonization and dispossession in other parts of the world.

Thus, 9/11, according to this analysis, did not really disrupt anti-Arab racism in any momentous way. Rather, it polarized attitudes that had been in place years before the word *terrorism* entered common parlance. . . .

Unreasonable and Pragmatic

. . . Post-9/11 racism . . . is not limited to politicians' blunders or marginal and/or jingoistic publications. It made its way, for instance, into what first appeared to be an evenhanded analysis of the Israeli–Palestinian conflict on the op-ed page of the *Washington Post* by former editor Stephen S. Rosenfeld. Displaying a remarkable, if unconscious, propensity for turn-of-the-century anthropological essentialism, Rosenfeld attacks what he dubs "the Palestinians' killing wing" by explaining, "The Palestinians' truest weapon is their high birthrate. It emits a seemingly unstoppable flow of adolescents trained in murder" (2003). Rosenfeld's statement is at base no different than that offered in 2002 by prominent writer Daniel Pipes: "In the most elemental terms, we see here [on college campuses] the contrast between the civilized nature of Israel and its friends and the raw barbarism of Israel's enemies" (2002). It is worth noting that Pipes, whose moral apparatus exemplifies the very worst facets of imperative patriotism, was generally dismissed as a zealot until 9/11, after which he became popular among media in search of sensationalistic evidence of Islamic aggression or "fifth-column" Arab Americans. (The "fifth-column" charge can be found all over Pipes's website, submitted by enraged readers who deplore the sensibilities of Arab and Arab American scholars.) In fact, Pipes, along with Stanley Kurtz, Martin Kramer, Steve Emerson, and Bill Kristol as well as a litany of fundamentalist Protestant leaders, exemplifies the stereotypical discourse inherent in the post-9/11 backlash against Arab Americans.

About Pipes, Ian Lustick observes that he "takes views that no responsible academic would ever articulate. He's so far outside the pale of mainstream scholarship, yet the [American news] networks need people to give this view because it's a popular view. A reasonable position they can get anywhere. What they're looking for is an unreasonable position" (quoted in Brook 2002). We can add to Lustick's analysis. What he calls an "unreasonable position" is, after 9/11, perfectly reasonable according to the pragmatism of a political culture that suddenly found in Arab Americans an excuse to increase federal interference in civilian privacy by inducing fear and then working to reduce that fear through what are justified as practical means—for example, ethnic profiling, surveillance, citizen spying, detention—things that have occurred recurrently throughout modern American history (with, most prominently, the American Indian Movement and Black Panthers). And all these means are, of course, purportedly used with great regret in order to preserve the impossibly abstract but highly compelling "American way of life" (a phrase Pipes and similar writers use incessantly). I would replace Lustick's use of the word *unreasonable* with *pragmatic*. Imperative patriotism relies on a perceived pragmatism in order to command moral legitimacy. Today, the most conspicuous feature of the pragmatism is the word *terrorism*, which is used uncritically to describe anybody (of the requisite Arab background) who contests either domestic or international American hegemony. A set of common assumptions must exist between speaker and audience when *terrorism* is employed without analysis or qualification. Those assumptions, based on the notion that terrorism is a morally repugnant and inexplicable act exclusive to the East, survive only in the framework of a corresponding assumption, that Arabs are inferior in culture and intellect to Americans (read: whites). . . .

. . . Much of the tension I have explored exists because of a specific vocabulary directed at Arab Americans. The vocabulary becomes particularly troublesome when it is used to explain Arab culture or, more causally, Arab "behavior" to a curious public. This is where anti-Arab racists, posing as responsible analysts, poison American–Arab American relations. When scholars and commentators denounce Arabs and Arab Americans as "terrorists" and threats to "American national security" and "the American way of life," to borrow from Campus Watch parlance, a profound defensiveness arises in the Arab American community. That defensiveness, coupled with a long-standing ambivalence about an identity that traverses the Atlantic, reinforces the inability of Arab Americans to fruitfully navigate the metaphorical spaces between center and margin in the United States. . . .

Arab Americans and Ethnic Studies

. . . Since what has been called decolonization of the mind is so central to the pedagogy of ethnic studies, Arab American concerns reach beyond the Arab American community. Yet the extensive reach of those concerns will not be acknowledged by chance. Arab Americans must force their recognition. Ethnic studies scholars, for their part, can find critical intersections of race, culture, and representation in the Arab American community. Minority scholarship has illustrated in the past twenty years that issues within different ethnic groups are never mutually exclusive, nor are the respective scholarly apparatuses in place to address those issues. If ethnic studies scholars are concerned with community activism in addition to professional work, then America's rapidly changing social dynamics after 9/11 are ripe for assessment with priority on response, especially if we manage to transform "the American way of life" into "American ways of life." It is not by accident that I see ethnic studies as a possible solution to the difference and the pragmatic strength of imperative patriotism because if there are no solutions to be found in the field, then the field will have failed in its stated mission.

Works Cited

Brook, Daniel. 2002. "Pipes' Dreams." *Philadelphia City Paper*, July 18. At http://www.danielpipes.org/434/pipes-dreams.

Obenzinger, Hilton. 1999. *American Palestine*. Princeton, NJ: Princeton Univ. Press.

Pipes, Daniel. 2002. "The War on Campus." *New York Post*, Sept. 17. At https://www.meforum.org/campus-watch/7859/the-war-on-campus.

Rosenfeld, Stephen S. 2003. "Beyond Slogans." *Washington Post*, Feb. 18. At https://www.washingtonpost.com/archive/opinions/2003/02/18/beyond-slogans/eca54a2b-9f79-4c38-b02f-b9a3afd832fd/.

17

The Limits of Muslim Cool

SU'AD ABDUL KHABEER

After settling into my economy-class seat for the long-haul flight to London in April 2014, I opened up my iPad to peruse, with a fair bit of chagrin, a recently released 104-page US Department of State digital publication entitled *American Muslims* (2014). The design quality of the color- and photo-filled report was impressive. Beyond its design, one of the first things that struck me about the report was how it represented the racial and ethnic diversity of US American Muslim communities. Specifically, the booklet included US Black Muslim narratives. This jumped out at me from the photos used, including one of Ibtihaj Muhammad, a member of the US national fencing team, to the individuals profiled, such as magazine editor Tayyibah Taylor. Likewise, a US Black American, the Harvard-trained historian Precious Muhammad, had penned one of the reflective autobiographical articles in the publication. Although she was the sole Black Muslim who had written for the booklet (and whose other publications were cited in the "Want to Know More?" reference section), this remains a significant inclusion that stands in stark contrast to the many ways in which Blackness is marginalized or rendered invisible in US Muslim communities and the broader US discourse about Muslims.

Another remarkable characteristic of the report—and this was the source of my chagrin—was that it explicitly highlighted Chicago and indirectly appropriated Muslim Cool. While the organizations and individuals profiled in the report came from across the United States, Chicago was the only city that was specifically highlighted as a symbol of American exceptionalism. For example, echoing the celebration of the United States as a multicultural nation, the report quoted a local Chicago Muslim leader heralding the city: "There is no other place where Muslims from different parts of the world have established one community with so much diversity" (US Department of State 2014, 38).[1] The booklet and the four short videos that accompanied it online (US Department of State 2014) also prominently feature IMAN [Inner-City Muslima Action Network], IMAN's executive director Dr. Rami Nashashibi, and Muslim hip hop artists, citing their contributions to US American society as symbols of successful Muslim integration in the multicultural fabric of the United States. In this report, then, the figures, institutions, and movements that I had identified as the vanguard of Muslim Cool—because they engage Blackness to offer a counternarrative to hegemonies that produce unequal power relations—were strategically deployed to reinforce the hegemonic power of the state.

This booklet was not designed for domestic consumption but for US embassies abroad, yet I first found out about it through postings on my Facebook timeline. Friends and colleagues, some of whom contributed to the publication, were celebrating the report as a symbol of inclusion and recognition by the US government. The

Excerpt from Su'ad Abdul Khabeer, *Muslim Cool: Race, Religion, and Hip Hop in the United States* (New York: New York Univ. Press, 2016), 178–218. A works cited list was added at the end of the chapter. Reprinted with corrections and press style changes for consistency throughout the volume by permission of New York University Press. The author's full set of footnotes may be located in the original source.

1. This narrative of Chicago began with immigration and ended with immigration, with only a casual reference to native-born converts and without any mention of the Nation of Islam. It thus differs from Muslim Cool's and IMAN's narrative of Islam in Chicago.

fortuitous timing of my reading of the report, on the eve of my UK trip, and its explicit and subtle references to my field sites and to Muslim Cool, gave fresh urgency to the questions that had led me to the United Kingdom. I was on my way to follow a multicity tour of US American artists, six of whom were Muslim, which was sponsored by the US embassy in the United Kingdom. I decided to follow these US American Muslim artists to a different context, that of the United Kingdom, in order to explore how Muslim Cool travels beyond the United States. My interest in the circulation of Muslim Cool outside the United States was sparked by my interactions with non-US Muslim artists who performed and participated in IMAN's arts and culture work while I was in the field. I found that although they were from different contexts, including the United Kingdom, they were still doing Muslim Cool; their identities as Muslims were being forged through the loop of hip hop, Islam, and Blackness.

I also met the US American artists on tour in the United Kingdom through my relationship with IMAN. Each of these artists had an individual music career, but they were on tour as members of the FEW [Fifth Element Warriors] Collective, a group of artists that had expanded in membership since the 2007 ISNA [Islamic Society of North America] convention [mentioned earlier]. These artists were politically conscious and had multiple motivations for participating in the tour—none of which was to endorse US foreign policies. The tour was an opportunity to do a gig, to expand their international audiences, and to connect with like-minded artists and activists in the United Kingdom. These were not the first US Muslims to participate in what scholars and the state call "hip hop diplomacy." The State Department's hip hop ambassador program began in 2005 with a non-Muslim US Black American female activist, Toni Blackman. But over the years these tours have taken US Muslim hip hop artists, predominantly US Black men, to a number of Muslim-majority locations such as Turkey, Morocco, Indonesia, Pakistan, and the Occupied Territories. Twenty-first-century hip hop diplomacy reenacts the jazz diplomacy of the Cold War era. At that time the US State Department deployed jazz artists as part of a cultural offensive against the Soviet Union. "Jazz ambassadors," particularly US Black American artists, were used to counter the perception that the United States was a racist nation, a perception the Soviets attempted to use to their advantage (Von Eschen 2004). In the post–civil rights and post-9/11 era, hip hop has similarly served as a tool of the broader agenda of cultural diplomacy. It has been deployed by the state to manage the US profile abroad but also to manage young Muslims who are perceived as potential terrorists (Aidi 2014, 225). Critically, in this management of an imperial relationship with the "Muslim world," US Muslims have become a strategic asset for the state's efforts to "reform" Islam outside the United States.

This chapter [of *Muslim Cool*], through a look at IMAN and the Muslim hip hop tours, examines Muslim Cool's relationship to the state on two scales—the domestic and the global. It also looks at this relationship temporally; specifically, I question how this post–civil rights and post-9/11 moment creates the possibility for Muslim Cool to tell a counternarrative to anti-Black racial and religious hegemonies while simultaneously telling the hegemonic narrative of the state. As Stuart Hall (1998) insightfully notes, popular cultural forms are always in a tactical relationship with power. Thus, the utility in investigating the possible limits of Muslim Cool lies not in declaring Muslim Cool, IMAN, or this cadre of US American Muslim artists complicit with the state—which would divert attention away from the real holders of power. Rather, it lies in charting the context that engenders the limits of Muslim Cool's alterity.

I illustrate how Muslim Cool's claim to alterity hits a stumbling block, a wall, or a tension in its encounters with the state. The state, [along with] the power it enacts, is not contained by the various arms of the US government but rather is a "complex formation" (Hall 1996, 429) that "has no institutional fixity" (Trouillot 2001, 126). Importantly, the state's lack of "fixedness" is not a weakness but the source of its power. Examining Gramsci's formulation as it relates to the modern state, Hall argues that the hegemony of the liberal democratic state is "sustained, not exclusively through the enforced instrumentality of the state [i.e., force and coercion], but, rather, it is grounded in the relations and institutions of civil society" (Hall 1996, 428).

Gramsci's formulation also insists on the recognition that hegemony is "historically specific" (Hall 1996, 424).

This is important because the US hegemony that Muslim Cool must contend with is post–civil rights and post-9/11. This periodization is critical because it is a marker of how regimes of surveillance and multiculturalism coexist and complement claims of US exceptionalism, and these are claims made through the incorporation of dissent. Institutions of civil society, nonprofits such as IMAN, are incorporated within the state's technologies of governmentality (Kwon 2013). Likewise, the symbols and signs of marginalized groups such as US Black Americans are incorporated to authenticate the "legitimacy and social completeness" of the United States (Greenhouse 2005, 359). At this historically specific moment, US American Muslims are deployed as a "critical component of the late American empire's cultural repertoire" (Aidi 2014, 257). They symbolize the success of US multicultural inclusion and are evidence of the fitness of the United States as the dominant global power.

In the first half of this chapter I address the limits of Muslim Cool within the United States. I look at the construction of Muslim Cool as an alternative and as resistance through the deployment of the Black radical tradition in the arts activism of IMAN. I show that because of the paradox of the post–civil rights era, IMAN's connection to the Black radical tradition is in tension with IMAN's status as a nonprofit and with its commitment to a rights-based discourse of critical engagement, which results in an alignment with state objectives of subjectification—the cultivation of citizens as subjects who reproduce the state's hegemonic power. In the second part of the chapter, I chart the contested context of US American Muslim participation in cultural diplomacy. I argue that the political realities of the post–civil rights and post-9/11 United States cut a hard bargain to belong for US American Muslims.

The Black Radical Genealogy of the Muslim Hip Hop Generation

On a yellow notepad I quickly jotted down some notes on Imam Talib's [Imam al-Hajj Talib Abdur Rashid] talk "Artists of the Hip Hop Generation and Liberation." I was still working at IMAN at this time, and Imam Talib was at the IMAN office for an "artists' brunch." The brunch had been designed by Nashashibi as an intimate conversation between Imam Talib and a select group of about fifteen young Muslims, including Man-O-Wax, Tasleem, and Tyesha. These artists had been invited to the brunch because of their long-standing relationship to IMAN's work and to the Muslim hip hop scenes in Chicago and beyond. For Nashashibi, closeness between scholars such as Imam Talib, artists such as Tasleem, and activists such as himself was the bedrock of IMAN's work. Yet he was not the only one invested in building these relationships. Imam Talib had been working since the 1990s to instruct and support musicians and performers who had converted to Islam and who, as Imam Talib explained, were seeking spiritual balance while working within an industry that was hostile to the moral code they struggled to live by. For the artists in the IMAN conference room that morning, the talk was like a port in a storm, a refuge from the kind of policing described earlier.

The central focus of Imam Talib's presentation was the hip hop generation. He drew on religious and secular texts to impress upon us that we were part of a generation—the hip hop generation—and had to be attentive to the opportunities and responsibilities that came with our generational location. Specifically, he cited the Qur'anic verse 2:141 (trans. M. Asad 2012): "Now those people who have passed away: unto them shall be accounted what they have earned; and unto you, what you have earned; and you will not be judged on the strength of what they did." He amplified the point by referencing Frantz Fanon: "Each generation must, out of relative obscurity, discover its mission, fulfill it or betray it" (Fanon 2004, 206).

During his lecture Imam Talib suggested that the hip hop generation should take its cues from earlier generations, such as the Salaf as-Salih and Black Power activists. The term "Salaf as-Salih," "the pious predecessors," is used by Muslims to denote the first three generations of Muslims—those who were companions of the Prophet Muhammad and the two generations that followed, all of whom are widely revered in Sunni Muslim tradition. Linking the Salaf to the hip hop generation, Imam Talib highlighted the role of the arts and artists among the Salaf: "The Rasul [Prophet] recited poetry at [the battle of] Uhud to lift the spirits of the troops. . . . Prophet Muhammad loved the poetry of Umayyah Ibn Abi as-Salt and Ka'b Ibn Malik and Hasan Ibn Thabit, whose skills were so sublime the Prophet had another *minbar* [pulpit] built for him." Likewise, Imam Talib linked the hip hop generation to the Black Power movement through the arts, specifically citing the poetry ensemble the Last Poets, established in the late 1960s, and the role it played as part of the Black Arts Movement.

His lecture was emphatic in its claim that artists play a critical role in the struggle against injustice. This role, Imam Talib argued, is described in the Qur'an (22:78, trans. M. Asad 2012): "And strive hard in God's cause with all the striving that is due to Him: It is He who has elected you [to carry his message], and has laid no hardship on you in [anything that pertains to] religion, [and made you follow] the creed of your forefather Abraham." Drawing on this verse and the model provided by the earlier generations of artist-activists, Imam Talib contended that the hip hop generation had a specific and momentous role to fulfill. He maintained that Muslim hip hop artists are a part of a historical "continuum . . . back through African American history, back to West Africa, back to the Prophet. There is no reason whatsoever why the young Muslim artists of this day and time, like their ancestors, the Last Poets, and like their ancestors, the Griots of Muslim West Africa, there is no reason why they should not be doing the same exact thing."

Imam Talib asserted that Muslim hip hop practice is genealogically linked to Muslim tradition because it participates in a history of Muslim artistic production as the work of liberation—*art as activism*. This genealogy of art as activism locates the Muslim hip hop generation within multiple lines of descent: as descendants of the transnational and transhistorical Islamic tradition by way of the Salaf but also as descendants of the African diaspora by way of the West African Griots and as inheritors of the Black radical tradition by way of the Last Poets. Imam Talib claimed this genealogy for Muslim hip hop artists irrespective of their contemporary racialized position. However, beyond the multiethnic Salaf, his genealogical narrative privileges Muslim arts rooted in Africa and the African diaspora. . . .

The paradox of the post–civil rights era is rooted primarily in the era's concurrent gains and losses in racial equality. As [Bakari] Kitwana argues, the hip hop generation is the beneficiary of the legal successes of the civil rights movement: "voting rights, affirmative action, rise of black elected officials," and the limited expansion of economic opportunity that has led to the growth of a small Black economic elite (2002, 147–48). This is an elite that comprises, among others, Black American entertainers and athletes whose success is a hallmark of what Cornel West has termed the "AfroAmericanization of White youth": a process through which styles originated by Black American youth "have become disproportionately influential in shaping popular culture" (West 1994, 10). I understand this AfroAmericanization as the instrumentalization of Blackness, described earlier, which extends the historic love and theft of Blackness (Lott 2013) into the twenty-first century so that Blackness becomes, once again, a globally traded commodity as a piece of Americana. Yet these signs of "progress" parallel, and often obscure, continued racial discrimination in the form of disparities in health, housing, education, and employment, punitive laws and policing practices that target Black and Latin@ youth, astronomical rates of Black and Latin@ incarceration (despite a general downward trend in crime rates), and the broader criminalization of Black youth in the popular imagination of the United States.

This paradox shapes hip hop activism in two specific ways. As a post–civil rights generation, the hip hop generation is unable to accept fully the easy binary of resistance and co-optation that defined the civil rights era (Kitwana 2002).[2] At the same time, hip hop activism is evaluated on the basis of the success—material, imagined, and commodified—of the civil rights and Black Power–era activists (Clay 2012). Hip hop activism, then, is located amid the tensions between the desire for a deeply equitable world, different levels of entanglement with the current political, economic, and social world orders, and nostalgia for a populist radicalism. This holds true for IMAN as it does for the broader hip hop generation; for them, the civil rights–Black Power era, particularly Black Power activism, is central to the engagement of art as activism.

2. I use the term "civil rights era" to refer to the period from the 1950s through the 1970s, not the activism specific to the civil rights movement.

Muslim Arts Activism and the Black Arts Movement

I see the role of the arts at IMAN and in the work of the Muslim hip hop artists I met in the field as a partial extension of the Black Arts Movement, the cultural arm of the Black Power movement. . . . The Black Power movement denotes the activists and organizations that emerged after the assassination of Malcolm X and whose "collective thrust . . . toward racial pride, strength and self-definition" positioned them as his heirs (Van Deburg 1993, 2). The Black Power movement is often presented as the counterpoint to the civil rights movement. Whereas the civil rights leadership advocated nonviolence, Black Power activists trained for self-defense; whereas civil rights tactics were often mired in respectability politics, Black Power activists took pride in vernacular and Afrocentric aesthetics; and while the civil rights movement demanded rights as citizens, Black Power activists organized for worldwide revolution (Van Deburg 1993).

The art of the Black Arts Movement, whether poetry, music, or literature, was oppositional at its core because it was explicitly designed to raise the consciousness of the masses by disrupting white-supremacist narratives about Black people–narratives circulating within as well as outside Black communities. This art was also generative: artists such as Amiri Baraka and Sonia Sanchez created new interpretations of the poetic form and articulated an aesthetic grounded in the US Black experience. The Black Arts Movement targeted "the cultural arena as the primary site of political action" and advocated "a cultural revolution in art and ideas" (Larry Neal, quoted in Ongiri 2009, 90–117). Like their Black Arts predecessors, my US American Muslim arts activist teachers also saw the arts as a critical field of contestation. The arts became a site where hip hop–generation Muslims could mount challenges to the interlocking hegemonies of white supremacy and of Arab and South Asian US American Muslims. Likewise, Man-O-Wax's Turntable *dhikr*, described earlier, and the Arabized graffiti that adorns the wall of IMAN's office are just two examples of how their art is also generative. These similarities showed me how Muslim Cool's alterity was constructed through the Black radical tradition.

To illustrate this dynamic I turn to two examples of IMAN's arts activism: Community Café (CC), a recurring performance event, and a summer program, Leaders of the New School (LONS). Community Café, which took place about every other month, was one of IMAN's signature events that showcased Muslim and/or socially conscious artists. Yet CC was always more than a pure performance event; it was designed to be a symbolically powerful space for making meaning and fostering unity among US Muslims—which is why all promotional materials for the event while I was in the field featured "unity" within the word "Community" in bold type. Crucially, this meaning and this unity were forged through symbolic uses of the Black radical tradition, exemplifying Muslim Cool's alterity.

. . . [T]he Black radical tradition was the centerpiece of a CC in celebration of Black history month. This CC was held in coordination with DePaul University at the university's Reskin Theater. The program for the CC featured a black-and-white collage of iconic images: a laughing Malcolm X and Martin Luther King Jr. at their first and only face-to-face meeting; Coretta Scott King speaking at an antiwar rally just weeks after her husband's assassination; a pensive Angela Davis in 1969; the classic H. Rap Brown donning black shades in 1967; an afroed Arthur Ashe holding his 1975 Wimbledon trophy; Chuck Berry posing for his 1959 single "Johnny B. Goode"; an early photo of Afrika Bambaataa throwing up the P-Funk sign; and MC Lyte in the early 1990s. Deploying Black US American icons for Black History Month has become so common that images like these are used in all corners from big business to the political Right in the United States. But whereas some corporations, pundits, and politicians use Black US American figures to reproduce their own economic and political power, I read the aim of this collage as one of alterity—evoking the Black radical tradition as resistance.

The collage linked the radical Black politics of figures such as Davis, Brown, and Malcolm X to Berry's musical genius, which stands as a counterpoint to histories that write Blackness out of rock and roll. The collage also featured Bambaataa and Lyte, who are hip hop pioneers—a status derived both from their musical consciousness raising and from their activist contributions to hip hop.

The inclusion of Bambaataa *and* Lyte departed from the tendency to represent hip hop as a male enterprise. It was also a visual representation of the hip hop generation's genealogical connection to the civil rights and Black Power activists through arts activism, which is key to the construction of Muslim Cool's alterity.

This construction of Muslim Cool as an alternative and as resistance also took place though the deployment of the Black radical tradition in the work of the artists who performed at the CC. These artists were often hip hop emcees and poets, known within Muslim circuits but also in underground and conscious hip hop circles. Over the years of my field research and beyond, the roster for Community Café included Amir Sulaiman, The Reminders, members of Jurassic 5, Cap D, MTeam, Brother Ali, Pop Master Fabel, and others. The lineups also included song and storytelling ensembles such as Three Generationz, who performed at the NYC CC, and the theater troupe Progress Theater, who performed at the Black History Month CC and also a year later at a CC honoring "Mothers of the Movement." These US American Muslim artists used their art as a form of activism. Their work is "consciousness raising" because they push their audiences to reconsider the dominant narratives of power. They challenge hegemonies in the footsteps of the Black Arts Movement.

For example, Amir Sulaiman, a spoken-word poet who came to prominence by appearing on Def Poetry Jam and performs frequently at CC and other IMAN events, always delivers work that is hard-hitting and boundary challenging—in both content and cadence. In verses that challenge the contemporary discourse that links acts of terrorism to Islam and Muslims, Sulaiman proclaims:

> From South Street to Central Road, we are shook in
> a trauma
> Of terrorism that precedes Al Qaeda and Osama
> Forget Bin Laden; Ben Franklin
> Enslaved my great-great-grandmamma, comma
> Great-great-grandfather, comma
> Indigenous nations of reservations, comma
> ([see] Sulaiman 2007 [in *Muslim Cool*'s discography]) . . .

. . . The use of the Black Arts Movement's consciousness-raising strategies was also central to IMAN's youth-development work while I was in the field. Participating in a national trend (Clay 2012) that uses hip hop and spoken-word poetry to empower and organize young people, this programming linked the arts and community organizing as a means of developing youth as leaders in their communities. At IMAN and some of its partner organizations on the Southwest Side, young people would discover and/or refine their writing and performance skills through freewriting workshops, paid writing internships, regularly scheduled open-mic events, and special events such as community forums in local schools. Most of these events took place in the neighborhood, but there were also times when my teachers were invited to suburban Muslim communities to perform at small youth-centered activities as well as large formal banquets.

Toward the end of my fieldwork I attended a few of the early group meetings of IMAN's then newly formed Leaders of the New School (LONS). LONS was a summer artist apprenticeship program that was designed to raise the consciousness of participants through a range of arts-based activities that "teach youth how ideology shapes" their lives and their neighborhoods (Clay 2012, 52). LONS was part of revamped youth-development programming at IMAN that focused on distinct levels of engagement, from drop-ins to the appointment of a youth member to IMAN's board of directors. These levels of progressive engagement were designed to keep youth involved in IMAN's work over a long trajectory. LONS brought together a group of mentors and young people who were interested in various artistic forms that aligned with the elements of hip hop: movement, vocal performance, music, and visual art. As an artist apprenticeship program, it connected youth with particular mentors based on their interests; thus, a young woman who was a poet and singer was mentored by two vocal-performance instructors, a poet and an emcee, both of whom had had formal theater training.

While giving youth the opportunity to explore their interests in the arts was a central organizing aspect of the program, LONS was about more than "just art." In line with the positive youth-development trend among nonprofits, LONS activities did promote youth self-expression, yet these activities were also geared toward getting young people to think collectively. Unity was repeatedly emphasized in the LONS sessions I attended, reflecting the implicit understanding of arts activism at IMAN as being in line with the Black radical tradition: consciousness raising for collective action. In this model, as in that of the Last Poets ensemble, it is not the singular artist who changes the world but rather the collective—which is not uniform but united like the fingers in a fist. . . .

Although LONS began toward the end of my time in Chicago, it stands as the culmination of IMAN's youth-focused programming that was being developed while I was in the field. The centrality of consciousness-raising art as a mobilizing precursor to collective action at IMAN is a marker of the imprint of the Black Arts Movement and illustrates how IMAN's arts activism—from its venues and publicity to its programs and performers—evoked the Black radical tradition. The claims made on the Black radical tradition by the Muslim hip hop generation, as exemplified by IMAN, do important discursive work—work that constitutes Muslim Cool as a counterpoint. However, IMAN's arts activism is only a partial extension of the Black Arts Movement and the Black radical tradition more broadly. Its partiality is rooted in a critical shift that defines the post–civil rights era: the domestication of racial politics in the United States.

Limiting Muslim Cool at Home

Looking back at my initial response to the State Department report I described at the beginning of this chapter, I should not have been too surprised to find IMAN featured in such a document. Its inclusion matches the narrative that has already been constructed around IMAN in mainstream media and some academic work—including, to a certain extent, this monograph. This storyline often centers on Rami Nashashibi's biography (much to his chagrin) and focuses primarily on IMAN's work with the arts, youth, and interfaith engagement in a way that positions the organization as a signpost of the coming of a "uniquely diverse, inclusive *American* Islam" (Warren 2010, emphasis mine). Critically, in this telling, the conditions of racial inequality that IMAN seeks to impact become just the backdrop to a triumphant American (Muslim) narrative.

Of course, for IMAN the conditions of racial inequality are not a backdrop but the organization's raison d'être. Yet, to be fair, this narrative of "the triumph to come" aligns in some ways with the story IMAN tells about itself. Nashashibi, who wrote an article on IMAN for the State Department publication, guides IMAN's work through the prism of what he calls "critical engagement" for US American Muslims (Nashashibi 2005). This theory of engagement is undergirded by the ever-present and urgent reality that Muslim claims to US belonging are contested. Nashashibi argues that in order to solidify their position as US Americans, US Muslims must engage the political process and the institutions of civil society, much as other historically marginalized groups have done and continue to do: "From 19th-century anti-slavery activists to 20th-century social reformers like Dorothy Day, Malcolm X and Martin Luther King, Jr., people of different faith communities have been at the center of such social activism. Today American Muslims are a growing part of this tradition" (in US Department of State 2014).

Two of the three references in Nashashibi's genealogy of faith-based activism are iconic leaders of the Black liberation struggle in the United States. This is reflective of his own thinking and the way IMAN's work and Muslim Cool more broadly are inspired by and seek to connect to Black freedom struggles. Nashashibi is, of course, a hip hop head, and so his nod to Malcolm X also reflects the esteemed position of Malcolm X and the Black radical tradition in hip hop and hip hop activism—an esteem that shapes Muslim Cool's alterity. During my time at IMAN it was clear that Martin Luther King Jr. was also a radical Black figure—IMAN's King marched through Chicago's Marquette Park to protest residential segregation and opposed the Vietnam War. Yet Nashashibi also includes the white female founder of the Catholic Worker Movement, Dorothy Day. This inclusion contests claims that US American Muslims do not belong to the nation by locating these Muslims within a multiracial and multifaith US American tradition of social activism. This is a move of conscious US American Muslim self-making that reflects not only the pressures of the exclusion of the post-9/11 context but the post–civil rights domestication of racial politics in the United States as well.

By the "domestication of racial politics" I am referring to the way the dominance of the rights-based discourse of the civil rights movement narrows the set of concerns of Blacks and other communities of color in the United States to the demand for full citizenship as *Americans*—a term that implies both the extension of the legal rights of citizenship but also affective modes of belonging as citizens. I consider this a narrowed set of concerns because claims to full citizenship by people of color in the United States require moving away from internationalist and transnational frameworks of belonging. This does not mean that communities of color give up their transnational attachments, but being legitimate citizens in the eyes of the state requires that move. In the specific case of the US Black American political imagination, domestication came by way of the explicit delinking of the domestic Black struggle from the anticolonial movements of the period by the civil rights establishment. This move, which Richard Iton calls "black realpolitik," meant that the civil rights establishment would fall into step with a vision of American exceptionalism as a concession for racial equality at home (Iton 2010).

The domestication of racial politics does not mean that marginalized racial communities no longer engage in forms of dissent. The concept of "cultural citizenship" as articulated by Renato Rosaldo (1994) is grounded in dissent—objecting to the institutionalized exclusion of Latin@ communities from the nation. Likewise, in her work on South Asian immigrant teenagers, Sunaina Maira defines "dissenting citizenship" as a form of cultural citizenship the basis of whose engagement with the state is "a critique of its [the state's] politics" (Maira 2009, 201). Yet as Maira illustrates, dissenting citizens are still seeking belonging *as citizens*. Thus, because citizenship is a site of subject making by citizens as well as by the state (Ong 1996), the post–civil rights era is defined by the ways in which this desire for belonging is taken up by the state, which co-opts dissent through its administration of dissent.

In her recent monograph *Uncivil Youth* (2013), Soo Ah Kwon traces how the expansion of the nonprofit sector in the late twentieth century has worked to limit the forms of political resistance available to racialized communities in the United States. Building on Hall's (1996) Gramscian analysis that state power is "grounded in the relations and institutions of civil society," Kwon argues that limits on political mobilization are not the result of violent state repression but of the incorporation of marginalized communities as a category of administration. Nonprofit organizations serve the state's administration through youth-development programming that "empowers" young people to self-actualize as individuals and future leaders of their communities, in the process becoming "ideal democratic subjects" (Kwon 2013, 58). Kwon notes that the growth of 501(c)(3)s is a consequence of civil rights–era mobilization and the concurrent rise of neoliberal governance as the dominant form of state power in the late twentieth-century United States. The nonprofitization of activism is a state objective under neoliberalism, enacting what Kwon terms an "affirmative governmentality that stresses neoliberal principles of self-responsibility and community governance" (Kwon 2013, 46). I do not call on Iton, Maira, and Kwon to make the point that the desire for citizenship, the work of nonprofits, and youth engagement are categorically "negative" but rather to critically consider what kinds of political possibilities are foreclosed to Muslim Cool by the post–civil rights commitment to a rights-based discourse and the cultivation of engaged citizens.

On the one hand, like most activist nonprofits whose work and perspective are explicitly concerned with the suffering of racialized communities, IMAN is at odds with the state, which upholds racial suffering. Yet, on the other hand, in a departure from the activist models of the Black radical tradition, IMAN is not in direct confrontation with the state. As a post-civil-rights-era nonprofit organization, IMAN has a much more complicated relationship to state power and governance. IMAN uses the critique of the Black radical tradition to shape the contours of the rhetoric of its dissent: how to levy a critique at the state, the importance of levying a critique at the state, and the necessity for US American Muslims to be critical. Yet the organization's theory of "critical engagement," which guides its work on the ground, turns more on the rights-based rhetoric of the civil rights movement.

Nashashibi articulates IMAN's work as critical engagement to set it apart from US American Muslims who engage with the broader US American society primarily through education and the marketplace but do not "analyze the intimate relationships they have with a broad set of political arrangements," on the one hand, and from US American Muslims who withdraw from broader US American society "as an articulation of deep Islamic principles or an expression of heightened piety . . . often couched in terms of renouncing or rejecting *dunya* [worldly affairs]," on the other hand (Nashashibi 2005, 2–4). By contrast, Nashashibi proposes for US American Muslims an engagement with the political process and with institutions of civil society that is critical of state power. For Nashashibi, this engagement is also attentive to the ways in which race and class position US American Muslims differently in relation to state power. Critical engagement is a form of dissenting cultural citizenship because at stake in Nashashibi's definition of engagement is the recognition of US American Muslims as *Americans*—which again implies both the extension of the legal rights of citizenship and affective modes of belonging as citizens.

IMAN's arts activism is an important part of a larger agenda for social change. Other projects include participation in rallies for immigration reform; Muslim legislative days at the Illinois state capitol and *iftar*s (Ramadan dinners) at the White House; reentry programs that provide jobs for formerly incarcerated Black Muslim men; a free health clinic for the underinsured; and working with Arab grocers to provide fresh-food options at local corner stores on the city's Southwest Side. All these projects come out of IMAN's commitment to critical engagement, which relies on a rights-based framework—IMAN dissents from the exclusion or the neglect of the rights of people of color as citizens—and accordingly responds through a series of programs that reflect the constraints of the post-civil-rights-era prioritization of one's status as a US citizen. This does not mean that IMAN as an organization or the individuals who participate in its work do not have visions of belonging beyond the state; but it means that the articulation of those linkages is often rendered secondary, if engaged in at all.

IMAN's relationship to state power and governance, which illustrates one of the limits of Muslim Cool, is not merely or even primarily about "where the funding comes from" but about how a commitment to social change through the expansion of the rights of a dissenting racialized citizenry can align with state objectives of subjectification. IMAN's arts activism, like all hip hop activism, is located within tensions between nostalgia for a populist radicalism, desires for a deeply equitable world, and uneasy alignments with the dominant political, economic, and social world orders. Again, I do not consider this a reflection of a desired compatibility with all forms of state power; IMAN consistently dissents from the state's practices of racialized inequality. But it does reflect the paradox of the post–civil rights era, a paradox that enables a neoliberal state hegemony—one that is itself flexible—to set limits on Muslim Cool both domestically and abroad.

Imperial Muslim Cool?

As stated earlier, the limits of Muslim Cool are born out of a context that is post–civil rights and post-9/11. The post–civil rights administration of dissent through the institutions of civil society is a technology of a broader, state-generated discourse of US multiculturalism. The narrative of US multiculturalism upholds the racial and ethnic diversity of the US population as the nation's most valuable asset. This asset is an achievement: the discourse configures the US Black American struggle to overcome slavery and Jim/Jane Crow as a testament to US American ideals and culture. Accordingly, multiculturalism, when deployed by the state, is a triumphant narrative of American exceptionalism.

However, in the lived experience of racial minorities, the state administration of dissent through the incorporation of Black freedom movements as quintessentially "American" is not a challenge to structural inequality. While the rhetoric of US multiculturalism allows for affective recognition as citizens, it does not displace the racial hierarchies that privilege the White Christian citizen but rather "remains appropriately hierarchal" (McAlister [2001] 2005, 259).

Parallel to the post–civil rights multicultural state is the post-9/11 surveillance state. Replicating the COINTELPRO [FBI Counter Intelligence Program] regime of the mid-twentieth century, the current domestic surveillance state legitimizes increased overt and covert monitoring of US citizens with reference to national security. . . . In a partial inversion of state multiculturalism in the United States, race is also central to the logic of the surveillance state. Racialization under regimes of surveillance determines who does not belong. As Junaid Rana has shown, the surveillance state "deploys the Muslim body as a concrete objective entity to control and regulate" (Rana 2011, 155). This marks the contemporary "racialization of Muslims," which scholars have noted in a post-9/11 shift of the designation "Muslim" from a religious to a racial category (Naber 2008; Rana 2011; Razack 2008; Volpp 2002). As a racial category, the "Muslim" is known through bodily and behavioral markers, such as "Middle Eastern looks," beards, and headscarves—markers that are signs of suspicion. . . . Accordingly, surveillance meets multiculturalism in what scholars refer to as the US government's support for "moderate Islam."

In her article "Secularism, Hermeneutics, and Empire: The Politics of Islamic Reformation," Saba Mahmood analyzes US government efforts to "foster what is now broadly called 'moderate Islam' as an antidote and prophylactic to fundamentalist interpretations of Islam" (Mahmood 2006, 331). Drawing on a broader intellectual critique of secularism's "unmarkedness" (T. Asad 2003), Mahmood argues that these efforts advance US hegemony through "secular normativity," which does not reject but rather reshapes religious subjectivity to fit US imperial aims (Mahmood 2006, 328). This religious subjectivity is that of the "autonomous individual believer [who] is a necessary protagonist in the plot of secular political rationality, one who owes his allegiance to the sovereign rule of the state rather than [to] the structures of traditional authority" (Mahmood 2006, 340). Importantly, Mahmood notes that some Muslims, too, seek the goals of this strategy as part of a "secular liberal Muslim agenda" (Mahmood 2006, 329).

Likewise, in his book *Rebel Music: Race, Empire, and the New Muslim Youth Culture*, political scientist Hisham Aidi (2014) traces the ways in which race, music, and diplomacy bring Muslims directly within Euro-American imperial agendas. He argues that music is "a key component of the Sufi counteroffensive" against the "Salafi" or "Islamist" articulations of Islam that, according to US and European policy makers, fuel so-called Islamic extremism (Aidi 2014, 75). . . . According to Aidi, this Sufi counteroffensive in the United Kingdom was openly backed by the United States and a host of prominent US scholars such as Hamza Yusuf, who, while not acting at the behest of the US government, preached messages of political and social integration that aligned with US interests. Music, including hip hop, also emerged as a part of the [UK] Prevent strategy ("Prevent Strategy" 2011). . . .

Muslim populations are geopolitically significant. Power over these populations enables access to significant natural resources and consumer markets, and control over these resources and markets is thus a key state objective for the United States. However, Muslims have their own objectives that may or may not align with those of the state—hence the need for the right input here and the right input there to reach the aggregate impact of US hegemony. This suggests that, as an effect of power, the low-impact cultural diplomacy strategy must be seen in the aggregate. Multiple low-impact events, small inputs, and each tidbit of information are pooled to spin a particular narrative of American exceptionalism in order to justify US empire. . . .

My focus on the state's administration of dissent is not meant to suggest that Muslim Cool consequently becomes devoid of all potential to resist state hegemony. Rather, I seek to elucidate the very real constraints on the forms of resistance used by a critical racial and religious minority. These constraints accommodate only a narrowed political vision and very particular political options, and divergence from these options is subject to the violence of the surveillance state. In a post-9/11 United States in which the term "radical" has become synonymous with "Muslim terrorist" and where even those US American Muslims who have chosen to cooperate with counterterrorism work are surveilled, what are the alternate choices for resistance and political vision? Indeed, while the hip hop generation is distinct from its civil rights and Black Power predecessors, the intensity of the state's repressive violence directed at Black Power activists—from the surveillance regime of COINTELPRO and its relationship to the assassination of Malcolm X to the police murders of youth activists such as Fred Hampton and of groups such as MOVE and to the ascendance of Assata Shakur to the top of the FBI's most-wanted list—seems to stand as a warning that should administration by civil society fail, state repressive violence will follow. This does not mean that Muslim Cool cannot find a way around the state, but it does mean that for it to do so, US American Muslim hip hop activists will continue to have to reconsider what it means to belong. *Pa'lante*!

Works Cited

Aidi, Hisham. 2014. *Rebel Music: Race, Empire, and the New Muslim Youth Culture*. New York: Vintage Books.

Asad, Muhammad, trans. 2012. *The Message of the Qur'an*. London: Book Foundation.

Asad, Talal. 2003. *Formations of the Secular: Christianity, Islam, Modernity*. Stanford, CA: Stanford Univ. Press.

Clay, Andreana. 2012. *The Hip-Hop Generation Fights Back: Youth, Activism, and Post–Civil Rights Politics*. New York: New York Univ. Press.

Fanon, Frantz. 2004. *The Wretched of the Earth*. Translated by Richard Philcox. Introductions by Jean-Paul Sartre and Homi K. Bhabha. New York: Grove Press. Orig. pub. in French in 1961.

Greenhouse, Carol J. 2005. "Hegemony and Hidden Transcripts: The Discursive Arts of Neoliberal Legitimation." *American Anthropologist* 107, no. 3: 356–68.

Hall, Stuart. 1996. "Gramsci's Relevance for the Study of Race and Ethnicity." In *Stuart Hall: Critical Dialogues in Cultural Studies*, edited by Kuan-Hsing Chen and David Morley, 411–41. New York: Routledge.

———. 1998. "What Is This 'Black' in Black Popular Culture?" In *Black Popular Culture*, edited by Gina Dent, 21–33. New York: New Press.

Iton, Richard. 2010. *In Search of the Black Fantastic: Politics and Popular Culture in the Post–Civil Rights Era*. Kindle ed. New York: Oxford Univ. Press.

Kitwana, Bakari. 2002. *The Hip Hop Generation: Young Blacks and the Crisis in African-American Culture*. New York: Basic Civitas Books.

Kwon, Soo Ah. 2013. *Uncivil Youth: Race, Activism, and Affirmative Governmentality*. Durham, NC: Duke Univ. Press.

Lott, Eric. 2013. *Love & Theft: Blackface Minstrelsy and the American Working Class*. New York: Oxford Univ. Press.

Mahmood, Saba. 2006. "Secularism, Hermeneutics, and Empire: The Politics of Islamic Reformation." *Public Culture* 18, no. 2: 323–47.

Maira, Sunaina. 2009. *Missing: Youth, Citizenship, and Empire after 9/11*. Durham, NC: Duke Univ. Press.

McAlister, Melani. [2001] 2005. *Epic Encounters: Culture, Media, and U.S. Interests in the Middle East since 1945*. Updated ed. with a post-9/11 chapter. Berkeley: Univ. of California Press.

Naber, Nadine. 2008. "'Look, Mohammed the Terrorist Is Coming!': Cultural Racism, Nation-Based Racism, and the Intersectionality of Oppressions after 9/11." In *Race and Arab Americans before and after 9/11: From Invisible Citizens to Visible Subjects*, edited by Amaney Jamal and Nadine Naber, 276–304. Syracuse, NY: Syracuse Univ. Press.

Nashashibi, Rami. 2005. "IMAN & Critical Engagement." Unpublished document. Photocopy.

Ong, Aihwa. 1996. "Cultural Citizenship as Subject-Making: Immigrants Negotiate Race and Cultural Boundaries in the United States." *Current Anthropology* 37, no. 5: 737–62.

Ongiri, Amy Abugo. 2009. *Spectacular Blackness: The Cultural Politics of the Black Power Movement and the Search for a Black Aesthetic*. Charlottesville: Univ. of Virginia Press.

"Prevent Strategy." 2011. Presented to Parliament by the Secretary of State for the Home Department by Command of Her Majesty. June. London.

Rana, Junaid. 2011. *Terrifying Muslims: Race and Labor in the South Asian Diaspora*. Durham, NC: Duke Univ. Press.

Razack, Sherene H. 2008. *Casting Out: The Eviction of Muslims from Western Law and Politics*. Toronto: Univ. of Toronto Press.

Rosaldo, Renato. 1994. "Cultural Citizenship in San Jose, California." *PoLAR* 17, no. 2: 57–63.

Trouillot, Michel-Rolph. 2001. "The Anthropology of the State in the Age of Globalization: Close Encounters of the Deceptive Kind." *Current Anthropology* 42, no. 1: 125–38.

US Department of State. 2014. *American Muslims*. Washington, DC: US Government Publication Office. At http://photos.state.gov.

Van Deburg, William L. 1993. *New Day in Babylon: The Black Power Movement and American Culture, 1965–1975*. Chicago: Univ. of Chicago Press.

Volpp, Leti. 2002. "The Citizen and the Terrorist." *UCLA Law Review* 49:1575–600.

Von Eschen, Penny M. 2004. *Satchmo Blows Up the World: Jazz Ambassadors Play the Cold War.* Cambridge, MA: Harvard Univ. Press.

Warren, James. 2010. "Using an Islamic View to Forge Connections." *New York Times*, Apr. 17. At www.nytimes.com.

West, Cornel. 2001. *Race Matters*. New York: Vintage Books.

18

The Racial Dilemma

ERIK LOVE

"Looking Muslim": The Middle Eastern American Racial Category

. . . It should go without saying that the world's 1.6 billion Muslims span the full range of human appearance. There is no way to *actually* "look Muslim." Nevertheless, race operates at the very core of Islamophobia. The process by which Islamophobia came to affect anyone who "looks Muslim" is an all-too-familiar process, one that has constantly roiled American life: the social construction of racial categories. Race is what links aspects of physical appearance (facial features, skin tone, attire, hair texture, etc.) to an ascribed social identity such as White, Black, or Asian. In America, as a fact of life, everyone gets ascribed with a racial identity. In today's America, "Muslim" or "Middle Eastern" is one of the most commonly ascribed racial categories. Most of the time, getting racially ascribed with this identity is quick and easy. But the violence in some Islamophobic hate crimes serves as a reminder that racial identification is not benign.

Somehow, Islamophobia remained largely under the radar until the 2000s. Despite decades of widespread, extremely damaging effects, Islamophobia did not attract a great deal of attention in America until recently. No doubt the new attention is due mainly to the unprecedented scale of the terrorist attacks of September 11, 2001, (or 9/11), which led to an extraordinary surge in Islamophobic hate crimes and discrimination. This led many analysts and scholars to conclude that a "new" wave of specifically anti-Muslim sentiment had appeared in the United States. A great many books and articles have described the challenges facing Muslim American communities and the specifically anti-Muslim components of "post-9/11" Islamophobia. But limiting the discussion of Islamophobia to the "post-9/11" era obscures the long history of racial discrimination affecting Arabs, Muslims, Sikhs, South Asians, and others in the United States.

This is because American Islamophobia developed in very much the same ways as all American social structures that involve race. As a form of racism, Islamophobia is built into American institutions. White supremacy and Islamophobia stem from the same root, and they both are burrowed into the foundations of American institutions. Therefore, any effective understanding of Islamophobia must take into account the full scope of American race and racism.

Drawing the connections between race and Islamophobia provides, among other insights, the only plausible explanation for why Christians, Sikhs, Hindus, and people of all faiths are vulnerable to Islamophobia. Moreover, shining a light on the intrinsically dehumanizing elements of racism enables an understanding of connections between hate crimes and discriminatory "counterterrorism" policies, both domestically in the United States and globally on the so-called battlefields of the "war on terror." All of these flow directly from the same source: Islamophobic racism. Seeing the links between them requires an understanding of how racism is embedded into American social institutions.

Excerpt from Erik Love, *Islamophobia and Racism in America* (New York: New York Univ. Press, 2017), selections from pp. 1–10. Reprinted with corrections and press style changes for consistency throughout the volume by permission of New York University Press.

The Race with No Name

To illustrate the difficult task of untangling the complex web that connects race and Islamophobia, consider that there is no name for the socially constructed racial category that has been used to collectively ascribe Arab, Muslim, Sikh, and South Asian Americans. This category is called by many names: "Muslim" or "Middle Eastern," or sometimes it is rendered with an acronym like "MENA" (Middle Eastern and North African). Even when there is acknowledgment that there is, in fact, a racial category here, it has been nearly impossible to find a generally accepted term for it, yet all the while it finds constant expression through everyday encounters and in structural Islamophobic discrimination.

Currently, the most common colloquialism for this racial category is probably "Muslim," but over the years the most popular term for this racial category has varied quite a bit. Thirty years ago, the term "Arab" referred to people from a broadly conceived Middle East, while at that time "Muslim" had a close association with Black American communities. That these terms have shifted is not at all unusual. The popular names for racial categories change all the time.

There are profound implications to recognizing that a single racial identity spans across Arabs, Muslims, Sikhs, and South Asians in America. Consider that when most Americans today use the term "Muslim" in conversation, they are probably not really talking about Muslims. Instead, they are calling up this long-standing racial category, one that haphazardly includes hundreds of ethnic groups containing both Muslims and non-Muslims. Because this particular racial term, "Muslim," also happens to connote a religion, it has the unfortunate confounding effect of ascribing both a religious and a racial identity to a seemingly indiscriminate collection of communities.

This is the awesome power, the terrible magic, and the ignoble wonder of race: to ignore diversity, to reject indigenous identity, and to promulgate its own version of history all at the same time. Apart from denying the heritage of so many people, numerous malicious stereotypes are closely associated with the socially constructed "Muslim" racial category. Most notably there is the bigoted assumption that "Muslims" are somehow predisposed to become "radicalized" terrorists. The racist and demonstrably false stereotype about terrorism and "Muslims" is so pervasive that openly asserting it has become a perfectly acceptable, mainstream opinion in the United States.

Defining the Middle Eastern Racial Category

Using the colloquial term "Muslim" to refer to the racial category is confusing, to say the least. Again, actual Muslim communities are extremely diverse and cannot be described as a singular, homogenous group. Therefore, the term "Muslim" will not suffice for an in-depth analysis in large part because it is not precise enough. At the same time, listing Arab, Muslim, Sikh, and South Asian Americans when referring to the racial category is cumbersome and still inaccurate because communities and individuals beyond those described even by that long list are swept into the racial category. Moreover, there is no other racial identity category commonly referred to by listing some of the various ethnic, religious, and panethnic groups swept under the umbrella of racial ascription. In short, the lack of a name for the racial category is a big problem.

Advocates have long struggled with this situation. Finding a widely agreed-upon identity term is often a crucial part of building an effective advocacy effort. For much of the latter half of the 1900s, the term "Arab American" was the preferred term for many advocates. It became a politically powerful identity category due to the successful organizing of advocates beginning in the mid-1900s. By the turn of the twenty-first century, however, "Arab American" had been largely (but not completely) replaced in mainstream discussions by the term "Muslim American."

Meanwhile, there have been several attempts by advocates to come up with a new, succinct collective term for the racial category, one that avoids singling out any group like "Arab" or "Muslim." Some have tried using the acronym AMEMSA (Arabs, Middle Easterners, Muslims, and South Asians). Others have promulgated a different acronym, SWANA (Southwest Asians and North Africans). Both of these have a certain pronounceable quality to them. Each provides a way to describe the various groups with ties to the vast geographical space across

North Africa and Southwest Asia, and SWANA does so without using the controversial term "Middle Eastern." These are noble efforts, but no other racial category is commonly referred to with an acronym. In any event, neither acronym has yet taken hold, and the term "Muslim" remains the most relevant one in common parlance in the mid-2010s. Every alternative to "Muslim" has significant drawbacks.

Despite these problems with it, here, I will use the term "Middle Eastern." Compare "Middle Eastern American" with "Asian American," which also denotes a racial category by making reference to a vast geographic region with unclear boundaries. I contend that saying "Middle Eastern American" evokes a racial image in exactly the same way, despite the lack of an accepted definition of "Middle Eastern."

To sum up, I join with a growing group of scholars who find that a Middle Eastern racial identity category exists in American culture. Like other socially constructed racial categories, it is unstable even as it firmly connects stereotypes and prejudices with physical appearances. It coexists with many overlapping social identities. As a result, perceptions of the Middle Eastern category depend on social context. Someone who "looks Middle Eastern" in one neighborhood might, for example, "look Latinx" in a different neighborhood. These contradictions and discontinuities do not nullify the existence of the racialized Middle Eastern category. On the contrary, these sorts of inconsistencies and illogical tensions always exist in the social construction of racial identity categories. These categories are necessarily arbitrary, volatile, and often bitterly contested by those they purport to describe. Yet racial identity categories are nonetheless quite real, and they retain a great deal of social power. Particularly in the area of counterterrorism policy, due to the racist stereotype that Middle Easterners are predisposed to commit acts of terrorism, there is a great deal of race-based discrimination built upon this racial category.

Confronting the Racial Dilemma

Strategically, does it benefit civil rights advocates to call out Islamophobia as racism? Or would it be wiser if they avoided the controversial issue of race? For example, they might instead describe Islamophobia as an infringement upon religious freedom or a violation of human rights, without bringing up race explicitly. On the other hand, using the language of race to link their efforts against Islamophobia to venerated, long-standing civil rights campaigns against racism might provide Middle Eastern American advocates with a powerful moral authority.

Civil rights advocates have always played a pivotal role in the development of American racial thinking. Now and in the decades ahead, Middle Eastern American civil rights advocates have a crucial role to play in determining how the nation deals with race and racism.

19

A Different Kind of Brown

Arabs and Middle Easterners as Anti-American Muslims

BRADLEY J. ZOPF

The steady growth and visibility of nonwhite/non-Black ethnoracial minority groups, especially Latina/os, Asians, and Arab/Middle Easterners, are redefining the racial landscape of the United States. Although we know that these "intermediate groups" (Bonilla-Silva 2015) defy straightforward racial classification, occupy different locations in the racial order, and are racialized through ethnicity, national origin, and/or religion, rather than strictly phenotype, we know less about how these groups experience racialization differently. In this research I examine how Egyptians articulate a sense of brown racialization that simultaneously homogenizes Latina/os, Asians (especially South Asians), and Arab/Middle Easterners as foreign and threatening yet distinguishes Arabs/Middle Easterners as anti-American terrorists on the basis of religion.

Although Arabs and Middle Easterners have not always been systematically included in mainstream scholarship on race, they represent an important case for examining the dynamic nature of race, the importance of religion to racialization, and the ongoing fluctuations in the US racial order (Cainkar 2009; Jamal 2008b; Naber 2008a). Officially classified as white but racialized as nonwhite, Arabs and Middle Easterners are in the unenviable position of being among the most "invisible of invisibles" (Gualtieri 2008, 149), existing in racially ambiguous space as neither fully white nor recognized as people of color (Cainkar 2009; Naber 2008a; Tehranian 2009). Despite relative invisibility in mainstream race scholarship, the literature on Arab and Middle Eastern racialization is extensive and generally finds that these groups are racialized as nonwhite; are targets of racial, ethnic, and religious prejudice; and are victims of interpersonal and institutional racial discrimination (Bakalian and Bozorgmehr 2009; Cainkar 2009; Garner and Selod 2015; Meer and Modood 2009; Rana 2011; Selod and Embrick 2013).

The racial formation of Arabs, Middle Easterners, and, increasingly, Muslims illustrates a complex interplay of race, ethnicity, national origin, religion, and US foreign policy that differs in historical timing and context from other racialized groups (Cainkar 2006, 2008). . . .

Interviews with [fifty-three] Egyptian and Egyptian Americans reveal complex racial narratives underscoring a racialization as brown, foreign, and threatening. The following sections . . . analyze how Egyptians describe and give meaning to their racialization as brown. Their racial narratives demonstrate racialization to be a layered process in which skin color operates as a first level of racialization homogenizing brown-skinned ethnoracial groups. Additionally, brown skin in combination with ethnic or national-origin differences result in a similar form of racialization among these groups that come to define them as neither citizens nor Americans. However, while shared skin color may result in a broad brown ethnoracial category that is viewed as neither white nor black as well as foreign, religion further distinguishes

Excerpt from Bradley J. Zopf, "A Different Kind of Brown: Arabs and Middle Easterners as Anti-American Muslims," *Sociology of Race and Ethnicity* 4, no. 2 (2017): 178–91. Reprinted with corrections and press style changes for consistency throughout the volume by permission of SAGE Publications, Inc.

Egyptians from these other groups, especially Latina/os and Asians. Egyptians articulate how race, ethnicity, national origin, and especially religion combine to demarcate Egyptians as a particular kind of brown: anti-American Muslim terrorists. . . .

Brown Racialization

Although Arab, Middle Eastern, and Muslim racialization "does not rely on phenotype alone" (Jamal 2008b, 318), Egyptians emphasize skin color and other phenotypic characteristics in the construction of a broad brown ethnoracial other. Sabrina says, "I think maybe sometimes there is a large brown racial category in the United States which is that in-between." Inez says, "There are brown people in the world. I'm Egyptian. I say brown because it's like the other. It's the not black and the not white." As neither white nor black, brown serves as a color-based language Egyptians use to situate themselves within hegemonic conceptualizations of race as skin color.

Many Egyptians evoked definitions of race that combined skin color and/or ancestry in complex ways. For example, Matthew says, "When I think of race . . . it marks, I don't know your skin color." Yet later in the interview, Matthew rationalizes racially identifying as white, saying, "When I think of race, like your descent . . . I feel that our descent is white." Like Matthew, many Egyptians use a combination of skin color and ancestry in conceptualizing race. Yet not all came to the same conclusion that they are white. In fact, most do not see themselves as white but use other terms, such as *Caucasian*, *Arab*, *Middle Eastern*, or *brown*, to describe their race. . . .

The notion that Egyptians are not white, even if they are lighter-skinned, is highlighted by Kaarim's experience with coworkers. Like Matthew above, Kaarim self-identifies as white yet through various interactions has found that others do not see him as white.

> I had this discussion with a few of my colleagues and then I was like "So what do you think I am?" . . . They were like, "Middle Eastern." Well why not white? Then they were like, "Look at the skin color you are not white, you are like kind of bronze color." So I see myself [as] white, among Egyptians at least I am in the lighter color, so I thought that I'm white you know. A little bit darker than a typical American but I felt I am white, but then it looks like they see me as bronze rather than white. [ellipses in all quotations from interlocutors indicate omitted material]

Despite his relatively light skin color, Kaarim is . . . not perceived to be white in part because his Egyptian heritage locates him outside the traditional boundaries of whiteness.

Although some Egyptians see themselves as white in part because they have lighter skin tones than other Egyptians, most describe their skin color as brown, tan, or in between. Mahmoud describes his skin color as *abyad* (the color of wheat), while Sarah says Egyptians have "dark skin color, [but] not dark dark skin." Molly, who describes her own skin color as brown, refers to Hispanics as sharing similar skin color, saying, "I am not white and not dark, that's why I kinda say brown. You could say there are some Latinos or Hispanics that have that same . . . skin color." . . .

Many other Egyptians recognize that having brown, rather than white, skin tone means they share a phenotypic characteristic with Latinos/Hispanics and South Asians. Although most Egyptians are identified as either Arab or Middle Eastern, having brown skin means they are sometimes mistaken for other ethnoracial groups. Jacob explains, " . . . I guess there's sort of this whole brown category. I get mistaken for Hispanic, I get mistaken for Indian, these are the people who are neither black nor white. . . . It's a visual thing more than anything else."

I found that Egyptians, especially men with light to medium skin tone, are often mistaken for Latina/o or Hispanic. John says that "eight out of ten times [people] thought maybe I was Mexican or Spanish or something." Matthew, who often makes people guess where he is from, says, "They would always think I'm Puerto Rican, or some Hispanic descent, or something." Even Egyptian women, especially those who are Christian, recall experiences where people speak to them in Spanish. Lizabeth remembers an interaction with an elderly woman at a grocery store in which she was accused of not knowing her "mother tongue" because she could not speak or understand Spanish.

Unlike Egyptian men, Egyptian Muslim women who are not immediately identified as Arab or Middle Eastern are often mistaken for South Asian, especially if they are wearing hijab. Samantha, who wears hijab, says, "Because of my skin tone, I've gotten Indian, Pakistani before. I usually get Pakistani or Indian for some reason." Maya, who has both worn and not worn hijab, reveals this, saying, "Before I covered my hair, I was always mistaken for Greek, Italian, Mexican, Puerto Rican. After I started covering my hair, I was always mistaken for Indian. . . ."

Their narratives demonstrate the powerful role that religion plays in differentiating brown-skinned ethnoracial groups. Egyptian Muslim women whose outward appearance marks them as Muslim are much more likely than Egyptian men to be mistaken for South Asian because of the assumption that Arabs/Middle Easterners and South Asians are Muslim (see Joshi 2006).

Despite recognizing the existence of a broader brown ethnoracial category, many Egyptians challenge the homogenization of these groups. Unlike O'Brien (2008), who found Latina/os and Asians often identified with other members of the racial middle, few Egyptians identified with Latina/os or South Asians, often differentiating themselves on the basis of cultural, ancestral, and religious grounds. Many Egyptians viewed their racialization as unique, resulting in a particular kind of brown defined by pervasive perceptions of Islam as radical, violent, and associated with terrorism. For example, Inez explains, "I think there's a brown look, but there's also a Middle Eastern look. I think that when they think of a Middle Eastern person they think of a man with a beard, someone who looks like bin Laden. . . ."

Inez emphasizes that Egyptians, as Middle Eastern, are not simply brown but are distinguishable by different phenotypical features. Yet by invoking Osama bin Laden, the terrorist most associated with 9/11, she highlights how "certain phenotypical features associated with a group and attached to a race in popular discourse become associated with a particular religion or religions" (Joshi 2006, 211).

Similarly, other Egyptians question the utility of the brown ethnoracial category by evoking differences in ethnonational background. Jacob suggests,

> Brown [is] not a good category 'cause it's like totally different groups. Hispanics, Indians, and Egyptians, you're talking about across the globe different cultures. They just happen to share a shade of color that's similar enough. So I don't think the brown category makes much sense.

Although Inez and Jacob's comments challenge the homogenization of brown-skinned ethnoracial groups as a singular category, the narratives above attest to its superficial existence. Their comments indicate racialization is a process, rather than a product, in which race, ethnicity, national origin, and religion interact in intricate ways. This layering of race, ethnicity, national origin, and religion suggests that brown represents not a singular but rather a multifaceted racial formation in which different kinds of brown ethnoracial groups exist. The following section examines how Egyptians articulate a brown racialization that defines them as neither citizen nor American.

Foreign Racialization

Egyptians recognize that they are often viewed as foreigners in the United States. For many, the combination of brown skin and ethnic signifiers such as national origin or language marks them as neither citizen nor American regardless of their citizenship status or nation of birth. Maya, a second-generation Muslim, says, "We're not white, we're not black, we're brown people. I think we are a different other that's kind of an immigrant other. Whereas white and black is usually something [American], brown refers to other and from somewhere else." Maya's comment reflects a form of "foreigner racialization" (Ancheta 2006) that conflates race with nationality and citizenship. Their narratives below reveal how brown-skinned ethnoracial groups often face nativism and xenophobia driven by twin logics of "cultural racism" and "nation-based racism" that defines Latina/os, Asians, and Arab/Middle Easterners as both foreign and non-American (Naber 2008b).

Because they do not fit the "typical white American" mold, Egyptians consistently face questions about where they are from. Echoing Maya's statement above, Megan says, "I think because of the color of our skin . . . people will automatically assume you're not your typical white American." Because brown skin tone cues nativism and xenophobia, questions like "What are you?" and "Where are you from?" often represent attempts to validate those concerns. For example, Lizabeth, who was born in the United States, says,

> When people meet me, the first question they ask is, "Where are you from?" I think a lot of times when you meet your typical white-skinned person, you don't necessarily jump to the where-are-you-from question because they don't look like they're necessarily from anywhere, you know? For me, because I'm darker, I think the automatic assumption is that I come from somewhere else.

Beyond skin color and phenotype, ethnonational ancestry, as indicated by national origin and/or linguistic cues, provides an additional layer of racialization confronting Egyptians. For some Egyptians, like Matta, this means hiding their Egyptian background in an attempt to avoid being seen as foreign:

> MATTA: I just feel like sometimes I just don't want to open up a conversation of "Oh, you're Egyptian." I think it just kind of highlights maybe something subconsciously, "OK, I am letting them know that I'm different." I think that maybe that's why I don't say it. I don't know.
>
> INTERVIEWER: When they find out, what do . . .
>
> MATTA: I mean, they assume I'm an immigrant.

Although Matta avoids mentioning his Egyptian ancestry, others take a more proactive approach when trying to dispel notions that they are foreigners. Samantha often leads with her identification as American, rather than Egyptian, to emphasize her American identity. When asked where she is from, she says, "I usually say my family is from Egypt because I don't want people to misunderstand and think that I was born and raised [in Egypt] and I don't know anything but Egypt. I want, first and foremost, [people to know] I am American."

Beyond divulging that they are from Egypt, some Egyptians mention that others may use linguistic cues to racialize them as foreign. Kaarim says, "I mean from the moment I speak, my accent just pops out, 'Where are you from?' Well, I'm from Egypt." Similarly, Abdul says,

> If I am with someone and we speak in Arabic . . . sometimes some people ask like 'What language is this?' I don't know if they ask because they are curious like they are worried, you know what I mean. 'Cause like when you speak Arabic people can recognize it from the movies [with] terrorists. Like people avoid you because you are dark, or because you are Arab, or because you are Muslim. You know people still have this kind of racism.

Because non-English languages and non-American accents lead others to assume they are foreign, Egyptians often have to account for where they are from. Abdul's comment, like Inez's comment earlier, demonstrates what Bloodsworth-Lugo and Lugo-Lugo (2008) described as the "browning of terror." By invoking an association between Arabic language, religion, and race, Abdul's comments articulate a particular kind of brown racialization faced by many Egyptians. The following section examines how Egyptians, along with other Arabs and Middle Easterners, are racialized as anti-American Muslim terrorists.

Anti-American Muslim Racialization

Many Egyptians reveal that their allegiance to America is not simply questioned but often summarily rejected by others who assume that because they are Muslim, they cannot also be American. Ismaael is a citizen and has lived in the United States for more than twenty years:

> ISMAAEL: I know a lot of people don't view me as American, and you know that's frustrating at times, but I accept it, but I definitely view myself as American . . .
>
> INTERVIEWER: Why don't others see you as American? . . .
>
> ISMAAEL: Like I said, it goes back to that definition of being normal and being white, and I don't fit that category, so I am automatically not a real American.

Although both Latina/os and Asians also have their Americanness challenged, Ismaael distinguishes Arabs and Middle Easterners from these groups, saying, "Having brown skin and being from the Middle East is different." Similarly, Maya believes her Americanness is questioned because of her ethnic and religious background. Maya, who was born and raised in the United States, says, "Your Americanness might be different than [mine]. I am also American, born here. It's just that no one has a problem with [yours] because you don't have a contentious part. Obviously now for Muslims and Arabs we do." What is questionable about both Ismaael's and Maya's Americanness is their Arab or Middle Eastern ancestry. Maya's comment also highlights her Muslim identity as well. Their comments reflect what Selod (2015) describes as "de-Americanization," a process by which one's loyalty to the United States is revoked primarily because of negative associations between Arab culture and Islam. Whereas Latina/os are viewed as illegal immigrants and Asians as foreigners, Arabs and Muslims are increasingly seen as anti-American in ways that challenge the legitimacy of their presence in the United States. No longer simply brown, Egyptians become what Jacob calls "brown Arab" as the conflation of race, ethnicity, and national origin with religion further distinguishes them from other brown-skinned ethnoracial groups.

The racialization of Islam as violent, radical, and connected to terrorism is driven by a rhetoric of fear. Sabrina, a second-generation Muslim, eloquently describes this, saying,

> I think a lot of it is very, very deep rooted in political history and a lot of people in the United States just understand that all those Muslims, Middle Easterners, they hate America. I think it is rooted in fear. . . . If that's all you see and hear and the only time you ever really interact with somebody who is Muslim or you see something about Muslims [is] on TV when they are . . . blowing up buildings somewhere. . . .

Such fear of Arabs and Muslims is not new. Polls have consistently shown that Americans hold prejudicial attitudes toward Arabs and Muslims, seeing them as untrustworthy, violent, and threatening (Cainkar 2016; Panagopoulous 2006). Immediately after 9/11, public-opinion polls showed "widespread support for special treatment of Arabs" and [that] "a majority of Americans favored profiling Arabs" (Cainkar 2002, 23). Oswald found that "perceptions of threat" alone are often enough to activate "anti-Arab reactions" (2005, 1792), and Jamal (2008a) found that Americans increasingly supported policies that infringed upon the civil liberties of Arab, Middle Eastern, and Muslim communities.

The idea that Arabs, Middle Easterners, and Muslims represent a potential threat is echoed throughout Egyptian narratives. Ismaael recalls that after 9/11 there was "a period everyone was a suspect unless you were proven otherwise." Similarly, Fareed recalls the emergence of an atmosphere of anxiety after 9/11. He says, "I felt a change of attitudes after September 11. I felt that people who didn't think about it before are now a little bit more sensitized to the fact that you're dealing with people who might be related to Arabs or Muslims. . . ."

Similarly, Salwa says that after 9/11 hate, racism, and bigotry "got amped up hardcore to the point where it was really frightening." She felt as if she had "zero rights" and everyone "considered [her] to be an alien and a danger." When asked how she came to be defined as a danger, Salwa points to the media in constructing Arabs, Middle Easterners, and Muslims as terrorists. The idea these groups are associated with terrorism in the media was repeated by many Egyptians, especially Muslims, who found it difficult to watch their communities being vilified. For example, Ermina says, "When they talk about terrorism, they have to say Islamic. . . . When there is an incident that has terror in it, and the perpetrator is not Muslim, they don't mention his religion." Similarly, Maya says the media portrays Arabs and Muslims as "a very violent culture" and religion. This association of Arabs, Middle Easterners, and Muslims with terrorism frames not just Muslims but also those who "look Muslim" (Elver 2012) or have an Arab/Middle Eastern ethnic background.

The conflation of Arab ethnicity with Islam, and thus terrorism, reveals a convergence of race, ethnicity, national origin, and religion that many Egyptians recognize as problematic, especially Coptic Christians, who because of their skin color, nationality, and/or Arabic-sounding names are often mistaken for Muslim. Jacob says that Americans "think coming from the Middle East automatically makes you Muslim." Mariam states that for "a lot of people, their first assumption when you say Egyptian [is] that you're Muslim." For all too many Copts, like Catherine, being mistaken for Muslim "happens all the time." Thus, Coptic Christians often seek out opportunities to dispel these mistaken assumptions. Sofia says that "when people ask me where I am from, I say I'm Coptic. . . . You want to distinguish that you know you are Christian." She goes on to explain that by saying she is Coptic Christian, she hopes to avoid being associated with Islam. The association of Islam with terrorism means that the stakes of being identified as Muslim, whether correct or incorrect, are high for Egyptians.

The atmosphere of fear and mistrust cuts both directions as many Egyptians, especially women, describe their anxiety about becoming targets of racial profiling because of their hijab. For example, Daphne says,

> . . . Like 9/11 that was a very difficult time. Although I did not experience any, um [discrimination], . . . it was a very difficult time, and I can tell you every time something happens, the Muslim community is always fearful that there would be retaliation or consequences. Yes, I feel that I could be targeted or I could be profiled.

Daphne's fear of being profiled, akin to what Naber (2006) called an "interment of the psyche," is justified by the history of racial profiling and hate crimes experienced by Arabs, Middle Easterners, and Muslims (Cainkar 2009; Henderson et al. 2006; Santoro and Azab 2015). On July 20, 2016, a Muslim man, Mohamed Ahmed, was singled out by an American Airlines flight attendant who announced his seat number and said, "I'll be watching you," and [he] was eventually removed from the plane (Revesz 2016). Events such as these happen frequently enough that Egyptians who fit the Arab/Middle Eastern/Muslim racial archetype feel the ever-present danger of racial profiling, especially when flying.

Their narratives reflect what Chon and Arzt described as "terror profiling . . . the selectively negative treatment by both government and private entities of individuals and groups thought to be associated with terrorist activity, based on race, ethnicity, national origin, and/or religion" (2005, 238). They argued that the incorporation of religion and religious appearance brings the practice of racial profiling in line with the war on terror. According to Schildkraut (2009), support for "counterterrorism profiling" is higher than traditional forms of racial profiling. Although relatively few Egyptians experienced terror profiling, many described it as an ever-present threat that loomed over their experiences at airports. Phrases [such as] "flying while brown" (Chandrasekhar 2003), "flying while Arab" (Baker 2002), and "flying while Muslim" (Blackwood, Hopkins, and Reicher 2015) have entered [the] common lexicon in the same way as "driving while black" (Baker 2002).

Egyptians recognize that observable cues, especially brown skin coupled with ethnic or religious signifiers, often identify them as Arab, Middle Eastern, and/or Muslim and therefore potential targets of profiling. For example, Sabrina says, "I mean a lot of them know OK these are Middle Eastern features, and they know what Arabs look like, but here there's also a very clear image of what Muslims look like." . . . Similarly, Tia expresses that profiling is more likely if you look Muslim. She describes conservative dress, hijab, and dark skin as signs of "being Arab or Muslim." Daphne, who personally does not wear hijab, says, "If I walk down the street, I don't think someone would point me out necessarily." Yet she describes the following experience, saying, "A friend of mine who does wear a scarf . . . she wasn't welcomed at certain stores, and people would treat her differently. . . . Although she carriers herself in a decent way, there was that sense of unwelcoming of her." Similarly, Inez, who is Coptic Christian, recalls the following experience she had with an African American Muslim friend:

> I did an experiment with my black friend. We decided I was going to put a scarf on my head to look like hijab to see what would happen. What was interesting was that no one was really worried or scared of her. They were looking at her and talking to her normally, but they were afraid of me. I just looked, yeah, normally when I'm walking down the street, I don't stand out. OK, I look like a brown person,

> but that definitely made a big difference. I will never forget the guy at the Blockbuster would not look me in the eye. He would talk to her and not look me in the eye.

. . . [Inez's] experiment suggests that the combination of skin color, perceived ethnic background, and religious dress influenced how she was racialized. Unlike her friend, who was likely perceived to be African American, Inez's brown skin interacts with perceived religious dress (scarf) by racializing her as Arab Muslim and therefore threatening. The above comments suggest the importance of religious signifiers in identifying Egyptians as Arab, Middle Eastern, and/or Muslim.

Beyond skin color and religious dress, ethnoreligious cues such as name and nationality also contribute to the terror profiling of Egyptians. Lizabeth says,

> Ever since 9/11, I think if you have facial hair, you know any of those characterizing features, or [if] they're dressed in a different way than someone else, people look at them. . . . I know that with everything that happened after 9/11, I think people do kind of look at you—you're dark skinned, you have a funny last name, I think after all that there's a lot of sensitivity around that.

Like Lizabeth, Tia remembers her father being singled out for extra security checks, saying, "Every single time it would be my father because his name is Mohammed." Salwa recalls being harassed several times at airports. Despite her proclamation that she does not "look like a terrorist," she recalls having been pulled off airplanes, forced to sit in the back away from the cockpit, and randomly selected for searches all because of her last name. She says, "I don't wear hijab, people don't know what I am, but it was my name. My last name is [Awad]." Lizabeth, Tia, and Salwa's comments illustrate that having an Arabic- or Muslim-sounding name may be enough [for some people] to become victims of terror profiling.

In addition to one's name, national origin background can contribute to Egyptians' being associated with terrorism. Catherine was once introduced as "my Egyptian legal clerk" and recalls the interaction that followed:

> And this man, I'll never forget, says, "Are you going to be flying anytime soon?" And I had no idea what he was talking about. I was just confused. Then it took me a couple of hours . . . then I was like, what did he just ask me!? Really! Like, I didn't, it's not like it was happening all the time so I wasn't aware all the time. But when it would happen, [I] just was like, "Wow, Why?!"

The above narratives illustrate what scholars have found concerning how observable traits, such as skin color, name, national origin, and religious appearance can be used to identify Arabs, Middle Easterners, and/or Muslims as potential threats (Elver 2012; Love 2009; Naber 2008b; Rana 2011). For example, Ramirez, Hoopes, and Quinlan argued that "Arab-Americans, and those with Arab appearances, increasingly [are] singled out for questioning and security checks based on their skin color, clothing, name, or religious beliefs" (2003, 1195). This conflation of race, ethnicity, national origin, and religion demonstrate racialization as a layered process in which their skin color and phenotype, ethnicity, national origin, and religion come to define Arabs and Middle Easterners as a different kind of brown: anti-American Muslim terrorists.

. . . The association of Arabs and Middle Easterners with terrorism has existed at least since the 1970s and was codified in Ronald Reagan's 1980s foreign policy (Semati 2010), yet 9/11 solidified the conflation of Arabs/Middle Easterners with Islam (Garner and Selod 2015; Joshi 2006; Rana 2011; Selod and Embrick 2013). In particular, Joshi argued that the racialization of Islam has reduced Muslims to a "homogeneous, undifferentiated" community associated with terrorism (2006, 212). Similarly, Bayoumi argued that the war on terror has "reinscribed, through a legal mechanism, the cultural assumption that a terrorist is foreign-born, an alien in the United States, and a Muslim" (2006, 275). This progression from "friendly foreigner" to "enemy race" (Tehranian 2009, 64) and anti-American Muslim terrorist continues to be facilitated by a rhetoric of fear that portrays Arabs, Middle

Easterners, and Muslims as the preeminent threat to national security.

Discussion

In this study I find that Arab and Middle Eastern Americans have been racialized not only as brown and foreign but more specifically as anti-American Muslim terrorists. The narratives presented challenge narrow conceptualizations of race based on skin color and phenotype and highlight how racial, ethnic, national origin, and religious cues identify them as Arab, Middle Eastern, and/or Muslim. Even though race scholars have moved away from strict color-based definitions of race by incorporating ethnicity, national origin, and religion (Alcoff 2009; Balibar 1991; Joshi 2006; Kibria 2002; Meer and Modood 2009; Naber 2008b; Rana 2011; Selod and Embrick 2013), there is limited theorizing on how these aspects result in different forms of racialization. Indeed, Emerson, Korver-Glenn, and Douds argued that "too often work in the study of race and ethnicity has not taken the influence of religion seriously enough, with the consequence being an incomplete understanding of racialization, racial and ethnic identity, and racial inequality" (2015, 349). In this article I address this shortcoming by explicitly examining how religion adds an additional axis of racialization. Thus, this research not only builds on existing scholarship that conceptualizes race as more than skin color but further contributes by theorizing racialization as a layered process in which skin color, ethnicity, national origin, and religion combine in complex ways to produce different kinds of brown ethnoracial groups with different experiences, locations in the racial order, and racializing experiences. I highlight the ways skin color and phenotype result in a broad yet problematic brown ethnoracial category; examine how ethnicity and national origin in combination with skin color and phenotype contribute to the racialization of brown-skinned ethnoracial groups as foreign and un-American; and analyze how the racialization of Islam constructs Arabs, Middle Easterners, and/or Muslims as the quintessential enemy to the United States. Unlike Latina/os, who share in the American Christian tradition, and Asians, whose religions are often viewed as peaceful, with many of their practices, such as meditation, having been co-opted in mainstream American culture, Arabs and Middle Easterners are associated with Islam, [which is perceived as] a violent, misogynist, and radical religion.

. . . There is . . . an increasing body of research that conceptualizes race as a multidimensional construct in which different racial dimensions are often not consistent . . . (see Roth 2016). More generally, however, the experiences of Arabs, Middle Easterners, and, increasingly, Muslims need to shape future theoretical and empirical research on race. Their experiences are far too complex and important to continue ignoring.

Works Cited

Volume editors' note: The works cited list includes sources cited in the original publication of this chapter but not in the excerpt given here.

Alcoff, Linda. 2009. "Latinos beyond the Binary." *Southern Journal of Philosophy* 47, no. 1: 112–28.

Ancheta, Angelo N. 2006. *Race, Rights, and the Asian American Experience*. 2nd ed. New Brunswick, NJ: Rutgers Univ. Press.

Bakalian, Anny, and Mehdi Bozorgmehr. 2009. *Backlash 9/11: Middle Eastern and Muslim Americans Respond*. Berkeley: Univ. of California Press.

Baker, Ellen. 2002. "Flying while Arab: Racial Profiling and Air Travel Security." *Journal of Air and Law Commerce* 67:1375–405.

Balibar, Étienne. 1991. "Is There Neo-racism?" In *Race, Nation, Class: Ambiguous Identities*, edited by Étienne Balibar and Immanuel Wallerstein, 17–28. New York: Verso.

Bayoumi, Moustafa. 2006. "Racing Religion." *New Centennial Review* 6, no. 2: 267–93.

Blackwood, Leda, Nick Hopkins, and Stephen Reicher. 2015. "'Flying while Muslim': Citizenship and Misrecognition in the Airport." *Journal of Social and Political Psychology* 32, no. 2: 148–70.

Bloodsworth-Lugo, Mary K., and Carmen R. Lugo-Lugo. 2008. "Citizenship and the Browning of Terror." *Peace Review: A Journal of Social Justice* 20:273–82.

Bonilla-Silva, Eduardo. 2015. "More Than Prejudice: Restatement, Reflections, and New Directions in Critical Race Theory." *Sociology of Race and Ethnicity* 1, no. 1: 73–87.

Cainkar, Louise. 2002. "No Longer Invisible: Arab and Muslim Exclusion after September 11." *Middle East Report*, no. 24: 22–29.

———. 2006. "Immigrants from the Arab World." In *New Chicago: A Social and Cultural Analysis*, edited by John Patrick Koval, 182–96. Philadelphia: Temple Univ. Press.

———. 2008. "Thinking outside the Box: Arab Americans and U.S. Racial Formations." In *Race and Arab Americans before and after 9/11: From Invisible Citizens to Visible Subjects*, edited by Amaney Jamal and Nadine Naber, 46–80. Syracuse, NY: Syracuse Univ. Press.

———. 2009. *Homeland Insecurity: The Arab American and Muslim American Experience after 9/11*. New York: Russell Sage Foundation.

———. 2016. "Race and Racialization: Trends and the Process of Reckoning Social Place." In *Handbook of Arab American Psychology*, edited by Mona M. Amer and Germine H. Awad, 19–34. New York: Routledge.

Chandrasekhar, Charu. 2003. "Flying while Brown: Federal Civil Rights Remedies to post 9/11 Airline Profiling of South Asians." *Asian American Law Journal* 10, no. 2: 215–52.

Chon, Margaret, and Donna Arzt. 2005. "Walking while Muslim." *Law and Contemporary Problems* 68:215–54.

Elver, Hilal. 2012. "Racializing Islam before and after 9/11: From Melting Pot to Islamophobia." *Transnational Law & Contemporary Problems* 21, no. 1: 119–74.

Emerson, Michael, Elizabeth Korver-Glenn, and Kiara W. Douds. 2015. "Studying Race and Religion: A Critical Assessment." *Sociology of Race and Ethnicity* 1, no. 3: 349–59.

Garner, Steve, and Saher Selod. 2015. "The Racialization of Muslims: Empirical Studies in Islamophobia." *Critical Sociology* 41, no. 1: 9–19.

Gualtieri, Sarah M. A. 2008. "Strange Fruit? Syrian Immigrants, Extralegal Violence, and Racial Formation in the United States." In *Race and Arab Americans before and after 9/11: From Invisible Citizens to Visible Subjects*, edited by Amaney Jamal and Nadine Naber, 147–69. Syracuse, NY: Syracuse Univ. Press.

Henderson, Nicole J., Christopher W. Ortiz, Naomi F. Sugie, and Joel Miller. 2006. *Law Enforcement & Arab American Community Relations after September 11, 2001: Engagement in a Time of Uncertainty*. New York: Vera Institute of Justice.

Jamal, Amaney. 2008a. "Civil Liberties and Otherization of Arab and Muslim Americans." In *Race and Arab Americans before and after 9/11: From Invisible Citizens to Visible Subjects*, edited by Amaney Jamal and Nadine Naber, 114–30. Syracuse, NY: Syracuse Univ. Press.

———. 2008b. "Conclusion: Arab American Racialization." In *Race and Arab Americans before and after 9/11: From Invisible Citizens to Visible Subjects*, edited by Amaney Jamal and Nadine Naber, 318–23. Syracuse, NY: Syracuse Univ. Press.

Joshi, Khyati. 2006. "The Racialization of Hinduism, Islam, and Sikhism in the United States." *Equity and Excellence in Education* 39, no. 3: 211–26.

Kibria, Nazli. 2002. *Becoming Asian American: Second-Generation Chinese and Korean American Identities*. Baltimore: Johns Hopkins Univ. Press.

Love, Erik. 2009. "Confronting Islamophobia in the United States: Framing Civil Rights Activism among Middle Eastern Americans." *Patterns of Prejudice* 43, nos. 3–4: 401–25.

Meer, Nasar, and Tariq Modood. 2009. "Refutations of Racism in the 'Muslim Question.'" *Patterns of Prejudice* 43, nos. 3–4: 335–54.

Naber, Nadine. 2006. "The Rules of Forced Engagement: Race, Gender, and the Culture of Fear among Arab Immigrants in San Francisco post 9/11." *Cultural Dynamics* 18, no. 3: 235–67.

———. 2008a. "Introduction: Arab Americans and U.S. Racial Formations." In *Race and Arab Americans before and after 9/11: From Invisible Citizens to Visible Subjects*, edited by Amaney Jamal and Nadine Naber, 1–45. Syracuse. NY: Syracuse Univ. Press.

———. 2008b. "'Look, Mohammed the Terrorist Is Coming!' Cultural Racism, Nation-Based Racism, and Intersectionality of Oppressions after 9/11." In *Race and Arab Americans before and after 9/11: From Invisible Citizens to Visible Subjects*, edited by Amaney Jamal and Nadine Naber, 276–304. Syracuse, NY: Syracuse Univ. Press.

O'Brien, Eileen. 2008. *The Racial Middle*. New York: New York Univ. Press.

Oswald, Debra L. 2005. "Understanding Anti-Arab Reactions post-9/11: The Role of Threats, Social Categories, and Personal Ideologies." *Journal of Applied Social Psychology* 35, no. 9: 1775–99.

Panagopoulous, Costas. 2006. "The Polls-Trend: Arab and Muslim Americans and Islam in the Aftermath of 9/11." *Public Opinion Quarterly* 70:608–24.

Ramirez, Deborah A., Jennifer Hoopes, and Tara Lai Quinlan. 2003. "Defining Racial Profiling in a post September 11 World." *American Criminal Law Review* 40:1195–233.

Rana, Junaid. 2011. *Terrifying Muslims: Race and Labor in the South Asian Diaspora*. Durham, NC: Duke Univ. Press.

Revesz, Rachael. 2016. "Muslim Passenger Kicked Off American Airlines Flight after Attendant Announces: 'I'll Be Watching You.'" *Independent*, July 21. At http://www.independent.co.uk/news/world/americas/muslim-kicked-off-plane-american-airlines-racial-discrimination-cair-uncomfortable-a7147311.html.

Roth, Wendy. 2016. "The Multiple Dimensions of Race." *Ethnic and Racial Studies* 39, no. 8: 1310–38.

Santoro, Wayne, and Marian Azab. 2015. "Arab American Protest in the Terror Decade: Macro- and Micro-level Response to post-9/11 Repression." *Social Problems* 62, no. 2: 219–40.

Schildkraut, Deborah. 2009. "The Dynamics of Public Opinion on Ethnic Profiling after 9/11: Results from a Survey Experiment." *American Behavioral Scientist* 53, no. 1: 61–79.

Selod, Saher. 2015. "Citizenship Denied: The Racialization of Muslim American Men and Women post 9/11." *Critical Sociology* 41, no. 1: 77–95.

Selod, Saher, and David G. Embrick. 2013. "Racialization and Muslims: Situating the Muslim Experience in Race Scholarship." *Sociology Compass* 7, no. 8: 644–55.

Semati, Mehdi. 2010. "Islamophobia, Culture, and Race in the Age of Empire." *Cultural Studies* 24, no. 2: 256–75.

Tehranian, John. 2009. *Whitewashed: America's Invisible Middle Eastern Minority*. New York: New York Univ. Press.

Tuan, Mia. 1998. *Forever Foreigners or Honorary Whites? The Asian Ethnic Experience Today*. New Brunswick, NJ: Rutgers Univ. Press.

20

Introduction

The Politics of Privilege

JOHN TOFIK KARAM

Nearing Avenida Paulista (Paulista Avenue) in uptown São Paulo on a cool evening in 2001, I follow the public signs of Arabness. I first come across Habib's Arab fast-food restaurant. Preparing almost half of the estimated 1.2 million *esfihas* ("Arab" meat pies) sold daily in the city, the chain is ignored by professionals who drive in the direction of posh Syrian-Lebanese restaurants up the street. I proceed toward Club Homs on the main avenue. Hailed as "the house of Arabs," it is one of a half-dozen Middle Eastern country clubs in the area. On this night, the club is hosting a chic commemoration of the National Day of Syria. Passing through the security gate, I join a cadre of mostly Arab and some non-Arab Brazilians. Among the eminent businessmen in attendance is a third-generation Syrian-Lebanese who has been praised by President Cardoso for training Brazilian executives in how to export to the Arab world. The Arab Brazilian Chamber of Commerce over which he presides is located just across the avenue. Also present are dozens of foreign dignitaries and national politicians, such as a second-generation Lebanese city councilor who leads the annual Lebanese independence-day event in the São Paulo city government. Her honored guests the previous year included physicians of Lebanese descent who practice at the award-winning Syrian-Lebanese Hospital just two blocks off the main avenue.

Excerpt from John Tofik Karam, "Introduction: The Politics of Privilege," in *Another Arabesque: Syrian-Lebanese Ethnicity in Neoliberal Brazil* (Philadelphia: Temple Univ. Press, 2007). A works cited list was created for this chapter. Reprinted with some corrections.

That such an arabesque winds through and beyond Avenida Paulista may seem puzzling. After all, Avenida Paulista is hardly an Arab space. Considered the "postcard of São Paulo," it guides the country's current neoliberal experiment. Attracting increased flows of foreign capital since the 1970s, Avenida Paulista today is home to headquarters of national and transnational groups in industry, trade, and finance, such as the Federation of the Industries of the State of São Paulo, Banco Itaú, Citibank, and the Bank of Boston. State and business elites from Brazil and the world pass through the many blocks of high-rise buildings that line the eight-lane avenue. Alongside traders and statesmen, prosperous doctors, lawyers, engineers, and other professionals meet in the upscale cosmopolitan restaurants and bars in the adjacent "noble" neighborhoods of os Jardins (the Gardens). How have apparent Arab elements and events attained such a marked visibility amid such dominant interests on Avenida Paulista? What does this say about the place of Middle Eastern descendants today in this Brazilian city and nation?

Nearly a half-century after the last major waves of immigration, Middle Easterners have attained an unprecedented kind of privilege throughout Brazil. They oversee multimillion-dollar business ventures, constitute an estimated 10 percent of both the city council in São Paulo and the federal Congress in Brasília, own advertising and television enterprises, star in the top-rated soap opera *O Clone* (The Clone), and run some of the most envied country clubs among national elites. [*Another Arabesque*] focuses on the greater recognition of Brazilians of Syrian-Lebanese descent during the neoliberal "transition." Through the 1970s to today, neoliberal initiatives—such as market liberalization, government downsizing, and consumer diversification—further linked Brazil into the world system. At this crossroads, second- and third-generation Syrian-Lebanese have ethnically projected themselves as export partners, ethical politicians, and diverse connoisseurs, shaping and reflecting the Brazilian nation-state in the late twentieth and early twenty-first centuries.

Drawing on the work of Michael Omi and Howard Winant (1986), my wider contention is that Syrian-Lebanese ethnicity has intensified as a project in Brazil. "Every project," writes Winant (1994, 139), "is necessarily both a discursive or cultural initiative, an attempt at . . . identity formation on the one hand; and a political initiative, an attempt at organisation . . . on the other." I show that second- and third-generation Syrian-Lebanese have articulated an "ethnic project" about the meaning and place of Arab business, politics, family life, social mobility, and leisure. Layered with contradictions and ambivalences, the Arab ethnic project is evident not necessarily in daily situations, but in "marked frames" of action for the "public sphere" (Habermas 1989; Lewis 1999), such as business seminars, political celebrations, dinner banquets, and heritage vacations. Represented in newspapers, television, advertising, or other media, these institutional practices guide my analysis of Arab ethnic recognition in Brazil. Throughout my book, "arabesque" is used to express this privileged design of Arabness today.

The Arab ethnic project is intricately part of Brazil's neoliberal experiment. In the open economy, Syrian-Lebanese descendants have fashioned themselves as Arab promoters of Brazilian exports to the Persian Gulf market. During a World Bank anticorruption program in the São Paulo city government, politicians of Lebanese descent have sponsored an [ethnic] celebration of Lebanese independence day. In consumer diversification, Syrian-Lebanese socialites have used the mainstream marketing appeal of "Arab food" to build social capital with non-Arab guests in their country clubs. Brazilians of Syrian-Lebanese descent have even been targeted as a market for homeland tourism in Syria and Lebanon. In short, Arab ethnicity has gained a novel force in the turn toward economic openness, state transparency, and consumer diversity. This focus on the novel formation of Arabness in Brazil is what I mean by "another" arabesque in the book's title. While attentive to its continuities with the past, I suggest, Syrian-Lebanese ethnicity has also undergone significant change in neoliberal Brazil. . . .

Numbers and Names in the Arab Americas

Addressing the construction of Arabness in nationalist ideologies and political economic agendas on the Brazilian periphery of the world system, a corollary aim in [*Another Arabesque*] is to redirect the study of Arabness outside the Middle East, Europe, and the United States. My focus on Brazilians of Syrian-Lebanese descent aims to call attention to another arabesque in the world today. But to highlight the particularity of this Brazilian formation of Arabness, my book makes brief comparisons with Arabs in the Americas, especially in the United States.

Mostly departing from present-day Syria and Lebanon, Middle Eastern immigrants in the Americas have been estimated at more than 300,000 between the 1870s and the 1930s (Himadeh 1936; Issawi 1966; Karpat 1985). Spreading evenly across Argentina, Brazil, and the United States,[1] these immigrants attained a striking presence as peddlers by the 1890s and were popularly caricatured as such for the next several decades.[2] In Brazil in 1945, the poet Carlos Drummond de Andrade rhymed: "The turcos [Turks] were born to sell / colorful knickknacks in canisters/ door-to-door. / . . . If they open the canister, who resists / the impulse to buy? / It's cheap! Cheap! Buy now! / Pay later! But buy!" (cited in Gattaz 2001, 15). Likewise, in the United States a Syrian peddler appears

1. Syrian-Lebanese immigrants numbered roughly 130,000 in the United States from the 1870s until the 1930s (Suleiman 1999, 2), 107,000 in Brazil during the same period (Lesser 1999, 49), and 108,000 in Argentina from 1882 to 1950 (Jozami 1996, 28). Smaller numbers of Middle Easterners also immigrated to other Latin American and Caribbean countries.

2. In Buenos Aires, 53 percent of resident Arabs were said to have engaged in peddling or small-scale businesses (Klich 1992, 273). In New York City, over 50 percent of resident Arabs traded goods (Miller [1905] 1969, 11, as cited in Khater 2001, 74).

in Lynn Riggs's play *Green Grow the Lilacs* (1931).[3] When Rodgers and Hammerstein turned the play into the musical *Oklahoma* in 1943, the figure became "the Persian" Ali Hakem (Baringer 1998, 452). Today, this peddling past remains striking in the public construction of Arabness in Brazil, but it has been replaced by the "reel bad Arab" stereotype in the United States (Shaheen 1984). Historians agree that the vast majority of Middle Eastern immigrants to Brazil arrived in the early twentieth century (Gattaz 2001; Lesser 1999; Nunes 1993; Truzzi 1997). Mostly stemming from present-day Syria and Lebanon, 140,464 Middle Easterners immigrated to Brazil from 1880 to 1969 (Lesser 1999, 8). From the 1970s onward, however, it appears that only 500 to 700 immigrants from mostly South Lebanon and Palestine arrived annually.[4] Despite such small numbers, news reportage and immigration museums have estimated that there are 6 million to 10 million Syrian and Lebanese descendants in present-day Brazil (Varella 2000). How could an ethnic group that totaled fewer than 200,000 grow to upward of 6 million within a century?

Such statistics must not be dismissed as misrepresentations but probed as social facts. Take, for example, an article published on Middle Easterners in the newsweekly *Veja* (Varella 2000). It "estimated" that 7 million citizens of Syrian-Lebanese origin now live in Brazil (Varella 2000). Within a month of its publication, a second-generation Lebanese (who owns an advertising agency) asked if I had read it. He then added, "It was me who gave much of the information." I suspect that he and others introduced such estimates in interviews for news reportage or academic research.[5] Maintaining a privileged presence in business and political circles, Middle Easterners have overestimated themselves as a way to strengthen their place in the Brazilian nation.

These numerical claims have gained greater legitimacy in public circulation, as made evident in the social life of an article from *Folha de S. Paulo*'s Sunday magazine in 2001, "O nosso lado árabe" (Our Arab Side). It "estimated" that "10 million immigrants and descendants live in Brazil" who "are basically of the nationalities Lebanese (7 million) and Syrian (3 million)." Citing the article as a source, the São Paulo state immigration museum, Memorial do Imigrante, publicized the statistics in an exposition about Lebanese immigration in 2002. Reflecting the intensification of Arab ethnicity, these figures have depicted Middle Eastern descendants as nearly 5 percent of the Brazilian population.

In comparison, a brief look at the numbers of Middle Easterners in the United States is revealing. From the 1870s through the 1930s, roughly 130,000 immigrants from present-day Syria and Lebanon went to the United States (Suleiman 1999, 2). Since 1967, however, more than 250,000 Middle Easterners have immigrated to the United States (Orfalea 1988), mostly from the Arabian Gulf, Egypt, Iraq, Jordan, Lebanon, and Palestine. But census and similar estimates for US Americans of Middle Eastern heritage have been criticized as "low" by activists and researchers during the past two decades (Schopmeyer 2000; Zogby 1990). A more accurate, if unsubstantiated, estimate today is 2.5 million (Suleiman 1999, 2). That Middle Easterners have been underrepresented in the United States and overrepresented in Brazil

3. A Tulsa, Oklahoma, blogger recently provided an interesting, and plausible, explanation for the character developed by Lynn Riggs: Immigrants from the southern Lebanese town of Marjeyoun had first come as peddlers during the Oklahoma land rush. They eventually established St. Anthony's Orthodox church in Tulsa. Sol Bayouth was one of the founders of the parish. He eventually became friends with Riggs, who used him as a "template for a character in his story 'Green Grow the Lilacs.'" See http://orthodox-okie.blogspot.com/2004_10_31_orthodox-okie_archive (accessed on November 11, 2004).

4. This is my estimate based on discussions with immigration officials in São Paulo and with Arab Brazilian journalists. It also bears mentioning that the latter agree that the estimated number of immigrants diminished greatly from the 1970s through the 1990s.

5. My colleagues often used the same calculations. In one memorable instance, Abdo, a well-to-do tourist industry executive, reflected that one of his colleagues once voiced skepticism about the population figures. "But these data," Abdo countered, "are collected by the consulates." I thus raised the question to a staff person in the Lebanese consulate in São Paulo. Upon hearing that 7 million Lebanese live in Brazil, I asked about the data's source. Disappearing for a few minutes, the employee returned with a book about the cuisine of immigrants in Brazil, titled *Correntes de imigrantes e invenções culinárias no 5o centenário do Brasil* (Roque 2000). Flipping to the chapter "Lebanon," the employee pointed to two lines of text that gave the number 7 million "Lebanese descendants in Brazil" with no reference.

speaks to the historic "invisibility" of Arabs in the United States (Naber 2000; Saliba 1999) and what I suggest is their growing visibility in Brazil.

"Middle Easterners" are identified by many labels in Brazil: *turco* (Turk), *sírio* (Syrian), *libanês* (Lebanese), *sírio-libanês* (Syrian-Lebanese), *árabe* (Arab), and *árabe brasileiro* (Arab Brazilian). What must be stressed is the degree of ambiguity and fluidity between them, like other racial and ethnic terminology in Brazil.[6] As a Middle Eastern descendant, for instance, I am regularly called a "Turk," "Lebanese," "Syrian-Lebanese," and "Arab." Historically, the *turco* designation was coined by Brazilian statesmen to classify sojourners who carried travel documents of the Ottoman Sultanate from the late nineteenth century until World War I.[7] After Syria and Lebanon were created as geopolitical entities under the French colonial mandate in the 1920s, the categories of *sírio* and *libanês* were added to Brazilian immigration rosters (Lesser 1999, 8). Yet, from the late nineteenth century to the present, *turco* has been commonly used by Brazilian elites and masses in reference to people of Middle Eastern origin. In earlier times, the label was seen as derogatory. But today Middle Easterners claim that *turco* is not discriminatory but a "joking" or "caring" term of reference, thus reflecting the nationalist ideology of racial democracy.

Conventionally, "Syrian-Lebanese" has been the term crafted and used by Middle Easterners themselves, which "included an implicit notion of Brazilianness" (Lesser 1999, 42). But the designation of "Arab" has gained increasing usage as well. Brazilians of Syrian-Lebanese descent who oversee the Arab Brazilian Chamber of Commerce (CCAB), for instance, have stressed an explicitly Arab identity to (non-Arab) Brazilian clients interested in exporting to primarily Arabian Gulf markets. Likewise, Habib's, the "Arab" fast-food chain, has been represented to consumers with an overt *apelo árabe* (Arab appeal), notwithstanding the fact that most of its menu is derived from "Syrian-Lebanese" cuisine. Even the *colônia árabe* (Arab community) has become a "target market" in airline advertising. Such currency of the Arab label reflects the culture of economic openness and consumer diversity in Brazil.

The politics of naming Middle Easterners in US history is instructive here, too. Like their counterparts in Brazil, Middle Eastern immigrants to the late nineteenth-century United States were classified as "Turks" (Samhan 1999, 216). The term continued to be used to insult "Syrian-Lebanese" until midcentury. But today, this etymological past has been forgotten. US Americans of Middle Eastern origin are generally identified by themselves and others as "Arab American" or "Middle Eastern," as well as by [their] nationalities of origin (such as "Lebanese"). Yet scholars have pointed out that labels like "Arab" and "Palestinian" are invariably constructed in a discursive relation to European Jews (Massad 1993; Saliba 1999). In the United States, one must speak of "Arabs" in reference to European Jews. Unlike the usage of the "Arab" designation in Brazilian racial and national economies, the US politics of identifying "Arabs" reflects the racial ideology of US nationalism and the historical privilege of European Jewish colonialism in US foreign policy. . . .

Arab Brazilianness, September 11 Notwithstanding

But, one may rightly ask, are the contrasts between Arabs in Brazil and [Arabs in] the United States still relevant in a post–September 11 world? Entering the final months of research in São Paulo in September 2001, I watched with incredulity news reportage of Arabs and Muslims being scrutinized and held incommunicado in the United States. Given the past discrimination against Middle Easterners and Muslims in the United States, such violence was tragic but predictable. But I was really shocked by news coverage of the alleged terrorist transnational connections of Middle Easterners in the Brazilian city of

6. Anthropologists initially found that Brazilians moved between dozens of labels that made racial identification thoroughly inconsistent (Harris 1964; Kottack 1983; Wagley 1952). In contrast, Roger Sanjek (1971) noted that numerous designations of race do not indicate what Harris called the "maximization of ambiguity" (Harris 1970, 1). My work asserts that there is a degree, and not "maximization," of ambiguity in racial and ethnic classification.

7. During this time period, these Middle Eastern sojourners included mostly Christians but also some Muslims and Magribi Jews. Lesser (1999: 45–47) noted that one of the first waves of Middle Easterners to Brazil were Jews from Morocco in the late nineteenth century.

Foz do Iguazu, located near Paraguay and Argentina in the so-called triborder region (*tríplice fronteira*). Within weeks after September 11, the BBC, the *New York Times*, and other global news agencies claimed that international and local authorities were monitoring triborder Middle Eastern communities for terrorist suspects.[8] By late September, these imaginary links had made prime-time news on the Globo television network in Brazil. Drawing special interest was the US military forces' discovery of a photograph of Brazil's famous Foz do Iguaçu waterfalls in an al-Qaeda training camp in Afghanistan.[9] With global and national media spotlights on this purported "proof," it seemed that Arabs across national borders in the Americas could become subsumed by the US American "war on terror."

In the first weeks of uncertainty in São Paulo following the September 11 attacks, the Arab Brazilian Chamber of Commerce (as well as the Syrian consulate, in the same building) received a bomb threat. An official government event honoring Arab immigration and culture in the nearby city of Guarulhos was postponed. Recent Lebanese migrants who operate stores on Rua 25 de Março (March 25 Street) in the city center were interviewed about the September 11 attacks on the eight o'clock news. Even a close friend, Leila, kept her daughter home from school for two days, fearing reprisals from classmates or even teachers. After more than a year of research with Arabs in Brazil, I harbored fears that the *colônia sirio-libanesa* was being abruptly reorganized according to US American national representations of Middle Easterners. Were Brazilians of Syrian-Lebanese descent, I anxiously wondered, experiencing a break with historical and current patterns of Arab ethnicity in Brazil? Had they been suddenly encompassed by the politics of Middle Easternness endemic to, and established before, the September 11 attacks in the United States?

As a reminder against any hasty prediction of a post–September 11 world, Leila herself stated, "I was really worried, but then the soap opera started." Already slotted to begin on the Globo TV network in September 2001, *O Clone* (The Clone) hit the airwaves as scheduled but in a context that its financiers, cast, and audience could never have imagined. . . . Its storyline was the "forbidden love" between a Brazilian boy, Lucas, and a Brazilian-raised Muslim Moroccan woman, Jade. Filmed and set between Brazil and Morocco, the first of three parts was lengthened from less than one hundred *capítulos* (episodes) to nearly two hundred. Capitalizing on tumultuous world events (including reprisals against Arabs in the United States), Globo media moguls reinvented the soap opera as a way to educate the Brazilian public about the Muslim Arab world. During the soap opera's premiere, the screenwriter Glória Perez was cited as saying: "We need to say no to prejudice, to stop feeding this ignorance, showing common people. There is terrorism in all countries and between all peoples, and the Muslims are people like us."[10] Despite such claims, however, *O Clone* touched off a consumption frenzy of "Middle Eastern" cultural commodities. As examined [here] . . . , belly dancing classes and "Moroccan" clothing accessories, among other products, gained popularity in the Brazilian public sphere. In such terms, the September 11 attacks provoked initial concern among Arab Brazilians, but—as Leila remarked—"then the soap opera started."[11]

Within weeks, on September 23, 2001, *Folha de S. Paulo*'s Sunday magazine published "Brasil das arábias" (Brazil of the Arabias), a cover story about Arab culture and immigration to Brazil. The magazine's caption began: "Our Arab Side: Portuguese legacy and Syrian-Lebanese

8. "Argentina, Paraguay, Brazil Step up Search for 'Terrorists' in Tri-Border Area," BBC Monitoring Service, United Kingdom, Sept. 15, 2001; Larry Rohter, "Terrorists Are Sought in Latin American Smugglers' Haven," *New York Times*, Sept. 27, 2001. These and other unsubstantiated reports were based on earlier US American and European news coverage that conflated Arab communities with terrorist cells in the Foz do Iguaçu region.

9. For instance, see "Casa usada pela al Qaeda tinha foto que seria das cataratas do Iguaçu," *Folha de S. Paulo*, Nov. 16, 2001.

10. Rodrigo Dionisio, "Muçulmanos ganham destaque em 'O Clone,'" *Folha de S. Paulo*, Sept. 23, 2001.

11. I do not mean to minimize the effects of September 11. But given the fact that both September 11 and *O Clone* were watched on television sets in Brazil, it should not seem surprising that a soap opera would have an equal effect on the lay public.

immigration inscribed the influence of Arab culture in the Brazilian quotidian." It continued: "The strong influence of Arab culture [is] in cuisine, music, architecture, fashion, and the Portuguese language." A half-dozen articles explained the reach of Islam across Brazil and the world, the Koran's central tenets, and Arab contributions to Brazil. One article spoke of Arab culture as "literally consumed" in the state of São Paulo: "According to the Syndicate of Hotels, Restaurants, Bars, and Equivalents of São Paulo, . . . almost 25 percent of the meals served daily in São Paulo city restaurants come out of Arab cuisine" (Yuri 2001, 8). Other news columns described the Moorish style of architecture in the city of São Paulo, the Moorish origins of many words in the Portuguese language, the "children of 25 de Março" who became international fashion designers, as well as the presence of Arab descendants in MPB (*música popular brasileira*, or Brazilian popular music). In the last editorial on cuisine, the food critic Josimar Melo evoked the words of Gilberto Freyre from *Casa grande e senzala*: "Much of what is in the Brazilian is not European [or] indigenous [or] even the result of direct contact with black Africa. . . . [I]t is still much of the Moor which persists in the intimate life of Brazilians through colonial times." In emphasizing "arabisms" in this nationalist narrative of a post–September 11 Brazil, Melo concluded, "*Ou seja, somos todos um pouco árabes* [In other words, we are all a bit Arab]."

These subtle references to the "mixture" of Arabness in Brazil were accompanied by explicit public claims of racial democracy. A "March for Peace" had been carried out in the SAARA, an acronym for a downtown commercial district (and association) in Rio de Janeiro. It was organized in response to both the September 11 attacks and the continuing violence between Israelis and Palestinians. Making the eight o'clock Globo news on September 25, the march was said to have been purposefully held in the SAARA, a "traditional" area of Arab and Jewish commerce in Rio de Janeiro. The Globo news anchors explained that since the early twentieth century, Arabs and Jews "have lived together" in the same neighborhood and that the only *briga* (fight) was over prices and customers. Showing images of middle-aged merchants grasping each other's hands and torsos, the television anchors concluded: "Brazil is a country of tolerance." In a world of violent acts and retaliations, the Brazilian notion of racial democracy has taken on a novel ideological, and potentially progressive, purpose.

A different scenario unfolded in the US American context. Amid the real fear that anyone perceived as Arab or Muslim would be made [a] scapegoat[] for September 11, mass media embarked on a campaign to educate the public at large about Islam and the Arab world, including television documentaries on the Public Broadcasting System (Howell and Shryock 2004, 455), one hundred questions and answers about "Arab Americans" on the Detroit Free Press website, and an op-ed piece in the *New Yorker* (Shryock 2002, 918), among others. Headed by John Ashcroft, the US Attorney General's Office also issued several calls to respect Muslims, Arabs, and South Asians. Made just two days after September 11, one such announcement declared that "any threats of violence or discrimination against Arab or Muslim Americans or Americans of South Asian descent . . . are not just wrong and un-American, but also are unlawful and will be treated as such" (US Department of Justice, cited in Howell and Shryock 2004, 447). At the same time that actual Arabs and Muslims were monitored and targeted by the Federal Bureau of Investigation and Central Intelligence Agency in the United States, Arab and Islamic differences were encompassed by US American multiculturalist ideology.

This anecdotal comparison between Arabs in Brazil and [Arabs in] the United States should suggest that September 11, 2001, and later events are not a homogenizing force whereby Arabs across the Americas have been encompassed by the US American "war on terror" and similar politics. While Arabs and Muslims in the United States continue to be identified and separated out by US American multiculturalism, Arabs and Muslims in Brazil remain acknowledged within the Brazilian nationalist ideas of "mixture" and "racial democracy." This not only suggests that Arabs have been contained by national projects (Howell and Shryock 2004, 455). It also demonstrates that September 11 and its after-effects have reinforced—at least for now—the historically specific formations of Arabness in US American and Brazilian nationalist frameworks.

Works Cited

Baringer, Sandra. 1998. "*Oklahoma!* and Assimilation." *Proceedings of the Modern Language Association* 113, no. 3: 452–53.

Gattaz, André Castanheira. 2001. "História oral da imigração libanesa para o Brasil, 1880–2000." PhD diss., Universidade de São Paulo.

Habermas, Jürgen. 1989. *The Structural Transformation of the Public Sphere: An Inquiry into a Category of Bourgeois Society.* Cambridge, MA: MIT Press.

Harris, Marvin. 1964. *Patterns of Race in the Americas.* New York: Walker.

———. 1970. "Referential Ambiguity in the Calculus of Brazilian Racial Identity." *Southwestern Journal of Anthropology* 14, no. 4: 1–14.

Himadeh, Sa'id. 1936. *The Economic Organization of Syria and Lebanon.* Beirut: American Press.

Howell, Sally, and Andrew Shryock. 2004. "Cracking Down on Diaspora: Arab Detroit and America's War on Terror." *Anthropological Quarterly* 76, no. 3: 443–62.

Issawi, Charles, ed. 1966. *The Economic History of the Middle East 1800–1914.* Chicago: Univ. of Chicago Press.

Jozami, Gladys. 1996. "The Return of the '*Turks*' in 1990s Argentina." *Patterns of Prejudice* 30:16–35.

Karpat, Kemal. 1985. "The Ottoman Emigration to America." *International Journal of Middle East Studies* 17:175–209.

Khater, Akram. 2001. *Inventing Home: Emigration, Gender, and the Middle Class in Lebanon, 1870–1920.* Berkeley: Univ. of California Press.

Klich, Ignácio. 1992. "*Criollos* and Arabic Speakers in Argentina: An Uneasy *Pas de Deux*, 1888–1914." In *The Lebanese in the World: A Century of Emigration,* edited by Albert Hourani and Nadim Shehadi, 243–83. London: I. B. Tauris.

Kottack, Conrad. 1983. *Assault on Paradise: Social Change in a Brazilian Village.* New York: Random House.

Lesser, Jeffrey. 1999. *Negotiating National Identity: Immigrants, Minorities, and the Struggle for Ethnicity in Brazil.* Durham, NC: Duke Univ. Press.

Lewis, J. Lowell. 1999. "Sex and Violence in Brazil: Carnival, Capoeira, and the Problem of Everyday Life." *American Ethnologist* 26, no. 3: 717–32.

Massad, Joseph. 1993. "Palestinians and the Limits of Racialized Discourse." *Social Text* 11, no. 1: 90–112.

Miller, Lucius Hopkins. [1905] 1969. *Our Syrian Population: A Study of the Syrian Communities of Greater New York.* San Francisco: Reed.

Naber, Nadine. 2000. "Ambiguous Insiders: An Investigation of Arab American Invisibility." *Ethnic and Racial Studies* 23:37–61.

Nunes, Heliane Prudente. 1993. "A imigração árabe em Goiás." PhD diss., Universidade de São Paulo.

Omi, Michael, and Howard Winant. 1986. *Racial Formation in the United States: From the 1960s to the 1980s.* New York: Routledge.

Orfalea, Gregory. 1988. *Before the Flames: A Quest for the History of Arab Americans.* Austin: Univ. of Texas Press.

Riggs, Lynn. 1931. *Green Grow the Lilacs.* New York: Samuel French.

Roque, Carlos. 2000. "Líbano." In *Correntes de imigrantes e invenções culinárias no 5o centenário do Brasil,* 155–64. São Paulo, Brazil: n.p.

Saliba, Therese. 1999. "Resisting Invisibility: Arab Americans in Academia and Activism." In *Arabs in America: Building a New Future,* edited by Michael Suleiman, 304–19. Philadelphia: Temple Univ. Press.

Samhan, Helen Hatab. 1999. "Not Quite White: Race Classification and the Arab-American Experience." In *Arabs in America: Building a New Future,* edited by Michael Suleiman, 209–26. Philadelphia: Temple Univ. Press.

Sanjek, Roger. 1971. "Brazilian Racial Terms: Some Aspects of Meaning and Learning." *American Anthropologist* 73:1126–43.

Schopmeyer, Kim. 2000. "A Demographic Portrait of Arab Detroit." In *Arab Detroit: From Margin to Mainstream,* edited by Nabeel Abraham and Andrew Shryock, 61–92. Detroit: Wayne State Univ. Press.

Shaheen, Jack. 1984. *The TV Arab.* Bowling Green, OH: Bowling Green State Univ. Popular Press.

Shryock, Andrew. 2002. "New Images of Arab Detroit: Seeing Otherness and Identity through the Lens of September 11." *American Anthropologist* 104:917–22.

Suleiman, Michael. 1999. "Introduction: The Arab Immigration Experience." In *Arabs in America: Building a New Future,* edited by Michael Suleiman, 1–22. Philadelphia: Temple Univ. Press.

Truzzi, Oswaldo. 1997. *Patrícios: Sírios e libaneses em São Paulo.* São Paulo, Brazil: Editora Hucitec.

Varella, Flávia. 2000. "Patrícios, dinheiro, diploma e voto: A saga da imigração Árabe." *Veja* 4 (Oct.): 122–29.

Wagley, Charles, ed. 1952. *Race and Class in Rural Brazil.* Paris: United Nations Educational, Scientific, and Cultural Organization.

Winant, Howard. 1994. *Racial Conditions: Politics, Theory, Comparisons.* Minneapolis: Univ. of Minnesota Press.

Yuri, Débora. 2001. "O nosso lado árabe." *Revista da Folha*, Sept. 23.

Zogby, John. 1990. *Arab America Today: A Demographic Profile of Arab Americans.* Washington, DC: Zogby International.

Part Four
Orientalism and Arab Americans
Troubling Ways of Knowing

In her Farhat J. Ziadeh Distinguished Lecture in Arab and Islamic Studies in 2010, Yvonne Haddad noted that when Casey Kasem assembled a list of prominent Arab Americans, he privileged politicians and performers and did not include any scholars. While that may not be surprising given Kasem's own status as an entertainer, it nevertheless offers important context about the politics of representation in relation to Arab Americans. In privileging politicians and entertainers, Kasem's list implies a preference for highlighting Arab Americans' legitimacy through mainstream political participation and recognition by the entertainment industry. Though such listings and celebrations of prominent Arab Americans usually do not directly name damaging stereotypes about Arabs, they invite consideration of the way that self-representation is necessarily bound up with already-existing orientalist narratives of Arabs as exotic and/or violent others who somehow fall outside legitimate frameworks of what constitutes being "American." Insofar as the list compiled by Kasem could be seen as a defensive response to predominantly negative assumptions and portrayals of Arabs in mainstream media, it highlights the way that representational practices themselves have often been overdetermined by orientalism and the false binary of "negative" versus "positive" images.

This part of the reader considers how Arabs have been constructed in discourses about them, and it explores how Arab Americans have participated in strategic engagements with these discourses in visual media, marketing, politics, literature, and the arts. It is therefore framed by a set of intersecting questions: How have Arab Americans and Arab America been imagined, represented, and understood? How have Arab Americans subverted, reformulated, contested, or exploited these discourses about them in response to changing cultural constraints and political pressures? What are some of the contradictions or limitations of such interventions? In *Decolonizing Methodologies* ([1999] 2012), Linda Tuhiwai Smith writes that "what makes ideas 'real' is the system of knowledge, the formations of culture, and the relations of power in which these concepts are located" (50). Many of the essays collected in this part explore how the material realities of Arab Americans' lives have been shaped by representational strategies drawn from the long history and malleability of orientalist ideas and images, made all the more "real" by the political and cultural contexts that have shaped them, including more recent contexts of the "war on terror." Given its focus on knowledge production as structured by power, this part is therefore critically engaged with Edward Said's influential work *Orientalism* (1978), in which he employs the notion of "imaginative geographies" to describe the representational strategies that defined the West in opposition to a constructed East. Using the metaphor of the "stage" (63), Said asserts that "the Orient is less a place than a *topos*, a set of references, a congeries of characteristics, that seems to have its origin in a quotation, or a fragment of a text" (177). In other words, the idea of the "Orient" is choreographed through citational practices that together form what Michel Foucault (1982), whose work Said engages, calls a "discursive formation"—that set of phrases, keywords, and assumptions that determine how the "East" comes to be understood. In more recent iterations, this imaginative geography has been linked to a binary construction of "cultural" or "civilizational" difference, between East and West, an idea that substitutes nineteenth century imagined "racialized difference" with an imagined entrenched and inherent "cultural" or "civilizational" quality that is somehow devoid of the very historical, political, and social contexts that inform it (see Said 2001). Importantly, Said also locates the project of orientalist knowledge production in direct relationship to colonialism. Noting, for example, that Napoleon deployed scholars along with the military during the invasion of Egypt in 1798, Said shows how orientalism gains its authority through the production of knowledge. Building on Said, Lisa Lowe argues that orientalism is a heterogeneous "apparatus" (1991, 8) that can be flexibly appropriated in the service of colonialist and imperialist power.

Scholars have also pointed to the gendered and sexualized dynamics of orientalist imaginative geographies, with the East configured as seductively exotic, subordinately effeminate, and ruled by passion and, in contrast, the West as masculine, disciplined, and rational (Abu-Lughod 1998; Alloula 1986; Kahf 1999). This gendered binary, seemingly without contradiction, intersects with fantasy and desire to also create representations of the East as either homoerotic (Afary and Anderson 2005; Boone 2014; Foucault 1990) or sexually repressive and backward. Maintaining the association with rationality, the West, meanwhile, promotes itself through narratives of sexual liberalism and the rubrics of tolerance and exceptionalism (Eisenstein 2007; Puar 2007). Narratives of Arab culture as sexually repressive play out, for example, in the United States and Israel through "pinkwashing" campaigns that portray Israel and the United States as bastions of LGBTQ democratic-liberal acceptance in order to deflect attention from or even justify military invasions and occupations of Southwest Asian and North African (SWANA) countries (Hochberg 2010).

Scholarly work that addresses the various permutations of orientalist tropes associated with Arab Americans inspire this part of the reader. Arabs have at times been linked to a primitive but familiar past in the mythology of the Holy Land (McAlister [2001] 2005; Obenzinger 1999; Salaita 2006; Shakir 1997). They have also and to some extent continue to be linked to an alluring yet exotic Muslim-defined East that invokes *The Arabian Nights* and its associated exoticized orientalist imagery, such as the harem (Homsi Vinson 2014, 2015; Jarmakani 2008; Kahf 1999; Nance 2009; Shohat 1997). While the associations of Arabs both with the Holy Land and with orientalist ideas about an exotic East serve imperial aims (see Jarmakani 2008; McAlister [2001] 2005), they also reveal an attraction to and fascination with the "East" (Boone 2014; Nance 2009; Shamma 2009). However, as the United States rose as a global imperial power, dominant narratives shifted, so that the Arab "East" has become increasingly equated with the figure of the terrorist and/or Muslim fundamentalist (Cainkar 2018; Joseph and D'Harlingue 2008; Naber 2008; Said 1978, [1981] 1997; Shaheen [2001] 2009), a hostile valuation akin to earlier orientalist European views of the menacing Muslim "other," the "Turk" (Matar 2000; Vitkus 2003).

After September 11, 2001 (9/11), liberal multicultural narratives celebrating diversity were combined with the long-standing conflation of Arabs with Muslims and the demonization of both as terrorists in US discourses to produce what Mahmood Mamdani (2004) calls the "good Muslim, bad Muslim" dichotomy. Charting a rhetorical shift in the US administration's characterization of the "enemy" after the events of 9/11, Mamdani notes that the dichotomy introduces a false choice between seemingly positive liberal incorporation and blanket vilification: "After an unguarded reference to pursuing a 'crusade,' President Bush moved to distinguish between 'good Muslims' and 'bad Muslims.'" As Mamdani demonstrates, "the central message of such discourse: unless proved to be 'good,' every Muslim was presumed to be 'bad.' All Muslims were now under obligation to prove their credentials by joining in a war against 'bad Muslims'" (15). As Evelyn Alsultany (in chapter 21 in this part) has shown, the "good Muslim, bad Muslim" binary finds resonance in TV representations of Arabs and Muslims, which reproduce many of the same stereotypes about Arabs and Muslims from earlier representational practices, even if they pretend to present more "positive" portrayals than in previous times.

In line with the work of Said and subsequent studies in orientalism, Arab American cultural studies scholarship critically interrogates the politics of representation in relation to the politics of knowledge production. Early interventions in this area of scholarship include Jack Shaheen's books *The TV Arab* (1984) and *Reel Bad Arabs* ([2001] 2009), which identified predominant stereotypes about Arabs in popular TV and film. They also include Ronald Stockton's article "Ethnic Archetypes and the Arab Image" (1994), which traced the evolution of caricatures of Arabs in popular media and noted their continuity with antisemitic portrayals, and Ella Shohat's work on orientalism in film, which is reworked and incorporated into her book *Unthinking*

Eurocentrism (1994), coauthored with Robert Stam. Scholars in this area have tirelessly detected negative portrayals of Arabs in US popular culture as "villains and terrorists; maidens; or sheikhs" (Shaheen [2001] 2009, 25–34) and have categorized and unpacked common stereotypes about Arab women as both hypersexualized and oppressed (Kahf 2011). Building on the work of naming and deconstructing stereotypes, scholars in this area have also analyzed representations of Arabs in relation to other ethnic and racial groups in the United States, notably in relation to portrayals of Native Americans (Jarmakani 2008; Salaita 2006), and they have charted the legacies of these representations in connection to colonialist, militaristic, and imperialist projects (Alsultany 2012; Jarmakani 2008, 2015; Mahdi 2020; Salaita 2016). Jack Shaheen can be credited with essentially inaugurating the subfield of Arab American media studies. His careful cataloging of negative representations of Arabs (including their conflation with Muslims) in TV and film productions demonstrates the relentless and pervasive nature of these stereotypical portrayals, and his conclusions demonstrate an ethical commitment to addressing the damage these portrayals inflict. As Shaheen reminds us, "Filmmaking is political" (2008, xviii). Statements like this one, which is characteristic of both his work and the field more generally, ground Arab American media and cultural studies in the question of how representations are shaped by and, in turn, shape our political realities.

Building on the project of identifying and cataloging orientalist representations in US popular culture, both the essays that we include in this part and those that inspired it are further interested in (1) complicating the binary of "negative" and "positive" portrayals that frames representations of Arabs and Muslims in the media; (2) elucidating what has been illegible and unrepresented in mainstream popular culture; and (3) unsettling and destabilizing stereotypical images of Arabs and Muslims by demonstrating the connections between those images, US imperialism, and white-supremacist heteropatriarchy. All of these themes demonstrate how discursive formations and representational strategies of Arabs and Muslims are integral to both definitions of Arab Americans, covered in part one, and discussions of empire, covered in part five.

One project of the essays in this part is to expand the critical framework of orientalism. Matthew Jaber Stiffler's essay (chapter 26), for example, explores the phenomenon of self-orientalism through the strategic deployment of orientalist imagery in Arab American foodways. Stiffler's contribution also provokes us to think about how Arab Americans have at turns internalized, grappled with, and even appropriated and manipulated for their own benefit the dominant representations and understandings of Arabs. Pauline Homsi Vinson's essay (chapter 27) builds on these ideas by exploring how invoking the figure of Shahrazad in Arab American literature—though often taken as self-orientalism—can also demonstrate creative, subversive, and critically recuperative potential. Waïl Hassan's piece (chapter 23) demonstrates the way writers of the *mahjar* (emigrants from Ottoman-ruled Greater Syria) spoke back to European orientalist conceptions, with some, such as Ameen Rihani, essentially questioning orientalist frameworks and others, such as Kahlil Gibran, incorporating self-orientalizing conventions. The work by Evelyn Alsultany (chapter 21), mentioned earlier, complicates the idea that "positive" representations of Arabs and Muslims in mainstream TV and film are all it takes to redress the long tradition of racist orientalist stereotypes. Analyzing how mainstream TV drama series offer what she calls "simplified complex representations" (p. 295), Alsultany demonstrates that these series rehash many long-standing orientalist stereotypes of exotic Arabs and Muslims driven by unruly passions while simultaneously inscribing the "good Muslim, bad Muslim" (Mamdani 2004) binary reinforced by imperialist discourses of the war on terror.

Yet another project of the essays in this part is to highlight what has been excluded or obscured from dominant frames of representation; epistemological work must attend to questions of refusal and impossibility. Mejdulene Shomali's essay (chapter 24) charts the exclusion of queer femmes in Arab American literature and in popular representation more broadly. In the orientalist frame that reifies the idea of SWANA sexuality as either exoticized through femininity or repressed through modes of hypermasculinity, Shomali identifies the troubling pattern that "queer women can't exist, and queer men are necessarily hypermasculine to make up for their homosexuality" (p. 320). The selection from Jacob Rama Berman's book *American Arabesque* (chapter 22) points to another form of illegibility—namely, the role that oblique references to Arabs, Muslims, and Indigenous Imazighen play in the consolidation of the American national narrative. Attending to the line "the shores of Tripoli" in the US Marine Corps hymn and in the Mameluke sword earned by US Marine Corps officers, Berman traces how an American fantasy of spreading freedom and democracy across the globe was constructed around encounters between US marines, Indigenous people, Arabs, and Ottoman rulers in the early 1800s on the Barbary Coast of North Africa. Much like Toni Morrison's work *Playing in the Dark* (1992), which demonstrates how an unacknowledged Black presence in US literature actually enables its literary whiteness, Berman's work uncovers the obscured and unacknowledged role of Arab cultural symbols in the mainstream US national imaginary.

Indeed, as demonstrated in essays included in other parts—by Christina Civantos, Hisham Aidi, Ella Shohat—orientalism manifests differently throughout the Americas and is also shaped by what Aidi (2003) has called the "Moorish Atlantic." If Christopher Columbus can be regarded as "the first Orientalist of the Americas" (Shohat, chapter 4, p. 87) insofar as the discovery doctrine had already orientalized Indigenous peoples as *los indios*, the concept of the "Moorish Atlantic" also foregrounds analyses of conquest and settler colonialism as central to interrogations of orientalism in the Americas.

Moreover, crossover popular-culture phenomena—such as the widespread popularity of Columbian Lebanese singer Shakira and the worldwide syndication of the originally Brazilian telenovela *O Clone* (Aidi 2014; Alsultany and Shohat 2013; Karam 2010)—underscore the necessity of fostering a broader perspective of orientalism as shaped by "the coloniality of power," a framework that decenters Eurocentric models of understanding colonialism and imperialism (Dussel 1995; Grosfoguel 2006; Lugones 2010; Quijano 2000;).

The aim of representation can also be to disrupt dominant narratives. For example, Wafaa Bilal's art installation project *Domestic Tension* (2007), which he chronicles in the book *Shoot an Iraqi: Art, Life, and Resistance under the Gun* (Bilal and Lydersen 2008), forces webcam viewers to engage with the reality of "living under fire" by inviting them to shoot a paintball gun at him. Simulating the circumstances of living under military fire during the US-led war on Iraq, Bilal enacts what Carol W. N. Fadda calls a "performative destabilization" (chapter 11, p. 171) of dehumanizing constructions of Arab/Muslim men. Directly confronting orientalist and imperialist portrayals, the pieces we have gathered in part four address how artistic and cultural works trouble dominant representational practices in ways that unsettle and destabilize them. Focusing on theater, Michael Malek Najjar (chapter 25) discusses how Arab American solo female performers embody and reenact their own experiences in ways that confront and challenge dominant US narratives about Arabs and the ramifications of US military intervention in Southwest Asia and North Africa. At the same time as art intervenes in dominant understandings of SWANA, it can also provide a forum for Arab Americans to grapple with feeling caught between essentializing narratives of cultural authenticity and orientalist representations. Umayyah Cable (chapter 13) addresses this issue in their discussion of Palestinian and Arab film festivals, as does Thea Abu El-Haj (2009) in her work.

In disrupting strict demarcations between "over there" and "over here," such scholarship and the art it analyzes force readers and viewers to confront the impacts of violent US military intervention and imperialism on the actual bodies and life experiences of people in and from SWANA.

Analyzing the impacts of representations and their power to shape, reflect, and justify imperialism and structural racism has been a major concern of the field of Arab American studies. Indeed, in his most recent book, *Guilty* (2008), Jack Shaheen reaffirms the conclusions of *Reel Bad Arabs* ([2001] 2009): "You, dear reader, should mull over this telling political-entertainment linkage: Long before the United States launched real expeditionary operations against Iraq in March 2003, Hollywood was already launching a reel war against reel [*sic*] Arabs" (xviii–xix). As important as the argument that stereotypical representations can materially support and justify the decision to invade Iraq (among other devastating military actions) is the fact that Arab American scholars have had to make this argument again and again. Indeed, in his introduction to the second edition of *Covering Islam* ([1981] 1997), Said notes that in the intervening fifteen years between the two editions, popular discourse about Arabs and Muslims had exhibited only "more highly exaggerated stereotyping and belligerent hostility" (xi) than what he had described in the first edition in 1981. Whether identifying, deconstructing, dismantling, or pushing back against the long-standing barrage of stereotypes about Arabs and Muslims, much of the research on ways of knowing, representing, and understanding Arabs in the Americas has sought to reveal and redress the deleterious effects of orientalist imagery on the peoples it purports to represent. At the same time, this work has produced critical interventions of incredible creativity, political power, and aesthetic appeal, and in so doing it has disrupted heteronormative, nation-bound, and racialized modes of seeing, understanding, and representing Arab Americans.

Works Cited

Abu El-Haj, Thea Renda. 2009. "Imagining Postnationalism: Arts, Citizenship Education, and Arab American Youth." *Anthropology & Education Quarterly* 40, no. 1: 1–19.

Abu-Lughod, Lila. 1998. "Feminist Longings and Postcolonial Conditions." In *Remaking Women: Feminism and Modernity in the Middle East*, edited by Lila Abu-Lughod, 3–31. Princeton, NJ: Princeton Univ. Press.

Afary, Janet, and Kevin Anderson. 2005. *Foucault and the Iranian Revolution: Gender and the Seductions of Islamism*. Chicago: Univ. of Chicago Press.

Aidi, Hisham. 2003. "The Moorish Atlantic: Moors, Aztecs, and the Invention of the Americas." Paper prepared for the seminar "Modernity and Its Others," taught by Paul Gilroy, Sociology Department, Yale Univ., New Haven, CT, May.

———. 2014. *Rebel Music: Race, Empire, and the New Muslim Youth Culture*. New York: Vintage.

Alloula, Malek. 1986. *The Colonial Harem*. Translated by Myrna Godzich and Wlad Godzich. Minneapolis: Univ. of Minnesota Press.

Alsultany, Evelyn. 2012. *Arabs and Muslims in the Media: Race and Representation after 9/11*. New York: New York Univ. Press.

Alsultany, Evelyn, and Ella Shohat, eds. 2013. *Between the Middle East and the Americas: The Cultural Politics of Diaspora*. Ann Arbor: Univ. of Michigan Press.

Bilal, Wafaa, and Kari Lydersen. 2008. *Shoot an Iraqi: Art, Life, and Resistance under the Gun*. San Francisco: City Lights Press.

Boone, Joseph Allen. 2014. *The Homoerotics of Orientalism*. New York: Columbia Univ. Press.

Cainkar, Louise. 2018. "Fluid Terror Threat: A Genealogy of the Racialization of Arab, Muslim, and South Asian Americans." In "Arab/Americas: Locations & Iterations," edited by Sarah M. A. Gualtieri and Pauline Homsi Vinson. Special issue of *Amerasia Journal* 44, no. 1: 27–60.

Dussel, Enrique. 1995. *The Invention of the Americas: Eclipse of "the Other" and the Myth of Modernity*. Translated by Michael D. Barber. New York: Continuum.

Eisenstein, Zillah. 2007. *Sexual Decoys: Gender, Race, and War in Imperial Democracy*. London: Zed Press.

Foucault, Michel. 1982. *The Archaeology of Knowledge*. Translated by A. M. Sheridan Smith. New York: Pantheon. Orig. pub. in French in 1969.

———. 1990. *The History of Sexuality*. Vol. 1: *An Introduction*. Translated by Robert Hurley. New York: Vintage Books. Orig. pub. in French in 1976.

Grosfoguel, Ramón. 2006. "World-Systems Analysis in the Context of Transmodernity, Border Thinking, and Global Coloniality." *Review* (Fernand Braudel Center) 29, no. 2: 167–87.

Hochberg, Gil Z. 2010. "Introduction: Israelis, Palestinians, Queers: Points of Departure." *GLQ* 16, no. 4: 493–516.

Homsi Vinson, Pauline. 2014. "Re-encountering Scheherazade: Gender, Cultural Mobility, and Narrative Transformations in Alia Yunis's *The Night Counter*." In "Gender and Mobility," edited by Sarah M. A. Gualtieri and Akram Khater. Special issue of *Mashriq & Mahjar* 2, no. 1: 55–76.

———. 2015. "Representations of Sexualities: United States." In *Encyclopedia of Women and Islamic Cultures (EWIC)*, edited by Suad Joseph, guest edited by Sarah Gualtieri. Leiden: Brill Online, Feb. At http://dx.doi.org/10.1163/1872-5309_ewic_COM_002015.

Jarmakani, Amira. 2008. *Imagining Arab Womanhood: The Cultural Mythology of Veils, Harems, and Belly Dancers in the U.S.* New York: Palgrave.

———. 2015. *An Imperialist Love Story: Desert Romances and the War on Terror.* New York: New York Univ. Press.

Joseph, Suad, and Benjamin D'Harlingue, with Alvin Ka Hin Wong. 2008. "Arab Americans and Muslim Americans in the *New York Times*, before and after 9/11." In *Race and Arab Americans before and after 9/11: From Invisible Citizens to Visible Subjects*, edited by Amaney Jamal and Nadine Naber, 229–75. Syracuse, NY: Syracuse Univ. Press.

Kahf, Mohja. 1999. *Western Representations of the Muslim Woman: From Termagant to Odalisque*. Austin: Univ. of Texas Press.

———. 2011. "The Pity Committee and the Careful Reader: How Not to Buy Stereotypes about Muslim Women." In *Arab & Arab American Feminisms: Gender, Violence, & Belonging*, edited by Rabab Abdulhadi, Evelyn Alsultany, and Nadine Naber, 111–23. Syracuse, NY: Syracuse Univ. Press.

Karam, John Tofik. 2010. "Belly Dancing and the (En)gendering of Ethnic Sexuality in the 'Mixed' Brazilian Nation." *Journal of Middle East Women's Studies* 6, no. 2: 86–114.

Lowe, Lisa. 1991. *Critical Terrains: French and British Orientalisms*. Ithaca, NY: Cornell Univ. Press.

Lugones, María. 2010. "Toward a Decolonial Feminism." *Hypatia* 25, no. 4: 742–59.

Mahdi, Waleed F. 2020. *Arab Americans in Film: From Hollywood and Egyptian Stereotypes to Self-Representation*. Syracuse, NY: Syracuse Univ. Press.

Mamdani, Mahmood. 2004. *Good Muslim, Bad Muslim: America, the Cold War, and the Roots of Terror.* New York: Pantheon.

Matar, Nabil. 2000. *Turks, Moors, and Englishmen in the Age of Discovery*. New York: Columbia Univ. Press.

McAlister, Melani. [2001] 2005. *Epic Encounters: Culture, Media, and U.S. Interests in the Middle East 1945–2000*. Berkeley: Univ. of California Press.

Morrison, Toni. 1992. *Playing in the Dark: Whiteness and the Literary Imagination.* Cambridge, MA: Harvard Univ. Press.

Naber, Nadine. 2008. "'Look, Mohammed the Terrorist Is Coming!': Cultural Racism, Nation-Based Racism, and the Intersectionality of Oppressions after 9/11." In *Race and Arab Americans before and after 9/11: From Invisible Citizens to Visible Subjects*, edited by Amaney Jamal and Nadine Naber, 276–304. Syracuse, NY: Syracuse Univ. Press.

Nance, Susan. 2009. *How* The Arabian Nights *Inspired the American Dream.* Chapel Hill: Univ. of North Carolina Press.

Obenzinger, Hilton. 1999. *American Palestine: Melville, Twain, and the Holy Land Mania.* Princeton, NJ: Princeton Univ. Press.

Puar, Jasbir. 2007. *Terrorist Assemblages: Homonationalism in Queer Times.* Durham, NC: Duke Univ. Press.

Quijano, Aníbal. 2000. "Coloniality of Power, Ethnocentrism, and Latin America." *Nepantla* 1, no. 3: 533–80.

Said, Edward. 1978. *Orientalism.* New York: Vintage Books.

———. [1981] 1997. *Covering Islam: How the Media and the Experts Determine How We See the Rest of the World.* New York: Pantheon.

———. 2001. "The Clash of Ignorance." *Nation*, Oct. 4. At https://www.thenation.com/article/archive/clash-ignorance/.

Salaita, Steven. 2006. *The Holy Land in Transit: Colonialism and the Quest for Canaan.* Syracuse, NY: Syracuse Univ. Press.

———. 2016. *Inter/Nationalism: Decolonizing Native America and Palestine.* Minneapolis: Univ. of Minnesota Press.

Shaheen, Jack G. 1984. *The TV Arab.* Bowling Green, OH: Bowling Green State Univ. Popular Press.

———. 2008. *Guilty: Hollywood's Verdict on Arabs after 9/11.* New York: Olive Branch Press.

———. [2001] 2009. *Reel Bad Arabs: How Hollywood Vilifies a People.* Updated ed. New York: Olive Branch Press.

Shakir, Evelyn. 1997. *Bint Arab: Arab and Arab American Women in the United States.* Westport, CT: Praeger.

Shamma, Tarek. 2009. *Translation and the Manipulation of Difference: Arabic Literature in Nineteenth-Century England.* New York: Routledge.

Shohat, Ella. 1997. "Gender and Culture of Empire: Toward a Feminist Ethnography of Cinema." In *Visions of the East: Orientalism in Film*, edited by Matthew Bernstein and Gaylyn Studlar, 19–66. New Brunswick, NJ: Rutgers Univ. Press.

Shohat, Ella, and Robert Stam. 1994. *Unthinking Eurocentrism: Multiculturalism and the Media.* New York: Routledge.

Smith, Linda Tuhiwai. [1999] 2012. *Decolonizing Methodologies: Research and Indigenous Peoples.* 2nd ed. New York: Zed Books.

Stockton, Ronald. 1994. "Ethnic Archetypes and the Arab Image." In *The Development of Arab-American Identity*, edited by Ernest McCarus, 119–53. Ann Arbor: Univ. of Michigan Press.

Vitkus, Daniel. 2003. *Turning Turk: English Theater and the Multicultural Mediterranean, 1570–1630.* New York: Palgrave McMillan.

21

How TV Dramas Legitimized Torture during the War on Terror

EVELYN ALSULTANY

> Am I crazy or is attacking torture by lobbying the producers of *24* almost as ridiculous as trying to make nuclear power plants safer by urging the producers of *The Simpsons* to stop letting Homer play with plutonium in the lunchroom of the Springfield nuke plant?
>
> —Peter Carlson, *Washington Post*

> Intentionally or not—and for better and for worse—fiction can play a real role in the construction of political reality. Amid the global war on terror, those in Hollywood and those in Washington would do well to take heed of this fact about fiction.
>
> —Kelly M. Greenhill, *Los Angeles Times*

In 2004 the Council on American–Islamic Relations (CAIR) accused the TV drama *24* of perpetuating stereotypes of Arabs and Muslims (*Free Republic* 2005). CAIR objected to the persistent portrayal of Arabs and Muslims in the context of terrorism, stating that "repeated association of acts of terrorism with Islam will only serve to increase anti-Muslim prejudice" (*BBC News* 2007).[1] CAIR's critics retorted that programs like *24* are cutting edge, reflecting one of the most pressing social and political issues of the moment, the war on terror. Some critics further contended that CAIR was trying to deflect the reality of Muslim-led terrorism by confining television writers to politically correct themes.[2]

The writers and producers of *24* responded to CAIR's concerns in a number of ways. For one, the show often included sympathetic portrayals of Arabs and Muslims, in which they are the "good guys" or in some way on the side of the United States. Representatives of *24* stated that the show had "made a concerted effort to show ethnic, religious and political groups as multi-dimensional, and political issues are debated from multiple viewpoints" (*Northern Territory News* 2007, 23). The villains on the eight seasons of *24* were Russian, German, Latino, Arab/Muslim, Euro-American, and African, even the fictional president of the United States. Rotating the identity of the "bad guy" is one of the many strategies used by TV dramas to avoid reproducing the Arab/Muslim terrorist

Excerpt from Evelyn Alsultany, *Arabs and Muslims in the Media: Race and Representation after 9/11* (New York: New York Univ. Press, 2012), 18–46; the chapter title has been changed for this publication. Full references in the original notes were converted to author-date citations in the text and notes here, and a works cited list was added. Reprinted with corrections and press style changes for consistency throughout the volume by permission of New York University Press.

1. CAIR has also created an advertising campaign to counteract negative stereotypes. For an analysis of its ad campaign, see Alsultany 2007 and chapter 5 [in *Arabs and Muslims in the Media*].

2. Critics of CAIR include www.jihadwatch.org and www.frontpagemag.com.

stereotype (or any other stereotypes, for that matter).[3] *24*'s responsiveness to such criticism even extended to creating a public-service announcement (PSA) that was broadcast in February 2005, during one of the program's commercial breaks. The PSA featured the lead actor, Kiefer Sutherland, staring deadpan into the camera, reminding viewers that "the American Muslim community stands firmly beside their fellow Americans in denouncing and resisting all forms of terrorism" and urging us to "please bear that in mind" while watching the program.[4]

CAIR is not the only organization that lobbied *24* to change its representations. Whereas CAIR objected to stereotyping Arabs and Muslims as terrorists, the Parents Television Council, Human Rights First, and faculty from West Point Military Academy objected to *24*'s portrayal of torture as an effective method of interrogation. The Parents Television Council was concerned that children would become desensitized to torture; Human Rights First was concerned that viewers might come to perceive certain human beings as deserving of torture, not worthy of human rights; and the West Point faculty were concerned that some of their cadets believed torture was an effective method of interrogation because of *24*'s portrayal of it. Tony Lagouranis, former army interrogator, stated, "Among the things that I saw people doing [in Iraq] that they got from television was water-boarding, mock execution, using mock torture" (*Democracy Now!* 2007).

Howard Gordon, one of the writers, responded by stating, "I think people can differentiate between a television show and reality" (quoted in Mayer 2007). The writers and producers of *24* explained that the show was fictional, that it was not intended as a documentary or military manual. They went on to say that the torture scenes are for dramatic, entertainment purposes only. Furthermore, the writers and producers of *24* stated that although the character Bauer uses torture and is a US hero, torture is not glamorized because Bauer is traumatized by his use of torture. However, Joel Surnow, executive producer, defended the use of torture in the show, claiming, "We've had all of these torture experts come by recently, and they say, 'You don't realize how many people are affected by this. Be careful.' They say torture doesn't work. But I don't believe that. I don't think it's honest to say that if someone you love was being held, and you had five minutes to save them, you wouldn't do it." In contrast, Sutherland expressed concern about the "unintended consequences of the show." Fox Television network executive David Nevins admitted that the show conveyed a clear message on the war on terror: "There's definitely a political attitude of the show, which is that extreme measures are sometimes necessary for the greater good. The show doesn't have much patience for the niceties of civil liberties or due process" (all quoted in Mayer 2007).

In November 2006 members of Human Rights First and West Point met with the writers and producers of *24* to address the potential impact of their representations of torture (Bauder 2007; Mayer 2007; Miller 2007). David Danzig, manager at Human Rights First, explained that the meeting was difficult for *24*'s writers and producers because "they have a hugely popular show, and we were suggesting to them that they do something actually a little bit risky, which is change their format. And there's obviously a lot of money at stake." Though the *24* crew insisted their depiction of torture should not have an influence on its viewers, it is interesting to note that the story line of the next season (which debuted on January 13, 2008, fourteen months after the meeting) involved Jack Bauer being tried by the US government for his illegal use of torture.

This [essay] explores this slippery realm between representations and their potential impacts. Through each facet of this discussion, what arises is a fact that is utterly taken for granted: television mediates the war on terror. Between 2001 and 2009 the fictional creations of a tiny number of artists and executives shaped the ways that viewers engaged with the very real war going on around us. As indicated in the opening epigraph, the journalist Peter Carlson thinks that it is ridiculous that a TV drama, rather than the US government, was criticized for its role in torture (and for its *representation* at that). Whether [that was] ridiculous or not, the journalist Kelly M. Greenhill (2007) asserts that it is important to take seriously the power of TV dramas to shape public

3. I use "Arab/Muslim" not to denote that these identities are one and the same but rather to point to how Arab and Muslim identities are conflated.

4. This PSA was broadcast during one of the program's commercial breaks on Monday, February 7, 2005, on Fox.

perceptions of the war on terror. Throughout the Bush years, TV shows became a crucial way that Americans saw, thought about, and talked about the United States in a state of emergency after 9/11. Public debate, it sometimes seemed, was displaced onto TV dramas. The slippage between debating a television show and debating a government's policies and practices demonstrates the significance of TV dramas during the war on terror.

After September 11, 2001, a number of TV dramas were created using the war on terror as their central theme. Dramas such as *24* (2001–11), *Threat Matrix* (2003–4), *The Grid* (2004), *Sleeper Cell* (2005–6), and *The Wanted* (2009) depict US government agencies and officials heroically working to make the nation safe by battling terrorism. A prominent feature of these television shows is Arab and Muslim characters, most of whom are portrayed as grave threats to US national security. But in response to increased popular awareness of ethnic stereotyping and the active monitoring of Arab and Muslim watchdog groups, television writers had to adjust their story lines to avoid blatant, crude stereotyping.

24 and *Sleeper Cell* were among the most popular of the fast-emerging post-9/11 genre of terrorism dramas. *24* centered on Jack Bauer, a brooding and embattled agent of the government's Counter-Terrorism Unit (CTU) who raced a ticking clock to subvert impending terrorist attacks on the United States. The title refers to a twenty-four-hour state of emergency, and each of a given season's twenty-four episodes represented one hour of "real" time. *Sleeper Cell* was not as popular as *24*, partly because it was broadcast on the cable network Showtime and therefore had a much smaller audience. While *24* lasted eight seasons, *Sleeper Cell* lasted two. *Sleeper Cell*'s story line revolved around an undercover African American Muslim FBI agent who infiltrates a group of homegrown terrorists (the "cell" of the show's title) in order to subvert their planned attack on the United States.

This chapter [of *Arabs and Muslims in the Media*] focuses on episodes of *24* that revolved around themes of terrorism. I begin by introducing the term "simplified complex representations," through which I map the representational strategies that have become standard since the multicultural movement of the 1990s. Analyzing the TV drama *24* as a case study, I address the concerns expressed by various organizations regarding representations of torture on TV dramas, demonstrating the impact of such fictional representations on actual military and torture strategies. I argue that terrorism TV dramas like *24* were central to normalizing logics that legitimized torturing Arab and Muslim men, conveying that torture is necessary and effective to winning the war on terror.

Simplified Complex Representations

Simplified complex representations are strategies used by television producers, writers, and directors to give the impression that the representations they are producing are complex. While I focus on television, film uses these strategies as well. Here I briefly describe the most common ways that writers and producers of television dramas depicted Arab and Muslim characters after 9/11 and during the years of the Bush administration. While some of these [ways] were used more frequently (and to greater narrative success) than others, they all helped to shape the many layers of simplified complexity. I argue that simplified complex representations are the representational mode of the so-called postrace era, signifying a new era of racial representation. These representations appear to challenge or complicate former stereotypes and contribute to a multicultural or postrace illusion. Yet at the same time most of the programs that employ simplified complex representational strategies promote logics that legitimize racist policies and practices, such as torturing Arabs and Muslims. The seven strategies include: (1) Inserting Patriotic Arab or Muslim Americans; (2) Sympathizing with the Plight of Arab and Muslim Americans after 9/11; (3) Challenging the Arab/Muslim Conflation with Diverse Muslim Identities; (4) Flipping the Enemy; (5) Humanizing the Terrorist; (6) Projecting a Multicultural US Society; and (7) Fictionalizing the Middle Eastern or Muslim Country. . . .

The seven representational strategies I have found are not exhaustive, nor are they all new to our post-9/11 world. Rather, these strategies collectively outline some of the ways in which writers and producers of television (and film) have sought to improve representations of Arabs (and other racial and ethnic groups). These strategies are an astounding shift in the mass-entertainment landscape.

They present an important departure from stereotypes into more challenging stories and characters. This new breed of terrorism programs reflects a growing sensitivity to the negative impact of stereotyping. These new representational strategies seek to make the point—indeed, often with strenuous effort—that not all Arabs are terrorists and not all terrorists are Arabs. However, for all their innovations, these programs remain wedded to a script that represents Arabs and Muslims only in the context of terrorism and therefore do not effectively challenge the stereotypical representations of Arabs and Muslims.

Stuart Hall has claimed that even those with the best intentions, liberal writers and producers who seek to subvert racial hierarchies, may inadvertently participate in inferential racism—that is, "apparently naturalized representations of events and situations relating to race, whether 'factual' or 'fictional,' which have racist premises and propositions inscribed in them as a set of unquestioned assumptions" ([1981] 2000, 273). The persistent unquestioned assumption in these TV dramas is that Arabs and Muslims are terrorists, despite writers' efforts to create a wider range of Arab and Muslim characters. The primary objective of commercial television networks is not education, social justice, or social change. Rather, the goal is financial, to keep as many viewers watching for as long as possible. Television must therefore strike a balance between keeping its products as engaging as possible and not offending potential viewers. Writers thus seem to be constrained and influenced by two factors: viewers have been primed to assume that Arabs/Muslims are terrorists, and therefore writers create what viewers expect and what will sell; at the same time, some viewers are particularly sensitive and fed up with stereotypes, and therefore writers must create a more diverse world of characters. The results are some modifications to avoid being offensive while perpetuating core stereotypes that continue to have cultural capital (see Bourdieu 1993 for his definition of cultural capital). Post-9/11 television is testimony to the fact that the stereotypes that held sway for much of the twentieth century are no longer socially acceptable—at least in their most blatant forms. But this does not mean that such stereotypes (and viewers' taste for them) have actually gone away; they have only become covert. Simplified complex representational strategies reflect the commodification of the civil rights and multiculturalist movements. The commodification of multiculturalism, while reflecting the sensibilities of some viewers, is submerged under the more prominent consumable message that Arabs and Muslims pose a terrorist threat to American life and freedom.

These strategies attempt to make representations complex yet do so in a simplified way; they are predictable strategies that can be relied on if the plot involves an Arab or Muslim terrorist but are a new standard alternative to (and seem a great improvement on) the stock ethnic villains of the past. Under the guise of complexity, these representational strategies construct "good" and "bad" Arabs and Muslims, reinforcing a narrow conception of what constitutes a "good" Arab or Muslim (Mamdani 2004). "Bad" Arabs or Muslims are the terrorists, and their "good" counterparts are those who help the US government fight terrorism. Despite the shift away from the more blatant stereotypes of previous decades, Arab and Muslim identities are still understood and evaluated primarily in relation to terrorism. This binary focus, in turn, overpowers the strategies described above. Though some television writers and producers might honestly desire to create innovative shows, devoid of stereotypes, any such efforts are overwhelmed by the sheer momentum of our current representational scheme. Thus, representations of Arab and Muslim identities in contexts that have nothing to do with terrorism remained strikingly unusual in the US commercial media in the decade after 9/11.[5] . . .

While these representational strategies that challenge the stereotyping of Arabs and Muslims were being broadcast, circulated, and consumed, real Arabs and Muslims were being detained, deported, held without due process, and tortured. Certainly not all Arabs and Muslims were subject to post-9/11 harassment. Nonetheless, what I am arguing is that simplified complex racial representations—a new representational mode collectively constructed by these multiple representational

5. Even recent films with positive representations of Arab and Muslim characters, such as *The Visitor* (2007) and *Sorry, Haters* (2005), are framed in the context of 9/11. *Little Mosque on the Prairie* (2007–12), a sitcom televised by the Canadian Broadcasting Corporation, has not crossed over into the United States.

strategies—perform the ideological work of producing a postrace moment in which denying the severity of the persistence of institutionalized racism becomes possible. These TV dramas produce reassurance that racial sensitivity is the norm in US society while simultaneously perpetuating the dominant perception of Arabs and Muslims as threats to US national security. . . .

Although the impact of their particular representational strategies is limited, the impact of the TV dramas themselves is far-reaching. Operating as sites to discuss and debate the war on terror, TV dramas have participated in mediating the war itself. They do this by producing a public around it, by lifting "people from the realm of their idiosyncratic interests, their 'particularity,' towards the realm of common interests, the 'universal' values that join them together and define a collectivity of spectators as precisely a 'public'" (Chouliaraki 2006, 30). TV dramas turn the war on terror into a common interest on at least two levels. First, TV dramas base their story lines on current events, thereby establishing a relationship to pressing political concerns. Despite being fictional, TV dramas are intimately involved with the particulars of the war on terror, creating a product that can feel more real to viewers than the news media. In other words, through TV dramas viewers can imagine the war on terror in a nonabstract way: they can watch US government agencies at work to combat terrorism; they get to know the terrorists and get to virtually visit Afghanistan and other sites where the war on terror is waged. Second, in addition to or as an extension of political forums, viewers discuss the war on terror on internet forums, which in turn become places where government policies are discussed and debated, which in turn further blurs the boundaries between the war on terror and its representation. The fact that various groups lobbied particular TV dramas to change their representation of Arabs/Muslims or of torture in order to manage the potential adverse impact on public perceptions demonstrates how powerfully television mediates the war on terror. Writers and producers of TV dramas were pressured to be accountable to the possibility of viewers consuming their representations as a clone of the war on terror.

TV dramas that represent the war on terror have an intimate relationship with what comes to be imagined and understood as "the real," by which I mean the "truth" produced by the US government about the war on terror. Because TV dramas have a semblance of "the real"—indeed, they take great pains to create a sense of authenticity—they can become an extension of it (see Sontag 1977). According to Jean Baudrillard (1994), it is not that the representation threatens to replace the original but rather that the distinction between the original and its representation has broken down. Representations of reality—images, symbols, signs, media—have come to stand in for "the real" to the extent that the representation becomes indistinguishable from the original, or what he terms "clones of the real." Some viewers experience and make sense of the war on terror through its simulation. As Susan Willis writes,

> America lives its history as a cultural production. The post-9/11 era, as one defined by individual uncertainty in the face of an over-certain but often mistaken and repressive state, has seen a tremendous burgeoning of cultural forms meant to explain and manage the crisis. Daily life in America is articulated across an array of competing popular fictions. (2005, 4–5)

Fictional TV dramas examined in this [essay] are cultural forms that participated in explaining and managing the war on terror. Viewers' experiences of the war on terror, in turn, were intimately linked to these cultural forms.

Prime-Time Torture

The controversy surrounding *24*'s depiction of torture arose shortly after the revelation that US military personnel had tortured inmates at Iraq's Abu Ghraib prison (Leung 2004). Leaked photos showed Iraqi prisoners being physically, psychologically, and sexually abused. The horrific photos intensified the debate about whether or not the US government was sanctioning torture. In the view of the right-wing commentator Rush Limbaugh, the photos did not reveal torture but rather the US military "blowing off steam"; he questioned what the public was so worried about since the torture victims "are trying to kill us" (in Meyer 2004).

Here I explore the extent to which TV dramas mediate the war on terror by normalizing logics that legitimize torture. The apparent contradiction here is a key example of how simplified complex representations operate: in the case of *24*, multiple strategies are employed to avoid a simple conflation of Arabs and Muslims with terrorism, yet at the same time for many Americans *24* has helped make the real torture of Arabs and Muslims seem like a necessary evil— regrettable, perhaps, but essential for the safety of our nation.

In *24* this process works in various ways, all of which ultimately create a sense of urgent realism, a sense that disaster could strike at any moment and thus that quick decisions must be made (even if they are difficult ones). One such device is the use of a split screen in order to present the show's multiple plotlines and a version of "real time." The most important of these techniques, however, is the "ticking time bomb scenario,"[6] one of the show's foundational plot devices. Agent Jack Bauer knows that a deadly bomb will be detonated within the next few hours; he therefore must make the difficult decision to torture a suspect in order to obtain the necessary information to disarm the bomb. The "real time" and ticking time bomb scenarios create an environment of immediate urgency. However, creating a sense of realism and a realistic portrayal are very distinct objectives; the ticking time bomb scenario as a symbol of the war on terror might effectively create dramatic realism but is not necessarily realistic. The ticking time bomb scenario has powerfully influenced the public discourse on the war on terror, particularly the debate on torture. Right-wing politicians and advocates reason that torture is necessary precisely because of this specter of an impending attack. President Bush in a nationally televised speech told citizens that the CIA, in successfully capturing and questioning terrorist Khalid Sheik Mohammed, extracted timely information using procedures that stopped further terrorist attacks (McCoy 2006). In other words, the ticking time bomb scenario represented in *24* was used as a justification for torture in the war on terror.

As I mentioned at the beginning of this [essay], the writers and producers of *24* repeatedly claimed that their show is entertainment as opposed to a realistic or educational program on the war on terror. And as I mentioned, the show has been criticized by a range of groups for its depiction of terror. These groups fear that the show will sway its viewers into perceiving torture as a necessary and effective technique. The frequency and intensity of these attacks are perhaps the most compelling evidence of just how gripping the show's depiction of torture is. Again and again in *24*, Jack Bauer employs any means necessary to capture terrorists and thwart terrorist attacks. Across the show's eight seasons, viewers witnessed Bauer choking, suffocating, electrocuting, stabbing, and shooting suspects in the hope of extracting information. As an outlaw hero, Bauer's heroism relies on his breaking the rules to save the day. Thus viewers are frequently reminded that Bauer's actions are illegal to heighten the dramatic quality of his actions. Furthermore, he doesn't *want* to be doing this, but he *has* to do it—for the sake of all of us. Jack Bauer breaks the law in order to (often single-handedly) stop terrorism and save lives. He is a stunningly successful manifestation of situational morality: he is the good guy who does bad things because they are justifiable. The show thus positions viewers to admire his bravery, even if repelled by his actions; Bauer's choices are portrayed as difficult and sad, perhaps even terrible, but nonetheless necessary (Sutherland and Swan 2007). According to the logic of *24*, we would all be dead if it weren't for Jack Bauer.

As mentioned, the Parents Television Council expressed concern that children who watch *24*'s torture scenes may become desensitized to violence and may perceive torture favorably. Human Rights First expressed concern that viewers might conclude that not all human beings are deserving of basic human rights. Military faculty from West Point expressed concern that *24* was having an undue influence on US interrogators in the field and on cadets in training. Because torture has been found to be an ineffective method of interrogation, they wanted the show to make torture scenes realistic: subjects do not necessarily "break" in a few minutes or hours—as they so often do under Bauer's coercion—and then provide truthful information (Miller 2007). West Point faculty

6. For more on these strategies, see Peacock 2007.

stated that it is not uncommon for a tortured suspect to provide false information in order to stop whatever is being done to him; it can take weeks or even months for a suspect to break, and some die in the process. They stated that a more realistic scenario would be to spend months with a prisoner establishing trust (which is how *Sleeper Cell* portrayed interrogation). West Point faculty witnessed military cadets disregard their training in order to mimic Jack Bauer. Tony Lagouranis, a former US Army interrogator at Abu Ghraib, stated that such programs can trump the military training that soldiers receive. Brigadier-General Patrick Finnegan, dean of West Point, stated that Bauer's illegal behavior, persistent violation of protocols, and use of torture were influencing young soldiers in the field: "The disturbing thing is that although torture may cause Jack Bauer some angst, it is always the patriotic thing to do" (quoted in Buncombe 2007). In other words, *24*, whether intended or not, has successfully linked torture to patriotism.

Following the Abu Ghraib scandal, debates ensued in newspapers on whether the torture scenes in *24* were influencing the public to support torture by representing it as an effective and therefore legitimate tactic in the war on terror. It became part of the public discourse. Kelly M. Greenhill, in an editorial in the *Los Angeles Times*, reported that during the May 15, 2007, Republican presidential debate, candidate Tom Tancredo said about the war on terror, "I am looking for Jack Bauer at this point"; and Rudolph Giuliani argued that interrogators should use "any method they can think of." Giuliani's statement was met with applause (Greenhill 2007). Supreme Court justice Antonin Scalia, in a speech defending the use of torture, stated, "Jack Bauer saved Los Angeles. . . . He saved hundreds of thousands of lives. . . . Are you going to convict Jack Bauer?" (quoted in Lithwick 2008). According to Dahlia Lithwick of *Newsweek*, the Bush administration lawyers who designed interrogation methods in the war on terror and redefined torture cited Jack Bauer more often than the US Constitution.[7] Secretary of Homeland Security Michael Chertoff gave a speech at a Heritage Foundation dinner, "Fact vs. Fiction in the War on Terror," on the ways in which *24* does and does not mirror real life.[8] Even an Arab American defended *24* in an editorial in the *Wall Street Journal*, stating, "Well, here's the hard cold truth: When Islamic terrorists stop being a threat to America's survival, viewers will lose interest in *24*, because it will have lost its relevancy. Until such time, I will continue to watch *24*—because, believe it or not, the idea that there are Jack Bauers out there in real life risking their lives to save ours does mean something to me. . . . Because terrorists and their supporters continue to hide amongst us in plain sight, we need Jack Bauer, now more than ever" (Dabul 2007). *24* became a vehicle for the government to discuss the war on terror and particularly to recognize the counterterrorism efforts of government agents, thus revealing how TV dramas mediated the war on terror, not only by representing current events but, more important, by normalizing the need for torture given the alleged impending threat Arab/Muslim terrorists pose to US national security.

Furthermore, Jack Bauer stands in for the US government: he confronts multiple dilemmas inherent in war and demonstrates the difficult necessity of his actions. He also brings comfort to Americans that everything possible is being done to protect them. It is not only his determination that brings comfort but also portrayals of the US government's technological capabilities. Caren Kaplan writes that since the Gulf War, the media has focused on technological advances during war, in particular precision targeting. She writes, "'Space power' and the vast resources of the military-industrial-media-entertainment network generated discourses

7. For examples of how the US government redefined torture, see Bloche and Marks 2005 and *Washington Post* 2007.

8. The Heritage Foundation is the largest right-wing think tank in Washington, DC. Its mission is to "formulate and promote conservative public policies based on the principles of free enterprise, limited government, individual freedom, traditional American values, and a strong national defense" (www.heritage.org/about/). The foundation supports faith-based initiatives, school vouchers, banning abortion, and overturning affirmative action. The Heritage Foundation is very influential on Capitol Hill and takes credit for much of Bush's foreign and domestic policies (Chertoff 2006).

of precision that obscured information about civilian deaths or rendered them inconsequential. The representations of the war were less embodied than previous representations of wars, with U.S. military casualties going undercover or under the radar, as it were, as well" (2006, 705). This concept of "precision war" has seeped into television shows. Despite the intense violence in many TV dramas, and even moments where government agencies are portrayed as making grave errors, technology is central to the ultimate heroism of the United States. *24* has high-tech means to defeat the terrorists—from tracking their locations to eavesdropping on important conversations to recovering crucial information from damaged hard drives and precision bombing of targets. This emphasis on precision extends from technology to torture techniques; Bauer's precision torture extracts needed information.

Human Rights First and the Parents Television Council documented that representations of torture on US television increased exponentially after 2000. They report that from 1996 to 2001 there were 102 scenes of torture. From 2002 to 2005 torture scenes increased to 624. The 67 torture scenes in *24*'s first five seasons placed it at the forefront of prime-time depictions (Miller 2007). In addition to an increase in representations of torture on prime-time television, there also has been a shift in the identity of the torturer. In the history of US television, the torturer had usually been the bad guy, not the good guy. Historically, torture was used as a technique by writers and producers to villainize a character; it was considered immoral and therefore a stock tool of the bad guys—who included the Russians during the Cold War, the Viet Cong during the Vietnam War, and Latin American and Middle Eastern dictators in the 1980s and 1990s. Since 9/11 and especially through the character of Jack Bauer, the hero has become the torturer. Torture is now used for the greater good, as opposed to being used in the service of evil or power.

Polls indicate that representing the good American hero as the torturer changed public opinion on torture (Siegel 2007). A poll conducted by *ABC News* and the *Washington Post* in 2004 revealed that the majority of Americans—65 percent—are against torture, while 35 percent believe that torture is acceptable in some cases.[9] However, it also indicated that the public made a distinction between torture and physical abuse. While the majority of respondents indicated that torture was unacceptable, 46 percent indicated that physical abuse is acceptable. Among the actions deemed acceptable were sleep deprivation (approved by 66 percent of respondents), hooding (57 percent), noise bombing (54 percent), threatening to shoot a suspect or expose him or her to extreme heat or cold (40 percent), punching and kicking (29 percent), and sexual humiliation (16 percent). The same poll revealed that 60 percent of the public perceived the Abu Ghraib prison scandal to constitute "abuse," not "torture." What emerges here is a wide gray area in which morality becomes a slippery slope [where] there are always exceptions to the rules. The news media aided this growing acceptance of torture, or at least of some of its manifestations. Brigitte L. Nacos and Oscar Torres-Reyna write, "An ironic consequence of the Abu Ghraib revelations was the drastic decline of the use of the T-word in pertinent news accounts. Instead, anchors, correspondents, and reporters themselves preferred terms like 'abuse,' 'alleged abuse,' 'mistreatment,' and 'wrongdoing'" (2007, 86). Government officials and journalists came to distinguish between "hard-core torture," "torture lite," and "coercion" (Bowden 2003). Nacos and Torres-Reyna note that after the Abu Ghraib prison scandal, "Americans were less inclined to agree with the statement that torture is 'never justified' as a means to force suspected terrorists to reveal important information. By December 2004, more than seven months after the Abu Ghraib story broke, only 27 percent of the public rejected the torture of terrorist suspects categorically, while 69 percent found it justified to varying degrees" (2007, 91). The operating cultural logic shifted from one in which torture was considered illegal and morally wrong to an exceptionalist logic in which torture was considered wrong but necessary and effective in moments of national crisis. But public-opinion polls also demonstrate an ideologically fractured populace, in which approximately half

9. See Morris and Langer 2004.

of the public agree and the other half disagree that there is a difference between "torture" and "abuse" or that either is acceptable.

Certainly *24* alone is not responsible for shifting perspectives in favor of justifying torture or "abuse." Representations of torture on *24* are part of a larger field of meaning and exist alongside the Bush administration's enormous public-relations efforts to make torture palatable to the American mainstream and make torture legally acceptable, often despite its clear violation of the Geneva Conventions. The news media and government officials succeeded in making torture acceptable and necessary, and TV dramas participated in doing the ideological work (even as they offered post-9/11 representational strategies that resisted stereotyping) to justify the US government's actions during the war on terror.

After the meeting in 2006 with Human Rights First, West Point faculty, and members of the FBI and CIA, the writers and producers of *24* introduced a new plot to the show. In season 7, which aired in 2008, the US government puts Bauer on trial for his use of torture. Bauer is depicted as a broken human being, seemingly haunted by all the people he has tortured. His actions are questioned throughout the season by other characters who maintain that torture is not only illegal but also morally wrong. The antitorture message, it seems, is clear. And yet this plotline becomes, in effect, another simplified complex representational strategy: this explicit portrayal of the terrible consequences of inflicting violence on others is continually called into question by the season's other, far more urgent events. As Bauer is confronted with one ticking time bomb scenario after another, the rest of the plot seems to be an advertisement for the unfortunate necessity of torture to divert terrorist attacks, consistent with simplified complex representational modes. These terrorist dramas are built on a basic paradox between representational strategies that project a postracial, multicultural United States and the logics that legitimize racism and torture. These processes are simultaneous and interlinked. Simplified complex representations enable logics that justify torture; or, more specifically, they make a successful case for torture because the suspension of Arab and Muslim American civil rights relies on them as evidence that racism is no longer a factor in the decisions most Americans make. Therefore, if the actions of the government, or the military, are not racist, then the people the United States fights must be the bad guys. TV dramas, by co-opting multiculturalism and standardizing these seemingly humanistic representations of the Other, produce a postrace illusion of good if problematic intentions. This illusion makes logics that legitimize racism appear as though they are not racist.

The television landscape shifted on 9/11 as the vague, ominous threat to US national security took center stage. The story lines in TV dramas such as *24* and *Sleeper Cell* reinforced the government's need for a war on terror; these shows have, in numerous guises, replayed the tragedy of 9/11 weekly to US audiences, keeping the trauma fresh in the collective memory. These cultural productions, despite employing a range of strategies to avoid reproducing stereotypes, offer a very specific story that keeps viewer-citizens living and reliving the war on terror. There is a fundamental contradiction [in] representational strategies that project an enlightened, postracial culture yet maintain the relevance of the threat. So long as Arabs and Muslims are represented primarily in the context of terrorism, our current crop of representational strategies—for all their apparent innovations—will have a minimal impact on viewers' perceptions of Arabs and Muslims and, far worse, will perpetuate a simplistic vision of good and evil under the guise of complexity and sensitivity.

What is most strongly conveyed by these post-9/11 TV dramas is that Arabs and Muslims pose a threat to US peace and security. The articulated fear, similar to that during the Cold War, is that the enemy is among "us," so that we must live in a state of constant fear and vigilance. According to Douglas L. Howard, "For all we know, our neighborhoods, our businesses, and our highways have been or are being targeted even as we speak, but we are (and we must feel) powerless to protect ourselves from what we cannot see and what we do not know. *24*, in all its violent glory, makes us believe that, if the terrorists are out here, something, everything, in fact, is being done to stop them and to keep us safe" (2007, 142). *24*, despite its representational strategies, does the ideological work of perpetually reenacting the Arab/Muslim threat.

Above all, what is depicted in these TV dramas is a nation in perpetual danger. As Melani McAlister has written, "The continuing sense of threat provides support for the power of the state, but it also provides the groundwork for securing 'the nation' as a cultural and social entity. The 'imagined community' of the nation finds continuing rearticulation in the rhetoric of danger" (2001, 6). Writers and producers create an "imagined community" (Anderson 1983) of viewers, many of whom are interpellated into a sense of impending threat that supports the state (see Althusser [1971] 2001 for his definition of interpellation). Television is the fundamental way such a threat can be conveyed to a nation. In addition to being the disseminator of this threat, television capitalizes on it, keeping viewers both fearful and captivated.

Works Cited

Alsultany, Evelyn. 2007. "Selling American Diversity and Muslim American Identity through Non-Profit Advertising Post-9/11." *American Quarterly* 59, no. 3 (Sept.): 593–622.

Althusser, Louis. [1971] 2001. "Ideology and Ideological State Apparatuses (Notes towards an Investigation)." In *Lenin and Philosophy and Other Essays*, 85–126. New York: Monthly Review Press.

Anderson, Benedict. 1983. *Imagined Communities: Reflections on the Origin and Spread of Nationalism*. New York: Verso.

Bauder, David. 2007. "Group: TV Torture Influencing Real Life." *USA Today*, Feb. 11. At https://www.usatoday.com/life/television/2007-02-11-tv-torture_x.htm.

Baudrillard, Jean. 1994. *Simulacra and Simulation: The Body, in Theory*. Translated by Sheila Faria Glaser. Ann Arbor: Univ. of Michigan Press. Orig. pub. in French in 1981.

BBC News. 2007. "*24* under Fire from Muslim Groups." Jan. 19. At http://news.bbc.co.uk/2/hi/entertainment/6280315.stm.

Bloche, M. Greg, and Jonathan Marks. 2005. "Doing unto Others as They Did unto Us: The Path to Torture." *New York Times*, Nov. 14.

Bourdieu, Pierre. 1993. *The Field of Cultural Production: Essays on Art and Literature*. New York: Columbia Univ. Press.

Bowden, Mark. 2003. "The Dark Art of Interrogation." *Atlantic*, Oct. 1. At https://www.theatlantic.com/magazine/archive/2003/10/the-dark-art-of-interrogation/302791/.

Buncombe, Andrew. 2007. "US Military Tells Jack Bauer: Cut Out the Torture Scenes . . . or Else!" *Independent*, Feb. 13. At https://www.independent.co.uk/news/world/americas/us-military-tells-jack-bauer-cut-out-the-torture-scenes-or-else-436143.html.

Carlson, Peter. 2007. "Jack Bauer of *24*, the Interrogator's Marquis de Sade?" *Washington Post*, Feb. 20.

Chertoff, Michael. 2006. Remarks at Heritage Foundation Discussion, "Fact vs. Fiction in the War on Terror." Ronald Reagan Building, Washington, DC. Major Leaders Special Transcripts, Federal News Service, June 23.

Chouliaraki, Lilie. 2006. *The Spectatorship of Suffering*. Thousand Oaks, CA: Sage.

Dabul, Emilio Karim. 2007. "In Defense of '24': An Arab-American Defends the Real-Life Bauers." *Wall Street Journal*, Feb. 7. At https://www.wsj.com/articles/SB117081835396500463.

Democracy Now!. 2007. "Is Torture on Hit Fox TV Show '24' Encouraging U.S. Soldiers to Abuse Detainees?" Feb. 22. At https://www.democracynow.org/2007/2/22/is_torture_on_hit_fox_tv.

Free Republic. 2005. "Fox TV Accused of Stereotyping American Muslims." Jan. 13. At http://www.freerepublic.com/focus/f-news/1320357/posts.

Greenhill, Kelly M. 2007. "'24' on the Brain." *Los Angeles Times*, May 28. At https://www.latimes.com/archives/la-xpm-2007-may-28-oe-greenhill28-story.html.

Hall, Stuart. [1981] 2000. "Racist Ideologies and the Media." In *Media Studies: A Reader*, 2nd ed., edited by Paul Marris and Sue Thornham, 271–82. New York: New York Univ. Press.

Howard, Douglas L. 2007. "'You're Going to Tell Me Everything You Know': Torture and Morality in FOX's *24*." In *Reading* 24: *TV against the Clock*, edited by Steven Peacock, 133–46. London: I. B. Tauris.

Kaplan, Caren. 2006. "Precision Targets: GPS and the Militarization of U.S. Consumer Identity." *American Quarterly* 58, no. 3: 693–714. At https://doi.org/10.1353/aq.2006.0061.

Leung, Rebecca. 2004. "Abuse of Iraqi POWs by GIs Probed." *60 Minutes II*, Apr. 27. At https://www.cbsnews.com/news/abuse-of-iraqi-pows-by-gis-probed/.

Lithwick, Dahlia. 2008. "Lithwick: How Jack Bauer Shaped U.S. Torture Policy." *Newsweek*, July 25. At https://www.newsweek.com/lithwick-how-jack-bauer-shaped-ustorture-policy-93159.

Mamdani, Mahmood. 2004. *Good Muslim, Bad Muslim: America, the Cold War, and the Roots of Terror.* New York: Pantheon Books.

Mayer, Jane. 2007. "Whatever It Takes: The Politics of the Man behind '24.'" *New Yorker*, Feb. 19. At https://www.newyorker.com/magazine/2007/02/19/whatever-it-takes.

McAlister, Melani. 2001. *Epic Encounters: Culture, Media, and U.S. Interests in the Middle East, 1945–2000.* Berkeley: Univ. of California Press.

McCoy, Alfred W. 2006. "The Myth of the Ticking Time Bomb." *Progressive*, Sept. 13. At https://progressive.org/%3Fq%3Dnode/3940/.

Meyer, Dick. 2004. "Rush: MPs Just 'Blowing Off Steam.'" *CBS News*, May 6. At https://www.cbsnews.com/news/rush-mps-just-blowing-off-steam/.

Miller, Martin. 2007. "'24' Gets a Lesson in Torture from the Experts." *Los Angeles Times*, Feb. 13. At https://www.latimes.com/archives/la-xpm-2007-feb-13-et-torture13-story.html.

Morris, David, and Gary Langer. 2004. "Terrorist Suspect Treatment: Most Americans Oppose Torture Techniques." *ABC News*, May 27. At http://abcnews.go.com/sections/us/polls/torture_poll_040527.html.

Nacos, Brigitte Lebens, and Óscar Torres-Reyna. 2007. *Fueling Our Fears: Stereotyping, Media Coverage, and Public Opinion of Muslim Americans.* Lanham, MD: Rowman & Littlefield.

Northern Territory News. 2007. "*24* Comes under Muslim Fire." Jan. 29.

Peacock, Steven, ed. 2007. *Reading* 24: *TV against the Clock.* New York: I. B. Tauris.

Siegel, Robert. 2007. "Torture's Wider Use Brings New Concerns." *All Things Considered*, NPR, Mar. 13. At https://www.npr.org/templates/story/story.php?storyId=8286003.

Sontag, Susan. 1977. *On Photography.* New York: Farrar, Straus and Giroux.

Sutherland, Sharon, and Sarah Swan. 2007. "'Tell Me Where the Bomb Is, or I Will Kill Your Son': Situational Morality on *24*." In *Reading* 24: *TV against the Clock*, edited by Steven Peacock, 119–32. London: I. B. Tauris.

Washington Post. 2007. "Bad Methods: President Bush's Alternative Techniques for Questioning Terrorism Suspects Have No Basis in Science or Law." *Washington Post*, June 1. At www.washingtonpost.com/wp-dyn/content/article/2007/05/31/AR2007053102007.html.

Willis, Susan. 2005. *Portents of the Real: A Primer for post-9/11 America.* London: Verso.

22

Introduction to *American Arabesque*

Arabs, Islam, and the 19th-Century Imaginary

JACOB RAMA BERMAN

. . . On April 27, 1805, the exiled ruler of Tripoli, Hamet Karamanelli, presented Lieutenant Neville Presley O'Bannon with a jeweled Mameluke sword in acknowledgment of the successful bayonet charge the young marine from Virginia had led earlier that day against the fortified city of Derne. The ceremony took place on North Africa's Mediterranean coast, and the larger event it commemorated was eventually incorporated into the marine hymn as a testament to the transatlantic reach of US military power and political influence: "from the halls of Montezuma to the shores of Tripoli." Soon after the sword ceremony, O'Bannon raised the Stars and Stripes over Derne. The event marked a turning point in the United States' first extracontinental military venture and, as marine lore holds, the first time the American flag had been carried and planted on the other side of the Atlantic. To this day, commission officers of the Marine Corps carry a replica of the same Mameluke sword that Hamet Karamanelli presented to O'Bannon on the shores of Tripoli.

The sword exchange still resonates in the American national memory as a heroic first chapter in the country's global crusade against despotism and its enduring commitment to spreading democracy to the far corners of the earth.[1] In other words, the Mameluke sword and the event it commemorates have been translated into an American national fantasy. Berlant, describing her definition of national fantasy, explains, "I mean to designate how national culture becomes local—through the images, narratives, monuments, and sites that circulate through personal/collective consciousness" (1991, 5). The marine hymn is one of these transformative narratives, and in it Barbary becomes a productive site of American national identity. It is in this "fantasy" sense that the invocation "to the shores of Tripoli" uses affect to bind the individual citizen to the collective notion of national honor, integrity, and military power. But what if we were to read this national fantasy dialectically through the filter of Arab history and the Arabic language? What if we took a philological approach to the

Excerpt from Jacob Rama Berman, introduction to *American Arabesque: Arabs, Islam, and the 19th-Century Imaginary*, (New York: New York Univ. Press, 2012), 11–15. Full references in the original notes were converted to author-date citations in the text and notes here, and a works cited list was added. Reprinted with corrections and press style changes for consistency throughout the volume by permission of New York University Press.

1. In the devastating aftermath of 9/11, the "Barbary analogy," as it came to be known, was invoked repeatedly as a historical precedent for waging war against stateless actors and the failed nation-states that give them refuge. Multiple writers, pundits, military analysts, and cultural critics posited a narrative of a historical continuum between Thomas Jefferson's refusal to pay tribute to Muslim pirates at the outset of the nineteenth century and George W. Bush's refusal to appease Islamic terrorists at the outset of the twenty-first century. For recent histories that endorse the "Barbary analogy," see Lambert 2007 and Oren 2011. Two other works of history published in the wake of 9/11 that establish a continuum between the US war on terror and the Barbary Wars by emphasizing the Manichean binaries I wish to avoid are Joseph Wheelan, *Jefferson's War: America's First War on Terror, 1801–1805* (2004), and Joshua E. London, *Victory in Tripoli: How America's War with Barbary Established the U.S. Navy and Shaped a Nation* (2005).

hymn's translation of the Mameluke sword into the marine sword?

O'Bannon was a member of a small expeditionary force of eight marines, a hundred or so European fortune fighters, and several hundred Bedouin Arabs. The group had been led across the Libyan Desert by an intrepid Revolutionary and Indian War veteran from Massachusetts, General William Eaton. Eaton's covert mission was to overthrow the acting ruler of Tripoli, Yusuf Karamanelli, and to replace him with his more pliable brother Hamet. The ultimate goal was to free the hundreds of American citizens held in Tripoli's slave prisons and rid the US government of the need to pay tribute to a piratical state. In a matter of days after Hamet had handed the Mameluke sword to Lt. O'Bannon in Derne, his brother Yusuf precipitously began negotiations for peace with the United States. Far from being "chastised for his temerity" (as Eaton preferred) or removed from his position of tyrannical power, Yusuf ultimately signed a treaty that established him as legitimate ruler of Tripoli in the eyes of the US government.[2] This treaty contained a secret proviso banishing Hamet from Tripoli and assuring his removal by securing his immediate family as Yusuf's hostages.[3]

In the years that followed the triumphant sword exchange in Derne, Eaton and Hamet remained connected through the written word. Hamet wrote many letters to the US Senate complaining of his exile on an obscure Mediterranean island, his penury, and the unpaid debt that America owed him. When informed of the treaty negotiations that ultimately made Hamet an exile, Eaton, still occupying the Derne camp, wrote in distress to Samuel Barron, the commander in chief of US forces in the Mediterranean. "Could I have apprehended this result of my exertions," Eaton complained, "certainly no consideration would have prevailed on me to have taken an agency in a tragedy so manifestly fraught with intrigue; so wounding to human feelings; and as I must view it, so degrading to our national honor" (quoted in Prentiss 1813, 356). In Eaton's view, the shores of Tripoli do not consolidate the righteous and masculine national subjectivity that so often affectively attaches itself to the marine hymn. Instead Eaton narrates the United States' surreptitious retreat in the dead of night from Derne as "unmanly."[4] As concerns Hamet, Eaton remarks in his journal, "He falls from the most flattering prospects of a kingdom, to beggary!" (quoted in Prentiss 1813, 364).

How do we interpret the results of the US military's actions in Barbary? Was it victory or defeat? Was it honorable or dishonorable? Tracking what Hamet's Mameluke sword signifies in both American and Arab cultural traditions provides a global perspective on the phrase "to the shores of Tripoli." Paying attention to the dynamics of translation, in other words, disturbs the exceptionalist national fantasy that the marine hymn invokes. What emerges in its place is a narrative on American identity in which belonging and alienation (enfranchisement and disenfranchisement) are intrinsically bound together.

[The term] [*m*]*ameluke* refers to the organized bodies of slave soldiers employed by various Islamic armies from as early as the ninth century. The members of this corps, captured or bartered during their childhoods and raised as military orphans, eventually gave birth to two Egyptian dynasties. The first dynasty had consolidated its control over the state by the end of the thirteenth century. This generation of Mamelukes replaced the Arabo-Islamic caliphate with a form of military rule that placed power in the hands of central Asian, Turkish, Kurdish, and Caucasian soldiers. The Mamelukes' dynastic power

2. Eaton, explaining his decision to undertake the dangerous mission with Hamet, declares, "I would rather yield my person to the danger of war in almost any shape, than my pride to the humiliation of treating with a wretched pirate for the ransom of men who are the rightful heirs of freedom" (quoted in Prentiss 1813, 267). Ultimately, "treat with a pirate" is exactly what the US government did, much to Eaton's dismay.

3. In a letter dated February 16, 1806, Eaton discusses this "secret proviso" that the State Department diplomat Tobias Lear inserted into the treaty. "Mr. Lear observed, that it would be useless at present to send for Hamet's family; for that it was expected by the reigning Bashaw, they were not to be claimed until Hamet should be so withdrawn and so situated, as to remove all apprehension of his further attempting to regain his kingdom. This I understood to be a secret engagement on the part of our commissioner of peace" (see US Senate 1806).

4. For more on the importance of manhood to the consolidation of US national identity, see Nelson 1998.

originated in seizure, and their political aim was self-interestedly to perpetuate that power through clientage. To the Arab historian Ibn Khaldun, the advent of Mameluke control of Egypt is a signal event in the decay of the Arab *asabiyya* (group loyalty) that created the pinnacles of Arabo-Islamic civilization, the Ummayad and Abassid Caliphates.[5] Ibn Khaldun argues that the Mameluke dynasty marks a historical shift whereby Arabs will no longer be rulers of the Islamic *umma* (community) but rather will become the ruled. Seen through the perspective of Ibn Khaldun's theory of history, the Mamelukes revived an older form of natural kingship (*mulk*) but changed the terms of loyalty from tribal/ethnic bonds to military bonds.[6] By the beginning of the nineteenth century, the second Mameluke dynasty had taken control of Egypt, following the same policies as its original Mameluke predecessors.

The word *mameluke* is derived from the Arabic verb *malaka* (ملك), "to take in possession, seize, take over, acquire, lay hands (on); to dominate, control, be master (of)" (Wehr 1993, 1081). A *mameluke* is a slave or possession of someone, but a *malik* (derived from the same verbal root) is a king, and *mulk* is something that Ibn Khaldun theorized as natural kingship. In practice, the Mameluke dynasty combined these seemingly opposed states of being: they were both slaves and kings, both victims and administrators of imperialism. No man could become a Mameluke ruler who had not first been a Mameluke slave. The janissary body of the Mamelukes was not hereditary and theoretically could only be refreshed with new orphans. The Mameluke system meant that a boy seized on a military raid into the Caucus Mountains and raised as a slave could become the ruler of an Egyptian population to which he was not ethnically, racially, or culturally attached.

The transformation of the Mameluke sword into the US Marine sword entails an act of transvaluation whereby an Arabo-Islamic symbol of slavery, imperialism, and dynastic hegemony becomes a symbolic expression of America's commitment to freedom and democracy. And yet O'Bannon himself hailed from a state in which slavery was legal. The larger conflict in North Africa that came to be known as the Tripoli War gave birth to the US Navy, impetus to the US Marines, and still provides a quilting point for subsequent narratives of the United States' extracontinental military interventions in the name of overthrowing tyrants rather than appeasing them. The other narrative, the narrative that suggests the United States' own history of slavery, hegemony, and imperial aggression, remains as a ghostly complement to the New World symbol that American historiography was to fashion out of Hamet's Mameluke sword.

The proceedings from the court-martial of an American sailor aboard a ship sent to the Barbary Coast during the war with Tripoli provides a telling example of the gap many Federal-era Americans felt existed between the promise of revolutionary freedom and the reality of continued American bondage, between the affect of national fantasy and the lived experience of those still occluded from the values the national fantasy promoted. On June 23, 1804, Robert Quinn, the president of the sailors aboard the US frigate *President*, was summoned to the bar at Hampton Roads for the crime of mutiny. The evidence against Quinn consisted of a letter he had written to Commodore Samuel Baron, commander of the US naval squadron deployed to the Mediterranean to free American slaves held captive in Barbary prisons. The letter lists a series of complaints the common sailors had with their treatment and meal allowances. In the letter, Quinn uses the pointed terms of revolutionary rhetoric:

> Tyranny is the beginning of all mischief and is generally attended with bad things at the latter end. Any Commodore or captain that had the least feeling or thought would not suffer this hard usage it is almost impossible for us to live. . . . Some of

5. The Umayyad Caliphate lasted from AD 661 to 750, when it was overthrown by the Abbasids. At the caliphate's greatest extent, the Umayyads controlled over five million square miles, making it one of the largest empires the world had ever seen. Named after Umayya Ibn Abd Shams, the Umayyads were originally from Mecca but made Damascus the capital of their caliphate. The Abbasids ruled the Islamic world from AD 750 to 1258. They were named after Abbas Ibn Abd al-Muttalib and made Baghdad the capital of their caliphate. The Abbasids slowly lost power to the army it had created, the Mamelukes.

6. Unlike pre-Islamic dynasties, however, the Mameluke *mulk* was infused with a respect for the Shari'a, or the code of Islamic law.

> our friends in America and other parts shall know
> of this shortly and in time we hope to get redress—
> death is always superior to slavery—we remain your
> unhappy slaves.[7]

Quinn received cold satisfaction for his invocation of the language of the Revolutionary War and his appeal to its metaphors of freedom. He was sentenced to have his eyebrows shaved and to be branded on the forehead with the word "Mutiny." He also received 326 lashes equally apportioned among the crew of the different ships of the squadron. Eaton was one of the judges. Quinn and his fellow sailors had deployed to Barbary aboard an American ship rhetorically positioned as fighting tyranny and freeing slaves. Yet it is American commodores and captains he accuses of tyranny and slave driving.

The marine hymn subsumes contradictions between the American rhetoric of liberty and the American history of bondage by appealing to the national fantasy of America's historical commitment to freedom. In other words, the hymn reinterprets the Mameluke sword, translating it into an affective iteration of American national identity. To put the marine sword in dialectic with the Mameluke sword is to think through exchanges between America and the Arab world not only in terms of martial conquest but also in terms of intercultural translation. It is to reconstruct our understanding of national symbols with an eye toward their etiology.

The cause of the sword exchange commemorated in the marine hymn was the installation of Hamet Karamanelli, with the aid of the United States, as ruler of Tripoli. The result of the sword exchange was his disenfranchisement, exile, and alienation. The larger cause that had brought US marines to the shores of Tripoli was the enslavement of American citizens, who had been promised life, liberty, and the pursuit of happiness by the Declaration of Independence. As white slaves in North Africa as well as the white seamen sent to rescue them were well aware, these universal rights were far from universally applied in their home country.

7. "The Tripolitan War Collection, 1804–5," Mss. Misc. Boxes T., American Antiquarian Society, Worcester, MA.

Works Cited

Berlant, Lauren Gail. 1991. *The Anatomy of National Fantasy: Hawthorne, Utopia, and Everyday Life*. Chicago: Univ. of Chicago Press.

Lambert, Frank. 2007. *The Barbary Wars: American Independence in the Atlantic World*. New York: Hill and Wang.

London, Joshua. 2005. *Victory in Tripoli: How America's War with the Barbary Pirates Established the U.S. Navy and Shaped a Nation*. Hoboken, NJ: Wiley.

Nelson, Dana D. 1998. *National Manhood: Capitalist Citizenship and the Imagined Fraternity of White Men*. Durham, NC: Duke Univ. Press.

Oren, Michael B. 2011. *Power, Faith, and Fantasy: America in the Middle East, 1776 to the Present*. New York: Norton.

Prentiss, Charles. 1813. *The Life of the Late General William Eaton; Principally Collected from His Correspondence and Other Manuscripts*. Brookfield, MA: Merriam.

US Senate, Committee on Application of Hamet Bashaw. 1806. *Documents Respecting the Application of Hamet Caramanelli, Ex-Bashaw of Tripoli*. Washington, DC: Duane and Son.

Wehr, Hans. 1993. *The Hans Wehr Dictionary of Modern Written Arabic*. 4th ed. Edited by J. M. Cowan. Ithaca, NY: Spoken Language Services.

Wheelan, Joseph. 2004. *Jefferson's War: America's First War on Terror, 1801–1805*. New York: Carroll & Graf.

23

The Rise of Arab American Literature

WAÏL S. HASSAN

We are not of the East or the West;
No boundaries exist in our breast:
We are free.
—Ameen Rihani

Cultural Translation and the "Nahda"

Ameen Rihani (1876–1940) is the author of the first Arab American poetry collection, *Myrtle and Myrrh* (1905), the first Arab American play, *Wajdah* (1909), and the first Arab American novel, *The Book of Khalid* (1911). . . . His first English-language publication, however, was a translation of selected poems by the great tenth-century Arab poet Abu al-ʿAla' al-Maʿarri (Rihani 1903). . . . In Arabic, Rihani published poetry, literary criticism, essays, history, books on his travels throughout the Arab world, and studies of nearly all of its heads of state. . . . He was the first to write prose poetry in Arabic, and he spearheaded an important literary movement known as Mahjar (immigrant) poetry, which introduced European Romantic themes in Arabic literature. . . .

What unites this prolific output in Arabic and English is an overarching project of cultural translation that ambitiously aimed to reinterpret the "East" and the "West" to each other and bring about a civilizational synthesis, coupled with Rihani's tireless pursuit of Arab independence—first from the Ottoman Empire then from European colonialism—and of political unity. Although Rihani shared those twin objectives with many of his contemporaries, his approach was shaped by his location in the United States. The first objective dates back to the beginnings of the Arab Nahda (or Renaissance) in the 1830s. In the wake of the French occupation of Egypt (1798–1801), it became all too clear to Egypt's ruler Muhammad Ali (1769–1849) that Europe's strength was the result of modern scientific knowledge, and it was in the interests of acquiring that knowledge that he began sending educational missions to France in the 1820s. In 1831, an Egyptian Islamic scholar called Rifa'a al-Tahtawi returned from one such mission in Paris to establish a school for translation that would disseminate modern European science and ideas. The core of Nahda reformism was selective appropriation: adopting modern European ideas, sciences, and institutions that would strengthen Arab societies while rejecting aspects of Europe that did not harmonize with Arab Islamic mores and values. Christian Levantine intellectuals who played an important role in the movement from the 1860s onward, and to whom Rihani was heir, contributed to the rise of secular Arab nationalism as an anti-Ottoman ideology.[1] But this impulse was not sectarian per se, for it was shared by many Muslim intellectuals and political leaders from the early part of the nineteenth century, contributing to the Arab Revolt of 1916, led by Sharif Husayn of Mecca and coordinated with the British invasion of Palestine in the final

Excerpt from Waïl S. Hassan, "The Rise of Arab-American Literature: Orientalism and Cultural Translation in the Work of Ameen Rihani," *American Literary History* 20, nos. 1–2 (2007): 245–75. Reprinted by permission of Oxford University Press.

1. See Hourani 1967, 51–102.

phase of World War I. In the McMahon–Husayn correspondence of 1915–16 leading up to the revolt, the British encouraged Arab aspirations to independence, only secretly to conclude the Sykes–Picot Agreement with the French in 1916 that effectively divided the Arab world in spheres of influence and then to issue the Balfour Declaration in 1917 promising the establishment of a Jewish state in Palestine.[2] None of this could have been seen by Arab nationalists as anything but a betrayal by the British, something that deepened the mistrust felt by many toward Europe and further complicated the task of social and political reform predicated on cultural translation and synthesis. Inspired by Woodrow Wilson's Fourteen Points, some Arabs hoped that the United States would play a more positive role in the Middle East than the European powers, whose colonial ambitions there had become obvious, and some even called for a US mandate in the region (Khalidi 2004, 32–33).

The Syrian intellectuals who came to the United States in the late nineteenth century and established a number of Arabic-language newspapers in the 1890s were products of the Nahda. They wrote in Arabic, and many were outspoken in their criticism of the Ottomans and of social conditions back home, especially religious superstition and the power of the clergy. Although many of those early immigrants imported with them local sectarian biases, espoused by the various newspapers at the time, gradually and under pressure from the larger society in which they became a racialized minority (Majaj 2000), those biases began to be fused into a "Syrian" identity in the United States and a nationalist politics with respect to events back home. . . . Rihani . . . advocated Arab unity and independence from the Ottomans and later from European colonialism, a goal he hoped would be achieved with the aid of the United States. He believed that because the ideals expressed in its Declaration of Independence and its historical experience as a former colony, the United States would be a natural ally in the Arab struggle for national liberation, which he hoped would come to fruition with the creation of the United Arab States, on the US model, after the demise of the Ottoman Empire. The task, therefore, was to explain both this historical affinity between the United States and the Arab world and the advantages of their forging an alliance. . . .

Rihani's literary, intellectual, and political project is captured in the title of the published proceedings of a symposium held a few months after 9/11 to celebrate his life's work, *Ameen Rihani: Bridging East and West*.[3] Heir to two literary and cultural traditions, Rihani not only contributed to both but also tried to fuse them together. [Because he wrote] in two languages throughout his life, such "bridging" involved constant translation, a process that immediately collided with the discourse of Orientalism. Rihani, [Kahlil] Gibran, and Abraham Rihbany knew that addressing American readers required more than just the ability to write in a foreign language. They had to situate themselves in relation to a powerful discourse through which their readers had already formed their ideas about that distant culture. The shift from Arabic to English meant that Anglophone Arab American literature was to be constrained by that antecedent discourse, in relation to which the nascent literary tradition must constantly define itself. Obviously, when writing in Arabic, Rihani and Gibran not only had a different agenda but also enjoyed a greater discursive latitude in that, first, they did not have to explain Arab culture to Arab readers; second, they were not expected by their readers to be Oriental spokesmen; and third, they did not have to abide by discursive strictures imposed on their cultures by a conquering knowledge system, with its stereotypes, typologies, and culturalist and racialist frames of reference, privileged texts and modes, and so forth—even when they could not free themselves entirely from its powerful imprint. They wrote within an Arabic cultural discourse and could ignore or dismiss simplistic or offensive Orientalist descriptions, or they could boldly and directly challenge their imperialistic underpinnings. When writing in English, however, they had to couch their message in ways that guaranteed or at least increased the likelihood of its acceptance—of *their* acceptance as writers—by

2. See Hourani 1991, 315–19.

3. The symposium was sponsored by the Ameen Rihani Institute, Washington, DC, and the American University Center for Global Peace, Washington, DC, April 19–20, 2002.

American readers. As Evelyn Shakir points out, "The first generation of Arab-American writers (as might be expected of immigrants in an age of rampant xenophobia) dressed carefully for their encounter with the American public, putting on the guise of prophet, preacher, or man of letters. They could not hide their foreignness, but they could make it respectable" (1996, 6). Some of those roles (such as Gibran's posture as mystic or Oriental sage) are, of course, among the stereotypes circulating within Orientalism's regime of truth, while others (Rihani as a man of letters and Abraham Rihbany as a Protestant minister) were carefully calculated to challenge aspects of it in an effort not only to "make foreignness respectable" but also to redefine the relationship between East and West. The implied message was, "Here we are, we can produce literature that draws upon the most distinguished Western writers, and we can minister to American Protestant congregations, but we, too, are Orientals."

Edward Said described the stance of the Orientalist as that of a translator: "The relationship between Orientalist and Orient was essentially hermeneutical: standing before a distant, barely intelligible civilization or cultural monument, the Orientalist scholar reduced the obscurity by translating, sympathetically portraying, inwardly grasping the hard-to-reach object. Yet the Orientalist remained outside the Orient, which, however much was made to appear intelligible, remained beyond the occident" (1978, 222). Early Arab American writers in English tried to appropriate that stance of Orientalist translator, and, in fact, their implicit claim was that they were better equipped to interpret the Orient than European Orientalists. . . . This attempt to replace the Orientalist as interpreter or translator of the Orient was a way of claiming cultural space and voice, countering the negativity associated with the Orient, and mediating between it and the West for the sake of greater cross-cultural understanding. Edward Said's *Orientalism* (1978) and the polemics it initiated, together with the areas of inquiry it opened up, such as postcolonial studies, represent a watershed in that contest over voice, representation, and discursive power in which early Arab Americans engaged. Said's critique of Orientalism and of the concept of the Orient puts into question the antithetical construct of the Occident or the West, but early Arab American writers did not go so far. They accepted the Orientalist distinction between the contrasting essences of East and West, the former seen as passive, mystical spiritual, traditional, backward and the latter correspondingly as aggressive, rational, materialistic, modern, progressive. What they wanted to contest was the hierarchy of value attached to the poles of this binary. They were angry at, and rebellious against, the oppressive rule of the Ottoman Empire and highly critical of social and political conditions in Syria and the rest of the Arab world. They correspondingly admired the social, political, and technological advances of western European countries and the United States. But they were also very conscious and proud of their great civilization's past and rich literary heritage, to which they contributed through their Arabic prose and poetry, written in the United States.[4] They could not, therefore, accept the idea of the East's inferiority. Moreover, the prevailing attitude toward Europe within what [Albert] Hourani [1967] calls the "liberal" school of Arabic thought from the 1830s onward emphasized critically selective borrowing from Europe: only those ideas and sciences deemed compatible with Arab culture and necessary for the reform of its social institutions were to be adopted, while decadent and materialistic aspects of Europe were in need of reform and to be rejected. Given the balance of power and the challenges of social reform in their countries, Nahda intellectuals never imagined themselves on a mission to reform Europe, but they discriminated sharply between what they considered to be advantages and disadvantages of its civilization and advocated borrowing selectively from it.

Because of their location in the United States, Arab intellectuals at the turn of the twentieth century saw themselves as reformers of East *and* West. The discursive challenge facing them was to replace Orientalist valuations with a model of duality without hierarchy, whereby the contrasting essences were seen as existing in a sort of metaphysical equilibrium and reciprocity: East and West complement, need, and have something to teach each other. Rihbany puts it succinctly: "The world needs a characteristic Oriental civilization as it needs a

4. On the contribution of the Mahjar writers to Arabic literature in the early twentieth century, see Badawi 1993, 41–47.

characteristic Occidental civilization" (1922, 159). Reform of the East depends on inspiration and material assistance from the West, but "if it is to be significantly of value to either the East or the West, a new Eastern civilization must be genuinely Eastern. It must not be a replica of Western civilization, which needs a hundred reforms" (299–300). A "better East" (289) would be more suitable to Western business interests (299) yet would remain free from the material and spiritual ravages of industrialization discernible in "New York, Chicago, and London" (300). By the same token, "the Oriental must never cease to teach his Occidental brother; nor ever allow himself to forget his own great spiritual maxims which have guided the course of his life for so many centuries" (301). At the end of the day, East would still be East, and West West.

Others like Rihani (and less explicitly Gibran) envisioned a Hegelian dynamic that would eventually blend East and West into a higher civilizational synthesis and saw themselves in the role of two-way reformers and facilitators of that process. Like Rihbany, they accepted the Orientalist distinction between East and West but rejected its historical immutability in favor of a conception of East and West as values and attitudes of mind that are not geographically determined and that can, therefore, circulate among cultures over long historical periods. This more plastic form of Orientalism can explain the erstwhile historical ascendancy of Phoenician and Arab civilizations. Thus, pride in an illustrious cultural and civilizational heritage that has much to offer their new country is the theme of Gibran's address "To Young Americans of Syrian Origin" (1926), which appeared in the inaugural issue of *The Syrian World*, the first English-language literary and cultural magazine in North America, launched specifically for the benefit of second-generation Arab Americans whose native language was English. Pride in Syrian heritage (or the "Syrian Race," as it was often described at the time) is also the theme of a series of articles by the Reverend W. A. Mansur, published in *The Syrian World* throughout its six-year life (1926–32). Rihani clearly articulated this reconstructed Orientalism in the June 1927 issue of the same magazine. In an address originally delivered two months earlier at the American University of Beirut and titled "Where East and West Meet," Rihani declares that his title "implies a partial denial of the dictum of Rudyard Kipling, megaphoned to the world in a line of verse, 'East is East and West is West, and never the twain shall meet.'" Rihani goes on:

> I admit, at the start, that, from a surface point of view, the evidence is in favor of Mr. Kipling. The East prays, the West dances; the East dreams, the West thinks; the East broods, the West plays. What is a mark of respect in the East, is considered an offense in the West: the Oriental, when he enters your house, slips off his shoes at the door; the Occidental finds a hat-rack for his hat. . . . [T]he one is suave and insidious, the other is blunt and often crude. The Oriental is imaginative and metaphoric, the Occidental is literal and "matter-of-fact." Kipling's dictum is in this, at least, wholly to the point. (8)

Rihani here validates Orientalist typology: East and West are homogenous, self-evident, autonomous, and antithetical to one another. However, those traits do not fall along the colonialist hierarchy of values that defines the East as primitive, childish, superstitious and the West as advanced, mature, rational. Some of Rihani's pairs of opposites are value-neutral (praying/dancing, dreaming/thinking, imaginative/literal, metaphoric/matter-of-fact), others are moral equivalents (suave/blunt, insidious/crude), and one actually reverses Orientalist valuations (brooding/playing). In other words, while endorsing duality, he is undermining the hierarchy. Moreover, those traits are not irrevocably wedded to symbolic geography but are variable and historical:

> Like all generalities, however, these traits are not without exception. They are characteristic, but not exclusive. Take, for instance, the fawning and florid Oriental, extravagant with the metaphor and the puff, he is not a type exclusive. He is a species produced by despotism and its pompous court. The aristocracy kowtows to the emperor; the lower classes kowtow to the aristocracy and to each other. . . .
>
> When absolute monarchies were the rule in Europe, the Europeans, on the whole, were quite Oriental in the art of fawning and adulation; while the extravagant manner, as much in evidence in the nation as around the throne, was revealed, not only in speech, but also in the dress of the period. Consider

> the ruffles and feathers of mylords at court; the flounces and trains of mylady in waiting; consider the dedications penned by needy scribes to their rich patrons. . . . As for the people, they follow, according to the Arabic proverb, their sovereign. (8–9)

A critical historical perspective relativizes Orientalist valuations, which become anything but timeless. If Europeans were at one time Orientals and Arabs Occidentals, those identities become variable, dynamic, and interchangeable. What matters ultimately is

> the highest ideal of the prophets and the poets—the ideal of the soul—which includes the ethical and the practical aspects of life, and which is neither Oriental nor exclusively Occidental. It is supremely human. Before it every mark of birth disappears; and customs and traditions are held in abeyance, and the differences in nationality and language cease to be a hindrance to understanding. The soul seeking expression, the soul reaching out for the truth, is one everywhere. Confucius might be American in his ideal, even as he is Chinese, and Emerson might be Chinese, even if he is American. Cotama [*sic*] Buddha made manifest in London might be mistaken for Carlyle and Carlyle revisiting the glimpses of the moon in Japan might be mistaken for Cotama. Jelal-ud-Din Rumi, were he born in Assisi would have been a St. Francis; and St. Francis, were he born in Shiraz would have been a Jelal-ud-Din. . . . And genius everywhere is one. In the Orient and in the Occident the deep thinkers are kin, the poets are cousins, the pioneers of the spirit are the messengers of peace and goodwill to the world. Their works are the open highways between nations, and they themselves are the ever living guardians and guides. (9–10)

This transcendentalist metaphysics of the spirit, prophecy, and poetry trivializes Orientalist hierarchies but also overlooks the material conditions of cultural and ideological production.[5] If "East and West meet" in a celestial sphere inhabited by Buddha, Rumi, St. Francis, Carlyle, and Emerson, they can remain safely and discreetly separated in the material world. (The very worldly and avowedly agnostic Confucius seems oddly out of place in this company!) In its conciliatory, nonconfrontational stance, [this metaphysics] offers itself as an alternative to the dominant discourses of difference, but without exposing their internal inconsistencies or their affiliations with power. In fact, it offers an illusory sense of freedom that sublimates the dialectics of history. The same idea is expressed in Rihani's poem "A Chant of Mystics," published in 1921 in a collection bearing the same title:

> Nor Crescent nor Cross we adore;
> Nor Budha [*sic*] nor Christ we implore;
> Nor Muslem [*sic*] nor Jew we abhor:
> We are free.
>
> We are not of Iran or of Ind,
> We are not of Arabia or of Sind:
> We are free.
>
> We are not of the East or the West;
> No boundaries exist in our breast:
> We are free. (84)

This passage is frequently quoted to illustrate the nobility of Rihani's endeavors to reconstruct a human community free from religious, ethnic, and cultural chauvinism. Yet the fact that the entire collection contains not a hint of the historical and political conditions that were radically transforming the map of the Middle East in 1921, and in which Rihani himself was fully embroiled as a speaker, writer, nationalist, activist, and delegate to postwar conferences, points to the unbridgeable chasm between this rarefied metaphysics and material reality. Rihani's negotiation of Orientalism vacillates between this Sufi ideal that transcends dualism and the material, worldly transactions that confront it—that is, between metaphysical unity and cultural translation.

Translation and Orientalist Knowledge

It is highly significant that Rihani's first English-language book was not only an effort at cultural translation but was itself a literary translation that directly challenged

5. See Dunnavent's (1991) study of Rihani and American transcendentalism.

Orientalist scholarship. In his preface to *The Quatrains of Abu'l-Ala* (1903), which was expanded and republished in *The Luzumiyat of Abu'l-Ala* (1918), Rihani describes the classical Arab poet (974–1058) as "the Lucretius of Al-Islam, the Diogenes of Arabia and the Voltaire of the East" (1903, vi). Abu al-'Ala' al-Ma'arri was a skeptic and a rationalist whose example represented, first of all, an implicit challenge to the idea of an exclusively spiritual East. Yet this skeptical rationalism is tempered by a mystical, nonsectarian, anticlerical religiosity that centers around a nonpartisan God whose love embraces all humanity regardless of creed.

> Another prophet will, they say, soon rise;
> But will he profit by his tricks, likewise?
> My prophet is my reason, aye, myself—
> From me to me there is no room for lies.
> (Rihani 1903, 57)

> These superstitions, Sacred Books and Creeds,
> These cults and Myths and other noxious Weeds—
> So many Lies are crowned, in every age,
> While Truth beneath the tyrant's heel still bleeds.
> (Rihani 1903, 59)

> Muhammad or Messiah! Hear thou me,
> The truth entire nor here nor there can be;
> How can our God who made the sun and moon
> Give all his light to one Sect, I can not see.
> (Rihani 1918, 35)

Rihani found in those beliefs a way to overcome religious and political schisms, including the polarity between a dreamy, stagnant, albeit spiritually rich East and a rationalist, progressive, yet drearily materialistic West. He believed that al-Ma'arri combined the best qualities of both and held out the hope of a future synthesis of civilizations. At the same time, al-Ma'arri demonstrates to the West that the germ of Enlightenment could be found in the East (and eight centuries before Europe, for that matter), the implication being that Orientalists either did not fully understand the East or deliberately misrepresented it. Secondly, through al-Ma'arri, Rihani questions Europe's fascination with Omar Khayyam—Persian author of *ruba'iyyat* (Arabic and Persian for "quatrains"), famous in Europe in Edward Fitzgerald's translation—a fascination that represents at once partial and partisan knowledge. Thus, Rihani's argument that Khayyam was an imitator of, and a lesser thinker than, al-Ma'arri directly challenged the authority of Orientalists by exposing the inadequacy of their representation. Khayyam

> was an imitator or a disciple of [al-Ma'arri]. The birth of the first and the death of the second . . . occurred about the middle of the eleventh century. . . . [T]he skepticism and pessimism of Omar are, to a great extent, imported from Märrah. In his religious opinions the Arabian philosopher is far more outspoken than the Persian poet. I do not say that Omar was a plagiarist, but I say this: Just as Voltaire, for instance, acquired most of his liberal and skeptical views from Hobbes, Locke and Bayle, so did Omar acquire his from Abu'l-Ala. (Rihani 1903, xviii–xix)

Moreover, Khayyam appealed to English readers because of his rebellion against Islam, which made him easy to enlist in the discourse on the backwardness and fanaticism of that religion. Al-Ma'arri, by contrast, attacks all creeds, as well as tribalism and chauvinism of all stripes, and can, therefore, only be subversive to Orientalist culturalism.

Yet al-Ma'arri also exposes a fundamental ambivalence in Rihani's Orientalism: on the one hand, al-Ma'arri undermines the binary model that structures Orientalism. If the Orient had its own Hobbes, Locke, Bayle, and Voltaire, then the entire distinction between the rationalist scientific West and the superstitious and fanatical East collapses. On the other hand, al-Ma'arri demonstrates Oriental influence on the Occident, something that Rihani finds extremely significant because it reinforces the idea of Europe's indebtedness to the wisdom of the East in general and to Arab civilization in particular, thereby undermining the supposed superiority of the West. Rihani's wavering between the impulse to deconstruct Orientalism and the temptation to play the game of cultural one-upmanship—his wanting to have it both ways—points to his own intellectual investment in the opposition East/West, which seemed unassailable in his age, but which also afforded him a platform from which to launch his revisionary discourse.

For the dichotomy East/West was not only culturally and intellectually reductive, it was also enabling for Rihani insofar as he could reinterpret or "expand" it to the point where it no longer sustained cultural and political hegemony, but in a nonconfrontational, conciliatory manner suited to his reformist project of civilizational synthesis. His hesitancy is no doubt also due to his sense of being a minority writer, an outsider to the American literary scene, or, as he puts it in the introduction to the first collection of his own English verse, *Myrtle and Myrrh*, published two years later, "a stranger at thy [the reader's] gate" (1905, 5) who "relies on the hospitality and cordiality due a guest" (6).

Rihani is careful, in the preface to the 1903 translation of al-Ma'arri, not to challenge Orientalist knowledge explicitly:

> The English-reading public, here and abroad, has already formed its opinion of Khayyam, and let it not, therefore, be supposed that in making this claim I aim to shake or undermine its great faith. Nor am I so presumptuous as to think that one could succeed in such a hazardous undertaking. My desire is to confirm and not to convulse, to expand and not to contract the Oriental influence on Occidental minds. (xix)

However, by the time he sits down to expand the 1903 preface into the version that appears in the 1918 volume of translation, that hesitancy has all but disappeared. The above statement about not wishing to challenge Orientalist knowledge is reproduced, but he goes on to do just that anyway. Elaborating on the neglect and distortion that al-Ma'arri suffered at the hands of Arab scholars who tried to turn him into a great Sufi whose heretical ideas were forced upon him by the strictures of Arabic prosody, Rihani registers his surprise "to find a European scholar like Professor [D. S.] Margoliouth giving countenance to such views, even repeating, to support his own argument, such drivel" (1918, 18). Sensing that the absurdity of such views may not necessarily be self-evident to his readers (given that inane pronouncements on the Arab mind, the Arabic language, Islam's responsibility for the backwardness of Arabs, and so on are not rare in either Orientalist scholarship or popular culture), Rihani turns to al-Ma'arri's prose works to show how his ideas of religion as a superstition prevail there too. Rihani goes on to offer this powerful indictment of European scholarship that anticipates the sweeping nature of Edward Said's critique of Orientalism's ideological investments:

> The East still remains the battle-ground of the creeds. And the Europeans, though they shook off their fetters of moral and spiritual slavery, would keep us in ours to facilitate the conquests of European commerce. And the terrible Dragon, which is fed by the foreign missionary and the native priest, by the theologians and the ulema, and which still preys upon the heart and mind of the Orient nations, is as active to-day as it was ten centuries ago. Let those consider this, who think [German Orientalist Alfred Freiherr] Von Kremer exaggerated when he said, "Abu'l-Ala is a poet many centuries ahead of his time." (1918, 20–21)

The neglect suffered by al-Ma'arri results from a conspiracy between Orientalists (with Von Kramer and Reynold A. Nicholson as exceptions that Rihani makes sure to mention) and conservative Arab scholars—two groups whose ideological imperatives require a monolithic and static conception of the Islamic tradition. As a rationalist and free thinker, al-Ma'arri did not fit with that conception: from an Orientalist perspective, an Oriental rationalist is an oxymoron; for conformist Arab scholars, al-Ma'arri was a heretical thinker whose difficult writings demanded the sort of misreading that blunted their incisive edge or co-opted them altogether. For Rihani, al-Ma'arri disturbs both regimes of truth and, therefore, serves as a model for the kind of progressive intellectual that Rihani himself aspired to be. Al-Ma'arri also becomes a particularly appropriate subject not only for interrogating Eastern and Western self-images and particularly Western views of the East but for renewing East–West dialogue as well, since he embodied the kind of synthesis between spiritual wisdom and skeptical rationalism that Rihani took for a civilizational ideal, one which he himself promoted and aspired to embody in his own work.

Within a few years of publishing his first translation of al-Ma'arri, Rihani attempted to extend this project of cultural translation through all three major genres, writing a poetry collection, a play, and a novel by 1911. . . . The poems gathered in *Myrtle and Myrrh* (1905) are on the same themes as his Arabic verse and written in anachronistic idiom and conventional forms and, together with his second collection, *The Chant of Mystics and Other Poems* (1921), came across as exotic, quaint, and mediocre. They were "either ignored . . . altogether or damned with faint praise" (Bushrui and Munro 1970, 16). As for his play *Wajdah* (written in 1909, published in 2001), it "seeks to convey to Western readers a topic that is neither familiar nor usual to them. . . . Perhaps it is the first time that an Arab-American portrays to the West a defiant Arab woman who questions everything and defies all norms" ("Publisher's Foreword," Rihani [1909] 2001, 9–10). Such a theme, however, must have seemed totally foreign, and what with the play's being heavily influenced by Shakespearean tragedy and anachronistic in its language, style, and form, it was never published or performed during Rihani's lifetime. . . . Rihani's poetry and drama may have exhibited more literary ambition than talent, but they nevertheless stand as a testimony to his effort to "expand" American consciousness of the Orient.

Translational Poetics

Much more complex and rewarding is *The Book of Khalid* (1911). Rihani goes one step further in that novel than in his translations, *Myrtle and Myrrh*, *Wajdah*, or *The Chant of Mystic*, in that he attempts to fuse Arabic and European literature thematically, linguistically, formally, and structurally. . . . Like other immigrant narratives, it is a story of coming to America; but like numerous fictional and autobiographical accounts of Arab intellectuals, from Rifa'a al-Tahtawi's *Takhlis al-ibriz fi talkhis bariz*, the text that inaugurated the Nahda in the mid-1830s, to the novels of Tayeb Salih and Ahdaf Soueif in the late twentieth century, it is also a story of returning home, of migration rather than immigration. . . . Furthermore, its English is not only archaic but also at times nearly unintelligible to readers unfamiliar with Arabic and its cultural frame of reference. In addition to the verbal humor and ironic tone characteristic of the Arabic *maqama* genre, Rihani's English is infused with Arabic words, expressions, proverbs, and even rhetorical strategies characteristic of nineteenth-century Arabic literature, such as parallelisms and rhymed prose.[6] It is a language radically deterritorialized, in Deleuze and Guattari's terms, availing itself liberally of the resources of another language with different cultural, rhetorical, and literary norms. Those strategies signal the emergence, in Arab immigrant writing, of what I call here "translational literature"—texts that dramatize the process of translation and foreground the limits of translatability. . . .

Works Cited

Allen, Roger. 1998. *The Arabic Literary Heritage: The Development of Its Genres and Criticism*. Cambridge: Cambridge Univ. Press.

Badawi, M. M. 1993. A *Short History of Modern Arabic Literature*. Oxford: Clarendon.

Bushrui, Suheil, and John Munro. 1970. Introduction to *A Chant of Mystics and Other Poems by Ameen Rihani*, edited by Suheil Bushrui and John Munro, 15–25. Beirut: Rihani House.

Dunnavent, Walter Edward, III. 1991. "Ameen Rihani in America: Transcendentalism in an Arab-American Writer." PhD diss., Indiana Univ.

Gibran, Kahlil. 1926. "To Young Americans of Syrian Origin." *The Syrian World* 1, no. 1: 4–5.

Hourani, Albert. 1967. *Arabic Thought in the Liberal Age 1789–1939*. London: Oxford Univ. Press.

———. 1991. *A History of the Arab Peoples*. Cambridge, MA: Belknap.

Khalidi, Rashid. 2004. *Resurrecting Empire: Western Footprints and America's Perilous Path in the Middle East*. Boston: Beacon.

6. An immensely popular narrative genre that emerged in the tenth century and continued till the beginning of the twentieth, involving the adventures of a wandering rogue who lives by his wits. For a brief introduction to the genre, see Allen 1998, 268–78; Abdelfattah Kilito's *Les séances* (1983) is the most thorough study of the genre in a European language.

Kilito, Abdelfattah. 1983. *Les séances: Récits et codes culturels chez Hamadhânî et Harîrî*. Paris: Sindbad.

Majaj, Lisa Suheir. 2000. "Arab Americans and the Meaning of Race." In *Postcolonial Theory and the United States: Race, Ethnicity, and Literature*, edited by Amritjit Singh and Peter Schmidt, 320–37. Jackson: Univ. Press of Mississippi.

Rihani, Ameen, trans. 1903. *The Quatrains of Abu'l-Ala*. New York: Doubleday, Page.

———. 1905. *Myrtle and Myrrh*. Boston: Gorham Press.

———. 1911. *The Book of Khalid*. New York: Dodd, Mead.

———, trans. 1918. *The Luzumiyat of Abu'l-Ala*. New York: James T. White.

———. 1921. *A Chant of Mystics and Other Poems*. New York: James T. White.

———. 1927. "Where East and West Meet." *The Syrian World* 1, no. 12 (June): 8–11.

———. [1909] 2001. *Wajdah: A Play in Four Acts*. Washington, DC: Platform International.

Rihbany, Abraham Mitrie. 1922. *Wise Men from the East and from the West*. Boston: Houghton Mifflin.

Said, Edward W. 1978. *Orientalism*. New York: Penguin.

Shakir, Evelyn. 1996. "Arab-American Literature." In *New Immigrant Literatures in the United States*, edited by Alpana Sharma Knippling, 3–18. Westport, CT: Greenwood.

24

The Pulse of Queer Life

Arab Bodies in Gay Bars

MEJDULENE B. SHOMALI

In June 2016, a Pakistani American security guard named Omar Mateen perpetrated a mass shooting at Pulse, a gay nightclub in Orlando, Florida. Mateen murdered forty-nine people and injured fifty-eight; his victims were mostly Latino men because it was the club's Latin night. At the same time mourners reeled from the violence inflicted on queer brown people by a brown man, many also grieved that violence was enacted in what many consider a safe space, the gay bar. This essay analyzes the discourses that circulated within queer communities about Mateen and about gay bars after the Pulse shooting in conjunction with Saleem Haddad's *Guapa* (2016), a novel about queer Arab life. The titular queer bar of the novel, Guapa, is central in the story and character development. *Guapa* follows twenty-four hours in the life of Rasa, a gay man living in an unnamed Arab country. On the day the novel's events take place, Rasa's lover, Taymour, will be married to a woman. The night before, Rasa's effeminate best friend Maj has been arrested in a police sting of known queer hangouts. The book opens with Rasa and Taymour discovered in bed together by Rasa's grandmother and follows Rasa as he copes with the fallout of the discovery, attends Taymour's wedding, and attempts to find and free Maj. The backdrop of the novel, the unnamed Arab country, is marked by some notable signifiers of the Arab Spring: protests occur in a central city square; as protests thin, the authoritarian regime maintains its stronghold; some pockets of the revolution take on increasingly Islamic fundamentalist agendas; and, finally, the protagonist experiences fatigue and disillusionment that the protests and sacrifices seem in vain. This tenuous post–Arab Spring political climate affects the queer subjects of the novel, in particular their inclusion/exclusion in the history and the future of the country.

There are compelling points of convergence between the fictional Guapa and the devastatingly real Pulse. In pairing Pulse and *Guapa*, I aim to discuss how gay bars produce and preclude safety for their subjects. The centrality of the gay bar is the topic of the first section. In the second section, I examine how masculinity and femininity are represented in anti-Arab, Islamophobic, and nationalist discourses and how those representations circumscribe the possibility of queer subjects, in particular queer women. In both Pulse and *Guapa*, the idea of a queer Arab and/or Muslim subject is seemingly impossible. In both, the primary bodies under discussion are bodies assigned male at birth and those that identify as men. I will suggest that this emphasis on men and masculinity is not incidental but rather a function of anti-Arab racism, Islamophobia, and Orientalism from without as well as of nationalist and authenticity politics from within. These discourses erase or obfuscate women and make women—though not femininity per se—marginal. In the third section, I discuss how security functions locally and globally in each case to make queer Arab and Muslim subjects impossible. In Pulse, Muslim queers are perceived as threats to US queer cultures via Islamophobia. In *Guapa*, Arab queers are perceived as inauthentic outsiders or threats to their ancestral cultures and to the future of the independent Arab nation. Specifically, Orientalist, Islamophobic, and anti-Arab discourses position queer Arab and Muslim subjects as threats to queer US cultures, while Arab nationalist discourses mark queers as threats to the postcolonial Arab nation. In other words, queer Arabs and Muslims are not safe either in the United States or "at home."

Orientalism, Islamophobia, anti-Arab racism, new Arab nationalisms, and authenticity politics are limiting discourses that circumscribe our capacity to see, imagine, and understand queer Arab and Muslim subjects. They limit the narratives available to us about queer Arab or Muslim life and position men as the central and most significant protagonists. Although this centralization is true of patriarchal cultures at large, the Orientalist and Islamophobic erasure of women makes a queer Arab or Muslim woman particularly unrepresentable. Limiting discourses affect not only narrations about queer Arab or Muslim life by noncommunity members but also those stories from within the community, such as in *Guapa*. I argue that a transnational framing is central to navigating these limiting discourses and understanding queer Arab characters. I juxtapose *Guapa* with coverage of Mateen and the Pulse shootings to demonstrate the utility of the transnational frame.

Though its central narrative unfolds in the unnamed Arab country, *Guapa* is written in English and was released in the United States and the United Kingdom. *Guapa*'s central character, Rasa, is back in the Arab country after college in the United States. As such, the production and content of the book fashion Rasa into a transnational Arab character, one whose queer coming-of-age takes place across and through contact with multiple cultural contexts. The events at Pulse are similarly transnational in scope: the club is in Orlando but on that night is dominated by Latinx queers, Puerto Ricans in particular. The shooter is a Pakistani American with several cultural and personal ties to Arab peoples and Muslim organizations.

I suggest the transnational brown spaces of Guapa and Pulse offer a unique frame from which to understand how Arab queer subjects are represented and formed. In her work on Arab American literature, Carol W. N. Fadda insists on the transnational character of Arab American literatures and identities, where the transnational "highlights the crucial ways the influences and factors shaping Arab American identities [lie] beyond the US nation-state" (Fadda-Conrey 2014, 8). I adopt Fadda's definition and insistence on the transnational because it captures the means by which Arab and Arab American subjects and texts are mutually constitutive and mutually constituted by discourses that circulate in the United States, the United Kingdom, Arab nations, and elsewhere. Looking toward transnational circuits allows queer subjects to articulate their experiences and emerge despite limiting discourses such as Orientalism and Islamophobia. I turn now to the points of convergence between *Guapa* and the Pulse shooting.

"I Want Take You to a Gay Bar"

After Rasa and Maj are reunited, they plan to hit the streets to protest.[1] But first they stop at the underground queer bar in the novel, Guapa. By way of its recurrence and role in the novel, Guapa functions as the central space from which queer characters understand and enact their identities and their revolutionary politics. The revolution of the novel, sexual and otherwise, unfolds in Guapa. At the same time, the state attempts to regulate and discipline its revolutionary queer subjects by raiding the bar in the hours just prior to the novel's opening scene. In many ways, then, the book begins and ends in the bar.

In the aftermath of the Pulse shooting, queer folks went online to mourn. One facet of this grief centered on the gay bar. Even though gay bars have been experiencing a national decline, the Pulse shooting was narrated as the experience of violence in an alleged space of acceptance and safety (Frohman 2016; Lopez 2016). On social media platforms, people posted about their first gay bars (Sykes 2016). They reminisced about the scenes of life in gay clubs, about the freedom gay bars afford life in general (*Guardian* Readers 2016). The gay bar emerged as a physical space and an archive of feeling for personal and national LGBT history in the United States (Cvetkovich

1. The section title comes from Detroit EDM band Electric Six's bizarre and political party anthem "Gay Bar" (2003).

2003). The gay bar was not only the scene of many individual comings-of-age but also the story of a national arrival at gay identity.

Guapa works similarly. Haddad paints Guapa as an oasis for queer love and expression. Guapa is the only public place where Rasa is free to love Taymour and Maj is free to perform femininity without being penalized (Haddad 2016, 128–31).[2] In other scenes of the book, Maj's feminine performances are immediately met with violence. For example, during Rasa and Maj's first meeting, Maj is accosted by a group of schoolboys for being beautiful "like a girl" (43). Whereas the Arab nation where the novel is set remains unnamed, the bar Guapa is also the book's title. The anonymity of the nation and the specificity of the bar decenter the national context and highlight instead sexual spaces as sites of meaning making in the novel.

Thus, in *Guapa* and in the United States, the gay bar is imagined as a safe space for queer subject formation. The bar's centrality to queer identity and culture is evident in queer coming-of-age literatures—for example, the canonical *Stone Butch Blues* (Feinberg 1993)—as well as in the responses to the Pulse shooting cited earlier. Maj and Rasa punctuate their days with visits to Guapa; the bar houses the best version of their intimate lives. The notion of queer bars as significant and safe spaces persists despite the violence that occurs in US gay bars and in *Guapa*. One of the most famous gay bars in the United States, Stonewall, was the object of police surveillance, violence, and harassment before it became a symbol of gay liberation. Guapa itself is subject to raids within the space of the novel (281). The violence visited upon gay bars by state and nonstate actors forces us to ask some questions: For whom is the bar safe, and what are the patrons safe from? I am particularly interested in what safety or welcome is available for queer Arab and Muslim subjects in both the US gay bar imaginary as told by the discourses around Pulse and in the imagined Guapa. What it looks like to be Arab and queer is discussed in the next section.

2. Subsequent citations to *Guapa* give page numbers only.

Desperately Seeking Sawsan

It is difficult to locate explicit representations of Arab or Muslim LGBT life in the United States or elsewhere.[3] This is in part due to the fact that LGBT identities are new even in the West. Theorists of sexuality in Arab and Middle East studies also contend that Western identity categories are inappropriate to Arab subjects, who may exchange and participate in same-sex practices but do not attach those practices to categorical identities such as gay or lesbian (Amireh 2010; Baron and Pursley 2013). In these communities, a richer archive of nonnormative sexuality can be located by thinking against identity and looking instead for desire and deviance (Arondekar 2009; Gopinath 2005; Shah 2011; Shomali 2019). At the same time, some Arab and Muslim subjects *do* adopt the language and identities under the LGBT spectrum. Over the past several years, there has been a small uptick in novels that feature or include gay Arab and Muslim characters.[4] Anglophone novels include Haddad's *Guapa*; Hasan Namir's *God in Pink* (2015); Karim Dimechkie's *Lifted by the Great Nothing* (2015); Alia Younis's *The Night Counter* (2009); Rabih Alameddine's *Koolaids* (1998) and *The Angel of History* (2016); and Randa Jarrar's *A Map of Home* (2008). Of these texts, only Jarrar's features a queer woman in any depth—namely, the bisexual protagonist, Nidali. *Guapa* briefly includes a lesbian character, Nora. What accounts for this emphasis on queer men and the scarcity of queer women? In a

3. Although I want to recognize the capaciousness and danger of pairing Arab and Muslim, many of the discourses that circulate about these communities do not. Thus, the framing of Arab queerness in Arab and American texts is affected by the same discourses that frame Mateen's actions at Pulse, though he is not Arab but rather Pakistani American and Muslim. The impact of Islamophobia and anti-Arab racism are mutually constitutive of Arab and Muslim experiences and are explored here as such.

4. Some Arabic-language texts explicitly center queer or LGBT characters, and, of them, three (that I am aware of) concern women primarily. Although it's not within the scope of this essay to exhaust all LBGTQ Arab or Muslim work, Orientalist and Islamophobic discourses translate in many languages, and I would tentatively suggest that many of the trends I describe here also occur across texts.

survey of these texts, a handful of conventions and repeating tropes emerged. They include:

1. Write about men.
2. Write about men who love femininity but not women.
3. Write about feminine men and male femininity and men in drag.
4. Write about hypermasculine men who can't bear the stigma.
5. Write about all the tenderness of hypermasculine men when they finally have sex with other men.
6. Write about men who are revolutionaries in the bed and the *balad*.[5]
7. Write about dysfunctional family dynamics, particularly with parents.
8. Write about Islam and queer Muslim men.
9. Write about beards.
10. Write about blowjobs.
11. Write about anal sex.
12. Write about being caught.
13. Write about prurient sex in dark alleys, cabs, and behind closed doors.
14. Write about men marrying women but having same-sex lovers on the side.
15. Write about masculine women and chain smokers.
16. Don't write about feminine women.
17. Don't write about women.
18. Definitely write about blowjobs.

This list, tongue-in-cheek though it is, reminds us of the several limiting discourses for Arab and Muslim subjects. First, Orientalism produces hypermasculine, oversexed men and pliant, quiet, veiled women (Abdulhadi, Alsultany, and Naber 2011). Second, anti-Arab sentiment in the United States and the West, particularly after September 11, 2001 (9/11), produces Arab subjects as hypersexual and seemingly queer insofar as their acts of aggression are read through a lens of repression (Puar 2007; Puar and Rai 2002). In this discourse, queer women can't exist, and queer men are necessarily hypermasculine to make up for their homosexuality. It is useful to recall here the sexual torture inflicted on prisoners at Abu Ghraib, the curious threats to sodomize Bin Laden when he was finally captured, and the accusations against Mateen as a frustrated homosexual engaging in vengeance at Pulse (Freccero 2002; Rao 2016; Tétreault 2006). Third, writers and artists of Arab or Muslim descent must contend with internal tropes around authenticity and identity that often designate nonnormative desire as antithetical to their cultures (Naber 2012).

Thus, the only lexicon that exists is one where queer men must emerge and reckon with their "cultural" repression in hypersexual and hypervisible ways. The bind of Orientalism and authenticity accounts for the proliferation of texts featuring queer Arab or Muslim men with relatively similar narrative arcs and for the scarcity of texts featuring queer women. Where the dominant representation of Arab and Muslim women is first about silence and repression by Arab and Muslim men, their available narratives circle not around their own sexuality, per se, but around their rejection of their sexist Arab or Muslim cultures at large. Of course, lesbianism would be an excellent way to achieve this! However, in both cases, the root of the repression is not men at large but Arab and Muslim men in particular in their exquisitely patriarchal Arab or Muslim culture. Arab and Muslim men and women are tasked thus with disregarding Arab or Muslim masculinity; for men, this disregard manifests as the ultimate rejection of masculinity—homosexuality. Women reorient to become the object of a white or Western male gaze rather than an Arab or Muslim one. This is why so many scenes of Arab and Muslim queer men feature sex explicitly, while the dominant trope for women is unveiling. As such, the space of representation between Orientalism, anti-Arab racism, and internal bids for cultural authenticity creates a horizon of impossibility for nonnormative subjects.

How does all this connect to Pulse? After the attack, many gay men in Orlando held that Mateen was himself gay and acting out of some mixture of resentment, repression, and general instability. He was upset that he wasn't more attractive to gay men in Orlando, in particular gay

5. *Balad* is an Arabic word for "country."

Latino men (Rao 2016). Some queer folks came forward to suggest they had seen him on Grindr and in the club itself (*Vice* 2016). Meanwhile, the FBI adamantly insisted that "no evidence" supported the theory of Mateen's nonnormative sexuality (Hennesey-Fiske 2016). Mateen's widow, Noor Salman, was put on trial in March 2018 for aiding and abetting the attack. In Salman's trial, Mateen was configured as a monster, abuser, and philanderer. Salman's defense portrayed her as a "woman of below average intelligence" who was incredibly susceptible to suggestion (Levenson et al. 2018). Salman remained silent during the trial, choosing not to testify in her own defense. Though her defense attorneys argued that the prosecution of her was an example of gendered Islamophobia, their own characterization of her relied on stereotyping Muslim and Arab women as oppressed and suffering—women in need of saving. According to her lawyers, she was basically too stupid and too disrespected by her husband to have ever been in on the attack (Jeltsen 2018). Based on these defenses, Salman was acquitted. Most evident in Mateen's and Salman's combined cases are two of the most dominant gender stereotypes for portraying Arab and/or Muslim subjects—the violent and repressive Muslim man, and the abused and silenced Muslim woman.

The reality of Mateen's sexual practices matter very little in the narratives produced about him. Multiple discourses proliferated, including the one Mateen set forward, in which he claimed the attack was a response to US imperial violence in the Middle East and North Africa region and attributed that violence to multiple Islamic fundamentalist groups (Visser and Couwels 2016). US responses to Mateen's attack were predictable: Islamophobes marshaled the violence in service of Muslim surveillance and stricter immigration policy; Muslim communities denounced him and often the homophobia implied in his actions; some feminist and queer communities urged the public to understand his actions through the lens of toxic masculinity or to resist Islamophobia. A small handful spoke about queer Arabs and Muslims as parties affected by the events. The strains that emerged suggested that there were good Muslims, and there was Mateen. There were queers, and there were Muslims. Naturally, these responses were not mutually exclusive—certainly some queers were Islamophobic, and some Muslims and Arabs defended homophobia, and so on. Ultimately, what animated Mateen was the figure of the "monster, terrorist, fag," one explicitly racialized into an Arab Muslim monolith (Puar and Rai 2002). The nuances of Mateen's actual identity were insignificant to US representations of him; he was simply a terrorist. Indeed, the trope of the "monster, terrorist, fag" collapses all nuance of identity or even factual aspects thereof—the trope overrides Mateen's non-Arab and non-Middle Eastern background, overrides his "real" or "alleged" sex life, and contributes instead to the neo-Orientalist repertory of images about Arabs, Islam, and the Middle East.

In *Guapa*, for Rasa and Maj, on the forefront of their nation's revolution, faggotry is the scene of terror. The novel demonstrates this: Rasa and Taymour are discovered in bed together by Rasa's grandmother, and Rasa spends the day agonizing over her response; Guapa is raided in an attempt to strengthen the state's chokehold on the revolution; when Rasa tries to pick up Maj at the police station and is interrogated by officers, they scream at him for crossing his legs and call him "she" (136–37). His feminization is an acknowledgment of his queerness. Rasa's compliance with the guards and his fear are contrasted with Maj's resistance and bravery (138–39). Maj has and always will perform femininity; he has and always will participate in the protests (122, 282–83). The subject of policing is always Maj—the gender nonconformant, the drag queen, the effeminate man. His femininity is lauded and exalted next to Rasa's seeming masculine compliance, especially during the scene of Rasa's interrogation. It is precisely because Maj's femininity exposes him to violence that he is narrated by Rasa as a revolutionary subject. Nora—the masculine lesbian, founder, and manager of Guapa—is never afforded these radical overtures or significance, despite her responsibility in creating Guapa in the first place. She is a marginal character, mentioned in only a few scenes of the novel.

Despite this oversight, Haddad's treatment of gender and sexual nonconformity achieves some remarkable points. By placing Maj and Rasa at the center of the uprising, Haddad affirms an understanding of nonnormative genders and sexualities as central to the revolutionary context of the novel. Centering queer subjects works against Orientalist framings that route Arab and Muslim unrest through allegedly repressed sexuality. Through Rasa and Maj's harassment and experiences of violence, the novel explores the homophobia that is indeed present in the Arab world. Against the flat representations of Arabs and Muslims in the Pulse coverage, *Guapa* upholds the simultaneous impossibility and necessity of queer Arab or Muslim subjects. But that subject—even that impossible subject—is a man.

Whither the Hummusexual?

The impossibility of the queer Arab or Muslim subject is further configured through the entangled languages of safety and security. Mateen, a security guard twice investigated by the FBI, attacks a "safe space," a US gay bar on Latin night. What does security entail in this context? In the United States, gay bars became safe from state-sponsored violence through processes of privatization, territorialization, and organization that ultimately reified white men as paradigmatic gay subjects (Hanhardt 2013). In more direct terms, as LGBT people organized in the United States, safety was achieved by designating some spaces as gay safe spaces, privatizing those spaces, and dissociating them from other "derelict" communities (poor, of color). As noted earlier, prior to the 1970s and 1980s, gay bars were focal points of police violence. Thus, the "safety" of the gay bar is predicated on the notion of an ideal gay citizen subject—one who is not criminal, not in the streets, not "un-American" in any way aside from homosexuality; this subject is not safe from homonormativity, racism, or classism per se. The gay safe space is simply spatially separated from the usual policing forces.

At the national level, security is a heteronormative tool of empire (Jarmakani 2015). The framework of US exceptionalism invokes the United States as free of homophobia compared to the locations it colonizes and invades. Simultaneously, communities of color in the United States are understood as exceptionally homophobic compared to white communities. At the national level, security also entails security from violence. If the gay bar imagines a subject safe from police violence, and the state imagines a citizen body secure from outsider attacks, Mateen punctures both safety and security in the United States. Mateen's brown skin and association with Islam consolidate his homophobia, born in the United States, as somehow *outside* the United States.[6] He obfuscates the violence of the heteronormative US state, often targeted at brown, Black, and Indigenous bodies, very much like those dancing at Pulse that night. Rather than locating the violence within the colonial and racist implementations of safety that create niche gay spaces and even "nicher" gay Latin spaces, we locate violence in the "monster, terrorist, fag" (Kalish and Shane 2016). This further frees the US normative or homonormative subject to respond with violence or benevolence.

The figure of the "monster, terrorist, fag" codifies Orientalism, anti-Arab racism, and Islamophobia to preclude Arab or Muslim subjects from visibility or inclusion in the LGBTQ community in the United States. Queer Arab or Muslims are at best invisible. More likely, Arab or Muslim subjects must renounce homophobia in their communities, become ambassadors against homophobia, or repeatedly affirm the existence of queers in those communities. Most realistically, however, Arab and Muslim subjects experience violence in defense of the "free" US subject, both domestically and transnationally. These options leave very few moments of queer Arab or Muslim possibility. Instead, as the coverage of Mateen's act indicated and our current political climate corroborates, safety and security in the United States eradicate Arab and Muslim bodies.

In *Guapa*, Maj and Rasa are policed not only because of their homosexuality but also because their bodies threaten the security of the Arab nation in the novel (284). That security threat is mutually constituted by their presence in the revolution and by Maj's obvious homosexuality as an effeminate character. The security of the "traditional or authentic" Arab nation seeks to eradicate queerness. The revolution imagined by the unnamed Arab state in the novel targets queerness as incompatible with its past and future national image. Although *Guapa* is fictional, the pattern of cracking down on gendered and sexual nonnormativity in the pursuit of an authentic

6. All evidence suggests that Mateen was not aware Pulse was a gay nightclub when he attacked it, calling into question the idea that the attack was rooted in homophobia. See Greenwald and Hussein 2018.

national identity is rooted in historical precedent—for example, Egyptian police crackdowns on known queer and gay spaces in 2001, 2014, and 2017 and Egypt's conversations regarding the criminalization of homosexuality. In *Guapa*, the gay bar is "safe" only insofar as it holds capacity for the expression of queer desire. It is not "safe" from state violence, as the contemporary US gay bar purports to be. As such, the queer Arab subject is neither secure nor safe in the Arab local and national contexts.

To conclude, I suggest that understanding Pulse and *Guapa* necessitates a transnational frame for thinking about queer Arab and Muslim subjects, no matter where they are geographically located, because Orientalist and neo-Orientalist frames and internal bids for authenticity affect the representation of queer transnational Arab and Muslim subjects. In Pulse and *Guapa*, we see the bar reoccur. The gay bar both produces and precludes queer Arab and Muslim subjects, particularly through discourses of safety.

Guapa's attempt to center Maj and Rasa and to center the bar rather than the nation is perhaps the way that Haddad imagines queer subjects are capable of eluding state violence and attaining a different kind of community organization. Like Pulse, Haddad's Guapa is a transnational space. Guapa's patrons are ex-pats and pats, men and women, queers and their kin. They are of the mainstream and simultaneously of its undercurrent, tugging the waters of the revolution in new directions. In a special issue of the journal *GLQ* devoted to considering Pulse, Eng Beng Lim (2018) imagines an "Orlando(s)cene" that resists the current political climate of the United States, recently presided over by Donald Trump. Lim articulates this vision of utopic queer nightlife by reflecting on the composition of Pulse that evening, where Mateen's victims and other attendees served as a testament to the multiple possible modes of engagement and queer visioning—that Pulse's transnational queer bodies of color constituted a corporeal response to white supremacy and toxic masculinity, that their presence and commitment to queer life in these distinctly dangerous times constituted not only a horizon of possibility but one of transformation. Indeed, this is the framing Haddad offers of Guapa. Guapa is threatened by the Arab nation because the gay bar questions the nation as the organizing entity.

Here we can return to the previous section's central question: Whither the hummusexual? Where does the queer Arab or Muslim subject exist? If a queer way forward for Muslim or Arab subjects exists, it is most likely in the transnational imaginary that Lim and Haddad articulate. At the same time, let us not forget about Nora from Guapa or the women who died at Pulse or the numerous queer Arab women and femmes whose stories seem impossibly foreclosed. The erasure of queer women and the fraught representations of queer men reveal the extent to which discourses about and by Arabs about what constitutes Arab culture are deeply informed by heteropatriarchy and heteronormativity. A breach in that horizon of impossibility is then possible only through feminist and queer challenges to it. Haddad's transnational Guapa and Lim's Orlando(s)cene will be radical spaces only if they resist imperial investments in the gendered and sexual enactments of Orientalism, Islamophobia, anti-Arab racism, and the politics of cultural authenticity.

If we bring Nora and her "army of lesbians" (273) to the foreground of Guapa as the center of its radical agenda, what new organizational and representational strategies might be revealed? If we study the women of Pulse, such as Brenda Lee Marquez McCool, a frequent visitor and Pulse club "mom" who shielded her own son during the shooting (Bloch, Hersher, and Domonoske 2016), what might we learn about love, care, and resilience? What stories of revolution and resistance do women and femmes live? How might we learn new modes of becoming from their stories? These questions, which foreground Arab women and femme-of-center subjects, will radically alter our vision of queer Arab subjectivity and transnational Arab politics.

Works Cited

Abdulhadi, Rabab, Evelyn Alsultany, and Nadine Naber, eds. 2011. *Arab & Arab American Feminisms: Gender, Violence, & Belonging*. Syracuse, NY: Syracuse Univ. Press.

Alameddine, Rabih. 1998. *Koolaids: The Art of War*. New York: Picador.

———. 2016. *The Angel of History*. New York: Atlantic Monthly Press.

Amireh, Amal. 2010. "Afterword" to "Queer Politics and the Question of Palestine/Israel," edited by Gil Z. Hochberg. Special issue of *GLQ* 16, no. 4: 635–48.

Arondekar, Anjali. 2009. *For the Record: On Sexuality and the Colonial Archive in India*. Durham, NC: Duke Univ. Press.

Baron, Beth, and Sara Pursley. 2013. Editorial foreword to "Queer Affects," edited by Beth Baron and Sara Pursley. Special issue of *International Journal of Middle East Studies* 45, no. 2: 203–4.

Bloch, Hannah, Rebecca Hersher, and Camila Domonoske. 2016. "'They Were so Beautiful': Remembering Those Murdered in Orlando." NPR, June 13. At https://www.npr.org/sections/thetwo-way/2016/06/12/481785763/heres-what-we-know-about-the-orlando-shooting-victims.

Cvetkovich, Ann. 2003. *An Archive of Feelings: Trauma, Sexuality, and Lesbian Public Cultures*. Durham, NC: Duke Univ. Press.

Dimechkie, Karim. 2015. *Lifted by the Great Nothing*. New York: Bloomsbury.

Electric Six. 2003. "Gay Bar." On *Fire*. XL Recordings.

Fadda-Conrey, Carol. 2014. *Contemporary Arab-American Literature: Transnational Reconfigurations of Citizenship and Belonging*. New York: New York Univ. Press.

Feinberg, Leslie. 1993. *Stone Butch Blues*. Ithaca, NY: Firebrand Books.

Freccero, Carla. 2002. "They Are All Sodomites!" *Signs* 28, no. 1: 453–55.

Frohman, Denice. 2016. "The Pulse Shooting: Grieving Safe Space and the Work We Have to Do." *HuffPost*, June 14. At https://www.huffingtonpost.com/entry/the-pulse-shooting-grieving-safe-space-and-the-work_us_575f53d4e4b072d1185b0a8d.

Gopinath, Gayatri. 2005. *Impossible Desires: Queer Diasporas and South Asian Public Cultures*. Durham, NC: Duke Univ. Press.

Greenwald, Glenn, and Murtaza Hussein. 2018. "As the Trial of Omar Mateen's Wife Begins, New Evidence Undermines Beliefs about the Pulse Massacre, Including Motive." *Intercept*, Mar. 5. At https://theintercept.com/2018/03/05/as-the-trial-of-omar-mateens-wife-begins-new-evidence-undermines-beliefs-about-the-pulse-massacre-including-motive/.

Guardian Readers. 2016. "'The People There Became a Kind of Family': What Gay Bars Mean to You." *Guardian*, June 16. At https://www.theguardian.com/commentisfree/2016/jun/16/gay-bars-mean-for-guardian-readers-pulse-nightclub-orlando-community.

Haddad, Saleem. 2016. *Guapa*. New York: Other Press.

Hanhardt, Christina B. 2013. *Safe Space: Gay Neighborhood History and the Politics of Violence*. Durham, NC: Duke Univ. Press.

Hennesey-Fiske, Molly. 2016. "FBI Investigators Say They Have Found No Evidence That Orlando Shooter Had Gay Lovers." *Los Angeles Times*, June 23.

Jarmakani, Amira. 2015. *An Imperialist Love Story: Desert Romances and the War on Terror*. New York: New York Univ. Press.

Jarrar, Randa. 2008. *A Map of Home*. New York: Other Press.

Jeltsen, Melissa. 2018. "Everyone Got the Pulse Massacre Story Completely Wrong." *Huffpost*, Apr. 4. At https://www.huffpost.com/entry/noor-salman-pulse-massacre-wrong_n_5ac29ebae4b04646b6454dc2.

Kalish, Blair, and Zachary Shane. 2016. "The Pulse Nightclub Shooting: Connecting Militarism, Neoliberalism, and Multiculturalism to Understand Violence." *North American Dialogue* 19, no. 2: 102–16.

Levenson, Eric, Nicole Chavez, Martin Savidge, and Ray Sanchez. 2018. "Pulse Gunman's Widow Found Not Guilty." *CNN*, Mar. 31. At https://www.cnn.com/2018/03/30/us/noor-salman-pulse-trial-verdict/index.html.

Lim, Eng Beng. 2018. "The Orlando (S)cene." *GLQ* 24, no. 1: 44–47.

Lopez, German. 2016. "Gay Clubs Are Meant to Be Safe Spaces. Now One Is the Site of the Worst US Mass Shooting." *Vox*, June 12. At https://www.vox.com/2016/6/12/11912758/orlando-florida-shooting-pulse-gay-safe-space.

Naber, Nadine. 2012. *Arab America: Gender, Cultural Politics, and Activism*. New York: New York Univ. Press.

Namir, Hasan. 2015. *God in Pink*. Vancouver: Arsenal Pulse Press.

Puar, Jasbir K. 2007. *Terrorist Assemblages: Homonationalism in Queer Times*. Durham, NC: Duke Univ. Press.

Puar, Jasbir K., and Amit Rai. 2002. "Monster, Terrorist, Fag: The War on Terrorism and the Production of Docile Patriots." *Social Text* 20, no. 3: 117–48.

Rao, Sameer. 2016. "Omar Mateen's Alleged Former Lover Describes Pulse Massacre as 'Revenge' for Rejection." *Colorlines*, June 23. At https://www.colorlines.com/articles/omar-mateens-alleged-former-lover-describes-pulse-massacre-revenge-rejection.

Shah, Nayan. 2011. *Stranger Intimacy: Contesting Race, Sexuality, and the Law in the North American West*. Berkeley: Univ. of California Press.

Shomali, Mejdulene. 2019. "Dancing Queens: Queer Desire in Golden Era Egyptian Cinema." *Journal of Middle East Women's Studies* 15, no. 2: 135–56.

Sykes, Charles. 2016. "'My First Gay Bar': Rachel Maddow, Andy Cohen, and Others Share Their Coming-Out Stories." *New York Times*, June 22. At http://time.com/4365403/orlando-shooting-gay-bar-pulse-nightclub/.

Tétreault, Mary Ann. 2006. "The Sexual Politics of Abu Ghraib: Hegemony, Spectacle, and the Global War on Terror." *NWSA Journal* 18, no. 3: 33–50.

Vice. 2016. "A Man Claims He Was Omar Mateen's Lover and the Orlando Shooting Was 'Revenge.'" June 22. At https://www.vice.com/en_us/article/kwkq7e/orlando-shooter-omar-mateen-gay-lover-said-attack-was-revenge-vgtrn.

Visser, Steve, and John Couwels. 2016. "Orlando Killer Repeatedly Referenced ISIS, Transcript Shows." *CNN*, Sept 24. At https://www.cnn.com/2016/09/23/us/orlando-shooter-hostage-negotiator-call/index.html.

Yunis, Alia. 2009. *The Night Counter.* New York: Shaye Areheart Books.

25

Female Arab American Solo Performance

A Bourgeoning Genre of Arab American Art

MICHAEL MALEK NAJJAR

One of the largest genres of Arab American theater is that of female Arab American solo performance and stand-up comedy. Since the 1990s, there has been a large cadre of female performers who have written and performed deeply personal material that deal with issues regarding biculturality, political protest, transnational issues, and Arab American feminism.[1] In addition, Arab American female stand-up comedians are carving a space for themselves in the stand-up comedy world.[2] This essay focuses on three seminal Arab American solo works: Heather Raffo's *9 Parts of Desire* (2006), Leila Buck's *ISite* (2014), and Jennifer Jajeh's *I Heart Hamas, and Other Things I'm Afraid to Tell You* (2012). These three plays are prime examples of works written and performed by Arab American solo theater performers who are contending with their bicultural upbringing, their return and rearrivals[3] as sojourners to the Arab world, and their trauma watching their country of birth assailing their ancestral homelands. These female performers occupy the space that transgresses many preconceived notions placed upon these women by both the Arab society and the American society they inhabit. By doing this they are creating what Nadine Naber calls "articulations of Arabness," or performances grounded in "Arab histories and sensibilities about family, selfhood, and ways of being in the world but are also hybrid, syncretic, and historically contingent" (2012, 8). In addition, these female solo performers are seeking what Evelyn Shakir calls a yearning "for new narratives about themselves, their mothers, their grandmothers, and for new readings of Arab culture" (1997, 3). Furthermore, these women defy American expectations of Arab women by rejecting what Amira Jarmakani calls "representations of veils, harems, and belly dancers" that have been perpetuated by Hollywood films and popular entertainment for decades (2010, xii). I would add that they also refute dangerous notions of Arab women as terrorists or unpatriotic Americans since their deeply political works confront notions of American exceptionalism, imperialism, and military supremacy. These highly educated, theatrically trained, and politically active women refuse simplistic categorizations that seek to pigeonhole them within the American theater and

Revision of Michael Malek Najjar, *Arab American Drama, Film, and Performance: A Critical Study, 1908 to the Present* (Jefferson, NC: McFarland, 2015), 204–30. Full references in the original notes were converted to author-date citations in the text and notes here, and a works cited list was added.

1. Writer/performers Elmaz Abinader (*Country of My Origin*), Soha Al-Jurf (*Pressing beyond In Between*), Andrea Assaf (*Eleven Reflections on September*, 2011), Leila Buck (*ISite*, 2014), Laila Farah ("Living in the Hyphen-Nation," 2002), Elizabeth Huffman (*Not My Revolution*, 2019), Jennifer Jajeh (*I Heart Hamas*, 2012), Rania Khalil (*Flag Piece*), Taous Claire Khazem (*In Algeria They Know My Name*, 2016), Heather Raffo (*9 Parts of Desire*, 2006), Lena Rizkallah (*Layla's Sahra*), Najla Said (*Looking for Palestine*, 2013), and Jameeleh Shelo (*My American Cousin*) are but a few making their mark as professional solo performers in the American theater.

2. The comedians include Eman El Husseini, Nour Hadidi, Dina Hashem, Maria Shehata, and Maysoon Zayid.

3. See Fadda-Conrey 2014, 67–68.

entertainment fields. Instead, they bring deeply empathetic portraits of Arab and Arab American women to the stage that contradict facile stereotypes placed upon them by a society that often seeks to orientalize, trivialize, or sexualize them.

These performances break traditional norms in several important ways. First, they embody Arab lives on stage at a time when those lives are taken for granted. Second, they create a performer–audience dynamic that forces otherwise apathetic audiences to revalue those they deem as the foreign, dangerous "Other." Third, they create a space where Americans are forced to confront their involvement with wars and political systems that are funded with their taxpayer dollars yet lead to occupations, renditions, indefinite detentions, drone warfare, torture, and death and destruction on an immense scale. I contend that these female Arab American solo performers are representing, through their performances, those who cannot represent themselves. By doing so, with great vulnerability, they are humanizing those whom most Americans would comfortably disregard as less than human and therefore worthy of destruction. In other words, their work is a determined attempt to make Arabs and Arab Americans human in a time when they are being systematically dehumanized by the government, the military, and the media.[4]

Several Arab American scholars have also studied female solo performance in this context. Somaya Sami Sabry categorizes this form as "performing Sheherazadian orality." She writes that Arab American female solo performance is a diasporic site where identifications are explored, reductive representations are undercut, and performances are sites of resistance. As attempts to break the silence surrounding the racialization these women experience in their daily lives, solo performances in theater and stand-up comedy help audiences "conceive how and why Arab and American identities are negotiated and articulated within the historical and political context of the 'war on terror'" (2011, 129). Dalia Basiouny and Marvin Carlson write that these performances were created to contradict Western stereotypes of Arab women as voiceless, oppressed individuals with no outlet for expression within Arab culture. Through the use of autobiographical solo performances, these women explore "the forces that encourage or discourage the formation of identity" (2009, 213). Hence, they utilize theater as a means of exploring and expressing identity at a time when their cultures are the subject of suspicion and misunderstanding. Hala Baki writes that stand-up performances by Arab American female comics explore subversive ways of tackling issues of identity through "a form of social resistance which I term comic resistance" (2015, 1). For Baki, this comic form is popular resistance that can inspire social change among the masses through activism. The use of this activism via comedy is a source of power for minorities, namely Arab American women. However, Baki adds, the task of this resistance is fraught with difficulty given the societal expectations specifically placed upon these women (27).

As these scholars have demonstrated, female Arab American solo performance is a form of political, theatrical, and comic resistance that is based on primarily autobiographical material that is written and performed by the women themselves. Unlike plays that are written from an author's invention, these plays are fundamentally based in the personal experiences of the writer/performers and are founded in a deep sense of political and moral ethics combined with a deep sense of empathetic understanding. To fully understand these works, it is helpful to examine the performers' perspectives on their plays, affording readers and spectators with another frame by which to understand these works.

Heather Raffo's 9 Parts of Desire: "A Psychic Civil War Onstage"

Raffo was initially not drawn to the genre of solo performance and was not naturally inclined to write it. For her, *9 Parts of Desire* was more about telling a story in a structure that "heightens what is being said" and finding a form that matched the function of the collected consciousness and spirit of one person playing nine Iraqi women in what she calls "a psychic civil war on stage" (interview by the author, May 20, 2010). The play required the solo performance

4. For more on this topic, see Judith Butler's *Precarious Life: The Powers of Mourning and Violence* (2006), chapter 2.

structure because the story she was telling required one person to inhabit nine different lives. For Raffo, *9 Parts of Desire* is more a play than a solo performance—or, in her words, a combination of "storytelling, performance art, and a play" (interview by the author, 2010). Raffo's assessment of her own work is confirmed by the fact that the play has been performed successfully both as a solo performance and with several actresses playing the various roles (interview by the author, 2010).

Raffo, who initially wrote and performed the monodrama, based her play on what she calls a "life-changing trip" to Iraq in 1992. There she met many Iraqi women who inspired her to write their stories. Instead of a formal interview process, Raffo spent time living with these women, who entrusted her with their personal accounts. She writes that these stories were not told to her verbatim but were composites that were based on research and later dramatized and written in a poetic style more akin to songwriting (Heather Raffo's Official Website 2020). Thus, the play does not read like a traditional drama; it is a series of monologues where the text reads like poetry.

Raffo also provides an Arab American perspective through the character titled only "The American." In the play, The American sits transfixed by the television, watching the grainy night-vision coverage of the attack on Baghdad by US forces, wondering if her family living in the city has survived while she goes about her life in America working out at the gym and getting pedicures. What is important about adding the Arab American diasporic perspective here is that Raffo humanizes the pain and fear that Americans of Arab descent (in this case Iraqi descent) experience when foreign wars funded by their own taxpayer dollars are fought against Arab states. For most Americans, the green-tinted video footage of US bombs being dropped on Baghdad signaled a victorious "shock and awe" campaign by the military on an evil Arab regime. For Iraqi Americans, however, it heralded a lethal war that targeted their innocent families. The American in Raffo's play dramatized the inner trauma Arab Americans experienced during "Operation Desert Storm," while many of their fellow countrymen were reveling in the violence of war. Raffo writes, "I wanted the audience to see these women not as the 'other' but much more like themselves than they would have initially thought" (Heather Raffo's Official Website 2020). Watching The American suffer a nervous breakdown onstage provides a moment of empathy for those helplessly watching the war on television.

Raffo's *9 Parts of Desire* and her later play *Noura* pay homage to Iraqi women who have suffered the brunt of the many difficulties faced by the Iraqi people over the past half century, including the Iran–Iraq War, the two major Gulf Wars, the American occupation of Iraq, the rise of ISIS [Islamic State of Iraq and Syria], and the ongoing Sunni/Shi'a/Kurdish conflicts. Raffo's writing and her performances in her own plays seek to create value for Arab lives, demonstrating that US involvement in these wars has very real and direct consequences on Arabs and Americans of Arab descent. By performing Iraqi women and dramatizing their struggles, Raffo offers a more human and humane dimension to a people who have suffered under decades of dictatorship, occupation, war, and sectarian conflict.

Leila Buck's *ISite*: "Touching so Many Shores at Once"

Leila Buck's play *ISite* is a monodrama that explores the tensions of growing up Arab American of mixed parentage. Buck's mother is Lebanese from a mixed Muslim and Christian family, and her father, Stephen Buck, has filial roots that date back to the Massachusetts Bay Colony in 1636 (personal correspondence from Buck to the author, March 19, 2014). Buck is a transnational to her very core, stating, "I took my first international flight in the womb. I guess that's why I've always loved takeoff. In a way, I was born in flight" (Buck 2014, 24). Even her name becomes a point of contention; her mother wished to put her English name "Kathryn" first because children would not make fun of her. When asked why she did this, the character named "Mom" replies, "Children are cruel. I want her to feel like she belongs, as an American just like you" (24). The question of naming is a complicated one for most Arabs and is a point of contention within the Arab American community. Buck writes, "I'm Katie Buck. But Leila is my . . . *middle* name" (24).

Over time, Leila has dropped "Kathryn" altogether and is now known only by "Leila."

ISite focuses primarily on Buck's cross-cultural experiences of living between worlds. Buck displays her writing and acting through portrayals of multiple perspectives of herself and her family at different points in their lives. Her experience of performing the play in front of audiences over many years prior to and after 9/11 has led to many conversations with audience members. Buck's plays are situated at the intersection of her parents' and grandparents' transgenerational trauma and Buck's own experiences as a bicultural Arab American who has experienced life in both the Arab world and the United States during times of political upheaval. Her plays offer a glimpse into the complicated allegiances, identities, and situational politics that face Arab Americans. By embodying the characters, as a performer Buck provides audiences with personal testimonial and theatrical storytelling. Although Buck plays "characters" in her solo works, they are based on her personal experiences and convictions. This, merged with her dynamic acting abilities, creates thoughtful and entertaining performances that take audiences into an empathetic space where they can be moved by her thoughts and ideas without feeling simultaneously threatened by them. Buck believes her work "moves us across barriers toward greater understanding and empathy—and from there, toward a more just and peaceful world" (Buck 2014, 23). This idealism is at the heart of the Arab American female solo performance genre and shared by many of its practitioners. Part of the difficulty of identity is rooted in the ability (or lack thereof) to speak Arabic. This struggle with the inability to speak Arabic is a major preoccupation with many Arab American playwrights. The Relative in the play, while speaking to Woman, says, "Why your mother didn't teach you the language of your country?!" The Woman replies, "Yes I want to talk to you! I just—don't know how" (Buck 2014, 26). This concept of the shamefulness of not understanding or speaking Arabic becomes a major preoccupation with many second- and third-generation Arab Americans because in Arab culture the ability to speak Arabic is intricately tied to the concept of heritage. The loss of Arabic is equal to the loss of culture.

In the section titled "Passing," Buck asks if she could pass as an Arab. Walking around the souks of Jeddah, Saudi Arabia, Woman dons an abaya and goes into the market fully covered for the first time in her life. Buck realizes that "as long as I remain silent, I belong. And I can watch this world with foreign yet familiar eyes . . . I am amazed at how well I pass for an Arab. But there is something beautiful in discovering what really makes you who you are. If everyone looks the same, you find another way to know them. So what makes me who I am?" (Buck 2014, 27). The same she says regarding family: one's position in the world is defined by one's position in a family "because that is where your *identity*—begins" (28). Another marker of Arab identity in this play is food. According to Woman, "In the Arab world, food is love. It is also a gesture of hospitality. . . . To refuse food is like a personal rejection of an Arab's culture, heritage, and family. No pressure!" (30). In this way Buck negotiates her Arabness with her Americanness. As an American of Arab descent, she must navigate the complicated social structures that dictate one's place in society through family ties, language acumen, and cultural markers such as food and hospitality.

Buck also addresses the Palestinian struggle in *ISite.* Woman's cousin, Lena, is originally Palestinian. When Lena attempts to go back to Palestine, she is placed in the line for Palestinians and not in the one for Americans. There, she witnesses soldiers beating an old woman. She says,

> In Arabic class in college my American professor taught me that Intifada literally means shaking off. And I think sometimes about what that means to my cousins over there. Shaking off—occupation? Frustration? Degradation? The more we share the more we fight, like brother and sister who can't stand seeing themselves in each other. Everyone always says that Arabs are anti-Semitic. Well that's impossible. Arabs can't be anti-Semitic. Arabs are Semites. We come from the same land—the one we're fighting for. (Buck 2014, 41)

Like others in this genre, Buck refuses to be tarred with the "anti-Semite" designation that some utilize to silence voices critical of US foreign policy.

Buck's experiences growing up in the Arab world, in places as diverse as Saudi Arabia, Iraq, and Oman, inform her entire existence. For Buck, she is the sum of all of these parts—the American diplomat father and the Lebanese mother, the Palestinian cousins, all of these diverse people and experiences inform her being. Buck brings all of these people, places, and experiences together in her final statement of the play:

> It's touching so many shores at once that forms the shape of who I am. We all take our shape from the lands that we touch. That's what home is I guess—where you make contact with the earth. And every time I touch down in new soil I see myself for the first time. (44)

Buck returns to these images in this play and in her other works. In *ISite*, she utilizes the metaphor of water touching many shores and trees being transplanted to new lands, and in her later work *In the Crossing*, she utilizes the metaphor of being a bridge between cultures. Buck sees herself living in the space between "Arab" and "American," and . . . she understands that she must translate the seemingly unbridgeable chasm between these two identities. Instead of feeling defeat, Buck finds this bridge building her calling. In her play *In the Crossing* she says, "I mean, what is a bridge, really? Something that connects things that wouldn't be connected otherwise" (Buck 2010, 121). Buck's writing and performance allow audiences to cross bridges she creates through her personal, intimate storytelling.

Jennifer Jajeh's *I Heart Hamas*: "Need of Humanization Stories"

Jennifer Jajeh, a female Christian Palestinian American performer, has been performing her monodrama *I Heart Hamas: And Other Things I'm Afraid to Tell You* since 2008. Jajeh explains that she created the play because she was tired of explaining herself and her thoughts about the Israel/Palestine conflict. In 2000 she traveled to her parents' hometown of Ramallah, where she lived for a year and a half. The 9/11 attacks occurred ten days after her return home. "I clearly had post-traumatic stress disorder from living in a war zone," she says. "'Why do these people hate us?' is what a lot of people were saying after September 11th. There's such a misunderstanding of Arabs and Muslims in general. . . . There was such a need of humanization stories" (quoted in Girmay 2010). For an actress who was frustrated with the limited choice of roles available to her, the performance became a means for opening up the conversation about Palestine, taking the fear out of the discourse, and being more playful about the ideas within the debate. She is clear that she is not speaking for all Palestinians in her work. "I'm not representing the Palestinian perspective," she says. "I'm representing my Palestinian perspective" (quoted in Girmay 2010). By saying this, Jajeh refuses to totalize the Palestinian experience in one play. Instead, she provides audiences with a very personal reflection of her own realization as a Palestinian American who has journeyed back to her ancestral homeland and has returned very much changed. Carol Fadda labels this phenomenon "returns and rearrivals" (Fadda-Conrey 2014, 68). For Fadda, Arab American female protagonists experience a revisionary negotiation of their Arab American identity through journeys to their Arab ancestral homelands. She notes,

> Renegotiating the place of the Arab-American body, specifically the female body, in light of such political relations inscribes transformative understandings of the Arab homeland onto the US terrain. For instead of the homeland being regarded as the root cause of Arab-Americans' foreignness in the US, a more complex, transnational, and less binary-based knowledge of this homeland becomes an important conduit for reimagining the place occupied by the Arab-American subject within the U.S. (2014, 68)

This transnational knowledge also challenges the simplistic notions Americans have about US foreign policy regarding Middle Eastern conflicts. Therefore, Jajeh could not help being transformed by the embodied knowledge she gains visiting Palestine, and she is forever changed because of it.

Jajeh labels her monodrama "a tragicomic solo show" (Jajeh 2012, 1).[5] The play's provocative title, given the US Department of State's designation of Hamas as a terrorist organization, along with Jajeh's asking audience members to "consider the current conflict in the Middle East from the Palestinian perspective," immediately asks the audience for empathy with the Palestinian "Other." Like other Arab American writers, she too prefaces the play with a plea to not accuse the writer/performer of being anti-Semitic, reminding the audience that the word "Semite" includes Arabs (2). In the play, Jajeh takes the audience through a journey of the frustrations she encounters being told that "there is no such thing as a Palestinian" and losing acting jobs because of being Middle Eastern. Jajeh tells the audience,

> I've spent my entire life defining myself for you. Trying to make my Palestinianness easier to digest, more fun, less threatening. But you see the more I do that, the more I feel like parts, huge parts of me are being erased. Like the real me just gets watered down into a tastier, easier to swallow version. (5)

Like some other Arab American performers, Jajeh reminds audiences that she is a Christian and that there are Christian Arabs in Palestine. She also attempts to show the audience where Palestine is on a map, but there is no map she can find that actually says the word "Palestine." In the play, Jajeh's agent tells her to be cautious performing in a show that mixes business with politics since she might want to be careful who she offends. Later, Jajeh takes a transformational journey to Palestine. On her journey she falls in love, is detained by Israeli forces at a checkpoint, and spits on an Israeli soldier. When she asks, rhetorically, if spitting on soldiers was the right thing to do, she replies,

> It's hard to separate things in your mind. You have to understand what it's like there. What it feels like to be assaulted everyday. They treat us like we don't exist or we're not even human. And I've only been here for a year. Imagine if you grew up here. It's like living in a pressure cooker. Not everyone can handle the pressure. (25)

When Jajeh arrives at a scene where children are throwing stones at Israeli soldiers, she decides to stay and film the scene. She witnessed a boy get shot, which drives her into a depression. Her boyfriend, Hakam, tells her she must be strong if she wishes to live in Palestine. Jajeh crosses the unimaginable line of actually empathizing with those who commit violence.

> Look, if I could snap anybody could. This idea we have of what terrorism, Hamas is. That it's some mad crazy radical person. Some religious fundamentalist driven by insane motives that we can't understand. But maybe in reality, it's just a person who's had enough and doesn't see any other options. Maybe it's just a normal human reaction against violence and oppression. After living in Ramallah for only a year and a half, I even reached a point where I could imagine blowing people up. But I had the option to leave. (30)

Like other Arab American writers, Jajeh retains a deep bond with Palestine but cannot conceive of living there. Her Palestinian identity is a part of her that she cannot forego in her work, in her relationships, or in her political views. The play's provocative title, especially considering the recurring wars between Hamas and Israel, is one that some would automatically reject as untenable. However, Jajeh refuses to reduce the argument into absolutes instead she embraces the complexity of the situation that faces Palestinians and Palestinian Americans daily.

What makes works by Palestinian American female solo performers such as Jajeh compelling is the fact that they empathize with the Palestinian point of view regardless of the exigencies of dominant US views on the conflict. Their direct confrontation with violence, poverty, and occupation as well as their ancestral connections to Palestine cause them to have feelings of anger and shame. These performances are their way of coping with the

5. Permission to quote from *I Heart Hamas* was granted by the author.

trauma they and their families experience. With these plays, they work through their postmemorial trauma by performing the experiences of their Palestinianness onstage, despite risks to their careers.

In this chapter I suggest that contemporary performers are attempting to revalue Arabs and Arab Americans in theater by utilizing the solo performance form that has traditionally been the domain of non-Arab/Arab American performers. They are the contemporary artistic counterparts to the important academic work that preceded them in response to the anti-Arab backlash of the 1967 Six-Day War. The Arab American scholars that preceded or are contemporaries of these artists have created the theoretical backdrop for the formation of these theater works. In fact, many of these artists cite these scholars when discussing their works with public. In some cases, this is a family matter. Arab American scholars such as Edward W. Said and Rashid Khalidi fathered Arab American solo performers Najla Said and Ismail Khalidi. However, other solo performers such as Heather Raffo, Leila Buck, and Jennifer Jajeh artistically convey the complex issues Arab American feminist scholars have been critically pursuing for decades. Like the Arab Americans writing during the 1967 war, who were mainly first-generation immigrants, this group of second-generation artists are dealing with the latest Arabophobic and Islamophobic blowback from conflicts in the Middle East. These hyphenated artists must contend with the so-called war on terror and the evolving anti-Arab, anti-Muslim fervor in the United States in the twenty-first century.

These theater makers have made the conscious decision to speak from and create works focused on their Arab American identity. After the 9/11 attacks and the subsequent wars fought to avenge that tragic event, Arab Americans were outed from whatever protections their pre-9/11 identities might have afforded them. Instead of denying or eschewing their Arabness, these writer/performers confronted issues such as governmental persecution, racial profiling, renditions, black sites, and torture. In addition, these works confront other issues that concern Arab Americans, such as the Israel/Palestine conflict, negative stereotyping of Arabs in popular entertainment, and intra-Arab conflicts within the United States. With these plays, this generation of Arab American performers will no longer play the "tiny, marginal, and unimportant role" Edward W. Said believed Arab Americans had been assigned to playing for more than a century in American culture (Orfalea 2006, 175).

Works Cited

"9 Parts of Desire." N.d. Heather Raffo's official website. At https://heatherraffo.com/projects/nine-parts-of-desire/.

Abinader, Elmaz. *Country of My Origin*. Unpublished play manuscript.

Ameri, Anan, and Holly Arida. 2007. *Etching Our Own Image: Voices from within the Arab-American Art Movement*. Newcastle, UK: Cambridge Scholars.

Assaf, Andrea. 2011. *Eleven Reflections on September*. CD. Art2Action.

Baki, Hala. 2015. *Female Voices of Comic Resistance in Arab-American Stand-Up Comedy*. At http://hdl.handle.net/10211.3/140313.

Basiouny, Dalia, and Marvin Carlson. 2009. "Current Trends in Arab-American Performance." In *Performance, Exile, and "America,"* edited by Yana Meerzon and Silvija Jestrovic, 208–19. New York: Palgrave Macmillan.

Buck. Leila. 2010. *In the Crossing*. Unpublished play manuscript, in author's files.

———. 2014. *ISite*. In *Four Arab American Plays*, edited by Michael Malek Najjar, 21–44. Jefferson, NC: McFarland.

Butler, Judith. 2006. *Precarious Life: The Powers of Mourning and Violence*. London: Verso.

Darraj, Susan Muaddi, ed. 2004. *Scheherazade's Legacy: Arab and Arab American Women on Writing*. Westport, CT: Praeger.

Fadda-Conrey, Carol. 2014. *Contemporary Arab-American Literature: Transnational Reconfigurations of Citizenship and Belonging*. New York: New York Univ. Press.

Farah, Laila. 2002. "Living in the Hyphen-Nation." *Counterpoints* 169:179–95.

Girmay, Weenta. 2010. "Jennifer Jajeh and *I Heart Hamas*." *Pittsburgh City Paper*, Oct. 20. At https://www.pghcitypaper.com/Blogh/archives/2010/10/20/jennifer-jajeh-and-i-heart-hamas.

Huffman, Elizabeth. 2019. *Not My Revolution*. Unpublished play manuscript, last modified Jan. 15, in author's files.

Jajeh, Jennifer. 2012. *I Heart Hamas: And Other Things I'm Afraid to Tell You*. Unpublished play manuscript, last modified Dec., in author's files.

Jarmakani, Amira. 2010. *Imagining Arab Womanhood: The Cultural Mythology of Veils, Harems, and Belly Dancers in the U.S.* New York: Palgrave Macmillan.

Al-Jurf, Soha. *Pressing Beyond in Between*. Unpublished play manuscript, in author's files.

Khazem, Taous Claire. 2016. *In Algeria They Know My Name*. Unpublished manuscript, last modified Apr. 8, in author's files.

Naber, Nadine. 2012. *Arab America: Gender, Cultural Politics, and Activism*. New York: New York Univ. Press.

Orfalea, Gregory. 2006. *The Arab Americans: A History*. Northampton, MA: Olive Branch Press.

Raffo, Heather. 2006. *Heather Raffo's 9 Parts of Desire: A Play*. Evanston, IL: Northwestern Univ. Press.

Rizkallah, Lena. *Layla's Sahra*. Unpublished play manuscript, in author's files.

Sabry, Somaya Sami. 2011. *Arab-American Women's Writing and Performance: Orientalism, Race, and the Idea of The Arabian Nights*. London: I. B. Tauris.

Said, Najla. 2013. *Looking for Palestine: Growing Up Confused in an Arab-American Family*. New York: Riverhead Books.

Shakir, Evelyn. 1997. *Bint Arab: Arab and Arab American Women in the United States*. Westport, CT: Praeger.

Shelo, Jameeleh. *My American Cousin*. Unpublished play manuscript, in author's files.

26

Consuming Orientalism

Public Foodways of Arab American Christians

MATTHEW JABER STIFFLER

Introduction

Elias and Joseph Kirdahy opened a restaurant on Washington Street in New York City's "Syrian Colony" in about 1913. The Kirdahy brothers, Christian immigrants from Greater Syria, named their restaurant, simply, Kirdahy Bros. Oriental Restaurant.[1] It was apparently successful, surviving on Washington Street for decades, nestled among dozens of other Arab American–owned cafés, grocery stores, linen shops, and dry-goods stores. Sometime in the mid-1920s, the Kirdahy brothers (now Simon and Joseph, after Elias moved to Ohio) changed the name of their restaurant to "The Sheik," after the 1921 Rudolph Valentino film of the same name. According to legend, the Kirdahy brothers donned "The Sheik" name at the suggestion of Hollywood star John Barrymore, who frequented the establishment.[2]

The Sheik restaurant was a prime ethnic destination for New Yorkers, as it was reviewed or mentioned by dozens of publications throughout its existence. One 1962 guide book, *New York on Five Dollars a Day*, said of The Sheik, "Your grandparents will probably remember this exotic Middle Eastern restaurant from the days when it was known as 'Kirdahy Brothers' and located on the lower East Side" (Feldman 1962, 157). This review was typical of the manner in which non-Arab Americans portrayed the restaurant: exotic and unusual, but inviting. The restaurant would live on at various locations and with various owners until the 1960s, a long life for a New York City restaurant.

The Kirdahy brothers' success spurred other Arab American restauranteurs to name their establishments after popular Hollywood depictions of Arab countries. The Son of the Sheik restaurant, arguably the most well-known Arab restaurant in New York in the mid-twentieth century, opened in the early 1930s. *The Son of the Sheik* (1926) was also a popular Rudolph Valentino film. Arab Americans would open Sheik and Son of the Sheik restaurants in other US cities, namely Detroit (The Sheik

Revised version of Matthew Jaber Stiffler, "Consuming Orientalism: Public Foodways of Arab American Christians," *Mashriq & Mahjar: Journal of Middle East and North African Migration Studies* 2, no. 2 (2014): 111–38. Full references in the original notes were converted to author-date citations in the text and notes here, and a works cited list was added.

The author thanks the Arab American National Museum in Dearborn, Michigan, for the use of archival materials and for supporting the writing of the article. He also thanks Nadine Naber for her continual guidance and for sharing her work and expertise. Finally, he thanks the reviewers and editors for invaluable feedback.

1. In 1922, there is an entry in the local New York City directory for Kirdahy Bros. Oriental Restaurant at 87 Washington St. (Abdou 1922). In a 1930 community directory, the Kirdahy restaurant is listed as "The Sheik" (*Nasib Arida's* 1930). In various directories, the restaurant is listed in the 1930s as being at 241 Fifth Avenue, remaining on Fifth Avenue through at least the early 1950s, finally ending up on Lexington Avenue in the 1960s.

2. The Sheik opened in 1913 on Washington Street. In her New York City guidebook, Kate Simon recounts the legend that the restaurant was renamed after John Barrymore suggested it (1959, 176).

restaurant, 1920s) and Miami (Son of Sheik restaurant, 1932), and Jacksonville (The Sheik, 1965), which became institutions in those cities as well.[3]

As businessmen, the Kirdahy brothers were capitalizing on the US public's fascination with the "exotic" Arab world. By the 1920s, as cafés and restaurants in New York City's Syrian Colony shifted from serving to more than just the Arab immigrant population, owners began offering menus in English as well as Arabic and changed the names of their establishments from simply "Khalil's" or "The Ladies and Gents Restaurant" to "The Cairo," "The Eastern Star," "Mecca," and "The Arabian Inn."[4] This was a conscious engagement with US popular-culture representations of Arabs and the Arab world, a way of grafting the Arab American experience onto the Orientalist legacy of an exotic Arabness, in order to serve "authentic" food in an "authentic" environment.[5]

My essay will demonstrate the long history of self-Orientalism within Christian Arab American public foodways (mainly through restaurants and church food festivals) and claims to an authentic Arabness within US multiculturalism, often utilizing imagery associated with *The Arabian Nights*. Building on Nadine Naber's (2012) placement of "authenticity" within the context of US multiculturalism, I argue that a constructed Arab cultural identity can be used to make claims to an authenticated Arabness when deployed within the liberal multicultural marketplace that commodifies identity. I use the term *authenticated* to describe an Arabness (a cultural identity) that Arab American Christians constructed, which was authentic only in that it reflected US popular-culture constructs of an authentic Arab.

Arab American Christians are a diverse group. Within Arab American Christendom are Coptic Catholics and Coptic Orthodox, who trace their heritage to Egypt; Maronite Catholics from Lebanon; Melkite Catholics, who come largely from Lebanon and Palestine; Chaldean Catholics from Iraq; Antiochian Orthodox (Greek Orthodox), mainly from Jordan, Lebanon, Palestine, and Syria. There are also a number of Arabic-speaking Protestant congregations in the United States. This essay focuses on the Antiochian Orthodox Archdiocese, as Antiochian Orthodox are the largest denomination of Arabic-speaking Christians in the United States who self-identify as Arab or Arab American.[6] The Antiochian Orthodox Archdiocese is representative of the Arab American Christian experience. The Antiochians share a similar history in the United States with the Maronite and Melkite Churches, which founded parishes at the end of the nineteenth century and tended to settle in industrial centers on the Eastern Seaboard and the Midwest. Antiochian parishes, like other Eastern-rite Christian communities, have continually celebrated their cultural identity through public ethnic festivals and have become known for their production and sale of Middle Eastern food in their respective localities.[7]

My analysis of the construction and maintenance of an Arab American Christian cultural identity in the US context takes into account the transnational positioning

3. In Detroit, The Sheik restaurant is thought to be the first Arab restaurant to cater to non-Arab clientele. In their essay "Continuity and Adaptation in Arab American Foodways" (2000), William Lockwood and Yvonne Lockwood claim, "For many old Detroiters, The Sheik was the place where their conception of Arab food was created" (517).

4. Ray Hanania mentions that a restaurant called The Mecca, owned by a Palestinian immigrant, opened around 1915, perhaps originally with a different name (2005, 12).

5. My argument here is that these restaurant owners not only were engaging with popular-culture representations of an imagined Arab past but were also building on what Melani McAlister ([2001] 2005) calls the "commodity Orientalism" of the late nineteenth and early twentieth century, where the US public's fascination with the Holy Land and the "Orient" was commodified through travel books, novels, and silent films about a mythical Orient.

6. Maronite Catholics and Chaldeans tend to shy away from the labels *Arab* and *Arab American*, instead choosing to celebrate a national identity (such as Iraqi or Lebanese) or the identity of the ancient civilization (such as Babylonian or Phoenician). See Shryock and Lin 2009. Melkite Catholics tend to identify as Arab, but their numbers are much smaller than the Antiochians. There are complex homeland cultural, religious, and political reasons for these disparities, which remain beyond the scope of this essay. See Naber and Stiffler 2013 for a more in-depth discussion of Arab American Christian identity politics.

7. Although I focus here on the Antiochian Orthodox, similar studies could easily be done featuring the Maronite, Coptic, and Melkite communities. For example, Yasmeen Hanoosh (2011) has delved into constructions of an ancient "Chaldean-ness" in her work on Iraqi Christians in the United States.

of Antiochian Orthodox Christians vis-à-vis US military and political interests in the Middle East, homeland events (such as political or humanitarian crises), and US popular, political, and media discourses about Arabs that structure their position within the US multiculture.[8] Antiochian Orthodox have continually constructed and reconstructed their cultural identity in response to this positionality. As Naber argues about Arabness and American-ness, which is similar to the scope of my work, these constructs shift and change along with contexts and power relationships (2012, 14).

Finally, this essay will argue for the importance of public foodways to the Arab American experience. Within Arab immigrant communities, eating ethnic food is the most common ethnic-related cultural practice.[9] Joe Kadi, in the introduction to the anthology *Food for Our Grandmothers*, describes cultural identity construction in relation to food and homeland: "Lebanon. I grew up tasting Lebanon and hearing its music, but not speaking and only rarely hearing its language" (1994, xv). Many Arab Christians, who may not speak Arabic or have not lived in the Middle East, still know its food well and identify eating it with their cultural identity. Randa Kayyali similarly places food as a main marker of cultural identity for Arab Americans. Kayyali writes that "some multigenerational Arab Americans describe their Arabic-language skills as 'kitchen Arabic,' meaning they only know the Arabic words for dishes cooked by their family in the home" (2006, 84).

Arab American Christian Foodways

Food and the celebration of food, or what Charles Camp (1989) labels the "food event," is a potent cultural form through which to analyze a group's identity construction. My focus on the food festival and ethnic restaurants as food events allows me to analyze how food and its associated imagery function both as markers of community identity and as cultural commodities for sale to the general public.

The consumption of cultural identity through food forms the basis of my argument about the importance of studying Arab American Christian food festivals and restaurants as spaces where the public encounters a constructed Arabness. Deborah Lupton speaks literally about the consumption of the other: on the "simplest, biological level . . . we become what we eat" (1994, 666). The consumption of "ethnic" foods by people outside of that cultural group speaks volumes about the larger context of multiculturalism and its celebration of depoliticized identity. As cultural critic Lisa Lowe has famously claimed, multiculturalism "is concerned with 'importation,' not 'immigration,'" as the US public loves to purchase cultural artifacts (such as food) but only outside of the social and political reality for the peoples who generate and sell those artifacts (1996, 87).

Public foodways, which I define here as ethnic restaurants and food festivals aimed at a general public (which may or may not include Arab Americans), are a rich site for understanding how an ethnic community constructs a cultural identity. Penny Van Esterik, whose work is based on fieldwork with urban ethnic festivals in the 1970s, writes that "the ethnic food festival is an example of the staging of ethnicity for American consumption" (1982, 217). Similarly, Lucy Long, noted scholar of "culinary tourism," argues that in the case of ethnic restaurants "it is about groups using food to 'sell' their histories and to construct marketable and publicly attractive identities" (2004, 20). Since foods are not "inherently strange or exotic" but are about the "experience of the individual" (i.e., consumer), "tourism depends on a perception of otherness rather than an objective reality of an item's relationship to that individual" (24). That perception of otherness is most often achieved through the framing of the food (advertising, menus, restaurant names, etc.), in which ethnic restaurants play up their perceived otherness in order to successfully sell food to the general US public. It is within this context that culinary tourism offers power to ethnic groups, as it "[allows] producers and consumers to elevate

8. For my work, cultural identity is not a watered-down version of race but a viable framework for analyzing articulations of racialized groups.

9. Paul Eid, in his study of second-generation Arabs in Canada, found that the "most common ethnic-related cultural practice . . . is eating ethnic food" (2007, 84). Eid says that this correlates with other researchers, mainly Wsevolod Isajiw, who says that eating ethnic food is maintained from generation to generation more than anything else.

food from being a mere sustenance to the realms of art and recreation, and therefore tools for the expression and manipulation of social power" (24). In the case of Arab Christians, they can market their ethnicity and frame their presentation of food against the majority group's frame of reference for Arabs and the Middle East. Although the whole of these images and rhetoric may look like an uncritical self-Orientalism, they may actually become a strategic representational practice.

As early as the 1890s, writers in New York City and other places in the United States were venturing to the Arabic-speaking areas of their cities and reporting on the "wondrous" and "exotic" foods they encountered as well as the people who made and served those foods. They often wrote about these encounters by comparing the ethnic enclaves to the times of "ancient Araby." Numerous feature articles in the first decade of the 1900s in the *New York Times*, the *Sun*, and the *New York Daily Tribune* tell all about the strange and exotic delicacies of the Syrian quarter. New York newspapers as well as those from as far away as Atlanta and Fort Wayne, Indiana, described the "mysterious" and "Oriental" nature of the Syrians and their food. Using Orientalist language that reflected European imperialism's exploration and ultimate colonization of Arab lands, the *New York Times*' 1902 feature on the Syrian community begins: "That explorer who penetrates to the interior of one of the Syrian restaurants . . ." ("Syrian Colony of New York and Its Characteristics," May 25). At the same time that the Syrians were being "discovered" by bohemians, writers, and other intrepid "explorers," Syrians were discovering their ability to play into the Orientalist rhetoric used to describe their restaurants and also entice people to their church-based festivals.

5. Flyer for a *ḥafli* in Altoona, Pennsylvania, in 1972. Author's collection.

Middle Eastern–themed food festivals are often the centerpiece of the year at most parishes, excluding the celebration of religious holidays of course. These well-planned, multiday community celebrations create a space of fellowship and fund-raising for the Arab Christian community.[10] In areas with historically sizeable Arab and Arab American populations, such as Pittsburgh, Pennsylvania; Worcester, Massachusetts; Toledo, Ohio; Houston, Texas; and the Detroit area, Antiochian Orthodox churches have been holding these annual events since ethnic festivals became popular in America in the 1970s and often way before. But what may be surprising is that in areas and cities not known for having an ethnic Arab population, Antiochian parishes have routinely held large festivals that successfully draw in large numbers from the surrounding non-Arab communities, such as in Lexington, Kentucky; Indianapolis, Indiana; Charleston, West Virginia; and Portland, Oregon. Liberal multiculturalism's focus on ethnic festivals, combined with the long history of fund-raising in US churches, helped to make the food festival a

10. For example, the 1979 food fair at St. George in Pittsburgh, Pennsylvania, netted the church more than $7,000, which was more than 50 percent of their net proceeds for the entire year. The 2009 Sahara Fest in Livonia, Michigan, despite the bad weather and poor economy, grossed $50,000 for the four-day festival.

viable fund-raising option for Antiochian Orthodox churches.[11]

The food festivals and their preparation have always attracted local media, who have often published or broadcasted lengthy cultural features on the churches, their histories and their unique or "exotic" cultural traditions, echoing the first written features on the Arab American community in New York City. For example, each year that the small but noticeable Syrian and Lebanese Christian community of Altoona, Pennsylvania, planned their annual food fair, the local newspaper, *Blair Press*, ran features with lead lines such as "Something of the unusual this month will be offered to the community in the form of an Arabic Hafli" ("Orthodox Church Plans 'Arabic Hafli' Night," May 3, 1972).

Another article in the August 19, 1963, issue of the *Altoona Mirror* entices the reader further: "Many Americans, in spite of the space age and jet flight, have never had an opportunity to visit an Oriental country, but on Saturday, Sept. 7 . . . a little of the Orient will come to Altoona [Pennsylvania]" ("Hafla to Include Arabic Music, Dancing, Food").

The articles typically had pictures of the food being served, recipes, or a group photo of the ladies society in charge of staging the *ḥafli*. The articles used "exotic" and "delights" and "different" to describe Arab communities and their festival. Outside of coverage about wars in the Middle East and their impact on the Arab communities here, the food festivals were one of the only ways these Arab Christian communities could draw attention. And they knew this.[12] They learned how to advertise their festivals effectively, often sensationalizing their Arab heritage in ways that can only be described as self-Orientalizing. For example, numerous parishes in Pennsylvania and Texas have called their festivals "Feast from the East," and in the case of St. George Church in El Paso, Texas, the name was used since at least 1966. The church in Little Falls, New Jersey, has used various incarnations of "Arabian Nights Festival" since 1978, and St. Mary's in Livonia, Michigan, called their festival "Sahara Fest" from about 2006 to 2010.

Arabian Nights and the Politics of Orientalism

Edward Said's *Orientalism* (1978), along with myriad scholarly works that have sprouted from it or in response to it, is crucial to my project. *Orientalism* establishes the long history of Western knowledge production about a Middle Eastern "other" within a binary framework that continues to operate in US popular and political discourses about Arabs and the Middle East.[13] Following the long line of scholars who have mobilized and modified Said's framework, my use of self-Orientalism aims to investigate the ways that Arab Americans retooled Orientalist imagery and rhetoric as a representational practice and a strategy for constructing an authentic cultural identity.

As a representational practice, self-Orientalism at times speaks back to popular US representations of Arabs and the Middle East in an attempt to privilege one over others (Hall 1997). As the popular representations of

11. A number of long-running ethnic food festivals at Antiochian parishes were begun or intensified in the American Bicentennial era. Festivals that have been around longer typically grew from the dinners that ladies societies started hosting as early as the 1920s and 1930s. A search of parish-sponsored websites, church publications, and newspapers in locales with active Antiochian Orthodox parishes found that at least ten parishes began hosting yearly festivals during the 1970s or intensified existing ones (such as expanding to a second or third day). Considering that in 1977 there were only 106 parishes in the archdiocese, that number is significant.

12. Many festival organizers tout the opportunity for the surrounding communities to have a positive image of Arabs and the Middle East by coming to the festival. Especially during times of heightened tension in the Middle East, when news coverage is saturated with unflattering portrayals of Arabs, the festivals are seen by Antiochians as an important intervention. At the twenty-second annual "Mideastern Festival" in Atlanta, hosted by St. Elias Antiochian parish, which coincided with the end of the intense fighting of the Lebanese Civil War in 1990, one of the food booth operators was quoted as saying, "We are trying to make the other face of Lebanon visible—the real one. A country that is a mixture of various peoples and nations, a country that is a major contributor to civilization" (quoted in "City's Arabs Celebrate Peace," *Atlanta Journal* and *Atlanta Constitution*, November 15, 1990).

13. Jarmakani uses "cultural mythologies" and focuses on the "civilizing mission" of the deployment of troops to Afghanistan under the pretense of "saving" the women (2008, 11–12).

Arabs in the United States shifted throughout the twentieth century, Arab American Christians, through their public deployment of self-Orientalist imagery, attempted to consistently reaffirm the more positive aspects of the representations of Arabs, mainly the legacy of *The Arabian Nights* as the representation of an exotically authentic other and the biblical positioning of the Middle East as the Holy Land. Self-Orientalism, at times, also reinforces the more undesirable dominant discourses of Arabs and the Middle East as premodern or backward in the attempt to assert an authentic Arabness.[14]

Especially in the second half of the twentieth century, Antiochian self-Orientalism hoped to claim the authentic cultural Arabness of "ancient Araby," removing the experiences of contemporary Arabs from the context of US imperial projects in the Middle East.[15] Beginning in the late 1960s, images of rich oil sheiks and kaffiyeh-wearing Palestinian "terrorists" were rampant in Hollywood movies, the evening news, and political cartoons, but Arab Americans attempted to privilege a more positive set of representations of Arabs. Though the use of *Arabian Nights*–style imagery was anachronistic and did not represent any "reality" of Arab American life, by self-Orientalizing through "exotic" and ahistorical imagery, Arab Americans could market their food and religion in the depoliticized space of multiculturalism. But at its most critical, self-Orientalism offers the power of selective participation within multiculturalism.

Arab American self-Orientalism is akin to Gayatri Chakravorty Spivak's (1988) concept of "strategic essentialism," especially in the given context of foodways within liberal multiculturalism. Spivak understood that within hegemonic discourses of race, citizenship, and belonging, minoritized groups have few avenues for exerting an identity that would circulate effectively within dominant discourses. As a representational strategy, self-Orientalism did allow Arab Americans a chance to speak back to dominant representations of their community by emphasizing the exotic elements instead of the ones associated with potential danger/terrorism. However, as other scholars, including Spivak, have argued about strategic essentialism, it ceases to be effective if the self-essentialized identity becomes fixed in the minds of the dominant group (Morton 2003, 75). In the case of Arab American self-Orientalism, particularly in a culinary/foodways context, the essentialized identity of Arabs as exotic others is often solidified in dominant narratives and reflected in the ways that non–Arab Americans write about Arab American ethnic foodways, with words such as *exotic*, *delicacy*, *ancient*, *desert*, *fantasy*, etc. being used often in restaurant reviews and write-ups about festivals.

Arab American Christian Self-Orientalism

A striking example of strategic self-orientalizing is a flyer for a public *ḥafli* at an Arab American church (specifically Antiochian Orthodox) in New Jersey in 2008. The flyer features an *Arabian Nights*–style palace in the background and the text "Arabian Night Hafli" overtop, with a tagline that reads "Join us for some fun at Palace St. George."[16] There is also an image of a Lebanese dancer in traditional dress and a photograph of Middle Eastern pastries, which highlight that the event will involve music, dancing, and food. The entire advertisement, one that this church used for consecutive years, is typical of flyers from other Arab American parishes. One reason this one stands out is that the main image of the palace is taken directly from Disney's *Aladdin*.

The second reason why the parish of St. George's use of *Aladdin* is so intriguing is that Arab American

14. My work is similar to Christina Civantos's (2006) study of Arab Argentines, as she argues that Argentinians of Arab descent have strategically engaged with discourses of Orientalism in their literary work, a process she refers to as "auto-Orientalism," in order to insert themselves into or to combat nationalist logics.

15. For this analysis, I draw from Phil Deloria (1998), who writes that "Indianness," as something culturally authentic, was constructed in relation to the perceived modernity of the American public, especially in relation to Indians and Indianness.

16. Holding ethnic food festivals was a structural component of the Little Falls, New Jersey, parish. A January 1976 article in *The Word* (the official publication of the Antiochian Orthodox Archdiocese) about the consecration of the parish's new church building mentioned that the new construction also included a separate banquet hall and kitchen, which was "custom designed" and "will serve the many activities sponsored by the parish, complete with sheesh-kabob charcoal stove."

6. Cover of program book for the St. George food fair in Pittsburgh in 1983. Author's collection.

advocacy groups took issue with Disney's adaptation of the story, and not for its unoriginality. Upon its theatrical release, Arab American advocacy groups were furious at the film's opening lines: "Oh I come from a land / From a faraway place/ Where the caravan camels roam / Where they cut off your ear / If they don't like your face / It's barbaric, but hey, it's home" (quoted in Shaheen 2001, 57). Eventually Disney's executives cut the "cut off your ear" line for the film's video release but left the "barbaric" reference. On their own, these references, particularly for such a popular film, are jarring enough. But as Michael Cooperson (2006) argues, the film is part of the context of the first Gulf War, a time, according to Nabeel Abraham, that anti-Arab racism and violence "reached an all time high" (1994, 204). The movie also features negative stereotypes of Arabs, such as the Americanizing of the protagonists of the movie versus the dark-skinned, hook-nosed, thick-accented villains (Cooperson 2006, 276; Shaheen 2001, 52).

Given the anti-Arab stereotyping in Disney's *Aladdin*, why would an Antiochian Orthodox Church of mostly Palestinian and Lebanese adherents use an image from the animated feature as their logo promoting their ethnic food festival? The use of the image by the parish of St. George was part of the larger history of the circulation of *The Arabian Nights* within Arab Christian circles and particularly the Antiochian Archdiocese. The self-Orientalizing, even through images that were once used to marginalize Arabs and the Middle East as violent and decidedly un-American, was now being used in a playful way to claim a cultural authenticity.[17] The festival organizers' strategic use of self-Orientalism is relatively straight forward: utilize familiar reference points to draw outsiders to their event. As the Arab Christians adopted these sometimes centuries-old depictions of their homelands, they were in a sense selling the American public the "Orient" that was created by and through the multiple, contextual, and Western-mediated incarnations of *The Arabian Nights*.

As part of their annual Middle Eastern food fair festivities in 1983, members of St. George Antiochian Orthodox Church (Pittsburgh, Pennsylvania) created and distributed a "souvenir book" of recipes, folklore, and selections and illustrations from well-known Arabic stories and folktales (Johnson, Khalil, and Nemy 1983).[18] As with most publications by Arab Christian parishes, the booklet also included the requisite advertisements and sponsorships from parishioners and local businesses, the majority of which were Middle Eastern themed. The cover image on the booklet, titled *A Thousand and One Delights: Arabian Nights Entertainments*, was taken from the cover of Andrew Lang's 1908 edition of the *Nights* and depicts the iconic frame story of the heroine Scheherazade occupying the king with magical tales. The booklet features a letter on the inside cover addressed to visitors, offering to "instill a little magic in [their] evening, for the flavor of Arabic foods is as vivid, as exotic and enchanting as Arabic dancing; as Arabic folklore in the tales told by Scheherazade to the King for a thousand and [one] nights." The letter further depicts the Arab American Christians as carriers of ancient Arab traditions of food and folklore: "While we live in the now, in today, our roots stretch back and we constantly draw strength and wisdom from what has gone before, be it a few years, centuries, or eons."[19] Here, the parishioners construct an authentic Arab Christian cultural identity as a legacy of *The Arabian Nights*.

The booklet for the 1983 food fair connects the food prepared and eaten by church members with the "Tales of Ancient Araby" by juxtaposing stories and illustrations with recipes that "have been handed down from generation to generation from times more ancient than history." Making a claim to Arab cultural authenticity from the space of the church is a double-edged sword. Antiochians, as Christians, are given more flexibility with which to shape their self-representation than Muslim Arabs, as Arab Christians have a solid claim to cultural citizenship and can be seen as white ethnics, totally meltable into an American multicultural society (Ong 1996, 758).

But their self-Orientalization is made more complex in light of their position as potentially more American than Arab Muslims but less authentically Arab, especially since, as Paul Eid argues, "Christian Arabs find that their relation to 'Arabness' is mediated by an Islam-laden categorizing frame of reference made up by the majority group" (2007, 25). Their self-Orientalizing, in order to be authentically Arab, has to speak to and through the proliferation of Muslim-themed imagery about the Arab

17. My understanding of "play" follows Roger Abrahams's (1980) folkloric use of the term as "stylized behavior" in a festive context.

18. I am indebted to the Very Rev. Fr. John Abdullah for mailing a copy of this booklet to me.

19. The earliest known Arabic manuscript of the collection of tales known as *The Arabian Nights* or *Alf laīla wa laīla* is of Syrian origin, as were many of the parishioners at St. George.

region. This is reflected in the numerous restaurants nationwide with names like "The Mecca" (New York, Pittsburgh, and Chicago all had restaurants owned by Arab Christians with this name by the 1950s), which conjure images of Muslims for an American public.

Self-Orientalism functions to market an Arab cultural identity within culturally essentialist historical processes that are inherently tied to consumerism as a means of experiencing the other, mainly "commodity Orientalism" and liberal multiculturalism. By recycling popular-culture representations of the Arab world, the Antiochians were presenting themselves within a familiar frame of reference. In order to draw in as many people as possible to their food festivals, Antiochian parishes had to market in stereotypes. Or in the words of Susan Nance, the Antiochians had to present a "comprehensible novelty" to an American audience, one that offered "new content," as in a Christian Arabness built on unique foods and exotic music, but "that still flattered preexisting attitudes" about Arabs and the Middle East (2009, 9–10), namely the referential imagery of *The Arabian Nights*.[20] Finally, a less critical but still important function of self-Orientalism serves to capture and construct a nostalgic Arabness using Western-mediated imagery of an Oriental precolonial past. Typically these Arab American Christians, many of whom by the 1970s did not speak Arabic or had never been to the Middle East, painted themselves into the Orientalist fantasy of *The Arabian Nights* as an opportunity to capture a cultural heritage. Their cultural Arabness was created in part by grafting their own understanding of their cultural heritage (mostly through food and music) onto representations of Arabs and the Middle East from US popular culture.[21] In the words of Nance (2009), who is drawing from Phil Deloria (1998), they were "playing Eastern"—constructing an authenticated Arabness, which was authentic only in that it reflected what popular culture constructed as an authentic other.[22]

But how did this work? How can predominantly Arab American parishes, especially in a postindustrial city like Pittsburgh, where the economic ills of the late 1970s and early 1980s could easily be blamed on the media's "greedy Arabs," celebrate their Arab culture and heritage and expect the community around the church to willingly support them? The parishioners constructed their Arabness based on earlier, less politicized representations of Arabs and the Middle East. As Ronald Stockton argues about the "essential quality of stereotypes," "They take people 'out of history'" (1994, 120). The Antiochians were not creating a "real" Arab with this self-Orientalizing because they knew who the real Arabs were: the priests and the parishioners of their faith as well as the other Arab activists, both Muslim and Christian, with whom they worked to obtain social justice for their people in the homeland and the hostland.

For example, at the same time that parishes were celebrating ethnic food festivals using self-Orientalizing imagery and rhetoric, there were significant and sustained politicized action and humanitarian efforts on behalf of the homeland. It was not unusual for weekly church bulletins as well as the archdiocese's official monthly magazine, *The Word*, to report on parish food festivals as well as on ongoing political and humanitarian support for Palestine and Lebanon in the same pages as religious news and debates on theological and doctrinal matters. All were treated as pertinent church issues.

Further, parishes across the country were consistently collecting donations for refugee children from Lebanon and Palestine via the church-sponsored and heavily promoted Arab Children's Relief Fund. Even if raising money to send to Palestinian refugee children was purely a humanitarian effort, in light of US discourses that figure Palestinians as enemies and Israelis as victims, the humanitarian effort becomes politicized. Though this

20. Although I draw on Susan Nance's (2009) important intervention and investigation of the practice of "playing Eastern," her approach is more capitalist deterministic.

21. The Antiochians' use of self-Orientalism as a representational practice is part of a larger tradition of the reclamation of Orientalist art by non-Westerners. Roger Benjamin, writing about the collecting of Orientalist paintings by privileged Arab collectors, says that these individuals "exerted control over the image of their past and of their heritage—an act of repossession" (1997, 33).

22. Deloria (1998) argues that to claim authenticity is to claim the position of other.

politicized humanitarian action on behalf of the collective homeland was occurring simultaneously as the production and celebration of the food festival, the food festivals remained depoliticized. The space of the ethnic food festival, even in this larger context of anti-Arab racism and violence of the 1970s and the post-9/11 period, was not the space where the Antiochians advanced their transnational commitments to their homelands. They had other outlets.

Conclusion

At the same time that the Kirdahy brothers were repackaging their restaurant to New Yorkers hungry for a taste of the exotic, Arab American restaurant owners nationwide were also packaging foods from their homeland in ways more palatable to the US public. For example, since as early as the 1920s and 1930s there have been restaurants across the United States named either "Aladdin" or "Ali Baba."

The self-Orientalist imagery of church-sponsored food festivals and Arab American Christian–owned restaurants attempted to market a safe and friendly ethnicity to an American public hungry for (depoliticized) diversity. Arab Americans have been successful at marketing their authenticity within the confines of liberal multiculturalism, as they have attempted to solidify a romantic image of Arabs in the minds of Americans (to paraphrase the title of Michael Suleiman's book from 1988), as opposed to the more negative discourses on Arabs, while taking the opportunity to teach the general public about their heritage through cultural symbols such as food and music, albeit sometimes in uncritical ways that simply reinforced popular-culture discourses.

To be Arab American is to construct an identity that is simultaneously part of but different from the nation. In other words, constructing a cultural identity is not only about holding onto a homeland identity but also about performing American-ness. Arab American Christians continue to utilize the space given to them by multiculturalism, based on their constructed authenticated difference, to construct an Arabness that is culturally engaging and profitable and one that speaks back to the proliferation of negative images of Arabs in popular culture.

Works Cited

Abdou, Nagib T. 1922. *Medicine and Commerce.* New York: Nagib T. Abdou.

Abraham, Nabeel. 1994. "Anti-Arab Racism and Violence in the United States." In *The Development of Arab American Identity*, edited by Ernest McCarus, 155–214. Ann Arbor: Univ. of Michigan Press.

Abrahams, Roger. 1980. "Play." In *Folklore Studies in the Twentieth Century: Proceedings of the Centenary Conference of the Folklore Society*, edited by Venetia J. Newall, 119–22. Totowa, NJ: Rowan and Littlefield.

Benjamin, Roger. 1997. "Post-colonial Taste? Non-Western Markets for Orientalist Art." In *Orientalism: Delacroix to Klee*, edited by Roger Benjamin, 32–40. Sydney: Art Gallery of New South Wales.

Camp, Charles. 1989. *American Foodways: What, When, Why, and How We Eat in America.* American Folklore series. Little Rock, AR: August House.

Civantos, Christina. 2006. *Between Argentines and Arabs: Argentine Orientalism, Arab Immigrants, and the Writing of Identity.* Albany: State Univ. of New York Press.

Cooperson, Michael. 2006. "The Monstrous Births of 'Aladdin.'" In *The* Arabian Nights *Reader*, edited by Ulrich Marzolph, 265–82. Detroit: Wayne State Univ. Press.

Deloria, Phil. 1998. *Playing Indian.* New Haven, CT: Yale Univ. Press.

Eid, Paul. 2007. *Being Arab: Ethnic and Religious Identity Building among Second Generation Youth in Montreal.* Studies in Ethnic History. Montreal: McGill-Queen's Univ. Press.

Feldman, Joan M. 1962. *New York on 5 Dollars a Day.* New York: Crown.

Hall, Stuart. 1997. "The Spectacle of the 'Other.'" In *Representation: Cultural Representations and Signifying Practices*, edited by Stuart Hall, 223–79. Thousand Oaks, CA: Sage.

Hanania, Ray. 2005. *Arabs of Chicagoland, Images of America.* Charleston, SC: Arcadia.

Hanoosh, Yasmeen. 2011. "Fighting Our Own Battles: Iraqi Chaldeans and the War on Terror." In *Arab Detroit 9/11: Life in the Terror Decade*, edited by Nabeel Abraham, Sally Howell, and Andrew Shryock, 126–50. Detroit: Wayne State Univ. Press.

Jarmakani, Amira. 2008. *Imagining Arab Womanhood: The Cultural Mythology of Veils, Harems, and Belly Dancers in the U.S.* New York: Palgrave.

Johnson, Theresa, John E. Khalil, and Philip Nemy. 1983. *A Thousand and One Delights: Arabian Nights Entertainments*. Souvenir book. Pittsburgh: St. George Antiochian Orthodox Church.

Kadi, Joe. 1994. Introduction to *Food for Our Grandmothers: Writings by Arab-American & Arab-Canadian Feminists*, edited by Joe Kadi, xiii–xx. Boston: South End Press.

Kayyali, Randa. 2006. *The Arab Americans*. New Americans series, edited by Ronald H. Bayor. Westport, CT: Greenwood Press.

Lang, Andrew, ed. 1908. *The* Arabian Nights *Entertainments*. London: Longmans, Green.

Lockwood, William, and Yvonne Lockwood. 2000. "Continuity and Adaptation in Arab American Foodways." In *Arab Detroit: From Margin to Mainstream*, edited by Nabeel Abraham and Andrew Shryock, 515–49. Detroit: Wayne State Univ. Press.

Long, Lucy. 2004. "Culinary Tourism: A Folkloristic Perspective on Eating and Otherness." In *Culinary Tourism*, edited by Lucy Long, 20–50. Lexington: Univ. Press of Kentucky.

Lowe, Lisa. 1996. *Immigrant Acts: On Asian American Cultural Politics*. Durham, NC: Duke Univ. Press.

Lupton, Deborah. 1994. "Food, Memory, and Meaning: The Symbolic and Social Nature of Food Events." *Sociological Review* 44, no. 4: 664–85.

McAlister, Melani. [2001] 2005. *Epic Encounters: Culture, Media, and U.S. Interests in the Middle East since 1945*. Updated ed. Berkeley: Univ. of California Press.

Morton, Stephen. 2003. *Gayatri Chakravorty Spivak*. Routledge Critical Thinkers. New York: Routledge.

Naber, Nadine. 2012. *Arab American: Gender, Cultural Politics, and Activism*. New York: New York Univ. Press.

Naber, Nadine, and Matthew Stiffler. 2013. "Maronite Catholics, Orthodox Christians, and Sunni Muslims from the Arab Region: Between Empire, Racialization, and Assimilation." In *Mis-reading America: Mimicry, Interruptions, Reorientation, and U.S. Communities of Color*, edited by Vincent Wimbush, 208–72. New York: Oxford Univ. Press.

Nance, Susan. 2009. *How the* Arabian Nights *Inspired the American Dream, 1790–1935*. Chapel Hill: Univ. of North Carolina Press.

Nasib Arida's and Sabri Andria's Syrian American Directory Almanac. 1930. New York: Aseeb and Arida.

Ong, Aihwa. 1996. "Cultural Citizenship as Subject Making: Immigrants Negotiate Racial and Cultural Boundaries in the U.S." *Current Anthropology* 37, no. 5: 737–62.

Said, Edward. 1978. *Orientalism*. New York: Vintage Books.

Shaheen, Jack. 2001. *Reel Bad Arabs: How Hollywood Vilifies a People*. New York: Olive Branch Press.

Shryock, Andrew, and Ann Chih Lin. 2009. "Arab American Identities in Question." In *Citizenship and Crisis: Arab Detroit after 9/11*, edited by the Detroit Arab American Study Team, 35–68. New York: Russell Sage Foundation.

Simon, Kate. 1959. *New York Places and Pleasures: An Uncommon Guidebook*. New York: Meridian Books.

Spivak, Gayatri Chakravorty. 1988. "Subaltern Studies: Deconstructing Historiography." In *Selected Subaltern Studies*, edited by Ranajit Guha and Gayatri Chakravorty Spivak, 3–32. New York: Oxford Univ. Press.

Stockton, Ronald. 1994. "Ethnic Archetypes and the Arab Image." In *The Development of Arab American Identity*, edited by Ernest McCarus, 119–53. Ann Arbor: Univ. of Michigan Press.

Suleiman, Michael W. 1988. *The Arabs in the Mind of America*. Brattleboro, VT: Amana Books.

Van Esterik, Penny. 1982. "Celebrating Ethnicity: Ethnic Flavor in an Urban Festival." *Ethnic Groups* 4 (Oct.): 207–28.

27

Arab American Literature, Storytelling, and the Paradox of Shahrazad

PAULINE HOMSI VINSON

A look at Arab American literature published in the late 1990s and early 2000s reveals a preoccupation with nostalgic remembrances, the life-sustaining potential of storytelling, and *The Thousand and One Nights*. This essay traces some of the ways in which contemporary Arab American writers evoke the lifesaving potential of storytelling enacted in *The Thousand and One Nights*, and it argues that such evocations present critical interventions in how we understand Arab American history and Arab American literary aesthetics.[1]

Whereas some works, such as Mohja Kahf's poetry collection *E-mails from Scheherazad* (2003), Susan Muaddi Darraj's collected volume *Scheherazade's Legacy: Arab and Arab American Women on Writing* (2004), and Alia Yunis's novel *The Night Counter* (2009) directly invoke and reinvent the figure of Shahrazad, others, such as Diana Abu-Jaber's novel *Crescent* (2003b), Rabih Alameddine's novel *The Hakawati* (2008), and Zeyn Joukhadar's novel *The Map of Salt and Stars* (2018) borrow narrative elements from the tales such as the frame narrative and the intertwining of the fantastical with the real. Still others, such as Jack Marshall's poetry collection *Arabian Nights* (1986), Hedy Habra's short-story collection *Flying Carpets* (2012), and Dunya Mikhail's poetry collection *The Iraqi Nights* (2014), evoke the *Nights* directly in their titles, while a subset highlights the problematic legacy of the *Nights* for Arab American writers. Among the latter are *Dinarzad's Children: An Anthology of Arab American Fiction* ([2004] 2009), edited by Pauline Kaldas and Khaled Mattawa, which highlights Arab American connections to Dinarzad, Shahrazad's occluded sister, and Laila Halaby's novel *Once in a Promised Land* (2007), which draws on Arab folk storytelling traditions and the figure of Shahrazad to present a cautionary tale on the seductions and limits of possibilities for Arabs in the United States. Yet another approach to the *Nights* is taken by Laila Lalami, who draws on the life-giving potential of Arab oral folk storytelling traditions but pointedly refrains from any

This essay extends ideas first presented in Pauline Homsi Vinson, "Representations of Sexualities: United States," in *Encyclopedia of Women and Islamic Cultures*, edited by Suad Joseph, guest edited by Sarah Gualtieri (Leiden: Brill Online, Feb. 2015), at http://dx.doi.org/10.1163/1872-5309_ewic_COM_002015. The revision is published here with the permission of Brill Online. The author also thanks Amira Jarmakani and Louise Cainkar for reading and commenting on early drafts of this expanded version.

1. This study joins a growing number of works that take note of the repeated references to storytelling and *The Thousand and One Nights* in Arab American literature. These works include my own prior publications (Homsi Vinson 2014, 2015) as well as contributions by Mejdulene Shomali (2018), who queers Arab American women writers' uses of Shahrazad; Atef Laouyene (2015), who discusses the uses of strategic orientalism in Abu-Jaber's work; Waïl Hassan (2011), who addresses the relationship between orientalism and translational poetics in Anglophone Arab writing; Mazen Naous (2020), who considers the link between storytelling and Arab American poetics; Somaya Sami Sabry (2011), who focuses on gender and storytelling in Arab American responses to the *Nights*; and Marie-Christin Sawires-Masseli (2018), who focuses on Arab American fiction and its relation to the *Nights*. Though not directly engaged with the *Nights*, Therí Pickens's edited collection *Arab American Aesthetics* (2018) also bears mention as it draws our attention to artistic choices in Arab American writing and its relationship to politics, history, and culture.

direct allusions either to Shahrazad or her famous tales in *Hope and Other Dangerous Pursuits* (2005) and *The Moor's Account* (2014).

Whether through direct allusion or pointed refusal to name *The Thousand and One Nights*, contemporary Arab American literary uses of oral storytelling motifs, as this essay demonstrates, present what amounts to a collective critical engagement with the orientalist legacy of the tales, the context of literary reception in the United States, and the enduring appeal of the power of oral storytelling to extend the life of the teller and transform the listener. Reconfigurations of the *Nights* in Arab American literature, this essay argues, reestablish connections between different generations and across different continents, redress elisions in accounts of Arab and Arab American history, and confront both the legacy of orientalist reception of the tales and the paradox of Shahrazad as a figure who presents a creative model of narrative agency but who also "bargains with patriarchy"—to borrow Deniz Kandiyoti's (1988) phrase—and gets co-opted by orientalist fantasy.[2]

Storytelling as Survival

In *The Thousand and One Nights*, storytelling saves lives. This idea is foregrounded in the frame tale, where Shahrazad uses her skillful storytelling to ensure her survival and rescue other women from the murderous misogyny of King Shahrayar, who, having witnessed his wife's infidelity, orders her death and demands to marry a new bride each day, only to have her executed the morning after.[3] Shahrazad insists on marrying Shahrayar, confident that she can put an end to his killing spree. Night after night, she spins tales within fantastical tales that remain unfinished at dawn, thereby prompting Shahrayar to postpone her death in order to hear the remainder of her stories. After 1,001 nights, Shahrayar regains his trust in women and recognizes Shahrazad as his wife and mother of his sons. Through the power of her storytelling, Shahrazad saves women's lives, reforms a tyrant king, and restores order to the kingdom, albeit all within the confines of authoritarianism and patriarchy, now reconfigured as responsible and benign.

Not only does Shahrazad fall in line with a process of empowerment through accommodation that Deniz Kandiyoti (1988) has described as "bargaining with patriarchy"—that is, she saves lives through "an uneasy compromise" that reforms without overturning the king's absolute authority—but she also recognizes that the power of her storytelling is conditional upon Shahrayar's willingness to hear more of her tales. Each night Shahrazad begins a story at the prompting of her sister Dinarzad, and each dawn she ceases her narration, causing her sister to ask for more, to which Shahrazad replies with a variation on the following: "Tomorrow night I shall tell you the rest [of the story], which is stranger and more wonderful [than what came before], if the king spares me and lets me live" (Haddawy 2010, 31).[4] As Roy Mottahedeh observes, "It is the promise that things more astonishing and strange, *aja'b and aghrab*, that lie ahead that sustains suspense" and propels the action in the tales of *The Thousand and One Nights* (1997, 35). Such a promise compels Shahrayar to delay Shahrazad's execution and exclaim: "I will not have her put to death until I hear what happened" (Haddawy 2010, 30). The power of storytelling is conditional on the listener's willingness to grant permission for the teller to speak, but in controlling the narrative, the teller also gains power over the listener. In *The Thousand and One Nights*, Ferial Ghazoul observes, Shahrazad "gains the upper hand" (1996, 24) through her storytelling. She manages this, moreover, by transforming Shahrayar from her would-be killer into a willing listener of her tales.

2. I thank Amira Jarmakani for reminding me of the aptness of Kandiyoti's term to my discussion of Shahrazad.

3. Shahrayar catches his wife "in the act" with a head Black slave named Mas'ud and watches as she leads a highly theatrical and scopic scene of infidelity with ten white female servants and ten Black male slaves. The perceived sexual transgression is thus tied to notions of gender, race, and class in the frame tale. I address this topic at greater length in my forthcoming book, *Transporting Tales: Echoes of* The Thousand and One Nights *in Contemporary Arab American Literature*. For discussions of race and racism in *The Thousand and One Nights*, see Beaumont 2002; Irwin n.d.; and Shamaa 2017. For the emphasis on seeing in the frame tale, see Malti-Douglas 1991.

4. For quotations from *The Thousand One Nights*, I use the translation by Husain Haddawy, *The Arabian Nights* (2010).

Shahrazad's storytelling thus does more than serve as a narrative device that launches a series of entertaining tales; it invests storytelling with power—the power to save lives, the power to captivate and rehabilitate the listener, and the power to enact domestic and political reform. As Somaya Sami Sabry remarks, "Transformation and change are central to Scheherazade's narrative" (2011, 50). In transforming Shahrayar into a listener, Shahrazad also transforms him from a murderous misogynist into an amenable husband and responsible ruler. In the words of Nawar al-Hassan Golley, Shahrazad "transforms narrative into life" (2003, 81). It is this lifesaving and transformative potential of storytelling that gets repeatedly evoked in contemporary Arab American writing. However, while Shahrazad rescues women from the king's misogyny and the kingdom from his tyranny, contemporary Arab American writers revive the subversive power of Arab oral storytelling traditions associated with Shahrazad in order to envision new ways for narrating Arab lives in the United States. For them, as for Shahrazad, the extent to which they succeed depends on their abilities to hold the reader's attention and subvert the very forces that would co-opt them: an orientalist reception environment and the patriarchal framework of the tales.

Storytelling and Reception Environments

Arab American literary reinventions of *The Thousand and One Nights* have proliferated in the two decades since the attacks of September 11, 2001 (9/11). This period not only witnessed a rise in anti-Arab and anti-Muslim sentiment and hate crimes (Alsultany 2012; Cainkar 2018; Naber 2008) but also presented opportunities for Arab, Muslim, and Southwest Asian and North African (SWANA) Americans—groups whose configurations overlap and are often conflated—to speak in venues that previously had shunned them (Jamal 2008).[5] This paradoxical positioning of Arab, Muslim, and SWANA Americans as simultaneously objects of curiosity and possible security threats coincides with persistent orientalist responses to *The Thousand and One Nights* both as an expression of Arabo-Muslim exoticism, luxurious excess, and seduction and as evidence of excessive violence, irrationality, and oppression in an ahistorical and geographically malleable construction of an Arab/Muslim East (Kabbani 1994; Makdisi and Nussbaum 2008; Ouyang 2003; Sallis 1999; Yamanaka and Nishio 2006).

In evoking *The Thousand and One Nights*, as this essay demonstrates, contemporary Arab American writers simultaneously reclaim and draw sustenance from Arab oral storytelling traditions. However, as is the case for Shahrazad, so too for contemporary Arab American writers: for storytelling to succeed, it requires reciprocity between teller and listener of the tales. For Arab American writers, to establish reciprocity they must overcome and reimagine both the patriarchal framework and the orientalist legacy of the tales, including a history of self-orientalism (see Shakir 1996; Stiffler 2018 and chapter 26 in this volume), and they must also navigate through a political climate that interprets Arabs and Muslims through the prism of racialized othering, terrorism, and religious fanaticism (see Cainkar 2018).

In *The Hakawati* (2008), Rabih Alameddine explicitly acknowledges the need for reciprocity between tellers and listeners of tales, highlighting the negotiated and ever-shifting power dynamic between the two. The novel opens and closes with the word *listen*, perhaps a secular literary echo of the imperative *iqra'*, or "read," in the Qur'an.[6] But as the opening line also reveals, the invitation to listen is also followed by a supplication for listeners to grant permission for the teller to become their guide: "Listen. Allow me to be your god. Let me take you on a journey beyond imagining. Let me tell you a story" (5). To gain the "upper hand" and become a god, the storyteller needs the listener's willingness to go along

5. For example, Diana Abu-Jaber discusses how she struggled to find a publisher for her book *Arabian Jazz* ([1993] 2003a), which was published in 1993, because, as one of the editors considering the work put it, "Arabs were inappropriate," but then when Abu-Jaber asked her own editor if they should pull the manuscript of *Crescent* from the publisher's, having submitted it right before 9/11, the editor told her, "No, you have to stick with it" because, her editor elaborated, "I think people are really going to be interested in this now. This is actually the time for this kind of story" (Abu-Jaber 2005).

6. I owe this observation to Amira Jarmakani.

for the journey of the tale. Diana Abu-Jaber emphasizes a similar point in *Crescent* (2003b) when the protagonist's uncle, an Iraqi immigrant to the United States, tells her, "You know, there's an art to listening to a story—it requires equal parts silence and receptivity" (274). The success of storytelling requires the listener's willingness to be receptive to the teller and the teller's tale, but as in *The Thousand and One Nights*, tellers of tales can shift this balance of power through the imaginative possibilities of fantasy, the allure of the marvelous and the strange, and the lifesaving potential of oral storytelling embodied in the figure of Shahrazad.

Storytelling, Survival, and Narrative Agency

The idea that storytelling is lifesaving is central to contemporary literary evocations of *The Thousand and One Nights*. In many of the stories, the motifs themselves become the very vehicles for survival, suggesting that it is not simply the content of the story but its Shahrazadian mode of narration that is life sustaining. In Diana Abu-Jaber's *Crescent* (2003b), for example, the character Han risks his life by returning to Iraq to reunite with his dying mother. He is captured and imprisoned in one of Saddam's notorious prisons but then manages his escape, crosses the desert on foot by following the path of migrating ibex, and emerges alive in the guise of the fantastical Abdelrahman Salahadin, a central character from the novel's fantastical secondary narrative as told to the protagonist by her uncle. This figure fakes his own drowning and is at one point abducted by a mermaid, but in each instance he manages to stay alive in ways as marvelous and strange as those in *The Thousand and One Nights*. His name, moreover, evokes Salah ad-Din al-Ayyubi (1138–93), better known in English as "Saladin," the legendary founder of the Ayyubid dynasty, suggesting both a continuity and a depth of history to Arab heroic figures as well as a recognition of the mythologizing and continued reinvention of such figures and how we understand them.

The power of narrative fantasy to intersect with historical legend and extend life to the present also occurs in Zeyn Joukhadar's novel *The Map of Salt and Stars* (2018). Like Abu-Jaber, Joukhadar uses a realistic frame narrative that is interwoven with a secondary fantastical one. In the frame storyline, a Syrian American girl named Nour survives her journey out of twenty-first-century war-torn Syria by retracing the path of the fictional character Rawiya, the storyteller adventurer, who is presented in a secondary narrative within the text as a travel companion to a historical figure, the twelfth-century mapmaker al-Idrissi. The intertwining of the historical and the fantastical in the embedded narrative of Joukhadar's novel, as in Abu-Jaber's, ensures the survival of the main character in the frame tale. Fantastical storytelling in these novels is not only capable of saving lives, as in the *Nights*, but also reimagines the past in ways that produce new possibilities for the present.

The power of storytelling to save lives is enacted at the narrative level in a number of contemporary Arab American literary echoes of *The Thousand and One Nights* and serves as a means of preserving connections historically, between generations, and spatially, across geographical expanses. In *Crescent*, for example, the protagonist Sirine learns about her Arab family and Arab heritage through the fantastical stories and family recollections that her paternal uncle relates to her. Similarly, in *The Map of Salt and Stars*, the young protagonist, Nour, maintains connections to her deceased father by remembering and retelling the stories he used to tell her. The life-sustaining potential of intergenerational storytelling is also emphasized in Alia Yunis's *The Night Counter* (2009), which presents an immortalized Scheherazade, who travels on a flying carpet from Baghdad to Los Angeles to coach a cantankerous octogenarian Lebanese immigrant named Fatima in how she can preserve her family by passing on to them her life stories. Emphasizing the life-sustaining power of storytelling, Scheherazade tells Fatima: "What is immortality if not the continuation of our stories?" (363). Similarly, in Rabih Alameddine's *The Hakawati* (2008), the young protagonist returns to Lebanon from Los Angeles to be by his father's side on his deathbed. There, he tells his father, "I know your stories. . . . And I can tell you my stories. If you want" (513). The stories he tells him, moreover, are variations on and extensions of tales his paternal grandfather and uncle, the "hakawatis" of the family, had told him. Storytelling in the novels by Yunis and Alameddine becomes life sustaining not so much because it literally saves the life of the storyteller, as in the *Nights*, but because it serves as a cross-cultural thread that maintains continuity across generational and geographical distance, thereby metaphorically sustaining lifelines between tellers and listeners of tales.

This is also the case in the work of Laila Lalami, who emphasizes the life-sustaining potential of oral storytelling traditions but pointedly mentions neither Shahrazad nor the tales of *The Thousand and One Nights*. In *Hope and Other Dangerous Pursuits* (2005), for example, the character Murad realizes at the end of the novella that "there was no use reading stories like this [a book in English full of inaccuracies about his hometown Tangiers] anymore; he needed to write his own. He thought about his father, who'd told stories to his children, and how they were almost forgotten today. . . . [H]e was already lost in the story he would start writing tonight" (186). Recognizing that his father's stories would be lost if not retold, Murad also recognizes that basing his own writing on his father's stories would sustain him and free him from the orientalist frames of books written by others about Tangiers. The recollection of times past rescues important family traditions from oblivion and empowers new storytellers to regain narrative agency and tell their own stories in their own voices.

Similarly, in the historical novel *The Moor's Account* (2014), Lalami retells the story of Estebanico, an enslaved Moroccan "black moor" who is taken to Florida and manages to survive by living among Native Americans. At the end of the novel, Estebanico relates:

> I remembered the stories my mother had told me so often when I was a young boy. I had taken them with me when I crossed the Ocean of Fog and Darkness. I had fed on them in the terrible years of deprivation and I have used them to find my way whenever I was lost. . . . I wanted to tell a story to my child, so that he might share the joy or the pain it contained, that he might learn something from it. . . . I wanted to tell him a story that he might remember me. . . . And in this relation I tried to tell the story of what really happened when I journeyed to the heart of the continent. (320)

In Lalami's work, storytelling, as in the *Nights*, ensures survival, giving sustenance to Mustafa/Estebanico as he "fed on them in the terrible years of deprivation," but stories in *The Moor's Account* also serve as a "guide," to help Mustafa/Estebanico "find [his] way whenever [he] was lost." The stories serve as a way to learn about the past and as a remembrance of earlier generations across geographies and gendered narrations; Mustafa/Estebanico remembers the stories his mother had told him and hopes to pass them on to his son so that his son may "learn something" and "remember" him. But the stories also have another function: "to tell the story of what really happened when" the Arab-Muslim-Moor "journeyed to the heart of the continent." That is, the story also operates as truth telling, writing Moorish/Arab/Muslim presence into existence and undoing orientalist and colonialist accounts of imperial conquest, as exemplified in Joseph Conrad's *Heart of Darkness* (1899). Storytelling in *The Moor's Account* saves lives, connects one generation with another across time and geographical distance, and helps us reenvision US history, reinscribing Arab-Muslim-SWANA presence within foundational narratives of the United States, which typically elide them.

Refusing to name Shahrazad, Lalami suggests that it is not necessary to engage with orientalism on its own terms, preferring instead to draw on the rich oral storytelling heritage to which *The Thousand and One Nights* belongs but does not delimit. In this, she can be understood to be using what Amira Jarmakani (2008 and chapter 6 in this volume) has called "the politics of invisibility," which "can mean using silence as a strategy" and "does not solely operate as a counterdiscourse since counternarratives run the risk of legitimating the problematic assumptions of the very discourses they resist" (p. 111). In this, Lalami deliberately sidesteps the paradox of Shahrazad, a point I develop more fully in the next section.

Storytelling and the Paradox of Shahrazad

In the frame tale of *The Thousand and One Nights*, Shahrazad is depicted as a self-possessed woman who "was intelligent, knowledgeable wise, and refined. She had read and learned" (Haddawy 2010, 13). Not only is Shahrazad learned, but she is also determined. When her father, the vizier, forbids her from marrying Shahrayar, she tells him, "If you don't take me to King Shahrayar, I shall go to him by myself behind your back" (17). And when her father tries to dissuade her from her plan by telling her stories of defiant women who are physically punished and subdued by men, she tells him: "Such tales don't deter me from my request. If you wish, I can tell you many such tales" (17). The opening frame tale thus presents Shahrazad as self-assured and intelligent, the teller of tales, not their object nor their impressionable audience; she is someone determined to take matters into her own hands, confident in her abilities to save the lives of women and reform a tyrannical king through the power of her own skillful storytelling.

In the epilogue to the tales, however, Shahrazad's image shifts. In one ending, she reveals three sons to Shahrayar, whom he acknowledges as his own while affirming Shahrazad's role as his wife and mother of his sons (Grotzfeld [1985] 2010, 473; Malti-Douglas 1991, 25). This ending, Fedwa Malti-Douglas remarks, reinscribes Shahrazad's feminist voice within patriarchy as she ceases her storytelling and Shahrayar orders that his scribes record the tales that she has relayed to him (1991, 27). Shahrazad, Malti-Douglas remarks, is "no longer a storyteller, since an anonymous narrator is talking about her. . . . [S]he has become the object, rather than the producer or even the controller, of literary discourse" (27). Shahrazad rescues women from murderous misogyny, but she herself becomes reinscribed within the confines of benign patriarchy.

If the ending of Arab renditions of *The Thousand and One Nights* reinscribes Shahrazad within patriarchy, orientalist translations and renditions of the tales deprive her of her agency, changing her from an erudite woman in command of her situation into a muted object of a desiring male gaze. In his nineteenth-century English translation of the *Nights*, for example, Edward Lane, according to Paulo Horta, "deprives the character [Shahrazad] of her agency" by "abandoning any reference to the frame tale after the introduction and arranging the stories into chapters that disrupt the nightly rhythms of Shahrazad's storytelling" (2017, 206). Similarly, Fatema Mernissi observes that the early twentieth-century production of *Schéhérazade* by the Ballets Russes erases the voice of its female heroine, Shahrazad.[7] As Mernissi exclaims, "To my surprise, the ballet's Scheherazade lacked the most powerful erotic weapon a woman has—her *nutq*, or capacity to think in words and penetrate a man's brain by using carefully selected terms" (2001, 38). In depriving Shahrazad of her speech, the orientalists reduce her, in the words of Susan Muaddi Darraj, to "nothing more than a harem sex kitten" (2004a, 2; see also Marzolph and van Leewuen 2004, 702; Ouyang 2003). Thus, whereas medieval Arab representations of Shahrazad endowed her with the power of storytelling only to recuperate it within the confines of patriarchal order, European orientalists celebrated her tales while subduing her speech. Hence, the paradox of Shahrazad and a central irony in Arab American reinventions of *The Thousand and One Nights*, which is that the site of agency is also the place of constraint. If the fictional Shahrazad must "bargain with patriarchy" and place herself at the mercy of Shahrayar in order to reform him, preserve her life, and save other women, in the lives of actual women, compromise, Kandiyoti explains, demonstrates how "contestation and resistance [are] possible but always circumscribed by the limits of the culturally conceivable" (1998, 147). What is conceivable for contemporary Arab American writers is circumscribed within a literary environment of reception that equates Arab writers with *The Thousand and One Nights* whether they choose such a connection or not (see Alameddine 2014; al-Shaykh 2013) and a political climate that regards Arabs and Muslims in relation to terrorism and women's oppression (see Abu-Lughod 2013; Alsultany 2012; Cainkar 2018; Fayad 1994; Hamilton 1994; Jarmakani, chapter 6 in this volume; Joseph and D'Harlingue 2008; McAlister [2001] 2005; Naber 2008). In order to lay claim to the legacy of subversive Arab oral storytelling embodied in the figure of Shahrazad, Arab American writers must navigate through the patriarchal containment of her voice as well as both its erasure and co-optation in orientalist discourse.

7. Mernissi's first name is spelled "Fatema" on the cover of *Scheherazade Goes West* (2001), though it is spelled "Fatima" in publications of her other works in English.

For the Lebanese writer Joumana Haddad, the paradox of Shahrazad is enough cause to put an end to her. As Haddad explains, Shahrazad "saves herself from death by bribing 'the man' with her endless stories, But . . . this 'bribing the man' scheme . . . does not teach women resistance and rebellion. . . . It rather teaches them concession and negotiation over their basic RIGHTS" (2011, 142, emphasis in original). And, "to make things worse," Haddad adds, Shahrazad "is nauseatingly cherished by the Orientalists" (142). In a gesture that echoes Virginia Woolf's need to kill the "angel in the house" in order to free her writing from Victorian constraint, so, too, Haddad, declares: "I killed Scheherazade," even though, she confesses, "I really loved reading and re-reading *The Arabian Nights*" (142). To unburden herself of the patriarchal and orientalist trappings that cling to Shahrazad, Haddad gets rid of Shahrazad, but in doing so also relinquishes a part of her own past that included her appreciation of Shahrazad's tales.

It would be tempting to consider Laila Lalami's refusal to name Shahrazad as akin to Haddad's. However, unlike Haddad, Lalami reclaims the lifesaving potential of storytelling associated with Shahrazad and reworks the gendered power dynamic between oral storyteller and scribe that Malti-Douglas has described. Whereas in her interpretation of the tales Malti-Douglas regards the inscription of Shahrazad's stories by a male scribe as a containment of her voice, in *The Moor's Account* (2014) Lalami reverses the process. Creatively reconstructing what Estebanico/Mustafa's account might have been had the Spanish viceroy deemed it worthy of recording (3), Lalami revives Estebanico/Mustafa's imagined speech and reinscribes it into her historical fiction, magnifying in the process her own literary voice and the possibilities for Arab American writing.

Unlike Lalami and in direct contrast to Haddad, the UK-based Lebanese writer Hanan al-Shaykh observes that even though in her youth she considered Shahrazad "a cliché," she now sees her as "the first feminist on earth" (2013). This revision of Shahrazad came about when al-Shaykh, who now resides in London, was urged to re-read the tales in Arabic after the playwright Tim Supple asked her to help him stage his theatrical production of *The Thousand and One Nights* (al-Shaykh 2011). Similarly, Susan Muaddi Darraj unabashedly claims Shahrazad as a precursor and literary model for Arab and Arab American literary agency. In explaining the title for her edited collection, for example, Darraj asserts that she chose *Scheherazade's Legacy: Arab and Arab American Women on Writing* as "a testament to the heroine of *The Thousand and One Nights*" and emphasizes that she, along with many of the contributors to the collection, "trace their affiliation to Arab culture" and "find Scheherazade to be a common ancestor" (Darraj 2004a, 3). Though Darraj would eventually rue the "exotic and orientalist design" (2011, 249) on the book cover that her title invited, she nonetheless finds in Shahrazad a powerful, if fictional, figure in Arab narrative history to whom she can trace a literary connection and from whom she can draw strength to sustain her own writing as an Arab American writer who must use her voice to correct wrongs and remedy political abuse.

In a similar vein, Zeyn Joukhadar, who borrows the frame-narrative technique and other elements from *The Thousand and One Nights*, such as the giant bird the Roc in *The Map of Salt and Stars*, also traces his narrative choices to a living Arab literary heritage that he associates with folk oral Arab storytelling traditions and the *Nights*. As he explains, "It's a traditional Arab storytelling technique to weave two stories together," adding, "That in itself is part of the heritage we can take with us" (Joukhadar 2018). Shahrazad and the literary traditions to which her tales belong, including both the *khurafat* (fantastical tales) and *asmar* (evening nightly entertainments) (Abbott 1949, 155; Pinault 1992, 3), provide a living and portable cultural-literary heritage that continues to inspire and empower contemporary writers of Arab backgrounds.

Clearly, Shahrazad presents a paradoxical figure for Arab and Arab American women's agency: on the one hand, she offers a powerful link to Arab literary heritage and empowered storytelling; on the other hand, she reinforces associations of Arabs and Arab Americans with orientalist fantasy and patriarchal tyranny. But whereas writers such as Haddad and Lalami refuse to acknowledge her or her tales, others, such as Darraj and al-Shaykh, wholeheartedly embrace her; still others, such as Abu-Jaber, Alameddine, and Joukhadar, emphasize the narrative motifs of the tales over Shahrazad's character; and some, such as Kahf and Yunis, transform and reinvent her. In their reinventions, Yunis and Kahf, this essay illustrates, draw on alternative trajectories within both Arab and American responses to Shahrazad's tales, interweaving the power of subversive distortions in Arab oral storytelling with the force of creative adaptation in US-centered modes of self-fashioning.

Creative Distortions and the Reinvention of Shahrazad

During the nineteenth and early twentieth centuries in the United States, *The Thousand and One Nights* not only contributed to orientalist representations of an indolent yet violent Arab-Muslim East but also supported subversive modes of creative self-fashioning. This is an idea promoted by Susan Nance, who argues that in the United States between 1790 and 1935 "the ethos of excessive, luxurious abundance people looked for in the ideology of consumption came straight from the *Arabian Nights*" (2009, 45). This abundance, Nance elaborates, provided the means for disrupting certain social boundaries. For example, "affluent Anglo-American women who played Oriental by making a cozy corner in the parlor in the 1880s" through the acquisition of "oriental" cushions, rugs, and textiles were eager to "embrace feminine products and practices branded Eastern because they put women at the center of attention as creative people" (77). To "play Eastern" in this sense transforms orientalist products into liberating modes of self-fashioning. What is adopted is not simply a commodity but a style, a way of being in the world that can be signaled through orientalist appropriations of *The Thousand and One Nights*.[8]

If the tales of *The Thousand and One Nights* inspire liberating forms of self-fashioning through material acquisition and theatrical display in the United States, the oral traditions to which the *Nights* belongs foster subversive retellings through creative revisions. *The Thousand and One Nights*, David Pinault remarks, belongs to the tradition of *asmar*, "oral evening-entertainments," but it also "survives as the crafted composition of authors who used various forms of written literary Arabic to capture the oral narrative tradition" (1992, 16). According to Muhsin al-Musawi, the oral dimension that is inscribed in the tales is "in keeping with an enormous corpus of women's narrative that is orally preserved and, if written, embedded in a male tradition" (2009, 40). It is this tradition of women's oral narration that Fatema Mernissi highlights when she recounts how her illiterate grandmother "used storytelling, that oral medium, to escape censorship" and introduced "heretical distortions into the tales" of the *Nights*, casting them in a feminist light that undermined the patriarchal emphasis of the written texts (2001, 5). It is this same subversive element of oral narration that Yunis and Kahf combine with specifically American modes of creative self-fashioning. Brief examples from their work illustrate the generative tension that the paradox of Shahrazad makes possible.

In her essay "My Arabian Superheroine" (2013), Alia Yunis explains her decision to evoke Shahrazad in her novel *The Night Counter* (2009) and recalls how she would dress up as Shahrazad for Halloween because she "didn't feel American enough to . . . get away with dressing up as the Bionic Woman or a Charlie's Angel" (395).[9] Highlighting her perceived difference from (white) American female heroines, the young Alia reaches for an Arab model. However, as she grew up in the United States in the 1970s, her conception of Shahrazad, she reveals, was influenced by both Hollywood representations of Arab women in reruns of TV shows such as *I Dream of Jeannie* and her mother's reminder that Shahrazad was an Arab woman who saved lives (396). And though Yunis

8. Matthew Jaber Stiffler (2014 and chapter 26 in this reader) discusses Nance in relation to Arab American foodways and the ways in which Arab church festivals make use of strategic orientalism. As Stiffler highlights, Nance's phrase "playing Eastern" is borrowed from Phil Deloria's (1998) phrase "playing Indian."

9. For an extended discussion of Yunis's reinvention of Shahrazad in *The Night Counter*, see my essay "Re-encountering Scheherazade: Gender, Cultural Mobility, and Narrative Transformations in Alia Yunis's *The Night Counter*" (2014).

imagined Shahrazad as someone "who went around being beautiful by swirling around in lots of diaphanous veils and telling stories of magical people" (396), her own costume, she relates, consisted of "a long dress some relative I had never met had sent me from Lebanon or Jordan or Palestine and . . . a colorful scarf with fake coins on it" (395). In this improbable costume, Yunis recalls, she felt that she had become "Scheherazade, the Wonder Woman of the Middle East, the prettiest and most powerful person I knew" (395). In combining the emphasis on beauty and physicality that Shahrazad's migration west had accrued to her with the Arab emphasis on Shahrazad's empowering agency, Yunis creates an Arab American hybrid that embodies elements of Arab as well as American fantasies of empowerment: the Arab storyteller who saves lives and the American comic book action hero.

Yunis's explanation of her childhood efforts to create a costume that suited her can be seen as a type of translational move similar to those that Waïl Hassan has described in *Immigrant Narratives: Orientalism and Cultural Translation in Arab American and Arab British Literature* (2011). However, I would argue that Yunis's reconfiguration of Shahrazad goes beyond making Arab forms comprehensible to American audiences, as Hassan's concept of translational practices suggests; in fact, her translational efforts do not succeed because her neighbors fail to recognize her as a transformed Shahrazad and think she is dressed as a fortune-teller (Yunis 2013, 395). What Yunis illustrates, I suggest, is a humorously innocent but radical process of creative reinvention wherein she makes use of an American type of extravagant creativity, "playing Eastern," as it were, but through Arab-inflected "subversive distortions" that sidestep both the shadow of orientalism/self-orientalism and its opposite, the imperative for Arab cultural "authenticity."

Like Yunis, Mohja Kahf draws on the figure of Shahrazad to offer radical re-visions of both Arab and American cultural constraints. In a poem entitled "*Thawrah* des Odalisques at the Matisse Retrospective" in her collection *E-mails from Scheherazad* (2003), Kahf arabizes the English language of her poem and announces a *thawrah* (revolution) by the female figures trapped and silenced within European orientalist paintings that continue to make their rounds in the United States, as evidenced in the retrospective exhibit of Matisse's work referenced in the poem's title. Starting the poem with the traditional opening of an Arabic fairy tale, Kahf's speaker declares:

> *Yown min al-ayyam* [Once upon a time] we just
> decided: Enough is enough
> . . . .
> I looked across the gallery at Red Culottes and gave
> the signal
> She passed it on to Woman in Veil and kicked
> through canvas.
> (64, lines 1, 3–5)

In a gesture of transnational solidarity, Kahf's speaker continues:

> Pink Nude wanted in though she wasn't an odalisque
> . . . .
> Woman with Goldfish came
> . . . .
> *Awwal shee* [first of all] we all wanted to pee
> Then Hindu Pose and With Tambourine
> led us in some stretches
> I helped With Turkish Chair rebraid her hair
> Most of the Culottes and With Magnolias wanted
> clothes
> (65, lines 29, 36, 49–53)

Animating and clothing the female nudes of orientalist art, Kahf at once highlights the embodied physical needs of actual women while discarding the voyeuristic languid eroticism of the painted odalisques.

At the end of her poem, Kahf positions the transnational feminist solidarity of the "*thawrah* of the odalisques" within a specifically Arab American frame of reference that combines both Arab and African American oral traditions:

> I, Small Odalisque, drew up my purple robe and
> ululated
> And we all ululated
> In post-odalisquesque
> Jube-jube-jube-jube-jubilation.
> (69, lines 237–40)

In echoing the Arabic ululation with the intimation of an African American spiritual jubilation, Kahf culminates the *thawrah* of the odalisques with a vocal celebration of life that recognizes orientalism as a form of racism under white hegemony and celebrates shared and intersecting modes of resistance, solidarity, and survival.

While Kahf's poem "*Thawrah*" responds to orientalist appropriations of Shahrazad, the titular poem of *E-mails* confronts Arab patriarchy. In this poem, Shahrazad has given birth to a daughter (not sons), and she has amicably divorced Shahrayar. Shahrazad, the speaker of the poem, asserts:

> I told a story. He began to listen and I found
> That story led to story. Powers unleashed, I wound
> The thread around the pirn of night. A thousand days
> Later, we got divorced. . . .
> (Kahf 2003, 43, lines 9–12)

Kahf's image of Shahrazad stands in stark contrast to both patriarchal recuperation and orientalist appropriations of her tales.[10] She is an immigrant to the United States who speaks in contemporary American idiom interspersed with Arabic words, a figure who creates a life independently of Shahrayar, telling her own tales and writing the stories that determine her own fate.

Through creative reinventions, Yunis and Kahf confront the paradox of Shahrazad and offer re-visions of her story that refuse either to completely idolize or to reject her. Along with the work of Laila Lalami, who conjures but does not name Shahrazad, or with that of Abu-Jaber, Alameddine, and Joukhadar, who strategically emulate narrative techniques associated with her, these works confront both the orientalist legacy and the patriarchal frameworks of *The Thousand and One Nights* and thread through the fraught political climate for Arab American writers in the United States. Whether through creative refusals or creative reimaginings, contemporary Arab American echoes of *The Thousand and One Nights* recover occluded Arab American history, confront both the orientalist legacy and patriarchal frameworks of the tales, and reestablish cultural, literary, and historical links between generations and across geographical distance. Collectively, they demonstrate the generative capacity of *The Thousand and One Nights* and its afterlives while also offering ways to move beyond the paradox of Shahrazad, providing new perspectives and critical interventions in how we understand Arab American history and Arab American literary aesthetics.

10. For a queer critique of Arab American feminist reconfigurations of Shahrazad, see Shomali 2018.

Works Cited

Abbott, Nabia. 1949. "A Ninth-Century Fragment of the *Thousand Nights*: New Light on the Early History of the *Arabian Nights*." *Journal of Near Eastern Studies* 8, no. 3: 129–64.

Abu-Jaber, Diana. [1993] 2003a. *Arabian Jazz*. New York: Norton.

———. 2003b. *Crescent*. New York: Norton.

———. 2005. "An Interview with Diana Abu-Jaber." Interviewed by Jay Stevens. *CutBank* 1, no. 63: art. 9. At https://scholarworks.umt.edu/cutbank/vol1/iss63/9.

Abu-Lughod, Lila. 2013. *Do Muslim Women Need Saving?* Cambridge, MA: Harvard Univ. Press.

Alameddine, Rabih. 2008. *The Hakawati*. New York: Knopf.

———. 2014. "Rabih Alameddine: *An Unnecessary Woman*." Author Talk. Book Passage, Larkspur, CA, Mar. 11.

Alsultany, Evelyn. 2012. *Arabs and Muslims in the Media: Race and Representation after 9/11*. New York: New York Univ. Press.

Beaumont, Daniel. 2002. *Slave of Desire: Sex, Love, and Death in* The 1001 Nights. Madison, NJ: Fairleigh Dickinson Univ. Press.

Cainkar, Louise. 2018. "Fluid Terror Threat: A Genealogy of the Racialization of Arab, Muslim, and South Asian Americans." In "Arab/Americas: Locations & Iterations," edited by Sarah M. A. Gualtieri and Pauline Homsi Vinson. Special issue of *Amerasia Journal* 44, no. 1: 27–60.

Darraj, Susan Muaddi. 2004a. Introduction to *Scheherazade's Legacy: Arab and Arab American Women on Writing*, edited by Susan Muaddi Darraj, 1–4. Westport, CT: Praeger.

———, ed. 2004b. *Scheherazade's Legacy: Arab and Arab American Women on Writing*. Westport, CT: Praeger.

———. 2011. "Personal and Political: The Dynamics of Arab American Feminism." In *Arab & Arab American Feminisms: Gender, Violence, & Belonging*, edited by Rabab

Abdulhadi, Evelyn Alsultany, and Nadine Naber, 248–60. Syracuse, NY: Syracuse Univ. Press.

Deloria, Phil. 1998. *Playing Indian*. New Haven, CT: Yale Univ. Press.

Fayad, Mona. 1994. "The Arab Woman and I." In *Food for Our Grandmothers: Writings by Arab-American & Arab-Canadian Feminists*, edited by Joe Kadi, 170–72. Boston: South End Press.

Ghazoul, Ferial. 1996. *Nocturnal Poetics:* The Arabian Nights *in Comparative Context*. Cairo: American Univ. of Cairo Press.

Golley, Nawar al-Hassan. 2003. *Arab Women's Lives Retold: Exploring Identity through Writing*. Syracuse, NY: Syracuse Univ. Press.

Grotzfeld, Heinz. [1985] 2010. "Neglected Conclusions of *The Arabian Nights*: Gleanings in Forgotten and Overlooked Recensions." In *The Arabian Nights*, translated by Husain Haddawy, edited by Daniel Heller-Roazen, 470–85. New York: Norton.

Habra, Hedy. 2012. *Flying Carpets*. Greensboro, NC: March Street Press.

Haddad, Joumana. 2011. *I Killed Scheherazade: Confessions of an Angry Arab Woman*. Chicago: Lawrence Hill Books.

Haddawy, Husain, trans. 2010. *The Arabian Nights*. Edited by Daniel Heller-Roazen. New York: Norton.

Halaby, Laila. 2007. *Once in a Promised Land*. Boston: Beacon Press.

Hamilton, Marsha J. 1994. "The Arab Woman in U.S. Popular Culture." In *Food for Our Grandmothers: Writings by Arab-American & Arab-Canadian Feminists*, edited by Joe Kadi, 173–80. Boston: South End Press.

Hassan, Waïl S. 2011. *Immigrant Narratives: Orientalism and Cultural Translation in Arab American and Arab British Literature*. New York: Oxford Univ. Press.

Homsi Vinson, Pauline. 2014. "Re-encountering Scheherazade: Gender, Cultural Mobility, and Narrative Transformations in Alia Yunis's *The Night Counter*." In "Gender and Mobility," edited by Sarah M. A. Gualtieri and Akram Khater. Special issue of *Mashriq & Mahjar* 2, no. 1: 55–76.

———. 2015. "Representations of Sexualities: United States." In *Encyclopedia of Women and Islamic Cultures*, edited by Suad Joseph, guest edited by Sarah Gualtieri. Leiden: Brill Online, Feb. At http://dx.doi.org/10.1163/1872-5309_ewic_COM_002015.

Horta, Paulo Lemos. 2017. *Marvellous Thieves: Secret Authors of the* Arabian Nights. Cambridge, MA: Harvard Univ. Press.

Irwin, Robert. N.d. "The Dark Side of *The Arabian Nights*." *Critical Muslim* 13, no. 1. At https://www.criticalmuslim.io/the-dark-side-of-the-arabian-nights/.

Jamal, Amaney. 2008. "Civil Liberties and the Otherization of Arab and Muslim Americans." In *Race and Arab Americans before and after 9/11: From Invisible Citizens to Visible Subjects*, edited by Amaney Jamal and Nadine Naber, 114–30. Syracuse, NY: Syracuse Univ. Press.

Jarmakani, Amira. 2008. *Imagining Arab Womanhood: The Cultural Mythology of Veils, Harems, and Belly Dancers in the U.S.* New York: Palgrave.

Joseph, Suad, and Benjamin D'Harlingue, with Alvin Ka Hin Wong. 2008. "Arab Americans and Muslim Americans in the *New York Times*, before and after 9/11." In *Race and Arab Americans before and after 9/11: From Invisible Citizens to Visible Subjects*, edited by Amaney Jamal and Nadine Naber, 229–75. Syracuse, NY: Syracuse Univ. Press.

Joukhadar, Zeyn. 2018. *The Map of Salt and Stars*. New York: Touchstone.

———. 2018. "Saratoga Springs Bookstore Talk with Author about Her Novel on Syria's Civil War." Interview by Massarah Mikati, *Times Union* , May 10. At https://www.timesunion.com/local/article/Saratoga-Springs-bookstore-hosts-book-talk-on-12904359.php.

Kabbani, Rana. 1994. *Imperial Fictions: Europe's Myths of Orient*. London: Pandora.

Kahf, Mohja. 2003. *E-mails from Scheherazad*. Gainesville: Univ. Press of Florida.

Kandiyoti, Deniz. 1988. "Bargaining with Patriarchy." *Gender and Society* 2, no. 3: 274–90.

———. 1998. "Gender and Contestation: Rethinking 'Bargaining with Patriarchy.'" In *Feminist Visions of Development: Gender Analysis and Policy*, edited by Cecile Jackson and Ruth Pearson, 135–53. New York: Routledge.

Lalami, Laila. 2005. *Hope and Other Dangerous Pursuits*. Orlando, FL: Harcourt.

———. 2014. *The Moor's Account*. New York: Pantheon Books.

Laouyene, Atef. 2015. "Politics of the Exotic in Diana Abu-Jaber's *Crescent*." *Critique* 56:586–601.

Makdisi, Saree, and Felicity Nussbaum, eds. 2008. The Arabian Nights *in Historical Context: Between East and West*. Oxford: Oxford Univ. Press.

Malti-Douglas, Fedwa. 1991. *Woman's Body, Woman's Word: Gender and Discourse in Arabo-Islamic Writing*. Princeton, NJ: Princeton Univ. Press.

Marshall, Jack. 1986. *Arabian Nights*. Minneapolis: Coffee House Press.

Marzolph, Ulrich, and Richard van Leeuwen, eds., with Hassan Wassouf. 2004. *The* Arabian Nights *Encyclopedia*. 2 vol. set. Oxford: ABC-CLIO.

McAlister, Melani. [2001] 2005. *Epic Encounters: Culture, Media, and U.S. Interests in the Middle East since 1945*. Berkeley: Univ. of California Press.

Mernissi, Fatema. 2001. *Scheherazade Goes West: Different Cultures, Different Harems*. New York: Washington Square Press.

Mikhail, Dunya. 2014. *The Iraqi Nights*. Translated by Kareem James Abu-Zeid. New York: New Directions Book.

Mottahedeh, Roy P. 1997. "*'Ajā'ib* in *The Thousand and One Nights*." In The Thousand and One Nights *in Arabic Literature and Society*, edited by Richard C. Hovannisian and Georges Sabagh, 29–39. Cambridge: Cambridge Univ. Press.

Al-Musawi, Muhsin. 2009. *The Islamic Context of* The Thousand and One Nights. New York: Columbia Univ. Press.

Naber, Nadine. 2008. "'Look, Mohammed the Terrorist Is Coming!': Cultural Racism, Nation-Based Racism, and the Intersectionality of Oppressions after 9/11." In *Race and Arab Americans before and after 9/11: From Invisible Citizens to Visible Subjects*, edited by Amaney Jamal and Nadine Naber, 276–304. Syracuse, NY: Syracuse Univ. Press.

Nance, Susan. 2009. *How* The Arabian Nights *Inspired the American Dream, 1790–1935*. Chapel Hill: Univ. of North Carolina Press.

Naous, Mazen. 2020. *Poetics of Visibility in the Contemporary Arab American Novel*. Columbus: Ohio Univ. Press.

Ouyang, Wen-Chin. 2003. "Metamorphosis of Scheherazade in Literature and Film." *Bulletin of the School of Oriental and African Studies* 66, no. 3: 402–18.

Pickens, Therí A., ed. 2018. *Arab American Aesthetics: Literature, Material Culture, Film, and Theatre*. London: Routledge.

Pinault, David. 1992. *Story-Telling Techniques in* The Arabian Nights. Leiden: Brill.

Sabry, Somaya Sami. 2011. *Arab-American Women's Writing and Performance: Orientalism, Race, and the Idea of* The Arabian Nights. New York: I. B. Tauris.

Sallis, Eva. 1999. *Scheherazade through the Looking Glass: The Metamorphosis of* The Thousand and One Nights. Surrey, UK: Curzon Press.

Sawires-Masseli, Marie-Christin. 2018. *Arab American Novels post-9/11: Classical Storytelling Motifs against Outsidership*. Heidleberg, Germany: Universitätsverlag Winter.

Shakir, Evelyn. 1996. "Arab American Literature." In *New Immigrant Literatures in the United States*, edited by Alpana Sharma Knippling, 3–18. Westport, CT: Greenwood.

Shamaa, Tarek. 2017. "Women and Slaves: Gender Politics in the *Arabian Nights*." *Marvels & Tales* 31, no. 2: 239–60.

Al-Shaykh, Hanan. 2011. *One Thousand and One Nights: A Retelling*. London: Bloomsbury.

———. 2013. "Scheherazade: From Storytelling 'Slave' to 'First Feminist." Interviewed by Rachel Martin. *Weekend Edition Sunday*, NPR, June 9. At https://www.npr.org/2013/06/09/189539866scheherazade-from-storytelling-slave-to-first-feminist.

Shomali, Mejdulene. 2018. "Scheherazade and the Limits of Inclusive Politics in Arab American Literature." *MELUS* 43, no. 1: 65–90.

Stiffler, Matthew Jaber. 2014. "Consuming Orientalism: Public Foodways of Arab American Christians." *Mashriq & Mahjar* 2, no. 2: 111–38.

———. 2018. "'Serving Arabness': Imagery and Imagination of Arab-Themed Restaurants." In *Arab American Aesthetics: Literature, Material Culture, Film, and Theatre*, edited by Therí A. Pickens, 63–86. London: Routledge.

Yamanaka, Yuriko, and Tetsuo Nishio. 2006. The Arabian Nights *and Orientalism: Perspectives from East & West*. London: I. B. Tauris.

Yunis, Alia. 2009. *The Night Counter*. New York: Shaye Areheart Books.

———. 2013. "Afterward: My Arabian Superheroine." In *Scheherazade's Children: Global Encounters with the* Arabian Nights, edited by Philip F. Kennedy and Marina Warner, 395–400. New York: New York Univ. Press.

Part Five

Security/Insecurity

Empire and the War on Terror

> The reason advanced [for surveillance and deportation of Arabs] is prevention of terrorism, but the real objective is to suppress the free expression of those who stand up against a one-sided policy motivated by political considerations.
>
> —M. Cherif Bassiouni, introduction to *The Civil Rights of Arab-Americans*

The "war on terror" commenced unofficially in the United States in the late 1960s. Referring to the surveillance and deportation of Arab students and activists opposing US policies toward Palestine in the wake of the Israel–Arab War in 1967, M. Cherif Bassiouni's statement demonstrates that the war on terror, in its multiple forms and locations, has always been tied to the policies of US empire. Arab American life has been substantially shaped by the war on terror and its epistemological, ideological, and disciplinary powers. Although the war on terror has materially inflicted tremendous injury and death across the globe, it is nonetheless built on a social construction manifested in the figure of the Arab terrorist. Just as the system of racial classification serves the project of white supremacy and rigid gender binaries serve heteropatriarchy, so too the war on terror serves the interests of the larger project of US empire. Ideologically, the war on terror relies on notions of a good "us" and a bad "them" to do its work. Drawing on orientalist tropes, it frames Arabs and by extension Arab Americans as barbaric people whose primary shared cultural attribute is a commitment to violence. This idea is encapsulated in the notion that Arabs are, first and foremost, a terrorist threat. As discussed in the general introduction to the reader, this narrative dominated American mainstream media during and after the Israeli–Arab War of 1967 and Israeli conquest of the rest of Palestine and parts of Egypt, Lebanon, and Syria. It served to valorize Israeli aggression against Palestinians and other Arabs using white-supremacist binaries of modern/backward cultures and superior/inferior people; to wit, Arabs could be justifiably subdued (by "our" modern forms of violence) because "they" are violent in an uncivilized way and incapable of "modernization," including in their use of natural resources (Naber 2008; Said [1981] 1997). US empire's claim to oil resources on Arab lands is also framed by conceptions of Arabs as inherently deceitful. Displaying the malleability of orientalist tropes, the FBI deployed the notion of greedy Arab sheikhs in its Abscam anticorruption sting operations of the late 1970s and early 1980s, signaling the traction of the idea that Arabs acting in control of oil resources on their lands (as in the oil boycott in 1973) were not only selfish but going beyond legality. Similarly, when US empire lost its dominance over Iranian oil after the Islamic Revolution of 1979, US state and media discourse reconfigured Iran as a demon to be taken down (Mamdani 2002; Said [1981] 1997).

The narratives of the war on terror argue not only that "we" need to be saved from "their" greed, barbarism, and terror but also by extension that "we" must also save "them" from themselves. If the image of the Arab terrorist generates fear that justifies expansive national-security policies, militarism, and war, then the gendered variant asserts that Arab (and Muslim) women are voiceless victims of a hyperpatriarchal culture who need to be saved through military invasion (Abu-Lughod 2013). In her critique of First Lady Laura Bush's claim that the war on terror and invasion of Afghanistan were "a fight for the rights and dignity of women," Lila Abu-Lughod notes, "It is problematic to construct the Afghan or Muslim woman as someone in need of saving. When you save someone, you imply that you are saving her from something. You are also saving her to something. What violences are entailed in this transformation? What presumptions are being made about the superiority of that to which you are saving her? Projects of saving other women depend on and reinforce a sense of superiority, and are a form of arrogance that deserves to be challenged" (2013, 46–47).

Savior narratives are updated versions of the classic colonialist "civilizing mission," which not only manifests itself through conquest but also through the logic of "soft" or "smart" power (Sheehi 2011, 187; Youmans 2009) and "humanitarian imperialism" (Atanasoski 2013; Grewal 2014). And although profoundly current, these narratives about Arabs (and Muslims) are also informed by the historical practices of western empire, as discussed in nearly every section of this reader and by numerous scholars: the Crusades and Reconquista (Grosfoguel and Mielants 2006; König 2018; Shohat 2013 and chapter 4 in this reader); European colonialism (Said 1978); the Barbary Wars (Berman, chapter 22 in this reader); the conquest of the Indigenous people of the Americas and the slave trade (Curtis 2009; McHeimech 2016; Salaita 2016; Shohat 2013 and chapter 4 in this reader).

This part of the reader addresses the following questions: In what ways is the war on terror about ideas, dissent, and the maintenance of racial, religious, and economic hegemonies rather than about terrorism? How does the war on terror enlist crossover technologies of control, such as those used for policing Black communities and border control? How does the war on terror mask policies of conquest and plunder, especially of natural resources such as oil, minerals, and water? Who gets caught up in the crosshairs of the war on terror, and how are they ensnared? How is the war on terror weaponized, both literally and figuratively? What weapons—including domestic surveillance, proxy wars, drone warfare, so-called surgical strikes, and unlawful detention—does it deploy, and how does it justify their use? How does the language of precision, deployed both domestically and globally as part of national-security discourse, mask the chaotic and catastrophic destruction inflicted on people, water, animals, and the land? In what ways do narratives intended to justify conquest and domination, including those of soft power, avert our gaze from the casualties of the war on terror, not only among humans but also to the environment?

The fabrications and fantasies of the war on terror do a considerable amount of work. They provide moral justifications for a wide range of policies and practices, including US military interventions, foreign-aid packages, weapons sales across Southwest Asia and North Africa (SWANA), a host of US-backed proxy wars, soft-power humanitarian efforts, environmentally destructive racial capitalism, and invasive domestic national-security policies—framing them all with good intentions for "us." This is a point that Steven Salaita emphasizes in his discussion of the US war in Iraq in chapter 16: "Politicians frequently speak about the need to occupy Arab countries and 'civilize' them by introducing the natives to 'democracy.' (Like the colonial discourse that preceded it, this one rarely mentions the actual motivation for intervention: the plunder of resources, in this case oil.) Americans today hear so much about the need for their government's 'leadership' in all areas of the world that most, like the Europeans before them, automatically equate colonization with generosity and moral strength" (p. 245).

The drive to save "brown women from brown men" (Spivak 1993, 93), the contemporary manifestations of colonialist "civilizing" missions, and the workings of the military-industrial complex demonstrate how the war on terror operates through discourses of bringing democracy, freedom, and security to SWANA regions.

Waging Benevolence: Neoimperialist Savior Complexes

"Benevolent supremacy"—a "white man's burden" version of US imperialism that disavows its own imperialism—is another discourse that shapes the practices of US empire. Melani McAlister's book *Epic Encounters* ([2001] 2005) traces how this discourse of "benevolent supremacy" shapes US foreign policies. Reading biblical epic films alongside an analysis of the National Security Council Document 68, which outlines post–World War II US security policy, McAlister argues, for example, that "consent and submission, faith and perversion of faith, slavery and freedom became the intertwined terms by which policymakers framed U.S. world power" (53). If McAlister draws our attention to the language of "benevolent supremacy" as a precursor to "soft power," neither of which overtly acknowledges the United States as an imperialist nation, Amy Kaplan highlights the shift to a more overt assertion of US empire after September 11, 2001 (9/11). In "Where Is Guantánamo?" (2005), Kaplan observes that "since September 11, 2001, neoconservatives and liberal interventionists have openly embraced the vision of an ascendant American Empire policing and transforming the world around it through military and political might and economic and cultural power" (832; see also Stoler 2006, 50, and Youmans 2009). As the metaphor of "policing the world" suggests, even if more overtly named, this mode of US empire maintains the idea of US exceptionalism by working around or changing the definitions of legal warfare. As Kaplan notes, this version of US empire is able to respond to the "changing demands of empire by creating new categories of persons before the law" (2005, 834), such as the racialized category of "enemy combatant," and by generally exploiting the mechanism of extralegality.

Exploring US military use of metadata to deploy "surgical strikes" against racialized, presumed terrorist targets, Keith Feldman's essay in this part of the reader (chapter 31) expands the scope of Kaplan's analysis to demonstrate how extralegality and the logic of preemption enable both detention and killing practices in the war on terror. Parallel to extralegal detention policies in the global war on terror is the extralegal killing enabled by drone warfare (Kapadia 2019; Miller 2017), with its racism-informed, imprecise targeting of civilians, who are then posthumously labeled as terrorists. Feldman argues in "Empire's Verticality" (2011) that drone warfare implements racialization "from above," which is inspired by the logic of borders and checkpoints at the same time that it extends their reach to a vertical plane. The war on terror transforms Arabs and Muslims into legitimate targets, whose lives and liberties can be sacrificed for "our" security. "Playing global cop" (Evans 2005), the United States and its allies skirt international human rights frameworks by technically operating outside of them. Drone strikes on wedding parties and so-called black sites holding civilians are justified through the rhetoric of precision and rationality—and, therefore, the logic goes, are more humane than conventional forms of warfare (Kapadia 2019; Parks and Kaplan 2017). In short, the soft power of white supremacy condescends and destroys while framing its actions as legitimate.

The founding narrative of US exceptionalism, whose logical extension is a "reluctant" empire, and the logic of national security, which creates a class of racialized "terrorist" enemies, together serve as an endless reservoir for justifying US intervention in SWANA. One powerful early iteration of US exceptionalism was the notion of the United States as its own "Promised Land," an idea that was solidified through what Hilton Obenzinger calls a Holy Land "mania" (1999, 5)—romanticized cultural engagements with the idea of the Holy Land, such as paintings, photographs, travel literature, and large-scale replicas, popular in the latter half of the nineteenth century and exemplified by the replica of Jerusalem at the St. Louis World's Fair in 1904. In these US cultural engagements with the Holy Land, Palestinians (and Arabs more generally) were either disappeared from the land or transformed into objects populating the landscape (Davis 1996; Jarmakani 2008). As "a crucial forum for negotiating American settler identity" (Obenzinger 1999, 5), the Holy Land mania coalesced with the genocidal impulse of US "expansionist" settler colonialism by reframing it as a divine civilizing mission. These cultural framings resonated with the positioning of Indigenous Americans as if at best nonexistent and at worst "barbaric" subjects who were deemed inept custodians of the land. Such logic easily resurges, for instance, in reports about the looting of the Iraq National Museum in the wake of the US invasion in 2003, which cast all Iraqis as primitive people incapable of protecting "our" western civilization from destruction (Jarmakani 2008, 16). Similarly, the language of Christian dispensationalism renews and extends the sense of stewardship over the Holy Land through an appeal to a divine plan that echoes earlier US justifications of "manifest destiny." Saving the "Holy Land" by protecting it from its "barbaric" inhabitants and neighbors is a manifestation of this logic and a key project of US empire. Christian dispensationalists "assume an urgent missionary zeal, and hope to save as many people as possible before the rapture" (Salaita 2006, 169), as demonstrated through the popularity of cultural products such as the *Left Behind* book series popular in the early 2000s (noted in McAlister 2007). According to dispensationalist logic, for salvation to occur, Israel and all of occupied Palestine "must be restored to the Chosen People" (Salaita 2006, 169) prior to their conversion to Christianity. Dispensationalists therefore not only oppose a Palestinian state but are also hostile to the very presence of Palestinians (even Christian Palestinians) in the Holy Land and view Arabs as impediments to God's plan (Salaita 2006, 172; see also Fink 2014). Such formulations draw on long-standing orientalist notions of the "Holy Land" as belonging to "western" Christian civilization, thereby disappearing Arabs from their homelands, and depend on a "good Christian, bad Muslim" binary that conflates Christian Arabs with Muslims and demonizes both (Jarmakani 2015, 26–27).

Operations of Empire

Essentializing binaries and their reliance on the supposed immutability of characteristics and inevitability of events erase the need for considerations of cause and effect or for close examinations of history; they effectively hide the operations of empire. Mahmood Mamdani, for example, has shown how US empire strategically instrumentalized its own distortions by forging alliances between Arab and South Asian Muslims to fight for US imperial interests in the name of jihad, which "was in reality an American jihad" (2004, 128). As Mamdani observes, in 1979, the same year as the Iranian Revolution took place, the Soviet Union invaded Afghanistan; the Reagan administration's strategy to combat the Soviet occupation and control of Afghanistan was to bankroll the idea of jihad, even while US officials and the US media were aggressively condemning Islamists in Iran. Hundreds of millions of dollars were spent by the CIA and its allies to recruit tens of thousands of foot soldiers, especially underpaid "guest" workers in Arab Gulf states, to be armed and trained in Pakistan to fight the Soviets in Afghanistan. According to Mamdani, the US government hoped "to unite a billion Muslims worldwide in a holy war, a crusade" against the Soviet Union (128). Mamdani notes that "the Islamic world had not seen an armed Jihad for nearly a century. But now the CIA was determined to create one in service of a contemporary political objective" (127). It did so with the substantial assistance of a wealthy Saudi named Osama bin Laden. This American-sponsored jihad was the historic precursor to al-Qaeda as well as to the formation of the Islamic State of Iraq and Syria (ISIS) that followed the US invasion and occupation of Iraq. Yet all of these developments are widely explained and understood as having no rational cause but rather as *natural* outgrowths of the inherent violence of Arabs and Islam.

As the United States expands its oil and mineral frontier in the SWANA region, US imperialism has at times shifted from the colonial model of conquest and occupation of an entire territory to the use of proxy political and military formations to defend its extraction of raw materials (Jarmakani 2015, 50). What is often called a "special relationship" between the United States and Saudi Arabia is narrated as a "deal" whereby Saudi Arabia trades oil for militarized security. Yet, as Timothy Mitchell argues, scratching the surface of this deal reveals "security" to be a front for arms sales, which are "useful for their uselessness" (2011, 155–58). The "rhetoric of security" about oil-rich regions (namely, Saudi Arabia and the United Arab Emirates) has been produced to justify arms sales that ultimately return US petro-dollars back to the United States. This project of racial capitalism, as Danielle Haque's essay in this part highlights, wreaks ecological devastation through resource extraction and the weapons of war, altering the means for human survival and preventing people from "inhabiting and interacting with land in the ways they choose" (chapter 30, p. 399). Reminding us that Arab Americans belong to many geographies to which they "cannot return because of occupation, war, or economic disenfranchisement" (p. 398), Haque's analysis highlights the relationships between humans and the biosphere, and it demonstrates how environmental destruction is not disconnected from "the slow violence of environmental racism, settler colonialism, and globalization" (p. 398). Alternately forcing and prohibiting human migration, the violence done to the environment completes the circle of empire's grasp; moving bodies are also then policed in their new locations or subject to policies (e.g., travel bans, watch lists, and detention centers) that force them to stay in place.

Domesticating and Weaponizing Security: Surveilling Arab America

Practices centered in the United States that constitute the domestic front of the war on terror entail the collaborative efforts of a wide range of institutions and actors. State disciplinary actions—such as surveillance, detentions, deportations, as well as visa and naturalization delays and denials—operate in partnership with private persons and institutions that orchestrate forms of silencing, such as social and political exclusion and censorship. Together, these practices provide the discursive fodder for hate crimes, murders, and bullying. With direct impacts on Arab Americans, they curtail freedom of expression and movement and establish a sense of insecurity, fear, and double consciousness, or the "sense of always looking at one's self through the eyes of others" (Du Bois 1903, 3). As the quote from Bassiouni at the beginning of this introduction asserts, domestic dissent against the policies and practices of US empire has been criminalized and securitized under the guise of fighting terrorism. Insecurity, surveillance, repression, and, at times, fear have not ceased being central features of the Arab American experience since 1967, their levels rising and falling depending on the moment.

US government activities monitoring Arab Americans—or, rather, the extent of those activities—were first uncovered when the Arab American attorney Abdeen Jabara sued the FBI for spying on him (Bassiouni 1974b). As his case unfolded, Jabara discovered that beginning shortly after the Israeli–Arab War of 1967, the National Security Agency was surveilling his home and business, recording his telephone conversations, and collecting his bank records. He also found that the FBI was interviewing his neighbors and professional contacts. In addition, Arab Americans discovered that beginning in 1967 the FBI and the Immigration and Naturalization Service (precursor to the Department of Homeland Security), with the assistance of local police, were conducting invasive interviews of Arab university students that contained threats of deportation (which were acted upon) if on college campuses they engaged in free-speech activities that criticized US foreign policies. These practices were institutionalized in Richard Nixon's Operation Boulder, a covert racial profiling scheme commenced in 1972 during the latter years of COINTELPRO (Counter Intelligence Program), another covert and illegal government program that spied on civil rights activists, the Black Panthers, and other domestic opposition movements. Operation Boulder tasked eight federal agencies, including the State Department, the CIA, the FBI, the Immigration and Naturalization Service, and the National Security Agency, with watching "ethnic Arabs" in the United States, impeding their entry into the country, deporting them as needed, and delaying and obstructing their naturalization (Bassiouni 1974b). Government documents referred to Arab student organizers as "potential terrorists" (a term still widely used, as we see in Cainkar's and Bayoumi's essays in chapters 28 and 29) who were supplied with overseas "Arab money" to conduct "intelligence operations" (Bassiouni 1974a, 78). As is well documented in Bassiouni's book *The Civil Rights of Arab-Americans: The Special Measures* (1974), the "Arab terrorist" narrative was repeated frequently in the mainstream news, effectively cementing the image in the public's mind. The FBI took its mission seriously; the book reports that in one single quarter of 1972 the FBI judged two thousand Arab students deportable, an additional forty-one left the country voluntarily, and sixty-eight were in deportation proceedings. Concurring with Bassiouni's assertion that "the real objective is to suppress the free expression of those who stand up" (Bassiouni 1974c, vi), a Justice Department official wrote that students' "organizational work" on college campuses "awakened the curiosity of many Americans about the Middle East, the Palestinian question and US foreign policy" (Gessert 1974, 23).

These government actions clearly intended to stifle the opposition expressed by Arab American activists and their allies; more such actions would follow, indicating a pattern of suppression that came to be known by activists as "the chill." The US government's continuing efforts to silence critiques of its policies included, for example, the "LA 8" case in 1987, in which seven Palestinians and a Kenyan active in Palestine solidarity work were arrested on "terrorism" charges (which were later changed to support for communism and changed again to support for the Popular Front for the Liberation of Palestine), a congressional revision of the McCarren Walter Act in 1990, which modified the ideological bars to US immigration for members of "totalitarian parties" but added new bars, such as "support for terrorism" and "representatives of the PLO" (US Senate 1990). These policies were not isolated incidents of suppression; they were part of a systemic effort of containment, as exposed by the revelation in 1987 of a multiagency "contingency plan" for the domestic internment of noncitizen Arabs and Muslims in the United States (see Wofford and Kelly 2016). As demonstrated in Bayoumi's contribution to this part as well as in recent scholarship on the government's Countering Violent Extremism program, multiagency surveillance practices focusing on policing communities of color remain in operation, even if some of them have been refigured through humanitarian imperialist logics of help and "care" (Nguyen 2019; Zahzah 2020). Nadine Naber and Junaid Rana argue these same points: "Hidden behind the phrases 'healthy communities' and 'safe spaces,' these programs contribute to the framing of Islam and Muslims as signifiers of potential criminality and terrorism" (2019). President Donald Trump's "Muslim Ban" also invoked the language of terror threat in order to deny entry into the United States to nationals of a range of mostly Muslim-majority countries (Cainkar 2020). Ideologies of Arab threat along with policing and surveillance practices mark the continuities between 1967 and the present.

Although Palestinian nationalism was constructed as a threat to Americans, indeed quite the opposite was true. Palestinians, Arabs, and their institutions have been the victims of numerous violent attacks, as in the bombings of American Arab Anti-Discrimination Committee (ADC) offices in 1985, presumed to have been conducted by the Jewish Defense League—which the Southern Poverty Law Center considers a violent extremist group—and the murder of ADC's regional director Alex Odeh (Abraham 1994). And although a white, Christian man perpetrated the Oklahoma City bombing in 1994, Arabs and Muslims and persons assumed to be in these groups suffered the repercussions, including 150 hate crimes against Arab Americans reported by the ADC and 222 incidents of harassment of Muslim Americans recorded by the Council on American Islamic Relations (Cainkar 2018). Statements by persons such as known anti-Arab and anti-Muslim activist Steven Emerson (identified by the US media as a "terrorism expert") contributed to this climate of hate. Emerson, for example, was observed on nationwide television stating: "This was done with the attempt to inflict as many casualties as possible. That is a Middle Eastern trait" (quoted in Doyle 2015). A malleable social construction that gained salience following the 1979 Revolution overthrowing the US-backed shah of Iran, the term *Middle Easterner* embraces an expandable group of "threats" to US empire and its allies. Narratives of the Arab/Muslim/Middle Eastern terrorist threat are thus not only deployed by government agents to make their "antiterror" activities appear logical and necessary but also exploited by a range of civil society actors to serve their political interests, as in Emerson's pro-Israel agenda (Szremski 2012). In addition to criminalizing dissent, such narratives further reduce the security and safety of Arab and Muslim Americans by generating a social climate of hate.

The US government waged its largest ever antiterror campaign against Arab and Muslim Americans, in particular those who are brown and Black, after 9/11 and did so with widespread media and public support. Cainkar reports in chapter 28 on the implementation after 9/11 of dozens of invasive domestic-security policies that targeted and disrupted the lives of Arab and Muslim Americans. These collective policies uncovered very few terrorists and instead ramped up levels of fear. As Sally Howell and Andrew Shryock report in chapter 32, after 9/11 Arab and Muslim Americans were "compelled, time and again, to apologize for acts they did not commit, to condemn acts they never condoned, and to openly profess loyalties that, for most US citizens, are merely assumed" (p. 410). The post-9/11 period also marked the heightened criminalization of personal remittances sent to support family and charitable donations to domestic organizations that might subject one to scrutiny, as Cainkar as well as Howell and Shryock observe in their contributions to this part. Focusing on the Detroit area, the location of the most concentrated Arab and Muslim communities in the United States, Howell and Shryock note, "Arabs in Detroit have been forced to distance themselves from Arab political movements, ideologies, causes, religious organizations, and points of view that are currently at odds with US policy" (p. 410). Their findings affirm our assertion that the domestic war on terror is deeply tied to dissent from the policies of empire.

The connection between the policies of empire and the so-called fight against domestic terrorism, however, extends beyond the silencing of dissent; both directly affect local policing practices and enable racialized surveillance in the United States. Recalling Operation Boulder, which mobilized eight federal agencies to spy on Arabs and Arab Americans in 1972, contemporary "fusion centers" extend the scope of cooperation to a wide range of federal, state, and local agencies, including tribal, campus, and transit police, through data-sharing platforms. Any time a "Suspicious Activity Report" (which can include innocent activities such as taking photographs or using binoculars) is uploaded to a fusion center database, it becomes immediately accessible to "tens of thousands of agencies in the country" (Stop LAPD Spying Coalition 2013). The counterterrorist practice of intelligence gathering expands into the logic of preemption (in both military strikes and predictive technologies of policing), widening the range of suspects and stamping them as already-criminals. Bayoumi's essay in this part, for example, demonstrates that the ongoing war on terror deeply informs the practices of the New York Police Department. He provides an elaborate rendering of the department's multifaceted program of spying on Muslims, including in their places of worship, at coffee shops, and on sports teams, as well as of the impacts of this program on those surveilled. He points out that the police used census data to locate these communities, relying yet again on categories of people and nations thought to be "bad" or a "threat." The so-called ISIS trials of nine Somali American young men in Minneapolis in 2016, who were "manufactured" as terrorists through FBI entrapment and subsequently convicted as such, demonstrate the ways in which the category of "terrorist" is used to fluidly criminalize communities of color (Bile 2019). In chapter 33, Leslie Quintanilla and Jennifer Mogannam examine a "transnational system of incarceration" by looking at immigration detention centers in relation to the prison-industrial complex. In that context, they discuss the training exchanges—focusing on technologies of "securitization"—between the San Diego and Israeli police forces. Such exchanges demonstrate the rise of what Paul Amar (2013) calls "human-security states," which regulate their dispossessed and displaced populations through surveillance, criminalization, and incarceration. The city of San Diego—as a site of immigration detention centers, US military presence, Countering Violent Extremism operations, and development of new military and surveillance technologies (at the University of California at San Diego)—demonstrates the intersections of the transnational prison- and military-industrial complexes in action. Quintanilla and Mogannam further connect the drones tested across the US–Mexico border to those used in Yemen, Iraq, Syria, and Pakistan, and they describe coalitional borderlands organizing between the Palestinian Youth Movement–San Diego and Colectivo Zapatista in response to this connection.

It is widely evident that the war on terror did not begin on 9/11, nor has it ever been what the US government has claimed: a rational, disinterested response to an objective phenomenon—Arab/Muslim/Middle Eastern acts of terrorism. The expression "war on terror," like similarly constructed expressions such as "war on drugs" and "war on poverty," uses the language of military combat to attack a disembodied noun, a word that can easily refer to a thing (drugs), a condition (poverty), or a tactic of aggression (terror). Making it at once easier to deploy and more difficult to implement, the phrase "war on" arouses strong emotion and an "us versus them" mentality that gives permission for a wide range of oppressive practices. The emotional resonance and malleability of the expression "war on terror" allow the policies and practices of US empire to continue and even expand with minimal dissent. These discursive practices and transnational crossover technologies of control highlight the need for coalitional organizing to oppose them, a topic we cover in part six.

Works Cited

Abraham, Nabeel. 1994. "Anti-Arab Racism and Violence in the United States." In *The Development of Arab-American Identity*, edited by Ernest McCarus, 155–214. Ann Arbor: Univ. of Michigan Press.

Abu-Lughod, Lila. 2013. *Do Muslim Women Need Saving?* Cambridge, MA: Harvard Univ. Press.

Amar, Paul. 2013. *The Security Archipelago: Human-Security States, Sexuality Politics, and the End of Neoliberalism*. Durham, NC: Duke Univ. Press.

Atanasoski, Neda. 2013. *Humanitarian Violence: The U.S. Deployment of Diversity.* Minneapolis: Univ. of Minnesota Press.

Bassiouni, M. Cherif. 1974a. "Appendix 3: Newspapers and Comments." In *The Civil Rights of Arab-Americans: The Special Measures*, edited by M. Cherif Bassiouni, 75–85. Belmont, MA: AAUG Press.

———, ed. 1974b. *The Civil Rights of Arab-Americans: The Special Measures*. Belmont, MA: AAUG Press.

———. 1974c. Introduction to *The Civil Rights of Arab-Americans: The Special Measures*, edited by M Cherif Bassiouni, v–vii. Belmont, MA: AAUG Press.

Bile, Ramla. 2019. "Parallels between the Central Park 5 and the Minnesota 'ISIS Trials.'" *Ubuntu: The Collective*, Sept. 12. At https://www.weareubuntu.com/race-politcs/2019/9/12/parallels-between-the-central-park-5-and-the-minnesota-isis-trials.

Cainkar, Louise. 2018. "Fluid Terror Threat: A Genealogy of the Racialization of Arab, Muslim, and South Asian Americans." In "Arab/Americas: Locations & Iterations," edited by Sarah M. A. Gualtieri and Pauline Homsi Vinson. Special issue of *Amerasia Journal* 44, no. 1: 27–60.

. 2020. "The Muslim Ban and Trump's War on Immigration." *Middle East Report* 294 (Spring). At https://merip.org/2020/06/the-muslim-ban-and-trumps-war-on-immigration/.

Curtis, Edward E. 2009. *Muslims in America: A Short History.* Oxford: Oxford Univ. Press.

Davis, John. 1996. *The Landscape of Belief: Encountering the Holy Land in Nineteenth-Century American Art and Culture.* Princeton, NJ: Princeton Univ. Press.

Doyle, Chris. 2015. "The Big Joke Is That Fox News' 'Terrorism Expert' Advises the FBI." *Al Arabiya News*, Jan. 14. At https://english.alarabiya.net/views/media/2015/01/14/The-big-joke-is-that-Fox-News-terrorism-expert-advises-the-FBI.

Du Bois, W. E. B. 1903. *The Souls of Black Folk*. Chicago: A. C. McClurg.

Evans, Linda. 2005. "Playing Global Cop: U.S. Militarism and the Prison-Industrial Complex." In *Global Lockdown: Race, Gender, and the Prison-Industrial Complex*, edited by Julia Sudbury, 215–27. New York: Routledge.

Feldman, Keith. 2011. "Empire's Verticality: The Af/Pak Frontier, Visual Culture, and Racialization from Above." *Comparative American Studies* 9, no. 4: 325–41.

Fink, Steven. 2014. "Fear under Construction: Islamophobia within American Christian Zionism." *Islamophobia Studies Journal* 2, no. 1: 27–43.

Gessert, Charles R. 1974. " A Non-Arab Looks at an Anti-Arab-American Policy." In *The Civil Rights of Arab-Americans: The Special Measures*, edited by M. Cherif Bassiouni, 16–27. Belmont, MA: AAUG Press.

Grewal, Inderpal. 2014. "American Humanitarian Citizenship: The 'Soft' Power of Empire." In *Postcolonial Conflict Zones*, edited by Sandra Pnzanesi, 64–81. New York: Routledge.

Grosfoguel, Ramón, and Eric Mielants. 2006. "The Long-Durée Entanglement between Islamophobia and Racism in the Modern/Colonial Capitalist/Patriarchal World-System: An Introduction." *Human Architecture* 5, no. 1: 1–12.

Jarmakani, Amira. 2008. *Imagining Arab Womanhood: The Cultural Mythology of Veils, Harems, and Belly Dancers in the U.S.* New York: Palgrave.

———. 2015. *An Imperialist Love Story: Desert Romances and the War on Terror.* New York: New York Univ. Press.

Kapadia, Ronak. 2019. *Insurgent Aesthetics: Security and the Queer Life of the Forever War.* Durham, NC: Duke Univ. Press.

Kaplan, Amy. 2005. "Where Is Guantánamo?" *American Quarterly* 57, no. 3: 831–58.

König, Daniel G. 2018. "The Making of a Christian Atlantic: The Role of Islam in the Early Modern Emergence of 'the West.'" In *Entre mers—Outre-mer: Spaces, Modes, and Agents of Indo-Mediterranean Connectivity*, edited by Nikolas Jaspert and Sebastian Kolditz, 219–46. Heidelberg, Germany: Heidelberg Univ.

Mamdani, Mahmood. 2002. "Good Muslim, Bad Muslim: A Political Perspective on Culture and Terrorism." *American Anthropologist* 104, no. 3: 766–75.

———. 2004. *Good Muslim, Bad Muslim: America, the Cold War, and the Roots of Terror.* New York: Pantheon.

McAlister, Melani. [2001] 2005. *Epic Encounters: Culture, Media, and U.S. Interests in the Middle East 1945-2000.* Berkeley: Univ. of California Press.

———. 2007. "Left Behind and the Politics of Prophecy Talk." In *Exceptional State: Contemporary U.S. Culture and the New Imperialism*, edited by Ashley Dawson and Malini Johar Schueller, 191–220. Durham, NC: Duke Univ. Press.

McHeimech, Zeinab. 2016. "Slavery: North America." In *Encyclopedia of Women and Islamic Cultures*, supplement 13, edited by Suad Joseph. Leiden: Brill Online. At http://dx.doi.org/10.1163/1872-53209_ewic_COM_002047.

Miller, Andrea. 2017. "(Im)Material Terror: Incitement to Violence Discourse as Racializing Technology in the War on Terror." In *Life in the Age of Drone Warfare*, edited by Lisa Parks and Caren Kaplan, 112–33. Durham, NC: Duke Univ. Press.

Mitchell, Timothy. 2011. *Carbon Democracy: Political Power in the Age of Oil.* New York: Verso.

Naber, Nadine. 2008. "'Look, Mohammed the Terrorist Is Coming!': Cultural Racism, Nation-Based Racism, and the Intersectionality of Oppressions after 9/11."

In *Race and Arab Americans before and after 9/11: From Invisible Citizens to Visible Subjects*, edited by Amaney Jamal and Nadine Naber, 276–304. Syracuse, NY: Syracuse Univ. Press.

Naber, Nadine, and Junaid Rana. 2019. "The 21st Century Problem of Anti-Muslim Racism." *Jadaliyya*, July 25. At https://www.jadaliyya.com/Details/39830.

Nguyen, Nicole. 2019. *Suspect Communities: Anti-Muslim Racism and the Domestic War on Terror.* Minneapolis, MN: Univ. of Minnesota Press.

Obenzinger, Hilton. 1999. *American Palestine: Melville, Twain, and the Holy Land Mania.* Princeton, NJ: Princeton Univ. Press.

Parks, Lisa, and Caren Kaplan, eds. 2017. *Life in the Age of Drone Warfare.* Durham, NC: Duke Univ. Press.

Said, Edward. 1978. *Orientalism.* New York: Vintage Books.

———. [1981] 1997. *Covering Islam: How the Media and the Experts Determine How We See the Rest of the World.* New York: Pantheon.

Salaita, Steven. 2006. *The Holy Land in Transit: Colonialism and the Quest for Canaan.* Syracuse, NY: Syracuse Univ. Press.

———. 2016. *Inter/Nationalism: Decolonizing Native America and Palestine.* Minneapolis: Univ. of Minnesota Press.

Sheehi, Stephen. 2011. *Islamophobia: The Ideological Campaign against Muslims.* Atlanta, GA: Clarity Press.

Shohat, Ella. 2013. "The Sephardi-Moorish Atlantic: Between Orientalism and Occidentalism." In *Between the Middle East and the Americas: The Cultural Politics of Diaspora*, edited by Evelyn Alsultany and Ella Shohat, 42–64. Ann Arbor: Univ. of Michigan Press.

Spivak, Gayatri Chakravorty. 1993. "Can the Subaltern Speak?" In *Colonial Discourse and Post-colonial Theory: A Reader*, edited by Patrick Williams and Laura Chrisman, 66–111. Hemel Hempstead, UK: Harvester Press.

Stoler, Ann Laura. 2006. "Imperial Formations and the Opacities of Rule." In *Lessons of Empire: Imperial Histories and American Power*, edited by Craig Calhoun, Frederick Cooper, and Kevin M. Moore, 48–60. New York: New Press.

Stop LAPD Spying Coalition. 2013. "To Observe and to Suspect: A People's Audit of the Los Angeles Police Department's Special Order 1." Mar. 19. At https://stoplapdspying.org/wp-contents/uploads/2013/04/PEOPLES-AUDIT-UPDATED-APRIL-2-2013-A.pdf.

Szremski, Kristin. 2012. "Why Is 'Terror Expert' Attacking US Solidarity Groups?" *Electronic Intifada*, Jan. 5. At https://electronicintifada.net/content/why-terror-expert-attacking-us-solidarity-groups/10779.

US Senate. 1990. Immigration Act of 1990. S.358. 101st Cong., 2nd sess. At https://www.congress.gov/bill/101st-congress/senate-bill/358.

Wofford, Ben, and Caroline Kelly. 2016. "The Forgotten Government Plan to Round Up Muslims." *Politico*, Aug. 19.

Youmans, William. 2009. "Humor against Hegemony: Al-Hurra, Jokes, and the Limits of American Soft Power." *Middle East Journal of Culture and Communication* 2:76–99.

Zahzah, Yazan. 2020. "Warcare Economies: Countering Violent Extremism in San Diego." Master's thesis, San Diego State Univ.

28

Whose Homeland Security?

LOUISE CAINKAR

> On September 11, the wheel of history turned and the world will never be the same. . . . The attacks of September 11 were acts of terrorism against America orchestrated and carried out by individuals living within our borders. Today's terrorists enjoy the benefits of our free society even as they commit themselves to our destruction. They live in our communities—plotting, planning and waiting to kill Americans again.
>
> —Attorney General John Ashcroft, "September 11, 2001: Attack on America" (October 25, 2001)

Attorney General John Ashcroft's declaration that "the world will never be the same" was a prescient script for the United States government's actions after the 9/11 attacks, whether in the United States, the Arab and Muslim majority worlds, or other outposts of the global "war on terror." In the United States, the notion that terrorists were hiding in American communities just waiting to attack, living undercover lives that had public veneers of normalcy, provoked fear in the hearts of Americans and cast an air of suspicion on Arab and Muslim Americans. Government statements were clear in their directives: "The federal government cannot fight this reign of terror alone. Every American must help us defend our nation against this enemy" (Ashcroft 2001a). Since terrorists were alleged to be inconspicuously residing in "our" communities, the message was apparent: Arabs and Muslims in the United States should be closely observed and their seemingly normal activities should be treated as suspect. Arabs and Muslims, who understood their position as subjects of watchdogs in a panoptical world, were to be placed under a microscope by their non-Arab or non-Muslim neighbors. Study data show that social relationships between themselves, their neighbors, and strangers were commonly perceived by Arab Muslims to have changed into a new set of roles: one party was looking out for danger, while the other was forced to behave in ways that would demonstrate innocence.

The government's statements and pleas for help thus socially constructed Arabs and Muslims living in the United States as persons who were likely to be connected to the 9/11 attacks and other future acts of terrorism. They were people who, if not terrorists themselves, might be hiding terrorists or covering up their knowledge of brewing terrorist plots. So constructed, Arabs and Muslims in the United States were reconstituted as people who were not really part of the American nation; they were "them" and thus not fully eligible for the nation's package of civil and constitutional rights. In fact, they were often described as persons whose presence in the United States was intended to take advantage of these very rights in order to plot its destruction, as in the Ashcroft statement above. As a result of the way they

Excerpt from Louise Cainkar, "Whose Homeland Security?," in *Homeland Insecurity: The Arab American and Muslim American Experience after 9/11* (New York: Russell Sage Foundation, 2009), 110–52. A works cited list was added to the end of this chapter.

were being represented by the US government, many of the persons interviewed in this study were visited by law enforcement authorities because a neighbor or co-worker had reported them as acting in a suspicious manner—whether because they made overseas phone calls, because they opened their trunk frequently, or because of the way they dressed. Some reported being removed from airplanes or denied boarding; some lost their jobs; and some simply reported that life in the United States was no longer the same. These and other aspects of the post-9/11 Arab and Muslim experience . . . contributed to a sense of "homeland insecurity." This feeling abated over time but never really went away during the period of this study (2002–6).

This chapter [of *Homeland Insecurity*] focuses on federal government statements and policies implemented after the 9/11 attacks. At the same time as it asked the American public to watch out for suspicious behavior, the government crafted an extensive set of policies aimed at "trimming the haystack" to find the needle that "resists discovery" (Leiken 2004, 136). These measures included mass arrests, preventive detentions, FBI interviews, registration and fingerprinting of tens of thousands of male foreign nationals, widespread wiretapping, secret hearings, closures of charities, criminal indictments, and reviews of private Internet, telecommunication, and financial records, which were secured through more than thirty thousand national-security letters issued annually to American businesses after the passage of the USA PATRIOT Act (Cole 2006). These measures were directed almost solely against persons of Arab ethnicity or the Muslim faith. Their ongoing reportage effectively sent a message to the American people that ethnic and religious profiling was acceptable, even necessary, so long as it was directed at these groups.

In the end, few terrorists posing a threat to the United States were actually uncovered by these extraordinary efforts of the US government. Not a single person was convicted of a terrorist crime after eighty thousand domestic special registrations, five thousand preventive detentions, and tens of thousands of FBI interviews, activities referred to by the Georgetown law professor David Cole as the "most aggressive national campaign of ethnic profiling since World War II" (2006, 17). The US government claimed to have broken up domestic terrorist cells in Buffalo (Lackawanna), Detroit, Portland, Seattle, and northern Virginia, but it could never prove that any of these groups had plans to inflict damage in the United States. Only one of the groups, the "Lackawanna Six," had an al-Qaeda connection. This group of young Yemeni American men was not new to the government. They had been reported to the FBI months before the 9/11 attacks by an Arab Muslim neighbor, who learned of their plans to join an al-Qaeda training camp in Afghanistan in the spring of 2001. Shortly after arriving at the camp, some of the young men fled in fear, wanting nothing to do with what was going on there, while others finished training and later returned home (Purdy and Bergman 2003). They resumed their lives in Lackawanna and were under FBI observation and wiretapping. Although there was no evidence that they ever had plans to stage an attack, they were arrested in September 2002 and heralded with much publicity as the government's key homegrown terrorist find.

Criminal indictments in "terrorism-related" cases fared slightly better than the outcomes of FBI interviews, mass registrations, charity closures, and detentions without charge: more than four hundred post-9/11 indictments produced some two hundred convictions, very few of which, however, were for terrorism (Eggen and Tate 2005). In fact, only thirty-nine of these "terrorism-related" cases ended in convictions on terrorism charges, and the majority of these convictions were for "support" (encompassing a wide range of noncriminal activities) of a terrorist group, not for actual terrorist activities. The Syracuse-based Transactional Records Access Clearinghouse (TRAC 2003) found that the median sentence handed down in cases the Justice Department identified as "terrorism related" was fourteen days. New York University's Center on Law and Security (2005) found upon review of "terror-related" cases that there were "almost no convictions on charges reflecting dangerous crimes" (1). According to Cole (2006, 18), "several of the government's most prominent 'terrorist' cases have disintegrated under close scrutiny." While some have argued that the government's dragnet antiterror tactics had deterrent value, such value is as immeasurable as the claimed deterrent value of the death penalty.

The government's highly rhetorical public statements, its claims concerning its arrests and roundups of terrorists that would never be substantiated, and the sensationalized media coverage that accompanied each government action, all led the public to believe that the government was acting intelligently. The government's announcements and actions stoked public fears, while granting it the leeway it wanted to sidestep the rule of law. They appeared to confirm the notion that Arabs and Muslims living in the United States posed a collective danger to other Americans, therein encouraging public retaliation against any perceived group member. Although the 9/11 Commission (National Commission on Terrorist Attacks upon the United States 2004) found no evidence of Arab American or Muslim American knowledge of, participation in, or support for the 9/11 attacks, its conclusion was never really given much play in the American media or by the Bush administration. The commission found that the persons held responsible for the 9/11 attacks were visitors to the United States on a deadly mission who took pains to stay separate from Arab and Muslim American communities; federal law enforcement authorities acted on a wholly different set of premises. After "about half a million interviews," according to one former FBI special agent in charge of counterterrorism, some in government concluded that there was no one "who had they stepped forward could have provided a clue to help us get out in front of this."[1] The FBI interviews stigmatized Arab and Muslim Americans in the presence of onlookers, who were likely to presume that the visit had been spurred by something serious—something more than a name or a look, a suspicious neighbor, an overseas phone call, or a way of dressing.

Many policy analysts (and many Arab and Muslim Americans) argued at the time that Arab and Muslim American communities should be among the government's primary allies in its domestic antiterrorism work (see, for example, Chishti et al. 2003). Such a strategy would have required a very different perspective, one that, instead of collective suspicion built on stereotypes, presumed that Arab and Muslim Americans also cared about the lives of others.

Instead, Human Rights Watch (2002) found that Arabs and Muslims who volunteered to help the federal authorities sometimes ended up in indefinite, incommunicado detention. Such arrests were based not on data, but on presumptions of suspicion, grounded in the notion that persons of the Muslim faith or of Arab origins were security threats. Human Rights Watch (2005, 6) concluded in "Witness to Abuse" that needless incarcerations "aggravated distrust towards the government in Muslim communities in the United States that have been repeatedly targeted by sweeping, ill-advised, and at times illegal post–September 11 investigation, arrest, and detention policies." If it had been true that terrorists were lurking inside Arab and Muslim American communities, the government's strategies were counterproductive to finding them because they instilled a deep fear of government agents (Cainkar 2004). In sum, despite nearly unrestricted power, dragnet policies, a cooperative citizenry, and the evidentiary leeway permitted by secret evidence and secret hearings, the government's allegation that Arab and Muslim terrorists were lurking in our communities, "plotting, planning and waiting to kill Americans"—as Attorney General Ashcroft told the US Mayors Conference in October 2001—was never proven correct. Yet the nearly 100 percent rate of false positives during this domestic-security roundup period created extensive anxiety among Arabs and Muslims in the United States, producing an understanding that really anything goes. Their fundamental human right to personal security had been sacrificed, and each person knew it deeply on an individual level.

"Homeland Insecurity"

> Let the terrorists among us be warned: If you overstay your visa—even by one day—we will arrest you. If you violate a local law, you will be put in jail and kept in custody as long as possible. We will use every available statute. We will seek every prosecutorial advantage. We will use all our weapons within the law and under the Constitution to protect life and enhance security for America. Some will

1. Michael E. Rolince, former FBI special agent in charge of counterterrorism and section chief of the International Terrorism Operations Section, in a speech delivered at the workshop "Muslim–Law Enforcement Partnership," MPAC convention, Long Beach Convention Center, Long Beach, CA, December 17, 2005.

> ask whether a civilized nation—a nation of law and not of men—can use the law to defend itself from barbarians and remain civilized. Our answer, unequivocally, is "yes." Yes, we will defend civilization.
>
> —Attorney General John Ashcroft, "September 11, 2001: Attack on America" (October 25, 2001)

Substitute "Arab and Muslim men" for the word "terrorists" in this statement by Attorney General Ashcroft, and you have a proximate rendering of the US government's antiterrorism policies in the aftermath of the 9/11 attacks and certainly the way those policies were understood by Arab and Muslim men. In this statement invoking the language of the clash of civilizations, where terrorists, barbarians, visa violators, and local lawbreakers are defined as the same, the missing link is supplied by Arab and Muslim male noncitizens, the primary subjects of these particular government strategies. A close reading of John Ashcroft's language in his October 25, 2001, speech shows how Arab and Muslim men who were *at most* visa violators were transformed into terrorist suspects. The trick is located in the vague definition of "the law," the positioning of the word "or," and the linkage of this blurred language to terrorists:

> In the "war on terror," this Department of Justice will arrest and detain any suspected terrorist who has violated *the law*. Our single objective is to prevent terrorist attacks by taking *suspected terrorists* off the street. If suspects are found not to have links to terrorism *or* not to have violated the law, they are released. But *terrorists who are in violation of the law* will be convicted, in some cases deported, and in all cases prevented from doing further harm *to* Americans. (Ashcroft 2001a, emphasis added)

In the subsequent paragraph of this statement, Ashcroft is able to leverage this vague language to claim that nearly one thousand terrorist arrests had been made:

> Within days of the September 11 attacks, we launched this antiterrorism offensive to prevent new attacks on our homeland. To date, our antiterrorism offensive has arrested or detained *nearly 1,000 individuals* as part of the September 11 terrorism investigation. Those *who violated the law* remain in custody. Taking *suspected terrorists in violation of the law* off the streets and keeping them locked up is our clear strategy to prevent terrorism within our borders. (emphasis added)

In fact, these detainees were overwhelmingly Arab and Muslim men who were arrested on the basis of their looks or on reports of suspicion and who could not prove *at that moment* that their presence in the United States was legal. Once detained, they were largely unable to obtain release from prison until a host of government agencies proved that they were *not* terrorists—a very lengthy process—only after which visa violators were deported and others were released (Human Rights Watch 2002, 2005). In the end, *none* of these post-9/11 detainees was found to have terrorist connections (Cole 2003; Human Rights Watch 2002, 2005). Yet these statements by government officials offered the American public a grossly exaggerated sense of government accomplishment as well as of domestic threat. Government spokespersons simply latched on to popular stereotypes in existence long before 9/11, that Arabs and Muslims were monolithic and inherently violent, and put them to work.

That these ideas about Arabs and Muslims were already in place is evidenced in Attorney General Ashcroft's report at a September 18, 2001, press briefing, only seven days after the attacks:

> To date, the FBI has received more than 96,000 tips and potential leads: more than 54,000 on the website, nearly 9,000 on the hot line, the toll-free WATTS line, and more than 33,000 leads that were generated in the FBI field offices. (Ashcroft 2001b)

These tips and leads singled out innocent Arab and Muslim Americans—citizens, permanent residents, and visitors alike—as suspects. Persons who received law enforcement visits based on these tips reported that their allegedly suspicious actions pertained to normal activities interpreted by onlookers as suspicious—for example, unpacking the trunk of the car or opening the mailbox. The award-winning documentary *Persons of Interest* (Alison Maclean and Tobias Perse, 2004) reported on a man arrested because a postcard of the World Trade Center was taped to his deli counter *and* he was Arab, while Human Rights Watch (2002) reported the arrest of a man who, with his family, was taking tourist photos; these were among many other arrests based on profiling alone. Despite President Bush's (2001) statement on September 20 that "no one should be singled out for unfair treatment or unkind words because of their ethnic background or religious faith," the US government was engaging in precisely such actions. While Ashcroft asserted that the rule of law and the Constitution would be respected, the constitutionality of many post-9/11 government strategies was legally challenged (Cole 2006; Chang and Kabat 2004).

This study found that fear of government far outweighed any other post-9/11 fears among Arab Muslim Americans. Their sense of "homeland insecurity" was driven less by the public's hostile behavior than by the government's.[2] During my research, a substantial number of Arab Muslim Americans expressed worry that they might be rounded up and sent to internment camps by agents of the American government—especially if another attack occurred, an event over which they would have no control—and believed that the American government had the power and mass-media influence to auger popular support for such an action. From their perspective, "democracy" and "the rule of law" had become hollow phrases that government spokespersons deployed to defend targeting Arab and Muslim communities. These interlocutors felt that the rule of law did not apply to them and that the government could do whatever it wished with them with widespread popular approval. Their citizenship had been rendered meaningless. This perspective is expressed in the following quote from an interview with an Arab American woman:

> I lost trust in American values, to put it very simply. I no longer have the serene sense that I will always be safe here. I feel that being an American citizen is meaningless. That it doesn't really protect you in any way. It's an immense sense of danger, and I've never gotten over it. . . . I think the way I approach things made me less surefooted, less confident even about the future of our family here. Can you believe it? I came home and told my husband, shouldn't we be putting our money in banks overseas? Maybe one of these days we'll end up being in concentration camps.

An Arab American man articulates the sense of arbitrariness that characterized what he calls the American "police state" as he reflects on the possibility that Arab Americans would find themselves repeating the Japanese American experience with camps.

> I suffered, physically no, but mentally and psychologically yes. And I would say, not because I'm Palestinian-born. Primarily because I'm an American citizen—i.e., this is the land of the free, rule of the law, democracy, etc.—and suddenly it became a police state. Human rights, laws, protection against individual [individual protections], and so on, are out of the window. Everybody becomes a target, for whatever reason the government decides. It doesn't have to be just violations. An edict by somebody in an office makes your life in jeopardy. It did affect me as a Palestinian in that the police state that prevailed after 9/11 reminded me of what happened to the Japanese in this country.

Few persons interviewed in this study said that their lives were unchanged after 9/11. A majority reported a sense of living on the edge in the United States, with lingering fears of government policies that might force their expulsion or internment. At the same time, there was broad recognition that the climate for their treatment as enemies of the United States had been established long before 9/11; as this Arab American woman notes, even American-born Arabs were viewed as foreigners:

> The attitude and outlook was always there, it was just exaggerated, making you feel like you're the enemy, that you're the bad one, and you're definitely a foreigner and do not belong in this country, when

2. Limited interviews with Arab American Christians produced the same findings because post-9/11 US government policies targeting Arabs did not distinguish between Christians and Muslims.

> I was born and raised in this country, and I'm just as much an American as anyone else. I feel like maybe I need to get the hell out of this country because something bad is going to happen to our people here. It's a horrible feeling.

This sense of uncertainty led many interviewees to take steps to protect themselves and their families; some sent their college-bound children to schools outside of the United States, for instance, and some accelerated their efforts to build a home overseas. Indeed, a November 2002 survey by the Chicago-based Muslim Civil Rights Center found that 25 percent of immigrant respondents reported seriously considering moving to their country of origin because of the post-9/11 climate. Some Arab and Muslim American families did choose to leave the United States, while others were forced to leave by the government policies enumerated in this chapter. Most, however, decided to wait and see what the American experience had in store for them.

> I don't feel this is a safe place. I don't know if I will be here in ten years, whereas at the beginning I had established that I was going to be here in this country. . . . I don't know what I'm going to do, because this is the country where I thought I would stay and that my daughter will grow up here. . . . I do not know what will happen to us here. Who knows what will happen to us here?

These findings about fear of the government and the abrogation of the rule of law have been replicated in other studies. The Vera Institute of Justice's national study of Arab Americans found that community members "expressed greater concern about being victimized by federal policies and practices than by individual acts of harassment" (Henderson et al. 2006, 184). Sally Howell and Andrew Shryock (2003, 449) report that government policies created "a climate in which Middle Easterners and South Asians in the U.S. can be treated as a special population to whom certain legal protections and civil rights no longer apply." Under such conditions, the homeland, whether adopted or by birth, was a very insecure place to live.

Government Domestic-Security Policies after 9/11

The rest of this chapter offers an inventory of some of the American government's known domestic-security policies following the 9/11 attacks, the methods by which these policies were used to target Arab and Muslim American communities, and their impacts. . . . After examining these policies, we look at some of the social-psychological outcomes of the government's secret surveillance on Arab and Muslim Americans. . . . Most of the government's post-9/11 national-security policies were designed and carried out by the executive branch of government with little or no a priori public discussion or debate. Twenty-five of the thirty-seven known US government security initiatives implemented in the first two years after the September 11 attacks either explicitly or implicitly targeted Arabs and Muslims living in the United States, who were singled out by the government as one conflated group (Tsao and Gutierrez 2003). These measures included mass arrests, secret and indefinite detentions, prolonged detention of "material witnesses," closed hearings and the use of secret evidence, government eavesdropping on attorney–client conversations, FBI home and work visits, wiretapping, seizures of property, removals of aliens with technical visa violations, freezing the assets of charities, and mandatory special registration. I have argued conservatively that at least two hundred thousand Arabs and Muslims living in the United States directly experienced one of these measures. Others, including the FBI agent quoted earlier, have cited much larger figures. The most severe measures were taken against noncitizens, who were accorded a lesser set of rights than Arab and Muslim American citizens and permanent residents, whose treatment, in turn, fell below the standard most would consider acceptable for US citizens.

Mass Arrests

The first to be caught in the post-9/11 "investigation dragnet" were some 1,200 Arab or Muslim males (presumably noncitizens) who were arrested shortly after the attacks and detained under high-security conditions. The exact identities and individual fates of these detainees are not known because the federal government has to this date (2008) refused to release specific information about them. . . . Males who matched an Arab/Muslim phenotype and were determined for any reason (or no reason) to be suspicious were the first to be locked up, *after* which the government looked for violations with which to charge them (Cole 2003). Being unable to prove legal residence in the United States at the moment of contact was a sufficient condition. Arab and Muslim men seen in rental cars or observed taking photos of buildings or tourist sites were arrested by government agents and eventually jailed for months as "persons of interest"—that is, as potential security threats. Detainees could not be released (or deported) until they were cleared of terrorist connections, a process that took many months. Attorney General Ashcroft announced a rule change on September 18, 2001, that gave government largely unlimited time to find and press charges on persons it had detained by expanding "the twenty four-hour time period to forty-eight hours, or to an additional reasonable time if necessary under an emergency or in other extraordinary circumstances" (Ashcroft 2001b). On September 21, 2001, in a document known as the Creppy memo, Ashcroft ordered that every immigration hearing designated "of special interest" be held in secret (Cole 2003). By 2003, it was assumed that most of these early detainees had been released and that at least five hundred had been deported. Deportations were based on violations of immigration law, and one [detainee] had to be cleared of terrorist connections to be deported. . . . The government netted not a single terrorist suspect from this dragnet operation.

Human Rights Watch (2002, 2005) issued two major investigative reports concerning these post-9/11 arrests. In its first report, "Presumption of Guilt" (Human Rights Watch 2002, 12), it found that government agents used stereotypes to determine who to arrest; "being a male Muslim non-citizen from certain countries became a proxy for suspicious behavior." Some men were incarcerated "simply because spouses, neighbors, or members of the public said they were 'suspicious' or accused them without any credible basis of being terrorists" (12). The Human Rights Watch report concluded: "Operating behind a wall of secrecy, the U.S. Department of Justice thrust scores of Muslim men living in the United States into a Kafkaesque world of indefinite detention without charges and baseless accusations of terrorist links." . . .

Human Rights Watch's second report, "Witness to Abuse" (2005), coauthored by the American Civil Liberties Union (ACLU), reported on its investigation of the cases of seventy persons it was able to locate who were picked up during this period and held on "material witness" charges. Its interviews uncovered aggressive armed arrests and persistent denials of due process rights. . . . Interviews also uncovered repeated verbal abuse and physical deprivation during extensive periods of incarceration and frequent use of leg chains, solitary confinement, and banging on cells all night. Some detainees reported recurring strip searches and intentional physical cruelty. These abuses were also investigated by the Justice Department's Office of the Inspector General (2003), which found that intense psychological pressure was used on suspects to extract confessions. . . . The Office of the Inspector General's (2003, 45) investigation of the treatment of post-9/11 detainees at the Metropolitan Detention Center in Brooklyn found a pattern of "unnecessary" body searches that appeared "intended to punish"; they were conducted in the presence of women and filmed in their entirety. . . .

These types of repeated, invasive strip searches were not serving security purposes; rather, they were degradation ceremonies intended to emasculate. Their repeated use on Arab and Muslim men in American custody became somewhat characteristic of the post-9/11 world, whether in New York, Abu Ghraib, Iraq, Guantánamo, or elsewhere. The additional features of female onlookers and filming suggest that extra efforts were made to intensify the humiliation based on shared understandings of Arab/Muslim culture: that these aspects would increase the detainee's pain by adding public shame.

Once released from jail, many of these so-called persons of interest found that they had been imprinted with a terrorist stigma, which made putting their lives back together extremely difficult. Among those who remained in the United States, follow-up investigative reports indicated that former detainees were shunned by clients, customers, coworkers, and fellow community members. Arab and Muslim Americans feared that a simple contact with a former suspect might render them the next person to disappear indefinitely in the hands of the American government and its web of prisons. Under the USA PATRIOT Act and in consort with aggressive federal agents and prosecutors, "contact" was used as evidence of aiding and abetting terrorism. Some former detainees intending to stay eventually left the United States because they could not reconstruct their lives—as in the case of the sensationally covered but wrongfully arrested "Evansville Eight." Human Rights Watch (2005, 98) provided the following account of Tarek Albasti, an Egyptian national arrested as a material witness in October 2001 as one of the Eight, a group that eventually received a government apology for the wrongful arrests:

> After we were released we were in hell, you tell yourself, okay, well they released us so everyone should understand we are innocent, but that was not the case. Because I mean there are some people who support you and stuff like this but everyone is curious: did you snitch on somebody else, or did you make a deal with the government, or why were you released, or did you really do something or not. It's just like all this doubt in people's mind. . . .

These arbitrary arrests signaled early on to Arab and Muslim Americans (both citizens and noncitizens) that American legal protections were easily circumvented and did not apply to them. In fact, it was the very secrecy and lack of transparency in these arrests that sparked fear in members of these communities. This fear was augmented by the statements of government officials: by referring to detainees as "terrorists," "suspected terrorists," and "barbarians," they seemed to ensure that there would be little public outcry over any action the government took. Taken together, these measures produced a frightening world for Arab and Muslim Americans.

The USA PATRIOT Act

On October 24, 2001, the US Congress passed the executive-branch-crafted USA PATRIOT (Uniting and Strengthening America by Providing Appropriate Tools Required to Intercept and Obstruct Terrorism) Act of 2001; President Bush signed it into law two days later (P.L. 107-56). Under intense pressure from Attorney General Ashcroft, who used the rhetoric of fear in his speech to Congress, the act was quickly passed through the circumvention of normal congressional procedures; only a few congresspeople had read the act in its entirety (Cole and Dempsey 2002). . . . Among a host of other provisions, the USA PATRIOT Act expanded the power of the US government to use surveillance and wiretapping without first showing probable cause, permitted secret searches and access to private records by government agents without oversight, authorized the detention of immigrants on alleged suspicions and the denial of admission to the United States based on a person's speech, and expanded the concept of guilt by association. . . .

These PATRIOT Act surveillance provisions sent a major chill through American Arab and Muslim communities and were another feature of the social context that caused many interviewees to feel unsafe in the United States. We return to this impact later when discussing how these laws in combination with the *feeling of being watched* produced in many Arab and Muslim Americans a type of double-consciousness (Du Bois [1903] 1995; Fanon 1963), a state in which they were watching themselves being watched by others.

Visa Holds

In an effort to gain control over the types of persons entering the United States from Arab and Muslim-majority countries, the State Department issued a classified cable in October 2001 imposing a mandatory twenty-day hold on all nonimmigrant visa applications submitted by men ages eighteen to forty-five from twenty-six (mostly Arab or Muslim-majority) countries, subjecting them to special security clearance. Over time their applications required approval in Washington, with no time limit imposed on the response. The impact of this policy was extensive and received substantial media attention. Foreign students were unable to return to school in the United States; professors, researchers, and Fulbright Scholars requiring nonimmigrant visas missed one to two semesters of university work; medical and chemotherapy patients being treated at facilities like the Mayo and Cleveland Clinics were forced out of their treatment cycles; and artists, musicians, and businessmen were forced to break contracts they had signed.

FBI Interviews

In November 2001, the Justice Department announced its intention to interview some five thousand individuals who had come to the United States from Arab and Muslim-majority countries since January 1, 2000, on nonimmigrant visas. It later announced a second round of interviews with an additional three thousand persons and then a third round with thousands of Iraqis living in the United States, including persons granted refugee status. The actual number of domestic-security interviews that were conducted with US citizens and noncitizens is unknown. John Tirman (2005), director of the Center for International Studies at MIT, estimated in April 2005 that the FBI had conducted at least two hundred thousand interviews. Retired FBI agent [Michael] Rolince, in charge of counterterrorism, spoke of some half a million interviews. Study interlocutors spoke about the disruptions and apprehension caused by the FBI interviews as well as about what was perceived as the FBI's unprofessional ways of getting information—offering to pay people to spy on others or blackmailing them into cooperating. . . . Many interviewees stressed that if they had learned of anything harmful to the United States, they would have been willing informants because this was their country too. Their lack of any such reporting was interpreted by the government, however, as indicating not an absence of terrorist plots but complicity in them.

The Absconders Initiative

In January 2002, the Immigration and Naturalization Service (INS) launched the "absconders initiative" to track down and deport 6,000 noncitizen males from (unnamed) "Middle Eastern" countries who had been ordered deported (usually for overstaying a visa) by an immigration judge but had never left the United States. At the time there were an estimated 314,000 so-called absconders in the United States, the vast majority from Latinx countries. Although fewer than 2 percent were "Middle Eastern," the government's ethnic profiling targeted this group. By May of the same year, the Justice Department reported that 585 "Middle Eastern" absconders had been caught, and a year later it reported that 1,100 persons had been detained under this initiative (Cole 2003).

The Enhanced Border Security and Visa Entry Reform Act and Other Border and Domestic Immigration-Control Procedures

On May 14, 2002, Congress passed the Enhanced Border Security and Visa Entry Reform Act. Among the many provisions of this act—which calls for the integration of INS databases, the development of machine-readable visas, the requirement that all airlines submit to US authorities a list of passengers who have boarded any plane bound for the United States, and stricter monitoring of foreign students—is a restriction on nonimmigrant visas for individuals from countries identified by the State Department as state sponsors of terrorism. In late June 2002, the Department of Justice issued an internal memo to the INS and to US Customs requesting that these two agencies seek out and search all Yemenis, including American citizens, entering the United States. Reports circulated that Yemeni Americans were being removed from planes and boarding lines and having to wait hours for security clearances. On July 14, 2002, the INS announced that it would begin enforcing section 265(a) of the Immigration and Nationality Act, which requires all aliens to register changes of address within ten days of moving. . . . Shortly thereafter, a Palestinian legal immigrant in North Carolina who was stopped for driving four miles over the speed limit was detained for two months and then charged with a misdemeanor for failing to report his address change. The INS was seeking his deportation, but a local immigration judge ruled that he could not be deported for this infraction because he did not willfully break this law. The policy change concerning enforcement of section 265(a) ultimately led to the special registration program for Arab and Muslim men.

The Special Registration Program

On September 11, 2002, the Immigration and Naturalization Service implemented the "special registration" program, which required "certain non-immigrant aliens" to register with the US immigration authorities, be fingerprinted and photographed, respond to questioning, and submit to routine reporting. The program was rolled out in phases and had both port-of-entry and domestic call-in components. [*Homeland Insecurity* provides extensive analysis of this program and its legal history.] Persons covered by the program were citizens and nationals of Iran, Iraq, Libya, Syria, Sudan, Afghanistan, Algeria, Bahrain, Eritrea, Lebanon, Morocco, North Korea, Oman, Qatar, Somalia, Tunisia, United Arab Emirates, Yemen, Pakistan, Saudi Arabia, Jordan, Kuwait, Bangladesh, Egypt, and Indonesia.

The special registration program (eventually renamed NSEERS, for National Security Entry and Exit Registry System) had a massive impact on Arab and Muslim American communities. Because the program worked by country of nationality and citizenship, the swoop included Muslims, Christians, Jews, and Baha'is, among others. According to the Department of Homeland Security, between September 11, 2002, and June 1, 2003, 127,694 men were initially registered at their US port of entry, and another 82,880 were registered in domestic call-in registration. Removal (deportation) orders were issued for 13,434 of the latter group, who had visa irregularities, although all were cleared of connections to terrorism. The number of Arabs, Muslims, and others from Muslim-majority countries eventually deported from the nearly 13,500 ordered deported under this program is not known, nor do we know the number of family members they took with them. Even prior to special registration, more Arabs and Muslims (none accused of terrorist connections) had been removed from the United States since the September 11 attacks than the number of foreign nationals deported for their political beliefs following the infamous 1919 Palmer Raids (Gourevitch 2003). The potential of an additional 13,000 deportees rounded up for visa violations through the special registration has few historic precedents, except for perhaps Operation Wetback of the 1950s, when more than 1 million US citizens and noncitizens of Mexican descent were deported to Mexico.

Thousands of Arab, Iranian, African, and South Asian families with a member whose immigration status was irregular left the country permanently rather than be subjected to registration, a pattern that particularly characterized the Pakistani American community. While the INS had estimated that 15,000 Pakistanis would be subject to call-in registration, the Pakistani embassy estimated the number at 65,000. In 2002 and 2003, FOR SALE signs were widely evident in Chicago's Pakistani neighborhoods, and many families were reported to have sold their homes at great financial loss. One Chicago attorney with Pakistani clients told me in March 2003: "I advise my clients who have no hope to adjust their status to leave with dignity before the registration program ends. They can't imagine that Americans would want to deport them. The dream of America is over for them. The only other option is to live as a psychological fugitive."

"Hey, Arab and Muslim Man: This Notice Is for You"

Domestic "call-in" registration for nonimmigrants already in the United States was implemented on November 6, 2002, when Attorney General Ashcroft published a call-in notice in the *Federal Register* for "certain visiting citizens and nationals" of Iran, Iraq, Libya, Syria, and the Sudan who had entered the United States and been inspected by the INS prior to September 11, 2002. . . . Since the *Federal Register* is not a commonly read publication, the INS produced flyers to advertise the call-in program with "THIS NOTICE IS FOR YOU" splayed across the top, eerily reminiscent of the notices posted for Japanese living in the western United States during World War II. . . . Upon appearing at an INS office, persons who reported for call-in special registration were required to: answer questions under oath before an immigration officer, who recorded them; present all travel documents, passports, and an I-94; present all government-issued identification; present proof of residence, including land title, lease, or rental agreement; present proof of matriculation at an educational institution or proof of employment, as required by the visa; and provide "such other information as is requested by the immigration officer." They were also subject to all of the other special registration requirements for port-of-entry registration, such as reporting in person annually, reporting changes of address within ten days, and undergoing exit registry upon departure. Willful noncompliers were subject to criminal charges, fines, and removal.

Attorney General Ashcroft amended the Code of Federal Regulations (CFR) to declare the willful failure to register and provide full and truthful disclosure of information a failure to maintain nonimmigrant status—a deportable offense. . . . The arrest and detention of hundreds of registrants, mostly Iranians, in southern California during this first period of special registration sparked nationwide protest as persons voluntarily acting in compliance with the new rules were handcuffed and led off to jail for visa violations. Some reported sleeping on concrete floors in rooms holding up to fifty prisoners. Others reported verbal abuse and strip and body-cavity searches. The director of the southern California chapter of the ACLU said the arrests were "reminiscent of the internment of Japanese Americans during World War II" (*BBC News Online* 2002). . . .

In the end, special registration was nothing short of a massive roundup of male Arab, African, and Asian foreign nationals from predominantly Muslim countries. While it launched the potential removal of some 13,400 of these men from the United States—the 16 percent of registrants who may have been out of legal immigration status, many of whom were placed in detention—it produced no terrorists. Indeed, it revealed an incredibly law-abiding population in which fewer than 1 percent of 80,000 registered men could be tarred with any record of predatory criminal activity. . . .

Policies Guided by Racialized Stereotypes

Homeland security policies cast a net so broadly and indiscriminately over Arab and Muslim men it is clear that they were guided by stereotypes rather than concrete information. . . . Over a period of decades, by commission and omission, interested parties, the mainstream media, and government officials helped to produce a common American understanding that Arabs, and later Muslims, were mostly, and almost innately, about violence and hatred of Americans. "Arabness" and being Muslim were put forth as nearly insurmountable genetic essences and collectively shared cultural systems that stood in opposition to American values and interests. Scores of scholars and pundits perpetuated this image with their own evidence of the existence of a generic Arab and Muslim "rage" (Said [1981] 1997).

Criticism of American foreign policies in the Arab world was equated with support for terrorism. Since the late 1960s, American government resources vis-à-vis these communities were used largely to silence their dissent. Law-abiding community members who criticized American foreign policies were criminalized. American government agencies focused their time and resources on wiretapping, interviewing, spying, banning, charging, and trying to deport Arab and Muslim Americans who were engaged in building nonviolent opposition to American foreign policies (Bassiouni 1974; Butterfield 1999; Akram and Johnson 2004). This history created the conditions for which government agents made no distinction between Arabs and Muslims living in the United States and persons who actually posed a threat to the United States. They were one and the same. . . . After the 9/11 attacks, the American government admitted that it knew almost nothing about Arab and Muslim American communities or about where to look for potential terrorists, and so, armed only with racialized stereotypes, it engaged in dragnet behavior.

At the intersection of the government's ignorance of the lives of Arab and Muslim Americans and the availability of a handy toolbox of stereotypes that endorsed the appropriateness of racial and religious profiling, a relationship between the 9/11 attackers and Arab and Muslim Americans was constructed and acted upon. These racialized notions, not information, guided the government's post-9/11 homeland security policies. After the most comprehensive and visible of the post-9/11 policies had run their course, government agencies commenced with a new approach, one of community engagement, although many at the top in Washington and many among Arab and Muslim Americans were never particularly convinced of its value. Throughout all these periods, silent spotlights focused on members of these communities have remained in place.

The Deceptive Calm of Surveillance

By late 2003, high-profile government activity in Arab and Muslim American communities appeared to slow down. Mass arrests and special registration had ended, and thousands of visa violators had been expelled from or left the United States (often accompanied by their US citizen family members). In January 2003, FBI director Robert Mueller ordered his field offices to develop wiretapping and undercover activity goals according to the number of mosques in the field area, thus shining hidden (and not so hidden, according to community members) spotlights on geographic areas with concentrations of Muslims (Isikoff 2003). There were still sensationalized arrests that more often than not fizzled into nonterrorism cases (Chang and Kabat 2004; but see Peled 2018), closures of Muslim charitable institutions, and documented patterns of delays in immigration and naturalization processing (CAIR-Chicago 2007). In his State of the Union Address, President Bush (2003) spoke of suspected terrorists around the world meeting with arrest or other unspecified fates—"Let's put it this way: They are no longer a problem to the United States and our friends and allies"—leaving little doubt that the rule of law was still elusive. The everyday concerns of Arab Americans turned to more subtle government security measures, like being watched, secretly wiretapped, or clandestinely searched. An Arab American woman describes this state of deceptive calm:

> Yeah. I mean, after September 11, I don't think anybody felt safe, not anyone in general. Nobody felt safe, but Muslims definitely did not feel safe. It's been a couple of years now, so people feel less of the fear and the shock than they did afterwards. I don't feel that somebody's going to physically hurt me. As far as infringing on my privacy, that's a different story. It's pretty much given that all our phone calls are tapped and our e-mails are read and all that stuff. Who knows if people watch us or not? We don't even know exactly what's happening, but we're very much aware that tabs are being kept on us to make sure that we're not doing anything anti-American.

Similarly, an Arab American man describes his compromised sense of safety as a loss of personal privacy:

> I guess I feel safe. Anyone could be at the house, you know. Anybody could get the key from the manager and get in my house if they want to check sometime in the house. I'm not talking about stealing, you know. The PATRIOT Act allows it, so I don't know if they were there or not. They can come even if I don't know it. They have the ability to come. It doesn't matter, because I have nothing to hide.

Arab Muslims described conducting routine activities with the sense that they might be watched. This double-consciousness (Du Bois [1903] 1995) is qualitatively different from the certainty of being watched. W. E. B. Du Bois expressed it as "this sense of always looking at one's self through the eyes of others" (45). Nadine Naber (2006) describes this phenomenon as "internment of the psyche," as the disciplinary effects of the state penetrate everyday actions. Hatem Bazian (2004) has argued that internment camps are unnecessary when people can be virtually interned, their every movement watched, their every sentence recorded, their every transaction noted by hidden cameras, microphones, internet tapping, and compilation of phone, bank, credit card, and library records. The government's power and secrecy and its call for citizens to be watching their Arab and Muslim neighbors produced a psychological state in which few ever felt fully safe or secure. Round-the-clock double-consciousness constructs a psychological jail.

> I think it affected the quality of my personal life and in terms of being connected to the broader community (other than Arab). Because I feel that the Arabs became labeled and I feel that it put us kind of on the defensive mode in trying to explain ourselves, that we're not "The Them" whatever "Them" was. I feel that has an impact on the quality of life, so the kids, when they go to school, the issues they had to deal

> with in terms of how Arabs were and are stereotyped and perceived. . . . It was like, we'd be standing out there to get the mail, you know, it was kind of like, "look what you people did to us." . . . I think people monitor themselves much closer because there's an issue going on presently in terms of who is a terrorist. Those are the issues that as Arabs, we feel a lot of pressure.

In May 2004, Attorney General Ashcroft and FBI director Mueller announced an intensification of domestic antiterrorism activity, although they said they had no new intelligence concerning a threat and were not raising the nation's terror-threat level. Another round of FBI interviews was announced, references were made to securing the upcoming 2004 elections, and the American public was kept on fear-alert and asked to be "extra vigilant about their surroundings, neighbors, and any suspicious activity." This initiative, later revealed as Operation Front Line, a multiagency effort spearheaded by Immigration and Customs Enforcement (ICE) that used the new NSEERS, SEIS (Student and Exchange Information System), and US-VISIT databases to identify targets, led to 2,556 investigations and 504 arrests of persons largely from Arab- and Muslim-majority countries; none was charged with a terrorism-related crime (Lichtblau 2008; Yale Law School and ADC 2008). . . .

Conclusion

National narratives of the tragedy of 9/11 speak to the grave injury that these violent attacks and the thousands of deaths caused by them delivered to the American nation and people, but these narratives largely exclude the related experiences of millions of Arab and Muslim Americans (who, according to some sources, died in disproportionate numbers on 9/11). Their experiences are instead found in a second body of literature: the reports of civil liberties defenders, hate-crimes reporters, attorneys, activists, and scholars who have documented the rights violations, assaults, and harassments they endured in the wake of the 9/11 attacks. These two separate narratives about the impact of 9/11 on American society seem to mirror the American government's concept of homeland security after the attacks: there was a de facto and often de jure dichotomy between persons who were part of "the homeland" and whose safety and rights were being protected and another group excluded from "the homeland" whose safety and rights were revocable. Arab and Muslim Americans and the immigrants within their communities observed that their rights and security were sacrificed so the rest of the nation could feel safer. This effective dichotomization of the American population also gave a green light to the violent expressions of bigots, who signaled this understanding of ingroups and outgroups by the flag waving that so commonly accompanied harassments of Arab and Muslim Americans after 9/11. This examination of the activities undertaken by the US Departments of Justice and Homeland Security and other federal agencies to preserve "our freedoms" in the years following the 9/11 attacks reveals that the rights of Arab and Muslims Americans, who were cast as threatening foreigners, were sacrificed for the freedoms of another set of Americans.

Works Cited

Akram, Susan M., and Kevin R. Johnson. 2004. "Race and Civil Rights pre–September 11, 2001: The Targeting of Arabs and Muslims." In *Civil Rights in Peril: The Targeting of Arabs and Muslims*, edited by Elaine C. Hagopian, 9–26. Chicago: Haymarket Books.

Ashcroft, John. 2001a. "September 11, 2001: Attack on America." Prepared remarks for the US Conference of Mayors, Oct. 25. Avalon Project, Yale Law School. At http://avalon.law.yale.edu/sept11/doj_brief003.asp.

———. 2001b. "September 11, 2001: Attack on America: Attorney General Remarks; September 18, 2001." Press briefing, FBI headquarters. At http://avalon.law.yale.edu/sept11/doj_brief020.asap.

Bassiouni, M. Cherif, ed. 1974. *The Civil Rights of Arab-Americans: The Special Measures*. Belmont, MA: AAUG Press.

Bazian, Hatem. 2004. "Virtual Internment: Arabs, Muslims, Asians, and the War on Terrorism." *Journal of Islamic Law and Culture* 9, no. 1: 1–26.

BBC News Online. 2002. "Mass Arrest of Muslims in LA." Dec. 19. At http//news.bbc.co.uk/2/Americas/2589317.stm.

Bush, George W. 2001. "President Declares 'Freedom at War with Fear': Address to a Joint Session of Congress and the American People." Sept. 20. At http://archives.cnn.com/2011/US/09.20/gen.bush.transcript.

———. 2003. "State of the Union Address." At http://www.cnn.com/2003/ALLPOLITICS/01/28/sotu.transcript.

Butterfield, Jeanne A. 1999. "Do Immigrants Have First Amendment Rights?" *Middle East Report* 212:4–7.

Cainkar, Louise. 2004. "US Muslim Leaders and Activists Evaluate post 9/11 Domestic Security Policies." Background paper. Reframing the Challenge of Migration and Security, Social Science Research Council. At http://programs.ssrc.org/gsc/publications/gsc_activities/migration/cainkar.pdf.

CAIR-Chicago. 2017. "Citizenship Delays Were Top Issue for U.S. Muslims in 2006." At https://www.cairchicago.org/blog/blog/2007/06/report-citizenship-delays-were-top-issue-for-u-s-muslims-in-2006.

Chang, Nancy, and Alan Kabat. 2004. *Summary of Recent Court Rulings on Terrorism-Related Matters Having Civil Liberties Implications*. New York: Center for Constitutional Rights.

Chishti, Muzaffar A., Doris Meissner, Demetrios G. Papademetriou, Jay Peterzell, Michael J. Wishnie, and Stephen W. Yale-Loehr. 2003. *America's Challenge: Domestic Security, Civil Liberty, and National Unity after September 11*. Washington, DC: Migration Policy Institute.

Cole, David. 2003. *Enemy Aliens*. New York: New Press.

———. 2006. "Are We Safer?" *New York Review of Books* 53, no. 4: 15–18.

Cole, David, and James Dempsey. 2002. *Terrorism and the Constitution: Sacrificing Civil Liberties in the Name of National Security*. New York: New Press.

Du Bois, W. E. B. [1903] 1995. *The Souls of Black Folk: Essays and Sketches*. New York: Signet.

Eggen, Dan, and Julie Tate. 2005. "U.S. Campaign Produces Few Connections on Terrorism Charges." *Washington Post*, June 12.

Fanon, Frantz. 1963. *The Wretched of the Earth*. Translated by Constance Farrington. Oxford: Oxford Univ. Press. Orig. pub. in French in 1961.

Gourevitch, Alex. 2003. "Detention Disorder." *American Prospect*, Jan. 31. At http://www.prospect.org/cs/articles?article=detention_disorder.

Henderson, Nicole, Christopher W. Ortiz, Naomi F. Sugie, and Joel Miller. 2006. *Law Enforcement and Arab American Community Relations after September 11, 2001*. New York: Vera Institute of Justice.

Howell, Sally, and Andrew Shryock. 2003. "Cracking Down on Diaspora: Arab Detroit and America's 'War on Terror.'" *Anthropological Quarterly* 76, no. 3: 443–62.

Human Rights Watch. 2002. "Presumption of Guilt: Human Rights Abuses of post–September 11 Detainees." *Human Rights Watch* 14, no. 4: 3–95.

———. 2005. "Witness to Abuse: Human Rights Abuses under the Material Witness Law since September 11." *Human Rights Watch* 97, no. 2: 1–100.

Isikoff, Michael. 2003. "The FBI Says, Count the Mosques." *Newsweek*, Feb. 3.

Leiken, Robert S. 2004. *Bearers of Global Jihad? Immigration and National Security after 9/11*. Washington, DC: Nixon Center.

Lichtblau, Eric. 2008. "Inquiry Targeted 2,000 Foreign Muslims in 2004." *New York Times*, Oct. 30. At http://www.nytimes.com/2008/10/31/us/31inquire.html.

Naber, Nadine. 2006. "The Rules of Forced Engagement: Race, Gender, and the Culture of Fear among Arab Immigrants in San Francisco post-9/11." *Cultural Dynamics* 18, no. 3: 235–67.

National Commission on Terrorist Attacks upon the United States. 2004. *The 9/11 Commission Report: Final Report of the National Commission on Terrorist Attacks upon the United States*. New York: Norton.

New York University, Center on Law and Security. 2005. *Terrorist Trials: A Report Card*. New York: Center on Law and Security, New York University School of Law.

Office of the Inspector General. 2003. *Supplemental Report on September 11 Detainees' Allegations of Abuse at the Metropolitan Detention Center in Brooklyn, NY*. Washington, DC: Office of the Inspector General.

Peled, Miko. 2018. *Injustice: The Story of the Holy Land Five*. Charlottesville, VA: Just World Books.

Purdy, Mathew, and Lowell Bergman. 2003. "Unclear Danger: Inside the Lackawanna Terror Case." *New York Times*, Oct. 12.

Said, Edward W. [1981] 1997. *Covering Islam: How the Media and the Experts Determine How We See the Rest of the World*. Rev. ed. New York: Vintage Books.

Tirman, John. 2005. "Security the Progressive Way." *Nation*, Apr. 11.

Transactional Records Access Clearinghouse (TRAC). 2003. *Criminal Terrorism Enforcement since the 9/11/01 Attacks*. Syracuse, NY: TRAC.

Tsao, Fred, and Rhoda Rae Gutierrez. 2003. *Losing Ground: The Loss of Freedom, Equality, and Opportunity for America's Immigrants since the September 11 Attacks*. Chicago: Illinois Coalition for Immigrant and Refugee Rights.

Yale Law School and the American-Arab Anti-Discrimination Committee. 2008. "Joint Press Release: ICE Targets Immigrants from Muslim Majority Countries prior to 2004." At http://www.adc.org/PDF/frontline.pdf.

29

Introduction to *This Muslim American Life*

Dispatches from the War on Terror

MOUSTAFA BAYOUMI

In August 2011, almost exactly ten years after the terrorist attacks of 2001, the Associated Press published an article titled "With CIA Help, NYPD Moves Covertly in Muslim Areas." The article's authors, Matt Apuzzo and Adam Goldman, described how the New York Police Department was working with officials "on loan" from the CIA to develop a massive and covert surveillance program that directly targeted the entire Muslim community in and around New York City. Initially, the NYPD flatly denied the reporters' findings. "Someone has a great imagination," NYPD spokesman Paul Browne said (Apuzzo and Goldman 2011). The AP then posted on their website a trove of leaked internal documents from the police department that proved not only the existence of the program but also that the department felt free to lie outright to its public about its actions. Veteran police reporter Len Levitt also gained access to internal documents and on September 5 published an article (reprinted two days later by the *Huffington Post*) on the scope of the surveillance (Levitt 2011a, 2011b). Levitt noted that the NYPD had placed confidential informants in seven Muslim student associations (MSAs) at local colleges and that Brooklyn College, where I teach, and Baruch College had been listed as MSAs "of concern." Levitt wrote about one confidential police report that listed "42 top tier 'persons of interest,'" which included "a lecturer at Brooklyn College." For weeks, people assumed that this lecturer must be me.

Frankly, I wondered the same while also thinking that it would be absurd for the police to waste their resources on me. The Associated Press called me to ask me if I thought I was being surveilled, and a *New York Times* columnist also interviewed me about the report. Later, someone I know and trust who was shown the file told me that it had identified someone else. Of course, just because I was not the person named in the report does not mean that the NYPD has not spied on me. It just means I don't know for sure.

Others have learned something different. Mohammad Elshinawy is a young Egyptian American from Brooklyn with a popular following among New York's devout Muslims. I know Mohammad, who was once my student, and he and I also spent some time together when I was writing my book about Brooklyn's Arab Muslim youth. I could tell even then that he was a rising star with religious conservatives. Always dressed in a *galabeyya* with a kufi on his head, a fist-length beard on his chin, and sneakers on his feet, Mohammad commanded the respect of Brooklyn's young Muslims with his eloquence, intelligence, scholarly knowledge, and mastery of Qur'anic Arabic. It wasn't just the young people who were attracted to Mohammad. He has also been

Excerpt from Moustafa Bayoumi, introduction to *This American Life: Dispatches from the War on Terror* (New York: New York Univ. Press, 2015), 1–15. Full references in the original notes were converted to author-date citations in the text and notes here, and a works cited list was added. Reprinted with corrections and press style changes for consistency throughout the volume by permission of New York University Press.

the subject of fastidious NYPD surveillance. According to Apuzzo and Goldman, Mohammad's popularity had initially attracted the interest of the FBI, which became concerned that he might have been recruiting young men to fight overseas. That investigation was concluded with no charges filed. Yet the NYPD decided to pursue the matter—and Mohammad—further (Apuzzo and Goldman 2013).

I wondered what it's like to know you've been surveilled by the police, so I contacted Mohammad to ask him. He invited me to one of the regular classes he offers on the Qur'an at Masjid al-Ansar, a simple storefront mosque in Bensonhurst, Brooklyn, that, as reports indicate, has also been under NYPD surveillance. After the class, we went to a quiet room in the mosque's basement to talk. Boxes of canned foods, ready to distribute to the needy, surrounded us as we sat on the carpeted floor. I asked Mohammad what he felt after learning about the surveillance on him and its extent.

"Apprehension," he said, after thinking a while. "To what degree is this going to affect me?" He shared that he carefully considered his actions and that he would "try to take a stand and get past this hump." Mohammad was referring to being a plaintiff in a lawsuit filed by the ACLU against the police department.[1] "There's no reason why we should consider ourselves second-class citizens," he said, speaking about Muslim Americans generally. "I'm born in this country like anybody else," he said.

From the documents leaked to the AP, we know the character of the surveillance practiced on Mohammad and the NYPD's views on the young man. Labeling his race as "ME," that is, Middle Eastern, the police files describe Mohammad's views as "hard-core Salafi ones" (NYPD Technical Operations Unit 2009). (Salafis are scriptural conservatives who seek a belief system based on their understanding of the early days of Islam, and the police department operates under the assumption that they are particularly prone to violence.) One report states that the "TIU [Terrorism Interdiction Unit] believes that [Mohammad] is a threat due to the fact that he is so highly regarded by so many young and impressionable individuals" (NYPD Technical Operations Unit 2009), as if charm were a weapon. In the same report and under the heading "Surveillance Objective" is written, "Target moves on a daily basis to many different spots. Every day of the week is beneficial. [Most beneficial would be] after 1500 (after target gets off of work)," revealing essentially that Mohammad is a hardworking young man. The spying even invaded his love life and followed him around the city. The report continues, "Surveillance has revealed many things re: this target. His change of auto, the fact that he was going to get married b/c surv[eillance] observed him shopping for diamond rings w/ a female in the diamond district." I asked him about this detail. "I took my fiancée to go buy her a diamond ring, and even then I'm being tailgated," he told me. "Many times we knew we were being tailgated," he explained, "it's just like, what are you going to do? Call the cops on the cops?" He laughed. "It's quite a predicament!"

Looking closely at the NYPD surveillance program, we can get a larger sense of its dangerous presumptions and misguided activities. The program began in 2002, when Police Commissioner Ray Kelly hired David Cohen, a former deputy director for operations at the CIA, as his deputy commissioner of intelligence. Cohen succeeded in getting a judge to relax provisions of the Handschu Agreement, a 1985 consent decree developed in response to a lawsuit against the NYPD for spying on the constitutionally protected activity of political groups in the 1960s and 1970s. The Handschu Agreement previously allowed police surveillance only when officers had specific information a crime would be committed or was being planned. Under the new rules adopted in 2003, police no longer needed evidence to begin an investigation, just the *possibility* of criminal activity.

Cohen established four units in his Intelligence Division—the Demographics Unit, the Intelligence Analysis Unit, the Cyber Intelligence Unit, and the Terrorism Interdiction Unit—and hired Lawrence Sanchez, a CIA analyst, to oversee intelligence. Using data from the 2000

1. The lawsuit was settled in 2017, and the settlement inaugurated greater protections against discriminatory policing and unconstitutional surveillance by the NYPD (Shamsi 2017).

US Census, the Intelligence Division proceeded to chart where the Muslims in New York lived.[2]

This mapping has precedents. It recalls a 1919 map of ethnic New York drafted by the NYPD and New York State Police that identified certain ethnic neighborhoods in an effort to root out socialists, communists, and anarchists (Harris 2012). It's reminiscent of when the Census Bureau provided the government with information on where Japanese Americans lived to assist the War Relocation Authority in interning them during World War II (Minkel 2007). And it bears a resemblance to specially tabulated statistics on Arab American populations, indicating zip-code-level breakdowns of Arab Americans by country of origin, which the Census Bureau produced for Homeland Security from August 2002 to December 2003 (Clemetson 2004).

The NYPD did more than exploit publicly available data, however. They also sent out "rakers," plainclothes officers who could blend in to the community, and "mosque crawlers," informants working for the police. (Rakers were so dubbed because Cohen described their actions as akin to "raking an extinguished fire pit" [Apuzzo and Goldman 2013].) The Intelligence Division viewed everything about ordinary Muslim life as suspicious and cataloged it all. They established sports leagues as a way to spy on Muslim youth (NYPD Intelligence Division n.d.b). They recorded license plate numbers from the cars of mosque visitors. They noted where Muslims got haircuts, and they eavesdropped on conversations in cafés (NYPD Intelligence Division 2007). They considered it suspicious, as the "Egyptian Locations of Interest Report" (NYPD Intelligence Division 2006) makes clear, when café televisions were tuned to al Jazeera and when they were not. The report states that in one café "the Al Jazeera news channel is prohibited inside this location because the owner feels it brings extra scrutiny from law enforcement." They made more than seventy-five visits to thirty-four "targeted" travel agencies in South Asian communities around New York to discover, as found in the "Pakistani Travel Agency Report" (NYPD Intelligence Division n.d.a), that there were four principal airlines to Pakistan: Pakistan International Airlines, Emirates Airlines, Kuwait Airways, and Gulf Air. They also often got facts wrong, identifying Sephardic Jews and Lebanese Christians as Syrian Muslims, Coptic Egyptians as more numerous than Muslim Egyptians in New York, and Sunni Muslims as Shi'i Muslims (Apuzzo and Goldman 2013).

More troubling still, the NYPD designated selected mosques as "Terrorism Enterprises," meaning any visitor to these Muslim houses of worship could be investigated and that speech, including sermons, would be monitored and recorded. "It was an unprecedented moment in the history of American law enforcement," Apuzzo and Goldman write in *Enemies Within*, their 2013 book about the surveillance program. "The NYPD regarded houses of worship—and everyone who prayed there—as possible criminal organizations" (180).

All of this netted, the NYPD was later forced to admit, not a single lead on suspected terrorist activity (Apuzzo and Goldman 2013, 181).[3] After the facts of the

2. The Demographics Unit was renamed the "Zone Assessment Unit" in 2010 out of concern for how the former would sound to the public if discovered (Apuzzo and Goldman 2013). The CIA paid Sanchez's salary from 2002 to 2004, despite the fact that the CIA is forbidden from having "any police, subpoena or law enforcement powers or internal security functions" (National Security Act of 1947). Sanchez remained in his post until 2010, and the NYPD paid his salary after 2004. After 2010, a former CIA clandestine officer, Lance Hamilton, replaced Sanchez until his identity became known, after which he was recalled (Apuzzo and Goldman 2013). Working out of an office in the Brooklyn Army Terminal, the Intelligence Division divided the community into what they called "Ancestries of Interest," twenty-eight countries mostly from the Middle East and South Asia as well as former Soviet states with large Muslim populations. They also included "American Black Muslim" on the list, as if being Muslim and Black meant your ancestry belonged to another nation (Apuzzo and Goldman 2013).

3. While testifying in a deposition on June 28, 2012, Assistant Chief Thomas Galati, commanding officer of the Intelligence Division, revealed that no leads had been discovered or investigations begun as a result of the Demographics Unit's work. Galati also revealed that the NYPD was suspicious of foreign languages. The department was concerned about "Islamics [*sic*] radicalized towards violence," and so it kept surveillance records on two Pakistani men who in a conversation in Urdu had complained about the mistreatment they felt Muslims received at the hands of airport security in the United States. When Galati was shown the document, he responded, "I'm seeing Urdu. I'm seeing them [the officers] identify the individuals involved

program were no longer deniable and due in large part to the mobilizing efforts of New York's Muslim communities and their allies, the department announced in April 2014 that they would disband the Demographics Unit. They did not, however, announce a halt to other aspects of their Muslim community surveillance, including designating mosques as "Terrorism Enterprises" (Yachot 2014).

Nor has the NYPD announced an end to using informants to monitor Muslim communities without any probable cause. We now know the inner workings of informant life. One informant, Shamiur Rahman, who was a regular attendee of Mohammad's lectures, emerged from the shadows in October 2012, revealing on his Facebook page that he had been sent by the NYPD to observe Muslims and "bait" them into saying inciting things, particularly statements containing "jihad" and "revolution" (Apuzzo and Goldman 2012a). For this he was paid as much as a thousand dollars a month and given leniency on misdemeanor marijuana possession charges. According to a *New York Times* report from May 2014, such practices are continuing (Goldstein 2014). The end of the Demographics Unit does not mean the end of bias-based policing of New York's Muslims, who can still count on being treated by the NYPD as harbingers of terrorism just by going about their everyday affairs.

Why would the NYPD expend such massive resources—the counterterrorism and intelligence units are staffed by nearly a thousand employees and operate with a combined budget of over a hundred million dollars (2010 figures)—to spy on the mundane and the ordinary? The reasoning behind their actions must be their belief that Muslims will almost necessarily become, if they aren't already, terrorists or supporters of terrorism. Testifying before the Senate Committee on Homeland Security and Governmental Affairs in 2007, Lawrence Sanchez, the CIA official who worked with the NYPD, explained how the NYPD aims to crawl not just into the mosques but into the souls of Muslims to reveal their true essence, even before they know themselves. "Rather than just protecting New York City citizens from terrorists," Sanchez said, "the New York Police Department believes that part of *its mission is to protect New York City citizens* from turning into terrorists" (US Senate, Committee on Homeland Security and Governmental Affairs 2007, emphasis added). From there, he explained how it was proper to trample on the constitutional rights of ordinary Muslims. Testifying that the NYPD now scrutinizes "what most people would say would be non-criminal, would be innocuous, behaviors that could easily be argued in a Western democracy, especially in the United States, [are] protected by First and Fourth Amendment rights," Sanchez said, "[we don't] look at them in a vacuum, but . . . look across to them as potential precursors to terrorism."

The same prejudicial assumptions of the inevitably violent Muslim have been found in training documents used by both the FBI, which also hired a former CIA official, Philip Mudd, to run its counterterrorism operations, and the US military (Ackerman 2010, 2011, 2012). (The manner in which domestic law enforcement generally has been integrated with the country's intelligence services during the war on terror also begs serious study.)

Nor is this assumption limited to the United States. In Guantánamo Bay, scores of prisoners have been cleared for release since 2010 by the US government's own Guantánamo Review Task Force, and yet [at the time of this writing, c. 2014] dozens of these men remain behind bars and bereft of hope, most having been incarcerated without charge or trial for more than twelve years. Why? Because Congress and the Pentagon have dragged their feet on releasing the men, arguing that they should not be freed due to the future possibility that they will return to their home countries only to take up hostilities against the United States. In this case, a past of abuse by the United States might make that argument more tenable, but even here a New American Foundation study found

in that [conversation] are Pakistani. I'm using that information for me to determine that this would be a kind of place that a terrorist would be comfortable in," adding that "most Urdu speakers from that region would be of concern, so that's why it's important to me." He says essentially the same thing about Bengali speakers later in the deposition (Galati 2012, 29, 85–86, 92). As the AP notes, "About 15 million Pakistanis and 60 million Indians speak Urdu. Along with English, it is one of the national languages of Pakistan" (Apuzzo and Goldman 2012b).

that 8.8 percent of returned captives have undertaken "militant activity," significantly below the Pentagon's official estimate of 14 percent (Bergen and Cahall 2013).

Then there are the drones. In 2012, the *New York Times* described President Obama's vastly expanded program of drone warfare during the war on terror and reported that when it authorizes a strike, the White House "in effect counts all military-age males in a strike zone as combatants . . . unless there is explicit intelligence posthumously proving them innocent" (Becker and Shane 2012). This partly reflects a shell game used by the White House to show how they are minimizing civilian casualties, and former CIA officials have expressed dismay at the concept. One called it "guilt by association" that has led to "deceptive" estimates of civilian casualties. "It bothers me when they say there were seven guys, so they must all be militants," a CIA official told the *New York Times*, adding, "They count the corpses and they're not really sure who they are" (quoted in Becker and Shane 2012). A year after this revelation, President Obama stated that "the high threshold that we've set for taking lethal action applies to all potential terrorist targets, regardless of whether or not they are American citizens" (Obama 2012). But what qualifies as a "potential terrorist" has never been delineated. And while the official line is that the US military does not target males in Afghanistan and other declared or undeclared war zones solely because they are of military age, the *Nation* has shown that the practice not only continues but is even recorded in internal reports that mention MAMs (military-age males) (Turse 2013), as if all males of that age are reducible (and thus justifiably killed due) to their potential for terrorism.

This idea that you are seen not as a complex human being but only as a purveyor of possible future violence illustrates the extraordinary predicament at the heart of contemporary Muslim American life. To be a Muslim American today is to be full of potential, and not in the sweet way that grandmothers and elementary school teachers use the word. The state has enveloped itself in a near religious task, to sneak and peek into the conscience of one set of its citizens and residents and their coreligionists abroad. In this *Minority Report* world, the police aim to patrol the minds of Muslims for what they believe they will think and not for their actions.

Nor is this point of view limited to government. [The idea] [t]hat Muslims will ultimately reveal themselves as usurpers and organizers of future chaos and terror exists in American society at large, where constructing a mosque is often viewed not innocently but as part of a larger plan for the future takeover of the country, despite how ridiculous that sounds and impossible that would be. This notion reached its media apex with massive demonstrations in 2010 against the planned construction of a Muslim cultural center in the vicinity of Ground Zero. . . . [B]ut Muslim communities around the country have faced uphill battles to establish Islamic centers and mosques for years. In 2012, the Pew Forum on Religion and Public Life published a study using media sources that cataloged fifty-three examples of community resistance to new mosques in twenty-one states (Pew Research Center 2012). Similarly, at least thirty-two state legislatures have drafted bills barring judges from considering foreign law, including sharia (Islamic legal principles), in their decisions. The guiding force behind these linked agitations is the notion of "creeping sharia"—that is to say, in their ordinary expressions of life, Muslims are both untrustworthy and conquest-minded, and soon the American Constitution will be superseded by Islamic law. In late August 2013 North Carolina became the seventh state to sign such a bill into law, and in November 2014 voters in Alabama overwhelmingly approved an antisharia ballot initiative. Behind both antisharia bills and antimosque agitation is the suspicion less of what Muslims are doing and more of what they will do with the law and their property in the future. In the grammar of Islamophobia, the future is tense.

The scary, duplicitous, and secret life of Muslims is perhaps most shamelessly displayed in Showtime's blockbuster series *Homeland*. Nick Brody is a returning marine who had been captured in Iraq and held for eight years by the terrorist Abu Nazir. Brody is essentially reprogrammed during his captivity while caring for Abu Nazir's son—who is subsequently killed in a drone strike—into adopting Islam, and when he returns to the United States, he seeks to avenge the boy's death and fight for his new faith. Brody leads a double life, a public one where he is an American hero who becomes a congressman and is eventually tapped as a vice presidential running mate and a private one where he is not only a secret Muslim but also a secret terrorist. *Homeland*'s whole suspense and momentum derive not from what Brody is but what he might become, an American hero or a Muslim terrorist. The show feeds off the same presumption of future malfeasance that is the essence of today's anti-Muslim prejudice.

"I am in the strenuous and far from dull position of having news to deliver to the Western world," James Baldwin wrote in 1979, and his news is simple and straightforward, "*black* is not a synonym for *slave*" (emphasis in original). The situation is disturbingly similar today. *Muslim* is not a synonym for *terrorist*. And yet the automatic association of Muslim Americans with terrorism has become completely institutionalized and thoroughly commonsensical, even though it flies in the face of the evidence. In fact, terrorist acts or attempts thereof by Muslim Americans in the years since the 2001 attacks have been extremely rare, far fewer than the number of attacks carried out by right-wing extremists. According to the Triangle Center on Terrorism and Homeland Security, terrorist acts perpetrated by Muslim Americans in the United States since 9/11 have killed thirty-seven people, and the majority of those deaths are attributed to two attacks: one by Major Nidal Hasan, who killed thirteen fellow soldiers in Fort Hood, Texas, and the other the series of shootings by the "Beltway snipers," who, unconnected to the war on terror (and mainline Islam), killed eleven people (Kurzman 2013). The Boston Marathon bombers were responsible for another four deaths in 2013. By contrast, 133 people were killed by non-Muslims in mass shootings in 2013 alone (Kurzman 2013). Another report, published by West Point's Combating Terrorism Center in 2012, found that between 1990 and 2012 non-Muslim far-right extremists have committed 4,420 violent acts in the United States that have killed 670 people and injured 3,053 more, and the number of attacks has risen precipitously since 2000 and especially since 2007 (Perliger 2012). Polling data also indicate that Muslim Americans are in fact the least likely major religious group in the country to support military attacks on civilians (Gallup 2011). And according to the investigative journalist Trevor Aaronson (2013), the vast majority of those Muslim Americans who have been arrested on terrorism or terrorism-related charges over the past dozen years have been vulnerable losers nabbed in sting operations that come perilously close to entrapment, small-time offenders with distant links to radicals overseas, or immigrants caught lying to federal officials. According to Aaronson, independent plots that have risen to credible threats number just five—rather amateurish—cases.

Terrorism is a serious issue, and five attempts are clearly five too many. All those who have been victims of terrorism should be mourned, and justice must be served. And yet some sense of perspective and proportionality surely ought to be maintained. Instead, however, the national-security apparatus routinely invokes the fear of terrorism, implicitly or explicitly by Muslims, to assume ever-expanding powers over American lives and to justify military intervention overseas. The image that the country is under siege by these Muslim terrorists and their sympathizers is regularly reinforced, and the minuscule amount of violence that can be associated with Muslim Americans is magnified and decontextualized, seen as a true expression of Islamic belief rather than occurring within the context of global warfare. In important ways, the constant promotion and creation of the Muslim American threat displaces the violence of the war on terror overseas back on[to] the image of the violent Muslim terrorists who must live among us (Kundnani 2014). Don't worry about facts. The image of the Muslim terrorist is a very useful one.

Such images and notions matter because, taken together, they create a kind of war-on-terror culture that is continuously reflected and reinforced across American society. It's important to understand not only what war-on-terror culture is but also the costs it has had on Muslim Americans specifically and on social and political life in the United States generally. War-on-terror culture assumes that Muslims collectively are responsible for and sympathetic to all acts of violence by individual Muslims everywhere, unless and until they explicitly say otherwise. But even then, their words are often doubted since Muslims are seen as doctrinally prone to lying and violence. If any Muslim commits a horrible act of violence, the action is automatically assumed to be a heinous political feat. With non-Muslim Americans, the situation is different, as Conor Friedersdorf explains. "When mass killers are native-born whites," he writes, "their motivations are treated like a mystery to [be] unraveled rather than a foregone conclusion" (2014). And there's more. A *Washington Post* columnist discovered that major news media won't even consider an act of violence as terrorism unless the government names it as such first, giving the government, apropos of war-on-terror culture, tremendous power over labels and abdicating the media's own independence (Farhi 2014).

War-on-terror culture also means that Muslim American history is forgotten, as if Muslims existed in the United States only after September 2001. War-on-terror culture represents Muslims always and only through the war-on-terror lens and never on their own terms. War-on-terror culture means that Muslim job applicants, according to a 2014 study by researchers at the University of Connecticut, receive "32 percent fewer emails and 48 percent fewer phone calls than applicants from the control group, far out-weighing measurable bias against the other faith groups" (Breen 2014). War-on-terror culture promotes the seductive synergy of militarism and entertainment (Remember when Michelle Obama, flanked by soldiers in dress uniforms in the White House, announced the Best Picture Oscar for *Argo*?) while rationalizing or ignoring the massive civilian death toll of the war on terror. War-on-terror culture means that the 9/11 Memorial, supposedly dedicated to ending intolerance and ignorance, offers pamphlets in nine languages but bizarrely not in Arabic, and the 9/11 Museum tour concludes with a film considered by many to be inflammatory toward Islam (Lekas Miller 2013). War-on-terror culture is essentially the deep institutionalization of George W. Bush's simplistic proclamation that "either you are with us, or you are with the terrorists" (Bush 2001), as if there can be no other options, as if one can't oppose the horrors that the war on terror delivers and the murderous nihilism of terrorism simultaneously.

Because war-on-terror culture ascribes a programmed and malevolent future to Muslims, it marks almost anything Muslims say about themselves as immediately suspect, part of a larger plot of apologetics at best or propaganda at worst. In this way, it not only denies the rich history of Islam in America but also sees Islam as always and forever a foreign and a foreigner's faith to the United States. The good news, however, is that war-on-terror culture is not the only game in town. Resistance to its simplistic worldview has motivated a small but growing war-on-terror counterculture, a large part of which is reflected in cultural production by and about Muslim Americans and probing scholarship on Muslim Americans in recent years. The audiences for this kind of work have also expanded and deepened.

Resistance to the dictates of war-on-terror culture can be found in novels such as Mohja Kahf's *The Girl in the Tangerine Scarf* (2006), Randa Jarrar's *A Map of Home* (2008), Mohsin Hamid's *The Reluctant Fundamentalist* (2007), and Amy Waldman's *The Submission* (2011), all serious attempts to ponder the complexities of contemporary Muslim life. Major cultural institutions such as New York's Poetry House and the National Endowment for the Humanities have developed programs to educate the broader public about the lives and traditions of Muslims, here and abroad. The *Daily Show* and the *Colbert Report* have frequently lampooned manifestations of Islamophobia through their invaluable satire. And universities, high schools, and houses of worship across the country have hosted countless speakers and held innumerable seminars with Muslim Americans in attempts to gain greater understanding of Muslim American lives.

Scholarly inquiry into Muslim American history, life, and realities has produced other probing work, including Hisham Aidi's *Rebel Music: Race, Empire, and the New Muslim Youth Culture* (2014), Evelyn Alsultany's *Arabs and Muslims in the Media* (2012), Louise Cainkar's *Homeland Insecurity* (2011), Sohail Daulatzai's *Black Star, Crescent Moon: The Muslim International and Black Freedom beyond America* (2012), Kambiz Ghaneabassiri's *A History of Islam in America* (2010), Zareena Grewal's *Islam Is a Foreign Country* (2013), Deepa Kumar's *Islamophobia and the Politics of Empire* (2012), Sunaina Maira's *Missing* (2009), Timothy Marr's *The Cultural Roots of American Islamicism* (2006), Junaid Rana's *Terrifying Muslims* (2011), Steven Salaita's *Anti-Arab Racism* (2006),

Denise Spellberg's *Thomas Jefferson's Qur'an* (2013), and many more. This war-on-terror counterculture reflects the desire to investigate Muslim American life beyond the clichés of law enforcement and popular culture, however overwhelming those may be, and represents a point of optimism in a general period of political pessimism. Much more, however, is needed.

Works Cited

Aaronson, Trevor. 2013. *The Terror Factory: Inside the FBI's Manufactured War on Terrorism*. Brooklyn, NY: Ig Publishing.

Ackerman, Spencer. 2010. "Al-Qaeda Expert Philip Mudd Retires from FBI." *Washington Independent*, Apr. 21. At http://washingtonindependent.com/82879/al-qaeda-expert-philip-mudd-retires-from-fbi.

———. 2011. "FBI Teaches Agents: 'Mainstream' Muslims Are 'Violent, Radical.'" *Wired*, Sept. 14. At http://www.wired.com/2011/09/fbi-muslims-radical/all/1.

———. 2012. "Exclusive: Senior US General Orders Top-to-Bottom Review of Military's Islam Training." *Wired*, Apr. 24. At http://www.wired.com/2012/04/ military-islam-training/.

Aidi, Hisham. 2014. *Rebel Music: Race, Empire, and the New Muslim Youth Culture*. New York: Pantheon.

Alsultany, Evelyn. 2012. *Arabs and Muslims in the Media: Race and Representation after 9/11*. New York: New York Univ. Press.

Apuzzo, Matt, and Adam Goldman. 2011. "With CIA Help, NYPD Moves Covertly in Muslim Areas." Associated Press, Aug. 23.

———. 2012a. "Informant: NYPD Paid Me to 'Bait' Muslims." Associated Press, Oct. 23.

———. 2012b. "NYPD: Muslim Spying Led to No Leads, Terror Cases." Associated Press, Aug. 21.

———. 2013. *Enemies Within: Inside the NYPD's Secret Spying Unit and Bin Laden's Final Plot against America*. New York: Touchstone.

Baldwin, James. 1979. "Open Letter to the Born Again." *Nation*, Sept. 29.

Becker, Jo, and Scott Shane. 2012. "Secret 'Kill List' Proves a Test of Obama's Principles and Will." *New York Times*, May 29.

Bergen, Peter, and Bailey Cahall. 2013. *How Many Guantanamo Detainees "Return to the Battlefield"?* Washington, DC: New America Foundation, May 7. At http://newamerica.net/sites/newamerica.net/files/profiles/attachments/GTMO_Appendix_5-7-2013.pdf.

Breen, Tom. 2014. "Great Resume, Too Bad about Your Religion." *UConnToday.com*, June 16. At http://today.uconn.edu/blog/2014/06/great-resume-too-bad-about-your-religion/.

Bush, George W. 2001. "Address to a Joint Session of Congress and the American People." Sept. 20. At http://georgewbush-whitehouse.archives.gov/news/releases/2001/09/20010920-8.html.

Cainkar, Louise. 2011. *Homeland Insecurity: The Arab American and Muslim American Experience after 9/11*. New York: Russell Sage Foundation.

Clemetson, Lynne. 2004. "Homeland Security Given Data on Arab-Americans." *New York Times*, July 30.

Daulatzai, Sohail. 2012. *Black Star, Crescent Moon: The Muslim International and Black Freedom beyond America*. Minneapolis: Univ. of Minnesota Press.

Farhi, Paul. 2014. "In the News Media, Are Muslims the Only Terrorists?" *Washington Post*, June 10.

Friedersdorf, Conor. 2014. "If the Las Vegas Killers Were Muslims, We'd Call Them Terrorists. But Should We?" *Atlantic*, June 10. At http://www.theatlantic.com/politics/archive/2014/06/if-these-killers-were-muslims-wed-call-them-terrorists/372472/.

Galati, Thomas. 2012. Deposition in 71CIV.2203. US District Court, Southern District of New York. June 28.

Gallup. 2011. *Muslim Americans: Faith, Freedom, and the Future*. Abu Dhabi, United Arab Emirates: Gallup Center.

Ghaneabassiri, Kambiz. 2010. *A History of Islam in America: From the New World to the New World Order*. New York: Cambridge Univ. Press.

Goldstein, Joseph. 2014. "New York Police Recruit Muslims to Be Informers." *New York Times*, May 10.

Grewal, Zareena. 2013. *Islam Is a Foreign Country*. New York: New York Univ. Press.

Hamid, Mohsin. 2007. *The Reluctant Fundamentalist*. New York: Harcourt.

Harris, Sam. 2012. "Police Demographics Unit Casts Shadows from Past." *New York Times*, *City Room* blog, Jan. 3. At http://cityroom.blogs.nytimes.com/2012/01/03/police-demographics-unit-casts-shadows-from-past/.

Jarrar, Randa. 2008. *A Map of Home*. New York: Penguin.

Kahf, Mohja. 2006. *The Girl in the Tangerine Scarf*. New York: PublicAffairs.

Kumar, Deepa. 2012. *Islamophobia and the Politics of Empire.* Chicago: Haymarket Books.

Kundnani, Arun. 2014. *The Muslims Are Coming! Islamophobia, Extremism, and the Domestic War on Terror.* New York: Verso.

Kurzman, Charles. 2013. *Muslim-American Terrorism: Declining Further.* Durham, NC: Triangle Center on Terrorism and Homeland Security, Feb. 1.

Lekas Miller, Anna. 2013. "Forgetting 'Little Syria' at the 9/11 Memorial." *Al Jazeera*, Aug. 2. At http://www.aljazeera.com/indepth/features/2013/07/2013730135344232174.html.

Levitt, Len. 2011a. "The NYPD: Spies, Spooks, and Lies." *NYPD Confidential*, Sept. 5.

———. 2011b. "The NYPD: Spies, Spooks, and Lies." *Huffington Post*, Sept. 7.

Maira, Sunaina. 2009. *Missing: Youth, Citizenship, and Empire after 9/11.* Durham, NC: Duke Univ. Press.

Marr, Timothy. 2006. *The Cultural Roots of American Islamicism.* New York: Cambridge Univ. Press.

Minkel, J. R. 2007. "Confirmed: The U.S. Census Bureau Gave Up Names of Japanese-Americans in WW II." *Scientific American*, Mar. 30.

National Security Act. 1947. P.L. 80–235, 61 Stat. 496. July 26.

New York Police Department (NYPD) Intelligence Division: Demographics Unit. 2006. *Egyptian Locations of Interest Report.* New York: NYPD, July 7.

———. 2007. *Internet Cafe Report.* New York: NYPD, June 15.

———. N.d.a. *Pakistani Travel Agency Report.* New York: NYPD.

———. N.d.b. *Sports Venues Report.* New York: NYPD.

New York Police Department (NYPD) Technical Operations Unit. 2009. "Surveillance Request: Mohammad Elshinawy." Feb. 2.

Obama, Barack. 2012. "Remarks by the President at the National Defense University." May 23. At https://obamawhitehouse.archives.gov/the-press-office/2013/05/23/remarks-president-national-defense-university.

Perliger, Arie. 2012. *Challengers from the Sidelines: Understanding America's Violent Far Right.* West Point, NY: Combating Terrorism Center at West Point.

Pew Research Center. 2012. *Controversies over Mosques and Islamic Centers across the U.S.* Forum on Religion & Public Life. Washington, DC: Pew Research Center, Sept. 27. At http://features.pewforum.org/muslim/2012Mosque-Map.pdf.

Rana, Junaid. 2011. *Terrifying Muslims: Race and Labor in the South Asian Diaspora.* Durham, NC: Duke Univ. Press.

Salaita, Steven. 2006. *Anti-Arab Racism.* London: Pluto.

Shamsi, Hina. 2017. "Revised Settlement Means Even Stronger Protections from NYPD Surveillance for New York's Muslims." American Civil Liberties Union blog, Mar. 6. At https://www.aclu.org/blog/national-security/privacy-and-surveillance/revised-settlement-means-even-stronger-protection.

Spellberg, Denise. 2013. *Thomas Jefferson's Qur'an: Islam and the Founders.* New York: Knopf.

Turse, Nick. 2013. "America's Lethal Profiling of Afghan Men." *Nation*, Sept. 18. At http://www.thenation.com/article/176253/americas-lethal-profiling-afghan-men.

US Senate, Committee on Homeland Security and Governmental Affairs. 2007. *The Role of Local Law Enforcement in Countering Violent Islamist Extremism.* 110th Cong., 2nd sess., Oct. 30. Washington, DC: US Government Publication Office. At http://www.gpo.gov/fdsys/pkg/ CHRG-110shrg34411/html/CHRG-110shrg34411.htm.

Waldman, Amy. 2011. *The Submission.* New York: Farrar, Straus and Giroux.

Yachot, Noa. 2014. "NYPD Shutters Muslim Mapping Unit—but What about Other Tactics?" American Civil Liberties Union blog, Apr. 15. At https://www.aclu.org/blog/national-security-religion-belief/nypd-shutters-muslim-spying-unit-what-about-its-tactics.

30

Water Occupation and the Ecology of Arab American Literature

DANIELLE HAQUE

> And the protests: "We have so many problems!—our identity to defend, our cultures under siege. We can't waste time admiring trees!"
>
> —Lisa Suhair Majaj, *Geographies of Light*

> Like you, we don't control our natural resources. Just as you were not consulted about the Dakota Access Pipeline that will traverse your land and contaminate your water supply if installed, we are not consulted by Israel, which wants to mine the gas supply in our harbor for its own use and monopolizes the water supply in the West Bank for the green lawns of its own residents—leaving Palestinians parched and dry. In Gaza, where I live, only 10 percent of our water supply is drinkable due to the conditions in which we must live. We too know that "water is life."
>
> —Israa Suliman, "A Letter from Gaza"

Settler-colonial states have long referred to Indigenous protestors as terrorists and treated them as combatants. As the Standing Rock Sioux Tribe continues to defend their water and land against the construction of the Dakota Access Pipeline, militarized police forces have attacked water protectors with mace, rubber bullets, tear gas, and water cannons, all familiar forms of state violence for Palestinians. The United Nations calls the water, sanitation, and hygiene situation in the Gaza Strip unsustainable, and the World Bank reports that 90 percent of residents do not have access to safe drinking water.[1]

In Laila Halaby's 2007 novel *Once in a Promised Land*, when the protagonist Jassim's uncle, Abu Jalal, speaks to him of water, Jassim thinks, "Imagine, in the face of Palestine being destroyed, of more people being made refugees, of their culture being stolen, of Jordan being placed on the brink of civil unrest as a result—imagine talking about water as the more important issue!" (41). The Dakota pipeline and Gaza's water occupation epitomize how the model of the nation-state and the Enlightenment narrative of historical progression that underpins it work to disenfranchise Indigenous peoples, transform them into peripheral citizens subject to

Excerpt from Danielle Haque, "Water Occupation and the Ecology of Arab American Literature," *Multi-ethnic Literature of the United States* 44, no. 1 (2019): 65–86. Full references in the original notes were converted to author-date citations in the text and notes here, and a works cited list was added. Reprinted with corrections and press style changes for consistency throughout the volume by permission of Oxford University Press.

1. For more comprehensive data on water access, see OCHA n.d. and "Water Situation Alarming in Gaza" (2016).

state terror, and terminate tribal and local sovereignties. Civil unrest, stolen culture, population displacement, and water theft are interrelated phenomena. The pipeline and Gaza's depleted water sources extend beyond issues of national sovereignty; after all, their fate is also determined by international alliances and corporate interests. The issue is also planetary: water cannot be bound by borders—it is connected above and below ground, continuously moving in a global cycle.

The relationship between humans and the biosphere is an essential component of human relationships with one another. Water links global communities literally, through shared oceans and waterways, but also through the unequal burden of pollution and rising seas on the Global South that is a direct result of settler colonialism and globalization. Arab American literature has made significant and often overlooked contributions to ecological aesthetics and praxis and to environmental justice. In 2016, *Mizna: Prose, Poetry, and Art Exploring Arab America*, a Minnesota-based literary journal, published an environment issue [volume 17, number 2], intending the pieces to be read relationally, in conversation with each other, even as they represent different geographies and perspectives. Contributors such as Suzan Boulad, Rasha Abdulhadi, Farah Kader, and Dawud Mulla, through their critique of settler-colonial legacies, environmental racism, and slow violence, express alternative modes of inhabiting and interacting with the biosphere.[2] Similarly, in Halaby's *Once in a Promised Land*, water, in the pipes beneath us and the reservoirs we share, is an allegory for the ways in which humans are reliant on one another. All these texts depict human relationships to the biosphere and how they oppose national frameworks defining what land (and water) is and how we should relate to it. Within their pages, the planet is not merely the setting in which human histories play out but also a place where nonhuman actors interact with humans and are simultaneously impacted by human practices.

Arab American literature has been overlooked as a source of ecological aesthetics, praxis, and ethics. However, a number of scholars are pioneering what Nadine A. Sinno calls the "greening of modern Arabic literature."[3] Sinno's project is straightforward: she advocates reading Arabic literature with careful attention to how the environment is represented and demonstrates the benefits of such a reading through conscientious analysis of novels by Yahya Yakhlif and Ghada Samman, showing how their works claim nature as essential to human identity. Sinno believes that the inclusion of diverse voices, which necessarily includes Middle Eastern literatures, fulfills and disseminates one of the principal premises of ecocriticism: "the inevitability of interconnectedness, not only among species, but also among various literary and cultural discourses" (2013, 143). By insisting on the inclusion of diverse voices without prescribing how those voices should be interpreted or claiming that there is a monolithic Arabic environmental voice, Sinno's analysis shows how human relationships with their environments are variegated and localized. Yet her wording in this passage also suggests that literary discourses do not only represent multispecies dependence in their pages but also embody our biosphere's connectedness through their own transcultural, transnational contingencies. Literature about biospheric interdependence is culturally specific yet relies on connections with other literary forms and histories for its reception and circulation; this cycle of influence and the continually changing, borrowing, adapting forms of literature embody how we depend on one another for the health and circulation of our waterways and ecosystems.

Postcolonial ecocriticism is a mode of reading that attends to what Graham Huggan and Helen Tiffin outline as "the need for a broadly materialistic understanding of the changing relationship between people, animals, and environment—one that requires attention, in turn, to the cultural politics of representation as well as to those more specific 'processes of mediation . . . that can be recuperated

2. I am taking the category of Arab American literature as a given entity and not reviewing discussions of how that category has developed or its implications as a discrete category. For scholarship on these debates, see Carol Fadda-Conrey (2014), Waïl Hassan (2011), and Steven Salaita (2007).

3. For examples of ecocritical readings of Arab and Arab American literature, see Hamoud Yahya Ahmed and Ruzy Suliza Hashim (2014), Ismet Bujupaj (2015), and Sharif S. Elmusa (2013). Halaby's novel takes up questions of sovereignty within and over the biosphere.

for anticolonial critique'" (2010, 12). The short stories and poems featured in *Mizna* and Halaby's novel foreground environmental issues "not only as central to the projects of European conquest and global domination, but also as inherent in the ideologies of imperialism and racism on which those projects historically—and persistently—depend" (Huggan and Tiffin 2010, 6). Foundational to European colonial conquest is the Enlightenment divide between nature and human culture, a binary underpinning settler-colonial logics.

The eighteenth-century European movement to enclose both common land and religion into private spheres made land secular and therefore fungible. The biblical notion of stewardship, that man has dominion over every living creature, is naturalized into secular understandings of private property. Western and US political secularism naturalizes Protestant values into civic (and eventually environmental) ones, including the separation of religious and secular, public and private, civilization and wilderness, and preservation and development into discrete spheres. Standing Rock, for example, demonstrates how US legal constructions of property and citizenship are linked, as both are rooted in a Protestant ethos that shapes the animating myth about what it means to be "American," which is to say a "white, property-owning body politic" (Simpson 2014, 8). It is also an example of environmental racism that indicates the ways in which racial minorities are excluded from decisions about land and water management, disproportionately exposed to toxic materials and pollutants, and denied access to sanitation and clean water. Environmental racism also describes the unequal relationship of the Global North and South, which amplifies ecological inequalities to national and regional scales.

Artists and scholars point to the contingencies that shape interconnectedness in cultural production to denote multispecies dependence more broadly, providing epistemologies of multispecies kinship through literary forms. I read, for example, the unlikely connections made across class and ethnicity in *Once in a Promised Land* as modeling human and biospheric kinship usually obscured (and obstructed) by racial capitalism. . . . Such regional contexts allow readers to see local challenges to a global system whose primary value is capital accumulation. The effect of reading works such as the ones in *Mizna* and *Once in a Promised Land* through postcolonial ecocritical frameworks is to build, text by text, relationship by relationship, local political strategies for equity and planetary care. Arab American literature offers vital critical perspectives for ecocritical studies in part because of the diversity of its origins and the multiple subject and geographic positions it represents.

In their critique of the Western bent of ecocriticism, Elizabeth DeLoughrey and George B. Handley note how much of

> recent scholarship theorizing the development of ecocriticism and environmentalism has positioned Europe and the United States as the epistemological centers, while the rest of the world has, for material and ideological reasons, been thought to have arrived belatedly, or with less focused commitment, to an ecologically sustainable future. (2011, 8)

Contrary to this historical focus on the West, however, they argue that the "global south has contributed to an ecological imaginary and discourse of activism and sovereignty that [are] not derivative of the Euro-American environmentalism of the 1960s and 1970s" (2011, 8). They suggest instead a genealogy of ecocriticism that includes "indigenous, ecofeminist, ecosocialist, and environmental justice scholars and activists, who have theorized the relations of power, subjectivity, and place for many decades" (2011, 9).

Therefore, the task of greening Arab American literature is not only to diversify ecocritical studies but also to investigate distinctive expressions of Arab and Arab American experiences of land and how specific texts articulate local ecological praxis. From communities that have been in the United States since the waves of migration from the Ottoman Empire in the 1880s through the 1920s to later immigrants from diverse regions and refugees of the Nakba, the Six-Day War, the Lebanese Civil War, the Gulf Wars, and so on, the map of Arab America is vast.[4] This diversity produces complex renderings

4. See Kemal H. Karpat (1985) for a discussion of Ottoman immigration to the United States.

of belonging to geographies and texts that grapple with transnational and hybrid identities. One perpetual refrain in Arab American literature is how US culture perceives Arab Americans as somehow not belonging to the land, not being truly and fully "American," and instead sees them as interlopers who must be kept under surveillance for a variety of threats. Nadine Naber argues that 9/11 was a turning point in "histories of anti-Arab racism in the United States," when Arab Americans shifted from invisible citizens to hypervisible (and policed) subjects (2008, 4). Both invisibility and hypervisibility describe ways in which Arab Americans are perceived as unattached to US geographies and histories. Furthermore, the landscape of the United States in much of Arab American literature is juxtaposed, often through memory and nostalgia, with other landscapes, perhaps from childhood or parental recollection. These are often lands to which one cannot return because of occupation, war, or economic disenfranchisement. Because Arab American literature traverses nations and cultures, it is particularly apt for the task of connecting regional and planetary ecological concerns.

This diversity of origins is significant because it resists a monolithic voice while providing political praxes around which to organize. Greening forces a shift away from Orientalist and colonial frameworks that portray Arabs as essentially belonging to an exotic (often desert) premodern landscape in need of civilization or as immigrant invaders of Western geographies. Instead, it links the complex history of racialization of Arab Americans and the experience of political, cultural, and legal exclusion in the United States to the slow violence of environmental racism, settler colonialism, and globalization. . . . [5]

If greening denotes careful attention to representations of land, *mizna* provides an apt metaphor for narrating political and cultural strategies for renewal and liberation. In its front matter, the literary journal defines *mizna* as an "Arabic word describing a desert cloud that holds the promise of rain and respite" ([vol. 17, no. 2] 2016, ii). . . . Arab American ecocritical literary practices can reveal the limitations of national frameworks for regulating human relationships with the biosphere. They can also model environmental justice, for example, through reading Abdulhadi's and Mulla's poems as demanding the decolonization of Palestine through characterization of sea and birds and with imagery of stolen water. . . . One challenge in reading Arab American literature in terms of ecology is that [ecology] is too often seen as peripheral to political turmoil instead of embroiled in it. Lisa Suhair Majaj's poem "Cadence" (in Majaj 2009), some of which prefaces this essay, addresses an audience that perceives nature writing or environmental activism as a secondary or even luxurious concern, coming after the more serious matters of exile, occupation, and racism. While Sinno uses an ecocritical framework to analyze novels, she also comments on the "absence of exclusive focus on the environment," which she attributes to the "more political nature of these texts whose themes include war, loss, and identity." Yet she notes how the authors use nature to develop these pressing themes, arguing that while the authors use nature thematically and as a way of "illuminating the human condition," they also depict nature as an entity in and of itself and a victim of war (2013, 127). Sinno's reading emphasizes that environmental degradation is intimately connected to violence, while Majaj's poem asserts the right of all people to love and defend nature.

Arab American literature often narrates movement across landscapes, including migration, displacement, and return, and is therefore transnational and transcultural. What can these literary mappings of movement tell us about how to transform human relationships to place without rearticulating the violence inherent in property and stewardship? It is at the juncture of movement and place that I locate the need for dialogue with Native American studies, which challenges the notion that the colonial project of occupation is complete. . . . The United States and the Middle East region have both been historically imagined as promised lands with inhospitable frontiers in need of taming. . . . There are numerous examples of hydrologists, archaeologists, and ethnographers describing biblical promised lands as expressions of capitalism. Settler-colonial logic continues to inform contemporary archaeological projects across Palestine

5. For a history of Arab American racialization, see Amaney Jamal and Nadine Naber (2008) and Ian Haney-López (2006).

that use biblical claims to dominion over a promised land to justify occupation.

Foregrounding these related colonial histories embeds Arab American literature in the US settler-colonial state from which it emerges, a state whose historical treatment of Native Americans underpins much of its logics regarding the Middle East.[6] It also underscores the persistence of that state, as the United States is entangled with other historical and persistent settler-colonial states globally, many of which figure prominently in the texts I analyze. In the past three decades, there are multiple ways in which racial capitalism and its accompanying political and military apparatuses impact Arab Americans, Arab immigrants, and refugees seeking asylum in the United States, including the Gulf War, the invasion and occupation of Afghanistan and Iraq, shadow warfare in Somalia, increased surveillance of US populations through legal and juridical systems, and the most recent travel visa ban.

Steven Salaita has worked to forge generative connections between Native American and Palestine studies; he describes "inter/nationalism" as demanding "commitment to mutual liberation based on the proposition that colonial power must be rendered diffuse across multiple hemispheres through reciprocal struggle" (2016, ix). His writing marks a significant shift in what he describes as "prioritizing matters of liberation rather than merely assessing the mechanics of colonization" (2016, xi). Among the many reasons Salaita articulates as to why Native American studies is important to Palestine studies is that scholars "can contribute to decolonial projects in the spaces we inhabit while simultaneously reinvigorating our commitment to global sites of injustice" (2016, 136). Scholars of Palestine studies, he suggests, should draw on Native American theorizations of colonialism, sovereignty, and dispossession, all of which underscore the "planetary nature of plutocratic and neoliberal dominion that maintains colonial structures" (2016, 170).

Salaita's framing of the connections between Native American and Palestine studies can apply to ecocritical readings of Arab American literature more generally, encouraging us to read the ways in which specific texts attend to the material, geographical politics of inter/nationalism and the possibility of mutual liberation. Arab American texts often articulate how racial capitalism and its resultant environmental racism make people unfree—keeping them from inhabiting and interacting with land in the ways they choose—and provide narrative models for resistance. Power is interrelated on a planetary level, and herein lies my impulse to expand on the connections Salaita makes, using his framework to read what Arab American literature tells us about the global outflow of slow violence and how to divert its course.

Mizna's environmental issue is concerned with both the immediate violence of war and displacement and the ensuing slow violence that follows in its wake, including the violence of climate change. Indeed, its guest editor, Gary Paul Nabhan, who describes himself as an Arab American nature writer, points out in his foreword that it is unsurprising that Arab Americans are writing about climate change: "After all, many of us are climate refugees, from meteorological droughts and local plagues, or from political droughts, such as water wars or the export of peasant-grown food to industrialized countries" (2016, vi). Rob Nixon defines slow violence as "a violence that occurs gradually and out of sight, a violence of delayed destruction that is dispersed across time and space, an attritional violence that is typically not viewed as violence at all." He writes about the challenges for narrative and visual art to represent these "long dyings," including the aftermath of war, climate change, and deforestation (2011, 2).

Nixon also provides a definition of displacement that corresponds with the literature I consider here: "Instead of referring solely to the movement of people from their places of belonging," he defines displacement as "the loss of the land and resources beneath them, a loss that leaves communities stranded in a place stripped of the very characteristics that make it inhabitable" (2011, 19). By expanding the definition of displacement to include sedentary people losing the land beneath them to slow violence, Nixon changes the defining terms of place so that it refers to how people and land flourish together and how that flourishing can be stolen. The ramifications are

6. For analysis of the connections between US settler colonialism and its policies with regard to the Middle East, see Susan Kollin (2015).

significant for Arab American writers, whose works often have multiple settings and are about movement and loss of place. Reconceptualizing place indicates a reconsideration of how theft and violence occur even when people are in place. If authors are writing while physically in the United States, it also draws attention to the occupied land on which those authors write, the American occupation of Arab lands, and how the United States funds an outpouring of slow violence elsewhere.

Underscoring connections between environmental injustices and human suffering is key to articulating postcolonial ecology. . . . The history of Palestinian displacement *in place*, the inability to flourish in mutual relationship with one's homeland, is the subject of Dawud Mulla's poem "Water Wars" (2016). The speaker is the hudhud or hoopoe, an endangered bird indigenous to the region. Unlike its human kin, who are dislocated from place while held captive by checkpoints and walls, the nonhuman speaker of "Water Wars" is in constant forced movement away from home. The hoopoe tells of how it "presided over the Conference of the Birds" (Mulla 2016, 3), a reference to the twelfth-century poem by Farid ud-Din Attar, in which the hoopoe, the wisest of all the birds, leads other birds on a journey toward enlightenment. This Sufi text frames the poem, yet readers do not journey toward illumination; instead, we follow the hoopoe as it is chased out of its lands. The hoopoe can be read as a metaphor for Palestinians forced into exile, yet it has more mobility than Palestinians in exile because of their need for official documents and acceptance as political refugees by other governments. The poem's refrain reiterates that the invisible boundaries imposed by humans cannot restrain nature's migration: "I fly across borders that refugees cannot cross" (Mulla 2016, 17). Yet, while flight gives [the hoopoe] more mobility, animals continuously migrate through human-influenced landscapes and waterways, their patterns often disrupted by obstacles such as fences or changed because of deforestation and pollution. This migration is overlaid with that of the Palestinian exile and exile in place, in which the first is driven out because of policies that make land uninhabitable and the other forced to stay where life is unsustainable. Both are restricted by the need for documentation and state-sanctioned asylum.

The theme of water dispossession infuses the poem as the hoopoe speaks of Israeli bombings to obtain water resources and to destroy irrigation canals and of crops dying, sewage seeping into water supplies, and polluted water killing children. Israel, the hoopoe says,

> diverted the Jordan River by building
> the National Water Carrier.
> All to make the desert bloom and put swimming
> pools
> and dishwashers in Israeli homes.
> As the Dead Sea dried up, I flew to the Lebanese
> coast.
>
> (Mulla 2016, 11–12, lines 13–17)

During the Mandate period, Zionists used slogans such as making the "desert bloom" in order to make it appear that Palestine was both uninhabited and underused agriculturally. Former Israeli president and prime minister Shimon Peres writes: "The country was mostly an empty desert, with only a few islands of Arab settlement, and Israel's cultivable land today was indeed redeemed from swamp and wilderness" (1970, 249). Under Peres's presidency in 2008, to commemorate Israel's sixtieth anniversary, the hoopoe was chosen as the national bird through a nationwide election held by the Society for the Protection of Nature in Israel. The initiative was headed by ornithologist Yossi Leshem, founder of the International Center for the Study of Bird Migration in Latrun, a site of Israeli atrocities in 1948. By using this endangered bird as its speaker, the poem gestures to Latrun's violent history and contemporary preservation projects. The figure of the hoopoe links 1948 to 2008, underscoring how the rhetoric of making the desert bloom persists unremitted through present-day greenwashing, in which Israel presents its water theft and abuse as environmentally and technologically progressive. These claims are belied by the luxurious imagery of swimming pools and dishwashers against the backdrop of a dying sea and disappearing life. . . .

The speaker describes the hoopoe as the national bird of Israel and as endangered, showing how not only the bird but also its displacement and threatened survival are apt emblems for Israel as a settler-colonial state.

Overlapping human and nonhuman migrations, as represented by this prominent avian symbol of the Israeli nation, driven farther and farther from its territories, press the reader to ask what forms conjoined environmental and human justice should take. Environmental justice means Palestinians must have collective control over the conditions of their existence, which requires confronting ethnonationalist and racial capitalist forces that profit from the status quo. It means letting go of the certainty that capitalism and nationalism are the ends of history and that alternatives such as ecosocialism or liberation movements must negotiate within the parameters that already exist. Instead we can imagine other modes of being, drawing on traditional practices and merging them with new technologies and practices that are replenished, not threatened, by human and planetary contingencies.

Works Cited

Ahmed, Hamoud Yahya, and Ruzy Suliza Hashim. 2014. "Resisting Colonialism through Nature: An Ecopostcolonial Reading of Mahmoud Darwish's Selected Poems." *Holy Land Studies* 13, no. 1: 89–107.

Bujupaj, Ismet. 2015. "Nature in Arab American Literature: Majaj, Nye, and Kahf." *European Journal of American Studies* 10, no. 2. At journals.openedition.org/ejas/11130.

DeLoughrey, Elizabeth, and George B. Handley. 2011. "Introduction: Toward an Aesthetics of the Earth." In *Postcolonial Ecologies: Literatures of the Environment*, edited by Elizabeth DeLoughrey and George B. Handley, 3–42. Oxford: Oxford Univ. Press.

Elmusa, Sharif S. 2013. "The Ecological Bedouin: Toward Environmental Principles for the Arab Region." *Alif: Journal of Contemporary Poetics* 33:9–35.

Fadda-Conrey, Carol. 2014. *Contemporary Arab-American Literature: Transnational Reconfigurations of Citizenship and Belonging*. New York: New York Univ. Press.

Halaby, Laila. 2007. *Once in a Promised Land: A Novel*. Boston: Beacon Press.

Haney López, Ian. 2006. *White by Law: The Legal Construction of Race*. 10th anniversary ed. New York: New York Univ. Press.

Hassan, Waïl S. 2011. *Immigrant Narratives: Orientalism and Cultural Translation in Arab American and Arab British Literature*. Oxford: Oxford Univ. Press.

Huggan, Graham, and Helen Tiffin. 2010. *Postcolonial Ecocriticism: Literature, Animals, Environment*. London: Routledge.

Karpat, Kemal H. 1985. "The Ottoman Immigration to America: 1860–1914." *International Journal of Middle East Studies* 17, no. 2: 175–209.

Kollin, Susan. 2015. *Captivating Westerns: The Middle East in the American West*. Lincoln: Univ. of Nebraska Press.

Majaj, Lisa Suhair. 2009. *Geographies of Light*. Washington, DC: Web del Sol Association.

Mulla, Dawud. 2016. "Water Wars." *Mizna* 17, no. 2: 11–12.

Naber, Nadine. 2008. "Introduction: Arab Americans and U.S. Racial Formations." In *Race and Arab Americans before and after 9/11: From Invisible Citizens to Visible Subjects*, edited by Amaney Jamal and Nadine Naber, 1–45. Syracuse, NY: Syracuse Univ. Press.

Nabhan, Gary Paul. 2016. Foreword to "The Environment Issue," edited by Gary Paul Nabhan. *Mizna* 17, no. 2: vi–vii.

Nixon, Rob. 2011. *Slow Violence and the Environmentalism of the Poor*. Cambridge, MA: Harvard Univ. Press.

OCHA: United Nations Office for the Coordination of Humanitarian Affairs, Occupied Palestinian Territory. N.d. "Water, Sanitation, and Hygiene." At www.ochaopt.org/theme/water%2C-sanitation-and-hygiene.

Peres, Shimon. 1970. *David's Sling: The Arming of Israel*. New York: Random House.

Salaita, Steven. 2007. *Arab American Literary Fictions, Cultures, and Politics*. New York: Palgrave Macmillan.

———. 2016. *Inter/Nationalism: Decolonizing Native America and Palestine*. Minneapolis: Univ. of Minnesota Press.

Simpson, Audra. 2014. *Mohawk Interruptus: Political Life across the Borders of Settler States*. Durham, NC: Duke Univ. Press.

Sinno, Nadine A. 2013. "The Greening of Modern Arabic Literature: An Ecological Interpretation of Two Contemporary Arabic Novels." *ISLE: Interdisciplinary Studies in Literature and the Environment* 20, no. 1: 125–43.

Suliman, Israa. 2016. "A Letter from Gaza to the Natives of Standing Rock." We Are Not Numbers, Nov. 15. At https://wearenotnumbers.org/home/Story/Gaza_stands_with_Standing_Rock.

"Water Situation Alarming in Gaza." 2016. *World Bank*, Nov. 22. At www.worldbank.org/en/news/feature/2016/11/22/water-situation-alarming-in-gaza.

31

You (Shall) Have the Body

Patterns of Life in the Shadow of Guantánamo

KEITH P. FELDMAN

> In order to function, that is, to be readable, a signature must have a repeatable, iterable, imitable form; it must be able to be detached from the present and singular intention of its production.
>
> —Jacques Derrida, "Signature Event Context"

> Are we witnesses who confirm the truth of what happened in the face of the world-destroying capacities of pain, the distortions of torture, the sheer unrepresentability of terror, and the repression of the dominant accounts? Or are we voyeurs fascinated with and repelled by exhibitions of terror and sufferance? What does the exposure of the violated body yield?
>
> —Saidiya Hartman, *Scenes of Subjection*

For three days in early October 2015, the Park Avenue Armory Museum in New York City staged *Habeas Corpus*, a work of installation art that exposed, if not a present-tense violation of the body, then the flickering visions of its immediate past (*Habeas Corpus Program* 2015). The writ of habeas corpus—Latin for "you (shall) have the body"—emanates from the Magna Carta and decrees that authorities holding a person captive must present the body of that person before a tribunal tasked with ruling on the legality of their captivity. This foundational principle of the rule of law was routinely denied the roughly 780 people held at the US detention camp at Guantánamo Bay, Cuba.

Excerpt of Keith P. Feldman, "You (Shall) Have the Body: Patterns of Life in the Shadow of Guantánamo," *Comparatist* 42 (Oct. 2018): 189–203. Full references in the original notes were converted to author-date citations in the text and notes here, and a works cited list was added.

In response to numerous petitions brought by Guantánamo's detainees, the US Supreme Court clarified first, in 2004, that the writ of habeas corpus did indeed apply to people held on the Caribbean island (Kaplan 2005) and, second, in 2008, that people held captive at Guantánamo Bay did indeed have the right to bring habeas cases (Paik 2016). The Park Avenue art installation critically commented upon this legal history, foregrounding the ways the detained body was obscured from the purview of law and refused entrance into the sovereign territory of the United States. Produced by the acclaimed US performance artist Laurie Anderson, the installation's centerpiece featured what Anderson called the "telepresencing" of one former detainee, Mohammed El Gharani (*Habeas Corpus Program* 2015, 3). Born in Chad and raised in Saudi Arabia, in 2002 the then fourteen-year-old El Gharani was taken captive in Pakistan and detained for two months at the US military prison in Bagram, Afghanistan, before being sent to Guantánamo, where he was held without charge (*Habeas Corpus Program* 2015, 6–7). The US state alleged that El Gharani had been part of an al-Qaeda cell in London, though El Gharani had never visited London, and even if he had, he would have been a preteen at the time alleged by the state. In 2009, US judge Richard J. Leon ruled that the allegations against El Gharani were meritless, and, later that year, US authorities at Guantánamo facilitated El Gharani's release to Chad (*Mohammed El Gharani v. George W. Bush, et al.* 2009).

For *Habeas Corpus*, the Park Avenue Armory's cavernous Drill Hall was crosshatched by a dazzling refraction of countless beams of light scattered throughout an otherwise darkened room. The play of light on the floors, walls, and ceiling signaled a sense of extraterrestrial transport to a site beyond all that our Earth-laden gravity seemingly holds in place. At the center of the installation was what one viewer described as "an apparition of ambiguous magnificence": a sixteen-foot-high sculpture of a chair, into which was projected a live video feed of El Gharani broadcast from an undisclosed location in West Africa (Ross 2015). The sculpture's dimensions and proportions echoed those of the Lincoln Memorial in the District of Columbia, an allusion underscored in the installation's printed program (*Habeas Corpus Program* 2015, 10). What had begun for Anderson as an aesthetic exploration of "telepresence, cameras, time, and prison" had transformed into a chance for those in attendance to hear directly from a former Guantánamo detainee.[1] As El Gharani put it in the exhibition's program, "Many people have told my story. Now I have the opportunity to speak for myself for the first time" (*Habeas Corpus Program* 2015, 2). And speak he did. The projection of El Gharani described the physical ordeal of his captivity, his relation to other detainees, his efforts to learn English, his captivity's relation to the history of slavery and the Middle Passage. In a video interview screened in another room, El Gharani recounted, among other things, his visit with Anderson to a West African slave fort, a site he suggests was laden with a sense of historical repetition and similitude: capture, forced transatlantic transit, indefinite captivity. A live video feed was transmitted from the hall to El Gharani's undisclosed location, though apparently without audio, rendering verbal communication unidirectional and nonreciprocal. Here was a former Guantánamo detainee, presented before the US public, in a sculptural allusion to the legacy of racialized captivity and state-authorized emancipation, whose virtual performance enacted what the US state had earlier refused. By ambivalently addressing the embodied violence faced by Arabs and Muslims in the war on terror, as one commentator put it, El Gharani was "present, absent, and never really there," leaving behind a spectral image of suffering that "has not, and cannot, be made whole" (Varon 2015).

What kinds of critical concerns are raised by representations of corporeality in the shadow of Guantánamo? How does *Habeas Corpus* seek to bring those subjected to state-authorized violence into what decolonial philosopher Sylvia Wynter, following sociologist Helen Fein, once called our "universe of moral obligation" (1994, 44)? In what follows, I argue that *Habeas Corpus* prompts studying Arab and Muslim representation beyond the purview of positive and negative tropes and identitarian frameworks. This is not to downplay the ways some representations of Arabs and Muslims in the war on terror are negative and others are positive—the distribution thereof is highly and consequentially uneven—but rather to emphasize that some cultural practices meant to prompt awareness, action, or ethical reorientation are buttressed by representational protocols that do as much to reinscribe normative notions of human community as they do to challenge their terms of reference.[2] To riff on Wynter, the universe, with its historically sedimented differential distribution of human value and valuelessness, is remarkably stubborn.

How, then, ought we to treat a work like *Habeas Corpus*, one that conveys through robust aesthetic intensity a sympathetic representation of Muslims positioned at the capillary limit of US imperial culture—a representation that seeks recognition, reveals duress, bears witness to torture and bodily degradation? How

1. Habeas Corpus Program, 18. In an earlier iteration of Anderson's telepresencing project, people incarcerated were silently projected into a sculpture, living but mute. Anderson notes that this was to be her approach for *Habeas Corpus* prior to meeting El Gharani and hearing how much he has to say.

2. For a foundational critique of reading only for positive and negative representations, see Alsultany 2012.

might we read in ways that denaturalize what feminist critic Grace Hong calls an "allure of legibility" that cannot not desire a sympathetic recognizable subject?[3] *Habeas Corpus* is surely a "critical" work insofar as its point of departure is a salient critique of the excesses of US state power. It renders a recognizable humanity for people detained at Guantánamo Bay, drawing close that which is purported to be distant. Yet bridging these relative locations—"bringing Guantánamo to Park Avenue," as Anderson's (2015) own essay on *Habeas Corpus* puts it—is neither natural nor neutral, and neither are their rhetorical or ideological effects. In order to enunciate its claim for a shared humanity, the exhibit foregrounds youth, innocence, fractured kinship, resilience, tearful expressions of interiority. *Habeas Corpus* performs proximity as a warrant for recognition by drawing from a storehouse of sentimental figures. Feminist literary critic Lauren Berlant's argument about sentimentality is instructive in this regard. Berlant contends that "humanization strategies . . . always traffic in cliché . . . indulg[ing] in the confirmation of the marginal subject's embodiment of *inhumanity* on the way to providing the privileged with heroic occasions of recognition, rescue, and inclusion" (2008, 35, emphasis in original). Foregrounding El Gharani's singular body as the locus of recognition deserved not only runs the risk of deepening a commonsense presumption that there are subjects who are not deserving of recognition, that there are, in political sociologist Mahmood Mamdani's singular phrase, "good Muslims" and "bad Muslims" (Mamdani 2004); it also leaves untroubled the presumption that attendees to the show are granted the authority to bestow recognition, a presumption freighted with a long genealogy of colonialism and racism.

Working through the "allure of legibility" requires bringing together critical genealogies that surface the contemporary security-oriented dispensation of imperial culture with those that take up the long-standing racialization of Islam as a salient thread in the cultures of US imperialism. It prompts accounting for the representation of the figure of the Guantánamo detainee as one that arises out of what Black studies scholar Alexander Weheliye calls "racializing assemblages." Weheliye, following in the pathbreaking work of Wynter and Hortense Spillers, views race as "a set of articulated political relations or assemblages, and not a biological or cultural descriptor" (2014, 19). Importantly, even as *Habeas Corpus* reveals the clichés at work in an aesthetics of recognition, it also undercuts the liberal genre of a selfsame autonomous body. The image flickers; it's noisy. The ambivalence of El Gharani's telepresence disrupts any sense that the rendering of his body goes unmediated. To the contrary. The material artifice in which his image is projected is "monumental," as one commentator puts it (Ross 2015). It reflexively signifies its own technological production and circulation. El Gharani's ephemeral presence is contingent on a network of media technologies. The installation points not so much to the complex composition of El Gharani's being and biography as it does to the assemblage that brings his image before us. In this way, the installation reveals what critical anthropologist Junaid Rana calls the "infrastructure" of raciality in the war on terror, one that is "fundamentally about bodies as a materiality, a discursive arrangement, and a relation of/to power" (2016, 124).

At the same time, while the *Habeas Corpus* installation foregrounds the recognizable body as entangled with contemporary media technologies, the visual logic of the war on terror's racializing procedures need not latch onto a body to render difference or alterity thinkable.[4] "Pattern-of-life" analysis is one important disembodied form of visuality, one that departs in important ways from the liberal paradigm of embodied autonomous subjectivity discussed previously. "Pattern-of-life" analysis rose to the fore in the Bush administration's distinction between "signature strikes" and "personality strikes" in authorizing drone attacks. A "personality strike" is, in ProPublica's terms, "a targeted attack on a particular individual identified as a terrorist leader." An individual is affirmatively

3. Hong is quoted in Cacho 2012, 13. My formulation is meant to resonate with Gayatri Chakravorty Spivak's argument that human rights are rights that one cannot not want. See Spivak 2004.

4. Indeed, Weheliye's own argument foundationally disrupts the prevailing focus on the body in critical studies of race.

known and identified as such, figured as an autonomous subject and individual agent. A "signature strike," by contrast, is an attack "against someone believed to be a militant whose identity isn't necessarily known." (See also Chamayou 2015.) In this sense, pattern-of-life analysis is avowedly productive, meaning that the security state creates the subjects it seeks to know and visualizes those subjects through a mix of corporeal and technoscientific data. The ostensibly rational calculability of pattern-of-life analysis hinges, at least in part, on a formal rendering of subjectivity that, for the purposes of risk assessment and threat perception, foregrounds rationality and ideological neutrality as its operative frame. As feminist security studies scholar Lauren Wilcox puts it, "'Signature strikes' are not aimed at targeting known individuals, but rather on producing packages of information that become icons for killable bodies on the basis of behavior analysis and a logic of preemption" (2017, 16). These icons are drawn from the traces a particular individual leaves behind, commonly called metadata: the congeries of biometric details, geospatial coordinates, and communications information (time and location of phone calls, emails, text messages, etc.) that persons of interest produce. The former director of the National Security Agency (NSA) once put it plainly: "We kill people based on metadata" (quoted in Cole 2014). Metadata are the traces of communication and transaction left behind in a richly constructed context. Subjects are construed through the "data exhaust" of geospatial coordinates, time stamps, and SIM cards.[5] The abstractions of "pattern-of-life" analysis visualize risk and threat through the structured traces of data and metadata, fastening onto the signatures that stand in for the individual body.

In this sense, "pattern-of-life" analysis is a practice not avowedly concerned with content in the first instance but rather treats content as epiphenomenal to what literary scholar Caroline Levine terms the "patternings, shapes, and arrangements" that come to constitute form (2015, 13). As the NSA general counsel once claimed, "Metadata absolutely tells [*sic*] you everything about somebody's life. If you have enough metadata, you don't really need content" (quoted in Rusbridger 2013). Yet as the information sciences make readily apparent, metadata are themselves content-rich data about data, construed through particular grids of intelligibility that are themselves genealogically contoured, calibrated, and revised (see Pomerantz 2015). Critical education scholar Ezekiel Dixon-Román's remarks are instructive here: "As an assemblage, data are formed, shaped, and entwined with the histor(icit)y of the human" (2017, 50). Patterns of life crystallize in a signature, an assemblage of bodies, networks, technologies, and spatiotemporal coordinates that has everything to do with coloniality's differential distribution of human value and valuelessness.[6]

Insofar as the "signature" is a formal rendering of abstraction that consequentially mediates the original or the real, it is not especially novel or innovative. An important precursor to the "signature" is the stereotype. The standard usage of the term "stereotype" refers to what the *Oxford English Dictionary* calls "a preconceived and oversimplified idea of the characteristics which typify a person." It is not incidental that this commonsensical meaning is in fact metaphorical. The stereotype emerged initially in the technical vocabulary of printing at the end of the eighteenth century as a form of new media. In the *OED*'s words, to "stereotype" first described "the method or process of printing in which a solid plate of type-metal, cast from a papier-mâché or plaster mould taken from the surface of a forme of type, is used for printing from instead of the forme itself." The surface of the original plate, in other words, would be translated into another medium, made of a wholly distinct material, and that new medium would become the basis from which other reproductions would be created. A major innovation in print culture at the time, the stereotype afforded quicker and cheaper reproduction of texts, lending ease to the nineteenth-century creation and circulation of (and increasing middle-class access to) novels, newspapers, pamphlets, advertising, etc.

5. As geographer Jeremy Crampton puts it, "Big Data creates an 'identity paradox.' Whereas individuals seek control over the formation of their identity, Big Data constitutes identity" (2015, 521).

6. For a wider treatment of the aesthetic dimension operating at the interface of human and technology, see Jagoda 2016.

The stereotype, in its crude logic of typification and its rigid lack of historical malleability, has readily lent itself to base forms of prejudice and social discrimination and has come to inform, among other things, the particular rise of racial profiling as a security strategy.[7] The signature, by contrast, is presumptively more labile, more scientific, more precise in its capacity to attach an individualized truth value to a subject. Even more, signatures supplement the past-tense forensics of fingerprints and DNA left behind at the scene with a pattern whose temporality is oriented toward the permanent present. Philosopher Jacques Derrida's gloss of the signature is pertinent here, for "pattern-of-life" analysis as a reading practice is concerned with the "repeatable, iterable, imitable form" (1988, 20). That there is someone called the "signer," whose agency in writing brings the signature into the world—Derrida's own signature is ironically attached to his published essay on the topic—only further unsettles the absence/presence binary Derrida destabilizes. In this way, the "signature" constructed to rationalize the identification of a security risk is not an absence constituted by the presence of one's own individual agential inscription; rather, in "pattern-of-life" analysis, one's disembodied technoscientific traces are unwittingly reconstructed into a signature, creating an aestheticized abstraction of one's activities without the conscious foreknowledge of the individual.

The formal orientation of "pattern-of-life" analysis provides a contemporary reminder that processes of producing what Wynter calls the "dysselected" draw from a capacious network of signifying ensembles to predicate their norm/deviance framework. We might juxtapose these iconic aestheticizations with those found in *Habeas Corpus*, suffused with sympathetic content to dramatize its own embodied patterns of life. Doing so renders the grieveability for forms of life in the crosshairs of state-authorized violence (see Butler 2010). Yet as Lauren Wilcox compellingly argues, liberal presumptions about the body preclude grasping the way bodies are "not natural or pre-political objects that are only acted upon." Importantly, bodies are "inherently unstable," and violence, as highlighted in transnational feminist insights, "is not something that is done to an already established body" but is rather "part and parcel of the production of the various bodies that are subjected to violence" (2015, 10). Wilcox's claim invites scholars in Arab American studies to historicize the propensity to reify the individual body as a prepolitical site of sentimentality, while also being attuned to the particular operations, such as pattern-of-life analysis, that produce, interconnect, and entangle subjects through a technoscientific rationality.

If the critique of pattern-of-life analysis offered above reminds us of the fatal artifice that can attach to formalist renderings of difference, how might that reminder animate a critique of more sympathetic representations of Muslim subjectivity in the war on terror? *Habeas Corpus* foregrounds Muslim subjects as a high-profile limit case of US imperial culture. It foregrounds bodily integrity and interiority, staging an overt offering of the body to be reckoned with and to be recognized. It offers proximity as a key expression of a recognition-oriented cultural politics, making the body hypervisible against the backdrop of a surreal aesthetics of decontextualization. It frames state-authorized violence as excessive or exceptional, relying on an assumed juridical norm that serves as the basis for a proper form of political recognition. The liberal democratic state would not, or ought not, behave in this way, the argument runs. Yet such a framing forgets the sedimented residues and active recombinations of colonial, imperial, and racial capitalist histories that condition recognizable figures of political subjectivity.[8] In comprehending the installation as operating in conjunction with juridically oriented claims for human status and political standing, interposed but

7. Narrative offers a counter to profiling as a form of racialized abstraction. As cultural critic Moustafa Bayoumi puts it, "What exactly is a profile? It's a sketch in charcoal, the simplified contours of a face, a silhouette in black and white, a textbook description of a personality. . . . Stories have the capacity to convert a line drawing into flesh, to dislodge the power of the presumption and prejudice" (2009, 4, 12).

8. On the unwitting obscuring in some left liberal response to the photos of torture at Abu Ghraib prison of the banal and quotidian forms of carceral violence in the US prison regime, see Rodríguez 2006. On the wider engagement with these enmeshed histories, see Elia et al. 2016.

nonidentical with such claims, *Habeas Corpus* also troubles a post-Enlightenment frame of human cognizability. Its aesthetic complexity—the noise in the signal, the nonreciprocal audio, the reflexive decontextualization—seizes on the problem of witnessing what Black feminist critic Saidiya Hartman (1997) calls the "violated body's exposure."

When we heed the "tradition of the oppressed," as philosopher Walter Benjamin reminds us, we learn much about the obscured continuities that traffic across the norm/exception binary. At the same time, as historian Nikhil Singh instructively argues, focusing our analytical acuity only on limit cases produces its own foreshortenings, "limit[ing] thinking (especially critical thinking) to the most austere conceptualizations of enduring, if not entirely unchanging, modalities of racial dominance and state violence (without hegemony) across time" (2012, 299). With these cautions in mind, we ought to understand representations of the detainee's body in Guantánamo's shadow as actively involved in racialization's enduring if also changeful historical complexity, part of both the shifting distribution of stigma and privilege across time and space and the struggles over legitimacy and racial common sense that contour the terrain of political contestation.[9] An operative question for scholars in Arab American studies is how to keep these prevailing tensions in full view. Just as scholars in Arab American studies have long problematized the production and effects of racial and gendered stereotypes, I have suggested a complementary approach, one that addresses the limitations of sympathetic embodied modes of representation as a presumptively ethical response to technoscientific modes of entanglement, stigmatized forms of racialized representation, or the enforced absence and invisibility of people detained at Guantánamo. Substituting the icons of pattern-of-life analysis with sentimental protocols of human being does not move beyond the representational logics of empire. Other critical tasks are required to enable scholars in Arab American studies to pluralize the subjects of violence, torture, and bodily evisceration and in so doing, perhaps, to grasp the multidirectional and reciprocal forms of sociality that might yet enable us to think relationality otherwise.

9. See Cacho 2012 and Melamed 2011.

Works Cited

Alsultany, Evelyn. 2012. *Arabs and Muslims in the Media: Race and Representation after 9/11*. New York: New York Univ. Press.

Anderson, Laurie. 2015. "Bringing Guantánamo to Park Avenue." *New Yorker*, Sept. 23. At https://www.newyorker.com/culture/cultural-comment/bringing-guantanamo-to-park-avenue.

Bayoumi, Moustafa. 2009. *How Does It Feel to Be a Problem? Being Young and Arab in America*. New York: Penguin Press.

Berlant, Lauren. 2008. *The Female Complaint: The Unfinished Business of Sentimentality in American Culture*. Durham, NC: Duke Univ. Press.

Butler, Judith. 2010. *Frames of War: When Is Life Grievable?* London: Verso.

Cacho, Lisa Marie. 2012. *Social Death: Racialized Rightlessness and the Criminalization of the Unprotected*. New York: New York Univ. Press.

Chamayou, Grégoire. 2015. *A Theory of the Drone*. New York: New Press.

Cole, David. 2014. "We Kill People Based on Metadata." *New York Review of Books*, May 10.

Crampton, Jeremy W. 2015. "Collect It All: National Security, Big Data, and Governance." *GeoJournal* 80:519–31.

Derrida, Jacques. 1988. "Signature Event Context." In *Limited Inc*, 1–21. Evanston, IL: Northwestern Univ. Press.

Dixon-Román, Ezekiel. 2017. "Toward a Hauntology on Data: On the Sociopolitical Forces of Data Assemblages." *Research in Education* 98, no. 1: 44–58.

Elia, Nada, David M. Hernández, Jodi Kim, Shana L. Redmond, Dylan Rodríguez, and Sarita Echavez See, eds. 2016. *Critical Ethnic Studies: A Reader*. Durham, NC: Duke Univ. Press.

Habeas Corpus Program. 2015. Park Avenue Armory, Oct. 2.

Hartman, Saidiya V. 1997. *Scenes of Subjection: Terror, Slavery, and Self-Making in Nineteenth-Century America*. New York: Oxford Univ. Press.

Jagoda, Patrick. 2016. *Network Aesthetics*. Chicago: Univ. of Chicago Press.

Kaplan, Amy. 2005. "Where Is Guantánamo?" *American Quarterly* 57, no. 3: 831–58.

Levine, Caroline. 2015. *Forms: Whole, Rhythm, Hierarchy, Network*. Princeton, NJ: Princeton Univ. Press.

Mamdani, Mahmood. 2004. *Good Muslim, Bad Muslim: America, the Cold War, and the Roots of Terror.* New York: Pantheon.

Melamed, Jodi. 2011. *Represent and Destroy: Rationalizing Violence in the New Racial Capitalism*. Minneapolis: Univ. of Minnesota Press.

Mohammed El Gharani v. George W. Bush, et al. 2009. 593 F. Supp. 2d 144, Jan. 14.

Paik, A. Naomi. 2016. *Rightlessness: Testimony and Redress in U.S. Prison Camps since World War II.* Chapel Hill: Univ. of North Carolina Press.

Pomerantz, Jeffrey. 2015. *Metadata*. Cambridge, MA: MIT Press.

Rana, Junaid. 2016. "The Racial Infrastructure of the Terror-Industrial Complex." *Social Text* 34, no. 4: 111–38.

Rodríguez, Dylan. 2006. "(Non)Scenes of Captivity: The Common Sense of Punishment and Death." *Radical History Review* 96:9–32.

Ross, Alex. 2015. "Monumental." *New Yorker,* Oct. 19. At https://www.newyorker.com/magazine/2015/10/19/monumental-musical-events-alex-ross.

Rusbridger, Alan. 2013. "The Snowden Leaks and the Public." *New York Review of Books*, Nov. 21.

Singh, Nikhil. 2012. "Racial Formation in an Age of Permanent War." In *Racial Formation in the Twenty-First Century,* edited by Daniel Martinez HoSang, Oneka LaBennett, and Laura Pulido, 276–301. Berkeley: Univ. of California Press.

Spivak, Gayatri Chakravorty. 2004. "Righting Wrongs." *South Atlantic Quarterly* 103, nos. 2–3: 523–81.

Varon, Jeremy. 2015. "The Guantánamo Saga in Laurie Anderson's 'Habeas Corpus.'" *Public Seminar,* Oct. At http://www.publicseminar.org/2015/10/the-guantanamo-saga-in-laurie-andersons-habeas-corpus/.

Weheliye, Alexander G. 2014. *Habeas Viscus: Racializing Assemblages, Biopolitics, and Black Feminist Theories of the Human*. Durham, NC: Duke Univ. Press.

Wilcox, Lauren B. 2015. *Bodies of Violence: Theorizing Embodied Subjects in International Relations.* Oxford: Oxford Univ. Press.

———. 2017. "Embodying Algorithmic War: Gender, Race, and the Posthuman in Drone Warfare." *Security Dialogue* 48, no. 1: 11–28.

Wynter, Sylvia. 1994. "'No Humans Involved': An Open Letter to My Colleagues." *Knowledge on Trial* 1, no. 1: 42–71.

32

Cracking Down on Diaspora

Arab Detroit and America's "War on Terror"

SALLY HOWELL AND ANDREW SHRYOCK

It is hard now to portray Arab Detroit outside the framework provided by the attacks of September 11, 2001. The idea, popular not so long ago, that the Arabs of metropolitan Detroit had finally entered the cultural mainstream, producing US senators (Spencer Abraham) and union bosses (Steve Yokich, president of the UAW) and captains of industry (Jacques Nasser, CEO of Ford), is likely to be dismissed today as wishful thinking. Once hailed as "an immigrant success story," as "the capital of Arab America," the image of Arab Detroit changed within hours of the 9/11 attacks. Suddenly, it was a scene of threat, "divided loyalties," and potential backlash. In the suburb of Dearborn, home to 30,000 Arab Americans, people began, after 9/11, to describe their neighborhoods as "ghettoes" and "enclaves," a terminology of Otherness that was popular in nineteenth-century newspaper accounts of Detroit's newly arrived immigrants from Mt. Lebanon. Non-Arabs, for their part, began to use terms like "you people" when talking to Arab neighbors, relatives, and friends. In the language of polite society, "you people" is replaced by unctuous, incessant references to "the Muslim American community" or "the Arab American community," a double-edged jargon that effectively subordinates individual citizens to a logic of collective responsibility even as it protects them from accusations of collective guilt. "The 9/11 attacks," Arabs in Detroit tell us, "set us back a hundred years."

The collapse of history is a powerful motif. It captures much of what is happening in Detroit. The Arab community has played a critical role in the development of Detroit's economy and culture throughout the twentieth century, and its influence on high politics and everyday life in the Arab homelands—which are linked to Detroit by an irregular flow of money, information, ideas, and people—is so pervasive, so taken for granted, that scholars of Arab immigration to the Americas are only now beginning to study it systematically (Khater 2001). As the Bush administration's "war on terror" expands, however, Arab Detroit's rich history of domestic integration and transnational connection is being truncated, questioned, repoliticized, Americanized, and selectively erased. This radical transformation is rooted in anxiety about boundaries: Arabs and Muslims are clearly "in Detroit," with "us," but their hearts might still be "over there," with "them." The opposition is stark, and unrealistic, yet having it both ways, cultivating an identity that is both "here" and "there"—a sensible option that, in an era of multicultural tolerance, is still possible for many immigrant and ethnic Americans—is no longer a position Arabs in Detroit can easily embrace. The defense of boundaries, we will argue, only accentuates the centrality of the state in placing them; it also points to the moral dimension of boundary maintenance, to "being on the right side" of the line and the law. Rules, regulations, security protocols, and law enforcement technologies are

Excerpt from Sally Howell and Andrew Shryock, "Cracking Down on Diaspora," *Anthropology Quarterly* 76, no. 3 (2003): 443–62. In this excerpt, all informational footnotes were removed, along with their bibliographic references to make the essay shorter. Reprinted with corrections and press style changes for consistency throughout the volume by permission of George Washington University.

never adequate to the task of moralizing national boundaries. Loyalty to the state (also known as "patriotism") is the affective medium in which proper identity placement is made and measured.

In the aftermath of 9/11, Arab and Muslim Americans have been compelled, time and again, to apologize for acts they did not commit, to condemn acts they never condoned, and to openly profess loyalties that, for most US citizens, are merely assumed. Moreover, Arabs in Detroit have been forced to distance themselves from Arab political movements, ideologies, causes, religious organizations, and points of view that are currently at odds with US policy. This coercive predicament, which thwarts scholarship as much as it curtails political activism, is the backdrop against which we write. To understand how this coercion works and what it is working on, we must reengage with the dimensions of Arab Detroit that are now being removed from the public language in which Arabs, *as Americans*, are allowed to speak of (and for) themselves. We must also acknowledge that the nation-state, once a construct to which cultural theorists attached such dismissive modifiers as "withering," "disintegrating," "eclipsed," and "vanishing," is (in its American imperial form) central to any understanding of what is happening in Detroit, where state oversight and American identification are most intense, are most openly called for, in those parts of "the community" that still have strong ties to Arab and Muslim worlds. The privilege of transnational identification—that is, the ability to sustain political and economic ties to sites of belonging and social reproduction that are not American and are not fully subject to US sovereignty—has been, for Arabs in Detroit, the first casualty of the war on terror.

Histories and Maps

Detroit and its suburbs are home to a large, diverse population of Arab immigrants and their descendants. Population estimates, always controversial, are routinely inflated by Arab American activists—who claim numbers as high as 400,000 for the Detroit community—but even sober demographic calculations suggest a population of roughly 125,000 people (Schopmeyer 2000, 89). Arabs in Detroit tend to reside in the suburbs. The most visible concentration is in Dearborn, where Lebanese, Yemenis, Iraqis, and Palestinians, most of them Muslim, have built a vibrant terrain of mosques, ethnic business districts, social service agencies, political action committees, village clubs, and neighborhood associations. . . .

In addition to newly arrived immigrants, there are large numbers of assimilated, second-, third-, and fourth-generation Arab Americans living throughout the metropolitan area. Immigrants from Ottoman Syria had established small enclaves in Detroit by the 1890s. Mostly Christians from what is today Lebanon, they worked as peddlers and shopkeepers. Detroit became a magnet for other Syrians in 1914, when Henry Ford began paying his factory workers five dollars a day. Political turmoil in Lebanon and economic opportunity in the United States have continued to draw new immigrants to Detroit. The most significant recent wave of immigration was precipitated by the Lebanese Civil War, which began in 1975. Between the years 1983 and 1990, just after the war's peak, over 30,000 immigrants came to the United States from Lebanon. Another 10,000 arrived from Africa, Canada, and Europe. Nearly 4,000 of them settled in greater Detroit (Schopmeyer 2000, 66).

The relationship between political and economic instability in the Middle East and migration to Michigan holds for each of the nationalities that make up Arab Detroit. While the Lebanese are the largest and most visible of Detroit's Arab communities, the city also includes America's largest Yemeni and Iraqi communities and sizable populations from Palestine, Egypt, Jordan, Syria, and other Arab countries. Each of these national groups represents an odd inversion of the demographics of their home country, giving some indication of the forces that have made migration possible and necessary. For example, Christians make up less than 5 percent of the Arab world, but in Detroit they are half the community. Detroit's Iraqi population is predominantly Catholic. The Lebanese, once overwhelmingly Christian, are now at least half Muslim, with Shi'a, a minority in Lebanon, outnumbering Sunnis three to one (Abraham and Shryock 2000, 199).

This broad range of lifestyles, national backgrounds, and levels of assimilation has made the Detroit Arab community hard to represent, both intellectually and politically. It is not simply an American ethnic community. Parts of it make sense only in relation to the Yemeni highlands, the Lebanese countryside, or the ravaged "no-fly zones" of Iraq. Nor is Arab Detroit an integral part of the Arab world. The city is home, for instance, to tens of thousands of Arabs who cannot speak Arabic and have never traveled to the Middle East. Likewise, the overrepresentation in Detroit of Arab minorities and politically disenfranchised populations (Palestinians, for instance, and thousands of Iraqi Shiʿa, displaced when their US-inspired uprising against Saddam Hussein failed in 1991) contributes greatly to its internal fragmentation. The inhabitants of Arab Detroit often find it difficult to imagine themselves as a unified "Arab American constituency," and the divide between Muslim and Christian Arabs is a stable feature of community politics.

Still, the interface between the newest Arab immigrants, the old-line Arab Americans, and the larger non-Arab society is administered by community organizations that represent and have struggled since the 1970s to create an Arab American ethnic identity compatible with American multiculturalism. This model of Arab American identity is secular, progressive, and pluralist. It treats religion (whether Christian or Muslim) as one aspect of an overarching Arab identity defined in national, cultural, ethnic, and historical terms. In the aftermath of 9/11, this model of community has been put to the test, along with the more localized and globalized identities available to Arabs in Detroit. The period of testing is far from over, but its effects on Arab Detroit are beginning to accumulate in trends that are ominous and contradictory.

Report from the War Zone

Nearly two years have passed since the 9/11 attacks. Today, the Arab and Muslim populations of Detroit have been transformed, by an elaborate array of legal and extralegal means, into a domestic front in the Bush administration's war on terror. Dearborn was the first American city to have its own office of Homeland Security, an honor it owes exclusively to the number of its Arab/Muslim residents. No government official has said it explicitly, but Arab Detroit is now a zone of threat, and its inhabitants have good reason to feel threatened by the mixed messages they have received from officialdom and society at large. The first months after the 9/11 attacks were a time of hate crimes and intimidation, but a simultaneous desire to "understand" and "protect" Arabs and Muslims flourished in America. The federal government quickly released statements (six coming before September 15, 2001) designed to prevent a domestic backlash. "Any threats of violence or discrimination against Arab or Muslim Americans or Americans of South Asian descent," warned the office of Attorney General John Ashcroft, "are not just wrong and un-American, but also are unlawful and will be treated as such" (US Department of Justice Memorandum 01-468, September 13, 2001).

Initial attempts to "reach out" to anyone who might suffer from scapegoating suggested, for some, that a solid decade of pluralist conditioning had finally paid off. The "pay off" was, in some cases, quite literal. The Arab Community Center for Economic and Social Services (ACCESS), the largest social service agency of its kind in the United States, has received over $5 million dollars in gifts since 9/11, mostly from corporate sponsors and private charitable foundations, to fund its cultural and educational programs, which now include "sensitivity training" for (among others) the very law enforcement agencies that monitor the Arab community. In the days following the 9/11 attacks, mosques throughout Detroit received a barrage of death threats, by mail and phone, but they also received visits from members of local Christian churches, who offered support and friendship. Several mosques held open houses to "introduce" themselves to curious neighbors, and these events were well attended and generally deemed to be successful. On the economic front, Middle Eastern restaurants and other small, Arab-owned businesses weathered months of reduced sales after 9/11, but Detroit's mayor, Kwame Kilpatrick, joined Arab American business leaders in welcoming a delegation of ambassadors and trade ministers from the Arab League, who, in November 2001, toured the city and discussed plans for promoting investment and trade between Detroit and the Arab world.

Gestures of support for Arabs and Muslims met with open, often vociferous assertions of patriotism by those who felt most vulnerable to hate crimes. Denunciations of the 9/11 attacks appeared on the websites of every major Arab and Muslim organization, in Detroit and nationally. Community leaders asserted publicly that Bin Laden was not a good Muslim or was not a Muslim at all and that "there is absolutely nothing about Arab or Muslim culture that condones or encourages violence" (ACCESS 2002). In all of these exchanges, problems of identification and doubt (about being Arab, about being American) were never far from view. The exaggerated display of American flags by Arabs in Detroit—on clothes, skin, cars, homes, storefront windows, and places of worship (Shryock 2002)—was part of a heightened desire, familiar among immigrants of manifold sorts, to "belong" or (failing that) to be sheltered from the brute consequences of not belonging. The singing of "The Star-Spangled Banner" and "God Bless America" became, for a time, a stage on which young Arab American vocalists could shine. They vied for spots on the podium at organizational events throughout Detroit. Photogenic young singers who wore the hijab attracted special media coverage, and one became the subject of a brief documentary video (Mandell 2002).

Though it now seems strange, it is nonetheless true that many Arab and Muslim American observers believed, in the first months of the post-9/11 era, that their community was "being inducted into a kind of collective citizenship ceremony" (Mattawa 2002, 160). As a Muslim cleric from Dearborn told a delegation of visitors to his mosque in May of 2002, "I would say that we have seen, in this congregation, more positive developments after September 11 than negative ones. People have never been so eager to learn about Islam. We cannot meet the demand for lectures and workshops. This is a good thing that has come from a very bad situation." These words came in response to a question about harassment and profiling, which the cleric acknowledged were daunting problems. His upbeat conclusion, however, is a refrain we hear often among Arabs in Detroit. It is partly a refusal to cower, but it is also testament to the adaptability with which many mosques and secular community groups have responded to the crisis.

This "positive" take on events has been related, from the very start, to parallel trends that undermine it and, as the United States prepares for war in Iraq, threaten to overwhelm it completely. The passage of the USA PATRIOT Act and policy decisions made by the Department of Justice, the Immigration and Naturalization Service (INS), and the Department of the Treasury have created a climate in which Middle Easterners and South Asians in the United States can be treated as a special population to whom certain legal protections and civil rights no longer apply. This set of policies has led to the detention of over 1,200 people in the United States (who were never named or charged with crimes), the deportation of over half these detainees, the interrogation of thousands of resident aliens from Arab and Muslim countries, and the arbitrary declaration (usually based on secret evidence) that certain religious and political organizations—particularly those accused of having links to groups that oppose the illegal, but US-backed, Israeli occupation of the West Bank and Gaza—are providing "material support to terrorists," a status that legitimizes the freezing of their financial assets and the criminalization of their leadership.

The PATRIOT Act II, now being assembled by the Department of Justice, will increase the government's power to revoke US citizenship (again, based on secret evidence), after which an accused person can be removed from the realm of civilian courts and legal protections, detained indefinitely, tried by military tribunal, deported, and even executed. Against powers of this magnitude—Hobbes himself could not have imagined a mightier Leviathan—the twentieth-century threat of "internment camps" seems inefficient and old-fashioned. In an age of credit cards, cell phones, and computers, Arabs and Muslims in America do not need to be rounded up en masse and held in detention camps, as Japanese Americans were during World War II. Instead, they can be placed under a tactically flexible "house arrest," monitored in the privacy of their homes or as they move about the country, their financial transactions, intellectual interests, and personal contacts tabulated, their bodies examined every time they board a plane or enter a federal building. When need arises, targeted groups can be arrested and, without due legal process, be loaded onto chartered flights and discreetly shipped back to their homelands (or to third countries, where they can be subjected to "further questioning").

Not everyone, of course, is traceable in this way. The US Border Patrol in Michigan is now using "unannounced, rotating checkpoints" to search automobiles for illegal aliens, drugs, and terrorists. And, lest you doubt that Arabs are being singled out, the FBI will reassure you that their Detroit office has more than doubled in size during the past year and that their agents are receiving full cooperation from "wary community leaders acting as cultural guides into the local Arab world" (*Detroit Free Press*, November 12, 2002). Mark Corallo, a US Justice Department spokesman, said of the probe: "It's the largest investigation in the history of the United States" (*Detroit Free Press*, November 12, 2002). The result, so far, has been dozens of arrests—mostly for graft, identity forgery, cigarette smuggling, and other black-market crimes—and the purported discovery of an "operational combat sleeper cell" of four "al-Qaida terrorists" (who might just be hapless immigrants who fit the profile; the evidence against them has not been made public, although federal prosecutors have "characterized" the evidence in a manner favorable to their case).

Appeals to common citizenship with Arabs and Muslims have been substantially degraded by this wartime regime and its rhetoric of suspicion. Historical reversions and relapses are occurring now with alarming frequency. Howard Coble, chairman of the House Committee on Homeland Security, recently defended the internment of Japanese Americans. He also said he did not support the internment of Arabs, but his wording was hardly convincing: "We were at war. They (Japanese Americans) were an endangered species. For many of the Japanese Americans, it wasn't safe for them to be on the street. Some probably were intent on doing harm to us, just as some of the Arab Americans are probably intent on doing harm to us" (Associated Press, February 5, 2003). The mass-mediated structures of public opinion, especially those that materialize on cable news networks, in the wide circulation press, and on talk radio—Coble's remarks were made on a call-in radio talk show—have performed well as a conduit for the anti-Arab, anti-Muslim views espoused by a complex network of conservative think tanks, pro-Israeli pundits, US (and other) government spokespeople, and retired military and State Department officials. It is ironic, and more than a bit depressing, to learn (from national pollsters like Knight Ridder) that Arab and Muslim Americans have a higher "approval rating" today than they did before the 9/11 attacks (*San Jose Mercury News*, September 11, 2002). Apparently, they have never been regarded more fondly. Meanwhile, the Arabs of Detroit, despite the monetary gifts, the publicity, and the well-wishes that continue to be showered on their prominent community organizations and leaders, must find ways to interpret the growing evidence that their place in America is more vulnerable than ever.

Going Out of (the Diaspora) Business

Evidence of vulnerability is abundant wherever Arab Detroit is connected to the Arab world by ties of kinship, structures of shared religious and political sentiment, and commercial relations. These linkages facilitate the flow of money, the lifeblood of Arab Muslim (and most other) diasporas, and the US government—which, before 9/11, was willing to "tolerate cultural pluralism, dual citizenship, and transnational activism as never before" (Werbner 2000, 6)—is now determined to regulate these material and ideological flows and, when they cannot be regulated, to cut them off entirely. Giving to international Muslim charities has declined radically as a result, but equally pervasive effects are being felt in Arab Detroit's commercial sector, a domain filled with conservative, pro-American businessmen, mostly Lebanese and Iraqi arrivistes who voted overwhelmingly for George Bush in the 2000 presidential elections.

Before 9/11, the success of Arab entrepreneurs in Detroit was a major selling point for the city. The booming Arab neighborhoods of Dearborn were expanding into Detroit and Dearborn Heights, reviving moribund local economies. Immigrant entrepreneurs, who had spent the 1980s channeling surplus income into houses, cars, financial support for relatives in the United States and abroad, and donations to churches and mosques, were beginning to flex their political muscle, contributing to municipal campaigns throughout the metropolitan area, backing and opposing mayors, placing their allies on school boards and town councils, and building their own political machines. By the late 1990s, these economic and political advances were attracting the attention of Arab governments and their trade representatives, who saw Detroit as a unique point of entrée. As a commercial zone, it was part of the American economy, yet it was Arabized in ways that would make transnational commerce more attractive to Middle Eastern investors.

Detroit's potential as a nexus for the flow of wealth between the Arab world and North America is now being used by federal authorities as a new context in which to reward and punish Arab entrepreneurs and the diasporas they support. The American Arab Chamber of Commerce, a high-profile, Dearborn-based business association, has been working in recent months to organize a major economic forum at which dignitaries from the Arab states and Detroit's business and government officials will negotiate new trade relations and investment deals. The chamber's partners in the project include the US Departments of State and Commerce as well as the League of Arab States and the Gulf Cooperation Council. "Our goal," says Ahmed Chebbani, president of the chamber, "is to make Detroit a hub of trade between the U.S. and the Middle East, similar to [the relationship between] Miami and Latin America" (*Detroit News*, May 7, 2002).

The American Arab Chamber of Commerce has vigorously promoted this event and wants to keep it as apolitical as possible. Still, a glitzy "show summit" attended by Gulf royals closely aligned with the United States—worse, a forum scheduled to coincide with a US invasion and occupation of Iraq—is a prospect many Arab businessmen are reluctant to endorse. The optimism that once marked planning for the summit has faded even among its key organizers, who have watched the Bush administration recast Arabs and Muslims as a threat to national security. Hamoud Rizk (pseudonym), a prominent Arab American business leader who spoke with us about the progress of the economic summit, feared that the old rationale for the event, which was based on a real sense of Arab American success and economic possibility, has evaporated.

"People have put a freeze on all their plans," Rizk observed. "Individuals are not investing right now. Not buying homes. Not starting new businesses. If anything, they are thinking more of buying or taking care of property overseas. People are scared. They are asking, 'Are we safe?'"

This climate, Rizk continued, is disastrous for business, which depends on stability and trust. Fear of internment camps and confiscation of assets is rampant among his friends and colleagues; everyone assumes the IRS is pouring over their financial statements, looking for signs of tax evasion.

"People are beginning to think about a future in the Middle East," Rizk told us. "They're worried that Arabs won't be treated like other Americans. They've lost their faith in the US legal system. It used to be America was thought of as a place for individual freedom. America prided itself on this. But now freedom is less certain. It depends on who you are. We're no longer innocent until proven guilty. Now, in our community, you have to prove you're innocent."

Increasingly, local and national news stories feature Arab Americans who are caught up in criminal investigations—for instance, "Operation Green Quest," conducted by the US Customs Office—that are clearly designed, both as propaganda and as policy, to discourage people from sending money to the Arab world. In January 2003, sixty federal and local agents raided five Yemeni American businesses in Dearborn, arresting six men for engaging in what officials called "illegal money transfers." Authorities told the media that up to $53 million is sent annually (and, it was strongly implied, illegally) from Detroit to Yemen, a claim that would seem ludicrous to anyone familiar with the small, working-class community of Yemeni immigrants that was said to generate this vast sum. The charges were quickly dismissed by a local magistrate for "lack of evidence." Similar arrests have been made among Iraqis in Detroit, a much larger and wealthier community, who were said by federal authorities to be sending over $20 million a year to relatives in Iraq via indirect routes through Jordan. Since 1991, it has been illegal for Iraqis to send money home to their families, but authorities did not enforce the policy rigorously until after 9/11.

"Regardless of whether the money is going for food or clothing," said James Dinkins, special agent in charge of US Customs investigations in Detroit, "ultimately some of the money makes its way back into the hands of Saddam" (*Detroit News*, January 31, 2003). Given the fact that most Iraqis in Detroit are staunch opponents of Saddam Hussein's regime, this claim seems disingenuous, but Dinkins reveals the larger agenda with his next statement: "Part of the embargo is to put pressure on people and the government to change their practices. The government only changes if the people put enough pressure on them" (*Detroit News*, January 31, 2003). Transnational flows are acceptable only if they connect the United States to regimes it supports; otherwise, they must be blocked with the explicit goal of causing human suffering and useful political instability.

These news stories (and the disciplinary strategies behind them) are followed closely by Arabs in Detroit, who realize the numbers are grossly exaggerated; they also realize that claims that Arabs in America are providing "material support" for terrorism have become as routine as they are unsubstantiated. Increased scrutiny and suspicion, economic instability in the United States and the Arab world, and an underreported but significant boycott of American products in the Middle East have created, according to Rizk, "a great reluctance to do business right now. Individuals are vulnerable. Where possible, they are keeping their assets liquid. Trade, commerce, shipping, these are all taking a tremendous hit. When sending $50 to a relative through Western Union provokes a federal inquiry, you question everything." The fate of the US-Arab Economic Forum is now on hold. "We are waiting to hear from the State Department," Rizk told us, without a trace of eagerness in his voice. "We should know any day now. This depends on when the strikes [on Iraq] begin and on whether their projected outcomes will be as they imagine or as we imagine."

American Carrot/American Stick

The fate of the economic summit has structural parallels in every quarter of Arab Detroit. Tremendous pressures of delegitimization and criminalization are paired with levels of public- and private-sector support that have never been higher. In exchange for organizing and hosting the US-Arab Economic Forum, for instance, the American Arab Chamber of Commerce will receive generous funding from the US government, state and local authorities, and American corporations. It will also solidify its role as intermediary between the Detroit business elite and big corporate and political interests in the Arab world, especially the Gulf states. The larger goal, says Nasser Beydoun, director of the chamber, is to increase Arab investment in the United States (which currently stands at $200 billion) and to bring more of that vast sum to Detroit, which, Beydoun claims, has so far attracted only $10 million in direct investment from the Arab world. Beydoun told reporters the summit would entice Arabs overseas to "funnel money into Detroit real estate, including the revitalization of the riverfront. Medical centers and universities could forge relationships with Arab counterparts, and General Motors Corp., Ford Motor Co., and DaimlerChrysler Corp. could increase their share of the Arab market" (*Detroit Free Press*, September 20, 2002). Talk of reciprocal US or Arab American investment in the Arab world is poorly developed in this discourse, and its lack is part of the tendency, exaggerated since 9/11, to locate Arab Muslim interests strictly within Americanizing frames of reference and control.

Attempts to regulate monetary flows between Arab Detroit and the Arab world have meant that resources once sent abroad are now flowing into US-based and US-focused ethnoreligious institutions. If contributions to global Islamic charities are falling, attendance and giving at local mosques are rising. "The only mosques that are suffering," a Dearborn cleric assured us, "are the ones that receive support from the Middle East. Praise God, we do not receive support from outside this country." New mosques (and Islamic schools) are being built, endowed, and enlarged in Detroit and across America, while Muslim advocacy groups in the United States—like the Council on American-Islamic Relations (CAIR) and the American Muslim Council—are awash in contributions from people who see great value in their mainstreaming agenda. "We're Americans," said a recent full-page ad in the *New York Times*, placed by CAIR, "and we're Muslims. We're American Muslims." For Muslims who are self-described "modernists" or "moderates," the post-9/11 climate has opened up new possibilities for creating an Islam that is unapologetically American, and this creation, all too often, is legitimized by contrasting it to an implicitly "bad" Islam that is associated not only with fanaticism but also, symbolically and spatially, with Arabs, the Middle East, and the cultures found there. Consider the representational window dressing in the following statement issued by CAIR: "Only about 18 percent of Muslims live in the Arabic-speaking world. The largest Muslim community is in Indonesia. Substantial parts of Asia and most of Africa have large Muslim populations, while significant minorities are to be found in the countries of the former Soviet Union, China, North and South America, and Europe" (2003).

At the household level, meanwhile, the movement of family members and liquid assets between (and around) national jurisdictions, once a highly fluid process, is being compulsively monitored and contained: the retired parents who might have come to the United States from Lebanon no longer want to; the extended family that moved regularly between Jordan and Detroit is now divided into "the ones who stay in Jordan" and "the ones who stay here"; the Yemeni whose visa is about to expire will not overstay but will return to Sanaa with his brother's wife and children, who are all citizens, but whose relatives in Yemen are pleading with them to come home, "until it is safe again in America." Buying property in Syria, sending a wedding gift of cash to a brother in Iraq, supplementing the budgets of family members living under house arrest in the West Bank, or discreetly funneling (undeclared) income into a business in Lebanon—all these quotidian transactions, which have their equivalents in other immigrant communities, are now more difficult, sometimes even endangering, for Arabs in Detroit.

Perhaps the greatest changes are occurring in realms of political and personal identification, where Arab and Muslim Americans must reimagine their communities in order to locate them securely in (national) space and represent them effectively to others. This political project is national in scope, and Arabs and Muslims are neither its principal targets nor its primary beneficiaries. The Public Broadcasting System (PBS), for instance, is now producing and promoting sympathetic, high-quality documentaries about Arabs and Islam in America; major initiatives are being devised and funded by elite US research foundations, institutes, and universities, where scholars who once had no interest in Arab and Muslim communities in the United States are now dividing up the research spoils; dozens of new books and special issues about Islam in America are in print, in press, or already on shelves; and Arab American and Muslim organizations are partners in this flurry of cultural production, all of which is animated, colored, and (too often) distorted by the necessity of knowing Arabs and Muslims in relation to the events of 9/11.

It is not surprising, in this moment of redefinition, that Arabs in Detroit would be eager to assert a sense of national belonging that is demanded of them and, at the same time, is denied to them. What is unexpected, however, is the odd way in which every attempt to assert American identity must involve a simultaneous stigmatization of any sense of Arab identity that includes a strong identification with religious beliefs, political ideologies, or cultural practices that are genuinely alternative to those prevalent in America today. To reassert their status as "good" and "loyal" and worthy of respect, Arab Americans must distance themselves not only from negative stereotypes but also from the people who are most likely to suffer from these images and their consequences. In an op-ed piece written by Jim Zogby (2001), head of the Arab American Institute, the scrutiny aimed at Arab Americans by journalists after the 9/11 attacks provides an opportunity to (re)assert the Americanness of Arabs in the United States. Note what counts here as evidence of "diversity."

> Arab Americans are being discovered, or should I say being rediscovered, by the same papers and networks that have discovered us twice before in just the past decade. As I speak to those assigned to do the story, they discover yet again the diversity of my community. The fact that we are not a new ethnic group in America (we've been here for 120 years). That most Arab Americans are not Muslims (in fact, only 20% are). That most Arab Americans are not recent immigrants (in fact, almost 80% are born in the U.S.). And that many Arab Americans have achieved prominence and acceptance in America (two proud Arab Americans, Spencer Abraham and Mitch Daniels, serve in President Bush's cabinet, and Donna Shalala served in Bill Clinton's cabinet).

The numbers, proportions, and terminology are all debatable, but Zogby's narrative is flawless in its ability to map the terrain of Otherness in which many Arab Americans, especially those in Detroit, now live. The Arab community Zogby does not speak to (and would encourage his readers not to dwell on) is new, Muslim, born overseas, unknown, unaccepted, accented, culturally peculiar, and politically untouchable. In Arab Detroit, people who belong to this zone of Otherness must keep their heads low and (just as often) their mouths shut as their own community leaders renegotiate the terms on which Arabs and Muslims will be tolerated in the American mainstream. The legal distinctions between "citizen" and "alien," between "legal alien" and "out of status," are gradually eroding, yet many Arab American spokespeople are publicly falling back on a set of binaries—an identity code spoken widely among Arabs in Detroit, but formerly as a kind of private, in-group classification system—that equates American-ness with security, loyalty, trustworthiness, and respect: "Arab Americans," "the Americanized," and "Arab Americans proper" are set apart from "Arabs," "immigrants," "temporaries," "illegals," and, in a more disparaging vein, "boaters." The fact that nearly every church, mosque, village club, and extended family in Arab Detroit is made up of people who belong on both sides of this taxonomy all but ensures that defensive labeling strategies will reinforce (and become part of) the marginalizing trends they are designed to combat.

To show the degree to which every gain in this process of remedial identification brings with it a setback, we have assembled the events of a three-day period in early November 2002, a time of national elections and the onset of Ramadan, when civic duty and religious sentiment were prominently on display in Arab Detroit and across the United States.

> On November 5, 2002, George and Laura Bush extend Ramadan greetings to Muslims everywhere: "Islam is a peace-loving faith that is practiced by more than one billion people, including millions of American Muslims. These proud citizens contribute to the diversity that makes our country strong, and the United States is grateful for the friendship and support of many Muslim Nations that are vital partners in the global coalition to fight against terrorism" (White House press release).
>
> On November 6, the American-Arab Anti-Discrimination Committee (ADC) requests that all Muslims currently held in US jails and military prisons receive proper accommodation for the Ramadan fast. ADC and the Arab American Institute (AAI) ask the White House for guidance on holiday charitable contributions. No one wants to have their property confiscated, their accounts frozen. No one wants to face detention or deportation because they gave money to the wrong people.
>
> On November 5, Imad Hamad, head of Detroit's ADC chapter, votes for the first time. He has spent the previous seven years fighting legal challenges, the use of secret evidence against him, and threats of deportation. His 2002 swearing-in as a US citizen was attended by FBI officials, who praised Hamad for his cooperation in recent months.
>
> On November 6, the AAI announces, on its website, that 70 percent of Arab American candidates were successful nationwide in the November 5 midterm elections. Ismael Ahmed, Democratic candidate for regent of the University of Michigan, is not one of them. A Republican activist ran a smear campaign against Ahmed, director of ACCESS, a social service agency based in Dearborn. The activist claimed Ahmed was a supporter of "Islamic terror groups." A public letter of support for Ahmed signed by Jewish members of Michigan's Democratic congressional delegation came too late to kill the rumor.
>
> On November 7, more than thirty Arab American activists from across the nation convened at ACCESS to discuss plans for a $9 million Arab American National Museum. The museum, the first of its kind in the country, will focus squarely on Arabs in America, not on ties to the Arab world, a separation that troubles some people, even as it thrills others. "This is the great divorce," one observer told us. "They're going to replace 2,000 years of culture with Casey Kasem's Top Forty Arab Americans." "It's time for us to define who we are where we are, which is in America," said another. "This is my home. I'm not foreign. We've got over a hundred years of history in this country. People need to hear that now more than ever."

Such is life on the margins of the American body politic, where acts of inclusion and exclusion are hard to distinguish. The Arabs and Muslims of Detroit must contend, for now—as Japanese, German, and Italian Americans have done in the past—with the dangers that accompany their status as political and cultural "dirt," what Mary Douglas so famously defined as "matter out of place."

Edward Said, in a recent (and pessimistic) essay, confesses that "I don't know a single Arab or Muslim American who does not now feel that he or she belongs to the enemy camp and that being in the United States at this moment provides us with an especially unpleasant experience of alienation and widespread, quite specifically targeted hostility" (quoted in Gabriel 2002, 23). Mainstream Arab American advocacy groups repeatedly remind us that although the conditions we explore in this essay are frightening, the majority of Arab Americans have not suffered direct abuse (though most know someone who has). Nonetheless, the alienation Said describes has forced many Arab Americans into a position reminiscent of the "double consciousness" W. E. B. Du Bois saw as a central aspect of African American life in the early 1900s. For Du Bois, this predicament brought about "a peculiar wrenching of the soul, a peculiar sense of doubt and bewilderment. Such a double life, with double thoughts, double duties, and double social classes, must give rise to double words and double ideals, and tempt the mind to pretense or to revolt, to hypocrisy or to radicalism" (1903, 202).

The range of options Du Bois laid out was not at all attractive, largely because it was (and still is) so effectively constrained by the defining, disdaining power of a dominant white society. The transnational and multicultural pluralism that became available to minority populations in the United States in the final decades of the twentieth century was, some would argue, an effective means by which to alleviate the most "wrenching" effects of double vision. The benefits of multicultural citizenship have never been fully extended to Arabs and Muslims in America, however, for reasons deeply embedded in popular religious sentiment and the logic of US foreign policy in the Middle East (McAlister 2001). As the United States prepares for another war—perhaps a series of wars—against Arab and Muslim people, the inhabitants of Arab Detroit are increasingly seen, and must increasingly see themselves, through a doubling lens.

Works Cited

Abraham, Nabeel, and Andrew Shryock. 2000. "Religion." In *Arab Detroit: From Margin to Mainstream*, edited by Nabeel Abraham and Andrew Shryock, 198–202. Detroit: Wayne State Univ. Press.

ACCESS Cultural Arts Program. 2002. *Understanding Arab Americans, the Arab World, & Islam*. Dearborn, MI: ACCESS.

Council on American-Islamic Relations (CAIR). 2003. "Islam in America National Ad Campaign." At www.americanmuslims.info/ad.asp?m= 02&d=16.

Du Bois, W. E. B. 1903. *The Souls of Black Folk*. Chicago: A. C. McClurg.

Gabriel, Judith. 2002. "Edward Said Speaks Out before and after 9-11: Muffling the Arab Voice." *Al-Jadid* 8, no. 39: 23–26.

Khater, Fouad. 2001. *Inventing Home: Immigration, Gender, and the Middle Class in Lebanon, 1870–1920*. Berkeley: Univ. of California Press.

Mandell, Joan. 2002. *I, Too, Sing America*. Detroit: Olive Branch.

Mattawa, Khaled. 2002. "Assimilation and Resistance in Arab Detroit." *Michigan Quarterly Review* 41, no. 1: 155–61.

McAlister, Melani. 2001. *Epic Encounters: Culture, Media, and U.S. Interests in the Middle East, 1945–2000*. Berkeley: Univ. of California Press.

Schopmeyer, Kim. 2000. "A Demographic Portrait of Arab Detroit." In *Arab Detroit: From Margin to Mainstream*, edited by Nabeel Abraham and Andrew Shryock, 61–92. Detroit: Wayne State Univ. Press.

Shryock, Andrew. 2002. "New Images of Arab Detroit: Seeing Otherness and Identity through the Lens of September 11." *American Anthropologist* 104:917–22.

Werbner, Pnina. 2000. "Introduction: The Materiality of Diaspora—between Aesthetic and 'Real' Politics." In "The Materiality of Diaspora," edited by Pnina Werbner. Special issue of *Diaspora* 9, no. 1: 5–20.

Zogby, James. 2001. "'Rediscovering' Arab Americans." Arab American Institute. At www.aaiusa.org/wwatch/111201.html.

33

Borders Are Obsolete

Relations beyond the "Borderlands" of Palestine and US–Mexico

LESLIE QUINTANILLA AND JENNIFER MOGANNAM

> I'm not going to confine myself to some narrow particularism. But I don't intend either to become lost in a disembodied universalism. . . . I have a different idea of a universal. It is a universal rich with all that is particular, rich with all the particulars there are, the deepening of each particular, the coexistence of them all.
>
> —Aimé Césaire, letter to Maurice Thorez, 1956, in *Discourse on Colonialism*

> We ask that you bring your word and use it to provoke thought, reflection, critique. We ask you to prepare your message, sharpen it, polish it. We ask that you use your message to honor those who will receive it, and not academia or its equivalents, even if that might come in the form of a shaking, a slap, or a scream.
>
> —SupGaleano, Mexico, April 2015

The Palestinian Youth Movement–San Diego (PYM) and Colectivo Zapatista (CZ) came together in the fall of 2013 after CZ approached PYM to work together on a 5K run along the US–Mexico border. This article aims to speak to how organizing, joint-struggles, and relationship-building processes around the Break Down Borders 5K function as possibilities against settler colonialism's manifestations at the US–Mexico border through the partnership of local Palestinian, Indigenous, Black, migrant, third world, and queer organizers on unceded Kumeyaay lands, otherwise known as San Diego, California. PYM was inspired by CZ's desire to work together and draw parallels between Palestine and Mexico. We began planning for this event knowing that we would have the autonomy to frame, expand, and deepen its meaning and political trajectory to focus on the connections between indigeneity in Palestine, Mexico, and the United States and the effects of settler-colonial displacement. Through organizing together for two years, we have learned from these experiences and, alongside each other, refined our joint political frameworks to include questions of the prison-industrial complex, land and water, spirituality, imperialism abroad, Blackness, and queerness.

A major point has been the politics of language in this border city. Break Down Borders is an annual event that includes speakers, food, facilitated group dialogues, dancing, and a 5K run/walk along the US border wall in San Ysidro, California.

The traction it has gained in the community has extended across other communities of struggle and across the border to Tijuana. Some community members in Tijuana were interested in joint organizing and learning more about Palestine. So members of PYM and CZ

This article first appeared in *American Quarterly* 64, no. 4 (Dec. 2015): 1039–46. Full references in the original notes were converted to author-date citations in the text and notes here, and a works cited list was added.

crossed the border and gave a bilingual presentation in English and Spanish. While trying to find linguistic translations for key Palestinian political language, we realized the importance of the politics of translation, the political language across and the distinctiveness of contexts. Through this critical multilingual conversation on Palestine and the US–Mexico border, we were able to translate, share a message, and ultimately build lasting relationships between Tijuana and San Diego. Social relationships rooted in a deep sense of camaraderie, illegible to both the hegemonic discourse of empire and the dominant discourse of solidarity movements, enabled people from across these contexts to come together through an anti-settler-colonialism framework. We refer to this space as the undercommons: an intimate social space that was never supposed to exist given the conditions of institutional marginalization between people's disparate conditions from which the border functions. The "undercommons" is a space that exists beyond the state, a collective space unmediated by the institution that can exist beyond the scope of capitalism because of its ability to be (temporarily) autonomous in its improvisational nature. This can be seen in the reweaving of the social relationships that exist in a capitalist system, structured by logistics, bureaucracy, and institutions. In this way, un/relearning connection, as Stefano Harney and Fred Moten (2014) put it, is an unmediated feeling of love that is misrecognized in the global capitalist cycle, where rejected subjectivities refuse the settler-colonial system and enact modes of living that work in tandem with decolonial thought.

Thinking through, reading, seeing, listening to on-the-ground movements through academic frameworks of the interconnected fields of border studies, ethnic studies, and American studies allow us to look to these events for a conjunctural analysis of movements and, even, revolution, but only through a myopic view since they are analyzed and written about only within the confines of an office in the corner of a campus. "Borderland" or "border" studies is not just about the physical or metaphorical border but about seeing around and through the holes in/of the border by living and creating these intimate social relationships in the undercommons. Reactionary political events, activism, or identitarian processes should not be the focus of "borderland" studies or American studies. Instead, we must shift to see/hear the proactive and creative processes and organizing happening through the border, permeating the loopholes of settler-colonial formations in interesting ways.

In *Undoing Border Imperialism* (2013), Harsha Walia explains a process of mobilizing where community organizing against oppression requires the offering of tangible resources by organizers and intellectuals along with direct engagement and involvement of marginalized communities whose lives are most affected by systematic oppression. She further proposes that "oppressed communities should be within the leadership of our movements precisely because those most impacted by systematic oppression . . . [are] also those who are most impacted by systems of border imperialism, capitalism and empire" (191). These steps in the decolonization process are part of what Walia terms *grassroots theory* (2013, 191). While academics might ponder the relevance of such strategies, these peoples, experiences, and relations are living the very concepts with which the academy is grappling, like racism, classism, sexism, colonialism, and empire. It is because of this that we believe these principles must be assumed as a means of accountability and of producing more meaningful and complex interventions that attend to and complement the experiences, articulations, and aims of communities subjected most to the oppressive regimes we so often discuss. And likewise, while written intellectual production is a contribution or tool that can be beneficial for decolonization, this production in and of itself is not sufficient for the project of decolonization.

The role of intellectuals working toward decolonization requires a questioning of position and relationship to organizing and movement work before giving it more weight than others or being hastily marked as a form of activism. For Walia, "Decolonization is, in essence, a subversion of border imperialism as it requires us to reimagine and reconfigure our communities based on shared ideals and visions" (2013, 256). This description suggests that a multitude of processes contribute to decolonization, but at the heart of decolonization are communities in struggle. By aiming for an understanding and articulation of grassroots theory and centering its producers and enactors, it is possible to strive for a community-based praxis whereby resistance to oppression is facilitated in various strategic ways.

Radical relation-building politics are not legible and cannot be understood only through the lens of settler colonialism at the border because although it is resistance, it is also in a space beyond the border itself. When multiple bodies that identify as queer, migrant, Palestinian, Lakota, Mexican, Black, Asian Pacific Islander, Central American, Iranian meet at the site called the US–Mexico borderland through dialogue at the Break Down Borders 5K, there are multiple temporalities and geographies, dislocated and connected, that are reacting to the imperial nation-state and how it positions these bodies. There is a necessity to create possibilities of life beyond the settler-colonial present of the United States, Israel, Mexico, and others, and while the border is present, it is not centered in these encounters. The energy of the border area is to build and create the spaces that intellectuals and academics can imagine existing only in a linear future, but we know are existing in the present. Danza azteca, dabke, Peace and Dignity Journeys, and the spirit of connectivity existed and intersected at the 5K border run.

While the Break Down Borders 5K takes place on the US–Mexico border, we find it important to remain grounded in the realities of each of our communities, and as such we find the language and study of borders limiting. Instead, we move toward understanding space and crossing geographies as more fluid ways to understand larger structures of oppression. We are concerned with creating a space where all peoples of struggle in San Diego (and their respective transnational struggles) could converge and organically exchange their own struggles' sensibilities, in turn fostering a process for understanding the linkages between one another. As organizers, we envisioned specific political framings for this action, including attempts to account for interconnected struggles locally and globally while diffusing any notion of oppression Olympics. One of our strategies was to be flexible through sharing and group reflection. We asked people to talk to others with whom they had just run/walked but not yet met, and we facilitated a large open circle where everyone could share their experiences and reasons for being there with everyone. This moment was laced with celebration and tears, as many participants shared the ideas and emotions that this action amplified. As a productive encounter, this action was found to be a most freeing and liberating moment ever experienced, so physically close to the border, by some in the undocumented community.

The location of this action was particular and strategic, and there was no shortcoming of community bases and allies. While we think about the connections between this border and Palestine, thousands of miles away, we also think about the parallels with other communities. We do not try to shy away from drawing the linkages between struggles for fear of exposing contradictions; rather, we note the parallels and work through the contradictions to foster a deeper understanding of the basis of our alliances. Concretely, the Israeli military and Mossad have trained local police departments like the San Diego Police Department. Therefore, limiting the parallel to Elbit Systems, the Israeli company that has been involved in both walls, and the construction of the walls in the spirit of border action would not only dilute the political framework but also oversimplify the many layers of oppression that go hand in hand with US and Zionist imperialisms, neoliberalism, and white supremacy. The wall, along with police, military, and intelligence exchange and the multinational security industry, produces a multifaceted conglomerate for oppression that affects Black, imprisoned/detained, and refugee populations as well.

San Diego is a unique site of oppression. In addition to being a border town, the city is an enormous military hub, which means that the military-industrial complex is foundational to the city's functioning. For example, San Diego is a politically conservative and increasingly "booming" city for science, technology, and engineering. These industries, as well as the academic-industrial complex (and specifically the University of California, San Diego), directly contribute to the expansion of the military-industrial complex in the United States and Israel. While displacing Indigenous folks, drone, security, weapons, and other technologies are developed in San Diego. As a result of the "boom" in these industries, a new wave of gentrification has hit the city. We also see that the drones tested across the US–Mexico border are the same drones striking Yemen, Syria, Iraq, and many other places around the world. Likewise, Zionist law enforcement tactics like tear gas and rubber bullets are being used against the small community of organizers and activists here in San Diego—tested on Palestinians by Israel and deployed on Black and brown bodies by the United States.

To make things more complicated, because of the heavy military presence in San Diego, refugee populations of the US war industry have strategically been relocated to this militarized city from Iraq and Somalia, the Philippines and Vietnam, and beyond. Consequently, not only are these refugees isolated and having to struggle to survive here, but their extreme poverty and quests for employment and other basic needs are leveraged by being offered economic stability if they work for the very force that created their refugeehood: the US military. Between military and local, federal, and international law enforcement, San Diego as a site produces a constellation of dynamics whereby transnational oppression and transnational struggles for justice converge. It is through this understanding and this shared space that we believe it necessary for the San Diego community to come together in joint-struggle and for academics to be more attentive to the convergences, rather than focusing only on ruptures, of joint-struggle among community bases. Thus, we call for not only attention to but also a moving beyond the question of the border and the limits that a conversation solely of borders might set.

Not only do borders complicate the question of indigeneity, but *this* border also complicates the question of the prison-industrial complex. We notice that language complicates the question of indigeneity and at times can reproduce divisions among Indigenous communities simply because of who got stuck on what side of the border and when. Conversely, because of activists' desire for the fluidity and/or abolition of borders, confusion around the term *indigeneity* arises where it often becomes disconnected from land, thus further reproducing the erasure of those whose lands we are on and of those who have preexisted this country's founding. The concept of the prison-industrial complex is also troubled here. While it disproportionately affects Black communities in the United States, in San Diego the prison population is a mix of Black and brown bodies as well as a mix of national backgrounds. Detention centers are overfilled with undocumented, queer, and trans peoples, and the same technologies and tactics are being used to further oppress them. By looking to San Diego's prison-industrial complex, we can see a transnational system of incarceration whereby the expendability of populations is no longer US specific; rather, it implicates all those who suffer at the hands of US imperialism and neoliberalism.

San Diego as a site offers us an understanding of the necessity of thinking transnationally as well as thinking together in the process of the struggle to defeat various systems by which we are affected in distinct and interconnected ways. Thus, we are calling not for conflating struggles but for opening up our specific struggles to each other so that we can clearly see our common oppressors and struggle against them together. We realize that this is not an easy task and that it is sometimes more convenient and tangible to focus our organizing on only each individual struggle. However, we are arguing that while this approach may feel more effective in the short term, we would be reproducing divisions perpetuated by our oppressors in the long run. It is therefore our responsibility as community organizers to bring our different communities together and brave through the contradictions that our collective work brings up. This is far preferable to maintaining divisions; no one struggle can be maintained, let alone achieve liberation, on its own. While moments of tipping the balance against oppression might be reached, the sustenance of liberation becomes increasingly difficult when repressive regimes are still intact elsewhere. Expanding the understandings and sites of oppression and struggle as well as opening channels for cross-movement relationship building in opposition to isolationism are necessary for liberation.

Notes

Our work is for the Palestinian Youth Movement, especially the San Diego chapter, Colectivo Zapatista San

Diego, and all the allies who continue to support and work in join-struggle everywhere.

Works Cited

Harney, Stefano, and Fred Moten. 2014. *The Undercommons: Fugitive Planning and Black Study.* Oakland, CA: AK Press.

Walia, Harsha. 2013. *Undoing Border Imperialism*. Oakland, CA: AK Press.

Part Six

Solidarities and Sites of Resistance, Theorizing Borders

On May 2, 2013, Assata Shakur became the first woman to be placed on the FBI's most-wanted terrorist list. As Angela Davis asks, "Why was it necessary to put a woman's face on terrorism, especially in the aftermath of the tragic bombing of the Boston marathon? Why was it necessary to put a Black face on terrorism, especially after initial news about the Boston bombing that the perpetrator was a Black man, or if not a Black man, at least a dark-skinned man in a hoodie—the ghost of Trayvon Martin?" (2016, 92). In her work, Davis underscores the facile criminalization of Black and brown people and of all oppressed people who are expected to accept their inferior status in a racist, sexist, ableist, and heteronormative carceral-security state. She highlights the connections between historic and ongoing state policies and practices that have ravaged communities of color by withdrawing social services while increasing surveillance and policing. In short, she demonstrates how the misappropriated charge of terrorism is used to criminalize resistance and dampen dissent against state violence.

Davis's questions invite us to explore the intersections, collusions, and interdependencies among policing, militarism, and US imperialism. Popular discourses that associate people identified as Southwest Asian and North African (SWANA) with terrorism dovetail into US state policies that attempt to criminalize social justice organizing—such as the Movement for Black Lives—by applying the charge of terrorism (Khan-Cullors and Bandele 2018). We can find connections as well between the prison- and military-industrial complexes and their parallel warehousing strategies in domestic prisons targeting Black communities, in military and domestic facilities imprisoning "enemy combatants" and "suspected terrorists," and in detention centers holding Latinx and SWANA immigrants. These connections highlight the potential for strategic solidarities between Arab Americans and other Black, Indigenous, and people-of-color (BIPOC) communities in the United States. They also open opportunities for exploring comparative settler colonialisms in the United States, Mexico, and Palestine (Lubin 2008; Salaita 2006, 2016), and they encourage the examination of the role of secrecy, redaction, and silence in arguably unlawful detentions of so-called enemy combatants. Quintanilla and Mogannam's contribution in part five (chapter 33) highlights coalitional organizing between the Palestinian Youth Movement–San Diego and Colectivo Zapatista in protesting the use of drones for unauthorized and unacknowledged military interventions and domestic policing and surveillance in the US–Mexico borderlands.

This sort of coalitional work has a long legacy. Islamophobia, or anti-Muslim racism, an issue we address in part three of this reader, contributes to the racialization of both Arabs and South Asians. Orientalism, which we discuss in part four, positions Arabs and both South Asians and East Asians as indistinguishably inferior to an imagined "civilized" West. Further, many of these parallels extend historically. Immigration bans in the 2000s recall the Chinese Exclusion Act of 1882, which suspended Chinese immigration to the United States and barred Chinese immigrants from acquiring US citizenship; detentions of Muslim and SWANA people in the aftermath of September 11, 2001 (9/11) in the United States evoke the internment of Japanese Americans during World War II. These historical connections are still present in our contemporary moment, as is evident in the work of organizations such as Tsuru for Solidarity, which mobilizes Japanese Americans against present-day immigration detention centers, and in refusals to accept xenophobic language, such as the racist label of COVID-19 as a "Chinese virus" (Arab American Studies Association 2020). These linkages point to the need for building strong coalitional work among BIPOC and other marginalized groups, recognized in the rallying calls "From Ferguson to Palestine" and "#NoBanNoWall."

This part of the reader asks: What are some of the roots and routes (Gilroy 1993) for solidarity between Arab and other BIPOC communities in the United States? What role do international alliances play in forging these solidarities? How do those alliances manifest themselves, and what forms do they take, including in activist, scholarly, and creative work? Recognizing intersections between various forms of state-sanctioned violence, imperialism, and neoliberal economies, this part also asks: What are the shared or parallel experiences that drive intergroup and transnational solidarity, and what is the work that must be done to develop practices that do not appropriate another's struggle simply to serve one's own or that reenact hierarchies of race, class, gender, sexuality, ability, religion, or national origin?

Tracing the increasingly pervasive ways that militarization of everyday life proliferates, the essays in this part are informed by the imperialist intersections of the "war on drugs" and the "war on terror." As mentioned earlier, Arab, Muslim, Latinx, Indigenous, and Black communities have been similarly and fluidly targeted through strategies of racial profiling and practices of delegitimizing protestors both by criminalizing them and by associating them with terrorism. Specifically referencing crossovers in the racialization and criminalization of Latinx and Arab communities, Lisa Marie Cacho argues that "to represent Middle Eastern immigrants as not only 'suspects of terrorism,' but also as 'illegal'" demonstrates how the figure of "'the terrorist' was grafted onto the 'illegal alien'"—a racist category that was "repurposed and rearticulated" (2012, 112–13). In an essay that also inspired the framing of this part, John Tofik Karam (2011) has written about the way that broadly conceived racist discourses of "terrorism," as defined through US rhetoric about the war on terror, were applied transnationally to the *triple frontera* (triple border) region between Argentina, Brazil, and Paraguay. Given that this region is home to many recent Lebanese Shiʿa migrants who have been accused by the United States of "being at the center of 'pirate networks' and of 'importing terrorism' from their compatriots in the militant Lebanese movement Hezballah" (Amar 2014a, 12), the narratives are clearly inflected by racist categorizations of the global war on terror. The "problem" of Somali piracy, for example, is commonly narrated as a result of the lawlessness of Somalia as a "failed state," a narrative that conveniently ignores the legacy of British and Italian colonialism as well as neocolonial intervention more recently in Somalia. Contemporarily, "the primary motivating event for the rise in piracy was illegal overfishing and illegal dumping of toxic waste" (Cowen 2014, 146) by outside international actors, which destroys the livelihoods of Somalians living in coastal communities. Labeling Somali "pirates" as the problem—and designating them as "universal criminals in international law" (Cowen 2014, 141)—therefore obscures how, in order to safeguard "the global circulation of stuff" (130) benefiting multinational corporations based in the global North, the label criminalizes Somalians who are just protecting their livelihoods. The fluid criminalizing of people as "terrorists" and "pirates" as well as the occasional collapsing of these two categories demonstrate how these figures are constructed as "enemies to *our common humanity*" (Cowen 2014, 135, italics in original), recalling the discussion in part five about how manipulations of legality are part of contemporary US imperialist techniques. The essays in this part ask what strategies can be imagined for organizing against white supremacy, militarism, and empire. They also highlight alliances that recognize the crossovers between "domestic" and "foreign" imperialist strategies of containment and repression and explore inventive and cross-cultural expressions of transnational resistance and solidarity.

The placement of Assata Shakur on the most-wanted terrorist list, Davis reminds us, is an expression of state power that indicates the importance of solidarity work connecting state violence as it has played out by similarly trained police forces in places such as Ferguson and Palestine; these are precisely the sorts of connections fostered in the Movement for Black Lives and the Boycott, Divestment, and Sanctions (BDS) movement (Bailey 2015; Pickens 2016; Ransby 2018). Further, this type of collaboration has roots in earlier collaborations between Black American struggles for liberation and struggles for justice in Palestine (Feldman 2015; Kelley 2019; Lubin 2014). At the same time, however, as Sarah M. A. Gualtieri and Pauline Homsi Vinson note, exclusionary policies also pit immigrants and other racialized groups against one another, as illustrated in Chinese exclusion laws and Arabs' efforts to distance themselves from "Asiatics" in order to become eligible for US citizenship at the turn of the twentieth century (2018, xii). Along similar lines, Therí Pickens has observed: "Whiteness operates as a ghostly presence that frames how communities of color interact with each other" (2016, 130). Such a "ghostly presence" acutely haunts the circumstances of George Floyd's killing by a Minneapolis police officer on May 25, 2020, because the call that brought Floyd into the hands of the police came from a corner store owned by a Palestinian Muslim American in order to abide by "'a state policy that requires stores' to notify the police about counterfeit bills" (Bayoumi 2020). These circumstances lay bare the mechanisms that make "middlemen minorities" (Bonacich 1973) agents of the state who, sometimes willingly, sometimes unwillingly, carry out its bidding (Bayoumi 2020). This positionality underscores the need for addressing systemic racism not only within state and civic institutions but also among Arab and Muslim American communities. Zena Salem (2020), for example, criticizes what she calls the "faux solidarity" of Arabs with the Black Lives Matter movement when ongoing racism in Arab countries toward Africans and Afro-Arabs is ignored (see also Abulhawa 2013; El-Hanan 2017). A number of scholars (Aidi [2003] 2005; Bayoumi 2020; Kashani 2018; West 2000)—including participants of a *Jadaliyya* "Roundtable on Anti-Blackness and Black–Palestinian Solidarity" (Erakat 2015) and contributors to a special issue of the *Journal of Palestine Studies* in 2019 on Black–Palestinian transnational solidarity—recognize the need for dismantling both anti-Black racism among Arabs and non-Black Muslims and anti-Muslim and anti-Arab sentiment in BIPOC communities more generally. Their work points to the important task of reenvisioning what Arab–Black solidarity might mean and the forms it might take. Such a "re-visioning" is evident in a growing body of Arab American scholarship (Abdulhadi and Olwan 2015; Abdul Khabeer 2016; Hartman 2019; Lubin 2014; Naber 2006; Pennock 2017; Pickens 2016 and chapter 3 in this reader). It is also evident in the work of Arab American organizations such as the Arab Resource and Organizing Center, the Arab Community Center for Economic and Social Services (ACCESS), and the Arab American Action Network. Far from reifying "divide and conquer" strategies and more in line with Arab/Arab American–Black transnational solidarity work exemplified by Angela Davis, the essays in this part work to illuminate the possibilities for cross-coalitional collaboration that can also attend to the differential histories and incommensurability of oppressions among communities of color in the United States.

Coalition Building in Arab American Communities

Despite a racial hierarchy that encourages the possessive investment in whiteness (Lipsitz 1998), particularly for ethnic groups who can claim whiteness even if they don't always enjoy its benefits, Arab Americans have built solidarities that aim to cut through the racial logics of divide and conquer.

Fundamentally shifting and rethinking the way the identity category "Arab American" has been marked "white" in official government documents such as the US Census, the essays we include here explore the simultaneity of racialization and oppression of SWANA, Latinx, Black, Indigenous, Asian, and Muslim American communities, and they look at comparative settler colonialisms in the United States, Mexico, and Palestine (Lubin 2008; Salaita 2006, 2016).

Foregrounding artistic and organizing spaces, this part spotlights the agency Arab Americans have found in creatively resisting oppression while at the same time critiquing settler colonialism, war, militarism, imperialism, and heteropatriarchy. The essays we include in it explore a range of alliances and affiliations, from the pan-African and anti-imperialist ties of post-1967 Arab students and activists (Khan, chapter 35) through more recent feminist alliances with Rasmea Odeh (Saliba, chapter 34), to alliances of colonized indigeneity in Palestine and the United States–Canada at Standing Rock (Olwan, chapter 39). Throughout this part, the essays raise trenchant questions about the politics and possibilities of solidarity (Kelley, chapter 36) as well as its limitations (Maira, chapter 38).

Connections across Domestic and Transnational State Violence

In its emphasis on collaborative and comparative work, this part is inspired by Arab American studies scholarship that joins with all voices silenced by white supremacy; global empire; religious, racial, and ethnic hierarchies; patriarchy; ableism; and heteronormativity. The banner that Kristian Davis Bailey held outside of Rasmea Odeh's federal court hearing read: "From Assata to Rasmea, We Fight for Freedom/Hurriya" (quoted in Clarno 2017, 2). This banner offers a contemporary example of solidarity that draws our attention to the transnational connections that such actions seek to assert across carceral and imperialist regimes. Encouraging us to analyze the slippages between "domestic" and "foreign" practices of state violence, the banner and the readings in this part remind us of the role of secrecy, redaction, and silence in arguably unlawful detentions of so-called enemy combatants. This example also accentuates the alliances and connections among the United States, Israel, and the Gulf states, such as the exchange programs between US police departments and the Israeli Defense Forces as well as the secret prisons and proxy wars funded by the United States but housed or executed by Saudi Arabia and the United Arab Emirates (Jewish Voice for Peace 2018).

The essays gathered here are grounded in transnational struggles for liberation and justice, and they are also rooted in a critique of transnationally figured state violences related to settler colonialism, migration-control regimes, state-sanctioned and enacted sexual violence, incarceration and other forms of violent enclosure, and the violent repression and criminalization of political dissent. As multiple scholars have shown, Arab Americans have built and participated in these sorts of trans-issue alliances particularly since the 1960s and 1970s (Feldman 2015; Khan 2018; Odeh 2018; Pennock 2017) and even earlier (Gualtieri 2020). Consciousness-raising in response to the Israeli–Arab War of 1967, in particular, helped consolidate the category "Arab American" as a strategic tool for organizing and forging solidarity with other communities of color against colonialism and state repression. As the prominent Arab American organizer Camille Odeh puts it, "Many of us got involved in social movements for social justice beyond the Arab world and against colonialism in Africa and Asia, Apartheid in South Africa, Central and Latin America, as well as the struggles of Native Americans, Indigenous people, and Chicanos here in the United States. It was an uplifting time and as Arab Americans, we felt transformed, affirmed, and uplifted from within" (2018, 24). This mode of uplift functioned especially in relation to "transnational alliances," particularly since, as Suraya Khan puts it in chapter 35, "Palestine was an issue that brought Arab Americans into conversation with other groups that grappled with racism, settler colonialism, and decolonization" (p. 451). In the 1970s, for instance, this sort of cross-coalitional work manifested in organizing by the Association of Arab American University Graduates against apartheid in South Africa (Khan, chapter 35, p. 454; Odeh 2018; Pennock 2018), work that was grounded in decolonial critiques. Decolonial critique is also central to Arab American feminism, a point that Therese Saliba, in her contribution to this reader, helps us contextualize when she argues for "feminism's expansive capacity to build a more inclusive transnational movement" (chapter 34, p. 445). Focusing on the case of Rasmea Odeh, Saliba offers feminist and comparative critiques of US and Israeli carceral regimes. Her essay traces how Arab American feminists, in solidarity with other feminists of color, "have sought to name, make visible, and confront intersectional forces of oppression" even as "they have also contributed to the reinvention of feminist movement strategies and discourses in defiance of heteropatriarchy and the new imperial logics of the state" (p. 437). As the readings in this part demonstrate, solidarity work begins with building alliances based on critical, transnational analysis of structural oppression.

Cross-Movement Organizing and the Complexities of Transnational Solidarity

Contemporary coalitional organizing calls upon us to grapple with the complexities of working together despite differential experiences of privilege and oppression. Both Standing Rock activism as well as unanswered calls for the clemency of Leonard Peltier at the close of Barack Obama's presidency invite us to investigate the connections between police and military use of detention to silence dissent. Yet investigating the parallels between Indigenous struggles for self-determination and other such struggles around the world also demands a critical reckoning with the inconsistencies of solidarity. Standing Rock resistance and activism against the Dakota Access Pipeline highlights the deputization of police forces to protect corporate and imperial interests while violently repressing peaceful protest. Dana Olwan's essay in this volume (chapter 39) explores the solidarities between Palestinian and Native American Indigenous struggles for rights and recognition, particularly with regard to repressive police and military action. Describing the Palestinian Youth Movement's presence in the fight to resist the pipeline, Nadya Tannous and Omar Zahzah explain that "the term 'solidarity' seems insufficient to describe the drive that moves us to take up coalitional work with Indigenous communities in the stolen lands of Turtle Island" (2018, 48). Instead, they propose a model of resistance that emphasizes "'joint struggle,' which . . . reflects our responsibility to foreground our Indigenous identities and attack the normalization of settler violence" (48). Taken together with the other essays in this part, these explorations of cross-movement organizing urge us to undertake a more thorough accounting of the model of solidarity than an emphasis on similarity of struggle alone might suggest.

Articulations of new models of solidarity are evident in the work of a number of scholars and activists in the Black–Palestinian transnational solidarity movement. For example, Marc Lamont Hill, who lost his contract with CNN in 2018 owing to his comments in support of Palestinians, uses the genre of life writing to anchor his discussion of solidarity in his experiences as a member of a solidarity delegation of Black activists and intellectuals to the West Bank. Pointing to the shortcomings of a "shared struggle" model of solidarity, Hill urges us instead to "embrace 'difference' as the central feature of our solidarity praxis" (2018, 955). Enacting a similar critique of "sameness" as a basis for transnational solidarity, Robin D. G. Kelley, whose work we excerpt in chapter 36, builds on a long history of transnational solidarity in Black liberation movements and argues for recognizing how struggles are not the same but rather linked, an observation that leads to an understanding of solidarity as a praxis "founded not on shared experience but [on] shared principles" (p. 464). Emphasizing the need for a "reckoning with history" in order to arrive at an understanding of "the deep roots of solidarity" (p. 464), Kelley proposes "a vision of worldmaking rather than a politics of analogy or identity" (p. 464–65) to provide space for imagining new ways of being with one another and in the world.

Mobilizing Dissent and the Forms of Cultural Adaptation

Hisham Aidi has illustrated how Arab and Islamic cultural symbols and traditions—from belly dancing in popular-music videos and telenovelas to transnational adaptations of the hip hop genre—demonstrate their importance to transnational consciousness, particularly in Central and South America, the

Caribbean, and the French *banlieues*. Aidi's essay in this part (chapter 37) begins with the galvanizing call *"Seamos moros!"* and charts how alliance building also draws on the cultural imaginary of symbolic figures. In the case of the Moorish Atlantic, the connection to Arab and Muslim rule in Andalusia and its links to the Americas provides cultural currency for fostering transnational and "South–South" political alliances (Amar 2014b; on the cultural politics of the Moorish Atlantic, see also Karam 2010 and Shohat 2013 as well as chapter 4 in this reader). Scholarship on Arab and Arab American hip hop has also highlighted precisely these sorts of transnational connections (Aidi 2014; Lubin 2014; Maira 2013; Youmans 2007). In "'A Strip, a Land, a Blaze,'" for example, Sunaina Maira discusses hip hop as an "Arab American CNN" for youth and shows how Arab American hip hop forges "transnational linkages among Arab communities and offers a critique of U.S. policies in the Middle East, particularly in Palestine and Iraq" (2013, 196). Describing Arab and Arab American rap as a "poetics of displacement and protest" (196), Maira also argues that the critique of US foreign policy embedded in the lyrics mirrors critiques made by BIPOC communities in the United States. As discussed in part four and highlighted here in relation to solidarity work, cultural representations can reflect and help shape social realities—for example, in the case of hip hop by offering a form of popular education, or what rapper KRS-One of Boogie Down Productions referred to as "edutainment" in the eponymous album of 1990. As politically conscious rappers such as KRS-One have demonstrated, hip hop was born out of a context of analyzing and lyrically protesting the Reagan-era criminalization and impoverishment of Black communities in the Bronx. As Meghan Drury argues, it is this aspect of the genre that a number of Arab artists draw on to "mobilize resistance" and to deploy "an articulation of diasporic sonic Arabness" (2017, 2). In other words, transnational connections, though they may entail elements of appropriation and distortion, also forge connections through creative borrowings that can act as a means for mobilizing to action. The appropriation of the rap form by SWANA communities builds on this tradition of social protest even as it underscores the complexities of solidarity. Su'ad Abdul Khabeer's concept of "Muslim Cool," included in chapter 17, describes this cultural practice as one in which Blackness as well as Black cultural forms are both "desired and devalued" (Abdul Khabeer 2016, 6). Any consideration of solidarity building must also attend to this paradox and commit to an honest accounting of the impact of such devaluation.

Probing new possibilities for collaboration and dissent, the essays in part six investigate the praxis of solidarity and resistance. In so doing, they cultivate grounded and situated solidarities that are nevertheless fluid and mobile—both in the sense of enacting critiques of heteronormative, settler, and imperialist logics and in the sense of developing creative, coalitional, and strategic modes of resistance. We hope these essays spark new conversations and modes of analysis that simultaneously expand and deepen the ways we envision cross-coalitional solidarity and scholarly practice in Arab American studies.

Works Cited

Abdulhadi, Rabab, and Dana Olwan. 2015. "Introduction: Shifting Geographies of Knowledge and Power: Palestine and American Studies." In "Palestine and American Studies," edited by Rabab Abdulhadi and Dana Olwan. Special issue of *American Quarterly* 67, no. 4: 993–1006.

Abdul Khabeer, Su'ad. 2016. *Muslim Cool: Race, Religion, and Hip Hop in the United States.* New York: New York Univ. Press.

Abulhawa, Susan. 2013. "Confronting Anti-Black Racism in the Arab World." *Al Jazeera*, July 7. At https://www.aljazeera.com/indepth/opinion/2013/06/2013 62472519107286.html.

Aidi, Hisham. [2003] 2005. "Let Us Be Moors: Islam, Race, and 'Connected Histories.'" *Souls* 7, no. 1: 36–51.

———. 2014. *Rebel Music: Race, Empire, and the New Muslim Youth Culture.* New York: Vintage.

Amar, Paul. 2014a. Introduction to *The Middle East and Brazil: Perspectives on the New Global South*, edited by Paul Amar, 1–14. Indianapolis: Univ. of Indiana Press.

———, ed. 2014b. *The Middle East and Brazil: Perspectives on the New Global South.* Indianapolis: Univ. of Indiana Press.

Arab American Studies Association. 2020. "Statement on COVID-19." At https://arabamericanstudies.org/aasa-statement-on-covid-19/.

Bailey, Kristian Davis. 2015. "Black–Palestinian Solidarity in the Ferguson–Gaza Era." *American Quarterly* 67, no. 4: 1017–26.

Bayoumi, Moustafa. 2020. "Why Did Cup Foods Call the Cops on George Floyd?" *New York Times*, June 17. At https://nyti.ms/3d8gr76.

Bonacich, Edna. 1973. "A Theory of Middleman Minorities." *American Sociological Review* 38, no. 5: 583–94.

Cacho, Lisa Marie. 2012. *Social Death: Racialized Rightlessness and the Criminalization of the Unprotected.* New York: New York Univ. Press.

Clarno, Andy. 2017. "The Thorns That Exist and Resist: Black–Palestine Solidarity in the Twenty-First Century." *Middle East Report* 282 (Spring): 2–9.

Cowen, Deborah. 2014. *Deadly Life of Logistics: Mapping Violence in Global Trade.* Minneapolis: Univ. of Minnesota Press.

Davis, Angela. 2016. *Freedom Is a Constant Struggle: Ferguson, Palestine, and the Foundations of a Movement.* Boston: Haymarket Books.

Drury, Meghan. 2017. "Counterorienting the War on Terror: Arab Hip Hop and Diasporic Resistance." *Journal of Popular Music Studies* 29:1–11.

Erakat, Noura, moderator. 2015. "Roundtable on Anti-Blackness and Black–Palestinian Solidarity." With Rabab Abdulhadi, Ahmad Abuznaid, Ebony Coletu, Bill Fletcher Jr., Che Gossett, Sarah Ihmoud, Robin D. G. Kelley, Aja Monet, Donna Murch, Nadine Naber, Linda Sarsour, Jared Sexton, and Nadera

Shalhoub. *Jadaliyya*, June 3. At https://www.jadaliyya.com/Details/32145/Roundtable-on-Anti-Blackness-and-Black-Palestinian-Solidarity.

Feldman, Keith. 2015. *A Shadow over Palestine: The Imperial Life of Race in America*. Minneapolis: Univ. of Minnesota Press.

Gilroy, Paul. 1993. *The Black Atlantic: Modernity and Double Consciousness*. London: Verso.

Gualtieri, Sarah M. A. 2020. *Arab Routes: Pathways to Syrian California*. Stanford, CA: Stanford Univ. Press.

Gualtieri, Sarah M. A., and Pauline Homsi Vinson. 2018. Introduction to "Arab/Americas: Locations & Iterations," edited by Sarah M. A. Gualtieri and Pauline Homsi Vinson. Special issue of *Amerasia Journal* 44, no. 1: vii–xxi.

El-Hanan, Lama. 2017. "Arab–Black Solidarity Shouldn't Erase Afro-Arabs & the Racism They Face in the Arab World." *Afropunk*, Sept. 5. At https://afropunk.com/2017/09/arab-black-solidarity-shouldnt-erase-afro-arabs-racism-face-arab-world/.

Hartman, Michelle. 2019. *Breaking Broken English: Black–Arab Literacy Solidarities and the Politics of Language*. Syracuse, NY: Syracuse Univ. Press.

Hill, Marc Lamont. 2018. "From Ferguson to Palestine: Reimagining Transnational Solidarity through Difference." *Biography* 41, no. 4: 942–57.

Jewish Voice for Peace. 2018. "About Deadly Exchange." At https://deadlyexchange.org/about-deadly-exchange/.

Karam, John Tofik. 2010. "Belly Dancing and the (En)gendering of Ethnic Sexuality in the 'Mixed' Brazilian Nation." *Journal of Middle East Women's Studies* 6, no. 2: 86–114.

———. 2011. "Crossing the Americas: The U.S. War on Terror and Arab Cross-Border Mobilizations in a South American Frontier Region." *Comparative Studies of South Asia, Africa, and the Middle East* 31, no. 2: 251–66.

Kashani, Maryam. 2018. "Habib in the Hood: Mobilizing History and Prayer towards an Anti-Racist Islam." In "Arab/Americas: Locations & Iterations," edited by Sarah M. A. Gualtieri and Pauline Homsi Vinson. Special issue of *Amerasia Journal* 44, no. 1: 61–84.

Kelley, Robin D. G. 2019. "From the River to the Sea to Every Mountain Top: Solidarity as Worldmaking." *Journal of Palestine Studies* 48, no. 4: 69–91.

Khan, Suraya. 2018. "Transnational Alliances: The AAUG's Advocacy for Palestine and the Third World." *Arab Studies Quarterly* 40, no. 1: 53–72.

Khan-Cullors, Patrisse, and Asha Bandele. 2018. *When They Call You a Terrorist: A Black Lives Matter Memoir.* New York: St. Martin's Press.

Lipsitz, George. 1998. *The Possessive Investment in Whiteness: How White People Profit from Identity Politics*. Philadelphia: Temple Univ. Press.

Lubin, Alex. 2008. "'We Are All Israelis': The Politics of Colonial Comparisons." *South Atlantic Quarterly* 107, no. 4: 671–90.

———. 2014. *Geographies of Liberation: The Making of an Afro-Arab Political Imaginary.* Chapel Hill: Univ. of North Carolina Press.

Maira, Sunaina. 2013. "'A Strip, a Land, a Blaze': Arab American Hip-Hop and Transnational Politics." In *Between the Middle East and the Americas: The Cultural Politics of Diaspora*, edited by Evelyn Alsultany and Ella Shohat, 195–213. Ann Arbor: Univ. of Michigan Press.

Naber, Nadine. 2006. "A Call for Consistency: Palestinian Resistance and Radical US Women of Color." In *Color of Violence: The INCITE! Anthology*, edited by INCITE! Women of Color against Violence, 74–80. Cambridge, MA: South End Press.

Odeh, Camille. 2018. "Arab American Activism." *Arab Studies Quarterly* 40, no. 1: 23–26.

Pennock, Pamela E. 2017. *The Rise of the Arab American Left: Activists, Allies, and Their Fight against Imperialism and Racism, 1960s–1980s*. Chapel Hill: Univ. of North Carolina Press.

———. 2018. "From 1967 to Operation Boulder: The Erosion of Arab Americans' Civil Liberties in the 1970s." *Arab Studies Quarterly* 40, no. 1: 41–52.

Pickens, Therí. 2016. "Blackness and Relationality: An ACLA Forum." *Comparative Literature* 68, no. 2: 130–40.

Ransby, Barbara. 2018. *Making All Black Lives Matter: Reimagining Freedom in the 21st Century*. Oakland: Univ. of California Press.

Salaita, Steven. 2006. *The Holy Land in Transit: Colonialism and the Quest for Canaan*. Syracuse, NY: Syracuse Univ. Press.

———. 2016. *Inter/Nationalism: Decolonizing Native America and Palestine*. Minneapolis: Univ. of Minnesota Press.

Salem, Zeina. 2020. "Anti-Black Racism in the Arab World: Denial, Ignorance, or Both?" *Egyptian Streets*, June 29. At https://egyptianstreets.com/2020/06/29/anti-black-racism-in-the-arab-world-denial-ignorance-or-both/.

Shohat, Ella. 2013. "The Sephardi-Moorish Atlantic: Between Orientalism and Occidentalism." In *Between the Middle East and the Americas: The Cultural Politics of Diaspora*, edited by Evelyn Alsultany and Ella Shohat, 42–64. Ann Arbor: Univ. of Michigan Press.

Tannous, Nadya Raja, and Omar Zahzah. 2018. "The Scarred Land: Settler Imprints and Indigenous Futures." *Funambulist: Politics of Space and Bodies* 20 (Nov.–Dec.): 46–49.

West, Stan. 2000. "An Afrocentric Look at the Arab Community." *Mizna* 2, no. 3: 20–22.

Youmans, William. 2007. "Arab American Hip Hop." In *Etching Our Own Image: Voices from within the Arab American Art Movement*, edited by Anan Ameri and Holly Arida, 42–61. Newcastle, UK: Cambridge Scholars.

34

Arab American Feminism

Historical Convergences and Transnational Solidarities

THERESE SALIBA

> It is the very capacity of feminism to embrace more and more complexity in response to historical circumstances that renders it so exciting [and] so radical.
>
> —Angela Davis, *The Meaning of Freedom*

In the 1960s, the watershed events of anticolonial nationalist struggles and the Arab defeat in the Israel–Arab War of 1967 also converged with the rise of feminist movements in the United States and throughout the world. From the Afro-Asian Women's Federation Conference in Cairo in 1961 to the United Nations Decade on Women (1975–85), the transnational conversations and debates spearheaded by women influenced an emergent Arab American feminism, which came to define itself in anti-imperialist and transnational terms. In this chapter, I examine the historical trajectories of Arab American feminism, situated in the imagined borderlands of US–Middle East geographies and relations, and how feminists and their allies have played a critical role in constructing and redefining US-Arab-Palestine relations, often in defiance of racialized and gendered imperialist logics. At critical historical junctures, transnational feminists have contributed to significant shifts in anti-imperialist feminist struggles, in the global movement for justice in Palestine, and in the struggles for gender justice in our communities. As these feminists have sought to name, make visible, and confront intersectional forces of oppression, they have also contributed to the reinvention of feminist movement strategies and discourses in defiance of heteropatriarchy and the new imperial logics of the state. I see in these debates and strategies key lessons that bring to light the imaginings and possibilities of feminist futures.

Sections of this essay were presented at the Arab American Studies conference "Waypoints and Watersheds: Arab American Activism and Memories, a Conference Marking the 50th Anniversary of the 1967 War," Dearborn, Michigan, March 26, 2017, and at the CASAR Transnational American Studies Conference, Beirut, Lebanon, January 7, 2014. Special thanks to my husband, Tom Wright, for his editorial guidance and to our daughter, Samia Saliba, for her youthful insights and inspiration.

The 1960s and 1970s: National Liberation, the First Step to True Solidarity

When Aisha Abdul-Rahman took to the podium to deliver her plenary address at Cairo's Afro-Asian People's Solidarity Conference in 1957, she argued against "the confines of imperialism" and how they rendered women "victims of ignorance, isolation, and slavery" (quoted in Prashad 2007, 54). In the "Cairo" chapter of *The Darker Nations* (2007), Vijay Prashad recounts how Abdul-Rahman, a journalist and professor, an advocate for women's rights, and an open critic of Gamel Abdel Nasser's state, asserted that the success of Third World revolutions depended on women's participation and liberation as central to the broader struggle for national sovereignty and class equality (56). In 1961, Cairo also hosted the Afro-Asian Federation of Women to develop a platform for women's struggles in the Third World (57). Participants argued that women's involvement in liberation struggles (as far back as the early 1900s), from street protests to guerrilla warfare, had earned them the right to social equality. They also asserted that women couldn't afford to ignore the fight against imperialism because "national independence was an essential prerequisite to women's rights" and women's progress (quoted on 294 n. 29). Moreover, it wasn't enough for states to promise equal education and equal wages, without giving women equal economic and political rights as well as rights over their bodies, health, and marriage, including the abolition of polygamy, medical care in pregnancy and childbirth, and the right to work, in order to "create the power for an engaged civil society that includes women," as Prashad points out (58). Yet Nasser's rise and ensuing forms of Arab nationalism tended to promote what Mervat Hatem has called "state feminism" in that they uphold the patriarchal order by increasing women's dependence on state services, while often maintaining the social conservatism of the family through personal status laws (Prashad 2007, 60). The limited gains for women under the nationalist leadership led Abdul-Rahman to conclude that national liberation "was only the first step to true solidarity" (quoted in Prashad 2007, 58). And one might argue that this quest for "true solidarity"—at times emergent, at others elusory—is still central to feminist anti-imperialist agendas today.

On the Palestine front, parallel social and political transformations to those in Egypt were occurring, nurtured by Arab nationalism and women's active participation in the nationalist struggle (Sharoni 1995, 61). In particular, the formation of the Palestinian Women's Association (1964) and the General Union of Palestinian Women (1965) sought to organize a progressive women's political agenda within the Palestine Liberation Organization (PLO) "to represent Palestinian women everywhere and to defend women's material and moral interests, as well as to improve their social, cultural, vocational and living standards in general, and above all to achieve equality in all areas of social and economic life" (quoted in Sharoni, 62). The harsh realities of the 1967 defeat and the Israeli military occupation placed additional burdens on women, and the period 1967–71 saw new forms of women's participation in the resistance, including demonstrations, sit-ins, and sabotage. Islah Jad states that by 1968 there were one hundred Palestinian women in Israeli prisons, "mainly accused of contacting fedayeen, concealing weapons, incitement, or membership in armed organizations" (1990, 129).

From Egypt to Palestine, women's movements formed a critical front in resistance to colonialism, occupation, war, and militarization. Their activism converged with a rising global feminist movement as well as with anticolonial and civil rights struggles; these movements also propelled an "epochal shift in the academy" that gave rise to women's studies, ethnic and race studies, and postcolonial studies (Shohat 2006, 361). Yet, as postcolonial feminists have pointed out, important critiques of imperialism have failed to "systematically explore the dynamics of gender as a critical aspect of the imperial project" (McClintock 1995, 14) or to acknowledge the ways in which a feminist anti-imperialist agenda sought to make visible and name the intersecting currents of power and domination, to complicate prevailing discourses, and to intervene in the construction of national and international policies, mandates, and narratives.

The United Nations Decade on Women (1975–85) became another platform for these transnational conversations and further fueled an emergent US Third World feminism that articulated an alliance of women of Asian, African, Middle Eastern, Latin American countries, and the diasporas as well as Native Americans against multiple exploitative structures and systems (Mohanty, Russo, and Torres 1991). Their multiedged, intersectional approach, influenced by radical US women of color, critiqued essentialist notions of "Third World women" and insisted that the politics of gender cannot be conceptualized apart from race, class, empire, nation, religion, and, later, sexuality and ability.

The transnational, antiracist, and anti-imperialist feminisms that have been central to Arab American feminist writing, theory, and activism were built upon this groundwork. The emergence of a more explicit "transnational feminism" in the 1990s expanded this critique to the hegemonic practices of western modernity, neoliberal economic structures, and the uneven exchanges of labor, culture, and militarized violence across national borders that have shaped the material conditions of women's lives in diverse locations (Grewal and Kaplan 1994). Arab American feminists have contributed to these radical critiques and transnational alliances as their writings and activism have sought to address wars and occupations in their homelands and discrimination in their communities. Moreover, the visibility and legitimacy of Arab American issues in general have benefited from solidarity with other feminists of color and Jewish feminist allies,[1] while also contributing to a more intersectional, complex, and radical construction of Arab American identity. As Angela Davis asserts, "It is the very capacity of feminism to embrace more and more complexity in response to historical circumstances that renders it so exciting [and] so radical" (2012, 192–93). Undoubtedly, the historical circumstances of the 1967 war, the Israeli invasion of Lebanon in 1982, and later the "war on terror" after September 11, 2001 (9/11), have tested the capacity of feminism for redefinition and inclusion of Arab, Muslim, and Palestinian issues.

1980s: The Reagan Era and Radical Feminist Alliances

In the era of Reagan–Thatcher conservatism, emerging Arab American feminism coincided not only with the rise of US Third World feminism but also with the Israeli invasion of Lebanon, which forced Arab and Palestinian concerns to the forefront. Feminist debates of the early 1980s are particularly critical to understanding the discursive and narrative shifts in Arab American identity formations over the past four decades. Arab American feminists began to challenge the discourses of Orientalism, liberal feminism, Zionism, nationalism, heteropatriarchy, and imperialism as well as to draw on their own lived experiences in order to rupture dominant narratives and to challenge the limits of academic and feminist discourses that have often placed Arab American feminists in the invisible borderlands of racialized categories or in zones of censorship and exclusion.

In the wake of Israel's invasion of Lebanon in 1982, the National Women's Studies Association (NWSA) considered a resolution put forth by the Third World Caucus "opposing Israel's 'genocidal' incursion" (Feldman 2015, 203). Carol Haddad describes how she was invited to speak on the Women of Color Caucus panel and presented the paper "Arab-Americans: The Forgotten Minority in Feminist Circles," but she also highlights the "hostility and parliamentary maneuvering" that went into defeating the resolution (1994, 220). Similarly, Azizah al-Hibri, who had initiated the NWSA resolution of 1982, critiqued the racism of western feminists for refusing to acknowledge the brutal bombing of her country of birth and their silencing of Muslim/Arab American women "not through coercion, but rather by their astounding inability to hear us regardless of how loudly we protest" (1994, 161). Al-Hibri stated: "We have been informed by some feminists that the topics we raised were sensitive ones which they did not want to touch" (163). As a result, the final NWSA 1982 resolution removed any mention of Israel and offered only a watered-down statement against genocide more broadly.

This response from liberal white feminists stood in contrast to women-of-color allies, who increasingly broadened their focus to include victims of US foreign policy, including the Palestinians. The radical feminist-of-color alliances of this period are perhaps best illustrated by the work of June Jordan, the African American poet and essayist who modeled transnational feminist solidarity long before it was in vogue and never retreated from speaking uncomfortable truths.[2] Jordan visited Palestinian refugee camps after the Israeli massacres at the Sabra and Shatilla camps in Lebanon in 1982 and returned to Lebanon after Israel's notorious massacre of refugees at a United Nations camp at Qana in 1996. Her haunting poetry (Jordan 1985) trenchantly indicted the US government and its citizens for the violence in Lebanon. Her writing bore witness to the strangulation of

1. The scholarship and activism of Jewish feminist allies have also been critical to supporting Arab American feminist issues but are beyond the scope of this analysis. Nevertheless, I draw on the insightful writings of Simona Sharoni, Judith Butler, Sarah Schulman, and others in this chapter.

2. My discussion of June Jordan is taken from my essay "June Jordan's Songs of Palestine and Lebanon" (Saliba 2016).

the US-backed Israeli occupation, linked Arab suffering to the terrors of anti-Black racism and police violence in the United States, and declared a collective struggle, resistance, and resilience.

Jordan clearly understood that to speak of Palestine was to commit "the ultimate taboo" (2002, 193). In the face of vicious charges of anti-Semitism, she exposed "the seemingly irreconcilable" divisions within feminist and leftist communities, between "those for whom Israel remained a sacrosanct subject exempt from rational discussion and dispute" and "those to whom Israel looked a whole lot like yet another country run by whitemen whose militarism tended to produce racist consequences" (193). Jordan saw the silencing of debate on this subject as an affront to the intellectual and moral life of the country. For this, Jordan—like so many others—experienced smears, censorship, and distortions of her words. A pioneer in moral courage on this issue, she cleared the way for those who followed (Feldman 2015; Saliba 2016).

Alice Walker drew inspiration from Jordan's work in her pointed reply to Letty Cottin Pogrebin, who accused the women's movement of anti-Semitism in the pages of *Ms. Magazine* (June 1982). Walker appealed to long-standing Jewish and Black alliances but also to broader issues of human oppression "because black people, to keep faith with their own ancestors, must struggle to resist all forms of oppression" ([1982] 1983, 349). Significantly, Walker faulted Pogrebin for not using the word *imperialism* and wrote: "To many people in the Third world [*sic*], Zionism doesn't equal racism so much as it equals Israeli imperialism" (351). She also drew on Jordan's essay in *Civil Wars* (Jordan 1981) to challenge the idea that alliance work meant "silent and uncritical loyalty." Strategically, Walker shifted the framework to an anti-imperialist critique, reframing alliances in terms of critical engagement with allies, and confronted charges of anti-Semitism as a direct attempt to censor those who had been too long silenced.

These groundbreaking writings and acts of solidarity from the early 1980s onward formed a radical politics of anti-imperialism, Palestine solidarity, and gender and sexual liberation that would continue to expand and forge deeper ties between women of color over the decades. In particular, they sought to dismantle the faulty connection between criticism of Israel and anti-Semitism that has perpetuated the silencing of Arab, Muslim, and Palestinian struggles for visibility, voice, and human rights. As Carol Haddad has written of these years, "The more we spoke and published, the more feminist publishers and conference organizers sought our viewpoints. Although scathing attacks and even threats continued, our voices began to be heard—and affirmed" (1994, 222–23). Yet, as Nadine Naber argues in *Arab America: Gender, Cultural Politics, and Activism* (2012), the predominant institutions of liberal multiculturalism continued to function as a hegemonic force, suppressing more radical civil rights agendas from the 1960s onward (45). Moreover, as Naber asserts, the near-exclusive focus of early Arab American organizations of the 1970s and 1980s on US-based discrimination also served to mute the more radical, transnational critiques that linked anti-Arab racism at home to US imperialist formations abroad (47–48).

Yet these more radical, transnational critiques became central to two collections of Arab American feminist writings, *Food for Our Grandmothers* (Kadi 1994) and *Arab and Arab American Feminisms* (Abdulhadi, Alsultany, and Naber 2011a), which arose in large part from the impetus of the Gulf War and 9/11, respectively, periods of resurgent US empire, and increased visibility, racism, state violence, and xenophobia against Arabs and Muslims. Both texts situate themselves within the tradition of radical US feminists of color and engage in feminist interventions rooted in anti-imperialist, antiracist, and queer politics as well as in transnational solidarities. These collections played a significant role in lending visibility and voice to Arab American feminism. They also articulated transformations of Arab American identity in ways that confronted Orientalist representations of "the oppressed Arab woman," examined the historically situated logics of anti-Arab and anti-Muslim racism, and exposed the limits of liberal multiculturalism (Abdulhadi, Alsultany, and Naber 2011b, xxi–xxiii), while foregrounding the continuities of colonial and imperialist violences within an intersectional feminist politics that drew lessons from and forged links with women of color in the United States and throughout the world.

By the turn of the millennium, Arab American feminism had well-established lines of solidarity with other feminist allies and could now deal more directly with internal questions of Arab identity. Arab American feminists had become increasingly critical of how anti-Orientalist critiques and their anti-imperialist variants had often served to silence internal critiques of sexism, homophobia, and violence within Arab families and community. Although feminist writings of the 1990s had taken on these issues, it wasn't until after 9/11 that Arab American Women Arising for Justice (AMWAJ) articulated a theory beyond anti-Orientalist critiques, with attention to "the inter-communal hierarchies" (Naber 2012, 23), particularly of sexism and homophobia, that shaped their lives as "Arab feminists, queers, and transgender people" (Naber 2011, 88). Although it was critical to understand how racism, war, and occupation exacerbated gender violence, it also had become increasingly important to address the material suffering of women as well as of queer and transgender folks, particularly when that suffering could not be attributed solely to militarized state power or to US empire.

The 9/11 Era: Imperialist Convergences, Captive Bodies, and Strategic Narrations

Following the attacks of September 11, 2001, the predicament of Arab American feminism became inextricably entangled with the problems faced by Arab and Muslim Americans as the global war on terror framed another critical juncture in world politics. With the hypermasculinization of US empire and the repressions of the expanding security state, unprecedented forms of militarized and state violence were inflicted particularly against Arab and Muslim bodies, with nearly half a million lives lost in post-9/11 wars.[3]

In this post-9/11 context, Louise Cainkar's *Homeland Insecurity* (2009) provided an important sociological and ethnographic study of Arab Muslim experiences in Chicago and contributed to understanding perceptions of Arabs and Muslims in the United States. Cainkar asserts, "Post-9/11 treatment of Arab and Muslim Americans was not about the attacks themselves but about the social construction of their relationship to the attacks" because they were seen as "an inherently volatile group" who would "readily conduct and approve of such attacks" (1–2). Moreover, Cainkar's incisive gender critique posits that while Arab men were seen as a threat to national security and American geopolitical interests, Arab Muslim women in hijab were seen as a potential threat to "American culture itself, in particular its core values of democracy and personal liberty" (2). Cainkar further asserts that while the majority of Arab Muslims of her study described their citizenship as inferior, they also saw their struggle in a positive light: "Just as those other groups [of immigrants] had been able to struggle and win the battle for social inclusion, so too would they" (7). Cainkar's interviews are nuanced and diverse, but she also sees the limitations of her project: "I believe that no amount of writing can ever fully reconstruct the flavor of those times for Arabs and Muslims in the United States" (21), and she impugns government policies for the damaging impacts of holding entire groups culpable for the 9/11 attacks (22). These post-9/11 policies cemented the massive transformation of the US security state, including increased surveillance, policing, detention, and deportation of Arabs, Muslims, and other immigrant communities that continue to this day.

Captive Palestinian (Women's) Bodies

The experiences of Palestinians subjected to Israel's carceral state have also affected feminist solidarity movements in the post-9/11 era. The case of Rasmea Odeh from 1969 to 2017 graphically exposed this harsh reality and prefigured the torture images coming out of Abu Ghraib, revealing similarities between Israel's post-1967 security state and the repressive state apparatus that grew so precipitously in the United States after 9/11.

In her inquiry into the representability of the human, Judith Butler examines how certain "frames of war" determine "what will and will not be a grievable life" (2010, 64). She also shows how torture exploits the "shame of sexuality" and, as in the case of the US military in Abu Ghraib, coerces sexual acts that seek

3. Estimates of deaths resulting from post-9/11 wars vary greatly, but Neta Crawford of the Watson Institute at Brown University estimated nearly a half-million dead in direct attacks and 800,000 more indirect war-related deaths. See Crawford 2018.

to decimate personhood (90). Israeli interrogators exploited this sexual shame in their brutal treatment of Rasmea Odeh, as her father described their ordeal in 1969: "Rasmiah couldn't stand on her own feet. She was lying on the floor and there were bloodstains on her clothes. Her face was blue and she had a black eye. . . . They were beating me and beating her, and we were both screaming. Rasmiah was still saying: 'I know nothing.' And they spread her legs and shoved the stick into her. She was bleeding from her mouth and from her face and from her end. Then I became unconscious" (quoted in Tolan 2006, 169).

Arrested as a college student, Odeh was beaten and tortured for twenty-five days, raped with sticks, subjected to electric shocks to her genitalia and breasts, denied food and sleep, and forced to watch her father being tortured. Under these conditions, she confessed to bombing charges and spent a decade in prison. She has testified before the United Nations in Geneva on her sexual torture and asserts that the US government was well aware of her case before she immigrated to the United States in 1994. In 2013, at that time the director of Chicago's Arab American Action Network, she was charged with falsifying immigration forms by omitting her jailing in Israel in 1969 (Naber 2014). A coalition of feminist scholars called on Barack Obama's Justice Department to drop charges against Odeh, by then sixty-nine years old. They wrote: "Rasmea's story encompasses some of the most urgent feminist struggles of our times—violence against women[,] the use of sexual violence as a tool of colonization and war . . . and the use of intimidation to thwart feminist activism" (Feminist Scholars 2014).

Denied the right to tell her story in court, Rasmea was convicted of lying on her immigration papers and stripped of her US citizenship. After continued activist efforts, she was given a new trial, but then the government added the new allegation of "terrorist activity" in 1969—the very charge confessed under torture and later rescinded.

In 2017, under Donald Trump's Justice Department, Rasmea accepted deportation to avoid prison. By then, her case had gained worldwide attention and brought together Arab American feminists, Palestine and civil rights activists, Jewish Voice for Peace, and others as she became a "symbol of deportation's many faces" (Ihejirika 2017). Rasmea's story brings into question the very limits of liberal democracy. Inevitably, the question arises: When the captive Arab/Muslim body, the Black body, the Mexican immigrant body, and the bodies of their families and the communities who fall outside the boundaries of national inclusion can be stripped of citizenship and denied any right to security, how do we measure the decline in equality and human rights under the empowered paternalistic, authoritarian security state?

Black–Palestinian Solidarities, Civil Rights, and BDS

Angela Davis, Alice Walker, and others have lent their support to Arab and Arab American struggles by drawing resonant analogies to African American experience and to the civil rights struggle, a link that is often obscured and appropriated by liberal multiculturalists. Their writings and activism highlight the strategic importance of transnational solidarities in confronting the structural violence of policies of segregation/apartheid, militarization, and the excesses of the prison/security state.

In her extended essay *Overcoming Speechlessness* (2010a), Walker bears witness to the horrific violence of Israel's attacks on Gaza in Operation Cast Lead in 2009. Significantly, Walker invokes resonant metaphors of the civil rights struggle, in particular the Montgomery bus boycott, and its moral authority to lend support to the Boycott, Divestment, Sanctions (BDS) movement: "It is time for us, en masse, to show up in front of our conscience, and sit down in the front of the only bus we have: our very lives" (2013, 279). Through her poetic, spiritual vision and the authority she carries from growing up in the Jim Crow South and as a participant in the civil rights movement, Walker frames Palestine as a struggle for civil rights within a future one-state solution and underscores our responsibility to "bring knowledge to the conscience of the global community" (2010b, xvii).

Yet in a *New York Times* interview in 2018, Walker's endorsement of David Icke's writing, which includes anti-Jewish conspiracy theories, was deeply disappointing to some feminists. This cast a shadow over her solidarity for Palestine and lent credence to the faulty connection made by conservative and liberal Zionists alike between advocacy for Palestinian human rights and anti-Semitism. As of this writing, it is difficult to say how this will shape Walker's legacy as one of the most celebrated African American feminist writers, but some Jewish feminists have weighed in on the debate. For example, Sarah Schulman (2018) acknowledges Walker's committed advocacy for Palestine but faults her for attributing Israeli brutality to Judaism itself; Rebecca Pierce reads Walker's comments as both anti-Jewish and anti-Black and argues for "principled solidarity and rejection of the tropes created by white supremacy" (2018).[4]

Angela Davis, in contrast, emerged from recent controversies around her engagement with Palestine and BDS as a model of this kind of principled solidarity. In her writings and philosophical insurgencies, Davis also appeals to the conscience of the global community as a grounding position for solidarity and probes the meaning of freedom and democracy as well as the role of feminism in the context of neoliberal capitalism. In drawing links between the record levels of imprisonment of people of color in the United States, indefinite detentions of Arabs and Muslims, and the practices in Guantánamo and Abu Ghraib, she asserts the transnational linkages between racialization and criminalization as well as between imprisonment practices and their affront to democracy, and she opens doors for transnational solidarity with the prison abolition movement. Davis has also been an advocate for Rasmea Odeh, visited the Palestinian territories, and issued statements in support of BDS. In *Freedom Is a Constant Struggle: Ferguson, Palestine, and the Foundations of a Movement* (2016), Davis condemns many forms of racist state violence from prisons to policing and draws links to the struggles to end violence against women, to end the occupation of Palestine, and to defend the rights of all immigrants (94). Moreover, she asserts that intersectional feminisms can help us "recognize a range of connections" (104) among discourses, institutions, identities, and ideologies, and she sees in these connections a "vast potential with respect to the forging of transnational solidarities" (137).

Yet Davis's solidarity with Palestine and the BDS movement led the Birmingham Civil Rights Institute to revoke her nomination for its annual Fred L. Shuttlesworth Human Rights Award in January 2019, largely due to pressure from some Jewish organizations and their supporters (Associated Press 2019; Chokshi 2019). But this move backfired, brought public reprimand to the institute, and fueled activist opposition, leading the institute to reoffer the award to Davis a few weeks later. In the interim, the controversy spurred extensive media coverage that gave more voice and validity to Davis's positions. The *New York Times*, for example, cited Palestine Legal's statement that the rescinded award puts Davis on "a long list of scholars and activists who have been censored, fired, de-funded, defamed, harassed and targeted with frivolous litigation because of concerted efforts by the Israeli government and anti-Palestinian organizations in the US to silence debate" (quoted in Associated Press 2019).[5] Speaking on the radio and television program *Democracy Now!*, Davis described the controversy as "quite exciting" because Palestinian human rights and its relation to the African American civil rights struggle "is finally being discussed in an open way" (quoted in Zonszein 2019). Moreover, Davis characterized the withdrawal of the award not as a personal assault but as "an assault against a whole generation of activists who have come to recognize how important internationalism is" (quoted in Zonszein 2019).

Arab American Feminist Strategic Narrations and Theory

The importance of internationalism has also been central to Arab American feminist writings, which have played a critical role in redefining Arab American studies and fueling transformations of Arab American identity. In the introduction to *Arab & Arab American Feminisms: Gender, Violence, & Belonging*, editors Rabab Abdulhadi,

4. See *New York Times* 2018a, 2018b. Both Schulman's (2018) and Pierce's (2018) articles are more complex and nuanced than I can examine here.

5. See also the Palestine Legal website at https://palestinelegal.org.

Evelyn Alsultany, and Nadine Naber theorize the diverse collection of poetry, essays, and narrative as "an act of strategic narration" that blends personal stories and theoretical analysis as Arab and Arab American writers seek to "transform lived experiences of discontent into critical knowledge and political consciousness" (2011b, xxx, quoting Kyla Wazana Tompkins). In taking on these "lived experiences of discontent" and drawing linkages between violent US policies at home and throughout the world, Arab American feminists formulate knowledge that challenges stereotypical representations and ruptures dominant narratives in order to tell a different story.

Arab American feminist writings often uncover "the systemic, institutionalized nature of the violence" of power/knowledge systems that have tried to censor their stories and silence their voices (Naber 2008, 3). They confront these silences, name the specificity of these exclusions, and contest the shifting currents of power these systems serve to obscure and protect. One such confrontational dialogue was ignited during the al-Aqsa Intifada, which converged with the editing of the anthology *This Bridge We Call Home* (2002) by Gloria Anzaldúa and AnaLouise Keating, a twentieth-year tribute and expansion of the groundbreaking collection *This Bridge Called My Back* (1981), edited by Cherríe Moraga and Gloria Anzaldúa. As contributors to the new volume shared messages and activist information over a listserv, one suggested writing a collective statement condemning Israel's violence against the Palestinians. According to Nada Elia (2011), that scholar was called racist, anti-Semitic, even a hatemonger; the efforts of Arab American feminists to intervene and offer critiques of Zionism, occupation, and Palestinian dispossession were consistently marginalized by a barrage of anti-Arab rhetoric that abated only when the listserv was shut down. But, as Elia describes, the Arab American contributors transformed themselves in the process: "We have given ourselves permission to narrate 'center-stage,'" and they refused to fade away despite the "immense backlash" (quoted on 155).

This refusal to be silenced is powerfully captured in Suheir Hammad's poetic insurgency "Beyond Words." Here, she describes the photos of rape, torture, and humiliation from Abu Ghraib (released in 2004) and Israeli military attacks on Gaza:

> I am told over and over
> Iraq is not Palestine
> Kabul is not New York
> . . . .
> Haiti is not Chechnya
> Chiapas is not East LA
> Iraq is not Palestine
> Over and over I am told
> . . . .
> No connections here
> No illuminated parallels
> Two different histories and two different peoples
> Make no links
> Do not confuse the issues
> (2011, 4–5)

Hammad confronts the denial of linkages across struggles—linkages often highlighted by transnational feminists. Drawing attention to these "illuminated parallels," she exposes the persistence and transnational reach of structural violences masked by discourses of denial, which also serve to suppress potential bonds of solidarity. This relationship between discourses and the structural systems they reinforce is laid bare in Edward Said's essay "Traveling Theory" (1982), where he argues that to attain a theory of a particular system is to threaten that system with destruction, as he did in his groundbreaking book *Orientalism* (1978).

In this spirit, a group of Arab American feminist scholars (some drawing lessons from the listserv controversy connected to the second *Bridge* anthology) wrote an influential theoretical analysis in 2001 confronting the feminist movement for its refusal to engage a critique of Zionism, which they termed "the forgotten -ism." Their essay, subtitled "An Arab American Women's Perspective on Zionism, Racism, and Sexism," was written in the midst of the al-Aqsa Intifada for the United Nations Third World Conference against Racism in South Africa and was then widely circulated after 9/11 and published in the *Color of Violence* anthology (Naber, Desouky, and Baroudi [2001/2006] 2016). Their uncompromising argument served as a kind of manifesto, exposing Zionism as a settler-colonial project and a system that promotes racism, sexism, discrimination, and censorship, particularly of those who speak up for Palestinian rights. They called on progressive activists and women-of-color allies to "be more consistent in their alliances with struggles against imperialism, colonialism, and racism" and invited allies "to learn our histories as we learn theirs, together demanding an end to all forms of oppression" (100, 112). In theorizing Zionism's racialized and gendered logics and foregrounding this "forgotten -ism," these Arab American feminists challenged its power and marginalizing impacts on their lives, on their activism, and on movements for global justice at this critical historical juncture of heightened visibility for Arab Americans.

The Trump Era: Historic Resistances and Emergent Movements

Today, as we stand against "the largest imperial military in the world [and] the largest national surveillance intelligence apparatus" (McClintock 2017) under the control of a hypermasculinist, white supremacist regime, I believe it is important to look to the legacy of women's and feminist struggles against imperialism, racism, and the exploitation of our planet for a way forward. In this historic moment, we witness feminism's expansive capacity to build a more inclusive transnational movement.

The persistent work of Arab American feminists and their allies, in concert with the BDS movement, has shifted public discourse on Palestine and strongly positioned Palestine solidarity as a feminist issue. For example, in 2015 the NWSA voted by nearly 90 percent in support of BDS. Rabab Abdulhadi, a coauthor of the initiative, described the NWSA resolution as "a long time in the making," reflecting the browning and radicalization of NWSA (quoted in Redden 2015). NWSA president Vivian M. May said the statement reflected the members' commitment "to an inclusive feminist vision, to contesting structural inequities on multiple fronts," as well as to their deep engagement "in anticolonial, antiwar and anti-imperialist feminist scholarship, teaching and activism" (quoted in Redden 2015).

The historic Women's Marches that swept the country after Trump's inauguration in January 2017 also sought to achieve this inclusive feminist vision. The massive mobilization and playful convergence of 3.7 million participants across the United States brought together a number of intersecting interests against the politics of Trumpism and shut down city streets even though people weren't engaged in direct action. These actions elevated the voices of Arab, Muslim, and Palestinian women, such as Linda Sarsour, who took leadership in planning the National Women's March and then took the stage to unapologetically claim her identity as Palestinian and Muslim. The diverse women's leadership articulated a new international feminist movement that has been decades in the making, one that has pushed gender politics, antiracism, and the question of Palestine to the center of struggles for global justice. As Angela Davis said in her speech at the first Women's March, "Women's rights are human rights all over the planet and that is why we say freedom and justice for Palestine" (quoted in Taylor 2019).

Shortly after the historic marches, on March 8, 2017, a coalition of feminist leaders, including Rasmea Odeh and Angela Davis, called for the International Women's Strike, with the stated goals of reproductive justice for all, labor rights, full social provisioning, environmental justice for all, and an end to gender violence. They also articulated an antiracist and anti-imperialist feminism that highlights the expanding solidarities across struggles, including "Black Lives Matter, the struggle against police brutality and mass incarceration, the demand for open borders and for immigrant rights, and for the decolonization of Palestine"—movements they described as "the beating heart of this new feminist movement."[6]

The day before the strike, an op-ed appeared in the *New York Times* titled "Does Feminism Have Room for Zionists?" (Shire 2017). Author Emily Shire questioned the emerging international feminist movement, particularly its call for "the decolonization of Palestine," as alienating to feminists like her, despite the movement's stated position against anti-Semitism. But the fact that Zionism is no longer a forgotten -ism but is central to the platforms of this newly reconfigured international feminism is due in large part to a long history of struggle, to the BDS movement, and to the unrelenting work of poets,

6. A description of the strike and statements were found at https://www.womenstrikeus.org/, accessed March 15, 2017, but are no longer available.

writers, and activists, many of whose names appear on these pages and many of whom have since passed on.

In many ways, the demands from the Women's March echo those of Third World feminists in Cairo in 1961, who appealed to their male nationalist leadership for "true solidarity"—with demands for equal pay, equal economic and political rights, and rights over their bodies, health, and family life, as they imagined a feminist future in which women are full partners in their newly liberated societies. And in the United States, feminists have long recognized the hard work and principled solidarity it takes to build a multiracial women's movement and to form productive alliances based on critical engagement with each other's stories and histories of struggle.

Still, in the third year of the Women's March, much media attention focused on charges of anti-Semitism against Women's March leaders, citing Tamika Mallory's relationship with the Nation of Islam and Linda Sarsour's support for the BDS movement. In the aftermath of a Pittsburg synagogue shooting of eleven Jewish members, Sarsour apologized for the leadership's belated response to anti-Semitism and evoked the challenges of trying to build an intersectional women's movement. She wrote, "We should have been faster and clearer in understanding our values and our commitment to fighting anti-semitism [*sic*]. We regret that" (Sarsour 2018). Sarsour and the other leaders also met with many Jewish groups and invited Jewish women into their organizing circle. In her speech at the third annual Women's March on January 19, 2019, in the midst of the controversy, she acknowledged that there are no perfect leaders; she also called on protestors to stand up for "free speech and our constitutional right to boycott, divestment and sanctions in these United States of America." Significantly, she did not back away from her support for Palestine and the BDS movement. And on the day of the third annual Women's March, celebrated African American legal scholar Michelle Alexander, author of *The New Jim Crow*, published a *New York Times* op-ed piece in honor of Dr. Martin Luther King Jr. titled "Time to Break the Silence on Palestine"—naming it one of the great moral challenges of our time (Alexander 2019).

Even as Palestine enters mainstream public discourse, the national and global contexts have undoubtedly posed new challenges to this new emergent feminist movement and to Arab American feminists in particular. Anti-BDS legislation, which Palestine Legal describes as twenty-first-century McCarthyism, has been passed in more than half the states and passed the Senate in 2019, although with growing opposition from Democrats (Weiss 2019). In addition, the Supreme Court ruling on the "Muslim Ban" instituted in June 2018, Trump's move of the US embassy in Israel to Jerusalem in May 2018, and his withdrawal of all US funding to the United Nations Works and Relief Agency for Palestinian Refugees in August 2018 flagrantly exposed his total disregard for Palestinian rights and his contempt for international law. In January 2020, Trump's so-called peace plan served as the final official US sanction and even celebration of the consolidation of Israel's apartheid policies.

Moreover, Trump's executive order on anti-Semitism in December 2019 exploited growing concerns about anti-Jewish rhetoric and hate crimes and conflated the definition of anti-Semitism with criticism of Israel. His authoritarian dictate aimed to censor free speech and suppress advocacy for Palestinian rights and freedom, particularly on college campuses. Yet as Dima Khalidi, director of Palestine Legal, pointed out, "The Trump administration is up against a diverse grass-roots movement that believes in freedom and equality for all in Israel and Palestine" (Khalidi 2019), even as Trump's own virulent rhetoric and policies have fueled white nationalists and heightened incidents of racism, anti-Semitism, and Islamophobia.

Yet these policies also impelled the forging of new alliances, solidarities, and historic levels of resistance. They fueled Women's Marches across the globe, the #MeToo and #Black Lives Matter movements, massive immigrant rights protests, and the election of unprecedented numbers of women and women of color to the US Congress in 2018, including Rashida Tlaib and Ilhan Omar, who publicly support BDS. In February 2019, as Omar apologized for using anti-Jewish tropes in her critique of the American-Israel Public Affairs Committee and was excoriated and misrepresented by many, her comments also fueled media and political critique of the committee's influence (Stolberg 2019b). Subsequently, a House resolution originally framed to condemn only anti-Semitism was rewritten to include white supremacy, racism, a host of other bigotries, and, for the first time, Islamophobia; it passed overwhelmingly and was hailed as an historic "victory for social justice and Palestinian rights" (Bennis 2019; Stolberg 2019a).

And in these hopeful moments of movement building and renewed solidarity, we hear echoes of the feminist voices that have refused silencing and witness the presence of defiant bodies in the streets, in our communities, and in the halls of power taking action to dismantle dehumanizing systems of violence and exclusion and to forge a future rooted in what Angela Davis calls "the indivisibility of justice" (quoted in Olmstead 2019).

Works Cited

Abdulhadi, Rabab, Evelyn Alsultany, and Nadine Naber, eds. 2011a. *Arab & Arab American Feminisms: Gender, Violence, & Belonging.* Syracuse, NY: Syracuse Univ. Press.

———. 2011b. "Arab and Arab American Feminisms: An Introduction." In *Arab & Arab American Feminisms: Gender, Violence, & Belonging*, edited by Rabab Abdulhadi, Evelyn Alsultany, and Nadine Naber, xix–xxxix. Syracuse, NY: Syracuse Univ. Press.

Alexander, Michelle. 2019. "Time to Break the Silence on Palestine." *New York Times*, Jan. 19. At https://www.nytimes.com/2019/01/19/opinion/sunday/martin-luther-king-palestine-israel.html.

Anzaldúa, Gloria, and AnaLouise Keating, eds. 2002. *This Bridge We Call Home: Radical Visions for Transformation.* New York: Routledge.

Associated Press. 2019. "Alabama Civil Rights Institute Rescinds Angela Davis Honor." *New York Times*, Jan. 7.

Bennis, Phyllis. 2019. "The Ilhan Omar Affair Was a Victory for Social Movements and Palestinian Rights." *Nation*, Apr. 1.

Butler, Judith. 2010. *Frames of War: When Is Life Grievable?* London: Verso.

Cainkar, Louise. 2009. *Homeland Insecurity: The Arab American and Muslim American Experience after 9/11.* New York: Russell Sage Foundation.

Chokshi, Niraj. 2019. "Angela Davis Says She's 'Stunned' After Award Is Revoked over Her Views on Israel." *New York Times*, Jan. 8.

Crawford, Neta. 2018. "Costs of War: 17 Years after 9/11, Nearly Half a Million Have Died in the 'Global War on Terror.'" Interviewed by Amy Goodman and Juan González, *Democracy Now!*, Nov. 21.

Davis, Angela Y. 2012. *The Meaning of Freedom: And Other Difficult Dialogues.* San Francisco: City Lights.

———. 2016. *Freedom Is a Constant Struggle: Ferguson, Palestine, and the Foundations of a Movement.* Chicago: Haymarket Books.

Elia, Nada. 2011. "The Burden of Representation: When Palestinians Speak Out." In *Arab & Arab American Feminisms: Gender, Violence, & Belonging*, edited by Rabab Abdulhadi, Evelyn Alsultany, and Nadine Naber, 141–58. Syracuse, NY: Syracuse Univ. Press.

Feldman, Keith P. 2015. *A Shadow over Palestine: The Imperial Life of Race in America.* Minneapolis: Univ. of Minnesota Press.

Feminist Scholars. 2014. "Feminist Scholars to Obama: End Prosecution of Palestinian Survivor of Sexual Torture." *Electronic Intifada*, Oct. 24. At https://electronicintifada.net/content/feminist-scholars-obama-end-prosecution-palestinian-survivor-sexual-torture/13973.

Grewal, Inderpal, and Caren Kaplan, eds. 1994. *Scattered Hegemonies: Postmodernity and Transnational Feminist Practices.* Minneapolis: Univ. of Minnesota Press.

Haddad, Carol. 1994. "In Search of Home." In *Food for Our Grandmothers: Writings by Arab-American & Arab-Canadian Feminists*, edited by Joe Kadi, 218–23. Boston: South End Press.

Hammad, Suheir. 2011. "Beyond Words." In *Arab & Arab American Feminisms: Gender, Violence, & Belonging*, edited by Rabab Abdulhadi, Evelyn Alsultany, and Nadine Naber, 3–9. Syracuse, NY: Syracuse Univ. Press.

Al-Hibri, Azizah. 1994. "Tear Off Your Western Veil!" In *Food for Our Grandmothers: Writings by Arab-American & Arab-Canadian Feminists*, edited by Joe Kadi, 160–64. Boston: South End Press.

Ihejirika, Maudlyne. 2017. "Political Activist Rasmea Odeh a Symbol of Deportation's Many Faces." *Chicago Sun Times*, Sept. 20.

Jad, Islah. 1990. "From Salons to Popular Committees: Palestinian Women 1919–1989." In *Intifada: Palestine at the Crossroads*, edited by Jamal R. Nassar and Roger Heacock, 125–42. West Bank: Birzeit Univ.; New York: Praeger.

Jordan, June. 1981. *Civil Wars: Selected Essays, 1963–80.* Boston: Beacon Press.

———. 1985. *Living Room: New Poems, 1980–1984.* New York: Thunder's Mouth Press.

———. 2002. "Life after Lebanon." In *Some of Us Did Not Die: New and Selected Essays of June Jordan*, 187–95. New York: Basic/Civitas Books.

Kadi, Joe, ed. 1994. *Food for Our Grandmothers: Writings by Arab-American & Arab-Canadian Feminists*. Boston: South End Press.

Khalidi, Dima. 2019. Letter to the editor. *Los Angeles Times*, Dec. 15.

McClintock, Anne. 1995. *Imperial Leather: Race, Gender, and Sexuality in the Colonial Contest*. New York: Routledge.

———. 2017. "What We Now Have . . ." Facebook post. Cited on Coldhearted Scientist blog, Jan. 23. At https://profacero.wordpress.com/2017/01/23/its-the-world-committing-suicide/.

Mohanty, Chandra, Ann Russo, and Lourdes Torres, eds. 1991. *Third World Women and the Politics of Feminism*. Bloomington: Indiana Univ. Press.

Moraga, Cherríe, and Gloria Anzaldúa, eds. 1981. *This Bridge Called My Back: Writings by Radical Women of Color*. San Francisco: Kitchen Table/Women of Color Press.

Naber, Nadine. 2008. "Introduction: Arab Americans and U.S. Racial Formations." In *Race and Arab Americans before and after 9/11: From Invisible Citizens to Visible Subjects*, edited by Amaney Jamal and Nadine Naber, 1–45. Syracuse, NY: Syracuse Univ. Press.

———. 2011. "Decolonizing Culture: Beyond Orientalist and Anti-Orientalist Feminisms." In *Arab & Arab American Feminisms: Gender, Violence & Belonging*, edited by Rabab Abdulhadi, Evelyn Alsultany, and Nadine Naber, 78–90. Syracuse, NY: Syracuse Univ. Press.

———. 2012. *Arab America: Gender, Cultural Politics, and Activism*. New York: New York Univ. Press.

———. 2014. "Justice for Rasmea Odeh." *Middle East Research and Information Project*, June 19. At https://www.merip.org/justice-rasmea-odeh.

Naber, Nadine, Eman Desouky, and Lina Baroudi. [2001/2006] 2016. "The Forgotten '-ism': An Arab American Women's Perspective on Zionism, Racism, and Sexism." In *Color of Violence: The INCITE! Anthology*, edited by INCITE! Women of Color against Violence, 97–112. Durham, NC: Duke Univ. Press.

New York Times. 2018a. "Alice Walker, Answering Backlash, Praises Anti-Semitic Author as 'Brave.'" Dec. 21.

———. 2018b. "Alice Walker: By the Book." Dec. 13.

Olmstead, Molly. 2019. "Why a Revoked Civil Rights Award for Angela Davis Is Causing an Uproar in Alabama." *Slate*, Jan. 8.

Pierce, Rebecca. 2018. "Alice Walker's Conspiracy Theories Aren't Just Anti-Semitic—They're Anti-Black." *Forward*, Dec. 19.

Prashad, Vijay. 2007. "Cairo." In *The Darker Nations: A People's History of the Third World*, 51–61. New York: New Press.

Redden, Elizabeth. 2015. "Another Association Backs Israel Boycott." *Inside Higher Ed*, Dec. 1.

Said, Edward. 1978. *Orientalism*. New York: Random House.

———. 1982. "Traveling Theory." *Raritan* 1, no. 3: 41–67.

Saliba, Therese. 2016. "June Jordan's Songs of Palestine and Lebanon." *Feminist Wire*, Mar. 24. At https://thefeministwire.com/2016/03/june-jordans-songs-of-palestine/.

Sarsour, Linda. 2018. "Women's March Response to Recent Criticism." Nov. 20. At https://womensmarch.com/newsroom.

Schulman, Sarah. 2018. "On Alice Walker, Judaism, and Palestine." *Mondoweiss*, Dec. 26.

Sharoni, Simona. 1995. *Gender and the Israeli–Palestinian Conflict: The Politics of Women's Resistance*. Syracuse, NY: Syracuse Univ. Press.

Shire, Emily. 2017. "Does Feminism Have Room for Zionists?" *New York Times*, Mar. 7. At https://www.nytimes.com/2017/03/07/opinion/does-feminism-have-room-for-zionists.

Shohat, Ella. 2006. *Taboo Memories, Diasporic Voices*. Durham, NC: Duke Univ. Press.

Stolberg, Sheryl Gay. 2019a. "House Votes to Condemn All Hate as Anti-Semitism Debate Overshadows Congress." *New York Times*, Mar. 7.

———. 2019b. "Ilhan Omar's Criticism Raises the Question: Is Aipac Too Powerful?" *New York Times*, Mar. 4.

Taylor, Keeanga-Yamahtta. 2019. "Turning the Women's March into a Mass Movement Was Never Going to Be Simple." *Nation*, Jan. 18.

Tolan, Sandy. 2006. *The Lemon Tree: An Arab, a Jew, and the Heart of the Middle East*. New York: Bloomsbury.

Walker, Alice. [1982] 1983. "To the Editors of *Ms. Magazine*." Reprinted in *In Search of Our Mother's Garden*, 347–54. New York: Harcourt Brace Jovanovich.

———. 2010a. *Overcoming Speechlessness: A Poet Encounters the Horror in Rwanda, Eastern Congo, and Palestine/Israel*. New York: Seven Stories Press.

———. 2010b. "What Changes the World? Bearing Witness to Truth." Foreword to Saree Makdisi, *Palestine Inside Out: An Everyday Occupation*, xvii–xxi. New York: Norton.

———. 2013. "You Will Have No Protection: Supporting BDS." In *The Cushion in the Road*, 277–80. New York: New Press.

Weiss, Philip. 2019. "'Combating BDS Act' Passes Senate, 77–23, as Dem Presidential Hopefuls Vote No." *Mondoweiss*, Feb. 5. At https://mondoweiss.net/2019/02/combating-presidential-paranoia/.

Zonszein, Mairav. 2019. "The Birmingham Civil Rights Institute's Insult to Angela Davis Has Boomeranged." *Nation*, Jan. 15.

35

Transnational Alliances

The AAUG'S Advocacy for Palestine and the Third World

SURAYA KHAN

> Never before have Americans of Arab background experienced the sense of alienation and bewilderment that they did in the Summer of 1967. The crisis was not simply the result of the defeat of Arab armies or the annexation of Arab territories, painful as these things may be. Rather, it was the consequence of a sudden awareness that a serious breakdown had indeed occurred in the political, ideological, and moral outlook of this country—a country we have adopted and loved. American jubilation over the Israeli victory . . . left most Arab-Americans aghast at the degree of insensitivity and even brutality that the U.S. had displayed. For a while, we all refused to believe that our country was capable of such inhumanity, yet we soon woke up to the reality of the situation and decided to adopt a positive rather than a negative response to the challenge.
>
> —Fauzi Najjar, "AAUG—the First Year"

Reflecting on the atmosphere after the Six-Day War of 1967, Fauzi Najjar described the Arab defeat to Israel as more than the *naksa*, or "setback," as it had become known. Najjar, a political scientist at Michigan State University, considered the defeat to be the darkest moment of both the "Arab nation" and US–Arab relations. He also articulated the conflicted emotions that many Arab Americans felt as they made the United States their home while the United States strengthened its relationship with Israel. Thus, in December 1967, Najjar and thirty-six Arab Americans formed a nonsectarian organization with two goals: to promote an understanding of "the Arab case" to the American public and to solidify "ties amongst Arab-Americans—of potential benefit to the Arab world" (Ad Hoc Conference Committee 1967). This organization became known as the Association of Arab American University Graduates (AAUG).

This article analyzes how the AAUG framed the Palestine question as both an Arab American and a Third World issue. As the first major Arab American organization to form after the 1967 War, the AAUG engaged in unprecedented educational and activist endeavors to promote the Palestinian case in the United States.[1] While doing so, the AAUG sought to forge transnational

Parts of this chapter appeared in Suraya Khan, "Transnational Alliances: The AAUG's Advocacy for Palestine and the Third World," *Arab Studies Quarterly* 40, no. 1 (Winter 2018): 53–72. Full references in the original notes were converted to author-date citations in the text and notes here, and a works cited list was added. Reprinted with corrections and press style changes for consistency throughout the volume by permission of California State University, San Bernadino.

1. While the scale of the AAUG's work, its wide membership, and its ideological underpinnings were unique, it is important to recognize earlier Arab immigrants' efforts to advocate for Palestine. Two noteworthy groups were the Arab National League, active from 1936 to 1939, and the Institute of Arab-American Affairs, which lasted from 1944 to 1950 (Bawardi 2014; Davidson 2001).

connections overseas and bolster a sense of community among Arab Americans.

To adopt Jean-François Sirinelli's term for intellectuals in France from the Dreyfus Affair to the Algerian Revolution, members of the AAUG represented an "intellectual generation" (1993, 86–87). They were a group of similarly aged individuals who may not have ascribed to the same ideologies but emerged in a similar cultural and educational milieu; they received their primary, secondary, and often even undergraduate education from institutions in the Middle East but then studied at prominent universities in the United States for advanced degrees. The "event" that was responsible for bringing this "generation" into existence was the consolidation of Israeli military hegemony in the Middle East, particularly after the Six-Day War of 1967.[2] As intellectuals in the United States who remained closely engaged with the Arab world, AAUG members did not claim to reflect the entire Arab American community's views. Nonetheless, they engaged in transnational debates and projects that shaped Arab and Arab American discourses on Arab nationalism, identity, and the Arab–Israeli conflict.

In analyses of the post-1967 era, several scholars have discussed the role that the AAUG played in the formation of Arab American identity and the field of Arab American ethnic studies. Yet only more recently have scholars begun to analyze the transnational character of both the AAUG and Arab American identities more broadly.[3] From its inception, the AAUG refused to limit its concerns to issues only affecting Arab Americans, although Palestine was its first and dearest cause. On the contrary, AAUG members constructed a transnational collective identity by standing in solidarity with Black Americans, Africans, South Asians, and Latin Americans. Thus, Palestine was an issue that brought Arab Americans into conversation with other groups that grappled with racism, settler colonialism, and decolonization.

Third Worldism

The AAUG's early leadership, including Ibrahim Abu-Lughod, Elaine Hagopian, Naseer Aruri, Abdeen Jabara, Edward Said, and many others, pushed the association into a transnational direction with their conscious commitment to the Third World. The concept of the Third World emerged in the context of Cold War interventions and indicated the struggle against colonial and postcolonial marginalization. By the 1970s, the Third World movement additionally involved a struggle against neocolonialism. According to Third World intellectuals and revolutionaries, "neocolonialism" entailed indigenous postcolonial regimes using nationalist discourse and economic attachment to superpowers to betray their country's well-being and independence (Westad 2005, 157).

AAUG members therefore occupied a unique position as recent migrants from the Arab world or second-generation Arab Americans who felt a connection to both the Middle East and the United States. Members of this generation closely monitored Israel's colonial practices and foreign engagements. They also disparaged Arab regimes that sought power by trading the welfare of their citizens for political or economic alliances with the United States or the Soviet Union. Prior to 1967, many Arab immigrants had engaged in leftist activism on American campuses by protesting the Vietnam War and civil rights infringements across the nation; activism for Palestine fit logically alongside these other movements. While concern for the Third World was not foreign to Arab Americans before 1967, the political marginalization that they encountered in American society in the following years provoked even greater empathy for those around the world who endured racism, dispossession, corrupt governments, and neocolonialism.

During the AAUG's first years, chapters sprung up throughout the United States. AAUG chapters played an

2. Sirinelli cites Jean Luchaire's definition of a generation as "a collection of individuals marked by one big event or by a series of such events" (1993, 86–87). Such an event brings a specific generation into existence when it is "the *determining* event" in the lives of those who had not been as affected by prior events.

3. The AAUG's first published monograph, entitled *The Arab Americans: Studies in Assimilation* (Hagopian and Paden 1969), engaged with questions of identity. Some scholars who have highlighted the role of the AAUG in Arab American identity formation and in the field of ethnic studies include Helen Hatab Samhan (1987), Michael Suleiman (1999), Gregory Orfalea (2006), Sarah M. A. Gualtieri (2009), Keith Feldman (2015), Salim Yaqub (2016), and Pamela Pennock (2017).

important role by organizing their own events, building ties with other local groups, and supporting Arab student organizations. While members often participated in protests and grassroots activism, the national organization primarily focused on academic endeavors. As Fauzi Najjar declared, the AAUG was "an organization where we can write. If you want a demonstration, there are other organizations to go to" (quoted in Ahmed-Fararjeh 2003, 107). The association thus concentrated on producing scholarly work as the most effective way to incite change. To that end, it published pamphlets, monographs, and newsletters. In 1978, Ibrahim Abu-Lughod, Edward Said, and Fouad Moughrabi also established the *Arab Studies Quarterly* under the auspices of the AAUG.[4]

Third Worldism is a persistent theme throughout the AAUG's publications and conventions. The association closely followed and supported the activism of various American and foreign groups concerned with fighting colonialism and racism in the global Third World. For instance, the AAUG's second annual convention in 1969 centered on the Palestinian struggle to regain the homeland. During this convention, the organizers released the following position statement, which was reprinted in its March 1970 *Newsletter*:

> The Association believes that the ideological direction and premises of the Palestinian Revolutionary Movement are humanistic, progressive, and consonant with the best traditions of Man. That it has related itself successfully to the revolutionary movements of the oppressed people of the world is natural and has enabled it to receive their moral and material support. Just as the Palestinian Revolution has publicly supported the just cause of the people of Asia, Africa, Latin America, and the Black Community in the U.S., the Association registers its gratitude for the continuing support of these communities to [*sic*] the legitimate aspirations of the Palestinian People.

The statement subsequently called on the American public to dissuade their government from further assisting "Israel's expansionism and totalitarianism" in order to prevent the destruction of US credibility in the Middle East and the world.

Later AAUG conventions often featured transnational themes, such as the third annual gathering in Detroit, titled "The Arabs and the World: Perspectives on a Troubled Relationship." The conference organizers' "Final Statement" adopted a more urgent tone as it noted with alarm that the United States was pursuing "a policy of duplicity and imperialism in the Middle East and the Third World" ("Final Statement" 1970). It condemned the US government's support of "racist settler, colonial and fascist regimes," which, the AAUG contended, ran counter to most Americans' wishes. The association urged a revision of American policy toward various African Third World movements, arguing that US military support for "Israel, Rhodesia, and South Africa and to the colonial regime of Portugal lies at the heart of the continued success of these colonial/Fascist regimes in thwarting the principles of liberty, dignity, and equality." The statement situated its appeals for a change in US government policy within a rhetoric that emphasized human rights, arguing that this military support was "an affront to the best ideals of the American people." They thus catered their Third World message to an American audience that read or watched segments about these conferences in several news outlets. The December 1969 issue of the *AAUG Newsletter* noted that the conference was covered in local NBC and CBS newscasts, the *Detroit Free Press*, the *Christian Science Monitor*, and the *New York Times* ("Press Coverage" 1969).

During its conventions, the AAUG invited established scholars and political activists from around the world and also encouraged its own members to contribute to the scholarly discourse on a variety of pressing subjects. In doing so, the AAUG provided a space for scholarly discussion that was perceived to be less hostile than other academic conferences focusing on the Middle

4. As Said and Abu-Lughod wrote in the introduction to the first issue in 1979, the *Arab Studies Quarterly* was to be enlisted in the AAUG's task of "combatting ignorance and prejudice where knowledge of Arabs is concerned" (Said and Abu-Lughod 1979, v). Its board of editors came from the AAUG's ranks, and it received financial backing from the organization.

East, such as the Middle East Studies Association (MESA).[5] Conferences often featured speakers who were not Arab American or even Arab as a way to forge transnational connections with others in the Third World. During the second convention, the Pakistani British leftist Tariq Ali was invited to give the keynote speech but was blocked from entering the United States because he had participated in a flag-burning protest outside the American embassy in London. The news outlets that reported on the event focused on this reason for Ali's absence, which had prompted the conference organizers to make A. L. Tibawi his replacement. As Ibrahim Abu-Lughod recalled, the media left after Tibawi's somewhat dry address on education reform in Mandatory Palestine and did not hear the fiery speech that Eqbal Ahmad gave next. Ahmad, a Pakistani leftist intellectual whose apartment had been searched by the FBI while [he was] en route to the conference, asked the audience whether they knew why the United States had barred Ali. He waited for the audience to shout, "No, we don't know why," and then exclaimed: "Because they accuse him of burning the American flag! But that is a lie! He did not burn the American flag; he cremated the American flag!" Thus, in Ahmad's view, the US flag and all it stood for had already been dead when Ali lit it on fire. Reflecting on the speech, Abu-Lughod said it spearheaded Ahmad's position as "the most important public speaker for the Arabs, especially the young generation, the students" (quotes from Eqbal Ahmad in Ahmed-Fararjeh 2003, 106–7).

Ahmad could also count on the AAUG for close support throughout its first decade. In 1971, Ahmad was indicted along with six antiwar activists for conspiring to kidnap President Nixon's national-security adviser Henry Kissinger and destroy government property. Ahmad was further charged with threatening the life of Kissinger. After the news broke, the AAUG issued a statement declaring that the US government had falsely accused Ahmad without evidence in order to suppress "all advocates of peace in Vietnam." Its March 1971 *Newsletter* urged readers to donate to his legal fund and featured Abu-Lughod calling Ahmad a "friend of the Arab community" who was devoted to "the Arab cause in the United States" ("Advocate of Peace" 1971, 6–7). Ahmad was eventually cleared of all charges.[6]

The third annual AAUG convention also featured another notable South Asian speaker: Krishna Menon, who served as the minister of defense in India and a member of the Indian Parliament. In his keynote address, titled "The Arabs and the Third World," Menon argued that all imperialism was "rooted in some form of superstition and in anachronistic racial and theocratic concepts." He further linked the Palestinian struggle to that of the people in Vietnam (quoted in "Annual Convention Draws Record Attendance" 1970). Later AAUG conventions and publications continually highlighted the connections between anti-imperial movements and reiterated the importance of transnational solidarity.

The AAUG and the Creation of an Arab–Black Coalition

During an era fraught with struggles for civil rights in the United States and self-determination in the decolonizing world, Arab Americans increasingly recognized the intersections between racialization and colonization. Therefore, many Arab American intellectuals and activists began to identify and cooperate with both Black Americans and Africans. While scholars have written extensively on Black positions on Zionism and the Arab–Israeli conflict, they have generally paid insufficient attention to intercommunal work between Arab Americans

5. Letters between Michael Suleiman and Ibrahim Abu-Lughod in 1970 discussed their concerns with MESA's treatment of Arab researchers of the Arab world. See specifically Michael Suleiman's letter to Ibrahim Abu-Lughod on December 5, 1970 (Michael Suleiman Collection 1970). In my personal communications with former AAUG member Janice Terry in 2015, she also reiterated that AAUG conferences highlighted pro-Palestinian perspectives that were not welcome at MESA during this era. For more on the AAUG and MESA, see Lockman 2004 and Mitchell 2004.

6. Ahmad was cleared of all charges in *United States of America, v. Eqbal Ahmad, Philip Berrigan, Elizabeth McAlister, et al.*, 347 F. Supp. 912. (Pennsylvania Dist. Court, 1972). For more on the trial, see Schaar 2015.

and African Americans.[7] Salim Yaqub (2016) has most recently analyzed this subject [for the period] from 1967 to 1980, arguing that scholars have failed to contextualize the evolution of Black Americans' criticism of Israel. He delineates a split on the issue along "radical" and "moderate" lines and contends that Black moderates began to criticize Israel only once Palestinian leadership signaled their hesitant willingness to accept the Israeli state if it would return the West Bank and Gaza to sovereign Palestinian control. While I contend that Yaqub overstates the dichotomy between both Black and Arab radicals and moderates, his work nevertheless contributes greatly to historians' understanding of transnational and interethnic activism.

Arab American members of the AAUG represented themselves as kindred to African and African American activists. Elaine Hagopian, the association's president in 1976, recalled that most of its members were "involved in demonstrations across the country against [South African] apartheid. And most were strongly involved with African American protest groups and arguing for civil rights" (personal communication, Sept. 30, 2015). Hagopian elaborated, "It was important to us to not become a one-issue organization. If you don't support other people's causes, why should they support yours? But it was more than just that; it was the commonality of the dehumanization. You have solidarity out of the commonality." The transnational identities of AAUG members, even if they did not grow up in the Arab world, thus allowed them to identify with both the decolonizing Third World and other minorities in the United States. This is a notable shift in self-identity given the historical efforts of early Syrian Americans to dissociate themselves from people of color in order to represent themselves as white and gain access to US citizenship (Gualtieri 2009).

Ibrahim Abu-Lughod's sway over the AAUG, beginning when he served as its second president, was evident in the organization's early concern with justice in Africa. In Abu-Lughod's view, unifying the study of the regions north and south of the Sahara was integral to understanding African history; he believed that promoting this analytical shift was his greatest contribution to the Program of African Studies at Northwestern University. Working with both students and AAUG members during a politically volatile era, Abu-Lughod attempted to foster links among various liberation movements by showing how Israel, South Africa, and Vietnam were "all connected" (Ahmed-Fararjeh 2003, 97–98).

Hagopian, Abu-Lughod, and like-minded AAUG members embodied this perspective in their support for decolonization and [their] opposition to neocolonialism throughout the continent, not just in North Africa. For instance, AAUG members were invited to attend the Sixth Pan African Congress in Dar Es Salaam, Tanzania, in 1974 ("Arab-American Community News" 1974). In 1977, AAUG member Hisham Sharabi joined Abu-Lughod at an Afro-Arab symposium in Sharjah, UAE. This gathering issued the "Declaration of Sharjah," which affirmed historical links between Arabs and Africans and endorsed Palestinian, Zimbabwean, Namibian, and African liberation movements' efforts to "dismantle the colonial-settler regimes of Rhodesia, South Africa, and Israel" ("Meetings in the Arab World" 1977). In 1979, the Washington, DC, AAUG chapter also organized a Day of Liberation of Africa and Palestine with the All African People's Revolutionary Party. The pan-African and pan-Arab organizers arranged demonstrations, discussions, and films about the Palestinian struggle and ended the affair with a luncheon honoring Shafiq al-Hout, who was visiting from the Beirut Office of the Palestine Liberation Organization (PLO) (Sahar 1979).

Notable Black figures also often spoke at AAUG national conventions and other events. In 1970, the AAUG invited Nation of Islam leader Louis Farrakhan and Shirley Graham Du Bois, activist and widow of W. E. B. Du Bois, to address its annual convention's banquet. The crowd met their comments on Black Nationalism with vibrant applause ("Annual Convention Draws Record Attendance" 1970, 2). Shirley Graham Du Bois's presence was especially noteworthy because of her deceased husband's previously sympathetic views toward Zionism

7. For critical engagement with the literature on Black Americans and Zionism, see Feldman 2015 and Lubin 2014. Both scholars shed new light on Black American leaders' engagement with Zionism and the Arab or Palestinian Nationalist movements. Pam Pennock (2017) has also closely analyzed solidarity movements across racial and ethnic boundaries.

(Sevitch 2009). Graham Du Bois's experience of living in Egypt after 1967 and her contact with numerous anti-Zionist thinkers transformed her perspective on Palestine. Three years after speaking to the AAUG audience, Graham Du Bois would tend to wounded Egyptian soldiers during the 1973 war in Cairo hospitals (Horne 2000). Seeing these crises firsthand prompted her to become a more vocal critic of Zionism. For instance, Graham Du Bois argued that the color line that stretched across America could be extended to the Middle East, where the "colored folk" were "battling with the 'white folk' of Israel" (1973, 32–37). Although at this point the PLO maintained a position that refused to accept the legitimacy of an Israeli state, Arab American organizations were nevertheless able to garner the support of some Black Americans who may have previously been supportive of (or at least indifferent to) the Zionist movement, like Shirley Graham Du Bois.

At the 1975 AAUG Convention, Stokely Carmichael argued that African Americans shared a deep opposition to Zionism with both Arabs and Africans. His statements spoke to a conscious effort of some Black civil rights activists to distance themselves from elements of the Jewish American population over the issue of Zionism. While many Jewish Americans were generally progressive on civil rights issues, their growing support for the Israeli establishment's exclusionary policies led some Black Americans to eschew this once close relationship. Carmichael noted that pro-Israeli groups had featured statements of support from Black elected officials in advertisements in major US newspapers because Zionists were "desperately aware that Black Americans increasingly condemn Israel as a racist state with political, economic, and military links with South Africa" (quoted in "Convention Is AAUG's Largest" 1975, 7). Carmichael later spoke at other AAUG events, such as a lecture [titled] "Angola and the Struggle for Liberation in Africa" at the Washington, DC, chapter in March 1976 ("Members and Chapters in the News" 1976).

Other Black American leaders further emphasized the kindred relationship between Blacks and Arabs, not just as victims of global imperialism but as American minorities. In 1972, Congresswoman Shirley Chisholm was the keynote speaker at the Washington, DC, AAUG chapter's annual banquet. Chisholm, a Democrat from New York, was in the midst of a difficult campaign to run as the first Black woman candidate for president. Although her underfunded campaign failed to garner enough votes during the Democratic primaries, she nevertheless ran with vigor and refused to temper her support for the radical wing of the civil rights movement. Speaking to more than two hundred guests, Chisholm disparaged the "treadmill of fruitless talks and new outbreaks of violence" that characterized American–Arab relations. She also predicted that American minorities would struggle with renewed fervor to gain true equality: "We are now entering an epoch that could bring the liberation of oppressed and deprived people of the world. There is now a social revolution in progress in this country. Black Power, Red Power, La Causa and La Huelga; and yes, Arab Power—these are a few of the slogans of that revolution" (quoted in "Americans Lose Arab Goodwill, Trust—Chisholm" 1972, 6).

In addition to inviting her to speak at their events, the AAUG closely followed Chisholm's campaign in its newsletter. Major media outlets often ignored Chisholm's campaign or described her in terms tinged with sexism by focusing on her "small stature" or calling her "feisty, pepper pot, or prim" (Winslow 2014, 116). The *AAUG Newsletter* eschewed these patronizing descriptors while covering her commitment to human rights and Palestinian issues. For instance, it highlighted Chisholm's comparison of Black youth who spent their early years in segregated urban neighborhoods to the Arab generation that had "grown up in the Palestinian ghetto." As she wrote in a position paper that the *Newsletter* quoted in full, Black Americans and Palestinians had both "made clear that they will no longer tolerate the injustice of their conditions" (quoted in "Shirley Chisholm Disavows Views of Black Caucus" 1972, 5). Chisholm's stance on the Middle East called for a renewed effort to resolve conflicts in the Middle East by focusing on the root cause: the dispute over Palestine.

However, the AAUG was not as proficient at building ties with some other Black members of Congress. In June 1972, the Congressional Black Caucus released a pro-Israel statement in response to the National Black Political Convention's radical critique of Zionism. At its Gary, Indiana, meeting, the National Black Political

Convention had called for the "dismantling" of Israel and a suspension of American aid to the state. Although eight thousand Black activists attended the convention and contributed to the resolution, the thirteen-member Black Caucus sought to distance itself from such sentiments. The caucus statement described the establishment of Israel as "a revolutionary development in the Middle East" and asserted that Israel had stimulated "the national inspirations of many Black people who were under colonial rule in Africa and the third-world nations in Asia." It furthermore called "special attention to the cordial relationship Israel has maintained with the developing Black nations in Africa and the third-world" because Israel had sent technical experts to many developing countries and allowed "hundreds of Africans" to travel to Israel for education (quoted in "Shirley Chisholm Disavows Views of Black Caucus" 1972, 1).

The AAUG subsequently participated in a two-day meeting that the Congressional Black Caucus sponsored at the 1972 African-American National Conference on Africa. Delegates from the AAUG and a number of African American organizations urged the passage of sanctions on American investments in "minority, white-ruled states or those that serve as conduits for South African products." It also requested that Africans gain control over the production, refining, and shipping of their own oil resources. The AAUG delegates requested a withdrawal of Israeli forces from the Sinai Peninsula and the reopening of the Suez Canal since its closure had "diverted shipping to South Africa and provided NATO with a pretext to provide military and financial aid" to the apartheid government in the name of protecting shipping routes. Finally, delegates encouraged a boycott of South African gems that were polished in Israel and sold throughout the United States ("Israel–South Africa Ties Exposed" 1972).

The latter demand was also the focus of a symposium that the Ohio AAUG and Organization of Arab Students chapters cosponsored at Ohio State University the same year on boycotting diamonds that were mined in South Africa, then cut in Israel, and sold in the US market. At this meeting, representatives of Arab American, African American, and socialist organizations formed a steering committee to adopt and pursue a plan of action to research and expose collusion between businesses and the governments of South Africa, Israel, and the United States.[8]

The AAUG backed up its claims about Israeli–South African ties with material produced by various advocacy groups and individuals. It welcomed news about other organizations that advocated for African decolonization, especially when such groups noted a connection between Israel and neocolonial regimes. In its March 1971 newsletter, the AAUG reported on a position paper that the Madison Area Committee on Southern Africa (MACSA) published about Israel and South Africa. In 1970, MACSA had led demonstrations at the University of Wisconsin–Madison against the American invasion of Cambodia, and the National Guard suppressed the protests. While MACSA initially omitted Israel from its discussion of worldwide repression in a position paper that sparked the campus protests, it subsequently organized a meeting to educate its members about Israeli policies in occupied Palestine. The AAUG noted that MACSA's resolutions were particularly newsworthy given the "active involvement of the U.S. government and Israel in the oppression and exploitation of the African people." The MACSA paper not only highlighted similarities between South Africa's treatment of its Black population and Israel's treatment of indigenous Palestinians but also explored Israel's strong ties to the South African regime. An AAUG member reported that Zionist and Israeli officials later asked MACSA to withdraw the paper from circulation: "The thrust of their objection was that it was 'anti-Semitic' not that the facts were wrong!" ("Madison Area Committee on Southern Africa" 1971).

By the mid-1970s, solidarity work between Arab Americans and African Americans reached unprecedented levels. In 1974 the AAUG again reported on the National Black Political Convention, which had taken place two years [earlier] in Gary, Indiana. This time, the convention attendees in Little Rock, Arkansas, passed a resolution that condemned Congress and President

8. The Arab American representatives on the steering committee were Abdeen Jabara of the AAUG, Riyad Mansour and Haidar al-Mustafawi of the Organization of Arab Students, and Hasan Husseini of the Arab-American Association of Ohio University ("Seminar on Israel, S. Africa Diamond Industries Held" 1972).

Nixon for giving $2.2 billion in aid to Israel while "ignoring the rights of Palestinian and African peoples struggling for self-determination and economic development" ("Arab-American Community News" 1974). During its October 1974 meeting in Chicago, the National Anti-Imperialist Conference in Solidarity with African Liberation also adopted similar resolutions that supported Arabs against Israeli colonialism. Speakers at its workshops compared Israel to Rhodesia, South Africa, and Portuguese colonists and portrayed the Arab struggle as "an integral part of the African continent's struggle for Liberation" ("Arab-American Community News" 1974). The idea of imitating the South African Boycott-Divestment-Sanction (BDS) movement to boycott corporations doing business with Israel and [with] trade unions that invested in Zionist institutions began to gain prominence.

In 1979, the AAUG invited a delegation of media representatives and leaders from the Black community in the United States to visit Lebanon. Its newsletter reported, "Members of this delegation, all of whom have been deeply involved in the political rights and community organizing efforts of the Black and Latino communities, had expressed interest in clarifying the context in which Palestinian and Lebanese Arabs are struggling for their rights and security in the face of Israeli military devastation." Jack O'Dell, a prominent civil rights organizer as part of the Southern Christian Leadership Conference (SCLC) and the head of Pacifica Radio, served as the chairman. Also on the delegation were Reverend Bennett Smith representing the SCLC; Pablo Sanchez and Lauri Parks, filmmakers from Washington, DC; Alfonso Gaskins, a student leader at Howard University Law School; Herb Boyd, a community activist in Detroit; and Jaqueline Jackson, who directed Operation PUSH (People United to Serve Humanity) with her husband, Jesse Jackson. This array of leaders met in Lebanon with PLO chairman [Yasser] Arafat and other PLO leaders such as Farouk al-Kaddoumi and Salah Khalaf. They then toured PLO SAMED (Palestine Martyrs Works Society) factories, Red Crescent hospitals, orphanages, and refugee camps near Beirut as well as in southern Lebanon. Jaqueline Jackson reportedly spoke of her "pain and embarrassment in realizing how much of the children's suffering had been inflicted through weapons and policies originating in the United States" (quoted in "American Blacks, Latinos, and Educators Form Delegation to Lebanon" 1979, 8). Jesse Jackson echoed his wife's views and became more outspoken about Arab issues. The following year, the *AAUG Newsletter* reprinted Jackson's assertion at the 1980 PUSH convention that "Blacks have a vital interest in peace in the Middle East because in a hot war we will die first and in a cold war over oil, we will be unemployed and freeze first" (quoted in "At the PUSH Convention" 1980).

Other Black leaders went on delegations to the Middle East and returned as more vocal critics of American foreign policy in the Middle East, particularly on Palestine. The 1979 AAUG convention featured three advocates of Arab–Black solidarity: Reverend Joseph E. Lowery, president of the Southern Christian Leadership Conference, Reverend Jesse Jackson, and Congressman Walter Fauntroy of Washington, DC. The spokesmen addressed a thousand participants at the annual convention with a message that could be summarized by Fauntroy's statement: "We are in Foreign Policy to stay." Lowery recalled his trip to the Middle East while speaking at the banquet. "When I was in Southern Lebanon, I saw 100,000 Black jobs flying faster than the speed of light over my head. We must turn these cluster bombs into biscuits. Foreign policy takes bread from the mouths of Black and Brown children" (quoted in "Twelfth AAUG Convention Highlights" 1979–80).

At the same 1979 AAUG convention, PLO chairman Yasser Arafat sent a message that Hatem Husseini, head of the Washington, DC, Palestine Information Office, read to the participants. In it, Arafat called upon the Arab American population to continue to "forge links of solidarity with Black Americans and other minority groups" who supported the Palestinian cause (quoted in "Chairman Arafat Sends Message" 1980, 8).

This represented a new era for the PLO, which had previously failed to build ties with mainstream Black American leaders. As Salim Yaqub has argued, the PLO was able to make more overt overtures to Black American politicians because by the mid-1970s Arafat and other PLO leaders had begun to articulate a more conciliatory position on Israel that would accept the establishment of an independent state "in any part of Palestine from which Israel will withdraw." Yaqub interprets this statement as "implying that Israel could exist in the remainder," a position that was "first unveiled in the summer of 1974" (2015, 21).

Arafat's message also indirectly referred to the Andrew Young controversy of 1978. The US ambassador to the United Nations had been fired after meeting with PLO contacts to discuss potential compromises between the Israeli and Palestinian leadership. The US policy against negotiating with the PLO was still in place, but the PLO's willingness to meet with American officials demonstrated a new openness toward a solution. Young's firing led to yet another area of common ground for Black and Arab Americans. The AAUG was especially vocal on the matter, with its Board of Directors issuing the following statement in 1978:

> The [AAUG] is deeply anguished over the resignation of Ambassador Andrew Young, and views with deep alarm the circumstances surrounding his resignation. We deplore the fact that Ambassador young's resignation resulted from his brief encounter with Mr. Zehdi Labib Terzi, the PLO's observer to the U.N. Not only was Ambassador Young unjustly reprimanded by Secretary of State Cyrus Vance, but he was also subjected to a chorus of verbal abuse by certain anti-Arab, anti–Third World public officials and organized groups. ("AAUG Statement on Andrew Young" 1978)

The statement went on to question the double standards that had led to Young's resignation after meeting with the PLO; the American ambassador to Austria, Milton A. Wolf, had held talks with a similarly high-level PLO official in Vienna with no consequences. The AAUG Board asked, "Was [Young] victimized because he chose to question the wisdom of sending millions of dollars in American arms to Israel as an inducement to peace in the Middle East? Was he victimized because he questioned Israeli annexation policies in the occupied West Bank and Gaza Strip?" ("AAUG Statement on Andrew Young" 1978). In the eyes of the AAUG leadership, Young was "victimized" because of his long history of standing against apartheid and racial inequality.

Conclusion

The mass movement the AAUG represented largely disintegrated by the late 1980s as members left or became less active in the organization. Many of the AAUG's "old guard" went in separate directions to advocate for Palestinians and Arabs in ways they thought were most effective. For instance, while the 1982 war in Lebanon, in particular, encouraged Ibrahim Abu-Lughod and Edward Said to engage in increased activism, their role in the AAUG diminished as they focused their work on other channels. Said retired as editor of the *Arab Studies Quarterly* in 1986 and became absorbed in other advocacy and academic work. Abu-Lughod concentrated his considerable energies in an effort to establish an Open University of Palestine in Beirut; after the 1982 war made that impossible, he joined other educational initiatives in the Middle East. In 1988, Elaine Hagopian and Naseer Aruri formed the Trans-Arab Research Institute to continue the kind of scholarly work on the Middle East that the AAUG had begun.

The AAUG's membership also declined as Arab American communities fractured over political conflicts. The association's criticism of the Camp David Accords led many Egyptian members to withdraw from the organization because they supported Anwar Sadat's unilateral move. The divisiveness in the aftermath of Israel's 1982 invasion of Lebanon and the expulsion of the PLO resulted in an exodus of many Lebanese AAUG members. As Ghada Talhami notes, "Having succeeded in implanting the Palestinian case in the consciousness of Third World intellectuals apparently did not mean that we have succeeded in transcending inter-Arab divisions, not even on an intellectual level" (2007, 131).

The AAUG failed to achieve its primary, ambitious goal; it was unable to stem the tidal wave of anti-Arab sentiments that prevailed, which were exacerbated by growing conflict between Israel and the Arab world after 1967. It could not impart enough knowledge to the larger American public to sway them to vote for politicians who would combat the growing influence of Israel's lobby. The vast majority of publications it produced would not reach the mainstream because of institutional obstacles that riddled the organization: its lack of funding, the overwork of its active members, and insufficient membership.[9]

Nevertheless, the post-1967 generation of activists engaged in unprecedented work, published prolifically, and facilitated a sense of belonging among disparate people who suffered from anti-Arab prejudice and felt distraught at events in the Middle East. Naseer Aruri, recalling the aftermath of the 1967 war, believed that the AAUG ultimately brought Arab immigrants and Americans born of Arab heritage together:

> For the longest time, quite a number of us recent immigrants could not bring ourselves to admit we were Americans. When we referred to ourselves as Arab-Americans, we could almost hear the Arab part quite loud, while the American part following the hyphen was barely audible. Thus, we remained Arabs in America rather than Arab-Americans. However, our rights as U.S. citizens were compromised because of our ethnicity, and not simply because of our commitment to identity. Not only those of us who were born abroad had their rights as citizens compromised, but those in AAUG who enjoyed birth citizenship were hassled and seen by the powers as Arab more than American. (2007, 36)

As Aruri's recollection demonstrates, transnational activism for Palestine and the Third World and the backlash it inspired in the United States in many ways strengthened Arab American identity.[10]

To conclude, I have examined the AAUG's advocacy for Palestine alongside its commitments to anticolonial (and anti-neocolonial) movements in the Third World during its first decade. In doing so, my work seeks to demonstrate that 1967 and subsequent moments in the Arab–Israeli conflict fostered the creation of a transnational intellectual generation that aligned itself with both the Palestinian revolutionary movement and the global postcolonial community. In the AAUG, representatives of an Arab American intellectual generation found like-minded individuals and created a community in exile.

9. Refer to some of the founders' reflections on the AAUG's achievements and shortcomings in the Summer–Fall 2007 special issue of the *Arab Studies Quarterly*. See in particular Rashid Bashshur, "Unfulfilled Expectations: The Genesis and Demise of the AAUG"; Michael Suleiman, "'I Come to Bury Caesar, Not to Praise Him': An Assessment of the AAUG as an Example of an Activist Arab-American Organization"; and Elaine Hagopian, "Reversing Injustice: On Utopian Activism."

10. For more on this backlash, as exemplified by the Nixon administration's "Operation Boulder," see Pennock 2017, Samhan 1987, and Yaqub 2016.

Works Cited

"AAUG Statement on Andrew Young." 1978. *AAUG Newsletter* 12, no. 3 (Sept.): 1.

Ad Hoc Conference Committee. 1967. "Minutes of December 9, 1967 Meeting in the Chicago Theological Seminary Chapel, University of Chicago, Chicago, Illinois." Box 23, folder 9, AAUG Papers. Eastern Michigan Univ., Ypsilanti.

"Advocate of Peace, Eqbal Ahmad, Accused by U.S. Government of Kidnapping Plot." 1971. *AAUG Newsletter* 4, no. 1 (Mar.): 6–7.

Ahmed-Fararjeh, Hisham. 2003. *Ibrahim Abu-Lughod: Resistance, Exile, and Return*. Palestine: Ibrahim Abu-Lughod Institute of International Studies at Birzeit Univ.

"American Blacks, Latinos, and Educators Form Delegation to Lebanon." 1979. *AAUG Newsletter* 12, no. 2 (July): 8.

"Americans Lose Arab Goodwill, Trust—Chisholm." 1972. *AAUG Newsletter* 5, no. 3 (July): 1, 6.

"Annual Convention Draws Record Attendance: AAUG Scholars Join U.S. & Foreign Specialists in Exploring Theme 'Arabs & the World.'" 1970. *AAUG Newsletter* 3, no. 4 (Dec.): 1–2, 4.

"Arab-American Community News." 1974. *AAUG Newsletter* 7, no. 1 (Mar.): 7.

Aruri, Naseer. 2007. "AAUG: A Memoir." *Arab Studies Quarterly* 29, nos. 3–4 (Summer–Fall): 33–46.

"At the PUSH Convention: A Push for Better Black–Arab Relations." 1980. *AAUG Newsletter* 13, no. 3 (Sept.–Oct.): 4.

Bawardi, Hani. 2014. *The Making of Arab Americans: From Syrian Nationalism to U.S. Citizenship*. Austin: Univ. of Texas Press.

"Chairman Arafat Sends Message to Convention." 1980. *AAUG Newsletter* 13, no. 1 (Dec. 1979–Mar. 1980): 3, 8.

"Convention Is AAUG's Largest." 1975. *AAUG Newsletter* 9, no. 4 (Dec.): 7.

Davidson, Lawrence. 2001. *America's Palestine: Popular and Official Perceptions from Balfour to Israeli Statehood.* Gainesville: Univ. Press of Florida.

Feldman, Keith. 2015. *A Shadow over Palestine: The Imperial Life of Race in America.* Minneapolis: Univ. of Minnesota Press.

"Final Statement." 1970. *AAUG Newsletter* 3, no. 4 (Dec.): 4, 6.

Graham Du Bois, Shirley. 1973. "Confrontation in the Middle East." *Black Scholar* 5, no. 3: 32–37.

Gualtieri, Sarah M. A. 2009. *Between Arab and White: Race and Ethnicity in the Early Syrian American Diaspora.* Berkeley: Univ. of California Press.

Hagopian, Elaine, and Ann Paden, eds. 1969. *The Arab Americans: Studies in Assimilation.* AAUG Monograph Series no. 1. Wilmette, IL: Medina Univ. Press International.

Horne, Gerald. 2000. *Race Woman: The Lives of Shirley Graham Du Bois.* New York: New York Univ. Press.

"Israel–South Africa Ties Exposed by AAUG Delegates at the Congressional Black Caucus." 1972. *AAUG Newsletter* 5, no. 3 (July): 1, 5.

Lockman, Zachary. 2004. *Contending Visions of the Middle East.* Cambridge: Cambridge Univ. Press.

Lubin, Alex. 2014. *Geographies of Liberation: The Making of an Afro- Arab Political Imaginary.* Chapel Hill: Univ. of North Carolina Press.

"Madison Area Committee on Southern Africa: Position Paper on Israel and Southern Africa." 1971. *AAUG Newsletter* 4, no. 1 (Mar.): 7–8.

"Meetings in the Arab World: Afro-Arab Symposium at Sharjah, UAE." 1977. *AAUG Newsletter* 11, no. 1 (Mar.): 10.

"Members and Chapters in the News." 1976. *AAUG Newsletter* 10, no. 3 (June): 10.

Michael Suleiman Collection. 1970. Michael Suleiman to Ibrahim Abu-Lughod, Dec. 5. Box 31A, folder 9. Arab American National Museum, Dearborn, MI.

Mitchell, Timothy. 2004. "The Middle East in the Past and Future of Social Science." In *The Politics of Knowledge,* edited by David Szanton, 74–118. Berkeley: Univ. of California Press.

Najjar, Fauzi. 1971. "AAUG—the First Year." *AAUG Newsletter* 4, no. 1 (Mar.): 1.

Orfalea, Gregory. 2006. *The Arab Americans: A History.* Northampton, MA: Olive Branch.

Pennock, Pamela. 2017. *The Rise of the Arab American Left: Activists, Allies, and Their Fight against Imperialism and Racism, 1960s–1980s.* Chapel Hill: Univ. of North Carolina Press.

"Press Coverage of Convention in U.S." 1969. *AAUG Newsletter* 2, no. 4 (Dec.): 5–6.

Sahar, Nadim. 1979. "Support for Palestine All across America." *AAUG Newsletter* 12, no. 2 (July): 12–13.

Said, Edward, and Ibrahim Abu-Lughod. 1979. "Why *ASQ*?" *Arab Studies Quarterly* 1, no. 1 (Winter): v–vi.

Samhan, Helen Hatab. 1987. "Politics and Exclusion: The Arab American Experience." *Journal of Palestine Studies* 16, no. 2 (1987): 20–28.

Schaar, Stuart. 2015. *Eqbal Ahmad: Critical Outsider in a Turbulent Age.* New York: Columbia Univ. Press.

"Seminar on Israel, S. Africa Diamond Industries Held." 1972. *AAUG Newsletter* 5, no. 3 (July): 4.

Sevitch, Benjamin. 2009. "W. E. B. Du Bois as America's Foremost Black Zionist." In *The Souls of W. E. B. Du Bois: New Essays and Reflections,* edited by Edward J. Blum, 233–53. Macon, GA: Mercer Univ. Press.

"Shirley Chisholm Disavows View of Black Caucus." 1972. *AAUG Newsletter* 5, no. 2 (June): 1, 5.

Sirinelli, Jean-François. 1993. "The Concept of an Intellectual Generation." In *Intellectuals in Twentieth-Century France: Mandarins and Samurais,* edited by Jeremy Jennings, 82–93. New York: St. Martin's Press.

Suleiman, Michael W., ed. 1999. *Arabs in America: Building a New Future.* Philadelphia: Temple Univ. Press.

Talhami, Ghada. 2007. "A Cultural, Not a Political Lobby: The Mixed Legacy of a Grand Plan." *Arab Studies Quarterly* 29, nos. 3–4 (Summer–Fall): 125–37.

"Twelfth AAUG Convention Highlights." 1979–80. *AAUG Newsletter* 13, no. 1 (Dec.–Mar.): 1–2.

Westad, Odd Arne. 2005. *The Global Cold War: Third World Interventions and the Making of Our Times.* New York: Cambridge Univ. Press.

Winslow, Barbara. 2014. *Shirley Chisholm: Catalyst for Change.* Boulder, CO: Westview Press.

Yaqub, Salim. 2015. "'Our Declaration of Independence': African Americans, Arab Americans, and the Arab-Israeli Conflict, 1967–1979." *Mashriq & Mahjar* 3, no. 1: 12–29.

———. 2016. *Imperfect Strangers: Americans, Arabs, and U.S.–Middle East Relations in the 1970s.* Ithaca, NY: Cornell Univ. Press.

36

From the River to the Sea to Every Mountain Top

Solidarity as Worldmaking

ROBIN D. G. KELLEY

I'll exist in a world that
fights against racism
like Martin and Malcolm
bleeds ghetto tales of Steve Biko
as a song that never dies
no matter what apartheid
makes of our bodies
feeds mouths in Belfast streets
and resurrects Bobby Sands' message
so that we will never
be hungry again
—Remi Kanazi, "Coexistence"

It is generally agreed that a resurgence of Black–Palestinian transnational solidarity (BPTS) began in the summer of 2014 when a wave of fatal police shootings of unarmed African Americans in the United States coincided with Israel's brutal fifty-one-day assault on Gaza. Much has been written about the expressions of solidarity between Black and Palestinian activists resisting racialized state violence, especially in Ferguson, Missouri, where mass protests erupted after police killed unarmed teenager Michael Brown and left his lifeless body in the streets for over four hours. (See, e.g., Baker 2014; Bailey 2015; Davis 2016; Kelley 2014; Gilbert 2014; Marcelin 2014; Obeidallah 2014; Yassin 2014.) These acts of solidarity were not merely spontaneous responses to coincidental and spectacular violence but the result of years of organizing. In the summer of 2011, for example, Rabab Abdulhadi and Barbara Ransby led a feminists-of-color delegation to Palestine that included Angela Davis, Gina Dent, Chandra Talpade Mohanty, Ayoka Chenzira, G. Melissa Garcia, Anna Romina Guevarra, Beverly Guy-Sheftall, and Premilla Nadasen. "We wanted to see for ourselves," they explained in a jointly written statement, "the conditions under which Palestinian people live and struggle against what we can now confidently name as the Israeli project of apartheid and ethnic cleansing. Each and every one of us—including those members of our delegation who grew up in the Jim Crow South, in apartheid South Africa, and on Indian reservations in the U.S.—was shocked by what we saw" (Ransby 2011).[1] The following year, inspired in

Excerpt from Robin D. G. Kelley, "From the River to the Sea to Every Mountain Top: Solidarity as Worldmaking," *Journal of Palestine Studies* 48, no. 4 (Summer 2019): 69–91. Full references in the original notes were converted to author-date citations in the text and notes here, and a works cited list was added. Reprinted with corrections and press style changes for consistency throughout the volume by permission of the University of California Press.

1. For an excellent reflection on building intersectional solidarities leading up to the summer of 2014, see, for example, Atshan and Moore 2014.

part by the absence of a coherent Black response to the Arab Spring and Israel's latest assault on Gaza, veteran labor leader and writer Bill Fletcher Jr., Felicia Eaves of the US Campaign to End the Israeli Occupation, Mark Harrison of Peace with Justice, and the Reverend D. A. Lams formed African Americans for Justice in the Middle East and North Africa (AAJMENA). Fifty-five Black activists and scholars signed its founding solidarity statement in support of "progressive struggles for national liberation, national sovereignty, justice and democracy" throughout the region and especially for Palestinians, whose struggles they hoped to "more fully integrate . . . into the lives and struggles of the African American people" ("African Americans for Justice" 2012).

In other words, we might think of the Ferguson–Gaza convergence as catalyzing rather than commencing the resurgence of BPTS. Thus, when Black4Palestine, born of this political firmament, issued its "Black Solidarity Statement with Palestine" in 2015, it garnered over eleven hundred signatures from activists, artists, and scholars. The document unflinchingly endorsed the Boycott, Divestment, and Sanctions (BDS) movement and condemned Israeli apartheid based "on ethnic cleansing, land theft[,] . . . the denial of Palestinian humanity and sovereignty," as well as racist attacks on African asylum seekers (Black4Palestine 2015). A new generation of young activists from Black Lives Matter, the Dream Defenders, Black Youth Project 100, and many other organizations visited the West Bank to bear witness to the intolerable conditions of Palestinian life under occupation.

Black activists quickly emerged as prominent advocates for Palestine. In August of 2016, the Movement for Black Lives (M4BL), a coalition of over sixty organizations, rolled out an ambitious policy statement aimed at dismantling racism, patriarchy, inequality, and militarism that included a forceful statement labeling Israel an "apartheid state" and characterizing the ongoing situation in Gaza and the West Bank as "genocide." Predictably, conservatives and liberals attacked the statement—especially the charge of genocide—as misleading, incendiary, and anti-Semitic. But even faced with the potential loss of funding, M4BL never backed down. Dream Defenders' codirector Rachel Gilmer drafted much of the statement after she and other members of her organization visited Palestine in the spring of 2016. Her takeaway: "We are never going to get free in the U.S. if the rest of the world is in chains" (Ransby 2018, 36).[2] The controversy over applying [the term] "genocide" to the condition of Palestinians under occupation generated some soul searching inside the progressive organization Jewish Voice for Peace (JVP), which not only came out in support of the statement but undertook a deeper interrogation of race and racism in Israel, [in] the United States, and among US Jews. In 2018, JVP launched its Deadly Exchange campaign, exposing and resisting the ongoing role of Israeli military and police in training US law enforcement in so-called counterterrorism and other tactics that reinforce racial profiling, hyperpolicing, and militarization (JVP 2018).[3]

Charges of Palestinian (or Arab) anti-Black racism soon followed these dramatic acts of BPTS.[4] The tensions surrounding anti-Blackness and, to a lesser degree, Black Islamophobia, often generated productive discussions, forums, debates, self-critique, and even new scholarship, reminding us that BPTS—like any solidarity—must be understood as a contingent political project rather than some kind of natural, essential, transhistorical alliance (Abulhawa 2013; Aidi 2014; Alhassen 2016; Daulatzai

2. See also Bailey 2016.

3. See also the Palestine Is Here database, which tracks Israeli military ties to US local government, police departments, corporations, and academic institutions, available at "Palestine Is Here," https://palestineishere.org/.

4. Accusations of Arab/Palestinian anti-Blackness and Black Islamophobia had been part of an ongoing debate long before the Ferguson/Gaza moment and in fact had begun to resurface in 2013 when professional academic organizations such as the American Studies Association were passing resolutions supporting the academic and cultural boycott of Israel. The popularity of Afropessimism and its emphasis on anti-Blackness as the foundational structure of the modern world fueled growing skepticism among some Black intellectuals about solidarity with Palestinians. For a good discussion of the post-Ferguson moment and charges of Arab anti-Blackness, see Alhassen 2016; Brady 2013; Erakat 2015; and Wilderson 2014. . . . [P]articipants [in a roundtable on anti-Blackness and Black–Palestinian solidarity (Erakat 2015)] included Rabab Abdulhadi, Ahmad Abuznaid, Ebony Coletu, Bill Fletcher Jr., Che Gossett, Sarah Ihmoud, Aja Monet, Donna Murch, Nadine Naber, Linda Sarsour, Jared Sexton, Nadera Shalhoub, and Robin D. G. Kelley.

2012; Erakat 2016; Feldman 2015; Fischbach 2018; Lubin 2013; Pickens 2015). Which raises the question: Why presume that racial or national identity, or racialized or colonial experience, should constitute the sole or even primary basis for solidarity? We know that there is no uniform Black or Palestinian sensibility, identity, or community. Class, gender, sexuality, location, generation, ideological differences, and so on—all dynamically shape and fracture Black and Palestinian identities, making solidarity within these communities difficult enough. Palestinian communities across Latin America, for example, have shown strong right-wing proclivities, particularly in El Salvador and Chile. And as I've written elsewhere, Zionism and strident support for Israel have been the default position of most African Americans, especially among elites (Kelley 2015, 2018). Anti-Blackness has never produced a united, uniform, unanimous Black antiracist response, nor have the depredations of Israeli settler colonialism generated a similarly unified Palestinian response. Hence, we should not be surprised to discover Palestinian anti-Black racism, Black anti-Arab racism and Islamophobia, reluctance to build alliances between these communities, or what is often the most common response: indifference.

Contemporary transnational solidarities are often built on analogies, what Timothy Seidel calls "a chain of equivalence" (2016, 1646), which is to say on identifying equivalent modalities of oppression, exploitation, and resistance. The Ferguson–Gaza convergence is a case in point. Activists highlighted the similarities in state violence, racialized histories of dispossession and enclosure, and tactics of popular resistance as an effective strategy for political mobilization and coalition building. However, it seems to me that analogies and "a chain of equivalence" are not the cement that holds transnational solidarities together. On the contrary, they can lead to historical distortion and muddled political intentions. For example, in 2011, inspired by the fiftieth anniversary of the US Freedom Rides organized by the Congress of Racial Equality to test federal laws prohibiting segregation on interstate bus travel, Palestinian "Freedom Riders" boarded Jewish-only buses in Jerusalem in order to challenge Israeli apartheid and the companies that run the transit system—notably Egged and Veolia—and therefore profit from the illegal occupation. However, by directly invoking parallels with the US civil rights movement, the organizers left some in the US media mistakenly believing that desegregation was the objective. The Palestinian Freedom Riders promptly issued a press release clarifying their goal and explaining the "significant differences" between the African American fight for desegregation and the Palestinian struggle for decolonization. They stated:

> In undertaking this action Palestinians do not seek the desegregation of settler buses, as the presence of these colonizers and the infrastructure that serves them is illegal and must be dismantled. As part of their struggle for freedom, justice and dignity, Palestinians demand the ability . . . to travel freely on their own roads, on their own land, including the right to travel to Jerusalem. Palestinian activists also aim to expose two of the companies that profit from Israel's apartheid policies and encourage global boycott of and divestment from them. (Alsaafin 2011)[5]

And yet the organizers continued to underscore the parallels between Birmingham, Alabama, in 1961 and Jerusalem in 2011 by emphasizing the structure of racist violence: "Palestinians understand that this act of nonviolent disobedience may result in violent attacks and even death at the hands of Israeli settlers that are to Israel what the Ku Klux Klan was to the Jim Crow South, or [at the hands of] the authorities that protect them" (Alsaafin 2011).

What mattered most to the Palestinian Freedom Riders and the organizers in and around Ferguson was not so much the parallels but their insistence that the struggles were *linked*, not only to each other but to injustice and oppression around the world. Which is to say that they echoed the same basic principles expressed by the women-of-color delegation in 2011, in the AAJMENA and Black4Palestine solidarity statements, in the M4BL policy statement on Palestine, and in JVP's Deadly Exchange campaign: namely, that justice is indivisible and global, that it knows no boundaries and is founded not

5. See also Greenberg 2011; Griffin 2015; and Joudah 2011.

on shared experience but [on] shared principles.[6] A commitment to other struggles based on internationalist principles of justice and human rights does not require reciprocity. Solidarity is neither a commodity to be exchanged [nor] collateral to be held nor a debt requiring repayment.

This more radical perspective that moves beyond analogies and toward a vision of the indivisibility of justice is powerfully and brilliantly illustrated in the three-minute video released in October of 2015, *When I See Them, I See Us*. Produced by Noura Erakat and written by Mari Morales-Williams, Remi Kanazi, and Kristian Davis Bailey, it deftly uses photographs, signs, and voice-over narrative to capture the common struggles of Black and Palestinian communities against state-sanctioned violence and oppression and culminates in a vision of a liberated future founded on "hope, strength, love / a place where our children can dream . . . a place where we can rise and be seen" (Black–Palestinian Solidarity 2015). Cultural studies scholar Olga Solombrino sees the film as establishing a new "geography of anger" as well as a geography of liberation by linking the United States and Palestine into a single landscape of violence that extends to a larger, global history of antiracist movements and decolonization. "In the eyes of the activists," Solombrino writes, "the same governing power that disciplines Blackness also disciplines Palestinianness, and unsuspectedly weaves vital connections creating solidarity. It re-activates the old tradition of decolonization and anti-racist movements, allowing them to be read with the same critical look" (2017, 82).

What Solombrino identifies as the reactivation of earlier traditions speaks to the ways in which activists seek to build solidarity on the basis of analogy in order to construct *a shared past*. In every catalyzing instance, there is a reckoning with history, a looking backward to understand the present catastrophe, the future possibility, and the deep roots of solidarity. Indeed, behind recent spectacular controversies or interventions involving Black intellectuals advocating for Palestine—namely, CNN's firing of Marc Lamont Hill, the decision of the Birmingham Civil Rights Institute (BCRI) to deny Angela Davis its highest honor, and Michelle Alexander's op-ed in the *New York Times* criticizing Israeli policies—lay a revisionist history that troubles the politics of analogy as well as the origins of BPTS. Each of these events pulls us back to the era surrounding 1967, when the convergence of Black urban rebellions and the Arab–Israeli War in June of that year birthed the first significant wave of Black–Palestinian solidarity and signaled the demise of the "Black–Jewish alliance" based on the notion of shared analogy of oppression rather than shared principles of liberation. Third World insurgencies and anti-imperialist movements, not just events in the United States and Palestine, created the conditions for radically reordering political alliances between 1967 and the mid-1970s.

Indeed, I would argue that what was being reordered was not just political alliances but a vision of the world. We are too quick to dismiss the post-1967 radical insurgencies as nationalist struggles dedicated to the creation of modern nation-states as the path to decolonization. Adom Getachew suggests, however, that the dominant strains of anticolonial nationalism should be understood as "worldmaking" rather than nation building. "Rather than foreclosing internationalism," she writes in her most recent book, "the effort to achieve national independence propelled a rethinking of state sovereignty, inspired a far-reaching reconstitution of the postwar international order, and grounded the twentieth century's most ambitious vision of global redistribution" (2019, 3). I argue that a vision of worldmaking rather than a politics of analogy

6. Of course, the idea that justice is global and indivisible is an old one: the Industrial Workers of the World (IWW) adopted the slogan "an injury to one is an injury to all" in the early twentieth century. But it is important to acknowledge the work of Rabab Abdulhadi, whose "Teaching Palestine" initiative builds upon and expands "the indivisibility of justice" as a framework for linking global resistance to race, class, gender, and sexual oppressions to opposition to Zionist logic undergirding the founding and management of the State of Israel based on racialization and colonial domination. These principles are best summed up in Martin Luther King's unforgettable words: "Injustice anywhere is a threat to justice everywhere. We are caught in an inescapable network of mutuality, tied in a single garment of destiny. Whatever affects one directly, affects all indirectly." The full text of King's "Letter from a Birmingham Jail" can be viewed at Martin Luther King Jr., "Letter from a Birmingham Jail [King, Jr.]," African Studies Center, University of Pennsylvania, at https://www.africa.upenn.edu/Articles_Gen/Letter_Birmingham.html.

or identity has been the real cement for BPTS and that the eruption of post-1967 history into present struggles to end occupation, dispossession, exploitation, and violence in Palestine and the United States has been a catalyst for imagining revolution as opposed to plotting coalition.

Breaking Silence

> It's possible that these men were afraid. You see, the Jericho road is a dangerous road.
>
> —Dr. Martin Luther King Jr., April 3, 1968

The growing strength of BDS and BPTS, the violent and continuing assault on Palestinian protesters taking part in weekly demonstrations under the banner of the Great March of Return, a resurgence of anti-Semitism, the Hill and Davis affairs, and the occasion of Dr. Martin Luther King Jr.'s ninetieth birthday inspired Michelle Alexander's powerful and incisive *New York Times* op-ed, "Time to Break the Silence on Palestine" (Alexander 2019). The essay is a tour de force, invoking King's iconic antiwar speech at Riverside Church on April 4, 1967, as a clarion call to oppose US material support for Israel's illegal occupation, settlement expansion, and violent repression of Gaza; to reject the smear tactic of silencing legitimate criticisms of Israel with charges of anti-Semitism; and to support the nonviolent tactic of BDS to advance justice in Palestine.

Alexander is correct to speculate that had King lived a bit longer, he would not have remained silent in the face of Israel's occupation and subjugation of Palestine. While King's record of support for Zionism is commonly invoked to defend current Israeli policies, his ideals and actions in the shadows of the 1967 war indicate a more complicated stance. King was never fully comfortable with the geopolitics surrounding the modern State of Israel. . . .

From the River to the Sea

> Any black person of national stature who speaks against Israel must expect a certain isolation from the press.
>
> —James Forman

On November 30, 2018, the US television conglomerate CNN summarily fired Marc Lamont Hill for making a speech at the United Nations on the International Day of Solidarity with the Palestinian People, held annually in recognition of the November 1947 partition that resulted in the Nakba and the creation of the modern State of Israel. In his address, Hill suggested that Israeli settlement policies left no alternative but a one-state solution, based either on apartheid or on a democratic model of equality, citizenship, and full political rights for Palestinians. Delivered at the "Special Meeting of the Committee on the Exercise of the Inalienable Rights of the Palestinian People" as part of the UN's annual commemoration, Hill's speech was powerful, evidence based, and judicious, leaving his critics little with which to level the standard accusation of anti-Semitism. So, they zeroed in on his use of the phrase "from the river to the sea, Palestine will be free" simply because Hamas uses it. That was all his critics needed to conclude that Hill wasn't just a Jew hater but a Hamas adherent.

Hill survived the attack with his reputation as a noted scholar intact. He received overwhelming international support, and efforts to have him fired from his faculty post at Temple University went nowhere. Nevertheless, the controversy surrounding Hill's speech is instructive. It has been framed in various ways, from an issue of academic freedom, an attack on BDS, [and] an example of the media's pro-Israel bias to further evidence that Black support for Palestinian rights is motivated by anti-Semitism (not unlike the recent attacks on Black and Muslim leadership of the Women's March). Indeed, less than twenty-four hours after CNN made its announcement, photos of Hill with Minister Louis Farrakhan circulated on the internet as "proof" that the Temple University professor is a closeted Jew hater. But once again, Hill's words and the particularity of the attacks against him demand a reckoning with history.

First, the odious phrase in question began as a *Zionist* slogan signifying the boundaries of Eretz Israel. . . . During the mid-1960s, the PLO embraced the slogan, but it meant something altogether different from the Zionist vision of Jewish colonization. Instead, the 1964 and 1968 charters of the Palestine National Council (PNC) demanded "the recovery of the usurped homeland in its entirety" and the restoration of land and rights—including the right of self-determination—to the Indigenous population. In other words, the PNC was calling for decolonization, but this did not mean the elimination or exclusion of all Jews from a Palestinian nation—only the settlers or colonists. . . .

Following the 1967 war, the Arab National Movement, led by Dr. George Habash, merged with Youth for Revenge and the Palestine Liberation Front to form the Popular Front for the Liberation of Palestine (PFLP). The PFLP embraced a Palestinian identity rooted in radical, Third World–oriented nationalism, officially identifying as Marxist-Leninist two years later. It envisioned a single, democratic, potentially socialist Palestinian state in which all peoples would enjoy citizenship. Likewise, Fatah leaders shifted from promoting the expulsion of settlers to embracing all Jews as citizens in a secular, democratic state. As one Fatah leader explained in early 1969, "If we are fighting a Jewish state of a racial kind, which had driven the Arabs out of their lands, it is not so as to replace it with an Arab state which would in turn drive out the Jews. . . . We are ready to look at anything with all our negotiating partners once our right to live in our homeland is recognized" (quoted in Chamberlin 2012, 97).[7] Thus by 1969, "Free Palestine from the river to the sea" came to mean one democratic secular state that would supersede the ethnoreligious State of Israel. Moreover, the Palestinian national movement had come to see itself as part of a global anti-imperialist movement in solidarity with other nonaligned or socialist nations or revolutionary movements like the Black Panthers.

The radicalization of the Palestinian national movement between 1967 and the mid-1970s also influenced the Arab student movement in the United States. At its August 1967 convention, the Organization of Arab Students (OAS) endorsed resolutions declaring solidarity with Black struggles in the United States, Africa, and throughout the diaspora as well as the National Liberation Front in Vietnam and the socialist countries supporting global revolutionary insurgencies; calling on Arab states to recognize the People's Republic of China and the People's Republic of Korea; and redoubling their commitment to Palestinian self-determination and Arab unity. The convention emphasized the indivisibility of all revolutionary, anti-imperialist movements in its opening statement. In that spirit, the OAS passed a resolution defending SNCC [Student Nonviolent Coordinating Committee] from charges of anti-Semitism and pointed to "the underlying similarities between the continuing struggle of the Palestinian Arabs in occupied Palestine against Zionist invasion and exploitation, and the ever-increasing resistance of the Afro-Americans in the United States to a power structure of inequality" (quoted in Pennock 2017, 86). The following year, the OAS invited Stokely Carmichael to address its convention in Ann Arbor, Michigan. There he vowed that Black revolutionaries would "help the struggle of the Arabs in any way we can, not only financially and morally, but with our very lives" (quoted in Pennock 2017, 87; see also Carmichael 1971, 131–43).

Carmichael, the leading proponent of Black Power and Third World internationalism, symbolized the deepening ideological divisions in the Black freedom movement—divisions, as we have seen, that left King in turmoil. Black liberals and the mainstream civil rights establishment remained lockstep behind Israel, that is until 1978 after Israel and Egypt signed the Camp David Accords. The treaty normalized relations between the two countries and demilitarized the Sinai Peninsula but left Palestinians without a key ally. This cleared the way for more aggressive Israeli rule over the Occupied Territories. But it also opened the door for Black liberals such as Andrew Young, then UN ambassador under US president Jimmy Carter, and Congressman Walter E. Fauntroy, to attempt to open a diplomatic back channel to the PLO in what was ultimately a failed effort to bring the warring parties to the table. Neither Young nor Fauntroy nor their allies saw their actions as "solidarity" with Palestinians but rather as an effort to bring peace to the region and establish a saner foreign policy in the interests of the United States and Israel. (And for this, they were labeled anti-Semitic and thoroughly rebuked by the mainstream political establishment.)[8]

7. See also Pennock 2017.

8. That Black "moderates" stood steadfast in their support of Israel should not surprise anyone. This observation has been made

So, when we talk about this moment as the high point of Black–Palestine solidarity, we must acknowledge that it was the Black Left, a political minority, that extended solidarity to the Palestinian Left based on a radical, anti-imperialist agenda. In fact, Black liberals and conservatives ramped up their support of Israel. . . .

And yet even the concept of a single democratic state falls short of capturing the worldmaking imagination of the Black and Palestinian Left in this moment, elements of which opposed both nationalist and statist solutions for a free Palestine. As Huey P. Newton explained during a press conference in 1970, national self-determination is impossible under US empire. National sovereignty and real democracy are a chimera in a world where the United States can overthrow regimes it doesn't like and prop up those it does. Our very survival, Newton insisted, depended not on creating new states but on completely transforming society. And creating a capitalist state, he went on, only buttresses imperialism. . . .

A Matter of Public Record

> I accept it on behalf of those who seek an end to apartheid in South Africa, to Pinochet's fascism in Chile, and to the continued violation of the sacred rights of the Palestinian people.
>
> —Angela Davis, upon receiving the Lenin Peace Prize, May 1, 1976

A little over a month after Hill's firing in December 2018, the BCRI announced that it would rescind its decision to give Davis its prestigious Fred L. Shuttlesworth Human Rights Award. The institute had named Davis as its 2018 recipient in September of 2018, so the sudden decision to withdraw the award and cancel the February [2019] gala was surprising and costly. The official statement of the BCRI's board of directors offered no explanation for the decision. "Upon closer examination of Ms. Davis' statements and public record, we concluded that she unfortunately does not meet all of the criteria on which the award is based. . . . While we recognize Ms. Davis' stature as a scholar and prominent figure in civil rights history, we believe this decision is consistent with the ideals of the award's namesake, Rev. Shuttlesworth" (quoted in Lartey 2019).[9]

Although the BCRI Board gave no formal explanation for its decision, [the decision had] followed soon after the publication of an article by Larry Brooks in the December 2018 issue of *Southern Jewish Life* attacking Davis for her critique of Israel's illegal occupation, support for BDS, and defense of former and current political prisoners Rasmea Odeh and Marwan Barghouti. Brooks did not stop there, however; he also included her Communist Party membership and dismissal from her faculty post at UCLA, her membership in the Black Panther Party, and her trial and imprisonment (Brooks 2018). Complaints started trickling into the BCRI's offices, and in no time the board caved to pressure. Populated primarily by corporate figures rather than civil rights veterans or activists, the board feared that honoring Davis would lead to a hemorrhaging of funds from wealthy donors. However, it all backfired. Instead, regular subscribers as well as big and small donors deluged the institute with letters and emails or quietly withdrew their support. Birmingham residents assembled in the streets to protest what they saw as a terrible injustice toward a native daughter. The BCRI came across as unprincipled, spineless, and petty, while Davis's reputation as a principled scholar-activist committed to human rights remained untarnished. Moreover, the controversy further elevated the question of Palestine, especially in African American communities and civil rights circles. The Birmingham Committee for Truth and Reconciliation, which had been leading demonstrations in Birmingham to protest the institute's recision, organized a homecoming event honoring Davis on February 16 (the day she was to receive the Shuttlesworth Award) that not only drew over three thousand people but featured a conversation about Palestine (Davis and Perry 2019). And as a result of global outrage, the BCRI reversed its decision again, announcing that it would grant Davis the Shuttlesworth Award after all.

before, including in the pages of [the *Journal of Palestine Studies*] nearly fifty years ago. See Young 1972.

9. The original statement by the BCRI has since been removed from its website.

. . . It is no accident that [Larry] Brooks and [Charles] Krulak laid out the full itinerary of Davis's career, presenting a veritable laundry list of alleged anti-Israel and *anti-American* crimes and misdemeanors in an effort to indict her in the court of public opinion. What is rendered as "a matter of public record" is actually part of a long and ongoing campaign of historical revisionism—or, better yet, antirevisionism. The old Cold War liberal model of civil rights history cannot account for Angela Davis as a central figure in the Black freedom movement because her conception of civil and human rights knows no boundaries.

. . . On the contrary, the old Cold War liberal framework ignores the internationalism that has long been at the core of the Black freedom movement. Decolonization; war; revolution; imperialism; the plight of the world's workers, migrants, refugees, and peasants—these are some of the issues that have occupied the work and imagination of the Black freedom movement.[10] Transnational solidarity is neither new nor marginal to Black movements. To take one example, few accounts of the Mississippi Freedom Democratic Party (MFDP) move beyond the 1964 showdown at the Democratic National Convention in Atlantic City, when President Lyndon B. Johnson and his acolytes refused to recognize the MFDP as the legitimate representatives of Mississippi's voters. Rarely do we talk about the MFDP's solidarity politics and foreign-policy agenda. Its 1968 platform, for example, called for an immediate end to the Vietnam War and the draft; renewed diplomatic ties with Cuba and China; cooperation with the UN "to eradicate tyranny in areas of the world—such as South Africa, Angola, Southern Rhodesia, Bolivia, Guatemala, and Greece"; and an arms embargo imposed on South Africa and the Middle East (Mississippi Freedom Democratic Party 1968).

As a matter of public record, Davis has fought for—and written about—Black liberation and Black lives; abolition democracy and socialism for all; Indigenous struggles for sovereignty; feminist struggles for freedom, autonomy, and power [for women] to do what they will with their bodies and identities; an end to the caging of human beings; and, of course, the struggles of all oppressed people for self-determination—including in Palestine.

Davis's radical, borderless activism and scholarship represent the highest expression of transnational solidarity, forged in radical political movements, through critical inquiry, via international travel, and under the pressure of state-sanctioned confinement. To her conservative critics and detractors, imprisonment was, at best, a mark of shame, at worst, evidence of criminality. . . . But for much of the world as well as the United States, Davis's imprisonment was a symbol of resistance and global solidarity. As an incarcerated political prisoner, she became the center of an international movement whose supporters pinned their own freedom to Davis's, concluding that to "Free Angela" was a blow to acts of state violence and racism around the world. . . .

Indeed, whereas sociologist Orlando Patterson described the condition of captivity as "social death" (Patterson 2018), the work that Davis initiated envisions the condition of captivity also as a basis of solidarity—in this instance, BPTS. In 2013, prisoners at Pelican Bay State Prison in California waged a sixty-day hunger strike to protest indefinite solitary confinement, just as Palestinian prisoners launched their own hunger strike against administrative detention. Three years later, Rabab Abdulhadi convened a US Prisoner, Labor, and Academic Solidarity Delegation to Palestine that included several former US political prisoners and prison activists (Block 2016; US Prisoner, Labor, and Academic Solidarity Delegation to Palestine 2016). But the event I want to highlight is the installation of a stunning art exhibit at the Abu Jihad Museum for the Prisoners Movement in Nablus [in the West Bank]. Curated by Black studies scholar Greg Thomas and [by] Mohammed Jamoos, a lecturer at Al Quds University, *George Jackson in the Sun of Palestine* not only revisits that critical moment in the early 1970s when Black–Palestinian solidarity was an expression of revolutionary global insurgency but also serves as a powerful example of multiple

10. See, for example, Bald 2013; Daulatzai 2012; Frazier 2014; Gore 2011; Guridy 2010; Horne 2005, 2009; Kelley 2012; Lubin 2013; Makalani 2011; Meriwether 2002; Mullen 2004; Onishi 2013; Plummer 1996; Polyné 2010; Ransby 2012; Slate 2012; Taylor 2002; Von Eschen 1997; West and Martin 2009; Wilkins 2001; and Wu 2013.

pasts erupting into and shedding new light on different presents. George Jackson had been in prison for a decade, having been sentenced to one year to life for petty robbery as a teenager. He became radicalized in prison, earned an international reputation as a writer and political thinker, and was appointed field marshal for the Black Panther Party. Regarded as a threat by prison authorities, in January of 1970 Jackson, together with John Clutchette and Fleeta Drumgo, was falsely charged with murdering a prison guard. The three men were dubbed the Soledad Brothers, and Davis joined their defense campaign and became intimately involved with Jackson and his family.[11] When San Quentin prison guards assassinated Jackson on August 21, 1971, protests erupted in prisons across the country, the most consequential being the Attica Correctional Facility in western New York State.

The exhibit itself, an outgrowth of Thomas's research on Jackson, centers around a generative mistake. After Jackson's death, prison authorities scoured his cell looking for evidence they might use to support the concocted story that he died trying to escape. What they mainly found were books and a fair amount of writing. Among the few things they were willing to release to his mother were two poems written in Jackson's hand, one titled "Enemy of the Sun," which the Black Panther Party newspaper promptly published as part of its George Jackson memorial issue. As it turned out, the author was not Jackson but noted Palestinian poet Samih al-Qasim. "Enemy of the Sun" first appeared in al-Qasim's 1958 debut collection titled *Procession of the Sun*. It was reprinted in 1970 in *Enemy of the Sun: Poetry of Palestinian Resistance*, a collection of poetry edited by Naseer Aruri and Edmund Ghareeb, published by the radical Black-run publishing house Drum and Spear Press. Jackson had the book and copied the poem by hand, probably to share with others. Thomas makes the profound observation that for years no one questioned Jackson's authorship because Palestinian [poetry] and Black poetry of resistance, especially in these revolutionary times, share a resemblance that reveals and reinforces the bases of solidarity. In Thomas's words, the exhibition was inspired by "a poetic 'mistake' of radical kinship and solidarity, even a magical 'mistake' that merged the identities of two writers of Black and Palestinian praxes of liberation." He then goes on to illuminate the multiple layers of resemblance and recognition, embedded in a brilliantly nuanced history of Black–Palestinian solidarity (Thomas 2015).

In March of 2018, I returned to the West Bank with a delegation organized by Abdulhadi around the theme of "teaching Palestine" and the indivisibility of justice. When we arrived in Nablus, we visited the Abu Jihad Museum for the Prisoners Movement, where I first encountered *George Jackson in the Sun of Palestine*. I had read about the exhibit, but nothing compared to seeing the poetry and the posters inspiring revolution, documenting a movement, and promoting an icon. What struck me most, however, was seeing the Jackson exhibit surrounded by hundreds of images of Palestinian prisoners along with their writings and artwork. I came away from the encounter convinced that it is not the condition of captivity that is the basis of solidarity but the *critique* of captivity from a place of confinement, the shared dream of liberation, and the mobilizing and planning to fulfill that dream. Here, in a small, underfunded museum in Nablus—a city renowned for its fierce resistance to occupation—we encountered the afterlives of the post-1967 moment in imprisoned men and women who left a record of looking ahead in order to produce a radically different future. This was worldmaking. Solidarity, in other words, is more than short-term alliances or coalitions but a sort of prefigurative politics that demands of us a deeper transformation of society and of our relationships to one another. What brought Palestinian and Black activists together in that moment was not just a recognition of parallel oppressions, humiliations, violence, and carcerality under occupation but a shared vision of liberation—a vision that extended beyond the nation-state and the transnational to the world.

11. On August 7, 1970, George Jackson's seventeen-year-old brother, Jonathan, entered a Marin County Courthouse armed, and he attempted to free William Christmas, James McClain, and Ruchell Magee to draw attention to the Soledad defendants, but he was killed, along with Christmas, McClain, and the judge they took as a hostage. Angela Davis was arrested because the guns were registered in her name since Jonathan was working as her bodyguard.

Works Cited

"2015 Black Solidarity Statement with Palestine." 2015. *Black for Palestine*. At http://www.blackforpalestine.com/read-the-statement.html.

Abulhawa, Susan. 2013. "Confronting Anti-Black Racism in the Arab World." *Al Jazeera*, July 7. At https://www.aljazeera.com/indepth/opinion/2013/06/201362472519107286.html.

"African Americans for Justice in the Middle East and North Africa: Solidarity Statement." 2012. *Pambazuka News*, July 26. At https://www.pambazuka.org/activism/african-americans-justice-middle-east-north-africa-solidarity-statement.

Aidi, Hisham D. 2014. *Rebel Music: Race, Empire, and the New Muslim Youth Culture*. New York: Random House.

Alexander, Michelle. 2019. "Time to Break the Silence on Palestine." *New York Times*, Jan. 19. At https://www.nytimes.com/2019/01/19/opinion/sunday/martin-luther-king-palestine-israel.html.

Alhassen, Maytha. 2016. "Engaged Witness: A post-1945 Transnational History of the Grammar and Geopolitics of Black–Arab Solidarity." PhD diss., Univ. of Southern California.

Alsaafin, Linah. 2011. "Palestinians Clarify Goal of 'Freedom Rides' Challenge to Segregated Israeli Buses." *Electronic Intifada*, Nov. 14. At https://electronicintifada.net/blogs/linah-alsaafin/palestinians-clarify-goal-freedom-rides-challenge-segregated-israeli-buses.

Atshan, Sa'ed, and Darnell L. Moore. 2014. "Reciprocal Solidarity: Where the Black and Palestinian Queer Struggles Meet." *Biography* 37, no. 2: 680–705.

Bailey, Kristian Davis. 2015. "Black–Palestinian Solidarity in the Ferguson–Gaza Era." *American Quarterly* 67, no. 4: 1017–26.

———. 2016. "Members of Dream Defenders' Delegation to Israel/Palestine Talk Segregation, Occupation, and That Massive Wall." *ColorLines*, June 17. At https://www.colorlines.com/articles/members-dream-defenders-delegation-israelpalestine-talk-segregation-occupation-and-massive.

Baker, Rana. 2014. "Palestinians Express 'Solidarity with the People of Ferguson' in Mike Brown Statement." *Electronic Intifada*, Aug. 15. At http://electronicintifada.net/blogs/rana-baker/palestinians-express-solidarity-people-ferguson-mike-brown-statement.

Bald, Vivek. 2013. *Bengali Harlem and the Lost Histories of South Asian America*. Cambridge, MA: Harvard Univ. Press.

Black4Palestine. 2015. "2015 Black Solidarity Statement with Palestine." At http://www.blackforpalestine.com/read-the-statement.html.

Black–Palestinian Solidarity. 2015. "*When I See Them, I See Us*." *Washington Post*, Oct. 14. At https://www.washingtonpost.com/video/world/when-i-see-them-i-see-us/2015/10/15/c8f8aa40-72c2-11e5-ba14-318f8e87a2fc_video.html?utm_term=.8fa637e3abb0.

Block, Diana. 2016. "Reflections on a Delegation to Imprisoned Palestine." *CounterPunch*, May 13. At https://www.counterpunch.org/2016/05/13/reflections-on-a-delegation-to-imprisoned-palestine/.

Brady, Nicholas. 2013. "The Void Speaks Back: Black Suffering as the Unthought of the American Studies Association's Academic Boycott of Israel." *Out of Nowhere*, Dec. 23. At https://outofnowhereblog.wordpress.com/2013/12/23/the-void-speaks-back-black-suffering-as-the-unthought-of-the-american-studies-associations-academic-boycott-of-israel/.

Brooks, Larry. 2018. "Prominent BDS Activist to Receive Civil Rights Institute's Shuttlesworth Award." *Southern Jewish Life*, Dec. 23. At https://sjlmag.com/2018/12/prominent-bds-activist-davis-to-receive.html.

Carmichael, Stokely. 1971. *Stokely Speaks: Black Power to Pan-Africanism*. New York: Random House.

Chamberlin, Paul Thomas. 2012. *The Global Offensive: The United States, the Palestine Liberation Organization, and the Making of the Post–Cold War Order*. New York: Oxford Univ. Press.

Daulatzai, Sohail. 2012. *Black Star, Crescent Moon: The Muslim International and Black Freedom beyond America*. Minneapolis: Univ. of Minnesota Press.

Davis, Angela Y. 1998. *The Angela Y. Davis Reader*. Edited by Joy James. Hoboken, NJ: Wiley Blackwell.

———. 2016. *Freedom Is a Constant Struggle: Ferguson, Palestine, and the Foundations of a Movement*. Chicago: Haymarket Books.

Davis, Angela, and Imani Perry. 2019. "Angela Davis Returns to Birmingham: Reflection on Palestinian Rights and Fight for Freedom Everywhere." *Democracy Now!*, Feb. 18. At https://www.democracynow.org/2019/2/18/angela_davis_returns_to_birmingham_reflecting.

Erakat, Noura, moderator. 2015. "Roundtable on Anti-Blackness and Black–Palestinian Solidarity." *Jadaliyya*, June 3. At https://www.jadaliyya.com/Details/32145/Roundtable-on-Anti-Blackness-and-Black-Palestinian-Solidarity.

———. 2016. "The Nakba and Anti-Blackness." *Jadaliyya*, May 19. At https://www.jadaliyya.com/Details/33280.

Feldman, Keith. 2015. *A Shadow over Palestine: The Imperial Life of Race in America*. Minneapolis: Univ. of Minnesota Press.

Fischbach, Michael R. 2018. *Black Power and Palestine: Transnational Countries of Color*. Stanford, CA: Stanford Univ. Press.

Frazier, Robeson Taj. 2014. *The East Is Black: Cold War China in the Black Radical Imagination*. Durham, NC: Duke Univ. Press.

Getachew, Adom. 2019. *Worldmaking after Empire: The Rise and Fall of Self-Determination*. Princeton, NJ: Princeton Univ. Press.

Gilbert, David. 2014. "Michael Brown Shooting: Gaza Strip Tweets Ferguson about How to Deal with Tear Gas." *International Business Times*, Aug. 14. At https://www.ibtimes.co.uk/gaza-strip-tweets-ferguson-about-how-deal-tear-gas-light-michael-brown-shooting-1461124.

Gore, Dayo F. 2011. *Radicalism at the Crossroads: African American Women Activists in the Cold War*. New York: New York Univ. Press.

Greenberg, Joel. 2011. "Palestinian 'Freedom Riders' Arrested on Bus to Jerusalem." *Washington Post*, Nov. 15. At https://www.washingtonpost.com/world/middle_east/palestinian-freedom-riders-arrested-on-bus-to-jerusalem/2011/11/15/gIQAQfkcPN_story.html.

Griffin, Maryam S. 2015. "Freedom Rides in Palestine: Racial Segregation and Grassroots Politics on the Bus." *Race and Class* 56, no. 4: 73–84.

Guridy, Frank Andre. 2010. *Forging Diaspora: Afro-Cubans and African Americans in a World of Empire and Jim Crow*. Chapel Hill: Univ. of North Carolina Press.

Horne, Gerald. 2005. *Black and Brown: African-Americans and the Mexican Revolution, 1910–20*. New York: New York Univ. Press.

———. 2009. *The End of Empires: African Americans and India*. Philadelphia: Temple Univ. Press.

Jewish Voice for Peace. 2018. "About Deadly Exchange." At https://deadlyexchange.org/about-deadly-exchange/.

Joudah, Nour. 2011. "From US South to Palestine, Freedom Rides Change History." *Electronic Intifada*, Nov. 16. At https://electronicintifada.net/content/us-south-palestine-freedom-rides-change-history/10599.

Kelley, Robin D. G. 2012. *Africa Speaks, America Answers: Modern Jazz in Revolutionary Times*. Cambridge, MA: Harvard Univ. Press.

———. 2014. "Another Freedom Summer." *Journal of Palestine Studies* 64, no. 1: 28–41.

———. 2015. "Apartheid's Black Apologists." In *Apartheid Israel: The Politics of an Analogy*, edited by Jon Soske and Sean Jacobs, 125–42. New York: Haymarket Books.

———. 2018. "Letter from a West Bank Refugee Camp." In *With Stones in Our Hands: Writings on Muslims, Racism, and Empire*, edited by Sohail Daulatzai and Junaid Rana, 298–305. Minneapolis: Univ. of Minnesota Press.

Lartey, Jamiles. 2019. "Birmingham Civil Rights Institute under Fire for Rescinding Angela Davis Honor." *Guardian*, Jan. 7. At https://www.theguardian.com/us-news/2019/jan/07/birmingham-civil-rights-institute-rescinds-honor-angela-davis.

Lubin, Alex. 2013. *Geographies of Liberation: The Making of an Afro-Arab Political Imaginary*. Chapel Hill: Univ. of North Carolina Press.

Makalani, Minkah. 2011. *In the Cause of Freedom: Radical Black Internationalism from Harlem to London, 1917–1939*. Chapel Hill: Univ. of North Carolina Press.

Marcelin, Megan French. 2014. "Linking Violence in Solidarity: Ferguson, Gaza, and the US State." *Jadaliyya*, Aug. 18. At https://www.jadaliyya.com/Details/31113/Linking-Violence-In-Solidarity-Ferguson,-Gaza,-and-the-US-State.

Meriwether, James. 2002. *Proudly We Can Be Africans: Black Americans and Africa, 1935–1961*. Chapel Hill: Univ. of North Carolina Press.

Mississippi Freedom Democratic Party. 1968. "Program of the Mississippi Freedom Democratic Party." Civil Rights Movement Veterans. At https://www.crmvet.org/docs/mfdp_program.pdf.

Mullen, Bill. 2004. *Afro-Orientalism*. Minneapolis: Univ. of Minnesota Press.

Obeidallah, Dean. 2014. "The Ties That Bind: Michael Brown, Gaza, and Muslim Americans." *Daily Beast*, Aug. 20. At https://www.thedailybeast.com/michael-brown-gaza-and-muslim-americans.

Onishi, Yuichiro. 2013. *Transpacific Antiracism: Afro-Asian Solidarity in 20th Century Black America, Japan, and Okinawa*. New York: New York Univ. Press.

Patterson, Orlando. 2018. *Slavery and Social Death: A Comparative Study*. 2nd ed. Cambridge, MA: Harvard Univ. Press.

Pennock, Pamela E. 2017. *The Rise of the Arab American Left: Activists, Allies, and Their Fight against Imperialism and Racism, 1960s–1980s*. Chapel Hill: Univ. of North Carolina Press.

Pickens, Therí A. 2015. *New Body Politics: Narrating Arab and Black Identity in the Contemporary United States.* London: Routledge.

Plummer, Brenda Gayle. 1996. *Rising Wind: Black Americans and Foreign Affairs, 1935–1960*. Chapel Hill: Univ. of North Carolina Press.

Polyné, Millery. 2010. *From Douglass to Duvalier: U.S. African Americans, Haiti, and Pan-Africanism*. Gainesville: Univ. of Florida Press.

Ransby, Barbara. 2011. "Why We, as Women of Color, Join the Call for Divestment from Israel." *ColorLines*, July 13. At https://www.colorlines.com/articles/why-we-women-color-join-call-divestment-israel.

———. 2012. *Eslanda: The Large and Unconventional Life of Mrs. Paul Robeson*. New Haven, CT: Yale Univ. Press.

———. 2018. *Making All Black Lives Matter: Reimagining Freedom in the 21st Century.* Oakland: Univ. of California Press.

Seidel, Timothy. 2016. "'Occupied Territory Is Occupied Territory': James Baldwin, Palestine, and the Possibilities of Transnational Solidarity." *Third World Quarterly* 37, no. 9: 1644–660.

Slate, Nico. 2012. *Colored Cosmopolitanism: The Shared Struggle for Freedom in the United States and India*. Cambridge, MA: Harvard Univ. Press.

Solombrino, Olga. 2017. "'When I See Them I See Us': Palestinianness, Blackness, and New Geographies of Resistance." *From the European South* 2:71–87.

Taylor, Ula Y. 2002. *The Veiled Garvey: The Life and Times of Amy Jacques Garvey.* Chapel Hill: Univ. of North Carolina Press.

Thomas, Greg. 2015. "Blame It on the Sun: George Jackson and Poetry of Palestinian Resistance." *Comparative American Studies* 13, no. 4: 236–53.

US Prisoner, Labor, and Academic Solidarity Delegation to Palestine. 2016. "We Stand with Palestine in the Spirit of 'Sumud,' March 24 to April 2, 2016." Freedom Archives. At https://www.freedomarchives.org/Pal/Delegation.We.Stand.pdf.

Von Eschen, Penny. 1997. *Race against Empire: Black Americans and Anticolonialism, 1937–1957.* Ithaca, NY: Cornell Univ. Press.

West, Michael O., and William G. Martin, eds. 2009. *From Toussaint to Tupac: The Black International since the Age of Revolution*. Chapel Hill: Univ. of North Carolina Press.

Wilderson, Frank B., III. 2014. "'We're Trying to Destroy the World': Anti-Blackness and Police Violence after Ferguson: An Interview with Frank B. Wilderson, III." Interviewed by Jared Ball, Todd Steven Burroughs, and Dr. Hate. *Ill Will Editions*, Nov. At https://illwilleditions.noblogs.org/files/2015/09/Wilderson-We-Are-Trying-to-Destroy-the-World-PRINT.pdf.

Wilkins, Fanon Che. 2001. "'In the Belly of the Beast': Black Power, Anti-Imperialism, and the African Liberation Solidarity Movement, 1968–1975." PhD diss., New York Univ.

Wu, Judy Tzu-Chun. 2013. *Radicals on the Road: Internationalism, Orientalism, and Feminism during the Vietnam Era*. Ithaca, NY: Cornell Univ. Press.

Yassin, Jaime Omar. 2014. "The Shortest Distance between Ferguson and Palestine." *CounterPunch*, Aug. 15. At http://www.counterpunch.org/2014/08/15/the-shortest-distance-between-palestine-and-ferguson/.

Young, Lewis. 1972. "American Blacks and the Arab–Israeli Conflict." *Journal of Palestine Studies* 2, no. 1: 70–85.

37

Let Us Be Moors

Islam, Race, and "Connected Histories"

HISHAM D. AIDI

"Seamos moros!" wrote the Cuban poet and nationalist José Martí in 1893, in support of the Berber uprising against Spanish rule in northern Morocco. "Let us be Moors . . . the revolt in the Rif . . . is not an isolated incident, but an outbreak of the change and realignment that have entered the world. Let us be Moors . . . we [Cubans] who will probably die by the hand of Spain" (Martí 1938, 201). Writing at a time when the scramble for Africa and Asia was at full throttle, Martí was accenting connections between those great-power forays and Spanish depredations in Cuba, even as the rebellion of 1895 germinated on his island. Throughout the past century, particularly during the Cold War, Latin American leaders from Cuba's Fidel Castro to Argentina's Juan Perón would express support for Arab political causes and call for Arab–Latin solidarity in the face of imperial domination, often highlighting cultural links to the Arab world through Moorish Spain. Castro, in particular, made a philo-Arab pan-Africanism central to his regime's ideology and policy initiatives. In his famous 1959 speech on race, the *jefe maximo* underlined Cuba's African and Moorish origins. "We all have lighter or darker skin. Lighter skin implies descent from Spaniards who themselves were colonized by the Moors that came from Africa. Those who are more or less dark-skinned came directly from Africa. Moreover, nobody can consider himself as being of pure, much less superior, race" (quoted in Dépestre 1967, 93).

With the launching of the "war on terror" and particularly with the invasion of Iraq, political leaders and activists in Latin America have been warning of a new imperial age and again declaring solidarity with the Arab world. Some refer rather quixotically to a Moorish past. Linking the war on Iraq to Plan Colombia and to the Bush administration's alleged support for a coup against him, the erratic Venezuelan strongman Hugo Chávez has repeatedly urged his countrymen to "return to their Arab roots" and attempted to mobilize the country's mestizo and Black majority against white supremacy. "They call me the monkey or Black," Chavez says of his domestic and international opponents. "They can't stand that someone like me was elected" (quoted in Ramonet 2002).

In less contentious terms, Brazil's left-leaning President Lula da Silva visited the Middle East in early December 2003 to seek "more objective" relations with the Arab world, to call for an "independent, democratic Palestinian state," and to launch a common market with the Arab world as an alternative to the North American market (particularly with many in Arab countries boycotting American products) (*Latin American Weekly Report* 2003). Brazil's largest trade union federation strongly denounced post–September 11 US intervention in Colombia, Venezuela, and the Middle East, praising the protest movements that have appeared against US and Israeli "militarism" and calling on Brazilian workers

Excerpt from Hisham D. Aidi, "Let Us Be Moors: Islam, Race, and 'Connected Histories,'" *Middle East Report* 33, no. 229 (Winter 2003): 42–53. Full references in the original notes were converted to author-date citations in the text and notes here, and a works cited list was added. Reprinted with corrections and press style changes for consistency throughout the volume by permission of the Middle East Research and Information Project (MERIP).

to join in the struggle "against Sharon's Nazi–Zionist aggression against the Palestinian people" and in support of the intifada.[1]

The Other September 11 Effect

In the age of the "war on terror," such expressions from the Western world of affinity with the Arab world are not confined to statements of political solidarity. In Latin America, Europe, and the United States, for example, there has been a sharp increase in conversion to Islam. At the first world congress of Spanish-speaking Muslims held in Seville in April 2003, the scholar Mansur Escudero, citing "globalization," said that there were 10 to 12 million Spanish speakers among the world's 1.2 billion Muslims (Deutsche Presse-Agentur 2003). In the United States, researchers note that usually 25,000 people a year become Muslim, but by several accounts that number has quadrupled since September 11.[2] In Europe, an Islamic center in Holland reported a tenfold increase, and the New Muslims Project in England reported a "steady stream" of new converts (Whittell 2002). Several analysts have noted that in the United Kingdom, many converts are coming from middle-class and professional backgrounds, not simply through the prison system or ghetto mosques, as is commonly believed (Compton 2002). The Muslim population in Spain is also growing, due to conversion as well as immigration and intermarriage.[3] Different explanations have been advanced to account for this intriguing phenomenon, known as "the other September 11 effect"—the primary effects being anti-Muslim and anti-immigrant backlash and infringements upon civil liberties. Commenting on how the accused "dirty bomber" José Padilla and the shoe bomber Richard Reid converted to Islam, French scholar Olivier Roy observes, "Twenty years ago such individuals would have joined radical leftist movements, which have now disappeared or become 'bourgeois'. . . . Now only two Western movements of radical protest claim to be 'internationalist': the anti-globalization movement and radical Islamists. To convert to Islam today is a way for a European rebel to find a cause; it has little to do with theology" (2003). This portrayal of Islam as an outlet for the West's political malcontents ignores the powerful allure of certain aspects of Islamic theology and begs the question of why for at least a century, even when communism was still in vogue, minorities in the West have seen Islam as a particularly attractive alternative. Roy's formulation also neglects the critical elements of racism and racialization. At least since Malcolm X, internationalist Islam has been seen as a response to Western racism and imperialism.

Though Westerners of different social and ethnic backgrounds are gravitating toward Islam, it is mostly the ethnically marginalized of the West—historically, mostly Black, but nowadays also Latino, Native American, Arab, and South Asian minorities—who, often attracted by the purported universalism and color blindness of Islamic history and theology, are asserting membership in a transnational *umma* and thereby challenging or "exiting" the white West. Even for white converts, like John Walker Lindh, becoming Muslim involves a process of racialization—renouncing their whiteness—because while the West stands for racism and white supremacy on a global scale, Islam is seen to represent tolerance and anti-imperialism. This process of racialization is also occurring in diasporic Muslim communities in the West, which are growing increasingly race conscious and "Black" as anti-Muslim racism increases. To cope, Muslims in the diaspora are absorbing lessons from the African American freedom movement, including from strains of African American Islam.

Over the past two years, Islam has provided an anti-imperial idiom and imaginary community of belonging for many subordinate groups in the West as Islamic culture and art stream into the West through minority and diaspora communities and, often in fusion with African

1. CUT National Plenary, Conjuntura Internacional e Nacional, Resolution 10, "Cresce a polaizacao politica a social em todo o mundo," accessible online at http://cutnacweb.cut.org.br/10plencut/conjtex5.htm.

2. New York Times, Oct. 22, 2001; *Economist*, Oct. 26, 2001. Imams and converts also made this claim in interviews carried out by Columbia University's Muslim Communities in New York Project on June 4 and June 16, 2003.

3. Christian Science Monitor, Oct. 2, 2002. See also Fernandez 2002.

American art forms, are slowly seeping into the cultural mainstream. Subsequently, many of the cultural and protest movements—antiglobalization, anti-imperialist, antiracist—in the West today have Islamic and/or African American undercurrents. At a time of military conflict and extreme ideological polarization between the West and the Muslim world, Islamic culture is permeating political and cultural currents, remaking identities and creating cultural linkages between Westerners and the Muslim world.

In sum, this article is about imagination and "culturalism" post-9/11. I consider why certain segments of the West are now choosing to remember their connections to the Muslim world and how the "remembering" and "imagined solidarity" are being expressed culturally and politically. I look at the conversion trends and the craze for Arab culture that has swept parts of Latin America and the United States in the past two years but focus on the cultural movements of "Islamic hip-hop" and the Arab European League that use the "frames" and "repertoires" of Islam and the African American struggle as examples of the political potential of "imagined solidarities" and as instances of what anthropologist Arjun Appadurai has called "culturalism": "[the] deliberate, strategic and populist mobilization of cultural material [and] cultural differences in the service of a larger national or transnational politics" (1996, 15). I also examine how Islamic culture and motifs are becoming central to the worldwide antiglobalization and antiwar movement and providing the cultural building blocks for an international "countermodernity" movement.

Latino Back Channels

Recent journalistic accounts have noted the growing rate of conversion to Islam in the southern Mexican state of Chiapas and the often violent clashes between Christian and Spanish Muslim missionaries proselytizing among the Indigenous Mayan community. The Muslim campaign in Chiapas is led by a Spaniard from Granada, Aureliano Perez, member of an international Sufi order called al-Murabitun, though he is contending with a rival missionary, Omar Weston, the Nation of Islam's local representative. Particularly interesting about the several hundred Mayan Muslims is the view of some of the converts that, though some of the missionaries are Spanish like the conquistadors, their embrace of Islam is a historic remedy for the Spanish conquest and the consequent oppression. "Five hundred years ago, they came to destroy us," said Anastasio Gomez, twenty-one, who now goes by Ibrahim. "Five hundred years later, other Spaniards came to return a knowledge that was taken away from us."[4] The view of 1492 as a tragic date signaling the end of a glorious era and the related idea that conversion to Islam entails a reclaiming of that past are common among the Latino Muslim community in the United States. That community, estimated in 2000 at 30,000 to 40,000 members, has grown in the past two years, with Latino Muslim centers and *da'wa* (proselytizing) organizations in New York, Los Angeles, Miami, Fresno, and Houston.[5] The banner hanging at the Alianza Islamica center in the South Bronx celebrates the African and Islamic roots of Latin America: against a red, white, and blue backdrop stands a sword-wielding Moor, flanked by a Taino Indian and a Black African. The Spanish conquistador is conspicuously absent. Imam (Omar Abduraheem) Ocasio of the Alianza Islamica speaks passionately about the continuity between Moorish Spain and Latin America: "Most of the people who came to Latin America and the Spanish Caribbean were from southern Spain, Andalusia—they were Moriscos, Moors forcefully converted to Christianity. The leaders, army generals, *curas* [priests] were white men from northern Spain . . . *sangre azul*, as they were called. The southerners, who did the menial jobs, . . . servants, artisans, foot soldiers, . . . were of mixed Arab and African descent. They were stripped of their religion, culture, brought to the so-called New World, where they were enslaved with African slaves. . . . But the Moriscos never lost their culture. . . . [W]e are the cultural descendants of the Moors."[6] The Puerto Rican imam writes, "Islamically inspired values were conveyed ever so subtly in the Trojan horse of Spanish heritage throughout the

4. Cox News Service, Aug. 11, 2002; see also Knight-Ridder News Service, June 20, 2003.

5. El Diario–La Prensa, Oct. 6, 2001. See also *Islamic Horizons*, July–Aug. 2002.

6. Interview with Rahim Ocasio, Apr. 16, 1999.

centuries and, after 500 years, Latinos were now ready to return" (Ocasio 1997).

In the past two years, Islam and the Arab–Muslim world seem to have entered even more poignantly into the Latin American imagination, gaining a presence in political discourse and strongly influencing Hispanic popular culture. This Arab cultural invasion of Latin America, which has reverberated in mainstream American culture, is often attributed to the Brazilian telenovela *El Clon* and Lebanese Colombian pop icon Shakira. *El Clon*, the highest-rated soap opera ever shown on Telemundo, a US Spanish-language channel, reportedly reaches 2.8 million Hispanic households in the United States as well as 85 million people in Brazil and tens of millions across Latin America. The series, which began broadcasting shortly after September 11, tells the story of Jade, a young Brazilian Muslim who returns to her mother's homeland of Morocco after her mother's death in Brazil. There she falls in love and settles down with Lucas, a Christian Brazilian, and adapts to life in an extended family setting in the old city of Fez. Filmed in Rio de Janeiro and Fez, the telenovela offers a profusion of Orientalist imagery—from veiled belly dancers swaying seductively behind ornate latticework to dazzling shots of Marrakesh and Fez spliced with footage of scantily clad women on Rio's beaches—and of course, incessant supplications of "Ay, por favor, Allah!" from Jade's neighbors in the medina. The Moroccan ambassador to Brazil, in a letter to a São Paolo newspaper, criticized the series for its egregious "cultural errors," "gross falsification," and "mediocre images" promoting stereotypes of Muslim women as submissive and men as polygamists leading lives of "luxury and indolence."

Despite the kitsch, *El Clon* has triggered what *Latin Trade* called "Mideast fever" across Latin America. Belly dancing and "Middle Eastern–style jewelry" became "the rage in Rio and Sao Paolo," Brazilians began throwing "A Thousand and One Nights" parties, "Talk to a Sheikh" chat rooms cropped up online, and two new agencies opened up to offer package tours to North Africa. (In his letter, the Moroccan ambassador acknowledged that Brazilian tourism to Morocco had increased by 300 percent thanks to *El Clon*.) A journalist visiting Quito, Ecuador, found viewers of the series "wide-eyed and drop-jawed for all things Arab" (Eisele 2002). Even in the United States, where *El Clon*'s broadcast was almost blocked due to alleged potential controversy, it has exerted cultural influence upon the Latino community and others. In New York, observers note the *El Clon*–triggered fashion for Arab jewelry and hip scarves, the overflowing belly-dancing classes, and a . . . beauty parlor called "El Clon" in Queens.[7]

Through the Latino back channel, the impact of Shakira in bringing Arab culture to the MTV audience has also been considerable. The Lebanese Colombian singer was bombarded with questions by the media about her views "as an Arab" on the September 11 attacks and advised to drop the belly dancing and the Arabic riffs from her music because it could hurt her album sales, but she refused. "I would have to rip out my heart or my insides in order to be able to please them," said the songstress and expressed horror at hate crimes against "everything that's Arab, or seems Arab" (quoted in O'Sullivan 2002). During the run-up to the Iraq War, Shakira's performances took on an explicitly political tone, with her dancers wearing masks of Tony Blair, George W. Bush, and Fidel Castro. Backdrop screens flashed images of Bush and Saddam Hussein as two puppets playing a sinister game of chess, with the Grim Reaper as the puppeteer. She also undertook a highly publicized tour of the Middle East (though her concerts in Casablanca, Tunis, and Beirut were postponed), during which she visited her father's ancestral village in the Bekaa Valley. Viewers across the region were delighted when Shakira appeared on Egyptian television singing the tunes of Fairuz. In Europe, the United States, South America, and even the Middle East, the belly-dancing star has fostered a reported mania for hip scarves with coins and tassels. In a random check of Cairo nightclubs, Egyptian government officials confiscated twenty-six Shakira outfits, "weighing no more than 150 grams [5 ounces]" and deemed "scandalous" ("L'habit de danse du ventre de Shakira" 2003), but local filmmakers are currently negotiating with government officials

7. Interview with Rosa Margarita of *El Diario–La Prensa*, Aug. 8, 2003. *El Clon*–inspired fashion can be viewed online at http://www.laoriginal.com/especiales.htm.

over rights to a film project called "Shakira fi al-Munira," about a young Egyptian girl infatuated with the Colombian chanteuse.

While the craze for Arab culture has occurred in the wake of September 11 and the ensuing war on terrorism, it is not necessarily political. Commenting on the popularity of shawarma and hookahs in Quito, one journalist observes that "the new fascination with Arabia comes at a time when there are new reasons for anti-American sentiment"—the recent policy of currency dollarization—but adds reassuringly that "*El Clon*'s following surely won't produce a new sect of Islamic fundamentalist terrorists in Latin America" (Eisele 2002). It is also not clear that conversion to Islam necessarily constitutes political or cultural resistance. Referring to the vogue for Islam and Arabic among Spanish youth, one Catalan journalist wryly observes: "It will take more than teenagers converting to an Islam lite to stop [Spanish prime minister José María] Aznar's Christian nationalism and Castilian imperialism. We need a civil dialogue about our relations with the Orient."[8] Belly dancing and learning elementary Arabic may not be acts of resistance, but such activities create important albeit imaginary cultural linkages that can be activated for political purposes. As Miles Copeland, head of the Mondo Melodia label, who will release a film on the American belly-dancing craze in January 2004, told PR Newswire: "Belly dancing is about art, not politics—but in experiencing the art, you also experience the culture, and that becomes political in and of itself." Interest in Arab culture and conversions are bringing Islam into the imagination of Western youth, feeding powerful movements and cultures of protest. . . .

"The specter of a storm is haunting the Western world," wrote the Black Power poet Askia Muhammad Toure in 1965. "The Great Storm, the coming Black Revolution, is rolling like a tornado; roaring from the East; shaking the moorings of the earth as it passes through countries ruled by oppressive regimes. . . . Yes, all over this sullen planet, the multi-colored 'hordes' of undernourished millions are on the move like never before in human history" (quoted in Kelley 2002, 60). Toure was pondering the appeal of "the East" to African American youth in the aftermath of the 1955 Bandung conference. There, President Sukarno of Indonesia had told the representatives of twenty-nine African and Asian nations that they were united "by a common detestation of colonialism in whatever form it appears. We are united by a common detestation of racialism." Those were the days when Malcolm X met with Fidel Castro at the famed Teresa Hotel in Harlem and when Malcolm, from his perspective of "Islamic internationalism," came to understand the civil rights movement as an instance of the struggle against imperialism, seeing the Vietnam war and the Mau Mau rebellion in Kenya as uprisings of the "darker races" and, like the African American struggle, part of the "tidal wave" against Western imperialism.

Some commentators, pointing to the current antiwar and antiglobalization movement, have suggested that a new era of Afro-Asian-Latin solidarity may be in the offing. In the United States, the past two years have seen a political ferment and coalition building between progressive groups—in particular between Arab and Muslim American groups and African American groups—not seen since the 1960s when the Black Panthers and the Student Nonviolent Coordinating Committee declared solidarity with the PLO, which in turn declared solidarity with Native Americans. September 11 and the subsequent backlash have led many African American leaders to stand with Muslim and Arab Americans, not least because African American Muslims are also targeted in the post–September 11 profiling and detention campaigns. Activists like Al Sharpton are mobilizing against the USA PATRIOT Act "because it is used to profile people of color" and "impacting Muslims everywhere, including Brooklyn and Harlem" (quoted in Davis 2002).

Given the centrality of Islam and the Arab world to the war on terror and the presence of kaffiyehs and (regrettably) Bin Laden T-shirts at protests from Porto Alegre to Barcelona, it appears that the new Bandung may have a distinct Arab or Islamic cast. In the past two years, a number of Latin American leaders have called

8. Interview with Fernando Casado Caneque, Sept. 8, 2003. Casado was referring to the conservative Aznar's effort to insert a reference to Europe's Christian roots in the EU's constitution, a measure that has provoked the Spanish Left and the regions of Andalusia and Catalunya, who resent how the Aznar government has made Catholicism so central to the state's identity. See *El País*, July 28, 2003.

for "concrete action" to establish a Palestinian state. Castro has signed agreements of bilateral cooperation with Algeria and the United Arab Emirates and continues to rail against "global apartheid" in general and "Israeli apartheid" in particular. Castro has also been accused of building ties with Iran and selling biotechnology in exchange for cheap oil. When he visited Iran in 2001, Castro spoke of his rapport with President Mohammad Khatami and reported that he "had the longest sleep of his life in Tehran." Most recently, he has been accused by the United States of jamming the satellite broadcasts of US-based Iranian opposition groups (Hamman 2003). Recent articles in right-leaning American newsmagazines claim to have discovered evidence that Venezuela is providing identity papers to suspicious numbers of people from Arab and South Asian "countries of interest" (as well as Colombians and Cubans). One article also features the claim of the former Venezuelan ambassador to Libya, Julio César Pineda, to possess correspondence from Hugo Chávez stating his desire to "solidify" ties between Latin America and the Middle East—including use of the oil weapon (Arostegui 2003a, 2003b). Chávez challenged the reporters in question to produce "one single shred of evidence" for their claims (Agence France-Presse 2003).

These stories of Cuban and Venezuelan ties to Middle Eastern radicals may be little more than partisan puffery, and Chávez's repeated calls for solidarity with the Arab world may be nothing more than petroleum diplomacy or an embattled leader's desperate plea for allies. Yet the Venezuelan leader's appeal to "Arab roots" is indicative of a trend in the West. Among Western subordinate groups and opposition movements that feel victimized or neglected by globalization, the Arabs are seen as bearing the brunt of the worldwide imperial assault in the era of the war on terror. As Western nationalists portray Islam as a threat to freedom and security and launch wars to bring democracy to the Muslim world, "the multi-colored hordes" of the West are reaching for teachings and precedents (like Moorish Spain) in Islam that they hope will make the West more compassionate and free.

Islam is leaking into the West through conversion, migration, and media-driven cultural flows, and, to many, the Islamic world is presenting a repertoire of alternative identities. As marginalized Westerners are finding inspiration in Islam, Muslims in the diaspora are inspired by the African American experience. The cross-fertilization taking place between Islamic, Black, and Latin cultures is creating fascinating trends and art forms. Many would argue that the fashion for Arabic tattoos, Allah chains, Orientalist soap operas, belly dancing, and hip scarves is just that—fashion. But as the Arab pride movement in Europe and Islamic hip-hop demonstrate, the vibrant cultural intermingling can have significant political implications. Cultural flows can spark forceful challenges to state policies, state-imposed identities, and the claims of Western nationalism.

For many of the minority convert communities and the diaspora Muslim communities, Islamic Spain has emerged as an anchor for their identity. Moorish Spain was a place where Islam was in and of the West and inhabited a Golden Age before the rise of the genocidal, imperial West, a historical moment that disenchanted Westerners can share with Muslims. Neither Muslim nostalgia for nor Western Orientalist romanticism about Andalusia is new, but it is new for different subordinate groups in the West to be yearning for "return" to Moorish Spain's multiracialism. In this worldview, the year 1492 is a historical turning point. On Columbus Day in October, Chávez urged Latin Americans to boycott celebrations of the "discovery," saying that Columbus was "worse than Hitler." That the longing for pre-1492 history is shared by many minorities throughout the West is an indication of their lasting exclusion and how the stridency of Western nationalism since September 11 has revived memories of centuries-old trauma. As one African American activist put it recently, "The profiling and brutalizing of African Americans didn't begin after September 11. It began in 1492."[9] In a similar spirit, after [Zacarias] Moussaoui was arrested in the United States and granted the right to represent himself in court, one of his first demands was "the return of Spain to the Moors."

9. Interview with Columbia's Muslim Communities of New York Project, July 21, 2003 (focus group for Muslims in NYPD and Fire Department).

With African American and Latino converts speaking of the tragedy of 1492, and with Muslim minorities in the West becoming increasingly race conscious and inspired by Black America ("l'autre Amerique"), the world is witnessing a new fusion between Islam and pan-Africanism. Today, however, this racialized Islamic internationalism contains elements of other cultures and diasporas as well. Islam is at the heart of an emerging global antihegemonic culture, which postcolonial critic Robert Young would say incarnates a "tricontinental counter-modernity" that combines diasporic and local cultural elements and blends Arab, Islamic, Black, and Hispanic factors to generate "a revolutionary black, Asian and Hispanic globalization, with its own dynamic counter-modernity . . . constructed in order to fight global imperialism" (2001, 2).

Works Cited

Appadurai, Arjun. 1996. *Modernity at Large: Cultural Dimensions of Globalization*. Minneapolis: Univ. of Minnesota Press.

Arostegui, Martin. 2003a. "From Venezuela, a Counterplot." *Insight on the News*, Mar. 4.

———. 2003b. "Terror Close to Home." *US News and World Report*, Oct. 6.

Compton, Nick. 2002. "The New Face of Islam." *Evening Standard*, Mar. 15. At https://www.standard.co.uk/news/the-new-face-of-islam-6308255.html.

Davis, Thulani. 2002. "Post 9-11 Civil Rights." *Village Voice*, Dec. 17. At https://www.villagevoice.com/2002/12/17/post9-11-civil-rights/.

Dépestre, René. 1969. "Carta de Cuba sobre el imperialismo de la mala fe." In *Por la revolución, por la poesía*, 71–130. Havana, Cuba: Institute del Libro.

Eisele, Kimi. 2002. "The Multicultural Power of Soap Operas." *Pacific News Service*, Nov. 25.

Fernandez, Yusuf. 2002. "Spain Returning to Islam." *Islamic Horizons*, July–Aug.

"L'habit de danse du ventre de Shakira ne fait pas le poids en Egypte." 2003. Agence France Presse French Wire, May 28.

Hamman, Henry. 2003. "Jamming of Satellite Broadcasts Puts Spotlight on Cuban-Iranian Ties: Source of Interference on the Expatriate Channels Has Been Traced to Havana. But Is It the Culprit? Henry Hamman Reports." *Financial Times*, July 21.

Kelley, Robin. 2002. *Freedom Dreams: The Black Radical Imagination*. Boston: Beacon Press.

Martí, José. 1938. "España en Melilla." In *Cuba: Letras*, vol. 2, 203–8. Havana, Cuba: Edición Trópico.

Ocasio, Rahim. 1997. "Latinos, the Invisible: Islam's Forgotten Multitude." *Message*, Aug.

O'Sullivan, Charlotte. 2002. "CHARLOTTE O'SULLIVAN's Column: DRESS-DOWN FRIDAY: [FOREIGN Edition]." *Independent*, July 19.

Ramonet, Ignacio. 2002. "The Conspiracy against Chávez." *El País* (English), Apr. 17.

Roy, Oliver. 2003. "Euro-Islam: The Jihad Within?" *National Interest*, Spring, 63–73.

Whittell, Giles. 2002. "'Allah Came Knocking at My Heart': Cover Story." *Times* (London), Jan. 7.

Young, Robert. 2001. *Postcolonialism: An Historical Introduction*. London: Blackwell.

38

From "Democracy and Its Others"

SUNAINA MAIRA

The war on terror has been fought in the name of "democracy," saving others unfit or incapable of the correct model of democracy required for Western, liberal governance or state building. "Democratization" and "democracy promotion" have been central alibis in US invasions and occupation of other regions and various forms of military and political intervention, from Iraq and Afghanistan to Yemen and Pakistan. Democracy is thus a core component of Western modernity, legitimizing a late-imperial project and globalized surveillance regime in conjunction with the framework of human and civil rights, women's rights, or gay rights. . . .

But it was apparent that the so-called Arab Spring and particularly Tahrir Square—as well as the later protests in Gezi Park in Istanbul—had seized the (liberal) American public imagination and the dominant narrative about democracy in the war on terror had been disrupted, if only for a brief moment.

The Egyptian revolution of 2011, in particular, and the visible presence of young, media-savvy activists such as Wael Ghonim, the Google executive who was one of many young Egyptians involved in the movement, became the symbol for many Americans of the "other" Middle East. These Arab cyberactivists, students, and "professional activists" became counterpoints to the images of Arab and Muslim youth that US publics had long been fed by the US mainstream media, especially after 9/11. Here, there were unarmed Egyptian youth facing down tanks in the streets, clean-shaven computer professionals organizing Facebook campaigns, young women in hijab leading hundreds of their peers in the streets and confronting the police, and nonviolent demonstrations organized in communal encampments. . . .

"Hack for Egypt"

In May 2011, I attended a . . . "solidarity event" [in Silicon Valley] related to the Arab uprisings . . . , one that demonstrated the ways that "democracy" is a moving target. The Hackathon for Egypt at Stanford University was billed as an "un-conference," a day-long event organized by a group of computer hackers and Stanford faculty and sponsored by the Center on Democracy, Development, and the Rule of Law (CDDRL), the Liberation Technology Program, and the Peace Innovation Lab at Stanford. It was cosponsored by Cloud to Street, a nonprofit organization inspired by the Egyptian movement to overthrow Mubarak that described itself as an "experiment in international digital activism."[1] The call for the conference stated, "Earlier this year, Egyptians combined technology and political activism to revolutionary effect. After overthrowing a thirty-year dictatorship, they face new challenges to establishing democracy. Can technology help them through the divisive times ahead? . . . Our aim is to build a community to show what digital activism

Excerpt from Sunaina Maira, "Democracy and Its Others," in *The 9/11 Generation: Youth, Rights, and Solidarity in the War on Terror* (New York: New York Univ. Press, 2016), 234–64. A works cited list was added to the end of this chapter. Reprinted with corrections and press style changes for consistency throughout the volume by permission of New York University Press.

1. "Lessons from an Experiment in International Digital Activism," Cloud to Street, Aug. 26, 2011, originally at http://www.cloudtostreet.org/?p=398, archived at https://web.archive.org/web/20120225075624/http://www.cloudtostreet.org/?p=398.

can achieve." The event was a fascinating example of the kind of solidarity projects emerging from the confluence of "hacktivists" (young and older), academics, and hi-tech entrepreneurs in Silicon Valley, all working in sites where democracy is defined, celebrated, and debated. The notion of the "professional activist" . . . merged at this event with the notion of the digital activist, showcasing an instance of transnational, techie solidarity politics centered on varied imaginings of democracy, solidarity, and resistance.

The hackathon was held in the d.school (Institute of Design) on the Stanford campus, in a chic, warehouse-like space with red-vinyl sofas and a large screen at the front of the room. The format of the "un-conference" was designed to connect Silicon Valley programmers with Egyptian activists and engineers and encourage an open-ended, "democratically designed" mix of hacking and activism. The participants that morning were an ethnically diverse crowd of people, some whites and South Asians in addition to a few Arabs—not an unusual mix for Silicon Valley—with many students but also several older people. . . . From the screen peered the faces of young Egyptian activists in Cairo who were waiting to talk to the audience via Skype, and in the room were young Egyptians who had come from Cairo, one of whom was the cofounder of the Kifaya movement, Ahmed Saleh, who had been involved in organizing the historic January 25 protest in Tahrir Square.

The event opened with remarks by Ben Roswell, the founder of Cloud to Street, a white Canadian and former diplomat to Afghanistan who had lived in Egypt and was now a visiting scholar at the CDDRL. Cloud to Street was launched by Roswell to support Egyptian activists who were using social media and who, according to the organization's mission statement, had "pioneered new methods of political change for the 21st century. In doing so they have not only transformed their country, but set an example for all countries seeking democratic change."[2]

2. "About: Working to Understand the Intersection of Cyberspace and Political Space," Cloud to Street, n.d. (ca. 2012), originally at http://www.cloudtostreet.org/?page_id=5, archived at https://web.archive.org/web/20210225161414/http://www.cloudtostreet.org/?page_id=5.

Digital media are not just viewed as a site for producing democracy in this discourse, but Egypt is actually offered as a possible political vanguard for media activism and for the West, rather than the other way around as in typical democracy-speak. Roswell had apparently been involved in organizing a digital town hall at Stanford in March on the Egyptian uprising, featuring young activists from Cairo, and a series of hackathons in solidarity with Egypt in partnership with the Liberation Technology Program. He commented that day that he and a small team had been visiting Cairo regularly since the fall of the Mubarak regime and meeting with Egyptian activists in order to find out how "technology was involved in dramatic change" and what support they could provide for this alternative "democracy promotion" movement. Roswell seemed to resist an overstatement of technology's revolutionary potential, saying, "What's driving their revolution is a huge amount of courage, it's not just technology." But he also acknowledged that the "incredible ingenuity and technological smarts" of the Egyptian activists had contributed to its success. For example, he noted that activists had installed web cameras around the protest camp at Tahrir Square to document violent attacks on the protesters, a strategic form of countersurveillance and one that was probably an important factor in the revolution's early success as images from Cairo were broadcast live to the world.

The goal of the hackathon at Stanford was for hackers to work together to develop digital tools and "apps" to support the democracy movement in Egypt, after presentations, including those by the activists from Cairo. One of the speakers was a young Egyptian American venture capitalist, in a red Egypt-solidarity T-shirt, who talked about being at a meeting at the US State Department concerning the use of social media on the very day that Mubarak finally resigned. He recollected, "People were floored in D.C. Few of the people there were Egyptian, but they were crying as they watched what was happening in Tahrir Square on CNN. It was bigger than Egypt, what was happening." I was struck by the irony submerged in this observation of US government officials apparently moved to tears by the protests in Cairo and rejoicing with Egyptians at the fall of the dictator that the United States had supported for so long. This comment crystallized for me the staging of a certain romance about the Egyptian revolution at the time, especially at that moment in spring 2011. The image of Tahrir Square had not yet been infused into the Occupy movement that exploded across the United States and around the world later that year (let alone been supplanted in Egypt itself by the conflict between the Muslim Brotherhood, the military, and popular revolutionaries), but it was already apparent that [this image] was deeply, if paradoxically, resonant for many Americans, not just those who were Arab or progressive.

The young Arab American entrepreneur went on to say, "We've already won, in a sense, because *you* are all here today. A big part of what will happen is what you want to do to help. Maybe you can start building some apps that we could use [in Egypt]." I think this seemingly simple statement captures part of what was romantic about Tahrir Square—a political fable of solidarity with a "good" revolution and a nonviolent, grassroots movement involving many clean-shaven youth, not just bearded males, against a "bad" ruler, who was finally acknowledged in the American public sphere as tyrannical, corrupt, and obsolete. The simplicity of this moral allegory about the triumph of the people's will in the struggle for democracy in Egypt resonated also with narratives of the US civil rights movement in the sanitized history of that struggle . . . and perhaps also with deep-seated national myths of America as a nation founded through the struggle for freedom and not through settler-colonial violence and genocide. But this political romance about Tahrir Square and Arab youth protesters was enabled by several evasions and contradictions pivoting on the trope of democracy.

I argue that this political allegory was effective because it allowed for a double move in the post-9/11 national culture and debates about the war on terror at that historical moment. On the one hand, it offered a redemptive moment for an American public wrestling with revelations of the violent excesses of US military force from Guantánamo to Abu Ghraib as well as [with] the failures of the Obama regime in following through on its promises to rehabilitate the view of US democracy and chart a "new beginning," as articulated in the president's "Address to the Muslim World" in Cairo in June 2009.[3] This allowed liberal Americans to express sympathy with the will of "the people" in an Arab nation that was not directly occupied by the United States and so alleviated, perhaps, some liberal guilt in response to the war on terror, if not anxieties about earlier imperial interventions overseas and settler violence at home whose repressed history is negotiated, or possibly recovered, through contemporary acts of US aggression (Pease 2009, 172–73). The participants at the hackathon were assured that their act of solidarity in the United States was a sign of victory for the Egyptian movement and that they could offer something tangible and positive to support this uprising for democracy. On the other hand, this romantic fable wiped clean the role of the United States in propping up the very dictatorship that the Egyptians had managed to overthrow, against all odds. It also erased other forms of US-sponsored violence that the protesters in Cairo were challenging, evident in the Egyptian protests in solidarity with Palestine and opposition to Egypt's collusion with Israel, [and] that were either evaded or downplayed in the US mainstream media (Abou-El-Fadl 2012). None of these complex issues of US imperialism and US-backed colonial violence that were tangled with the Egyptian revolution was discussed at the hackathon that day. . . .

The redemptive allegory of Tahrir Square, at least as it emerged in the early weeks of the Egyptian revolution, was also a gendered narrative, offering an opportunity to rethink or reinscribe powerful tropes about women's rights, freedom, and progress in the post-9/11 culture wars. The images of Egyptian women—old and young, wearing hijabs, abayas, jeans, T-shirts, or blue bras—on the streets and battling the police demonstrated that Muslim and Arab women could also be legible through the framework of democracy, even if they sometimes looked different and might have wanted different things than what American viewers of the revolution imagined. At the Stanford un-conference, one of the speakers was

3. "President Obama Speaks to the Muslim World from Cairo, Egypt," White House, June 4, 2009, at https://www.whitehouse.gov/video/President-Obama-Speaks-to-the-Muslim-World-from-Cairo-Egypt.

Sabah Hamamou, a young Egyptian journalist who was wearing a long black skirt and a headscarf with black stars, who founded Masrawyya, a media platform used to broadcast news and images of Tahrir Square that spread virally across the world. She traced the emergence of the protests in Egypt to the year 2003, a moment when the Second Intifada in Palestine was just ending and the war in Iraq was just beginning, alluding to the role of the United States and Israel in suppressing democracy in the region. I was struck that Hamamou was the only speaker at the event who situated the Egyptian revolution in the context of war and occupation in the region.

Hamamou also stressed that the revolution was not just for human rights embedded in liberal democratic governance but for an alternative political and economic structure that would address the people's "basic needs," such as "health care, education." Her talk thus extended beyond the horizon of democracy and civil rights, touching also on the question of economic and social rights and demands for the state to provide a "structure of redistribution, welfare, and constitutionality" that have been eroded in postcolonial states in the Global South and by neoliberalism at large (Spivak, in Butler and Spivak [2007] 2010, 90). Hamamou's talk was followed by a presentation by an Indian digital activist from the Liberation Technology Program on digital platforms for constitutional reform and a project for web-based discussions of the human rights principles in the Egyptian Constitution, convened by Egyptian opposition leader Mohamed ElBaradei. The goal of this crowdsourcing project, the Indian activist said, was that "constitutions could be changed for democracy" and that the uploading of constitutions from around the world on the internet would allow people to think about "different ways to organize political rights around the world."

While the presenters were speaking, the activists in Cairo peeking out from the projection screen appeared disconnected from the proceedings in the room. . . . Finally, . . . [t]he voice of Ahmed Boguta suddenly burst into the room from Cairo with a loud crackle. Boguta discussed his proposal for a website and interactive database to monitor the Egyptian Parliament and upcoming elections and inform citizens about the Parliament's role and responsibility. Other projects proposed by the Cairo activists also focused on harnessing technology to pave the way for democracy. Abdallah Helmy, of the Revolutionary Youth Union, suggested a mobile phone app that would connect activists to a larger social network and also "raise awareness about civic rights and duties." This was framed as a key issue for a society preparing for electoral democracy after decades of repression and debating the procedural challenges ahead. Rights education is thus central to this discourse of digital democracy and (de)democratization, whether in its liberal or leftist variants. . . .

The Skype talks were followed by presentations by the hackers and activists in the room as people in the audience pitched their ideas, some using a whiteboard. A slightly older white man from the Peace Innovation Lab greeted the room with "A salaam aleikum!" He went on to propose a project to "build apps that incentivize cooperation" that could be used to address "conflicts building between Copts and Salafis [Muslims]" in Egypt. Ossama Hassanein, a middle-aged Egyptian American entrepreneur from Silicon Valley, said he wanted to create a mobile app to generate "apolitical, nonpartisan communities of interest." Hassanein, who was wearing a red T-shirt with the Egyptian flag and the word "Freedom" emblazoned across his chest, was the chairman of TechWadi, a Silicon Valley–based organization of approximately two thousand Arab American entrepreneurs and CEOs. . . . One of the last proposals was from Hamamou herself; she remarked, "In 1798, Napoleon went to Egypt and compiled information about Egypt in twenty volumes. I have a dream to do the same with Egyptian stories." She said she wanted to create a database with audio files of Egyptian narratives, about Egypt by Egyptians. However, the audience seemed oblivious to Hamamou's strikingly overt challenge to the imperial and Orientalist desires of Western rulers and experts to document and catalog the colonized. In fact, one of the white male hackers present immediately suggested that her project could be merged with an American documentary film project. The irony of this appropriative response to the anticolonial thrust of Hamamou's archival project was, perhaps not surprisingly, lost on those present. The dominant language of countering sectarianism and creating apolitical communities for electoral participation and reconciliation, as well as market logics of incentivization and interest, instead shaped many of the local presentations while discussions of US foreign policy and US(-backed) repression were almost entirely absent. The talks by speakers from Cairo and Stanford completed, the audience was then asked to start working on projects during the "open space format" in the afternoon, in the presumably democratic spirit of creative collaboration.

Imperial Democracy

The "un-conference" in Silicon Valley, representing the confluence of technology, knowledge production, and global solidarity projects, is a fascinating example of one strand of politics that attempts to seize liberal democracy as a platform for mobilization and entrepreneurship. The event staged a certain performance of transnational, digital solidarity that was strikingly disconnected from local solidarity movements, given the absence of Arab American community activists, and featured instead Silicon Valley entrepreneurs and a select group of youth from the area. Also, some of the Arab Americans present had class interests that would probably not be aligned with those of left activists in the streets of Cairo challenging neoliberal capitalism. The racial and class schisms evident at the hackathon were not unexpected, given its location at an elite university in the heart of Silicon Valley, but the event seemed emblematic of a pervasive, liberal discourse of solidarity and rights activism that has emerged in tandem with Obama's war on terror and that obscures the difficult and pressing issues of imperial militarism, racial violence, surveillance, and repression. The question of democracy *within* the United States was not raised at all by the hacktivists at Stanford that day, nor, of course, [were] the contradictions of US support for repressive regimes, such as Egypt and Israel. The issue of human rights, or even civil rights, seemed to be located over *there*, but not in California or right here in Silicon Valley, where the FBI had been targeting antiwar activists and Muslim community leaders and secretly placing tracking devices on cars belonging to Egyptian American youth. There was no mention at all of the post-9/11 repression, including digital surveillance, that had so deeply affected Arab and Muslim American communities, including young activists.

I do not want to dismiss completely the desires of the various individuals present at the hackathon for real or even "radical" democracy, for there was a diverse group of people in the room, some of whom may indeed have had political orientations at odds with the general tenor of the public discussion or critiques of the format and nature of the event. When I spoke to one of the event organizers later at Stanford and asked her what the goal of the hackathon was, she was careful not to be "prescriptive" in suggesting a political agenda. She commented that the mission of the CDDRL was "to promote democracy, but not George Bush's notion of democratization. Democracy is different for each place; we want to support what people are doing in different regions." But the fact remains that the focus of "Hack for Egypt" was definitely on democracy outside the United States and only on Egypt. The project thus seems to illustrate what Stephen Sheehi (2011) describes as Obama's deployment of "soft power," which has been "a counter-narrative to the hard power of the Bush administration" and has co-opted the language of social change movements (for example, the slogan "Yes We Can"); this discourse "promises to assimilate Muslim communities into U.S.-driven and dominated globalization" through neoliberal, democratic reform, backed by coercion and violence (182).

One of the questions the hackathon immediately raised for me was what made Tahrir Square so appealing to a liberal American public as a site for reimagining the future of "democracy" in the post-9/11 era. This imaginary of democracy and rights was constituted through both the form and content of the un-conference as a presumably open, collaborative, and democratic space. The discussions by digital activists of nonviolent conflict resolution, civic education, and democratic "civil disobedience," with the help of technology, represent a "good," acceptable politics for Muslim and Arab subjects globally. This discourse of permissible politics during the early phase of the Arab uprisings did not completely alleviate liberal American fears that the overthrow of Mubarak would allow the Muslim Brotherhood or "bad" Arab and Muslim politics to run rampant in Egypt—as Hassanein's comment about the local solidarity rallies hinted—and that US strategic interests in the region were now going to be compromised. But Tahrir Square as an imperial allegory enshrined good Arab and Muslim activists, entrepreneurs, and youth as partners in the project for global (and digital) democratization.

Tahrir Square also provided a moment of redemption for Arab Americans, in a sense, and many young Egyptian and Arab Americans I met felt a surge of pride, mixed with hope and fear, as the protests overthrew Ben Ali in Tunisia and Mubarak in Egypt. Abed, whose family is from Cairo, talked to me in February 2011 about how he and many others in the Egyptian American community were "embracing their Egyptian pride" since the uprising in Tahrir Square. The frustration and anger among Egyptians with the dictatorship and its collusion with Israel was released, if for a moment, in a surge of genuine and deep hope for change, at last, for Egypt, Tunisia, and the region. Abed also acknowledged that the revolution was being embraced by Americans who were neither Egyptian nor Arab, citing the example of a video that was circulating on YouTube at the time, posted by a white American family who had lived in Egypt; it featured their four young daughters marching with the Egyptian flag in their living room and chanting, "Down with Mubarak!" Abed was cautious, however, about claiming pride in a national identity that would be exclusivist or chauvinistic, pointing to the role of Western colonialism in crafting national identities in the Arab world and insisting that the Egyptian revolution should not take precedence over movements in Tunisia or other Arab nations. This was a desire for democracy and pan-Arab solidarity that I heard from many young Arab American activists and that did not emerge from a conservative nationalism but from a yearning for sovereignty and liberation from the ravages of imperialism and neoliberal capitalism.

Yet the internationalizing of Tahrir Square also created contradictory responses from Arab American youth, who had perhaps become accustomed to Orientalist imaginaries of Arabs and Muslims and who felt redeemed by the shift in representation, if only for a brief moment. Abed said he was happy to see a column in the *New York Times*, written by the ubiquitous journalist Nicholas Kristof, titled "We Are All Egyptians." Abed read the title as an expression of solidarity with global struggles against "injustice" condensed into the symbol of Tahrir Square—but less so [with] the self-immolation of the Tunisian street vendor, Mohamed Bouazizi, that sparked the uprising in Tunisia. An important trope that made the allegory of Tahrir Square so effective in the early months of 2011 was the image of the Egyptian revolution as a nonviolent movement, based on peaceful protest. The theme of nonviolence also ran through some of the talks at the Stanford hackathon, but Abed pointed out the protests in Cairo did involve violence of various forms and by different groups. Noting that looters had targeted homes and museums and were sometimes armed, Abed was also angry about police brutality against protesters.[4] So while the protesters may have been nonviolent, this was certainly not a bloodless revolution. However, the romance of Tahrir Square at the time allowed for a liberal narrative that evaded the connections between the violence of the Mubarak regime—the physical violence perpetrated by its policemen, spies, and thugs as well as the social and economic violence it inflicted on Egyptians and others—and the violence of the imperial state that had propped up this and other antidemocratic regimes in the region and around the world.

In Abed's view, Arab and Muslim Americans were not immune to the appeal of a liberal allegory about democracy, which he critiqued as obscuring the question of imperialism and sovereignty. For example, CNN's Anderson Cooper quickly became the American face of this allegory for many viewers of his live reports from Tahrir Square, particularly after he was assaulted by Mubarak's thugs; he became the intrepid white American male hero who was on the "right" side of the war for democracy and the post-9/11 culture wars, at last. But Abed was skeptical of this Indiana Jones–like tale, observing trenchantly that

> a lot of Muslims and Arabs are applauding Anderson Cooper. . . . I give them [CNN] credit, they're doing an amazing job but . . . I mean, Anderson Cooper said, "The Egyptian government is, they've been evil

4. In fact, our conversation took place soon after an Egyptian academic teaching at UC Davis, Noha Radwan, had given a televised interview on the *Democracy Now!* show from Tahrir Square and subsequently been beaten up by pro-Mubarak thugs.

> for thirty years," and everybody's like, "Oh, mash 'Allah [praise be to God], Anderson Cooper! *Good job*!" Nobody's taking a step back and saying, okay, well, the only reason they have been in power is because of the US government [giving Mubarak] 1.3 billion dollars annually. . . . What bothers me is that the US is meddling in all of this, again . . . and it's not just Obama's administration, this is something the US has been doing since the 1800s, that whenever they see a country of interest . . . maybe there's political change and they are not sure where's it gonna go, they say, . . . "Well, let us help you," and it's just—Keep your hands off other people's business! It's none of their business!

Abed astutely situated US military, financial, and political support for the Mubarak regime and the Obama administration's concerns about whether Egypt would remain a US ally in the context of a much longer, imperial history of US and Western intervention in the affairs of other, sovereign nations, often in the guise of humanitarianism. He went on to critique the hypocrisy in official American narratives about spreading "democracy" globally while preserving US strategic interests:

> I don't care how strategic Egypt is; whatever happens, it is up to the people. If the people democratically elect the Muslim Brotherhood, then so be it, . . . it's their choice, you can't . . . call for a democracy and then when people democratically elect a certain— . . . Exactly like it happened in Palestine, like in Gaza, Hamas was democratically elected, but we said, "Oh no, we're not [interested in] democracy anymore, we wanna place our own people!" You can't do this, you can't have one hand in front of you and one hand behind your back, and say, "Oh okay, go ahead have democracy, no okay, we're gonna give you *this* option, this is what you *really* wanted to have . . . since you guys are not smart enough to choose the right people, we'll put them in place for you!"

Abed's ironic commentary—prescient in its observations about the election of the Muslim Brotherhood after Mubarak's fall and the US response—was laced with outrage over the selective deployment of democracy as a switch and bait in US foreign policy, as [was] apparent in the American (and Israeli) unwillingness to accept that Hamas was the democratically elected national government in Palestine in 2005.

I cite at some length Abed's critique of the inconsistent and shifting invocations of democracy by the United States not only because he was passionate about the events unfolding in Egypt as an Egyptian American student activist but also because he incisively articulated the problem of imperial democracy, in contrast to the discourse of digital democracy and solidarity at the hackathon. "Democratization" and "democracy promotion," the vocabulary favored by the Bush administration and adopted by the Obama regime, are imperial code words for regime change, the promotion of the free market, and the consolidation of US economic and strategic interests with the help of the US military. In some instances, young people like Abed were able to grasp the colonialist and also racialized logic of democracy as a touchstone of benevolent imperialism. For example, Abed critiqued the colonialist assumption that Palestinians, Arabs, or Muslims were not "smart enough to choose the right people" as their leaders in the eyes of the US state, but he also understood that this image of presumably backward, antidemocratic Arab and Muslim societies was embedded in the "strategic" interests of the US in maintaining its own hegemony and network of client states. The discourse of the post-9/11 culture wars focuses on Muslim and Arab American subjects who must be made "safe" for imperial multicultural democracy by inserting them into the grid of legibility of the "good" and "bad" Muslim or Arab. . . . This, then, is what democracy looks like when it passes the test of permissible Arab and Muslim American political subjecthood. . . .

Democracy, Imperial or Otherwise?

The long war against terrorism has been accompanied by racial and cultural wars that involve a battle over the meaning of democracy accompanied by a turn to rights. The dilemma of "democracy" in the current moment is that it has been deployed as an imperial political category throughout the Reagan–Cheney–Bush era of aggressive neoliberal interventionism as well as during the Obama regime's "open hand/clenched fist" policy of democratization and co-optation accompanied by military force, so it is naturally a suspect word for many on the left (Gaines 2010, 197; Sheehi 2011, 185). This is also true of the notion of "rights," particularly liberal civil rights and institutionalized human rights, . . . which represent political possibilities as well as failures for young activists. In the post–civil rights era, "democracy" has become a dirty word for some progressives and leftists, sullied by its co-optation by imperial, neoliberal governmentality. As Dean (2009) observes, "When democracy appears as both the condition of politics and the solution to the political condition, neoliberalism can't appear as the violence it is. Right and left share the same rhetoric of democracy. So preemptive war is fought in the name of democracy even as critics of the same war use the terms to voice, to imagine, their opposition" (18). She asks, "Is democracy the fallback position for left politics, all that remains of our wounded and diminished political aspirations? Or does the hope its evocation promises mark instead a pervasive left despair?" (76). . . .

The shifting narrative of democracy is part of a longer process of transformation of the US state into a liberal, officially antiracist state—a process that Alain Badiou (2005) suggests is, in fact, a "lengthy counter-revolutionary intellectual and political sequence" that began in the mid-1970s (xxxiv). On the one hand, Badiou points out that the period since the mid-1990s has been marked by "dramatic reactionary phenomena" including "racism, hostility toward the Arab world, . . . unchained Zionism," and a "violent defense" of US economic interests and neoliberal global capitalism. On the other hand, the "long 'war against terrorism'" has been accompanied by "massive hostility" and growing resistance to US hegemony globally as well as the eruption of Occupy protests and public-worker strikes at home (xxxv). During this same period, however, the liberal democratic state has been strengthened as the desired locus of political inclusion and recognition and as the arbiter of rights. . . . So the crux of the matter is not just that Muslim Americans desire political recognition through civil rights mobilization but that the state also desires this movement for rights and democracy (Reddy 2011, 193). The counter-revolutionary national consensus needs people to need liberal democracy as the endpoint of their struggles. Yet there are cracks in this consensus about democracy and legal egalitarianism. . . .

The concepts of democracy and rights—civil, women, gay, or human—are increasingly deployed (and mutated) by the Right, but the problem is also that they have been ceded by the liberal Left. As political theorists argue, democracy has come to represent a limited political horizon for resistance to imperialism and neoliberal capitalism not just because it is appropriated and deformed by the Right but because as a liberal political ideal or practice it is actually a symptom of a current impasse in politics (Dean 2009, 76–77). Žižek (2007), however, argues: "The true victory . . . occurs when the enemy talks your language. In this sense, a true victory is a victory in defeat. It occurs when one's specific message is accepted as a universal ground, even by the enemy" (17). Žižek suggests that the universalization of concepts historically associated with the Left is a moment of triumph, but I want to point out that the co-optation of these ideals occurs through a blurring and redefinition of their meaning, as when democracy becomes an alibi for totalitarianism and universalism a guise for repression of aspirations for equality and emancipation (Rancière 2006, 12). So when the Right uses the language of democracy or of rights, I think this moment actually has the potential to be a true defeat for the Left. Dean (2009) rightly observes that, in certain cases, "when one's enemy accepts one's terms, one's point of critique and resistance is lost, subsumed. The dimension of antagonism (fundamental opposition) vanishes" (9).

The shift to rights-talk is dangerous because it sometimes slips into "assertions of difference" and victimhood as the basis for claims to civil rights or gay rights, succumbing to a liberal multicultural politics of injury (Dean 2009, 5–9). Duggan (2003), however, has a nuanced analysis of the discourse of injury invoked by groups claiming rights as minorities or queers, arguing that this does not necessarily have to represent a politics of recognition, as pitted against a politics of (downward) redistribution. Struggles for racial, economic, or social justice can still offer a powerful critique of the "felicity of inclusion" into the liberal democratic order (Reddy 2011, 181). Reframing Žižek's optimistic pronouncement, it is useful to consider Spivak's (1995) insistence on "the continuing need for collective struggle," given that "there is no victory, but only victories that are also warnings" (xxv). This debate, which is not simply a theoretical one but has real implications for movements and people on the ground, is crucial . . . because it suggests that there is no easy way out of this political impasse of democracy and rights, but a resolution need not mean either defeatism or triumphalism for those concerned with radical transformation of the social order. The co-optation and deformation of democracy—and [of] concepts such as "radicalism," not to mention human rights, antiracism, feminism, and sexual equality—require a continuous pressing on these concepts and resistance to their appropriation by those in power. They necessitate collective organizing to challenge the retreat to politics defined as individualized consumption of political ideas and demands and a constant production of alternative knowledges and imaginaries of change. Furthermore, as the roots of the Arab uprisings should remind us, these alternative imaginaries are indeed being produced in other parts of the world, though they remain largely invisible in the United States, including even among US progressives, as is particularly true of the repressed histories of the Left in Afghanistan and Pakistan.

The caution in allegories about liberal democracy is also fundamentally about the question of the state as the horizon of political struggle, as reflected in the struggles of youth from communities targeted in the war on terror who turn to civil rights campaigns, attempting to oppose the state by appealing to the state. As Nivedita Menon (2004) has argued, in the context of movements coalescing around women's rights in India, rights-talk has ended up in many instances strengthening the state, through legal discourses, and in particular the power of Western states shrouded by the discourse of liberal universalism (38, 224). Moreover, she points out that the "continual recourse to the law" and to rights often becomes a substitute for "the other harder option of building a movement for an alternative vision" (6). The experiences of young activists in Silicon Valley demonstrate how a liberal civil rights discourse redirects a radical critique of the state and the institutionalized human rights apparatus suppresses, rather than supports, resistance to violence against racialized segments of humanity. Menon importantly argues that the investment in rights-based activism happens at the expense of developing other forms of resistance. It is worth noting that the critiques of these young people did spill over into radical challenges to imperialism, settler colonialism, global capitalism, and white supremacy, even if they did not use this terminology, in part because it was not as accessible to them as [were] the commonsensical paradigms of "civil rights" or "human rights."

Critical legal studies has emphasized that rights are "unstable and indeterminate," but there are disagreements between those, on the one hand, who suggest that rights-talk is important to expose nationalist rights mythologies and to continue to struggle for rights "in a world of no rights" for disenfranchised and disposable groups and those, on the other hand, who argue that the oppression of these groups has historically occurred *through* the law and that an alternative politics must be imagined and enacted (see Williams 2000; Spann 2000). Angela Davis (2005) argues that it is possible to engage in rights-based activism with a "dual strategy of taking up the law and recognizing its limitations in order to address that which the law cannot apprehend" (94). In this vein of not ceding but transforming the language of rights and democracy, it is inspiring to consider the statements of youth such as the radical young poet Amir Sulaiman, . . . who reflected on his experience of racial profiling and FBI surveillance:

> My position wasn't "I'm an American and therefore I have the right to speak and I am petitioning for this right." My position was that my right to speak is God-given, that it's a truly inalienable right, and not just because some men agree it's inalienable. I wasn't interested in surrendering that right, and I wasn't interested in humiliating myself in front of people by begging for a right that they neither have the power to give or revoke. (cited in Malek 2011, 145–46)

Sulaiman's articulation of rights as "inalienable" and ontological is profound, and while I depart from a divine justification of rights, I think his unequivocal rejection of the arbitrary power of certain groups of humans to bestow rights on others goes to the heart of the critique of rightlessness by prominent political theorists, articulated here in powerful and unapologetic terms. Sulaiman also offers an important course of action—a call for neither "begging" and "humiliating" oneself to the racist legal apparatus of the liberal democratic state nor "surrendering" one's right to have rights. . . .

I want to emphasize that the point is not to rush into post-statism but to think about what it means to actually engage in the other form of mass politics, the "harder option" Menon alludes to, that is not so readily available or sanctioned by the liberal democratic state but that also requires that we do not abdicate political struggle altogether out of a desire for a "pure politics." As Rancière (2010) argues, [both] those who bemoan the "end of politics" [and those who] celebrate the "return of politics" . . . end up participating in the repression of the political and consolidation of an existing political "consensus" (42). But it this *paradox* at the core of politics in imperial democracy that is crucial. Radical movements need to expose the "incoherence and gap inside the state, between the institutions charged with making laws and those charged with preserving or reinforcing them," according to Reddy (2011, 228), and bringing forth this contradiction is what is so threatening to the neoliberal democratic order. The gaps in civil rights activism that cannot address the criminalization of civil disobedience and denial of civil rights to Palestine solidarity activists or in human rights talk that cannot account for the imperial devastation in Af-Pak or Iraq are precisely the site of a dissensus, that is, "the demonstration (manifestation) of a gap in the sensible itself" (Rancière 2010, 38). This is where politics happens as "an intervention in the visible and sayable," an attempt by the targets of the war on terror and objects of surveillance to "mobilize" the gap between the promise of freedom by the existing international legal order and its realization (Rancière 2010, 37; Butler, in Butler and Spivak [2007] 2010, 68–69). As with all areas of political praxis, this is not just a conceptual debate but an actual, ongoing struggle on the ground, and the current struggle being waged by youth and people around the globe in the gaps between the state, democracy, and rights-talk is a difficult, frustrating, disillusioning, and risky one.

Arrested and Alternative Politics

. . . Departing from the trend in most studies of Muslim, Arab, and South Asian American youth, I suggest a different way to address the dilemma of democracy and the impasse of rights for the objects of imperial violence, situating the question of democracy squarely in relation to the foundational genocidal violence of the empire-state, to a politics of life and death in the settler colony, as well as to the "rule of difference" and inclusion through arrested politics. . . .

It should not be surprising that some young Arab, South Asian, and Afghan Americans articulated their response to the war on terror through the language of multicultural belonging and a desire for recognition as ethnic and religious subjects, given the commonsensical national framework provided by postpolitical, neoliberal democracy. This is one of the dilemmas of imperial modernity that is constituted by the paradigms of liberal civil rights and multicultural inclusion that young South Asian, Arab, and Afghan Americans must grapple with even while imagining resistance to the war on terror and challenging post-9/11 racism and repression. As Mmembe (2003) has demonstrated in his analysis of necropolitics, the reinsertion of race and colonialism into a discussion of exceptional state violence makes it apparent that a colonialist and racialized logic of sovereignty regulates the management of life and death in late modernity. Yet this is perhaps the most difficult argument to make in the heart of empire, which is why it seems almost impossible for many to present the predicament of Arab, South Asian, and Afghan Americans after 9/11 as a problem not of civil or human rights but of self-determination in a condition of late imperialism.

Resistance and Justice in the Age of Obama

How, then, to express dissent in the war on terror and what is the alternative form of the "political" in a moment in which anti-imperial politics has been arrested and the vocabulary of the Left seems to have been in so many cases deformed or defanged by the Right? What frameworks can young people use when "democracy" is the language of US statecraft and expansionism, "women's rights" and "gay rights" are the alibis of imperial interventions and occupation, and cultural and religious difference is promoted by the neoliberal, multicultural state, particularly under Obama? For many Americans, as Angela Davis (2012) observes, the election of Obama was used to suggest that "U.S. democracy has reached a zenith, change has come" for the disenfranchised, the deported, the incarcerated, the foreclosed, or the unemployed (179). Obama's presidency facilitated an exceptionalist narrative of US democracy, as Davis suggests, and allowed a nationalist consensus to be rebuilt on the telos of democracy among progressives and leftists, not just among liberal and conservative nationalists. . . .

In fact, it was the early phase of the Arab revolutions that galvanized mass movements across the United States and brought a different kind of "hope" for an alternative politics to the American liberal-Left, for a brief moment. In an only fitting interruption of the racialized, anti-Arab, and Islamophobic narrative of the war on terror, it was Arab protesters that inspired many across the United States, including youth, to take to their own streets and challenge "the radical redistribution of wealth to the very, very rich and the radical reconstruction of the state into the authoritarian tool for their protection"—the "radical" politics that Dean (2009, 9) observes was actually implemented by the Obama regime. As I have argued . . . [elsewhere], it is important to reclaim the meaning of radicalism in the post-9/11 era and situate it in the context of struggles for social transformation, wresting it away from the lexicon of counterterrorism and surveillance. Yet is also true that radical movements such as Occupy did not, in all instances, make the connections to US imperialism or to the violence of the settler-colonial state, even if there were some events led by Occupy activists in solidarity with Egyptian and Palestinian struggles, as in the Bay Area. The concept of "occupation" refers to a political tactic but also rests uneasily on the histories and realities of occupied regions in the settler-colonial present, from North America to Palestine. In some locations, such as UC Davis, student activists adopted the credo "Occupy/Decolonize" to incorporate this anticolonial critique, and when I was in Palestine, I noticed that young activists stenciled the slogans "#Un-Occupy" and "Occupy Wall Street, Not Palestine!" on walls in the West Bank to make the same point (Maira 2013).

These revolutionary acts by youth against the social order reframe the horizon of radical struggles and force us to think not (just) of rights and legal equality, but of justice. Against a liberal or bourgeois parliamentarian notion of consensual democracy as the acceptable object of emancipatory politics, Badiou (2005) poses the notion of equality not as an "objective of action" but as its "axiom" and emphasizes an "old, worn-out word"—"justice" (94, 98). For Badiou, to create a rupture in the status quo, "justice" cannot be a state project or a "category of statist and social order" but must be an "egalitarian moment of politics," one that is crucial and yet also difficult to easily locate in "spectacle" or "sentiment"; that is, one presumably knows what injustice looks like, and it can be dramatized through affective testimonials of suffering, but "justice is obscure" and yet at the core of "principles at work in rupture and disorder. . . . To seek refuge in history and statecraft is to return to the comfort of the familiar. This is what most of us prefer to do" (96–99, 175). Furthermore, against a notion of "formal, abstract democracy" confined to electoral politics and "legal equality" in "bourgeois democracy," Angela Davis, drawing on the work of W. E. B. DuBois, has argued for "abolition democracy," which would actually challenge the imperial, carceral state by building alternative social institutions and "insist on economic, racial, gender, and sexual justice and equality" (Davis 2005, 85, 95; 2012, 106).

The principles of justice and of a radical and truly emancipatory or abolition democracy, beyond a liberal, universalist conception of democratic rights, then, offer a horizon for left political movements that do not want to take refuge in the familiar. It is the negotiation of the meanings of justice, of equality not confined to the law, and of collective (not individual) freedom that must drive the rethinking of the discourse of civil rights, women's rights, gay rights, human rights, and even economic rights. In other words, this does not mean "giving up" on a discourse of rights or democracy but redefining it through a politics that returns to the core question of justice and that is open to the uncertainty, contradictions, and also creativity of imagining and establishing an alternative political order. . . .

Works Cited

Abou-El-Fadl, Reem. 2012. “The Road to Jerusalem through Tahrir Square: Anti-Zionism and Palestine in the 2011 Egyptian Revolution.” *Journal of Palestine Studies* 41, no. 2: 6–26.

Badiou, Alain. 2005. *Metapolitics*. Translated by Jason Barker. London: Verso.

Butler, Judith, and Gayatri C. Spivak. [2007] 2010. *Who Sings the Nation-State? Language, Politics, Belonging.* London: Seagull.

Davis, Angela Y. 2005. *Abolition Democracy: Beyond Empire, Prisons, and Torture*. New York: Seven Stories Press.

———. 2012. *The Meaning of Freedom: And Other Difficult Dialogues*. San Francisco: City Lights.

Dean, Jodi. 2009. *Democracy and Other Neoliberal Fantasies: Communicative Capitalism and the Failure of the Left.* Durham, NC: Duke Univ. Press.

Duggan, Lisa. 2003. *The Twilight of Inequality: Neoliberalism, Cultural Politics, and the Attack on Democracy.* Boston: Beacon Press.

Gaines, Kevin. 2010. “Of Teachable Moments and Specters of Race.” *American Quarterly* 62, no. 2: 195–213.

Maira, Sunaina. 2013. *Jil Oslo: Palestinian Hip-Hop, Youth Culture, and the Youth Movement*. Washington, DC: Tadween.

Malek, Alia. 2011. *Patriot Acts: Narratives of post-9/11 Injustice*. San Francisco: McSweeney’s/Voice of Witness.

Menon, Nivedita. 2004. *Recovering Subversion: Feminist Politics beyond the Law.* Ranikhet, India: Permanent Black.

Mmembe, Achille. 2003. “Necropolitics.” Translated by Libby Meintjes. *Public Culture* 15, no. 1: 11–40.

Pease, Donald. 2009. *The New American Exceptionalism*. Minneapolis: Univ. of Minnesota Press.

Rancière, Jacques. 2006. *Hatred of Democracy.* Translated by Steve Corcoran. London: Verso.

———. 2010. *Dissensus: On Politics and Aesthetics*. Edited and translated by Steve Corcoran. London: Continuum. [Electronic version.]

Reddy, Chandan. 2011. *Freedom with Violence: Race, Sexuality, and the US State*. Durham, NC: Duke Univ. Press.

Sheehi, Stephen. 2011. *Islamophobia: The Ideological Campaign against Muslims*. Atlanta, GA: Clarity Press.

Spann, Girardeau A. 2000. “Pure Politics.” In *Critical Race Theory: The Cutting Edge*, 2nd ed., edited by Richard Delgado and Jean Tefancic, 21–34. Philadelphia: Temple Univ. Press.

Spivak, Gayatri Chakravorti. 1995. Introduction to Mahasweta Devi, *Imaginary Maps: Three Stories*, xxiii–xxxi. New York: Routledge.

Williams, Patricia J. 2000. *The Divided World: Human Rights and Its Violence*. Minneapolis: Univ. of Minnesota Press.

Žižek, Slavoj. 2007. *Slavoj Žižek Presents Mao: On Practice and Contradiction*. London: Verso.

39

Complex Solidarities

Native Communities, Environmental Injustice, and the Struggle against the North Dakota Access Pipeline

DANA M. OLWAN

In September 2016, Standing Rock Sioux Tribe mobilized thousands of people to protect their land and water resources in Cannon Ball, North Dakota, against a proposed $3.88 billion pipeline intended to transport at least 570,000 barrels of crude oil daily. The would-be line is expected to cross four states, plunging under a section of the Missouri River, beneath the Standing Rock Sioux Reservation's main drinking-water supply and cutting through the community's burial ground. Efforts to stop the pipeline have brought together what Nick Estes describes as "the largest, mass-gathering of Natives and allies in more than a century" (2016). This nonviolent movement was met with National Guard deployments, police crackdowns and arrests, FBI investigations, and private-security forces that attacked protesters with dogs. This state-sanctioned violence compelled Maina Kai of the United Nations Human Rights Office of the High Commissioner's special rapporteur on the rights of freedom of association and peaceful assembly to issue a powerful statement against the excessive use of force against protestors "taking action to protect natural resources and ancestral territory in the face of profit-seeking activity" (quoted in United Nations Human Rights Office 2016). In November 2016, the police and military violently clashed with the protesters, arresting 141 Indigenous Water Protectors, marking them with numbers, and putting them into dog-kennel-like holding cells (Fragoso 2016). As Estes explains, "The camp and the Standing Rock reservation [were] under constant surveillance. The reason: Native bodies stand between corporations and their money. Halting the accumulating of capital, which in this context is the exploitation of our river and lands, has piqued settler ire and spite" (2016).

The Stop the Dakota Access Pipeline campaign, known as NoDAPL, emerged from a context of targeted legislative attacks on Indigenous governance, sovereignty, and life resources. It is shaped in relation to the US state's past and ongoing legacies of colonization of Indigenous lands, lives, and bodies. This movement opposes the settler-colonial vision of economic extraction, environmental destruction, and untethered corporate greed driving the interest in the theft and destruction of Indigenous lands. Reflecting on the longer histories of Indigenous struggles, Nick Estes notes that the NoDAPL campaign "practiced an unsettling countersovereignty" that "drew the support and solidarity of more than three hundred Native Nations and countless thousands of allied forces, sending a clear message to corporate interests" (2017, 119). This chapter focuses on the Indigenous fight against environmental destruction and exploitation to explore historical, emerging, and continuing solidarity efforts between Native and Palestinian communities. I analyze this recent and historic example of solidarity in order to demonstrate how Palestinians located in the United States have reflected on their own positioning within this settler state and how the North Dakota campaign represents an ongoing effort on the part of Palestinian activists and scholars to critically interrogate the deep, complicated, and intersecting web of relations, powers, and positionalities that form the bedrock of settler colonialism in which

Palestinians living in the United States and Canada are invariably implicated. I do this not to exceptionalize or romanticize this moment of solidarity or to dislodge it from longer historical relationships and connections between Palestinians and Native people in the United States and Canada (Krebs and Olwan 2012; Bhandar and Ziadeh 2016). My aim here is rather to show the contours of a new and unfolding theory and praxis of solidarity that is powerfully transforming relationships between Palestinians and Native people in the transnational circuitries of the United States, Canada, and Palestine.

My analysis in this chapter is informed by observations made about this historic event at a distance from the actual encampment at Standing Rock. As such, it is necessarily limited to a discursive analysis of the statements and actions of individual and group activists and organizations whose work demonstrates the inspiring possibilities of critical solidarities informed by the goals of radical geopolitical transformations and grounded in a commitment to liberation and decolonization. In writing this chapter, I am aware of both the limits and possibilities of discourse in shaping the praxis of relational and engaged forms of solidarity. In analyzing these narratives, I show what an investment in decolonial strategies of resistance and solidarity can offer in times of global upheaval and change. This decolonial form of solidarity has the potential to resist what Eve Tuck and K. Wayne Yang have labeled as "the too-easy adoption of decolonizing discourse (making decolonization a metaphor)" that repeatedly "get[s] in the way of more meaningful potential alliances" (2012, 3).

At Standing Rock, this intersectional, cross-racial, local movement with national and transnational reverberations in support of native sovereignty, land and treaty rights, and environmental justice succeeded when the Obama administration announced that the US Army Corps would not grant Dakota Access LLC, the corporation responsible for the construction of the pipeline, the last remaining easement it needs to drill under the Missouri River at Lake Oahe and complete construction of the pipeline (Meyer 2016). Responding to this victory, Tara Houska, national campaigns director of Honor the Earth, said, "The original peoples of these lands fought with all of our hearts against injustice and won. We have been maced, tased, demeaned, hit with water cannons in below freezing temperatures, we stand with the strength of our ancestors before us. The inaction from the administration and media was answered by our refusal to back down. Let this send a message around the world: we are still here. We are empowered. We are not sacrifice zones. Mni wiconi, water is life" (quoted in Knight 2016). Houska's centering of Native resistance and resilience in the face of state-supported corporate injustice is instructive, pointing to the high stakes of the struggle and standoff that took place in Standing Rock and continues today. As Erich Steinman notes, "Coalitions are born of threats, and the DAPL is a multidimensional threat both in material terms as well as being a symbol of multiple destructive and unjust processes. The pipeline constitutes a threat to both the particular place and its ecological system, and to the planet via its impact on climate" (2018, 12–13).

Proponents of the pipeline and their beneficiaries tout nationalist rhetoric, claiming that the pipeline would help the United States become "energy independent" from importing energy from other regions of the world. At the Standing Rock in Real Time teach-in during the American Studies Association Conference held in Chicago in 2017, Phil Deloria made the important connection between US president Donald Trump's signing of the executive order regarding the construction of the Keystone XL Pipeline on January 24, 2017, and his remarks a day earlier when he lamented the lost US opportunity to ransack Iraq's oil reserves in contravention of international law. Trump stated in his interview with CBS, "We go in, we spent three trillion dollars. We lose thousands and thousands of lives, and then look what happens is we get nothing. You know, it used to be to the victor belong the spoils. . . . There was no victor there, believe me. There was no victory. But I always said, 'Take the oil'" (quoted in Wright 2017). Read in relation to one another, as Deloria suggests we do, these statements and events render apparent the transnational connections between the "war on terror" abroad and the war on Native peoples and their lands and resources within the US settler-colonial nation-state.

Masking their investments in an estimated 7.4 billion barrels of undiscovered oil in the Bakken formation area, proponents argue that the pipeline is the safest, most cost-effective, and environmentally responsible way to move crude oil (Dakota Access Pipeline 2016; Levin 2016). As the campaign and the Native people in Standing Rock and elsewhere continue their mobilization efforts in preparation for new confrontations and struggles for land sovereignty, it is important to remember, as Nick Estes states, that NoDAPL is part of a much broader and much longer history of Native resilience "to protect water and land from inevitable spoliation in the name of profit" (2016).

NoDAPL is a nonviolent movement that links a critique of global capitalism with a resistance of settler colonialism, teaching us about the transnational politics and practices of decolonization at a time of empire and war. Emphasizing the transnational aspect of both the DAPL and the struggle against it, Katie Mazer and Martin Danilyuk state in their detailed report on DAPL, *Mapping a Many Headed Hydra: The Struggle over the North Dakota Access Pipeline* (2017):

> Dakota Access is fundamentally transnational not only for its entrenchment in transnational networks of infrastructure, commodity flows, and finance, but also in a much more basic way. This transnationalism is manifest through the local, international, and global ecologies on which we all rely and which are at stake in the expansion of this and other pipeline infrastructure. It is clear in the geographies of Indigenous territories and assertions of Indigenous sovereignty that defy and supersede the international boundaries of Canada and the United States through which the pipeline passes. And it is perhaps most evident in the social infrastructures and solidarity efforts that have coalesced around the fight at Standing Rock. (6)

The transnational analytical framework adopted here serves to remind us that the targeting of Native lands and resources is never an isolated event but part of a structural worldview that sees Native lands and peoples as usable, replaceable, and destroyable and thus undeserving of basic rights, such as the right to clean drinking water and other resources. Bringing our attention to the situated contexts in which colonial oppression becomes articulated and resisted, a focus on the transnational iterations and intersectional manifestations and consequences of the pipeline and of other forms of environmental destruction for the purpose of corporate profit shows the importance of political solidarity centered on environmental justice, which is understood and practiced to be part and parcel of resistance to intertwined forms of racism and settler colonialism (Mays 2016).

The complexities of solidarity as a theory and praxis have been explored by various scholars from several fields who have discussed the problems with the term *solidarity* itself and have reflected on ethical and meaningful forms of solidarity. Scholars on the left have grappled with the term, excavating its genealogies—both past and present. This includes the works of feminist scholars and activists and, in the academy, the work of transnational feminists of color, such as Chandra Talpade Mohanty (2003) and Sara Ahmed (2000), who have theorized the politics of solidarity and the work of making "common ground" without presuming sameness and without reconciling or overlooking differences. Some recent and important efforts can also be seen in the work of Markus Kip in his entry on solidarity in the edited collection *Keywords for Radicals: The Contested Vocabulary of Late-Capitalist Struggle* (2016), where Kip troubles the uptake of the term *solidarity* as "self-evident," exploring that an analysis of the term can help us better understand "how current expressions and longings for solidarity could be strategically related for radical transformation" (392). David Roedinger, in his keynote address to the American Studies Association in 2015 and later in a much needed intervention on the history of solidarity and its turns in American studies, called "for more scholarly consideration of solidarity but also for more sober and uneasy reflection on the difficulties of thinking through its promises and difficulties" (2016, 224), noting that in spite of its circulation *solidarity* remains a "surprisingly neglected" term in cultural studies that ought to be historicized. In their response to David Roediger's essay, Glen Coulthard and Leanne Betasamosake Simpson urge us to ensure that in our solidarity work and theorizations "we are not standing on the backs of Indigenous peoples but instead engaged as related comrades joined in critical co-resistance against the convergence of forces that divide and conquer us and the Earth on which we depend" (2016, 250).

Extending these engagements to the transnational, in his work *Inter/Nationalism: Decolonizing Native America and Palestine* (2016), the scholar and activist Steven Salaita formulates a theory and praxis for decolonization that are founded on the recognition of the relations and connections between struggles for justice in a number of geopolitical and historical sites. Salaita's work engages the radical activist and scholarly politics that animate mutual liberatory struggles from North America to Palestine in a way that is highly attuned to the "practices and possibilities of decolonization" (7). Salaita develops a methodology of critique that moves beyond a comparative approach to Native struggles against imbricated forms of settler colonialism. As he writes, "More than anything, [inter/nationalism] requires advocates of Palestine solidarity in the United States and Canada to divest themselves from the false promises of manifest destiny and turn their attention to extracting themselves from complicity, however tenuous it may seem, in forms of colonization they deplore when practiced by Israel. Doing so is not simply a matter of proclaiming support for Natives, but incorporating that support into material and intellectual action" (146). Salaita provides a deep and materially situated analysis invested in the pursuit of decolonial futures. For more than a decade and at a deep personal, intellectual, and material cost, Salaita's work has modeled for many Arabs and Palestinians and people of color in the United States and Canada what it means to think through imbricated dispossessions and the mutual liberation of Native and Palestinian peoples at the local, global, and the transnational levels.

Adopting a politics of solidarity attuned to the connections between struggles against different and interconnected forms of settler colonialism and racism, as articulated by Salaita and other scholars and activists, and in support of the campaign to stop the pipeline and in solidarity with Native people, Palestinian activists in Palestine and from across the United States and Canada have issued statements that iterate their support and respect for the NoDAPL mobilization efforts. From Gaza, Palestinian youth Israa Suliman penned an open letter in 2016 that accompanied a video titled *We Stand with Standing Rock* in which a Palestinian graffiti artist paints a picture of a Native woman with headgear, a drawing that is meant to symbolize, memorialize, and honor the Native people of Standing Rock. The one-minute video ends with several Palestinians stating their support for Native people and their struggles at Standing Rock: "We Stand with Standing Rock; we are not numbers," each of the video participants states.

Accompanying this video is Suliman's letter, which begins:

> Dear Native Americans,
>
> Although we are of different color, religion, culture and place, I have learned, as I read about the protests at Standing Rock, that we have much more in common than differences. When I read your history, I can see myself and my people reflected in yours. I feel in my core that your fight is my fight, and that I am not alone in the battle against injustice.

Drawing on the similarities between the struggles of Native people in the United States and those of Palestinians, Suliman's letter centers its analysis on the theft and destruction of natural resources in both settler-colonial contexts.

> Like you, we don't control our natural resources. Just as you were not consulted about the Dakota Access Pipeline that will traverse your land and contaminate your water supply if installed, we are not consulted by Israel, which wants to mine the gas supply in our harbor for its own use and monopolizes the water supply in the West Bank for the green lawns of its own residents—leaving Palestinians parched and dry. In Gaza, where I live, only 10 percent of our water supply is drinkable due to the conditions in which we must live. We too know that "water is life." (Suliman 2016)

Suliman's letter is based, in large part, on a recognition that Native solidarity does not rest only on assumed, romanticized, or metaphorical similarities between struggles and peoples. Instead, solidarity recognizes the *material conditions* of settler colonialism that structure, delimit, and make Native lives (and deaths) across national and transnational contexts.

Although Palestinians living in Palestine experience the ravages of settler coloniality in Palestine in ways that are distinct and separate from how Native peoples experience them in the United States and Canada, Suliman's letter is shaped by the well-documented history of water struggles of both Palestinians and Natives, who are prevented from access to clean water, running water, or safe water-pipe infrastructure in their own lands and territories through comparable and interconnected processes of settler colonialism that target Indigenous environments. In Gaza, according to the United Nations, 95 percent of the water to which Gaza residents have access is not safe to drink. In 2013, settler use of water in Palestine was six times higher than Palestinians' usage (Nieuwhof 2013). A United Nations Conference Trade and Development report warned in 2015 that the Gaza Strip could become "uninhabitable" by 2020 due to the Israeli government's destructive bombing campaigns and stifling blockade, which target Palestinian lands, peoples, and their resources. For both peoples, then, the phrase "water is life" is not an analogy or a metaphor.

This centering of environmental justice in mobilization efforts in support of Standing Rock is also readily apparent in the statements of solidarity and reflections from activists and scholars. From the United States, Palestinians and Palestinian Americans also responded to the Standing Rock Tribe's stand against environmental destruction by issuing statements that iterated support for Native rights and by sending caravans of Palestinian solidarity activists to the encampment itself. Writing on her reasons for joining Standing Rock Sioux to protest the Dakota Access Pipeline, Aida Najar explains how this resistance campaign brought together supporters from all across the world. Situating her own participation within a politics of solidarity and support premised on an opposition of settler colonialism and corporate greed, Najar writes: "My own caravan set out from California the 2nd week of September, preceding the Palestinian Youth Movement–USA Caravan that arrived soon after. As a contingent of Indigenous peoples in diaspora and recent settlers on Turtle Island, we attest that those standing at Standing Rock are standing for our present and future as well. We must in turn stand for each other against the present, future, and historical supremacies of erasure, the active legacy of settler-colonialism, and the viciousness of greed" (2016).

Najar's articulation showcases her commitment to exploring the intersections of struggles at the frontlines of Native resistance. At the encampment, Najar met various protectors and defenders of the land who unequivocally reminded her that solidarity between Natives and Palestinians is not only about similarities and convergences and that it is, in essence, about Native sovereignty and survival and all people's interdependence on water for life. Palestinian support of the NoDAPL campaign is striking because of its ability to draw on comparisons between the two sites of struggle without drawing attention *away* from the specificities and significance of the mobilization at Standing Rock and its insistence on environmental justice for all Native communities.

This powerful point is also made by the Palestinian activist-scholar Nada Elia, who in her observations about the campaign and the reasons why it matters writes that "these reasons are not 'about us,' they are not about the intersections of our struggles with those of the Standing Rock Sioux. . . . Standing Rock matters, even if we were not all impacted" (2016). By refusing to center Palestine in the solidarity campaigns with Standing Rock, Elia foregrounds a political form of solidarity that focuses on and analyzes Standing Rock and Native resistance without overlooking intersectionalities of joint struggle. This work helps promote a form of solidarity premised on a commitment to Native resistance and informed by what Clare Land describes as an "awareness of the politics of the basis for their involvement and their relationship to Indigenous struggles" (2015, 211). Understanding these struggles is not, however, immediate or automatic. It is an understanding that is not only shaped by the politics of location and place but also honed through the intention of learning, interrogating, and, ultimately, rejecting the logics of settler coloniality and seductive invitations to inclusion and belonging, as Elia demonstrates. While drawing on connections and similarities between Native and Palestinian movements, such an awareness necessitates that Native experience, interests, and leadership remain the focus and center of solidarity agendas and efforts and that Native priorities and concerns are constantly foregrounded in both our analyses and our praxis.

Extending this framework, and in addition to being physically present at the Standing Rock mobilization, the Palestinian Youth Movement–USA (PYM) chapter offered its unequivocal support for Standing Rock in a moving statement on September 7, 2016 that was widely circulated online and through social media forums:

> We, the Palestinian Youth Movement–United States Branch, stand in solidarity with Standing Rock Sioux, the Great Sioux Nation, and our other Native sisters, brothers, and siblings in the fight against the Dakota Access Pipeline (DAPL), which will span across four states, North Dakota, South Dakota, Iowa, and Illinois, and cross over the Missouri River. While supporters of the pipeline claim that the DAPL will benefit workers and communities alike with environmentalism as a focal point, both through job opportunities and increased availability of fuel and energy, we see that the DAPL is another opportunity to destroy Native environment and is an example of the continued invasion and violence upon Native land and against Native people. We condemn all forms of state violence against our First Nation siblings and denote that the undermining of their sovereignty and livelihood is a part of the continuing dialectic of settler-colonialism transnationally. . . .
>
> As Palestinians in the United States, we are exiled from our homeland while living as settlers upon Turtle Island. It is imperative that we demand recognition of the rights of Native nations and their people while building movements together with one another so that we can strengthen our collective call for justice. We call for an end of the Dakota Access Pipeline. We demand that the United States honor the treaties as the supreme law of the land and payment of governmental reparations.
>
> Water is life for all of us.
> Free the land.
> Free the people.
> Long live International Solidarity. (PYM 2016)

Drawing links between the struggles of Native peoples in Palestine and Native peoples on Turtle Island, the statement is informed by an understanding of settler colonialism not as an isolated "event" but as a "structure" that transgresses geographies of the local, connecting sites of struggles and injustice across space and time (Kauanui 2016; Wolfe 2006). The authors of the solidarity statement call for the recognition of the rights of Native peoples, while emphasizing the importance of building movements with one another and engaging collectively in conjoined political forms of solidarity. In this vision, the statement points out both the responsibility to honor Native sovereignty on its own terms and the simultaneous need to work together to set up and enact liberatory movements based on a transnational analytic and practical framework of support and engagement. In other words, PYM sets the recognition of Native sovereignty as a prerequisite for collective and transnational justice movements that are anchored in mutual struggle and international solidarity.

Importantly, the Palestine Youth Movement's statement makes clear its awareness that Palestinians, while exiled from their homes in Palestine, live in the United States as settlers and arrivants and thus as beneficiaries of the structures of dispossession, displacement, and destruction targeting the people they wish to be in solidarity with—however reluctantly or precariously they may live within the settler-colonial state. PYM's engagement with the concepts of settlers and arrivants showcases an awareness of the debates animating scholarship and activism on the position of non-Black people of color and their relationship to the process of settler colonialism in the United States and Canada, an awareness informed by an understanding of how the logics of anti-Arab and anti-Muslim racism intersect with the logics of anti-Native and anti-Black racism in the United States and their transnational articulations through imperial and militaristic projects outside of US borders.

In an article on the intricate and complicated ties between Indigenous struggles and futures from Turtle Island to Palestine, PYM general coordinator Nadya Raja Tannous and internal development coordinator Omar Zahzah note that "our identity as displaced Indigenous Palestinians is further complicated in the US by the fact that our forced itinerancy has driven us onto Turtle Island, where, as one among many variously racialized and repressed 'arrivant' communities (to use Chickasaw intellectual Jodi Byrd's phrase), our presence as non-Native people carries the weight of inherently reifying the settler hegemony of the colonial state if not critically engaged and challenged through meaningful joint struggle work" (2018, 47–48).

In this work, Tannous and Zahzah identify as "non-Native" arrivants who have been "driven" through "forced itinerancy" into settler colonialism in Canada and the United States. As these authors make clear, this places them as Palestinians in the specific position of having to directly engage and challenge settler colonialism so that they do not become participants in a process that normalizes violence on the Native peoples, lands, and resources. In other words, the position the authors stake here refuses a politics of "assumptive solidarity" or a solidarity that assumes sameness at the expense of difference or centers innocence while evading responsibility (Olwan 2015). In directly citing Jodi Byrd's work and her discussion of the arrivant/settler (Byrd 2011), Tannous and Zahzah make an important intervention in debates about the imbrication of non-Black people of color in the processes of settler colonialism (Lawrence and Dua 2005; Sharma and Wright 2008–9). In her writing, Byrd theorizes the "degrees to which indigenous people, settlers, and arrivants" have "functioned within and have resisted the historical project of the colonization of the 'New World'" (2011, xix). Byrd borrows the term *arrivant* from the African Caribbean poet Kaamau Brathwaite, exploring how the settler-colonial systems that constitute places such as the United States "have created internally contradictory quagmires where human rights, equal rights, recognitions are predicated on the very systems that propagate and maintain the dispossession of indigenous peoples for the common good of the world" (xix). Byrd's use of the term *arrivant* helps shed light on the powerful but also contradictory ways in which those of us who "arrive" in places such as the United States can become drawn and seduced into its liberal politics of recognition that are fundamentally premised on anti-Blackness and the erasures and dispossessions of Native peoples.

As Iyko Day notes in an essay that explores the links between indigeneity, anti-Blackness, and settler-colonial critique, "In a nation with such fraught contexts of forced migration, immigrant exclusion, relocation, and deportation, questions inevitably arise over whether non-Indigenous but racialized peoples—such as slaves, refugees, or the undocumented—are unequivocally 'settlers'" (2015, 105). PYM's statement does not bracket these complexities or engage in uncritical ways in discussions that contribute to the erasure of Native sovereignty or the perpetuation of the violent myth of "voluntary" arrival that erases the history of slavery and contributes to anti-Black racism. What is striking about Tannous and Zahzah's intervention outlined earlier—and by extension PYM's adoption of this rhetoric in its statements and in ongoing collaborative solidarity work with Native people—is its resolute unwillingness to stake for Palestinians a position of distance, innocence, or erasure in relation to settler coloniality and the founding violences of slavery and genocide.

In their work, PYM activists do not use their Palestinian identity to absolve themselves from the work of "International Solidarity" with Native people. Instead, it is precisely their identity as Palestinians and their "forced itineracies" in the United States that compel their activism against the uneven, contradictory, and violent circuits of war, empire, racism, and settler colonialism that structure their lives and the lives of the communities they seek to be in solidarity with. Their call to solidarity is neither ahistorical or overly celebratory; rather, it is a form of solidarity that is relational, premised on a critical approach to its practices and articulations—both in historical and contemporary forms. As such, the work of such groups helps set a new agenda for Arab American communities living in the United States, one that draws together an opposition to the logics of both slavery and genocide, compelling a form of solidarity that enacts what Noura Erakat and Marc Lamont Hill label as the need for "critical and nuanced analysis of contemporary Black–Palestinian solidarity politics" (2018). As Palestinian activists and scholars living in the settler-colonial state of the United States, they do this while simultaneously centering Native and Palestinian solidarities as forms of "solidarity as engaged praxis." (2019, 10).

Organized mainly by PYM, a transnational, independent, grassroots movement of young Palestinians in

Palestine and in exile worldwide as a result of the ongoing Israeli colonization and occupation of Palestine, activists joined a caravan from California to North Dakota in support of NoDAPL. There they witnessed and supported the campaign and Indigenous people's right to oppose the Dakota pipeline and assert their right to sovereignty, writing analogies of joint struggle into the very spaces where people rallied, camped, slept, and ate together. Commenting on what she witnessed at the encampment, activist Aida Najar wrote:

> At the end of one of the rows is the Palestinian flag. Seeing it filled me equally with joy and sadness because it confirmed two things. . . . [T]he first thought is that the power of collective resistance against greed and settler-colonialism is a mighty force. That thought was embodied by my joy to see a representation of will by the presently unseen Palestinian siblings who had come to take a stand against destructive powers. The second thought was embodied by sadness[,] for, if the struggle for protection of water, culture, land, heritage, and livelihood is truly mirrored in Standing Rock and Palestine, then the struggle ahead is both vast and uncompromising. (2016)

Najar would go on to articulate her reasons for going to Standing Rock, engaging the uncomfortable politics of being a Palestinian who lives on the stolen Indigenous lands of Indigenous people in a settler-colonial state.

> Why did I go in the first place? Because somewhere in the awkward power dynamic of being a US citizen, a non-native inhabitant of Turtle Island, and a Palestinian in the Diaspora, I saw the struggle for livelihood and culture, the struggle against settler-colonialism, the struggle to protect the sacred and maintain your own legitimacy, and the ever ominous force of erasure and historical amnesia. What I later saw at Standing Rock both embodied this and became bigger than it; as a Mohawk Elder said to me, without water, we [humans] are infertile dust. (2016)

What is at stake in such statements, utterances, and acts of solidarity? What do these moments of solidarity tell us about Native communities confronting settler colonialism across transnational borders and their struggles to work in solidarity with one another? What hopes do they offer about this nexus of ongoing and joint struggle? What might they reveal about the politics of solidarity between and among Native peoples? And how might we read such instances of solidarity in ways that, in the words of David Roediger, will "encourage an unease with the magic seemingly worked by such a word [as *solidarity*]" (2016, 225)? In responding to the calls by Indigenous scholars and activists in the United States and Canada, we are reminded that engaging in relational forms of solidarity—however consciously, ethically, or responsibly—will not exonerate us from responding to Indigenous calls for sovereignty and land protection and reclamation. Being in solidarity with Native people, as the example of Palestinian and Native solidarity at NoDAPL indicates, requires that we engage the complexities of genocide, racism, occupation, and colonialism in the settler-colonial states of Canada and the United States. Nadya Raja Tannous states, "As the dominant powers of the world maintain that our resistance as oppressed peoples and communities poses a greater threat to society than the immeasurable and all-encompassing violence of our oppressors, the partnership between Palestinians and Native Americans is neither surprising nor random. However, it does necessitate the question of how to best advocate and partner for collective liberation" (2016).

Keeping in mind Tannous's statement leads us to see that theorizing settler-colonial links across disparate but interconnected geographies of settler violence is critically needed, but it must be done as a process *with*—rather than *for*—others who are engaged in potentially mutual but possibly incommensurate liberation struggles (Byrd 2011). Here it is useful to heed the words of Harsha Walia, who reminds us that decolonial work requires "cultivating an ethic of responsibility within the Indigenous solidarity movement [which] begins with non-natives understanding ourselves as beneficiaries of the illegal settlement of Indigenous peoples' land and unjust appropriation of Indigenous peoples' resources and jurisdiction" (2012). Walia urges activists to move beyond a politics of solidarity toward the praxis of decolonization, which, in her analysis, is always moored to the interrogation of positionality and the rooting of ourselves in cultural kinships and economic systems that "serve[] rather than threaten[] our collective life on this planet" (2012). Similarly, Steven Salaita states that "solidarity is performed in the interest of better human relationships and for a world that allows societies to be organized around justice rather than profit. It happens across the communities with whom we are in contact—on behalf of the many we have never met" (2016, xix).

In the case of Palestinians living in the United States and Canada, this work may often involve recognizing and confronting our own complicated positionalities as migrants who live on occupied Indigenous lands and who have, at times, been invited, seduced, and sometimes even reluctantly and precariously incorporated into the settler-colonial states of the United States and Canada. As Nada Elia states, such recognition and confrontation would necessitate that we "understand that our own liberation is incomplete, without the liberation of the Indigenous people who view us as their relatives. Together, we can model and enact accountability, as we redefine indigenous sovereignty and self-determination, against white supremacy and Zionism" (2018). Palestinians' efforts to support the NoDAPL campaign offer Palestinian scholars and activists who are situated on Native lands in settler-colonial states hopeful signposts for responsible, ethical, and mutual forms of solidarity that are historically situated, materially grounded, and politically conscious. By stating Palestinians' collusions with and contestations of both settlement and coloniality as well as our differential and complicated roles in these systems and processes, these movements model forms of solidarity that are not premised on innocence, evasion, or denial. These movements are rooted in environmental justice and challenge corporate and settler-colonial attacks on Native lands and resources, recognizing the imbrications within longer and transnational trajectories of genocide, racism, and violence. Conjoined in an ongoing struggle around Native sovereignty and just environmental futures as well as in the battle against the interconnected logics of slavery and racism that sustain settler coloniality in its local and transnational formations, these movements are built on relational understandings of one another's past and current dreams and desires—ones that simultaneously recognize the potential mutualities and various incommensurabilities of struggles for justice against settler-colonial states and their divisive powers.

Works Cited

Ahmed, Sarah. 2000. *Strange Encounters: Embodied Others in Post-coloniality.* New York: Routledge.

Bhandar, Brenna, and Rafeef Ziadeh. 2016. "Acts and Omissions: Framing Settler Colonialism in Palestine Studies." *Jadaliyya*, Jan. 14. At http://www.jadaliyya.com/Details/32857.

Byrd, Jodi A. 2011. *The Transit of Empire: Indigenous Critiques of Colonialism.* Minneapolis: Univ. of Minnesota Press.

Coulthard, Glen, and Leanne Betasamosake Simpson. 2016. "Grounded Normativity / Place-Based Solidarity." *American Quarterly* 68, no. 2 (June): 249–55.

Dakota Access Pipeline. 2016. "Dakota Access: Pipeline Facts." At https://daplpipelinefacts.com/.

Day, Iyko. 2015. "Being or Nothingness: Indigeneity, Antiblackness, and Settler Colonial Critique." *Critical Ethnic Studies* 1, no. 2 (Fall): 102–21.

Elia, Nada. 2016. "Why Standing Rock Matters." *Mondoweiss*, Oct. 31. At https://mondoweiss.net/2016/10/standing-rock-matters/.

Erakat, Noura, and Marc Lamont Hill. 2018. "From Palestine to Turtle Island: Musings on Border Crossings." *Mondoweiss*, Apr. 2. At https://mondoweiss.net/2018/04/palestine-musings-crossings/.

———. 2019. "Black–Palestinian Transnational Solidarity: Renewals, Returns, and Practice." *Journal of Palestine Studies* 48, no. 4 (Summer): 7–16.

Estes, Nick. 2016. "Fighting for Our Lives: #NoDAPL in Historical Context." *Red Nation*, Sept. 18. At https://therednation.org/2016/09/18/fighting-for-our-lives-nodapl-in-context/.

———. 2017. "Fighting for Our lives: #NODAPL in Historical Context." *Wicazo Sa Review* 32, no. 2 (Fall): 115–22.

Fragoso, Alejandro Davila. 2016. "Dakota Access Protesters Say They Were Held in 'Dog Kennels' Following Mass Arrests." *Think Progress*, Oct. 31. At https://thinkprogress.org/dakota-access-activists-say-they-were-kept-in-dog-kennels-after-mass-arrests-1a38b63ea7d4/.

Kauanui, J. Kēhaulani. 2016. "'A Structure, Not an Event': Settler Colonialism and Enduring Indigeneity." *Lateral* 5, no. 1 (Spring). At https://doi.org/10.25158/l5.1.7.

Kip, Markus. 2016. "Solidarity." In *Keywords for Radicals: The Contested Vocabulary of Late-Capitalist Struggle*, edited by Kelly Fritsch, Clare O'Connor, and Ak Thompson, 391–98. Oakland, CA: AK Press.

Knight, Nika. 2016. "Dakota Access Pipeline Permit Denied." *Common Dreams*, Dec. 4. At https://www.commondreams.org/news/2016/12/04/dakota-access-pipeline-permit-denied.

Krebs, Mike, and Dana M. Olwan. 2012. "'From Jerusalem to the Grand River, Our Struggles Are One': Challenging Canadian and Israeli Settler Colonialism." *Journal of Settler and Colonial Studies* 2, no. 2: 138–64.

Land, Clare. 2015. *Decolonizing Solidarity: Dilemmas and Directions for Supporters of Indigenous Struggles*. London: Zed Books.

Lawrence, Bonita, and Enakshi Dua. 2005. "Decolonizing Antiracism." *Social Justice* 32, no. 4: 120–43.

Levin, Sam. 2016. "Dakota Access Pipeline: The Who, What, and Why of Standing Rock Protests." *Guardian*, Nov. 3. At https://www.theguardian.com/us-news/2016/nov/03/north-dakota-access-oil-pipeline-protests-explainer.

Mays, Kyle T. 2016. "From Flint to Standing Rock: The Aligned Struggles of Black and Indigenous People." Hot Spots, Society for Cultural Anthropology website, Dec. 22. At https://culanth.org/fieldsights/from-flint-to-standing-rock-the-aligned-struggles-of-black-and-indigenous-people.

Mazer, Katie, and Martin Danilyuk. 2017. *Mapping a Many Headed Hydra: The Struggle over the Dakota Access Pipeline*. Infrastructure Otherwise Report 001. At http://infrastructureotherwise.org/DAPL_Report_20170921_FINAL.pdf.

Meyer, Robinson. 2016. "The Obama Administration Temporarily Blocks the Dakota Access Pipeline." *Atlantic*, Sept. 9. At https://www.theatlantic.com/science/archive/2016/09/the-obama-administration-temporarily-blocks-the-dakota-access-pipeline/499454/.

Mohanty, Chandra Talpade. 2003. "'Under Western Eyes' Revisited: Feminist Solidarity through Anticapitalist Struggles." *Signs* 28, no. 2: 499–535.

Najar, Aida. 2016. "Palestinians Join Standing Rock Sioux to Protest Dakota Access Pipeline." *Mondoweiss*, Oct. 24. At https://mondoweiss.net/2016/10/palestinians-standing-pipeline/.

Nieuwhof, Adri. 2013. "Israeli Settlers Use Six Times More Water Than Palestinians—New Report." *Electronic Intifada*, Apr. 8. At https://electronicintifada.net/blogs/adri-nieuwhof/israeli-settlers-use-six-times-more-water-palestinians-new-report.

Olwan, Dana M. 2015. "On Assumptive Solidarities in Comparative Settler Colonialisms." *Feral Feminisms* 4 (Summer): 89–102.

Palestinian Youth Movement–USA (PYM). 2016. "PYM-USA Stands with Standing Rock. No to the Dakota Access Pipeline." Sept. 7. At https://www.pymusa.com/pym-usa-stands-with-standing-rock/.

Roediger, David. 2016. "Making Solidarity Uneasy: Cautions on a Keyword from Black Lives Matter to the Past." *American Quarterly* 68, no. 2 (June): 223–48.

Salaita, Steven. 2016. *Inter/Nationalism: Decolonizing Native America and Palestine*. Minnesota: Univ. of Minnesota Press.

Sharma, Nanditha, and Cynthia Wright. 2008–9. "Decolonizing Resistance, Challenging Colonial States." *Social Justice* 35, no. 3: 120–38.

Steinman, Erich. 2018. "Why Was Standing Rock and the #NoDAPL Campaign so Historic? Factors Affecting American Indian Participation in Social Movement Collaborations and Coalitions." *Ethnic and Racial Studies* 2018:1–21.

Suliman, Israa. 2016. "A Letter from Gaza to the Natives of Standing Rock." We Are Not Numbers, Nov. 15. At https://wearenotnumbers.org/home/Story/Gaza_stands_with_Standing_Rock.

Tannous, Nadya Raja. 2016. "How the Fight for Water Unites Palestine and Dakota." *Telesur English*, Nov. 24. At https://www.telesurenglish.net/opinion/How-the-Fight-for-Water-Unites-Palestine-and-Dakota-20161122-0039.html.

Tannous, Nadya Raja, and Omar Zahzah. 2018. "The Scarred Land: Settler Imprints and Indigenous Futures." *Funambulist* 20 (Nov.–Dec.): 46–49.

Tuck, Eve, and K. Wayne Yang. 2012. "Decolonization Is Not a Metaphor." *Decolonization: Indigeneity, Education, & Society* 1, no. 1: 1–40.

United Nations Conference on Trade and Development. 2015. "Gaza Could Become Uninhabitable in Less Than Five Years in Wake of 2014 Conflict and Ongoing De-development, according to New UNCTAD Report." Sept. 1. At https://unctad.org/en/Pages/PressRelease.aspx?OriginalVersionID=260.

United Nations Human Rights Office of the High Commissioner. 2016. "Native Americans Facing Excessive Force in North Dakota Pipeline Protests—UN Expert." Nov. 15.

At https://www.ohchr.org/EN/NewsEvents/Pages/DisplayNews.aspx?NewsID=20868&LangID=E.

Walia, Harsha. 2012. "Decolonizing Together: Moving beyond a Politics of Solidarity toward a Practice of Decolonization." *Briarpatch*, Jan. 1. At https://briarpatchmagazine.com/articles/view/decolonizing-together.

Wolfe, Patrick. 2006. "Settler Colonialism and the Elimination of the Native." *Journal of Genocide Research* 8, no. 4: 387–409.

Wright, Robin. 2017. "Donald Trump, Pirate-in-Chief." *New Yorker*, Jan. 20. At https://www.newyorker.com/news/news-desk/donald-trump-pirate-in-chief.

Contributors

Index

Contributors

Su'ad Abdul Khabeer is a scholar-artist-activist and senior editor at sapelosquare.com. She is the author of *Muslim Cool: Race, Religion, and Hip Hop in the United States* and curator of *Umi's Archive*, an interdisciplinary research project that critically engages everyday Black women as people who know things we all need to know. She is currently associate professor of American culture and Arab and Muslim American studies at the University of Michigan.

Hisham D. Aidi is senior lecturer at Columbia University's School of International and Public Affairs. He is the author of *Redeploying the State* (2008), a comparative study of market reform and labor movements in Latin America; coeditor, with Manning Marable, of *Black Routes to Islam* (2009); and author of *Rebel Music: Race, Empire, and the New Muslim Youth Culture* (2014). His work as a cultural reporter has appeared in the *Atlantic*, the *Nation*, and the *New Yorker*. Aidi is the recipient of the Carnegie Scholar Award (2008), the American Book Award (2015), and the Hip Hop Scholar Award (2015). He is currently a scholar-in-residence at the Schomburg Center for Research in Black Culture, working on a project titled "W. E. B. Du Bois and the Afro-Arab World." His most recent documentary short is titled *Malcolm X and the Sudanese*.

Evelyn Alsultany is associate professor in the Department of American Studies and Ethnicity at the University of Southern California. Prior to her appointment at USC, she taught at the University of Michigan for thirteen years, where she cofounded and served as the director of the Arab and Muslim American Studies Program within the Department of American Culture. She is the author of *Arabs and Muslims in the Media: Race and Representation after 9/11* (2012). She is coeditor of two volumes: *Arab & Arab American Feminisms: Gender, Violence, & Belonging* (Syracuse University Press, 2011), winner of the Arab American National Museum's Evelyn Shakir Non-Fiction Award, and *Between the Middle East and the Americas: The Cultural Politics of Diaspora* (2013). She served as the guest curator for the Arab American National Museum's online exhibit *Reclaiming Identity: Dismantling Arab Stereotypes*, which can be viewed at www.arabstereotypes.org. For more information on Alsultany, see http://evelynalsultany.com/.

Moustafa Bayoumi is the author of *How Does It Feel to Be a Problem? Being Young and Arab in America* (2009), which won an American Book Award and the Arab American Book Award for Non-Fiction, and of *This Muslim American Life: Dispatches from the War on Terror* (2015), which was chosen as a Best Book of 2015 by *Progressive Magazine* and awarded the Arab American Book Award for Non-Fiction. A regular contributor to the *Guardian*, Bayoumi has also written for the *New York Times*, *New York*, the *Nation*, CNN.com, the *London Review of Books*, the *Chronicle of Higher Education*, and many other periodicals. He is also the editor of *Midnight on the Mavi Marmara* (2010) and the coeditor (with Andrew Rubin) of *The Selected Works of Edward W. Said: 1966–2006* ([2000] 2019). Bayoumi is professor of English at Brooklyn College, City University of New York.

Jacob Rama Berman is an associate professor of English at Louisiana State University who specializes in the intersections of American literature and Islamic, Arab, and Arab American culture. His first book, *American Arabesque: Arabs and Islam in the Nineteenth Century Imaginary* (2012), deploys English- and Arabic-language source material to analyze the influence of Arab and Islamic references on the formation of American national identity. His current project, "Neither Here nor There: War on Terror's Other Fictions," focuses on the representation of trauma in fiction written in both English and Arabic about the war on terror. Through categories such as "cannibal democracy," "zombie citizenship," and "PTSD poetics" he locates a literary lingua franca that disrupts the either/or political rhetoric of the war on terror and reconfigures national narratives through international contexts. Dr. Berman has published scholarly articles on the Arab American *mahjar*,

Edgar Allan Poe, shipwreck narratives, and the Middle Eastern gothic. He also writes for the *Los Angeles Review of Books* and recently contributed an essay to the Denver Art Museum's catalog for the upcoming show *Near East to the Far West: French Orientalism and the American Frontier.* He currently lives with his wife and daughter in the Crescent City, New Orleans.

Umayyah Cable is assistant professor in the Departments of American Culture and Film, Television, and Media at the University of Michigan, Ann Arbor. Their research has been supported by a Mellon Postdoctoral Fellowship at Northwestern University and a Faculty Fellowship at the Charles Warren Center for Studies in American History at Harvard University. Their work has been published in journals such as *GLQ: A Journal of Lesbian and Gay Studies* as well as in the edited volume *Arab American Women: Representation and Refusal* (Syracuse University Press, 2021). They are currently completing a book manuscript on the history of Arab American media activism in the mobilization of Palestine solidarity politics in the United States.

Louise Cainkar is professor of sociology and social welfare and justice at Marquette University in Milwaukee, where she also directs the major in peace studies and the minor in Arab and Muslim American studies. She has published widely on Arab Americans and Muslim Americans in scholarly journals and books as well as in public scholarship. She is coeditor with Suad Joseph and Michael Suleiman of *Arab American Women: Representation and Refusal* (Syracuse University Press, 2021). Her book *Homeland Insecurity: The Arab American and Muslim American Experience after 9/11* (2009) was honored as Outstanding Adult Non-Fiction by the Arab American National Museum. She is a past president of the Arab American Studies Association and a current board member of the Association for Middle East Women's Studies. Cainkar has served on the editorial boards of a number of scholarly journals as well as on committees of the Middle East Studies Association and American Sociological Association. In 2021, she won Marquette University's Community Engaged Teaching Award.

Madeline Otis Campbell is associate dean of distance and global education at Worcester State University. A cultural anthropologist, Campbell specializes in Middle East refugee migration in urban contexts. Her award-winning book *Interpreters of Occupation: Gender and the Politics of Belonging in an Iraqi Refugee Network* was published in 2016 (Syracuse University Press). A forthcoming book, *Mobile Frontiers: Syrian Refugees Navigate Displacement*, is expected soon. She has published widely in scholarly journals and news outlets on the topics of Iraqi and Syrian refugee migration. Prior to joining the faculty at Worcester State University, Campbell worked in the field of refugee resettlement.

Christina Civantos is a professor in the Department of Modern Languages and Literatures at the University of Miami. She holds a PhD in comparative literature from the University of California at Berkeley and specializes in modern Hispanic and Arabic literary and cultural studies, with a focus on Arab immigrants and their descendants in Hispano-America and Spain, South–South relations between Latin America and the Arab world, empire and postcolonial studies, nationalisms, language ideologies, memory studies, and tolerance. Her publications include numerous articles and the books *Between Argentines and Arabs: Argentine Orientalism, Arab Immigrants, and the Writing of Identity* (2006), *The Afterlife of al-Andalus: Muslim Iberia in Contemporary Arab and Hispanic Narratives* (2017), and Jamón *and* Halal: *Lessons in Tolerance from Rural Andalucía* (2022).

Carol W. N. Fadda is associate professor of English at Syracuse University, where she teaches courses on critical race and ethnic studies, transnational and diasporic studies, and Arab American studies. She is a recipient of a National Endowment for the Humanities summer grant, a Future of Minority Studies Fellowship, and a Syracuse University Humanities Center faculty fellowship, and her essays on gender, race, ethnicity, war trauma, and transnational citizenship have appeared in a variety of journals and edited collections. She is the author of *Contemporary Arab-American Literature: Transnational Reconfigurations of Citizenship and Belonging* (2014), and her current book project is titled "Carceral States and Dissident Citizenships: Narratives of Resistance in an Age of 'Terror.'" She serves as the editor of the Critical Arab American Studies Book series published by Syracuse University Press.

Keith P. Feldman is associate professor of ethnic studies at the University of California, Berkeley. An interdisciplinary cultural studies scholar, he examines the interface between race, knowledge, and imperial cultures, with a focus on the United States, the so-called Middle East, and North Africa. Feldman is the author of *A Shadow over Palestine: The Imperial Life of Race in America* (2015), which was named Best Book in Humanities and Cultural Studies by the Association for Asian American Studies and was a Finalist for the Romero Best First

Book Prize in American Studies. Feldman is also the coeditor of *#identity: Hashtagging Race, Gender, Sexuality, and Nation* (2019), coeditor of a special issue of *Social Text* titled "Race/Religion/War," and the editor of the forum "Blackness and Relationality" for the journal *Comparative Literature.*

Sarah M. A. Gualtieri is the author of *Between Arab and White: Race and Ethnicity in the Early Syrian American Diaspora* (2009) and *Arab Routes: Pathways to Syrian California* (2019, which won the Arab American National Museum's Evelyn Shakir Non-Fiction Award. She is an historian who specializes in Arab America, racial formation, and archival theory and praxis. Gualtieri is professor in the Department of American Studies and Ethnicity at the University of Southern California, where she teaches courses on Middle Eastern feminisms, modern Arab revolutions, and the cultures of diaspora. She is also the adviser to graduate students in critical Middle Eastern American studies. She holds an Honors BA in history from McGill University, an MA in Middle East studies, and PhD in Middle East history from the University of Chicago.

Danielle Haque is associate professor of English at Minnesota State University at Mankato. She is the author of *Interrogating Secularism: Race and Religion in Arab Transnational Art and Literature* (Syracuse University Press, 2019).

Michelle Hartman is professor of Arabic literature and director of the Institute of Islamic Studies at McGill University as well as a literary translator of Arabic fiction into English. Her most recent book, *Breaking Broken English: Black Arab Solidarities and the Politics of Language* (Syracuse University Press, 2019) won the College Language Association prize in 2019 for creative scholarship. She has published work in critical Arab American studies in *MELUS*, the *Journal of Critical Race Inquiry*, the *College Language Association Journal*, and elsewhere.

Waïl S. Hassan is a professor in the Program in Comparative and World Literature and the Department of English at the University of Illinois at Urbana–Champaign. A specialist in modern Arabic literature and intellectual history, he is the author of *Tayeb Salih: Ideology and the Craft of Fiction* (2003) and *Immigrant Narratives: Orientalism and Cultural Translation in Arab American and Arab British Literature* (2011). He has translated Abdelfattah Kilito's *Thou Shalt Not Speak My Language* (2008) from Arabic into English and Alberto Mussa's *Lughz al-qāf* (2015) from Portuguese into Arabic. He has edited several books and special issues, including *Approaches to Teaching the Works of Naguib Mahfouz* (2012, with Susan Muaddi Darraj), *The Oxford Handbook of the Arab Novelistic Traditions* (2017), and *Literatura e (i)migração no Brasil* (2020, with Rogério Lima), and is currently writing a book on Brazilian literature. He is a past president of the American Comparative Literature Association.

Pauline Homsi Vinson teaches in the English Department at Diablo Valley College. Her publications and scholarly interests include translations from Arabic to English and scholarly articles on literary migrations, gender, race, and representation in Arab American literature, Shakespeare, and *The Thousand and One Nights*. She has taught in the United States, Malaysia, and the United Arab Emirates and is cofounder of the Arab American Studies Association and the Modern Language Association's forum on Global Arab and Arab American Literature. She is coeditor of special issues on Arab American studies in publications such as *Amerasia*, *Mashriq & Mahjar*, and *The Encyclopedia of Women and Islamic Cultures*. Homsi Vinson holds an honors BA in English from the University of California at Berkeley, an MA from the University of California at Santa Barbara, and a PhD from Northwestern University. Her current project explores the subversive potential of storytelling in Arab American reconfigurations of *The Thousand and One Nights*.

Sally Howell is associate professor of history at the University of Michigan–Dearborn, and director of the Center for Arab American Studies. She is a coeditor of *Citizenship and Crisis: Arab Detroit after 9/11* (2009) and *Arab Detroit 9/11: Life in the Terror Decade* (2011) and is the author of *Old Islam in Detroit: Rediscovering the Muslim American Past* (2014), which received the 2015 Arab American Book Award from the Arab American National Museum. Howell is currently curating *Halal Metropolis*, a research and public-arts project exploring the politics and aesthetics of Muslim visibility in Detroit.

Amira Jarmakani is professor of women's, gender, and sexuality studies and affiliated faculty with the Center for Islamic and Arabic Studies at San Diego State University. Her most recent book, *An Imperialist Love Story: Desert Romances and the War on Terror* (2015), explores the crucial role of desire in understanding how the war on terror works and how it perseveres. She is also the author of *Imagining Arab Womanhood: The Cultural Mythology of Veils, Harems, and Belly Dancers in the U.S.* (2008), which won the National Women's Studies

Association Gloria E. Anzaldúa Book Prize. She is past president of the Arab American Studies Association and an adviser for the Critical Arab American Studies series published by Syracuse University Press. She is a past assistant editor for *The Encyclopedia of Women and Islamic Cultures.*

Joe Kadi lives in the territories of the people of the Treaty 7 region in southern Alberta, which includes the Blackfoot Confederacy (comprising the Siksika, Piikani, and Kainai First Nations), the Tsuut'ina First Nation, and the Stoney Nakoda (including the Chiniki, Bearspaw, and Wesley First Nations). The City of Calgary is also home to Métis Nation of Alberta, Region III. A disabled trans man, he is part of the SWANA community and writes regularly for *Mizna: A Journal for Arab Americans.* He teaches in the Gender and Sexuality Studies Program of the University of Calgary.

John Tofik Karam is director of the Lemann Center for Brazilian Studies and professor in the Department of Spanish and Portuguese at the University of Illinois, Urbana–Champaign. His first book, *Another Arabesque: Syrian–Lebanese Ethnicity in Neoliberal Brazil* (2007), won awards from the Arab American National Museum and the Brazilian Studies Association and has been translated into both Arabic and Portuguese. His latest book is *Manifold Destiny: Arabs at an American Crossroads of Exceptional Rule* (2021). Supported in part by the National Endowment of the Humanities, this work casts Muslim Lebanese, Palestinians, and Syrians as circumstantial protagonists of a hemispheric saga. At the border where Brazil, Paraguay, and Argentina meet, Arabs animate and abide in a hemisphere where the United States once purportedly possessed a "manifest destiny." Their many folds or ways of accommodating states that suspend laws and norms by fiat reveal a hemispheric history of exceptional rule.

Charlotte Karem is an assistant professor of American culture and women's studies at the University of Michigan, Ann Arbor, where she is also a faculty member for the Arab and Muslim American Studies Program and affiliated faculty for the Center for Middle Eastern and North African Studies. Her research interests include Arab American history, sexuality, gender, and interdisciplinary historicist methods. Her current book manuscript proposes that sexuality is at the root of Arab American racialization. She holds a PhD in feminist studies from the University of Minnesota. Her work has been published in *Arab Studies Quarterly, Gender & History,* and the *Journal of American Ethnic History.*

Robin D. G. Kelley is the Gary B. Nash Endowed Chair in US History at the University of California, Los Angeles. His books include *Africa Speaks, America Answers: Modern Jazz in Revolutionary Times* (2012); *Freedom Dreams: The Black Radical Imagination* (2002); *Race Rebels: Culture Politics and the Black Working Class* (1994); *Yo' Mama's DisFunktional! Fighting the Culture Wars in Urban America* (1997); and *Hammer and Hoe: Alabama Communists during the Great Depression* (1990). He has written broadly on Black–Palestinian solidarity, boycott/divestment/sanctions and cultural boycott, and the history of Black movements and Zionism. His essays on Palestine have appeared in *Mondoweiss, Counterpunch, Social Text, Boston Review,* and *Journal of Palestine Studies* as well as in the anthologies *Apartheid Israel: The Politics of an Analogy* (2015), *Letters to Palestine: Writers Respond to War and Occupation* (2015), and *With Stones in Our Hands: Reflections on Racism, Muslims, and U.S. Empire* (2018).

Suraya Khan is assistant professor of history at San Antonio College. She received her PhD in US and Middle Eastern history at Rice University in 2018. Her research investigates the ways in which the issue of Palestine nurtured a spectrum of Arab American identities from the 1930s to the 1980s. By tracing Arab American activism for Palestine on regional, national, and transnational scales, her work explores the intersections between politics and migrant identities.

Akram Fouad Khater is University Faculty Scholar and professor of history and holds the Khayrallah Chair in Diaspora Studies at North Carolina State University, where he also serves as the director of the Khayrallah Center for Lebanese Diaspora Studies. His books include *Inventing Home: Emigration, Gender and the Making of a Lebanese Middle Class, 1770–1920* (new ed., 2001), *A History of the Middle East: A Sourcebook for the History of the Middle East and North Africa* (1991), and *Embracing the Divine: Passion and Politics in the Christian Middle East* (2011). He has produced several documentaries, including *Cedars in the Pines* (2015) and *The Romey Lynchings* (2020). He has curated several exhibits on early Arab American history, including *The Lebanese in America* (2018) and *Turath: An Exhibition of Early Arab American Culture* (2021). He is past editor of the *International Journal of Middle East Studies* and current coeditor of *Mashriq & Mahjar: Journal of Middle East and North African Migrations.*

Erik Love is the author of *Islamophobia and Racism in America* (2017). He is associate professor and chair of sociology at Dickinson College in Pennsylvania, where he also previously served as chair of Middle East studies. His research on civil rights advocacy has been published in various academic journals and presented at conferences around the world. His work has been supported by the National Science Foundation and the James Weldon Johnson Institute for the Study of Race and Difference.

Sunaina Maira is professor of Asian American studies at the University of California, Davis, and was a Mellon/ACLS Scholars and Society Fellow in 2019–20. Her new research project focuses on Arab refugees and immigrants, in particular Yemeni Americans, and the impact of the pandemic, the Muslim Ban, and the war in Yemen on Yemeni corner store owners in Oakland, California. She is the author of five monographs, including *The 9/11 Generation: Youth, Rights, and Solidarity in the War on Terror* (2016) and *Boycott! The Academy and Justice for Palestine* (2018). She also published a book based on ethnographic research in Palestine, *Jil Oslo: Palestinian Hip Hop, Youth Culture, and the Youth Movement* (2013). Maira launched a new section on West Asian American studies in the Association for Asian American Studies and coedited a special issue on Asian/Arab American studies for the *Journal of Asian American Studies*.

Lisa Suhair Majaj is a scholar of Arab American literature as well as a creative writer and freelance editor. She earned her PhD in American culture from the University of Michigan. In addition to publishing critical articles on Arab American topics, she has coedited three collections of essays on international women writers: *Going Global: The Transnational Reception of Third World Women Writers* (2000), *Etel Adnan: Critical Essays on the Arab-American Writer and Artist* (2002), and *Intersections: Gender, Nation, and Community in Arab Women's Novels* (2002). Her poetry volume *Geographies of Light* (2009) won the Del Sol Press Poetry Prize. She has taught and lectured at various institutions, and her creative writing has been translated into Arabic, Greek, Hebrew, Mayalam, and Indonesian. She has also written two children's books. Her poetry was used in the photography exhibition *Aftermath: The Fallout of War—America & the Middle East* at the Harn Museum of Art, University of Florida, in 2016. She lives in Nicosia, Cyprus.

Jennifer Mogannam is a University of California President's Postdoctoral Fellow in the Department of Anthropology and the Department of Gender, Sexuality, and Women's Studies at the University of California, Davis. Her research examines twentieth and twenty-first century Palestinian and Arab transnational movements and Third World solidarities, with an eye to analyzing movement praxis for liberated futures. She earned her PhD in ethnic studies at the University of California, San Diego, and is a longtime organizer in transnational Palestinian movements.

Nadine Naber is professor in the Gender and Women's Studies Program and the Global Asian Studies Program at the University of Illinois (UIC) at Chicago. Dr. Naber came to UIC from the University of Michigan, Ann Arbor, where she cofounded Arab and Muslim American studies. At UIC, she is the faculty founder of the Arab American Cultural Center. Dr. Naber is author of *Arab America: Gender, Cultural Politics, and Activism* (2012). She is coeditor of the books *Race and Arab Americans before and after 9/11* (Syracuse University Press, 2008); *Arab & Arab American Feminisms* (Syracuse University Press, 2010), winner of the Arab American Book Award 2012; and *The Color of Violence* (2006). Dr. Naber is a board member of the *Critical Ethnic Studies Journal*, the *Journal of Palestine Studies*, and *al-Shabakah*. She has served as an international fellow with the Open Society Foundation, an expert author for the United Nations Economic and Social Commission for Western Asia, and a board member of the Arab American Action Network. Dr. Naber is founder of the Liberate Your Research Workshops and cofounder of the organization Mamas Activating Movements for Abolition and Solidarity (MAMAS).

Alixa Naff is an oral historian who was key to the foundation of Arab American studies in the academy. During the summer of 1962, Naff drove across the United States and eastern Canada, conducting interviews with and collecting artifacts, newspapers, and pictures from as many members of the first wave of Arabic-speaking immigrants to North America as she could find. Her work documenting the lives of these immigrants continued, culminating in her book *Becoming American: The Early Arab Immigrant Experience* (1985), based on hundreds of such interviews. She established the Faris and Yamna Naff Arab American Collection at the Smithsonian Institution in Washington, DC, to preserve this history and to encourage ongoing research in the field of Arab American studies. The Arab American National Museum in Dearborn, Michigan, digitized her oral history interviews after her death on June 1, 2013, to honor her and to make them more accessible.

Michael Malek Najjar is associate professor in the Department of Theater Arts at the University of Oregon. He holds a PhD in theater and performance studies from the University of California, Los Angeles, and an MFA in directing from York University. He is an associate member of the Stage Directors and Choreographers Society and an alumnus of the British/American Drama Academy, Lincoln Center Directors Lab, Directors Lab West, and RAWI Screenwriters' Lab (in Jordan). He is the author of *Middle Eastern American Theatre: Communities, Cultures, and Creators* (2021) and *Arab American Drama, Film, and Performance: A Critical Study, 1908 to the Present* (2015). He has edited *Heather Raffo's Iraq Plays: The Things That Can't Be Said* (2021), *The Selected Works of Yussef El Guindi* (2019), and *Four Arab American Plays: Works by Leila Buck, Jamil Khoury, Yussef El Guindi, and Lameece Issaq & Jacob Kader* (2014). He is also coeditor of *Six Plays of the Israeli–Palestinian Conflict* (2018, with Jamil Khoury and Corey Pond).

Dana M. Olwan is associate professor in the Department of Women's and Gender Studies and affiliate faculty member in the Native American and Indigenous Studies Program at Syracuse University. Her work is located at the nexus of feminist theorizations of gender violence, transnational solidarities, and critical feminist pedagogies. She is the recipient of a Mellon Emerging Faculty Award and a Palestinian American Research Council grant. Her work has appeared in *Signs*, *Feminist Formations*, the *Journal of Settler Colonial Studies*, and *Feral Feminisms*. Her first book, *Gender Violence and the Transnational Politics of the Honor Crime* (2021), examines how certain forms of violence become known, recognized, and contested across multiple geopolitical contexts. She is coeditor with Chandra Talpade Mohanty of *Reimagining Comparative Feminist Studies*.

Therí A. Pickens is the author of *Black Madness :: Mad Blackness* (2019) and *New Body Politics* (2014). She edited *Arab American Aesthetics* (2018) and guest-edited the special issue of *African American Review* on Blackness and Disability (2017). You can find her at her website www.tpickens.org. She is professor of English.

Leslie Quintanilla organizes around the goal of autonomy beyond borders and seeks decolonial possibilities with a network of grassroots organizations at the US–Mexico border. She received her PhD in ethnic studies, with a certificate in critical gender studies, from the University of California, San Diego, and is currently an assistant professor at San Francisco State University in the Women and Gender Studies Department. She is also the cofounder of the Center for Interdisciplinary Environmental Justice, currently working alongside Indigenous communities resisting lithium-mining extraction in South America.

Steven Salaita is author of eight books, most recently *Uncivil Rites: Palestine and the Limits of Academic Freedom* (2015). He writes at stevesalaita.com.

Therese Saliba is faculty of Third World feminist studies at Evergreen State College, Washington, and is a former Fulbright scholar in Palestine. She is the author of numerous essays and coeditor of *Gender, Politics, and Islam* (2002) and *Intersections: Gender, Nation, and Community in Arab Women's Novels* (2002). Saliba is on the advisory board of the online *Encyclopedia of Women and Islamic Cultures* and works locally with the Rachel Corrie Foundation for Peace & Justice.

Ella Shohat is professor of cultural studies at New York University and since the 1980s has written on Orientalism, Eurocentrism, and the decolonization of knowledge. Her books include *On the Arab-Jew, Palestine, and Other Displacements: Selected Writings* (2017); *Taboo Memories, Diasporic Voices* (2006); *Israeli Cinema: East/West and the Politics of Representation* (1989; 2010); *Talking Visions: Multicultural Feminism in a Transnational Age* (1998); *Dangerous Liaisons: Gender, Nation, and Postcolonial Perspectives* (coedited 1997); *Between the Middle East and the Americas: The Cultural Politics of Diaspora* (coedited with Evelyn Alsultany, 2013); and, with Robert Stam, *Unthinking Eurocentrism* (1994; 2014), *Race in Translation: Culture Wars around the Postcolonial Atlantic* (2012), *Flagging Patriotism: Crises of Narcissism and Anti-Americanism* (2007), and *Multiculturalism, Postcoloniality, and Transnational Media* (2003). Shohat has served on the editorial boards of *Critique* and *Social Text*, coediting the special issues "911—A Public Emergency?," "Palestine in a Transnational Context," "Corruption in Corporate Culture," and "Edward Said: A Memorial Issue."

Mejdulene B. Shomali is a queer Palestinian poet and assistant professor of gender, women's, and sexuality studies at the University of Maryland, Baltimore County. Her poetry can be read in *Cosmonauts Avenue*, *Copper Nickel*, *Tinderbox*, *Diode Press*, *Mizna*, and other journals. Her academic prose can be read in *Multi-Ethnic Literatures of the US*, the *Journal of Middle East Women's Studies*, and several other journals and edited collections. Her book *Between Banat: Queer Arab Critique and Transnational Arab Archives* is forthcoming.

ANDREW SHRYOCK is Arthur F. Thurnau Professor of Anthropology at the University of Michigan. He studies political culture in the Middle East, Arab and Muslim immigrants in North America, and new approaches to history writing. His books include *Deep History: The Architecture of Past and Present* (2011), *Islamophobia/Islamophilia: Beyond the Politics of Enemy and Friend* (2010), and *Arab Detroit: From Margin to Mainstream* (2000, coedited with Nabeel Abraham).

MATTHEW JABER STIFFLER is the research and content manager at the Arab American National Museum in Dearborn, Michigan. He also leads a national research initiative through the Arab Community Center for Economic and Social Services (ACCESS), the largest Arab American community nonprofit in the country, to secure better data about the Arab American community. Stiffler received his PhD in American culture from the University of Michigan in 2010, where he serves as a lecturer in Arab and Muslim American studies. He is a former board member of the Arab American Studies Association and serves on the executive board of Michigan Humanities.

BRADLEY J. ZOPF is assistant professor of sociology at Carthage College. His research focuses on the experiences and understandings of race and racialization of Arab and Muslim Americans in the United States.

Index

Printed in the USA
CPSIA information can be obtained
at www.ICGtesting.com
CBHW080934231124
17904CB00005B/272

9 780815 637219